ROAD BRITAIN

GW00672214

2024

Scale 1:200,000
or 3.16 miles to 1 inch

37th edition June 2023 © AA Media Limited 2023
Original edition printed 1986.

All cartography in this atlas edited, designed and produced by the Mapping Services Department of AA Media Limited (A05845).

This atlas contains Ordnance Survey data © Crown copyright and database right 2023 and Royal Mail data © Royal Mail copyright and database right 2023. Contains public sector information licensed under the Open Government Licence v3.0.
Ireland mapping and distance chart contains data available from openstreetmap.org © under the Open Database License found at opendatacommons.org

Published by AA Media Limited, whose registered office is Grove House, Lutyens Close, Basingstoke, Hampshire RG24 8AG, UK. Registered number 06112600

All rights reserved. No part of this publication may be reproduced, stored in a retrieval system, or transmitted in any form or by any means – electronic, mechanical, photocopying, recording or otherwise – unless the permission of the publisher has been given beforehand.

ISBN: 978 0 7495 8340 8

A CIP catalogue record for this book is available from The British Library.

Disclaimer: The contents of this atlas are believed to be correct at the time of the latest revision, it will not contain any subsequent amended, new or temporary information including diversions and traffic control or enforcement systems. The publishers cannot be held responsible or liable for any loss or damage occasioned to any person acting or refraining from action as a result of any use or reliance on material in this atlas, nor for any errors, omissions or changes in such material. This does not affect your statutory rights.

The publishers would welcome information to correct any errors or omissions and to keep this atlas up to date. Please write to the Atlas Editor, AA Media Limited, Grove House, Lutyens Close, Basingstoke, Hampshire RG24 8AG, UK.
E-mail: *roadatlasfeedback@aamediagroup.co.uk*

Acknowledgements: AA Media Limited would like to thank the following for information used in the creation of this atlas:
Cadw, English Heritage, Forestry Commission, Historic Scotland, National Trust and National Trust for Scotland, RSPB, The Wildlife Trust, Scottish Natural Heritage, Natural England, The Countryside Council for Wales. Award winning beaches from 'Blue Flag' and 'Keep Scotland Beautiful' (summer 2022 data): for latest information visit *www.blueflag.org* and *www.keepscotlandbeautiful.org*. Road signs are © Crown Copyright 2023. Reproduced under the terms of the Open Government Licence. Transport for London (Central London Map), Nexus (Newcastle district map).
Ireland mapping: Republic of Ireland census 2016 © Central Statistics Office and Northern Ireland census 2016 © NISRA (population data); Irish Public Sector Data (CC BY 4.0) (Gaeltacht); Logainm.ie (placenames); Roads Service and Transport Infrastructure Ireland
Printed by 1010 Printing International Ltd, China

* The UK's most up-to-date atlases based on a comparison of 2023 UK Road Atlases available on the market in November 2022.

Contents

Map pages and distance chart	inside front cover
Route planning	**II–XVII**
Route planner	II–VII
Ferries and port plans	VIII–XI
Caravan and camping sites in Britain	XII–XV
Traffic signs	XVI–XVII
Motorways	**XVIII–XXV**
Restricted junctions	XVIII–XXI
M25 London Orbital motorway	XXII
M6 Toll motorway	XXIII
Smart motorways	XXIV–XXV
Map pages	**XXVI**
Road map symbols	**1**
Road maps	**2–173**
Britain 1:200,000 scale Some islands are shown at slightly smaller scales	2–169
Ireland 1:1,000,000 scale	170–173
District maps	**174–185**
Birmingham	174–175
Glasgow	176–177
London	178–181
Manchester	182–183
Tyne & Wear	184–185
Street map symbols	**186**
Towns, ports and airports	**187–237**
Town plans	188–234
Major airports	235–237
Port plans	VIII–XI
Channel Tunnel terminals	27
Central London street map and index	**238–253**
Index to place names	**254–302**
County, administrative area map	254
Place name index	255–302
Map pages and distance chart	**inside back cover**

Discover quality and friendly B&Bs at RatedTrips.com

REPUBLIC
OF
IRELAND

Legend

═══	Motorway
═══	Toll motorway
═══	Primary route dual carriageway
───	Primary route single carriageway
───	Other A road
⛴ or Ⓥ	Vehicle ferry
⛴	Fast vehicle ferry or catamaran
	National Park
◼	City with clean air or low/zero emission zone
16	Atlas page number

Isles of Scilly inset — 2

Channel Islands inset

ENGLISH

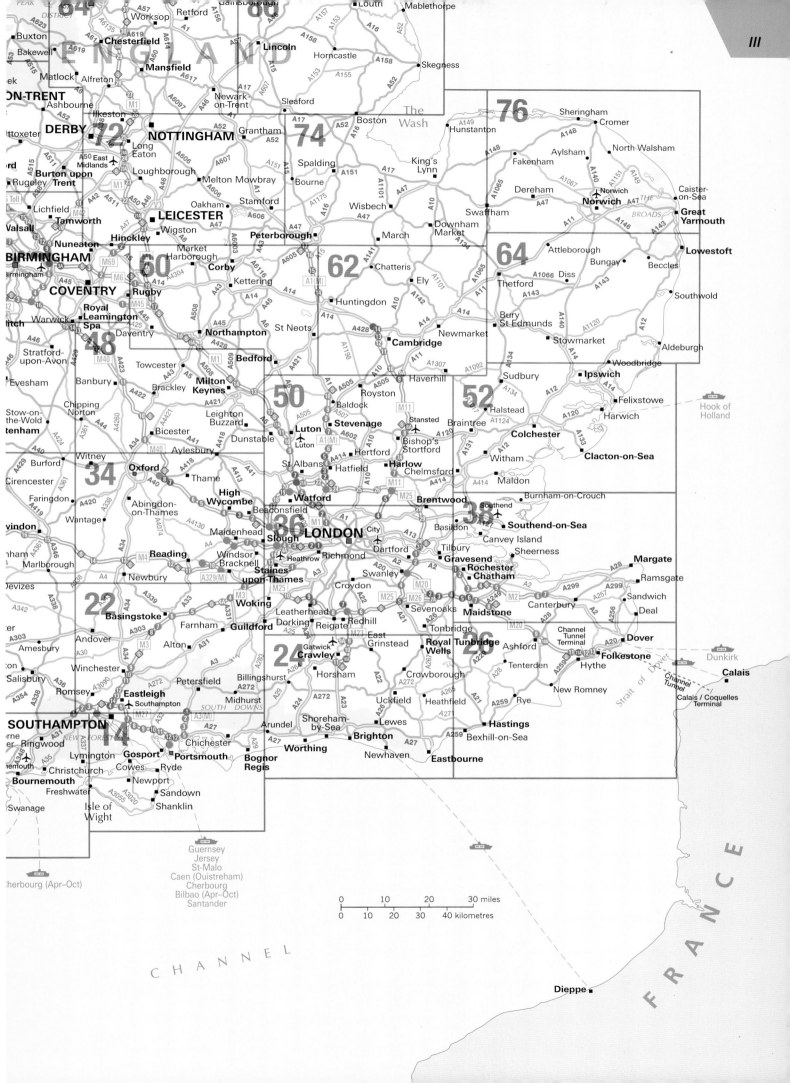

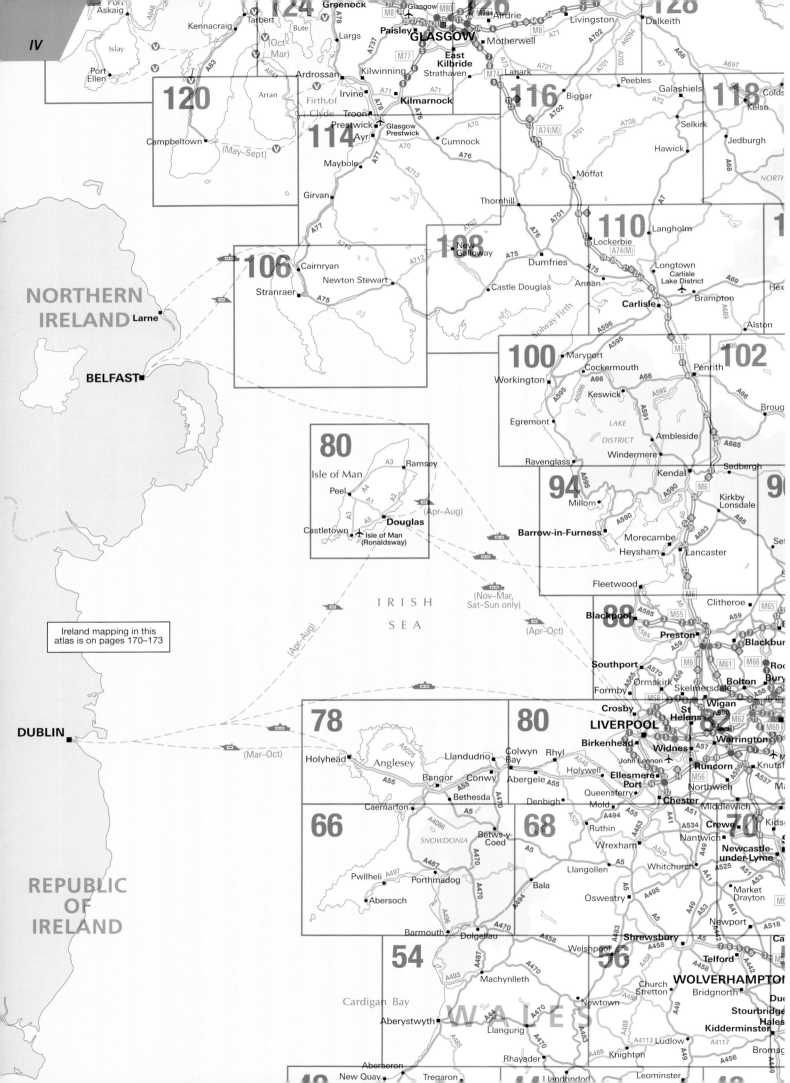

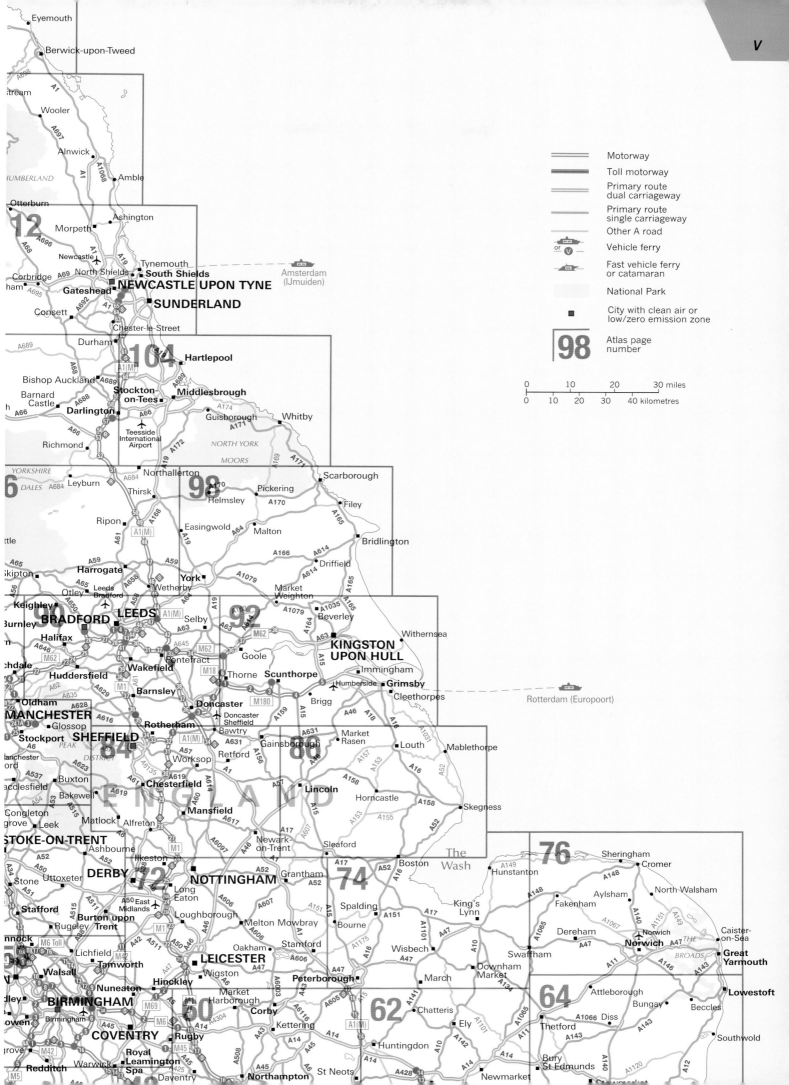

Motorway

Toll motorway

Primary route
dual carriageway

Primary route
single carriageway

Other A road

or Ⓥ Vehicle ferry

Fast vehicle ferry
or catamaran

National Park

■ City with clean air or
low/zero emission zone

98 Atlas page
number

0   10   20   30 miles
0   10   20   30   40 kilometres

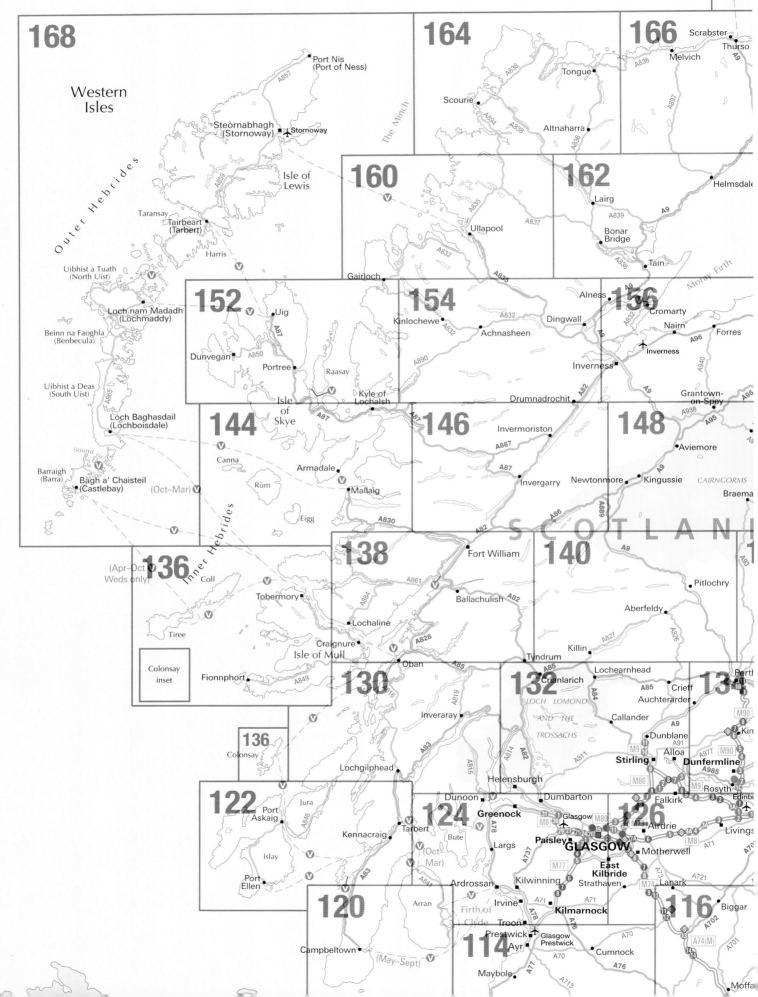

Strom

168

Western
Isles

Port Nis
(Port of Ness)

Steòrnabhagh
(Stornoway) • Stornoway

Isle of
Lewis

O u t e r   H e b r i d e s

Taransay

Tairbeart
(Tarbert)

Harris

Uibhist a Tuath
(North Uist)

Beinn na Faoghla
(Benbecula)

Loch nam Madadh
(Lochmaddy)

Uibhist a Deas
(South Uist)

Loch Baghasdail
(Lochboisdale)

Barraigh
(Barra)
Bàgh a' Chaisteil
(Castlebay)   (Oct–Mar)

164

166   Scrabster
        Thurso
      Melvich
Tongue

Scourie

Altnaharra

160

Ullapool

Gairloch

152

Uig

Dunvegan

Portree

Raasay

Isle
of
Skye

Kyle of
Lochalsh

162   Helmsdale

Lairg

Bonar
Bridge

Tain

Moray Firth

154

Kinlochewe

Achnasheen

156
Cromarty
Alness
Nairn   Forres
Dingwall

Inverness

Inverness

Drumnadrochit

Grantown-
on-Spey

144

Canna

Rùm

Armadale

Mallaig

Eigg

146

Invermoriston

Invergarry

148

Aviemore

Newtonmore   Kingussie   CAIRNGORMS

Braema

S C O T L A N

(Apr–Oct
Weds only)

136

Coll

Tobermory

Tiree

Colonsay
inset

Fionnphort

I n n e r   H e b r i d e s

Lochaline

Craignure

Isle of Mull

Oban

138

Fort William

Ballachulish

140

Pitlochry

Aberfeldy

Killin

Tyndrum

Lochearnhead

130

Inveraray

132
Crianlarich
LOCH LOMOND
AND THE
TROSSACHS

Callander

Perth

Crieff

Auchterarder

13

M90

Kin

136

Colonsay

122

Port
Askaig

Jura

Kennacraig

Islay

Port
Ellen

Tarbert

Bute

Helensburgh

Dunoon

124

Greenock

Largs

Ardrossan

120

Arran

Firth
of
Clyde

Campbeltown   (May–Sept)

Dumbarton

Glasgow

Paisley

GLASGOW

Kilwinning

Irvine

Troon
Prestwick
Ayr

Dunblane

Alloa

Stirling   Dunfermline

Rosyth

Falkirk

126
Airdrie   Livings

Motherwell

East
Kilbride

Strathaven   Lanark

Kilmarnock

Glasgow
Prestwick

Cumnock

Maybole

116   Biggar

Moffa

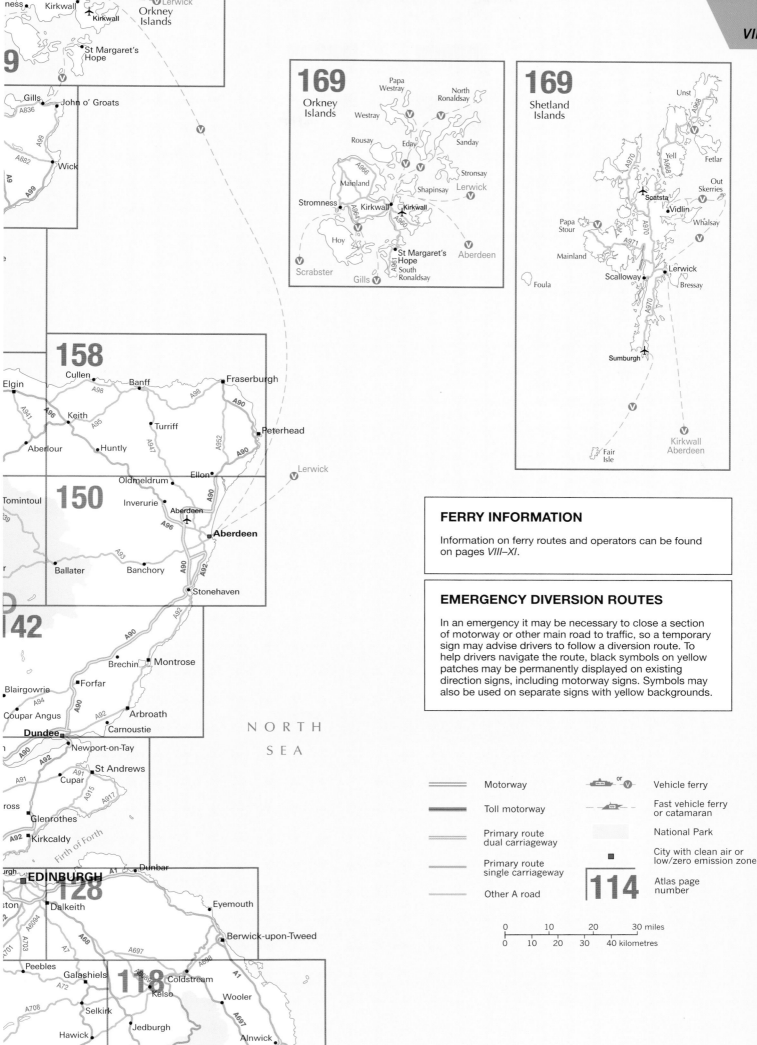

169
Orkney Islands

169
Shetland Islands

158

150

142

128

118

NORTH
SEA

FERRY INFORMATION

Information on ferry routes and operators can be found on pages *VIII–XI*.

EMERGENCY DIVERSION ROUTES

In an emergency it may be necessary to close a section of motorway or other main road to traffic, so a temporary sign may advise drivers to follow a diversion route. To help drivers navigate the route, black symbols on yellow patches may be permanently displayed on existing direction signs, including motorway signs. Symbols may also be used on separate signs with yellow backgrounds.

Motorway	Vehicle ferry
Toll motorway	Fast vehicle ferry or catamaran
Primary route dual carriageway	National Park
Primary route single carriageway	City with clean air or low/zero emission zone
Other A road	**114** Atlas page number

0   10   20   30 miles
0   10   20   30   40 kilometres

Channel hopping and the Isle of Wight

For business or pleasure, hopping on a ferry across to France, the Channel Islands or Isle of Wight has never been easier.

The vehicle ferry services listed in the table give you all the options, together with detailed port plans to help you navigate to and from the ferry terminals. Simply choose your preferred route, not forgetting the fast sailings (see 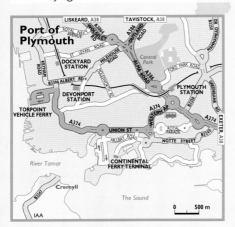).
Bon voyage!

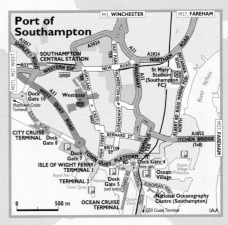

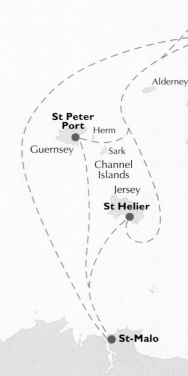

ENGLISH CHANNEL AND ISLE OF WIGHT FERRY CROSSINGS

From	To	Journey time	Operator website
Dover	Calais	1 hr 30 mins	dfdsseaways.co.uk
Dover	Calais	1 hr 30 mins	poferries.com
Dover	Dunkirk	2 hrs	dfdsseaways.co.uk
Folkestone	Calais (Coquelles)	35 mins	eurotunnel.com
Lymington	Yarmouth (IOW)	40 mins	wightlink.co.uk
Newhaven	Dieppe	4 hrs	dfdsseaways.co.uk
Plymouth	Roscoff	5 hrs 30 mins	brittany-ferries.co.uk
Poole	Cherbourg	4 hrs 30 mins (Apr–Oct)	brittany-ferries.co.uk
Poole	Guernsey	3 hrs	condorferries.co.uk
Poole	Jersey	4 hrs	condorferries.co.uk
Poole	St-Malo	6 hrs 20 mins–12 hrs (via Channel Is.)	condorferries.co.uk
Portsmouth	Caen (Ouistreham)	5 hrs 45 mins–7 hrs	brittany-ferries.co.uk
Portsmouth	Cherbourg	8 hrs	brittany-ferries.co.uk
Portsmouth	Fishbourne (IOW)	45 mins	wightlink.co.uk
Portsmouth	Guernsey	7 hrs	condorferries.co.uk
Portsmouth	Jersey	8–11 hrs	condorferries.co.uk
Portsmouth	St-Malo	11 hrs	brittany-ferries.co.uk
Southampton	East Cowes (IOW)	1 hr	redfunnel.co.uk

The information listed is provided as a guide only, as services are liable to change at short notice and are weather dependent. Services shown are for vehicle ferries only, operated by conventional ferry unless indicated as a fast ferry service ( ). Please check sailings before planning your journey.

Travelling further afield? For ferry services to Northern Spain see brittany-ferries.co.uk.

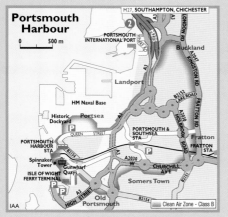

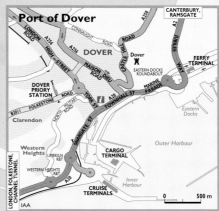

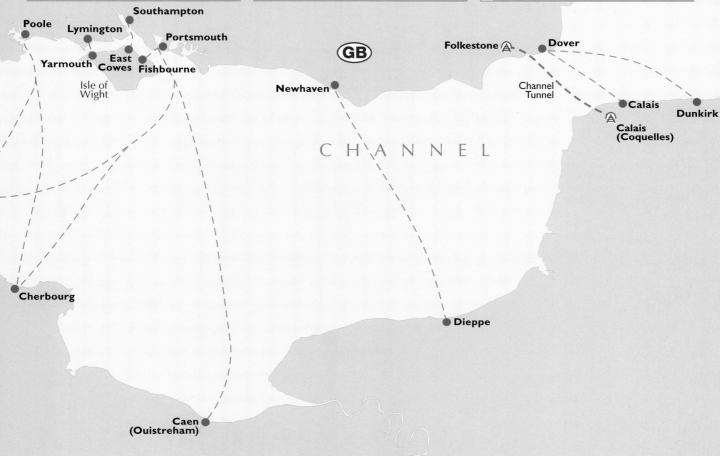

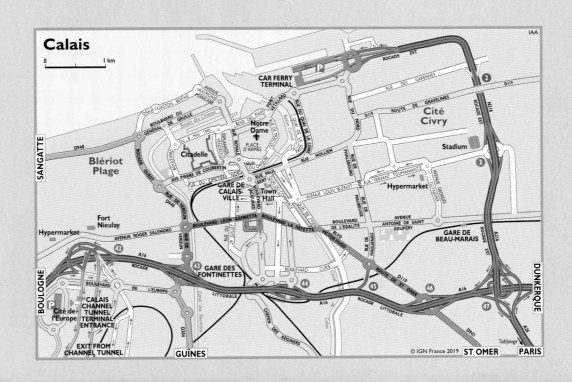

Ferries to Ireland and the Isle of Man

With so many sea crossings to Ireland and the Isle of Man the information provided in the table to the right will help you make the right choice.

IRISH SEA FERRY CROSSINGS

From	To	Journey time	Operator website
Cairnryan	Belfast	2 hrs 15 mins 🚢	stenaline.co.uk
Cairnryan	Larne	2 hrs	poferries.com
Douglas	Belfast	2 hrs 45 mins (April–Aug) 🚢	steam-packet.com
Douglas	Dublin	2 hrs 55 mins (April–Aug) 🚢	steam-packet.com
Fishguard	Rosslare	3 hrs 15 mins	stenaline.co.uk
Heysham	Douglas	3 hrs 45 mins	steam-packet.com
Holyhead	Dublin	2 hrs (Mar–Oct) 🚢	irishferries.com
Holyhead	Dublin	3 hrs 15 mins	irishferries.com
Holyhead	Dublin	3 hrs 15 mins	stenaline.co.uk
Liverpool	Douglas	2 hrs 45 mins (Apr–Oct) 🚢	steam-packet.com
Liverpool	Dublin	8 hrs–8 hrs 30 mins	poferries.com
Liverpool (Birkenhead)	Belfast	8 hrs	stenaline.co.uk
Liverpool (Birkenhead)	Douglas	4 hrs (Nov–Mar, Sat–Sun only)	steam-packet.com
Pembroke Dock	Rosslare	4 hrs	irishferries.com

The information listed is provided as a guide only, as services are liable to change at short notice and are weather dependent. Services shown are for vehicle ferries only, operated by conventional ferry unless indicated as a fast ferry service (🚢). Please check sailings before planning your journey.

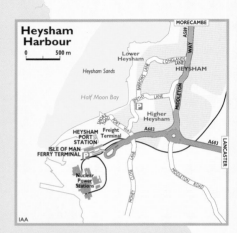

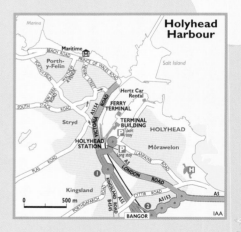

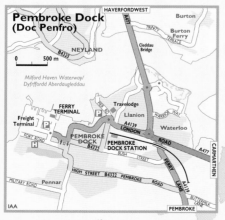

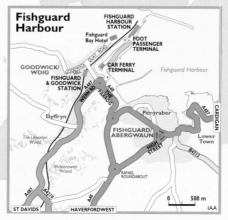

SCOTLAND FERRIES

From	To	Journey time	Operator website
Scottish Islands/west coast of Scotland			
Gourock	Dunoon	20 mins	western-ferries.co.uk
Glenelg	Skye	20 mins (Easter–Oct)	skyeferry.co.uk
Numerous and varied sailings from the west coast of Scotland to Scottish islands are provided by Caledonian MacBrayne. Please visit calmac.co.uk for all ferry information, including those of other operators.			
Orkney Islands			
Aberdeen	Kirkwall	6 hrs–7hrs 15mins	northlinkferries.co.uk
Gills	St Margaret's Hope	1 hr	pentlandferries.co.uk
Scrabster	Stromness	1 hr 30 mins	northlinkferries.co.uk
Lerwick	Kirkwall	5 hrs 30 mins	northlinkferries.co.uk
Inter-island services are operated by Orkney Ferries. Please see orkneyferries.co.uk for details.			
Shetland Islands			
Aberdeen	Lerwick	12 hrs	northlinkferries.co.uk
Kirkwall	Lerwick	7 hrs 45 mins	northlinkferries.co.uk
Inter-island services are operated by Shetland Island Council Ferries. Please see shetland.gov.uk/ferries for details.			

Please note that some smaller island services are day and weather dependent and reservations are required for some routes. Book and confirm sailing schedules by contacting the operator.

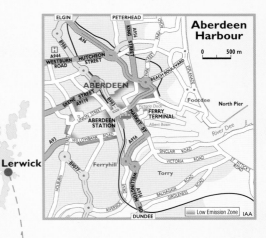

Aberdeen Harbour

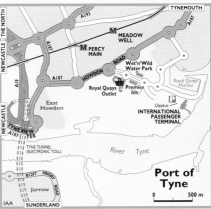

Port of Tyne

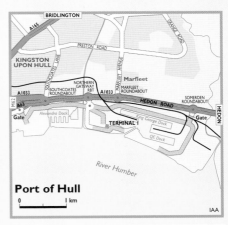

Port of Hull

For a port plan of Harwich see atlas page 53

NORTH SEA FERRY CROSSINGS

From	To	Journey time	Operator website
Harwich	Hook of Holland	6 hrs 30 mins	stenaline.co.uk
Kingston upon Hull	Rotterdam (Europoort)	11 hrs	poferries.com
Newcastle upon Tyne	Amsterdam (IJmuiden)	15 hrs 30 mins	dfdsseaways.co.uk

The information listed on this page is provided as a guide only, as services are liable to change at short notice. Services shown are for vehicle ferries only, operated by conventional ferry. Please check sailings before planning your journey as many are weather dependent.

Caravan and camping sites in Britain

These pages list the top 300 AA-inspected Caravan and Camping (C & C) sites in the Pennant rating scheme. **Five Pennant Premier sites are shown in green,** Four Pennant sites are shown in blue.

Listings include addresses, telephone numbers and websites together with page and grid references to locate the sites in the atlas. The total number of touring pitches is also included for each site, together with the type of pitch available. The following abbreviations are used: **C = Caravan CV = Campervan T = Tent**

To discover AA-rated caravan and camping sites not included on these pages please visit **RatedTrips.com**

ENGLAND

Alders Caravan Park
Home Farm, Alne, York
YO61 1RY
Tel: 01347 838722   **97 R7**
alderscaravanpark.co.uk
Total Pitches: 87 (C, CV & T)

Andrewshayes Holiday Park
Dalwood, Axminster
EX13 7DY
Tel: 01404 831225   **10 E5**
andrewshayes.co.uk
Total Pitches: 150 (C, CV & T)

Atlantic Bays Holiday Park
Padstow, Cornwall
PL28 8PY
Tel: 01841 520855   **4 D7**
atlanticbaysholidaypark.co.uk
Total Pitches: 70 (C, CV & T)

Ayr Holiday Park
St Ives, Cornwall
TR26 1EJ
Tel: 01736 795855   **2 E5**
ayrholidaypark.co.uk
Total Pitches: 100 (C, CV & T)

Back of Beyond Touring Park
234 Ringwood Road,
St Leonards, Dorset
BH24 2SB
Tel: 01202 876968   **13 K4**
backofbeyondtouringpark.co.uk
Total Pitches: 80 (C, CV & T)

Bagwell Farm Touring Park
Knights in the Bottom,
Chickerell, Weymouth
DT3 4EA
Tel: 01305 782575   **11 N8**
bagwellfarm.co.uk
Total Pitches: 320 (C, CV & T)

Bardsea Leisure Park
Priory Road, Ulverston
LA12 9QE
Tel: 01229 584712   **94 F5**
bardsealeisure.co.uk
Total Pitches: 83 (C & CV)

Bath Chew Valley Caravan Park
Ham Lane,
Bishop Sutton
BS39 5TZ
Tel: 01275 332127   **19 Q3**
bathchewvalley.co.uk
Total Pitches: 45 (C, CV & T)

Bay View Farm C & C Park
Croyde, Devon
EX33 1PN
Tel: 01271 890501   **16 G4**
bayviewfarm.co.uk
Total Pitches: 70 (C, CV & T)

Bay View Holiday Park
Bolton le Sands, Carnforth
LA5 9TN
Tel: 01524 732854   **95 K7**
holgates.co.uk
Total Pitches: 100 (C, CV & T)

Beacon Cottage Farm Touring Park
Beacon Drive, St Agnes
TR5 0NU
Tel: 01872 552347   **3 J3**
beaconcottagefarmholidays.co.uk
Total Pitches: 60 (C, CV & T)

Beaconsfield Holiday Park
Battlefield,
Shrewsbury
SY4 4AA
Tel: 01939 210370   **69 P11**
beaconsfieldholidaypark.co.uk
Total Pitches: 60 (C & CV)

Beech Croft Farm C & C Park
Beech Croft,
Blackwell in the Peak,
Buxton
SK17 9TQ
Tel: 01298 85330   **83 P10**
beechcroftfarm.co.uk
Total Pitches: 30 (C, CV & T)

Bellingham C & C Club Site
Brown Rigg,
Bellingham
NE48 2JY
Tel: 01434 220175   **112 B4**
campingandcaravanning
club.co.uk/bellingham
Total Pitches: 64 (C, CV & T)

Beverley Park C & C Park
Goodrington Road, Paignton
TQ4 7JE
Tel: 01803 843887   **7 M7**
beverley-holidays.co.uk
Total Pitches: 149 (C, CV & T)

Birchwood Tourist Park
Bere Road, Coldharbour,
Wareham
BH20 7PA
Tel: 01929 554763   **12 E6**
birchwoodtouristpark.co.uk
Total Pitches: 175 (C, CV & T)

Blue Rose Caravan & Country Park
Star Carr Lane, Brandesburton
YO25 8RU
Tel: 01964 543366   **99 N11**
bluerosepark.com
Total Pitches: 58 (C & CV)

Briarfields Motel & Touring Park
Gloucester Road, Cheltenham
GL51 0SX
Tel: 01242 235324   **46 H10**
briarfields.net
Total Pitches: 72 (C, CV & T)

Bridge House Marina & Caravan Park
Nateby Crossing Lane,
Nateby, Garstang
PR3 0JJ
Tel: 01995 603207   **95 K11**
bridgehousemarina.co.uk
Total Pitches: 50 (C & CV)

Broadhembury C & C Park
Steeds Lane, Kingsnorth,
Ashford
TN26 1NQ
Tel: 01233 620859   **26 H4**
broadhembury.co.uk
Total Pitches: 100 (C, CV & T)

Brook Lodge Farm C & C Park
Cowslip Green, Redhill,
Bristol, Somerset
BS40 5RB
Tel: 01934 862311   **19 N2**
brooklodgefarm.com
Total Pitches: 29 (C, CV & T)

Burnham-on-Sea Holiday Village
Marine Drive, Burnham-on-Sea
TA8 1LA
Tel: 01278 783391   **19 K5**
haven.com/burnhamonsea
Total Pitches: 75 (C, CV & T)

Burns Farm C & C
St Johns in the Vale, Keswick
CA12 4RR
Tel: 01687 79225   **101 K6**
burns-farm.co.uk
Total Pitches: 32 (C, CV & T)

Burrowhayes Farm C & C Site & Riding Stables
West Luccombe, Porlock,
Minehead
TA24 8HT
Tel: 01643 862463   **18 A5**
burrowhayes.co.uk
Total Pitches: 120 (C, CV & T)

Burton Constable Holiday Park & Arboretum
Old Lodges, Sproatley, Hull
HU11 4LJ
Tel: 01964 562508   **93 L3**
burtonconstableholidaypark.co.uk
Total Pitches: 105 (C, CV & T)

Caistor Lakes
99a Brigg Road, Caistor
LN7 6RX
Tel: 01472 859626   **93 K10**
caistorlakes.co.uk
Total Pitches: 28 (C & CV)

Cakes & Ale
Abbey Lane, Theberton,
Leiston
IP16 4TE
Tel: 01728 831655   **65 N9**
cakesandale.co.uk
Total Pitches: 55 (C, CV & T)

Calloose C & C Park
Leedstown, Hayle
TR27 5ET
Tel: 01736 850431   **2 F7**
calloose.co.uk
Total Pitches: 109 (C, CV & T)

Camping Caradon Touring Park
Trelawne, Looe
PL13 2NA
Tel: 01503 272388   **5 L11**
campingcaradon.co.uk
Total Pitches: 75 (C, CV & T)

Capesthorne Hall
Congleton Road, Siddington,
Macclesfield
SK11 9JY
Tel: 01625 861221   **82 H10**
capesthorne.com/caravan-park
Total Pitches: 50 (C & CV)

Carlyon Bay C & C Park
Bethesda, Cypress Avenue,
Carlyon Bay
PL25 3RE
Tel: 01726 812735   **3 R3**
carlyonbay.net
Total Pitches: 180 (C, CV & T)

Carnevas Holiday Park
Carnevas Farm, St Merryn,
Cornwall
PL28 8PN
Tel: 01841 520230   **4 D7**
carnevasholidaypark.com
Total Pitches: 195 (C, CV & T)

Cartref C & C
Cartref, Ford Heath,
Shrewsbury, Shropshire
SY5 9GD
Tel: 01743 821688   **56 G2**
cartrefcaravansite.co.uk
Total Pitches: 44 (C, CV & T)

Carvynick Holiday Park
Summercourt, Newquay
TR8 5AF
Tel: 01872 510716   **4 D10**
carvynick.co.uk
Total Pitches: 47 (C, CV & T)

Castlerigg Hall C & C Park
Castlerigg Hall, Keswick
CA12 4TE
Tel: 017687 74499   **101 J6**
castlerigg.co.uk
Total Pitches: 68 (C, CV & T)

Cheddar Mendip Heights C & C Club Site
Townsend, Priddy, Wells
BA5 3BP
Tel: 01749 870241   **19 P4**
campingandcaravanning
club.co.uk/cheddar
Total Pitches: 90 (C, CV & T)

Chy Carne Holiday Park
Kuggar, Ruan Minor, Helston,
Cornwall
TR12 7LX
Tel: 01326 290200   **3 J10**
chycarne.co.uk
Total Pitches: 30 (C, CV & T)

Clippesby Hall
Hall Lane, Clippesby,
Great Yarmouth
NR29 3BL
Tel: 01493 367800   **77 N9**
clippesbyhall.com
Total Pitches: 120 (C, CV & T)

Cofton Holidays
Starcross, Dawlish
EX6 8RP
Tel: 01626 890111   **9 N8**
coftonholidays.co.uk
Total Pitches: 450 (C, CV & T)

Concierge Camping
Ratham Estate, Ratham Lane,
West Ashling, Chichester
PO18 8DL
Tel: 01243 573118   **15 M5**
conciergecamping.co.uk
Total Pitches: 27 (C & CV)

Coombe Touring Park
Race Plain, Netherhampton,
Salisbury
SP2 8PN
Tel: 01722 328451   **21 L9**
coombecaravanpark.co.uk
Total Pitches: 50 (C, CV & T)

Cornish Farm Touring Park
Shoreditch,
Taunton
TA3 7BS
Tel: 01823 327746   **18 H10**
cornishfarm.com
Total Pitches: 48 (C, CV & T)

Cosawes Park
Perranarworthal, Truro
TR3 7QS
Tel: 01872 863724   **3 K6**
cosawes.co.uk
Total Pitches: 59 (C, CV & T)

Cote Ghyll C & C Park
Osmotherley, Northallerton
DL6 3AH
Tel: 01609 883425   **104 E11**
coteghyll.com
Total Pitches: 95 (C, CV & T)

Country View Holiday Park
Sand Road, Sand Bay,
Weston-super-Mare
BS22 9UJ
Tel: 01934 627595   **19 K2**
cvhp.co.uk
Total Pitches: 190 (C, CV & T)

Crealy Theme Park & Resort
Sidmouth Road,
Clyst St Mary, Exeter
EX5 1DR
Tel: 01395 234888   **9 P6**
crealy.co.uk
Total Pitches: 120 (C, CV & T)

Crows Nest Caravan Park
Gristhorpe,
Filey
YO14 9PS
Tel: 01723 582206   **99 M4**
crowsnestcaravanpark.com
Total Pitches: 43 (C, CV & T)

Deepdale Backpackers & Camping
Deepdale Farm,
Burnham Deepdale
PE31 8DD
Tel: 01485 210256   **75 R2**
deepdalebackpackers.co.uk
Total Pitches: 80 (CV & T)

Dibles Park
Dibles Road, Warsash,
Southampton, Hampshire
SO31 9SA
Tel: 01489 575232   **14 F5**
diblespark.co.uk
Total Pitches: 11 (C, CV & T)

Dornafield
Dornafield Farm, Two Mile Oak,
Newton Abbot
TQ12 6DD
Tel: 01803 812732   **7 L5**
dornafield.com
Total Pitches: 135 (C, CV & T)

East Fleet Farm Touring Park
Chickerell, Weymouth
DT3 4DW
Tel: 01305 785768   **11 N9**
eastfleet.co.uk
Total Pitches: 400 (C, CV & T)

Eastham Hall Holiday Park
Saltcotes Road,
Lytham St Annes,
Lancashire
FY8 4LS
Tel: 01253 737907   **88 D5**
easthamhall.co.uk
Total Pitches: 113 (C & CV)

Eden Valley Holiday Park
Lanlivery, Nr Lostwithiel
PL30 5BU
Tel: 01208 872277   **4 H10**
edenvalleyholidaypark.co.uk
Total Pitches: 56 (C, CV & T)

Exe Valley Caravan Site
Mill House, Bridgetown,
Dulverton
TA22 9JR
Tel: 01643 851432   **18 B8**
exevalleycamping.co.uk
Total Pitches: 48 (C, CV & T)

Eye Kettleby Lakes
Eye Kettleby,
Melton Mowbray
LE14 2TN
Tel: 01664 565900   **73 J7**
eyekettlebylakes.com
Total Pitches: 130 (C, CV & T)

Fennwood Caravan Park
Lyneal, Ellesmere,
Shropshire
SY12 0QF
Tel: 01948 710221   **69 N8**
fennwoodpark.co.uk
Total Pitches: 60 (C & CV)

Fields End Water Caravan Park & Fishery
Benwick Road, Doddington,
March
PE15 0TY
Tel: 01354 740199   **62 E2**
fieldsendwater.co.uk
Total Pitches: 80 (C, CV & T)

Flaxton Meadows
York Lane, Flaxton, York
YO60 7QZ
Tel: 01904 393943   **98 D8**
flaxtonmeadows.co.uk
Total Pitches: 35 (C, CV & T)

Flower of May Holiday Park
Lebberston Cliff, Filey,
Scarborough
YO11 3NU
Tel: 01723 584311   **99 M4**
flowerofmay.com
Total Pitches: 300 (C, CV & T)

Forest Glade Holiday Park
Near Kentisbeare, Cullompton,
Devon
EX15 2DT
Tel: 01404 841381   **10 C3**
forest-glade.co.uk
Total Pitches: 80 (C, CV & T)

Freshwater Beach Holiday Park
Burton Bradstock, Bridport
DT6 4PT
Tel: 01308 897317   **11 K6**
freshwaterbeach.co.uk
Total Pitches: 500 (C, CV & T)

Glenfield Caravan Park
Blackmoor Lane, Bardsey,
Leeds
LS17 9DZ
Tel: 01937 574657   **91 J2**
glenfieldcaravanpark.co.uk
Total Pitches: 30 (C, CV & T)

Globe Vale Holiday Park
Radnor, Redruth
TR16 4BH
Tel: 01209 891183   **3 J5**
globevale.co.uk
Total Pitches: 138 (C, CV & T)

Glororum Caravan Park
Glororum Farm, Bamburgh
NE69 7AW
Tel: 01670 860256   **119 N4**
northumbrianleisure.co.uk
Total Pitches: 43 (C & CV)

Golden Cap Holiday Park
Seatown, Chideock,
Bridport
DT6 6JX
Tel: 01308 422139   **11 J6**
wdlh.co.uk
Total Pitches: 108 (C, CV & T)

Golden Coast Holiday Park
Station Road,
Woolacombe
EX34 7HW
Tel: 01271 872302   **16 H3**
woolacombe.com
Total Pitches: 89 (C, CV & T)

Golden Sands Holiday Park
Quebec Road,
Mablethorpe
LN12 1QJ
Tel: 01507 477871   **87 N3**
haven.com/goldensands
Total Pitches: 172 (C, CV & T)

Golden Square C & C Park
Oswaldkirk,
Helmsley
YO62 5YQ
Tel: 01439 788269   **98 C5**
goldensquarecaravanpark.com
Total Pitches: 129 (C, CV & T)

Golden Valley C & C Park
Coach Road, Ripley,
Derbyshire
DE55 4ES
Tel: 01773 513881   **84 F10**
goldenvalleycaravanpark.co.uk
Total Pitches: 45 (C, CV & T)

Goosewood Holiday Park
Sutton-on-the-Forest,
York
YO61 1ET
Tel: 01347 810829   **98 B8**
flowerofmay.com
Total Pitches: 100 (C & CV)

Greenacre Place Touring Caravan Park
Bristol Road, Edithmead, Highbridge
TA9 4HA
Tel: 01278 785227   **19 K5**
greenacreplace.com
Total Pitches: 10 (C & CV)

Green Acres Caravan Park
High Knells, Houghton, Carlisle
CA6 4JW
Tel: 01228 675418   **110 H8**
caravanpark-cumbria.com
Total Pitches: 35 (C, CV & T)

Greenhill Farm C & C Park
Greenhill Farm, New Road, Landford, Salisbury
SP5 2AZ
Tel: 01794 324117   **21 Q11**
greenhillfarm.co.uk
Total Pitches: 160 (C, CV & T)

Greenhills Holiday Park
Crowhill Lane, Bakewell, Derbyshire
DE45 1PX
Tel: 01629 813052   **84 B7**
greenhillsholidaypark.co.uk
Total Pitches: 172 (C, CV & T)

Grouse Hill Caravan Park
Flask Bungalow Farm, Fylingdales, Robin Hood's Bay
YO22 4QH
Tel: 01947 880543   **105 P10**
grousehill.co.uk
Total Pitches: 175 (C, CV & T)

Gunvenna Holiday Park
St Minver, Wadebridge
PL27 6QN
Tel: 01208 862405   **4 F6**
gunvenna.com
Total Pitches: 75 (C, CV & T)

Haggerston Castle Holiday Park
Beal, Berwick-upon-Tweed
TD15 2PA
Tel: 01289 381333   **119 K2**
haven.com/haggerstoncastle
Total Pitches: 140 (C & CV)

Harbury Fields
Harbury Fields Farm, Harbury, Nr Leamington Spa
CV33 9JN
Tel: 01926 612457   **48 C2**
harburyfields.co.uk
Total Pitches: 59 (C & CV)

Harford Bridge Holiday Park
Peter Tavy, Tavistock
PL19 9LS
Tel: 01822 810349   **8 D9**
harfordbridge.co.uk
Total Pitches: 125 (C, CV & T)

Haw Wood Farm Caravan Park
Hinton, Saxmundham
IP17 3QT
Tel: 01502 359550   **65 N7**
hawwoodfarm.co.uk
Total Pitches: 60 (C, CV & T)

Heathfield Farm Camping
Heathfield Road, Freshwater, Isle of Wight
PO40 9SH
Tel: 01983 407822   **13 P7**
heathfieldcamping.co.uk
Total Pitches: 81 (C, CV & T)

Heathland Beach Holiday Park
London Road, Kessingland
NR33 7PJ
Tel: 01502 740337   **65 Q4**
heathlandbeach.co.uk
Total Pitches: 63 (C, CV & T)

Hendra Holiday Park
Newquay
TR8 4NY
Tel: 01637 875778   **4 C9**
hendra-holidays.com
Total Pitches: 548 (C, CV & T)

Herding Hill Farm Touring & Camping Site
Shield Hill, Haltwhistle, Northumberland
NE49 9NW
Tel: 01434 320175   **111 P7**
herdinghillfarm.co.uk
Total Pitches: 22 (C, CV & T)

Hidden Valley Park
West Down, Braunton, Ilfracombe, Devon
EX34 8NU
Tel: 01271 813837   **17 J3**
hiddenvalleypark.com
Total Pitches: 114 (C, CV & T)

Highfield Farm Touring Park
Long Road, Comberton, Cambridge
CB23 7DG
Tel: 01223 262308   **62 E9**
highfieldfarmtouringpark.co.uk
Total Pitches: 120 (C, CV & T)

Highlands End Holiday Park
Eype, Bridport, Dorset
DT6 6AR
Tel: 01308 422139   **11 K6**
wdlh.co.uk
Total Pitches: 195 (C, CV & T)

Hill of Oaks & Blakeholme
Windermere
LA12 8NR
Tel: 015395 31578   **94 H3**
hillofoaks.co.uk
Total Pitches: 263 (C & CV)

Hillside Caravan Park
Canvas Farm, Moor Road, Knayton, Thirsk
YO7 4BR
Tel: 01845 537349   **97 P3**
hillsidecaravanpark.co.uk
Total Pitches: 60 (C & CV)

Holiday Resort Unity
Coast Road, Brean Sands, Brean
TA8 2RB
Tel: 01278 751235   **19 J4**
hru.co.uk
Total Pitches: 453 (C, CV & T)

Hollins Farm C & C
Far Arnside, Carnforth
LA5 0SL
Tel: 01524 701767   **95 J5**
holgates.co.uk
Total Pitches: 12 (C, CV & T)

Hylton Caravan Park
Eden Street, Silloth
CA7 4AY
Tel: 016973 32666   **109 P10**
stanwix.com
Total Pitches: 90 (C, CV & T)

Island Lodge C & C Site
Stumpy Post Cross, Kingsbridge
TQ7 4BL
Tel: 01548 852956   **7 J9**
islandlodgesite.co.uk
Total Pitches: 30 (C, CV & T)

Isle of Avalon Touring Caravan Park
Godney Road, Glastonbury
BA6 9AF
Tel: 01458 833618   **19 N7**
avaloncaravanpark.co.uk
Total Pitches: 120 (C, CV & T)

Jasmine Caravan Park
Cross Lane, Snainton, Scarborough
YO13 9BE
Tel: 01723 859240   **99 J4**
jasminepark.co.uk
Total Pitches: 68 (C, CV & T)

Kennford International Holiday Park
Kennford, Exeter
EX6 7YN
Tel: 01392 833046   **9 M7**
kennfordinternational.co.uk
Total Pitches: 22 (C, CV & T)

Killiwerris Touring Park
Penstraze, Chacewater, Truro, Cornwall
TR4 8PF
Tel: 01872 561356   **3 K4**
killiwerris.co.uk
Total Pitches: 17 (C, CV & T)

King's Lynn C & C Park
New Road, North Runcton, King's Lynn
PE33 0RA
Tel: 01553 840004   **75 M7**
kl-cc.co.uk
Total Pitches: 150 (C, CV & T)

Kneps Farm Holiday Caravan Park
River Road, Stanah, Thornton-Cleveleys, Blackpool
FY5 5LR
Tel: 01253 823632   **88 D2**
knepsfarm.co.uk
Total Pitches: 40 (C & CV)

Knight Stainforth Hall Caravan & Campsite
Stainforth, Settle
BD24 0DP
Tel: 01729 822200   **96 B7**
knightstainforth.co.uk
Total Pitches: 100 (C, CV & T)

Ladycross Plantation Caravan Park
Egton, Whitby
YO21 1UA
Tel: 01947 895502   **105 M9**
ladycrossplantation.co.uk
Total Pitches: 130 (C & CV)

Lady's Mile Holiday Park
Dawlish, Devon
EX7 0LX
Tel: 01626 863411   **9 N9**
ladysmile.co.uk
Total Pitches: 570 (C, CV & T)

Lakeland Leisure Park
Moor Lane, Flookburgh
LA11 7LT
Tel: 01539 558556   **94 H6**
haven.com/lakeland
Total Pitches: 177 (C, CV & T)

Lamb Cottage Caravan Park
Dalefords Lane, Whitegate, Northwich
CW8 2BN
Tel: 01606 882302   **82 D11**
lambcottage.co.uk
Total Pitches: 45 (C & CV)

Langstone Manor C & C Park
Moortown, Tavistock
PL19 9JZ
Tel: 01822 613371   **6 E4**
langstonemanor.co.uk
Total Pitches: 40 (C, CV & T)

Lanyon Holiday Park
Loscombe Lane, Four Lanes, Redruth
TR16 6LP
Tel: 01209 313474   **2 H6**
lanyonholidaypark.co.uk
Total Pitches: 25 (C, CV & T)

Lickpenny Caravan Site
Lickpenny Lane, Tansley, Matlock
DE4 5GF
Tel: 01629 583040   **84 D9**
lickpennycaravanpark.co.uk
Total Pitches: 80 (C & CV)

Lime Tree Park
Dukes Drive, Buxton
SK17 9RP
Tel: 01298 22988   **83 N10**
limetreeparkbuxton.com
Total Pitches: 106 (C, CV & T)

Lincoln Farm Park Oxfordshire
High Street, Standlake
OX29 7RH
Tel: 01865 300239   **34 C4**
lincolnfarmpark.co.uk
Total Pitches: 90 (C, CV & T)

Littlesea Holiday Park
Lynch Lane, Weymouth
DT4 9DT
Tel: 01305 774414   **11 P9**
haven.com/littlesea
Total Pitches: 141 (C, CV & T)

Little Trevothan C & C Park
Trevothan, Coverack, Helston, Cornwall
TR12 6SD
Tel: 01326 280260   **3 K10**
littletrevothan.co.uk
Total Pitches: 80 (C, CV & T)

Long Acres Touring Park
Station Road, Old Leake, Boston
PE22 9RF
Tel: 01205 871555   **87 L10**
long-acres.co.uk
Total Pitches: 40 (C, CV & T)

Long Hazel Park
High Street, Sparkford, Yeovil, Somerset
BA22 7JH
Tel: 01963 440002   **20 B9**
longhazelpark.co.uk
Total Pitches: 46 (C, CV & T)

Longnor Wood Holiday Park
Newtown, Longnor, Nr Buxton
SK17 0NG
Tel: 01298 83648   **71 K2**
longnorwood.co.uk
Total Pitches: 47 (C, CV & T)

Manor Wood Country Caravan Park
Manor Wood, Coddington, Chester
CH3 9EN
Tel: 01829 782990   **69 M4**
cheshire-caravan-sites.co.uk
Total Pitches: 45 (C, CV & T)

Marsh House Holiday Park
Marsh House Farm, Carnforth, Lancashire
LA5 9JA
Tel: 01524 732854   **95 K6**
holgates.co.uk/our-parks/
marsh-house
Total Pitches: 74 (C & CV)

Marton Mere Holiday Village
Mythop Road, Blackpool
FY4 4XN
Tel: 01253 767544   **88 C4**
haven.com/martonmere
Total Pitches: 82 (C & CV)

Mayfield Park
Cheltenham Road, Cirencester
GL7 7BH
Tel: 01285 831301   **33 K3**
mayfieldpark.co.uk
Total Pitches: 105 (C, CV & T)

Meadow Lakes Holiday Park
Hewas Water, St Austell, Cornwall
PL26 7JG
Tel: 01726 882540   **3 P4**
meadow-lakes.co.uk
Total Pitches: 190 (C, CV & T)

Meadowbank Holidays
Stour Way, Christchurch
BH23 2PQ
Tel: 01202 483597   **13 K6**
meadowbank-holidays.co.uk
Total Pitches: 41 (C & CV)

Mena Farm: Touring, Camping, Glamping
Bodmin, Lanivet
PL30 5HW
Tel: 01208 831845   **4 G9**
menafarm.co.uk
Total Pitches: 25 (C, CV & T)

Middlewood Farm Holiday Park
Middlewood Lane, Fylingthorpe, Robin Hood's Bay, Whitby
YO22 4UF
Tel: 01947 880414   **105 P10**
middlewoodfarm.com
Total Pitches: 100 (C, CV & T)

Mill Farm C & C Park
Fiddington, Bridgwater, Somerset
TA5 1JQ
Tel: 01278 732286   **18 H6**
millfarm.biz
Total Pitches: 275 (C, CV & T)

Mill Park Touring C & C Park
Mill Lane, Berrynarbor, Ilfracombe, Devon
EX34 9SH
Tel: 01271 882647   **17 K2**
millpark.com
Total Pitches: 125 (C, CV & T)

Minnows Touring Park
Holbrook Lane, Sampford Peverell
EX16 7EN
Tel: 01884 821770   **18 D11**
minnowstouringpark.co.uk
Total Pitches: 59 (C, CV & T)

Monkey Tree Holiday Park
Hendra Croft, Scotland Road, Newquay
TR8 5QR
Tel: 01872 572032   **3 L3**
monkeytreeholidaypark.co.uk
Total Pitches: 700 (C, CV & T)

Monkton Wyld Holiday Park
Scott's Lane, Charmouth, Dorset
DT6 6DB
Tel: 01297 631131   **10 G5**
monktonwyld.co.uk
Total Pitches: 155 (C, CV & T)

Moon & Sixpence
Newbourn Road, Waldringfield, Woodbridge
IP12 4PP
Tel: 01473 736650   **53 N2**
moonandsixpence.co.uk
Total Pitches: 50 (C & CV)

Moss Wood Caravan Park
Crimbles Lane, Cockerham
LA2 0ES
Tel: 01524 791041   **95 K11**
mosswood.co.uk
Total Pitches: 25 (C & CV)

Naburn Lock Caravan Park
Naburn
YO19 4RU
Tel: 01904 728697   **98 C11**
naburnlock.co.uk
Total Pitches: 115 (C, CV & T)

New Lodge Farm C & C Site
New Lodge Farm, Bulwick, Corby
NN17 3DU
Tel: 01780 450493   **73 P11**
newlodgefarm.com
Total Pitches: 72 (C, CV & T)

Newberry Valley Park
Woodlands, Combe Martin
EX34 0AT
Tel: 01271 882334   **17 K2**
newberryvalleypark.co.uk
Total Pitches: 110 (C, CV & T)

Newlands Holidays
Charmouth, Bridport
DT6 6RB
Tel: 01297 560259   **10 H6**
newlandsholidays.co.uk
Total Pitches: 240 (C, CV & T)

Ninham Country Holidays
Ninham, Shanklin, Isle of Wight
PO37 7PL
Tel: 01983 864243   **14 G10**
ninham-holidays.co.uk
Total Pitches: 140 (C, CV & T)

Northam Farm Caravan & Touring Park
Brean, Burnham-on-Sea
TA8 2SE
Tel: 01278 751244   **19 K3**
northamfarm.co.uk
Total Pitches: 350 (C, CV & T)

North Morte Farm C & C Park
North Morte Road, Mortehoe, Woolacombe
EX34 7EG
Tel: 01271 870381   **16 H2**
northmortefarm.co.uk
Total Pitches: 180 (C, CV & T)

Oakdown Country Holiday Park
Gatedown Lane, Weston, Sidmouth
EX10 0PT
Tel: 01297 680387   **10 D6**
oakdown.co.uk
Total Pitches: 150 (C, CV & T)

Old Hall Caravan Park
Capernwray, Carnforth
LA6 1AD
Tel: 01524 733276   **95 L6**
oldhallcaravanpark.co.uk
Total Pitches: 38 (C & CV)

Old Oaks Touring & Glamping
Wick Farm, Wick, Glastonbury
BA6 8JS
Tel: 01458 831437   **19 P7**
theoldoaks.co.uk
Total Pitches: 88 (C, CV & T)

Orchard Farm Holiday Village
Stonegate, Hunmanby, Filey, North Yorkshire
YO14 0PU
Tel: 01723 891582   **99 N5**
orchardfarmholidayvillage.co.uk
Total Pitches: 91 (C, CV & T)

Ord House Country Park
East Ord, Berwick-upon-Tweed
TD15 2NS
Tel: 01289 305288   **129 P9**
maguirescountryparks.co.uk
Total Pitches: 79 (C, CV & T)

Otterington Park
Station Farm, South Otterington, Northallerton, North Yorkshire
DL7 9JB
Tel: 01609 780656   **97 N3**
otteringtonpark.com
Total Pitches: 62 (C, CV & T)

Oxon Hall Touring Park
Welshpool Road, Shrewsbury
SY3 5FB
Tel: 01743 340868   **56 H2**
morris-leisure.co.uk
Total Pitches: 105 (C, CV & T)

Park Cliffe C & C Estate
Birks Road, Tower Wood, Windermere
LA23 3PG
Tel: 015395 31344   **94 H2**
parkcliffe.co.uk
Total Pitches: 60 (C, CV & T)

Parkers Farm Holiday Park
Higher Mead Farm, Ashburton, Devon
TQ13 7LJ
Tel: 01364 654869   **7 K4**
parkersfarmholidays.co.uk
Total Pitches: 100 (C, CV & T)

Park Foot Holiday Park
Howtown Road, Pooley Bridge
CA10 2NA
Tel: 017684 86309 **101 N6**
parkfootullswater.co.uk
Total Pitches: 323 (C, CV & T)

Parkland C & C Site
Sorley Green Cross, Kingsbridge
TQ7 4AF
Tel: 01548 852723 **7 J9**
parklandsite.co.uk
Total Pitches: 50 (C, CV & T)

Pebble Bank Caravan Park
Camp Road, Wyke Regis,
Weymouth
DT4 9HF
Tel: 01305 774844 **11 P9**
pebblebank.co.uk
Total Pitches: 40 (C, CV & T)

Perran Sands Holiday Park
Perranporth, Truro
TR6 0AQ
Tel: 01872 573551 **4 B10**
haven.com/perransands
Total Pitches: 341 (C, CV & T)

Petwood Caravan Park
Off Stixwould Road,
Woodhall Spa
LN10 6QH
Tel: 01526 354799 **86 G8**
petwoodcaravanpark.com
Total Pitches: 98 (C, CV & T)

Plough Lane Touring Caravan Site
Plough Lane, Chippenham,
Wiltshire
SN15 5PS
Tel: 01249 750146 **32 H9**
ploughlane.co.uk
Total Pitches: 52 (C & CV)

Polladras Holiday Park
Carleen, Breage, Helston
TR13 9NX
Tel: 01736 762220 **2 G7**
polladrasholidaypark.co.uk
Total Pitches: 39 (C, CV & T)

Polmanter Touring Park
Halsetown, St Ives
TR26 3LX
Tel: 01736 795640 **2 E6**
polmanter.com
Total Pitches: 294 (C, CV & T)

Porthtowan Tourist Park
Mile Hill, Porthtowan, Truro
TR4 8TY
Tel: 01209 890256 **2 H4**
porthtowantouristpark.co.uk
Total Pitches: 80 (C, CV & T)

Primrose Valley Holiday Park
Filey
YO14 9RF
Tel: 01723 513771 **99 N5**
haven.com/primrosevalley
Total Pitches: 35 (C & CV)

Ranch Caravan Park
Station Road, Honeybourne,
Evesham
WR11 7PR
Tel: 01386 830744 **47 M6**
ranch.co.uk
Total Pitches: 120 (C & CV)

Ripley Caravan Park
Knaresborough Road, Ripley,
Harrogate
HG3 3AU
Tel: 01423 770050 **97 L8**
ripleycaravanpark.com
Total Pitches: 60 (C, CV & T)

River Dart Country Park
Holne Park, Ashburton
TQ13 7NP
Tel: 01364 652511 **7 J5**
riverdart.co.uk
Total Pitches: 170 (C, CV & T)

River Valley Holiday Park
London Apprentice, St Austell
PL26 7AP
Tel: 01726 73533 **3 Q3**
rivervalleyholidaypark.co.uk
Total Pitches: 45 (C, CV & T)

Riverside C & C Park
Marsh Lane, North Molton Road,
South Molton
EX36 3HQ
Tel: 01769 579269 **17 N6**
exmoorriverside.co.uk
Total Pitches: 58 (C, CV & T)

Riverside Caravan Park
High Bentham, Lancaster
LA2 7FJ
Tel: 015242 61272 **95 P7**
riversidecaravanpark.co.uk
Total Pitches: 61 (C & CV)

Riverside Meadows Country Caravan Park
Ure Bank Top, Ripon
HG4 1JD
Tel: 01765 602964 **97 M6**
flowerofmay.com
Total Pitches: 80 (C)

Robin Hood C & C Park
Green Dyke Lane, Slingsby
YO62 4AP
Tel: 01653 628391 **98 E6**
robinhoodcaravanpark.co.uk
Total Pitches: 32 (C, CV & T)

Rose Farm Touring & Camping Park
Stepshort, Belton, Nr Great
Yarmouth
NR31 9JS
Tel: 01493 738292 **77 P11**
rosefarmtouringpark.com
Total Pitches: 145 (C, CV & T)

Rosedale Abbey Caravan Park
Rosedale Abbey, Pickering
YO18 8SA
Tel: 01751 417272 **105 K11**
rosedaleabbeycaravanpark.co.uk
Total Pitches: 100 (C, CV & T)

Rudding Holiday Park
Follifoot, Harrogate
HG3 1JH
Tel: 01423 870439 **97 M10**
ruddingholidaypark.co.uk
Total Pitches: 86 (C, CV & T)

Run Cottage Touring Park
Alderton Road, Hollesley,
Woodbridge
IP12 3RQ
Tel: 01394 411309 **53 Q3**
runcottage.co.uk
Total Pitches: 45 (C, CV & T)

Rutland C & C
Park Lane, Greetham, Oakham
LE15 7FN
Tel: 01572 813520 **73 N8**
rutlandcaravanandcamping.co.uk
Total Pitches: 130 (C, CV & T)

St Helens in the Park
Wykeham, Scarborough
YO13 9QD
Tel: 01723 862771 **99 K4**
sthelenscaravanpark.co.uk
Total Pitches: 250 (C, CV & T)

St Ives Bay Beach Resort
73 Loggans Road, Upton
Towans, Hayle
TR27 5BH
Tel: 01736 752274 **2 F6**
stivesbay.co.uk
Total Pitches: 240 (C, CV & T)

Salcombe Regis C & C Park
Salcombe Regis, Sidmouth
EX10 0JH
Tel: 01395 514303 **10 D7**
salcombe-regis.co.uk
Total Pitches: 100 (C, CV & T)

Sand le Mere Holiday Village
Southfield Lane, Tunstall
HU12 0JF
Tel: 01964 670403 **93 P4**
sand-le-mere.co.uk
Total Pitches: 72 (C & CV)

Searles Leisure Resort
South Beach Road, Hunstanton
PE36 5BB
Tel: 01485 534211 **75 N3**
searles.co.uk
Total Pitches: 255 (C, CV & T)

Seaview Holiday Park
Preston, Weymouth
DT3 6DZ
Tel: 01305 832271 **11 Q8**
haven.com/parks/dorset/seaview
Total Pitches: 82 (C, CV & T)

Severn Gorge Park
Bridgnorth Road, Tweedale,
Telford
TF7 4JB
Tel: 01952 684789 **57 N3**
severngorgepark.co.uk
Total Pitches: 12 (C & CV)

Shamba Holidays
East Moors Lane, St Leonards,
Ringwood
BH24 2SB
Tel: 01202 873302 **13 K4**
shambaholidays.co.uk
Total Pitches: 82 (C, CV & T)

Shrubbery Touring Park
Rousdon, Lyme Regis
DT7 3XW
Tel: 01297 442227 **10 F6**
shrubberypark.co.uk
Total Pitches: 120 (C, CV & T)

Silverdale Caravan Park
Middlebarrow Plain, Cove Road,
Silverdale, Nr Carnforth
LA5 0SH
Tel: 01524 701508 **95 K5**
holgates.co.uk
Total Pitches: 80 (C, CV & T)

Skelwith Fold Caravan Park
Ambleside,
Cumbria
LA22 0HX
Tel: 015394 32277 **101 L10**
skelwith.com
Total Pitches: 150 (C & CV)

Skirlington Leisure Park
Driffield, Skipsea
YO25 8SY
Tel: 01262 468213 **99 P10**
skirlington.com
Total Pitches: 280 (C & CV)

Sleningford Watermill Caravan Camping Park
North Stainley,
Ripon
HG4 3HQ
Tel: 01765 635201 **97 L5**
sleningfordwatermill.co.uk
Total Pitches: 150 (C, CV & T)

Somers Wood Caravan Park
Somers Road, Meriden
CV7 7PL
Tel: 01676 522978 **59 K8**
somerswood.co.uk
Total Pitches: 48 (C & CV)

Southfork Caravan Park
Parrett Works, Martock,
Somerset
TA12 6AE
Tel: 01935 825661 **19 M11**
southforkcaravans.co.uk
Total Pitches: 27 (C, CV & T)

South Lytchett Manor C & C Park
Dorchester Road, Lytchett
Minster, Poole
BH16 6JB
Tel: 01202 622577 **12 G6**
southlytchettmanor.co.uk
Total Pitches: 150 (C, CV & T)

South Meadows Caravan Park
South Road, Belford
NE70 7DP
Tel: 01668 213326 **119 M4**
southmeadows.co.uk
Total Pitches: 169 (C, CV & T)

Stanmore Hall Touring Park
Stourbridge Road,
Bridgnorth
WV15 6DT
Tel: 01746 761761 **57 N6**
morris-leisure.co.uk
Total Pitches: 129 (C, CV & T)

Stanwix Park Holiday Centre
Greenrow, Silloth
CA7 4HH
Tel: 016973 32666 **109 P10**
stanwix.com
Total Pitches: 121 (C, CV & T)

Stroud Hill Park
Fen Road, Pidley, St Ives
PE28 3DE
Tel: 01487 741333 **62 D5**
stroudhillpark.co.uk
Total Pitches: 60 (C, CV & T)

Summer Valley Touring Park
Shortlanesend, Truro,
Cornwall
TR4 9DW
Tel: 07933 212643 **3 L4**
summervalley.co.uk
Total Pitches: 55 (C, CV & T)

Sumners Ponds Fishery & Campsite
Chapel Road, Barns Green,
Horsham
RH13 0PR
Tel: 01403 732539 **24 D5**
sumnersponds.co.uk
Total Pitches: 86 (C, CV & T)

Swiss Farm Touring & Camping
Marlow Road,
Henley-on-Thames
RG9 2HY
Tel: 01491 573419 **35 L8**
swissfarmhenley.co.uk
Total Pitches: 140 (C, CV & T)

Tanner Farm Touring C & C Park
Tanner Farm, Goudhurst Road,
Marden
TN12 9ND
Tel: 01622 832399 **26 B3**
tannerfarmpark.co.uk
Total Pitches: 120 (C, CV & T)

Tehidy Holiday Park
Harris Mill, Illogan,
Portreath
TR16 4JQ
Tel: 01209 216489 **2 H5**
tehidy.co.uk
Total Pitches: 18 (C, CV & T)

Tencreek Holiday Park
Polperro Road, Looe
PL13 2JR
Tel: 01503 262447 **5 L11**
dolphinholidays.co.uk
Total Pitches: 254 (C, CV & T)

The Inside Park
Down House Estate,
Blandford Forum,
Dorset
DT11 9AD
Tel: 01258 453719 **12 E4**
theinsidepark.co.uk
Total Pitches: 125 (C & CV)

The Laurels Holiday Park
Padstow Road, Whitecross,
Wadebridge
PL27 7JQ
Tel: 01208 813341 **4 F7**
thelaurelsholidaypark.co.uk
Total Pitches: 30 (C, CV & T)

The Old Brick Kilns
Little Barney Lane, Barney,
Fakenham
NR21 0NL
Tel: 01328 878305 **76 E5**
old-brick-kilns.co.uk
Total Pitches: 65 (C, CV & T)

The Orchards Holiday Caravan Park
Main Road, Newbridge,
Yarmouth,
Isle of Wight
PO41 0TS
Tel: 01983 531331 **14 D9**
orchards-holiday-park.co.uk
Total Pitches: 120 (C, CV & T)

The Quiet Site
Ullswater, Watermillock
CA11 0LS
Tel: 07768 727016 **101 M6**
thequietsite.co.uk
Total Pitches: 100 (C, CV & T)

Thornton's Holt Camping Park
Stragglethorpe Road,
Stragglethorpe,
Radcliffe on Trent
NG12 2JZ
Tel: 0115 933 2125 **72 G3**
thorntons-holt.co.uk
Total Pitches: 155 (C, CV & T)

Thornwick Bay Holiday Village
North Marine Road,
Flamborough
YO15 1AU
Tel: 01262 850569 **99 Q6**
haven.com/parks/yorkshire/thornwick-bay
Total Pitches: 67 (C, CV & T)

Thorpe Park Holiday Centre
Cleethorpes
DN35 0PW
Tel: 01472 813395 **93 P9**
haven.com/thorpepark
Total Pitches: 134 (C, CV & T)

Treago Farm Caravan Site
Crantock, Newquay
TR8 5QS
Tel: 01637 830277 **4 B9**
treagofarm.co.uk
Total Pitches: 90 (C, CV & T)

Treloy Touring Park
Newquay
TR8 4JN
Tel: 01637 872063 **4 D9**
treloy.co.uk
Total Pitches: 223 (C, CV & T)

Trencreek Holiday Park
Hillcrest, Higher Trencreek,
Newquay
TR8 4NS
Tel: 01637 874210 **4 C9**
trencreekholidaypark.co.uk
Total Pitches: 194 (C, CV & T)

Trethem Mill Touring Park
St Just-in-Roseland,
Nr St Mawes, Truro
TR2 5JF
Tel: 01872 580504 **3 M6**
trethem.com
Total Pitches: 84 (C, CV & T)

Trevalgan Touring Park
Trevalgan, St Ives
TR26 3BJ
Tel: 01736 791892 **2 D6**
trevalgantouringpark.co.uk
Total Pitches: 135 (C, CV & T)

Trevarrian Holiday Park
Mawgan Porth, Newquay,
Cornwall
TR8 4AQ
Tel: 01637 860381 **4 D8**
trevarrian.co.uk
Total Pitches: 185 (C, CV & T)

Trevarth Holiday Park
Blackwater, Truro
TR4 8HR
Tel: 01872 560266 **3 J4**
trevarth.co.uk
Total Pitches: 30 (C, CV & T)

Trevedra Farm C & C Site
Sennen, Penzance
TR19 7BE
Tel: 01736 871818 **2 B8**
trevedrafarm.co.uk
Total Pitches: 100 (C, CV & T)

Trevornick
Holywell Bay, Newquay
TR8 5PW
Tel: 01637 830531 **4 B10**
trevornick.co.uk
Total Pitches: 575 (C, CV & T)

Trewan Hall
St Columb Major, Cornwall
TR9 6DB
Tel: 01637 880261 **4 E9**
trewan-hall.co.uk
Total Pitches: 200 (C, CV & T)

Tudor C & C
Shepherds Patch, Slimbridge,
Gloucester
GL2 7BP
Tel: 01453 890483 **32 D4**
tudorcaravanpark.com
Total Pitches: 75 (C, CV & T)

Twitchen House Holiday Park
Mortehoe Station Road,
Mortehoe, Woolacombe
EX34 7ES
Tel: 01271 872302 **16 H3**
woolacombe.com
Total Pitches: 252 (C, CV & T)

Two Mills Touring Park
Yarmouth Road, North Walsham
NR28 9NA
Tel: 01692 405829 **77 K6**
twomills.co.uk
Total Pitches: 81 (C, CV & T)

Ulwell Cottage Caravan Park
Ulwell Cottage, Ulwell, Swanage
BH19 3DG
Tel: 01929 422823 **12 H8**
ulwellcottagepark.co.uk
Total Pitches: 77 (C, CV & T)

Upper Lynstone Caravan Park
Lynstone, Bude
EX23 0LP
Tel: 01288 352017 **16 C10**
upperlynstone.co.uk
Total Pitches: 65 (C, CV & T)

Vale of Pickering Caravan Park
Carr House Farm, Allerston,
Pickering
YO18 7PQ
Tel: 01723 859280 **98 H4**
valeofpickering.co.uk
Total Pitches: 120 (C, CV & T)

Waldegraves Holiday Park
Mersea Island, Colchester
CO5 8SE
Tel: 01206 382898 **52 H9**
waldegraves.co.uk
Total Pitches: 126 (C, CV & T)

Waleswood C &C Park
Delves Lane, Waleswood,
Wales Bar, Wales,
South Yorkshire
S26 5RN
Tel: 07825 125328 **84 G4**
waleswood.co.uk
Total Pitches: 163 (C, CV & T)

Wareham Forest Tourist Park
North Trigon, Wareham
BH20 7NZ
Tel: 01929 551393 **12 E6**
warehamforest.co.uk
Total Pitches: 200 (C, CV & T)

Waren C & C Park
Waren Mill, Bamburgh
NE70 7EE
Tel: 01668 214366 **119 N4**
meadowhead.co.uk/parks/waren
Total Pitches: 150 (C, CV & T)

Warren Farm Holiday Centre
Brean Sands, Brean,
Burnham-on-Sea
TA8 2RP
Tel: 01278 751227 **19 J3**
warrenfarm.co.uk
Total Pitches: 575 (C, CV & T)

Waterfoot Caravan Park
Pooley Bridge, Penrith,
Cumbria
CA11 0JF
Tel: 017684 86302   **101 N6**
waterfootpark.co.uk
Total Pitches: 34 (C, CV & T)

Watergate Bay Touring Park
Watergate Bay, Tregurrian
TR8 4AD
Tel: 01637 860387   **4 D8**
watergatebaytouringpark.co.uk
Total Pitches: 171 (C, CV & T)

Waterrow Touring Park
Wiveliscombe, Taunton
TA4 2AZ
Tel: 01984 623464   **18 E9**
waterrowpark.co.uk
Total Pitches: 42 (C, CV & T)

Wayfarers C & C Park
Relubbus Lane, St Hilary,
Penzance
TR20 9EF
Tel: 01736 763326   **2 F7**
wayfarerspark.co.uk
Total Pitches: 32 (C, CV & T)

Wells Touring Park
Haybridge, Wells
BA5 1AJ
Tel: 01749 676869   **19 P5**
wellstouringpark.co.uk
Total Pitches: 56 (C & CV)

Westbrook Park
Little Hereford, Herefordshire
SY8 4AU
Tel: 01584 711280   **57 J11**
westbrookpark.co.uk
Total Pitches: 53 (C, CV & T)

Wheathill Touring Park
Wheathill, Bridgnorth
WV16 6QT
Tel: 01584 823456   **57 L8**
wheathillpark.co.uk
Total Pitches: 50 (C & CV)

Whitefield Forest Touring Park
Brading Road, Ryde,
Isle of Wight
PO33 1QL
Tel: 01983 617069   **14 H9**
whitefieldforest.co.uk
Total Pitches: 90 (C, CV & T)

Whitehill Country Park
Stoke Road, Paignton, Devon
TQ4 7PF
Tel: 01803 782338   **7 M7**
whitehill-park.co.uk
Total Pitches: 260 (C, CV & T)

Whitemead Caravan Park
East Burton Road, Wool
BH20 6HG
Tel: 01929 462241   **12 D7**
whitemeadcaravanpark.co.uk
Total Pitches: 105 (C, CV & T)

**Widdicombe Farm
Touring Park**
Marldon, Paignton, Devon
TQ3 1ST
Tel: 01803 558325   **7 M6**
widdicombefarm.co.uk
Total Pitches: 180 (C, CV & T)

**Willowbank Holiday Home
& Touring Park**
Coastal Road, Ainsdale,
Southport
PR8 3ST
Tel: 01704 571566   **88 C8**
willowbankcp.co.uk
Total Pitches: 87 (C & CV)

Willow Valley Holiday Park
Bush, Bude, Cornwall
EX23 9LB
Tel: 01288 353104   **16 C10**
willowvalley.co.uk
Total Pitches: 41 (C, CV & T)

Wilson House Holiday Park
Lancaster Road, Out Rawcliffe,
Preston, Lancashire
PR3 6BN
Tel: 07807 560685   **88 E2**
whhp.co.uk
Total Pitches: 40 (C & CV)

Wolds View Country Park
115 Brigg Road, Caistor
LN7 6RX
Tel: 01472 851099   **93 K10**
woldsviewtouringpark.co.uk
Total Pitches: 60 (C, CV & T)

Wooda Farm Holiday Park
Poughill, Bude
EX23 9HJ
Tel: 01288 352069   **16 C10**
wooda.co.uk
Total Pitches: 200 (C, CV & T)

Woodclose Caravan Park
High Casterton,
Kirkby Lonsdale
LA6 2SE
Tel: 01524 271597   **95 N5**
woodclosepark.com
Total Pitches: 22 (C & CV)

Woodhall Country Park
Stixwold Road, Woodhall Spa
LN10 6UJ
Tel: 01526 353710   **86 G8**
woodhallcountrypark.co.uk
Total Pitches: 141 (C, CV & T)

**Woodland Springs Adult
Touring Park**
Venton, Drewsteignton
EX6 6PG
Tel: 01647 231648   **8 G6**
woodlandsprings.co.uk
Total Pitches: 93 (C, CV & T)

Woodlands Grove C & C Park
Blackawton, Dartmouth
TQ9 7DQ
Tel: 01803 712598   **7 L8**
woodlandsgrove.com
Total Pitches: 350 (C, CV & T)

Woodovis Park
Gulworthy, Tavistock
PL19 8NY
Tel: 01822 832968   **6 C4**
woodovis.com
Total Pitches: 50 (C, CV & T)

**Yeatheridge Farm
Caravan Park**
East Worlington, Crediton,
Devon
EX17 4TN
Tel: 01884 860330   **9 J2**
yeatheridge.co.uk
Total Pitches: 103 (C, CV & T)

York Caravan Park
Stockton Lane, York,
North Yorkshire
YO32 9UB
Tel: 01904 424222   **98 C10**
yorkcaravanpark.com
Total Pitches: 55 (C & CV)

York Meadows Caravan Park
York Road, Sheriff Hutton, York,
North Yorkshire
YO60 6QP
Tel: 01347 878508   **98 C7**
yorkmeadowscaravanpark.com
Total Pitches: 45 (C, CV & T)

SCOTLAND

Auchenlarie Holiday Park
Gatehouse of Fleet
DG7 2EX
Tel: 01556 506200   **107 P7**
swalwellholidaygroup.co.uk
Total Pitches: 49 (C, CV & T)

Banff Links Caravan Park
Inverboyndie, Banff,
Aberdeenshire
AB45 2JJ
Tel: 01261 812228   **158 G5**
banfflinkscaravanpark.co.uk
Total Pitches: 93 (C, CV & T)

Beecraigs C & C Site
Beecraigs Country Park,
The Visitor Centre, Linlithgow
EH49 6PL
Tel: 01506 284516   **127 J3**
westlothian.gov.uk/
stay-at-beecraigs
Total Pitches: 36 (C, CV & T)

Belhaven Bay C & C Park
Belhaven Bay, Dunbar,
East Lothian
EH42 1TS
Tel: 01368 865956   **128 H4**
meadowhead.co.uk
Total Pitches: 52 (C, CV & T)

Blair Castle Caravan Park
Blair Atholl, Pitlochry
PH18 5SR
Tel: 01796 481263   **141 L4**
blaircastlecaravanpark.co.uk
Total Pitches: 184 (C, CV & T)

Brighouse Bay Holiday Park
Brighouse Bay, Borgue,
Kirkcudbright
DG6 4TS
Tel: 01557 870267   **108 D11**
gillespie-leisure.co.uk
Total Pitches: 190 (C, CV & T)

Cairnsmill Holiday Park
Largo Road, St Andrews
KY16 8NN
Tel: 01334 473604   **135 M5**
cairnsmill.co.uk
Total Pitches: 62 (C, CV & T)

Craig Tara Holiday Park
Ayr
KA7 4LB
Tel: 0800 975 7579   **114 F4**
haven.com/craigtara
Total Pitches: 44 (C & CV)

**Craigtoun Meadows
Holiday Park**
Mount Melville, St Andrews
KY16 8PQ
Tel: 01334 475959   **135 M4**
craigtounmeadows.co.uk
Total Pitches: 56 (C, CV & T)

Faskally Caravan Park
Pitlochry
PH16 5LA
Tel: 01796 472007   **141 M6**
faskally.co.uk
Total Pitches: 300 (C, CV & T)

Glenearly Caravan Park
Dalbeattie,
Dumfries & Galloway
DG5 4NE
Tel: 01556 611393   **108 H8**
glenearlycaravanpark.co.uk
Total Pitches: 39 (C, CV & T)

Glen Nevis C & C Park
Glen Nevis, Fort William
PH33 6SX
Tel: 01397 702191   **139 L3**
glen-nevis.co.uk
Total Pitches: 380 (C, CV & T)

Hoddom Castle Caravan Park
Hoddom, Lockerbie
DG11 1AS
Tel: 01576 300251   **110 C6**
hoddomcastle.co.uk
Total Pitches: 200 (C, CV & T)

Huntly Castle Caravan Park
The Meadow, Huntly
AB54 4UJ
Tel: 01466 794999   **158 D9**
huntlycastle.co.uk
Total Pitches: 90 (C, CV & T)

Invercoe C & C Park
Ballachulish, Glencoe
PH49 4HP
Tel: 01855 811210   **139 K6**
invercoe.co.uk
Total Pitches: 60 (C, CV & T)

Linwater Caravan Park
West Clifton, East Calder
EH53 0HT
Tel: 0131 333 3326   **127 L4**
linwater.co.uk
Total Pitches: 60 (C, CV & T)

Milton of Fonab Caravan Park
Bridge Road, Pitlochry
PH16 5NA
Tel: 01796 472882   **141 M6**
fonab.co.uk
Total Pitches: 154 (C, CV & T)

Sands of Luce Holiday Park
Sands of Luce, Sandhead,
Stranraer
DG9 9JN
Tel: 01776 830456   **106 F7**
sandsofluce.com
Total Pitches: 80 (C, CV & T)

**Seal Shore Camping and
Touring Site**
Kildonan, Isle of Arran,
North Ayrshire
KA27 8SE
Tel: 01770 820320   **121 K7**
campingarran.com
Total Pitches: 43 (C, CV & T)

Seaward Holiday Park
Dhoon Bay, Kirkudbright
DG6 4TJ
Tel: 01557 870267   **108 E11**
gillespie-leisure.co.uk
Total Pitches: 25 (C, CV & T)

Seton Sands Holiday Village
Longniddry
EH32 0QF
Tel: 01875 813333   **128 C4**
haven.com/setonsands
Total Pitches: 40 (C & CV)

Shieling Holidays Mull
Craignure, Isle of Mull,
Argyll & Bute
PA65 6AY
Tel: 01680 812496   **138 C10**
shielingholidays.co.uk
Total Pitches: 90 (C, CV & T)

Silver Sands Holiday Park
Covesea, West Beach,
Lossiemouth
IV31 6SP
Tel: 01343 813262   **157 N3**
silver-sands.co.uk
Total Pitches: 111 (C, CV & T)

Thurston Manor Leisure Park
Innerwick, Dunbar
EH42 1SA
Tel: 01368 840643   **129 J5**
thurstonmanor.co.uk
Total Pitches: 120 (C & CV)

Witches Craig C & C Park
Blairlogie, Stirling
FK9 5PX
Tel: 01786 474947   **133 N8**
witchescraig.co.uk
Total Pitches: 60 (C, CV & T)

WALES

**Bron Derw Touring
Caravan Park**
Llanrwst
LL26 0YT
Tel: 01492 640494   **67 Q2**
bronderw-wales.co.uk
Total Pitches: 48 (C & CV)

**Caerfai Bay Caravan
& Tent Park**
Caerfai Bay, St Davids,
Haverfordwest
SA62 6QT
Tel: 01437 720274   **40 E6**
caerfaibay.co.uk
Total Pitches: 106 (C, CV & T)

Cenarth Falls Resort Limited
Cenarth,
Newcastle Emlyn
SA38 9JS
Tel: 01239 710345   **41 Q2**
cenarth-holipark.co.uk
Total Pitches: 30 (C, CV & T)

Commonwood Leisure
Buck Road, Holt,
Wrexham
LL13 9TF
Tel: 01978 664547   **69 L4**
commonwoodleisure.com/
cabins-tents
Total Pitches: 5 (C & CV)

Daisy Bank Caravan Park
Snead, Montgomery
SY15 6EB
Tel: 01588 620471   **56 E6**
daisy-bank.co.uk
Total Pitches: 64 (C, CV & T)

Dinlle Caravan Park
Dinas Dinlle,
Caernarfon
LL54 5TW
Tel: 01286 830324   **66 G3**
thornleyleisure.co.uk
Total Pitches: 175 (C, CV & T)

Eisteddfa
Eisteddfa Lodge, Pentrefelin,
Criccieth
LL52 0PT
Tel: 01766 522696   **67 J7**
eisteddfapark.co.uk
Total Pitches: 100 (C, CV & T)

Fforest Fields C & C Park
Hundred House, Builth Wells
LD1 5RT
Tel: 01982 570406   **44 G4**
fforestfields.co.uk
Total Pitches: 120 (C, CV & T)

Fishguard Bay Resort
Garn Gelli, Fishguard
SA65 9ET
Tel: 01348 811415   **41 J3**
fishguardbay.com
Total Pitches: 50 (C, CV & T)

Greenacres Holiday Park
Black Rock Sands,
Morfa Bychan, Porthmadog
LL49 9YF
Tel: 01766 512781   **67 J7**
haven.com/greenacres
Total Pitches: 39 (C & CV)

Hafan y Môr Holiday Park
Pwllheli
LL53 6HJ
Tel: 01758 612112   **66 G7**
haven.com/hafanymor
Total Pitches: 75 (C & CV)

**Hendre Mynach
Touring C & C Park**
Llanaber Road, Barmouth
LL42 1YR
Tel: 01341 280262   **67 L11**
hendremynach.co.uk
Total Pitches: 240 (C, CV & T)

Home Farm Caravan Park
Marian-glas,
Isle of Anglesey
LL73 8PH
Tel: 01248 410614   **78 H8**
homefarm-anglesey.co.uk
Total Pitches: 102 (C, CV & T)

Islawrffordd Caravan Park
Talybont, Barmouth
LL43 2AQ
Tel: 01341 247269   **67 K10**
islawrffordd.co.uk
Total Pitches: 105 (C & CV)

Kiln Park Holiday Centre
Marsh Road, Tenby
SA70 8RB
Tel: 01834 844121   **41 M10**
haven.com/kilnpark
Total Pitches: 146 (C, CV & T)

Pencelli Castle C & C Park
Pencelli, Brecon
LD3 7LX
Tel: 01874 665451   **44 F10**
pencelli-castle.com
Total Pitches: 80 (C, CV & T)

Penisar Mynydd Caravan Park
Caerwys Road, Rhuallt,
St Asaph
LL17 0TY
Tel: 01745 582227   **80 F9**
penisarmynydd.co.uk
Total Pitches: 71 (C, CV & T)

Plassey Holiday Park
The Plassey, Eyton,
Wrexham
LL13 0SP
Tel: 01978 780277   **69 L5**
plassey.com
Total Pitches: 90 (C, CV & T)

Pont Kemys C & C Park
Chainbridge, Abergavenny
NP7 9DS
Tel: 01873 880688   **31 K3**
pontkemys.com
Total Pitches: 65 (C, CV & T)

**Presthaven Beach
Holiday Park**
Gronant, Prestatyn
LL19 9TT
Tel: 01745 856471   **80 F8**
haven.com/presthaven
Total Pitches: 50 (C & CV)

Red Kite Touring Park
Van Road, Llanidloes
SY18 6NG
Tel: 01686 412122   **55 L7**
redkitetouringpark.co.uk
Total Pitches: 66 (C & CV)

Riverside Camping
Seiont Nurseries, Pont Rug,
Caernarfon
LL55 2BB
Tel: 01286 678781   **67 J2**
riversidecamping.co.uk
Total Pitches: 73 (C, CV & T)

**The Trotting Mare
Caravan Park**
Overton, Wrexham
LL13 0LE
Tel: 01978 711963   **69 L7**
thetrottingmare.co.uk
Total Pitches: 54 (C, CV & T)

Trawsdir Touring C & C Park
Llanaber,
Barmouth
LL42 1RR
Tel: 01341 280999   **67 K11**
barmouthholidays.co.uk
Total Pitches: 70 (C, CV & T)

Tyddyn Isaf Caravan Park
Lligwy Bay, Dulas,
Isle of Anglesey
LL70 9PQ
Tel: 01248 410203   **78 H7**
tyddynisaf.co.uk
Total Pitches: 80 (C, CV & T)

**Wern Farm Caravan &
Glamping Park**
Ty'n-y-Groes,
Conwy
LL32 8SY
Tel: 01492 650257   **79 P10**
wernfarmcaravanpark.co.uk
Total Pitches: 24 (C & CV)

White Tower Holiday Park
Llandwrog,
Caernarfon
LL54 5UH
Tel: 01286 830649   **66 H3**
whitetowerpark.co.uk
Total Pitches: 52 (C & CV)

CHANNEL ISLANDS

La Bailloterie Camping
Bailloterie Lane, Vale,
Guernsey
GY3 5HA
Tel: 01481 243636   **10 c1**
campinginguernsey.com
Total Pitches: 100 (C, CV & T)

Traffic signs

Signs giving orders

Signs with red circles are mostly prohibitive. Plates below signs qualify their message

Entry to 20mph zone

End of 20mph zone

Maximum speed

National speed limit applies

School crossing patrol

Stop and give way

Give way to traffic on major road

Manually operated temporary STOP and GO signs

No entry for vehicular traffic

No vehicles except bicycles being pushed

No cycling

No motor vehicles

No buses (over 8 passenger seats)

No overtaking

No towed caravans

No vehicles carrying explosives

No vehicle or combination of vehicles over length shown

No vehicles over height shown

No vehicles over width shown

Give priority to vehicles from opposite direction

No right turn

No left turn

No U-turns

No goods vehicles over maximum gross weight shown (in tonnes) except for loading and unloading

No vehicles over maximum gross weight shown (in tonnes)

Parking restricted to permit holders

No stopping during period indicated except for buses

No stopping during times shown except for as long as necessary to set down or pick up passengers

No waiting

No stopping (Clearway)

Signs with blue circles but no red border mostly give positive instruction.

Ahead only

Turn left ahead (right if symbol reversed)

Turn left (right if symbol reversed)

Keep left (right if symbol reversed)

Vehicles may pass either side to reach same destination

Mini-roundabout (roundabout circulation - give way to vehicles from the immediate right)

Route to be used by pedal cycles only

Segregated pedal cycle and pedestrian route

Minimum speed

End of minimum speed

Buses and cycles only

Trams only

Pedestrian crossing point over tramway

One-way traffic (note: compare circular 'Ahead only' sign)

With-flow bus and cycle lane

Contraflow bus lane

With-flow pedal cycle lane

Warning signs

Mostly triangular

Distance to 'STOP' line ahead

Dual carriageway ends

Road narrows on right (left if symbol reversed)

Road narrows on both sides

Distance to 'Give Way' line ahead

Crossroads

Junction on bend ahead

T-junction with priority over vehicles from the right

Staggered junction

Traffic merging from left ahead

The priority through route is indicated by the broader line.

Double bend first to left (symbol may be reversed)

Bend to the right (or left if symbol reversed)

Roundabout

Uneven road

Plate below some signs

Two-way traffic crosses one-way road

Two-way traffic straight ahead

Opening or swing bridge ahead

Low-flying aircraft or sudden aircraft noise

Falling or fallen rocks

Traffic signals not in use

Traffic signals

Slippery road

Steep hill downwards

Steep hill upwards

Gradients may be shown as a ratio i.e. 20% = 1:5

Tunnel ahead

Trams crossing ahead

Level crossing with barrier or gate ahead

Level crossing without barrier or gate ahead

Level crossing without barrier

School crossing patrol ahead (some signs have amber lights which flash when crossings are in use)

Frail (or blind or disabled if shown) pedestrians likely to cross road ahead

No footway for 400 yds
Pedestrians in road ahead

Zebra crossing

Safe height 16ʹ6″ (5.0 m)
Overhead electric cable; plate indicates maximum height of vehicles which can pass safely

Available width of headroom indicated

Sharp deviation of route to left (or right if chevrons reversed)

STOP when lights show
Light signals ahead at level crossing, airfield or bridge

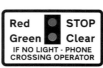
Red ● **STOP**
Green ● **Clear**
IF NO LIGHT - PHONE CROSSING OPERATOR
Minature warning lights at level crossings

Cattle

Wild animals

Wild horses or ponies

Accompanied horses or ponies

Cycle route ahead

Ice
Risk of ice

Queues likely
Traffic queues likely ahead

Humps for ½ mile
Distance over which road humps extend

Hidden dip
Other danger; plate indicates nature of danger

Soft verges for 2 miles
Soft verges

Side winds

Hump bridge

Ford
Worded warning sign

Quayside or river bank

Risk of grounding

Direction signs

Mostly rectangular
Signs on motorways - blue backgrounds

At a junction leading directly into a motorway (junction number may be shown on a black background)

On approaches to junctions (junction number on black background)

Route confirmatory sign after junction

Downward pointing arrows mean 'Get in lane'
The left-hand lane leads to a different destination from the other lanes.

The panel with the inclined arrow indicates the destinations which can be reached by leaving the motorway at the next junction.

Signs on primary routes - green backgrounds

On approaches to junctions

At the junction

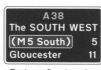
Route confirmatory sign after the junction

On approaches to junctions

On approaches to junction in Wales (bilingual)

Blue panels indicate that the motorway starts at the junction ahead.
Motorways shown in brackets can also be reached along the route indicated.
White panels indicate local or non-primary routes leading from the junction ahead.
Brown panels show the route to tourist attractions.
The name of the junction may be shown at the top of the sign.
The aircraft symbol indicates the route to an airport.
A symbol may be included to warn of a hazard or restriction along that route.

Signs on non-primary and local routes - black borders

On approaches to junctions

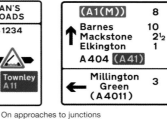

At the junction

Direction to toilets with access for the disabled

Green panels indicate that the primary route starts at the junction ahead.
Route numbers on a blue background show the direction to a motorway.
Route numbers on a green background show the direction to a primary route.

Emergency diversion routes

In an emergency it may be necessary to close a section of motorway or other main road to traffic, so a temporary sign may advise drivers to follow a diversion route. To help drivers navigate the route, black symbols on yellow patches may be permanently displayed on existing direction signs, including motorway signs. Symbols may also be used on separate signs with yellow backgrounds.

Note: The signs shown in this road atlas are those most commonly in use and are not all drawn to the same scale. In Scotland and Wales bilingual versions of some signs are used, showing both English and Gaelic or Welsh spellings. Some older designs of signs may still be seen on the roads. A comprehensive explanation of the signing system illustrating the vast majority of road signs can be found in the AA's handbook *Know Your Road Signs*. Where there is a reference to a rule number, this refers to *The Highway Code*.

Restricted junctions

Motorway and primary route junctions which have access or exit restrictions are shown on the map pages thus:

M1 London - Leeds

Northbound
Access only from A1
(northbound)

Southbound
Exit only to A1
(southbound)

Northbound
Access only from A41
(northbound)

Southbound
Exit only to A41
(southbound)

Northbound
Access only from M25
(no link from A405)

Southbound
Exit only to M25
(no link from A405)

Northbound
Access only from A414

Southbound
Exit only to A414

Northbound
Exit only to M45

Southbound
Access only from M45

Northbound
Exit only to M6
(northbound)

Southbound
Exit only to A14
(southbound)

Northbound
Exit only, no access

Southbound
Access only, no exit

Northbound
No exit, access only

Southbound
Access only from
A50 (eastbound)

Northbound
Exit only, no access

Southbound
Access only, no exit

Northbound
Exit only to M621

Southbound
Access only from M621

Northbound
Exit only to A1(M)
(northbound)

Southbound
Access only from A1(M)
(southbound)

M2 Rochester - Faversham

Westbound
No exit to A2
(eastbound)

Eastbound
No access from A2
(westbound)

M3 Sunbury - Southampton

Northeastbound
Access only from A303,
no exit

Southwestbound
Exit only to A303,
no access

Northbound
Exit only, no access

Southbound
Access only, no exit

Northeastbound
Access from M27 only,
no exit

Southwestbound
No access to M27
(westbound)

M4 London - South Wales

For junctions 1 & 2 see London district map
on pages 178–181

Westbound
Exit only to M48

Eastbound
Access only from M48

Westbound
Access only from M48

Eastbound
Exit only to M48

Westbound
Exit only, no access

Eastbound
Access only, no exit

Westbound
Exit only, no access

Eastbound
Access only, no exit

Westbound
Exit only to A48(M)

Eastbound
Access only from A48(M)

Westbound
Exit only, no access

Eastbound
No restriction

Westbound
Access only, no exit

Eastbound
No access or exit

M5 Birmingham - Exeter

Northeastbound
Access only, no exit

Southwestbound
Exit only, no access

Northeastbound
Access only from A417
(westbound)

Southwestbound
Exit only to A417
(eastbound)

Northeastbound
Exit only to M49

Southwestbound
Access only from M49

Northeastbound
No access, exit only

Southwestbound
No exit, access only

M6 Toll Motorway

See M6 Toll motorway map on page *XXIII*

M6 Rugby - Carlisle

Northbound
Exit only to M6 Toll

Southbound
Access only from M6 Toll

Northbound
Exit only to M42
(southbound) and A446

Southbound
Exit only to A446

Northbound
Access only from M42
(southbound)

Southbound
Exit only to M42

Northbound
Exit only, no access

Southbound
Access only, no exit

Northbound
Exit only to M54

Southbound
Access only from M54

Northbound
Access only from M6 Toll

Southbound
Exit only to M6 Toll

Westbound
Exit only to A483

Eastbound
Access only from A483

Northbound
No restriction

Southbound
Access only from M56
(eastbound)

Northbound
Exit only to M56
(westbound)

Southbound
Access only from M56
(eastbound)

Northbound
Access only, no exit

Southbound
Exit only, no access

Northbound
Exit only, no access

Southbound
Access only, no exit

Northbound
Access only from M61

Southbound
Exit only to M61

Northbound
Exit only, no access

Southbound
Access only, no exit

Northbound
Exit only, no access

Southbound
Access only, no exit

M8 Edinburgh - Bishopton

For junctions 7A to 29A see Glasgow district
map on pages 176–177

Westbound
Exit only, no access

Eastbound
Access only, no exit

Westbound
Access only, no exit

Eastbound
Exit only, no access

Westbound
Access only, no exit

Eastbound
Exit only, no access

M9 Edinburgh - Dunblane

Northwestbound
Access only, no exit

Southeastbound
Exit only, no access

Northwestbound
Exit only, no access

Southeastbound
Access only, no exit

Northwestbound
Access only, no exit

Southeastbound
Exit only to A905

Northwestbound
Exit only to M876
(southwestbound)

Southeastbound
Access only from M876
(northeastbound)

M11 London - Cambridge

Northbound
Access only from A406
(eastbound)

Southbound
Exit only to A406

Northbound
Exit only, no access

Southbound
Access only, no exit

Northbound
Exit only, no access

Southbound
No direct access,
use jct 8

Northbound
Exit only to A11

Southbound
Access only from A11

Northbound
Exit only, no access

Southbound
Access only, no exit

Northbound
Exit only, no access

Southbound
Access only, no exit

M20 Swanley - Folkestone

Northwestbound
Staggered junction; follow
signs - access only

Southeastbound
Staggered junction; follow
signs - exit only

Northwestbound
Exit only to M26
(westbound)

Southeastbound
Access only from M26
(eastbound)

Northwestbound
Access only from A20

Southeastbound
For access follow signs -
exit only to A20

Northwestbound
No restriction

Southeastbound
For exit follow signs

Westbound
Access only, no exit

Eastbound
Exit only, no access

Northwestbound
Access only, no exit

Southeastbound
Exit only, no access

M23 Hooley - Crawley

Northbound
Exit only to A23
(northbound)

Southbound
Access only from A23
(southbound)

Northbound
Access only, no exit

Southbound
Exit only, no access

M25 London Orbital

See M25 London Orbital motorway map on
page *XXII*

M26 Sevenoaks - Wrotham

Westbound
Exit only to clockwise
M25 (westbound)

Eastbound
Access only from
anticlockwise M25
(eastbound)

Westbound
Access only from M20
(northwestbound)

Eastbound
Exit only to M20
(southeastbound)

M27 Cadnam - Portsmouth

Westbound
Staggered junction; follow
signs - access only from
M3 (southbound). Exit
only to M3 (northbound)

Eastbound
Staggered junction; follow
signs - access only from
M3 (southbound). Exit
only to M3 (northbound)

Westbound
Exit only, no access

Eastbound
Access only, no exit

Westbound
Staggered junction; follow
signs - exit only to M275
(southbound)

Eastbound
Staggered junction; follow
signs - access only from
M275 (northbound)

M40 London - Birmingham

Northwestbound
Exit only, no access

Southeastbound
Access only, no exit

Northwestbound
Exit only, no access

Southeastbound
Access only, no exit

Northwestbound
Exit only to M40/A40

Southeastbound
Access only from
M40/A40

Northwestbound
Exit only, no access

Southeastbound
Access only, no exit

Northwestbound
Exit only, no access

Southeastbound
Exit only, no access

Northwestbound
Access only, no exit

Southeastbound
Exit only, no access

M42 Bromsgrove - Measham

See Birmingham district map on pages
174–175

M45 Coventry - M1

Westbound
Access only from A45
(northbound)

Eastbound
Exit only, no access

Westbound
Access only from M1
(northbound)

Eastbound
Exit only to M1
(southbound)

M48 Chepstow

Westbound
Access only from M4
(westbound)

Eastbound
Exit only to M4
(eastbound)

Westbound
No exit to M4 (eastbound)

Eastbound
No access from M4
(westbound)

M53 Mersey Tunnel - Chester

Northbound
Access only from M56
(westbound). Exit only to
M56 (eastbound)

Southbound
Access only from M56
(westbound). Exit only to
M56 (eastbound)

M54 Telford - Birmingham

Westbound
Access only from M6
(northbound)

Eastbound
Exit only to M6
(southbound)

M56 Chester - Manchester

For junctions 1,2,3,4 & 7 see Manchester
district map on pages 182–183

Westbound
Access only, no exit

Eastbound
No access or exit

Westbound
No exit to M6
(southbound)

Eastbound
No access from M6
(northbound)

Westbound
Exit only to M53

Eastbound
Access only from M53

Westbound
No access or exit

Eastbound
No restriction

M57 Liverpool Outer Ring Road

Northwestbound
Access only, no exit

Southeastbound
Exit only, no access

Northwestbound
Access only from A580
(westbound)

Southeastbound
Exit only, no access

M60 Manchester Orbital

See Manchester district map on pages
182–183

M61 Manchester - Preston

Northwestbound
No access or exit

Southeastbound
Exit only, no access

Northwestbound
Exit only to M6
(northbound)

Southeastbound
Access only from M6
(southbound)

M62 Liverpool - Kingston upon Hull

Westbound
Access only, no exit

Eastbound
Exit only, no access

Westbound
No access to A1(M) (southbound)

Eastbound
No restriction

M65 Preston - Colne

Northeastbound
Exit only, no access

Southwestbound
Access only, no exit

Northeastbound
Access only, no exit

Southwestbound
Exit only, no access

M66 Bury

Northbound
Exit only to A56 (northbound)

Southbound
Access only from A56 (southbound)

Northbound
Exit only, no access

Southbound
Access only, no exit

M67 Hyde Bypass

Westbound
Access only, no exit

Eastbound
Exit only, no access

Westbound
Exit only, no access

Eastbound
Access only, no exit

M69 Coventry - Leicester

Northbound
Access only, no exit

Southbound
Exit only, no access

M73 East of Glasgow

Northbound
No exit to A74 and A721

Southbound
No exit to A74 and A721

Northbound
No access from or exit to A89. No access from M8 (eastbound)

Southbound
No access from or exit to A89. No exit to M8 (westbound)

M74 and A74(M) Glasgow - Gretna

Northbound
Exit only, no access

Southbound
Access only, no exit

Northbound
Access only, no exit

Southbound
Exit only, no access

Northbound
No access from A74 and A721

Southbound
Access only, no exit to A74 and A721

Northbound
Access only, no exit

Southbound
Exit only, no access

Northbound
No access or exit

Southbound
Exit only, no access

Northbound
No restriction

Southbound
Access only, no exit

Northbound
Access only, no exit

Southbound
Exit only, no access

Northbound
Exit only, no access

Southbound
Access only, no exit

Northbound
Exit only, no access

Southbound
Access only, no exit

M77 Glasgow - Kilmarnock

Northbound
No exit to M8 (westbound)

Southbound
No access from M8 (eastbound)

Northbound
Access only, no exit

Southbound
Exit only, no access

Northbound
Access only, no exit

Southbound
Exit only, no access

Northbound
Access only, no exit

Southbound
No restriction

Northbound
Exit only, no access

Southbound
Exit only, no access

M80 Glasgow - Stirling

For junctions 1 & 4 see Glasgow district map on pages 176–177

Northbound
Exit only, no access

Southbound
Access only, no exit

Northbound
Access only, no exit

Southbound
Exit only, no access

Northbound
Exit only to M876 (northeastbound)

Southbound
Access only from M876 (southwestbound)

M90 Edinburgh - Perth

Northbound
No exit, access only

Southbound
Exit only to A90 (eastbound)

Northbound
Exit only to A92 (eastbound)

Southbound
Access only from A92 (westbound)

Northbound
Access only, no exit

Southbound
Exit only, no access

Northbound
Access only, no exit

Southbound
Access only, no exit

Northbound
No access from A912
No exit to A912 (southbound)

Southbound
No access from A912 (northbound).
No exit to A912

M180 Doncaster - Grimsby

Westbound
Access only, no exit

Eastbound
Exit only, no access

M606 Bradford Spur

Northbound
Exit only, no access

Southbound
No restriction

M621 Leeds - M1

Clockwise
Access only, no exit

Anticlockwise
Exit only, no access

Clockwise
No exit or access

Anticlockwise
No restriction

Clockwise
Access only, no exit

Anticlockwise
Exit only, no access

Clockwise
Exit only, no access

Anticlockwise
Access only, no exit

Clockwise
Exit only to M1 (southbound)

Anticlockwise
Access only from M1 (northbound)

M876 Bonnybridge - Kincardine Bridge

Northeastbound
Access only from M80 (northbound)

Southwestbound
Exit only to M80 (southbound)

Northeastbound
Exit only to M9 (eastbound)

Southwestbound
Access only from M9 (westbound)

A1(M) South Mimms - Baldock

Northbound
Exit only, no access

Southbound
Access only, no exit

Northbound
No restriction

Southbound
Exit only, no access

Northbound
Access only, no exit

Southbound
No access or exit

A1(M) Pontefract - Bedale

Northbound
No access to M62
(eastbound)

Southbound
No restriction

Northbound
Access only from M1
(northbound)

Southbound
Exit only to M1
(southbound)

A1(M) Scotch Corner - Newcastle upon Tyne

Northbound
Exit only to A66(M)
(eastbound)

Southbound
Access only from A66(M)
(westbound)

Northbound
No access. Exit only to
A194(M) & A1
(northbound)

Southbound
No exit. Access only from
A194(M) & A1
(southbound)

A3(M) Horndean - Havant

Northbound
Access only from A3

Southbound
Exit only to A3

Northbound
Exit only, no access

Southbound
Access only, no exit

A38(M) Birmingham
Victoria Road (Park Circus)

Northbound
No exit

Southbound
No access

A48(M) Cardiff Spur

Westbound
Access only from M4
(westbound)

Eastbound
Exit only to M4
(eastbound)

Westbound
Exit only to A48
(westbound)

Eastbound
Access only from A48
(eastbound)

A57(M) Manchester
Brook Street (A34)

Westbound
No exit

Eastbound
No access

A58(M) Leeds
Park Lane and Westgate

Northbound
No restriction

Southbound
No access

A64(M) Leeds
Clay Pit Lane (A58)

Westbound
No exit (to Clay Pit Lane)

Eastbound
No access (from Clay Pit
Lane)

A66(M) Darlington Spur

Westbound
Exit only to A1(M)
(southbound)

Eastbound
Access only from A1(M)
(northbound)

A194(M)
Newcastle upon Tyne

Northbound
Access only from A1(M)
(northbound)

Southbound
Exit only to A1(M)
(southbound)

A12 M25 - Ipswich

Northeastbound
Access only, no exit

Southwestbound
No restriction

Northeastbound
Exit only, no access

Southwestbound
Access only, no exit

Northeastbound
Exit only, no access

Southwestbound
Access only, no exit

A74(M) Gretna - Abington

Northbound
Exit only, no access

Southbound
Access only, no exit

Northeastbound
Access only, no exit

Southwestbound
Exit only, no access

Northeastbound
No restriction

Southwestbound
Access only, no exit

Northeastbound
Exit only, no access

Southwestbound
Access only, no exit

Northeastbound
Access only, no exit

Southwestbound
Exit only, no access

Northeastbound
Exit only, no access

Southwestbound
Access only, no exit

Northeastbound
Exit only (for Stratford
St Mary and Dedham)

Southwestbound
Access only

A14 M1 - Felixstowe

Westbound
Exit only to M6 & M1
(northbound)

Eastbound
Access only from M6 &
M1 (southbound)

Westbound
Exit only, no access

Eastbound
Access only, no exit

Westbound
Access only, no exit

Eastbound
Exit only, no access

Westbound
Exit only, no access

Eastbound
Access only from A1
(southbound)

Westbound
Access only, no exit

Eastbound
Exit only, no access

Westbound
No restriction

Eastbound
Access only, no exit

Northeastbound
No access, no exit

Southwestbound
Exit only, no access

Northeastbound
No restriction

Southwestbound
Access only, no exit

Northeastbound
Exit only, no access

Southwestbound
Access only, no exit

Northeastbound
Exit only, no access

Southwestbound
Access only, no exit

Northeastbound
Exit only (for Stratford
St Mary and Dedham)

Southwestbound
Access only

A55 Holyhead - Chester

Westbound
Exit only, no access

Eastbound
Access only, no exit

Westbound
Access only, no exit

Eastbound
Exit only, no access

Westbound
Exit only, no access

Eastbound
No access or exit.

Westbound
No restriction

Eastbound
No access or exit

Westbound
Exit only, no access

Eastbound
No access or exit

Westbound
Exit only, no access

Eastbound
Access only, no exit

Westbound
Exit only to A5104

Eastbound
Access only from A5104

Refer also to atlas pages 36–37 and 50–51. In August 2023 the Ultra Low Emission Zone is due to be extended.
For further information visit www.tfl.gov.uk/modes/driving/ultra-low-emission-zone

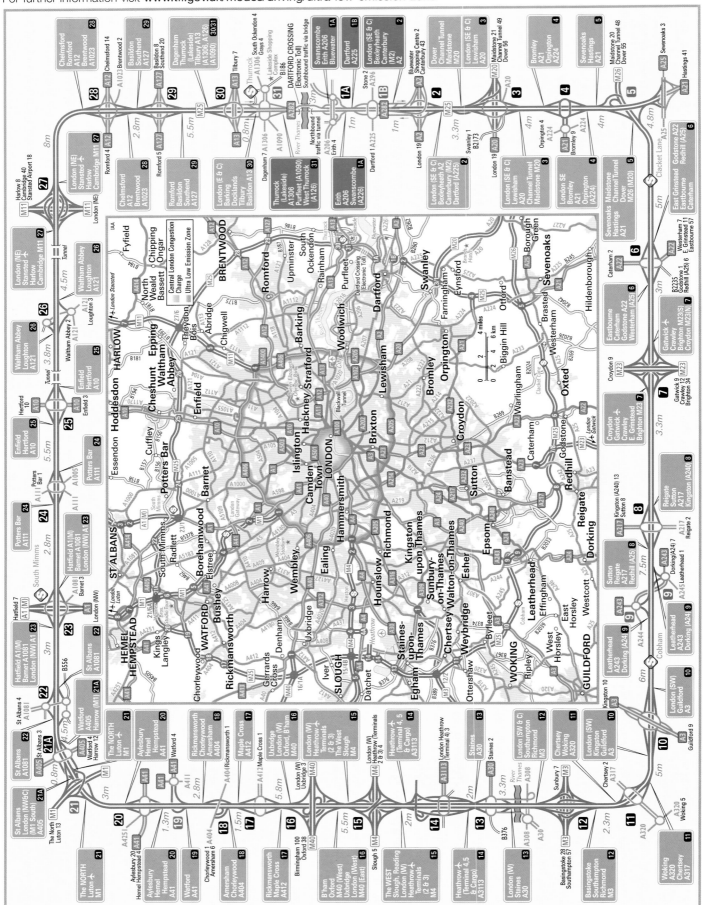

Refer also to atlas pages 58–59

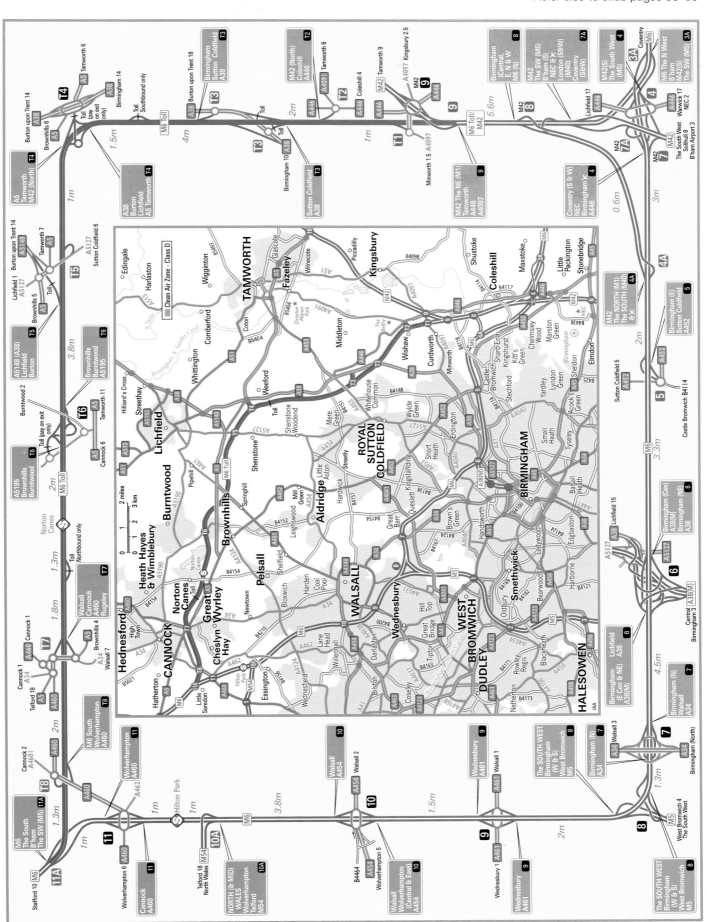

Smart motorways

Since Britain's first motorway (the Preston Bypass) opened in 1958, motorways have changed significantly. A vast increase in car journeys over the last 64 years has meant that motorways quickly filled to capacity. To combat this, the recent development of **smart motorways** uses technology to monitor and actively manage traffic flow and congestion.

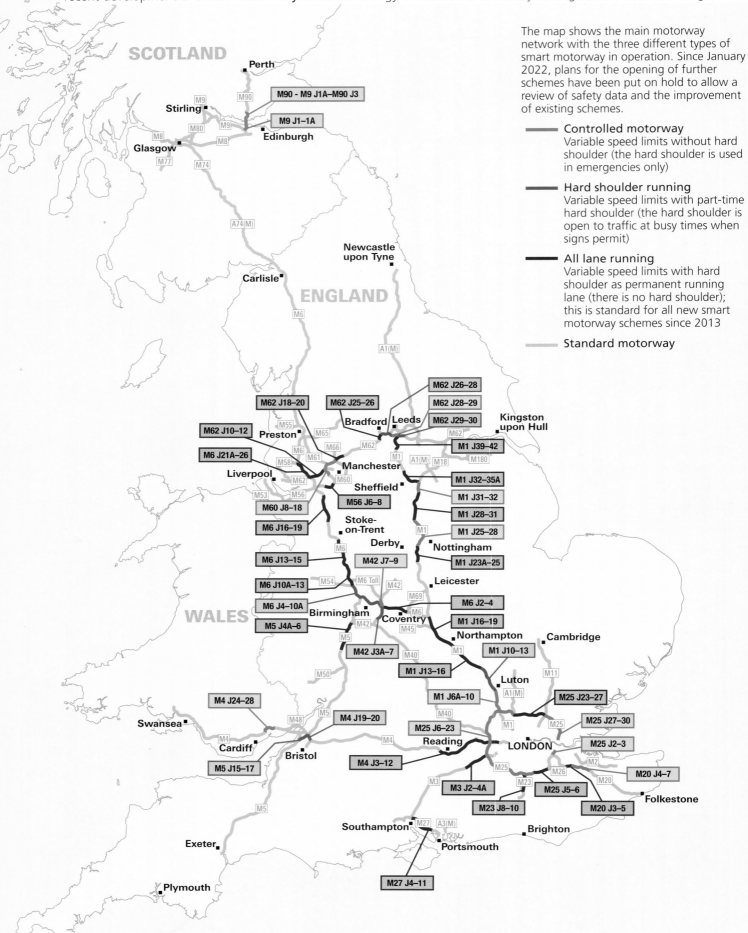

The map shows the main motorway network with the three different types of smart motorway in operation. Since January 2022, plans for the opening of further schemes have been put on hold to allow a review of safety data and the improvement of existing schemes.

— **Controlled motorway**
Variable speed limits without hard shoulder (the hard shoulder is used in emergencies only)

— **Hard shoulder running**
Variable speed limits with part-time hard shoulder (the hard shoulder is open to traffic at busy times when signs permit)

— **All lane running**
Variable speed limits with hard shoulder as permanent running lane (there is no hard shoulder); this is standard for all new smart motorway schemes since 2013

— Standard motorway

Smart motorways (*Intelligent Transport Systems* in Scotland) are the responsibility of National Highways, Transport Scotland and Transport for Wales

How they work

Smart motorways utilise various active traffic management methods, monitored through a regional traffic control centre:

- Traffic flow is monitored using CCTV
- Speed limits are changed to smooth traffic flow and reduce stop-start driving
- Capacity of the motorway can be increased by either temporarily or permanently opening the hard shoulder to traffic

- Warning signs and messages alert drivers to hazards and traffic jams ahead
- Lanes can be closed in the case of an accident or emergency by displaying a red X sign
- Emergency refuge areas are located regularly along the motorway where there is no hard shoulder available

In an emergency

On a smart motorway there is often no hard shoulder so in an emergency you will need to make your way to the nearest **emergency refuge area** or motorway service area.

Emergency refuge areas are lay-bys marked with blue signs featuring an orange SOS telephone symbol. The telephone connects to the regional control centre and pinpoints your location. The control centre will advise you on what to do, send help and assist you in returning to the motorway.

If you are unable to reach an emergency refuge area or hard shoulder (if there is one) move as close to the nearside (left hand) boundary or verge as you can.

If it is not possible to get out of your vehicle safely, or there is no other place of relative safety to wait, stay in your vehicle with your seat-belt on and dial 999 if you have a mobile phone. If you don't have a phone, sit tight and wait to be rescued. Once the regional traffic control centre is aware of your situation, via the police or CCTV, they will use the smart motorway technology to set overhead signs and close the lane to keep traffic away from you. They will also send a traffic officer or the police to help you.

Sign indicating presence of emergency refuge areas ahead

This sign is located at each emergency refuge area

Signs

Motorway signals and messages advise of abnormal traffic conditions ahead and may indicate speed limits. They may apply to individual lanes when mounted overhead or, when located on the central reservation or at the side of the motorway, to the whole carriageway.

Where traffic is allowed to use the hard shoulder as a traffic lane, each lane will have overhead signals and signs. A red cross (with no signals) displayed above the hard shoulder indicates when it is closed. When the hard shoulder is in use as a traffic lane the red cross will change to a speed limit. Should it be necessary to close any lane, a red cross with red lamps flashing in vertical pairs will be shown above that lane. Prior to this, the signal will show an arrow directing traffic into the adjacent lane.

These signals are mounted above the carriageway with a signal for each traffic lane; each signal has two pairs of lamps that flash. You should obey the signal for your lane

Move to adjacent lane (arrow may point downwards to the right)

Leave motorway at next exit

Red lamps flashing from side to side in pairs, together with a red cross, mean 'do not proceed in the traffic lane directly below'. More than one lane may be closed to traffic

Where variable speed limit signs are mounted over individual lanes and the speed limit is shown in a red ring, the limit is mandatory. You will be at risk of a driving offence if you do not keep to the speed limit. Speed limits that do not include the red ring are the maximum speeds advised for the prevailing conditions.

Speed limits of 60, 50 and 40mph are used on all types of smart motorways. When no speed limit is shown the national speed limit of 70mph is in place (this is reduced to 60mph for particular vehicles such as heavy or articulated goods vehicles and vehicles towing caravans or trailers).

Quick tips

- Never drive in a lane closed by a red X
- Keep to the speed limit shown on the gantries
- A solid white line indicates the hard shoulder – do not drive in it unless directed or in the case of an emergency
- A broken white line indicates a normal running lane

- Exit the smart motorway where possible if your vehicle is in difficulty. In an emergency, move onto the hard shoulder where there is one, or the nearest emergency refuge area
- Put on your hazard lights if you break down

Motoring information

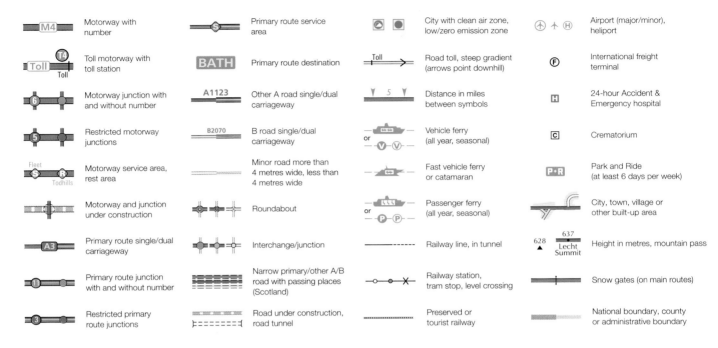

M4	Motorway with number	Primary route service area	City with clean air zone, low/zero emission zone	Airport (major/minor), heliport
Toll	Toll motorway with toll station	BATH — Primary route destination	Road toll, steep gradient (arrows point downhill)	International freight terminal
6	Motorway junction with and without number	A1123 Other A road single/dual carriageway	Distance in miles between symbols	24-hour Accident & Emergency hospital
5	Restricted motorway junctions	B2070 B road single/dual carriageway	Vehicle ferry (all year, seasonal)	Crematorium
Fleet Todhills	Motorway service area, rest area	Minor road more than 4 metres wide, less than 4 metres wide	Fast vehicle ferry or catamaran	Park and Ride (at least 6 days per week)
	Motorway and junction under construction	Roundabout	Passenger ferry (all year, seasonal)	City, town, village or other built-up area
A3	Primary route single/dual carriageway	Interchange/junction	Railway line, in tunnel	Height in metres, mountain pass
	Primary route junction with and without number	Narrow primary/other A/B road with passing places (Scotland)	Railway station, tram stop, level crossing	Snow gates (on main routes)
3	Restricted primary route junctions	Road under construction, road tunnel	Preserved or tourist railway	National boundary, county or administrative boundary

Touring information

To avoid disappointment, check opening times before visiting

Scenic route	Garden	Waterfall	Motor-racing circuit
Tourist Information Centre	Arboretum	Hill-fort	Air show venue
Tourist Information Centre (seasonal)	Country park	Roman antiquity	Ski slope (natural, artificial)
Visitor or heritage centre	Showground	Prehistoric monument	National Trust site
Picnic site	Theme park	Battle site with year	National Trust for Scotland site
Caravan site (AA inspected)	Farm or animal centre	Preserved or tourist railway	English Heritage site
Camping site (AA inspected)	Zoological or wildlife collection	Cave or cavern	Historic Scotland site
Caravan & camping site (AA inspected)	Bird collection	Windmill, monument or memorial	Cadw (Welsh heritage) site
Abbey, cathedral or priory	Aquarium	Beach (award winning)	Other place of interest
Ruined abbey, cathedral or priory	RSPB site	Lighthouse	Boxed symbols indicate attractions within urban area
Castle	National Nature Reserve (England, Scotland, Wales)	Golf course	World Heritage Site (UNESCO)
Historic house or building	Local nature reserve	Football stadium	National Park and National Scenic Area (Scotland)
Museum or art gallery	Wildlife Trust reserve	County cricket ground	Forest Park
Industrial interest	Forest drive	Rugby Union national stadium	Sandy beach
Aqueduct or viaduct	National trail	International athletics stadium	Heritage coast
Vineyard, brewery or distillery	Viewpoint	Horse racing, show jumping	Major shopping centre

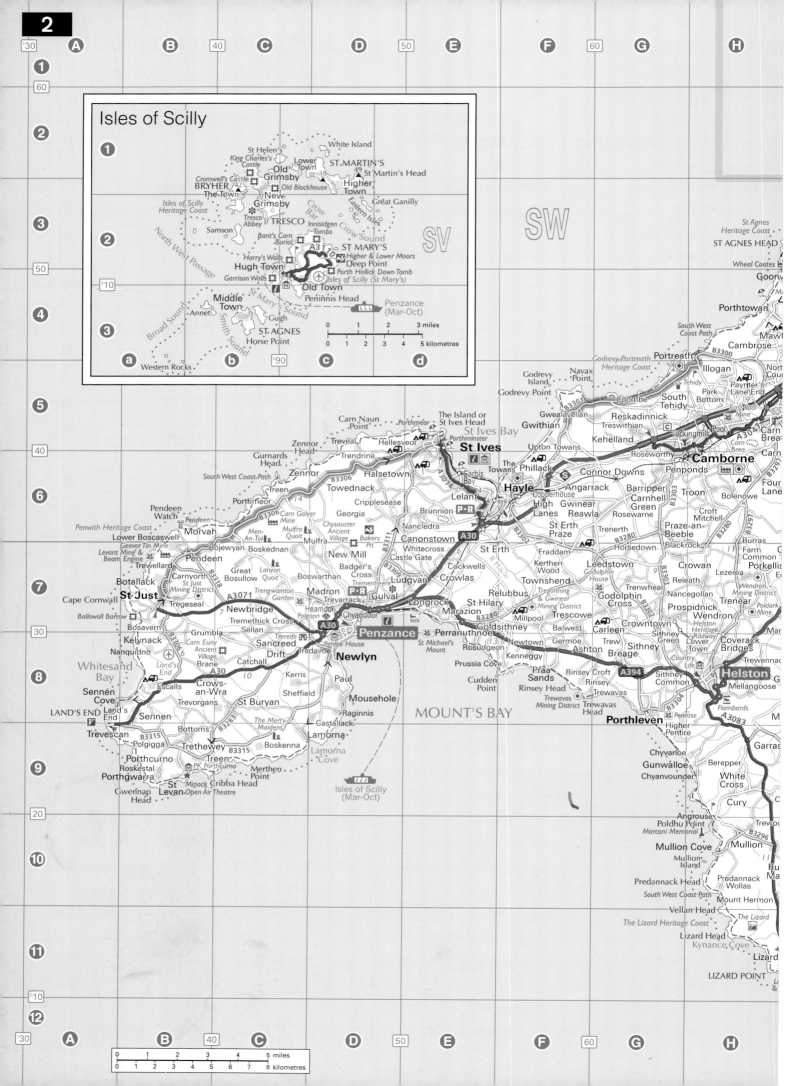

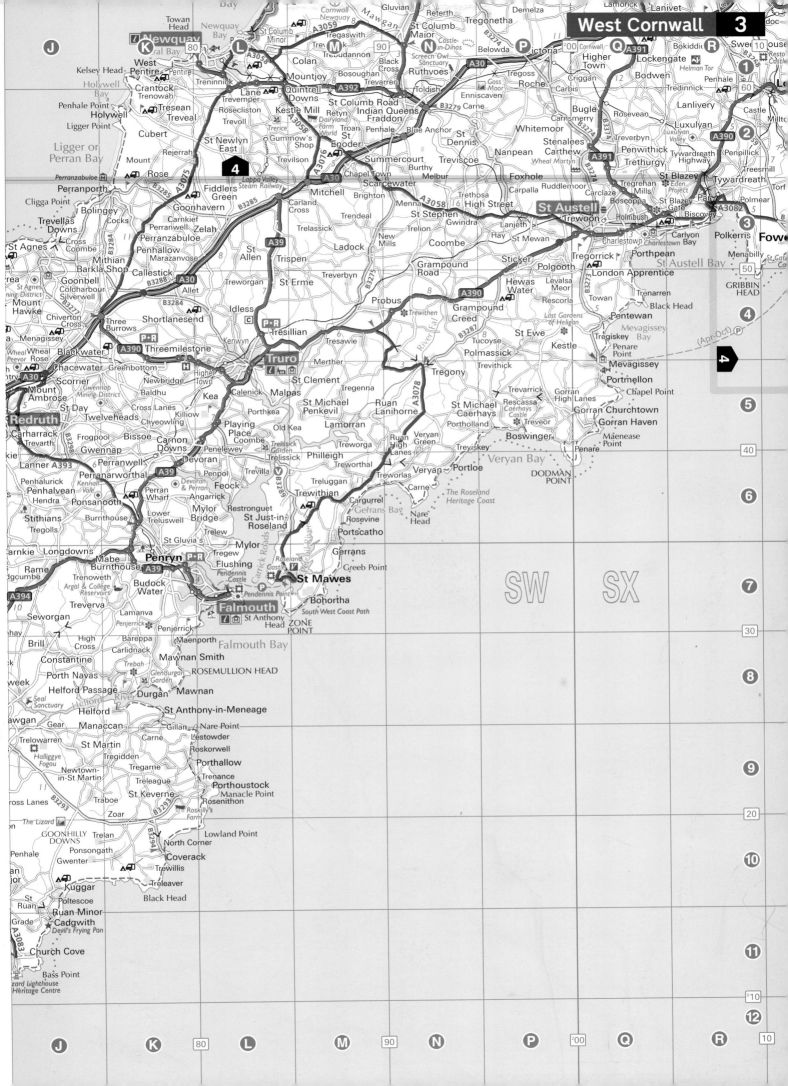

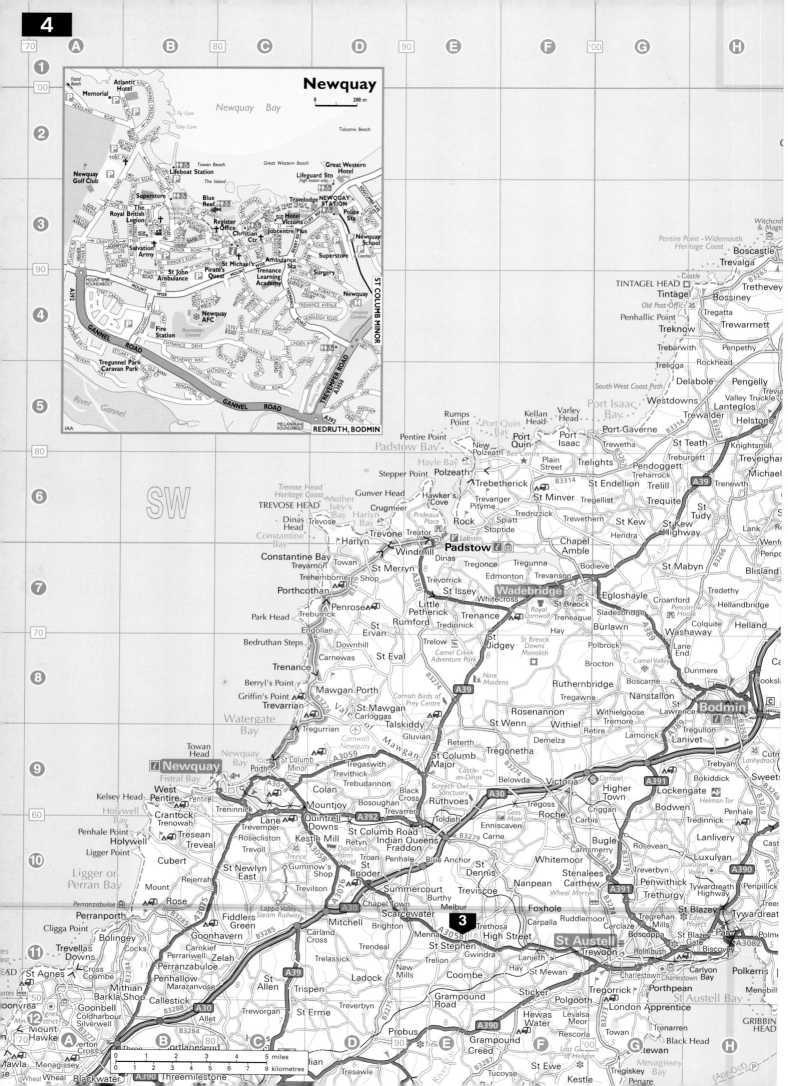

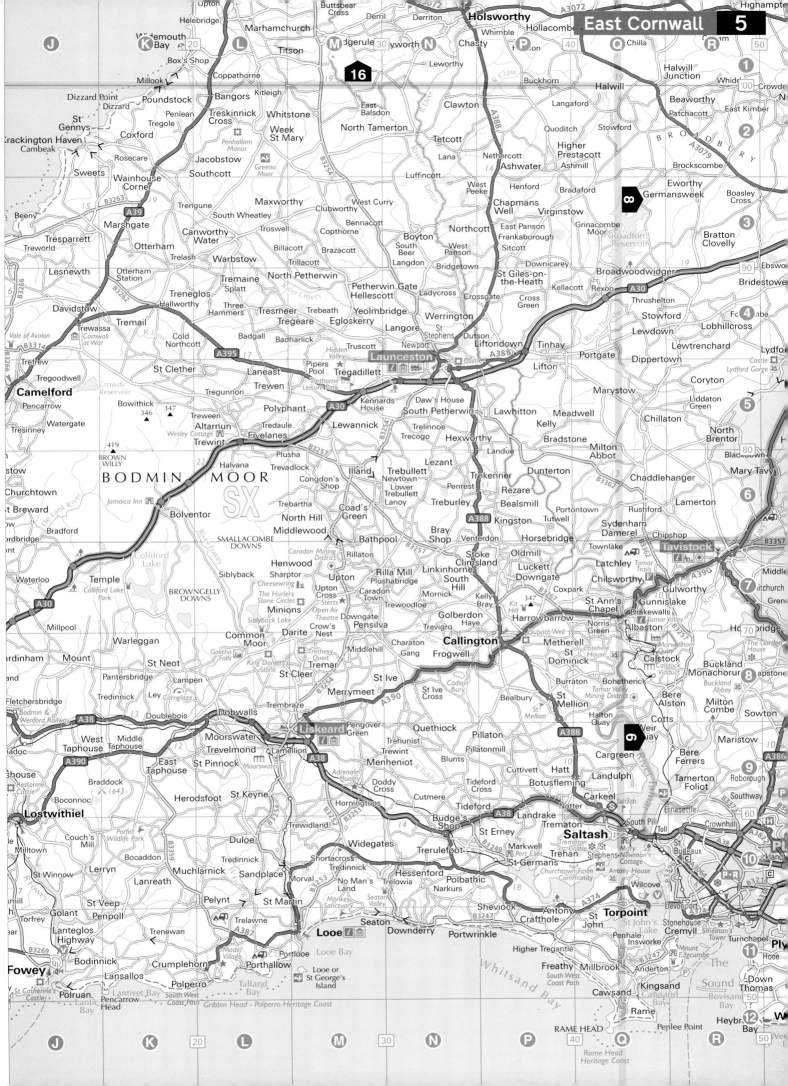

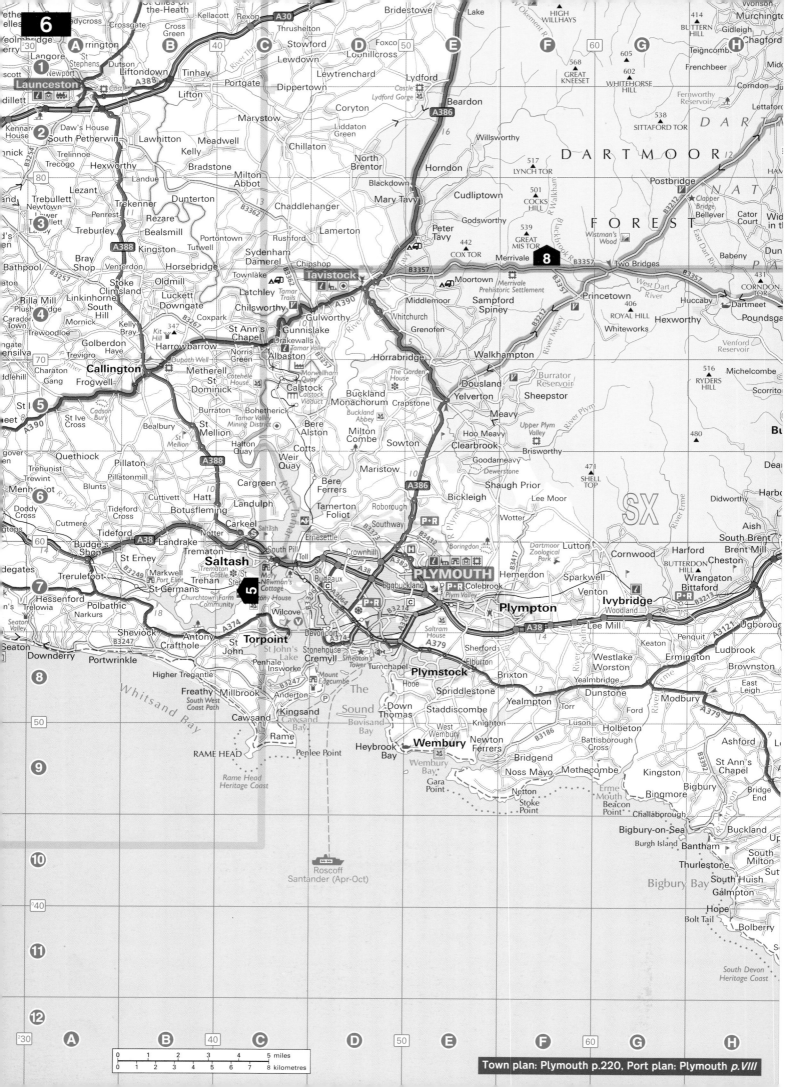

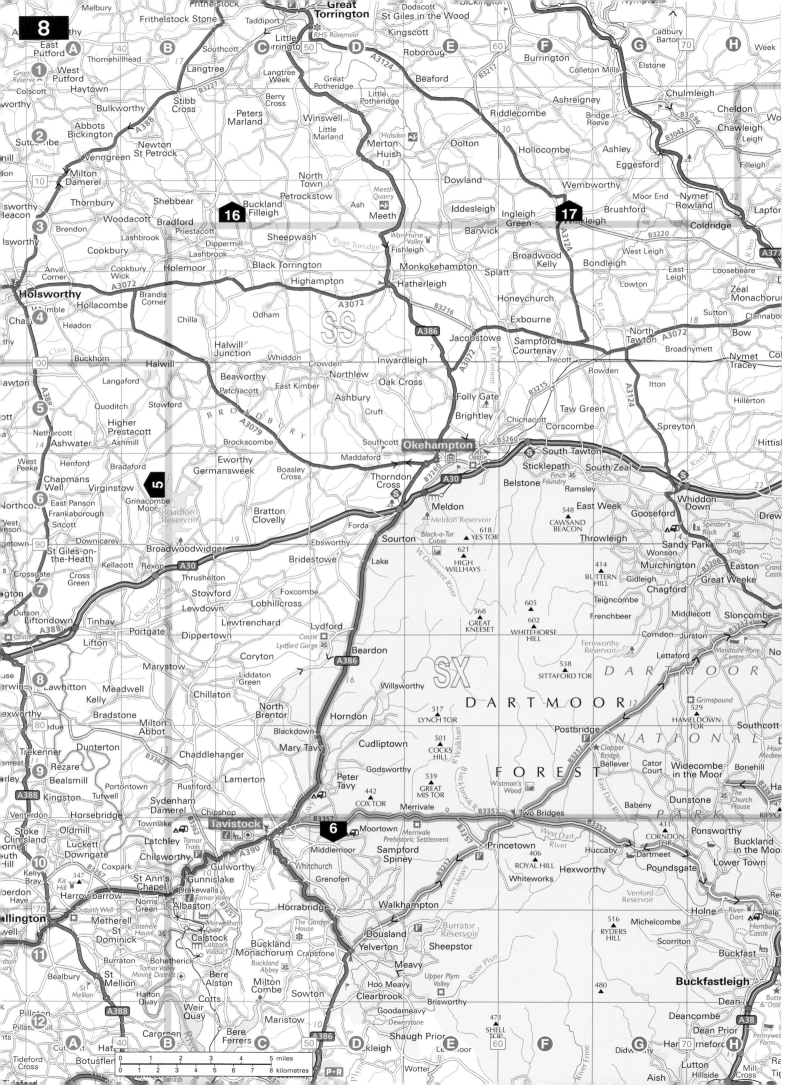

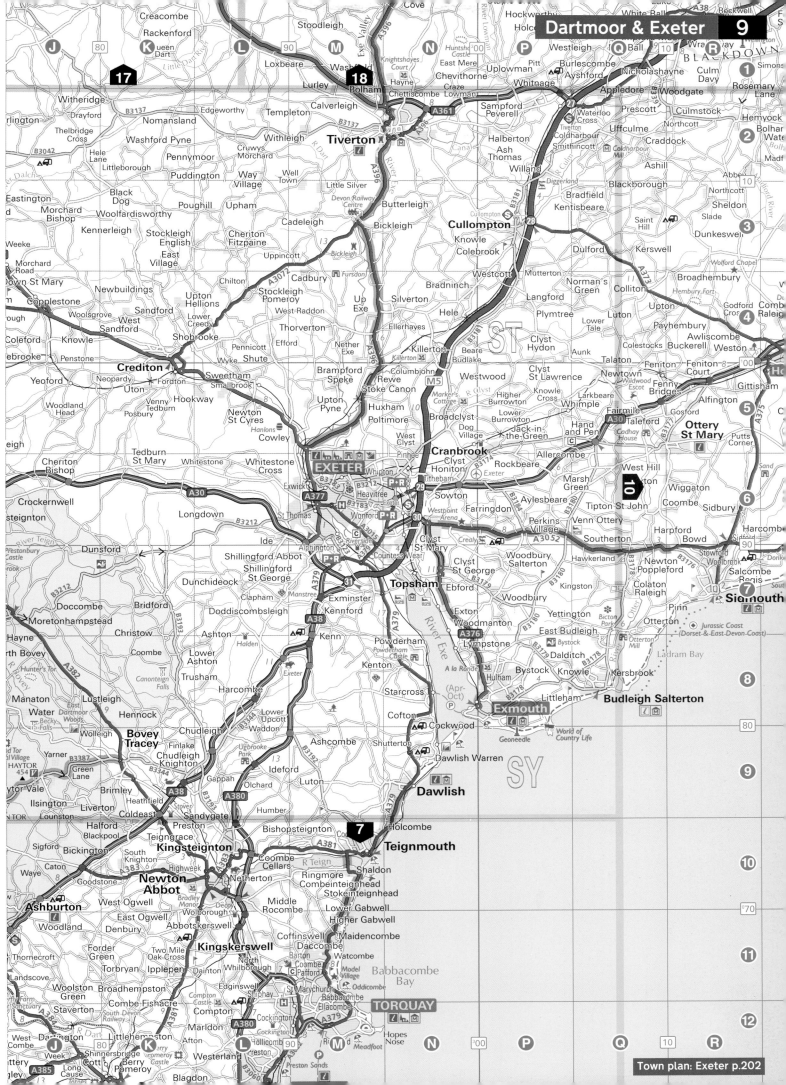

Town plan: Exeter p.202

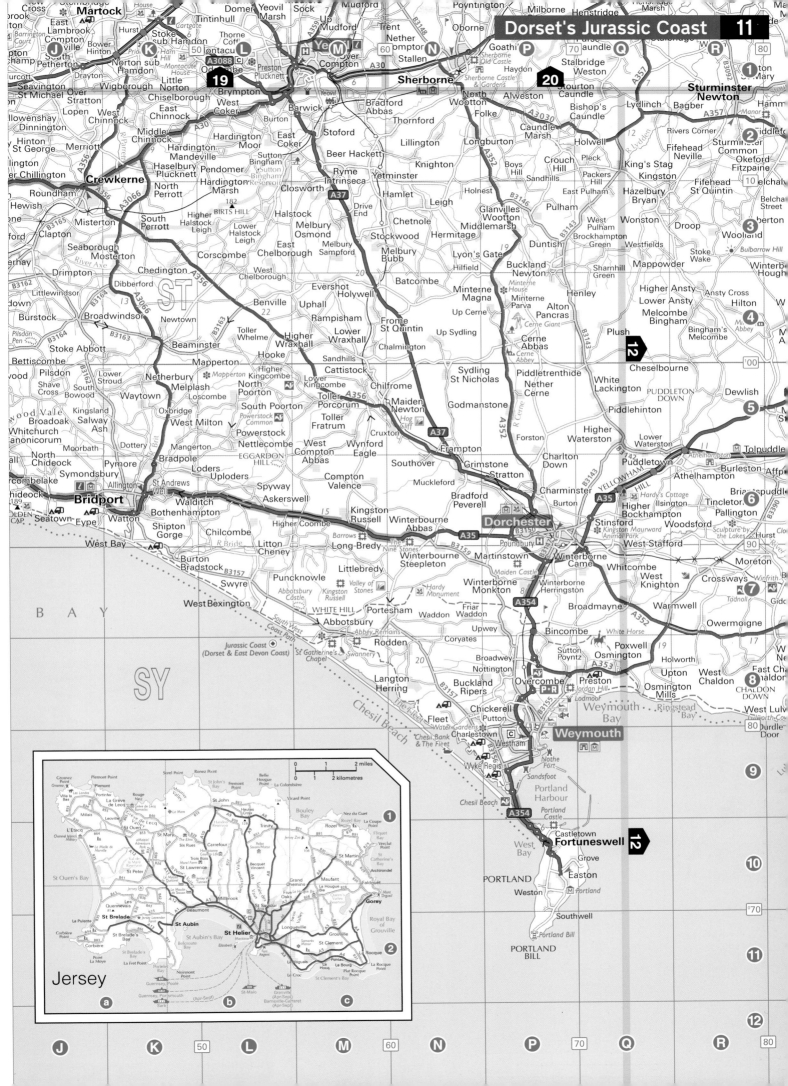

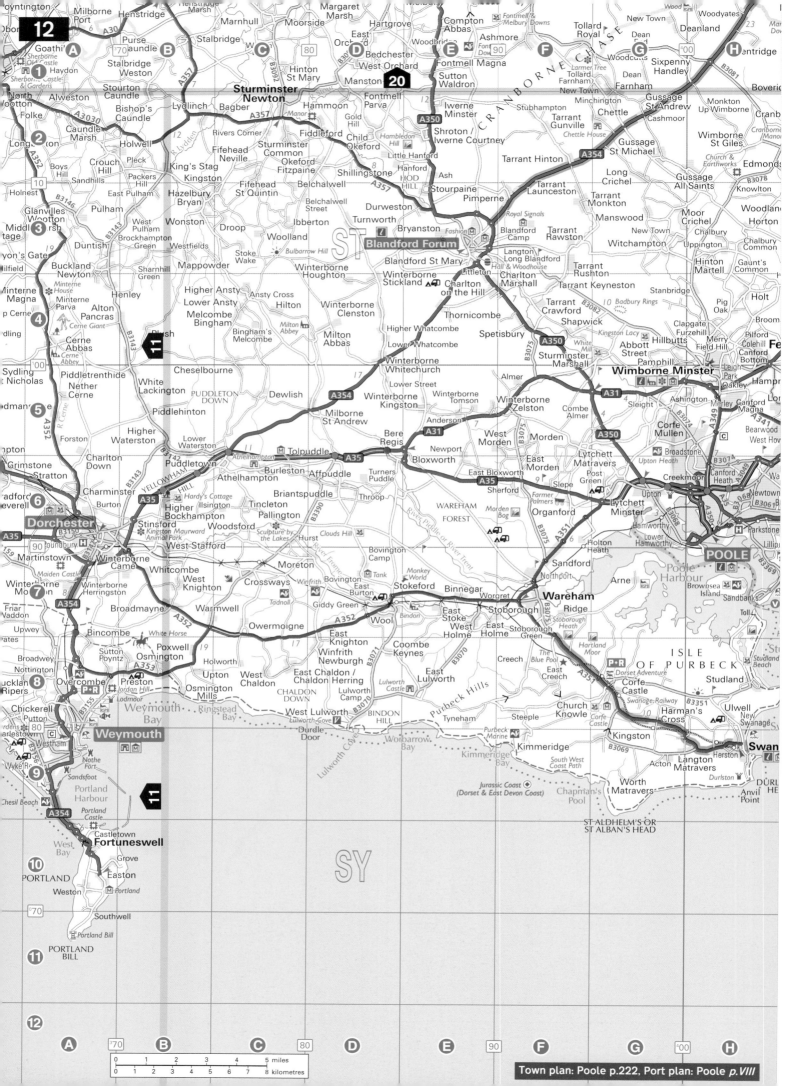

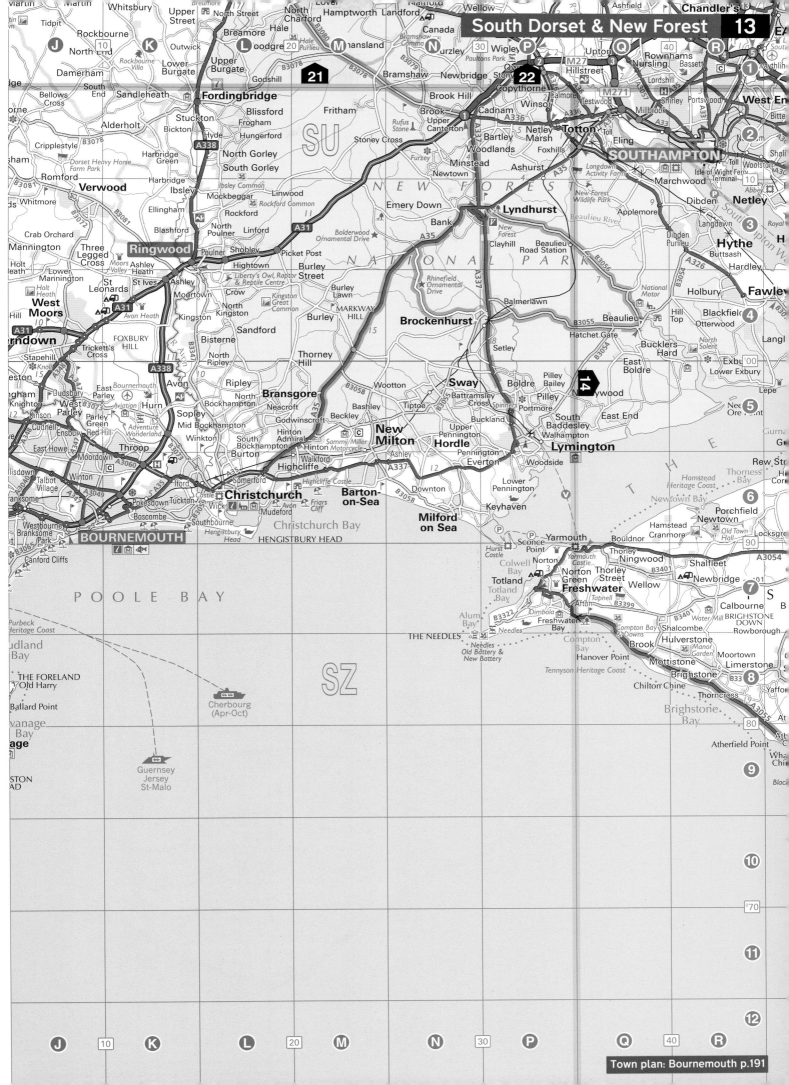

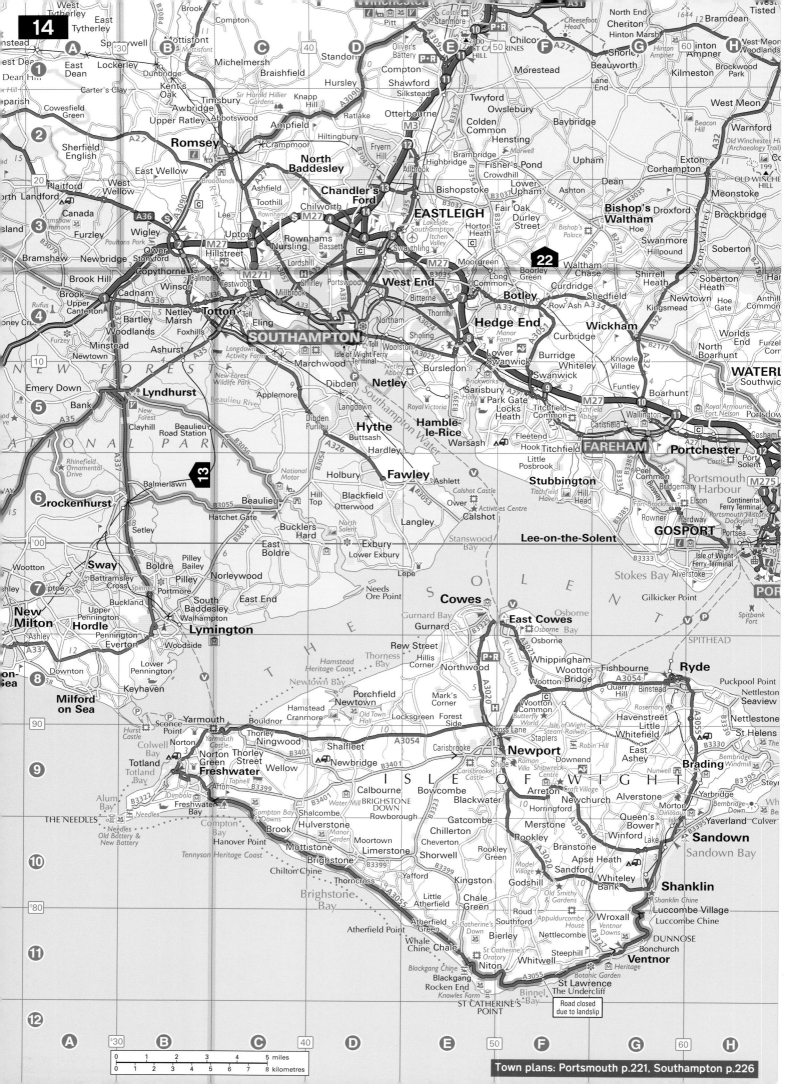

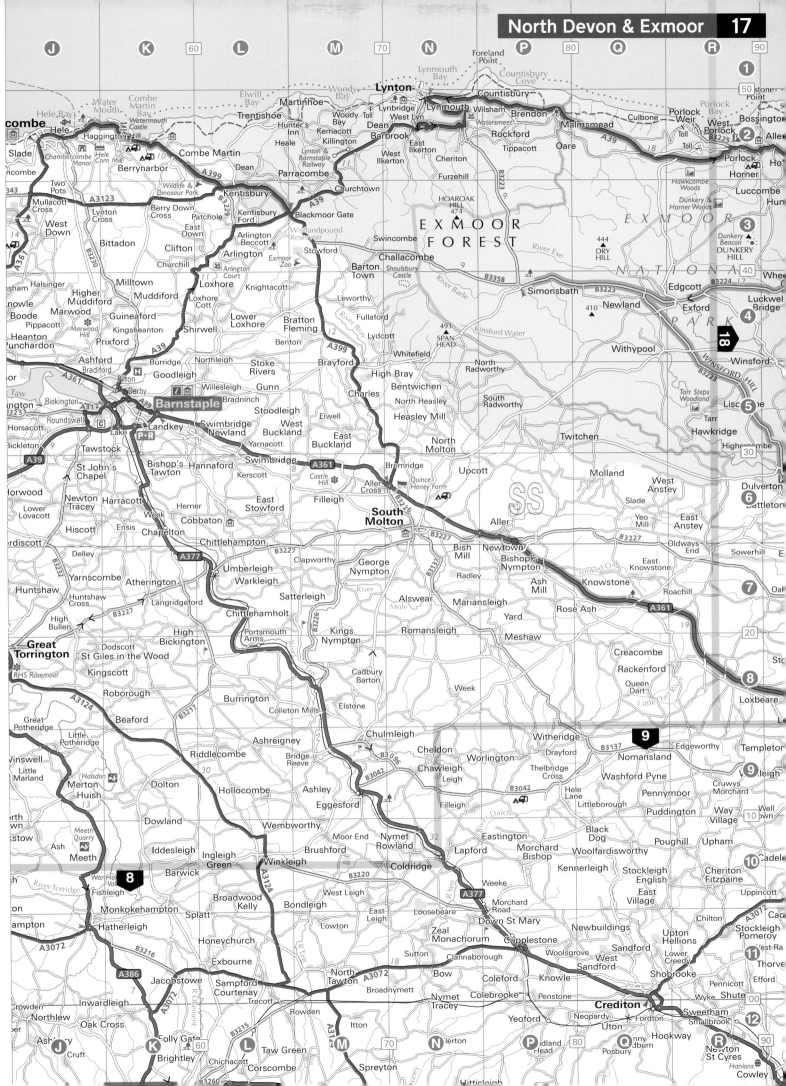

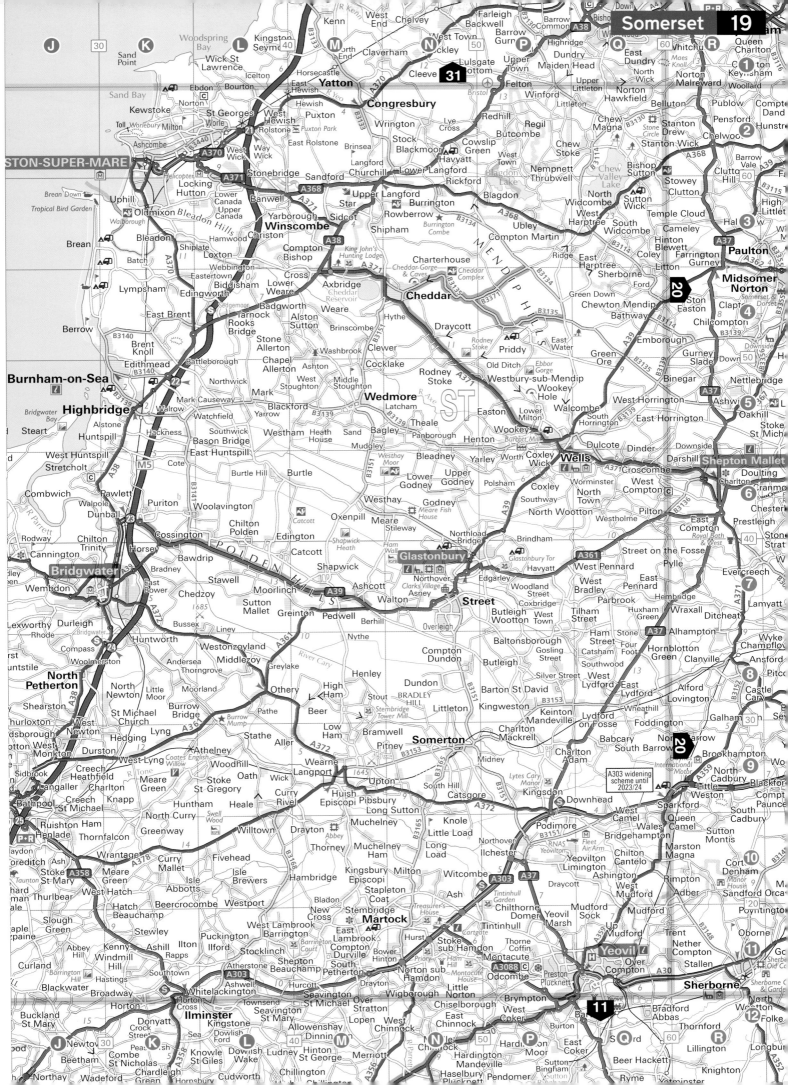

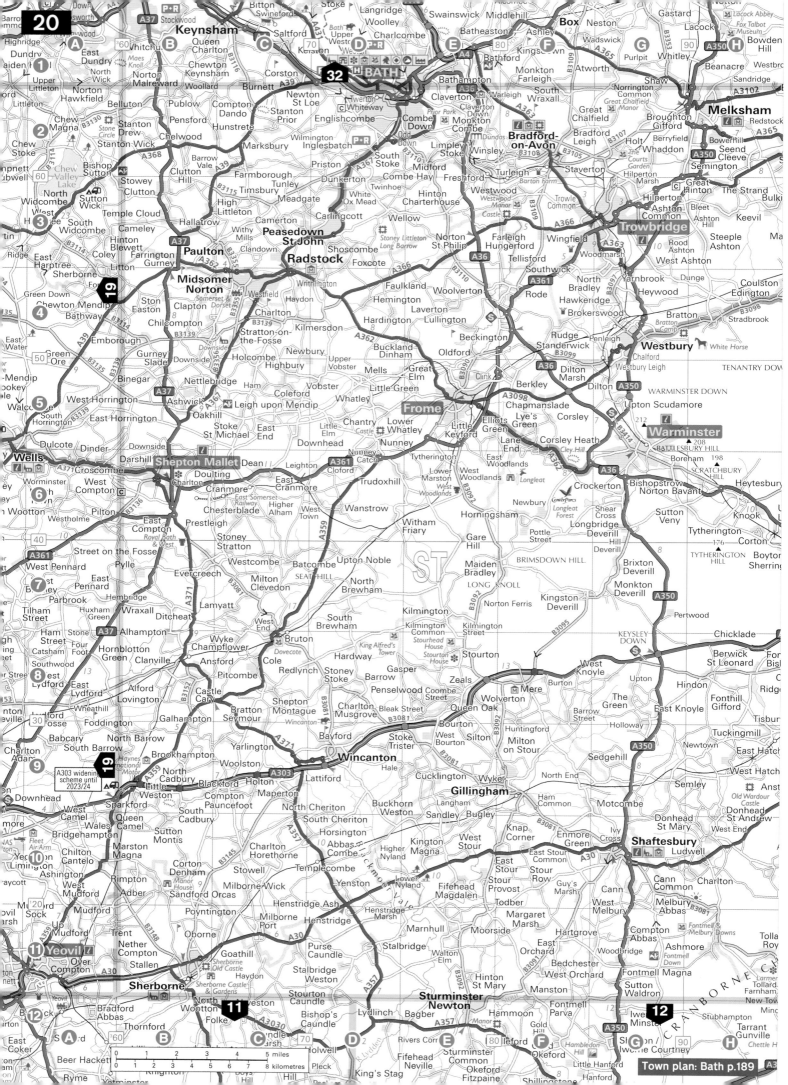

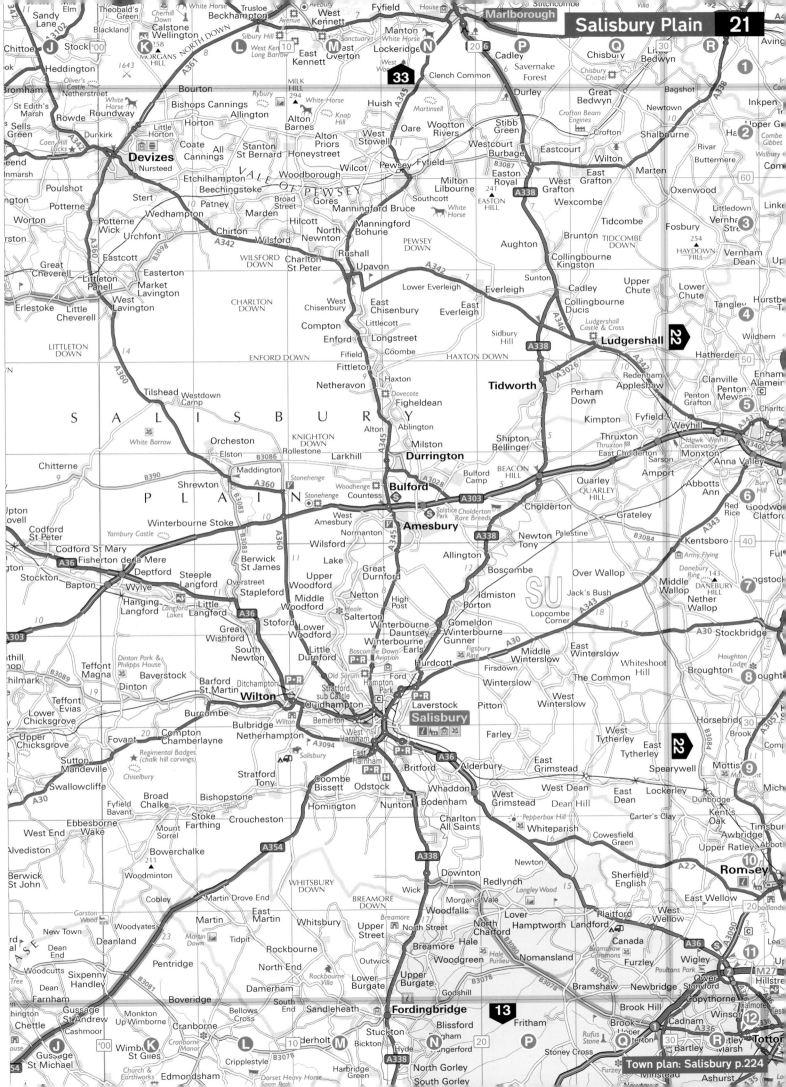

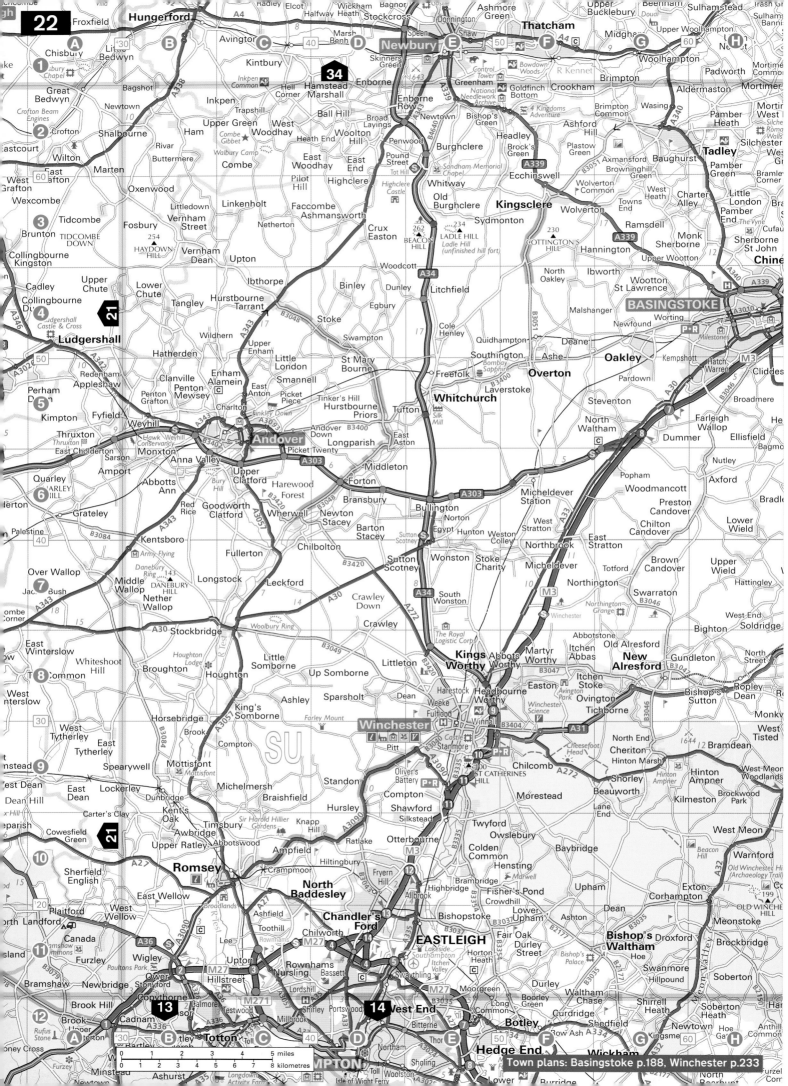

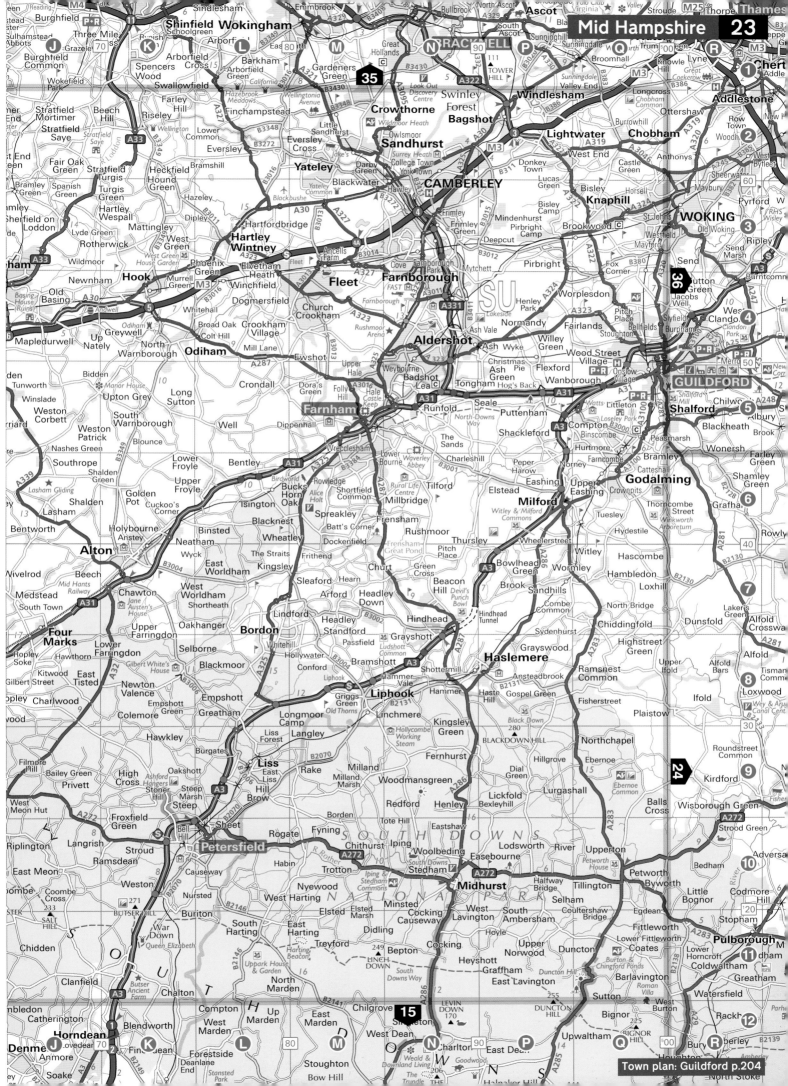

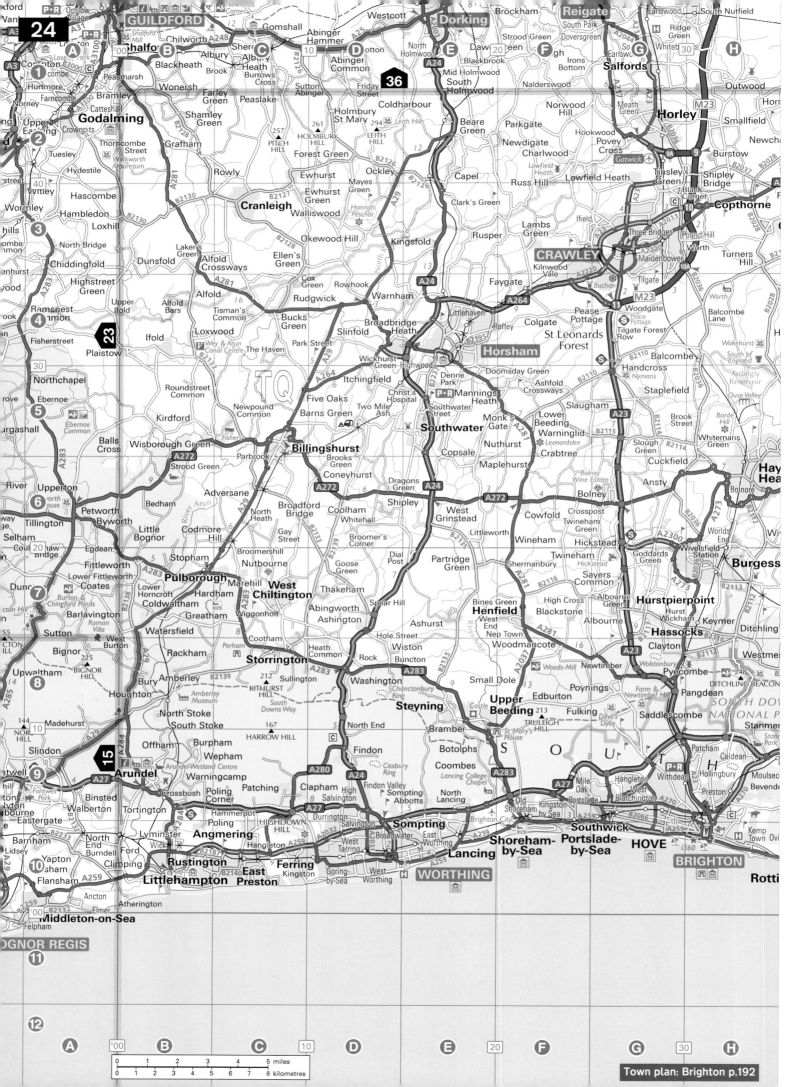

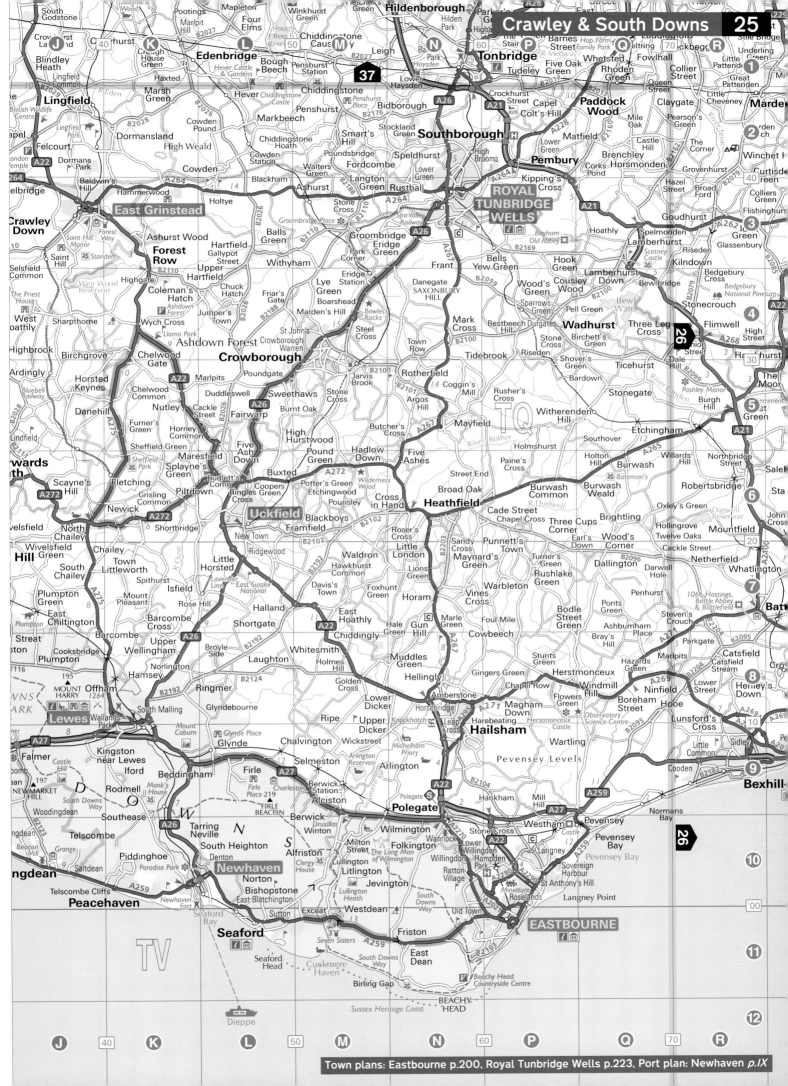

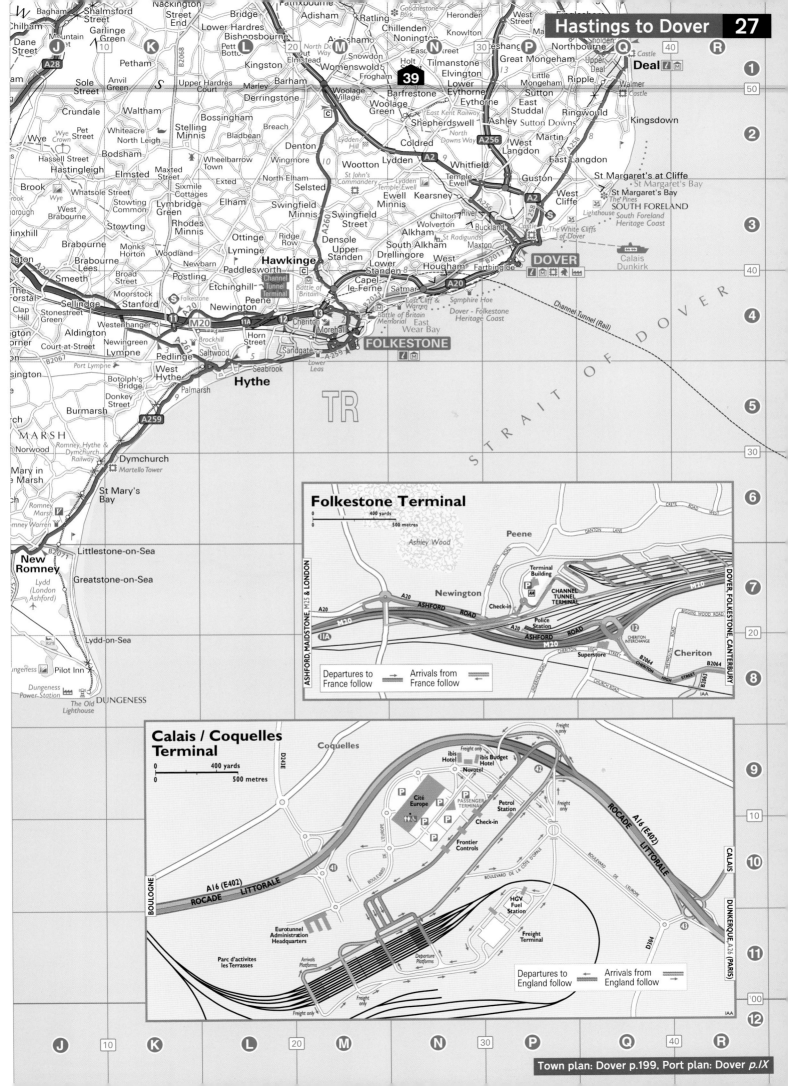

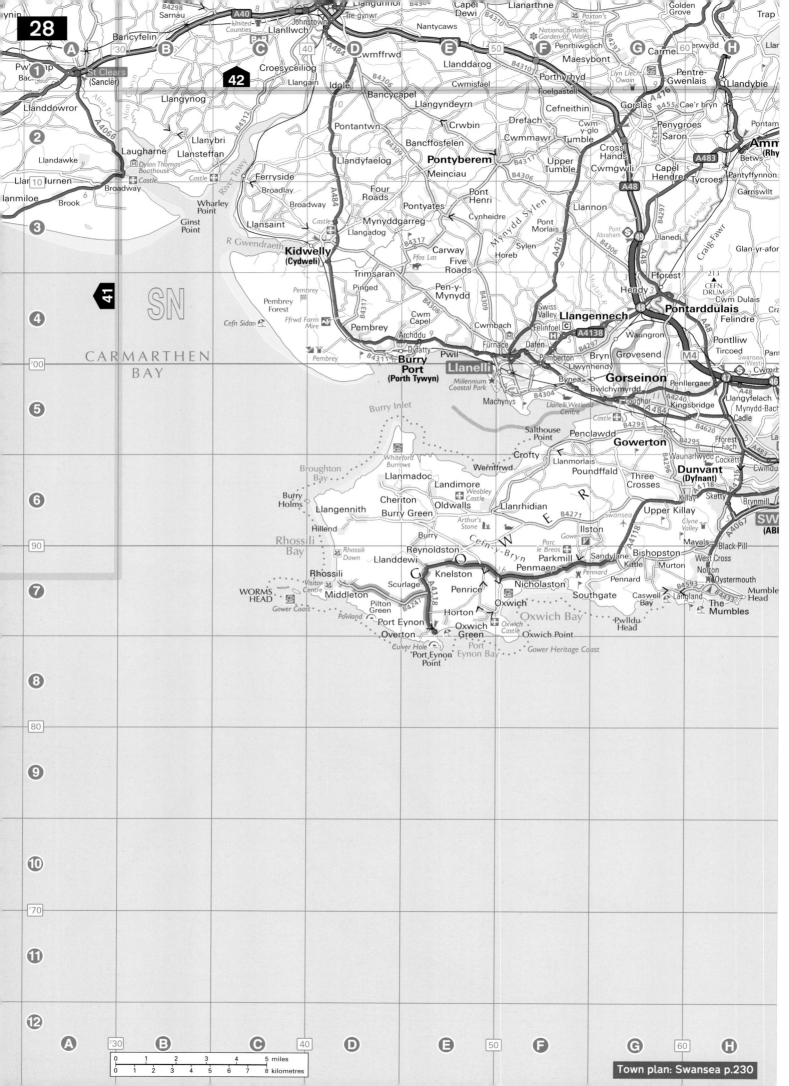

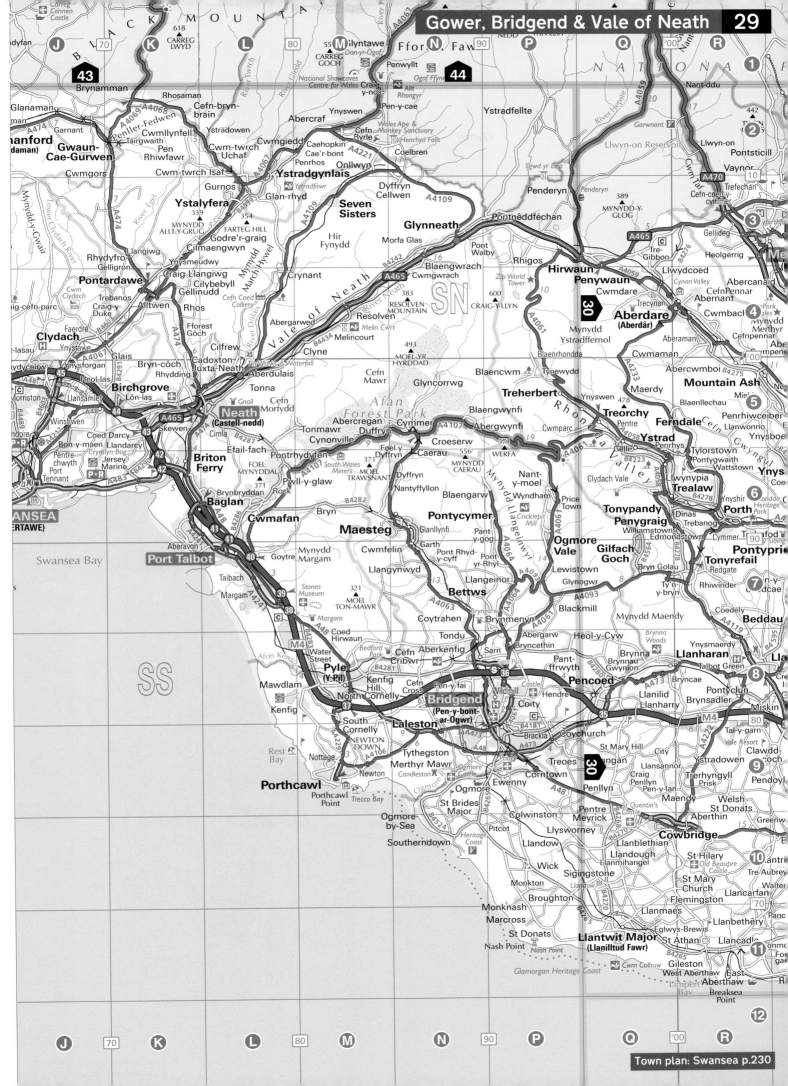

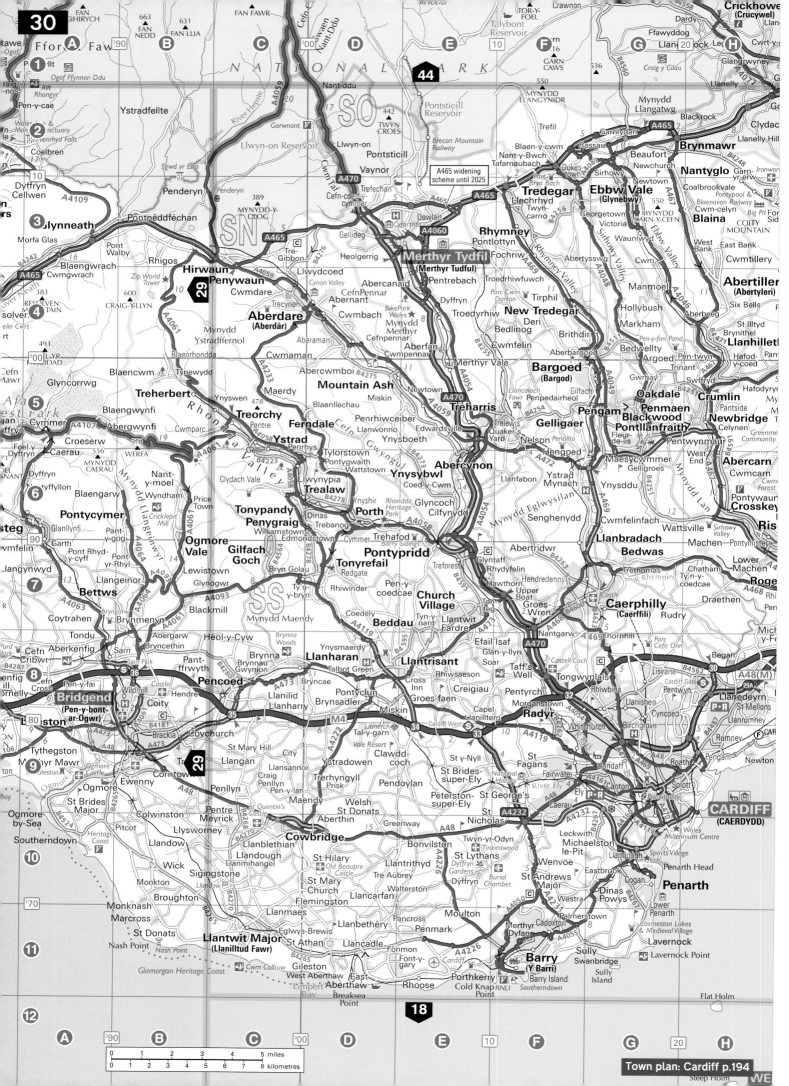

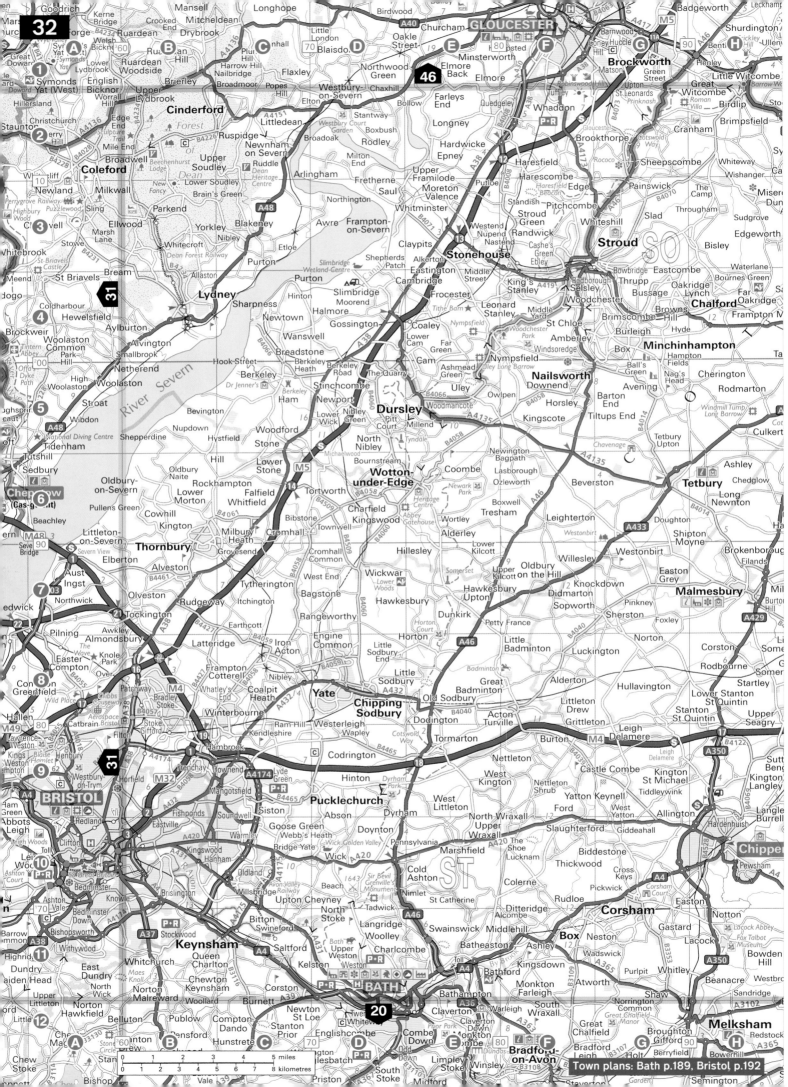

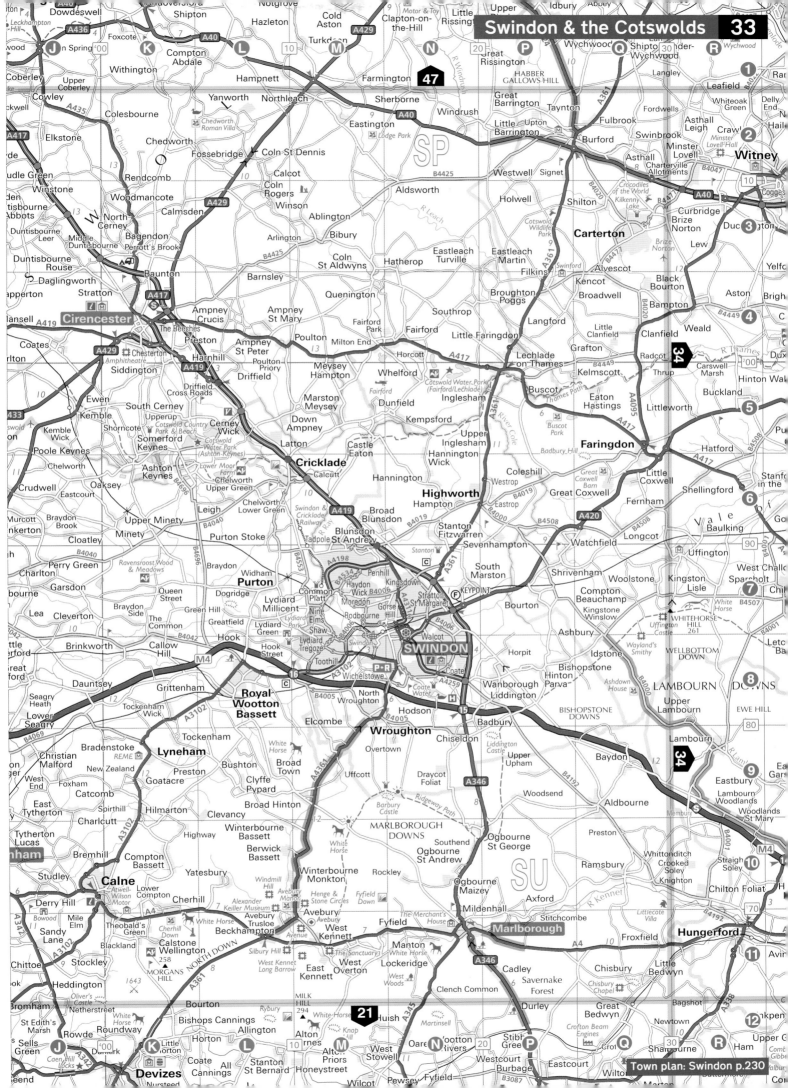

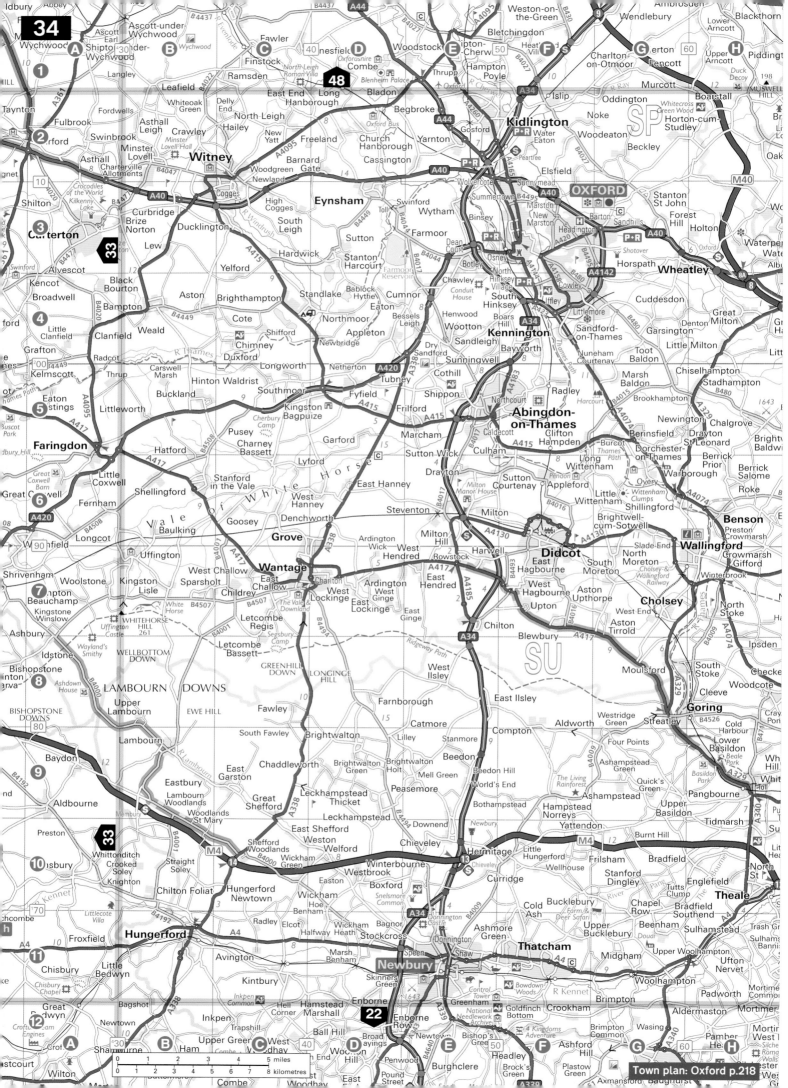

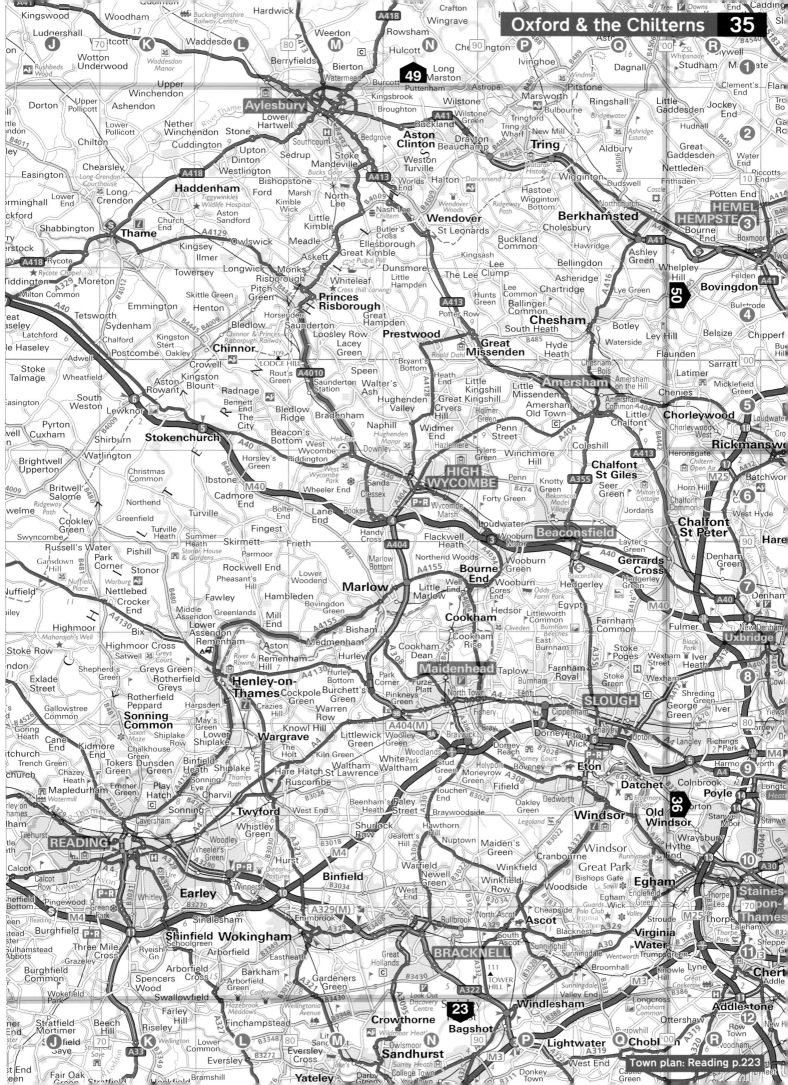

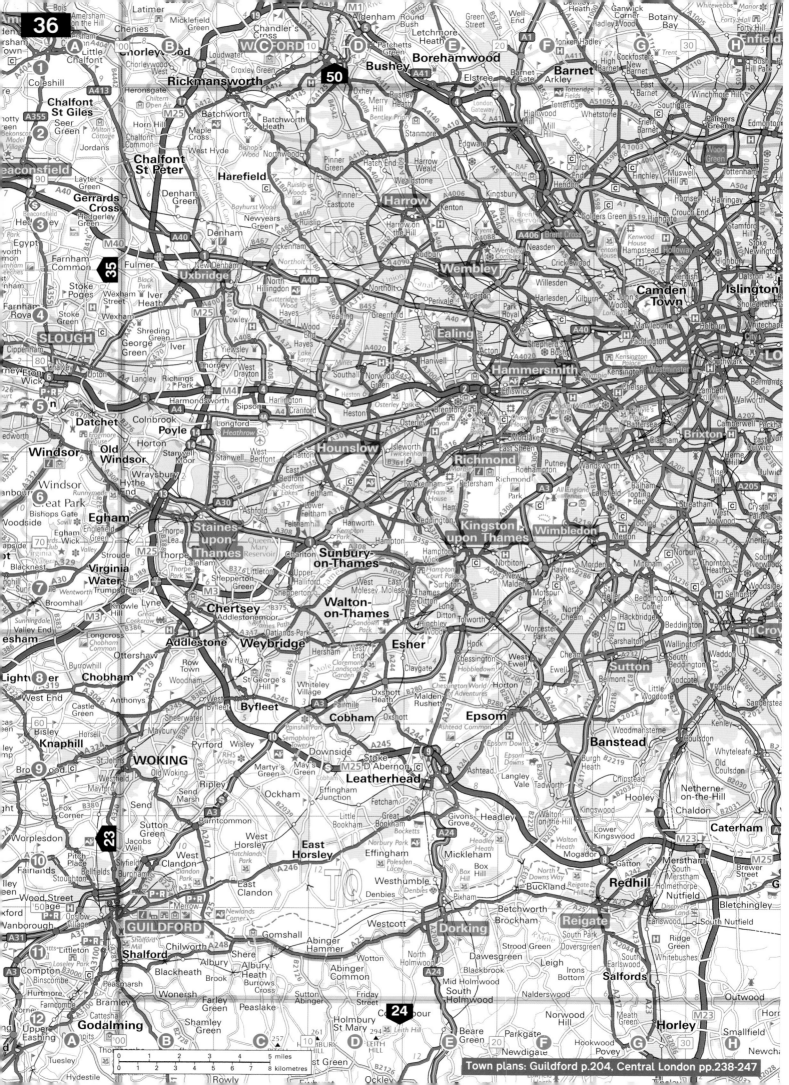

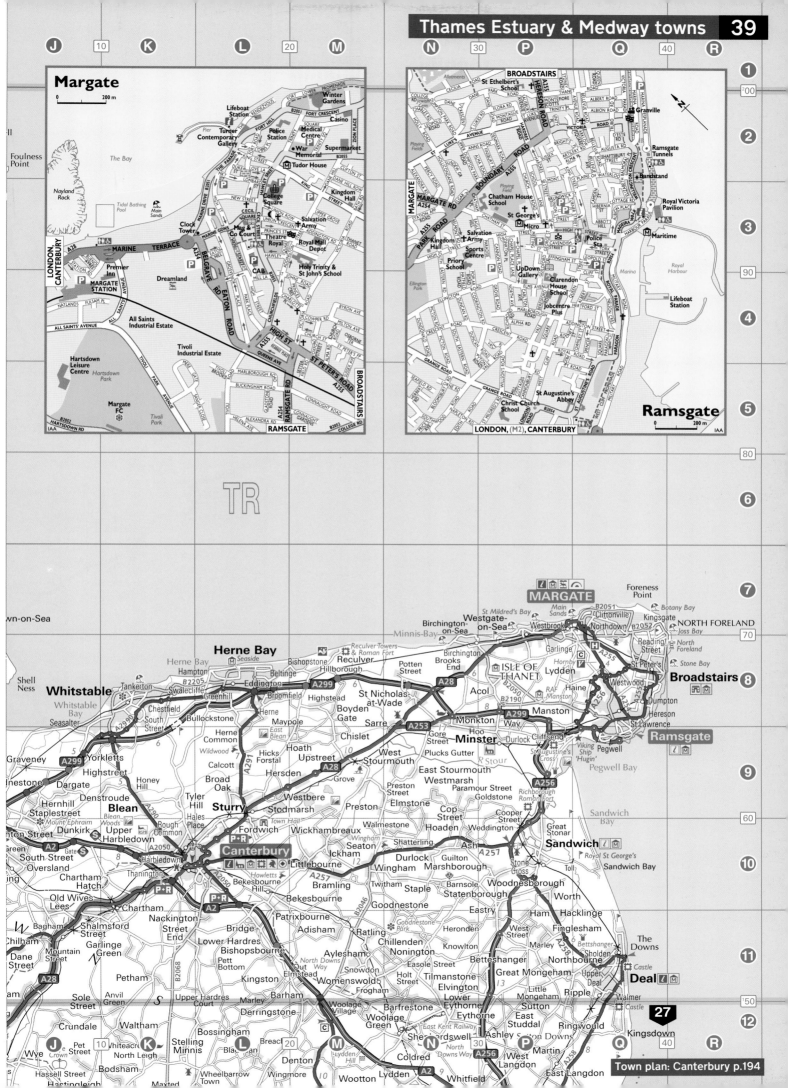

Margate

0   200 m

- Winter Gardens
- Lifeboat Station
- FORT CRESCENT
- Casino
- Turner Contemporary Gallery
- Police Station
- Medical Centre
- Supermarket
- War Memorial
- ZION PLACE
- Tudor House
- Kingdom Hall
- College Square
- UPPER GROVE
- Salvation Army
- Royal Mail Depot
- Theatre Royal
- Mag & Co Court
- Clock Tower
- CAB
- Holy Trinity & St John's School
- Premier Inn
- MARGATE STATION
- Dreamland
- All Saints Industrial Estate
- Tivoli Industrial Estate
- Hartsdown Leisure Centre
- Hartsdown Park
- Margate FC
- Tivoli Park

LONDON, CANTERBURY

The Bay
Nayland Rock
Foulness Point
Tidal Bathing Pool
Main Sands

MARINE TERRACE
BELGRAVE RD
EATON RD
HIGH ST
ST PETER'S ROAD
RAMSGATE RD
BROADSTAIRS
RAMSGATE

Ramsgate

0   200 m

- BROADSTAIRS
- St Ethelbert's School
- Granville
- Chatham House School
- St George's
- Ramsgate Tunnels
- Bandstand
- Micro
- Salvation Army
- Sports Centre
- Kingdom Hall
- Priory School
- UpDown Gallery
- Police Sta
- Royal Victoria Pavilion
- Maritime
- Ellington Park
- Clarendon House School
- Jobcentre Plus
- Marina
- Royal Harbour
- Lifeboat Station
- Christ Church School
- St Augustine's Abbey

MARGATE RD
BOUNDARY ROAD
GRANGE ROAD
LONDON, (M2), CANTERBURY

TR

- Foulness Point
- Shell Ness
- Whitstable
- Whitstable Bay
- Seasalter
- Graveney
- Yorkletts
- Highstreet
- Dargate
- Denstroude
- Hernhill
- Staplestreet
- Dunkirk
- Mount Ephraim
- Upper Harbledown
- Blean
- Rough Common
- Bean Woods
- Harbledown
- Thanington
- Chartham
- Chartham Hatch
- Nackington
- Old Wives Lees
- Shalmsford Street
- Chilham
- Mountain Street
- Bagham
- Petham
- Crundale
- Waltham
- Sole Street
- Anvil Green
- Upper Hardres Court
- Bossingham
- Stelling Minnis
- North Leigh
- Hassell Street
- Bodsham
- Wheelbarrow Town

- Herne Bay
- Hampton
- Tankerton
- Swalecliffe
- Chestfield
- South Street
- Bullockstone
- Broomfield
- Greenhill
- Eddington
- Herne
- Maypole
- Herne Common
- Wildwood
- Hicks Forstal
- Hoath
- Broad Oak
- Tyler Hill
- Sturry
- Hales Place
- Fordwich
- Howletts
- Bekesbourne Hill
- Bekesbourne
- Patrixbourne
- Bridge
- Lower Hardres
- Bishopsbourne
- Kingston
- Barham
- Derringstone
- Pett Bottom
- Womenswold
- Woolage Village
- Woolage Green
- Denton
- Wootton
- Lydden

- Reculver
- Reculver Towers & Roman Fort
- Beltinge
- Bishopstone
- Hillborough
- Highstead
- Boyden Gate
- St Nicholas at-Wade
- Sarre
- Chislet
- Upstreet
- West Stourmouth
- Plucks Gutter
- East Stourmouth
- Westmarsh
- Grove
- Preston Street
- Preston
- Elmstone
- Stodmarsh
- Westbere
- Wickhambreaux
- Ickham
- Littlebourne
- Seaton
- Bramling
- Twitham
- Adisham
- Aylesham
- Nonington
- Chillenden
- Knowlton
- Easole Street
- Snowdon
- Elvington
- Eythorne
- Frogham
- Barfrestone
- Shepherdswell
- Eythorne
- Coldred
- Whitfield

- Birchington-on-Sea
- Minnis Bay
- Westgate-on-Sea
- Garlinge
- Westbrook
- Birchington
- Brooks End
- Potten Street
- Acol
- ISLE OF THANET
- Manston
- RAF Manston
- Monkton
- Minster
- Gore Street
- Durlock
- Cliffsend
- Richborough Roman Fort
- Goldstone
- Paramour Street
- Cop Street
- Hoaden
- Weddington
- Ash
- Durlock
- Guilton
- Wingham
- Marshborough
- Staple
- Statenborough
- Woodnesborough
- Goodnestone
- Eastry
- Heronden
- Nonington
- Tilmanstone
- Betteshanger
- Sutton
- East Studdal
- Ringwould
- Ashley

- MARGATE
- Main Sands
- Cliftonville
- Kingsgate
- Northdown
- Botany Bay
- NORTH FORELAND
- Joss Bay
- North Foreland
- Reading Street
- Stone Bay
- Lydden
- Hornby
- Haine
- St Peter's
- Westwood
- Broadstairs
- Dumpton
- Hereson
- St Lawrence
- Ramsgate
- Pegwell
- Viking Ship 'Hugin'
- St Augustine's Cross
- Pegwell Bay
- Sandwich Bay
- Great Stonar
- Sandwich
- Royal St George's
- Stone Cross
- Toll
- Ham
- Hacklinge
- Finglesham
- Marley
- Sholden
- Northbourne
- Worth
- Great Mongeham
- Upper Deal
- The Downs
- Deal
- Castle
- Walmer
- Castle
- Ripple
- Kingsdown
- West Langdon
- East Langdon

27

Foreness Point

Town plan: Canterbury p.194

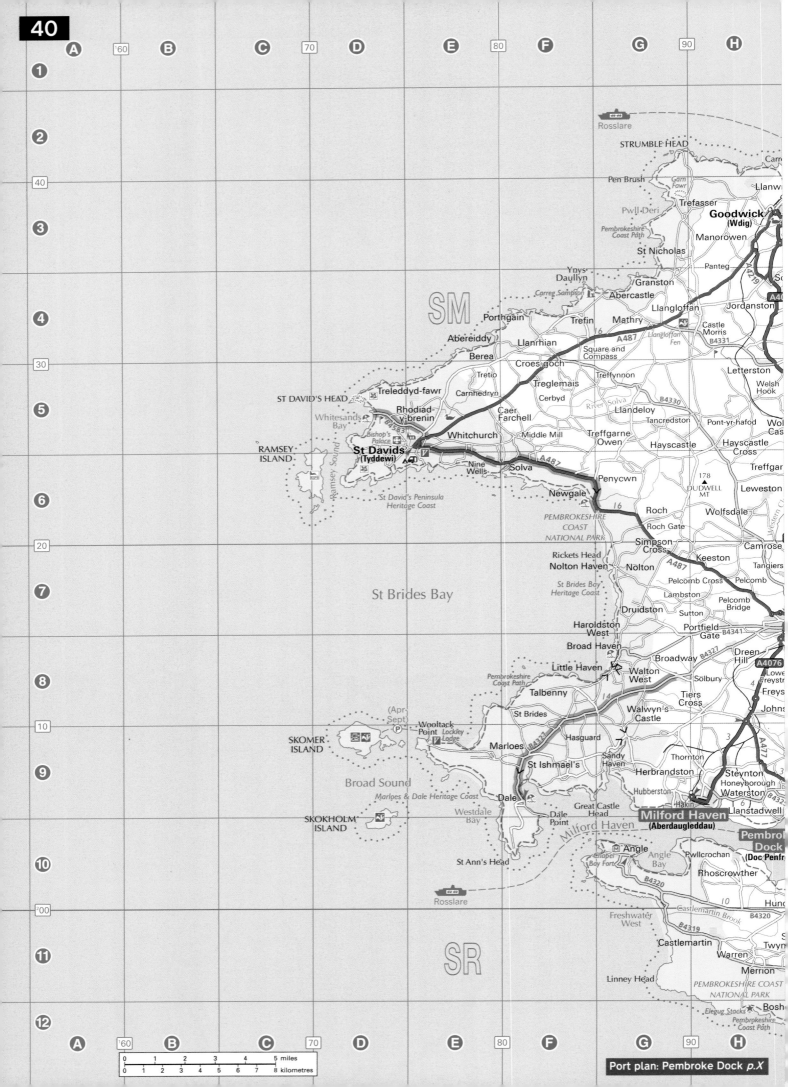

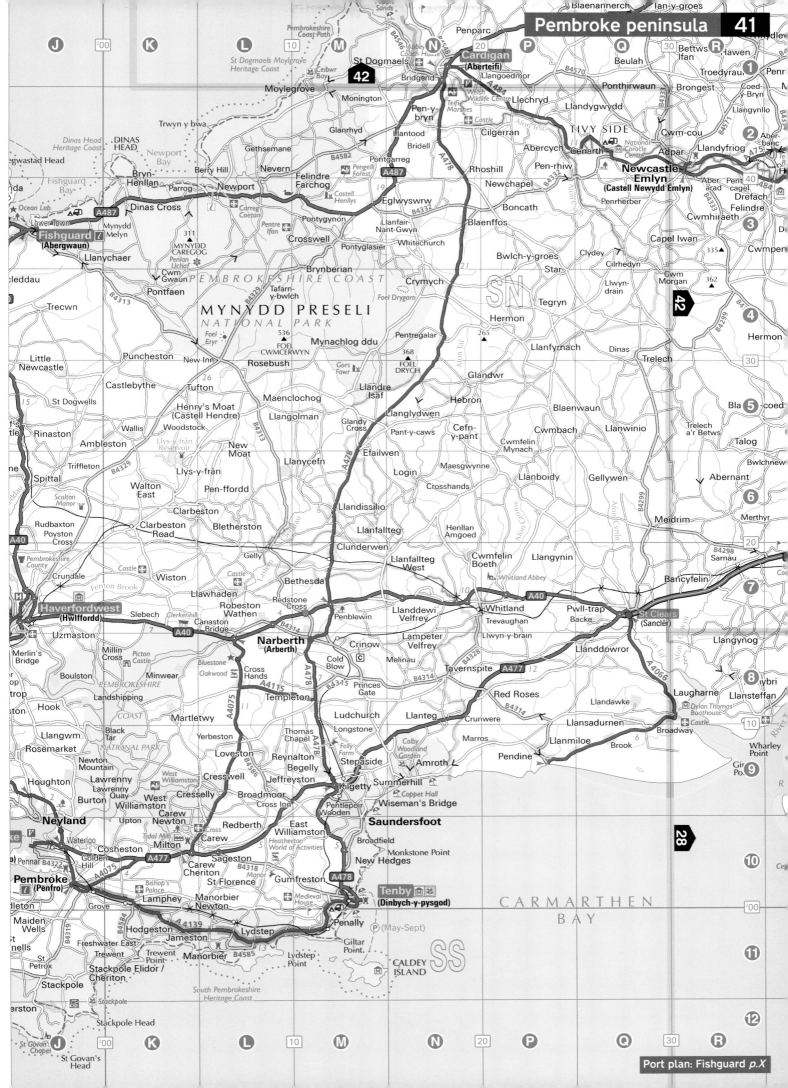

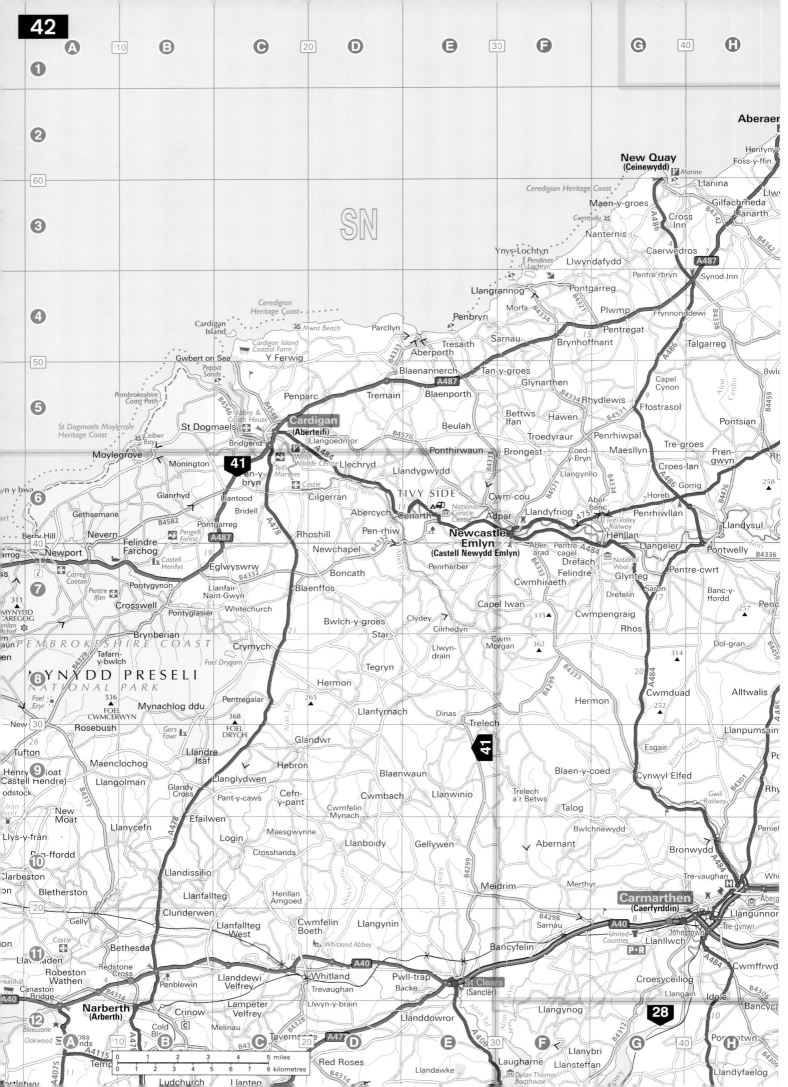

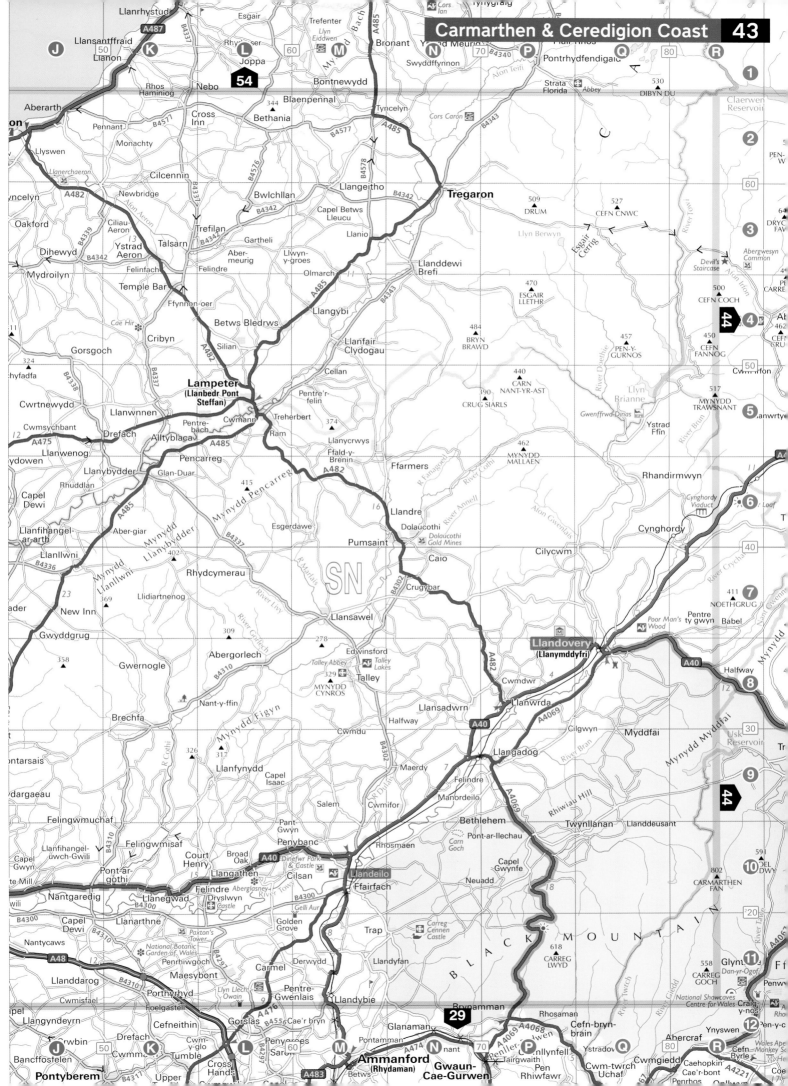

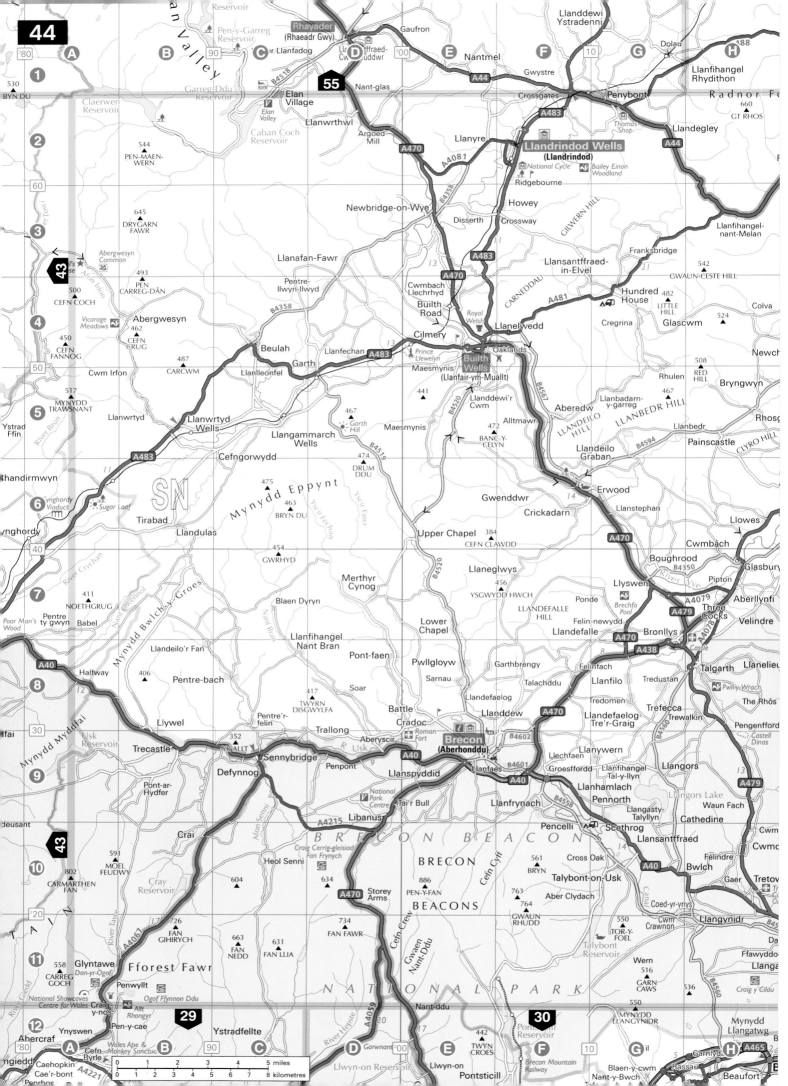

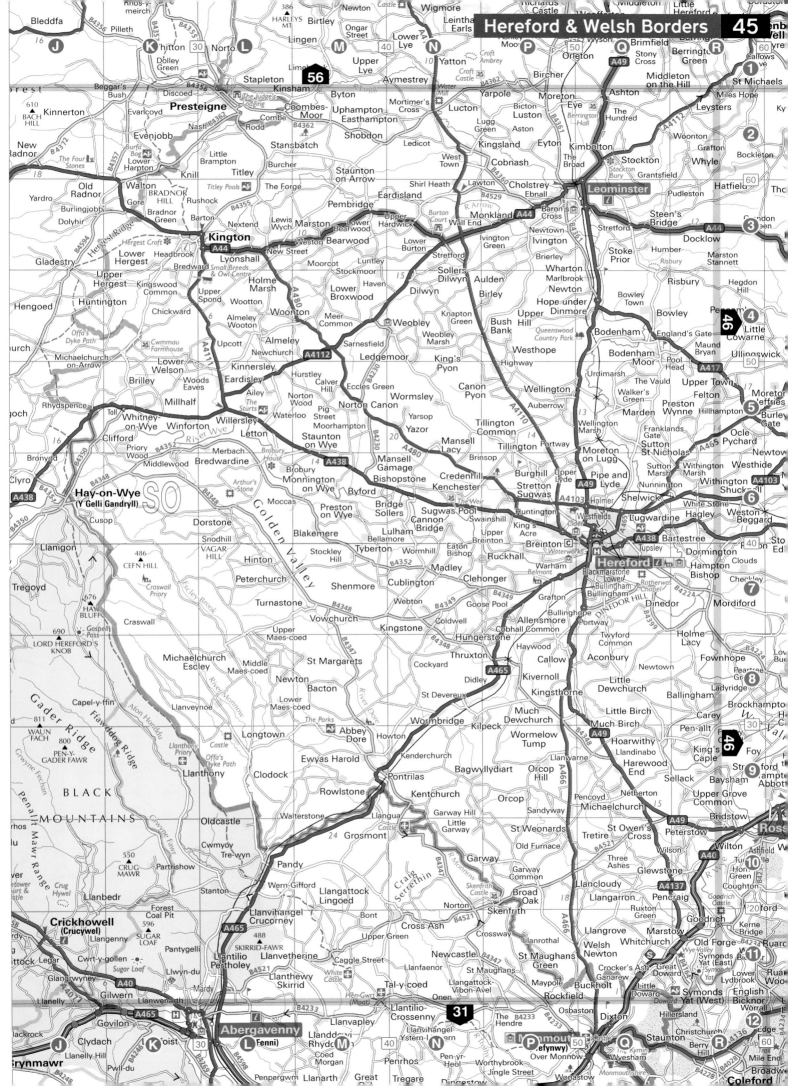

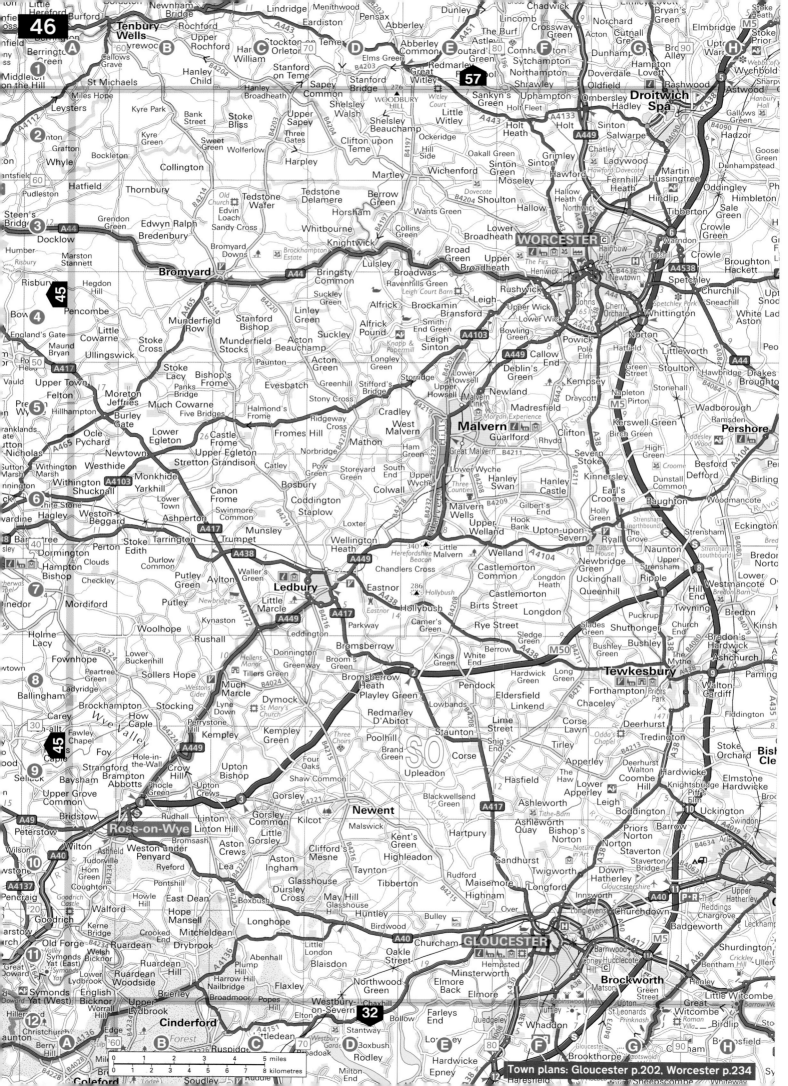

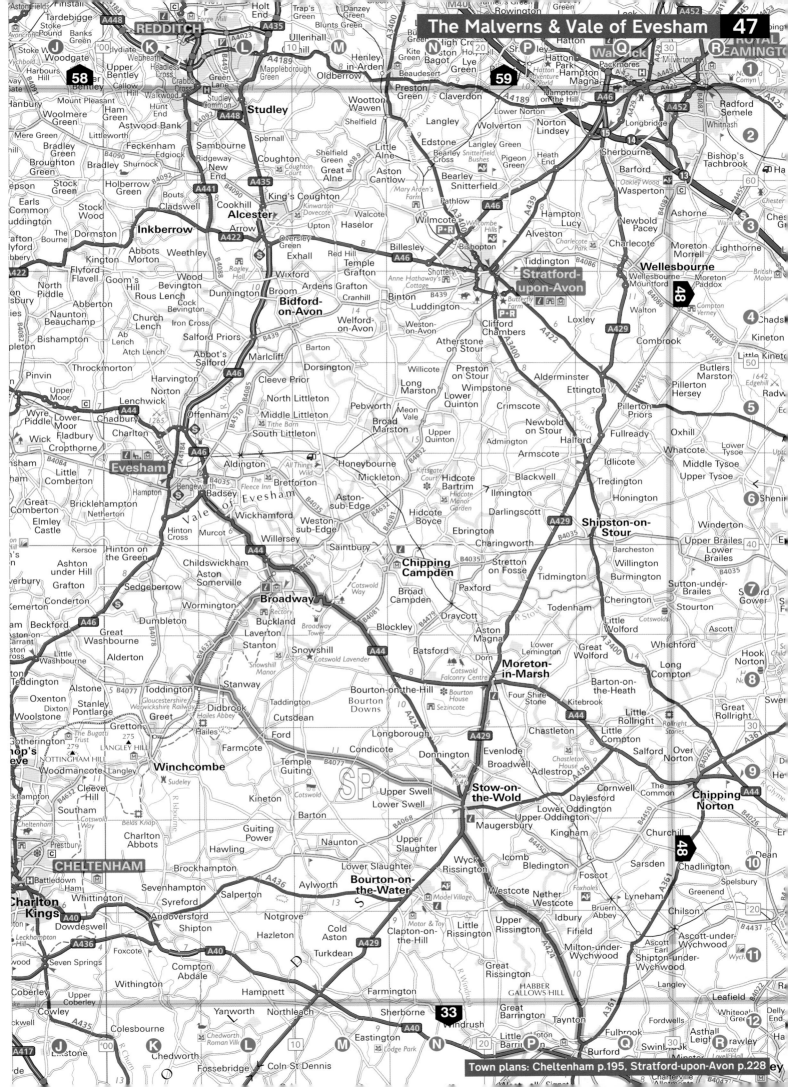

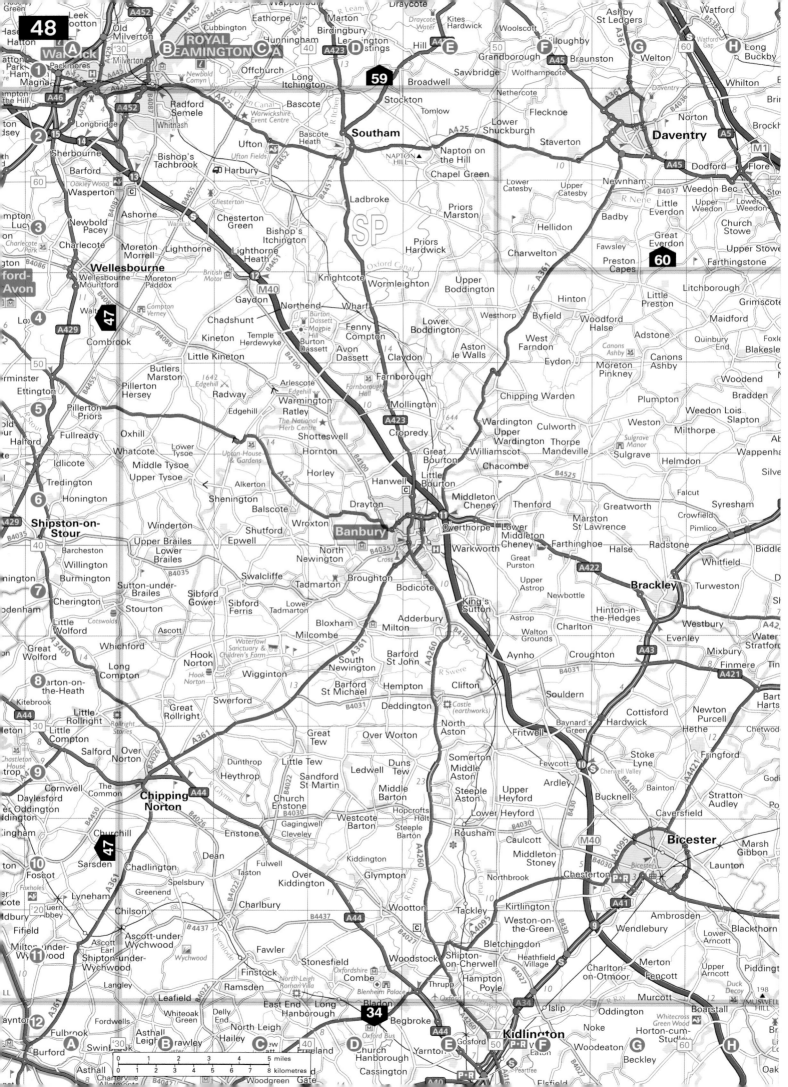

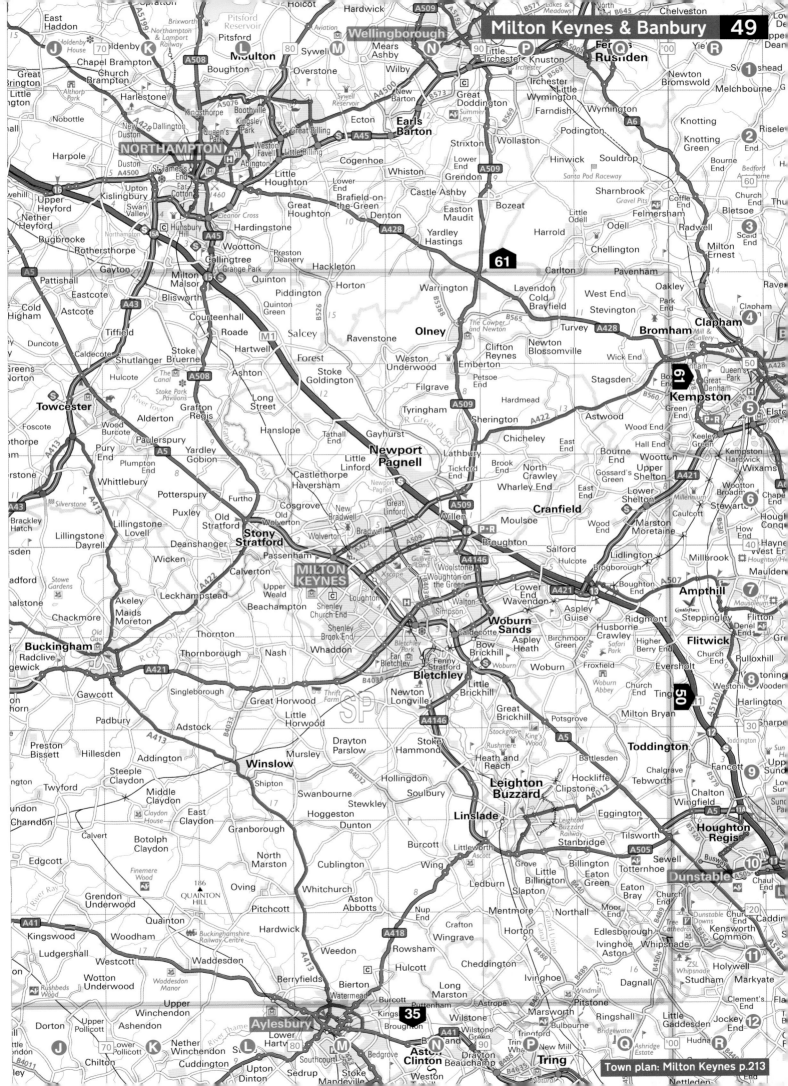

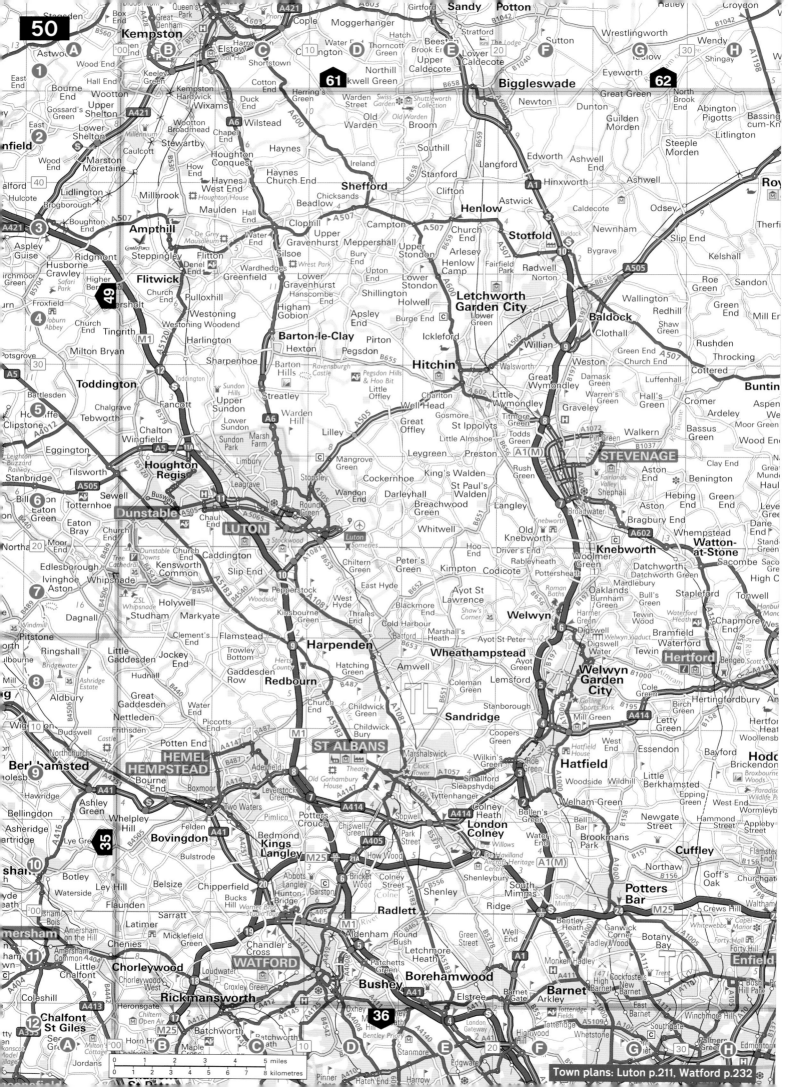

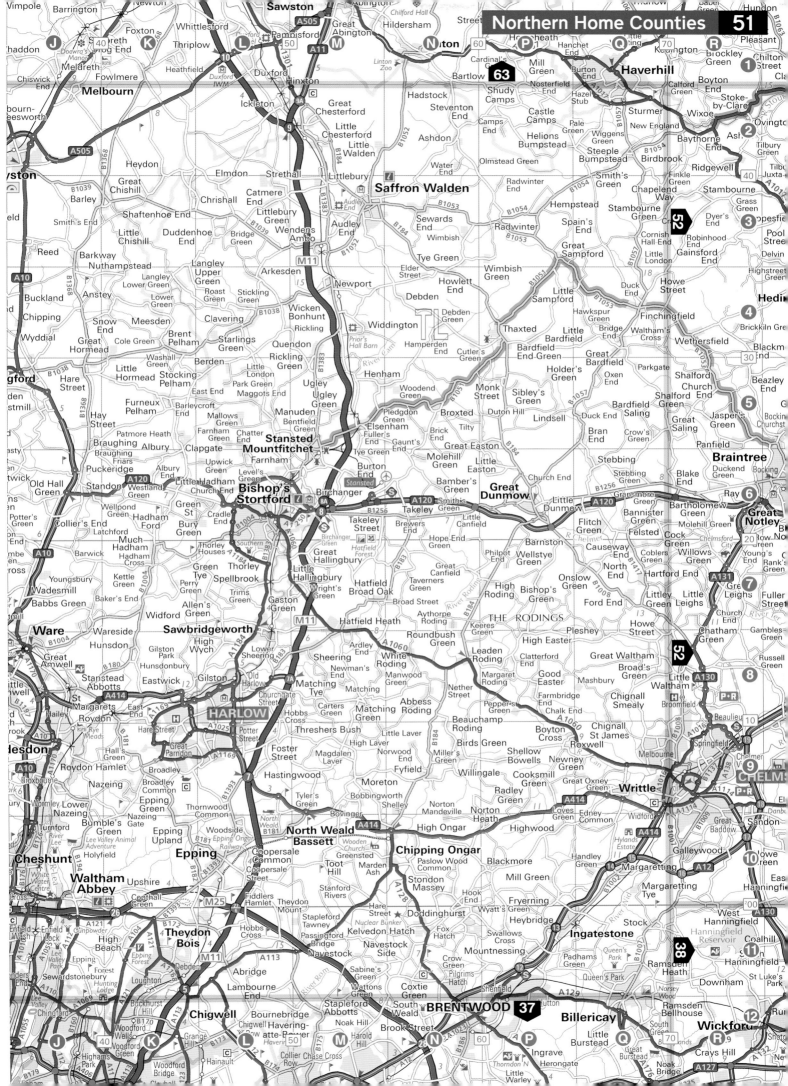

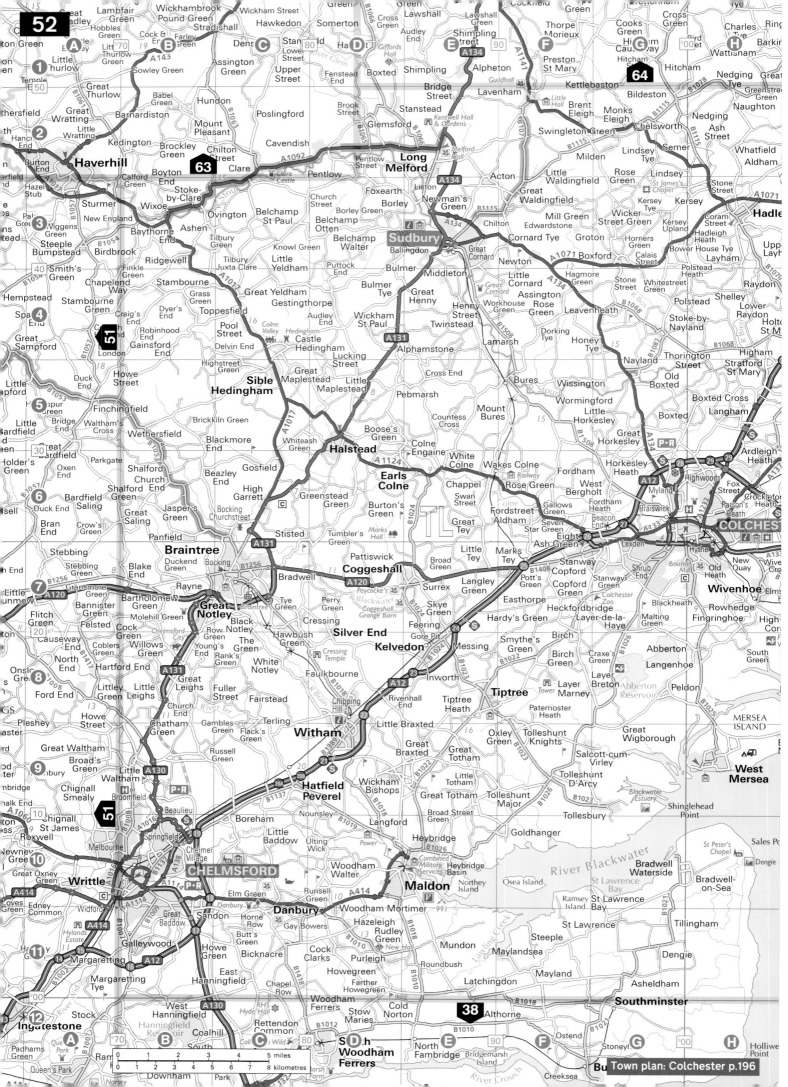

Harwich International Port

PASSENGER & CRUISE TERMINAL
HARWICH INTERNATIONAL STATION
CAR FERRY TERMINAL
FREIGHT TERMINAL
EAST DOCK ROAD
WEST DOCK ROAD
REFINERY ROAD
Parkeston
Harwich Industrial Estate
Superstore
PARKESTON ROUNDABOUT
ST NICHOLAS ROUNDABOUT
Superstore
Premier Inn
HARWICH
A120
Dovercourt
IPSWICH, COLCHESTER
Upper Dovercourt
MAIN ROAD
FRONK'S ROAD
IAA
0   400 m

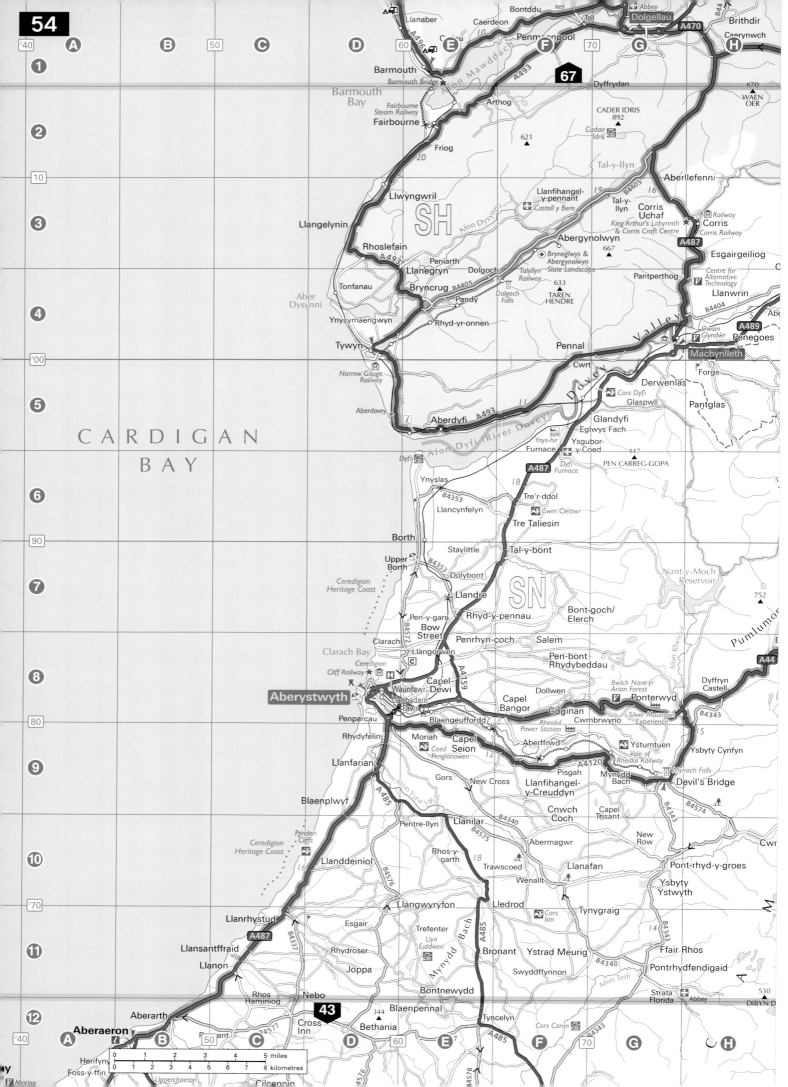

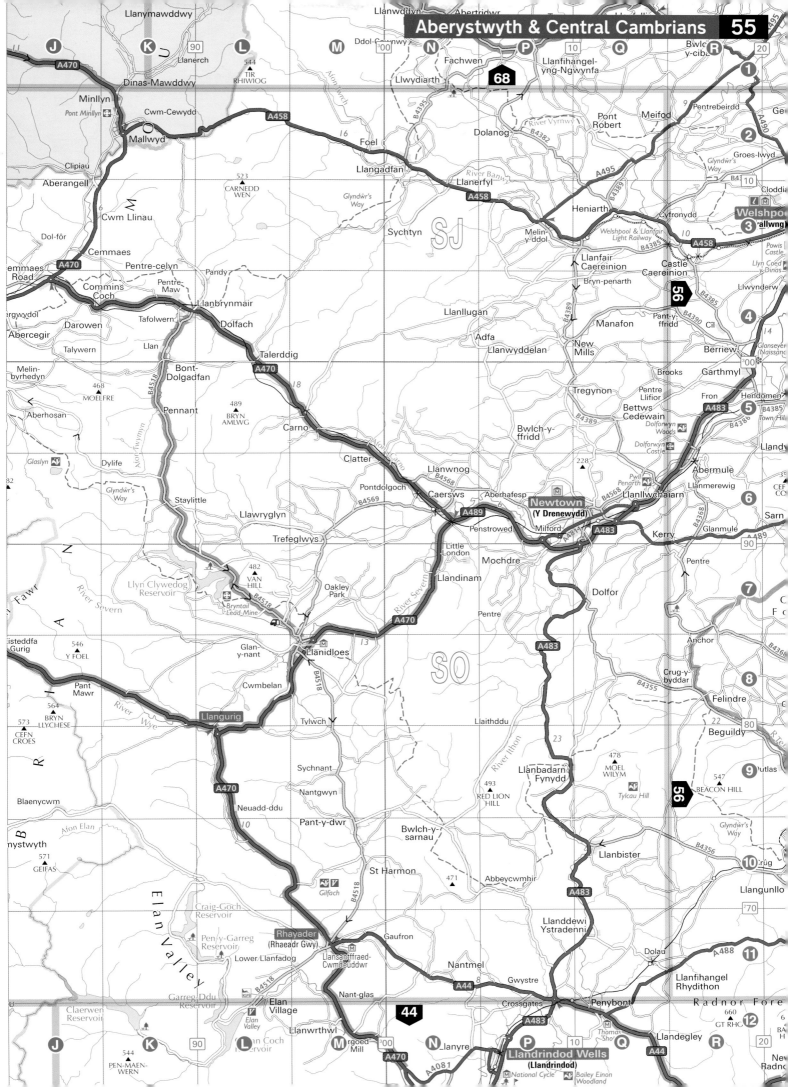

Llanymawddwy
Llanwddyn Abertridwr
J K Llanerch 90 L M Ddol-Cownwy N Fachwen P Q R
Dinas-Mawddwy 544 **68** Llanfihangel- Bwlch-y-cibau 20
TIR yng-Ngwynfa
Minllyn RHIWIOG Llwydiarth 1
Pont Minllyn Cwm-Cewydd Afon Twrch Meifod Pentrebeirdd 9 A490
Mallwyd A458 16 Foel Dolanog Pont 2
Clipiau Robert B4382 Glyndŵr's Groes-lwyd
Llangadfan River Banw Way B4
Aberangell A470 523 Llanerfyl A495 10 Cloddia
CARNEDD A458 Heniarth B4389 Welshpool
WEN Glyndŵr's SJ Cyfronydd rallwng
Cwm Llinau Way Welshpool & Llanfair 3
Dol-fôr Sychtyn Melin- Light Railway 10 A458 Powis
y-ddol B4385 Castle
Cemmaes Pentre-celyn Llanfair Castle Llyn Coed
rgwydol A470 Pandy Caereinion Caereinion y Dinas
Cemmaes Commins Pentre- Bryn-penarth 56 B4385 Llwynderw
Road Coch Maw Llanbrynmair Llanllugan B4389 4
Darowen Tafolwern Dolfach Manafon Pant-y- A4390 Cîl 14
Abercegir Talywern Llan Adfa New ffridd Berriew Glanseve
Talerddig Llanwyddelan Mills 00 (Naiss
Melin- Bont- A470 Brooks Garthmyl Hendomen
byrhedyn 468 Dolgadfan 18 Tregynon Pentre Fron A483 5 B4385
MOELFRE Pennant 489 Llifior Bettws Dolforwyn Town Hill B4386
Aberhosan BRYN Carno Cedewain Woods Llandi
AMLWG B4389 Dolforwyn
Dylife Clatter Castle Abermule 3
Glaslyn Afon Carno Llanwnog 228 Llanmerewig CEF
Staylittle Pontdolgoch B4568 Pwll 6
Glyndŵr's B4569 Caersws Aberhafesp Penarth Llanllwchaiarn
82 Way Llawryglyn 5 A489 Newtown A483 Sarn
Trefeglwys Penstrowed (Y Drenewydd) Kerry Glanmule 90 A489
N Little Milford A4814 A483 Pentre 7
Fawr River Severn 482 London Mochdre Dolfor
VAN HILL Oakley Llandinam Anchor Fo
Llyn Clywedog Park Pentre A483 Crug-y- 8
Reservoir Bryntail River Severn byddar B4355
Lead Mine A470 13 Felindre
isteddfa 546 Glan- Llanidloes SO 22 80
Gurig Y FOEL y-nant B4518 Beguildy
564 Cwmbelan Llanbadarn 478 547 9 utlas
Pant BRYN Fynydd MOEL BEACON HILL
Mawr LLYCHESE Llangurig Tylwch WILYM Glyndŵr's
573 A470 Sychnant Llaithddu Tylcau Hill 56 Way
CEFN River Wye Nantgwyn River Ithon Llanbister
CROES R 23
Blaenycwm Neuadd-ddu Bwlch-y- B4356 10 rug
Afon Elan A470 10 Pant-y-dwr sarnau 70
ystwyth 571 493 Llangunllo
GEIFAS St Harmon RED LION 471 Abbeycwmhir Llanfihangel
B HILL Llanddewi A488 11
Elan Gilfach Ystradenni Dolau A490
Valley B4518 44 Gaufron Nantmel Penybont 660 12
Craig-Goch Rhayader Llansantffraed- GT RHO
Reservoir (Rhaeadr Gwy) Cwmdeuddwr A44 8 Gwystre Llandegley 20 Rad
Pen-y-Garreg Lower Llanfadog A483 N Radnor Fore
Reservoir Crossgates Q R
J K 90 L M N P Llandrindod Wells A44 Nant
544 Garreg-Ddu Elan A470 A483 (Llandrindod) Radnor
PEN-MAEN- Reservoir Village rgoed lanyre Thomas National Cycle
WERN Claerwen Llanwrthwl Mill n Coch A4081 Bailey Einon
Reservoir Elan eservoir Woodland
Valley

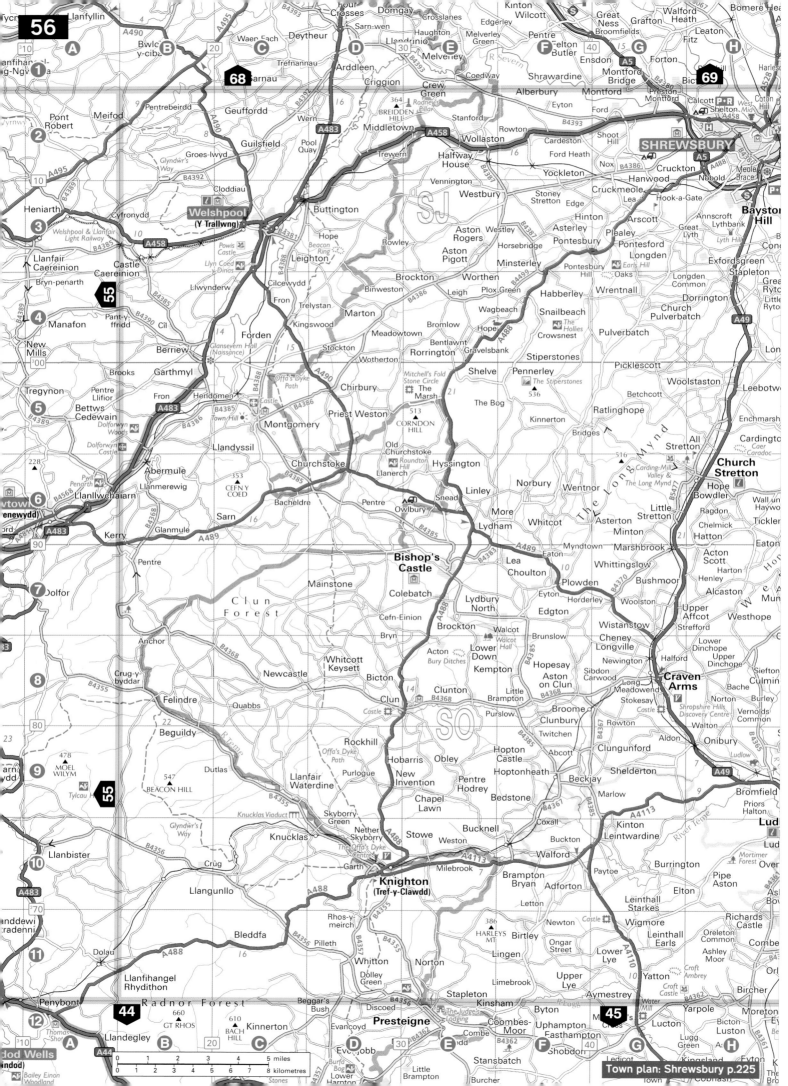

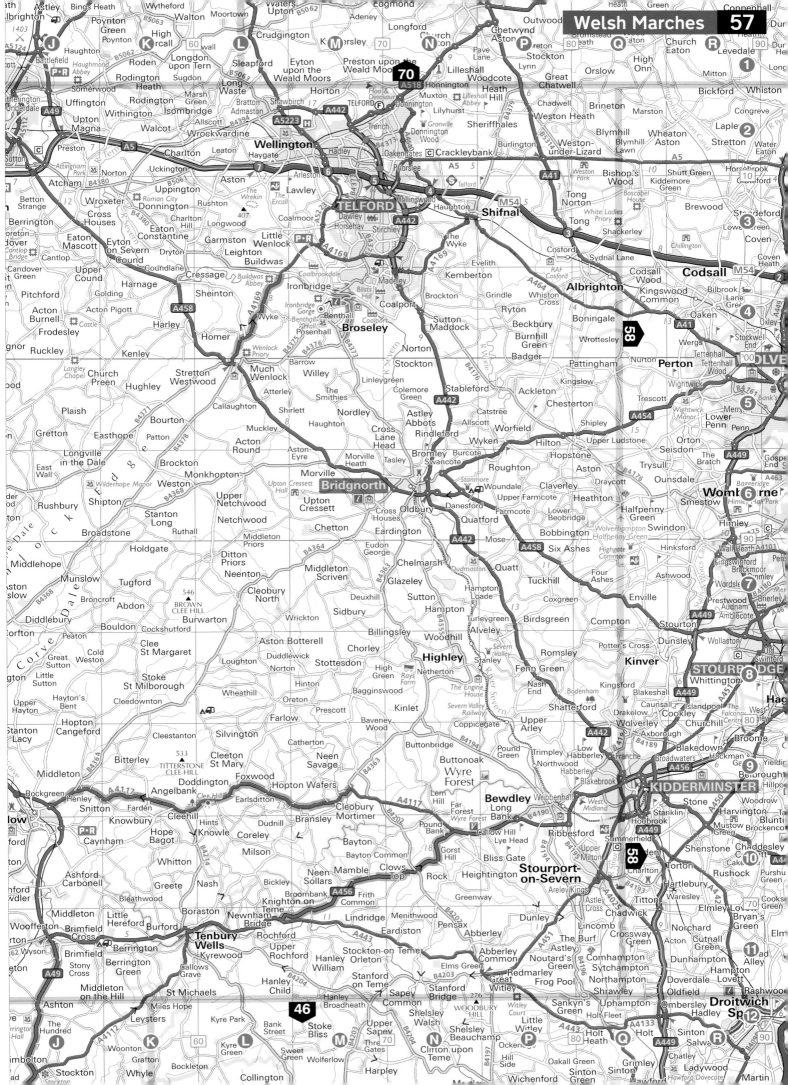

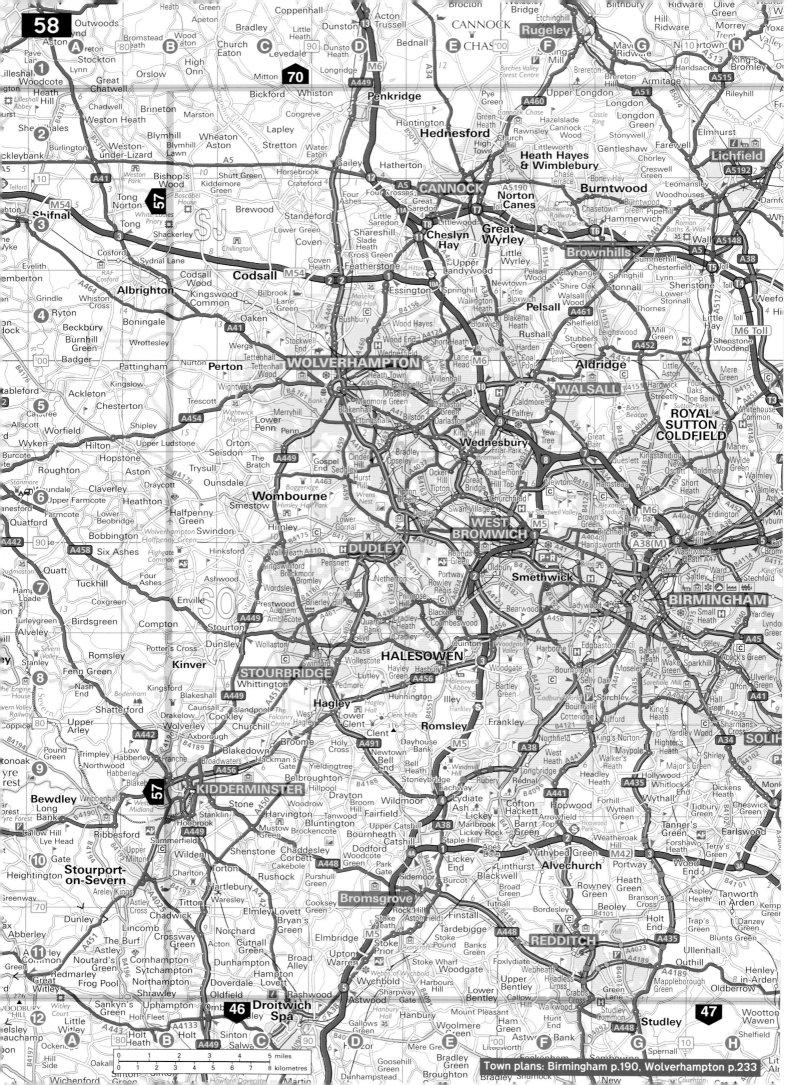

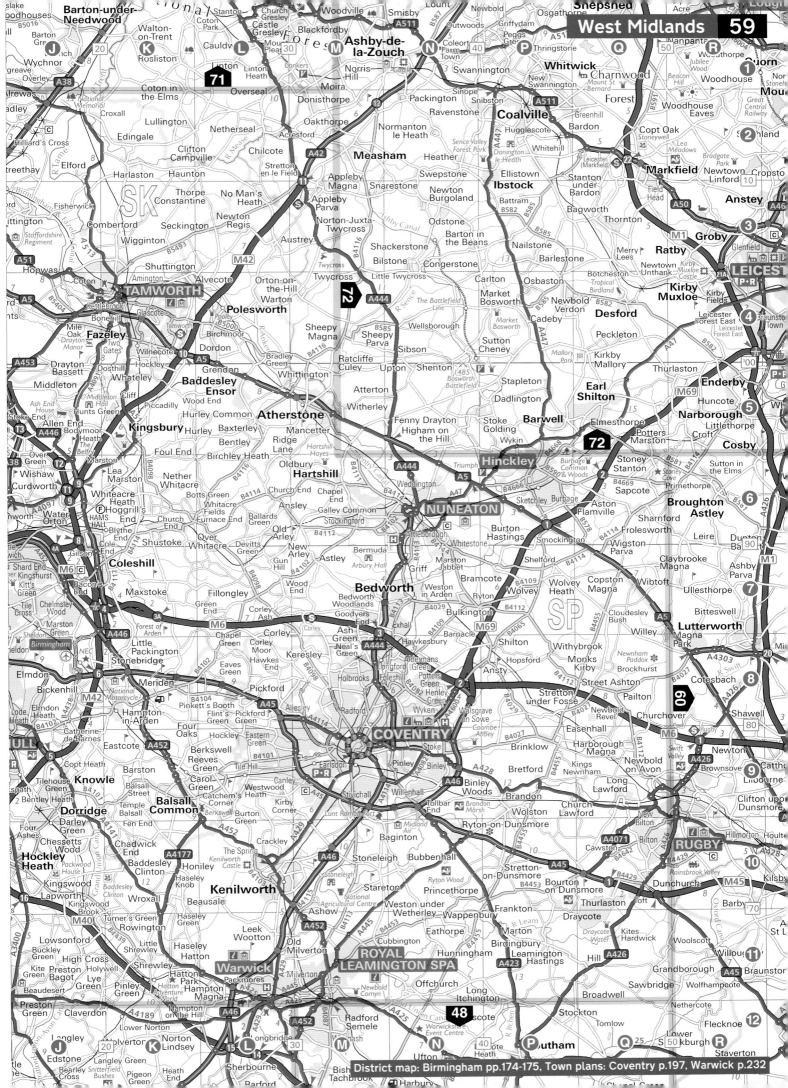

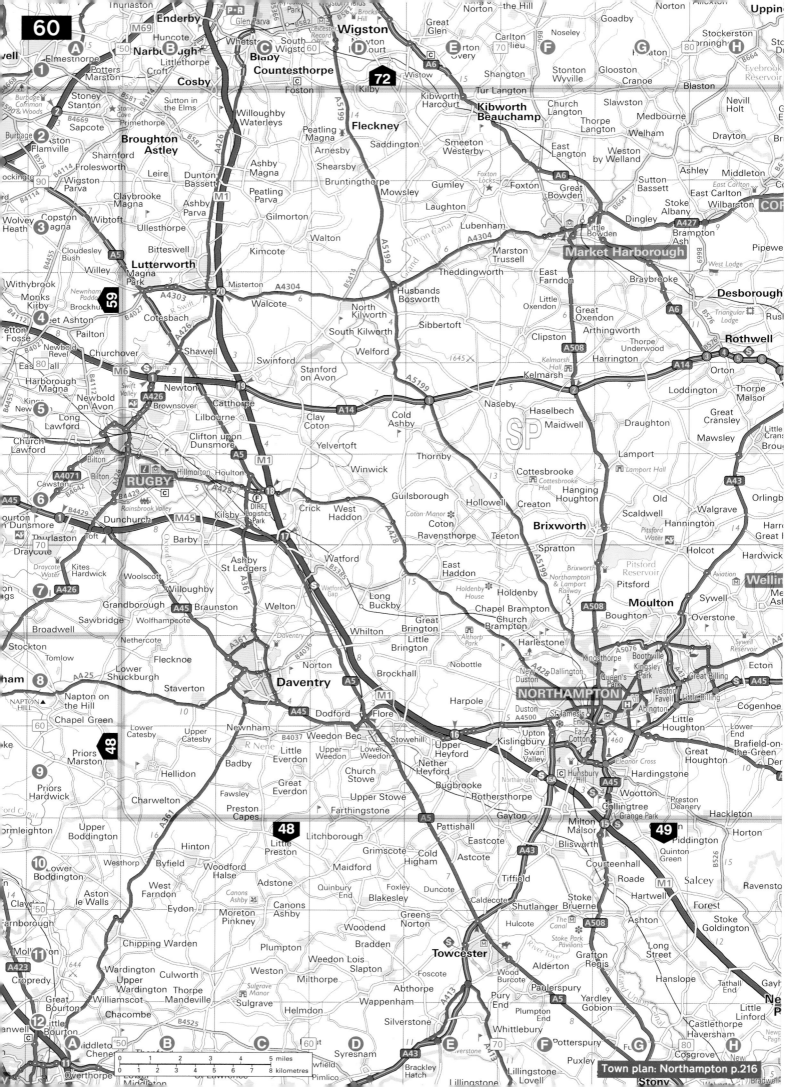

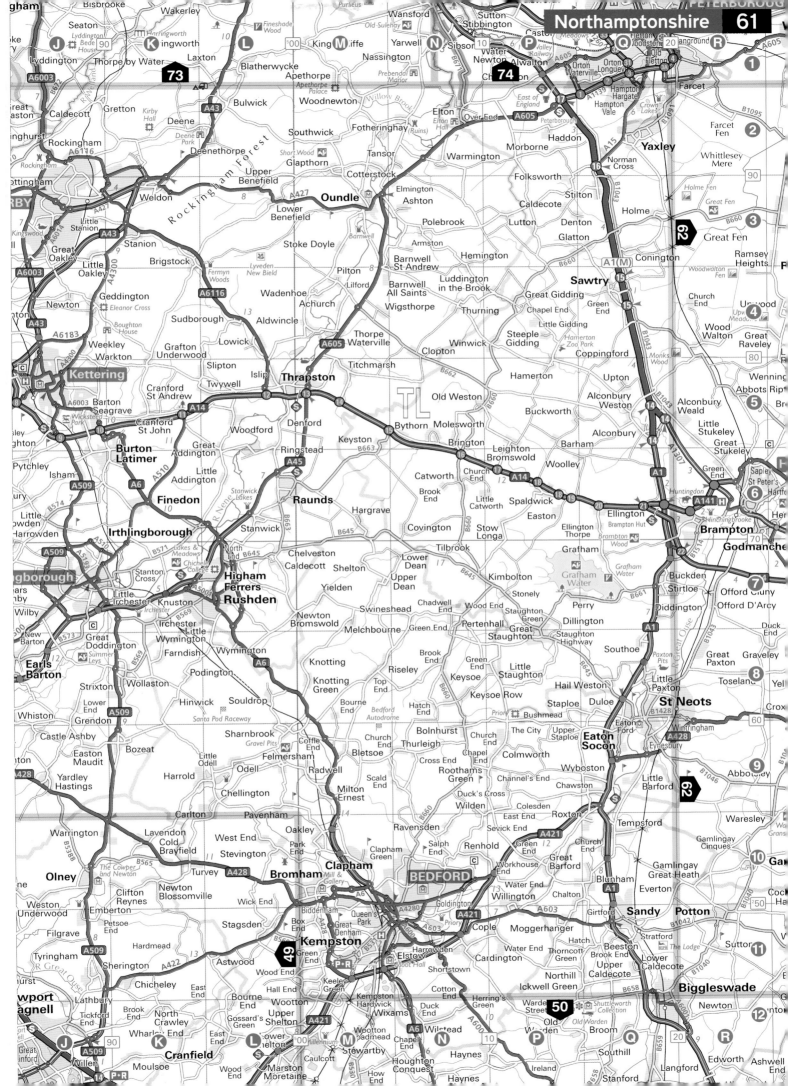

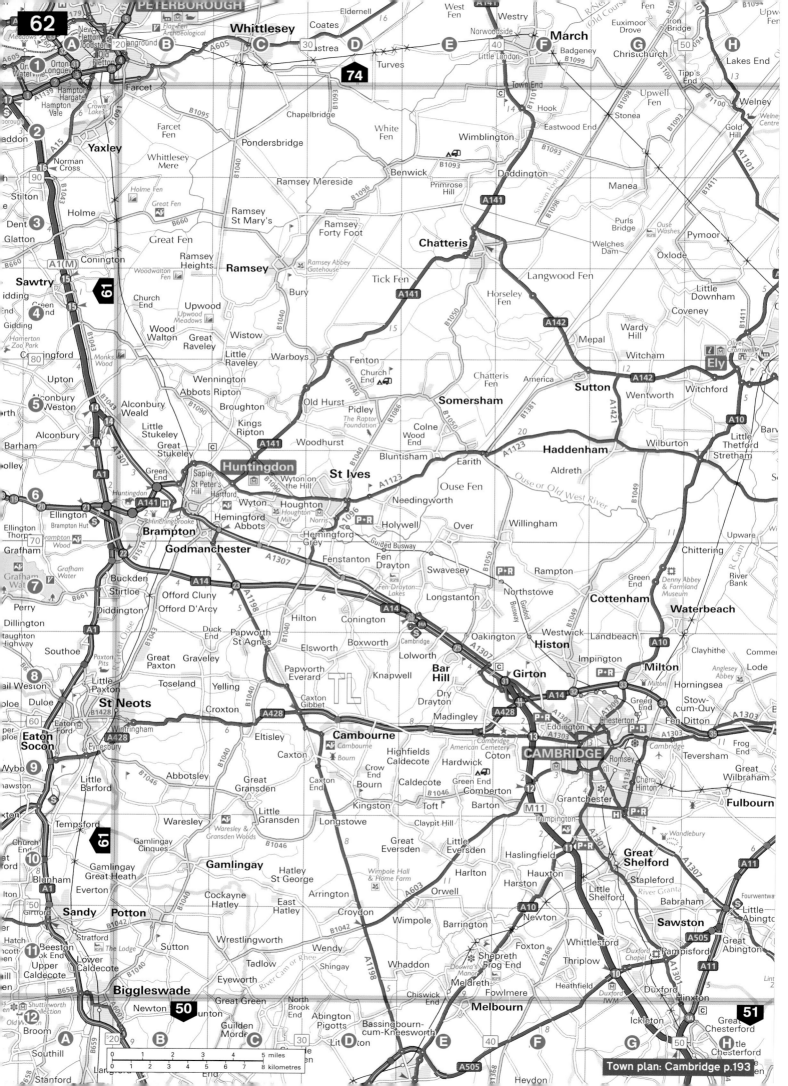

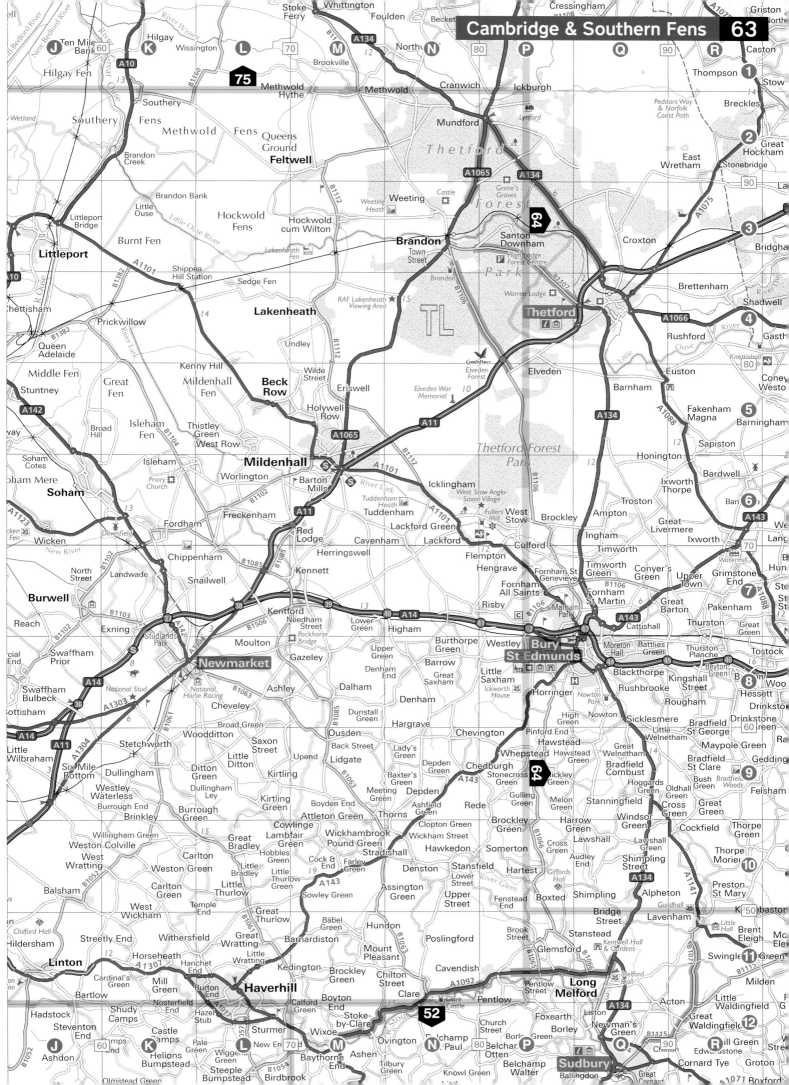

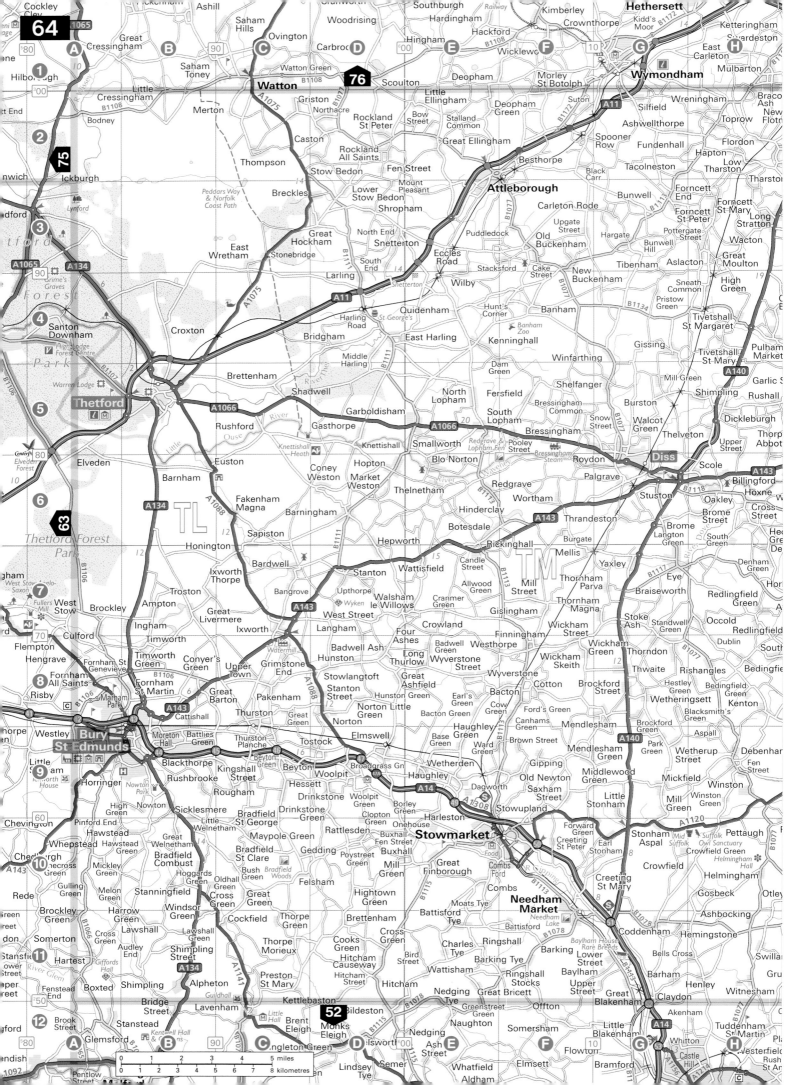

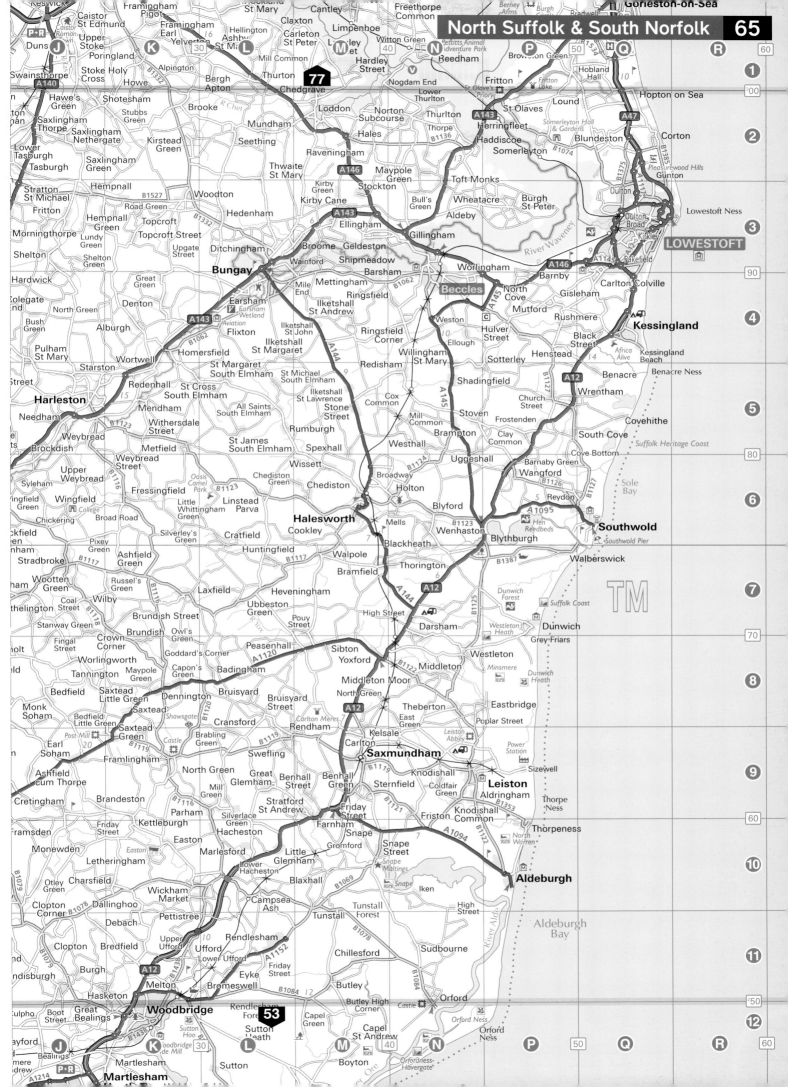

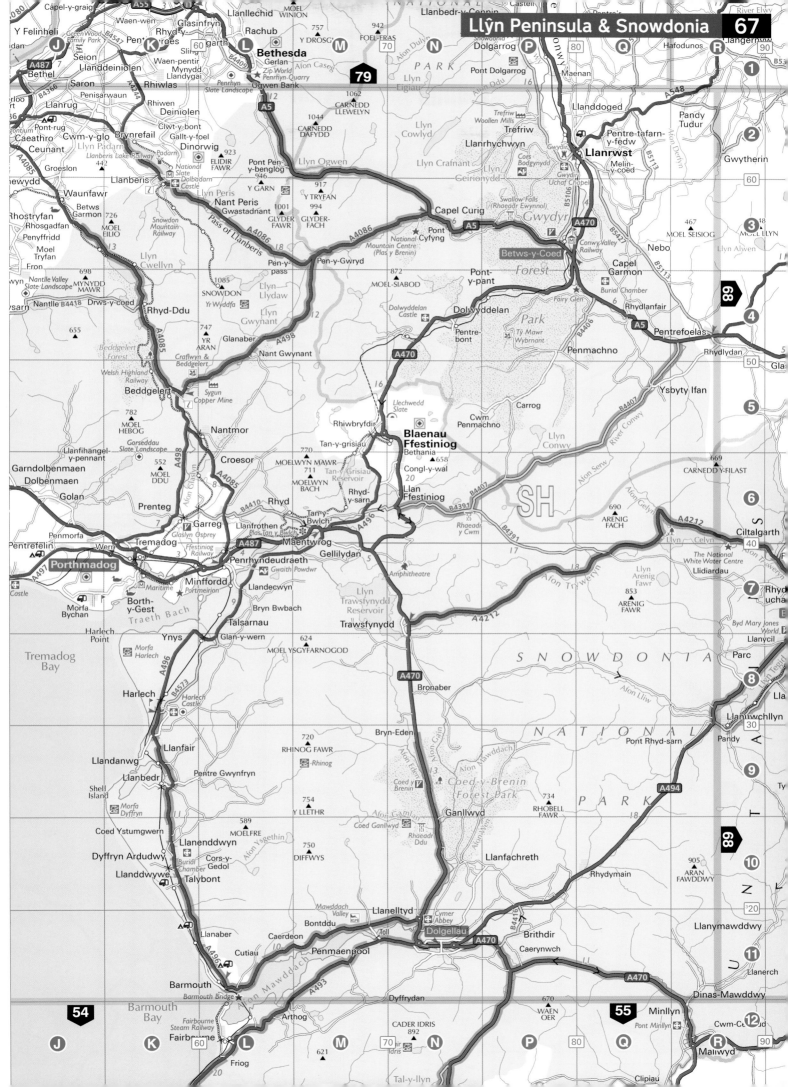

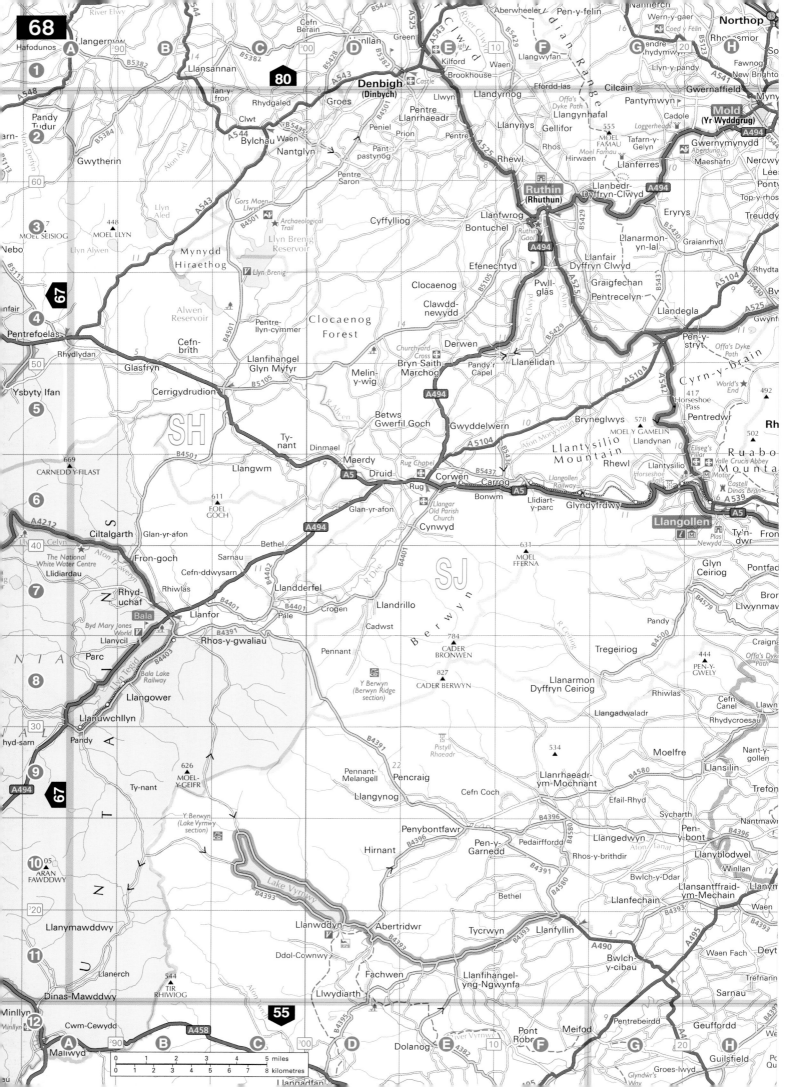

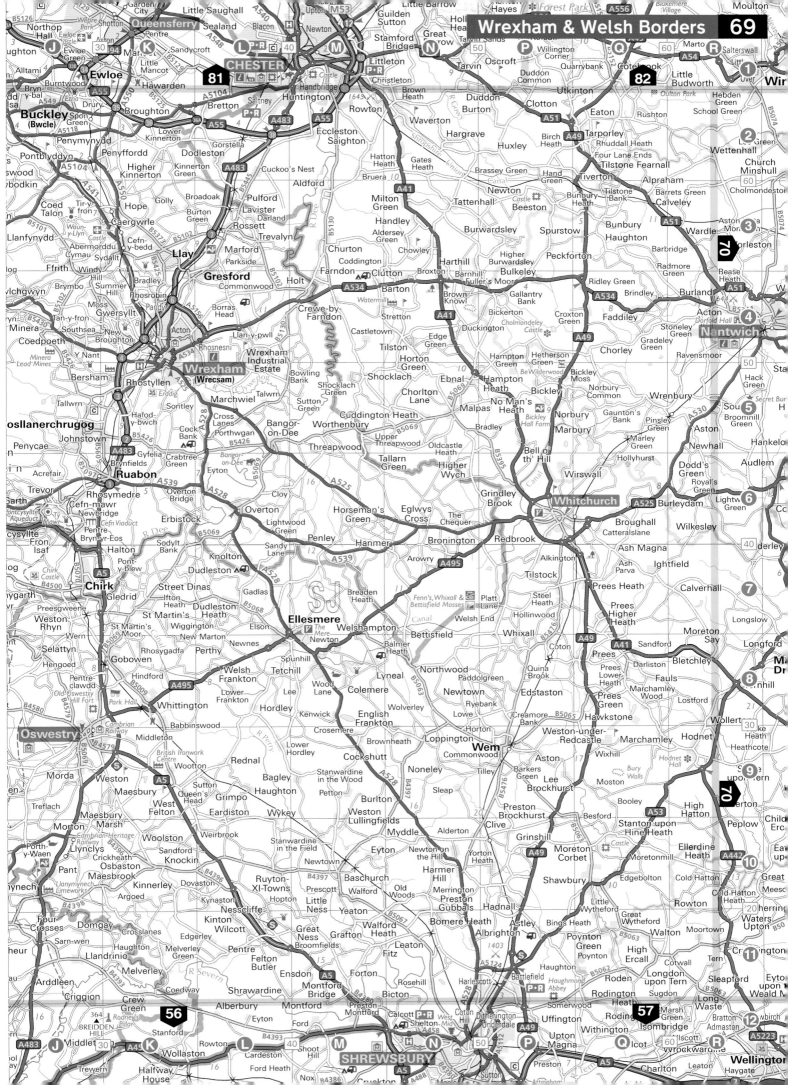

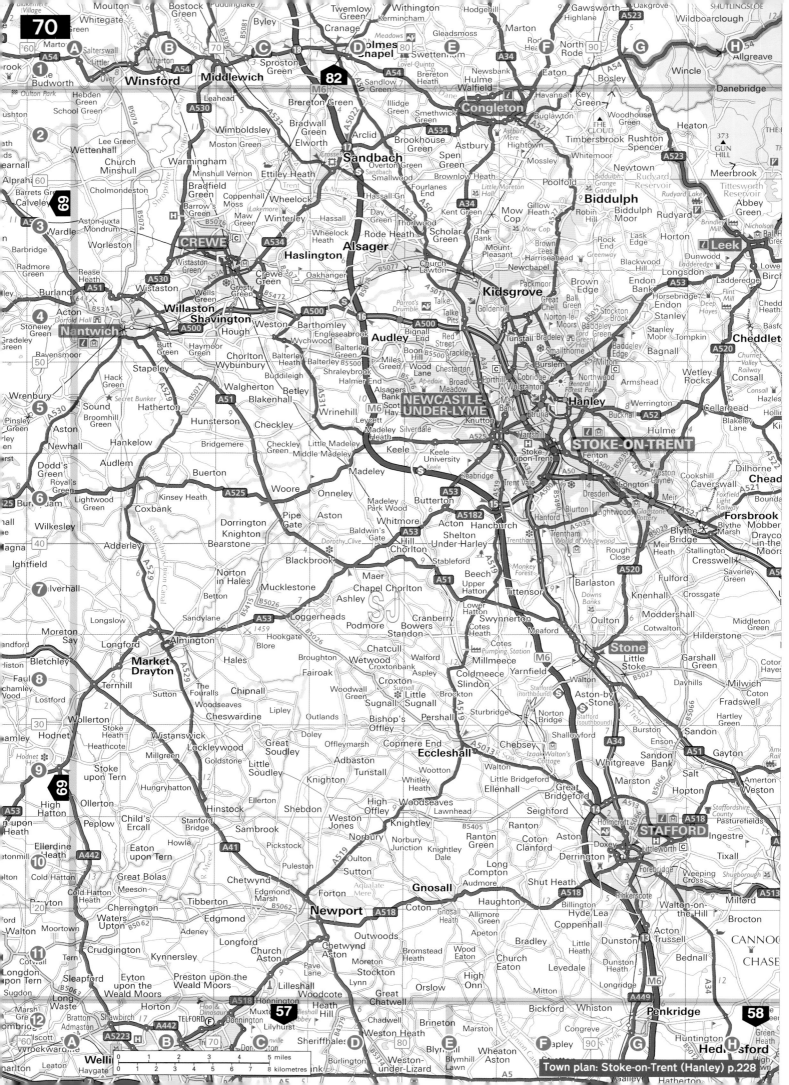

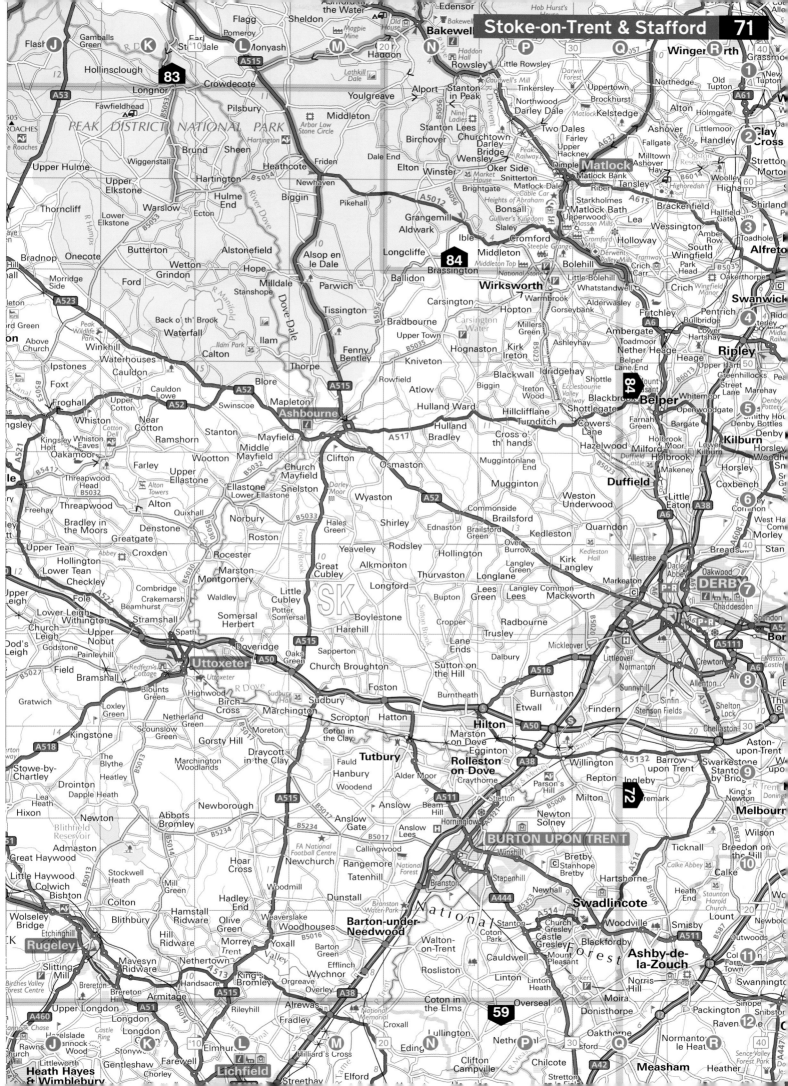

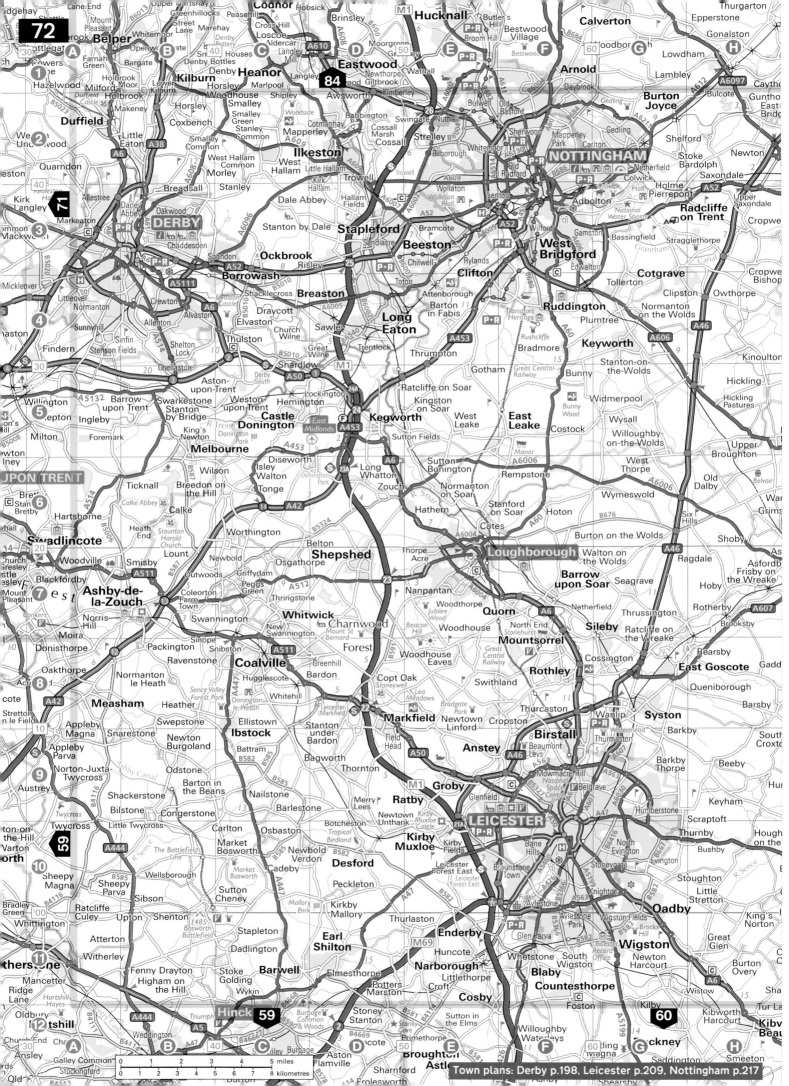

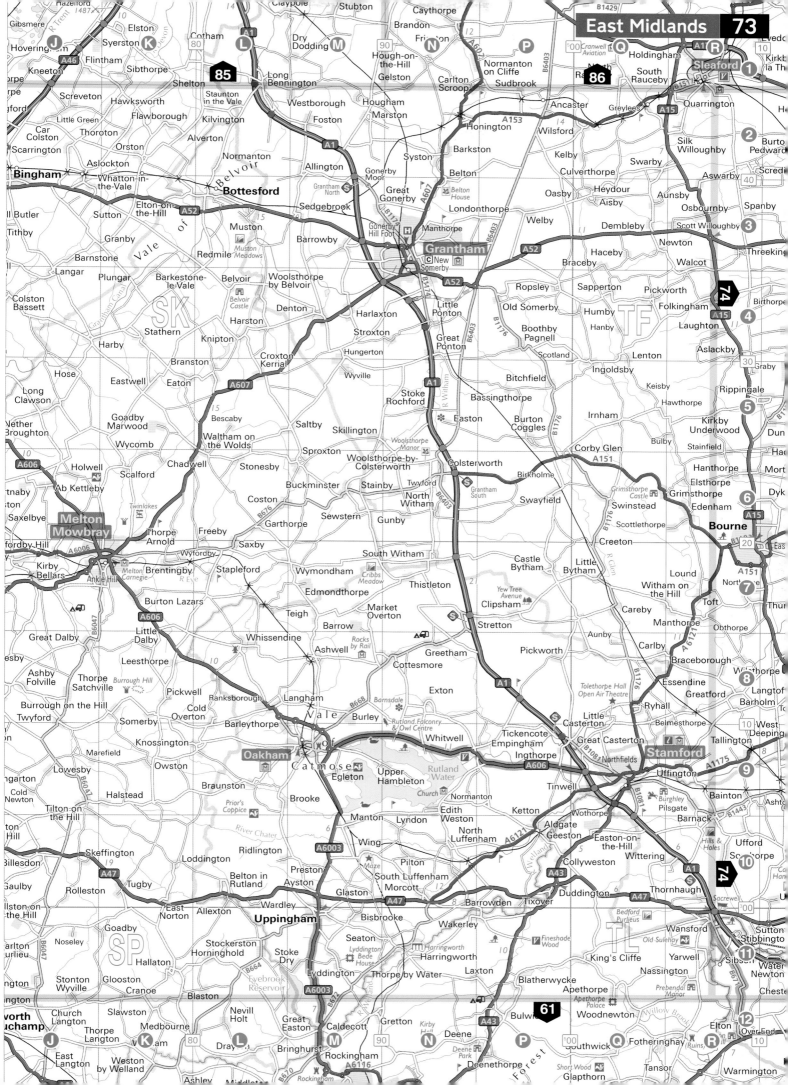

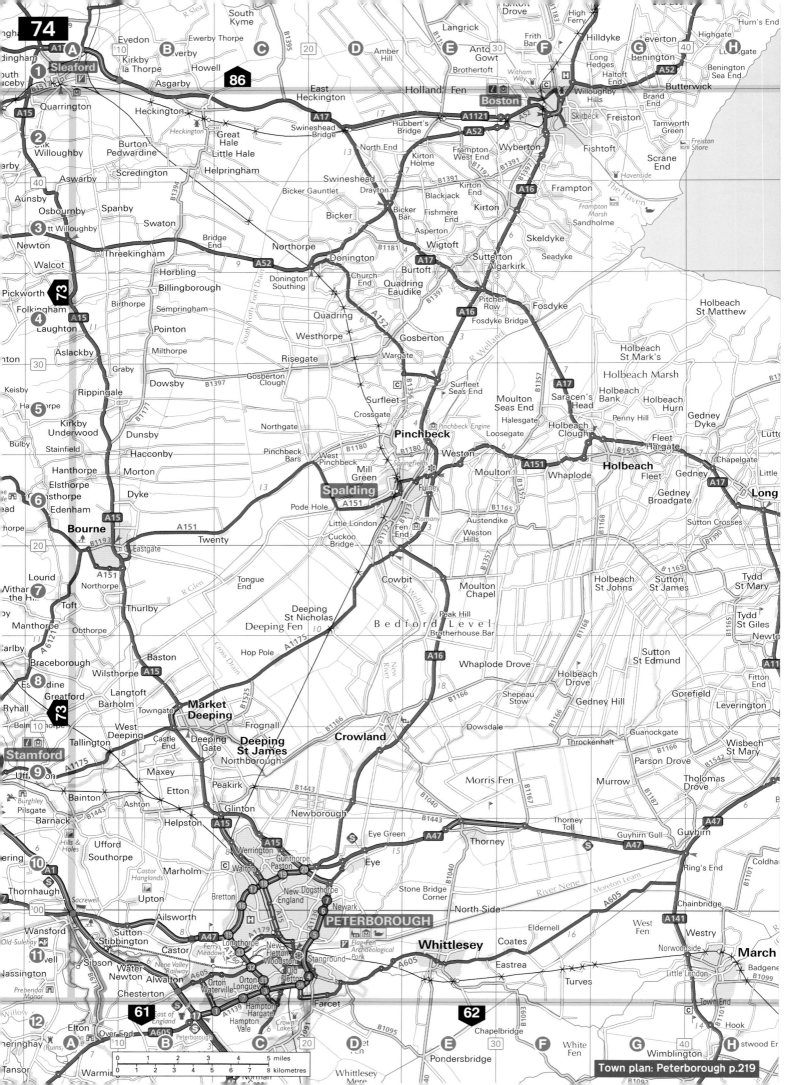

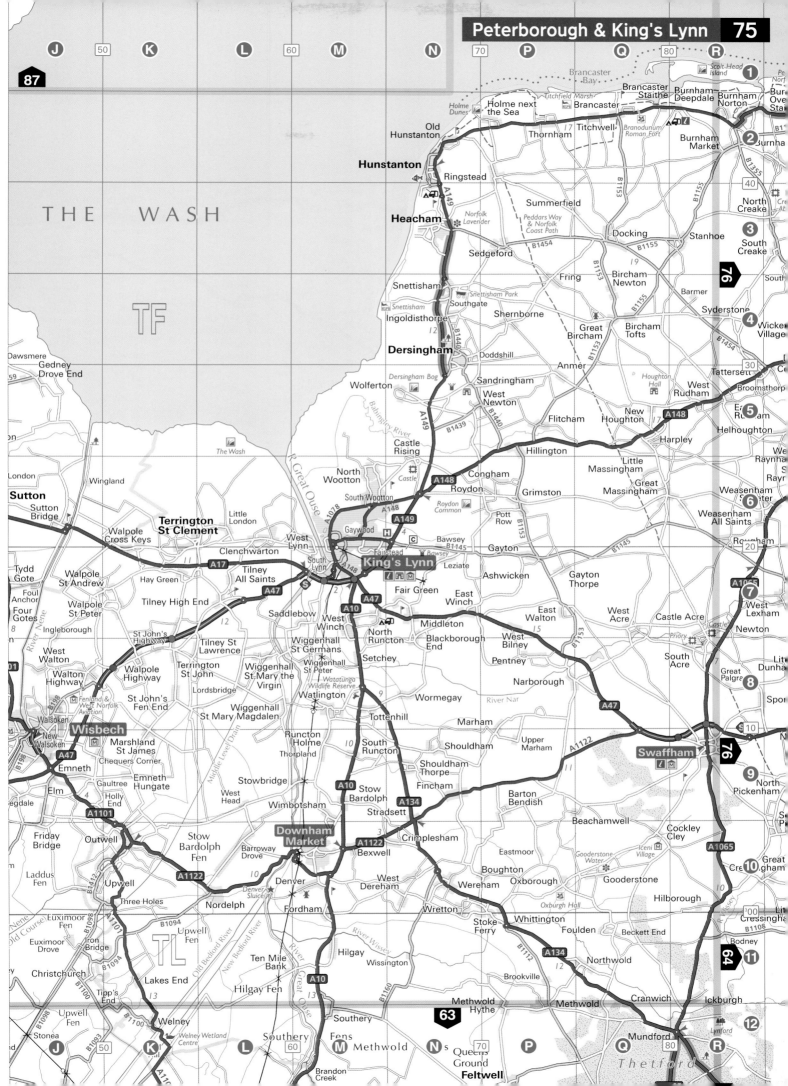

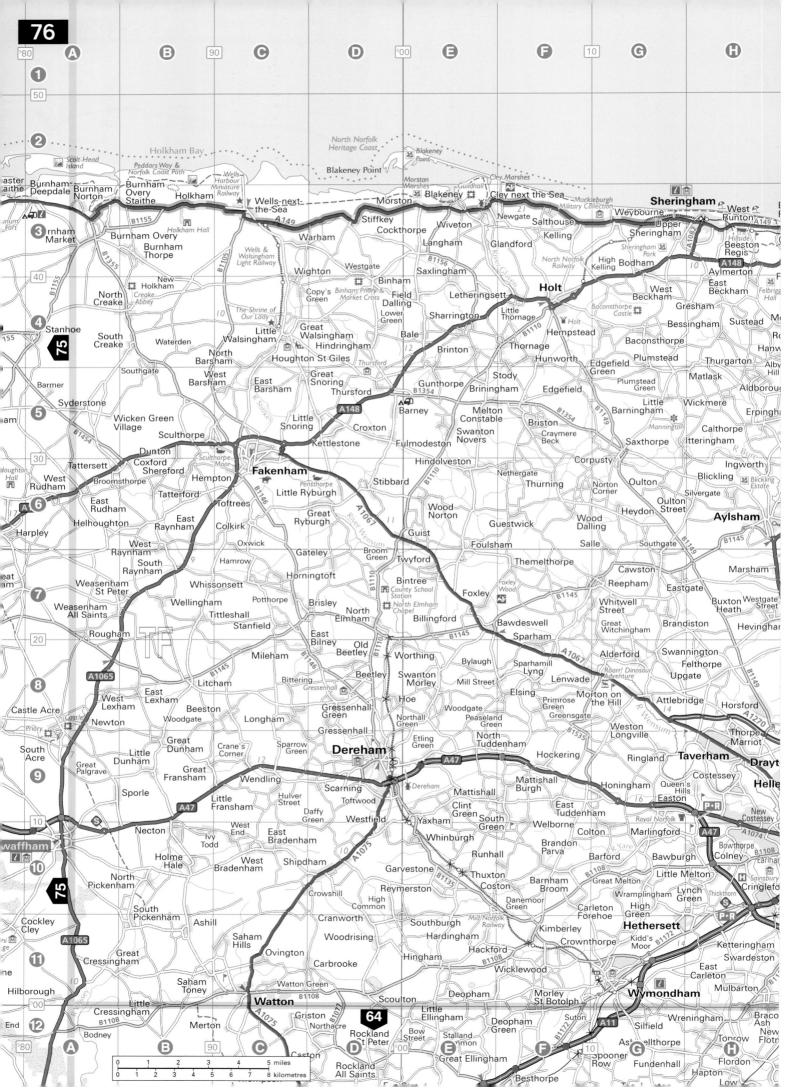

J   K 30   L   M 40   N   P 50   Q   R 60

1
50
2
3
40
4
5
30
6
20
7
8
10
9
10
00
11
12

TG

East Runton
Cromer
Overstrand
Sidestrand
Northrepps
Trimingham
Felbrigg
A149
B1436
Crossdale Street
Gimingham
Mundesley
Southrepps
Lower Street
Stow Mill
Knapton
Paston
Bacton
Walcott
Trunch
Bradfield
Old Hall Street
Edingthorpe
Antingham
Swafield
Pollard Street
Happisburgh
Thorpe Market
A140
A149
Suffield
Edingthorpe Green
Witton
Ridlington
Colby
North Walsham
Spa Common
Ridlington Street
Whimpwell Green
Banningham
B1145
Meeting House Hill
Crostwight
Happisburgh Common
Eccles on Sea
Hempstead
Felmingham
Tungate
Norfolk Motorcycle
Honing
Lessingham
Ingham Corner
Sea Palling
Tuttington
Skeyton Corner
Westwick
Briggate
East Ruston
Ingham
Waxham
Burgh next Aylsham
Bengate
Worstead
Stalham
Calthorpe Street
Skeyton
B1150
Dilham
The Broads
Stalham Green
Hickling
Horsey Corner
Swanton Abbott
Sloley
Frankfort
Low Street
Barton Turf
Sutton
Hickling Green
Horsey
Oxnead
Lamas
Scottow
Smallburgh
Wood Street
Hickling Heath
Hill Common
Horsey Windpump
Brampton
Badersfield
Little Hautbois
Fairstead
Pennygate
Barton Broad
Sutton Fen
Hickling Broad
Martham Broad
Buxton
Sco Ruston
Tunstead
Crowgate Street
Neatishead
Catfield
Catfield Common
West Somerton
East Somerton
Stratton Strawless
St James
Irstead
Sharp Green
Potter Heigham
Waterloo
Horstead
Coltishall
Wroxham Barns
Threehammer Common
Ludham
Martham
Winterton-on-Sea
Hainford
Frettenham
Belaugh
Hoveton
RAF Radar
Johnson Street
Bastwick
Cess
Hemsby Hole
A140
Newton St Faith
Wroxham
BeWILDerwood
Upper Street
A1062
Repps
Thurne
Rollesby
Hemsby
Newport
Horsham St Faith
Crostwick
A1151
Horning
Upper Street
R Thurne
Martham Broad
Ormesby Broad
Scratby
Spixworth
A1270
Rackheath
Woodbastwick
Bure Marshes
Broads Wildlife Centre
Clippesby
Burgh St Margaret
Ormesby St Michael
California
New Rackheath
Salhouse
Ranworth
Pilson Green
Thurne
Fleggburgh/
Ormesby St Margaret
Caister-on-Sea
Norwich
Old Catton
Sprowston
Little Plumstead
Panxworth
Ranworth Broad
Fairhaven
South Walsham
Cargate Green
Billockby
Filby
Thrigby
Mautby
Caister
West Caister
NORWICH
Thorpe End
Great Plumstead
Town Green
Hemblington
Burlingham Green
Upton
Stokesby
Thrigby Hall
West End
West Caister
Caister Roman Fort
Thorpe St Andrew
Witton
Blofield Heath
North Burlingham
Acle
Runham
A1042
A11
Blofield
Lingwood
Damgate
Stracey Arms Windpump
A47
Runham
Scroby Sands
Brundall
Postwick
Strumpshaw
Beighton
Tunstall
THE BROADS
River Yare
Elizabeth House
GREAT YARMOUTH
Whitlingham
Norwich
Trowse Newton
South Burlingham
Moulton St Mary
Halvergate
Berney Marshes
Burgh Castle
Southtown
Gorleston-on-Sea
Keswick
Kirby Bedon
Surlingham
Buckenham
Freethorpe
Berney Arms Windmill
Burgh Castle
Eaton
Old Lakenham
Arminghall
Bramerton
Hassingham
Southwood
Freethorpe Common
Wickhampton
Bradwell
Belton
Caistor St Edmund
Framingham Pigot
Rockland St Mary
Cantley
Carleton St Peter
Limpenhoe
Witton Green
Pettitts Animal Adventure Park
Dunston
Upper Stoke
Poringland
Framingham Earl
Yelverton
Ashby St Mary
Hellington
Langley Street
Browston Green
Hobland Hall
Swainsthorpe
Stoke Holy Cross
Alpington
Mill Common
Hardley Street
Fritton
Hopton on Sea
A140
Howe
Bergh Apton
Thurton
Chedgrave
Nogdam End
Lower Thurlton
Fritton Lake
St Olave's Priory
Lound
Hawe's Green
Shotesham
Brooke
R Chet
Loddon
Norton Subcourse
Thurlton
St Olaves
Somerleyton Hall & Gardens
Blundeston
A47
Corton
Saxlingham
Stubbs Green
Mundham
Raveningham
Herringfleet
Haddiscoe
Saxlingham Nethergate
Kirstead Green
Seething
Hales
Corton
Thwaite
Maypole
Pleasurewood Hills

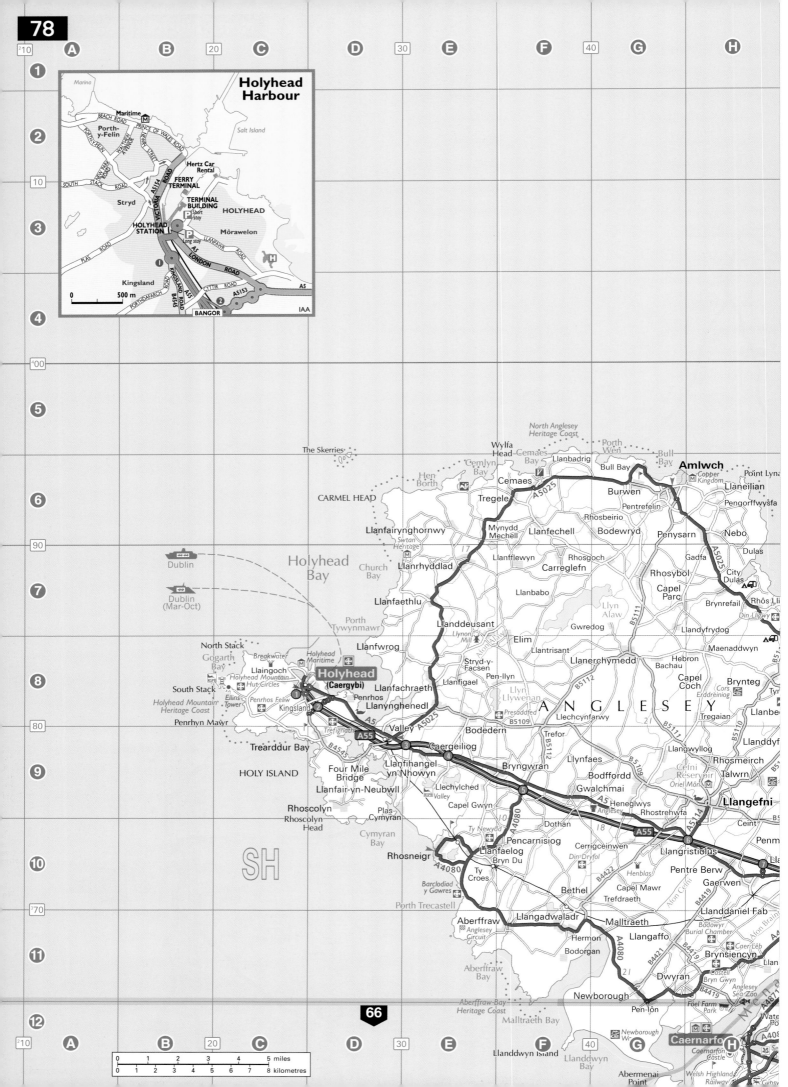

Holyhead Harbour

Marina
Maritime
BEACH ROAD
Porth-y-Felin
NEW PARK
WYNTHRY AVENUE
PENRHOS STREET
PRINCE OF WALES ROAD
VICTORIA A5154
SOUTH STACK ROAD
Stryd
Salt Island
Hertz Car Rental
FERRY TERMINAL
TERMINAL BUILDING
Short stay
P
HOLYHEAD
Môrawelon
LLANFAWR ROAD
HOLYHEAD STATION
P Long stay
PLAS ROAD
A5 LONDON ROAD
Kingsland
KINGSLAND ROAD
PORT YR AFARCH B4545
CYTTIR ROAD
A5153
A5
IAA
BANGOR

0   500 m

The Skerries
CARMEL HEAD
Llanfairynghornwy
Holyhead Bay
Church Bay
Hen Borth
Swtan Heritage
North Anglesey Heritage Coast
Wylfa Head
Cemaes Bay
Cemaes
Tregele
A5025
Llanbadrig
Porth Wen
Bull Bay
Amlwch
Copper Kingdom
Point Lyna
Llaneilian
Pengorffwysfa
Burwen
Pentrefelin
Rhosbeirio
Penysarn
Nebo
Mynydd Mechell
Llanfechell
Bodewryd
Gadfa
Dulas
Llanfflewyn
Rhosgoch
Rhosybol
City Dulas
Llanrhyddlad
Carreglefn
Capel Parc
Brynrefail
Rhôs Lli
Llanfaethlu
Llanbabo
Llyn Alaw
Din Lligwy
Llanddeusant
Llynon Mill
Gwredog
Llandyfrydog
Elim
Maenaddwyn
Llanfwrog
Stryd-y-Facsen
Llantrisant
Hebron
Bachau
Din Lligwy
North Stack
Gogarth Bay
Breakwater
Llaingoch
Holyhead Mountain
Hut Circles
Pen-llyn
Llyn Llywenan
Llanerchymedd
Capel Coch
Brynteg
Tyr
Holyhead (Caergybi)
Llanfachraeth
Llanfigael
Presaddfed
B5112
Erddreiniog
Llanbe
South Stack
Holyhead Mountain Heritage Coast
Ellins Tower
Penrhos Feilw
Kingsland
Penrhos
Llanynghenedl
Llechcynfarwy
A N G L E S E Y
Tregaian
Penrhyn Mawr
Trefignath
A5
Valley
A5025
Bodedern
Trefor
B5109
Llangwyllog
B5110
Llanddyf
Treaddur Bay
B4545
Caergeiliog
Bryngwran
Llynfaes
Bodffordd
Rhosmeirch
Talwrn
HOLY ISLAND
Four Mile Bridge
Llanfihangel yn Nhowyn
A55
Gwalchmai
Cefni Reservoir
Oriel Môn
Rhosmeirch
Llanfair-yn-Neubwll
Llechylched
Valley
Capel Gwyn
A5
Heneglwys
Anglesey
Rhostrehwfa
Llangefni
A5114
Rhoscolyn
Rhoscolyn Head
Plas Cymyran
Dothan
A4080
Pencarnisiog
Cerrigceinwen
Din-Dryfol
Llangristiolus
Ceint
Penm
SH
Cymyran Bay
Ty Newydd
Llanfaelog
Bryn Du
Capel Mawr
Henblas
Pentre Berw
Rhosneigr
A4080
Ty Croes
Bethel
Trefdraeth
B4422
Gaerwen
Barclodiad y Gawres
Aberffraw Circuit
Hermon
Bodorgan
Llangadwaladr
Llangaffo
Bodwyr Burial Chamber
Brynsiencyn
Porth Trecastell
Aberffraw
Mallraeth
A4080
A4421
B4419
Caer Lêb
Castell Bryn Gwyn
Anglesey Sea Zoo
Aberffraw Bay
Newborough
Pen-lôn
Foel Farm Park
Water
Aberffraw Bay Heritage Coast
Malltraeth Bay
Newborough W
Caernarfon
Dublin
Dublin (Mar-Oct)
Porth Tywynmawr

Llanddwyn Island
Llanddwyn Bay
Abermenai Point
Caernarfon Castle
Welsh Highlands Railway
A408

0   1   2   3   4   5 miles
0 1 2 3 4 5 6 7 8 kilometres

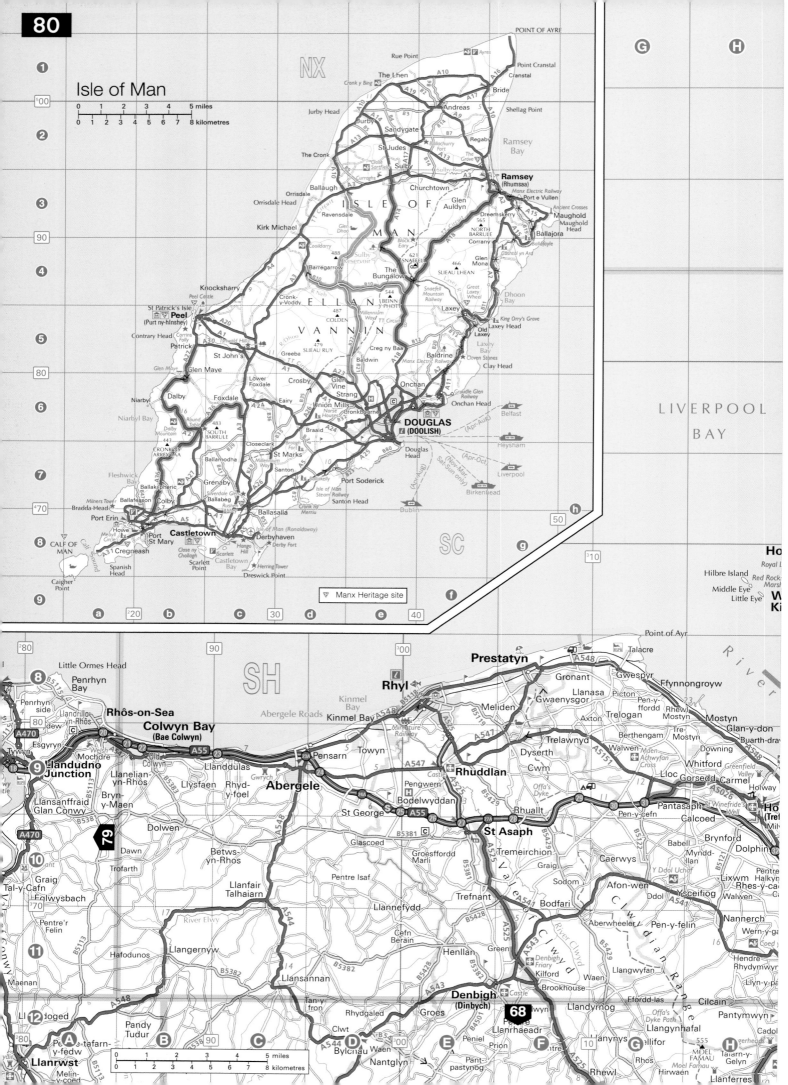

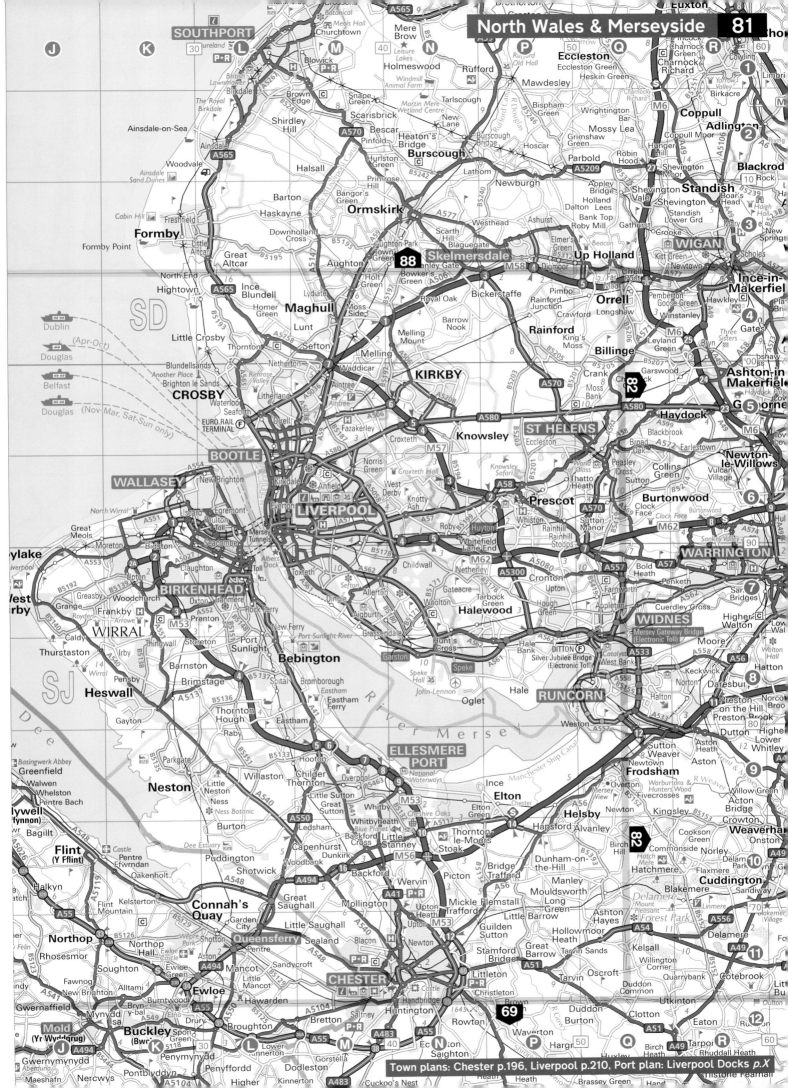

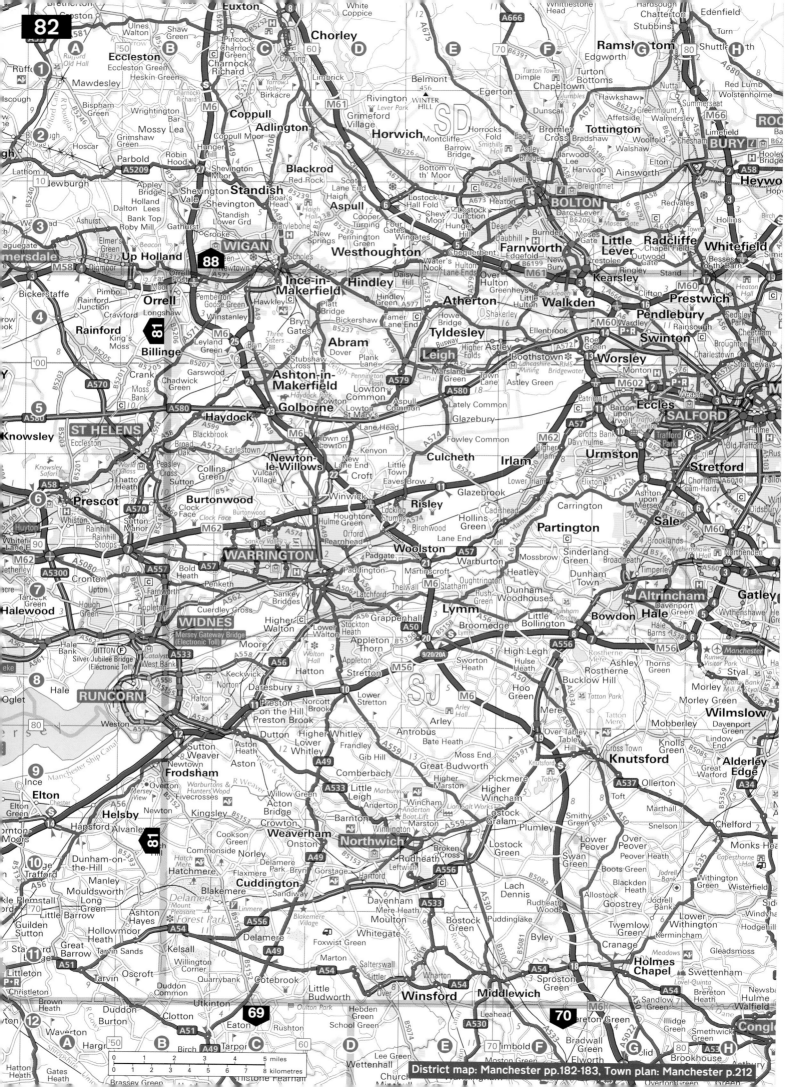

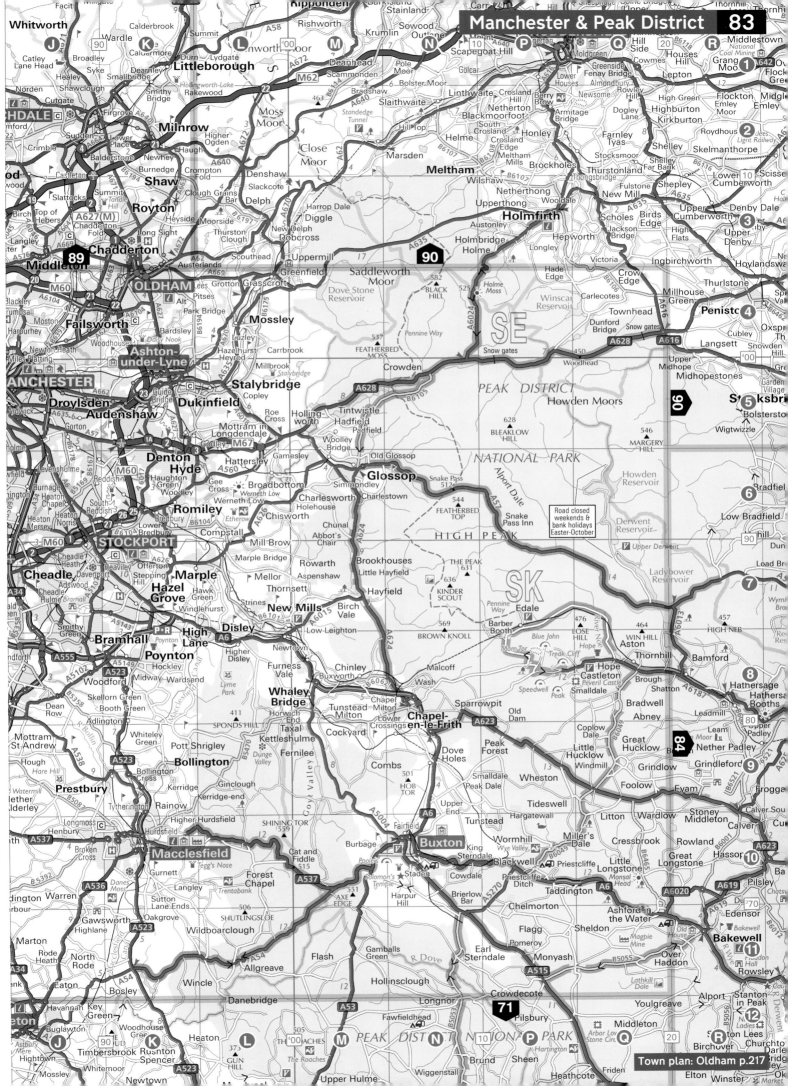

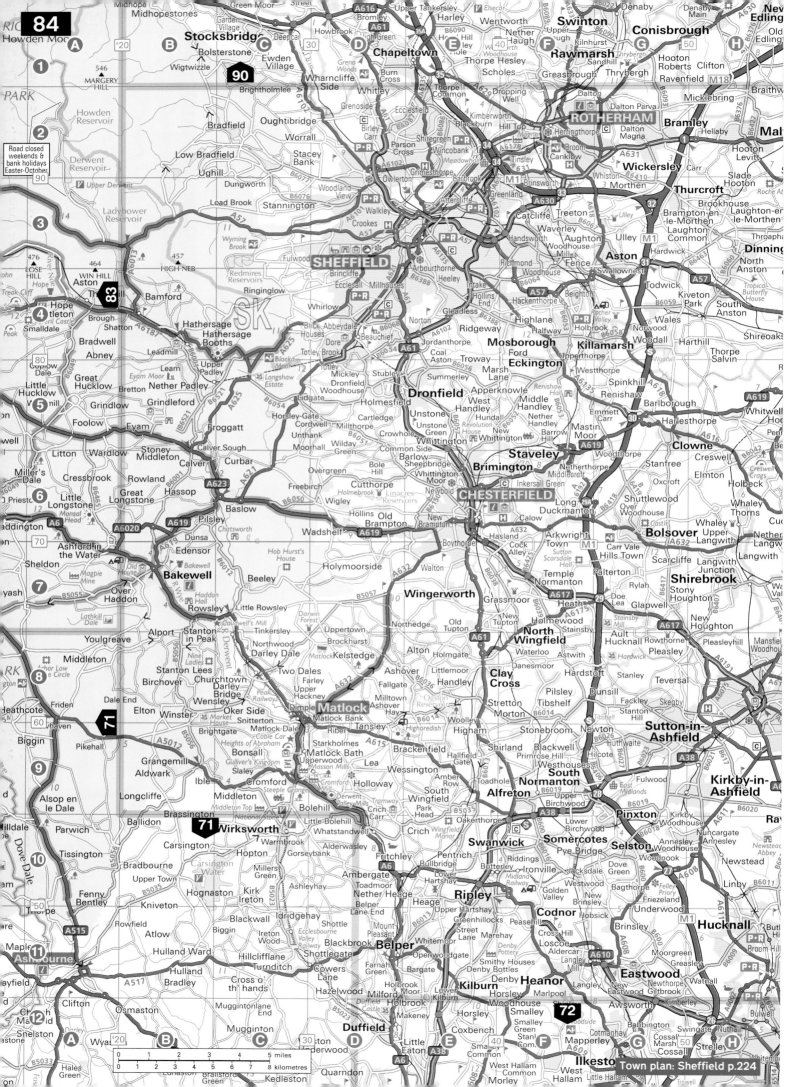

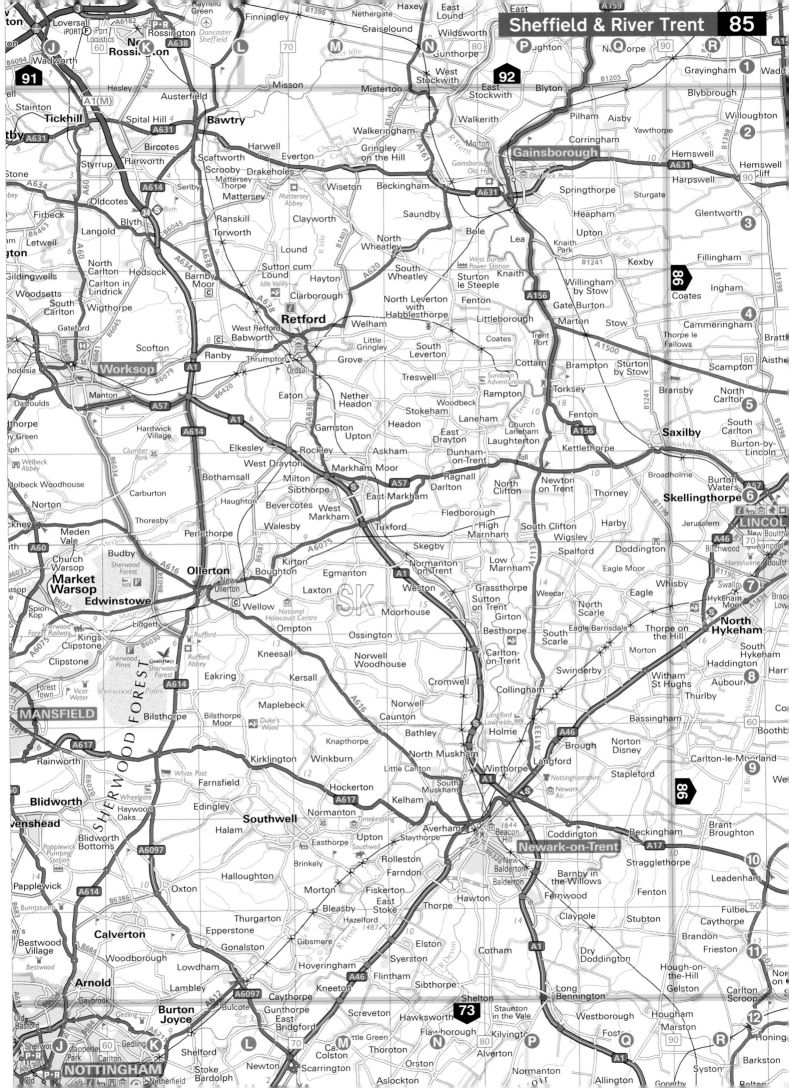

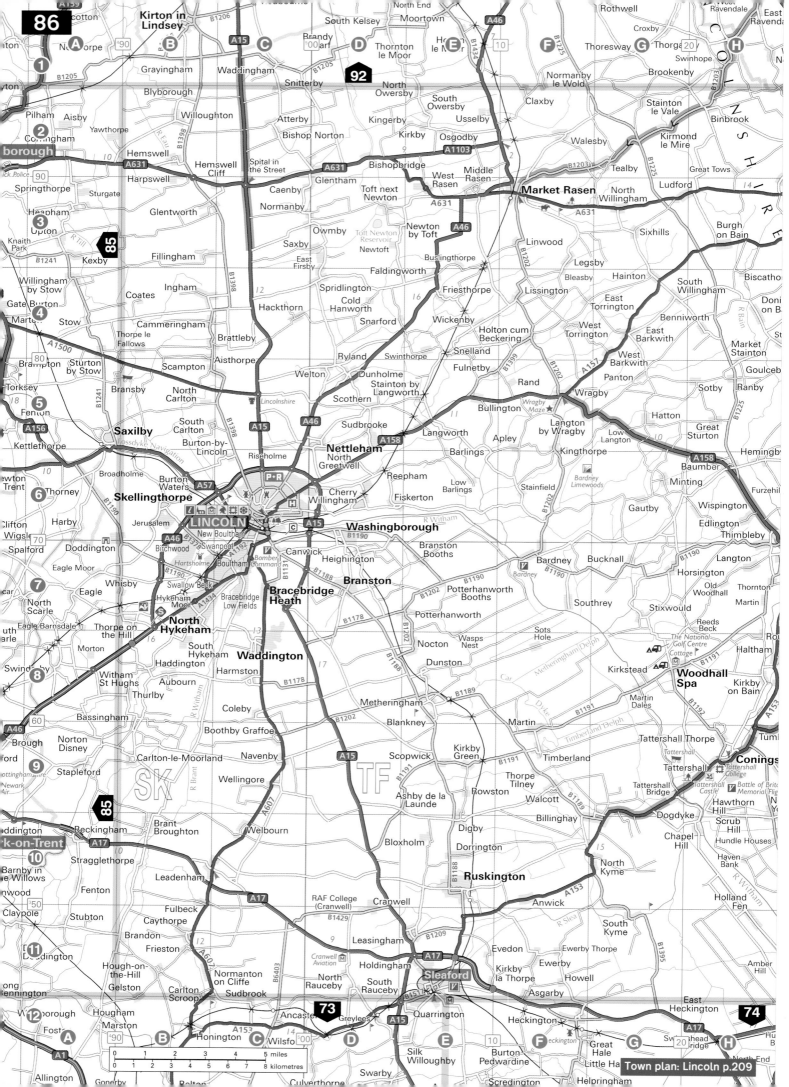

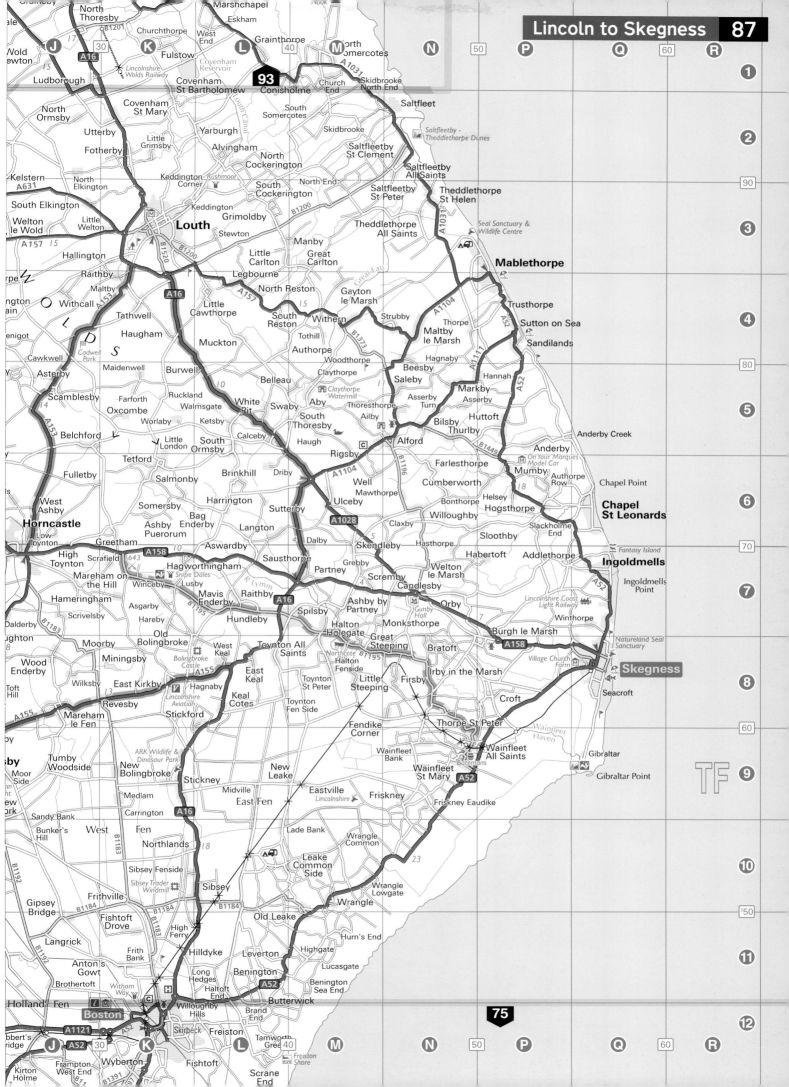

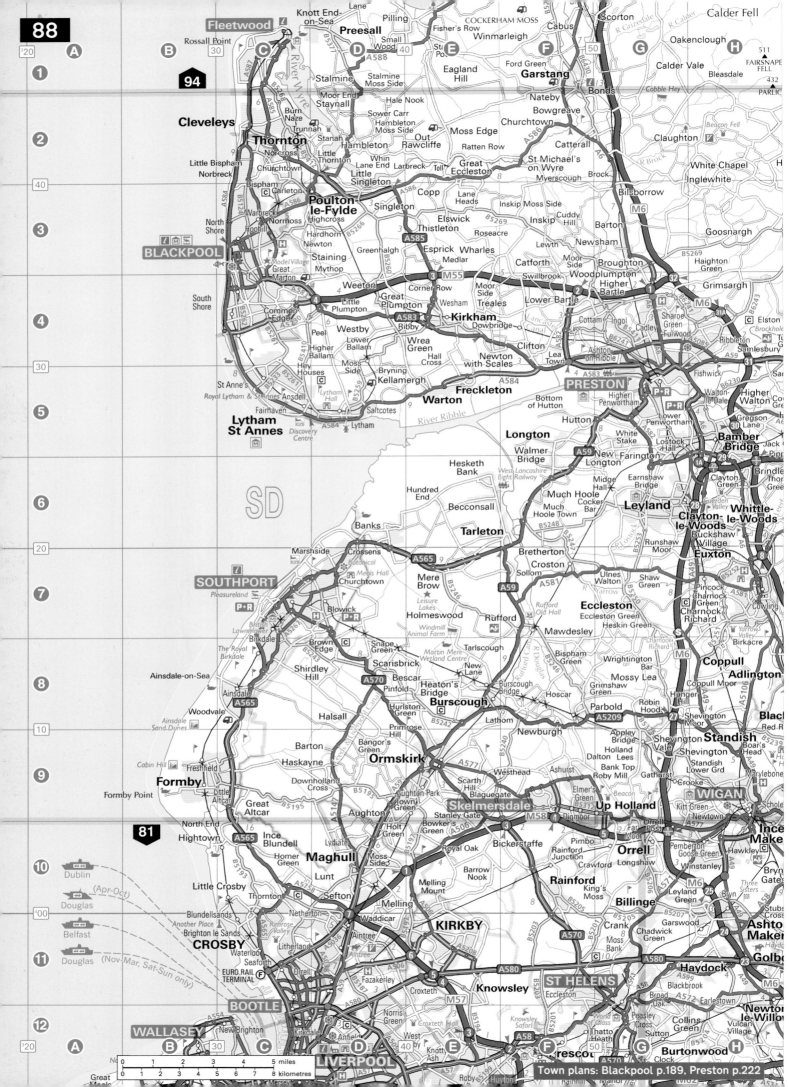

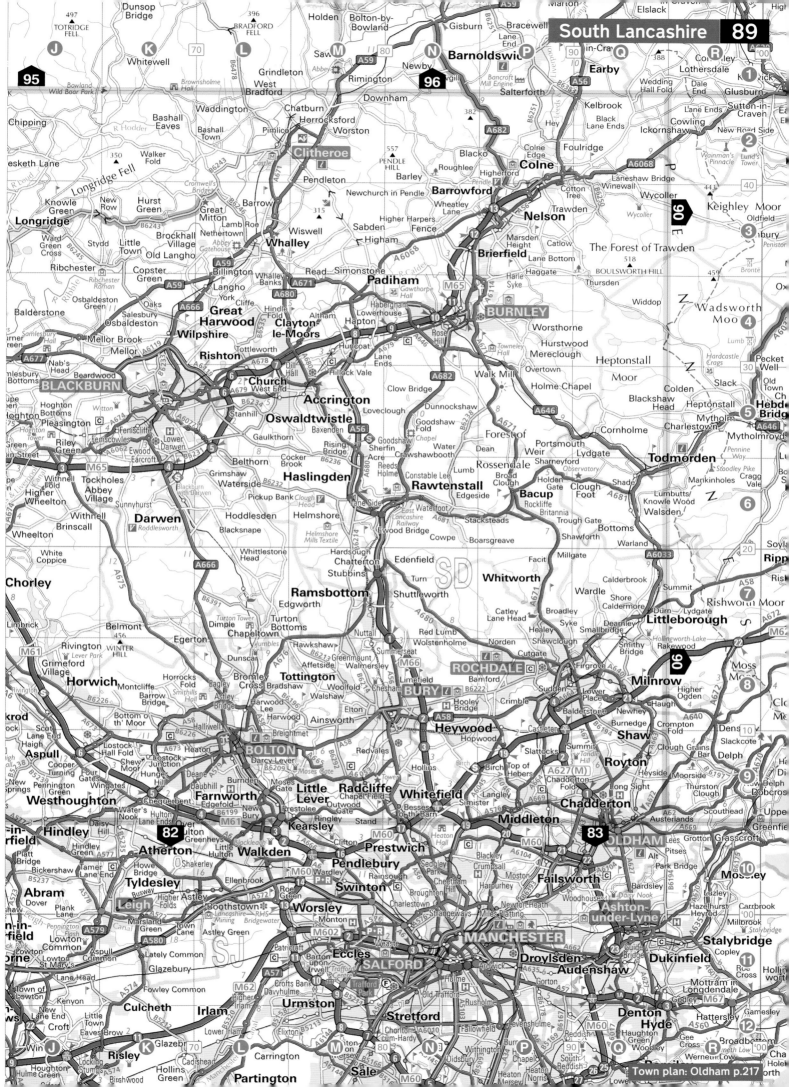

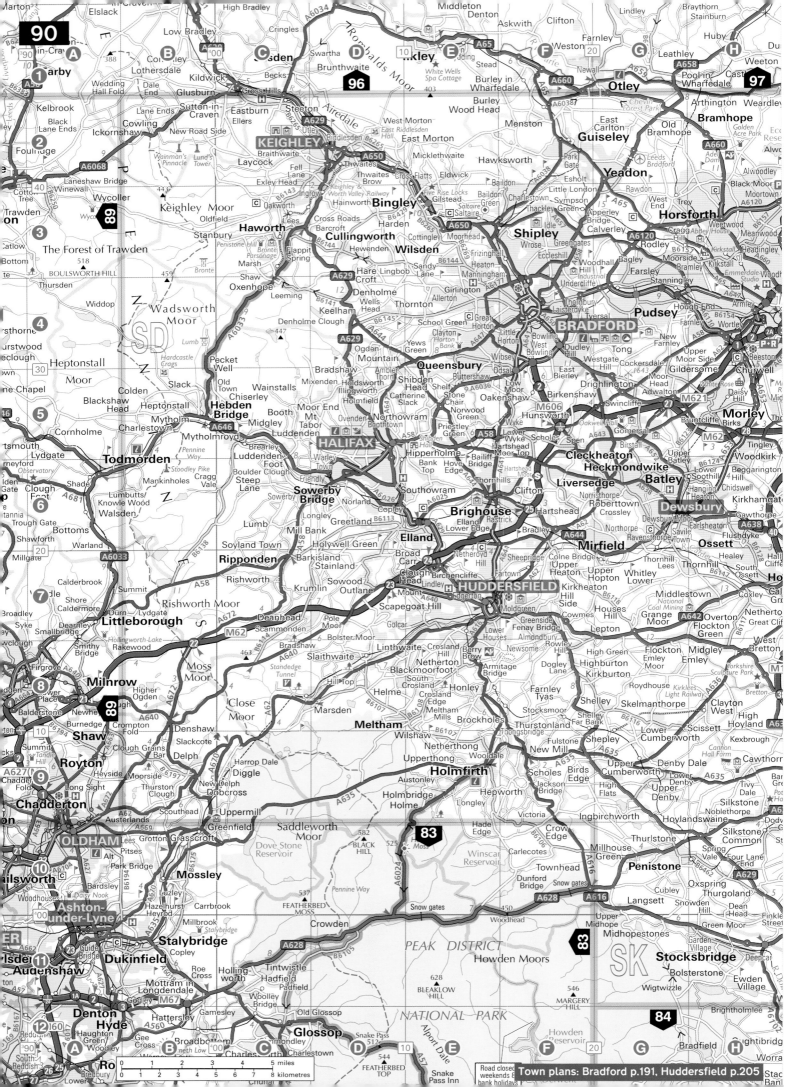

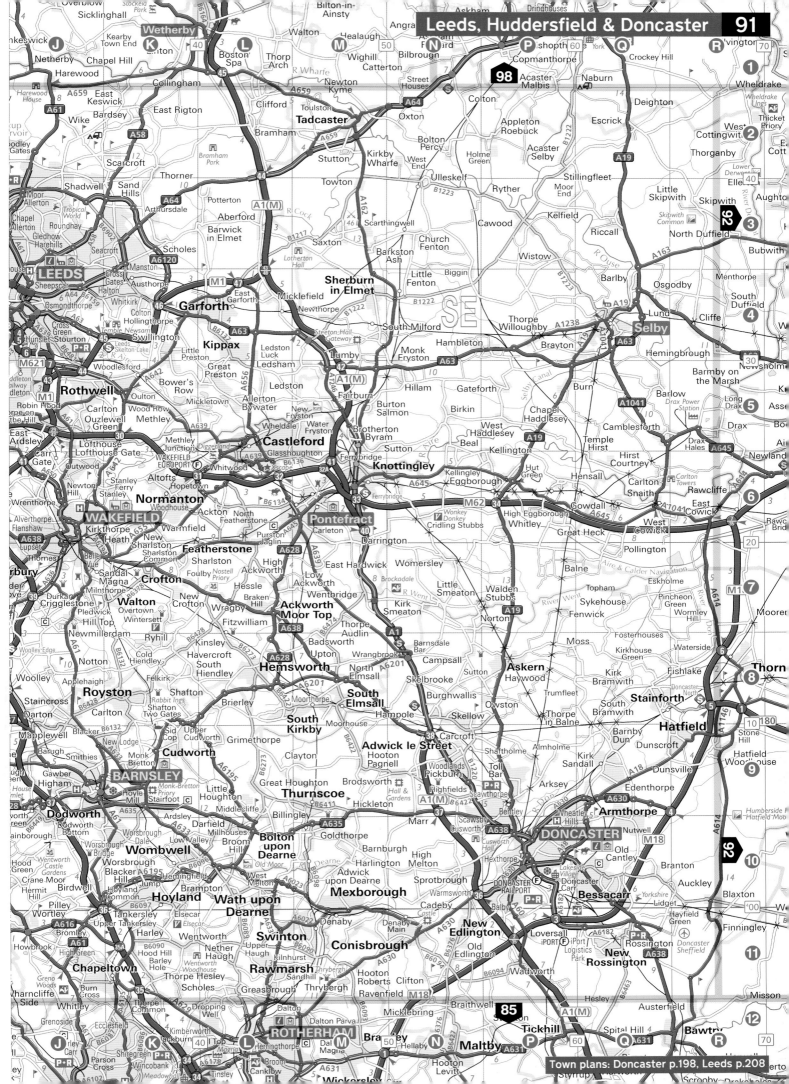

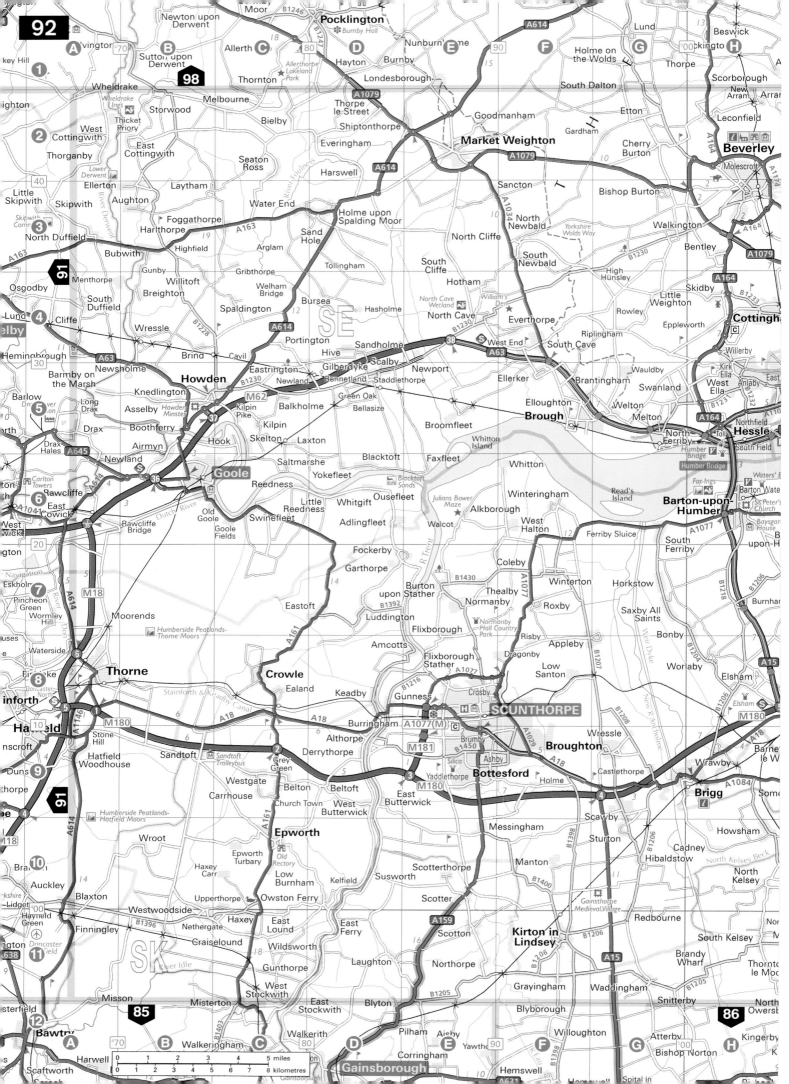

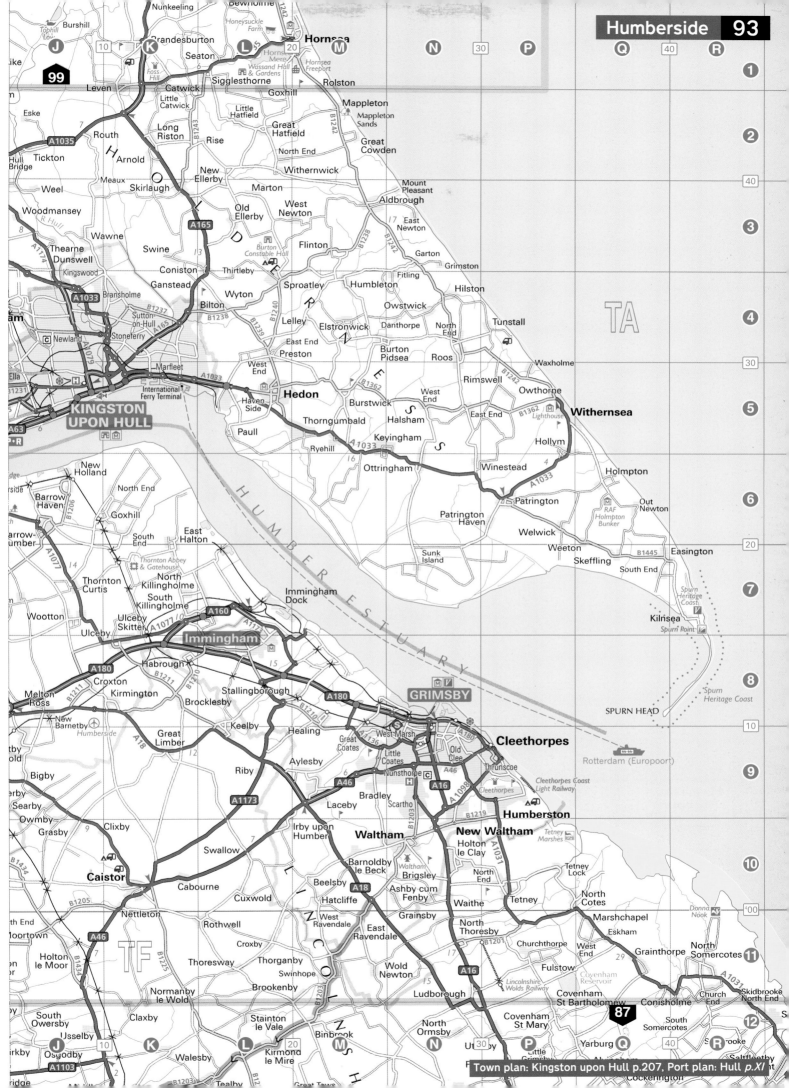

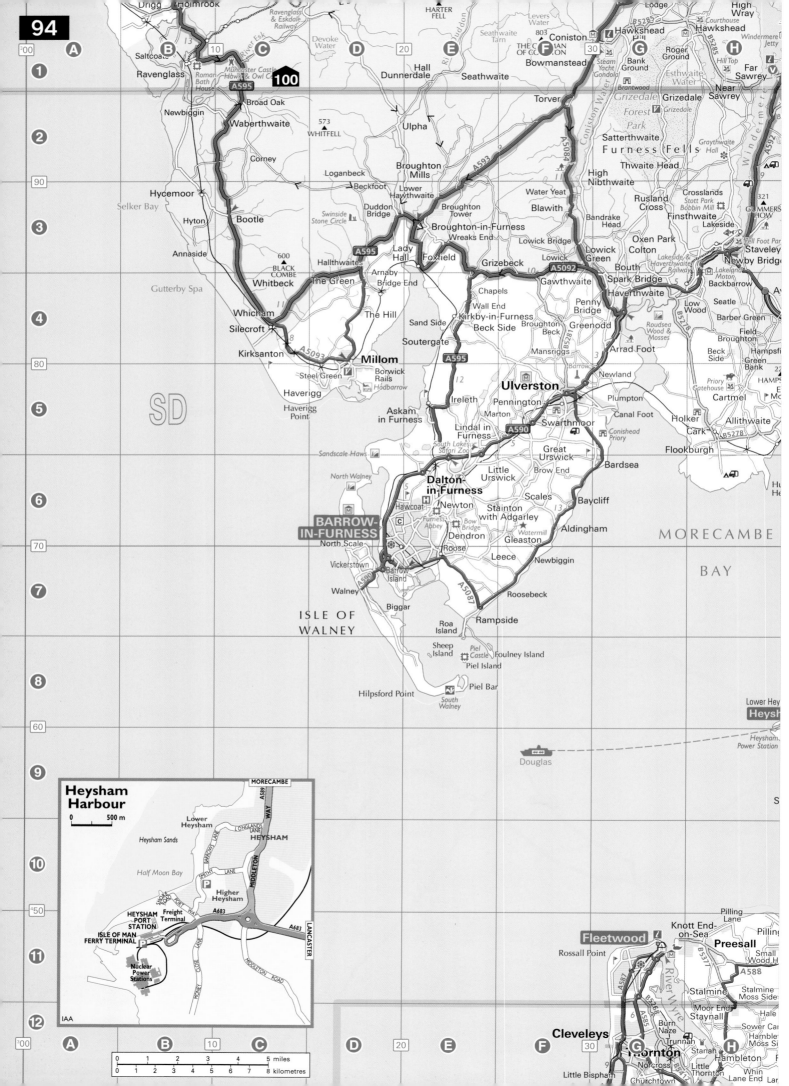

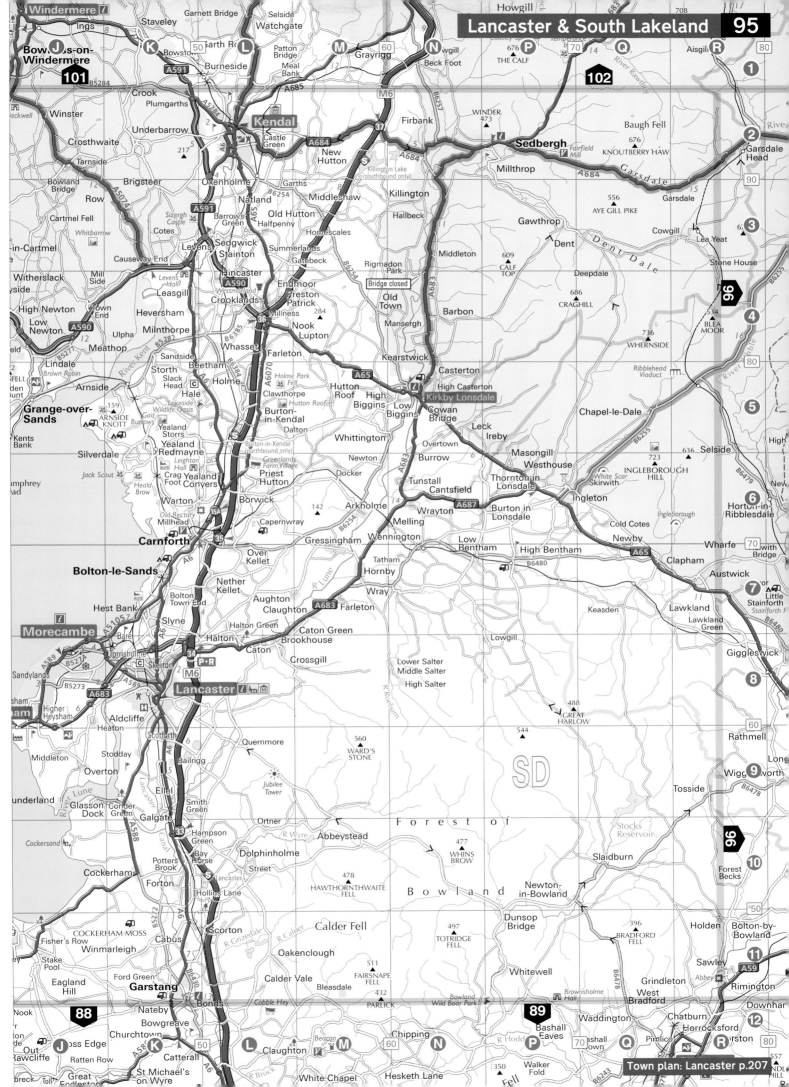

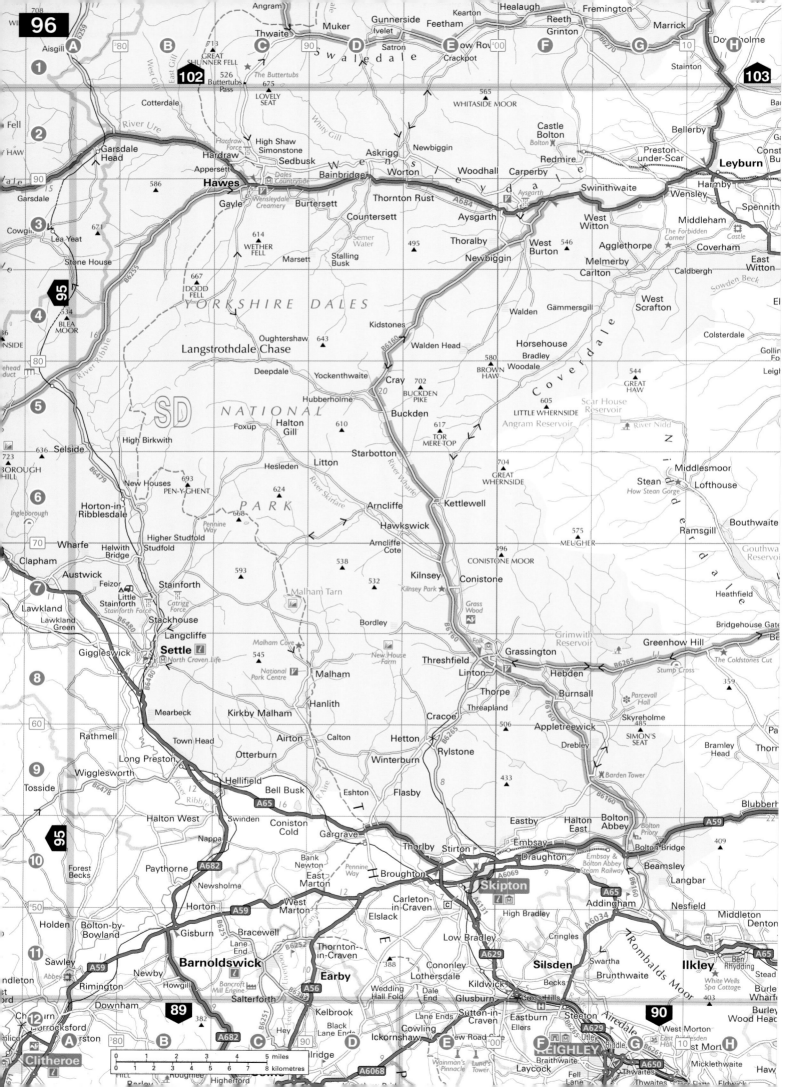

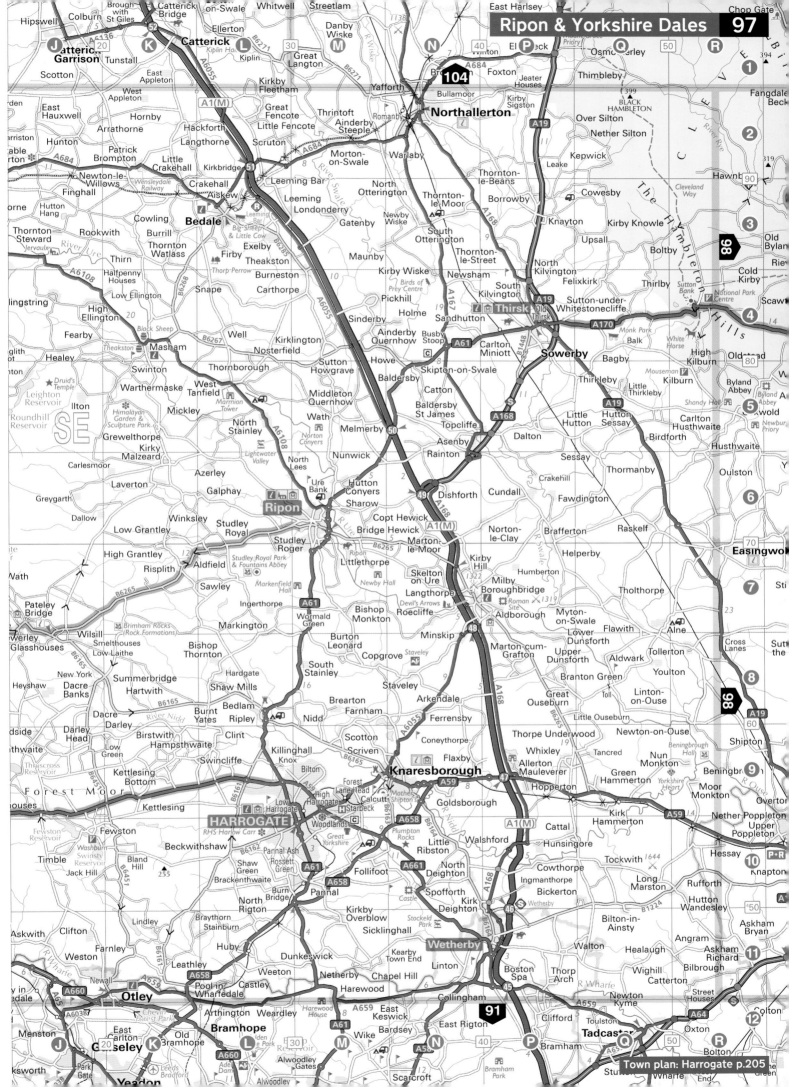

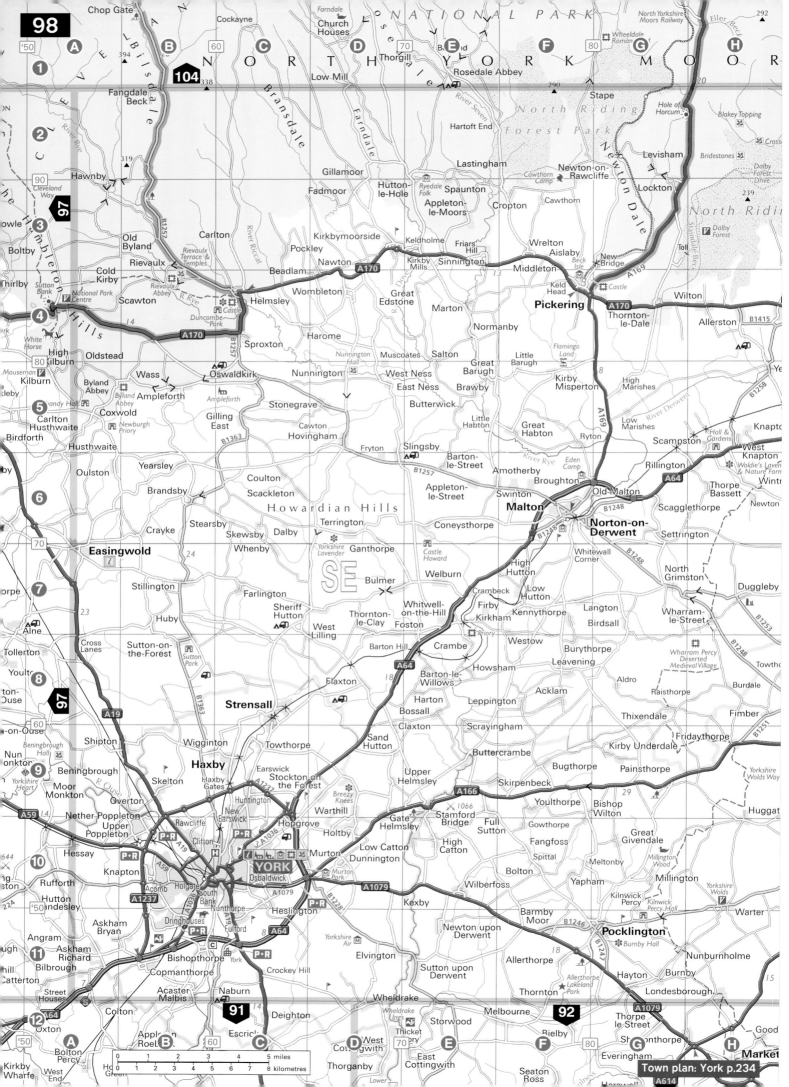

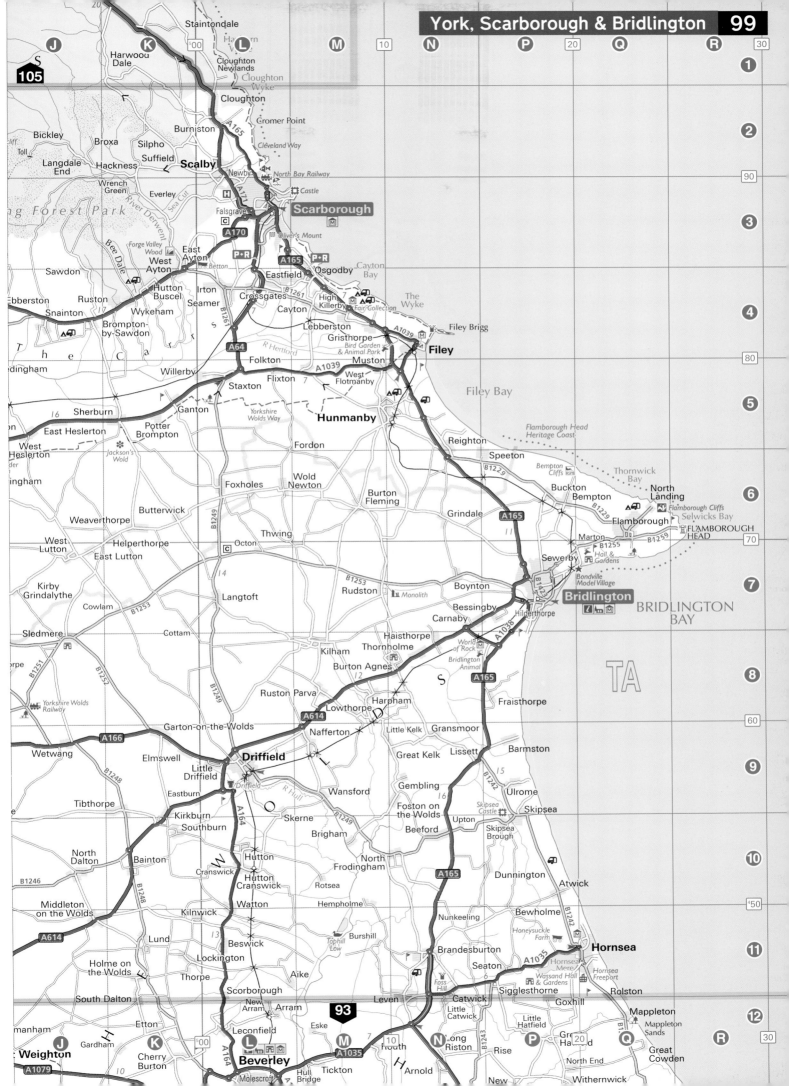

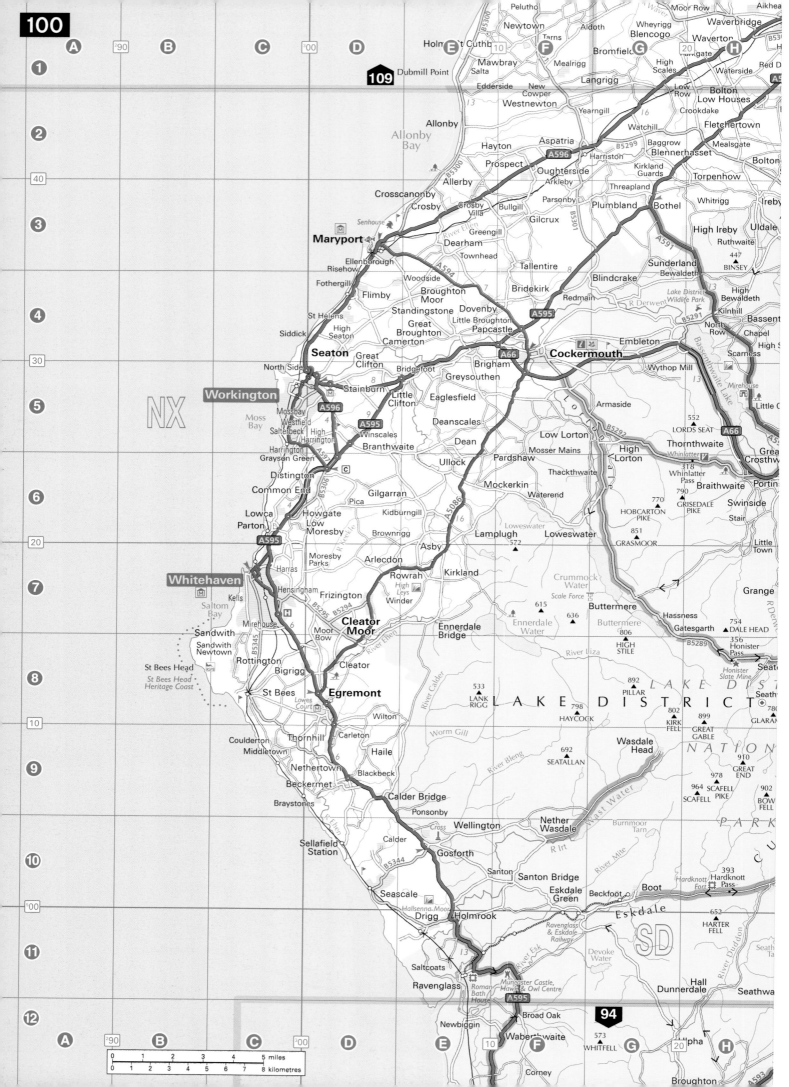

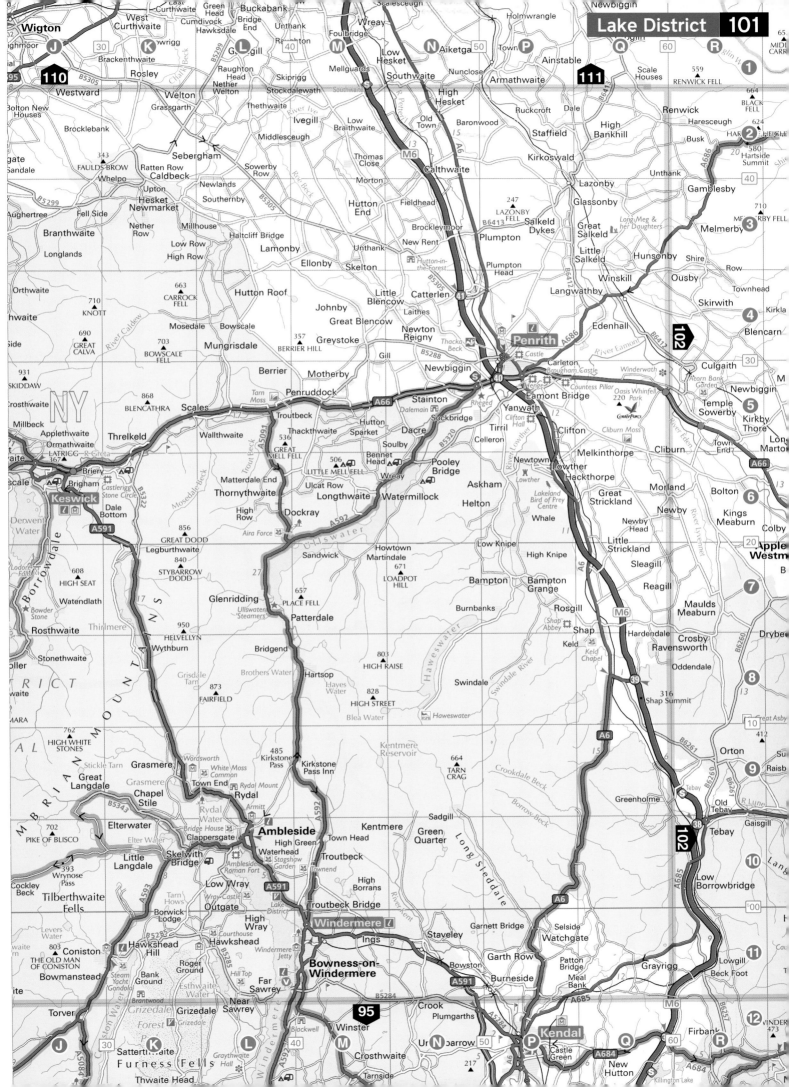

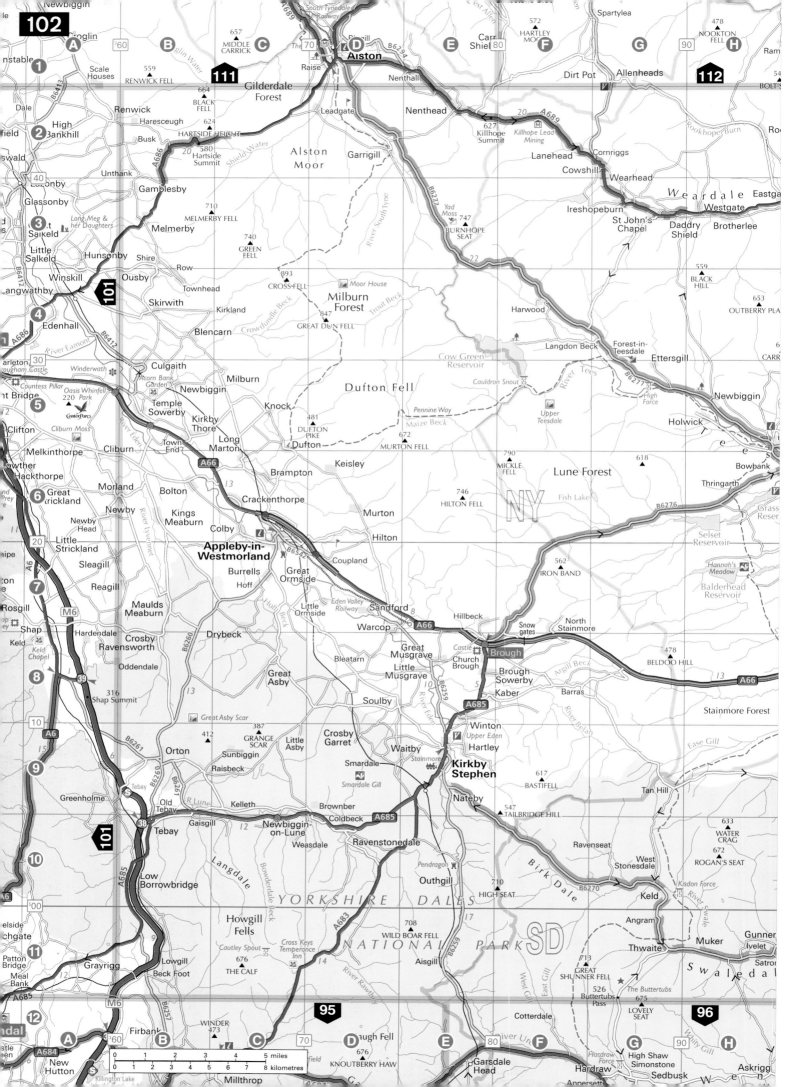

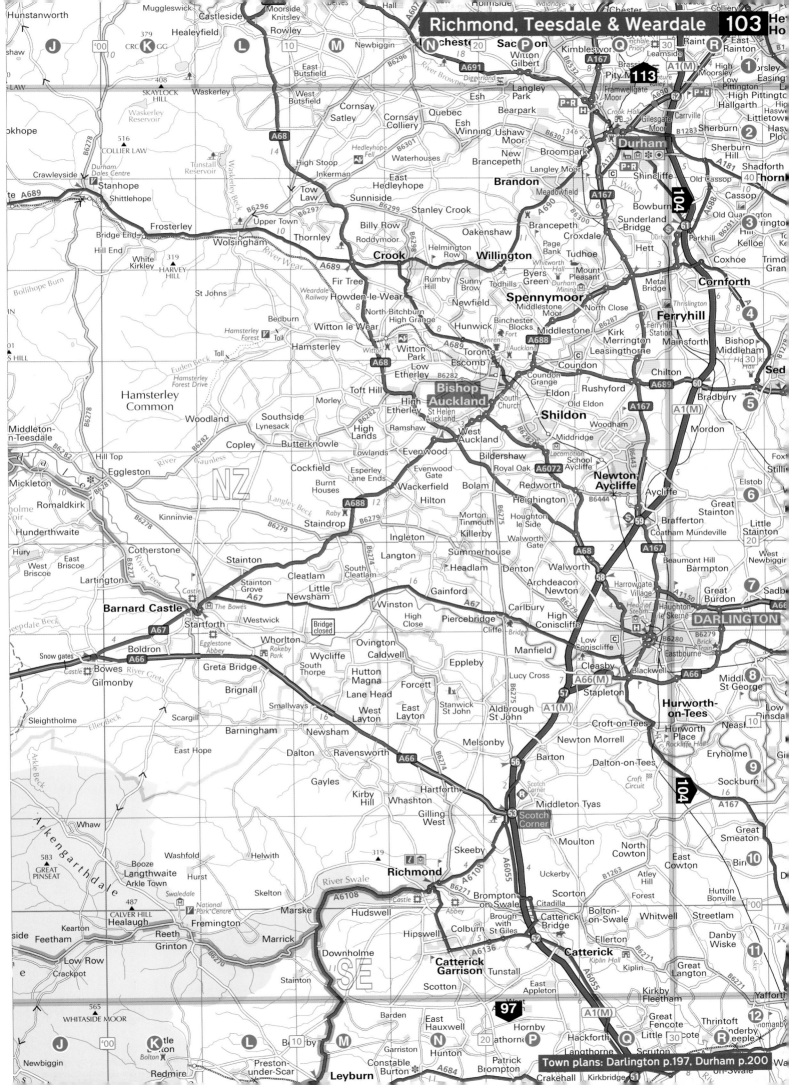

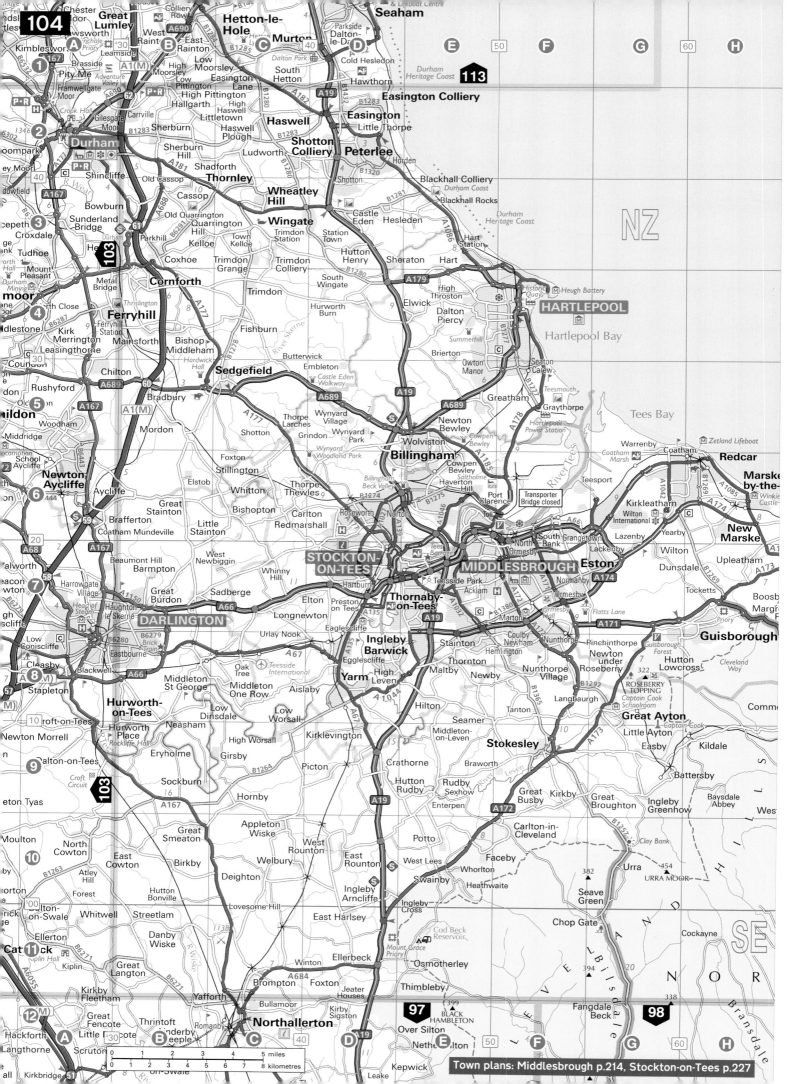

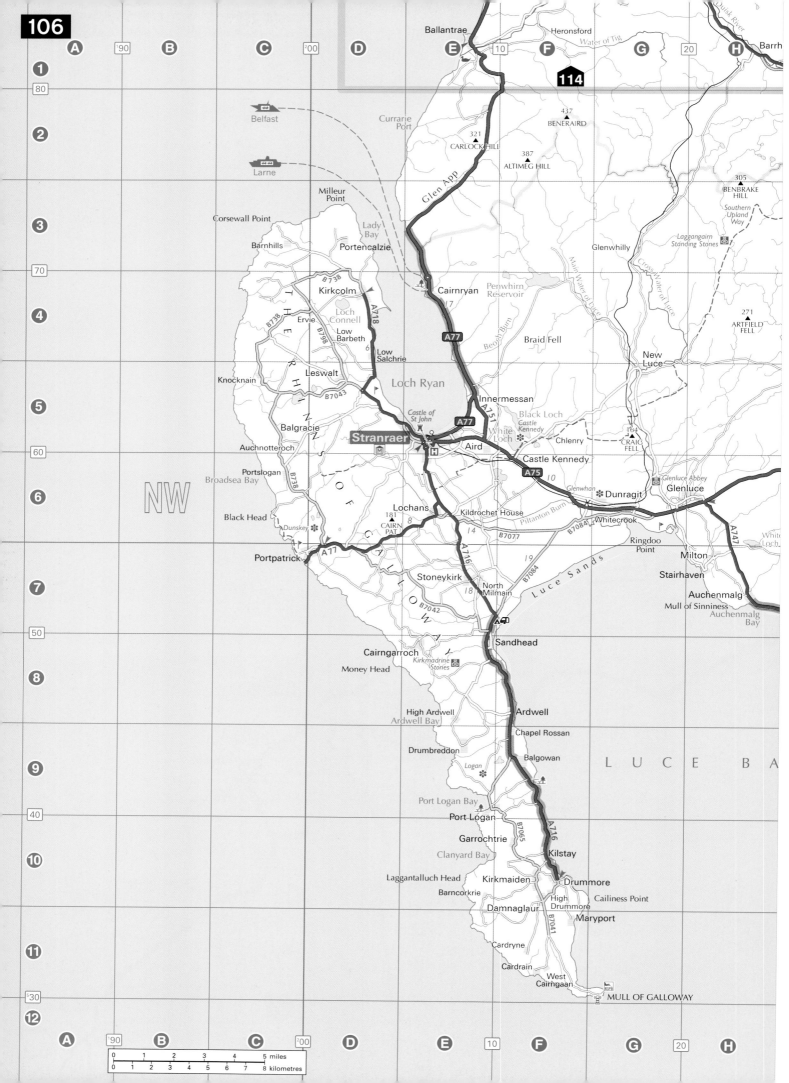

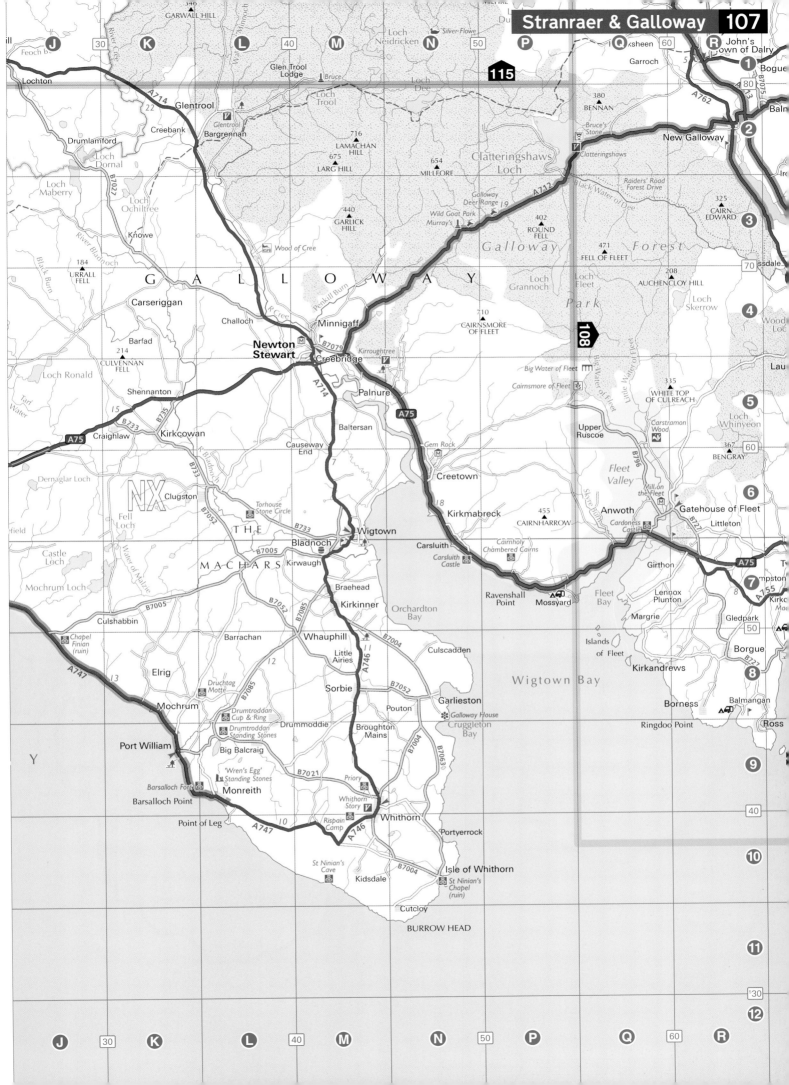

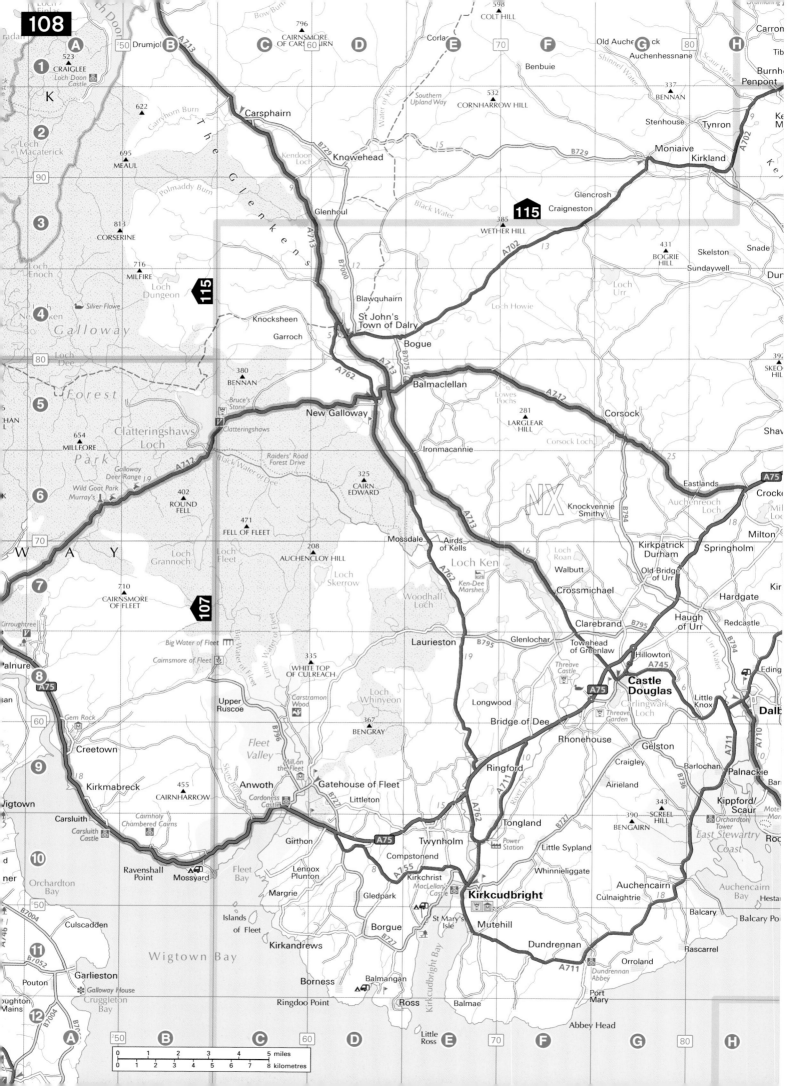

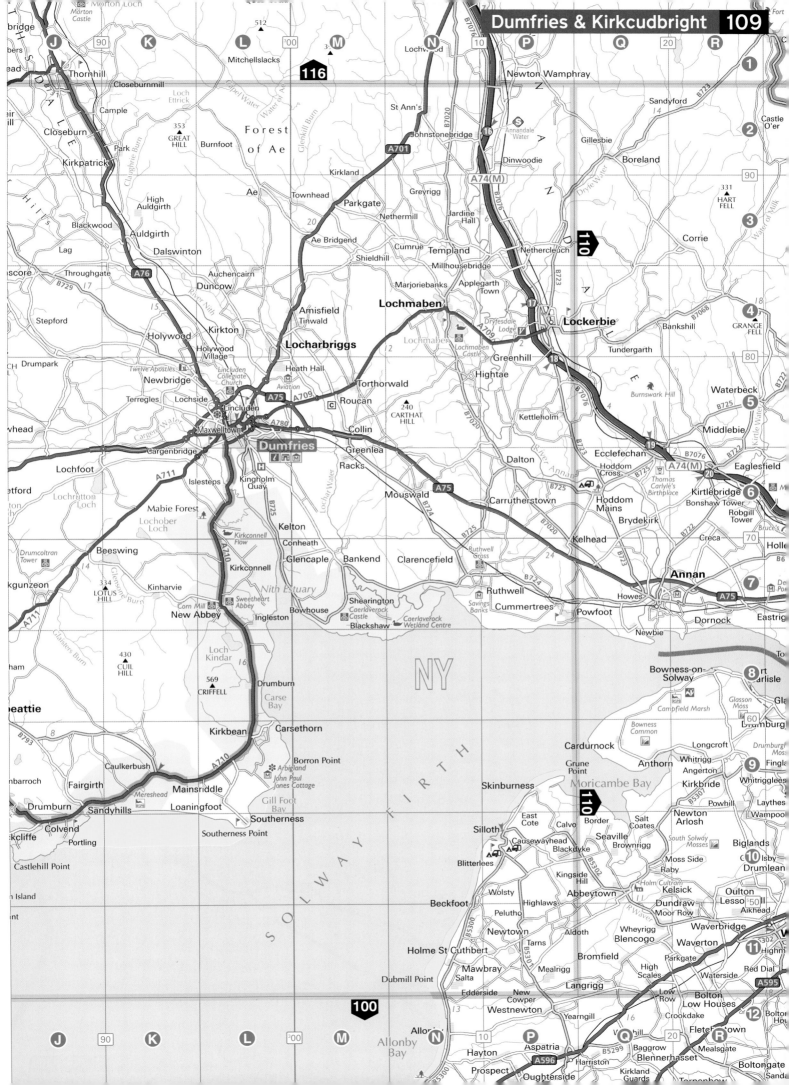

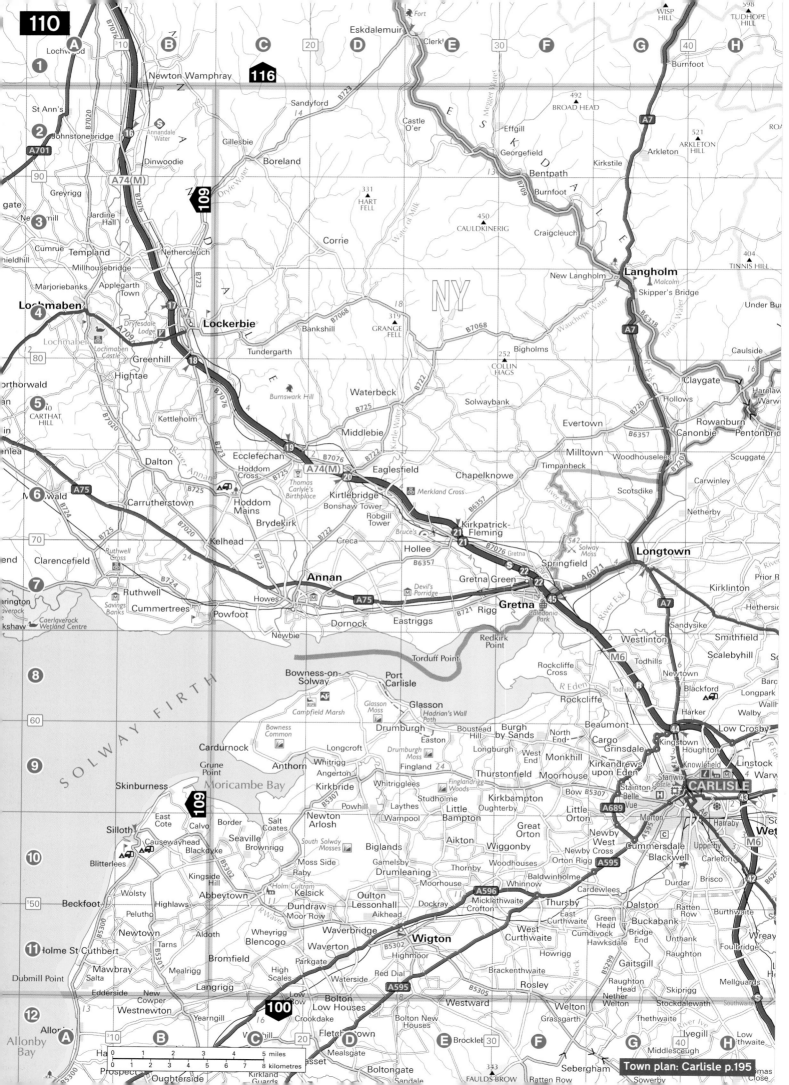

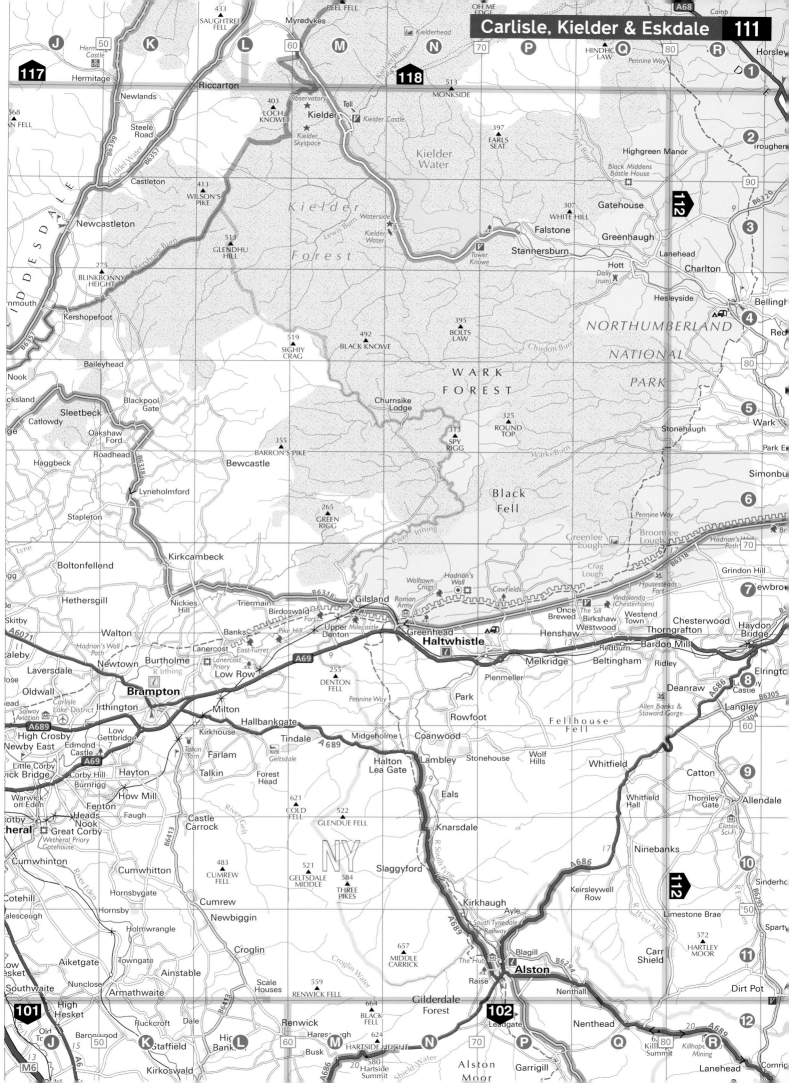

A68 Camp
Horsley
117
118
112
101
102
112

J K L M N P Q R

Hermit
Castle
Hermitage
Newlands
Riccarton
SAUGHTREE FELL 433
PEEL FELL
Myredykes
Kielderhead
Kielderburn
MONKSIDE 513
HINDHOPE LAW
Pennine Way
1
Troughen
2
Highgreen Manor
Black Middens Bastle House
3
B6320
Gatehouse
WHITE HILL 307
Falstone
Greenhaugh
Lanehead
Charlton
Hesleyside
Bellingha
Red
NORTHUMBERLAND
NATIONAL
PARK
4
5
Wark
Park E
Simonbu
6
Stonehaugh

Steele Road
Castleton
WILSON'S PIKE 413
LOCH KNOWE 403
Observatory
Kielder
Toll
Kielder Castle
Kielder Skyspace
Kielder Water
EARLS SEAT 397
Newcastleton
Kielder
Forest
Waterside
Lewis Burn
Kielder Water
Tower Knowe
Stannersburn
Hott
Dally (ruin)
568
N FELL
275
BLINKBONNY HEIGHT
GLENDHU HILL 513
Kershopefoot
Baileyhead
SIGHTY CRAG 519
BLACK KNOWE 492
BOLTS LAW 395
Chirdon Burn
Nook
ckland
Sleetbeck
Catlowdy
Blackpool Gate
Oakshaw Ford
Roadhead
Haggbeck
ge
Lyneholmford
Stapleton
Bewcastle
BARRON'S PIKE 355
WARK FOREST
Churnsike Lodge
ROUND TOP 325
SPY RIGG 313
Warks Burn
Broomlee Lough
Greenlee Lough
Pennine Way
Hadrian's Path
B6318
7
ewbro

Lyne
Boltonfellend
Hethersgill
Kirkcambeck
GREEN RIGG 265
River Irthing
Black Fell
Walltown Crags
Hadrian's Wall
Cawfields
Crag Lough
Housesteads Fort
Grindon Hill
Skitby
Nickies Hill
Triermain
Birdoswald
B6318
Gilsland
Roman Army
Vindolanda (Chesterholm)
Westend Town
Chesterwood
Thorngrafton
Haydon Bridge
A6071
Walton
Banks
Pike Hill
Upper Denton
East-Turret
Greenhead
Haltwhistle
Once Brewed
The Sill
Westwood
Birkshaw Westwood
Redburn
Bardon Mill
Elringt
8
aleby
Newtown
Burtholme
Lanercost
Lanercost Priory
Low Row
A69
Milton
DENTON FELL 255
Pennine Way
Plenmeller
Henshaw
Melkridge
Beltingham
Ridley
Deanraw
Langley
B6305
Laversdale
Oldwall
Irthington
Brampton
Hallbankgate
Park
Rowfoot
Allen Banks & Staward Gorge
Fellhouse Fell
High Crosby
Newby East
Edmond Castle
Low Gettbridge
Kirkhouse
Tindale
A689
Midgeholme
Coanwood
Lambley
Stonehouse
Wolf Hills
Whitfield
Catton
9
ck Bridge
Little Corby
Corby Hill
Burnrigg
Hayton
Farlam
Talkin
Talkin Tarn
Geltsdale
Forest Head
Halton Lea Gate
Eals
Knarsdale
Whitfield Hall
Thornley Gate
Allendale
Classic Sci-Fi
otby
Warwick-on-Eden
Heads Nook
Fenton
Faugh
Castle Carrock
COLD FELL 621
GLENDUE FELL 522
Ninebanks
10
heral
Cumwhinton
Cumwhitton
CUMREW FELL 483
GELTSDALE MIDDLE 521
THREE PIKES 584
Slaggyford
R South Tyne
A686
Keirsleywell Row
Limestone Brae
HARTLEY MOOR 572
11
Sinderho
Cotehill
Hornsbygate
Hornsby
Cumrew
Newbiggin
NY
MIDDLE CARRICK 657
Kirkhaugh
Ayle
Blagill
Carr Shield
Sparty
Aiketgate
Towngate
Holmwrangle
Ainstable
Croglin
Croglin Water
South Tynedale Railway
The Hub
Alston
B6294
Dirt Pot
12
ow sket
Southwaite
High Hesket
Nunclose
Armathwaite
Ruckcroft
Dale
Scale Houses
RENWICK FELL 559
Haresceugh
BLACK FELL 664
Gilderdale Forest
Raise
Leadgate
Nenthall
Nenthead
A689
Cornrig

J K L M N P Q R

M6
A6
Old Tc
Baronwood
Staffield
Kirkoswald
Hig Bank
Renwick
Busk
HARTSIDE HEIGHT 624
HARTSIDE HEIGHT
Hartside Summit 580
A686
Alston Moor
Garrigill
Gilderdale
Killhope Summit
Killhope Mining
Lanehead

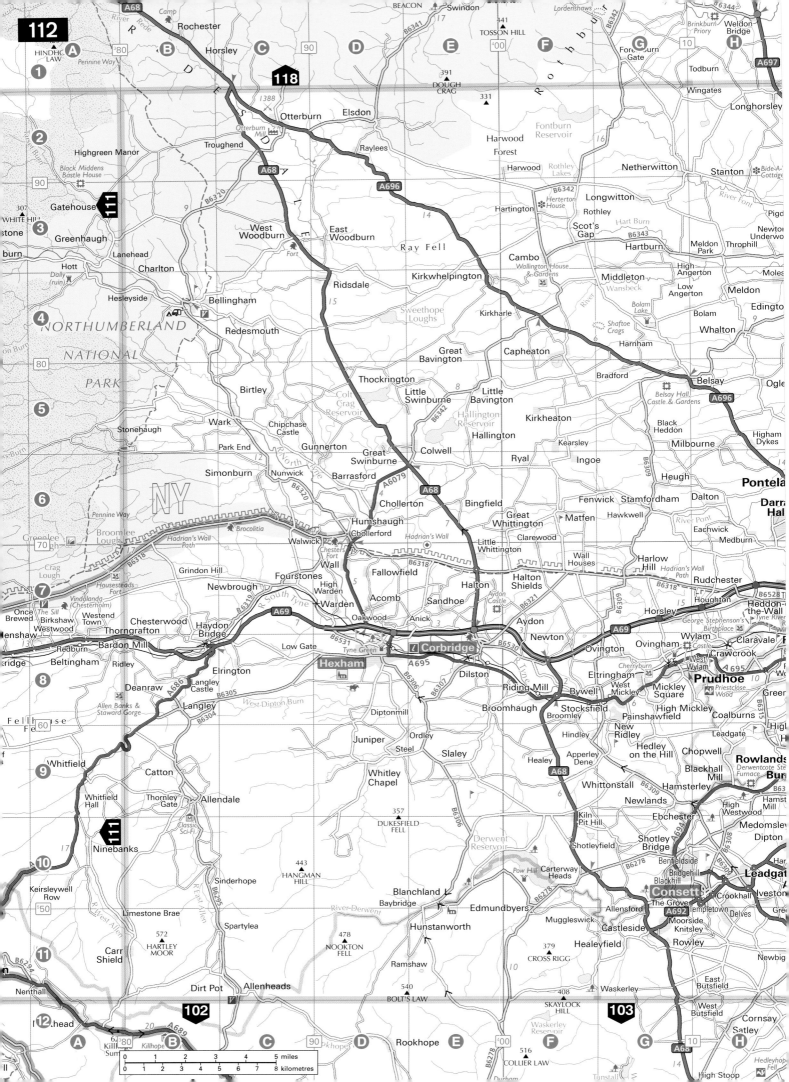

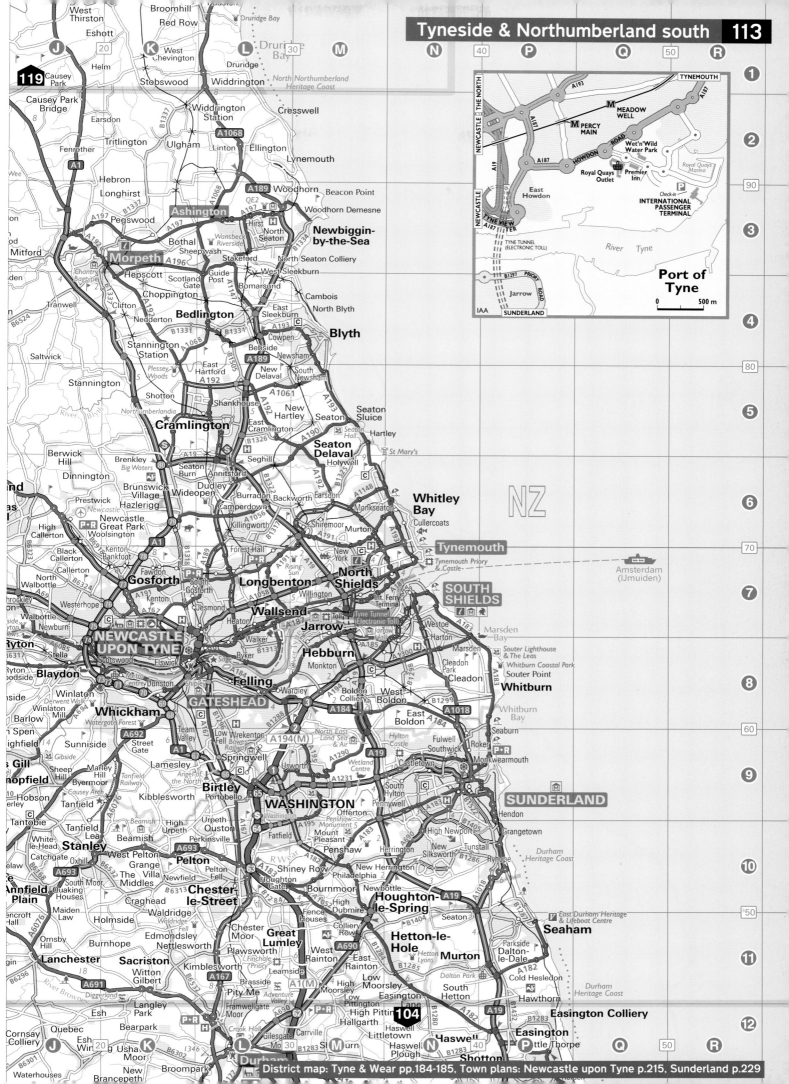

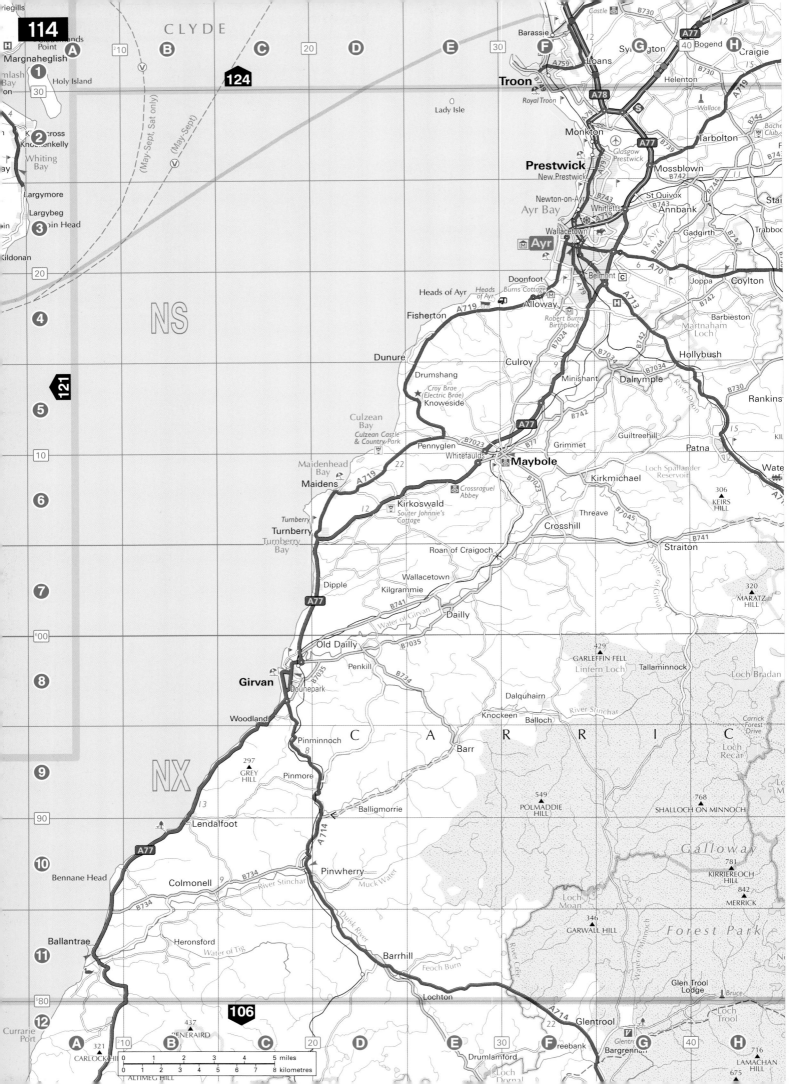

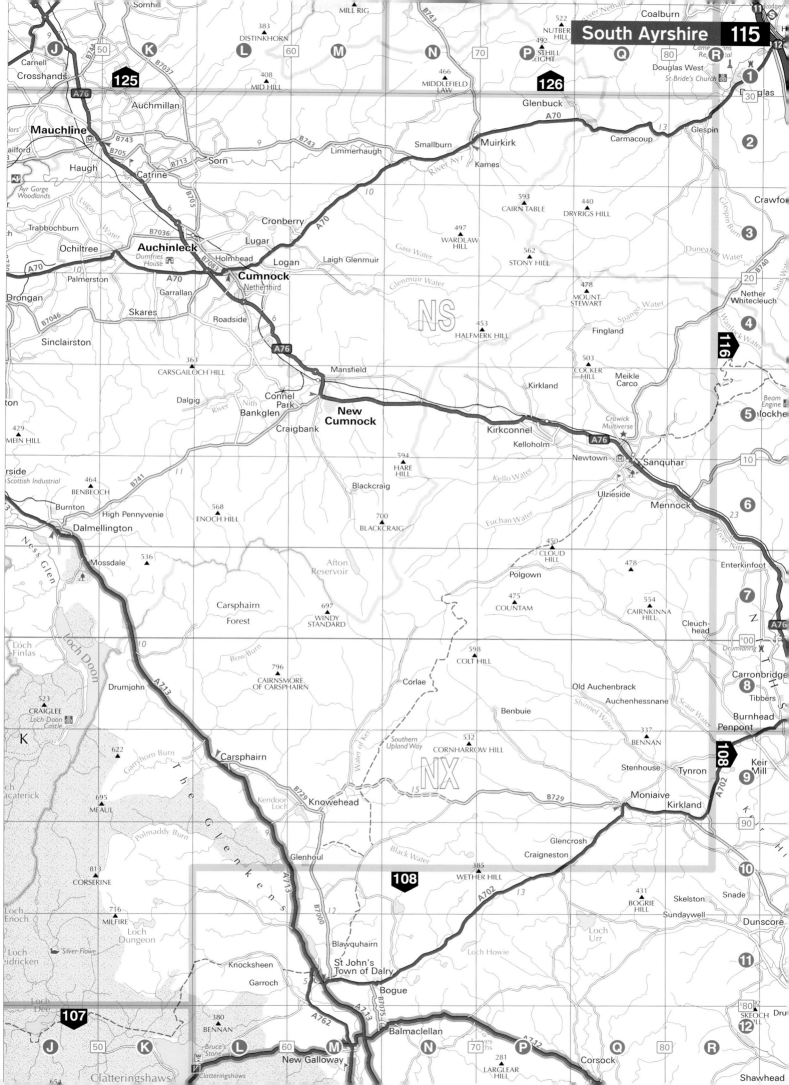

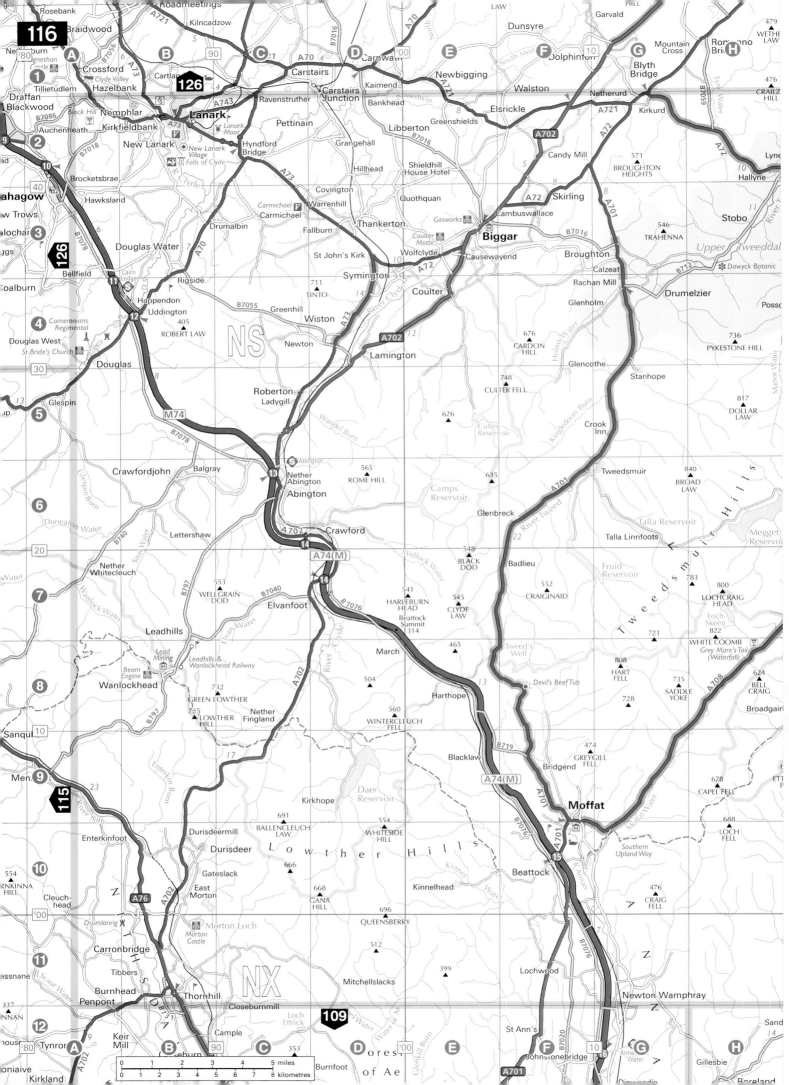

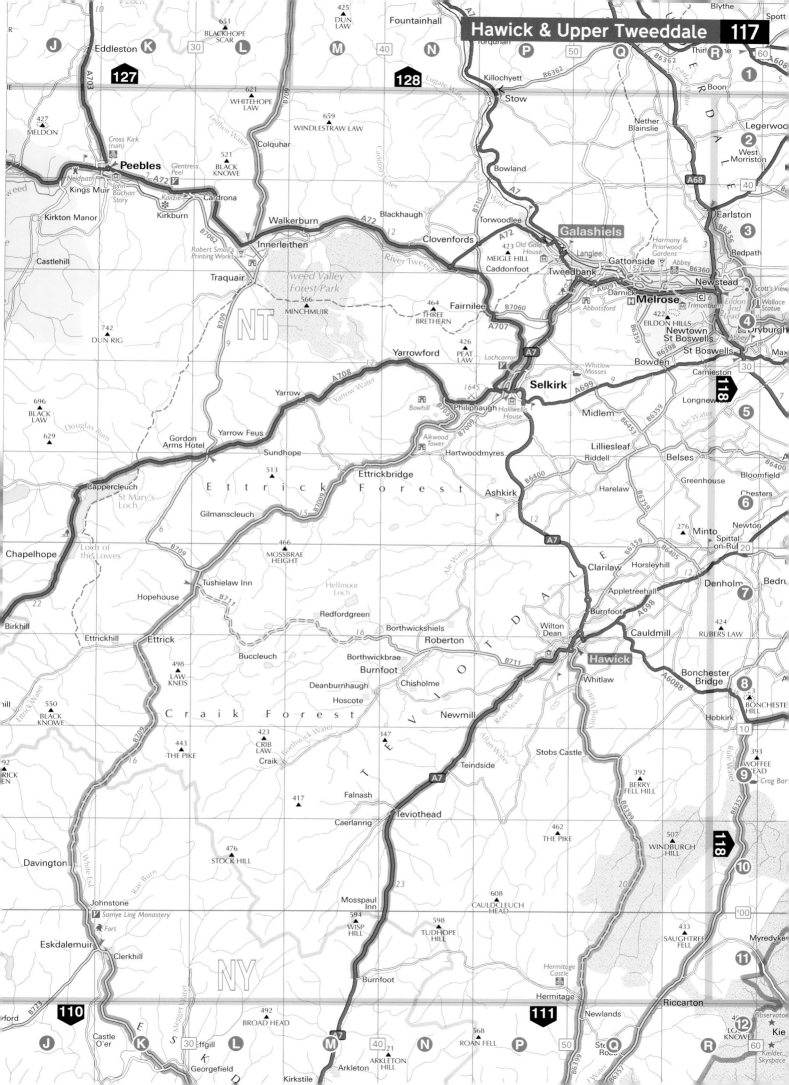

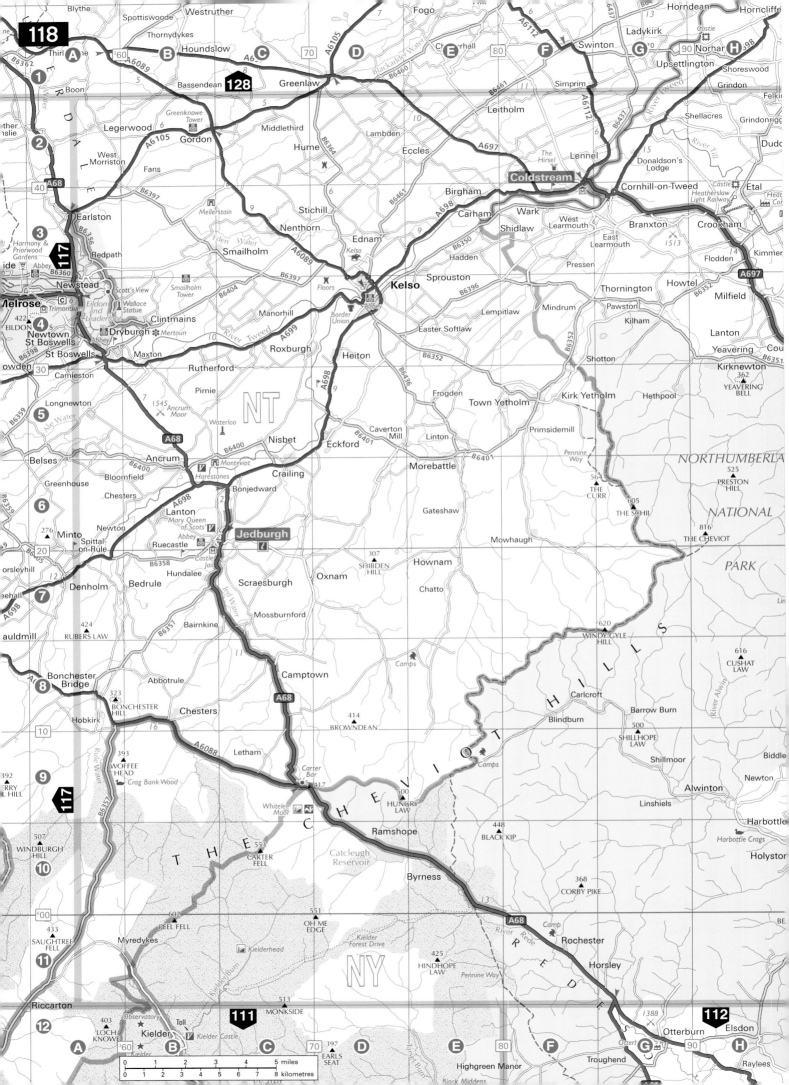

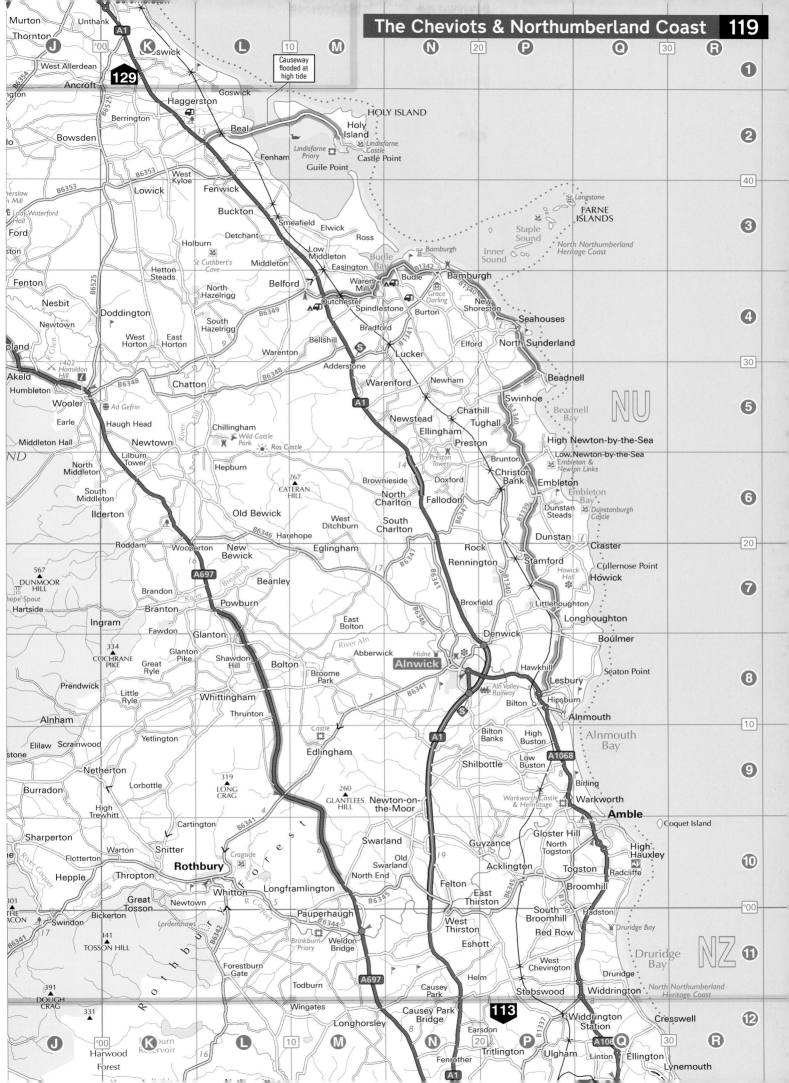

Causeway flooded at high tide

129

113

A1

J K L M N P Q R

Murton
Thornton
Unthank
West Allerdean
Ancroft
Bowsden
Berrington
Goswick
Haggerston
Goswick
Beal
Fenham
HOLY ISLAND
Holy Island
Lindisfarne Priory
Lindisfarne Castle
Castle Point
Guile Point
Lowick
West Kyloe
Fenwick
Buckton
Smeafield
Elwick
Ross
Detchant
Holburn
Low Middleton
Easington
Budle Bay
Bamburgh
FARNE ISLANDS
Longstone
Staple Sound
Inner Sound
North Northumberland Heritage Coast
St Cuthbert's Cave
Middleton
Belford
Waren Mill
Budle
Spindlestone
Burton
New Shoreston
Grace Darling
Seahouses
Outchester
Bradford
Lucker
Elford
North Sunderland
Bellshill
Warenton
Adderstone
Warenford
Newham
Swinhoe
Beadnell
Beadnell Bay
NU
Chatton
Chillingham
Wild Cattle Park
Ros Castle
Newstead
Chathill
Tughall
Ellingham
Preston
High Newton-by-the-Sea
Low Newton-by-the-Sea
Embleton & Newton Links
Hepburn
Brownieside
North Charlton
Doxford
Fallodon
Brunton
Christon Bank
Embleton
Embleton Bay
Dunstanburgh Castle
Old Bewick
West Ditchburn
South Charlton
Dunstan Steads
Harehope
Eglingham
Rock
Rennington
Stamford
Dunstan
Craster
New Bewick
Wooperton
Beanley
Howick Hall
Cullernose Point
Howick
Powburn
Broxfield
Littlehoughton
Longhoughton
Brandon
Branton
East Bolton
Denwick
Boulmer
Fawdon
Glanton
Glanton Pike
Shawdon Hill
Bolton
Abberwick
Alnwick
Hulne Park
Hawkhill
Lesbury
Seaton Point
Whittingham
Thrunton
Broome Park
Aln Valley Railway
Hipsburn
Alnmouth
Edlingham
Bilton
Alnmouth Bay
Bilton Banks
High Buston
Shilbottle
Low Buston
Newton-on-the-Moor
Birling
Warkworth
Amble
Coquet Island
Swarland
Old Swarland
North End
Guyzance
North Togston
Gloster Hill
High Hauxley
Rothbury
Cragside
Longframlington
Whitton
Newtown
Acklington
Togston
Radcliffe
Broomhill
Felton
East Thirston
South Broomhill
Hadston
Pauperhaugh
West Thirston
Red Row
Druridge Bay
NZ
Weldon Bridge
Eshott
Druridge
Forestburn Gate
Todburn
Causey Park
Helm
West Chevington
Widdrington
North Northumberland Heritage Coast
Wingates
Stobswood
Widdrington Station
Longhorsley
Causey Park Bridge
Earsdon
Cresswell
Harwood Forest
Tritlington
Ulgham
Linton
Ellington
Lynemouth
Fenrother

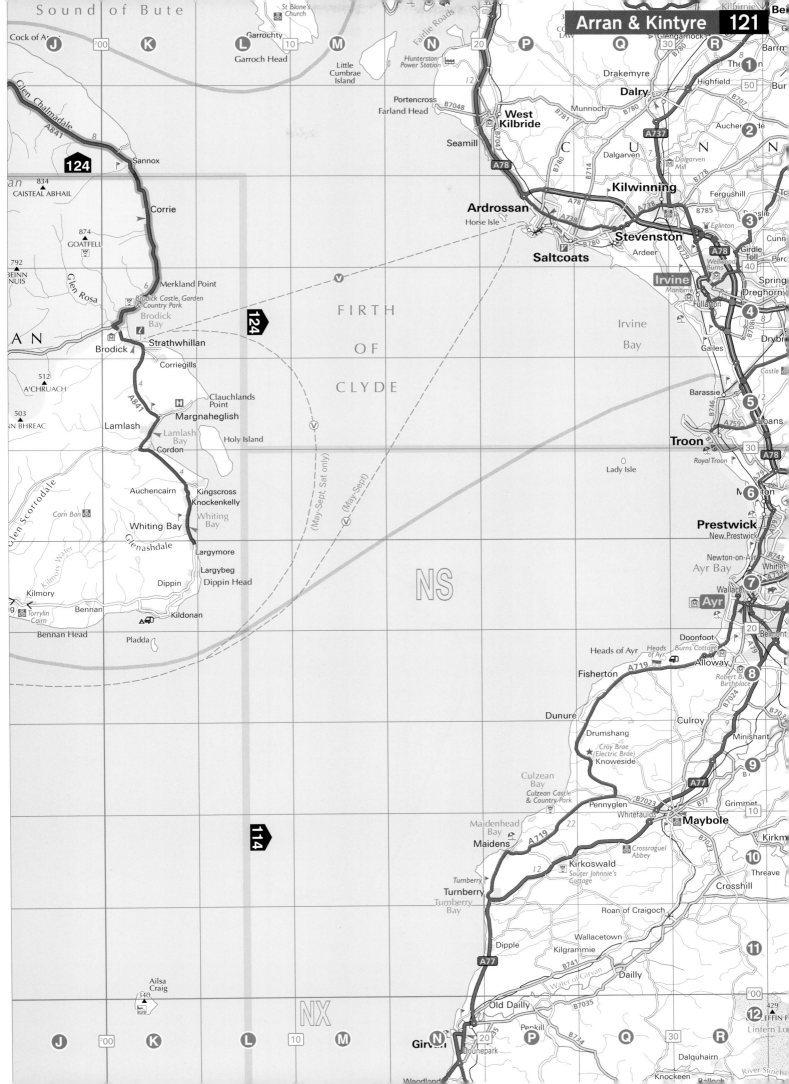

Sound of Bute

J K L M N P Q R

Cock of Arran
Garrochty
10
Garroch Head
Little Cumbrae Island
Fairlie Roads
Hunterston Power Station
St Blane's Church
Kilbirnie
Beith
Glengarnock
Barrmill
The Den
Drakemyre
Highfield
50
Dalry
Munnoch
Dalgarven Mill
Aucheniebrie
Kilwinning
Fergushill
Roslie
Eglinton

834 CAISTEAL ABHAIL
124
Sannox
Corrie
Portencross
Farland Head
West Kilbride
Seamill
Ardrossan
Horse Isle
Saltcoats
Stevenston
Ardeer
Girdle Toll
40
Wellwood Burns
Irvine
Dreghorn
Springside

Glen Chalmadale
A841
8
874 GOATFELL
792 BEINN NUIS

Glen Rosa
Merkland Point
Brodick Castle, Garden & Country Park
Brodick Bay
124
FIRTH
OF
CLYDE
Irvine Bay
Maritime
Fullarton
Gailes
Drybridge

Brodick
Strathwhillan
Corriegills
512 A'CHRUACH
503 BEINN BHREAC
A841
Clauchlands Point
Margnaheglish
Lamlash
Lamlash Bay
Holy Island
Cordon
NS
Barassie
Castle
5
12
Loans
Troon
A759
A78
Royal Troon
Lady Isle
6
Monkton

Glen Scorrodale
Carn Ban
Auchencairn
Kingscross
Knockenkelly
Whiting Bay
Whiting Bay
Glenashdale
Largymore
Largybeg
Dippin
Dippin Head
(May-Sept, Sat only)
(May-Sept)
Prestwick
New Prestwick
Newton-on-Ayr
Whitletts
Ayr Bay
Wallacetown
7

Kilmory Water
Kilmory
Torrylin Cairn
Bennan
Kildonan
Bennan Head
Pladda

114

Ailsa Craig
340
NX

Heads of Ayr
Heads of Ayr
Burns Cottage
Doonfoot
Ayr
Alloway
Robert Burns Birthplace
8
Belmont

Fisherton
Dunure
Culroy
Culzean Bay
Culzean Castle & Country Park
Drumshang
Croy Brae (Electric Brae)
Knoweside
Minishant
9
A77

Maidenhead Bay
Maidens
A719
Pennyglen
B7023
Whitefaulds
Crossraguel Abbey
Maybole
Kirkmic
10
Threave

Turnberry
Turnberry Bay
Kirkoswald
Souter Johnnie's Cottage
Roan of Craigoch
Crosshill

Dipple
Wallacetown
Kilgrammie
Dailly
11

Old Dailly
Penkill
B7035
Water of Girvan
River Stinchar
12

Girvan
Dounepark
Woodlands
Dalquhairn
Knockeen

J K L M N P Q R

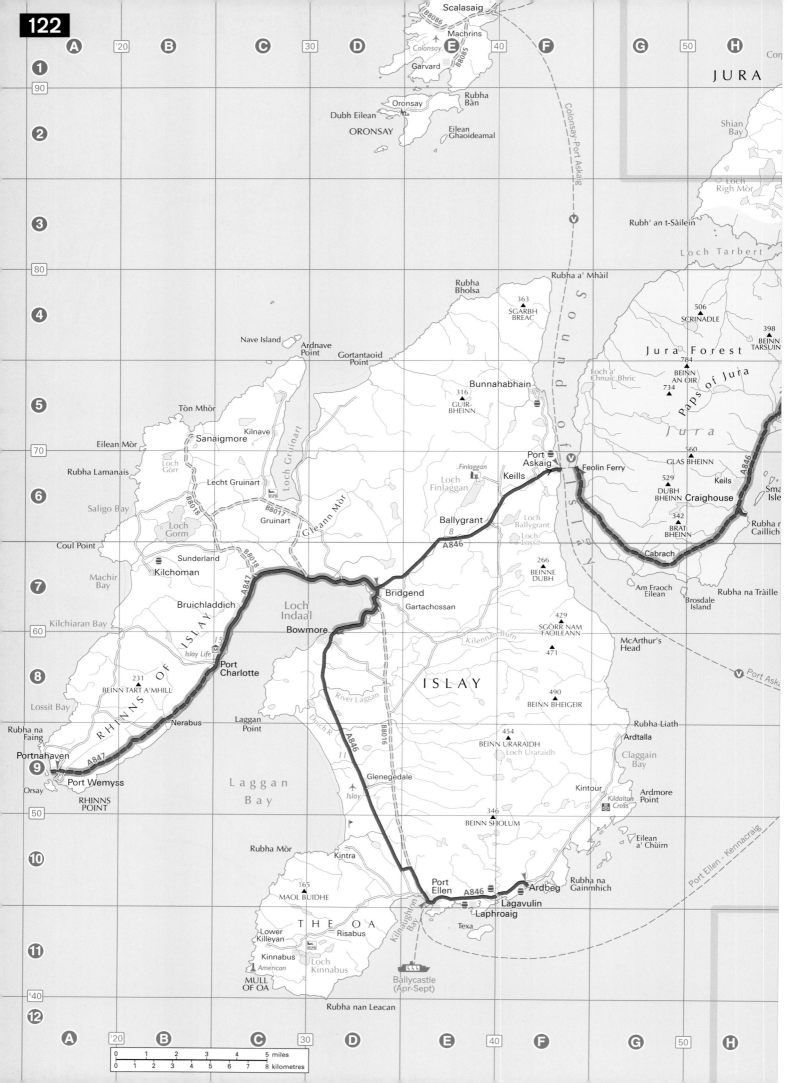

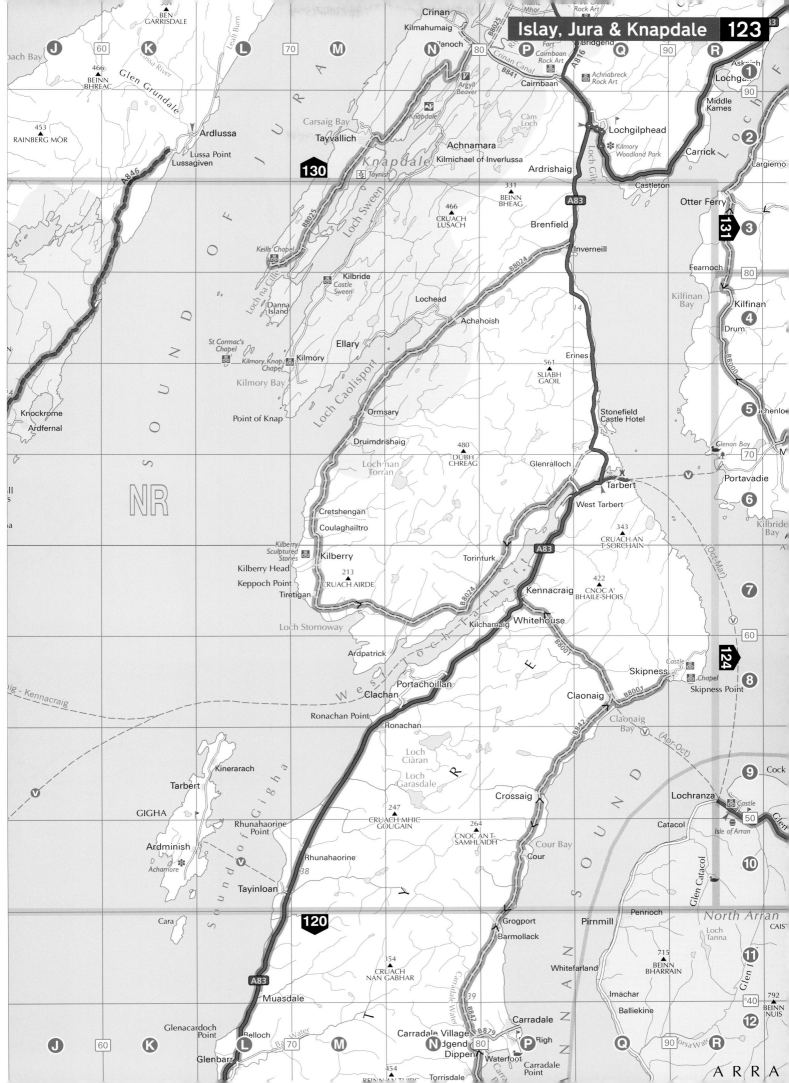

J `60` K `70` L M N `80` P Q `90` R

BEN GARRISDALE

Crinan
Kilmahumaig
N'anoch
Fort Cairnbaan Rock Art
Cairnbaan
`1` Lochga...
Askaig
Bridgend
Crinan Canal
Achnabreck Rock Art
`2` Middle Kames
Lochgilphead
Kilmory Woodland Park
Carrick
Largiemo...

466 BEINN BHREAC
Glen Grundale
Lussa River
Carsaig Bay
Knapdale
Argyll Beaver
Castleton
Ardrishaig
`3` Otter Ferry

453 RAINBERG MÒR
Ardlussa
Tayvallich
Achnamara
Kilmichael of Inverlussa
Kilmory Woodland Park
Taynish
`130`
Knapdale
Brenfield
A83
Fearnoch `80`
Lussa Point
Lussagiven

331 BEINN BHEAG
Loch Sween
466 CRUACH LUSACH
Inverneill
Kilfinan Bay
`4` Kilfinan
Drum

B8025
Keills Chapel
Kilbride Castle Sween
Lochead
B8024
14
B8000
`5` uchenlo...

Loch na Cille
Danna Island
Achahoish
Erines
561 SLIABH GAOIL
Glenan Bay
`70`

St Cormac's Chapel
Ellary
Kilmory Knap Chapel
Kilmory
Kilmory Bay
Loch Caolisport
Stonefield Castle Hotel
`6` Portavadie
Kilbride Bay

Knockrome
Ardfernal
Point of Knap
Ormsary
480 DUBH CHREAG
Glenralloch
Tarbert
West Tarbert

NR
Druimdrishaig
Loch nan Torran
343 CRUACH AN T-SORCHAIN
(Oct-Mar)

Cretshengan
Coulaghailtro
A83
Kilberry Sculptured Stones
Kilberry
Torinturk
422 CNOC A' BHAILE-SHOIS
`7` `60`

213 CRUACH AIRDE
B8024
Kennacraig
Kilberry Head
Keppoch Point
Tiretigan
Kilchamaig
Whitehouse
Castle
`124`
`8`

Loch Stornoway
Ardpatrick
B8001
Skipness
Chapel
Skipness Point

Craig - Kennacraig
Portachoillan
Clachan
Claonaig
B8001

Ronachan Point
Ronachan
Claonaig Bay
(Apr-Oct)

Kinerarach
Loch Ciaran
Loch Garasdale
`9` Cock
Lochranza
Castle

Tarbert
GIGHA
Rhunahaorine Point
Crossaig
247 CRUACH MHIC GOUGAIN
Catacol
Isle of Arran
`50`
Glen Catacol

Ardminish
Achamore
Rhunahaorine
38
264 CNOC AN T-SAMHLAIDH
Cour Bay
Cour
`10`

Cara
`120`
Grogport
Barmollack
Pirnmill
Penrioch
Loch Tanna
North Arran
CAIS...

A83
354 CRUACH NAN GABHAR
Whitefarland
715 BEINN BHARRAIN
`11`

Glenacardoch Point
Muasdale
Carradale
792 BEINN NUIS
`12`
Imachar
Balliekine
`6` `40`

J `60` K L `70` M N `80` P Q `90` R
Belloch
Glenbarr
Carradale Village
...dgend
Dippen
Waterfoot
Righ
Carradale Point
Torrisdale
A R R A

A846

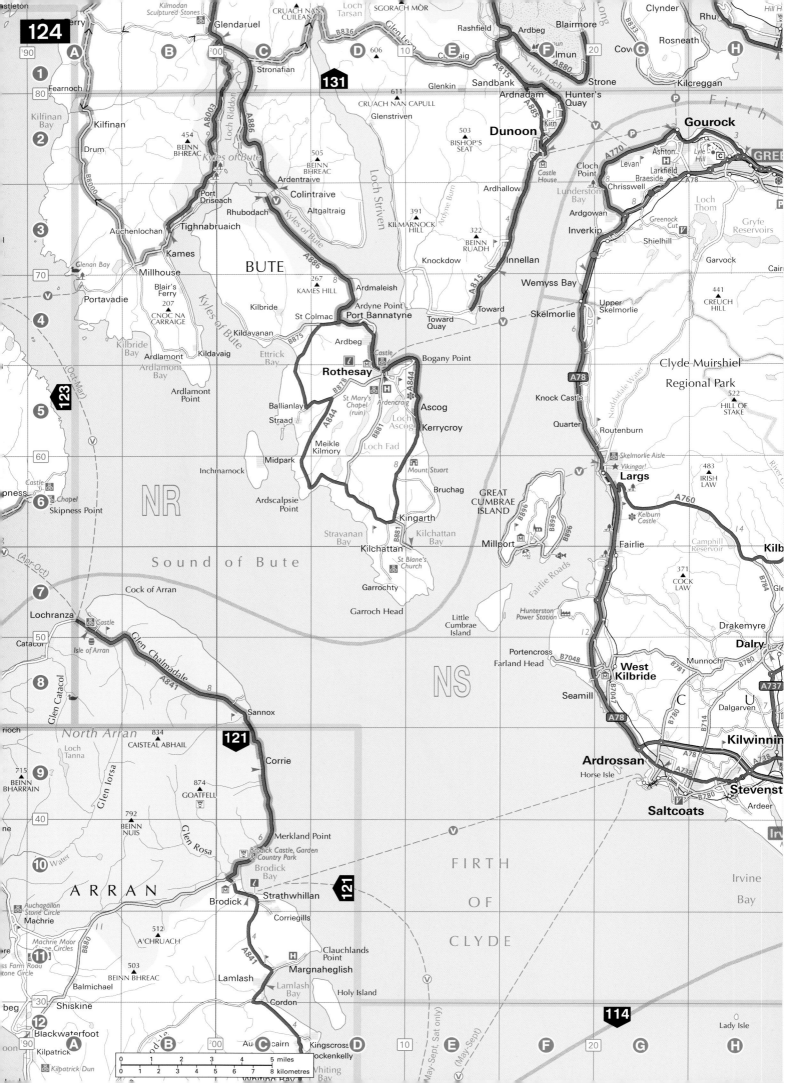

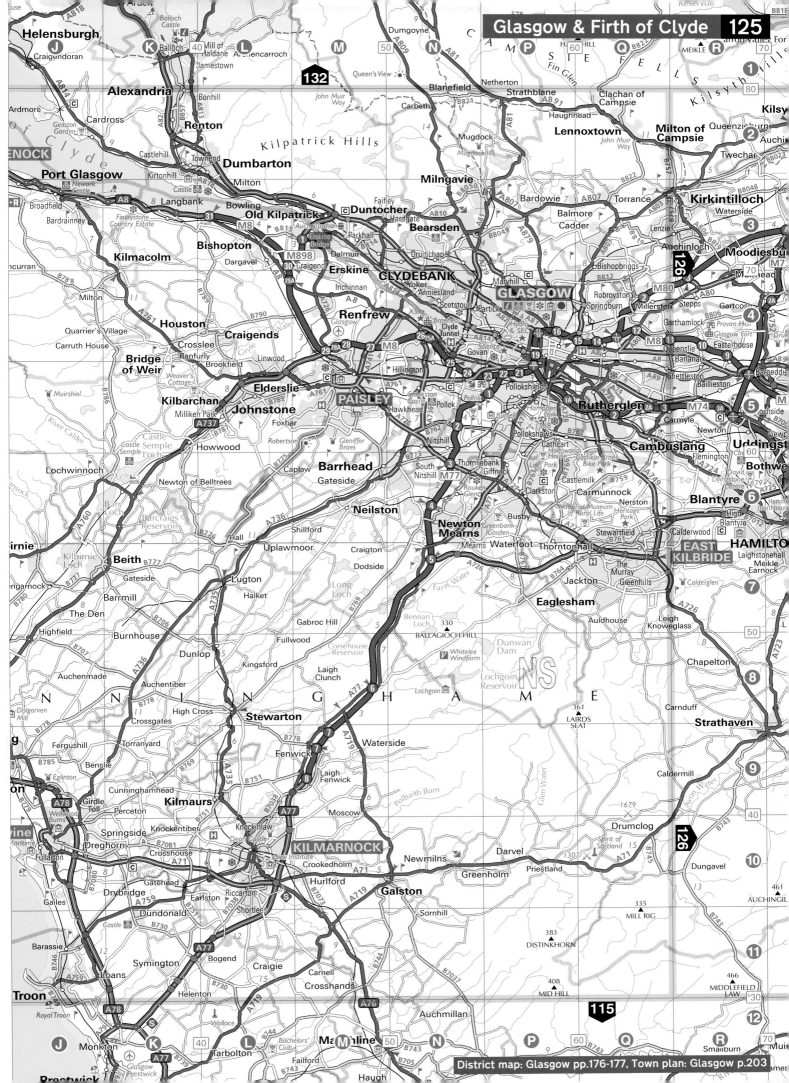

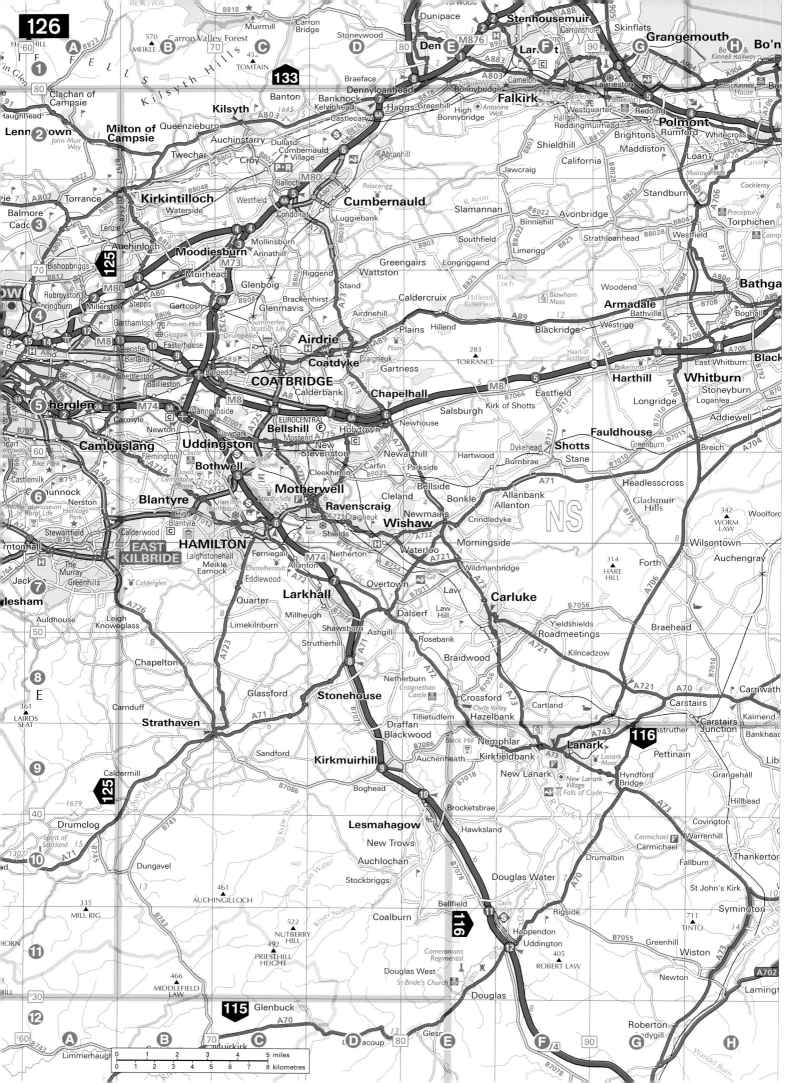

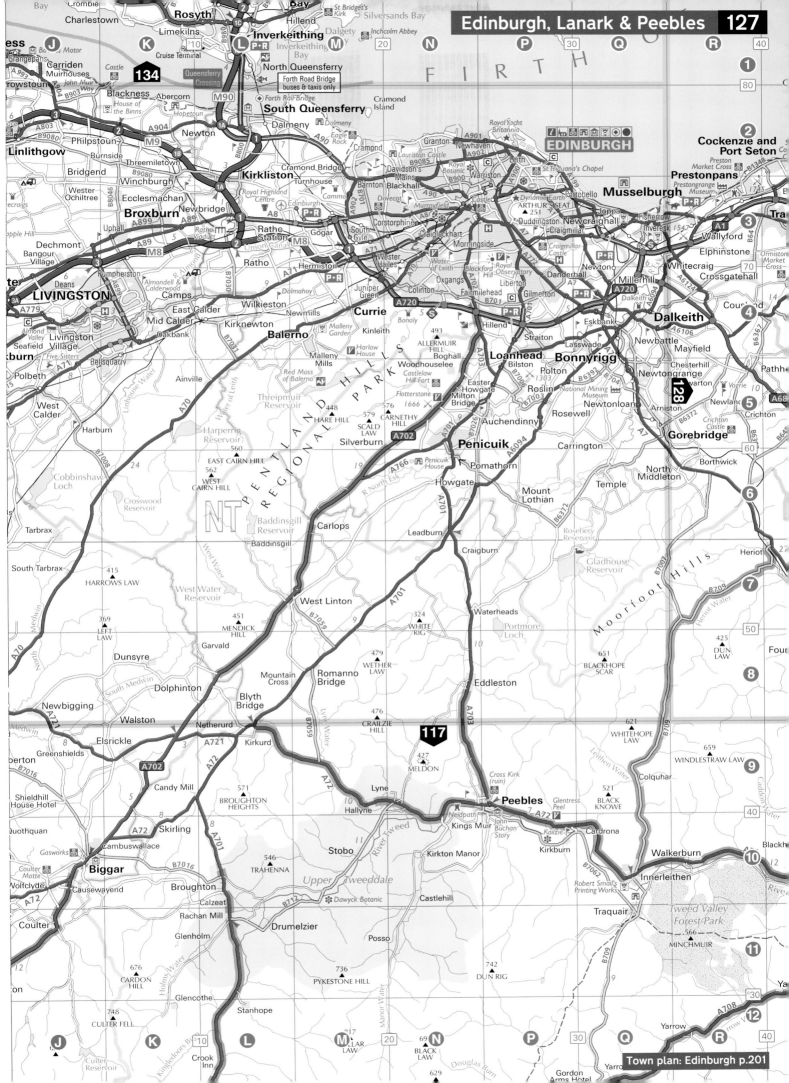

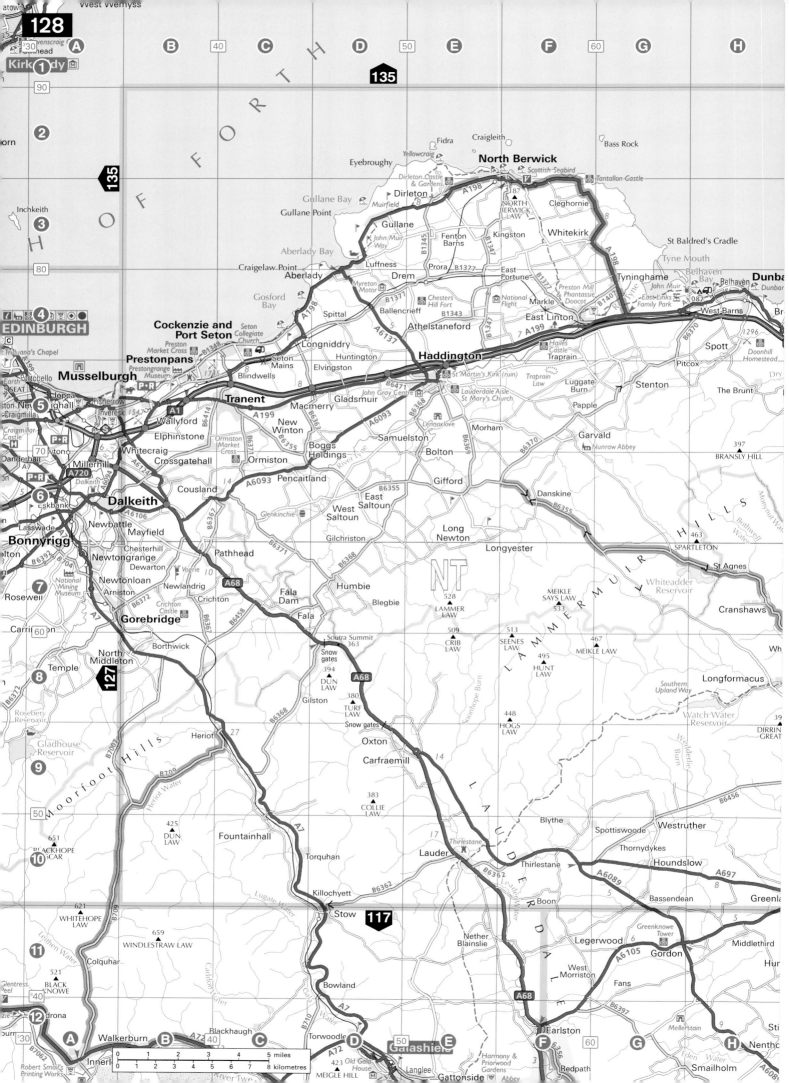

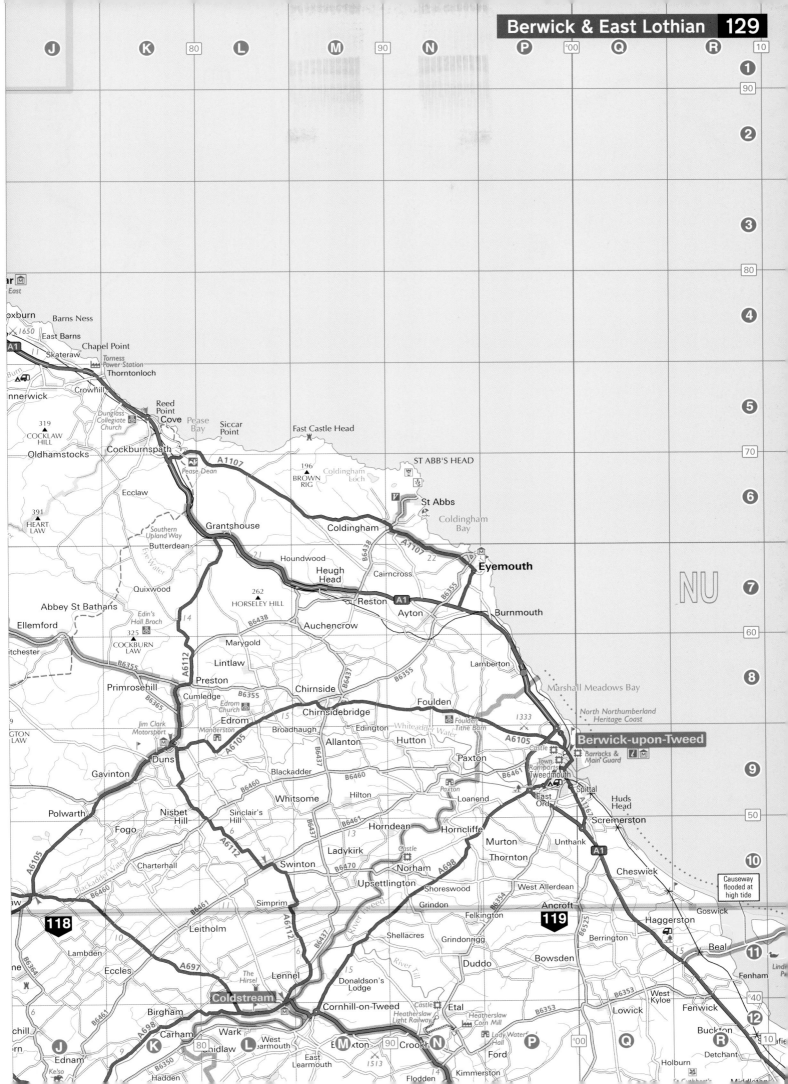

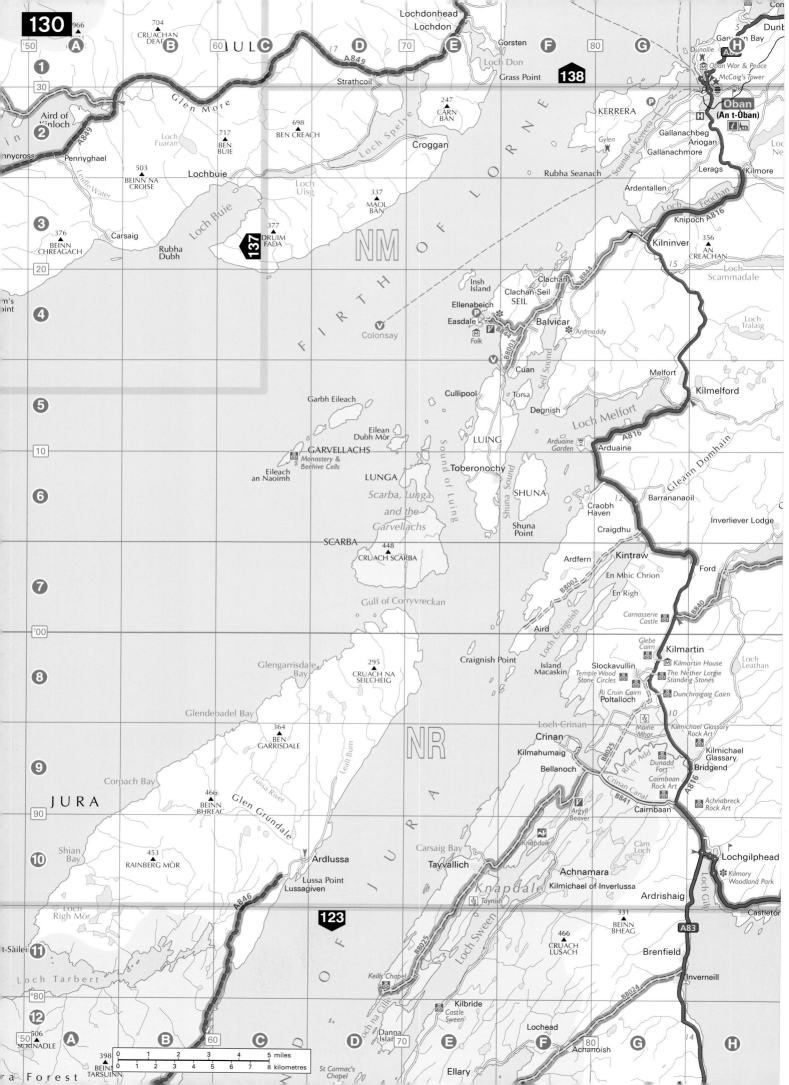

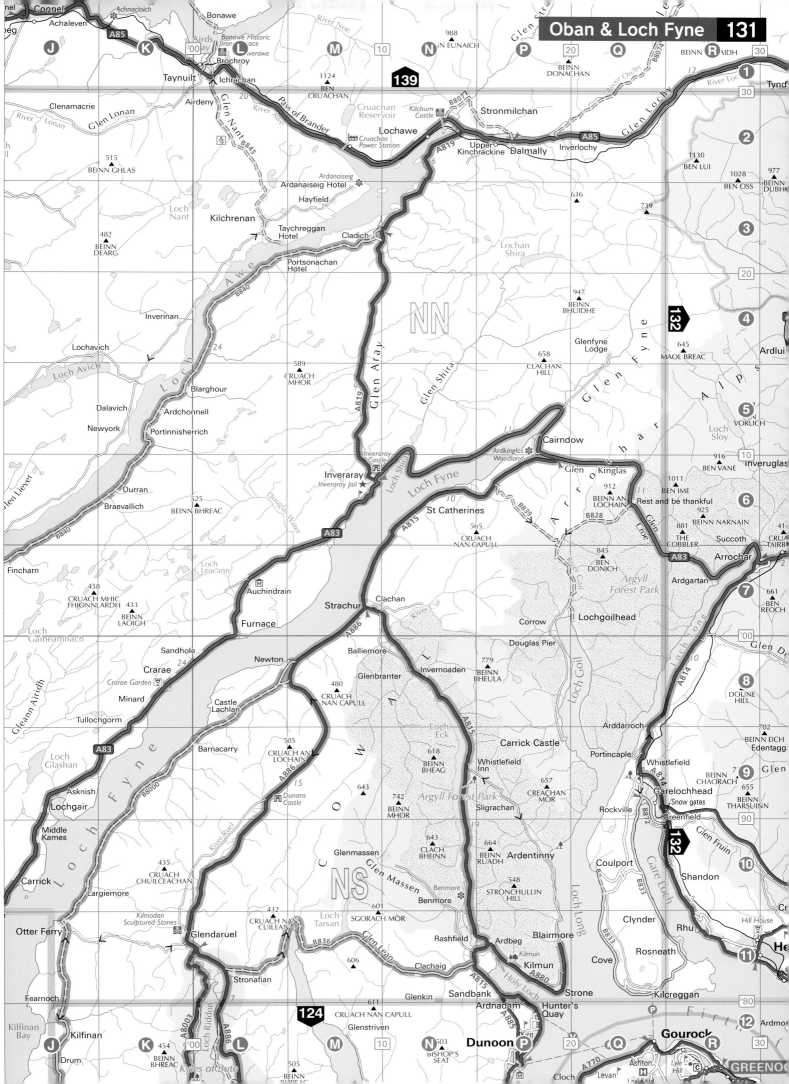

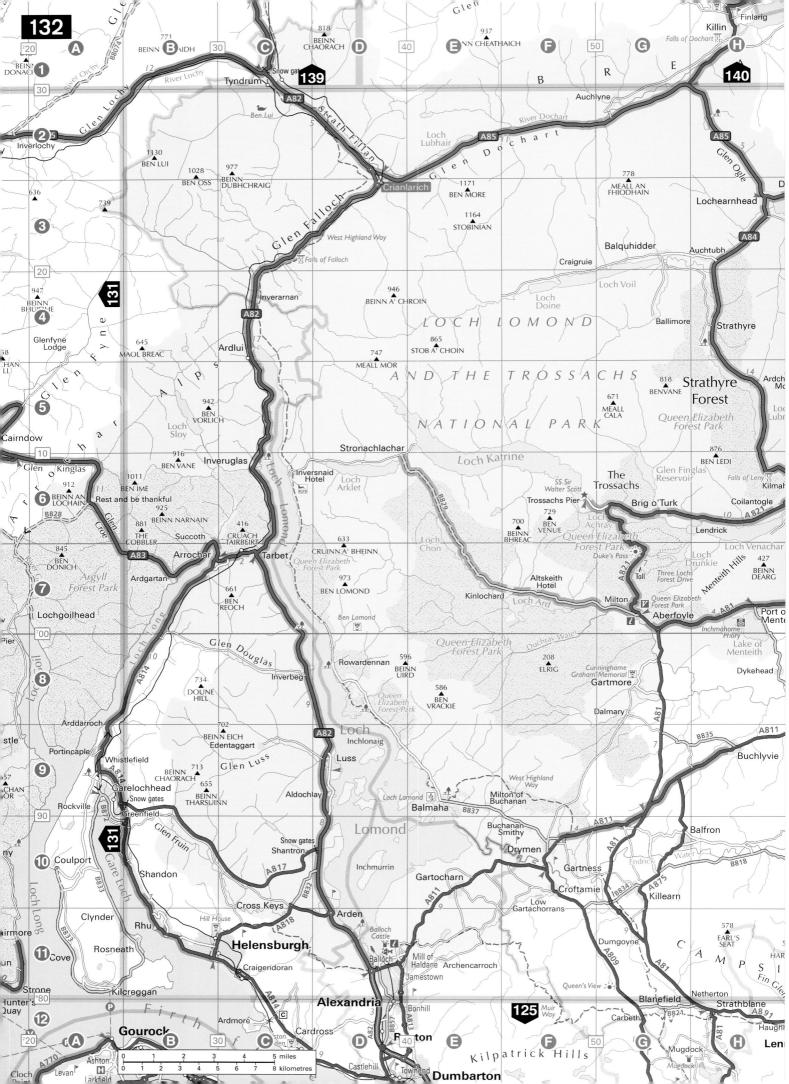

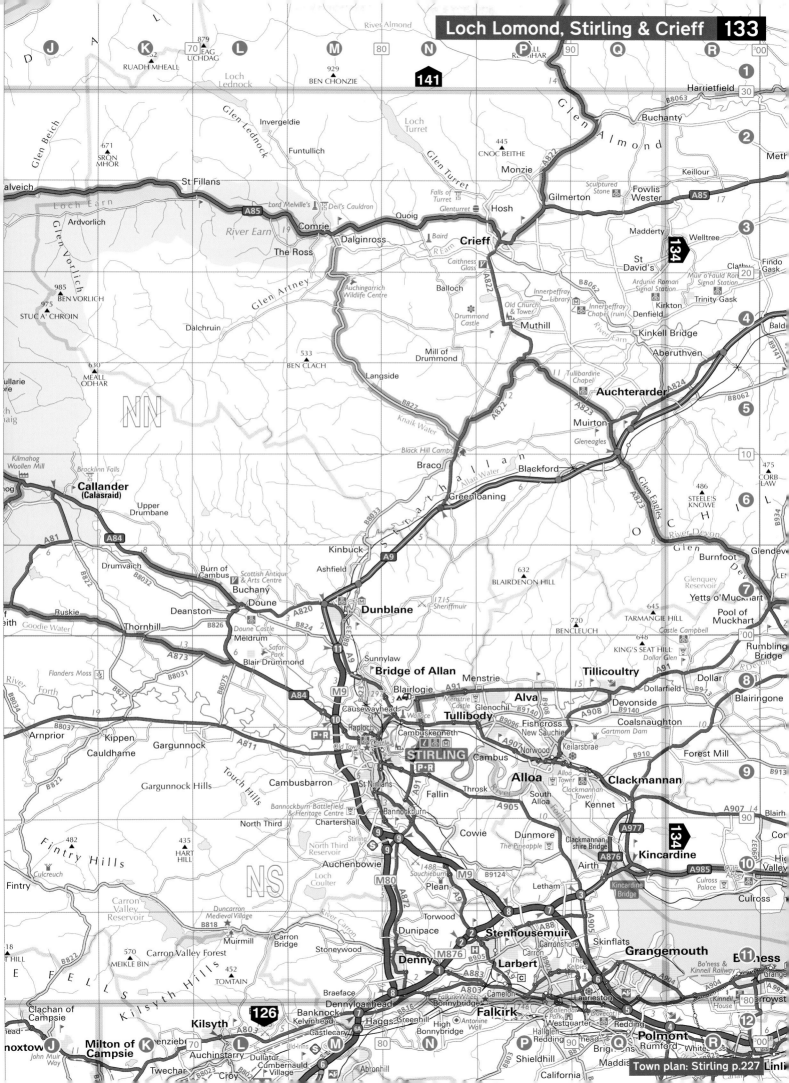

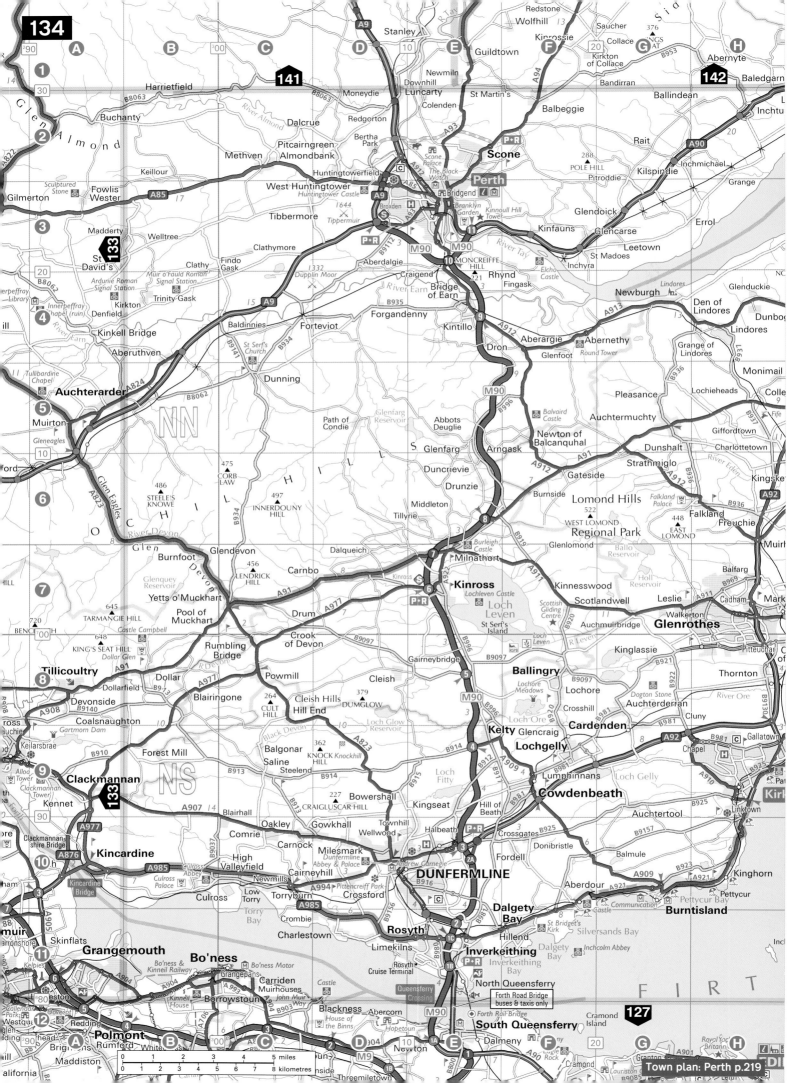

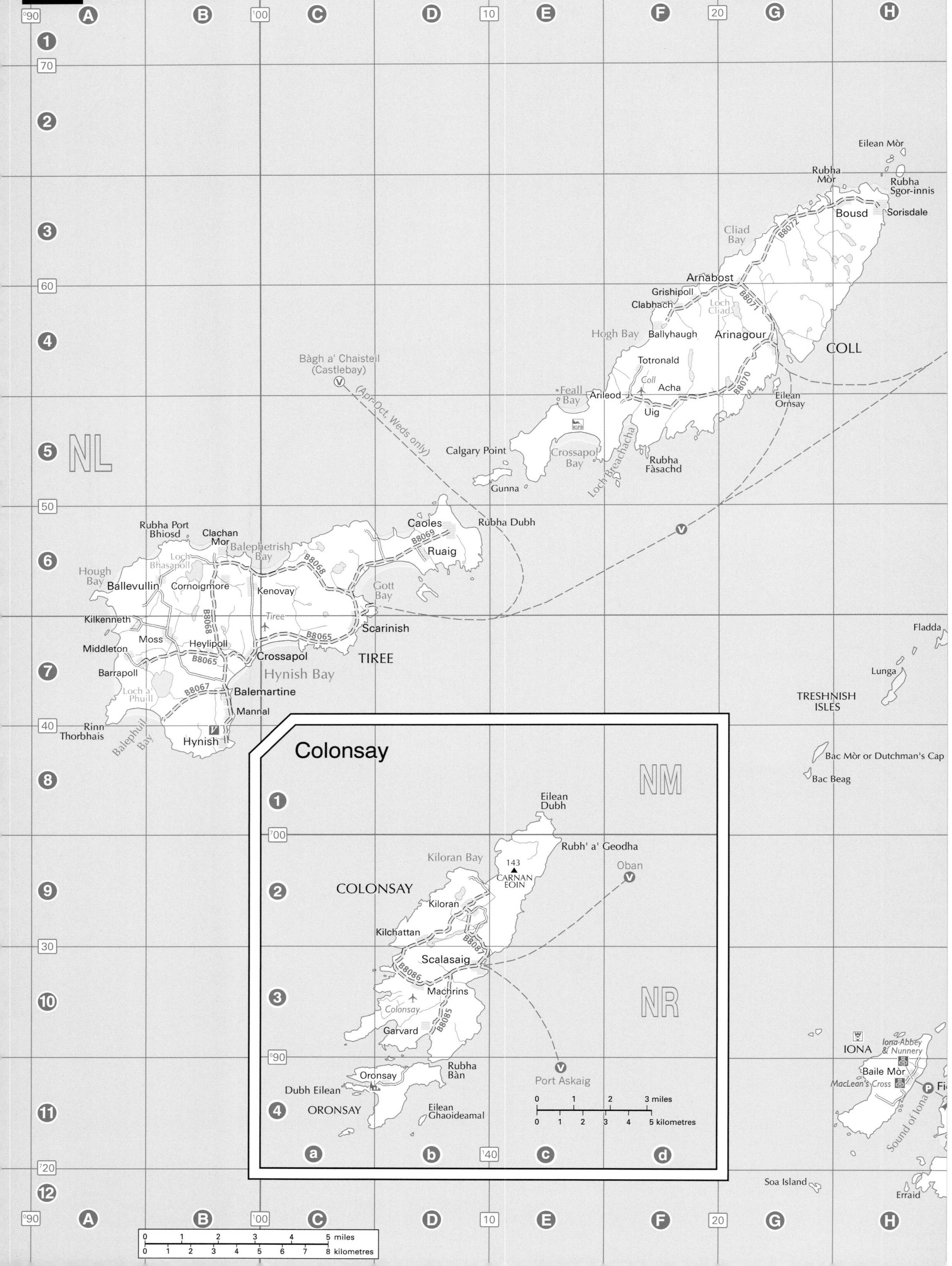

A   B   00   C   D   10   E   F   20   G   H

1

70

2

3

60

NL

4

5

50

6

7

40

8

9

30

10

90

11

20

12

90   A   B   00   C   D   10   E   F   20   G   H

COLL

Eilean Mòr
Rubha Mòr
Rubha Sgor-innis
Bousd
Sorisdale
Cliad Bay
B8072
Arnabost
Grishipoll
Clabhach
Loch Cliad
B8071
Hogh Bay
Ballyhaugh
Arinagour
Totronald
Coll
Acha
B8070
Feall Bay
Arileod
Uig
Eilean Ornsay
RSPB
Calgary Point
Crossapol Bay
Loch Breachacha
Rubha Fàsachd
Gunna

Bàgh a' Chaisteil
(Castlebay)
(Apr-Oct, Weds only)

Caoles
Rubha Dubh
B8069
Ruaig
Rubha Port Bhiosd
Clachan Mor
Balephetrish Bay
B8068
Hough Bay
Loch Bhasapoll
Ballevullin
Cornoigmore
Kenovay
Gott Bay
Kilkenneth
B8068
Tiree
Moss
Heylipoll
B8065
Scarinish
Middleton
Crossapol
TIREE
Barrapoll
B8065
Hynish Bay
Loch a' Phuill
Balemartine
B8067
Mannal
Rinn Thorbhais
Hynish
Balephuil Bay

Fladda
TRESHNISH ISLES
Lunga
Bac Mòr or Dutchman's Cap
Bac Beag

NM

NR

IONA
Iona Abbey & Nunnery
Baile Mòr
MacLean's Cross
Sound of Iona
Soa Island
Erraid

Colonsay

1

700

2

9

30

3

10

90

11

a   b   40   c   d

720

Eilean Dubh
Rubh' a' Geodha
143
CARNAN EOIN
Oban
Kiloran Bay
COLONSAY
Kiloran
Kilchattan
B8087
B8086
Scalasaig
Machrins
Colonsay
B8085
Garvard
Oronsay
Rubha Bàn
Dubh Eilean
ORONSAY
Eilean Ghaoideamal
Port Askaig

0   1   2   3 miles
0   1   2   3   4   5 kilometres

0   1   2   3   4   5 miles
0   1   2   3   4   5   6   7   8 kilometres

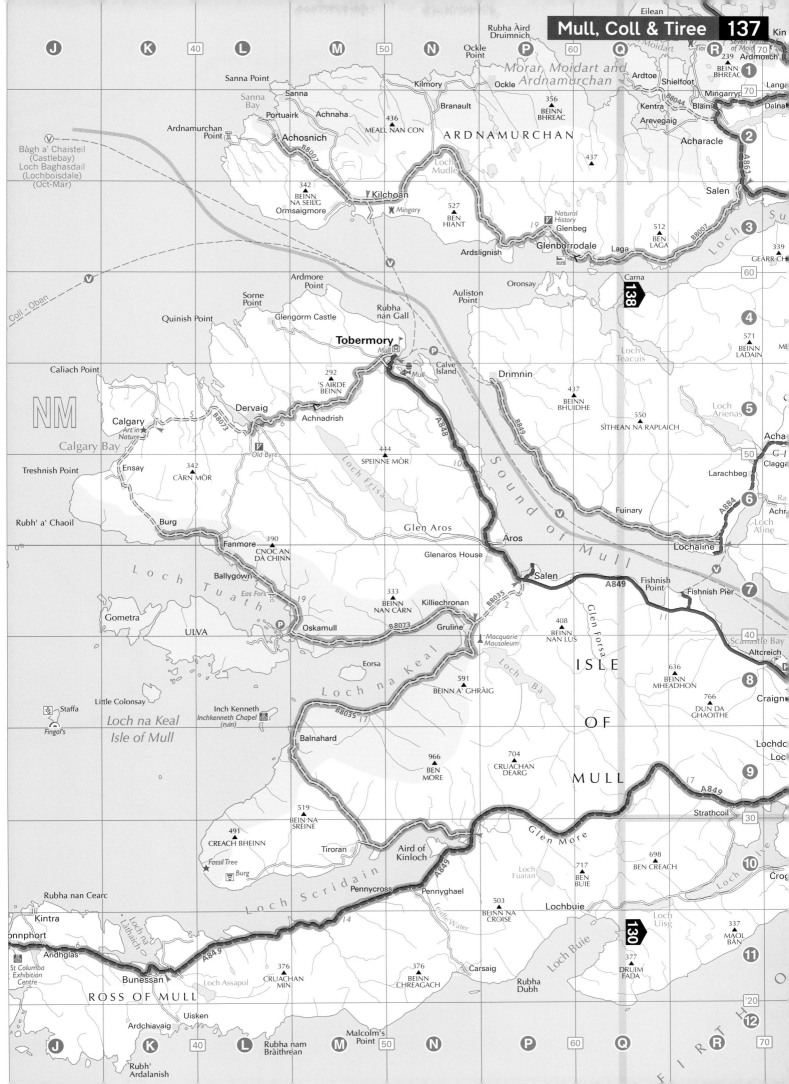

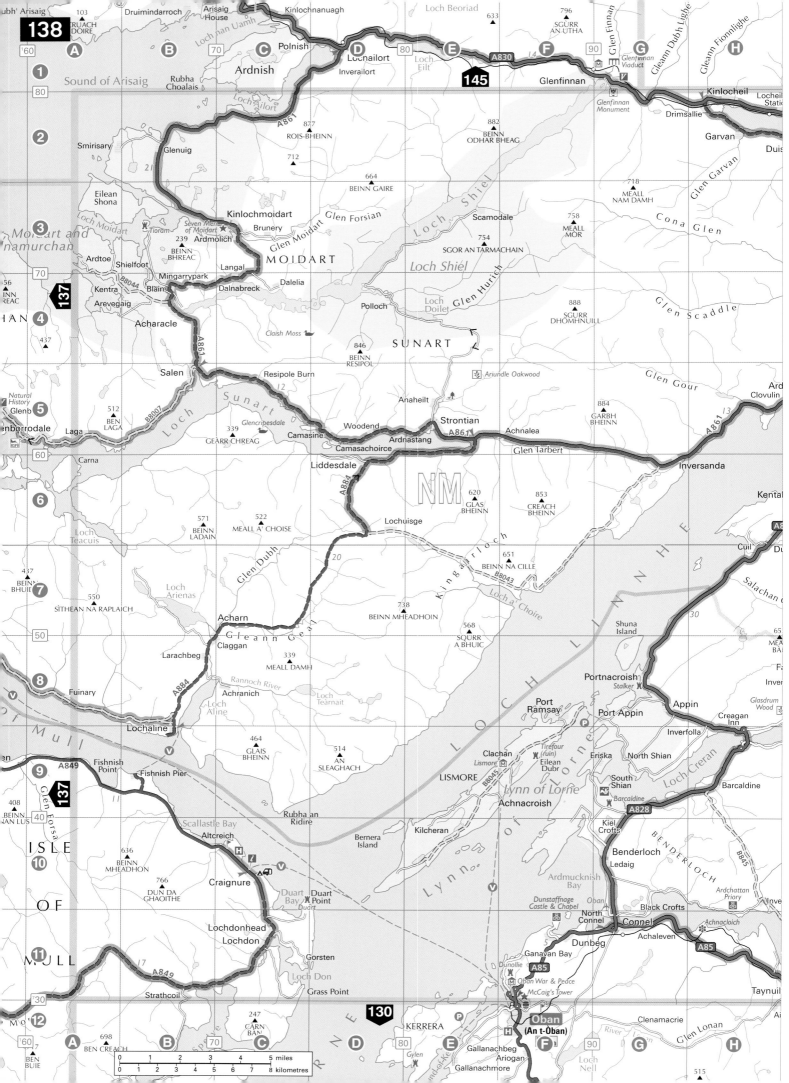

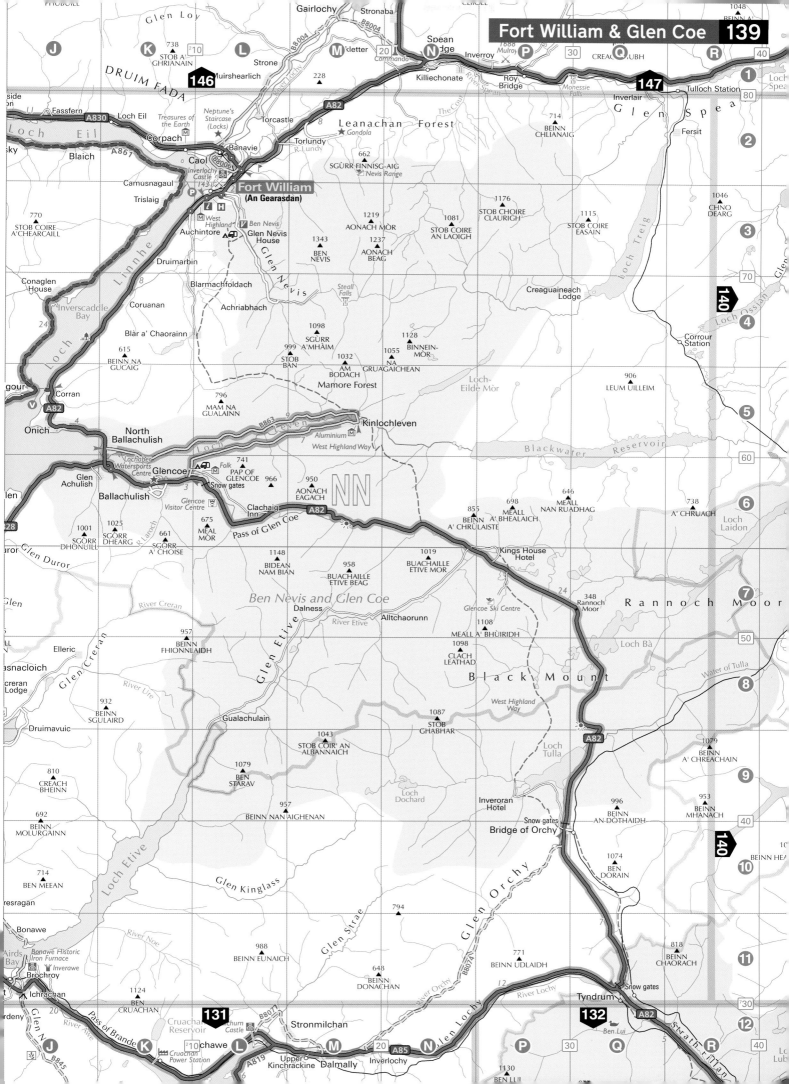

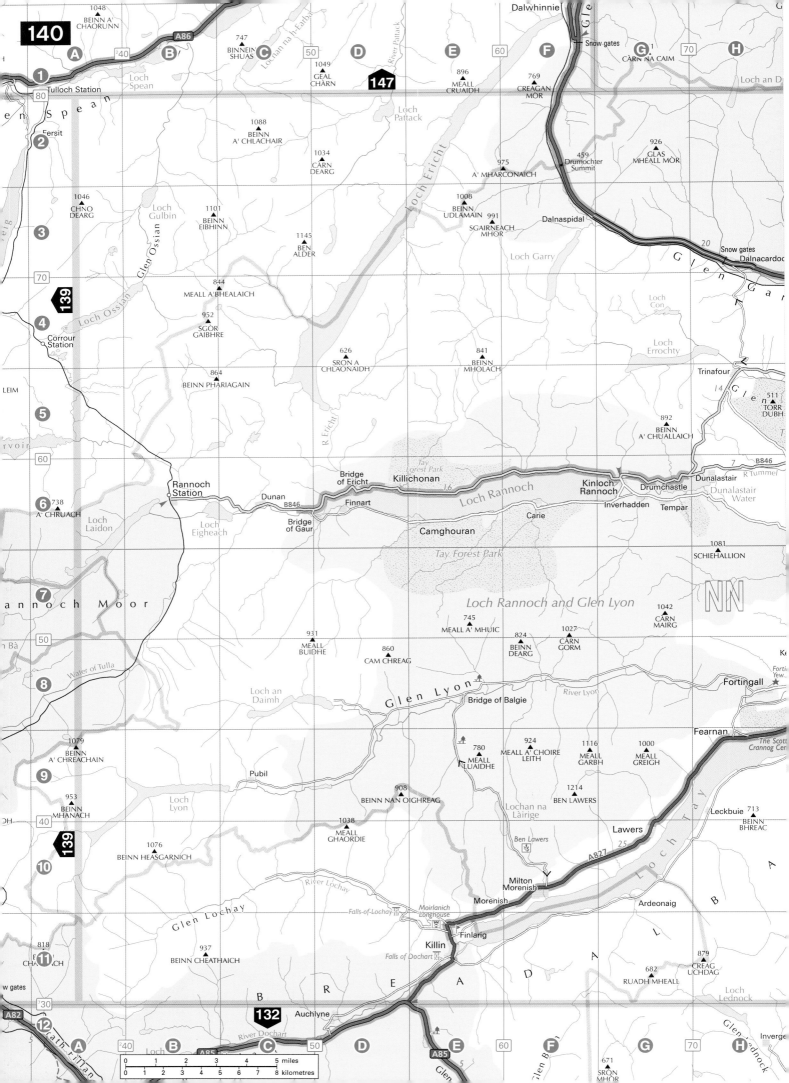

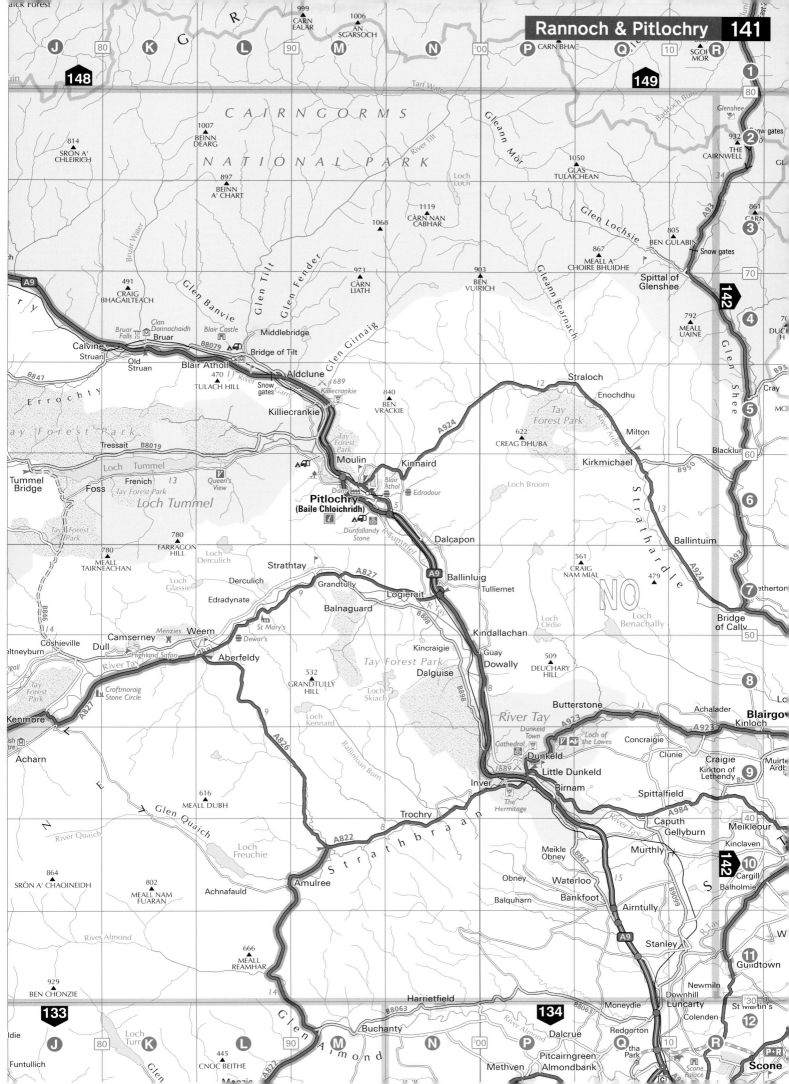

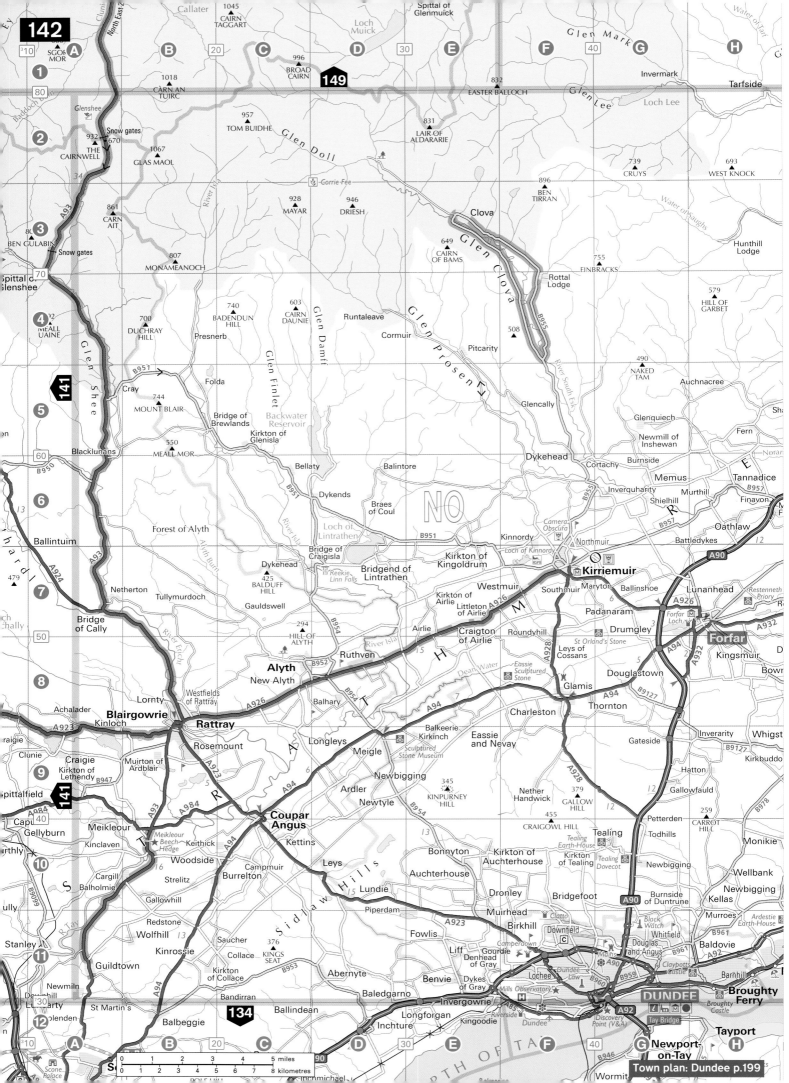

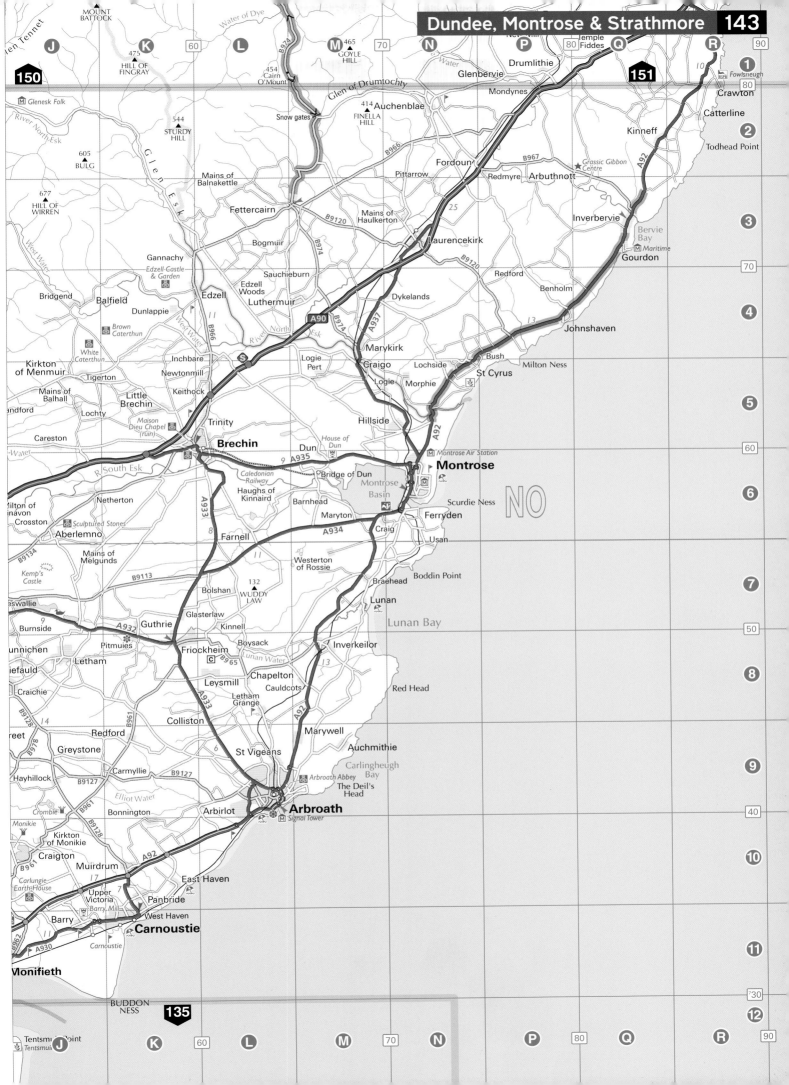

1

30

152 Talisker Bay

2

Rubha nan Clach

Fernilea
Carbost
ARNAVAL 369
Drynoch
Merkadale
Talisker

Glen Drynoch
A863
Sligachan
Sligachan
GLAMAIG 773

BEN LEE 444
Peinchorra

conser
A87

SKYE

Minginish

Talisker
Glen Eynort

Glen Brittle Forest

BEINN BHREAC 447

Grula

BEINN BHREAC 369

SGURR NAN GILLEAN 965

Fairy Pools

3

Loch Eynort

AN CRUACHIN 434

Glenbrittle
Bualintur

SGURR A' GHEADAIDH 974

Cuillin Hills

SGURR ALASDAIR 1009

The Cuillin Hills

Loch Coruisk

BLAVEN 927

20

4

Loch Brittle

CEANN NA BEINNE 225

GARS BHEINN 894

Rubha an Dùnain

Soay Sound

BEINN BHREAC 139

Mol-chlach

Loch Scavaig

Loch na Crèitheach

Kirkibost

BEN MEABOST 344

Elgol

Glasn

5

V Loch Baghasdail (Lochboisdale)

SOAY

Rubh' Aonghais

Strathaird Point

10

6

NG

CUILLIN SOUND

CANNA

Garrisdale Point

CÀRN A' GHAILL 210

A'Chill

Canna Harbour

Kilmory Bay

Rubha Shamhnan Insir

Sanday

7

Sound of Canna

MULLACH MÒR 302

Rubha na Roinne

00

A' Bhrìdeanach

ORVAL 570

Kinloch

Loch-Scresort

8

Oigh-sgeir

RÙM

ASKIVAL 810

Harris Bay

All vehicles must have the relevant island permit prior to travel to The Small Isles. Services are seasonal, day & weather dependent.

9

SGÙRR NAN GILLEAN 763

The Small Isles

90

Rubha nam Meirleach

Sound of Rùm

Bay of Laig

Cleadale

10

NM

Rubha an Fhasaidh

Laig

AN CRUACHAN 299

EIGG

Kildonnan

AN SGÙRR 393

Galmisdale

11

Eilean nan Each

Eilean Chathastail

80

MUCK

Sound of Eigg

12

Port Mòr

| 0 | 1 | 2 | 3 | 4 | 5 miles |
| 0 | 1 | 2 | 3 | 4 | 5 | 6 | 7 | 8 kilometres |

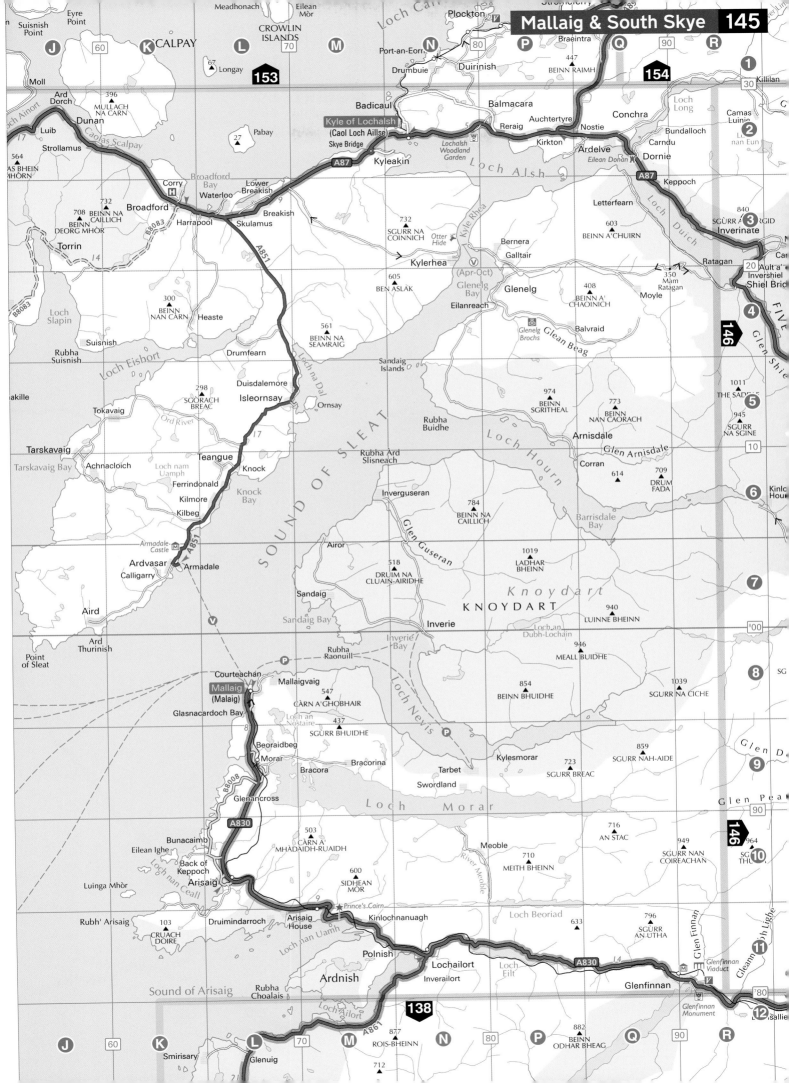

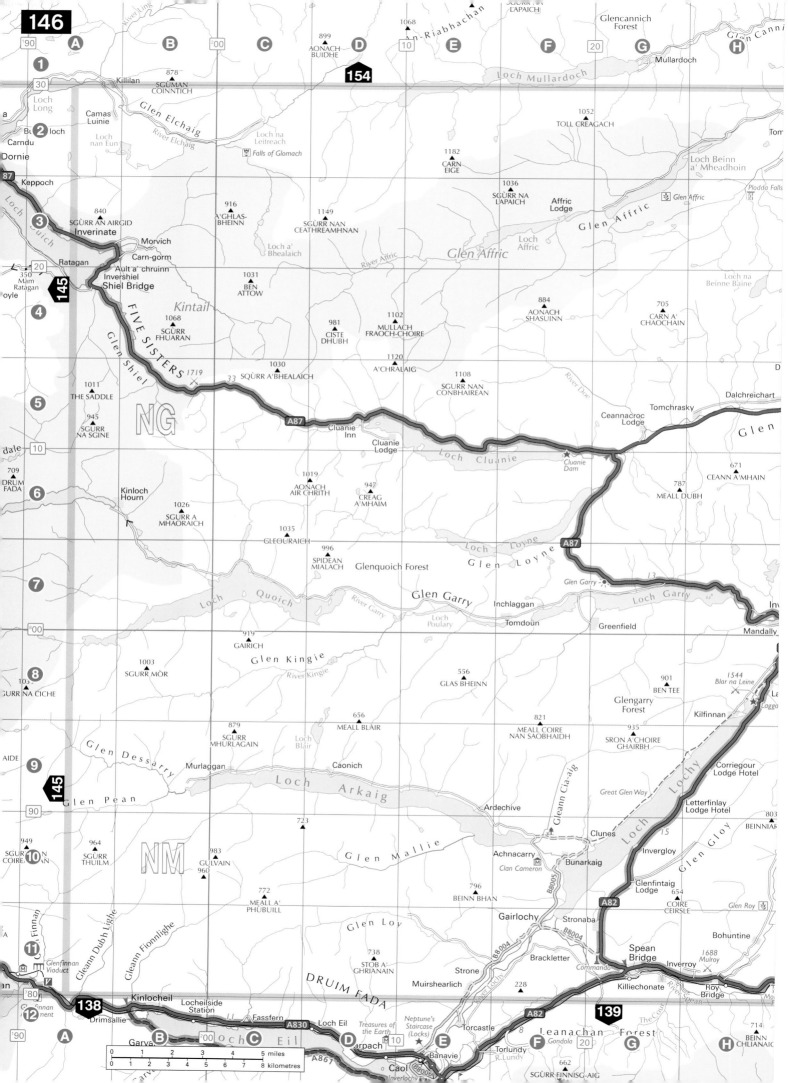

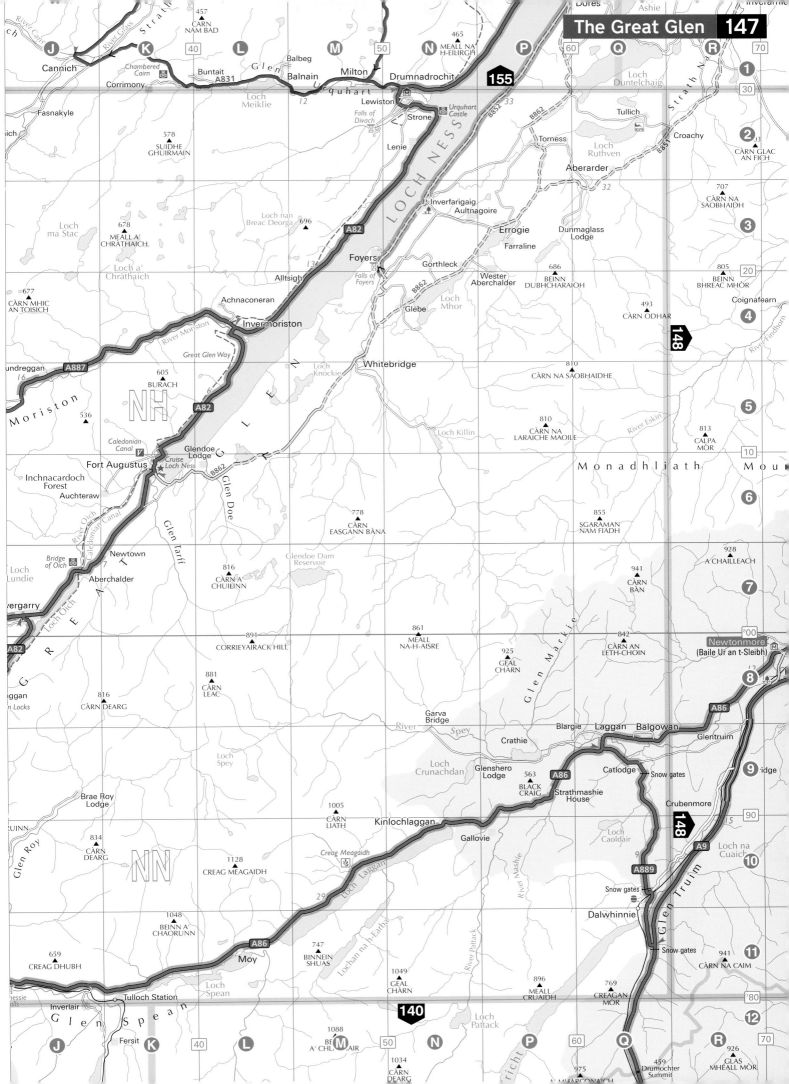

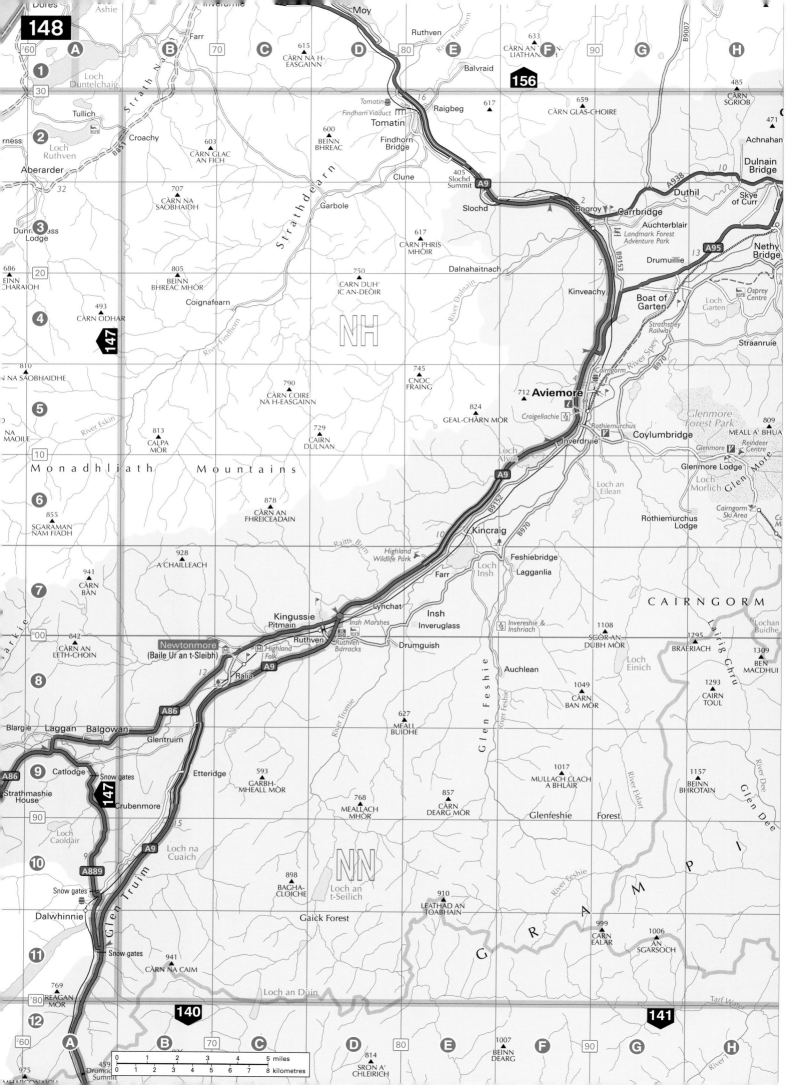

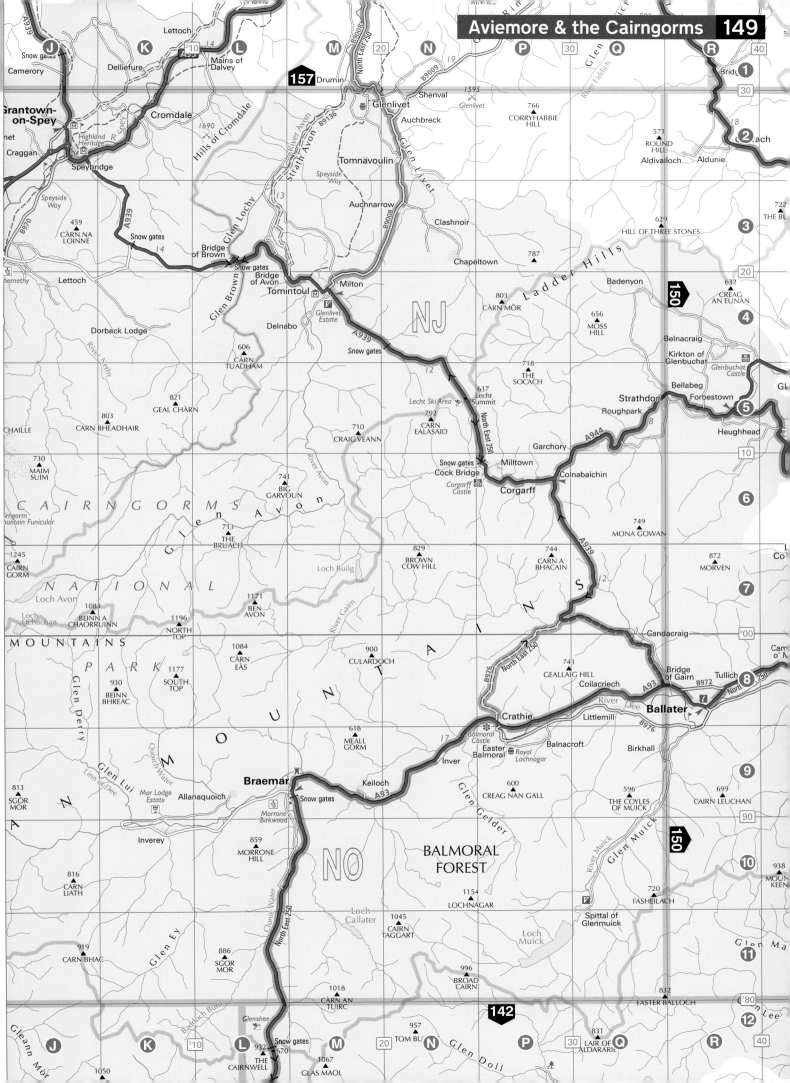

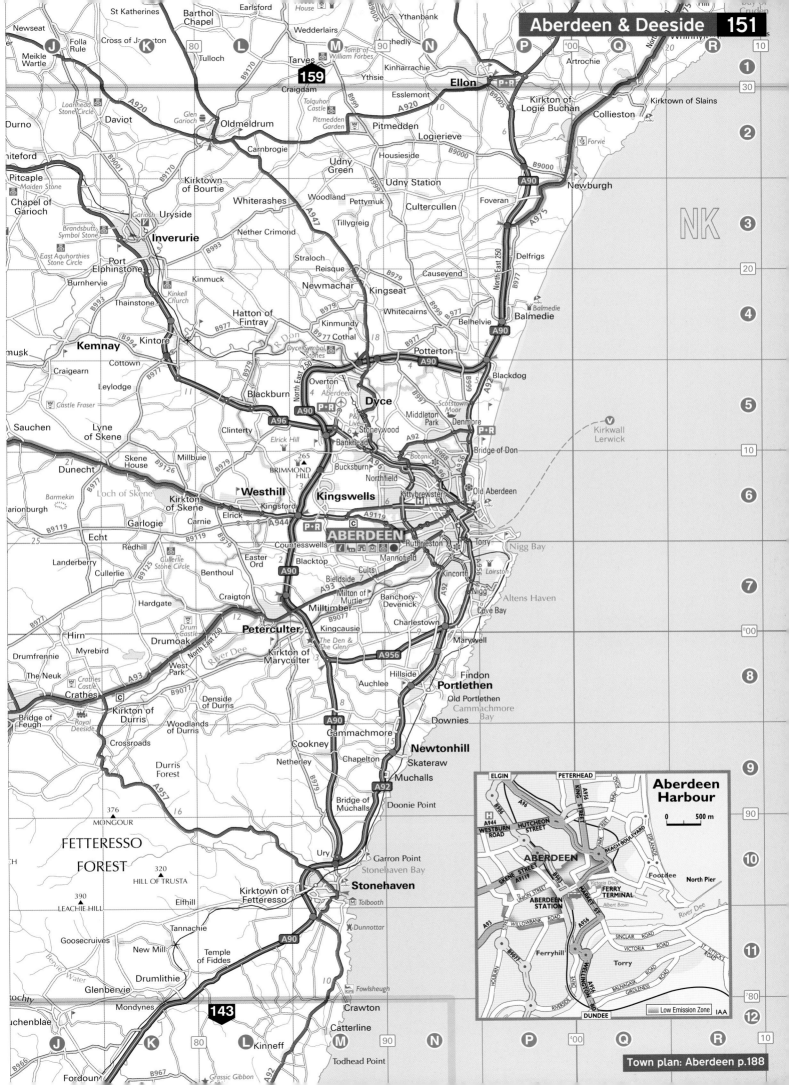

NK

159

143

Aberdeen Harbour

ELGIN PETERHEAD

H
WESTBURN ROAD HUTCHEON STREET
A944

ABERDEEN

SKENE STREET

KING STREET
PARK ROAD

BEACH BOULEVARD
ESPLANADE

UNION STREET A9119
B981

Victoria Dock
FERRY TERMINAL Albert Basin

North Pier
Footdee

River Dee

ABERDEEN STATION

A93
A956
HARRIET ST

WILLOWBANK ROAD

Ferryhill
HOLBURN

WELLINGTON RD
A956

SINCLAIR ROAD

VICTORIA ROAD
Torry
BALNAGASK ROAD
GIRDLENESS ROAD
ST FITTICKS ROAD

RIVERSIDE DR

DUNDEE

0 500 m

Low Emission Zone IAA

Town plan: Aberdeen p.188

J   K   60   L   M   70   N   B8021   P   80   Q   R   90   250
1
FALL NA

CNOC
BREAC   293

Garden   13
Londubh
Poolewe   80

North Erradale

Big Sand   A832
160   Strath
Smithstown   Heritage   Auchtercairn   2
Longa   Lonemore   Gairloch   Gairloch & Loch Ewe
Island   Loch   Charlestown   421   Loch
Gairloch   MEALL AN
DOIREIN

Eilean   3
Port   Horrisdale   River Kerry   Loch Bad
Henderson   B8056   an Sgalaig
Badachro   Victoria Falls   19
Opinan   70   Tallac

South Erradale   Loch Ghaineamhach   4
875   Loch na
BAOSBHEINN   h-Oidhc
Red Point   Loch a'   855
Ghodhainn   619   Loch a'   BEINN
Red   BEINN BHREAC   Bhealaich   AN EÒIN
Point   5
985   914
NG   Loch   BEINN   BEINN DEARG
Torridon   ALLIGIN   60
Rubha   Fearnmore   Lower
na Fearn   Diabaig   Allilgin Shuas   Inveralligin   6
Fearnbeg   Loch Diabaig   Torridon   Torri
odigarry   Ob   Arrina   House
Chuaig   Upper Loch Torridon   Deer
ffin Island   Cuaig   Kenmore   Loch   Annat
Callakille   Ardheslaig   Shieldaig   Shieldaig   Weste oss   7
Kilt Rock
ffin   Ellishader   Lonbain   492   493   Loch   902
AN GARBH-   CRÒIC-   Damph   B   50
Valtos   MHEALL   BHEINN   DAMPH
Rubha nam Brathairean   RONA   Glenshieldaig   Forest   8
Culnaknock   Eilean
Tigh   North Coast 500   Loch Lundie
ealt   Tote   Eilean   Loch Coultrie   730
Fladday   River Applecross   895   SGURR A
Old Man   Manish   Loch   BEINN BHAN   Rassal   GHARAIDH   9
of Storr   Point   Arnish   Torran   Applecross   Ashwood
Loch   Arnish   Applecross Bay   626   Kirkton
Leathan   Brochel   Milltown   Pass of the   40
da   RAASAY   Cattle   774   Kishorn   Lochcarron   154
312   Camusteel   Bealach na Bà   SGÙRR A CHAORACHAIN   Ardarroch   Slumbay   10
rvaig   Camusterrach   Achintraid   394
412   Aird Dhubh   Kishorn   BAD A
BEN   444   Culduie   Island   CHREAMHA   Ardnarff
TIANAVAIG   DÙN CAAN   Toscaig   Ardaneaskan   Strome
er   Rubha na' Leac   Stromeferry   Achmore   11
Camastianavaig   Oskaig   310   Eilean   447
Tianavaig   Inverarish   BEINN NA LEAC   Meadhonach   Eilean   Plockton   BEINN RAIMH   30
Bay   Clachan   Mòr   Port-an-Eorna   Braeintra
Ollach   Inverarish   SCALPAY   Duirinish   Balmacara   12
he Braes   Suisnish   Eyre   Drumbuie   Auchtertyre
444   Peinchorran   Point   Eilean   Conchra
N LEE   Point   Longay   Badicaul   Rera   Nostie   Ardelve
Sconser   67   145   Kyle of Lochalsh   Kirkton   Carndu
773   Moll   396   Pabay   N   Loch Aillse   P   Q   R   Dornie
GLAMAIG   Ard   MULLACH   Skye Bridge   Lochalsh   Eilean Donan
A87   Dorch   NA CARN   70   Woodland
J   L   K   Dunan   M   Garden   90
564   Strollamus   60   L   Kyleakin
A87

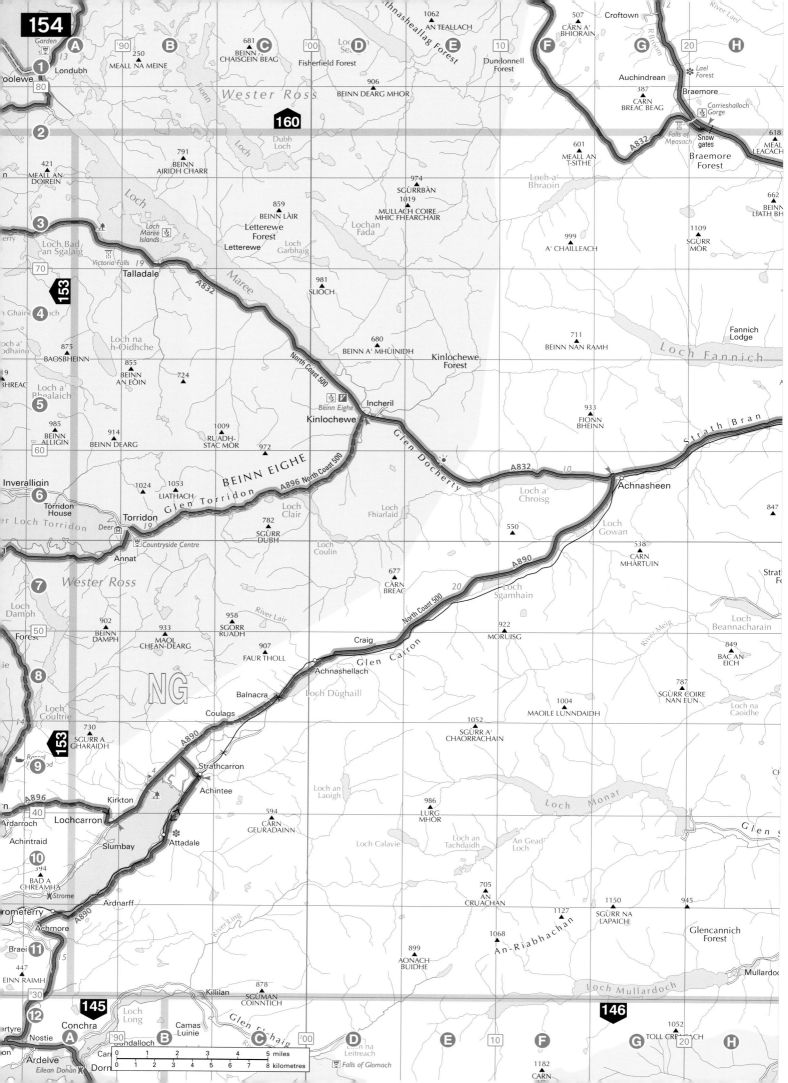

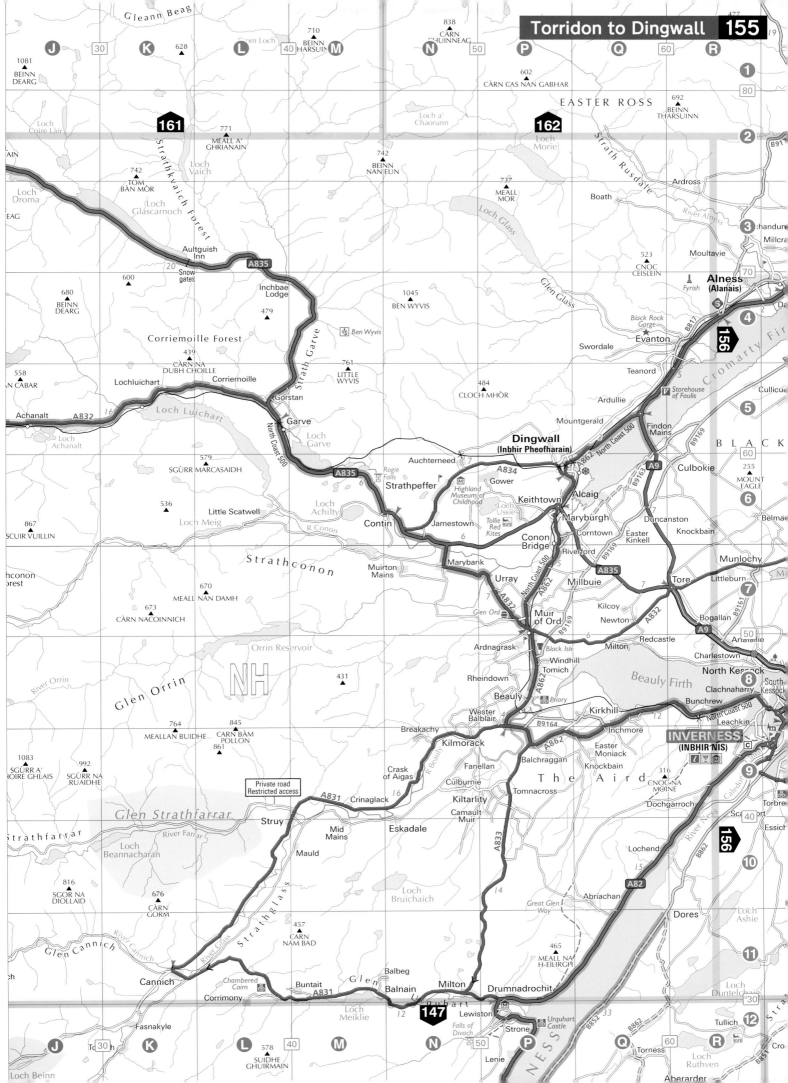

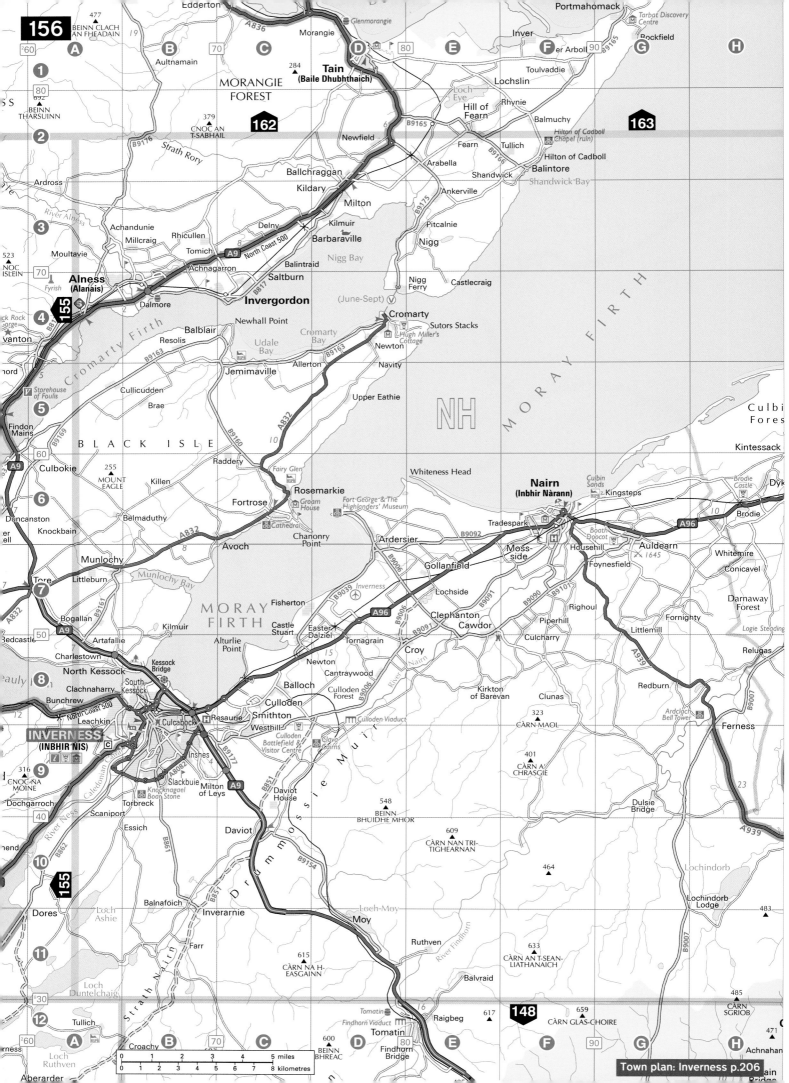

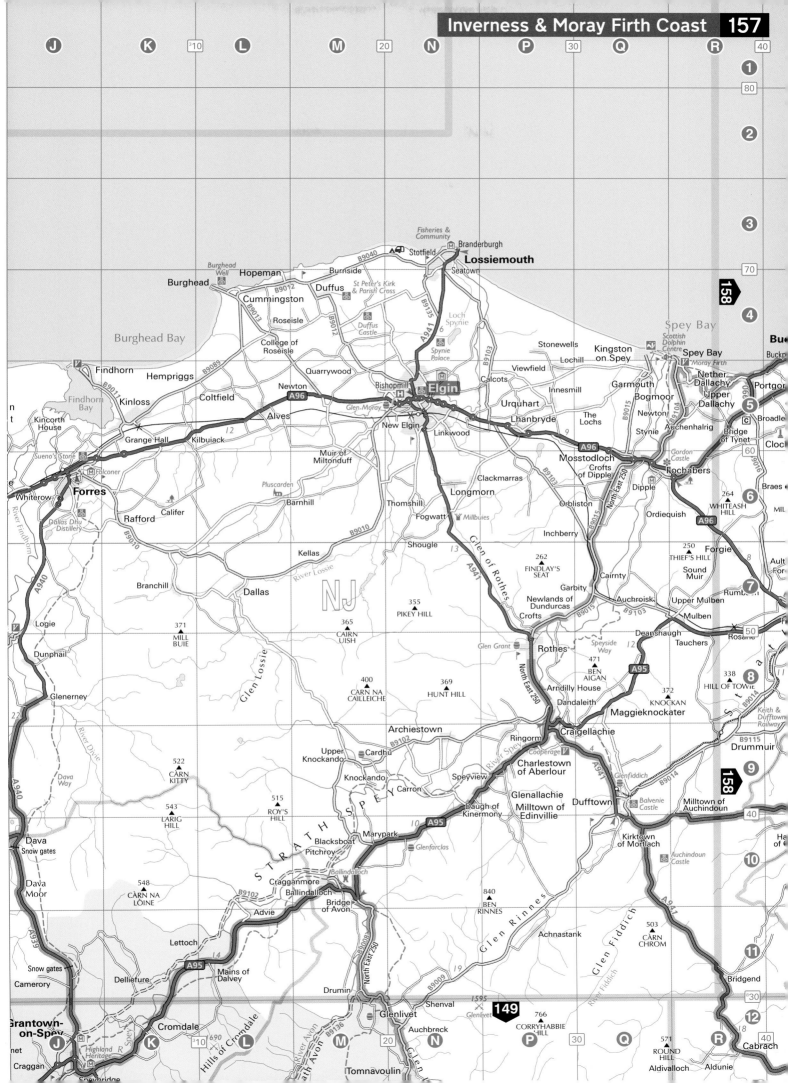

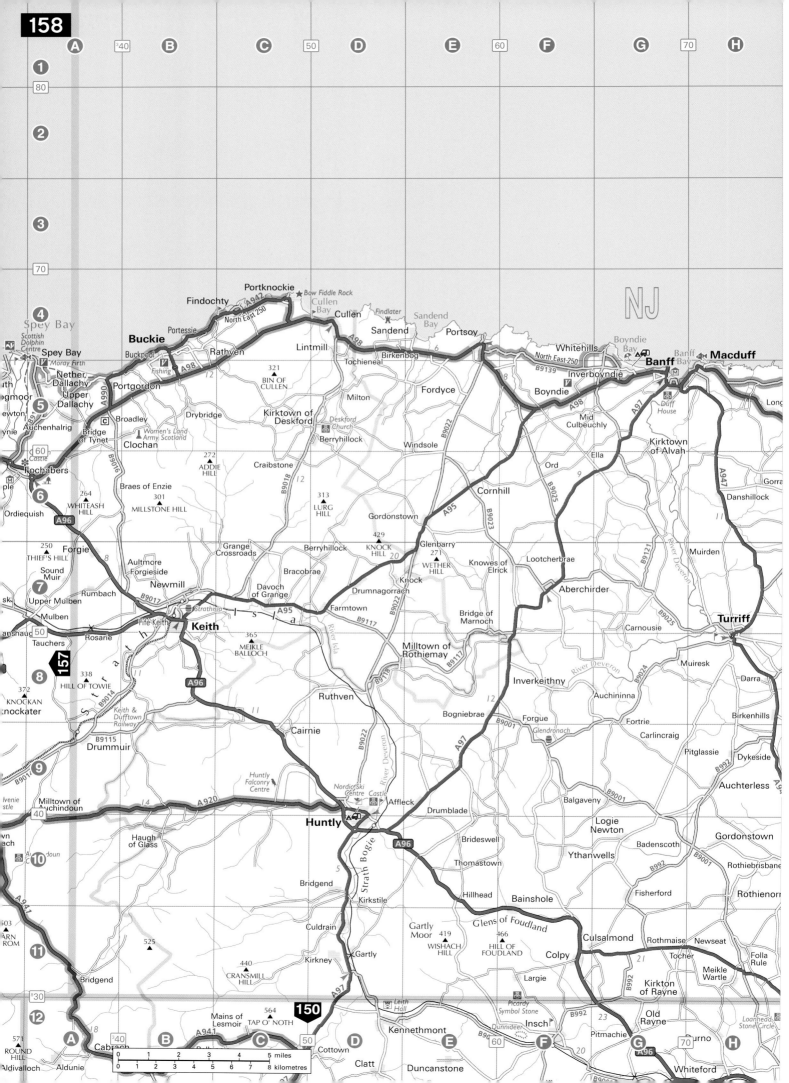

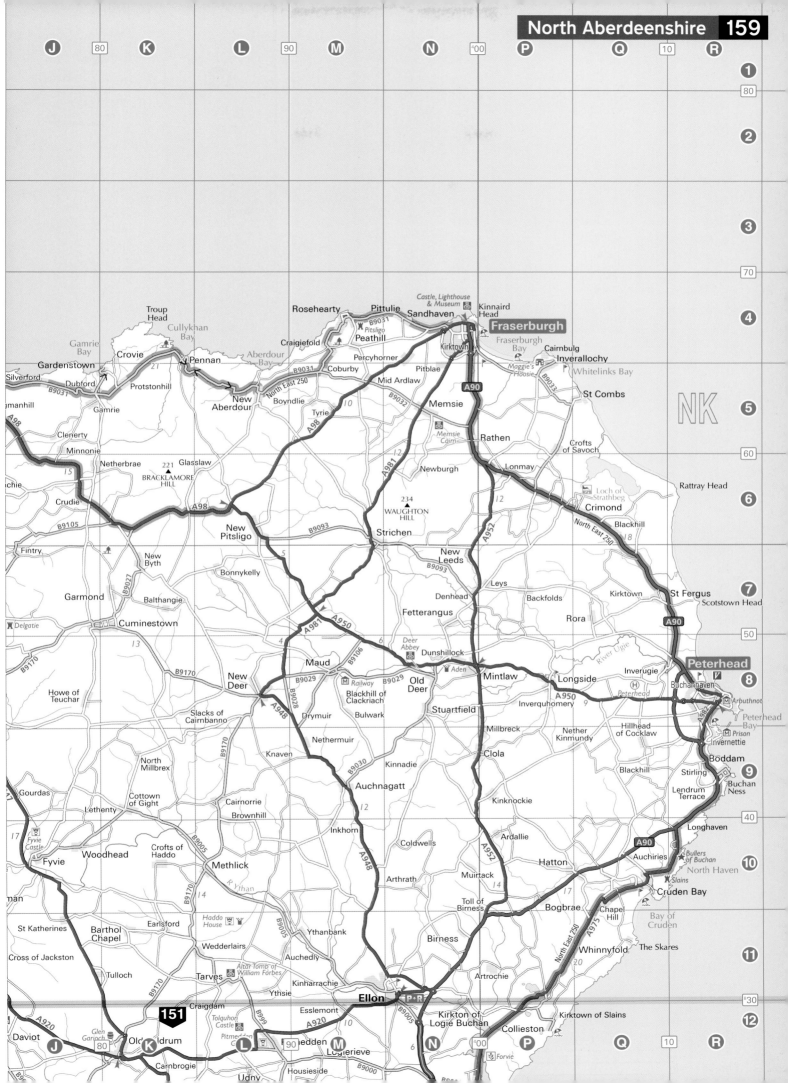

NK

Troup Head
Cullykhan Bay
Gamrie Bay
Gardenstown
Crovie
Pennan
Silverford
Dubford
Gamanhill
B9031
Protstonhill
Clenerty
Minnonie
Netherbrae
Crudie
B9105
Fintry
Garmond
Cuminestown
Delgatie
B9170
Howe of Teuchar
Gourdas
Lethenty
Fyvie Castle
Fyvie
Woodhead
B9005
St Katherines
Cross of Jackston
Barthol Chapel
Tulloch
Daviot
A920
Oldmeldrum
Carnbrogie
Udny

Rosehearty
Pittulie
Sandhaven
Kinnaird Head
Castle, Lighthouse & Museum
Fraserburgh
Craigiefold
Peathill
Pitsligo
Kirktown
Fraserburgh Bay
Cairnbulg
Inverallochy
Coburby
Percyhorner
Maggie's Hoosie
Whitelinks Bay
New Aberdour
Boyndlie
Mid Ardlaw
Pitblae
St Combs
Aberdour Bay
North East 250
Tyrie
Memsie
A90
Glasslaw
BRACKLAMORE HILL 221
Memsie Cairn
Rathen
Newburgh
Lonmay
Crofts of Savoch
New Pitsligo
WAUGHTON HILL 234
Strichen
Loch of Strathbeg
Crimond
Rattray Head
Blackhill
New Byth
Bonnykelly
B9093
New Leeds
North East 250
Balthangie
B9027
Leys
Kirktown
St Fergus
Scotstown Head
A90
Denhead
Backfolds
Fetterangus
Rora
New Deer
Maud
Deer Abbey
Dunshillock
A981 A950
Railway
Blackhill of Clackriach
Old Deer
Mintlaw
Aden
Longside
Inverugie
Peterhead
Drymuir
Bulwark
Peterhead
Buchanhaven
Nethermuir
Stuartfield
A950
Inverquhomery
Arbuthnot
Slacks of Cairnbanno
Knaven
Kinnadie
Millbreck
Nether Kinmundy
Hillhead of Cocklaw
Peterhead Bay
North Millbrex
Cottown of Gight
Cairnorrie
Brownhill
Auchnagatt
Clola
Prison
Invernettie
Boddam
Blackhill
Stirling
Buchan Ness
Lendrum Terrace
Methlick
Inkhorn
Coldwells
Kinknockie
Ardallie
Longhaven
A90
Auchiries
Bullers of Buchan
Arthrath
Muirtack
Hatton
North Haven
Slains
Cruden Bay
St Katherines
Haddo House
Wedderlairs
Ythanbank
Toll of Birness
Bogbrae
Chapel Hill
Bay of Cruden
Whinnyfold
The Skares
Altar Tomb of William Forbes
Auchedly
Birness
Artrochie
North East 250
Tarves
Kinharrachie
Ythsie
Ellon
Esslemont
Kirkton of Logie Buchan
Kirktown of Slains
Craigdam
Glen Garioch
Tolquhon Castle
Pitmedden
Udny
Logierieve
Colliestone
Forvie
Housieside
B9000

151

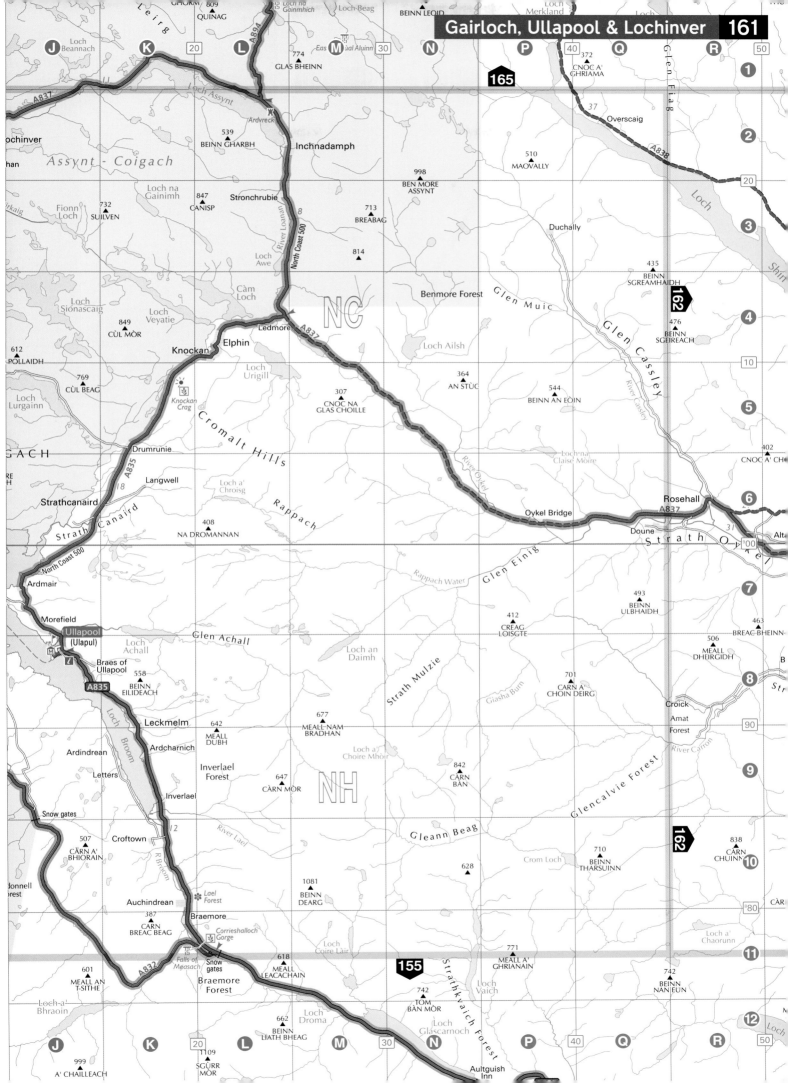

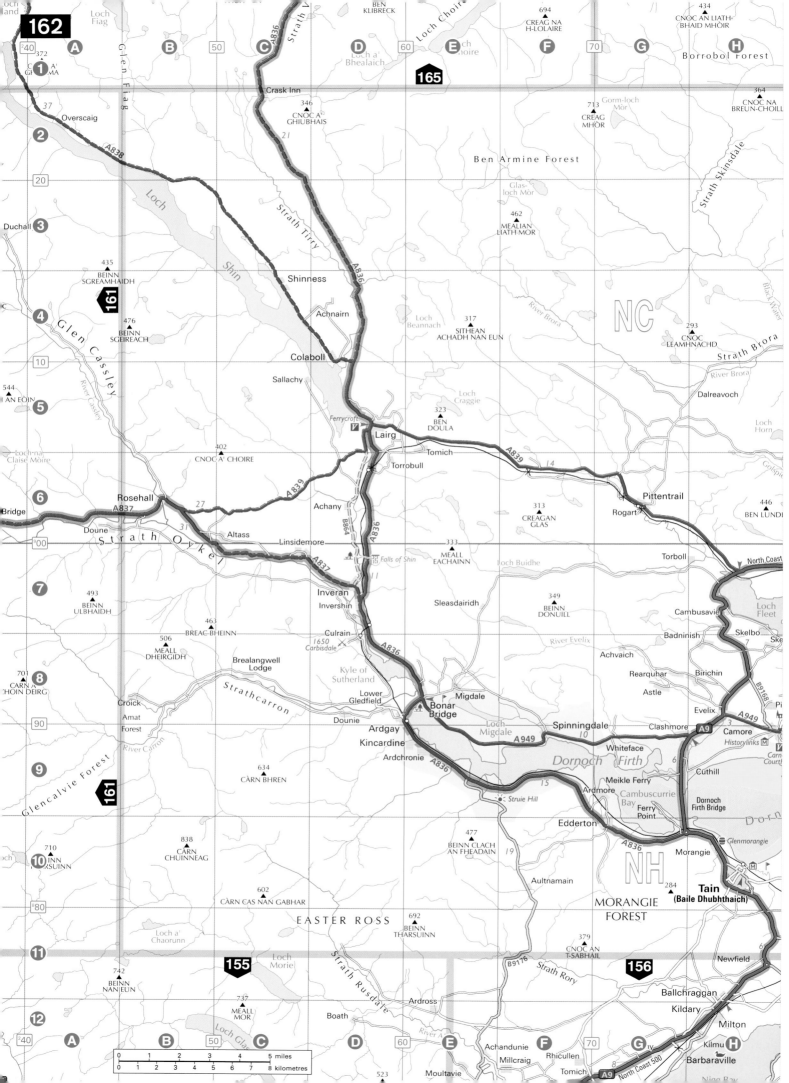

CNOC COIRE
NA FEÀRNA

484

Braemore

Dunbeath
Heritage

202
CNOC DAIL-
CHAIRN

J

K

90

Suisgill

L

518
CNOC AN
EIREANNAICH

M

300

N

705
MORVEN

626
SCARABEN

P

10

Q

mscraigs

R

20

Strath Free

Loch
Ascaig

Langwell Forest

167

Borgue

1

166

Learable Hill
Cairns, Stone Row
& Stone Circles

17

388
CREAG NAM FIADH

Kildonan Lodge

554
CREAG
SCALABSDALE

Newport

Langwell
House

Berriedale

North Coast 500

20

2

20

Kildonan

416
BEINN
DUBHAIN

A897

401
CNOC NA
MAOILE

A9

Badbea
Historic Village

20

3

337
CNOC NA H-
INNSE MOIRE

Strath of Kildonan

River Helmsdale

Torrish

404
CREAG
THORARAIDH

Ord of Caithness

421
CNOC NAN CRÙBAG MÒR

624
BEINN
DHORAIN

Navidale

Timespan

Snow gates

West
Helmsdale

East Helmsdale

Helmsdale

ND

4

Balnacoil

539
COL-
BHEINN

591
BEINN
MHEALAICH

Glen Loth

Gartymore

Portgower

Lothmore

10

520
BEN
HORN

Loch
Brora

Lothbeg

21

5

Burn

378
CAGAR
FEOSAIG

Clynelish

Dalchalm

Brora

Doll

6

Backies

A9

383
BEN BHRAGGIE

Rhives

Dunrobin
Castle

Carn
Liath

00

500

Golspie

7

Littleferry

lbo Street

Fourpenny

Embo

8

Embo Street

tgrudy

Royal Dornoch

90

Dornoch

egie
house

Dornoch Firth

Tarbat Ness

9

Dornoch
Point

Innis Mhor

Wilkhaven

Portmahomack

Tarbat Discovery
Centre

10

NJ

Inver

Rockfield

Lower Arboll

B9165

Toulvaddie

80

Lochslin

Loch
Eye

Rhynie

Hill of
Fearn

Balmuchy

11

B9165

Hilton of Cadboll
Chapel (ruin)

Fearn

Tullich

Hilton of Cadboll

Arabella

B9166

Shandwick

Balintore

Ankerville

Shandwick Bay

12

B9175

Pitca

Nigg

J

K

90

L

M

300

N

P

10

Q

R

20

Faraid Head

Balnakeil Bay
Balnakeil Craft Village
Balnakeil
Durness
(May-Sept) P
Keoldale
Sangomore
Sango Bay
Smoo Smoo

Whiten Head

Eilean Hoan

Eilean Nan Ròn

Ardmore Point
Kirtomy Point
Farr Point
Kirtomy

Sangobeg
Ceannabeinne

A838

408 ▲ BEN HUTIG
Strathan

Rabbit Islands
Tongue Bay

Neave or Coomb Island

Swordly
Farr

Loch Meadaidh

423 ▲ MEALL MEADHONACH

Talmine

Melness
Midtown

Skerray

Achtoty
Torrisdale

Torrisdale Bay
Farr Bay

Scullomie

Bettyhill

Invernaver

Achina

M
Bettyhill

Portnancon

A838

North Coast 500

Kyle of Tongue

Coldbackie

Strathnaver

489 ▲ MEALL NA CRÀ
Laid

230 ▲ BEN ARNABOLL

Borgie

13

A836

Skelpick

773 ▲ BEINN SPIONNAIDH
STACKIE

Loch Eriboll

262 ▲ DRUIM NAN CLIAR

Tongue

310 ▲ MEALL LEATHAD NA CRAOIBHE

River Borgie

Skelpick Burn

12

Strath Naver

Strath Beag

A838

31

Loch Hope

Kinloch

318 ▲ CNOC CRAGGIE

Loch Craggie

166

520 ▲ AN LÈAN-CHÀRN

Loch na Seilg

Kyle of Tongue

17

527 ▲ BEINN STUMANADH

213 ▲ CNOC MALPELLY

B871

Strathmore River

598 ▲ MEALLAN LIATH

927 ▲ BEN HOPE

A836

763 ▲ BEN LOYAL

Loch Loyal

NC

335 ▲ MEALL NA CUA

463 ▲ FEINNE-BHEINN MHÒR

Loch an Dherue

Loch Loyal Lodge

River Naver

Loch S

Strath More

557 ▲ CNOC NAN CUILEAN

Loch Syre

Dun Dornaigil Broch

Syre

729 ▲ SÀBHAL BEAG

Glen Golly

656 ▲ CNOC AN DÀIMH MÒR

294 ▲ POLE HILL

259 ▲ BEINN ROSAIL

B871

B MH

40

Loch Meadie

800 ▲
796 ▲ CÀRN DEARG
757 ▲ CARN AN TIONAIL

Loch Coire na Saidhe Duibhe

230 ▲ MEALL A' BHROLLAICH

Strath Naver

Loch Naver

270 ▲ BEADAIG

Loch Rimsdale

Loch nan Cla

Altnaharra

B873

12

873 ▲ BEN HEE

680 ▲ MEALL AN LIATH MÒR

Loch a' Ghorm-choire

Loch Truderscaig

Loch an Alltan na

10

30

Kinloch

613 ▲
L AN FHEUR LOCH

Loch Merkland

472 ▲ MEALL AN FHUARAIN

Loch Fiag

Strath Vagastie

959 ▲ BEN KLIBRECK

Loch Choire Forest

694 ▲ CREAG NA H-LOLAIRE

434 ▲ CNOC AN L BHAID MH

11

Borrol

372 ▲ CNOC A' GHRIAMA

Glen Fiag

A836

Loch a' Bhealaich

Loch Choire

713 ▲ CREAG M R

Gorm-loch Mòr

12

Overscaig

37

A838

Crask Inn

162

346 ▲ CNOC A' GHIUBHAIS

21

510

Ben Armine Forest

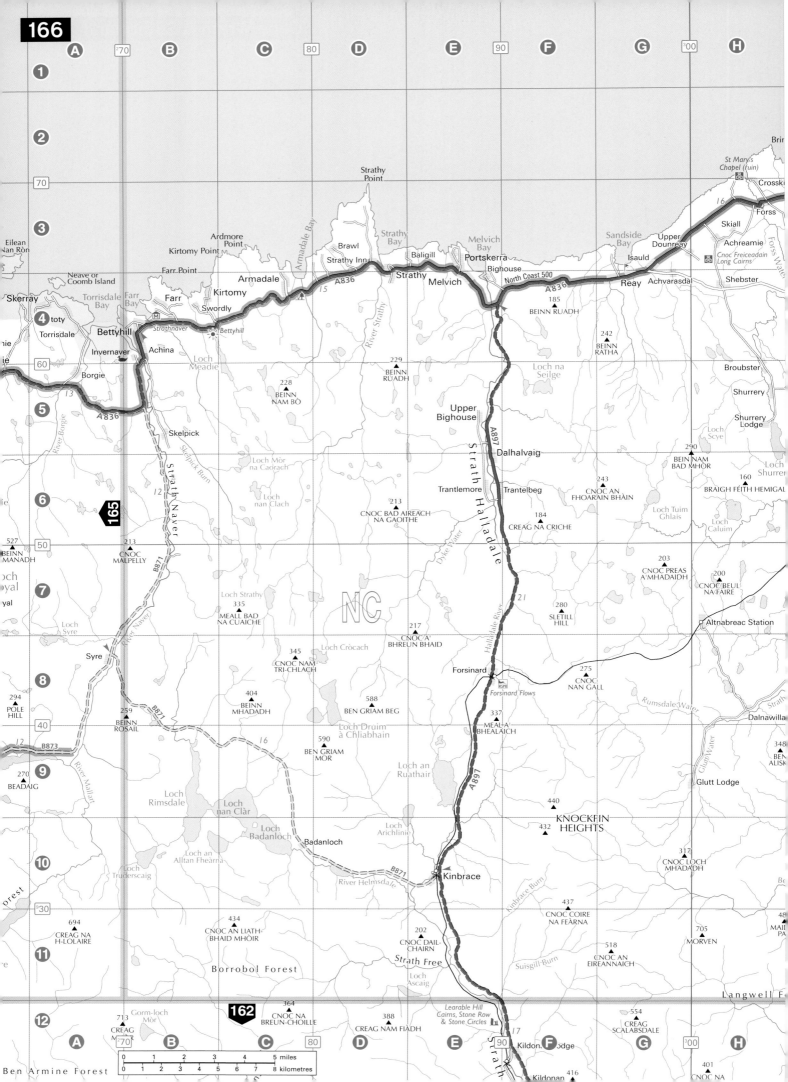

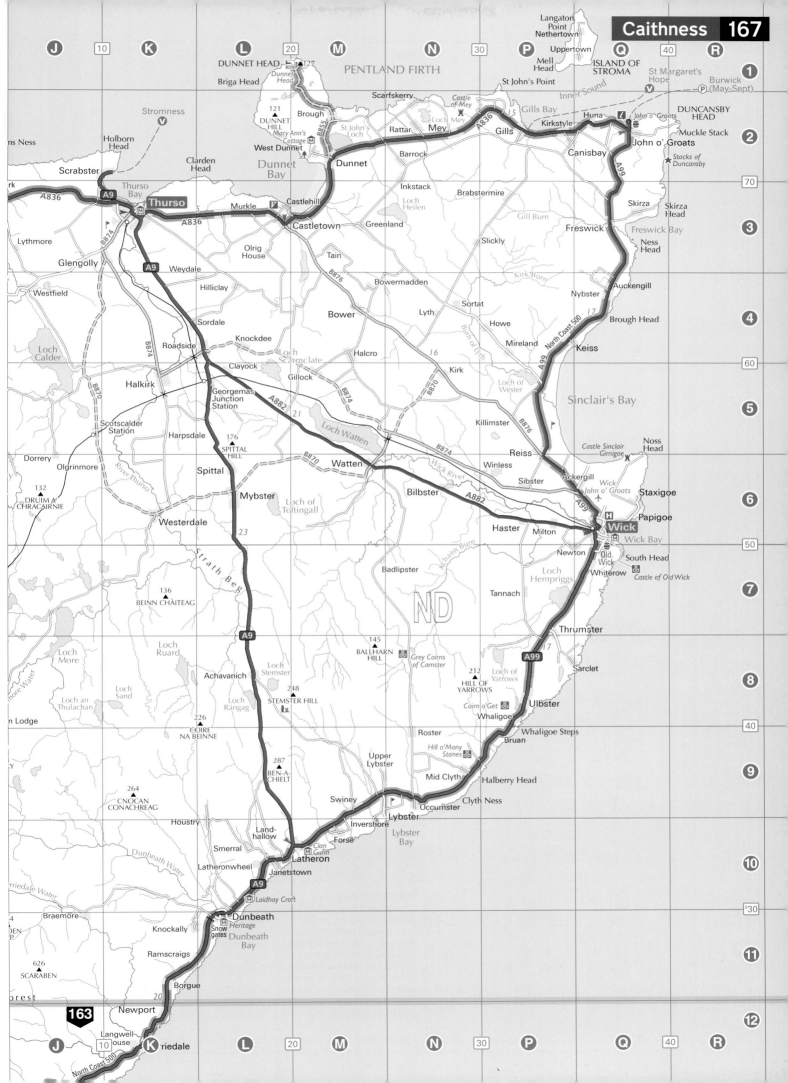

PENTLAND FIRTH

Langaton Point
Nethertown
Uppertown
Mell Head
ISLAND OF STROMA

St Margaret's Hope
Burwick (May-Sept)

DUNNET HEAD
127
Briga Head
Dunnet Head
121
DUNNET HILL
Mary Ann's Cottage
West Dunnet
Brough
Clarden Head
Stromness
Holborn Head
Scrabster
Thurso Bay
Thurso
A9
A836
Murkle
Castlehill
Castletown

St John's Point
Scarfskerry
Castle of Mey
Loch Mey
Rattar
Mey
Gills Bay
Gills
Kirkstyle
Huna
John o' Groats
DUNCANSBY HEAD
Muckle Stack
Stacks of Duncansby
Inner Sound

Canisbay
Skirza
Skirza Head
Freswick Bay
Ness Head
Freswick
Auckengill
Nybster
Brough Head
Keiss
North Coast 500

Inkstack
Brabstermire
Slickly
Mireland
Howe

Sinclair's Bay

Noss Head
Castle Sinclair Girnigoe
Ackergill
Reiss
Wick John o' Groats
Staxigoe
Papigoe
Wick Bay

A9
Glengolly
Lythmore
Westfield
B874
Weydale
Hilliclay
Sordale
Roadside
Clayock
Halkirk
B870
Scotscalder Station
Harpsdale
Dorrery
Olrginmore
132 DRUIM A' CHRACAIRNIE
Spittal
Westerdale
River Thurso
Strath Beg
23

Olrig House
Tain
Bower
Knockdee
Loch Scarmclate
Gillock
Georgemas Junction Station
A882
Loch Watten
21
176 SPITTAL HILL
Mybster
Loch of Toftingall
Watten
B870

Greenland
Lyth
Sortat
Bowermadden
Halcro
Kirk
16
Loch of Wester
Killimster
B876
Winless
Sibster
B874
Haster
Milton
Newton
Old Wick
Whiterow
Castle of Old Wick
South Head

Badlipster
ND
Tannach
Loch Hempriggs

Loch Calder
Loch Ruard
Loch More
Loch Sand
Loch an Thulachan
Lodge

136 BEINN CHÀITEAG
A9
Achavanich
Loch Stemster
Loch Rangag
226 COIRE NA BEINNE
248 STEMSTER HILL
287 BEN-A-CHIELT
264 CNOCAN CONACHREAG

145 BALLHARN HILL
Grey Cairns of Camster
212 HILL OF YARROWS
Cairn o'Get
Loch of Yarrows

Thrumster
A99
17
Sarclet
Ulbster
Whaligoe
Whaligoe Steps
Bruan
Halberry Head
Clyth Ness
Mid Clyth
Hill o'Many Stanes
Roster
Upper Lybster
Swiney
Occumster
Lybster
Clyth Ness
Invershore
Lybster Bay
Forse
Clan Gunn
Smerral
Landhallow
Latheron
Janetstown
Laidhay Croft
A9
Houstry
Latheronwheel
Snow gates
Dunbeath
Heritage
Dunbeath Bay
Knockally
Ramscraigs
626 SCARABEN
Borgue
Newport
163
Langwell House
Berriedale
North Coast 500

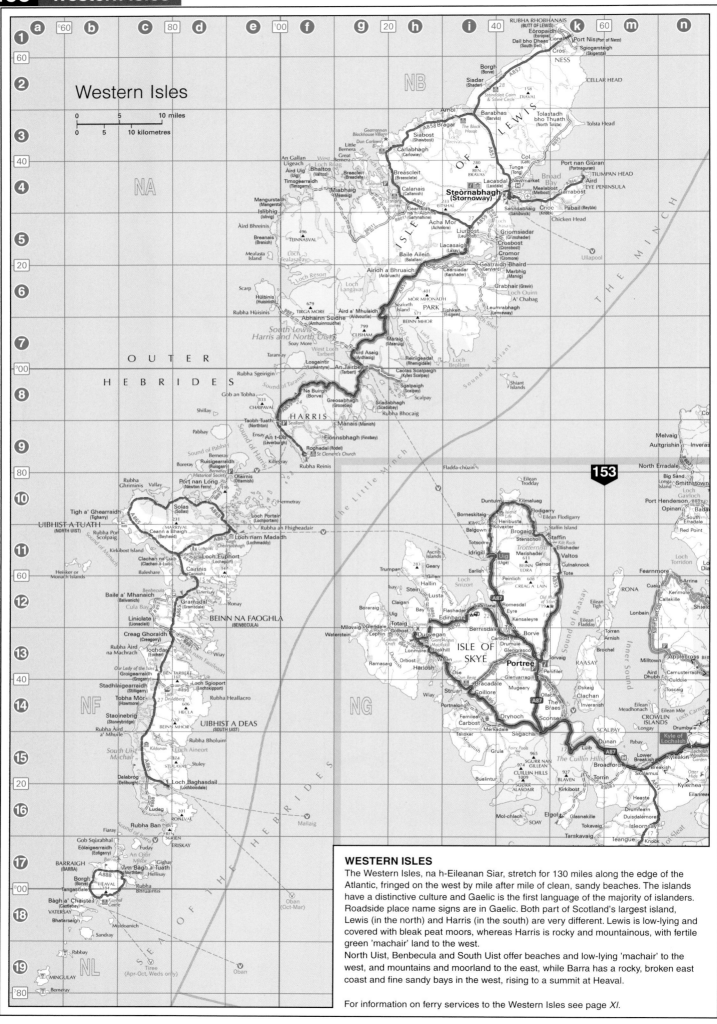

Western Isles

0 — 5 — 10 miles
0 — 5 — 10 kilometres

WESTERN ISLES

The Western Isles, na h-Eileanan Siar, stretch for 130 miles along the edge of the Atlantic, fringed on the west by mile after mile of clean, sandy beaches. The islands have a distinctive culture and Gaelic is the first language of the majority of islanders. Roadside place name signs are in Gaelic. Both part of Scotland's largest island, Lewis (in the north) and Harris (in the south) are very different. Lewis is low-lying and covered with bleak peat moors, whereas Harris is rocky and mountainous, with fertile green 'machair' land to the west.

North Uist, Benbecula and South Uist offer beaches and low-lying 'machair' to the west, and mountains and moorland to the east, while Barra has a rocky, broken east coast and fine sandy bays in the west, rising to a summit at Heaval.

For information on ferry services to the Western Isles see page XI.

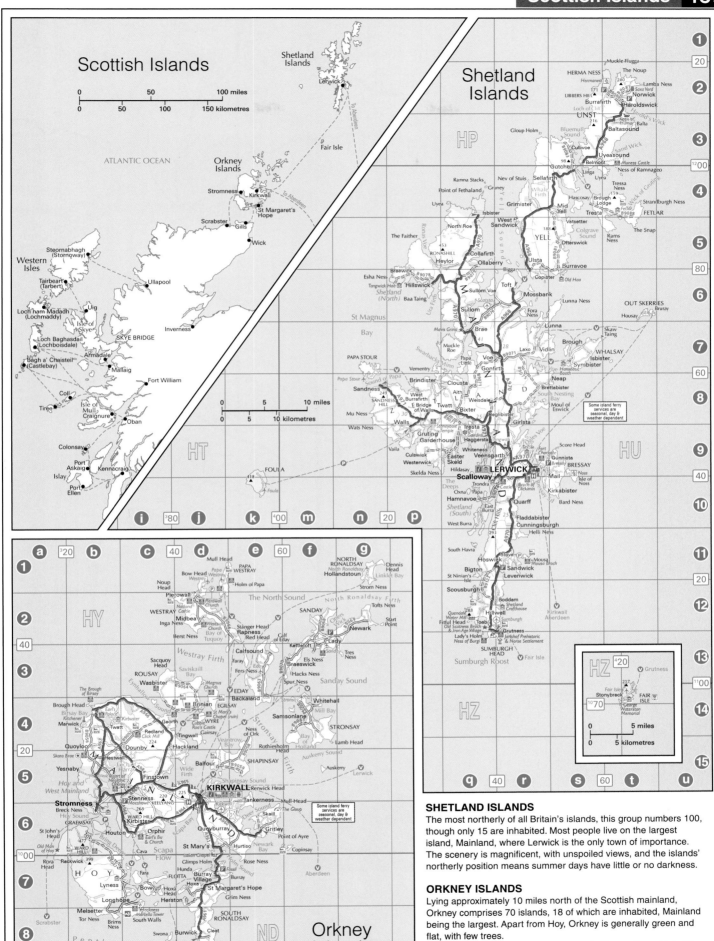

Scottish Islands

ATLANTIC OCEAN

Western Isles

Shetland Islands

Orkney Islands

Some island ferry services are seasonal, day & weather dependent

SHETLAND ISLANDS

The most northerly of all Britain's islands, this group numbers 100, though only 15 are inhabited. Most people live on the largest island, Mainland, where Lerwick is the only town of importance. The scenery is magnificent, with unspoiled views, and the islands' northerly position means summer days have little or no darkness.

ORKNEY ISLANDS

Lying approximately 10 miles north of the Scottish mainland, Orkney comprises 70 islands, 18 of which are inhabited, Mainland being the largest. Apart from Hoy, Orkney is generally green and flat, with few trees.

The islands abound with prehistoric antiquities and rare birds. The climate is one of even temperatures and 'twilight' summer nights, but with violent winds at times.

For information on ferry services to the Shetland and Orkney Islands see page *XI*.

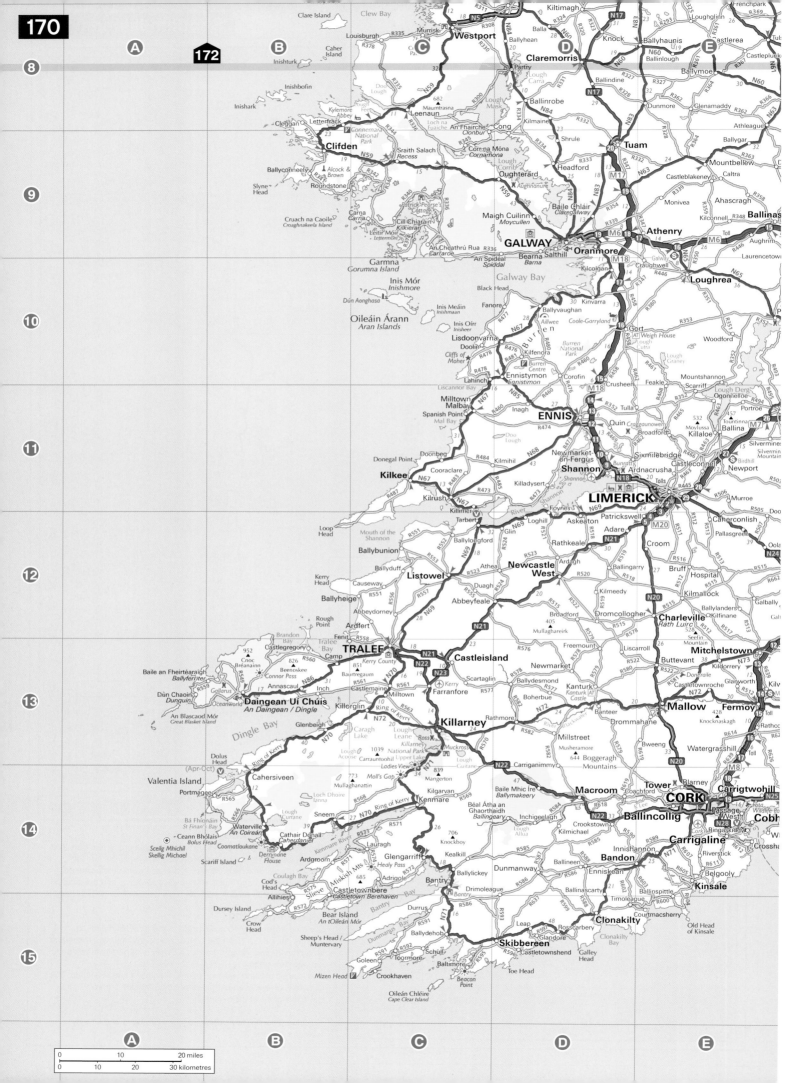

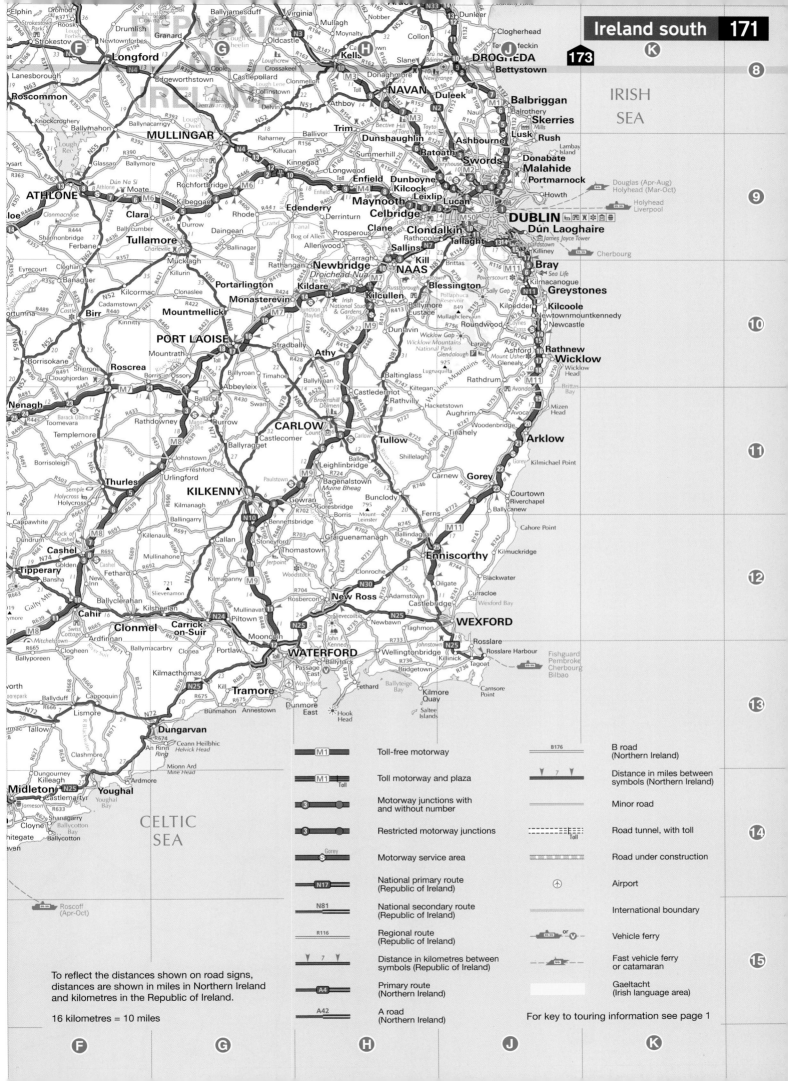

Ireland index

Abbeydorney C12
Abbeyfeale D12
Abbeyleix G11
Adamstown H12
Adare D12
Adrigole C14
Aghalee J5
Ahascragh E9
Ahoghill J4
Allenwood H9
Allihies B15
An Bun Beag E4
An Charraig E5
An Cheathrú Rua C9
An Clochán Liath E4
An Coireán B14
An Daingean B13
An Fál Carrach F3
An Fhairche C9
Annahilt J6
Annalong J6
Annascaul B13
Annestown G13
An Rinn G13
An Spidéal D9
Antrim J5
Ardagh D12
Ardara E5
Ardee H8
Ardfert C12
Ardfinnan F12
Ardglass K6
Ardgroom B14
Ardmore F14
Ardnacrusha E11
Arklow J11
Armagh H6
Armoy J3
Arvagh G7
Ashbourne J9
Ashford J10
Askeaton D12
Athboy H8
Athea D12
Athenry E9
Athleague E8
Athlone F9
Athy H10
Augher G6
Aughnacloy H6
Aughrim E9
Aughrim J11
Avoca J11

Bagenalstown H11
Baile an Fheirtéaraigh B13
Baile Chláir D9
Baile Mhic Íre D14
Baile na Finne F4
Bailieborough H7
Balbriggan J8
Balla D8
Ballacolla G11
Ballaghaderreen E7
Ballina D7
Ballina E11
Ballinafad E7
Ballinagar G9
Ballinagh G7
Ballinamallard G6
Ballinamore F7
Ballinascarty D14
Ballinasloe E9
Ballincollig E14
Ballindaggan H12
Ballindine D8
Ballineen D14
Ballingarry D12
Ballingarry G12
Ballingeary D14
Ballinlough E8
Ballinrobe D8
Ballinspittle E14
Ballintra F5
Ballivor H9
Ballon H11
Ballybay H6
Ballybofey F5
Ballybunion C12
Ballycanew J11
Ballycarry K5

Ballycastle J3
Ballycastle C6
Ballyclare J5
Ballyclerahan F12
Ballyconneely B9
Ballyconnell G7
Ballycotton F14
Ballycumber F9
Ballydehob C15
Ballydesmond D13
Ballyduff C12
Ballyduff F13
Ballyfarnon E7
Ballyferriter B13
Ballygally J4
Ballygar E9
Ballygawley H6
Ballygawley E6
Ballygowan K5
Ballyhaise G7
Ballyhalbert K5
Ballyhaunis E8
Ballyhean D8
Ballyheige C12
Ballyjamesduff G8
Ballylanders E12
Ballylickey C14
Ballyliffin G3
Ballylongford C12
Ballylynan H10
Ballymacarbry F13
Ballymahon F8
Ballymakeery D14
Ballymena J4
Ballymoney H4
Ballymore F9
Ballymore Eustace H10
Ballymote E7
Ballynacarrigy G8
Ballynahinch J6
Ballynure J5
Ballyporeen F13
Ballyragget G11
Ballyroan G10
Ballysadare E6
Ballyshannon F5
Ballyvaughan D10
Ballywalter K5
Balrothery J8
Baltimore C15
Baltinglass H10
Banagher F10
Banbridge J6
Bangor K5
Bangor Erris C7
Bansha F12
Banteer D13
Bantry C14
Barna D9
Béal an Mhuirthead B6
Béal Átha an Ghaorthaidh D14
Bearna D9
Belcoo F6
Belfast J5
Belgooly E14
Bellaghy H4
Belleek F6
Belmullet B6
Belturbet G7
Benburb H6
Bennettsbridge G12
Beragh G5
Bessbrook J6
Bettystown J8
Birr F10
Blacklion F6
Blackwater J12
Blarney E14
Blessington H10
Boherbue D13
Borris H11
Borris-in-Ossory F10
Borrisokane F10
Borrisoleigh F11
Boyle E7
Bray J10
Bridgetown H12

Brittas J9
Broadford E11
Broadford D12
Brookeborough G6
Broughshane J4
Bruff E12
Bunbeg E4
Bunclody H11
Buncrana G3
Bundoran E6
Bunmahon G13
Bunnyconnellan D7
Bushmills H3
Buttevant E13
Bweeng E13

Cadamstown F10
Caherconlish E12
Caherdaniel B14
Cahersiveen B14
Cahir F12
Caledon H6
Callan G12
Caltra E9
Camp B13
Carndonagh G3
Cappawhite F12
Cappoquin F13
Carlanstown H8
Carlingford J7
Carlow H11
Carna C9
Carnew J11
Carnlough J4
Carragh H9
Carraig Airt F3
Carraroe C9
Carrick E5
Carrickfergus K5
Carrickmacross H7
Carrickmore G5
Carrick-on-Shannon F7
Carrick-on-Suir G12
Carrigaline E14
Carrigallen F7
Carriganimmy D13
Carrigart F3
Carrigtwohill E14
Carryduff J5
Cashel F12
Castlebar D8
Castlebellingham J7
Castleblakeney E9
Castleblayney H6
Castlebridge J12
Castlecomer G11
Castleconnell E11
Castlederg G5
Castledermot H11
Castlegregory B13
Castleisland C13
Castlemaine C13
Castlemartyr F14
Castleplunket E8
Castlepollard G8
Castlerea E8
Castlerock H3
Castletownbere B15
Castletownroche E13
Castletownshend D15
Castlewellan J6
Cathair Dónall B14
Causeway C12
Cavan G7
Celbridge H9
Charlestown D7
Charleville E12
Cill Charthaigh E5
Cill Chiaráin C9
Clady H4
Clane H9
Clara G9
Claregalway D9
Claremorris D8
Clashmore F13
Claudy G4
Cleggan B8
Clifden B9
Cliffoney E6
Cloghan F10
Clogheen F13

Clogher G6
Clogherhead J8
Clogh Mills J4
Clonakilty D15
Clonaslee G10
Clonbur C9
Clondalkin J9
Clonea G13
Clones G7
Clonmany G3
Clonmel F12
Clonmellon H8
Clonroche H12
Clough K6
Cloughjordan F10
Cloyne F14
Coachford D14
Coagh H5
Coalisland H5
Cobh E14
Coleraine H3
Collinstown G8
Collon H8
Collooney E6
Comber K5
Cong D9
Convoy F4
Cookstown H5
Coole G8
Cooraclare C11
Cootehill G7
Cork E14
Cornamona C9
Corofin D10
Corr na Móna C9
Courtmacsherry E15
Courtown J11
Craigavon J6
Craughwell E10
Creeslough F4
Croithlí E4
Crolly E4
Crookhaven C15
Crookstown D14
Croom E12
Crossakeel H8
Crosshaven E14
Crossmaglen H7
Crossmolina D7
Crumlin J5
Crusheen D10
Culdaff G3
Cullybackey J4
Culmore G4
Curracloe J12
Curry E7
Cushendall J4
Cushendun J3

Daingean G9
Daingean Uí Chúis B13
Delvin H9
Derrinturn H9
Derry G4
Derrygonnelly F6
Derrylin G6
Dervock H4
Dingle B13
Doagh J5
Donabate J9
Donaghadee K5
Donaghmore H5
Donaghmore G11
Donegal F5
Donemana G4
Doolin C10
Doon E12
Doonbeg C11
Downings F3
Downpatrick K6
Downra F6
Draperstown H5
Drimoleague D14
Drogheda J8
Droichead Nua H10
Dromahair E6
Dromara J6
Dromcolliher D12
Dromiskin J7
Drommahane E13
Dromod F8
Dromore J6

Dromore G5
Dromore West D6
Drumaness K6
Drumfries G3
Drumkeeran F7
Drumlish F8
Drumquin G5
Drumshanbo F7
Drumsna F7
Duagh C12
Dublin J9
Duleek J8
Dunboyne J9
Dún Chaoin A13
Dundalk J7
Dundonald K5
Dundrum F12
Dunfanaghy F3
Dungannon H5
Dungarvan G13
Dunglow E4
Dungourney F14
Dunkineely E5
Dún Laoghaire J9
Dunlavin H10
Dunleer J8
Dunmanway D14
Dunmore E8
Dunmore East H13
Dunquin A13
Dunshaughlin H9
Durrow G11
Durrow G9
Durrus C15
Dysart E9

Easky D6
Edenderry H9
Edgeworthstown G8
Eglinton G4
Elphin E7
Emyvale H6
Enfield H9
Ennis D11
Enniscorthy H12
Enniscrone D6
Enniskean D14
Enniskillen F6
Ennistymon D10
Eyrecourt F10

Fahan G4
Falcarragh F3
Fanore D10
Farranfore C13
Feakle E11
Fenagh F7
Fenit B13
Ferbane F9
Fermoy E13
Ferns J12
Fethard F12
Fethard H13
Fintona G6
Fintown F4
Fivemiletown G6
Foxford D7
Foynes D12
Freemount D13
Frenchpark E8
Freshford G11

Galbally E12
Galway D9
Garrison F6
Garvagh H4
Gilford J6
Glandore D15
Glanworth E13
Glaslough H6
Glassan F9
Gleann Cholm Cille E5
Glenamaddy E8
Glenarm J4
Glenavy J5
Glenbeigh B13
Glencolumbkille E5
Glenealy J10
Glengarriff C14
Glenties E5

Glin D12
Golden F12
Goleen C15
Goresbridge H11
Gorey J11
Gort D10
Gorteen E7
Gortin G5
Gowran H11
Graiguenamanagh H12
Granard G8
Grange E6
Greencastle H3
Greencastle G5
Greenore J7
Greyabbey K5
Greystones J10
Gulladuff H4

Hacketstown H11
Headford D9
Hillsborough J6
Hilltown J6
Holycross F11
Holywood K5
Hospital E12
Howth J9

Inagh D11
Inch B13
Inchigeelagh D14
Inishcrone D6
Innishannon E14
Irvinestown F6

Johnstown G11

Kanturk D13
Keadue F7
Keady H6
Kealkill C14
Keel B7
Kells J4
Kells H8
Kenmare C14
Kesh F5
Kilbeggan G9
Kilcar E5
Kilcock H9
Kilcolgan D10
Kilconnell E9
Kilcoole J10
Kilcormac F10
Kilcullen H10
Kildare H10
Kildorrery E13
Kilfenora D10
Kilfinane E12
Kilgarvan C14
Kilkee C11
Kilkeel J7
Kilkenny G11
Kilkieran C9
Kill H9
Kill G13
Killadysert D11
Killala D6
Killaloe E11
Killarney C13
Killashandra G7
Killeagh F14
Killenaule F12
Killimer C11
Killiney J9
Killinick J13
Killorglin C13
Killough K6
Killucan G9
Killurin G10
Killybegs E5
Killyleagh K6
Kilmacanogue J10
Kilmacrenan F4
Kilmacthomas G13
Kilmaganny G12
Kilmaine D8
Kilmallock E12
Kilmanagh G11
Kilmeedy D12
Kilmichael D14
Kilmihil C11
Kilmore Quay H13

Kilmuckridge J12
Kilpedder J10
Kilrea H4
Kilrush C11
Kilsheelan G12
Kiltegan H11
Kiltimagh D8
Kilworth E13
Kingscourt H7
Kinlough E6
Kinnegad G9
Kinnitty F10
Kinsale E14
Kinvarra D10
Kircubbin K5
Knock D8
Knockcroghery F8

Lahinch C10
Lanesborough F8
Laragh J10
Larne K4
Lauragh C14
Laurencetown F10
Leap D15
Leenaun C8
Leighlinbridge H11
Leitrim F7
Leixlip H9
Letterfrack B8
Letterkenny F4

Lifford G4
Limavady H4
Limerick E11
Lisbellaw G6
Lisburn J5
Liscarroll D13
Lisdoonvarna D10
Lismore F13
Lisnaskea G6
Listowel C12
Loghill D12
Londonderry G4
Longford F8
Longwood H9
Loughbrickland J6
Loughglinn E8
Loughrea E10
Louisburgh C8
Lucan J9
Lurgan J6
Lusk J9

Macroom D14
Maghera H4
Magherafelt H5
Maguiresbridge G6
Maigh Cuilinn D9
Malahide J9
Málainn Mhóir E5
Malin G3
Malin More E5

170

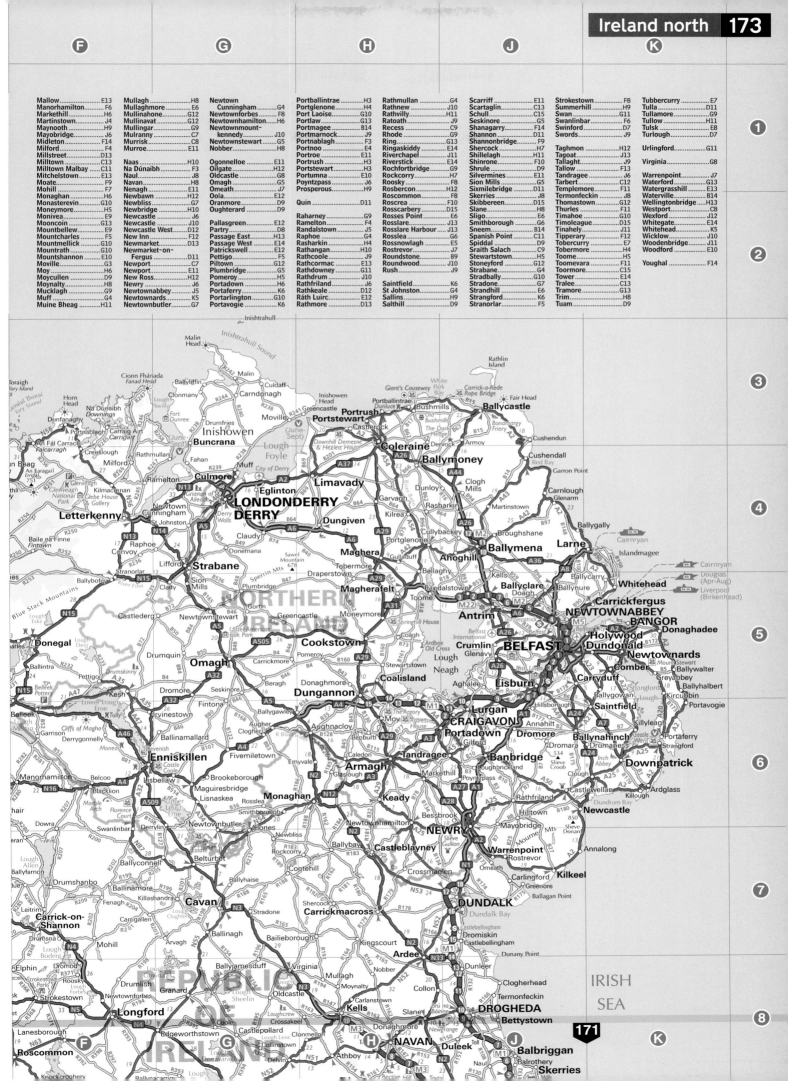

Mallow E13	Mullagh H8	Newtown	Portballintrae H3	Rathmullan G4	Scarriff E11	Strokestown F8	Tubbercurry E7
Manorhamilton F6	Mullaghmore E6	Cunningham G4	Portglenone H4	Rathnew J10	Scartaglin C13	Summerhill H9	Tulla D11
Markethill H6	Mullinahone G12	Newtownforbes ..F8	Port Laoise G10	Rathvilly H11	Schull C15	Swan G11	Tullamore G9
Martinstown J4	Mullinavat G12	Newtownhamilton ..H6	Portlaw G13	Ratoath J9	Seskinore G5	Swanlinbar F6	Tullow H11
Maynooth H9	Mullingar G9	Newtownmount-	Portmagee B14	Recess C9	Shanagarry F14	Swinford D7	Tulsk E8
Midleton F14	Mulranny C8	kennedy J10	Portmarnock J9	Rhode G9	Shannon D11	Swords J9	Turlough D7
Milford F4	Murrisk C8	Newtownstewart ..G5	Portnablagh F3	Ring G13	Shannonbridge F9		
Millstreet D13	Murroe E11	Nobber H8	Portnoo E4	Ringaskiddy E14	Shercock H7	Taghmon H12	Urlingford G11
Milltown C13			Portroe E11	Riverchapel J11	Shillelagh H11	Tagoat J13	
Milltown Malbay ..C11	Naas H10	Ogonnelloe E11	Portrush H3	Riverstick E14	Shinrone F10	Tallaght J9	Virginia G8
Mitchelstown E13	Na Dúnaibh F3	Oilgate H12	Portstewart H3	Rochfortbridge G9	Shrule D9	Tallow F13	
Moate F9	Naul J8	Oldcastle G8	Portumna E10	Rockcorry G6	Silvermines E11	Tandragee H6	Warrenpoint J7
Mohill F7	Navan H8	Omagh G5	Poyntzpass J6	Roosky F8	Sion Mills G5	Tarbert C12	Waterford G13
Monaghan H6	Nenagh E11	Omeath J7	Prosperous H9	Roscommon F8	Sixmilebridge D11	Templemore F11	Watergrasshill E13
Monasterevin E9	Newbawn H12	Oola E12		Roscrea F10	Skerries J8	Termonfeckin J8	Waterville B14
Moneymore H5	Newbliss G7	Oranmore D9	Quin D11	Rosscarbery D15	Skibbereen D15	Thomastown G12	Wellingtonbridge ..H13
Monivea E9	Newbridge H10	Oughterard D9		Rosses Point E6	Slane H8	Thurles F11	Westport C8
Mooncoin G13	Newcastle J6		Raharney G9	Rosslare J13	Sligo E6	Timahoe G10	Wexford J12
Mountbellew C11	Newcastle J10	Pallasgreen E12	Ramelton F4	Rosslare Harbour ..J13	Smithborough G6	Timoleague D15	Whitegate E14
Mountcharles F5	Newcastle West ..D12	Partry D8	Randalstown J5	Rosslea G6	Sneem B14	Tinahely J11	Whitehead K5
Mountmellick G10	New Inn F12	Passage East H13	Raphoe G4	Rossnowlagh E5	Spanish Point C11	Tipperary F12	Wicklow J10
Mountrath G10	Newmarket D13	Passage West E14	Rasharkin H4	Rostrevor J7	Spiddal D9	Tobercurry E7	Woodenbridge J11
Mountshannon E10	Newmarket-on-	Patrickswell E12	Rathangan H10	Roundstone B9	Sraith Salach C9	Tobermore H4	Woodford E10
Moville G3	Fergus D11	Pettigo F5	Rathcoole J9	Roundwood J10	Stewartstown H5	Toome H5	
Moy H6	Newport C7	Piltown G12	Rathcormac E13	Rush J9	Stoneyford G12	Toomevara F11	Youghal F14
Moycullen D9	Newport E11	Plumbridge G5	Rathdowney G11		Strabane G4	Toormore C15	
Moynalty H8	New Ross H12	Pomeroy H5	Rathdrum J10	Saintfield K6	Stradbally G10	Tower E14	
Mucklagh G9	Newry J6	Portadown H6	Rathfriland J6	St Johnston G4	Stradone G7	Tralee C13	
Muff G4	Newtownabbey J5	Portaferry K6	Rathkeale D12	Sallins H9	Strandhill E6	Tramore G13	
Muine Bheag H11	Newtownards K5	Portarlington G10	Ráth Luirc E12	Salthill D9	Strangford K6	Trim H8	
	Newtownbutler G7	Portavogie K6	Rathmore D13		Stranorlar F5	Tuam D9	

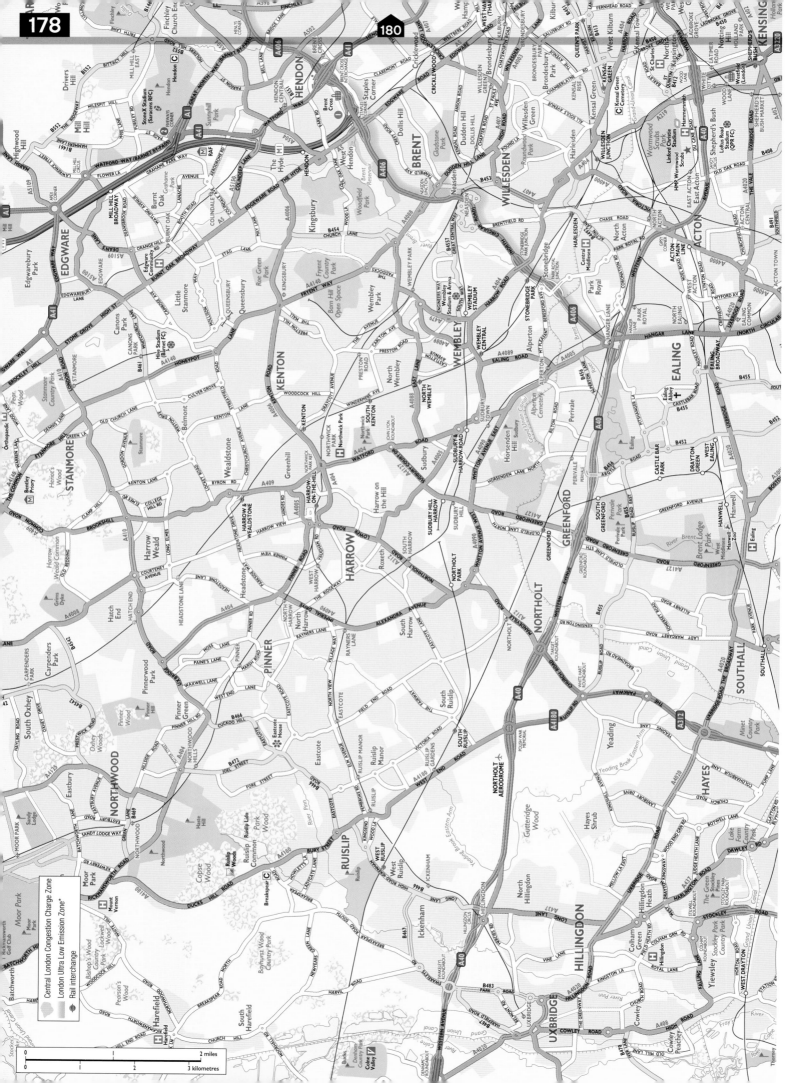

The Ultra Low Emission Zone is due to be extended in August 2023 to cover all London boroughs.

For further information visit www.tfl.gov.uk/modes/driving/ultra-low-emission-zone

For Central London see pages 238–247

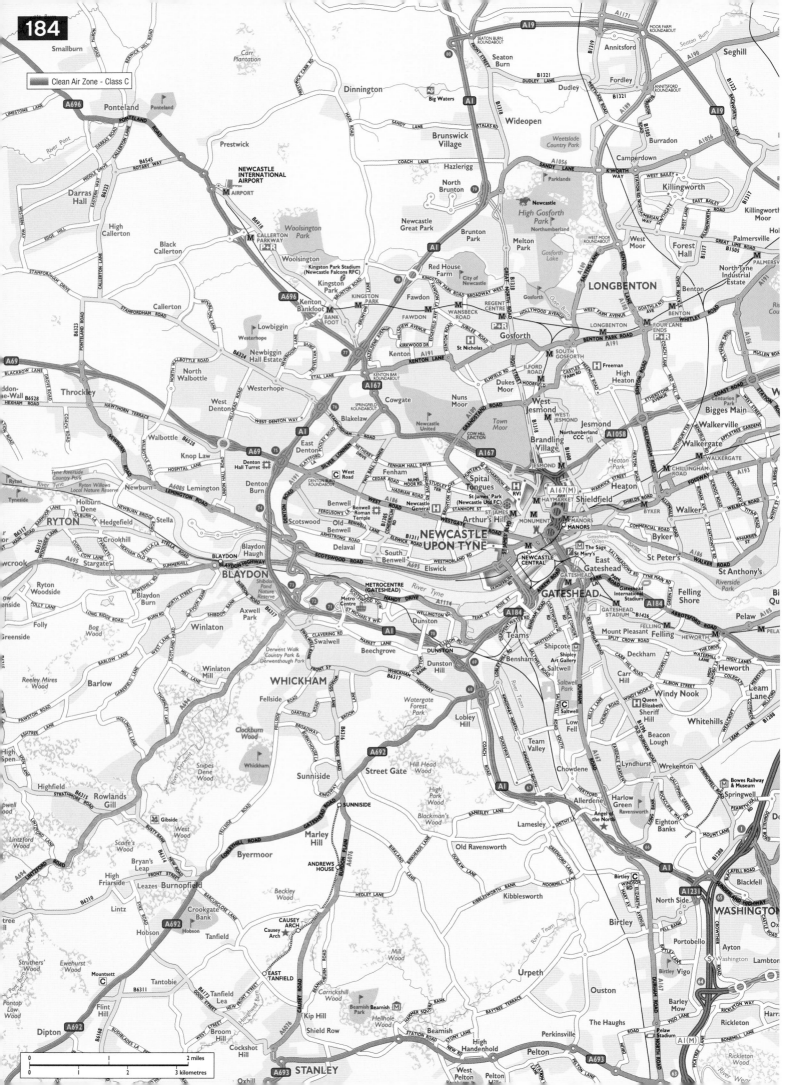

NORTH

SEA

Town, port and airport plans

2 Motorway and junction	One-way, gated/ closed road	Railway station	Toilet, with facilities for the less able
4 Primary road single/ dual carriageway and numbered junction	Restricted access road	Preserved or tourist railway	Car park, with electric charging point
37 A road single/ dual carriageway and numbered junction	Pedestrian area	Light rapid transit system station	Park and Ride (at least 6 days per week)
B road single/ dual carriageway	Footpath	Level crossing	Bus/coach station
Local road single/ dual carriageway	Road under construction	Tramway	Hospital, 24-hour Accident & Emergency hospital
Other road single/ dual carriageway, minor road	Road tunnel	Airport, heliport	Beach (award winning)
Building of interest	Lighthouse	Railair terminal	City wall
Ruined building	Castle	Theatre or performing arts centre	Escarpment
Tourist Information Centre	Castle mound	Cinema	Cliff lift
Visitor or heritage centre	Monument, memorial, statue	Abbey, chapel, church	River/canal, lake
World Heritage Site (UNESCO)	Post Office	Synagogue	Lock, weir
Museum	Public library	Mosque	Viewpoint
English Heritage site	Shopping centre	Golf course	Park/sports ground
Historic Scotland site	Shopmobility	Racecourse	Cemetery
Cadw (Welsh heritage) site	Football stadium	Nature reserve	Woodland
National Trust site	Rugby stadium	Aquarium	Built-up area
National Trust for Scotland site	County cricket ground	Showground	Beach

Central London street map (see pages 238–247)

London Underground station	London Overground station
Docklands Light Railway (DLR) station	Central London Congestion Charge boundary

Royal Parks

Green Park	Park open 5am–midnight. Constitution Hill and The Mall closed to traffic Sundays and public holidays 8am–dusk.
Hyde Park	Park open 5am–midnight. Park roads closed to traffic midnight–5am.
Kensington Gardens	Park open 6am–dusk.
Regent's Park	Park open 5am–dusk. Park roads closed to traffic midnight–7am, except for residents.
St James's Park	Park open 5am–midnight. The Mall closed to traffic Sundays and public holidays 8am–dusk.
Victoria Tower Gardens	Park open dawn–dusk.

Traffic regulations in the City of London include security checkpoints and restrict the number of entry and exit points.

Note: Oxford Street is closed to through-traffic (except buses & taxis) 7am–7pm Monday–Saturday.

Bishopsgate Streetspace Scheme: Temporary traffic restrictions are in operation between Shoreditch and London Bridge, 7am–7pm Monday–Friday. Follow local road signs for changes to permitted routes.

Central London Congestion Charge Zone (CCZ)
You need to pay a £15 daily charge for driving a vehicle on public roads in this central London area. Payment permits entry, travel within and exit from the CCZ by the vehicle as often as required on that day.

The daily charge applies 07:00–18:00 Mon–Fri, 12:00–18:00 Sat–Sun and bank holidays. There is no charge between Christmas Day and New Year's Day bank holiday (inclusive).

For up to date information on the CCZ, exemptions, discounts or ways to pay, visit **www.tfl.gov.uk/modes/driving/congestion-charge**

Ultra Low Emission Zone (ULEZ)
Most vehicles in Central London, including cars and vans, need to meet minimum exhaust emission standards or drivers must pay a daily charge to drive within the zone. From 29 August 2023 the ULEZ is due to be expanded from central and inner London, to include all London boroughs. The ULEZ operates 24 hours a day, every day of the year, except Christmas Day (25 December). The charge is £12.50 for motorcycles, cars and vans and is in addition to the Congestion Charge.

Please note the maps in this atlas show the zone in operation at the time of going to print.

For further information visit **www.tfl.gov.uk/modes/driving/ultra-low-emission-zone**

In addition the Low Emission Zone (LEZ) operates across Greater London, 24 hours every day of the year and is aimed at the most heavy-polluting vehicles. It does not apply to cars or motorcycles.

For details visit **www.tfl.gov.uk/modes/driving/low-emission-zone**

Town Plans

Central London

Ferry Ports

Channel Tunnel

Airports

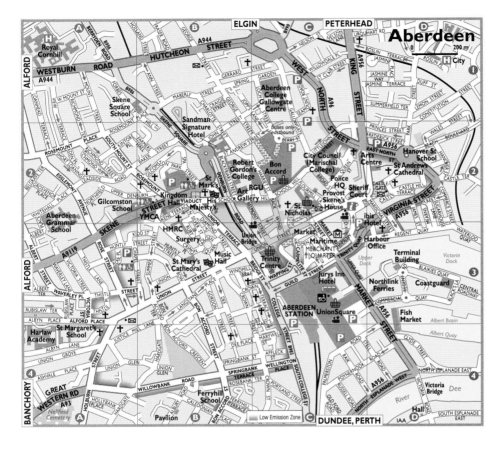

Aberdeen

Aberdeen is found on atlas page **151 N6**

Affleck Street	C4	Maberly Street	B1
Albert Street	A3	Marischal Street	D2
Albury Road	B4	Market Street	C3
Alford Place	A3	Nelson Street	C1
Ann Street	B1	Palmerston Road	C4
Beach Boulevard	D2	Park Street	D2
Belgrave Terrace	A2	Portland Street	C4
Berryden Road	A1	Poynernook Road	C4
Blackfriars Street	B2	Regent Quay	D3
Blaikies Quay	D3	Richmond Street	A2
Bon Accord Crescent	B4	Rose Place	A3
Bon Accord Street	B3	Rose Street	A3
Bridge Street	C3	Rosemount Place	A2
Caledonian Place	B4	Rosemount Viaduct	A2
Carmelite Street	C3	St Andrew Street	B2
Chapel Street	A3	St Clair Street	C1
Charlotte Street	B1	School Hill	C2
College Street	C3	Skene Square	B2
Constitution Street	D1	Skene Street	A3
Crimon Place	B3	Skene Terrace	B2
Crown Street	B3	South College Street	C4
Dee Street	B3	South Esplanade East	D4
Denburn Road	B2	South Mount Street	A2
Diamond Street	B3	Spa Street	B2
East North Street	D2	Springbank Street	B4
Esslemont Avenue	A2	Springbank Terrace	B4
Gallowgate	C1	Summer Street	B3
George Street	B1	Summerfield Terrace	D1
Gilcomston Park	B2	Thistle Lane	A3
Golden Square	B3	Thistle Place	A3
Gordon Street	B3	Thistle Street	A3
Great Western Road	A4	Trinity Quay	C3
Guild Street	C3	Union Bridge	B3
Hadden Street	C3	Union Grove	A4
Hanover Street	D2	Union Street	B3
Hardgate	B4	Union Terrace	B2
Harriet Street	C2	Upper Denburn	A2
Holburn Street	A4	Victoria Road	D4
Huntly Street	A3	Victoria Street	A3
Hutcheon Street	B1	View Terrace	A1
Jasmine Terrace	D1	Virginia Street	D2
John Street	B2	Wapping Street	C3
Justice Mill Lane	A4	Waverley Place	A3
King Street	C1	Wellington Place	C4
Langstane Place	B3	West North Street	C1
Leadside Road	A2	Westburn Road	A1
Loanhead Terrace	A1	Whitehall Place	A2
Loch Street	C1	Willowbank Road	A4

Basingstoke

Basingstoke is found on atlas page **22 H4**

Alencon Link	C1	London Street	C3
Allnutt Avenue	D2	Lower Brook Street	A2
Basing View	C1	Lytton Road	D3
Beaconsfield Road	C4	Market Place	B3
Bounty Rise	A4	May Place	C3
Bounty Road	A4	Montague Place	C4
Bramblys Close	A3	Mortimer Lane	A2
Bramblys Drive	A3	New Road	B3
Budd's Close	A3	New Road	C2
Castle Road	C4	New Street	B3
Chapel Hill	B1	Penrith Road	A3
Chequers Road	C2	Rayleigh Road	A2
Chester Place	A4	Red Lion Lane	C3
Churchill Way	B2	Rochford Road	A2
Churchill Way East	D1	St Mary's Court	C2
Churchill Way West	A2	Sarum Hill	A3
Church Square	B2	Seal Road	C2
Church Street	B2	Solby's Road	A2
Church Street	B3	Southend Road	A2
Cliddesden Road	C4	Southern Road	B4
Clifton Terrace	C1	Stukeley Road	A3
Cordale Road	A4	Sylvia Close	B4
Council Road	B4	Timberlake Road	B2
Crossborough Gardens	D3	Victoria Street	B3
Crossborough Hill	D3	Victory Roundabout	A2
Cross Street	B3	Vyne Road	B1
Devonshire Place	A4	Winchcombe Road	A3
Eastfield Avenue	D2	Winchester Road	A4
Eastrop Lane	D2	Winchester Street	B3
Eastrop Roundabout	C1	Winterthur Way	A1
Eastrop Way	D2	Worting Road	A3
Essex Road	A2	Wote Street	C3
Fairfields Road	B4		
Festival Way	C2		
Flaxfield Court	A2		
Flaxfield Road	A3		
Flaxfield Road	B3		
Frances Road	A4		
Frescade Crescent	A4		
Goat Lane	C2		
Hackwood Road	C4		
Hamelyn Road	A4		
Hardy Lane	A4		
Hawkfield Lane	A4		
Haymarket Yard	C3		
Joices Yard	B3		
Jubilee Road	B4		
London Road	D3		

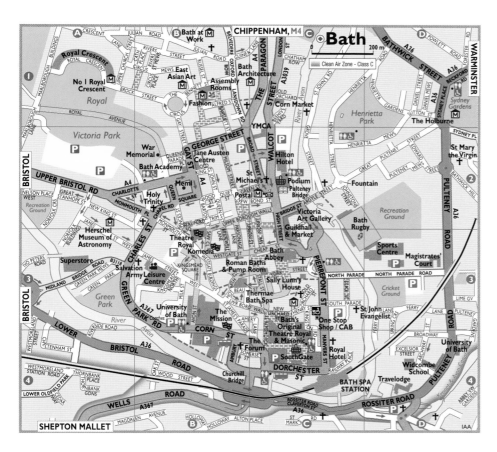

Bath

Bath is found on atlas page **20 D2**

Archway Street	D4	Lower Borough Walls	B3
Argyle Street	C2	Lower Bristol Road	A3
Avon Street	B3	Lower Oldfield Park	A4
Bartlett Street	B1	Manvers Street	B3
Barton Street	B2	Midland Bridge Road	A3
Bathwick Street	D1	Milk Street	B3
Beauford Square	B2	Milsom Street	B2
Beau Street	B3	Monmouth Place	A2
Beckford Road	D1	Monmouth Street	B2
Bennett Street	B1	New Bond Street	B2
Bridge Street	C2	New King Street	A2
Broad Street	C2	New Orchard Street	C3
Broadway	D4	Norfolk Buildings	A3
Brock Street	A1	North Parade	C3
Chapel Road	B2	North Parade Road	D3
Charles Street	A3	Old King Street	B2
Charlotte Street	A2	Oxford Row	B1
Cheap Street	C3	Pierrepont Street	C3
Cheltenham Street	A4	Princes Street	B2
Circus Mews	B1	Pulteney Road	D2
Claverton Street	C4	Queen Square	B2
Corn Street	B4	Queen Street	B2
Daniel Street	D1	Railway Place	D3
Dorchester Street	C4	Rivers Street	B1
Edward Street	D2	Rossiter Road	C4
Ferry Lane	D3	Royal Avenue	A1
Gay Street	B1	Royal Crescent	A1
George Street	B2	St James's Parade	B3
Great Pulteney Street	C2	St John's Road	C1
Great Stanhope Street	A2	Saw Close	B3
Green Park Road	A3	Southgate Street	C4
Green Street	B2	South Parade	C3
Grove Street	C2	Stall Street	C3
Guinea Lane	B1	Sutton Street	D1
Henrietta Gardens	D1	Sydney Place	D1
Henrietta Mews	C2	The Circus	B1
Henrietta Road	C1	The Paragon	C1
Henrietta Street	C2	Thornbank Place	A4
Henry Street	C3	Union Street	B2
High Street	C2	Upper Borough Walls	B2
Hot Bath Street	B3	Upper Bristol Road	A2
James Street West	B3	Upper Church Street	A1
John Street	B2	Walcot Street	C2
Julian Road	B1	Wells Road	A4
Kingsmead North	B3	Westgate Buildings	B3
Kingston Road	C3	Westgate Street	B2
Lansdown Road	B1	Westmoreland Station Road	A4
London Street	C1	York Street	C3

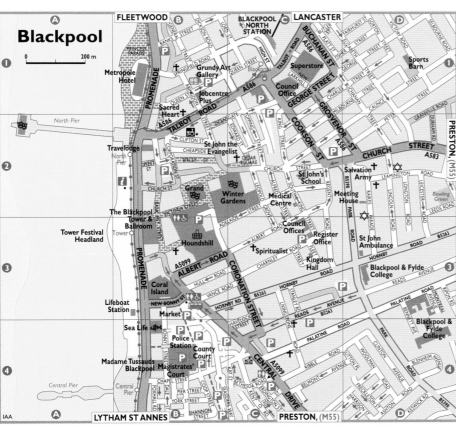

Blackpool

Blackpool is found on atlas page **88 C3**

Abingdon Street	B1	Havelock Street	C4
Adelaide Street	B3	High Street	C1
Albert Road	B3	Hornby Road	B3
Albert Road	C3	Hornby Road	D3
Alfred Street	C2	Hull Road	B3
Ashton Road	D4	Kay Street	C4
Bank Hey Street	B2	Kent Road	C4
Banks Street	B1	King Street	C2
Belmont Avenue	C4	Leamington Road	D2
Bennett Avenue	D3	Leicester Road	D2
Bethesda Road	C4	Leopold Grove	C2
Birley Street	B2	Lincoln Road	D2
Blenheim Avenue	D4	Livingstone Road	C3
Bonny Street	B4	Lord Street	B1
Buchanan Street	C1	Louise Street	C4
Butler Street	C1	Milbourne Street	C1
Caunce Street	D1	Montreal Avenue	D3
Cedar Square	C2	New Bonny Street	B3
Central Drive	C4	New Larkhill Street	C1
Chapel Street	B4	Palatine Road	C4
Charles Street	C1	Palatine Road	D3
Charnley Road	C3	Park Road	C4
Cheapside	B2	Park Road	D4
Church Street	B2	Peter Street	D2
Church Street	C2	Pier Street	B4
Church Street	D2	Princess Parade	B1
Clifton Street	B2	Promenade	B1
Clinton Avenue	D4	Queen Street	B1
Cookson Street	C2	Raikes Parade	D2
Coop Street	B4	Reads Avenue	C3
Coronation Street	C3	Reads Avenue	D3
Corporation Street	B2	Regent Road	C2
Dale Street	B4	Ribble Road	C4
Deansgate	B2	Ripon Road	D3
Dickson Road	B1	Seasiders Way	B4
Edward Street	C2	Selbourne Road	D1
Elizabeth Street	D1	South King Street	C2
Fairhurst Street	D1	Springfield Road	B1
Fisher Street	C1	Stanley Road	C3
Fleet Street	C3	Talbot Road	B1
Foxhall Road	B4	Talbot Road	C1
Freckleton Street	D4	Topping Street	C2
General Street	B1	Vance Road	B3
George Street	C1	Victoria Street	B2
Gorton Street	D1	Victory Road	D1
Granville Road	D2	West Street	B2
Grosvenor Street	C1	Woolman Road	D4
Harrison Street	D4	York Street	B4

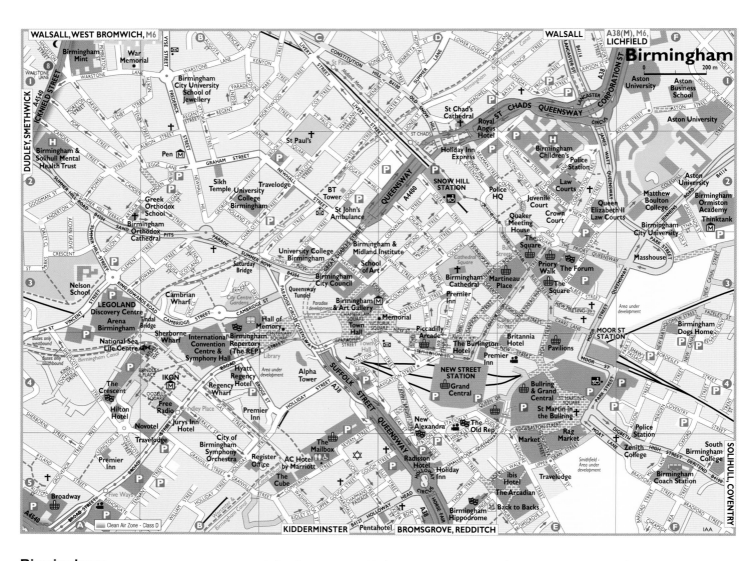

Birmingham

Birmingham is found on atlas page **58 G7**

Acorn Grove A2
Albert Street E3
Albert Street F3
Albion Street B2
Allison Street F4
Anderton Street A2
Arthur Place A2
Aston Street F1
Atlas Way B4
Banbury Street F3
Barford Street F5
Bartholomew Street F3
Barwick Street D3
Bath Street E1
Beak Street D4
Benacre Drive F4
Bennetts Hill D3
Berkley Street B4
Bishopgate Street A5
Blucher Street C5
Bond Street C1
Bordesley Street F4
Bow Street D5
Bradford Street F5
Bridge Street B4
Brindley Drive B3
Brindley Place B4
Broad Street A5
Bromsgrove Street E5
Brook Street C2
Brunel Street C4
Bull Street E3
Cambridge Street B3
Camden Drive B2
Camden Street A2
Cannon Street D3

Caroline Street B1
Carrs Lane E3
Carver Street A1
Chamberlain Square C3
Chapmans Passage C5
Charlotte Street B3
Cheapside F5
Cherry Street D3
Church Street D2
Civic Close B3
Clement Street A3
Cleveland Street D1
Coleshill Street F2
Colmore Circus Queensway E2
Colmore Row D3
Commercial Street C5
Constitution Hill C1
Cornwall Street D3
Corporation Street E1
Corporation Street E3
Coventry Street F4
Cox Street C1
Dale End E3
Daley Close A3
Dalton Street E2
Dean Street E5
Digbeth E4
Dudley Street D4
Eden Place C3
Edgbaston Street E4
Edmund Street D3
Edward Street B3
Ellis Street D5
Essington Street A5
Ethel Street D4
Etna Street F2

Exeter Street D5
Fazeley Street F3
Fleet Street C3
Fox Street F3
Frederick Street B1
Gas Street B4
George Street B2
Gloucester Street E5
Goodman Street A2
Gough Street C5
Graham Street B2
Granville Street B5
Great Charles Street
  Queensway C3
Grosvenor Street F2
Grosvenor Street West A5
Hall Street B1
Hampton Street D1
Helena Street B3
Henrietta Street C1
High Street E4
High Street Deritend F5
Hill Street C4
Hinckley Street D4
Hingeston Street A1
Holland Street B2
Holliday Street B5
Holloway Circus D5
Holloway Head C5
Holt Street F1
Horse Fair D5
Hospital Street D1
Hurst Street D5
Icknield Street A1
Inge Street D5
James Street B2
James Watt Queensway E2
Jennens Road F2
John Bright Street D4
Kenyon Street B1
King Edward's Drive A4

King Edwards Road A3
Ladywell Walk D5
Lancaster Circus E1
Lancaster Street E1
Lawson Street E1
Legge Lane B2
Lighthouse Avenue A3
Lionel Street C2
Livery Street C1
Louisa Street B3
Loveday Street E1
Lower Loveday Street D1
Lower Temple Street D4
Ludgate Hill C2
Margaret Street C3
Marshall Street C5
Martineau Way E3
Mary Ann Street C1
Mary Street C1
Meriden Street F4
Mill Lane F5
Moat Lane E4
Moor Street E4
Moor Street Queensway E4
Moreton Street A1
Navigation Street C4
Needless Alley D3
Nelson Street A3
New Bartholomew Street F4
New Canal Street F4
Newhall Hill B2
Newhall Street C2
New Meeting Street E3
New Street D3
Newton Street E2
Northwood Street C1
Old Snow Hill D1
Old Square E3
Oozells Square B4
Oxford Street F5
Parade B3

Paradise Circus Queensway C3
Paradise Street C4
Park Street E4
Pemberton Street A1
Pershore Street E5
Pope Street A1
Powell Street A2
Price Street E1
Princip Street E1
Printing House Street E2
Queens Drive D4
Queensway Tunnel C3
Rea Street F5
Regent Parade B1
Regent Place B1
Regent Street B1
Ridley Street C5
Ruston Street A5
Ryland Street A5
St Chads Queensway E1
St Jude's Pass D5
St Marks Crescent A3
St Martin's Square E4
St Paul's Square C1
St Philip's Place D3
St Vincent Street A3
Sand Pitts A2
Saturday Bridge B3
Scotland Street B3
Severn Street C5
Shadwell Street D1
Shaw's Passage F4
Sheepcote Street A4
Sherborne Street A4
Sloane Street B2
Smallbrook Queensway D5
Snow Hill Queensway D2
Spencer Street B1
Staniforth Street E1
Station Street D5
Steelhouse Lane E2

Stephenson Street D4
Suffolk Street Queensway.......C4
Summer Hill Road....................A2
Summer Hill Street A2
Summer Hill Terrace A2
Summer Lane D1
Summer Row B3
Swallow Street C4
Temple Row D3
Temple Row West D3
Temple Street D3
Tenby Street A1
Tenby Street North A1
Tennant Street A5
The Priory Queensway E3
Thorp Street D5
Tindal Bridge B3
Trent Street F4
Union Street E3
Upper Dean Street...................E5
Upper Gough Street.................C5
Vesey Street E1
Victoria Square C3
Vittoria Street B1
Vyse Street B1
Warstone Lane A1
Washington Street....................C5
Waterloo Street D3
Water Street C2
Weaman Street D2
Whittall Street E2
William Street B5
Woodcock Street F1

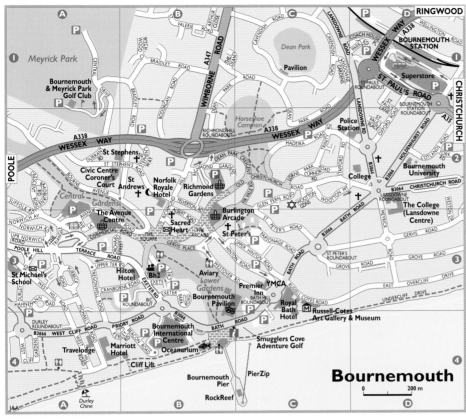

Bournemouth

Bournemouth is found on atlas page **13 J6**

Albert Road	B3	Old Christchurch Road	C2
Avenue Lane	A3	Orchard Street	A3
Avenue Road	A3	Oxford Road	D2
Bath Hill Roundabout	C3	Park Road	D1
Bath Road	B4	Parsonage Road	C3
Beacon Road	B4	Poole Hill	A3
BIC Roundabout	B3	Priory Road	A4
Bodorgan Road	B2	Purbeck Road	A3
Bourne Avenue	A2	Richmond Gardens	B2
Bournemouth Street		Richmond Hill	B3
Roundabout	D1	Richmond Hill Roundabout	B2
Bradburne Road	A2	Russell Cotes Road	C3
Braidley Road	B1	St Michael's Road	A3
Cavendish Road	C1	St Paul's Lane	D1
Central Drive	A1	St Paul's Place	D2
Christchurch Road	D2	St Paul's Road	D1
Coach House Place	D1	St Pauls Roundabout	D1
Commercial Road	A3	St Peter's Road	C3
Cotlands Road	D2	St Peter's Roundabout	C3
Cranborne Road	A3	St Stephen's Road	A2
Crescent Road	A2	St Stephen's Way	B2
Cumnor Road	C2	St Valerie Road	B1
Dean Park Crescent	B2	Stafford Road	C2
Dean Park Road	B2	Suffolk Road	A2
Durley Road	A3	Terrace Road	A3
Durley Roundabout	A4	The Arcade	B3
Durrant Road	A2	The Deans	B1
East Overcliff Drive	D3	The Square	B3
Exeter Crescent	B3	The Triangle	A3
Exeter Park Road	B3	Tregonwell Road	A3
Exeter Road	B3	Trinity Road	C2
Fir Vale Road	C2	Undercliff Drive	D3
Gervis Place	B3	Upper Hinton Road	C3
Gervis Road	D3	Upper Norwich Road	A3
Glen Fern Road	C2	Upper Terrace Road	A3
Grove Road	C3	Wellington Road	D1
Hahnemann Road	A3	Wessex Way	A2
Hinton Road	B3	West Cliff Gardens	A4
Holdenhurst Road	D2	West Cliff Road	A4
Kerley Road	A4	West Hill Road	A3
Lansdowne Gardens	C1	Weston Drive	D2
Lansdowne Road	C1	Westover Road	B3
Lansdowne Roundabout	D2	Wimborne Road	B1
Lorne Park Road	C2	Wootton Gardens	C2
Madeira Road	C2	Wootton Mount	C2
Meyrick Road	D3	Wychwood Close	B1
Norwich Avenue	A3	Yelverton Road	B2
Norwich Road	A3	York Road	D2

Bradford

Bradford is found on atlas page **90 F4**

Aldermanbury	B3	Lower Kirkgate	C2
Bank Street	B2	Lumb Lane	A1
Barkerend Road	D2	Manchester Road	B4
Barry Street	B2	Manningham Lane	A1
Bolling Road	C4	Manor Row	B1
Bolton Road	C2	Market Street	B3
Bridge Street	C3	Midland Road	B1
Broadway	C3	Morley Street	A4
Burnett Street	D2	Neal Street	B4
Canal Road	C1	Nelson Street	B4
Carlton Street	A3	North Brook Street	C1
Centenary Square	B3	Northgate	B2
Chandos Street	C4	North Parade	B1
Chapel Street	D3	North Street	C2
Cheapside	B2	North Wing	D1
Chester Street	A4	Otley Road	D1
Church Bank	C2	Paradise Street	A2
Claremont	A4	Peckover Street	D2
Croft Street	C4	Piccadilly	B2
Darfield Street	A1	Pine Street	C2
Darley Street	B2	Princes Way	B3
Drewton Road	A2	Randall Well Street	A3
Dryden Street	D4	Rawson Road	A2
Duke Street	B2	Rawson Square	B2
East Parade	D3	Rebecca Street	A2
Edmund Street	A4	St Blaise Way	C1
Edward Street	C4	St Thomas's Road	A2
Eldon Place	A1	Sawrey Place	A4
Filey Street	D3	Senior Way	B4
George Street	C3	Shipley Airedale Road	C1
Godwin Street	B2	Stott Hill	C2
Grattan Road	A2	Sunbridge Road	A2
Great Horton Road	A4	Tetley Street	A3
Grove Terrace	A2	Thornton Road	A3
Hallfield Road	A1	Trafalgar Street	B1
Hall Ings	B4	Tyrrel Street	B3
Hammerton Street	D3	Upper Park Gate	D2
Hamm Strasse	A1	Upper Piccadilly	B2
Holdsworth Street	C1	Valley Road	C1
Houghton Place	A1	Vicar Lane	C3
Howard Street	A4	Wakefield Road	D4
Hustlergate	B3	Wapping Road	D1
Infirmary Street	A1	Water Lane	A2
John Street	B2	Wellington Street	C2
Lansdowne Place	A4	Westgate	A2
Leeds Road	D3	Wharf Street	C1
Little Horton	A4	Wigan Street	A2
Little Horton Lane	B4	Wilton Street	A4

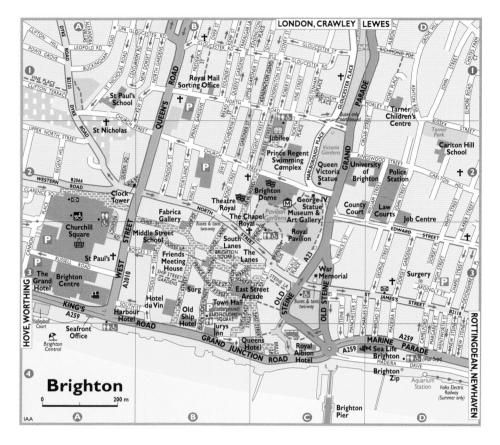

Brighton

Brighton

Brighton is found on atlas page **24 H10**

Ardingly Street	D3	Madeira Place	D4
Ashton Rise	D1	Manchester Street	C4
Bartholomew Square	B3	Margaret Street	D4
Black Lion Street	B3	Marine Parade	D4
Blaker Street	D3	Market Street	B3
Bond Street	B2	Marlborough Place	C2
Boyces Street	A3	Meeting House Lane	B3
Brighton Place	B3	Middle Street	B3
Broad Street	D4	Morley Street	D1
Buckingham Road	A1	New Dorset Street	B1
Camelford Street	D4	New Road	B2
Cannon Place	A3	New Steine	D4
Carlton Hill	D2	Nile Street	B3
Centurion Road	A1	North Gardens	B1
Chapel Street	D3	North Place	C2
Charles Street	C4	North Road	B1
Cheltenham Place	C1	North Street	B2
Church Street	A1	Old Steine	C3
Church Street	B2	Portland Street	B2
Circus Street	C2	Powis Grove	A1
Clifton Hill	A1	Prince Albert Street	B3
Clifton Terrace	A1	Prince's Street	C3
Devonshire Place	D3	Queen's Gardens	B1
Dukes Lane	B3	Queen Square	A2
Duke Street	B2	Queen's Road	B2
East Street	C3	Regency Road	A2
Edward Street	D3	Regent Hill	A2
Elmore Road	D1	Regent Street	C2
Foundry Street	B1	Robert Street	C1
Frederick Street	B1	St James's Street	D3
Gardner Street	B2	St Nicholas Road	A1
George Street	D3	Ship Street	B3
Gloucester Place	C1	Spring Gardens	B1
Gloucester Road	B1	Steine Street	C4
Gloucester Street	C1	Sussex Street	D2
Grand Junction Road	B4	Sydney Street	C1
Grand Parade	C2	Tichborne Street	B2
High Street	D3	Tidy Street	C1
Ivory Place	D1	Upper Gardner Street	B1
John Street	D2	Upper Gloucester Road	A1
Jubilee Street	C2	Upper North Street	A2
Kensington Gardens	C1	Vine Street	C1
Kensington Street	C1	Wentworth Street	D4
Kew Street	B1	Western Road	A2
King's Road	A3	West Street	A3
Kingswood Street	C2	White Street	D3
Leopold Road	A1	William Street	D2
Little East Street	B4	Windsor Street	B2

Bristol

Bristol is found on atlas page **31 Q10**

Anchor Road	A3	Passage Street	C2
Avon Street	D3	Pembroke Street	C1
Baldwin Street	B2	Penn Street	C1
Bath Bridge	D4	Pero's Bridge	B3
Bond Street	C1	Perry Road	A2
Bond Street	D2	Philadelphia Street	C2
Broadmead	C1	Portwall Lane	C4
Broad Plain	D2	Prewett Street	C4
Broad Quay	B3	Prince Street	B3
Broad Street	B2	Queen Charlotte Street	B3
Broad Weir	C2	Queen Square	B3
Canons Way	A3	Redcliffe Parade West	B4
Canynge Street	C3	Redcliffe Way	C4
Castle Street	C2	Redcliff Hill	C4
College Green	A3	Redcliff Mead Lane	C4
Colston Avenue	B2	Redcliff Street	C3
Colston Street	B2	Royal Fort Road	A1
Commercial Road	B4	Rupert Street	B2
Corn Street	B2	St Augustine's Parade	B3
Countership	B3	St George's Road	A3
Cumberland Road	A4	St Matthias Park	D1
Deanery Road	A3	St Michael's Hill	A1
Denmark Street	A3	St Stephen's Street	B2
Explore Lane	A3	St Thomas Street	C3
Fairfax Street	C2	Small Street	B2
Ferry Street	C3	Somerset Street	C4
Friary	D3	Southwell Street	A1
Frogmore Street	A2	Tankards Close	A1
Great George Street	A3	Telephone Avenue	B3
Great George Street	D1	Temple Back	C3
Guinea Street	B4	Temple Back East	D3
Haymarket	C1	Temple Gate	D4
Hill Street	A2	Temple Street	C3
Horfield Road	B1	Temple Way	D3
Jacob Street	D2	The Grove	B4
King Street	B3	The Horsefair	C1
Lewins Mead	B2	The Pithay	C2
Lodge Street	B2	Tower Hill	D2
Lower Castle Street	D2	Trenchard Street	A2
Lower Church Lane	A2	Tyndall Avenue	A1
Lower Maudlin Street	B1	Union Street	C1
Marlborough Hill	B1	Upper Maudlin Street	B1
Marlborough Street	B1	Victoria Street	C2
Marsh Street	B3	Wapping Road	B4
Museum Street	A4	Welsh Back	B3
Newgate	C2	Whitson Street	B1
Old Market Street	D2	Wine Street	C2
Park Street	A2	Woodland Road	A1

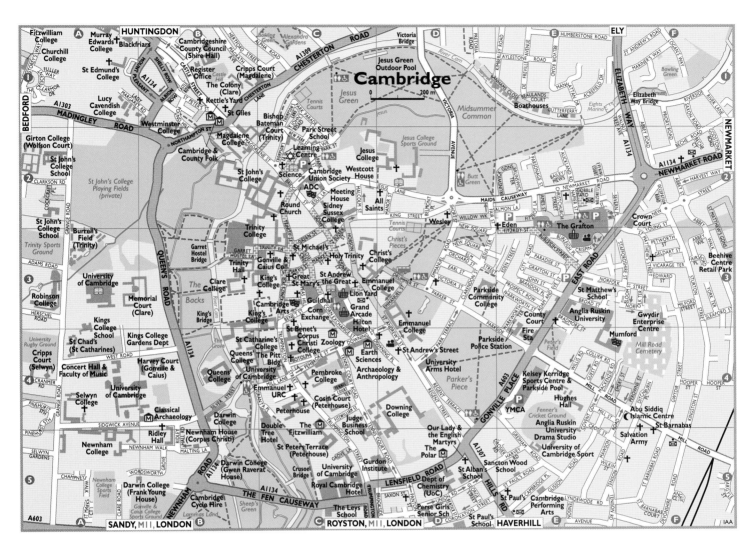

Cambridge

Cambridge is found on atlas page **62 G9**

Abbey Road	F1
Abbey Street	F2
Abbey Walk	F3
Acrefield Drive	E1
Adam and Eve Street	E3
Albion Row	B1
Alpha Road	C1
Auckland Road	E2
Aylestone Road	E1
Bailey Mews	E2
Banhams Close	D1
Beaulands Court	E1
Beche Road	F2
Belmont Place	D2
Belvoir Road	E1
Bene't Street	C3
Bloom Street	F3
Bradmore Street	E3
Brandon Place	E3
Bridge Street	C2
Broad Street	E3
Brookside	D5
Brunswick Gardens	E2
Brunswick Terrace	E2
Burleigh Place	E3
Burleigh Street	E3
Cambridge Place	E5
Castle Row	B1
Castle Street	B1
Champneys Walk	A5
Chesterton Lane	B1
Chesterton Road	C1
Christchurch Street	E2
City Road	E3
Clarendon Street	D3
Cobble Yard	E2

Collier Road	E4
Corn Exchange Street	C3
Coronation Street	D5
Covent Garden	E4
Crispin Place	E3
Cross Street	E4
Crusoe Bridge	B5
Cutler Ferry Close	E1
Cutterferry Lane	E1
De Freville Avenue	E1
Devonshire Road	F4
Ditchburn Place	F4
Downing Place	C4
Downing Street	C4
Drosier Road	D5
Drummer Street	D3
Earl Street	D3
East Road	E3
Eden Street	E3
Eden Street Back	E3
Edward Street	F3
Elizabeth Way	F1
Elm Street	D3
Emery Street	F4
Emmanuel Road	D3
Emmanuel Street	D3
Evening Court	E2
Fairsford Place	F3
Fair Street	D2
Fitzroy Lane	E2
Fitzroy Street	E3
Fitzwilliam Street	C4
Garret Hostel Bridge	B3
Garret Hostel Lane	B3
Geldart Street	F3
George IV Street	D5

Glisson Road	E5
Godstone Road	F2
Gonville Place	D4
Grange Road	A3
Grange Road	A4
Granta Place	B4
Green Street	C3
Gresham Road	E5
Gwydir Street	F4
Harvest Way	F2
Harvey Road	E5
Hertford Street	B1
Hills Road	D5
Hobson Street	C3
Humberstone Road	E1
James Street	E2
Jesus Lane	C2
Jesus Terrace	D3
John Street	E3
Kimberley Road	E1
King's Bridge	B3
King's Parade	C3
Kingston Street	F4
King Street	D2
Lady Margaret Road	A1
Lensfield Road	D5
Logan's Way	F1
Lwr Park Street	C2
Lyndewode Road	E5
Mackenzie Road	E4
Madingley Road	A1
Magdalene Street	B2
Magrath Avenue	B1
Maids Causeway	D2
Malcolm Street	C2
Malting Lane	B5
Manhattan Drive	E1
Manor Street	D2
Mariner's Way	F1
Market Street	C3
Mawson Road	E5

Milford Street	F3
Mill Lane	C4
Mill Road	E4
Mill Street	E4
Mortimer Road	E4
Mount Pleasant	B1
Napier Street	E2
Newmarket Road	E2
Newnham Road	B5
Newnham Walk	A5
New Park Street	C2
New Square	D3
New Street	F2
Norfolk Street	E3
Norfolk Terrace	F3
Northampton Street	B2
Occupation Road	F2
Orchard Street	D3
Panton Street	D5
Paradise Street	D3
Parker Street	D3
Park Parade	C1
Parkside	D3
Park Street	C2
Park Terrace	D4
Parsonage Street	E2
Peas Hill	C3
Pembroke Street	C4
Perowne Street	F4
Petworth Street	F3
Pound Hill	B1
Priory Road	F1
Prospect Row	E3
Queen's Road	B3
Regent Street	D4
Regent Terrace	D4
River Lane	F1
Riverside	F1
St Andrew's Road	F1
St Andrew's Street	D3
St Barnabas Road	F5

St Mary's Street	C3
St Matthew's Gardens	F2
St Matthew's Street	F3
St Paul's Road	E5
St Peter's Street	B1
Salmon Lane	E2
Saxon Road	F1
Saxon Street	D5
Severn Place	F2
Shelly Row	B1
Short Street	D2
Sidgwick Avenue	A4
Sidney Street	C2
Silver Street	B4
Staffordshire Street	F3
Sturton Street	F3
Sussex Street	C3
Tenison Avenue	E5
Tenison Road	E5
Tennis Court Road	C4
Tennis Court Terrace	C4
The Fen Causeway	B5
Thompson's Lane	C2
Trinity Lane	C3
Trinity Street	C2
Trumpington Road	C5
Trumpington Street	C4
Union Road	D5
Vicarage Terrace	F3
Victoria Avenue	D1
Victoria Bridge	D1
Victoria Road	D3
Warkworth Street	E3
Warkworth Terrace	E4
Wellington Street	E2
West Road	A4
Wilkin Street	E5
Willis Road	E4
Willow Walk	D2
Wordsworth Grove	A5
Young Street	F3

University Colleges

Christ's College	C3
Clare College	A3
Clare College	B1
Clare College	B3
Corpus Christi College	C4
Darwin College	B4
Downing College	D4
Emmanuel College	C3
Emmanuel College	D3
Fitzwilliam College	A1
Girton College (Wolfson Court)	A2
Gonville & Caius College	C3
Gonville & Caius College	B4
Jesus College	C2
King's College	B3
Lucy Cavendish College	A2
Magdalene College	B2
Murray Edwards College	A1
Newnham College	A5
Pembroke College	C4
Peterhouse	C4
Queens' College	B4
Robinson College	A3
St Catharine's College	C4
St Edmund's College	A1
St John's College	B2
Selwyn College	A4
Sidney Sussex College	C2
Trinity College	B3
Westminster College	B1

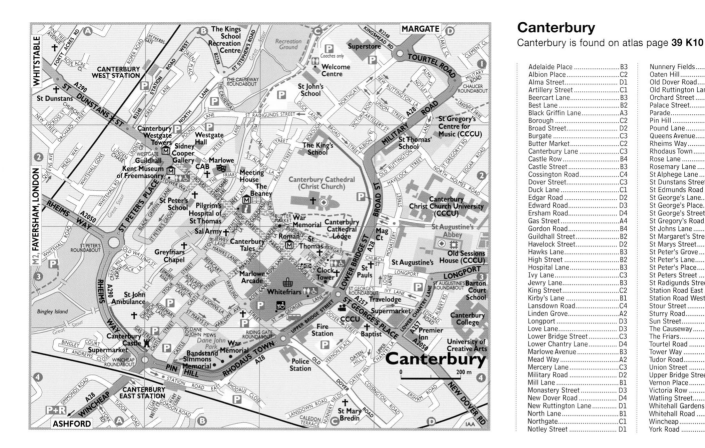

Canterbury

Canterbury is found on atlas page **39 K10**

Adelaide Place	B3
Albion Place	C2
Alma Street	D1
Artillery Street	C1
Beercart Lane	B3
Best Lane	B2
Black Griffin Lane	A3
Borough	C2
Broad Street	D2
Burgate	C3
Butter Market	C2
Canterbury Lane	C3
Castle Row	B4
Castle Street	B3
Cossington Road	C4
Dover Street	C3
Duck Lane	C1
Edgar Road	D2
Edward Road	D3
Ersham Road	D4
Gas Street	A4
Gordon Road	B4
Guildhall Street	B2
Havelock Street	D2
Hawks Lane	B3
High Street	B2
Hospital Lane	B3
Ivy Lane	C3
Jewry Lane	B3
King Street	C2
Kirby's Lane	B1
Lansdown Road	C4
Linden Grove	A2
Longport	D3
Love Lane	D3
Lower Bridge Street	C3
Lower Chantry Lane	D4
Marlowe Avenue	B3
Mead Way	A2
Mercery Lane	C3
Military Road	D2
Mill Lane	B1
Monastery Street	D3
New Dover Road	D4
New Ruttington Lane	D1
North Lane	B1
Northgate	C1
Notley Street	D1
Nunnery Fields	C4
Oaten Hill	C4
Old Dover Road	C4
Old Ruttington Lane	D2
Orchard Street	A2
Palace Street	C2
Parade	C3
Pin Hill	B4
Pound Lane	B2
Queens Avenue	A2
Rheims Way	A3
Rhodaus Town	B4
Rose Lane	B3
Rosemary Lane	B3
St Alphege Lane	B2
St Dunstans Street	A1
St Edmunds Road	B3
St George's Lane	C3
St George's Place	C3
St George's Street	C3
St Gregory's Road	D2
St Johns Lane	B3
St Margaret's Street	B3
St Marys Street	B3
St Peter's Grove	B3
St Peter's Lane	B2
St Peter's Place	A3
St Peters Street	B2
St Radigunds Street	B1
Station Road East	B4
Station Road West	A1
Stour Street	B3
Sturry Road	D1
Sun Street	C2
The Causeway	B1
The Friars	B2
Tourtel Road	D1
Tower Way	B2
Tudor Road	A4
Union Street	D1
Upper Bridge Street	C4
Vernon Place	C4
Victoria Row	C1
Watling Street	B3
Whitehall Gardens	A2
Whitehall Road	A2
Wincheap	A4
York Road	A4

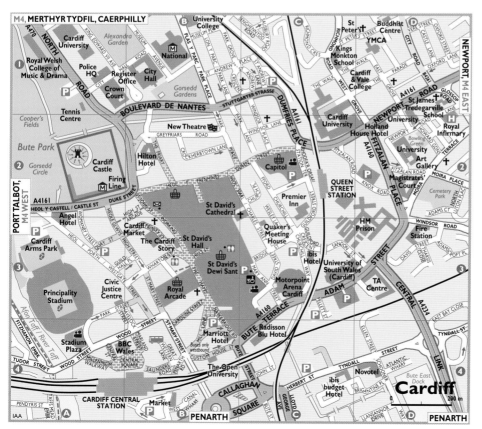

Cardiff

Cardiff is found on atlas page **30 G9**

Adam Street	C3
Adams Court	D2
Adamscroft Place	D3
Atlantic Wharf	D4
Boulevard de Nantes	B1
Bridge Street	C3
Brigantine Place	D4
Bute Street	C4
Bute Terrace	C3
Callaghan Square	B4
Caroline Street	B3
Castle Lane	D1
Castle Street	A2
Central Link	D3
Charles Street	B2
Churchill Way	C2
City Hall Road	A1
City Road	D1
Crockherbtown Lane	B2
Custom House Street	B4
David Street	C3
Davis Street	D3
Duke Street	A2
Dumfries Place	C2
East Bay Close	D3
East Grove	D1
Fford Churchill	C2
Fitzalan Place	D2
Fitzalan Road	D2
Fitzhamon Embankment	A4
Glossop Road	D1
Greyfriars Road	B2
Guildford Street	C3
Guildhall Place	A3
Havelock Street	B3
Hayes Bridge Road	B3
Heol Siarl	B2
Herbert Street	C4
High Street	B3
High Street Arcade	B2
Hills Street	B3
King Edward VII Avenue	A1
Knox Road	D2
Lloyd George Avenue	C4
Mary Ann Street	C3
Mill Lane	B4
Moira Place	D2
Moira Terrace	D2
Museum Avenue	B1
Museum Place	B1
Newport Road	D1
Newport Road Lane	D2
North Luton Place	D2
North Road	A1
Oxford Lane	D1
Oxford Street	D1
Park Grove	B1
Park Lane	B1
Park Place	B1
Park Street	A3
Pellett Street	C3
Pendyris Street	A4
Quay Street	A3
Queen Street	B2
Richmond Crescent	C1
Richmond Road	C1
St Andrew's Crescent	B1
St Andrew's Lane	C1
St Andrew's Place	B1
St John Street	B2
St Mary Street	B3
St Peter's Street	C1
Salisbury Road	C1
Sandon Street	C3
Saunders Road	B4
Schooner Way	D4
Stuttgarter Strasse	B1
The Friary	B2
The Hayes	B3
The Parade	D1
The Walk	C1
Trinity Street	B3
Tudor Street	A4
Tyndall Street	D4
Vere Street	D1
Wesley Lane	C2
West Canal Wharf	B4
West Grove	C1
Westgate Street	A3
Wharton Street	B3
Windsor Lane	C2
Windsor Place	C1
Windsor Road	D3
Womanby Street	A3
Wood Street	A4
Working Street	B3

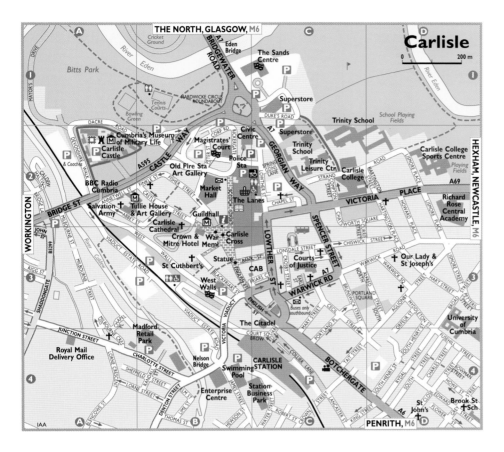

Carlisle

Carlisle is found on atlas page **110 G9**

Abbey Street	A2	Howard Place	D2
Aglionby Street	D3	Howe Street	D4
Annetwell Street	A2	James Street	B4
Bank Street	B3	John Street	A3
Blackfriars Street	B3	Junction Street	A4
Blencowe Street	A4	King Street	C4
Botchergate	C4	Lancaster Street	C4
Bridge Lane	A2	Lime Street	B4
Bridge Street	A2	Lismore Place	D2
Bridgewater Road	B1	Lismore Street	D3
Broad Street	D3	Lonsdale Street	C3
Brunswick Street	C3	Lorne Crescent	A4
Caldew Maltings	A2	Lorne Street	A4
Castle Street	B2	Lowther Street	C3
Castle Way	B2	Mary Street	C3
Cecil Street	C3	Mayor's Drive	A1
Chapel Place	A3	Milbourne Crescent	A3
Chapel Street	C2	Milbourne Street	A3
Charles Street	D4	Myddleton Street	D3
Charlotte Street	B4	North Alfred Street	D3
Chatsworth Square	C2	Orfeur Street	D3
Chiswick Street	C3	Peter Street	B2
Close Street	D4	Petteril Street	D3
Collier Lane	C4	Portland Place	C4
Compton Street	C2	Portland Square	C3
Corp Road	B2	Randall Street	B4
Court Square Brow	C4	Rickergate	B2
Crosby Street	C3	Rigg Street	A3
Crown Street	C4	Robert Street	C4
Currie Street	C3	Rydal Street	D4
Dacre Road	A1	Scotch Street	B2
Denton Street	B4	Shaddongate	A3
Devonshire Walk	A2	Sheffield Street	A4
Duke's Road	C1	South Alfred Street	D3
Edward Street	D4	South Henry Street	D4
Elm Street	B4	Spencer Street	C2
English Street	B3	Spring Gardens Lane	C2
Finkle Street	B2	Strand Road	C2
Fisher Street	B2	Tait Street	C4
Flower Street	D4	Thomas Street	B4
Friars Court	C3	Viaduct Estate Road	A3
Fusehill Street	D4	Victoria Place	C2
Georgian Way	C2	Victoria Viaduct	B4
Grey Street	D4	Warwick Road	C3
Hartington Place	D2	Warwick Square	D3
Hartington Street	D2	Water Street	C4
Hart Street	D3	West Tower Street	B2
Hewson Street	B4	West Walls	B3

Cheltenham

Cheltenham is found on atlas page **46 H10**

Albion Street	C2	Montpellier Parade	B4
All Saints' Road	D2	Montpellier Spa Road	B4
Ambrose Street	B1	Montpellier Street	A4
Argyll Road	D4	Montpellier Terrace	A4
Back Montpellier Terrace	A4	Montpellier Walk	A4
Bath Road	B4	New Street	A1
Bath Street	C3	North Street	B2
Bayshill Road	A3	Old Bath Road	D4
Bayshill Villas Lane	A3	Oriel Road	B3
Bennington Street	B1	Parabola Lane	A3
Berkeley Street	C3	Parabola Road	A3
Burton Street	A1	Park Street	A1
Carlton Street	D3	Pittville Circus	D1
Church Street	B2	Pittville Circus Road	D1
Clarence Parade	B2	Pittville Street	C2
Clarence Road	C1	Portland Street	C1
Clarence Street	B2	Prestbury Road	C1
College Road	C4	Priory Street	D3
Crescent Terrace	B2	Promenade	B3
Devonshire Street	A1	Queens Parade	A3
Duke Street	D3	Regent Street	B2
Dunalley Street	B1	Rodney Road	B3
Evesham Road	C1	Royal Well Lane	A2
Fairview Road	C2	Royal Well Road	B2
Fairview Street	D2	St Anne's Road	D2
Fauconberg Road	A3	St Anne's Terrace	D2
Glenfall Street	D1	St George's Place	B2
Grosvenor Street	C3	St George's Road	A2
Grove Street	A1	St George's Street	B1
Henrietta Street	B1	St James' Square	A2
Hewlett Road	D3	St James Street	C3
High Street	A1	St Johns Avenue	C2
High Street	C2	St Margaret's Road	B1
Imperial Lane	B3	St Paul's Street South	B1
Imperial Square	B3	Sandford Street	C3
Jersey Street	D1	Selkirk Street	D1
Jessop Avenue	A2	Sherborne Street	C2
Keynsham Road	D4	Station Street	A1
King Street	A1	Suffolk Parade	B4
Knapp Road	A1	Swindon Road	B1
Lansdown Road	A4	Sydenham Villas Road	D3
Leighton Road	D2	Trafalgar Street	B4
London Road	D3	Union Street	D2
Malden Road	D1	Wellington Street	C3
Market Street	A1	Winchcombe Street	C2
Milsom Street	A1	Winstonian Road	D1
Monson Avenue	B1	Witcombe Place	C3
Montpellier Grove	B4	York Street	D1

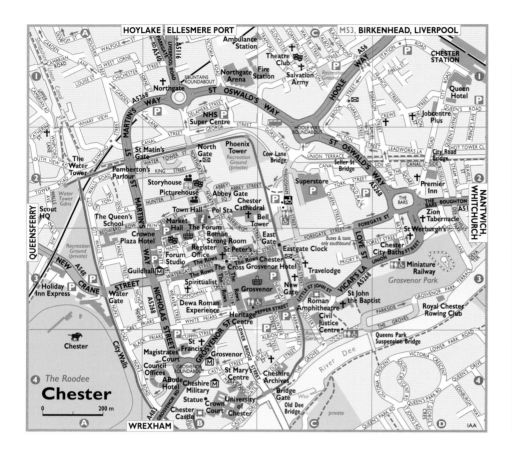

Chester

Chester is found on atlas page **81 N11**

Albion Street.....................C4	Nicholas Street B3
Bath Street.......................D2	Northgate Street................B2
Black Diamond Street C1	Nun's Road A3
Boughton..........................D2	Parkgate Road...................B1
Bouverie Street..................A1	Park Street........................C3
Bridge Street.....................B3	Pepper Street.....................C3
Brook Street......................C1	Princess Street...................B2
Canal Side.........................C2	Priory Place........................C3
Castle Street......................B4	Queen's Park Road..............C4
Charles Street....................C1	Queen's Road......................D1
Chichester Street...............A1	Queen Street......................C2
City Road..........................D2	Raymond Street..................A2
City Walls Road..................A2	Russell Street.....................D2
Commonhall Street..............B3	St Anne Street....................C1
Cornwall Street...................C1	St John's Road....................D4
Crewe Street......................D1	St John Street....................C3
Cuppin Street.....................B4	St Martin's Way A2
Dee Hills Park....................D2	St Mary's Hill.....................B4
Dee Lane...........................D2	St Olave Street....................C4
Delamere Street B1	St Oswald's Way.................B1
Duke Street........................C4	St Werburgh Street..............B2
Eastgate Street...................B3	Samuel Street.....................C2
Egerton Street....................C1	Seller Street.......................D2
Foregate Street...................C2	Shipgate Street...................B4
Forest Street......................C3	Souter's Lane.....................C3
Francis Street.....................D1	South View Road.................A2
Frodsham Street..................C2	Stanley Street.....................A3
Garden Lane.......................A1	Station Road.......................D1
George Street.....................B2	Steam Mill Street................D2
Gloucester Street.................C1	Steele Street.......................C4
Gorse Stacks......................C2	Talbot Street......................C1
Grosvenor Park Terrace.........D3	Tower Road........................A2
Grosvenor Road..................B4	Trafford Street....................C1
Grosvenor Street.................B4	Trinity Street......................B3
Hamilton Place....................B3	Union Street.......................D3
Hoole Way C1	Union Terrace.....................C2
Hunter Street.....................B2	Upper Cambrian Road A1
King Street........................B2	Vicar's Lane.......................C3
Leadworks Lane...................D2	Victoria Crescent.................D4
Little St John Street C3	Victoria Road......................B1
Liverpool Road....................B1	Volunteer Street..................C3
Lorne Street.......................A1	Walpole Street....................A1
Love Street........................C3	Walter Street......................C1
Lower Bridge Street..............B4	Watergate Street.................B3
Lower Park Road..................D4	Water Tower Street...............B2
Milton Street......................C2	Weaver Street.....................B3
New Crane Street A3	White Friars.......................B3
Newgate Street...................C3	York Street.........................C2

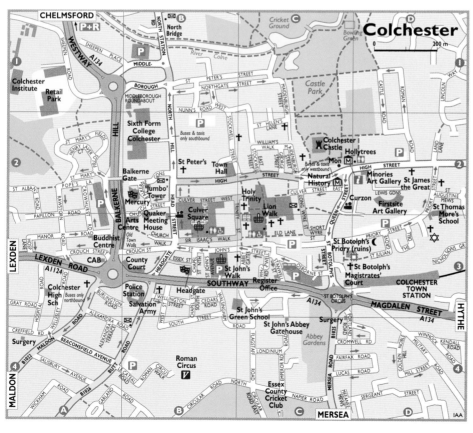

Colchester

Colchester is found on atlas page **52 G6**

Abbey Gates C3	Middleborough Roundabout ...A1
Alexandra Road......................A3	Military Road D4
Balkerne Hill.........................A3	Mill Street...........................D4
Beaconsfield Avenue...............A4	Napier Road........................C4
Burlington Road.....................A3	Nicholsons Green.................D3
Butt Road.............................A4	North Bridge........................B1
Castle Road..........................D1	Northgate Street...................B1
Cedars Road.........................B3	North Hill............................B1
Chapel Street North B3	North Station Road...............B1
Chapel Street South B3	Nunn's Road........................B1
Church Street........................B3	Osborne Street.....................C3
Church Walk.........................B3	Papillon Road.......................A3
Circular Road East C4	Pope's Lane.........................A2
Circular Road North B4	Portland Road......................C4
Creffield Road.......................A4	Priory Street........................D3
Cromwell Road......................C4	Queen Street.......................C3
Crouch Street........................A3	Rawstorn Road.....................A2
Crouch Street........................B3	Roman Circus Walk...............B4
Crowhurst Road.....................A2	Roman Road........................D1
Culver Street East.................C2	St Alban's Road....................A2
Culver Street West.................B2	St Augustine Mews...............D2
East Hill..............................D2	St Botolph's Circus................C3
East Stockwell Street..............C2	St Botolph's Street................C3
Essex Street.........................B3	St Helen's Lane....................C2
Fairfax Road.........................C4	St John's Avenue..................B3
Flagstaff Road......................C4	St John's Street....................B3
Garland Road........................A4	St Julian Grove....................D3
George Street........................C2	St Mary's Fields...................A2
Golden Noble Hill..................D4	St Peter's Street...................B1
Gray Road............................A3	Salisbury Avenue..................A4
Headgate.............................B3	Sheepen Place.....................A1
Head Street..........................B2	Sheepen Road......................A1
Henry Laver Court..................A2	Short Wyre Street..................C3
High Street...........................B2	Sir Isaac's Walk...................B3
Hospital Road A4	South Street.........................B4
Hospital Lane........................A3	Southway............................B3
Land Lane............................D2	Stanwell Street.....................C3
Le Cateau Road.....................B4	Trinity Street.......................B2
Lewis Gardens......................D2	Walsingham Road.................B3
Lexden Road.........................A3	Wellesley Road.....................A4
Long Wyre Street...................C2	Wellington Street..................B3
Lucas Road...........................C4	West Stockwell Street............B1
Magdalen Street....................D3	West Street..........................B4
Maidenburgh Street................C1	Westway..............................A1
Maldon Road.........................A4	Whitewell Road.....................C3
Manor Road A3	Wickham Road......................A4
Mersea Road........................C4	William's Walk......................C2
Middleborough......................B1	Winnock Road......................D4

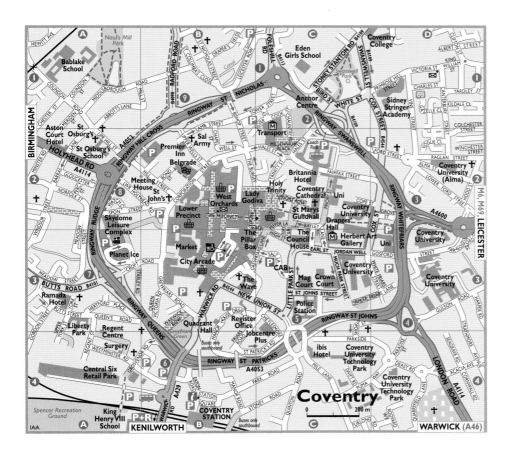

Coventry

Coventry is found on atlas page **59 M9**

Abbotts Lane	A1	Much Park Street	C3
Acacia Avenue	D4	New Union Street	B3
Alma Street	D2	Norfolk Street	A2
Barras Lane	A2	Park Road	B4
Bayley Lane	C2	Parkside	C4
Bird Street	C1	Primrose Hill Street	D1
Bishop Street	B1	Priory Row	C2
Broadgate	B2	Priory Street	C2
Butts Road	A3	Puma Way	C4
Butts Street	A3	Quarryfield Lane	D4
Canterbury Street	D1	Queen's Road	A3
Chester Street	A2	Queen Victoria Road	B3
Cheylesmore	C3	Quinton Road	C4
Cornwall Road	D4	Radford Road	B1
Corporation Street	B2	Raglan Street	D2
Coundon Road	A1	Regent Street	A4
Cox Street	D1	Ringway Hill Cross	A2
Cox Street	D2	Ringway Queens	A3
Croft Road	A3	Ringway Rudge	A3
Earl Street	C3	Ringway St Johns	C3
Eaton Road	B4	Ringway St Nicholas	B1
Fairfax Street	C2	Ringway St Patricks	B4
Foleshill Road	C1	Ringway Swanswell	C1
Gloucester Street	A2	Ringway Whitefriars	D2
Gosford Street	D3	St Johns Street	C3
Greyfriars Lane	B3	St Nicholas Street	B1
Greyfriars Road	B3	Salt Lane	C3
Grosvenor Road	A4	Seagrave Road	D4
Gulson Road	D3	Spon Street	A2
Hales Street	C2	Starley Road	A3
Hertford Place	A3	Stoney Road	B4
High Street	C3	Stoney Stanton Road	C1
Hill Street	B2	Strathmore Avenue	D3
Holyhead Road	A2	Swanswell Street	C1
Jordan Well	C3	The Burges	B2
Lamb Street	B2	Tower Street	B1
Leicester Row	B1	Trinity Street	C2
Little Park Street	C3	Upper Hill Street	B2
London Road	D4	Upper Wells Street	A4
Lower Ford Street	D2	Victoria Street	D1
Lower Holyhead Road	A2	Vine Street	D1
Manor House Drive	B4	Warwick Road	B3
Manor Road	B4	Warwick Road	B4
Meadow Street	A3	Westminster Road	A4
Meriden Street	A1	White Friars Street	D3
Middleborough Road	A1	White Street	C1
Mile Lane	C4	Windsor Street	A3
Mill Street	A1	Yardley Street	D1

Darlington

Darlington is found on atlas page **103 Q8**

Abbey Road	A3	Maude Street	A2
Albert Street	D4	Melland Street	D3
Appleby Close	D4	Neasham Road	D4
Barningham Street	B1	Northgate	C2
Bartlett Street	B1	North Lodge Terrace	B2
Beaumont Street	B3	Northumberland Street	B4
Bedford Street	C4	Oakdene Avenue	A4
Beechwood Avenue	A4	Outram Street	A2
Blackwellgate	B3	Parkgate	D3
Bondgate	B2	Park Lane	D4
Borough Road	D3	Park Place	C4
Brunswick Street	C3	Pendower Street	B1
Brunton Street	D4	Pensbury Street	D4
Chestnut Street	C1	Polam Lane	B4
Cleveland Terrace	A4	Portland Place	A3
Clifton Road	C4	Powlett Street	B3
Commercial Street	B2	Priestgate	C3
Coniscliffe Road	A4	Raby Terrace	B3
Corporation Road	B1	Russell Street	C2
Crown Street	C2	St Augustine's Way	B2
Dodds Street	B1	St Cuthbert's Way	C2
Duke Street	A3	St Cuthbert's Way	C4
Easson Road	B1	St James Place	D4
East Mount Road	D1	Salisbury Terrace	A1
East Raby Street	B3	Salt Yard	B3
East Street	C3	Scarth Street	A4
Elms Road	A2	Skinnergate	B3
Elwin Lane	B4	Southend Avenue	A4
Feethams	C4	Stanhope Road North	A2
Fife Road	A3	Stanhope Road South	A3
Four Riggs	B2	Stonebridge	C3
Freeman's Place	C2	Sun Street	B2
Gladstone Street	B2	Swan Street	C4
Grange Road	B4	Swinburne Road	A3
Greenbank Road	A1	Trinity Road	A2
Greenbank Road	B2	Tubwell Row	B3
Hargreave Terrace	C4	Uplands Road	A3
Haughton Road	D2	Valley Street North	C2
High Northgate	C1	Vane Terrace	A2
High Row	B3	Victoria Embankment	C4
Hollyhurst Road	A1	Victoria Road	B4
Houndgate	B3	Victoria Road	C4
John Street	C1	West Crescent	A2
John Williams Boulevard	D3	West Powlett Street	A3
Kendrew Street	B2	West Row	B3
Kingston Street	B1	West Street	B4
Langholm Crescent	A4	Woodland Road	A2
Larchfield Street	A3	Yarm Road	D3

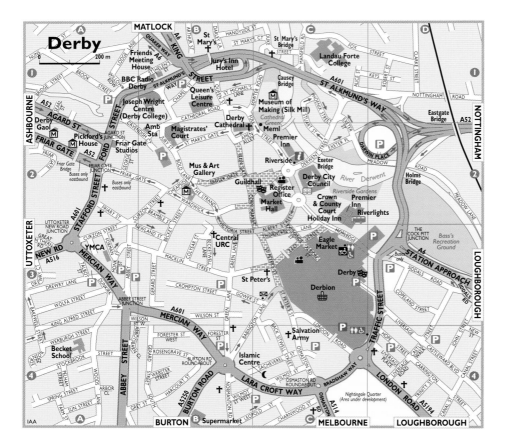

Derby

Derby is found on atlas page **72 B3**

Abbey Street	A4	King Alfred Street	A3
Agard Street	A1	King Street	B1
Albert Street	C3	Lara Croft Way	B4
Babington Lane	B4	Leopold Street	B4
Back Sitwell Street	C4	Liversage Road	D4
Becket Street	B3	Liversage Street	D3
Bold Lane	B2	Lodge Lane	A1
Bradshaw Way	C4	London Road	C3
Bramble Street	B2	Macklin Street	B3
Bridge Street	A1	Mansfield Road	C1
Brook Street	A1	Meadow Lane	D2
Burton Road	B4	Meadow Road	D2
Canal Street	D4	Mercian Way	B3
Carrington Street	D4	Morledge	C3
Cathedral Road	B1	Newland Street	A3
Cavendish Court	A2	New Road	A3
Chapel Street	B1	New Street	D4
Clarke Street	D1	Nottingham Road	D1
Copeland Street	D3	Osmaston Road	C4
Corn Market	B2	Phoenix Street	C1
Crompton Street	B3	Queen Street	B1
Curzon Street	A2	Robert Street	D1
Curzon Street	A3	Rosengrave Street	B4
Darwin Place	C2	Sacheverel Street	C4
Derwent Street	C2	Sadler Gate	B2
Drewry Lane	A3	St Alkmund's Way	C1
Duke Street	C1	St Helen's Street	B1
Dunkirk	A3	St Mary's Gate	B2
East Street	C3	St Peter's Street	C3
Exchange Street	C3	Siddals Road	D3
Exeter Place	C2	Sowter Road	C1
Exeter Street	C2	Spring Street	A4
Ford Street	A2	Stafford Street	A3
Forester Street West	B4	Station Approach	D3
Forman Street	A3	Stockbrook Street	A4
Fox Street	C1	Stuart Street	C1
Friary Street	A2	Sun Street	A4
Full Street	B1	The Cock Pitt	D3
Gerard Street	B3	The Strand	B2
Gower Street	B3	Thorntree Lane	C3
Green Lane	B3	Traffic Street	D4
Grey Street	A4	Trinity Street	D4
Handyside Street	B1	Victoria Street	B2
Harcourt Street	B4	Wardwick	B2
Iron Gate	B2	Werburgh Street	A4
John Street	D4	Wilmot Street	C4
Jury Street	B2	Wolfa Street	A3
Keys Street	D1	Woods Lane	A4

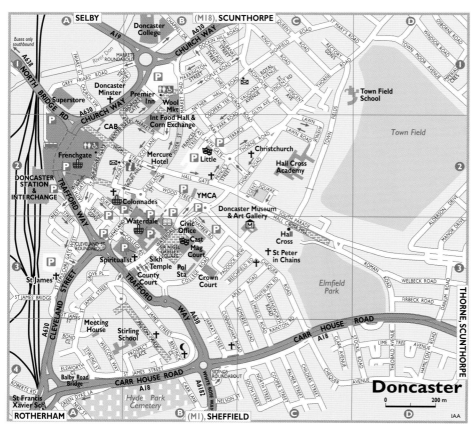

Doncaster

Doncaster is found on atlas page **91 P10**

Alderson Drive	D3	Nelson Street	B4
Apley Road	B3	Nether Hall Road	B1
Balby Road Bridge	A4	North Bridge Road	A1
Beechfield Road	B3	North Street	C4
Broxholme Lane	C1	Osborne Road	D1
Carr House Road	C4	Palmer Street	C4
Carr Lane	B4	Park Road	B2
Chamber Road	B3	Park Terrace	B2
Chequer Avenue	C4	Prince's Street	B2
Chequer Road	C3	Priory Place	A2
Childers Street	C4	Prospect Place	B4
Christ Church Road	B1	Queen's Road	C1
Church View	A1	Rainton Road	C4
Church Way	B1	Ravensworth Road	C3
Clark Avenue	C4	Rectory Gardens	C1
Cleveland Street	A4	Regent Square	C2
College Road	B3	Roman Road	D3
Cooper Street	C4	Royal Avenue	C1
Coopers Terrace	B2	St Georges Gate	B2
Copley Road	B1	St James Street	B4
Cunningham Road	B3	St Mary's Road	C1
Danum Road	D3	St Sepulchre Gate	B2
Dockin Hill Road	B1	St Sepulchre Gate West	A3
Duke Street	A2	St Vincent Avenue	C1
East Laith Gate	B2	St Vincent Road	C1
Elmfield Road	C3	Scot Lane	B2
Firbeck Road	D3	Silver Street	B2
Frances Street	B2	Somerset Road	B3
Glyn Avenue	C1	South Parade	C2
Green Dyke Lane	A4	South Street	C4
Grey Friars' Road	A1	Spring Gardens	A2
Hall Cross Hill	C2	Stirling Street	A4
Hall Gate	B2	Stockil Road	C4
Hamilton Road	D4	Theobald Avenue	D4
Harrington Street	B1	Thorne Road	C1
High Street	A2	Town Fields	C2
Highfield Road	C1	Town Moor Avenue	D1
Jarratt Street	B4	Trafford Way	A2
King's Road	C1	Vaughan Avenue	C1
Lawn Avenue	C2	Waterdale	B3
Lawn Road	C2	Welbeck Road	D3
Lime Tree Avenue	D4	Welcome Way	A4
Manor Drive	D3	West Laith Gate	A2
Market Place	A2	West Street	A3
Market Road	B1	Whitburn Road	C3
Milbanke Street	B1	White Rose Way	B4
Milton Walk	B4	Windsor Road	D1
Montague Street	B1	Wood Street	B2

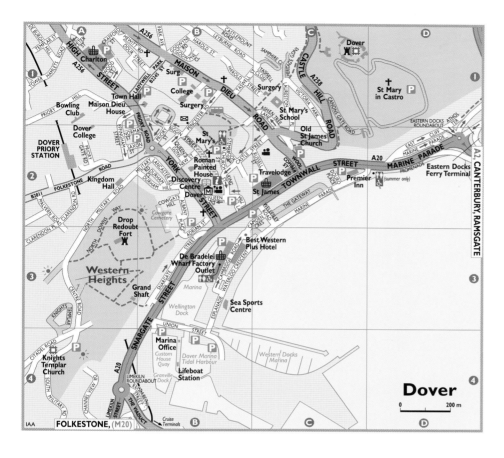

Dover

Dover is found on atlas page **27 P3**

Adrian Street B3
Albany Place B2
Ashen Tree Lane..................C1
Athol Terrace......................D1
Biggin Street B2
Cambridge Road B3
Camden Crescent C2
Canons Gate Road C1
Castle Hill Road C1
Castlemount Road B1
Castle Street......................B2
Centre Road A3
Channel View Road A4
Church Street B2
Citadel Road A4
Clarendon Place A3
Clarendon Road A2
Cowgate Hill B2
Crafford Street A1
De Burgh Hill A1
Douro Place C2
Dour Street A1
Durham Close B2
Durham Hill........................B2
East Cliff D2
Eastern Docks
    Roundabout D2
Effingham Street A2
Elizabeth Street A4
Esplanade B3
Folkestone Road A2
Godwyne Close B1
Godwyne Road..................B1
Harold Street B1
Harold Street B1
Heritage Gardens..............C1
Hewitt Road A1
High Street A1
King Street B2
Knights Templar A3
Ladywell A1
Lancaster Road B2
Laureston Place C1
Leyburne Road..................B1
Limekiln Roundabout........A4
Limekiln Street A4
Maison Dieu Road............B1
Malvern Road....................A2

Marine Parade....................C2
Marine Parade....................D2
Military Road B2
Mill Lane B2
New Street B2
Norman Street A2
North Downs Way A3
North Military Road A3
Park Avenue......................B1
Park Street B1
Pencester Road B2
Peter Street A1
Priory Gate Road..............A2
Priory Hill..........................A1
Priory Road A1
Priory Street B2
Promenade D2
Queen's Gardens..............B2
Queen Street B2
Russell Street....................B2
Samphire Close..................C1
Saxon Street A2
Snargate Street A4
South Military Road A4
Stembrook B2
Taswell Close C1
Taswell Street B1
Templar Street A1
The Viaduct A4
Tower Hamlets Road..........A1
Townwall Street C2
Union Street B3
Victoria Park C1
Waterloo Crescent B3
Wellesley Road C2
Wood Street......................A1
Woolcomber Street............C2
York Street........................B2

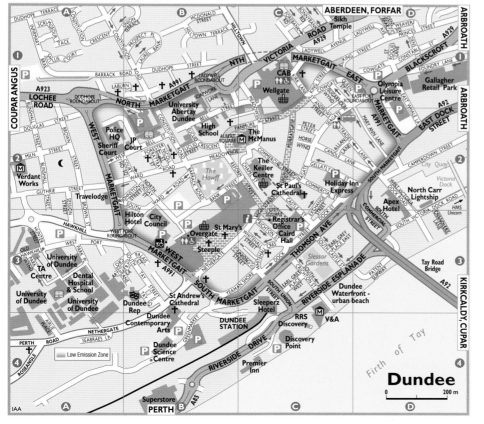

Dundee

Dundee is found on atlas page **142 G11**

Albert Square......................B2
Bank Street B2
Barrack Road A1
Barrack Road B1
Bell Street B2
Blackscroft D1
Blinshall Street A1
Blinshall Street A2
Bonnybank Road C1
Brown Street A2
Candle Lane C2
Castle Street......................C2
Chapel Street C2
City Square C3
Commercial Street............C2
Constable Street D1
Constitution Crescent........A1
Constitution Road A1
Constitution Road B2
Court House Square A2
Cowgate............................C1
Cowgate............................D1
Crichton Street C3
Dock Street........................C3
Douglas Street A2
Dudhope Street B1
East Dock Street D2
East Marketgait C1
East Whale Lane D1
Euclid Crescent B2
Euclid Street......................B2
Exchange Street................C3
Forebank Road..................C1
Foundry Lane D1
Gellatly Street C2
Greenmarket......................B4
Guthrie Street A2
Hawkhill A3
High Street C3
Hilltown B1
Hilltown Terrace................B1
Hunter Street A3
Infirmary Brae A1
Johnston Street B2
King Street C1
Kirk Lane C1
Laburn Street A1
Ladywell Avenue................C1

Laurel Bank B1
Lochee Road A1
McDonald Street D2
Meadowside........................B2
Miln Street A2
Murraygate C2
Nethergate A4
North Lindsay Street B2
North Marketgait................B1
North Victoria Road C1
Old Hawkhill......................A3
Panmure Street B2
Perth Road A4
Princes Street D1
Prospect Place B1
Queen Street C1
Reform Street B2
Riverside Drive..................B4
Riverside Esplanade..........C3
Roseangle A4
St Andrews Street C1
Scrimgeour Place..............A1
Seabraes Lane A4
Seagate..............................C2
Session Street A2
South Castle Street............C3
South Commercial Street ..D3
South Crichton Street........C3
South Marketgait B3
South Tay Street................B3
South Union Street............C3
South Victoria Dock Road ..D3
South Ward Road..............B2
Sugarhouse Wynd..............C1
Tay Road Bridge D3
Tay Square B3
Thomson Avenue C3
Trades Lane C2
Union Street B3
Union Terrace B1
Ward Road B2
Weavers Yard....................D1
West Marketgait................A2
West Port A3
West Victoria Dock Road ..D3
Whitehall Crescent............C3
Whitehall Street................C3
Yeaman Shore....................B3

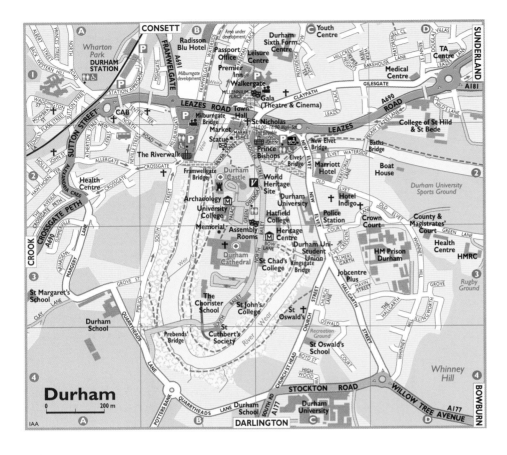

Durham

Durham

Durham is found on atlas page **103 Q2**

Albert Street A1	Mayorswell Close D1
Alexandria Crescent...............A2	Milburngate Bridge B1
Allergate A2	Millburngate..........................B2
Atherton Street......................A2	Millennium Place B1
Back Western Hill...................A1	Mowbray Street A1
Bakehouse Lane......................C1	Neville Street A2
Baths Bridge...........................C2	New Elvet...............................C2
Bow Lane C3	New Elvet Bridge....................C2
Boyd Street C4	New Street..............................A2
Briardene A3	North Bailey C3
Church Lane............................C3	North Road A1
Church Street C4	Old Elvet................................C2
Church Street Head................C4	Oswald Court C3
Clay Lane A3	Owengate................................B2
Claypath.................................C1	Palace Green...........................B2
Court Lane C3	Palmers Garth.........................C3
Crossgate A2	Pelaw Leazes Lane D2
Crossgate Peth.......................A3	Pimlico...................................A3
Douglas Villas........................ D1	Potters Bank...........................B4
Elvet Bridge............................C2	Prebends' Bridge.....................B4
Elvet Crescent.........................C3	Princes' Street A1
Elvet Waterside......................C2	Providence Row.......................C1
Finney Terrace........................C1	Quarryheads Lane A3
Flass Street.............................A2	Redhills Lane A2
Framwelgate...........................B1	Renny Street D1
Framwelgate Waterside...........B1	Saddler Street B2
Framwellgate Bridge..............B2	St Hild's Lane D1
Freeman Place B1	Silver Street............................B2
Gilesgate................................C1	South Bailey B3
Green Lane D3	South Road C4
Grove Street...........................A3	South Street B3
Hallgarth Street......................C3	Station Approach....................A1
Hawthorn Terrace...................A2	Stockton Road C4
Highgate.................................B1	Summerville............................A3
High Street C2	Sutton Street A2
High Wood View.....................C1	Tenter Terrace A1
Hillcrest..................................C1	Territorial Lane........................C2
Holly Street A2	The Avenue.............................A2
Illingworth Grove................... D3	The Hallgarth D3
John Street A2	Waddington Street A1
Keiper Heights C1	Wear View C1
Kingsgate Bridge....................C3	Whinney Hill D3
Leazes Lane D1	Willow Tree Avenue D4
Leazes Place C1	
Leazes Road B1	
Margery Lane..........................A3	
Market Place B2	
Mavin Street C3	

Eastbourne

Eastbourne is found on atlas page **25 P11**

Arlington Road.......................A2	Langney Road D1
Ashford Road B2	Langney Road C2
Ashford Road C1	Lascelles Terrace B4
Ashford Square B1	Latimer Road D1
Avenue Lane A1	Leaf Road...............................B1
Belmore Road C1	Lismore Road..........................B2
Blackwater Road A4	Longstone Road.......................C1
Bolton Road B3	Lushington Road.....................B3
Bourne Street..........................C1	Marine Parade D2
Burlington Place......................B3	Marine Road D1
Burlington Road......................C3	Mark Lane B2
Camden Road A2	Meads Road A3
Carew Road B1	Melbourne Road C1
Carlisle Road...........................A4	Old Orchard Road A2
Carlisle Road...........................B4	Old Wish Road A4
Cavendish Avenue...................C1	Pevensey Road........................C2
Cavendish Place C1	Promenade..............................C3
Ceylon Place C2	Queen's Gardens..................... D2
Chiswick Place B3	Saffrons Road A2
College Road...........................B3	St Anne's Road A1
Colonnade Gardens................. D2	St Aubyn's Road D1
Commercial Road B1	St Leonard's Road....................B1
Compton Street B4	Seaside...................................D1
Compton Street C3	Seaside Road C2
Cornfield Lane.........................B3	Southfields Road......................A2
Cornfield Road B2	South Street A3
Cornfield Terrace.....................B3	South Street B3
Devonshire Place B3	Spencer Road...........................B3
Dursley Road...........................C1	Station Parade A2
Elms Road C3	Station Street B2
Enys Road A1	Susan's Road C2
Eversfield Road A1	Sutton Road B2
Furness Road A3	Sydney Road C1
Gildredge Road B2	Terminus Road A2
Grand Parade C3	Terminus Road C3
Grange Road A3	The Avenue.............................A1
Grassington Road A3	Tideswell Road........................C2
Grove Road A3	Trinity Place C3
Hardwick Road........................B3	Trinity Trees............................B3
Hartfield Lane A1	Upper Avenue.........................B1
Hartfield Road A1	Upperton Gardens...................A1
Hartington Place......................C3	Upperton Road........................A1
Howard Square........................C4	West Street..............................A3
Hyde Gardens.........................B2	West Terrace...........................A2
Hyde Road A2	Willowfield Road..................... D1
Ivy Terrace A2	Wilmington Square..................B4
Jevington Gardens..................A4	Wish Road B3
Junction Road.........................B2	York Road A3

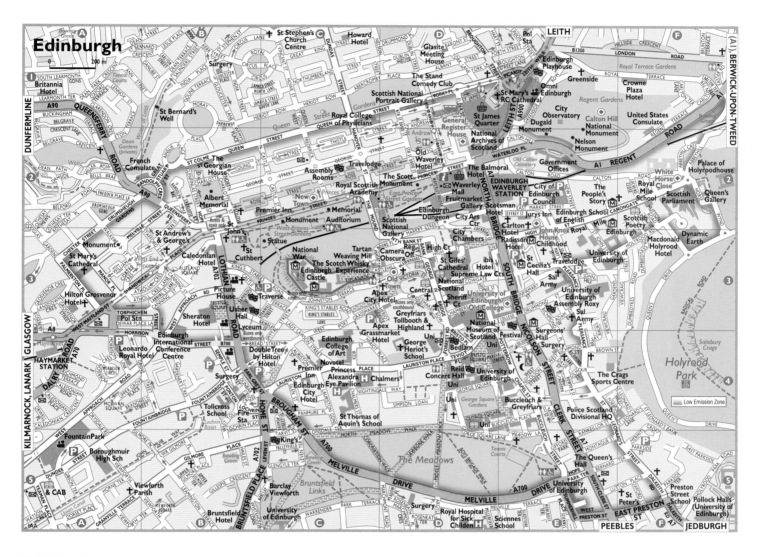

Edinburgh

Edinburgh is found on atlas page **127 P3**

Abbeyhill F2
Abercromby Place C1
Adam Street E3
Albany Street D1
Ann Street A1
Argyle Place D5
Atholl Crescent Lane A3
Bank Street D3
Barclay Terrace C5
Belford Road A2
Belgrave Crescent A2
Bernard Terrace E5
Boys Brigade Walk D5
Brandfield Street A4
Bread Street B4
Bristo Place D4
Brougham Street C4
Broughton Street D1
Broughton Street Lane E1
Bruntsfield Place B5
Buccleuch Place D4
Buccleuch Street E4
Caledonian Place A4
Caledonian Road A4
Caledonian Street A4
Calton Road E2
Candlemaker Row D3
Canning Street B3
Canongate E2
Carlton Terrace F1
Castle Hill C3
Castle Street C2
Castle Terrace B3
Chalmers Street C4
Chambers Street D3

Chapel Street E4
Charlotte Square B2
Chester Street Gardens A3
Circus Lane B1
Circus Place B1
Clarendon Crescent A1
Clerk Street E4
Cockburn Street D2
Cowan's Close E4
Cowgate D3
Coronation Walk C5
Dalkeith Road F5
Dalry Road A4
Danube Street B1
Davie Street E4
Dean Park Crescent A1
Dean Street A1
Dewar Place Lane A3
Douglas Gardens A3
Doune Terrace B1
Drummond Street E3
Dublin Street D1
Dumbiedykes Road F3
Dunbar Street B4
Dundas Street C1
Dundee Street A5
Earl Grey Street B4
Easter Road F1
East Market Street E2
East Parkside F5
East Preston Street F5
Elder Street D1
Forth Street D1
Fountainbridge A4
Frederick Street C2

Gardener's Crescent B4
George IV Bridge D3
George Square D4
George Square Lane D5
George Street B2
George Street C2
Gifford Park E5
Gillespie Crescent B5
Gilmore Park A5
Gilmore Place B5
Gilmour Street E4
Glenfinlas Street B2
Gloucester Lane B1
Granville Terrace A5
Great King Street C1
Great Stuart Street B2
Greenmarket C3
Greenside Row E1
Grindlay Street B3
Grosvenor Street A3
Grove Street A4
Haddon's Court E4
Hanover Street C2
Haymarket Terrace A4
Heriot Row C1
Hermits Croft F5
High Street D3
High Street E3
Hillside Crescent E1
Hill Street C2
Holyrood Park Road F5
Holyrood Road E3
Home Street C4
Hope Street B2
Horse Wynd F2
Howden Street E4
Howe Street C1
India Place B1
India Street B1
Jamaica Street South Lane B1
Jawbone Walk D5

Jeffrey Street E2
Johnston Terrace C3
Keir Street C4
Kerr Street B1
King's Stables Road B3
Lady Lawson Street C4
Lansdowne Crescent A3
Lauriston Gardens C4
Lauriston Place C4
Lauriston Street C4
Lawnmarket D3
Leamington Terrace B5
Leith Street E1
Leith Walk E1
Lennox Street A1
Leven Place C5
Lochrin Place B4
Lochrin Street B4
London Road E1
Lothian Road B3
Lower Gilmore Place B5
Lutton Place E5
Lynedoch Place Lane A2
Manor Place A2
Marchmont Crescent D5
Marchmont Road D5
Market Street D2
Meadow Lane E5
Melville Drive C5
Melville Street A3
Melville Terrace D5
Middle Meadow Walk D5
Millerfield Place D5
Miller Row A2
Moncrieff Terrace E5
Montague Street E5
Moray Place B1
Morrison Link A4
Morrison Street A4
Mound Place D3
Nelson Street C1

New Street E2
Nicolson Square E4
Nicolson Street E4
Nightingale Way C4
North Bridge D2
North Castle Street C2
North Meadow Walk C5
North St Andrew Street D1
North St David Street D1
Northumberland Street C1
Oxford Street F5
Palmerston Place A3
Panmure Place C4
Pleasance E3
Ponton Street B4
Potterrow E4
Princes Street C2
Queens Drive F3
Queensferry Road A1
Queensferry Street B2
Queen Street B2
Radical Road F3
Ramsay Lane C3
Randolph Crescent B2
Randolph Lane B2
Rankeillor Street E5
Regent Road E2
Richmond Place E3
Rose Street B2
Roseneath Place D5
Rothesay Place A3
Royal Circus B1
Royal Terrace E1
St Andrew Square D1
St Bernard's Crescent A1
St Colme Street B2
St James Place D1
St Leonard's Bank F4
St Leonard's Hill E4
St Leonard's Lane F4
St Leonard's Street E4

St Patrick Street E4
St Stephen Street B1
St Vincent Street C1
Saunders Street B1
Sciennes E5
Semple Street B4
Shandwick Place A3
Simpson Loan D4
South Bridge E3
South Charlotte Street B2
South Clerk Street E5
South Learmonth Gardens A1
South St Andrew Street D2
South St David Street D2
Spittal Street C4
Stafford Street B3
Tarvit Street C5
The Mound C2
Thistle Street C2
Torphichen Street A3
Union Street E1
Upper Gilmore Place B5
Victoria Street D3
Viewcraig Gardens E4
Viewcraig Street F3
Viewforth A5
Walker Street A3
Warrender Park Terrace C5
Waterloo Place D2
Waverley Bridge D2
West Approach Road A5
West Maitland Street A3
West Nicolson Street E4
West Port C4
West Richmond Street E4
West Toll Cross B4
William Street A3
Yeaman Place A5
York Lane D1
York Place D1
Young Street B2

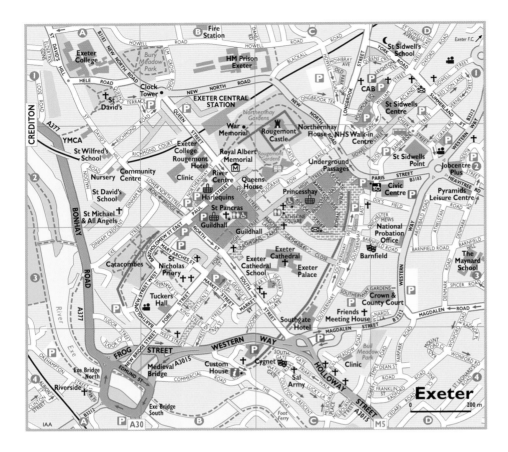

Exeter

Exeter is found on atlas page **9 M6**

Acland Road	D1	King Street	B3
Archibald Road	D3	King William Street	D1
Athelstan Road	D3	Longbrook Street	C1
Bailey Street	C2	Lower North Street	B2
Bampfylde Lane	C2	Magdalen Road	D3
Bampfylde Street	D2	Magdalen Street	C4
Barnfield Road	D3	Market Street	B3
Bartholomew Street East	B3	Martins Lane	C2
Bartholomew Street West	B3	Mary Arches Street	B3
Bear Street	C3	Musgrave Row	C2
Bedford Street	C2	New Bridge Street	A4
Belgrave Road	D2	New North Road	A1
Blackall Road	C1	Northernhay Street	B2
Bonhay Road	A2	North Street	B3
Bude Street	D2	Old Park Road	C1
Bull Meadow Road	C4	Oxford Road	D1
Castle Street	C2	Palace Gate	C3
Cathedral Close	C3	Paris Street	D2
Cathedral Yard	B3	Paul Street	B2
Cedars Road	D4	Preston Street	B4
Cheeke Street	D1	Princesshay	C2
Chichester Mews	C3	Queens Crescent	C1
Commercial Road	B4	Queen's Terrace	A1
Coombe Street	B3	Queen Street	B1
Deanery Place	C3	Radford Road	D4
Dean Street	D4	Richmond Court	B2
Denmark Road	D3	Richmond Road	A2
Dinham Crescent	A3	Roberts Road	C4
Dinham Road	A2	Roman Walk	C2
Dix's Field	D2	St David's Hill	A1
Eastgate	C2	Sidwell Street	C2
Edmund Street	A4	Sidwell Street	D1
Elm Grove Road	B1	Smythen Street	B3
Exe Street	A3	Southernhay East	C3
Fairpark Road	D4	Southernhay Gardens	C3
Fore Street	B3	Southernhay West	C3
Franklin Street	D4	South Street	B3
Friernhay Street	B3	Spicer Road	D3
Frog Street	A4	Summerland Street	D1
George Street	B3	Temple Road	D4
Guinea Street	B3	Tudor Court	A4
Haldon Road	A2	Tudor Street	A3
Heavitree Road	D2	Verney Street	D1
Hele Road	A1	Well Street	D1
High Street	C2	Western Way	B4
Holloway Street	C4	West Street	B4
Howell Road	B1	Wonford Road	D4
Iron Bridge	B2	York Road	D1

Gloucester

Gloucester is found on atlas page **46 F11**

Albert Street	D4	Millbrook Street	D4
Albion Street	B4	Montpellier	B4
All Saints' Road	D4	Napier Street	D4
Alvin Street	C2	Nettleton Road	C3
Archdeacon Street	B2	New Inn Lane	C3
Arthur Street	C4	Norfolk Street	B4
Barbican Road	B3	Northgate Street	C3
Barrack Square	B3	Old Tram Road	B4
Barton Street	D4	Over Causeway	A1
Bedford Street	C3	Oxford Road	D1
Belgrave Road	C4	Oxford Street	D2
Berkeley Street	B3	Park Road	C4
Black Dog Way	C2	Park Street	C2
Blenheim Road	D4	Parliament Street	B3
Brunswick Road	B4	Pembroke Street	C4
Brunswick Square	B4	Pitt Street	B2
Bruton Way	D3	Priory Road	B1
Bull Lane	B3	Quay Street	B2
Castle Meads Way	A2	Royal Oak Road	A2
Clarence Street	C3	Russell Street	B3
Clare Street	B2	St Aldate Street	C2
College Court	B2	St Catherine Street	C1
Commercial Road	B3	St John's Lane	B3
Cromwell Street	C4	St Mark Street	C1
Cross Keys Lane	B3	St Mary's Square	B2
Deans Walk	C1	St Mary's Street	B2
Eastgate Street	C3	St Michael's Square	B3
Gouda Way	B1	St Oswald's Road	B1
Great Western Road	D2	Sebert Street	C1
Greyfriars	B3	Severn Road	A3
Hampden Way	C3	Sherborne Street	D2
Hare Lane	C2	Sinope Street	D4
Heathville Road	D2	Southgate Street	B4
Henry Road	D1	Spa Road	B4
Henry Street	D2	Station Road	C3
High Orchard Street	A4	Swan Road	C1
Honyatt Road	D1	Sweetbriar Street	C1
Kings Barton Street	C4	The Cross	B3
Kingsholm Road	C1	The Oxebode	C3
King's Square	C3	The Quay	A2
Ladybellegate Street	B3	Union Street	C1
Llanthony Road	A4	Upper Quay Street	B2
London Road	D2	Vauxhall Road	D4
Longsmith Street	B3	Wellington Street	C3
Market Parade	C3	Westgate Street	A2
Merchants' Road	A4	Widden Street	D4
Mercia Road	B1	Worcester Parade	C2
Metz Way	D3	Worcester Street	C2

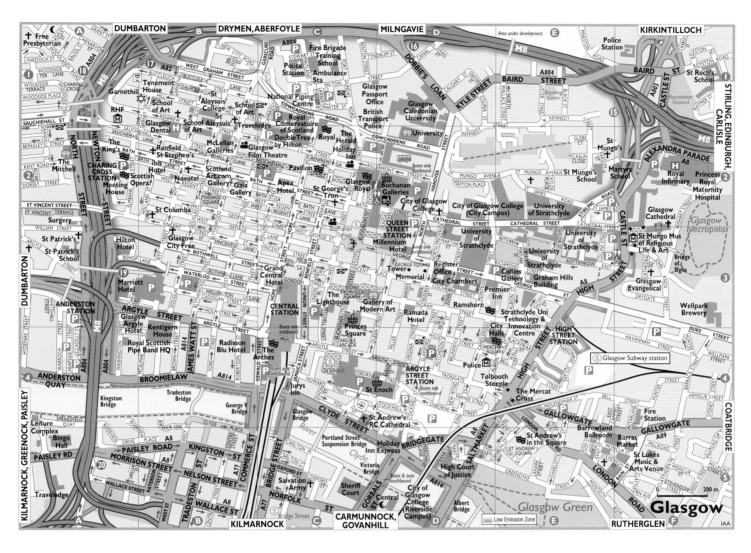

Glasgow

Glasgow is found on atlas page **125 P4**

Albert Bridge	D5	Candleriggs	D4	Gallowgate	E4	Lanark Street	E5	Paterson Street	B5	Steel Street	D5
Albion Street	D4	Carlton Place	C5	Garnethill Street	B1	Larbert Street	C1	Pinkston Road	E1	Stevenson Street	F5
Albion Street	E3	Carnarvon Street	A1	Garnet Street	B2	Lister Street	E1	Pitt Street	B2	Stewart Street	C1
Alexandra Parade	F2	Castle Street	F1	Garscube Road	C1	London Road	E4	Port Dundas Road	C1	Stirling Road	E2
Anderston Quay	A4	Castle Street	F2	Garth Street	D3	Maitland Street	C1	Portland Street		Stockwell Place	D4
Argyle Arcade	C4	Cathedral Square	F3	George Square	D3	Martha Street	D3	Suspension Bridge	C5	Stockwell Street	D4
Argyle Street	A3	Cathedral Street	D2	George Street	E3	Mart Street	D5	Queen Street	C4	Suffolk Street	E5
Armour Street	F4	Centre Street	B5	George V Bridge	B4	Maxwell Street	C4	Renfield Lane	C3	Sydney Street	F4
Ashley Street	A1	Chalmer Street	F5	Glasgow Bridge	C5	McAlpine Street	B4	Renfield Street	C3	Taylor Place	E2
Bain Street	F5	Charing Cross	A1	Glassford Street	D4	McAslin Close	E2	Renfrew Lane	C2	Taylor Street	E2
Baird Street	E1	Charles Street	F1	Glebe Court	E2	McFarlane Street	F4	Renfrew Street	B1	Tradeston Bridge	B4
Baliol Street	A1	Charlotte Street	E5	Gorbals Street	C5	McPhater Street	C1	Renton Street	C1	Tradeston Street	B5
Barrack Street	F4	Cheapside Street	A4	Gordon Street	C3	Merchant Lane	D5	Rhymer Street	F1	Trongate	D4
Bath Lane	B2	Claythorn Avenue	F5	Grafton Place	D2	Miller Street	D4	Richmond Street	E3	Turnbull Street	D5
Bath Street	A2	Claythorn Park	F5	Granville Street	A2	Millroad Drive	F5	Riverview Drive	A4	Tyndrum Street	C1
Bell Street	E4	Clyde Place	B4	Greendyke Street	E5	Millroad Street	F5	Robertson Street	B4	Union Street	C3
Berkeley Street	A2	Clyde Street	C4	Green Street	F5	Milton Street	C1	Rose Street	B2	Virginia Street	D4
Blackfriars Street	E4	Cochrane Street	D3	Hanover Street	D3	Mitchell Street	C4	Ross Street	E5	Wallace Street	A5
Black Street	E1	Collins Street	E3	High Street	E4	Moir Street	E5	Rottenrow	E3	Walls Street	E4
Blythswood Square	B2	Commerce Street	B5	Hill Street	B1	Molendinar Street	E5	Rottenrow East	E3	Warroch Street	A4
Blythswood Street	B3	Couper Street	D1	Holland Street	B2	Moncur Street	E5	Royal Exchange Square	C3	Washington Street	A4
Bothwell Lane	B3	Cowcaddens Road	C1	Holm Street	B3	Monteith Row	E5	Royston Road	F1	Waterloo Street	B3
Bothwell Street	B3	Dalhousie Lane	B1	Hope Street	C3	Montrose Street	D3	Royston Square	F1	Wellington Lane	B3
Bridgegate	D5	Dixon Street	C4	Howard Street	C4	Morrison Street	A5	St Andrew's Square	E5	Wellington Street	B3
Bridge of Sighs	F3	Dobbie's Loan	D1	Hunter Street	F4	Nelson Street	B5	St Andrew's Street	E4	Wellpark Street	F4
Bridge Street	C5	Dorset Street	A2	Hutcheson Street	D4	New City Road	B1	St James Road	E2	West Campbell Street	B3
Broomielaw	B4	Douglas Street	B3	Hydepark Street	A4	Newton Street	A2	St Mungo Avenue	D2	West George Lane	B2
Brown Street	B4	Drury Street	C3	Ingram Street	D3	New Wynd	D4	St Vincent Lane	B3	West George Street	B2
Brunswick Street	D4	Drygate	F3	Jamaica Street	C4	Norfolk Street	C5	St Vincent Place	C3	West Graham Street	B1
Buccleuch Lane	B1	Duke Street	F4	James Watt Street	B4	North Frederick Street	D3	St Vincent Street	A2	West Nile Street	C3
Buccleuch Street	B1	Dundas Street	D3	John Knox Street	F3	North Hanover Street	D3	St Vincent Terrace	A2	West Regent Lane	C2
Buchanan Street	C4	Dunlop Street	D4	John Street	D3	North Portland Street	E3	Saltmarket	D5	West Regent Street	B2
Cadogan Street	B3	Dyer's Lane	E5	Kennedy Street	D2	North Street	A2	Sauchiehall Lane	A2	West Street	B5
Calgary Street	D1	East Campbell Street	E4	Kennedy Street	E1	North Wallace Street	E1	Sauchiehall Street	A1	William Street	A3
Cambridge Street	C1	Elmbank Street	A2	Kent Road	A2	Osborne Street	C4	Sauchiehall Street	B2	Wilson Street	D4
Canal Street	D1	Fox Street	C4	Kent Street	E5	Oswald Street	C4	Scott Street	B1	Wishart Street	F3
				Killermont Street	C2	Oxford Street	C5	Shipbank Lane	D5	Woodlands Road	A1
				Kingston Bridge	A5	Paisley Road	A5	Shuttle Street	E3	Woodside Crescent	A1
				Kingston Street	B5	Parnie Street	D4	South Frederick Street	D3	Woodside Terrace	A1
				King Street	D4	Parsonage Square	E4	Springfield Quay	A4	Woodside Terrace Lane	A1
				Kyle Street	D1	Parson Street	E2	Stafford Street	D1	York Street	B4

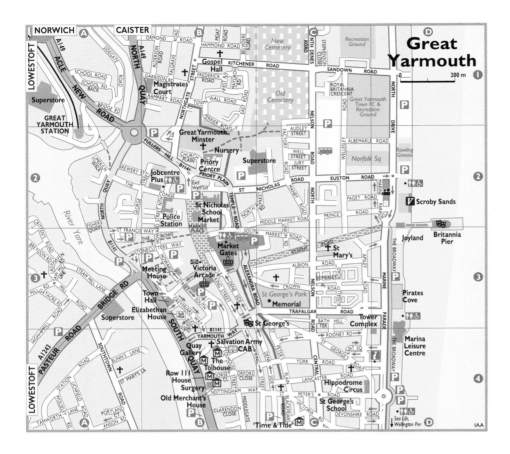

Great Yarmouth

Great Yarmouth is found on atlas page **77 Q10**

Acle New Road	A1	North Drive	D1
Albemarle Road	C2	North Market Road	C2
Albion Road	C3	North Quay	A2
Alderson Road	B1	Northgate Street	B1
Alexandra Road	B3	Nottingham Way	B4
Apsley Road	C3	Ormond Road	B1
Belvidere Road	B1	Paget Road	C2
Blackfriars Road	C4	Palgrave Road	B1
Brewery Street	A2	Pasteur Road	A4
Breydon Road	A3	Prince's Road	C2
Bridge Road	A1	Priory Plain	B2
Bridge Road	A3	Queen Street	B4
Bunn's Lane	A4	Rampart Road	B1
Church Plain	B2	Regent Road	C3
Critten's Road	A3	Rodney Road	C4
Crown Road	C3	Russell Road	C3
Dene Side	B3	St Francis Way	A3
Devonshire Road	C4	St George's Road	C4
East Road	B1	St Nicholas Road	B2
Euston Road	C2	St Peter's Plain	C4
Factory Road	C2	St Peter's Road	C4
Ferrier Road	B1	Sandown Road	C1
Fishers Quay	A2	Saw Mill Lane	A3
Frederick Road	B1	School Road	A1
Fullers Hill	B2	School Road Back	A1
Garrison Road	B1	Sidegate Road	A1
Gatacre Road	A3	South Market Road	C3
George Street	A2	South Quay	B3
Greyfriars Way	B3	Southtown Road	A4
Hammond Road	B1	Station Road	A4
High Mill Road	A3	Steam Mill Lane	A3
Howard Street North	B2	Stephenson Close	C1
Howard Street South	B3	Stonecutters Way	B3
King Street	B3	Tamworth Lane	A4
Kitchener Road	B1	Temple Road	B2
Ladyhaven Road	A3	The Broadway	D3
Lancaster Road	C4	The Conge	A2
Lichfield Road	A4	The Rows	B3
Limekiln Walk	A2	Tolhouse Street	B4
Manby Road	C2	Town Wall Road	B1
Marine Parade	D3	Trafalgar Road	C3
Maygrove Road	B1	Union Road	C3
Middle Market Road	C2	Victoria Road	C4
Middlegate	B4	Wellesley Road	C2
Moat Road	B1	West Road	B1
Nelson Road Central	C3	Wolseley Road	A4
Nelson Road North	C1	Yarmouth Way	B4
North Denes Road	C1	York Road	C4

Guildford

Guildford is found on atlas page **23 Q5**

Abbot Road	C4	Millmead	B3
Angel Gate	B3	Millmead Terrace	B4
Artillery Road	B1	Mount Pleasant	A4
Artillery Terrace	C1	Nightingale Road	D1
Bedford Road	A2	North Street	B3
Bridge Street	A3	Onslow Road	C1
Bright Hill	C3	Onslow Street	B2
Brodie Road	D3	Oxford Road	C3
Bury Fields	B4	Pannells Court	C2
Bury Street	B4	Park Street	B3
Castle Hill	C4	Pewley Bank	D3
Castle Street	C3	Pewley Fort Inner Court	D4
Chapel Street	B3	Pewley Hill	C3
Chertsey Street	C2	Pewley Way	D3
Cheselden Road	D2	Phoenix Court	B3
Church Road	B1	Porridge Pot Alley	B4
College Road	B2	Portsmouth Road	A4
Commercial Road	B2	Poyle Road	D4
Dene Road	D2	Quarry Street	B3
Drummond Road	B1	Sandfield Terrace	C2
Eagle Road	C1	Semaphore Road	D3
Eastgate Gardens	D2	South Hill	C3
Epsom Road	D2	Springfield Road	C1
Falcon Road	C1	Station Approach	D1
Farnham Road	A3	Station View	A2
Fort Road	C4	Stoke Fields	C1
Foxenden Road	D1	Stoke Grove	C1
Friary Bridge	A3	Stoke Road	C1
Friary Street	B3	Swan Lane	B3
George Road	B1	Sydenham Road	C3
Guildford Park Road	A2	Testard Road	A3
Harvey Road	D3	The Bars	C2
Haydon Place	C2	The Mount	A4
High Pewley	D4	The Shambles	B3
High Street	C3	Tunsgate	C3
Jeffries Passage	C2	Upperton Road	A3
Jenner Road	D2	Victoria Road	D1
Laundry Road	B2	Walnut Tree Close	A1
Leapale Lane	B2	Ward Street	C2
Leapale Road	B2	Warwicks Bench	C4
Leas Road	B1	Wherwell Road	A3
London Road	D2	William Road	B1
Mareschal Road	A4	Wodeland Avenue	A3
Market Street	C3	Woodbridge Road	B1
Martyr Road	C2	York Road	B1
Mary Road	A1		
Millbrook	B3		
Mill Lane	B3		

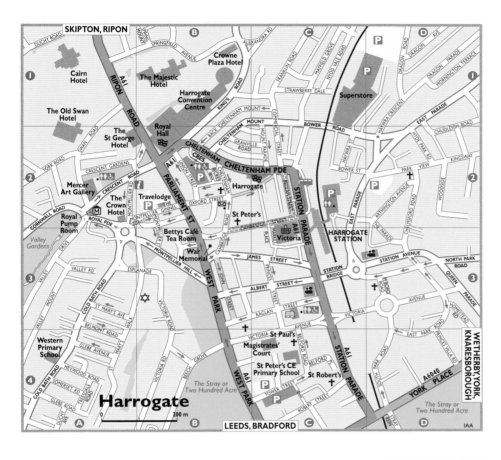

Harrogate

Harrogate is found on atlas page **97 M9**

Albert Street	C3	Montpellier Hill	B3
Alexandra Road	B1	Montpellier Road	A2
Arthington Avenue	D2	Montpellier Street	B2
Back Cheltenham Mount	B2	Mornington Terrace	D1
Beech Grove	B4	Mount Parade	C2
Belford Place	C4	North Park Road	D3
Belford Road	C4	Nydd Vale Road	C1
Belmont Road	A3	Oxford Street	B2
Beulah Street	C2	Park View	D2
Bower Road	C1	Parliament Street	B2
Bower Street	C2	Princes Street	C3
Cambridge Road	B3	Princes Villa Road	D4
Cambridge Street	C2	Queen Parade	D3
Chelmsford Road	D3	Raglan Street	C3
Cheltenham Crescent	B2	Ripon Road	A1
Cheltenham Mount	B2	Robert Street	C4
Cheltenham Parade	B2	Royal Parade	A2
Chudleigh Road	D2	St Mary's Avenue	A3
Cold Bath Road	A3	St Mary's Walk	A4
Commercial Street	C1	Somerset Road	A4
Cornwall Road	A2	South Park Road	D4
Crescent Gardens	A2	Springfield Avenue	B1
Crescent Road	A2	Spring Mount	B1
Dragon Avenue	D1	Station Avenue	D3
Dragon Parade	D1	Station Bridge	C3
Dragon Road	D1	Station Parade	C2
Duchy Avenue	A4	Strawberry Dale	C1
Duchy Road	A1	Stray Rein	D4
East Parade	C2	Swan Road	A2
East Park Road	D4	The Ginnel	B2
Esplanade	A3	The Parade	D2
Franklin Road	C1	Tower Street	C4
Glebe Avenue	A4	Treesdale Road	A4
Glebe Road	A4	Union Street	B2
Granville Road	B2	Valley Drive	A3
Haywra Street	C2	Valley Mount	A3
Heywood Road	A4	Valley Road	A3
Homestead Road	D3	Victoria Avenue	B4
Hyde Park Road	D2	Victoria Road	B3
Haywra Crescent	D2	West Park	B3
James Street	B3	West Park Street	B4
John Street	B3	Woodside	D2
King's Road	B1	York Place	D4
Kingsway	D2	York Road	A2
Market Place	C3		
Marlborough Road	D3		
Mayfield Grove	C1		
Montpellier Gardens	B2		

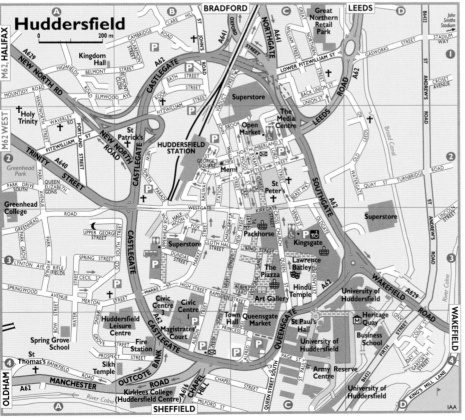

Huddersfield

Huddersfield is found on atlas page **90 E7**

Albion Street	B4	New North Road	A2
Alfred Street	C4	New Street	B4
Back Union Street	C1	Northgate	C1
Bankfield Road	A4	Northumberland Street	C2
Bath Street	B1	Old Leeds Road	D2
Belmont Street	A1	Old South Street	B3
Brook Street	C2	Outcote Bank	B4
Byram Street	C2	Oxford Street	C1
Cambridge Road	B1	Page Street	A2
Carforth Street	D4	Park Avenue	A2
Castlegate	B1	Park Drive South	A2
Chancery Lane	B3	Peel Street	C4
Chapel Hill	B4	Portland Street	A2
Chapel Street	B4	Princess Street	B4
Church Street	C2	Prospect Street	A4
Clare Hill	B1	Quay Street	D2
Claremont Street	B1	Queen Street	C3
Cloth Hall Street	B3	Queen Street South	C4
Cross Church Street	C3	Queensgate	C4
Dundas Street	B3	Railway Street	B2
Elizabeth Queen Gardens	A2	Ramsden Street	B3
Elmwood Avenue	A1	Rook Street	B1
Firth Street	D4	St Andrew's Road	D2
Fitzwilliam Street	A2	St George's Square	B2
Fitzwilliam Street	B2	St John's Road	B1
Gasworks Street	D1	St Peter's Street	C2
Great Northern Street	C1	Southgate	C2
Greenhead Road	A3	Spring Grove Street	A4
Half Moon Street	B3	Spring Street	A3
High Street	B3	Springwood Avenue	A3
Highfields Road	A1	Stadium Way	D1
John William Street	B2	Station Street	B2
King Street	C3	Trinity Street	A2
King's Mill Lane	D4	Turnbridge Road	D2
Kirkgate	C3	Union Street	C1
Leeds Road	C2	Upper George Street	A3
Lincoln Street	D3	Upperhead Row	B3
Lord Street	C2	Viaduct Street	B2
Lower Fitzwilliam Street	C1	Victoria Lane	C3
Lynton Avenue	A3	Wakefield Road	D3
Manchester Road	A4	Water Street	A3
Market Place	C3	Watergate	D2
Market Street	B3	Waverley Road	A2
Merton Street	A3	Wentworth Street	A2
Milford Street	B4	Westgate	B3
Mountjoy Road	A1	William Street	C1
New North Parade	B2	Wood Street	C1
New North Road	A1	Zetland Street	C3

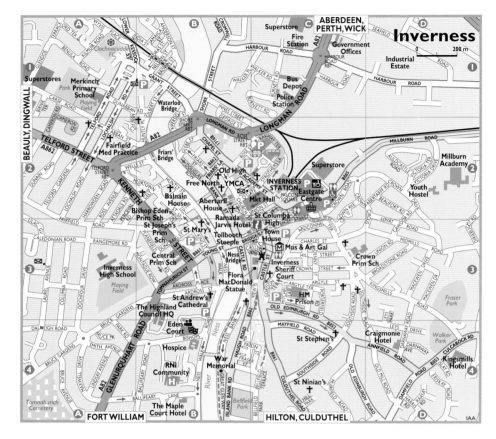

Inverness

Inverness is found on atlas page **156 B8**

Abertaff Road	D2	Glenurquhart Road	A4
Academy Street	B2	Gordon Terrace	C3
Anderson Street	B1	Grant Street	B1
Annfield Road	D4	Great Glen Way	B4
Ardconnel Terrace	C3	Harbour Road	C1
Ardross Street	B3	Harris Road	D4
Argyle Street	C3	Harrowden Road	A2
Argyle Terrace	C3	Haugh Road	B4
Ballifeary Lane	A4	High Street	C3
Ballifeary Road	B4	Hill Park	C4
Bank Street	B2	Hill Street	C3
Bellfield Terrace	C4	Huntly Street	B2
Benula Road	A1	Innes Street	B1
Birnie Terrace	A1	Kenneth Street	A2
Bishops Road	B4	King Street	B3
Bridge Street	B3	Kingsmills Road	D3
Broadstone Road	D3	Laurel Avenue	A3
Bruce Gardens	A4	Lindsay Avenue	A4
Bruce Park	A4	Lochalsh Road	A2
Burnett Road	C1	Longman Road	C2
Caledonian Road	A3	Lovat Road	D3
Cameron Road	A2	Lower Kessock Street	A1
Cameron Square	A2	Maxwell Drive	A4
Carse Road	A1	Mayfield Road	C4
Castle Road	B3	Midmills Road	D3
Castle Street	C3	Millburn Road	D2
Chapel Street	B2	Mitchell's Lane	C3
Charles Street	C3	Muirfield Road	C4
Columba Road	A3	Ness Bank	B4
Crown Circus	C2	Old Edinburgh Road	C3
Crown Drive	D2	Park Road	A4
Crown Road	C2	Planefield Road	B3
Crown Street	C3	Porterfield Road	C3
Culcabock Road	D4	Raasay Road	D4
Culduthel Road	C4	Rangemore Road	A3
Dalneigh Road	A4	Ross Avenue	A2
Damfield Road	D4	Seafield Road	D1
Darnaway Road	D4	Shore Street	B1
Denny Street	C3	Smith Avenue	A4
Dochfour Drive	A3	Southside Place	C3
Dunabban Road	A1	Southside Road	C4
Dunain Road	A2	Telford Gardens	A2
Duncraig Street	B3	Telford Road	A2
Eriskay Road	D4	Telford Street	A2
Fairfield Road	A3	Tomnahurich Street	B3
Falcon Square	C2	Union Road	D3
Friars' Lane	B2	Walker Road	C1
Glendoe Terrace	A1	Young Street	B3

Ipswich

Ipswich is found on atlas page **53 L3**

Alderman Road	A3	Key Street	C3
Anglesea Road	B1	King Street	B2
Argyle Street	D2	London Road	A2
Austin Street	C4	Lower Brook Street	C3
Barrack Lane	A1	Lower Orwell Street	C3
Belstead Road	B4	Museum Street	B2
Berners Street	B1	Neale Street	C1
Black Horse Lane	B2	Neptune Quay	D3
Blanche Street	D2	New Cardinal Street	B3
Bolton Lane	C1	Newson Street	A1
Bond Street	D3	Northgate Street	C2
Bramford Road	A1	Norwich Road	A1
Bridge Street	C4	Old Foundry Road	C2
Burlington Road	A2	Orchard Street	D2
Burrell Road	B4	Orford Street	A1
Cardigan Street	A1	Orwell Place	C3
Carr Street	C2	Orwell Quay	D4
Cecil Road	B1	Portman Road	A3
Cemetery Road	D1	Princes Street	A3
Chancery Road	A4	Quadling Street	B3
Charles Street	B1	Queen Street	B3
Christchurch Street	D1	Ranelagh Road	A4
Civic Drive	B2	Russell Road	A3
Clarkson Street	A1	St George's Street	B1
Cobbold Street	C2	St Helen's Street	D2
College Street	C3	St Margaret's Street	C2
Commercial Road	A4	St Matthews Street	B2
Constantine Road	A3	St Nicholas Street	B3
Crown Street	B2	St Peter's Street	B3
Cumberland Street	A1	Silent Street	B3
Dalton Road	A2	Sir Alf Ramsey Way	A3
Dock Street	C4	Soane Street	C2
Duke Street	D4	South Street	A1
Eagle Street	C3	Star Lane	C3
Elm Street	B2	Stoke Quay	C4
Falcon Street	B3	Suffolk Road	D1
Fonnereau Road	B1	Tacket Street	C3
Foundation Street	C3	Tavern Street	B3
Franciscan Way	B3	Tower Ramparts	B2
Geneva Road	A1	Tuddenham Avenue	D1
Grafton Way	B3	Turret Lane	C3
Great Gipping Street	A2	Upper Orwell Street	C3
Great Whip Street	C4	Vernon Street	C4
Grey Friars Road	B3	West End Road	A3
Grimwade Street	D3	Westgate Street	B2
Handford Road	A2	Willoughby Road	B4
Hervey Street	D1	Wolsey Street	B3
High Street	B1	Woodbridge Road	D2

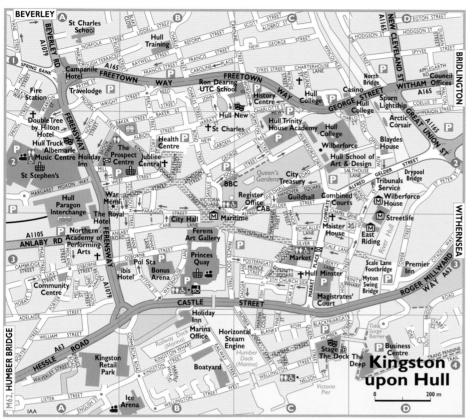

Kingston upon Hull

Kingston upon Hull is found on atlas page **93 J5**

Adelaide Street A4	Market Place C3
Albion Street B2	Mill Street A2
Alfred Gelder Street.................C2	Myton Street B3
Anlaby Road A3	New Cleveland Street D1
Baker Street B2	New Garden Street B2
Beverley Road A1	New George Street C1
Blackfriargate.........................C4	Norfolk Street A1
Blanket Row C4	Osborne Street B3
Bond Street B2	Osborne Street A3
Brook Street A2	Paragon Street B2
Caroline Street B1	Percy Street B1
Carr Lane B3	Porter Street A3
Castle Street B3	Portland Place A2
Chapel Lane C2	Portland Street A2
Charles Street B1	Posterngate C3
Charterhouse Lane...................C1	Princes Dock Street B3
Citadel Way D3	Prospect Street A1
Commercial Road B4	Queen Street C4
Dagger Lane C3	Railway Street B4
Dock Office Row D2	Raywell Street B1
Dock Street B2	Reform Street B1
Durban Street D1	Russell Street A1
Egginton Street B1	St Luke's Street A3
Ferensway A2	St Peter Street D2
Freetown Way A1	Saville Street B2
Gandhi Way D2	Scale Lane...............................C3
Garrison Road D3	Scott Street C1
George Street B2	Silver Street C3
George Street D1	South Bridge Road D4
Great Union Street................... D1	South Church Side C3
Grimston Street C2	South Street B2
Guildhall Road C2	Spring Bank.............................A1
Hanover Square C2	Spyvee Street D1
Hessle Road A4	Sykes Street C1
High Street C3	Tower Street D3
Hodgson Street........................ D1	Upper Union Street...................A3
Humber Dock Street.................C4	Victoria Square B2
Humber Street C4	Waterhouse Lane B3
Hyperion Street C4	Wellington Street......................C4
Jameson Street B2	Wellington Street West.............B4
Jarratt Street B2	West Street A2
King Edward Street B2	Whitefriargate C3
Kingston Street B4	Wilberforce Drive C2
Liddell Street B1	William Street A4
Lime Street C1	Wincolmlee..............................C1
Lister Street A4	Witham D1
Lowgate C3	Worship Street.........................C1
Margaret Moxon Way A2	Wright Street...........................A1

Lancaster

Lancaster is found on atlas page **95 K8**

Aberdeen Road D4	Lincoln Road A3
Aldcliffe Road..........................B4	Lindow Street B4
Alfred Street C2	Lodge Street C2
Ambleside Road D1	Long Marsh Lane A2
Balmoral Road D4	Lune Street B1
Bath Street D3	Market Street B3
Blades Street A3	Meeting House Lane A3
Bond Street D3	Middle Street B3
Borrowdale Road D2	Moor Gate D3
Brewery Lane C3	Moor Lane................................C3
Bridge Lane.............................B2	Morecambe Road......................B1
Brock Street C3	Nelson Street C3
Bulk Road D2	North Road C2
Bulk Street C3	Owen Road C1
Cable Street B2	Park Road D3
Castle Hill B3	Parliament Street C2
Castle Park A3	Patterdale Road D2
Caton Road C2	Penny Street B4
Cheapside C3	Portland Street B4
China Street B3	Primrose Street D4
Church Street B2	Prospect Street D4
Common Garden Street............B3	Quarry Road C4
Dale Street D4	Queen Street B4
Dallas Road B3	Regent Street B4
Dalton Road D2	Ridge Lane D1
Dalton Square C3	Ridge Street D1
Damside Street B2	Robert Street C3
Derby Road C1	Rosemary Lane C2
De Vitre Street C2	St George's Quay A1
Dumbarton Road D4	St Leonard's Gate C2
East Road D3	St Peter's Road C4
Edward Street C3	Sibsey Street A3
Fairfield Road..........................A3	South Road C4
Fenton Street B3	Station Road A3
Gage Street C3	Stirling Road D4
Garnet Street D2	Sulyard Street C3
George Street C3	Sun Street B3
Grasmere Road D3	Thurnham Street C4
Great John Street C3	Troutbeck Road D2
Gregson Road D3	Ulleswater Road D3
Greyhound Bridge Road.......... B1	West Road A3
High Street B4	Westbourne Road A3
Kelsey Street A3	Wheatfield Street......................A3
Kentmere Road D2	Williamson Road...................... D3
King Street B3	Wingate-Saul Road A3
Kingsway.................................C1	Wolseley Street D2
Kirkes Road D4	Woodville Street D3
Langdale Road D1	Wyresdale Road....................... D3

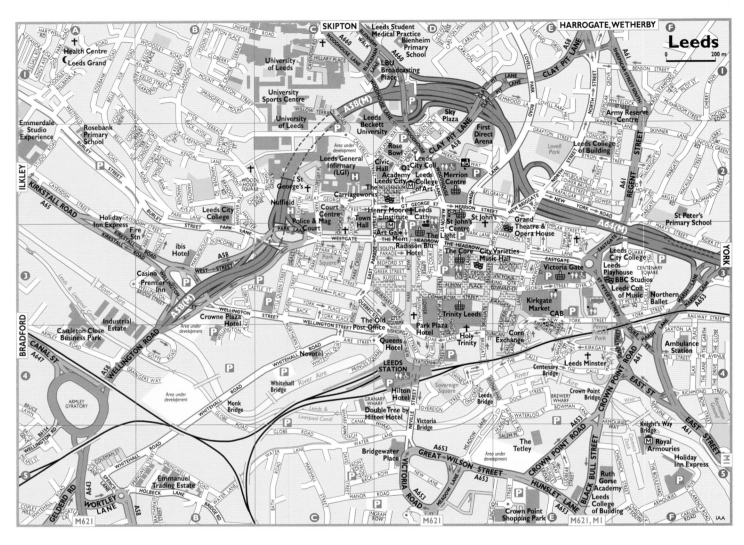

Leeds

Leeds is found on atlas page **90 H4**

Abbey Street	B3	Calverley Street	C2	Duke Street	F4	King's Avenue	A1	Northern Street	C4	Springfield Mount	B1
Aire Street	C4	Canal Street	A4	Duncan Street	D4	King Street	C3	North Street	E2	Springwell Road	B5
Albion Place	D3	Canal Wharf	C4	Duncombe Street	B3	Kirkgate	E3	Oxford Place	C3	Springwell Street	B5
Albion Street	D2	Carlton Hill	D1	Dyer Street	E3	Kirkstall Road	A2	Oxford Row	C3	Studio Road	A2
Alexandra Road	A1	Carlton Rise	D1	Eastgate	E3	Lady Lane	E3	Park Cross Street	C3	Swinegate	D4
Argyle Road	F2	Castle Street	B3	East Parade	C3	Lands Lane	D3	Park Lane	B2	Templar Street	E3
Armley Gyratory	A4	Cavendish Road	C1	East Street	F4	Leighton Street	C2	Park Place	C3	The Avenue	F4
Armley Road	A4	Cavendish Street	A2	Elmwood Lane	E1	Leylands Road	F2	Park Row	D3	The Boulevard	F5
Armouries Drive	F5	Centenary Square	F3	Flax Place	F4	Lifton Place	B1	Park Square East	C3	The Calls	E4
Armouries Way	E4	Central Road	E3	Front Street	C5	Lincoln Green Road	F2	Park Square North	C3	The Headrow	D3
Back Hyde Terrace	B2	Chadwick Street	F5	Gelderd Road	A5	Lisbon Street	B3	Park Square West	C3	Thoresby Place	C2
Back Row	C5	Cherry Row	F1	George Street	E3	Little Queen Street	C3	Park Street	C3	Trafalgar Street	E2
Bath Road	C5	Chorley Lane	B2	Globe Road	B4	Lovell Park Hill	E1	Pilot Street	F1	Upper Basinghall Street	D3
Bedford Street	D2	City Square	D3	Gotts Road	B4	Lovell Park Road	E1	Portland Crescent	D2	Vicar Lane	E3
Belgrave Street	D2	Claremont	B2	Gower Street	E2	Lower Basinghall Street	D3	Portland Way	D2	Victoria Road	D5
Belle Vue Road	A1	Clarence Road	F5	Grace Street	C3	Lower Brunswick Street	E2	Princes Square	C4	Victoria Street	B2
Belmont Grove	C2	Clarendon Road	B1	Grafton Street	E2	Lyddon Terrace	B1	Quarry Hill	F3	Victoria Terrace	B2
Benson Street	F1	Clay Pit Lane	D2	Graingers Way	A4	Mabgate	F2	Quebec Street	C3	Wade Lane	D2
Bingley Street	B3	Cloberry Street	B1	Great George Street	C2	Macauley Street	F2	Queen Square	D2	Water Lane	B5
Bishopgate Street	D4	Commercial Street	D3	Great Wilson Street	D5	Manor Road	C5	Queen Square Court	D2	Waterloo Street	E4
Black Bull Street	E5	Concordia Street	D4	Greek Street	D3	Mark Lane	D3	Queen Street	C3	Wellington Bridge Street	B3
Blackman Lane	C1	Concord Street	E2	Hanover Avenue	B2	Marlborough Street	B3	Railway Street	F3	Wellington Road	A4
Blenheim Walk	C1	Consort Street	B2	Hanover Lane	B2	Marshall Street	C5	Regent Street	F2	Wellington Road	A5
Boar Lane	D4	Consort View	A1	Hanover Square	B2	Marsh Lane	F4	Richmond Street	F4	Wellington Street	B3
Bowman Lane	E4	County Arcade	E3	Harewood Street	E3	Maude Street	E4	Rider Street	F3	Westfield Road	A1
Bow Street	F4	Cromer Terrace	B1	Harper Street	E4	Meadow Lane	D5	Rillbank Lane	A1	Westgate	C3
Brandon Road	B2	Cromwell Street	F2	Harrison Street	E3	Melbourne Street	E2	Rosebank Road	A1	West Street	B3
Bridge End	D4	Cross Arcade	E3	Hartwell Road	A1	Merrion Street	D2	St Cecilia Street	F3	Wharf Approach	C4
Bridge Road	B5	Cross Kelso Road	B1	High Court	E4	Merrion Way	D2	St John's Road	B1	Wharf Street	E4
Bridge Street	E2	Cross Stamford Street	F1	Holbeck Lane	B5	Millennium Square	D2	St Mary's Street	F3	Whitehall Quay	C4
Bridge Street	E3	Crown Point Road	E5	Hope Road	F2	Mill Street	F4	St Paul's Street	C3	Whitehall Road	A5
Briggate	D4	Crown Street	E4	Hunslet Lane	D4	Millwright Street	F2	St Peter's Square	E3	Whitehall Road	A5
Burley Street	A2	Cudbear Street	E5	Hunslet Road	E5	Mount Preston Street	B1	St Peter's Street	E3	Whitelock Street	F1
Butts Court	D3	David Street	C5	Hyde Park Road	A1	Mushroom Street	F1	Salem Place	E5	Willow Terrace Road	C1
Byron Street	E2	Dock Street	E4	Hyde Street	B2	Neptune Street	F4	Saxton Lane	F3	Woodhouse Lane	C1
Call Lane	E4	Duke Street	F4	Hyde Terrace	B1	Neville Street	D4	Sheepscar Grove	E1	Woodhouse Square	B2
				Infirmary Street	D3	New Briggate	E3	Sheepscar Street South	F1	Woodsley Road	A1
				Junction Street	D5	New Lane	D5	Skinner Lane	E1	Wortley Lane	A5
				Kelso Road	B1	New Station Street	D4	South Parade	D3	Wortley Lane	A5
				Kendal Lane	B2	New York Road	E2	Sovereign Street	D4	York Place	C3
				King Edward Street	E3	New York Street	E3	Spence Lane	A5	York Street	F3

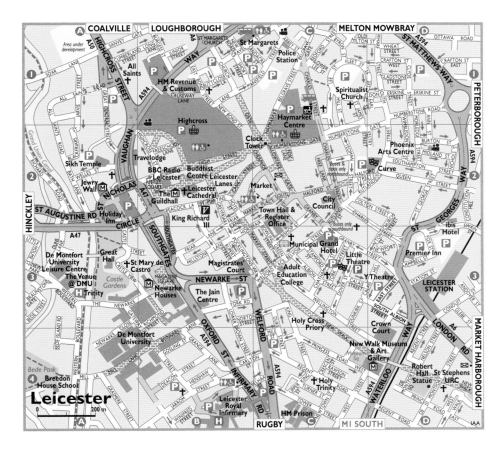

Leicester

Leicester is found on atlas page **72 F10**

Albion Street	C3	Infirmary Road	B4
All Saints Road	A1	Jarrom Street	B4
Bath Lane	A2	Jarvis Street	A1
Bedford Street	C1	King Street	C3
Belgrave Gate	C1	Lee Street	C1
Belvoir Street	C3	London Road	D3
Bishop Street	C3	Lower Brown Street	B3
Bonners Lane	B4	Magazine Square	B3
Bowling Green Street	C3	Mansfield Street	B1
Burgess Street	B1	Market Place South	B2
Burton Street	D2	Market Street	C3
Calais Hill	C3	Mill Lane	A4
Campbell Street	D3	Morledge Street	D1
Cank Street	B2	Newarke Street	B3
Castle Street	A3	New Walk	C3
Charles Street	C1	Oxford Street	B3
Chatham Street	C3	Peacock Lane	B2
Cheapside	C2	Pocklingtons Walk	B3
Church Gate	B1	Princess Road East	D4
Clyde Street	D1	Princess Road West	C4
Colton Street	C2	Queen Street	D2
Conduit Street	D3	Regent Road	C4
Crafton Street West	D1	Regent Street	D4
Deacon Street	B4	Richard III Road	A2
De Montfort Street	D4	Rutland Street	C2
Dover Street	C3	St Augustine Road	A3
Duke Street	C3	St George Street	D2
Duns Lane	A3	St Georges Way	D2
East Bond Street Lane	B1	St James Street	C1
Erskine Street	D1	St Matthews Way	D1
Fleet Street	C1	St Nicholas Circle	A2
Friar Lane	B3	Sanvey Gate	A1
Gallowtree Gate	C2	Soar Lane	A1
Gateway Street	A3	South Albion Street	D3
Granby Street	C2	Southampton Street	D2
Grasmere Street	A4	Southgates	B3
Gravel Street	B1	Station Street	D3
Great Central Street	A1	The Newarke	A3
Greyfriars	B2	Tower Street	C4
Halford Street	C2	Vaughan Way	A2
Haymarket	C2	Waterloo Way	D4
Highcross Street	A1	Welford Road	C3
Highcross Street	B2	Welles Street	A2
High Street	B2	Wellington Street	C3
Hill Street	C1	Western Boulevard	A4
Horsefair Street	B3	West Street	C4
Humberstone Gate	C2	Wharf Street South	D1
Humberstone Road	D1	Yeoman Street	C2

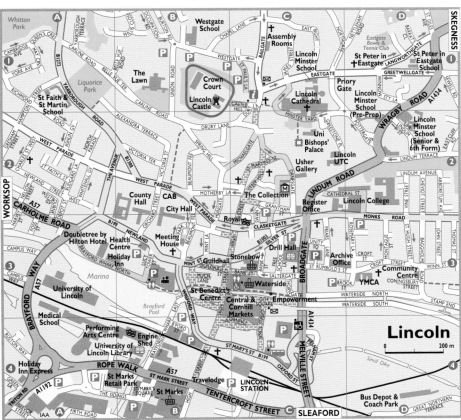

Lincoln

Lincoln is found on atlas page **86 C6**

Alexandra Terrace	B2	Montague Street	D3
Arboretum Avenue	D2	Motherby Lane	B2
Baggholme Road	D3	Nelson Street	A2
Bailgate	C1	Newland	B3
Bank Street	C3	Newland Street West	A2
Beaumont Fee	B3	Northgate	C1
Belle Vue Terrace	A1	Orchard Street	B3
Brayford Way	A4	Oxford Street	C4
Brayford Wharf East	B4	Park Street	B3
Brayford Wharf North	A3	Pelham Street	C4
Broadgate	C3	Pottergate	D2
Burton Road	B1	Queen's Crescent	A1
Carholme Road	A2	Richmond Road	A1
Carline Road	A1	Rope Walk	A4
Cathedral Street	C2	Rosemary Lane	D3
Chapel Lane	B1	Rudgard Lane	A2
Charles Street West	A2	St Hugh Street	D3
Cheviot Street	D2	St Mark Street	B4
City Square	C3	St Martin's Street	C2
Clasketgate	C3	St Mary's Street	B4
Cornhill	B4	St Rumbold's Street	C3
Croft Street	D3	Saltergate	C3
Danesgate	C2	Silver Street	C3
Depot Street	A3	Sincil Street	C4
Drury Lane	B2	Spring Hill	B2
East Bight	C1	Steep Hill	C2
Eastgate	C1	Swan Street	C3
Free School Lane	C3	Tentercroft Street	B4
Friars Lane	C3	The Avenue	A2
Grantham Street	C2	The Sidings	A4
Greetwellgate	D1	Thorngate	C3
Gresham Street	A2	Triton Road	A4
Guildhall Street	B3	Union Road	B1
Hampton Street	A1	Unity Square	C3
High Street	B3	Victoria Street	B2
Hungate	B3	Victoria Terrace	B2
John Street	D3	Vine Street	D2
Langworthgate	D1	Waterside North	C3
Lindum Road	C2	Waterside South	C3
Lindum Terrace	D2	Westgate	B1
Lucy Tower Street	B3	West Parade	A2
May Crescent	A1	Whitehall Grove	A2
Melville Street	C4	Wigford Way	B3
Michaelgate	C2	Winnow Sty Lane	D1
Minster Yard	C2	Winn Street	D3
Mint Lane	B3	Wragby Road	D2
Mint Street	B3	Yarborough Terrace	A1
Monks Road	D3	York Avenue	A1

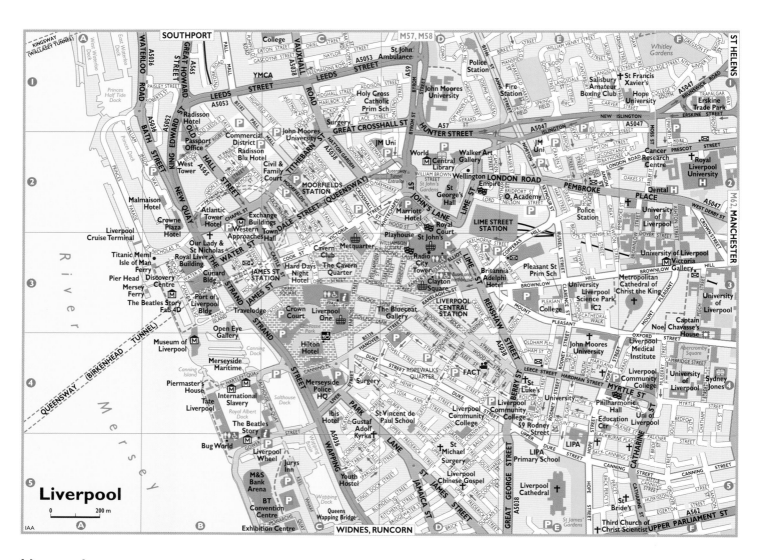

Liverpool

Liverpool is found on atlas page **81 L6**

Addison Street......................C1
Anson Street........................E2
Argyle Street........................C4
Arrad Street.........................F4
Ashton Street........................F2
Audley Street........................E2
Back Canning Street.............E5
Baltimore Street...................E4
Bath Street...........................B2
Beckwith Street....................C4
Bedford Street South.............F5
Benson Street.......................E3
Berry Street..........................E4
Bidder Street........................E1
Birkett Street........................D1
Bixteth Street.......................B2
Blackburne Place..................E5
Blundell Street......................C5
Bold Street...........................D3
Bosnett Street......................D3
Bridgewater Street...............D5
Bridport Street......................E2
Brook Street.........................B2
Brownlow Hill........................E3
Brownlow Street....................F3
Brunswick Road....................F1
Brunswick Street...................B3
Byrom Street.........................D1
Cambridge Street..................F4
Camden Street......................D2
Canada Boulevard.................B3
Canning Place.......................C4
Canning Street......................E5
Canterbury Street..................E1
Carver Street........................E1
Castle Street.........................C3

Catharine Street....................F5
Cathedral Walk......................E3
Chapel Street........................B2
Chatham Street.....................F4
Cheapside.............................C2
Christian Street.....................D1
Church Street........................C3
Churchill Way........................D2
Clarence Street.....................E3
Cockspur Street.....................C1
College Lane..........................C3
College Street North..............F1
College Street South..............F1
Colquitt Street.......................D4
Constance Street...................E2
Cook Street...........................C3
Copperas Hill........................E3
Cornhill.................................C5
Cornwallis Street...................D5
Craven Street........................E2
Cropper Street.......................D3
Crosshall Street....................C2
Crown Street.........................F2
Dale Street (Queensway).......C2
Dansie Street........................E3
Daulby Street........................F2
Derby Square........................C3
Devon Street.........................E2
Dover Street..........................F3
Drury Lane............................B3
Duke Street...........................D4
East Street............................B1
Eaton Street..........................B1
Edmund Street......................B2
Egerton Street.......................F5
Elliot Street...........................D3

Epworth Street......................F1
Erskine Street.......................F1
Falkner Street........................E4
Fazakerley Street..................B2
Fenwick Street......................B3
Fleet Street...........................D3
Fontenoy Street....................D1
Fraser Street.........................E2
Gascoyne Street....................B1
Gilbert Street.........................D4
Gildart Street.........................E2
Gill Street..............................E2
Gower Street.........................B5
Gradwell Street.....................D4
Great Crosshall Street...........C1
Great George Street...............E5
Great Howard Street..............B1
Great Newton Street..............E2
Greek Street..........................E2
Gregson Street......................F1
Grenville Street South............D5
Hackins Hey..........................C2
Hanover Street......................C4
Hardman Street.....................E4
Harker Street.........................E1
Hartley Quay..........................B4
Hart Street............................E2
Hatton Garden.......................C2
Hawke Street.........................E2
Henry Street..........................D4
Highfield Street......................B1
Hood Street...........................D2
Hope Place............................E4
Hope Street...........................E5
Hotham Street.......................E2
Hunter Street........................D1
Huskisson Street...................F5
Islington...............................E2
Jamaica Street......................D5
James Street.........................B3
Johnson Street......................C2

Keel Wharf............................C5
Kempston Street...................E2
Kent Street............................D5
Kinder Street.........................F1
King Edward Street................B2
Kingsway (Wallasey Tunnel)...A1
Knight Street.........................E4
Lace Street............................C1
Langsdale Street...................E1
Leece Street..........................E4
Leeds Street..........................B1
Lime Street...........................D2
Liver Street...........................C4
London Road.........................D2
London Road.........................E2
Lord Nelson Street................D2
Lord Street............................C3
Lydia Ann Street....................D4
Mann Island..........................B3
Mansfield Street....................E1
Marybone.............................C1
Maryland Street.....................E4
Midghall Street......................C1
Moorfields.............................C2
Moor Street...........................B3
Moss Street...........................F1
Mount Pleasant.....................E3
Mount Street.........................E4
Mulberry Street.....................F4
Myrtle Street.........................E4
Naylor Street.........................C1
Nelson Street........................D5
Newington............................D4
New Islington.........................E1
New Quay..............................B2
North John Street..................C2
Norton Street.........................E2
Old Hall Street.......................B2
Oldham Street.......................E4
Old Haymarket......................C2
Old Leeds Street...................B1

Ormond Street.......................B2
Oxford Street.........................F4
Paisley Street........................B1
Pall Mall...............................B1
Paradise Street.....................C3
Parker Street.........................D3
Park Lane..............................C4
Parr Street............................D4
Peech Street.........................F3
Pembroke Place....................E2
Pembroke Street...................F2
Percey Street........................E5
Pilgrim Street........................E4
Pleasant Street.....................E3
Pomona Street......................E3
Prescot Street.......................F2
Princes Parade.....................A2
Prospect Street.....................F1
Queensway
  (Birkenhead Tunnel)...........A4
Ranelagh Street....................D3
Redcross Street....................C3
Renshaw Street.....................D3
Richmond Lane.....................C3
Rigby Street..........................B2
Rodney Street.......................E4
Roscoe Street.......................E4
Rose Hill..............................D1
Russell Street........................E3
St Anne Street.......................D1
St James Street.....................D5
St John's Lane.......................D2
St Josephs Crescent..............D1
St Nicholas Place..................B3
St Paul's Street.....................B2
Salisbury Street....................E1
Salthouse Quay.....................C4
Sandon Street.......................F5
School Lane..........................C3
Seel Street............................D4
Seymour Street......................E2

Shaw Street..........................F1
Sir Thomas Street..................C2
Skelhorne Street...................D3
Slater Street..........................D4
Soho Street...........................E1
Sparling Street......................C5
Springfield............................E1
Stafford Street.......................E2
Stanley Street........................C2
Strand Street.........................B3
Suffolk Street........................D4
Tabley Street.........................C5
Tarleton Street......................D3
Temple Street........................C2
The Strand............................B3
Tithe Barn Street...................C2
Trafalgar Way........................F1
Trowbridge Street..................E3
Trueman Street......................C2
Upper Duke Street.................E5
Upper Frederick Street..........D4
Upper Parliament Street.........F5
Upper Pitt Street...................D5
Vauxhall Road........................C1
Vernon Street........................C2
Victoria Street.......................C3
Wakefield Street....................E1
Wall Street............................C3
Wapping...............................C5
Waterloo Road......................A1
Water Street.........................B3
West Derby Street..................F2
Westmorland Drive................C1
Whitechapel..........................D2
William Brown Street.............D2
William Henry Street..............E1
William Jessop Way...............A2
Williamson Square.................D3
Williamson Street..................D3
Wood Street..........................D3
York Street............................C4

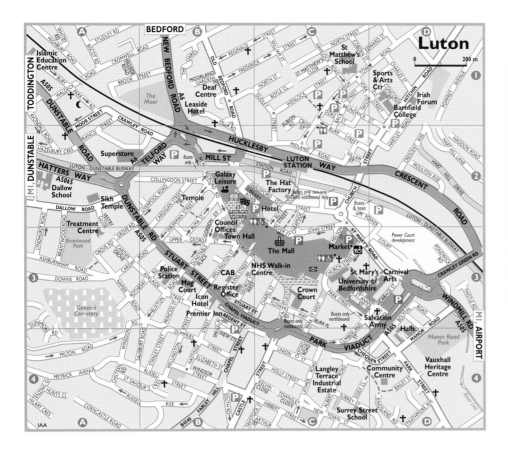

Luton

Luton is found on atlas page **50 C6**

Adelaide Street	B3	Hibbert Street	C4
Albert Road	C4	Highbury Road	A1
Alma Street	B2	High Town Road	C1
Arthur Street	C4	Hitchin Road	D1
Ashburnham Road	A3	Holly Street	C4
Biscot Road	A1	Hucklesby Way	B2
Brantwood Road	A3	Inkerman Street	B3
Brunswick Street	C1	John Street	C3
Burr Street	C2	King Street	B3
Bury Park Road	A1	Latimer Road	C4
Bute Street	C2	Liverpool Road	B2
Buxton Road	B3	Manor Road	D4
Cardiff Road	A3	Meyrick Avenue	A4
Cardigan Street	B2	Midland Road	C2
Castle Street	B4	Mill Street	B2
Chapel Street	B4	Milton Road	A4
Chapel Viaduct	B3	Moor Street	A1
Charles Street	D1	Napier Road	A3
Chequer Street	C4	New Bedford Road	B1
Church Street	C2	New Town Street	C4
Church Street	C3	Old Bedford Road	B1
Cobden Street	C1	Park Street	C3
Collingdon Street	B2	Park Street West	C3
Concorde Street	D1	Park Viaduct	C4
Crawley Green Road	D3	Princess Street	B3
Crawley Road	A1	Regent Street	B3
Crescent Road	D2	Reginald Street	B1
Cromwell Road	A1	Rothesay Road	A3
Cumberland Street	C4	Russell Rise	A4
Dallow Road	A2	Russell Street	B4
Dudley Street	C1	St Mary's Road	C3
Dumfries Street	B4	St Saviour's Crescent	A4
Dunstable Road	A1	Salisbury Road	A4
Farley Hill	B4	Stanley Street	B4
Flowers Way	C3	Station Road	C2
Frederick Street	B1	Strathmore Avenue	D4
George Street	B3	Stuart Street	B3
George Street West	B3	Surrey Street	C4
Gordon Street	B3	Tavistock Street	B4
Grove Road	A3	Telford Way	B2
Guildford Street	B2	Upper George Street	B3
Hart Hill Drive	D2	Vicarage Street	D3
Hart Hill Lane	D2	Waldeck Road	A1
Hartley Road	D2	Wellington Street	B4
Hastings Street	B4	Wenlock Street	C1
Hatters Way	A2	Windmill Road	D3
Havelock Road	C1	Windsor Street	B4
Hazelbury Crescent	A2	Winsdon Road	A4

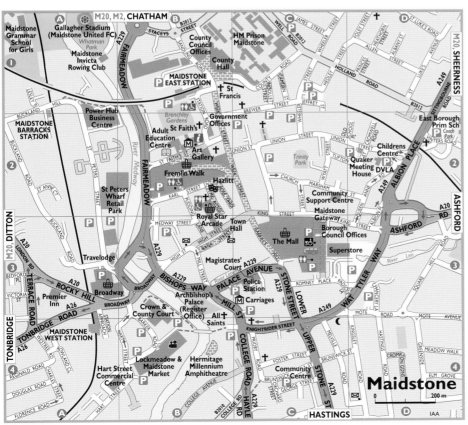

Maidstone

Maidstone is found on atlas page **38 C10**

Albany Street	D1	Market Buildings	B2
Albion Place	D2	Marsham Street	C2
Allen Street	D1	Meadow Walk	D4
Ashford Road	D3	Medway Street	B3
Bank Street	B3	Melville Road	C4
Barker Road	B4	Mill Street	B3
Bedford Place	A3	Mote Avenue	D3
Bishops Way	B3	Mote Road	D3
Brewer Street	C2	Old School Place	D2
Broadway	A3	Orchard Street	C4
Broadway	B3	Padsole Lane	C3
Brunswick Street	C4	Palace Avenue	B3
Buckland Hill	A2	Princes Street	D1
Buckland Road	A2	Priory Road	C4
Camden Street	C1	Pudding Lane	B2
Chancery Lane	D3	Queen Anne Road	D2
Charles Street	A4	Reginald Road	A4
Church Street	C2	Rocky Hill	A3
College Avenue	B4	Romney Place	C3
College Road	C4	Rose Yard	B2
County Road	C1	Rowland Close	A4
Crompton Gardens	A4	St Anne Court	A2
Cromwell Road	D2	St Faith's Street	B2
Douglas Road	A4	St Luke's Avenue	D1
Earl Street	B2	St Luke's Road	D1
Elm Grove	D4	St Peters Street	A2
Fairmeadow	B1	Sandling Road	B1
Florence Road	A4	Sittingbourne Road	D1
Foley Street	D1	Square Hill Road	D3
Foster Street	C4	Staceys Street	B1
Gabriel's Hill	C3	Station Approach	A4
George Street	C4	Station Road	B1
Greenside	D4	Terrace Road	A3
Hart Street	A4	Tonbridge Road	A4
Hastings Road	D4	Tufton Street	C2
Hayle Road	C4	Union Street	C2
Heathorn Street	D1	Upper Stone Street	C4
Hedley Street	C1	Victoria Street	A3
High Street	B3	Vinters Road	D2
Holland Road	D1	Wat Tyler Way	C3
James Street	C1	Week Street	B1
Jeffrey Street	C1	Well Road	C1
King Street	C2	Westree Road	A4
Kingsley Place	D4	Wheeler Street	C1
Knightrider Street	C4	Woollett Street	C1
Lesley Place	A1	Wyatt Street	C2
London Road	A3		
Lower Stone Street	C3		

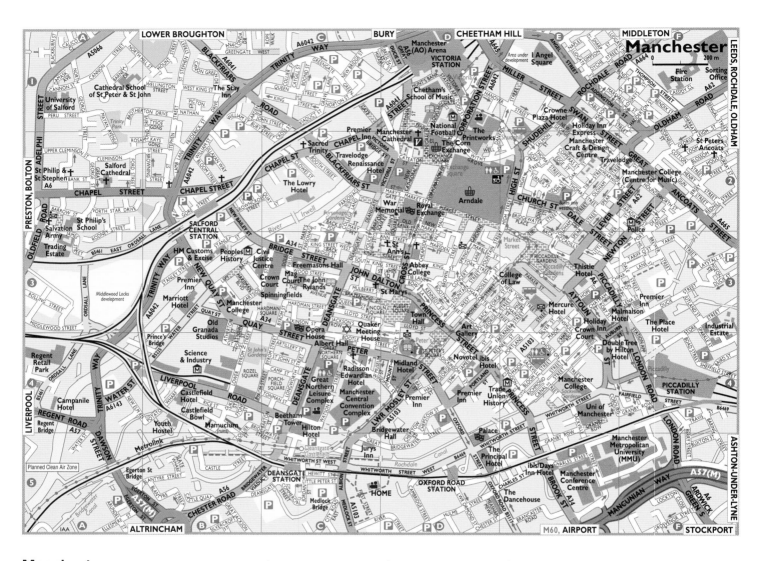

Manchester

Manchester is found on atlas page **82 H5**

Abingdon Street E4
Addington Street E1
Adelphi Street A2
Albion Street C5
Angel Street E1
Ardwick Green South F5
Artillery Street C4
Atherton Street B4
Atkinson Street C3
Auburn Street E4
Aytoun Street E3
Back Piccadilly E3
Bank Street A2
Baring Street F4
Barton Street C4
Berry Street F4
Blackfriars Road B1
Blackfriars Street C2
Blantyre Street B5
Bloom Street B2
Bloom Street E4
Blossom Street F2
Boad Street F4
Boond Street C1
Booth Street D3
Bootle Street C4
Brancaster Road E5
Brazennose Street C3
Brewer Street F3
Bridge Street C3
Bridgewater Place E2
Bridgewater Street B4
Bridgewater Viaduct B5
Brook Street E5
Brotherton Drive A1
Browncross Street B2

Browning Street B2
Brown Street D3
Bury Street B1
Byrom Street B4
Cable Street E1
Cambridge Street D5
Camp Street C4
Canal Street E4
Cannon Street A1
Canon Green Drive B1
Castle Street B5
Cathedral Street D2
Chadderton Street F1
Chapel Street A2
Charles Street E5
Charlotte Street D3
Chatham Street E3
Cheapside D3
Chester Road B5
China Lane E3
Chorlton Street E4
Church Street E2
City Road East C5
Cleminson Street A2
College Land C2
Collier Street C1
Commercial Street E2
Copperas Street E2
Cornell Street F1
Corporation Street D2
Cotton Street F2
Crosskeys Street F1
Cross Street C2
Cross Street D3
Dale Street E2
Dantzic Street D2

Dawson Street A5
Deansgate C4
Dickinson Street D4
Duke Street B4
Dulcie Street F3
East Ordsall Lane A3
Egerton Street A5
Exchange Square D2
Fairfield Street F4
Faulkner Street D4
Fennel Street D1
Ford Street A2
Fountain Street D3
Frederick Street B2
Garden Lane B1
Gartside Street B3
George Leigh Street F2
George Street D4
Gore Street B2
Granby Row E5
Gravel Lane C1
Great Ancoats Street F2
Great Bridgewater Street C5
Great Ducie Street D1
Great George Street A2
Great Jackson Street B5
Great John Street B4
Greengate C1
Greengate West B1
Gun Street F2
Hanover Street D1
Hardman Street C3
Hewitt Street C5
High Street E2
Hood Street F2
Hope Street E3
Houndsworth Street F2
Hulme Street D5
James Street A3
Jersey Street F2
John Dalton Street C3

John Street D1
John Street E2
Joiner Street E2
Jutland Street F3
Kennedy Street D3
King Street C1
King Street C3
King Street West C3
Lamb Lane B2
Laystall Street F3
Left Bank B3
Lena Street F3
Lever Street E2
Little Lever Street E3
Little Peter Street C5
Liverpool Road B4
Lloyd Street C3
London Road E4
Long Millgate D1
Longworth Street B4
Lower Byrom Street B4
Lower Mosley Street C4
Lower Ormond Street D5
Ludgate Street E1
Major Street E4
Mancunian Way E5
Marble Street D3
Market Street D2
Marsden Street D3
Marshall Street E1
Mason Street E1
Mayan Avenue A1
Medlock Street C5
Middlewood Street A3
Miller Street E1
Minshull Street D4
Mirabel Street C1
Mosley Street D3
Mount Street B1
Mount Street D4
Museum Street C4

Nathan Drive B1
New Bailey Street B2
New Bridge Street C1
New Cathedral Street D2
New Elm Road A4
New George Street E2
New Quay Street B3
Newton Street E3
New York Street E3
Nicholas Street D3
North George Street A1
North Hill Street A1
North Star Drive A2
Norton Street C1
Oldfield Road A3
Oldham Road F1
Oldham Street E2
Ordsall Lane A4
Oxford Road D5
Oxford Street D4
Pall Mall D3
Parker Street E3
Peru Street A1
Peter Street C4
Piccadilly E3
Piccadilly Gardens E3
Portland Street D4
Port Street F3
Potato Wharf A5
Princess Street D3
Quay Street B3
Queen Street C1
Queen Street C3
Redhill Street F2
Regent Road A4
Reyner Street D4
Rice Street B4
Richmond Street E4
Rochdale Road E1
Rodney Street A3
Rosamond Drive A2

Sackville Street E4
St Anns Square C2
St Ann Street C3
St James Square C3
St James Street D4
St Mary's Parsonage C3
St Stephen Street B2
Store Street F3
Sharp Street E1
Shudehill E2
Silk Street A1
Simpson Street E1
South King Street C3
Spear Street E3
Spring Gardens D3
Station Approach F3
Swan Street E1
Tariff Street F3
Thomas Street E2
Thompson Street F1
Tib Lane D3
Tib Street E2
Todd Street D1
Tonman Street C4
Travis Street F4
Trinity Way A4
Turner Street E2
Victoria Bridge Street C2
Victoria Station Approach D1
Victoria Street D2
Warwick Street E2
Watson Street C4
Well Street D2
West King Street B1
West Mosley Street D3
Whitworth Street D5
Whitworth Street West C5
Windmill Street C4
Withy Grove D2
Wood Street C3
York Street D3

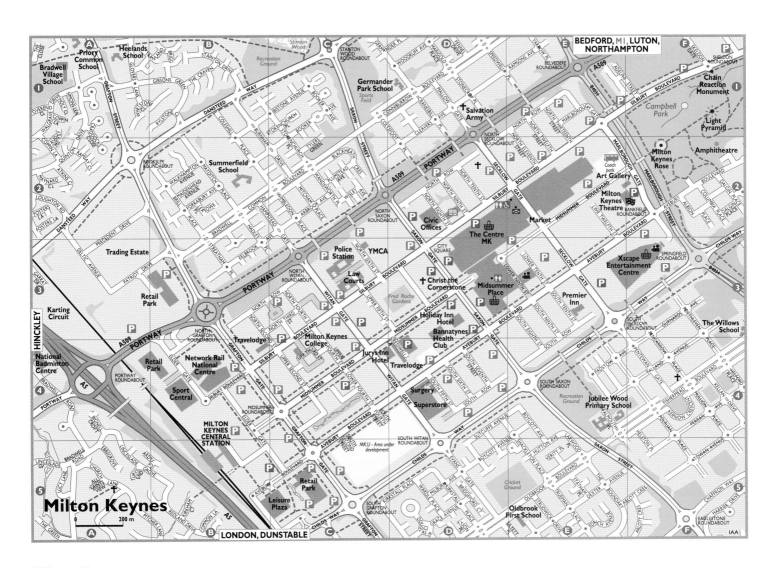

Milton Keynes

Milton Keynes is found on atlas page **49 N7**

Adelphi Street......................E1
Albion Place.........................F2
All Saints View.....................A5
Arbrook Avenue....................C2
Ardys Court..........................A5
Arlott Crescent.....................F5
Atkins Close.........................A2
Audley Mews........................A2
Avebury Boulevard................C5
Bankfield Roundabout...........E2
Belvedere Roundabout..........E1
Bignell Croft.........................A4
Blackheath Crescent.............C2
Booker Avenue.....................C1
Boycott Avenue....................D5
Boycott Avenue....................E4
Bradwell Common
    Boulevard........................B2
Bradwell Road......................A4
Bradwell Road......................A5
Bridgeford Court...................D5
Brill Place............................B2
Burnham Drive.....................B1
Chaffron Way........................F5
Childs Way...........................C5
Childs Way...........................F3
Church Lane.........................A5
City Square..........................D3
Cleavers Avenue...................D1
Coleshill Place......................B1
Coltsfoot Place.....................C1
Columbia Place.....................F2
Common Lane.......................B5
Conniburrow Boulevard.........C1
Coppin Lane.........................A2
Craddocks Close...................A1

Cranesbill Place...................D1
Cresswell Lane.....................D3
Dalgin Place.........................F2
Dansteed Way......................A2
Dansteed Way......................B1
Deltic Avenue.......................A3
Dexter Avenue.....................E5
Douglas Place.......................D5
Eaglestone Roundabout.........F5
Ebbsgrove...........................A5
Edrich Avenue......................E5
Eelbrook Avenue..................B3
Elder Gate...........................B4
Evans Gate...........................D5
Falmouth Place.....................E4
Fennel Drive........................D1
Fishermead Boulevard..........F4
Forrabury Avenue.................B2
Fosters Lane........................A2
Garrat Drive.........................A3
Germander Place...................C1
Gibsons Green.......................B1
Glovers Lane........................A1
Grace Avenue.......................D5
Grafton Gate........................B4
Grafton Street......................A1
Grafton Street......................C5
Gurnards Avenue..................F3
Hadley Place........................B2
Hampstead Gate...................B2
Harrier Drive........................F5
Helford Place........................F4
Helston Place.......................F4
Holy Close...........................A1
Hutton Avenue.....................E5
Ibistone Avenue...................C1

Kellan Drive.........................F4
Kernow Crescent..................F4
Kirkham Court......................B5
Kirkstall Place......................C5
Larwood Place......................E5
Leasowe Place......................B2
Linceslade Grove..................A5
Loughton Road.....................A2
Lower Fourth Street..............C4
Lower Ninth Street...............E3
Lower Tenth Street...............E3
Lower Twelfth Street............E2
Lucy Lane............................A5
Maidenhead Avenue.............B2
Mallow Gate.........................D1
Marigold Place......................D1
Marlborough Gate..................E1
Marlborough Gate..................E2
Marlborough Street...............F2
Mayditch Place.....................B2
Maynard Close......................A2
Midsummer Boulevard...........C4
Midsummer Boulevard...........E2
Midsummer Roundabout.........B4
Milburn Avenue....................D5
Mitcham Place......................C2
Mullion Place.......................F4
North Eighth Street...............D2
North Eleventh Street...........E1
North Fourth Street...............C3
North Grafton
    Roundabout.....................B3
North Ninth Street................D2
North Row............................B3
North Row............................D2
North Saxon Roundabout.......C2

North Secklow
    Roundabout.....................D1
North Second Street..............B3
North Sixth Street.................C3
North Tenth Street................D2
North Third Street.................C3
North Thirteenth Street.........E1
North Twelfth Street..............E1
North Witan Roundabout........C3
Oldbrook Boulevard...............E5
Overend Close......................A1
Padstow Avenue...................E4
Patriot Drive.........................A3
Pencarrow Place...................F3
Pentewan Gate.....................F4
Perran Avenue......................F4
Pitcher Lane.........................A5
Plumstead Avenue................C2
Polruan Place.......................F4
Porthleven Place...................F3
Portway...............................A4
Portway Roundabout.............A4
Precedent Drive....................A3
Quinton Drive.......................A2
Ramsay Close.......................A2
Ramsons Avenue..................E1
Redland Drive......................B5
Rooksley Roundabout...........A2
Rylstone Close......................B1
Saxon Gate...........................D2
Saxon Street.........................C1
Secklow Gate.......................D2
Shackleton Place...................E5
Sheldon Roundabout.............F1
Silbury Boulevard.................B4
Silbury Roundabout...............B4

Simons Lea..........................A1
Skeldon Gate........................F1
South Eighth Street...............E3
South Fifth Street.................D4
South Fourth Street..............C4
South Grafton Roundabout.....C5
South Ninth Street................E3
South Row............................D4
South Saxon Roundabout.......E4
South Secklow Roundabout....E3
South Second Street..............C5
South Seventh Street............D4
South Sixth Street.................D4
South Tenth Street................E3
South Witan Roundabout.......D5
Speedwell Place...................D1
Springfield Roundabout.........F3
Stainton Drive......................B1
Stanton Wood
    Roundabout.....................C1
Statham Place......................E5
Stokenchurch Place...............C1
Stonecrop Place....................D1
Streatham Place....................B3
Strudwick Drive....................E5
Sutcliffe Avenue...................D4
Talland Avenue....................F4
The Boundary.......................E5
The Close.............................A1
The Craven...........................B1
The Green............................A5
Towan Avenue......................F5
Tranlands Brigg....................B1
Trueman Place......................E5
Turvil End............................A5
Tylers Green........................C2

Tyson Place..........................D5
Ulyett Place..........................D5
Upper Fifth Street.................C3
Upper Fourth Street..............C4
Upper Second Street.............C4
Upper Third Street................C4
Verity Place..........................E5
Walgrave Drive.....................A1
Walkhampton Avenue...........B2
Wandsworth Place.................C2
Wardle Place........................D5
Whetstone Close...................A1
Wimbledon Place..................C2
Wisely Avenue......................C2
Witan Gate...........................C3
Woodruff Avenue..................D1
Yarrow Place........................E1

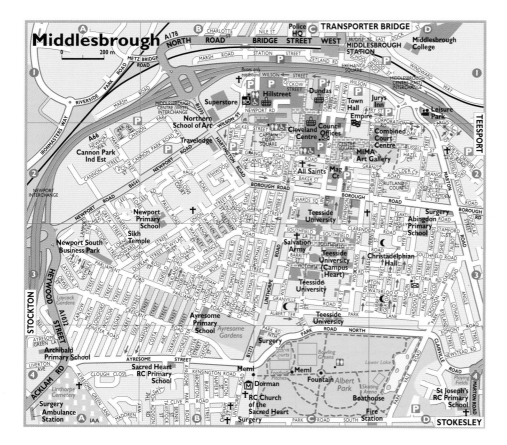

Middlesbrough

Middlesbrough is found on atlas page **104 E7**

Acklam Road	A4	Heywood Street	A3
Acton Street	C3	Ironmasters Way	A2
Aire Street	B4	Kensington Road	B4
Albert Road	C2	Kildare Street	A4
Amber Street	C2	Laurel Street	D3
Athol Street	B3	Lees Road	A2
Aubrey Street	D3	Linthorpe Road	B4
Ayresome Park Road	B4	Longford Street	A4
Ayresome Street	A4	Lorne Street	A3
Borough Road	C2	Lothian Road	D3
Bretnall Street	B2	Marsh Street	A2
Bridge Street East	C1	Marton Road	D2
Bridge Street West	C1	Melrose Street	D2
Bush Street	B4	Metz Bridge Road	A1
Cadogen Street	B3	Myrtle Street	D3
Camden Street	D2	Newlands Road	D3
Cannon Park Road	A2	Newport Road	A2
Cannon Park Way	A2	Palm Street	D3
Cannon Street	A2	Park Lane	C3
Carlow Street	A3	Park Road North	C4
Centre Square	C2	Park Vale Road	D4
Clairville Road	D4	Parliament Road	A3
Clarendon Road	C3	Pearl Street	C2
Clifton Street	B3	Pelham Street	C3
Corporation Road	D1	Portman Street	B3
Costa Street	B4	Princes Road	B3
Craven Street	B3	Riverside Park Road	A1
Crescent Road	A3	Ruby Street	C2
Croydon Road	D3	Russell Street	D2
Derwent Street	A2	St Pauls Road	B2
Diamond Road	B3	Southfield Road	C3
Egmont Road	D4	Station Street	C1
Emily Street	C2	Stowe Street	B3
Errol Street	D3	Tavistock Street	B4
Essex Street	A4	Tennyson Street	B3
Fairbridge Street	C2	Union Street	A3
Falmouth Street	D3	Victoria Road	C3
Finsbury Street	B3	Victoria Street	A3
Fleetham Street	B2	Warren Street	B2
Garnet Street	B2	Waterloo Road	D3
Glebe Road	B3	Waverley Street	B3
Grange Road	B2	Wembley Street	A3
Grange Road	D2	Wilson Street	B2
Granville Road	C3	Wilton Street	C3
Gresham Road	B3	Windsor Street	B2
Harewood Street	B3	Woodlands Road	C3
Harford Street	B4	Worcester Street	B4
Hartington Road	B2	Zetland Road	C1

Newport

Newport is found on atlas page **31 K7**

Albert Terrace	B3	Jones Street	B3
Allt-Yr-Yn Avenue	A2	Keynsham Avenue	C4
Bailey Street	B3	King Street	C4
Bedford Road	D2	Kingsway	C2
Blewitt Street	B3	Kingsway	C4
Bond Street	C1	Llanthewy Road	A3
Bridge Street	B2	Locke Street	B1
Bryngwyn Road	A3	Lower Dock Street	C4
Brynhyfryd Avenue	A4	Lucas Street	B1
Brynhyfryd Road	A4	Market Street	B2
Caerau Crescent	A4	Mellon Street	C4
Caerau Road	A3	Mill Street	B2
Cambrian Road	B2	North Street	B3
Caroline Street	D3	Oakfield Road	A3
Cedar Road	D2	Park Square	C4
Charles Street	C3	Queen's Hill	B1
Chepstow Road	D1	Queen's Hill Crescent	A1
Clarence Place	C1	Queen Street	C4
Clifton Place	B4	Queensway	B2
Clifton Road	B4	Risca Road	A4
Clyffard Crescent	A3	Rodney Road	C2
Clytha Park Road	A2	Rudry Street	D1
Clytha Square	C4	Ruperra Lane	C4
Colts Foot Close	A1	Ruperra Street	D4
Commercial Street	C3	St Edward Street	B3
Corelli Street	D1	St Julian Street	B4
Corn Street	C2	St Mark's Crescent	A2
Corporation Road	D2	St Mary Street	B3
Devon Place	B2	St Vincent Road	C2
Dewsland Park Road	B4	St Woolos Road	B3
Dumfries Place	D4	School Lane	C3
East Street	B3	Serpentine Road	A2
East Usk Road	C1	Skinner Street	C2
Factory Road	B1	Sorrel Drive	A1
Fields Road	A2	Spencer Road	A3
Friars Field	B4	Stow Hill	B3
Friars Road	B4	Stow Hill	B4
Friar Street	C3	Stow Park Avenue	A4
George Street	D4	Talbot Lane	C3
Godfrey Road	A2	Tregare Street	D1
Gold Tops	A2	Tunnel Terrace	A3
Grafton Road	C2	Upper Dock Street	B3
Granville Lane	D4	Upper Dock Street	C3
Granville Street	D4	Usk Way	D3
High Street	B2	Victoria Crescent	B3
Hill Street	C3	West Street	B3
John Frost Square	C3	Wyndham Strret	C1
John Street	D4	York Place	A4

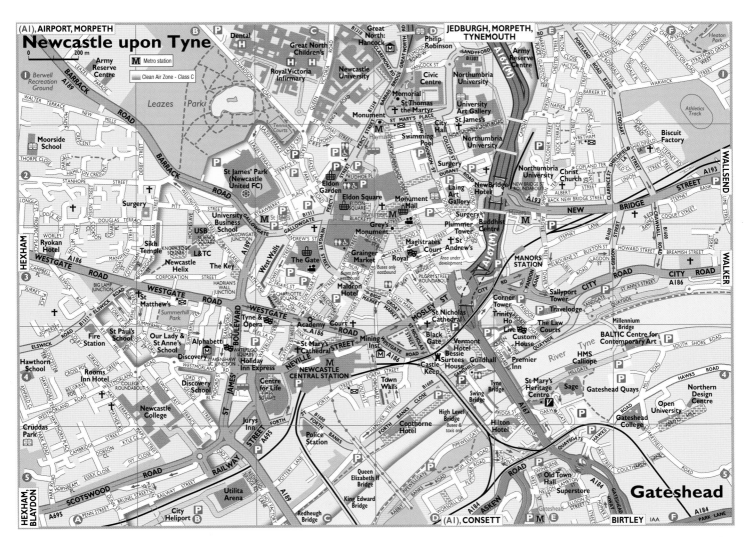

Newcastle upon Tyne

Newcastle upon Tyne is found on atlas page **113 K8**

Abbots Hill F4	Clayton Street West..............C4	Fenkle Street C3	King Edward Bridge C5	Oxford Street D2	Scotswood Road A5
Albert Street..........................E2	Cloth Market D3	Field Close F2	King Street.............................E4	Pandon..................................E3	Shieldfield Lane F2
Argyle Street..........................E2	Colby Court............................A4	Fletcher Road.........................D5	Kirkdale Green A4	Pandon Bank E3	Shield Street.........................E2
Askew Road D5	College Roundabout A4	Forth Banks C4	Kyle Close A5	Park Lane F5	Shot Factory Lane.................C5
Avision Street A2	College Street D2	Forth Banks Close D5	Lambton Street.......................E5	Park Road A5	Simpson Terrace....................E2
Back New Bridge Street E2	Cookson Close A3	Forth Street C4	Leazes Crescent C2	Peel Lane B4	Somerset Place......................A4
Barker Street..........................E1	Copland Terrace E2	Friars Street C3	Leazes Lane C2	Penn Street A5	South Shore Road...................F4
Barrack Road..........................A1	Coppice Way E1	Gallowgate B2	Leazes Park Road C2	Percy Street C2	South Street C4
Barras Bridge D1	Coquet Street F2	Gallowgate Junction B3	Leazes Terrace C2	Pilgrim Street D2	Stanhope Street.....................A2
Bath Lane B3	Corporation Street B3	Gateshead Highway E5	Liddle Road A2	Pink Lane C4	Stepney Bank F2
Belgrave Parade A4	Cottenham Street A3	George Street B4	Lime Street F2	Pipewellgate...........................D5	Stepney Lane E3
Big Lamp Junction A3	Coulthards Lane.....................F5	Gibson Street F3	Lombard Street.......................E4	Pitt Street B2	Stepney Road.........................F2
Blackett Street C2	Crawhall Road........................F2	Gladstone Terrace E1	Longley Street A2	Portland Road E1	Stoddart Street......................F1
Blagdon Street E3	Cross Parade A4	Gloucester Terrace A4	Lord Street.............................B4	Portland Road F1	Stowell Street C3
Blandford Square B4	Cross Street C3	Grainger Street C3	Low Friar Street......................C3	Pottery Lane C5	Stratford Grove West F1
Blandford Street B4	Darnell Place A2	Grantham Road E1	Maiden Street B5	Prospect Place A2	Strawberry Place....................C2
Bottle Bank E4	Dean Street D3	Great North Road D1	Mansfield Street.....................A3	Prudhoe Place........................C2	Summerhill Grove B3
Boyd Street F2	Derby Street B2	Grey Street D3	Maple Street B5	Quarryfield Road F5	Summerhill Street A3
Breamish Street F3	Diana Street B3	Groat Market C3	Maple Terrace.........................A4	Quayside E5	Summerhill Terrace................B4
Bridge Street E4	Dinsdale Place F1	Hamilton Crescent A2	Market Street D3	Quayside F3	Swinburne Street...................E5
Broad Chare E3	Dinsdale Road F1	Hanover Street C5	Mather Road A4	Quayside E4	Tarset Road F3
Brunel Street A5	Dobson Close A5	Harrison Place........................E1	Melbourne Street E3	Queen Street E4	Terrace Place C2
Buckingham Street B3	Douglas Terrace A2	Hawks Road E5	Mill Road F4	Queen Victoria Road C1	Tindal Street A3
Buxton Street E3	Duke Street B4	Hawthorn Place......................A4	Milton Close E1	Rabbit Banks Road D5	Tower Street E3
Byron Street...........................E1	Dunn Street A5	Hawthorn Terrace...................A4	Milton Place E1	Railway Street........................B5	Tyne Bridge E4
Cambridge Street A5	Durant Road D2	Helmsley Road E1	Monday Crescent A1	Red Barnes F2	Union Street F2
Camden Street E2	East Street E5	Henry Square E2	Mosley Street D3	Redheugh Bridge Road B5	Vallum Way A3
Campbell Place.......................A3	Edward Place A3	High Bridge D3	Napier Street E1	Richardson Road.....................B1	Victoria Street B4
Carliol Square D3	Eldon Square C2	High Level Road D5	Nelson Street C3	Rock Terrace E2	Walter Terrace........................A1
Charlotte Square C3	Ellison Street E5	High Street E5	Nelson Street E5	Rosedale Terrace E1	Warwick Street F1
Chelmsford Grove F1	Elswick East Terrace..............B4	Hillgate E4	Neville Street C4	Rye Hill A4	Waterloo Square B4
Chester Street E1	Elswick Road A3	Hood Street D3	New Bridge Street...................E2	St Andrew's Street C3	Waterloo Street C4
City Road E3	Elswick Row A3	Hopper Street E5	Newgate Street C3	St Ann's Street F3	Wellington Street....................B2
Claremont Road D1	Essex Close A5	Hornbeam Place A5	Newington Road F1	St James' Boulevard B4	Westgate Road A3
Clarence Street E2	Falconer's Court......................C3	Houston Street A4	New Mills A1	St Mary's Place D1	Westmorland Road A4
Clayton Street C3	Falconer Street E2	Howard Street F3	Northumberland Road D2	St Nicholas Street D4	West Street E5
		Hudson Street E5	Northumberland Street...........D2	St Thomas' Crescent C2	West Walls C3
		Ivy Close A5	Nun Street C3	St Thomas' Street C1	Worley Close A3
		Jesmond Road West..............D1	Oakwellgate E4	Sandgate E3	Worsdell Drive D5
		John Dobson Street................D2	Orchard Street C4	Sandhill D4	Wretham Place E2
		Jubilee Road...........................E3	Ord Street B5	Sandyford Road D1	York Street A3

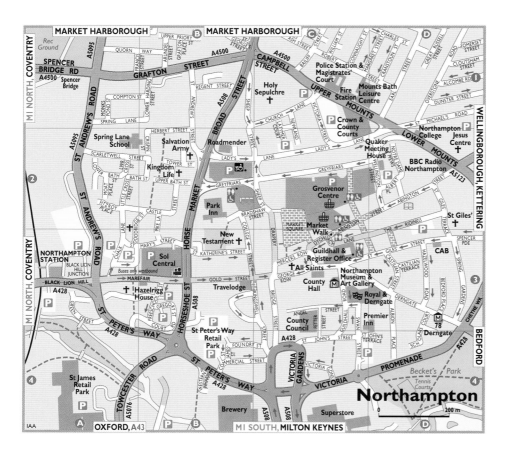

Northampton

Northampton is found on atlas page **60 G8**

Abington Street	C2	Little Cross Street	A2
Albert Place	D2	Lower Bath Street	A2
Albion Place	D3	Lower Cross Street	A2
Angel Street	C3	Lower Harding Street	B1
Arundel Street	B1	Lower Mounts	D2
Ash Street	C1	Marefair	A3
Bailiff Street	C1	Margaret Street	C1
Black Lion Hill	A3	Market Square	C2
Bradshaw Street	B2	Mercers Row	C3
Bridge Street	C3	Moat Place	A2
Broad Street	B1	Monkspond Street	A1
Campbell Street	C1	Newland	C1
Castilian Street	D3	Notredame Mews	D2
Castle Street	B2	Overstone Road	D1
Chalk Lane	A3	Pike Lane	B3
Cheyne Walk	D3	Quorn Way	A1
Church Lane	C1	Regent Street	B1
College Street	B2	Robert Street	C1
Commercial Street	B4	St Andrew's Road	A2
Connaught Street	C1	St Andrew's Street	B1
Court Road	B3	St Giles' Street	D3
Cranstoun Street	D1	St Giles' Terrace	D2
Crispin Street	B2	St John's Street	C4
Derngate	D3	St Katherine's Street	B3
Doddridge Street	A3	St Mary's Street	A3
Drapery	C3	St Michael's Road	D1
Dunster Street	D1	St Peter's Way	B4
Dychurch Lane	C3	Scarletwell Street	A2
Earl Street	D1	Scholars Court	D4
Fetter Street	C3	Sheep Street	B1
Fitzroy Place	A2	Sheep Street	C2
Foundry Street	B4	Spencer Bridge Road	A1
Francis Street	A1	Spencer Parade	D3
Freeschool Street	B3	Spring Gardens	D3
George Row	C3	Spring Lane	A1
Gold Street	B3	Swan Street	C3
Grafton Street	A1	Tanner Street	A4
Great Russell Street	D1	The Ridings	D2
Green Street	A3	Towcester Road	A4
Gregory Street	B3	Tower Street	B2
Greyfriars	B2	Upper Bath Street	B2
Guildhall Road	C3	Upper Mounts	C1
Hazelwood Road	D3	Upper Priory Street	B1
Herbert Street	B2	Victoria Gardens	C4
Horse Market	B3	Victoria Promenade	C4
Horseshoe Street	B3	Victoria Street	C1
Kingswell Street	C3	Wellington Street	D2
Lady's Lane	B2	Western Wharf	B4

Norwich

Norwich is found on atlas page **77 J10**

All Saints Green	B4	Pottergate	A2
Bank Plain	C2	Prince of Wales Road	C2
Barn Road	A1	Princes Street	C2
Bedding Lane	C1	Quay Side	C1
Bedford Street	B2	Queens Road	B4
Ber Street	C4	Queen Street	C2
Bethel Street	A3	Rampant Horse Street	B3
Bishopgate	D1	Recorder Road	D2
Brigg Street	B3	Red Lion Street	B3
Calvert Street	B1	Riverside Road	D3
Castle Meadow	C3	Riverside Walk	D1
Cathedral Street	D2	Rose Lane	C3
Cattle Market Street	C3	Rouen Road	C3
Chantry Road	B3	Rupert Street	A4
Chapelfield East	A3	St Andrews Street	B2
Chapelfield North	A3	St Benedicts Street	A2
Chapelfield Road	A3	St Faiths Lane	D2
Cleveland Road	A3	St Georges Street	B1
Colegate	B1	St Giles Street	A2
Convent Road	A2	St Julians Alley	C4
Coslany Street	B2	St Marys Plain	B1
Cow Hill	A2	St Peters Street	B3
Davey Place	B3	St Stephens Road	B4
Dove Street	B2	St Stephens Square	A4
Duke Street	B1	St Stephens Street	B4
Elm Hill	C2	St Swithins Road	A2
Exchange Street	B2	St Verdast Street	D2
Farmers Avenue	C3	Surrey Street	B4
Ferry Lane	D2	Ten Bell Lane	A2
Fishergate	C1	Theatre Street	B3
Friars Quay	B1	Thorn Lane	C4
Gaol Hill	B3	Tombland	C2
Gentlemans Walk	B3	Unicorn Yard	A1
Goldenball Street	C3	Union Street	A4
Grapes Hill	A2	Unthank Road	A3
Haymarket	B3	Upper Goat Lane	B2
Heigham Street	A1	Upper King Street	C2
King Street	C2	Upper St Giles Street	A2
London Street	B2	Vauxhall Street	A3
Lower Goat Lane	B2	Walpole Street	A3
Magdalen Street	C1	Wensum Street	C1
Market Avenue	C3	Wessex Street	A4
Mountergate	D3	Westlegate	B3
Music House Lane	D4	Westwick Street	A1
Muspole Street	B1	Wherry Road	D4
New Mills Yard	A1	Whitefriars	C1
Oak Street	A1	White Lion Street	B3
Palace Street	C1	Willow Lane	A2

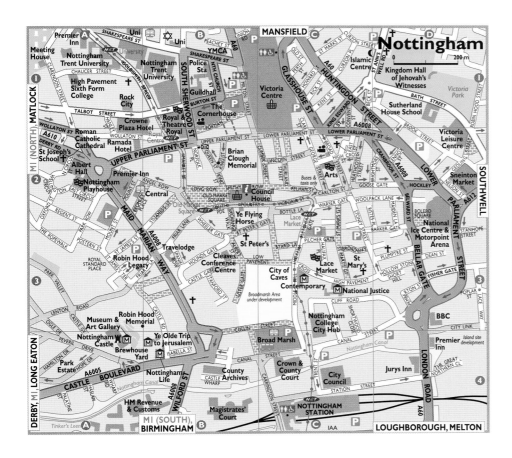

Nottingham

Nottingham is found on atlas page **72 F3**

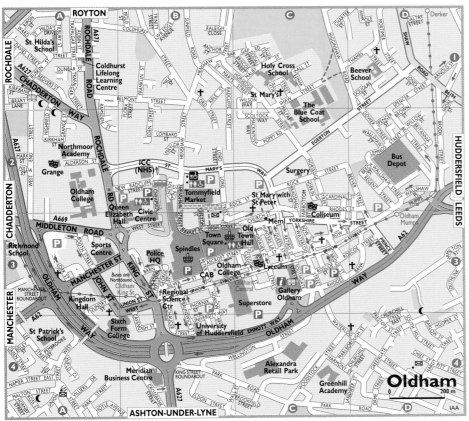

Oldham

Oldham is found on atlas page **83 K4**

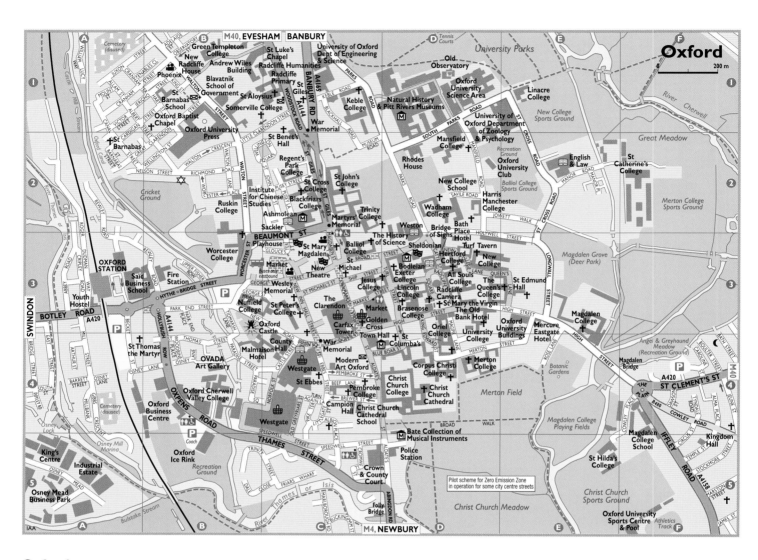

Oxford

Oxford is found on atlas page **34 F3**

Abbey Road............................A3	Cromwell Street....................C5	Marston Street.....................F5	St Barnabas Street................A2
Abingdon Road D5	Dale Close............................B5	Merton Street D4	St Clement's Street F4
Adelaide Street......................B1	Dawson Street......................F4	Millbank A4	St Cross Road E1
Albert Street.........................A1	East Street............................A4	Mill Street............................A4	St Cross Road E2
Albion Place.........................C4	Folly Bridge..........................C5	Mount Street........................A1	St Ebbes Street.....................C4
Allam Street.........................A1	Friars Wharf C5	Museum Road C2	St Giles................................C2
Alma Place...........................F4	George Street B3	Nelson Street........................A2	St John Street C2
Arthur Street........................A4	George Street Mews B3	New College Lane.................D3	St Michael's Street................C3
Banbury Road C1	Gibbs Crescent.....................A4	New Inn Hall Street...............C3	St Thomas' Street.................B4
Barrett Street........................A4	Gloucester Street..................C3	New Road B3	Savile Road D2
Bath Street...........................F4	Great Clarendon Street..........A2	Norfolk Street C4	Ship Street...........................C3
Beaumont Street...................C3	Hart Street............................B1	Observatory Street................B1	South Parks Road D2
Becket Street........................A3	High Street D3	Osney Lane A4	South Street..........................A4
Beef Lane C4	High Street E4	Osney Lane B4	Speedwell Street...................C5
Blackhall Road C1	Hollybush Row B3	Osney Mead A5	Stockmore Street...................F5
Blue Boar Street....................C4	Holywell Street D2	Oxpens Road B4	Temple Street F5
Bonn Square C4	Hythe Bridge Street...............B3	Paradise Square B4	Thames Street.......................C5
Botley Road A3	Iffley Road F4	Paradise Street B4	The Plain..............................F4
Boulter Street F4	James Street F5	Park End Street B3	Tidmarsh Lane B3
Brewer Street........................C4	Jericho Street A1	Parks Road C1	Trinity Street B5
Bridge Street.........................A4	Jowett Walk D2	Parks Road D2	Turl Street D3
Broad Street.........................C3	Juxon Street A1	Pembroke Street....................C4	Turn Again Lane....................C4
Broad Walk..........................D4	Keble Road C1	Pike Terrace C4	Tyndale Road F4
Buckingham Street C5	King Edward Street...............D3	Pusey Lane C2	Upper Fisher Row.................B3
Canal Street..........................A1	King Street............................B1	Pusey Street C2	Venables Close......................A1
Cardigan Street.....................A2	Little Clarendon Street B2	Queen's Lane D3	Victor Street A1
Caroline Street......................F4	Littlegate Street.....................C4	Queen Street.........................C4	Walton Crescent B2
Castle Street..........................C4	Longwall Street.....................E3	Radcliffe Square....................D3	Walton Lane..........................B2
Catte Street D3	Magdalen Bridge E4	Rewley Road A2	Walton Street........................B1
Circus Street.........................F5	Magdalen Street....................C3	Rewley Road B3	Wellington Square B2
Cornmarket Street C3	Magpie Lane D3	Richmond Road B2	Wellington Street...................B2
Cowley Place........................F4	Manor Place E2	Roger Dudman Way..............A3	William Lucy Way.................A1
Cowley Road F4	Manor Road E2	Rose Lane E4	Woodbine Place....................B4
Cranham Street A1	Mansfield Road D2	St Aldate's C4	Woodstock Road...................C1
Cranham Terrace A1	Market Street........................C3	St Aldate's D5	Worcester Place.....................B2
Cripley Road A3	Marlborough Road C5	Worcester Street....................B3	

University Colleges

All Souls College...................D3	
Balliol College......................C3	
Brasenose College D3	
Christ Church College............D4	
Corpus Christi College...........D4	
Exeter College......................D3	
Harris Manchester College D2	
Hertford College D3	
Jesus College........................C3	
Keble College.......................C1	
Linacre College.....................E1	
Lincoln College D3	
Magdalen College E3	
Mansfield College D2	
Merton College D4	
New College D3	
Nuffield College B3	
Oriel College........................D3	
Pembroke College.................C4	
Ruskin College B2	
St Catherine's College F2	
St Cross College C2	
St Hilda's College..................E5	
St John's College C2	
St Peter's College..................C3	
Somerville College.................B1	
The Queen's College..............D3	
Trinity College......................C2	
University College..................D3	
Wadham College...................D2	
Worcester College..................B3	

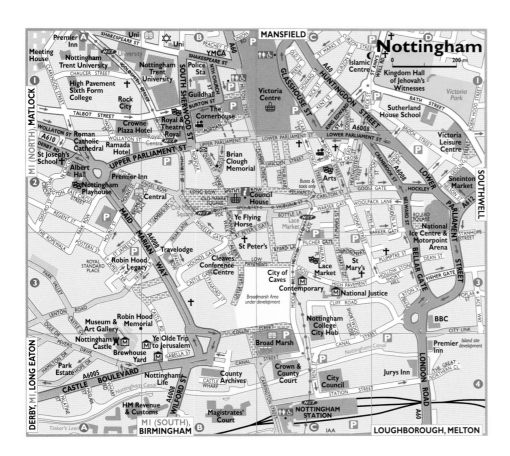

Nottingham

Nottingham is found on atlas page **72 F3**

Albert Street	B3	King Street	B2
Angel Row	B2	Lenton Road	A3
Barker Gate	D2	Lincoln Street	C2
Bath Street	D1	Lister Gate	B3
Bellar Gate	D3	London Road	D4
Belward Street	D2	Long Row	B2
Broad Street	C2	Lower Parliament Street	C2
Broadway	C3	Low Pavement	B3
Bromley Place	A2	Maid Marian Way	A2
Brook Street	D1	Market Street	B2
Burton Street	B1	Middle Hill	C3
Canal Street	C4	Milton Street	B1
Carlton Street	C2	Mount Street	A3
Carrington Street	C4	Norfolk Place	B2
Castle Boulevard	A4	North Circus Street	A2
Castle Gate	B3	Park Row	A3
Castle Road	B3	Pelham Street	C2
Chaucer Street	A1	Peveril Drive	A4
City Link	D3	Pilcher Gate	C3
Clarendon Street	A1	Popham Street	C3
Cliff Road	C3	Poultry	B2
Collin Street	B4	Queen Street	B2
Cranbrook Street	D2	Regent Street	A2
Cumber Street	C2	St Ann's Well Road	D1
Curzon Place	C1	St James's Street	A3
Derby Road	A2	St Marks Gate	C3
Exchange Walk	B2	St Marks Street	C1
Fisher Gate	D3	St Mary's Gate	B3
Fletcher Gate	C3	St Peter's Gate	B3
Forman Street	B1	Shakespeare Street	A1
Friar Lane	A3	Smithy Row	B2
Gedling Street	D2	South Parade	B2
George Street	C2	South Sherwood Street	B1
Glasshouse Street	C1	Spaniel Row	B3
Goldsmith Street	A1	Station Street	C4
Goose Gate	C2	Stoney Street	C2
Halifax Place	C3	Talbot Street	A1
Heathcote Street	C2	Thurland Street	C2
High Cross Street	C2	Trent Street	C4
High Pavement	C3	Upper Parliament Street	A2
Hockley	D2	Victoria Street	C2
Hollow Stone	D3	Warser Gate	C2
Hope Drive	A4	Weekday Cross	C3
Hounds Gate	B3	Wellington Circus	A2
Howard Street	C1	Wheeler Gate	B2
Huntingdon Street	C1	Wilford Street	B4
Kent Street	C1	Wollaton Street	A1
King Edward Street	C1	Woolpack Lane	C2

Oldham

Oldham is found on atlas page **83 K4**

Ascroft Street	B3	Napier Street East	A4
Bar Gap Road	B1	New Radcliffe Street	A2
Barlow Street	D4	Oldham Way	A3
Barn Street	B3	Park Road	B4
Beever Street	D2	Park Street	A4
Bell Street	D2	Peter Street	B3
Belmont Street	B1	Prince Street	D3
Booth Street	A3	Queen Street	C3
Bow Street	C3	Radcliffe Street	B1
Brook Street	D2	Ramsden Street	A1
Brunswick Street	B3	Regent Street	D2
Cardinal Street	C2	Rhodes Bank	C3
Chadderton Way	A1	Rhodes Street	C2
Chaucer Street	B3	Rifle Street	B1
Clegg Street	C3	Rochdale Road	A1
Coldhurst Road	B1	Rock Street	B2
Crossbank Street	B4	Roscoe Street	C3
Curzon Street	B2	Ruskin Street	A1
Dunbar Street	A1	St Hilda's Drive	A1
Eden Street	B2	St Marys Street	B1
Egerton Street	C2	St Mary's Way	B2
Emmott Way	C4	Shaw Road	D1
Firth Street	C3	Shaw Street	C1
Fountain Street	B2	Shore Street	D1
Franklin Street	B1	Siddall Street	C1
Gower Street	D2	Silver Street	B3
Grange Street	A2	Southgate Street	C3
Greaves Street	C3	South Hill Street	D4
Greengate Street	D4	Spencer Street	D2
Hardy Street	D4	Sunfield Road	B1
Harmony Street	C4	Thames Street	D1
Henshaw Street	B2	Trafalgar Street	A1
Higginshaw Road	C1	Trinity Street	B1
Highfield Street	A2	Tulbury Street	A1
High Street	B3	Union Street	B3
Hobson Street	B3	Union Street West	A4
Horsedge Street	C1	Union Street West	B3
John Street	A3	University Way	B4
King Street	B3	Wallshaw Street	D2
Lemnos Street	D2	Wall Street	B4
Malby Street	C1	Ward Street	A1
Malton Street	A4	Waterloo Street	C3
Manchester Street	A3	Wellington Street	B4
Market Place	B3	West End Street	A2
Marlborough Street	C4	West Street	B3
Middleton Road	A3	Willow Street	D2
Mortimer Street	D1	Woodstock Street	C4
Mumps	D2	Yorkshire Street	C3

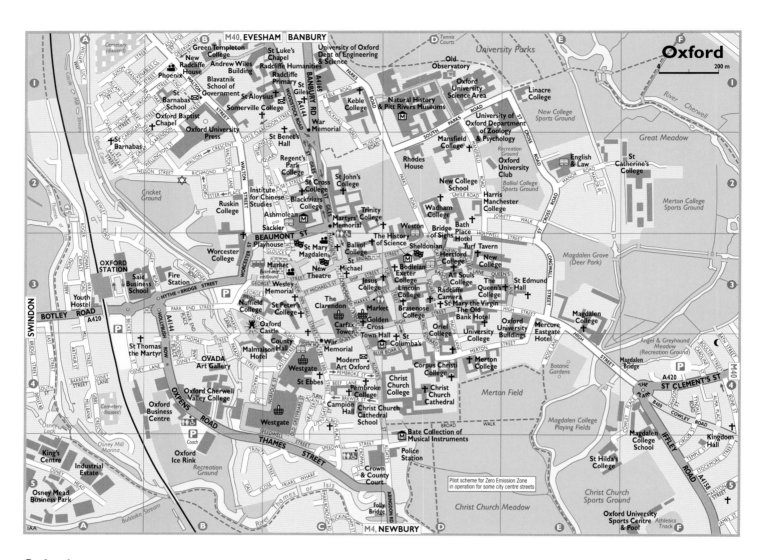

Oxford

Oxford is found on atlas page **34 F3**

Abbey Road	A3	Cromwell Street	C5
Abingdon Road	D5	Dale Close	B5
Adelaide Street	B1	Dawson Street	F4
Albert Street	A1	East Street	A4
Albion Place	C4	Folly Bridge	C5
Allam Street	A1	Friars Wharf	C5
Alma Place	F4	George Street	B3
Arthur Street	A4	George Street Mews	B3
Banbury Road	C1	Gibbs Crescent	A4
Barrett Street	A4	Gloucester Street	C3
Bath Street	F4	Great Clarendon Street	A2
Beaumont Street	C3	Hart Street	B1
Becket Street	A3	High Street	D3
Beef Lane	C4	High Street	E4
Blackhall Road	C1	Hollybush Row	B3
Blue Boar Street	C4	Holywell Street	D2
Bonn Square	C4	Hythe Bridge Street	B3
Botley Road	A3	Iffley Road	F4
Boulter Street	F4	James Street	F5
Brewer Street	C4	Jericho Street	A1
Bridge Street	A4	Jowett Walk	D2
Broad Street	C3	Juxon Street	A1
Broad Walk	D4	Keble Road	C1
Buckingham Street	C5	King Edward Street	D3
Canal Street	A1	King Street	B1
Cardigan Street	A2	Little Clarendon Street	B2
Caroline Street	F4	Littlegate Street	C4
Castle Street	C4	Longwall Street	E3
Catte Street	D3	Magdalen Bridge	E4
Circus Street	F5	Magdalen Street	C3
Cornmarket Street	C3	Magpie Lane	D3
Cowley Place	F4	Manor Place	E2
Cowley Road	F4	Manor Road	E2
Cranham Street	A1	Mansfield Road	D2
Cranham Terrace	A1	Market Street	C3
Cripley Road	A3	Marlborough Road	C5

Marston Street	F5	St Barnabas Street	A2
Merton Street	D4	St Clement's Street	F4
Millbank	A4	St Cross Road	E1
Mill Street	A4	St Cross Road	E2
Mount Street	A1	St Ebbes Street	C4
Museum Road	C2	St Giles	C2
Nelson Street	A2	St John Street	C2
New College Lane	D3	St Michael's Street	C3
New Inn Hall Street	C3	St Thomas' Street	B4
New Road	B3	Savile Road	D2
Norfolk Street	C4	Ship Street	C3
Observatory Street	B1	South Parks Road	D2
Old Greyfriars Street	C4	South Street	A4
Osney Lane	A4	Speedwell Street	C5
Osney Lane	B4	Stockmore Street	F5
Osney Mead	A5	Temple Street	F5
Oxpens Road	B4	Thames Street	C5
Paradise Square	B4	The Plain	F4
Paradise Street	B4	Tidmarsh Lane	B3
Park End Street	B3	Trinity Street	B5
Parks Road	C1	Turl Street	D3
Parks Road	D2	Turn Again Lane	C4
Pembroke Street	C4	Tyndale Road	F4
Pike Terrace	C4	Upper Fisher Row	B3
Pusey Lane	C2	Venables Close	A1
Pusey Street	C2	Victor Street	A1
Queen's Lane	D3	Walton Crescent	B2
Queen Street	C4	Walton Lane	B2
Radcliffe Square	D3	Walton Street	B1
Rewley Road	A2	Wellington Square	B2
Rewley Road	B3	Wellington Street	B2
Richmond Road	B2	William Lucy Way	A1
Roger Dudman Way	A3	Woodbine Place	B4
Rose Lane	E4	Woodstock Road	C1
St Aldate's	C4	Worcester Place	B2
St Aldate's	D5	Worcester Street	B3

University Colleges

All Souls College	D3
Balliol College	C3
Brasenose College	D3
Christ Church College	D4
Corpus Christi College	D4
Exeter College	D3
Harris Manchester College	D2
Hertford College	D3
Jesus College	C3
Keble College	C1
Linacre College	E1
Lincoln College	D3
Magdalen College	E3
Mansfield College	D2
Merton College	D4
New College	D3
Nuffield College	B3
Oriel College	D3
Pembroke College	C4
Ruskin College	B2
St Catherine's College	F2
St Cross College	C2
St Hilda's College	E5
St John's College	C2
St Peter's College	C3
Somerville College	B1
The Queen's College	D3
Trinity College	C2
University College	D3
Wadham College	D2
Worcester College	B3

Perth

Perth is found on atlas page **134 E3**

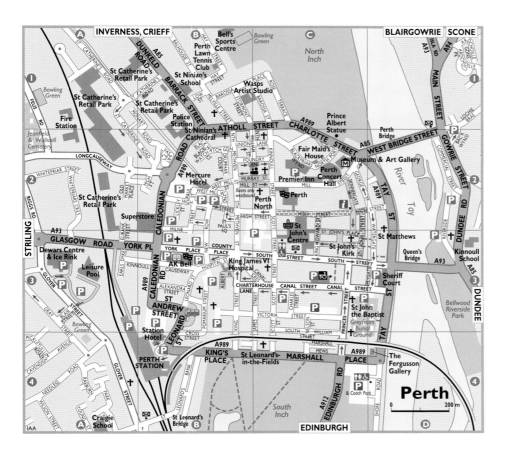

Albert Place	B3	Melville Street	B1
Alexandra Street	B3	Mill Street	C2
Atholl Street	B1	Milne Street	B2
Back Wynd	D2	Monart Road	A1
Balhousie Street	B1	Murray Street	B2
Barossa Place	B1	Needless Road	A4
Barrack Street	B1	New Row	B3
Blackfriars Wynd	C2	North Methven Street	B2
Black Watch Garden	B2	North Port	C2
Caledonian Road	B2	North William Street	B2
Caledonian Road	B3	Old Market Place	A2
Canal Street	C3	Paul Street	B2
Cavendish Avenue	A4	Perth Bridge	D2
Charles Street	C3	Pickletullum Road	A4
Charlotte Street	C2	Pomarium Street	B3
Charterhouse Lane	B3	Princes Street	C3
Commercial Street	D2	Queen's Bridge	D3
County Place	B3	Raeburn Park	A4
Cross Street	B4	Riggs Road	A2
Dundee Road	D3	Riverside	D3
Dunkeld Road	B1	Rose Terrace	C1
Earls Dykes	A3	St Andrew Street	B3
Edinburgh Road	C4	St Catherine's Road	A1
Elibank Street	A3	St John's Place	C3
Feus Road	A1	St John Street	C3
Foundry Lane	B2	St Leonard's Bank	B4
George Street	C2	St Paul's Square	B2
Glasgow Road	A3	Scott Street	C3
Glover Street	A3	Shore Road	D4
Glover Street	A4	Skinnergate	C2
Gowrie Street	D2	South Methven Street	B2
Gray Street	A3	South Street	C3
Hay Street	B1	South William Street	C4
High Street	B2	Speygate	D3
High Street	C2	Stormont Street	B1
Hospital Street	B3	Tay Street	D2
Isla Road	D1	Tay Street	D4
James Street	C3	Union Lane	B2
King Edward Street	C3	Victoria Street	C3
King's Place	B4	Watergate	D2
King Street	B3	West Bridge Street	D2
Kinnoull Causeway	A3	West Mill Street	B2
Kinnoull Street	C2	West Mill Wynd	B2
Leonard Street	B3	Whitefriars Crescent	A2
Lochie Brae	D1	Whitefriar Street	A2
Longcauseway	A2	Wilson Street	A4
Main Street	D1	York Place	A3
Marshall Place	C4	York Place	B3

Peterborough

Peterborough is found on atlas page **74 C11**

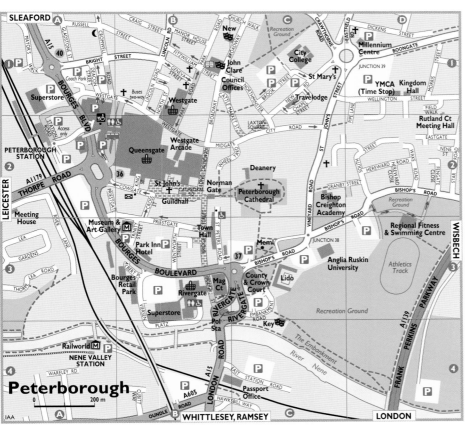

Albert Place	B3	New Road	C1
Bishop's Road	C3	Northminster	C1
Boongate	D1	North Street	B1
Bourges Boulevard	A1	Oundle Road	B4
Bridge Street	B3	Park Road	B1
Bright Street	A1	Pipe Lane	D2
Broadway	B2	Priestgate	A2
Brook Street	C1	Rivergate	B3
Cathedral Square	B2	River Lane	A2
Cattle Market Street	B1	Russell Street	A1
Chapel Street	C1	St John's Street	C2
Church Street	B2	St Peters Road	B3
Church Walk	C1	South Street	D2
City Road	C1	Star Road	D2
Cowgate	B2	Station Road	A2
Craig Street	B1	Thorpe Lea Road	A3
Crawthorne Road	C1	Thorpe Road	A2
Cromwell Road	A1	Trinity Street	B3
Cross Street	B2	Viersen Platz	B3
Cubitt Way	B4	Vineyard Road	C3
Deacon Street	A1	Wake Road	D2
Dickens Street	D1	Wareley Road	A4
Eastfield Road	D1	Wellington Street	D1
Eastgate	D2	Wentworth Street	B3
East Station Road	C4	Westgate	A1
Embankment Road	C3		
Exchange Street	B2		
Fengate Close	D2		
Field Walk	D1		
Fitzwilliam Street	B1		
Frank Perkins Parkway	D4		
Geneva Street	B1		
Gladstone Street	A1		
Granby Street	C2		
Hawksbill Way	B4		
Hereward Close	D2		
Hereward Road	D2		
King Street	B2		
Laxton Square	C2		
Lea Gardens	A3		
Lincoln Road	B1		
London Road	B4		
Long Causeway	B2		
Manor House Street	B1		
Mayor's Walk	A1		
Midgate	B2		
Morris Street	D1		
Nene Street	D2		

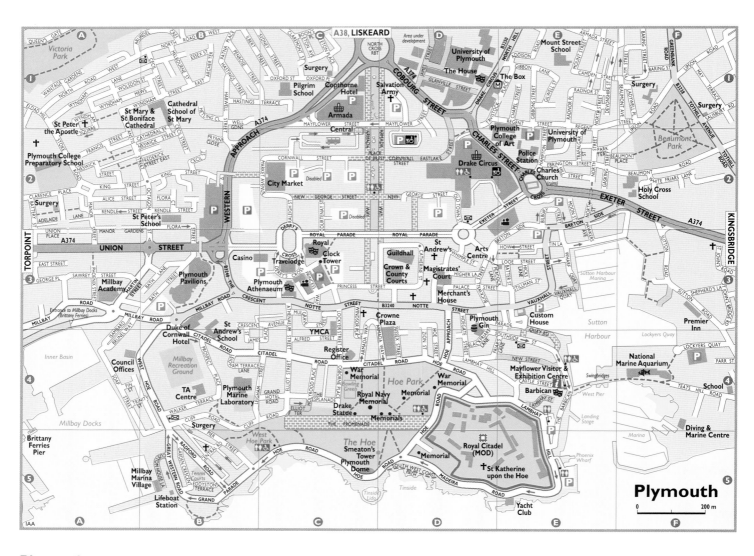

Plymouth

Plymouth is found on atlas page **6 D8**

Addison Road....................E1	Claremont Street.................C1	Grand Hotel Road..............C4	Martin Street.....................A3	Queen's Gate....................A1	Vauxhall Street...................E3
Adelaide Lane....................A2	Clarence Place...................A2	Grand Parade.....................B5	Mayflower Street................C1	Radford Road....................B5	Walker Terrace..................B4
Alfred Street.....................C4	Cliff Road...........................B4	Great Western Road...........B5	Mayflower Street................D1	Radnor Place.....................E1	Wantage Gardens.............A1
Alice Street.......................A2	Cobourg Street...................D1	Greenbank Road.................F1	May Terrace.......................F1	Radnor Street....................E1	Well Gardens.....................B1
Anstis Street.....................A2	Cornwall Street..................C2	Hampton Street..................E2	Melbourne Street...............B1	Raleigh Street....................C2	Western Approach.............B2
Archer Terrace..................B1	Courtenay Street................C3	Harwell Street....................B1	Millbay Road.....................A3	Regent Street....................E1	West Hoe Road.................A4
Armada Street...................E1	Crescent Avenue...............B3	Hastings Street...................B1	Moon Street.......................E2	Rendle Street.....................A2	Wharf Quay.......................E3
Armada Way......................C2	Custom House Lane...........B5	Hastings Terrace................B1	Mount Street......................E1	Royal Parade.....................C3	Whimple Street..................D3
Armada Way......................C4	Derry's Cross.....................C3	Hawkers Avenue................E2	Mulgrave Street.................C3	St James Place..................B4	Windsor Place...................C3
Arundel Crescent..............A1	Devonshire Street..............E1	Hetling Close.....................B1	Neswick Street..................A2	St John's Bridge Road.......F3	Wolsdon Street.................A1
Athenaeum Street.............C3	Drake Circus......................D1	Hicks Lane.........................E3	New George Street............C2	St John's Road..................F3	Wyndham Lane..................A1
Baring Street.....................F1	Eastlake Street...................D2	Higher Lane.......................D3	New Street.........................E4	Salisbury Road..................F3	Wyndham Mews.................A1
Bath Lane..........................B3	East Street..........................A3	Hill Street...........................E2	North Cross Roundabout....C1	Sawrey Street....................A3	Wyndham Square..............A1
Bath Street........................B3	Ebrington Street.................E2	Hoe Approach....................D4	North Hill...........................E1	Shepherd's Lane................F3	Wyndham Street East........A1
Batter Street......................E3	Eddystone Terrace..............B5	Hoegate Street...................D3	North Road West................A1	Soap Street........................A4	Zion Street.........................D4
Battery Street....................A2	Eldad Hill...........................A1	Hoe Road...........................C5	North Street.......................E2	Southside Street.................D4	
Beaumont Avenue.............F1	Elliot Street........................C4	Hoe Street..........................D3	Notte Street.......................C3	South West Coast Path......D5	
Beaumont Place.................E2	Elliot Terrace......................C4	Holyrood Place...................C4	Octagon Street..................B2	Stillman Street...................D4	
Beaumont Road..................F2	Essex Street........................B1	How Street.........................E3	Old Town Street.................D2	Stoke Road........................A2	
Bilbury Street....................E2	Eton Avenue......................C1	Ilbert Street.......................B1	Osborne Place....................C4	Sussex Street.....................D3	
Blackfriars Lane................D4	Eton Place..........................C1	Isambard Brunel Way.........A4	Oxford Street.....................C1	Sutton Road.......................F3	
Boon's Place.....................C1	Exeter Street......................D2	James Street.......................D1	Palace Street......................D3	Sydney Street....................B1	
Breton Side........................D3	Exeter Street......................E2	King Street.........................A2	Park Terrace.......................E2	Tavistock Place..................D1	
Brunel Way........................A4	Fin Street...........................A4	Ladywell Place...................F1	Parr Street.........................F4	Teats Hill Road..................F4	
Buckwell Street.................D3	Flora Court........................B2	Lambhay Hill......................D4	Patna Place.......................B1	The Barbican......................E4	
Camden Street...................E1	Flora Street........................B2	Lambhay Street..................E4	Peacock Lane....................D3	The Crescent......................B3	
Castle Street.......................E4	Francis Street.....................A2	Leigham Street...................B4	Penrose Street...................B1	The Esplanade....................C4	
Cathedral Street................A2	Frederick Street East..........A2	Leigham Terrace Lane.........B4	Phoenix Street...................A3	The Promenade..................C4	
Catherine Street................D3	Friar's Lane........................D4	Lipson Road.......................F1	Pier Street.........................B5	Tin Lane.............................E3	
Cecil Street........................B1	Garden Crescent................B5	Lockyers Quay....................F4	Place de Brest....................C2	Tothill Avenue....................F1	
Central Road......................B5	Gasking Street...................E2	Lockyer Street...................C3	Plym Street........................F1	Tothill Road........................F2	
Chapel Street.....................E1	George Place......................A3	Looe Street........................E3	Princess Street...................C3	Trafalgar Street..................E2	
Charles Cross.....................E2	Gibbon Lane.......................E1	Madeira Road.....................D5	Princess Way.....................C3	Trinity Street......................A4	
Charles Street....................D2	Gibbons Street...................E1	Manor Gardens..................A3	Prospect Place...................B4	Union Place........................A3	
Citadel Road......................B4	Gilwell Street......................E1	Manor Street......................A2	Prynne Close.....................B2	Union Street.......................A3	
Citadel Road......................C4	Glanville Street...................D1	Market Avenue...................C2	Quay Road.........................E4	Vauxhall Quay...................E3	

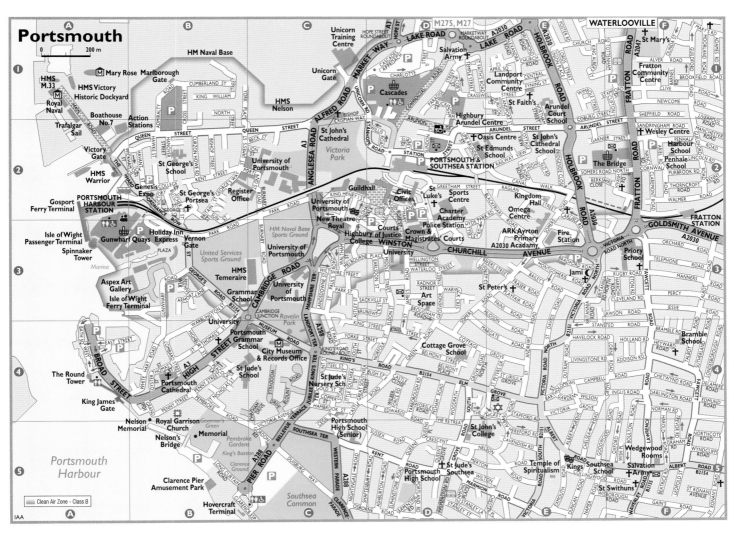

Portsmouth

Portsmouth is found on atlas page **14 H7**

Admiralty Road B2
Albany Road E5
Albert Grove E5
Albert Road E5
Alec Rose Lane D3
Alexandra Road E1
Alfred Road C1
Alver Road F1
Anglesea Road C2
Ariel Road F2
Armory Lane B3
Arundel Street D2
Arundel Street E2
Ashburton Road D5
Bailey's Road E3
Bath Square A4
Bellevue Terrace C5
Belmont Place D4
Bishop Crispian Way C2
Bishop Street B2
Blackfriars Road E2
Blount Road C4
Boulton Road F5
Bramble Road F1
Bridgeside Close E2
Britain Street B2
Broad Street A4
Brookfield Road F1
Brunswick Street C3
Buckingham Street D1
Cambridge Road C3
Campbell Road E4
Canal Walk E2
Carlisle Road E2
Cascades Approach D1
Castle Road C4

Cavendish Road E5
Central Street E1
Charlotte Street D1
Chelsea Road E5
Chester Place E5
Chetwynd Road F4
Church Road E1
Claremont Road F2
Clarence Parade C5
Cleveland Road F3
Clive Road F1
Clock Street B2
College Street B2
Collingwood Road E5
Commercial Road D1
Cornwall Road F2
Cottage Grove D4
Cottage View E2
Crasswell Street D1
Cross Street B2
Cumberland Street B1
Curzon Howe Road B2
Darlington Road F4
Drummond Road E1
Duisburg Way C5
Duncan Road E5
Earlsdon Street D3
East Street A4
Eldon Street D4
Elm Grove D4
Elphinstone Road D5
Exmouth Road E5
Fawcett Road E3
Fawcett Road F4
Flint Street C4

Foster Road E1
Fratton Road F2
Gain's Road F5
Garnier Street E2
Goldsmith Avenue F3
Gold Street C4
Goodwood Road E5
Gordon Road C5
Great Southsea Street C4
Green Road D4
Greetham Street D2
Grosvenor Street D3
Grove Road North D4
Grove Road South D5
Guildford Road F1
Guildhall Walk C2
Gunwharf Road B3
Hambrook Street C4
Hampshire Terrace C3
Harold Road F5
Havant Street B2
Havelock Road E4
Hawke Street B2
Hereford Road E5
Highbury Street B4
High Street B4
Holbrook Road E1
Holland Road F4
Hudson Road E3
Hyde Park Road D3
Inglis Road F4
Jessie Road F3
Jubilee Terrace C4
Kent Road D5
Kent Street B2
King Albert Street E1
King Henry I Street C2
King's Road C4
King's Terrace C4
King Street C4
King William Street B1

Lake Road D1
Landport Street E1
Landport Terrace C3
Landsdowne Street C3
Lawrence Road F5
Lawson Road F3
Leopold Street F5
Lincoln Road F2
Little Southsea Street C4
Livingstone Road E4
Lombard Street B4
Londesborough Road F4
Lords Street E1
Lorne Road F4
Main Road A1
Manners Road F3
Margate Road D4
Market Way C1
Marmion Road D5
Mary Rose Street D2
Melbourne Place C3
Merton Road D5
Middle Street D3
Milford Road E2
Montgomerie Road E3
Moorland Road F1
Museum Road C4
Napier Road E5
Nelson Road D5
Newcome Road F1
Nightingale Road C5
Norfolk Street D4
Norman Road F4
Olinda Street F1
Orchard Road F3
Ordnance Row B2
Osborne Road C5
Outram Road E4
Oxford Road F5
Oyster Street B4
Pains Road E3

Palmerston Road D5
Paradise Street D1
Park Road B3
Pelham Road D4
Pembroke Road B4
Penhale Road F2
Penny Street B4
Percy Road F3
Pier Road C5
Playfair Road D5
Portland Road D5
Purbrook Road F2
Queens Crescent D5
Queen Street B2
Raglan Street E2
Railway View E2
Richmond Place D5
Rivers Street D3
Rugby Road F3
Sackville Street C3
St Andrews Road E4
St Bartholomews Gardens ... E4
St Davids Road E4
St Edwards Road D4
St Faith's Road D1
St George's Road B3
St George's Square B2
St George's Way B2
St James's Road D3
St James's Street B2
St Nicholas Street B4
St Paul's Road C3
St Peters Grove E4
St Thomas's Street B4
Sandringham Road F2
Shaftesbury Road C5
Somers Road D4
Somers Road E3
Somers Road North E2
Southsea Terrace C5
Stafford Road E4

Stamford Street E1
Stanhope Road D2
Stansted Road E4
Station Street D2
Steel Street C4
Stone Street C4
Sussex Road D5
Sutherland Road F4
Talbot Road F4
Telephone Road F3
Temple Street D1
The Hard A2
The Retreat D5
The Thicket D4
Thorncroft Road F2
Tottenham Road F1
Trevor Road F4
Unicorn Road C1
Upper Arundel Street D2
Victoria Avenue C5
Victoria Grove E4
Victoria Road North E4
Victoria Road North F3
Victoria Road South E5
Vivash Road F2
Walmer Road E5
Warblington Street B4
Warwick Crescent D3
Waterloo Street D3
Waverley Road E5
Western Parade C5
West Street B4
White Hart Road B4
Wilson Grove E4
Wiltshire Street E5
Winston Churchill Avenue D3
Wisborough Road E5
Woodpath D4
Woodville Drive C4
Yarborough Road D4
Yorke Street C4

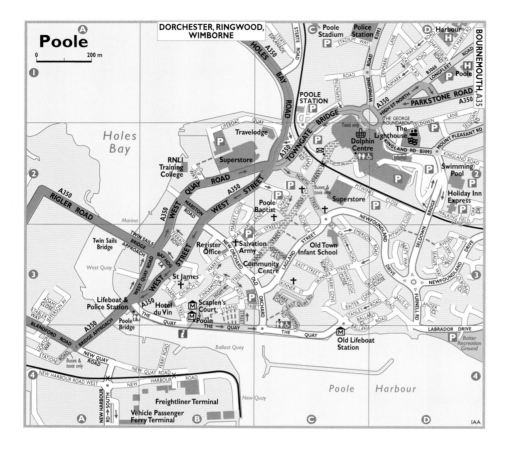

Poole

Poole is found on atlas page **12 H6**

Adams Close	A3	New Harbour Road West	A4
Avenel Way	D3	New Orchard	B3
Baiter Gardens	C3	New Quay Road	A4
Ballard Close	C3	New Street	B3
Ballard Road	C4	North Street	C2
Bay Hog Lane	B3	Norton Way	A4
Blandford Road	A3	Oak Drive	D2
Bridge Approach	A4	Old Orchard	B3
Castle Street	B3	Parkstone Road	D1
Chapel Lane	C2	Perry Gardens	C3
Church Street	B3	Pitwines Close	C2
Cinnamon Lane	B3	Poole Bridge	A3
Colborne Close	D3	Rigler Road	A2
Dear Hay Lane	B3	St Mary's Road	D1
Denmark Lane	D1	Seager Way	D3
Denmark Road	D1	Seldown Bridge	D3
Drake Road	C3	Seldown Lane	D2
Durrell Way	D3	Seldown Road	D2
East Quay Road	C3	Serpentine Road	C1
East Street	C3	Shaftesbury Road	D1
Elizabeth Road	D1	Skinner Street	C3
Emerson Road	C3	Slip Way	B2
Ferry Road	B4	South Road	C3
Fisherman's Road	C3	Stabler Way	A3
Furnell Road	D3	Stadium Way	C1
Globe Lane	C2	Stanley Road	C3
Green Close	D3	Sterte Esplanade	C1
Green Road	C3	Sterte Road	C1
High Street	B3	Strand Street	B3
High Street North	D1	Terrace Row	B3
Hill Street	C3	Thames Street	B3
Holes Bay Road	C1	The Quay	B3
Jefferson Avenue	A3	Towngate Bridge	C2
Kingland Road	D2	Twin Sails Bridge Approach	A3
Labrador Drive	D4	Twin Sails Bridge	A3
Lagland Street	C3	Vallis Close	D3
Lander Close	D3	Vanguard Road	C2
Liberty Way	D3	Walking Field Lane	D2
Lifeboat Quay	B2	Westons Lane	C3
Longfleet Road	D1	West Quay Road	B2
Maple Road	D1	West Street	B3
Market Close	B2	Whatleigh Close	C3
Market Street	B2	Wimborne Road	D1
Marston Road	B2		
Mount Pleasant Road	D2		
Newfoundland Drive	C2		
New Harbour Road	A4		
New Harbour Road South	A4		

Preston

Preston is found on atlas page **88 G5**

Adelphi Street	A1	Holstein Street	D1
Arthur Street	A3	Hopwood Street	D2
Avenham Lane	C4	Jutland Street	D1
Avenham Road	C3	Lancaster Road	C2
Avenham Street	C3	Lancaster Road North	C1
Berwick Road	C4	Latham Street	C4
Birley Street	C2	Lawson Street	B1
Boltons Court	C3	Leighton Street	A2
Bow Lane	A3	Lund Street	C1
Butler Street	B3	Lune Street	B3
Cannon Street	C3	Main Sprit Weind	C3
Carlisle Street	C2	Manchester Road	D3
Chaddock Street	C4	Market Street	C2
Chapel Street	B3	Market Street West	B2
Charlotte Street	D4	Marsh Lane	A2
Cheapside	C3	Maudland Road	A1
Christ Church Street	A3	Meadow Street	C1
Church Street	C3	Moor Lane	B1
Clarendon Street	D4	Mount Street	B3
Corporation Street	B2	North Road	C1
Corporation Street	B3	Oak Street	D3
Craggs Row	B1	Ormskirk Road	C2
Cross Street	C3	Oxford Street	C3
Crown Street	B1	Pedder Street	A1
Deepdale Road	D1	Percy Street	D2
Derby Street	D2	Pitt Street	A3
Earl Street	C2	Pole Street	D2
East Cliff	B4	Pump Street	D1
East Street	D1	Queen Street	D3
Edmund Street	D2	Ribblesdale Place	B4
Edward Street	A2	Ring Way	B2
Elizabeth Street	B1	Rose Street	D3
Fishergate	B3	St Austin's Road	D3
Fishergate Hill	A4	St Paul's Road	D1
Fleet Street	B3	St Paul's Square	D1
Fox Street	B3	St Peter's Street	B1
Friargate	B2	Sedgwick Street	C1
Friargate	C2	Selborne Street	D4
Fylde Road	A1	Shepherd Street	D3
Glover's Court	C3	Snow Hill	B2
Glover Street	C3	Syke Street	C3
Great Avenham Street	C4	Tithebarn Street	C2
Great Shaw Street	B2	Walker Street	B1
Grimshaw Street	D2	Walton's Parade	A3
Guildhall Street	C3	Ward's End	C2
Harrington Street	B1	Warwick Street	B1
Heatley Street	B2	West Cliff	A4
Herschell Street	D4	Winkley Square	B3

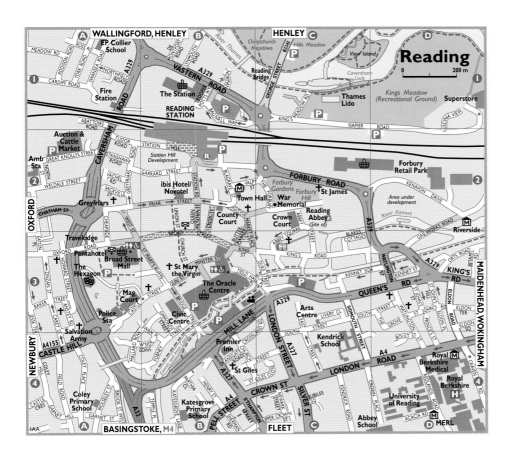

Reading

Reading is found on atlas page **35 K10**

Abbey Square	C3	King's Meadow Road	C1
Abbey Street	C2	King's Road	D3
Addison Road	A1	King Street	B3
Anstey Road	A3	Livery Close	C3
Baker Street	A3	London Road	C4
Blagrave Street	B2	London Street	C3
Blakes Cottages	C3	Mallard Row	A4
Boult Street	D4	Market Place	B2
Bridge Street	B3	Mill Lane	B4
Broad Street	B3	Minster Street	B3
Brook Street West	A4	Napier Road	C1
Buttermarket	B3	Newark Street	C4
Cardiff Road	A1	Northfield Road	A1
Carey Street	A3	Oxford Road	A3
Castle Hill	A4	Parthia Close	B4
Castle Street	A3	Pell Street	B4
Caversham Road	A2	Prince's Street	D3
Chatham Street	A2	Queen's Road	C3
Cheapside	A2	Queen Victoria Street	B2
Church Street	B3	Redlands Road	D4
Church Street	B4	Ross Road	A1
Coley Place	A4	Sackville Street	A2
Craven Road	D4	St Giles Close	B4
Crossland Road	B4	St John's Road	D3
Cross Street	B2	St Mary's Butts	B3
Crown Street	C4	Sidmouth Street	C3
Deansgate Road	B4	Silver Street	C4
Duke Street	C3	Simmonds Street	B3
East Street	C3	Southampton Street	B4
Eldon Road	D3	South Street	C3
Field Road	A4	Station Hill	B2
Fobney Street	B4	Station Road	B2
Forbury Road	C2	Swan Place	B3
Friar Street	B2	Swansea Road	A1
Garnet Street	A4	The Forbury	C2
Garrard Street	B2	Tudor Road	A2
Gas Works Road	D3	Union Street	B2
George Street	C1	Upper Crown Street	C4
Great Knollys Street	A2	Vachel Road	A2
Greyfriars Road	A2	Valpy Street	B2
Gun Street	B3	Vastern Road	B1
Henry Street	B4	Watlington Street	D3
Howard Street	A3	Weldale Street	A2
Katesgrove Lane	B4	West Street	A2
Kenavon Drive	D2	Wolseley Street	A4
Kendrick Road	C4	Yield Hall Place	B3
Kennet Side	C3	York Road	A1
Kennet Street	D3	Zinzan Street	A3

Royal Tunbridge Wells

Royal Tunbridge Wells is found on atlas page **25 N3**

Albert Street	C1	Lansdowne Road	C2
Arundel Road	C4	Lime Hill Road	B1
Bayhall Road	D2	Linden Park Road	A4
Belgrave Road	C1	Little Mount Sion	B4
Berkeley Road	B4	London Road	A2
Boyne Park	A1	Lonsdale Gardens	B2
Buckingham Road	C4	Madeira Park	B4
Calverley Park	C2	Major York's Road	A4
Calverley Park Gardens	D2	Meadow Road	B1
Calverley Road	C2	Molyneux Park Road	A1
Calverley Street	C2	Monson Road	C2
Cambridge Gardens	D4	Monson Way	B2
Cambridge Street	D3	Mount Edgcumbe Road	A3
Camden Hill	D3	Mount Ephraim	A2
Camden Park	D3	Mount Ephraim Road	B1
Camden Road	C1	Mountfield Gardens	C3
Carlton Road	D2	Mountfield Road	C3
Castle Road	A2	Mount Pleasant Avenue	B2
Castle Street	B3	Mount Pleasant Road	B2
Chapel Place	B4	Mount Sion	B4
Christchurch Avenue	B3	Nevill Street	B4
Church Road	A2	Newton Road	B1
Civic Way	B2	Norfolk Road	C4
Claremont Gardens	C4	North Street	D2
Claremont Road	C4	Oakfield Court Road	D3
Clarence Road	B2	Park Street	D3
Crescent Road	C2	Pembury Road	D2
Culverden Street	B1	Poona Road	C4
Dale Street	C1	Prince's Street	D3
Dudley Road	B1	Prospect Road	D3
Eden Road	B4	Rock Villa Road	B1
Eridge Road	A4	Royal Chase	A1
Farmcombe Lane	C4	St James' Road	D1
Farmcombe Road	C4	Sandrock Road	D1
Ferndale	D1	Somerville Gardens	A1
Frant Road	A4	South Green	B3
Frog Lane	B4	Station Approach	B3
Garden Road	C1	Stone Street	D1
Garden Street	C1	Sussex Mews	A4
George Street	D3	Sutherland Road	C3
Goods Station Tunbridge	B1	Tunnel Road	C1
Grecian Road	C4	Upper Grosvenor Road	B1
Grosvenor Road	B1	Vale Avenue	B3
Grove Hill Gardens	C3	Vale Road	B3
Grove Hill Road	C3	Victoria Road	C1
Guildford Road	C3	Warwick Park	B4
Hanover Road	B1	Wood Street	C1
High Street	B4	York Road	B2

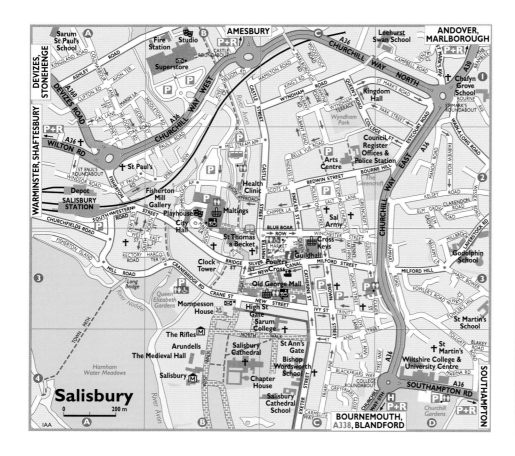

Salisbury

Salisbury is found on atlas page **21 M9**

Albany Road	C1	Kingsland Road	A1
Ashley Road	A1	King's Road	C1
Avon Approach	B2	Laverstock Road	D3
Bedwin Street	C2	Malthouse Lane	B3
Belle Vue Road	C2	Manor Road	D2
Blackfriars Way	C4	Marlborough Road	C1
Blue Boar Row	C3	Meadow Road	A1
Bourne Avenue	D1	Middleton Road	A1
Bourne Hill	C2	Milford Hill	D3
Bridge Street	B3	Milford Street	C3
Brown Street	C3	Mill Road	A3
Campbell Road	D1	Minster Street	C3
Castle Street	B1	Nelson Road	B1
Catherine Street	C3	New Canal	B3
Chipper Lane	C2	New Street	B3
Churchfields Road	A2	North Street	B3
Churchill Way East	D3	Park Street	D1
Churchill Way North	C1	Pennyfarthing Street	C3
Churchill Way South	C4	Queen's Road	C1
Churchill Way West	B2	Queen Street	C3
Clarendon Road	D2	Rampart Road	D3
Clifton Road	A1	Rectory Road	A3
Coldharbour Lane	A1	Rollestone Street	C2
College Street	C1	St Ann Street	C4
Cranebridge Road	B3	St Edmund's Church Street	C4
Crane Street	B3	St Mark's Avenue	D1
Devizes Road	A1	St Mark's Road	D1
Dew's Road	A3	St Paul's Road	B2
East Street	B3	Salt Lane	C2
Elm Grove	D2	Scots Lane	C2
Elm Grove Road	D2	Sidney Street	A1
Endless Street	C2	Silver Street	B3
Estcourt Road	D2	Southampton Road	D4
Exeter Street	C4	South Street	A3
Eyres Way	D4	South Western Road	A2
Fairview Road	D2	Spire View	B2
Fisherton Street	A2	Summerlock Approach	B2
Fowler's Road	D3	Tollgate Road	D4
Friary Lane	C4	Trinity Street	C3
Gas Lane	A1	Wain-A-Long Road	D1
George Street	A1	Wessex Road	D2
Gigant Street	C3	West Street	A3
Greencroft Street	C2	Wilton Road	A2
Guilder Lane	C3	Winchester Street	C3
Hamilton Road	C1	Windsor Road	A2
High Street	B3	Woodstock Road	C1
Ivy Street	C3	Wyndham Road	C1
Kelsey Road	D2	York Road	A2

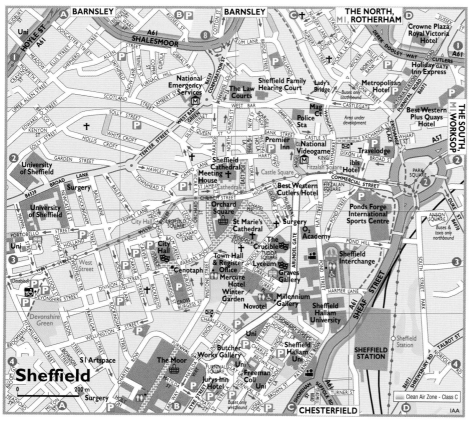

Sheffield

Sheffield is found on atlas page **84 E3**

Angel Street	C2	Hoyle Street	A1
Arundel Gate	C3	King Street	C2
Arundel Street	C4	Lambert Street	B1
Backfields	B3	Leopold Street	B3
Bailey Street	A2	Mappin Street	A3
Balm Green	B3	Meetinghouse Lane	C2
Bank Street	C2	Mulberry Street	C2
Barkers Pool	B3	Newcastle Street	A2
Broad Lane	A2	New Street	C2
Broad Street	D2	Norfolk Street	C3
Brown Street	C4	North Church Street	B2
Cambridge Street	B3	Orchard Street	B3
Campo Lane	B2	Paradise Street	B2
Carver Street	B3	Pinstone Street	B3
Castlegate	C1	Pond Hill	C3
Castle Street	C2	Pond Street	C3
Charles Street	B4	Portobello Street	A3
Charter Row	B4	Queen Street	B2
Church Street	B2	Rockingham Street	A2
Commercial Street	C2	St James Street	B2
Corporation Street	B1	Scargill Croft	C2
Cross Burgess Street	B3	Scotland Street	A1
Cutlers Gate	D1	Shalesmoor	B1
Derek Dooley Way	D1	Sheaf Street	D4
Devonshire Street	A3	Shoreham Street	C4
Division Street	A3	Shrewsbury Road	D4
Dixon Lane	C2	Silver Street	B2
Duke Street	D2	Smithfield	A1
Exchange Street	D2	Snig Hill	C2
Eyre Street	B4	Solly Street	A2
Fig Tree Lane	C2	South Street Park	D3
Fitzwilliam Street	A4	Suffolk Road	C4
Flat Street	C3	Surrey Street	C3
Furnace Hill	B1	Talbot Street	D4
Furnival Gate	B4	Tenter Street	B2
Furnival Road	D1	Townhead Street	B2
Furnival Street	C4	Trafalgar Street	A4
Garden Street	A2	Trippet Lane	B3
George Street	C2	Union Street	B4
Harmer Lane	C3	Vicar Lane	B2
Harts Head	C2	Victoria Station Road	D1
Hawley Street	B2	Waingate	C2
Haymarket	C2	Wellington Street	A4
High Street	C2	West Bar	B2
Holland Street	A3	West Bar Green	B2
Hollis Croft	A2	West Street	A3
Holly Street	B3	White Croft	A2
Howard Street	C4	York Street	C2

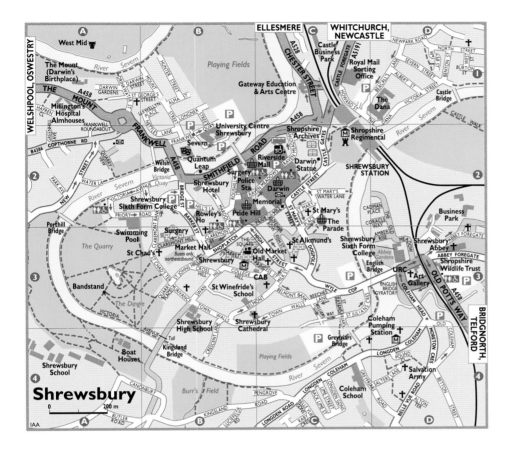

Shrewsbury

Shrewsbury

Shrewsbury is found on atlas page **56 H2**

Abbey Foregate	D3	Longner Street	B1
Albert Street	D1	Mardol	B2
Alma Street	B1	Market Street	B3
Amber Rise	D3	Milk Street	C3
Barker Street	B2	Moreton Crescent	D4
Beacall's Lane	D1	Mount Street	B1
Beeches Lane	C3	Murivance	B3
Belle Vue Gardens	C4	Nettles Lane	B1
Belle Vue Road	D4	Newpark Road	D1
Belmont	B3	New Street	A2
Belmont Bank	C3	North Street	D1
Benyon Street	D1	Old Coleham	D3
Betton Street	D4	Old Potts Way	D3
Bridge Street	B2	Park Avenue	A2
Burton Street	D1	Pengrove	C4
Butcher Row	C2	Pound Close	D4
Cadman Place	C2	Pride Hill	C2
Canonbury	A4	Princess Street	B3
Castle Foregate	C1	Priory Road	A2
Castle Gates	C2	Quarry Place	B3
Castle Street	C2	Quarry View	A2
Chester Street	C1	Raven Meadows	B2
Claremont Bank	B3	Roushill	B2
Claremont Hill	B3	St Chad's Terrace	B3
Claremont Street	B3	St George's Street	A1
Coleham Head	D3	St Johns Hill	B3
College Hill	B3	St Julians Crescent	C3
Copthorne Road	A2	St Julians Friars	C3
Coracle Way	D2	St Mary's Place	C2
Crescent Lane	B4	St Mary's Street	C2
Cross Hill	B3	St Mary's Water Lane	C2
Darwin Gardens	A1	Salters Lane	D4
Darwin Street	A1	Severn Street	D1
Dogpole	C3	Shoplatch	B3
Drinkwater Street	A1	Smithfield Road	B2
Fish Street	C3	Swan Hill	B3
Frankwell	A2	The Dana	D1
Frankwell Quay	B2	The Mount	A1
Greenhill Avenue	A2	The Old Meadow	D3
Greyfriars Road	C4	The Square	B3
High Street	C3	Town Walls	B3
Hill's Lane	B2	Victoria Avenue	A2
Howard Street	C1	Victoria Street	D1
Hunter Street	B1	Water Lane	A2
Kingsland Road	B4	Water Street	D1
Lime Street	C4	West Street	D1
Longden Coleham	C4	Williams Way	C3
Longden Road	C4	Wyle Cop	C3

Southend-on-Sea

Southend-on-Sea is found on atlas page **38 E4**

Albert Road	C3	Lancaster Gardens	C2
Alexandra Road	A3	Leamington Road	D2
Alexandra Street	A3	London Road	A2
Ambleside Drive	D2	Lucy Road	C4
Ashburnham Road	A2	Luker Road	A2
Baltic Avenue	B3	Marine Parade	C4
Baxter Avenue	A1	Milton Street	B1
Beach Road	D4	Napier Avenue	A2
Boscombe Road	C1	Nelson Street	A3
Bournemouth Park Road	D1	Oban Road	D1
Cambridge Road	A3	Old Southend Road	D3
Capel Terrace	A3	Outing Close	D3
Chancellor Road	B3	Pitmans Close	B2
Cheltenham Road	D2	Pleasant Road	C3
Chichester Road	B1	Portland Avenue	B3
Christchurch Road	D1	Princes Street	A2
Church Road	B3	Prittlewell Square	A3
Clarence Road	A3	Quebec Avenue	B2
Clarence Street	B3	Queen's Road	A2
Clifftown Parade	A4	Queensway	A1
Clifftown Road	B3	Queensway	C3
Coleman Street	B1	Royal Terrace	B4
Cromer Road	C2	Runwell Terrace	A3
Devereux Road	A4	St Ann's Road	B1
Eastern Esplanade	D4	St Leonard's Road	C3
Elmer Approach	A2	Scratton Road	A3
Elmer Avenue	A2	Short Street	B1
Essex Street	B1	Southchurch Avenue	D2
Ferndown Close	D1	Southchurch Road	C2
Fowler Close	D2	Stanier Close	D2
Gordon Place	A2	Stanley Road	C3
Gordon Road	A2	Sutton Road	C1
Grange Gardens	C2	Swanage Road	C1
Grover Street	B3	Toledo Road	C2
Guildford Road	B1	Tylers Avenue	B3
Hamlet Road	A3	Tyrrel Drive	C2
Hartington Place	C4	Victoria Avenue	A1
Hartington Road	C3	Warrior Square East	B2
Hastings Road	C2	Warrior Square North	B2
Hawtree Close	D4	Warrior Square	B2
Herbert Grove	C3	Wesley Road	C3
Heygate Avenue	B3	Western Esplanade	A4
High Street	B2	Weston Road	B3
Hillcrest Road	A2	Whitegate Road	B2
Honiton Road	D2	Wimborne Road	C1
Horace Road	C3	Windermere Road	D2
Kilworth Avenue	C2	Woodgrange Drive	D3
Kursaal Way	D4	York Road	B3

Southend-on-Sea

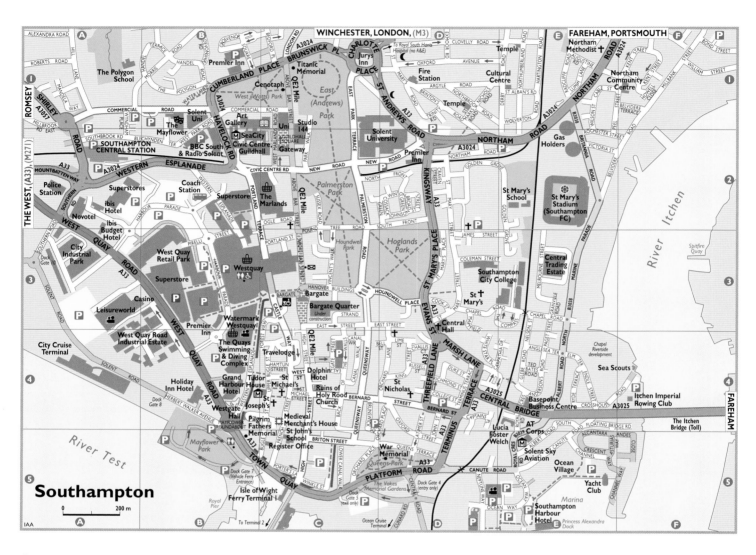

Southampton

Southampton is found on atlas page **14 D4**

Above Bar Street....................C1
Albert Road North.................E4
Albert Road South.................E5
Alcantara Crescent................E5
Alexandra Road.....................A1
Anderson's Road...................E4
Andes Close..........................F5
Anglesea Terrace...................E4
Argyle Road D1
Asturias Way.........................E5
Augustine Road.....................E1
Back Of The Walls C4
Bargate Street........................C3
Bedford Place........................C1
Bell Street D4
Belvidere Road......................E2
Belvidere Terrace...................F1
Bernard Street.......................C4
Blechynden Terrace...............B2
Bond Street...........................F1
Brinton's Road D1
Britannia Road E1
Briton Street C5
Broad Green......................... D2
Brunswick Place....................C1
Brunswick Square C4
Bugle Street..........................C5
Cable Street..........................E1
Canal Walk C4
Canute Road......................... D5
Captains Place D4
Carpathia Drive.....................D4
Castle Way............................C3
Central Bridge.......................D4
Central Road......................... D5
Challis Court D4

Channel Way.........................E5
Chapel Road......................... D3
Charlotte Place......................C1
Civic Centre Road B2
Clovelly Road D1
Coleman Street..................... D3
College Street........................D4
Commercial Road A1
Cook Street D3
Cossack Green D2
Craven Street........................ D2
Crosshouse Road E4
Cumberland Place..................B1
Cunard Road......................... D5
Derby Road E1
Devonshire Road...................A1
Duke Street D4
Eastgate Street......................C4
East Park Terrace...................C1
East Street C3
Elm Terrace E4
Endle Street E4
Evans Street.......................... D3
Exmoor Road D1
Floating Bridge Road E5
Forest View C4
French Street..........................C5
Glebe Road E4
Golden Grove D2
Granville Road E3
Grosvenor Square B1
Hamtun Street C4
Handel Road B1
Handel Terrace B1
Hanover Buildings..................C3
Harbour Parade......................B2

Hartington Road E1
Havelock Road B1
Herbert Walker Avenue B4
High Street C4
Hill Lane A1
Houndwell Place D3
Howell Close F1
Itchen Bridge F4
James Street D3
Johnson Street...................... D2
John Street D5
Kent Street F1
King Street D4
Kingsway............................... D2
Latimer Street....................... D5
Lime Street D4
London Road..........................C1
Lower Canal Walk C5
Lumpy Lane E1
Mandela Way A1
Marine Parade........................E3
Marsh Lane D4
Maryfield...............................E5
Mayflower Roundabout...........B4
Melbourne Street...................E3
Millbank Street......................F1
Millbrook Road East...............A1
Morris Road B1
Mountbatten Way A2
Nelson Street.........................E4
Neptune Way D5
New Road C2
Nichols Road......................... D1
Northam Road D2
Northbrook Road................... D1
North Front............................C2

Northumberland Road E1
Ocean Way............................ D5
Ogle Road C2
Orchard Place C5
Oxford Avenue D1
Oxford Street D4
Paget Street E4
Palmerston Road C2
Park Walk...............................C2
Peel Street E1
Pirelli Street...........................B3
Platform Road C5
Porter's Lane C5
Portland Street C3
Portland Terrace.....................B2
Pound Tree Road C3
Queens Terrace D5
Queensway.............................C4
Radcliffe Road E1
Richmond Street.....................D4
Roberts Road A1
Rochester Street.....................E2
Royal Crescent Road..............E5
Russell Street........................ D4
Ryde Terrace E1
St Alban's Road......................E1
St Andrews Road D1
St Marks Road....................... D1
St Mary's Place D3
St Mary's Road...................... D1
St Mary Street D2
St Michael Street....................C4
Shirley Road A1
Solent Road A3
Southbrook Road....................A2
Southern Road........................A2

South Front............................C2
Strand C3
Sussex Road..........................C2
Ted Bates Road E4
Terminus Terrace................... D5
The Compass D3
The Polygon B1
Threefield Lane D4
Town Road B5
Trinity Road D1
Upper Bugle Street C4
Victoria Street E2
Vincent's Walk C3
Water Lane B1
Western Esplanade A2
Western Esplanade B4
West Marlands Road...............C2
West Park Road B2
West Quay Road A2
West Street C4
White Star Place D4
William Street F1
Wilson Street E1
Winkle Street C5
Winton Street D2
Wolverton Road......................E1
Wyndham Place A1

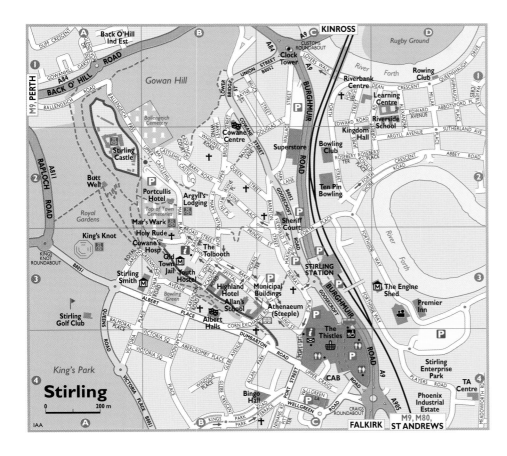

Stirling

Stirling is found on atlas page **133 M9**

Abbey Road	D2	James Street	C2
Abbotsford Place	D1	Kings Knot Roundabout	A3
Abercromby Place	B4	Kings Park Road	B4
Academy Road	B3	King Street	C3
Albert Place	A3	Lovers Walk	C1
Alexandra Place	D1	Lower Bridge Street	B1
Allan Park	B4	Lower Castlehill	B2
Argyll Avenue	D2	Mar Place	B2
Back O' Hill Road	A1	Maxwell Place	C3
Baker Street	B3	Meadowforth Road	D4
Ballengeich Road	A1	Millar Place	D1
Ballengeich Pass	A1	Morris Terrace	B3
Balmoral Place	A3	Murray Place	C3
Bank Street	B3	Ninians Road	C4
Barn Road	B2	Park Lane	C2
Barnton Street	C2	Park Terrace	B4
Bayne Street	B1	Players Road	D4
Bow Street	B3	Port Street	C4
Broad Street	B3	Princes Street	B3
Bruce Street	B1	Queenshaugh Drive	D1
Burghmuir Road	C1	Queens Road	A3
Castle Court	B2	Queen Street	B2
Clarendon Place	B4	Raploch Road	A2
Clarendon Road	B3	Ronald Place	C2
Corn Exchange Road	B3	Rosebery Place	C2
Cowane Street	B1	Rosebery Terrace	C2
Craigs Roundabout	C4	Royal Gardens	A3
Crofthead Court	B2	St John Street	B3
Customs Roundabout	C1	St Mary's Wynd	B2
Dean Crescent	D1	Shiphaugh Place	D1
Douglas Street	C2	Shore Road	C2
Dumbarton Road	B4	Spittal Street	B3
Edward Avenue	D1	Sutherland Avenue	D2
Edward Road	C1	Tannery Lane	B2
Forrest Road	D2	Union Street	B1
Forth Crescent	C2	Upper Bridge Street	B2
Forthside Way	C3	Upper Castlehill	A2
Forth Street	C1	Upper Craigs	C4
Forth Place	C3	Victoria Place	A4
Forth View	C1	Victoria Road	B3
Glebe Avenue	B4	Victoria Square	A4
Glebe Crescent	B4	Viewfield Street	C2
Glendevon Drive	A1	Wallace Street	C2
Goosecroft Road	C2	Waverley Crescent	D1
Gowanhill Gardens	A1	Wellgreen Lane	C4
Greenwood Avenue	A3	Wellgreen Road	C4
Harvey Wynd	B1	Whinwell Road	B2
Irvine Place	B2	Windsor Place	B4

Stockton-on-Tees

Stockton-on-Tees is found on atlas page **104 D7**

1825 Way	B4	Massey Road	D3
Allison Street	B1	Melbourne Street	A2
Alma Street	B1	Middle Street	B2
Bath Lane	C1	Mill Street West	A2
Bedford Street	A1	Nelson Terrace	B2
Bishop Street	B2	North Shore Road	D2
Bishopton Lane	A1	Northport Road	D1
Bishopton Road	A1	North Shore Link	C2
Bowesfield Lane	A4	Norton Road	B1
Bridge Road	B3	Palmerston Street	A2
Bridge Road	C4	Park Road	A4
Bright Street	B2	Park Terrace	C3
Britannia Road	A1	Parkfield Road	B4
Brunswick Street	B3	Parliament Street	B4
Bute Street	A2	Portrack Lane	D1
Church Road	D1	Prince Regent Street	B3
Clarence Row	C1	Princess Avenue	C1
Corporation Street	A2	Princeton Drive	D4
Council of Europe		Quayside Road	C3
Boulevard	C2	Raddcliffe Crescent	D3
Cromwell Avenue	B1	Ramsgate	B3
Dixon Street	A2	Riverside	C3
Dovecot Street	A3	Russell Street	B2
Dugdale Street	D1	St Paul's Street	A1
Durham Road	A1	Silver Street	B2
Durham Street	A2	Skinner Street	B3
Edwards Street	A4	Station Street	D4
Farrer Street	B1	Sydney Street	B2
Finkle Street	B3	The Square	D2
Frederick Street	B1	Thistle Green	C2
Fudan Way	D3	Thomas Street	B1
Gooseport Road	D1	Thompson Street	B1
Hartington Road	A3	Tower Street	B4
Harvard Avenue	D3	Union Street East	C1
High Street	B2	University Boulevard	C3
Hill Street East	D1	Vane Street	B2
Hume Street	B1	Vicarage Street	A1
Hutchinson Street	A2	Wellington Street	A2
John Street	B2	West Row	B3
King Street	B2	Westbourne Street	A4
Knightport Road	D1	Westpoint Road	C3
Knowles Street	C2	William Street	B3
Laing Street	B1	Woodland Street	A4
Leeds Street	B2	Worthing Street	A3
Lobdon Street	B2	Yale Crescent	C4
Lodge Street	B3	Yarm Lane	A4
Mandale Road	D4	Yarm Road	A4
Maritime Road	C1	Yarm Street	B3

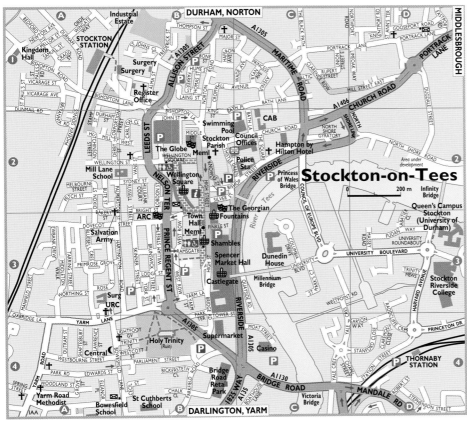

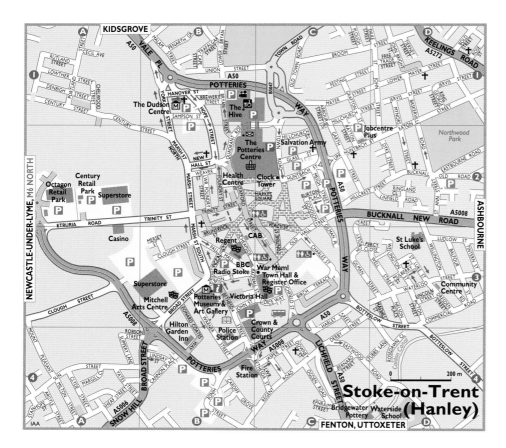

Stoke-on-Trent (Hanley)

Stoke-on-Trent (Hanley) is found on atlas page **70 F5**

Albion Street	B3	Linfield Road	D2
Bagnall Street	B3	Lower Mayer Street	D1
Balfour Street	D3	Lowther Street	A1
Baskerville Road	D1	Ludlow Street	D3
Bathesda Street	B4	Malam Street	B1
Bernard Street	C4	Marsh Street	B2
Bethesda Street	B3	Marsh Street North	B2
Birch Terrace	C3	Marsh Street South	B3
Botteslow Street	C3	Mayer Street	C1
Broad Street	B4	Mersey Street	B3
Broom Street	C1	Milton Street	A4
Brunswick Street	B3	Mount Pleasant	A4
Bryan Street	B1	Mynors Street	D1
Bucknall New Road	C2	New Hall Street	B2
Bucknall Old Road	D2	Ogden Road	C4
Cardiff Grove	B4	Old Hall Street	C3
Century Street	A1	Old Town Road	C1
Charles Street	C3	Pall Mall	B3
Cheapside	B3	Percy Street	C2
Chelwood Street	A1	Piccadilly	B3
Clough Street	A3	Portland Street	A1
Clyde Street	A4	Potteries Way	B1
Commercial Road	D3	Potteries Way	B4
Denbigh Street	A1	Quadrant Road	B2
Derby Street	C4	Regent Road	C4
Dyke Street	D2	Rutland Street	A1
Eastwood Road	C4	St John Street	D1
Eaton Street	D2	St Luke Street	D3
Etruria Road	A2	Sampson Street	B1
Foundry Street	B2	Sheaf Street	A4
Garth Street	C2	Slippery Lane	A4
Gilman Street	C3	Snow Hill	A4
Goodson Street	C2	Stafford Street	B2
Grafton Street	C1	Sun Street	A4
Hanover Street	B1	Tontine Street	C3
Harley Street	C4	Town Road	C2
Hillchurch	C2	Trafalgar Street	B1
Hillcrest Street	C2	Trinity Street	B2
Hinde Street	B4	Union Street	B1
Hope Street	B1	Upper Hillchurch Street	C2
Hordley Street	C2	Upper Huntbach Street	C2
Huntbach Street	C2	Warner Street	B3
Jasper Street	A4	Waterloo Street	D3
Jervis Street	D1	Well Street	D3
John Street	B3	Wellington Road	D3
Keelings Road	D1	Wellington Street	D3
Lichfield Street	C3	Yates Street	A4
Lidice Way	C3	York Street	B1

Stratford-upon-Avon

Stratford-upon-Avon is found on atlas page **47 P3**

Albany Road	A3	Narrow Lane	B4
Alcester Road	A2	New Broad Street	B4
Arden Street	B2	New Street	B4
Avenue Road	C1	Old Red Lion Court	C2
Bancroft Place	C2	Old Town	C4
Bell Court	B2	Orchard Way	A4
Birmingham Road	B1	Payton Street	C2
Brewery Street	B1	Percy Street	C1
Bridge Foot	D2	Rother Street	B3
Bridge Street	C2	Rowley Crescent	D1
Bridgeway	D2	Ryland Street	B4
Broad Street	B4	St Andrew's Crescent	A3
Brookvale Road	A4	St Gregory's Road	C1
Brunel Way	A2	St Martin's Close	A3
Bull Street	B4	Sanctus Drive	B4
Cedar Close	D1	Sanctus Road	A4
Chapel Lane	C3	Sanctus Street	B4
Chapel Street	C3	Sandfield Road	A4
Cherry Orchard	A4	Scholars Lane	B3
Cherry Street	B4	Seven Meadows Road	A4
Chestnut Walk	B3	Shakespeare Street	B1
Church Street	B3	Sheep Street	C3
Clopton Bridge	D3	Shipston Road	D4
Clopton Road	B1	Shottery Road	A3
College Lane	B4	Shrieves Walk	C3
College Mews	B4	Southern Lane	C3
College Street	B4	Swan's Nest	D3
Ely Gardens	B3	The Willows	A3
Ely Street	B3	Tiddington Road	D3
Evesham Place	B3	Tramway Bridge	D3
Evesham Road	A4	Tyler Street	C2
Garrick Way	A4	Union Street	C2
Great William Street	C1	Warwick Court	C1
Greenhill Street	B2	Warwick Crescent	D1
Grove Road	B3	Warwick Road	C2
Guild Street	C2	Waterside	C3
Henley Street	C2	Welcombe Road	D1
High Street	C3	Wellesbourne Grove	B2
Holtom Street	B4	Western Road	B1
John Street	C2	West Street	B4
Kendall Avenue	B1	Willows Drive North	A2
Lock Close	C2	Windsor Street	B2
Maidenhead Road	C1	Wood Street	B2
Mansell Street	B2		
Mayfield Avenue	C1		
Meer Street	B2		
Mill Lane	C4		
Mulberry Street	C1		

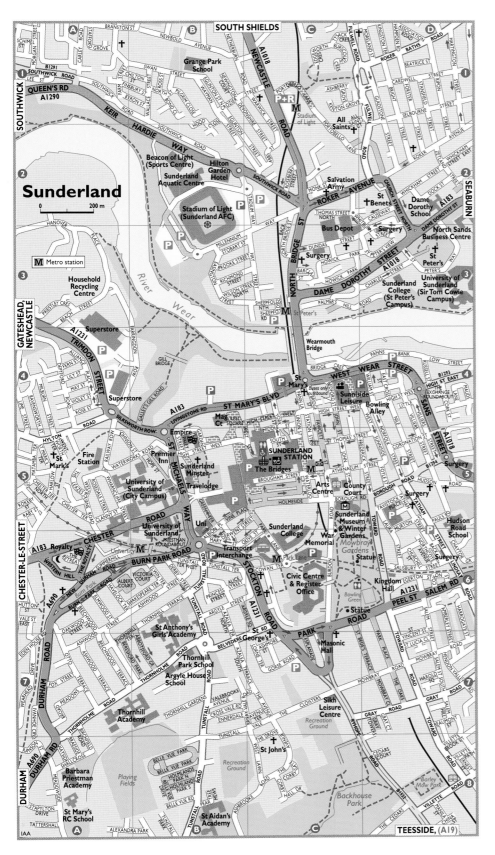

Sunderland

Sunderland is found on atlas page **113 N9**

Abbotsford Green B7
Abbs Street..........................C2
Albion Place..........................B6
Alice Street...........................B6
Alliance Place.......................A4
Amberley Street....................D6
Argyle Square.......................B6
Argyle Street.........................B6
Ashbrooke Road....................B8
Ashmore Street.....................C7
Ashwood Street A7
Ashwood Terrace...................A7
Association Road D1
Athenaeum Street..................C5
Azalea Terrace North..............B6
Azalea Terrace South..............B7
Back North Bridge Street........C3
Beach Street A3
Bedford Street C4
Beechwood Street..................A6
Beechwood Terrace A7
Belvedere Road......................B7
Beresford Park A7
Birchfield Road......................A7
Borough Road D5
Bridge Crescent C4
Bridge Street..........................C4
Briery Vale Road....................C7
Bright Street D1
Brooke Street B3
Brougham Street C5
Burdon Road C5
Burn Park Road B6
Cardwell Street......................D3
Carley Road A1
Charles Street........................D3
Chester Road A6
Churchill Street......................D6
Church Street North D2
Clanny Street.........................A5
Cork Street D4
Coronation Street D5
Cowan Terrace.......................C6
Cross Vale Road B7
Crozier Street B1
Dame Dorothy Street.............C3
Deptford Road A4
Derby Street B6
Derwent Street B6
Devonshire Street..................B1
Dock Street............................D2
Dundas Street C3
Durham Road A7
Easington Street B3
East Cross Street D4
Eden House Road A7
Egerton Street D6
Eglinton Street.......................B1
Eglinton Street North B1
Elmwood Street A6
Ennerdale..............................B7
Farm Street............................A1
Farringdon Row B4
Fawcett Street C4
Forster Street D1
Fox Street A7
Foyle Street D5
Frederick Street D5
Fulwell Road C1
Galley's Gill Road B4
Gladstone Street....................D1
Gorse Road C7
Gray Road D7
Green Terrace B5
Hampden Road D1
Hanover Place........................A2
Harlow Street.........................A5
Harrogate Street....................D6
Hartington Street...................D1
Havelock Terrace....................A6
Hay Street..............................C3
Hendon Valley Road D7
High Street East......................D4
High Street West.....................B5
Holmeside..............................C5
Hope Street B5
Howick Park C3
Hudson Road D5
Hylton Road A5
Johnson Street A5
John Street............................C4
Keir Hardie Way A1
Laura Street D5
Lindsay Road.........................D6
Little Villiers Street D4
Livingstone Road B4
Low Street D4
Mary Street D6
Mauds Lane D4
Meadowside..........................A8
Middle Street C5

Milburn Street........................A4
Millennium Way B3
Monk Street C2
Moreland Street D1
Morgan Street A1
Mowbray Road D7
Netherburn Road B1
Newbold Avenue B1
Newcastle Road C1
New Durham Road..................A6
Nile Street D4
Norfolk Street D5
North Bridge Street C3
Northcote Avenue D6
North Street............................B1
Oakwood Street A6
Olive Street B6
Otto Terrace A7
Palmer's Hill Road C3
Panns Bank D4
Park Lane C5
Park Place D6
Park Road C6
Pauls Road D5
Peel Street D6
Portobello Lane......................C1
Queen's Road A1
Railway Row A5
Ravensworth Street A4
Richmond Street.....................B3
Ripon Street D1
Roker Avenue C2
Roker Baths Road..................D1
Rosedale Street A5
Ross Street B1
Russell Street D4
Ryhope Road..........................C7
St Bede's Terrace....................D7
St Mary's Boulevard B4
St Michaels Way B5
St Peter's View D3
St Thomas' Street...................C5
St Vincent Street D7
Salem Road D6
Salem Street D6
Salem Street South D7
Salisbury Street D6
Sans Street D4
Selbourne Street....................D1
Shakespeare Terrace A6
Shallcross..............................A8
Sheepfolds Road C3
Silksworth Row A4
South Street C5
Southwick Road A1
Southwick Road C2
Stadium Way C2
Stansfield Street D1
Station Street C4
Stobart Street B3
Stockton Road C6
Swan Street B1
Tatham Street D5
Tatham Street Back...............D5
The Avenue............................C7
The Cloisters C7
The Royalty A6
Thomas Street North C2
Thornhill Terrace B6
Thornholme Road A7
Toward Road D5
Trimdon Street.......................A4
Tunstall Road B7
Tunstall Terrace B6
Tunstall Terrace West B6
Tunstall Vale B8
Union Street C4
Valebrooke Avenue................B7
Villette Road D8
Villiers Street D4
Vine Place B5
Wallace Street B1
Warwick Street C1
Waterloo Place C5
Waterworks Road...................A5
Wayman Street B1
Wearhead Drive A7
Westbourne Road A5
Western Hill A6
West Lawn C8
West Street C5
West Sunniside D4
West Wear Street C4
Wharncliffe Street..................A5
Whickham Street D2
Whickham Street East D2
Whitburn Street......................D3
William Street D4
Wilson Street North................B3
York Street C4
Zetland Street........................D2

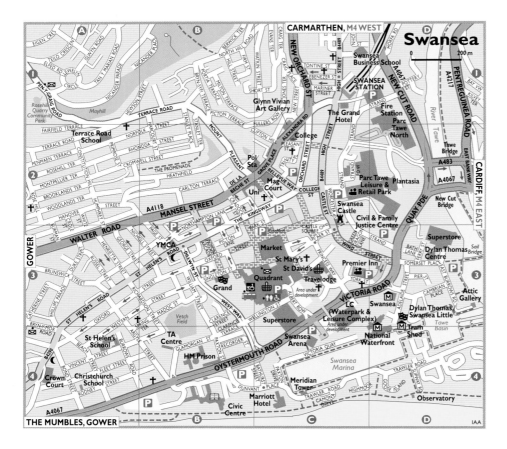

Swansea

Swansea is found on atlas page **29 J6**

Adelaide Street	D3	Mount Pleasant	B2
Alexandra Road	C2	New Cut Road	D1
Argyle Street	A4	New Orchard Street	C1
Bath Lane	D3	New Street	C1
Beach Street	A4	Nicander Parade	A1
Bellevue Way	C2	Nicholl Street	A3
Bond Street	A4	Norfolk Street	A2
Brunswick Street	A3	North Hill Road	B1
Burrows Road	A4	Northampton Lane	B2
Caer Street	C3	Orchard Street	C2
Carlton Terrace	B2	Oxford Street	A3
Castle Street	C2	Oystermouth Road	B4
Catherine Street	A3	Page Street	B3
Clarence Street	B3	Park Street	B3
Clifton Hill	C2	Paxton Street	B4
College Street	C2	Pentreguinea Road	D1
Constituion Hill	A2	Pen-Y-Graig Road	A1
Cradock Street	B2	Picton Lane	B3
Craig Place	C1	Pier Street	D3
Cromwell Street	A2	Primrose Street	A2
De La Beche Street	B2	Princess Way	C3
Dillwyn Street	B3	Quay Parade	D2
Duke Street	A3	Recorder Street	B4
Dunvant Place	B4	Rhondda Street	A2
East Bank Way	D2	Richardson Street	A3
East Burrows Road	D3	Rodney Street	A4
Ebenezer Street	C1	Russel Street	A3
Elfed Road	A1	St Helen's Road	A3
Ferry Street	D3	Short Street	B1
Firm Street	B1	Singleton Street	B3
Fleet Street	A4	Somerset Place	D3
George Street	A3	Strand	C1
Glamorgan Street	B4	Tan Y Marian Road	A1
Green Dragon Lane	C3	Terrace Road	A2
Grove Place	C2	The Kingsway	B2
Hanover Street	A2	Tontine Street	C1
Harcourt Street	B2	Trawler Road	C4
Heathfield	B2	Victoria Quay	C4
Henrietta Street	A3	Victoria Road	C3
Hewson Street	A1	Vincent Street	A4
High Street	C2	Walter Road	A3
Hill Street	B1	Watkin Street	C1
Humphrey Street	A2	Wellington Street	C2
Islwyn Road	A1	West Way	B3
Llewelyn Circle	A1	Western Street	A4
Madoc Street	B3	William Street	B3
Mansel Street	B2	Wind Street	C3
Mariner Street	C1	York Street	C3

Swindon

Swindon is found on atlas page **33 M8**

Albion Street	A4	Islington Street	C3
Alfred Street	C2	John Street	B3
Ashford Road	B4	King Street	B3
Aylesbury Street	B2	London Street	A3
Bathurst Road	C2	Manchester Road	C2
Beckhampton Street	C3	Market Street	B3
Bridge Street	B2	Maxwell Street	A3
Bristol Street	A3	Medgbury Road	C2
Broad Street	C2	Milford Street	B2
Cambria Bridge Road	A4	Milton Road	B3
Canal Walk	B3	Morley Street	B3
Carr Street	B3	Morse Street	B4
Chester Street	A3	Newcastle Street	D3
Church Place	A3	Newcombe Drive	A1
Cirencester Way	D1	Newhall Street	B4
Clarence Street	C3	Northampton Street	D3
College Street	B3	North Star Avenue	B1
Commercial Road	B3	Ocotal Way	D1
Corporation Street	C2	Park Lane	A3
County Road	D2	Plymouth Street	D3
Crombey Street	B4	Polaris Way	B1
Curtis Street	A4	Ponting Street	C2
Deacon Street	B4	Portsmouth Street	D3
Dixon Street	B4	Princes Street	C3
Dover Street	B4	Prospect Hill	C4
Dowling Street	B4	Queen Street	B3
Drove Road	D4	Radnor Street	A4
Dryden Street	A4	Regent Place	C3
Eastcott Hill	C4	Regent Street	B3
East Street	B2	Rosebery Street	C2
Edgeware Road	B3	Salisbury Street	C2
Elmina Road	C1	Sanford Street	B3
Emlyn Square	A3	Sheppard Street	B2
Euclid Street	C3	Southampton Street	D3
Faringdon Road	A3	Stafford Street	B4
Farnsby Street	B3	Stanier Street	B4
Fire Fly Avenue	A2	Station Road	B2
Fleet Street	B2	Swindon Road	C4
Fleming Way	C3	Tennyson Street	A3
Gladstone Street	C2	Theobald Street	A3
Gooch Street	C2	Victoria Road	C4
Graham Street	B4	Villett Street	B3
Great Western Way	A1	Westcott Place	A4
Groundwell Road	C3	Western Street	C4
Havelock Street	B3	Whitehead Street	B4
Hawksworth Way	A1	Whitney Street	B4
Haydon Street	C2	William Street	A4
Holbrook Way	B2	York Road	D3

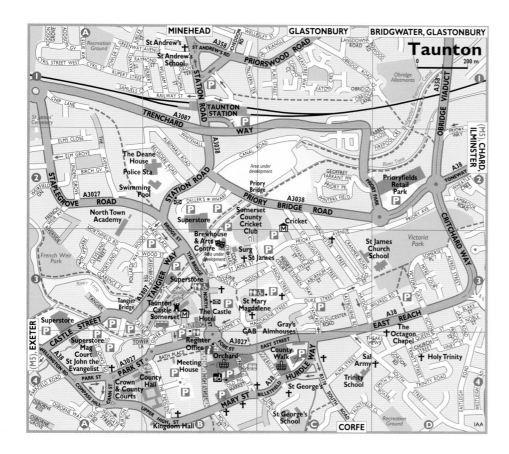

Taunton

Taunton is found on atlas page **18 H10**

Abbey Close	D2	Middle Street	B3
Albemarle Road	B2	Northfield Road	A3
Alfred Street	D3	North Street	B3
Alma Street	C4	Obridge Road	C1
Belvedere Road	B2	Obridge Viaduct	D2
Billetfield	C4	Old Pig Market	B4
Billet Street	C4	Parkfield Road	A4
Bridge Street	B2	Park Street	A4
Canal Road	B2	Paul Street	B4
Cann Street	A4	Plais Street	C1
Canon Street	C3	Portland Street	A3
Castle Street	A4	Priorswood Road	B1
Cheddon Road	B1	Priory Avenue	C3
Chip Lane	A1	Priory Bridge Road	B2
Church Street	D4	Queen Street	D4
Clarence Street	A3	Railway Street	B1
Cleveland Street	A3	Raymond Street	A1
Compass Hill	A4	Rupert Street	A1
Cranmer Road	C3	St Andrew's Road	B1
Critchard Way	D2	St Augustine Street	C3
Cyril Street	A1	St James Street	B3
Deller's Wharf	B2	St John's Road	A4
Duke Street	C3	Samuels Court	A1
Eastbourne Road	C3	South Road	C4
Eastleigh Road	D4	South Street	D4
East Reach	D3	Staplegrove Road	A2
East Street	C4	Station Road	B2
Fore Street	B4	Stephen Street	C3
Fowler Street	A1	Stephen Way	C3
French Weir Avenue	A2	Tancred Street	C3
Gloucester Road	C3	The Avenue	A2
Grays Road	D3	The Bridge	B3
Greenway Avenue	A1	The Crescent	B4
Gyffarde Street	C3	The Triangle	C1
Hammet Street	B4	Thomas Street	B1
Haydon Road	C3	Toneway	D2
Herbert Street	B1	Tower Street	B4
High Street	B4	Trenchard Way	B1
Hugo Street	C4	Trinity Street	D4
Hurdle Way	C4	Upper High Street	B4
Laburnum Street	C3	Victoria Gate	D3
Lansdowne Street	C1	Victoria Street	D3
Leslie Avenue	A1	Viney Street	D4
Linden Grove	A2	Wellington Road	A4
Lower Middle Street	B3	Wilfred Road	C3
Magdalene Street	B3	William Street	B1
Mary Street	B4	Winchester Street	C2
Maxwell Street	A1	Wood Street	B3

Torquay

Torquay is found on atlas page **7 N6**

Abbey Road	B1	Middle Warbury Road	D1
Alexandra Road	C1	Mill Lane	A1
Alpine Road	C2	Montpellier Road	D3
Ash Hill Road	C1	Morgan Avenue	B1
Avenue Road	A1	Palm Road	B1
Bampfylde Road	A2	Parkhill Road	D4
Beacon Hill	D4	Pembroke Road	C1
Belgrave Road	A1	Pennsylvania Road	D1
Braddons Hill Road East	D3	Pimlico	C2
Braddons Hill Road West	C2	Potters Hill	C1
Braddons Street	D2	Princes Road	C1
Bridge Road	A1	Queen Street	C2
Camden Road	D1	Rathmore Road	A2
Cary Parade	C3	Rock Road	C2
Cary Road	C3	Rosehill Road	D1
Castle Lane	C1	St Efride's Road	A1
Castle Road	C1	St Luke's Road	B2
Cavern Road	D1	St Marychurch Road	C1
Chestnut Avenue	A2	Scarborough Road	B2
Church Lane	A1	Seaway Lane	A4
Church Street	A1	Shedden Hill Road	B3
Cleveland Road	A1	Solbro Road	A3
Croft Hill	B2	South Hill Road	D3
Croft Road	B2	South Street	A1
East Street	A1	Stentiford Hill Road	C2
Ellacombe Road	C1	Strand	D3
Falkland Road	A2	Sutherland Road	D1
Fleet Street	C3	Temperance Street	C2
Grafton Road	D2	The King's Drive	A3
Hennapyn Road	A4	The Terrace	D3
Higher Union Lane	B1	Torbay Road	A4
Hillesdon Road	D2	Tor Church Road	A1
Hoxton Road	D1	Tor Hill Road	B1
Hunsdon Road	D3	Torwood Street	D3
Laburnum Street	A1	Trematon Ave	B1
Lime Avenue	A1	Trinity Hill	D3
Lower Ellacombe		Union Street	B1
Church Road	D1	Upper Braddons Hill	D2
Lower Union Lane	C2	Vanehill Road	D4
Lower Warbury Road	D2	Vansittart Road	A1
Lucius Street	A1	Vaughan Parade	C3
Lymington Road	B1	Victoria Parade	D4
Magdalene Road	B1	Victoria Road	C1
Market Street	C2	Vine Road	A1
Marion View	D3	Walnut Road	A2
Meadfoot Lane	D4	Warberry Road West	C1
Melville Lane	C2	Warren Road	B2
Melville Street	C2	Wellington Road	C1

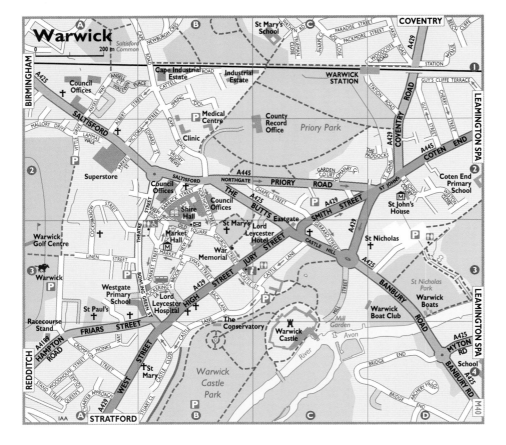

Warwick

Warwick is found on atlas page **59 L11**

Albert Street	A2	Old Square	B3
Ansell Court	A1	Packmore Street	C1
Ansell Way	A1	Paradise Street	C1
Archery Fields	D4	Parkes Street	A2
Back Lane	B3	Priory Mews	B2
Banbury Road	D3	Priory Road	C2
Barrack Street	B2	Puckering's Lane	B3
Beech Cliffe	D1	Queen's Square	A4
Bowling Green Street	B3	Roe Close	C1
Bridge End	D4	St Johns	D2
Brook Street	B3	St Johns Court	D2
Cape Road	B1	Saltisford	A1
Castle Close	B4	Sharpe Close	C1
Castle Hill	C3	Smith Street	C2
Castle Lane	B4	Spring Pool	B1
Castle Street	B3	Stand Street	A4
Cattell Road	B1	Station Avenue	D1
Chapel Street	C2	Station Road	D1
Charter Approach	A4	Stuart Close	B4
Cherry Street	D1	Swan Street	B3
Church Street	B3	Theatre Street	B3
Cocksparrow Street	A3	The Butts	B2
Coten End	D2	The Paddocks	D2
Coventry Road	D2	Trueman Close	C1
Crompton Street	A4	Victoria Street	A2
Edward Street	B2	Vittle Drive	A2
Friars Street	A4	Wallwin Place	A1
Garden Court	C2	Wathen Road	C1
Gerrard Street	C3	Weston Close	D2
Guy's Cliffe Terrace	D1	West Street	A4
Guy Street	D1	Woodcote Road	D1
Hampton Road	A4	Woodhouse Street	A4
High Street	B3	Yeomanry Close	C2
Jury Street	B3		
Lakin Road	D1		
Lammas Walk	A2		
Linen Street	A3		
Mallory Drive	A2		
Market Place	B3		
Market Street	B3		
Mill Street	C3		
Monks Way	A4		
Myton Road	D4		
New Bridge	B2		
Newburgh Crescent	B1		
New Street	B3		
Northgate	B2		
Northgate Street	B2		

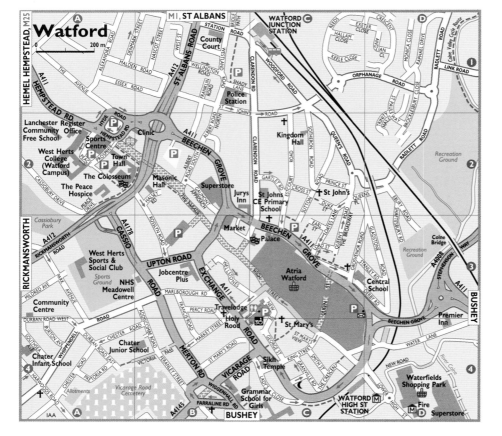

Watford

Watford is found on atlas page **50 D11**

Addiscombe Road	B3	Merton Road	B4
Albert Road North	B2	Mildred Avenue	A3
Albert Road South	B2	Monica Close	D1
Alexandra Road	A1	Nascot Street	B1
Anglian Close	D1	New Road	D4
Beechen Grove	C3	New Street	C3
Brocklesbury Close	D2	Orphanage Road	C1
Burton Avenue	A4	Park Avenue	A3
Cassiobury Drive	A2	Peace Drive	A2
Cassio Road	A3	Peace Prospect	A2
Chester Road	A4	Percy Road	B3
Clarendon Road	C1	Pretoria Road	A4
Cross Street	C2	Prince Street	C2
Denmark Street	A1	Queen's Road	C2
Derby Road	C3	Queen Street	C3
Duke Street	C2	Radlett Road	D2
Durban Road East	A4	Raphael Drive	D1
Durban Road West	A4	Reeds Crescent	C1
Earl Street	C3	Rickmansworth Road	A3
Ebury Road	D2	Rosslyn Road	B3
Essex Road	A1	St Albans Road	B1
Estcourt Road	C2	St John's Road	B1
Exchange Road	B3	St Mary's Road	B4
Farraline Road	B4	St Pauls Way	D1
Feranley Street	B4	Shady Lane	B1
Francis Road	B3	Shaftesbury Road	D2
Franklin Road	B1	Smith Street	C4
Gartlet Road	C2	Sotheron Road	C2
Gaumont Approach	B2	Southsea Avenue	A4
George Street	C2	Stanley Road	C3
Gladstone Road	D3	Station Road	B1
Granville Road	C4	Stephenson Way	D3
Grosvenor Road	C3	Sutton Road	C2
Halsey Road	B2	The Avenue	A1
Harwoods Road	A4	The Broadway	C3
Hempstead Road	A1	The Crescent	C4
High Street	C3	The Parade	B2
Hyde Road	A2	Upton Road	B3
Keele Close	C1	Vicarage Road	B4
King Street	C4	Victoria Passage	B4
Lady's Close	C4	Water Lane	D4
Link Road	D1	Wellington Road	B1
Loates Lane	C3	Wellstones	B3
Lord Street	C3	Westland Road	B1
Lower High Street	D4	West Street	B1
Malden Road	A1	Whippendell Road	A4
Market Street	B4	Wiggenhall Road	B4
Marlborough Road	B3	Woodford Road	C1

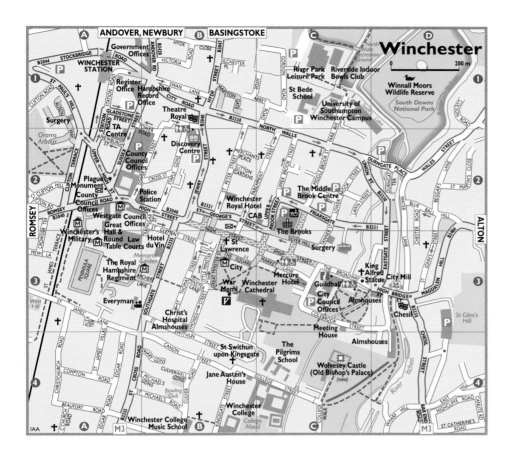

Winchester

Winchester is found on atlas page **22 E9**

Alex Terrace	A3	Market Lane	C3
Alison Way	A1	Marston Gate	B1
Andover Road	B1	Merchants Place	B2
Archery Lane	A3	Mews Lane	A3
Bar End Road	D4	Middle Brook Street	C2
Beaufort Road	A4	Minster Lane	B3
Beggar's Lane	D2	Newburgh Street	A2
Blue Ball Hill	D2	North Walls	C1
Bridge Street	D3	Parchment Street	B2
Canon Street	B4	Park Avenue	C2
Canute Road	D4	Romsey Road	A2
Chesil Street	D3	St Clement Street	B2
Chester Road	D2	St Cross Road	A4
Christchurch Road	A4	St George's Street	B2
City Road	B1	St James' Lane	A3
Clifton Hill	A2	St James Terrace	A3
Clifton Road	A1	St James' Villas	A4
Clifton Terrace	A2	St John's Street	D3
Colebrook Street	C3	St Martin's Close	D2
College Street	B4	St Michael's Gardens	B4
College Walk	C4	St Michael's Road	B4
Colson Road	D1	St Paul's Hill	A1
Compton Road	A4	St Peter Street	B2
Cross Street	B2	St Swithun Street	B3
Crowder Terrace	A3	St Thomas Street	B3
Culver Road	B4	Silchester Place	B1
Culverwell Gardens	B4	Silver Hill	C3
Durngate Place	D2	Southgate Street	B3
Durngate Terrace	D2	Staple Gardens	B2
Eastgate Street	D3	Station Road	A1
East Hill	D4	Stockbridge Road	A1
Edgar Road	A4	Sussex Street	A2
Friarsgate	C2	Sutton Gardens	B2
Friary Gardens	B4	Swan Lane	B1
Gladstone Street	A1	Symonds Street	B3
Gordon Road	C1	Tanner Street	C3
Great Minster Street	B3	The Broadway	C3
Highcliffe Road	D4	The Square	B3
High Street	B2	Tower Road	A1
Hyde Abbey Road	B1	Tower Street	A2
Hyde Close	B1	Trafalgar Street	B3
Hyde Street	B1	Union Street	C2
Jewry Street	B2	Upper Brook Street	C2
Kingsgate Street	B4	Upper High Street	A2
Lawn Street	C2	Victoria Road	B1
Little Minster Street	B3	Wales Street	D2
Lower Brook Street	C2	Water Lane	D3
Magdalen Hill	D3	Wharf Hill	D4

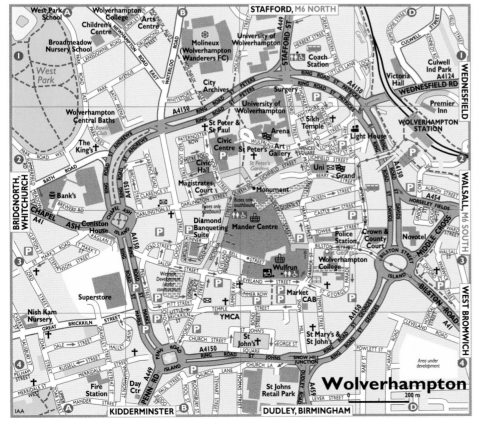

Wolverhampton

Wolverhampton is found on atlas page **58 D5**

Bath Avenue	A1	Peel Street	B3
Bath Road	A2	Penn Road	B4
Bell Street	B3	Piper's Row	D2
Berry Street	C2	Pitt Street	B3
Bilston Road	D3	Powlett Street	D4
Bilston Street	C3	Princess Street	C2
Birch Street	B2	Queen Square	B2
Broad Street	C2	Queen Street	C2
Castle Street	C3	Raby Street	D4
Chapel Ash	A3	Raglan Street	A3
Church Lane	B4	Red Lion Street	B2
Church Street	B4	Retreat Street	A4
Clarence Road	B2	Ring Road St Andrews	A2
Clarence Street	B2	Ring Road St Davids	D2
Cleveland Road	D4	Ring Road St Georges	C4
Cleveland Street	B3	Ring Road St Johns	B4
Corn Hill	D2	Ring Road St Marks	B3
Culwell Street	D1	Ring Road St Patricks	C1
Dale Street	A4	Ring Road St Peters	B2
Darlington Street	B3	Russell Street	A4
Dudley Road	C4	St George's Parade	C3
Dudley Street	C2	St John's Square	C4
Fold Street	B3	St Mark's Road	A3
Fryer Street	C2	St Mark's Street	A3
Garrick Street	C3	Salop Street	B3
Graiseley Street	A4	School Street	B3
Great Brickkiln Street	A4	Skinner Street	B3
Great Western Street	C1	Snow Hill	C3
Grimstone Street	D1	Stafford Street	C1
Horseley Fields	D2	Stephenson Street	A3
Hospital Street	D4	Stewart Street	B4
Lansdowne Road	A1	Summer Row	B3
Lever Street	C4	Tempest Street	C3
Lichfield Street	C2	Temple Street	B3
Little's Lane	C1	Thomas Street	B4
Long Street	C2	Tower Street	C3
Lord Street	A3	Vicarage Road	D4
Mander Street	A4	Victoria Street	B3
Market Street	C3	Walsall Street	D3
Merridale Street	A4	Warwick Street	D3
Middle Cross	D3	Waterloo Road	B1
Mitre Fold	B2	Wednesfield Road	D1
Molineux Street	B1	Westbury Street	C2
Newhampton Road East	A1	Whitmore Hill	B1
North Street	B2	Whitmore Street	C2
Park Avenue	A1	Worcester Street	B4
Park Road East	B1	Wulfruna Street	C2
Park Road West	A2	Zoar Street	A4

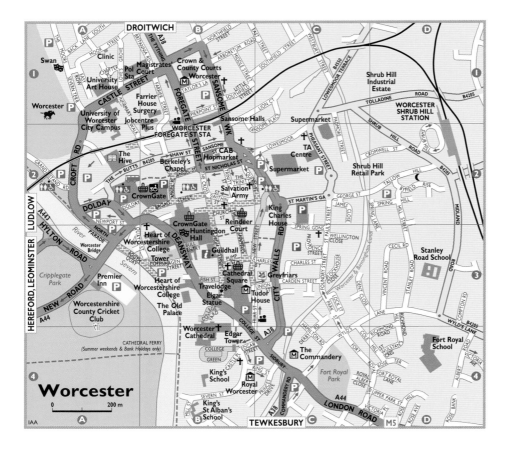

Worcester

Worcester

Worcester is found on atlas page **46 G4**

Albert Road	D4	Middle Street	B1
Angel Street	B2	Midland Road	D2
Arboretum Road	B1	Mill Street	B4
Back Lane South	A1	Moor Street	A1
Blockhouse Close	C3	Newport Street	A2
Britannia Road	A1	New Road	A3
Broad Street	B2	New Street	C3
Byfield Rise	D2	Northfield Street	B1
Carden Street	C3	North Parade	A3
Castle Street	A1	Padmore Street	C1
Cathedral Ferry	A4	Park Street	C3
Cecil Road	D3	Pheasant Street	C2
Charles Street	C3	Pierpoint Street	B1
Charter Place	A1	Providence Street	C3
Church Street	B2	Pump Street	B3
City Walls Road	C3	Quay Street	A3
Cole Hill	C4	Queen Street	B2
College Street	B3	Richmond Road	D4
Commandery Road	C4	Rose Hill	D4
Compton Road	D3	Rose Terrace	D4
Copenhagen Street	B2	St Martin's Gate	C2
Croft Road	A2	St Nicholas Street	B2
Cromwell Street	D2	St Paul's Street	C3
Deansway	B3	St Swithin Street	B2
Dent Close	C3	Sansome Walk	B1
Derby Road	C4	Severn Street	B4
Dolday	A2	Severn Terrace	A1
East Street	B1	Shaw Street	B2
Edgar Street	B4	Shrub Hill Road	D2
Farrier Street	B1	Sidbury	C4
Fish Street	B3	Southfield Street	C1
Foregate Street	B1	Spring Hill	D2
Fort Royal Hill	C4	Stanley Road	D3
Foundry Street	C3	Tallow Hill	D2
Friar Street	C3	Taylor's Lane	B1
George Street	C2	The Butts	A2
Grandstand Road	A2	The Cross	B2
Hamilton Road	C3	The Moors	A1
High Street	B3	The Shambles	B2
Hill Street	D2	The Tything	B1
Hylton Road	A3	Tolladine Road	C1
King Street	B4	Trinity Street	B2
Little Southfield Street	B1	Union Street	C3
Lock Street	C3	Upper Park Street	D4
London Road	C4	Vincent Road	D3
Love's Grove	A1	Wellington Close	C3
Lowesmoor	C2	Westbury Street	C1
Lowesmoor Terrace	C1	Wyld's Lane	C4

York

York is found on atlas page **98 C10**

Aldwark	C2	Lord Mayor's Walk	C1
Barbican Road	D4	Lower Ousegate	C3
Bishopgate Street	B4	Lower Priory Street	B3
Bishophill Senior	B3	Low Petergate	C2
Black Horse Lane	D2	Margaret Street	D3
Blake Street	B2	Market Street	C2
Blossom Street	A4	Micklegate	A3
Bootham	B1	Minster Yard	B1
Bridge Street	B3	Monkgate	C1
Buckingham Street	B3	Museum Street	B2
Cemetery Road	D4	Navigation Road	D3
Church Street	C2	New Street	B2
Clifford Street	C3	North Street	B2
College Street	C1	Nunnery Lane	A3
Colliergate	C2	Ogleforth	C1
Coney Street	B2	Palmer Street	D2
Coppergate	C3	Paragon Street	D4
Cromwell Road	B4	Parliament Street	C2
Davygate	B2	Pavement	C2
Deangate	C1	Peasholme Green	D2
Dove Street	B4	Percy's Lane	D3
Duncombe Place	B2	Piccadilly	C3
Dundas Street	D2	Price's Lane	B4
Fairfax Street	B3	Priory Street	C3
Fawcett Street	D4	Queen Street	A3
Feasegate	C2	Rougier Street	B2
Fetter Lane	B3	St Andrewgate	C2
Finkle Street	C2	St Denys' Road	D3
Fishergate	D4	St Leonard's Place	B1
Foss Bank	D1	St Martins Lane	B3
Fossgate	C2	St Maurice's Road	C1
Foss Islands Road	D2	St Saviourgate	C2
George Street	D3	St Saviours Place	C2
Gillygate	B1	Scarcroft Road	A4
Goodramgate	C2	Shambles	C2
Hampden Street	B4	Skeldergate	B3
High Ousegate	C3	Spen Lane	C2
High Petergate	B1	Spurriergate	B2
Holgate Road	A4	Station Road	A3
Hope Street	D4	Stonegate	B2
Hungate	D2	Swinegate	C2
Jewbury	D1	The Stonebow	C2
Kent Street	D4	Toft Green	A3
King Street	C3	Tower Street	C4
Kings Pool Walk	D2	Trinity Lane	B3
Kyme Street	B4	Victor Street	B4
Lendal	B2	Walmgate	D3
Long Close Lane	D4	Wellington Road	B2

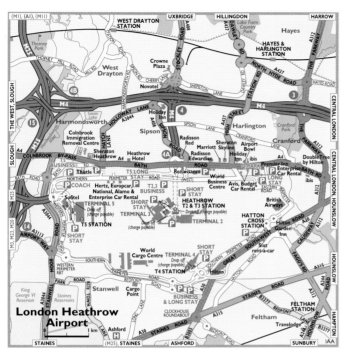

London Heathrow Airport – 17 miles west of central London, M25 junction 14 and M4 junction 4A

Satnav Location: TW6 1EW (Terminal 2), TW6 1QG (T3), TW6 3XA (T4), TW6 2GA (T5)
Information: visit www.heathrow.com
Parking: short-stay, long-stay and business parking is available.
Public Transport: coach, bus, rail and London Underground.
There are several 4-star and 3-star hotels within easy reach of the airport.
Car hire facilities are available.

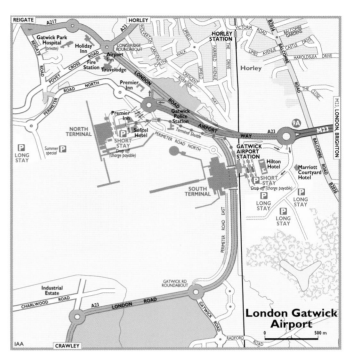

London Gatwick Airport – 29 miles south of central London, M23 junction 9A

Satnav Location: RH6 0NP (South terminal), RH6 0PJ (North terminal)
Information: visit www.gatwickairport.com
Parking: short and long-stay parking is available at both the North and South terminals.
Public Transport: coach, bus and rail.
There are several 4-star and 3-star hotels within easy reach of the airport.
Car hire facilities are available.

London Stansted Airport – 36 miles north-east of central London, M11 junction 8/8A

Satnav Location: CM24 1RW
Information: visit www.stanstedairport.com
Parking: short, mid and long-stay open-air parking is available.
Public Transport: coach, bus and direct rail link to London (Liverpool Street Station) on the Stansted Express.
There are several hotels within easy reach of the airport.
Car hire facilities are available.

London Luton Airport – 34 miles north of central London

Satnav Location: LU2 9QT
Information: visit www.london-luton.co.uk
Parking: short-term, mid-term and long-stay parking is available.
Public Transport: coach, bus and rail.
There are several 3-star hotels within easy reach of the airport.
Car hire facilities are available.

London City Airport

London City Airport – 8 miles east of central London

Satnav Location: E16 2PX
Information: visit *www.londoncityairport.com*
Parking: short and long-stay open-air parking is available.
Public Transport: easy access to the rail network, Docklands Light Railway and the London Underground.
There are 5-star, 4-star and 3-star hotels within easy reach of the airport.
Car hire facilities are available.

Birmingham Airport and The NEC

Birmingham Airport – 10 miles east of Birmingham, M42 junction 6

Satnav Location: B26 3QJ
Information: visit *www.birminghamairport.co.uk*
Parking: short and long-stay parking is available.
Public Transport: Monorail service (Air-Rail Link) operates to and from Birmingham International Railway Station.
There are several 4-star and 3-star hotels within easy reach of the airport.
Car hire facilities are available.

East Midlands Airport

East Midlands Airport – 14 miles south-west of Nottingham, M1 junction 23A/24

Satnav Location: DE74 2SA
Information: visit *www.eastmidlandsairport.com*
Parking: short-term, mid-term and long-stay parking is available.
Public Transport: bus and coach services to major towns and cities in the East Midlands.
There are several 4-star and 3-star hotels within easy reach of the airport.
Car hire facilities are available.

Manchester Airport

Manchester Airport – 10 miles south of Manchester, M56 junction 5

Satnav Location: M90 1QX
Information visit *www.manchesterairport.co.uk*
Parking: short-term, mid-term and long-stay parking is available.
Public Transport: coach, bus, rail and tram (Metrolink).
There are several 4-star and 3-star hotels within easy reach of the airport.
Car hire facilities are available.

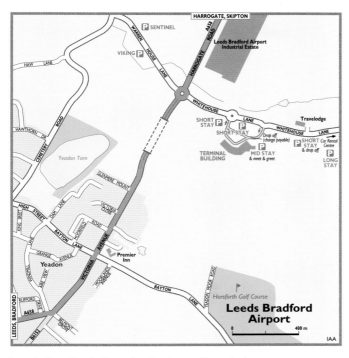

Leeds Bradford Airport – 8 miles north-east of Bradford and 8 miles north-west of Leeds

Satnav Location: LS19 7TU
Information: visit *www.leedsbradfordairport.co.uk*
Parking: short, mid-term and long-stay parking is available.
Public Transport: regular bus services to Bradford, Leeds and Harrogate.
There are several 4-star and 3-star hotels within easy reach of the airport.
Car hire facilities are available.

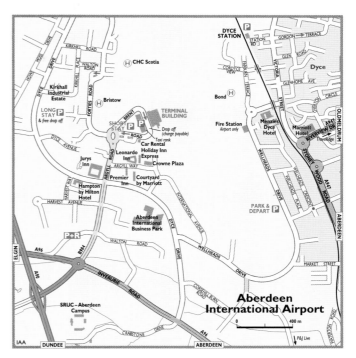

Aberdeen Airport – 7 miles north-west of Aberdeen

Satnav Location: AB21 7DU
Information: visit *www.aberdeenairport.com*
Parking: short and long-stay parking is available.
Public Transport: regular bus services to central Aberdeen.
There are several 4-star and 3-star hotels within easy reach of the airport.
Car hire facilities are available.

Edinburgh Airport – 9 miles west of Edinburgh

Satnav Location: EH12 9DN
Information: visit *www.edinburghairport.com*
Parking: short and long-stay parking is available.
Public Transport: regular bus services to Scottish cities including central Edinburgh, Glasgow, Dundee and Fife and a tram service to central Edinburgh.
There are several 4-star and 3-star hotels within easy reach of the airport.
Car hire and valet parking facilities are available.

Glasgow Airport – 10 miles west of Glasgow, M8 junction 28/29

Satnav Location: PA3 2SW
Information: visit *www.glasgowairport.com*
Parking: short and long-stay parking is available.
Public Transport: regular direct bus services to central Glasgow.
There are several 3-star hotels within easy reach of the airport.
Car hire facilities are available.

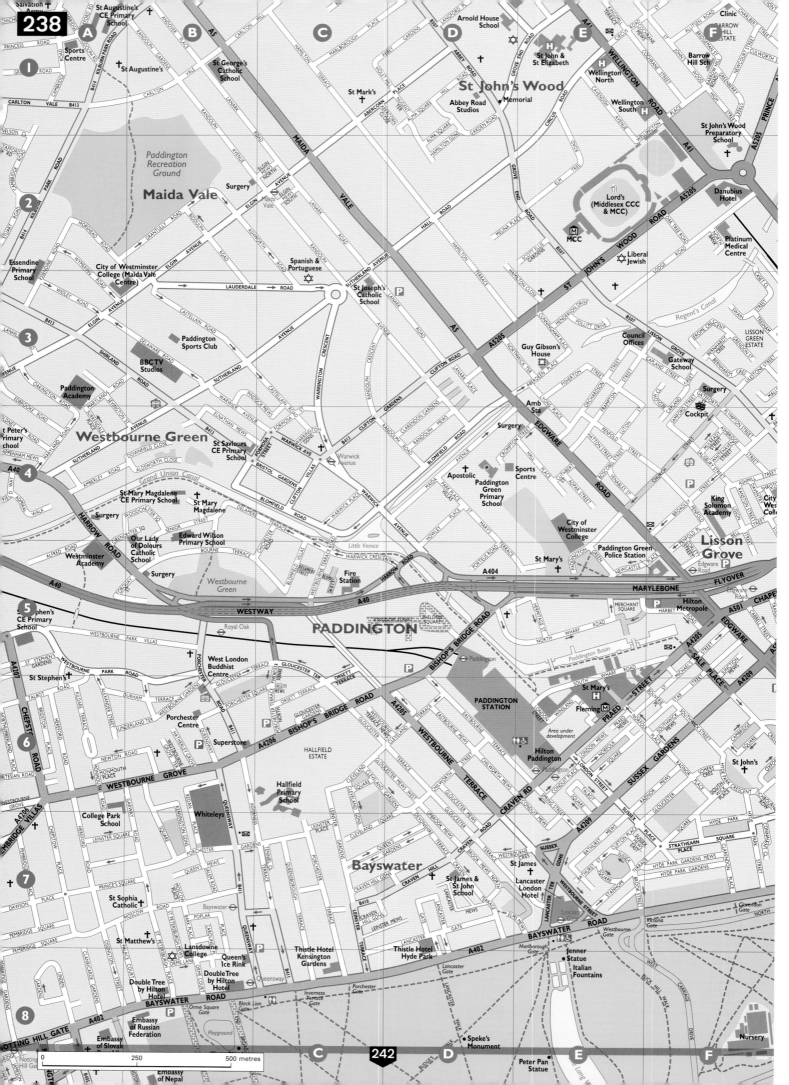

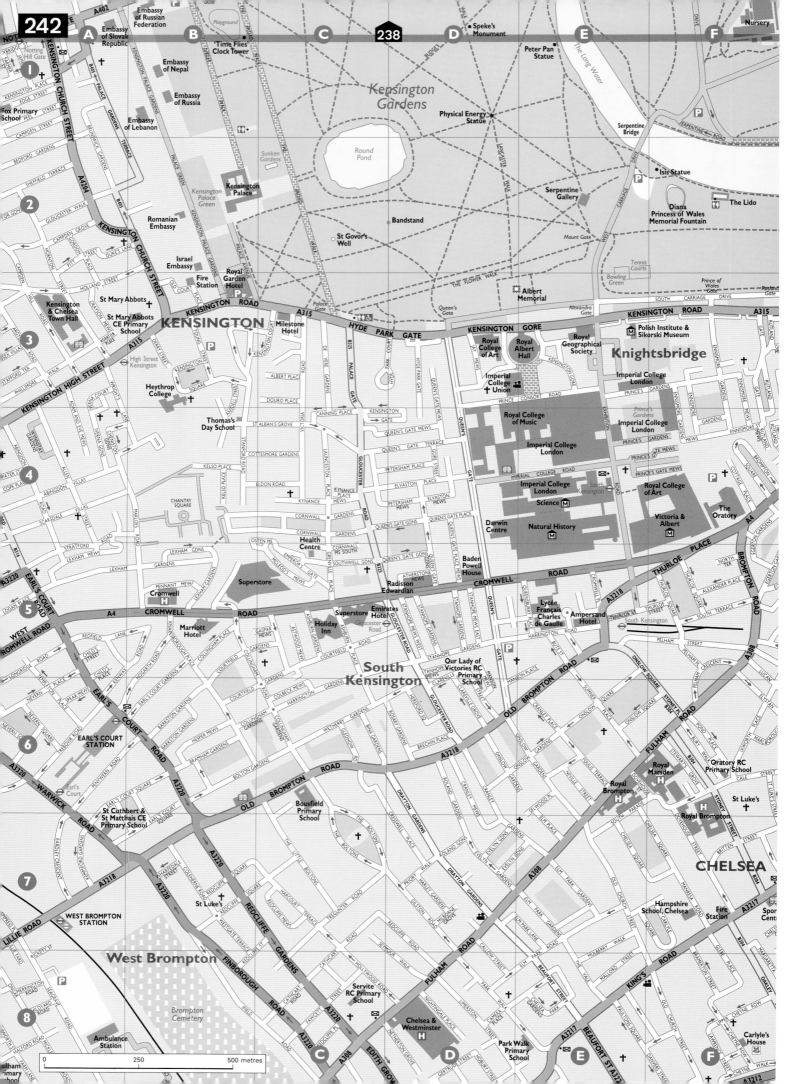

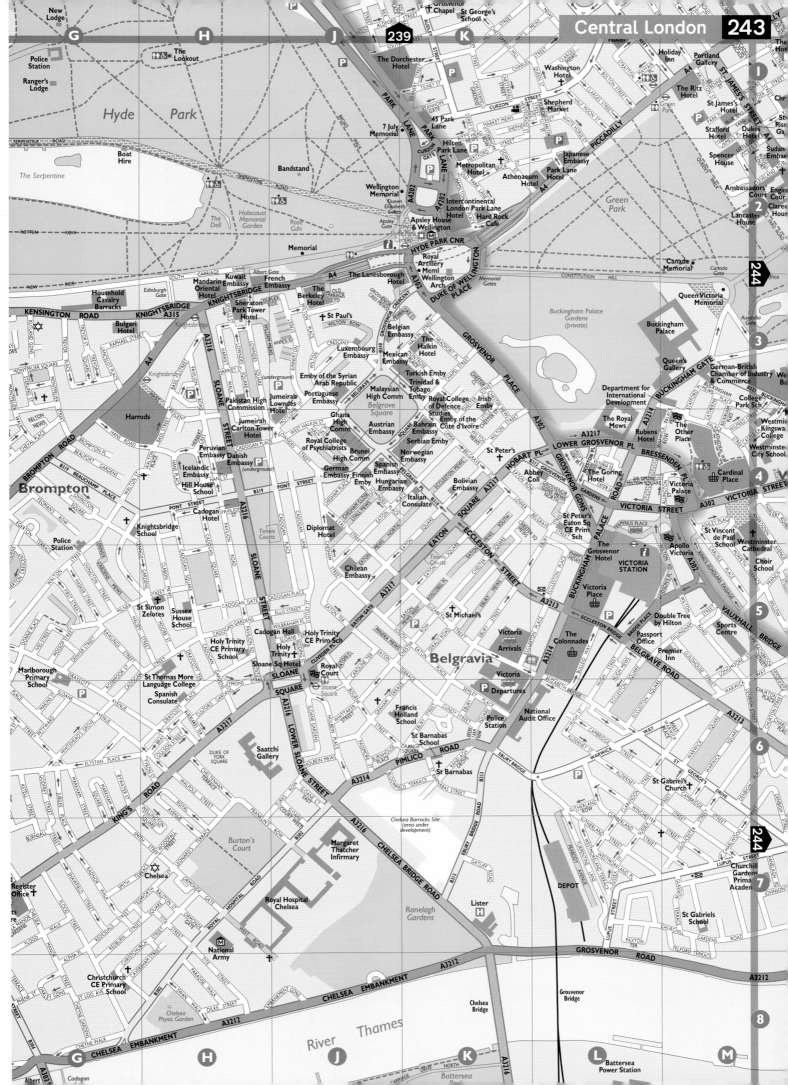

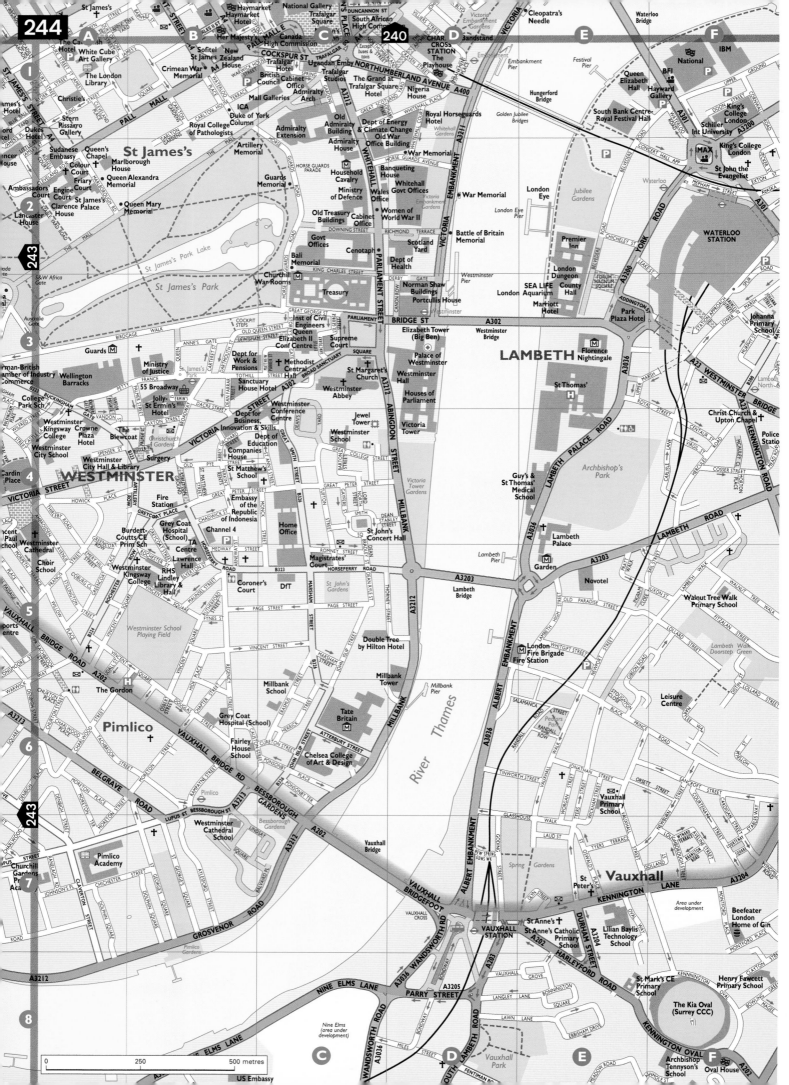

This index lists street and station names, and top places of tourist interest shown in red. Names are listed in alphabetical order and written in full, but may be abbreviated on the map. Each entry is followed by its Postcode District and then the page number and grid reference to the square in which the name is found. Names are asterisked (*) in the index where there is insufficient space to show them on the map.

A

Abbey Gardens NW8	238	C1
Abbey Orchard Street SW1P	244	B4
Abbey Road NW8	238	D1
Abbey Street SE1	246	B7
Abchurch Lane EC4N	241	L7
Abercorn Close NW8	238	C1
Abercorn Place NW8	238	C1
Aberdeen Place NW8	238	E3
Aberdour Street SE1	245	M5
Abingdon Road W8	242	A4
Abingdon Street SW1P	244	C4
Abingdon Villas W8	242	A4
Ackroyd Drive E3	247	L1
Acorn Walk SE16	247	K5
Acton Street WC1X	240	E2
Adam and Eve Mews W8	242	A3
Adam's Row W1K	239	K8
Adam Street WC2N	240	D8
Addington Street SE1	244	E3
Addle Hill EC4V	241	H7
Adelina Grove E1	246	F1
Adeline Place WC1B	240	B5
Adler Street E1	246	D2
Admiral Place SE16	247	K5
Admiral Walk W9	238	A4
Adpar Street W2	238	E4
Agar Street WC2N	240	D8
Agdon Street EC1V	241	H3
Agnes Street E14	247	L2
Ainsty Street SE16	247	G6
Air Street W1B	240	A8
Alaska Street SE1	244	F2
Albany Road SE5	245	L8
Albany Street NW1	239	L1
Albemarle Street W1S	239	L8
Alberta Street SE17	245	H6
Albert Bridge SW3	243	G8
Albert Embankment SE1	244	D7
Albert Gardens E1	247	H3
Albert Gate SW1X	243	H2
Albert Place W8	242	C3
Albion Gate W2	239	G7
Albion Place EC1M	241	H4
Albion Street SE16	247	G7
Albion Street W2	239	G7
Aldenham Street NW1	240	A1
Aldermanbury EC2V	241	K6
Alderney Mews SE1	245	K4
Alderney Street SW1V	243	L6
Aldersgate Street EC1A	241	J4
Aldford Street W1K	239	J8
Aldgate EC3M	246	B3
Aldgate ⊖ EC3N	246	B3
Aldgate East ⊖ E1	246	C2
Aldgate High Street EC3N	246	B3
Aldgate Square EC3N	246	B3
Aldsworth Close W9	238	B4
Aldwych WC2E	240	E7
Alexander Place SW7	242	F5
Alexander Street W2	238	A6
Alexandra Gate SW7	242	E2
Alfred Mews WC1E	240	B4
Alfred Place WC1E	240	B4
Alfred Road W2	238	A5
Alice Street SE1	245	M4
Alie Street E1	246	C3
Allen Street W8	242	A4
Allhallows Lane EC4R	241	L8
Allington Street SW1E	243	M4
Allitsen Road NW8	238	F1
Allsop Place NW1	239	H4
Alma Square NW8	238	D1
Alpha Place SW3	243	G8
Alsace Road SE17	245	M7
Alscot Road * SE1	246	C8
Alvey Street SE17	245	M6
Ambergate Street SE17	245	H7
Amberley Road W9	238	A4
Ambrosden Avenue SW1P	244	A4
Amelia Street SE17	245	J6
America Square EC3N	246	B3
America Street SE1	245	J2
Ampton Street WC1X	240	E2
Amwell Street EC1R	240	F2
Anchorage Point E14	247	M6
Andover Place NW6	238	B1
Angel ⊖ N1	241	G1
Angela Hooper Place * SW1E	244	A4
Angel Junction N1	241	G1
Angel Lane EC4R	241	L8
Angel Street EC1A	241	J6
Ann Moss Way SE16	246	F8
Ann's Close SW1X	243	J3
Ansdell Street W8	242	B4
Antill Terrace E1	247	H2
Antizan Street E1	246	B2
Apple Tree Yard SW1Y	240	A8
Appold Street EC2A	241	M4
Apsley Gate W1J	243	J2
Apsley House & Wellington Museum W1J	243	K2
Aquinas Street SE1	245	G1
Arbour Square E1	247	H2
Archangel Street SE16	247	J7
Archer Street W1B	240	B7
Arch Street SE1	245	J4
Arden Estate N1	241	M1
Argyle Square WC1H	240	D2
Argyle Street WC1H	240	D2
Argyll Road W8	242	A3
Argyll Street W1F	239	M6
Arlington Street SW1A	243	M1
Arlington Way EC1R	241	G2
Arne Street WC2H	240	D6
Arneway Street SW1P	244	B5
Arnhem Place E14	247	M8
Arnold Estate SE1	246	C7
Arnside Street SE17	245	K8
Artesian Road W11	238	A6
Arthur Street EC4V	241	L7
Artichoke Hill E1W	246	E4
Artillery Lane E1	246	A1
Artillery Row SW1P	244	B4
Arundel Street WC2R	240	F7

Ashbridge Street NW8	238	F4
Ashburn Gardens SW7	242	C5
Ashburn Place SW7	242	C5
Ashby Street EC1V	241	H2
Asher Way E1W	246	D4
Ashfield Street E1	246	E2
Ashford Street N1	241	M2
Ashley Place SW1P	243	M4
Ashmill Street NW1	238	F4
Ashmole Street SW8	244	F8
Ashworth Road W9	238	B2
Assam Street E1	246	C2
Assembly Passage E1	247	G1
Astell Street SW3	243	G6
Aston Street E14	247	K1
Astwood Mews SW7	242	C5
Atherstone Mews SW7	242	D5
Atterbury Street SW1P	244	C6
Attneave Street WC1X	240	F3
Augustus Street NW1	239	L1
Aulton Place SE11	245	G7
Austin Friars EC2N	241	L6
Australia Gate SW1A	243	M3
Austral Street SE11	245	H5
Aveline Street SE11	244	F7
Ave Maria Lane EC1A	241	H6
Avery Farm Row SW1W	243	K6
Avery Row W1K	239	L7
Aybrook Street W1U	239	J5
Aylesbury Road SE17	245	L7
Aylesbury Street EC1R	241	H4
Aylesford Street SW1V	244	B7
Aylward Street E1	247	G2
Ayres Street SE1	245	K2

B

Babmaes Street SW1Y	240	B8
Bache's Street N1	241	L2
Back Church Lane E1	246	D3
Back Hill EC1R	241	G4
Bacon Grove SE1	246	B8
Bainbridge Street WC1A	240	C6
Bakers Mews W1U	239	J6
Baker's Row EC1R	241	G4
Baker Street NW1	239	H4
Baker Street W1U	239	J5
Baker Street ⊖ NW1	239	H4
Balcombe Street NW1	239	G3
Balderton Street W1K	239	J7
Baldwin's Gardens EC1N	240	F5
Baldwin Street EC1V	241	L2
Bale Road E1	247	J1
Balfe Street N1	240	D1
Balfour Mews W1K	239	K8
Balfour Place W1K	239	J8
Balfour Street SE17	245	K5
Baltic Street East EC1Y	241	J3
Baltic Street West EC1Y	241	J4
Balvaird Place SW1V	244	C7
Bank ⊖ EC2R	241	L6
Bank End SE1	245	K1
Bankside SE1	241	J8
Banner Street EC1Y	241	K3
Banqueting House SW1A	244	C2
Banyard Road SE16	246	E8
Barbican EC1A	241	J4
Barbican Estate EC2Y	241	J5
Barge House Street SE1	245	G1
Bark Place W2	238	B7
Barkston Gardens SW5	242	B6
Barley Corn Way E14	247	L4
Barlow/Congreve Estate SE17	245	M5
Barlow Place W1J	239	L7
Barlow Street SE17	245	L5
Barnardo Street E1	247	H3
Barnby Street NW1	240	A1
Barnes Street E14	247	J2
Barnham Street SE1	246	A6
Baron's Place SE1	245	G3
Baron Street N1	241	G1
Barrett Street W1U	239	K6
Barrow Hill Estate NW8	238	F1
Barrow Hill Road NW8	238	F1
Barter Street WC1A	240	D5
Bartholomew Close EC1A	241	J5
Bartholomew Lane EC2R	241	L6
Bartholomew Street SE1	245	L5
Bartlett Court EC4A	241	G6
Barton Street SW1P	244	C4
Basil Street SW3	243	H4
Basin Approach E14	247	K3
Basinghall Avenue EC2V	241	K5
Basinghall Street EC2V	241	K5
Bastwick Street EC1V	241	J3
Bateman's Buildings W1D	240	B6
Bateman Street W1D	240	B6
Bath Street EC1V	241	K2
Bath Terrace SE1	245	J4
Bathurst Mews W2	238	E7
Bathurst Street W2	238	E7
Battle Bridge Lane SE1	245	M1
Batty Street E1	246	D2
Bayley Street WC1B	240	B5
Baylis Road SE1	244	F3
Bayswater ⊖ W2	238	B7
Bayswater Road W2	238	E7
Baythorne Street E3	247	L1
Beaconsfield Road SE17	245	M7
Beak Street W1F	240	A7
Bear Gardens SE1	241	J8
Bear Lane SE1	245	H1
Beauchamp Place SW3	243	G4
Beaufort Gardens SW3	243	G4
Beaufort Street SW3	242	E8
Beaumont Place W1T	240	A3
Beaumont Street W1G	239	K4
Beccles Street E14	247	M3
Beckett Street SE1	245	L3
Beckway Street SE17	245	M6
Bedale Street SE1	245	L1
Bedford Avenue WC1B	240	C5
Bedfordbury WC2N	240	C7
Bedford Gardens W8	242	A2
Bedford Place WC1N	240	D4
Bedford Row WC1R	240	E4

Bedford Square WC1B	240	B5
Bedford Street WC2E	240	D7
Bedford Way WC1H	240	C3
Bedlow Close NW8	238	F3
Beech Street EC2Y	241	J4
Beeston Place SW1W	243	L4
Belgrave Mews North * SW1X	243	J3
Belgrave Mews South * SW1X	243	K4
Belgrave Place SW1X	243	J4
Belgrave Road SW1V	243	L5
Belgrave Road SW1V	244	A6
Belgrave Square SW1X	243	J3
Belgrave Street E1	247	J2
Belgrove Street WC1H	240	D2
Bell Lane E1	246	B1
Bell Street NW1	238	F4
Bell Yard WC2A	240	F6
Belvedere Road SE1	244	E2
Benjamin Street EC1M	241	H4
Ben Jonson Road E1	247	J1
Bennett Street SW1A	243	M1
Ben Smith Way SE16	246	D7
Benson Quay E1W	246	F4
Bentinck Mews W1U	239	K6
Bentinck Street W1U	239	K6
Bere Street E1W	247	H3
Bergen Square SE16	247	K8
Berkeley Mews W1H	239	H6
Berkeley Square W1J	239	L8
Berkeley Street W1J	239	L8
Bermondsey ⊖ ⊖ SE16	246	E7
Bermondsey Spa SE16	246	C8
Bermondsey Square SE1	246	A8
Bermondsey Street SE1	246	A6
Bermondsey Wall East SE16	246	E7
Bermondsey Wall Estate SE16	246	D7
Bermondsey Wall West SE16	246	C6
Bernard Street WC1N	240	D4
Berners Mews W1T	240	A5
Berners Place W1F	240	A6
Berners Street W1T	240	A5
Bernhardt Crescent NW8	238	F3
Berryfield Road SE17	245	J6
Berry Street EC1V	241	H3
Berwick Street W1F	240	A6
Bessborough Gardens SW1V	244	C6
Bessborough Street SW1V	244	B6
Betterton Street WC2H	240	D6
Bevenden Street N1	241	L2
Bevin Close SE16	247	J5
Bevington Street SE16	246	D7
Bevin Way WC1X	240	F1
Bevis Marks EC3A	246	A2
Bewley Street E1	246	F3
Bickenhall Street W1U	239	H4
Bidborough Street WC1H	240	C2
Biddulph Road W9	238	B2
Big Ben (Elizabeth Tower) SW1A	244	D3
Bigland Street E1	246	E3
Billiter Square EC3M	246	A3
Billiter Street EC3M	246	A3
Bina Gardens SW5	242	C6
Bingham Place W1U	239	J4
Binney Street W1K	239	K7
Birchfield Street E14	247	M3
Birchin Lane EC3V	241	L7
Birdcage Walk SW1H	244	A3
Birde Lane EC4Y	241	H6
Bird Street W1U	239	K6
Birkenhead Street N1	240	D1
Bishop's Bridge Road W2	238	C6
Bishopsgate EC2M	246	A2
Bishops Square E1	246	B1
Bishop's Terrace SE11	245	G5
Bittern Street SE1	245	J3
Blackall Street EC2A	241	M3
Blackburne's Mews W1K	239	J7
Blackfriars ⇌ ⊖ EC4V	241	H7
Blackfriars Bridge SE1	241	H8
Blacklands Terrace SW3	243	H6
Black Friars Lane EC4V	241	H7
Blackfriars Road SE1	245	H3
Blackhorse Court SE1	245	L4
Black Lion Gate W2	238	B8
Black Prince Road SE11	244	E6
Blackwood Street SE17	245	K6
Blandford Street W1U	239	H5
Blenheim Street W1S	239	L7
Bletchley Street N1	241	K1
Blomfield Mews W2	238	C5
Blomfield Road W9	238	C4
Blomfield Street EC2M	241	M5
Blomfield Villas W2	238	C5
Bloomfield Terrace SW1W	243	J6
Bloomsbury Square WC1A	240	D5
Bloomsbury Street WC1B	240	C5
Bloomsbury Way WC1A	240	C5
Blount Street E14	247	K2
Blue Ball Yard SW1A	243	M1
Bohn Road E1	247	J1
Bolsover Street W1W	239	L4
Bolton Gardens SW5	242	B6
Bolton Street W1J	243	L1
Bond Street ⊖ W1C	239	K6
Bondway SW8	244	D8
Bonhill Street EC2A	241	L4
Bonnington Square SW8	244	E8
Boot Street N1	241	M2
Borough ⊖ SE1	245	K3
Borough High Street SE1	245	K3
Borough Road SE1	245	H3
Boscobel Place SW1W	243	K5
Boscobel Street NW8	238	E4
Boss Street SE1	246	B6
Boston Place NW1	239	G3
Botolph Lane EC3R	241	M7
Boundary Lane SE17	245	K8
Boundary Row SE1	245	G2
Bourdon Street W1K	239	L7
Bourlet Close W1W	239	M5
Bourne Estate EC1N	240	F4
Bourne Street SW1W	243	J6
Bourne Terrace W2	238	B5
Bouverie Place W2	238	F6
Bouverie Street EC4Y	241	G6
Bowland Yard * SW1X	243	J3
Bow Lane EC4M	241	K6
Bowling Green Lane EC1R	241	G3

Bowling Green Place SE1	245	L2
Bowling Green Street SE11	244	F8
Bowling Green Walk N1	241	M2
Bow Street WC2E	240	D7
Bowsell Street WC1N	240	D4
Boyd Street E1	246	D3
Boyfield Street SE1	245	H3
Boyle Street W1S	239	M7
Boyson Road SE17	245	K8
Brackley Street EC1Y	241	J4
Brad Street SE1	245	G2
Bradenham Close SE17	245	K8
Braganza Street SE17	245	H7
Braham Street E1	246	C3
Bramerton Street SW3	242	F7
Bramham Gardens SW5	242	B6
Branch Road E14	247	J3
Brandon Estate SE17	245	H8
Brandon Street SE17	245	K6
Brangton Road SE11	244	F7
Bray Crescent SE16	247	H6
Bray Place SW3	243	H6
Bread Street EC4M	241	K7
Bream's Buildings EC4A	240	F6
Brechin Place SW7	242	D6
Breezer's Hill E1W	246	D4
Brendon Street W1H	239	G5
Bressenden Place SW1W	243	L4
Brettell Street SE17	245	L7
Brewers Green SW1H	244	A3
Brewer Street W1F	240	A7
Brewhouse Lane E1W	246	F6
Brewhouse Walk SE16	247	J5
Brick Court WC2R	240	F7
Brick Lane E1	246	C1
Brick Street W1J	243	K2
Bridewell Place EC4V	241	H7
Bridgeman Street NW8	238	F1
Bridge Place SW1V	243	L5
Bridgeport Place E1W	246	D4
Bridge Street SW1A	244	D3
Bridgewater Street EC2Y	241	J4
Bridgeway Street NW1	240	A1
Bridle Lane W1F	240	A7
Bridstow Place W2	238	A6
Brightlingsea Place E14	247	L4
Brill Place NW1	240	C1
Briset Street EC1M	241	H4
Bristol Gardens W9	238	B4
Britannia Street WC1X	240	E2
Britannia Walk N1	241	L2
Britannia Way N1	241	L1
Britten Street SW3	242	F7
Britton Street EC1M	241	H4
Broadbent Street W1K	239	L7
Broadgate Circle EC2M	241	M5
Broadley Street NW8	238	F4
Broadley Terrace NW1	238	F4
Broadstone Place W1U	239	J5
Broad Walk NW1	239	K1
Broad Walk W2	239	H7
Broadwall SE1	245	G1
Broadway SW1H	244	B4
Broadwick Street W1F	240	A7
Brockham Street SE1	245	K4
Brodlove Lane E1W	247	H3
Bromley Street E1	247	J2
Brompton Place SW3	243	G4
Brompton Road SW3	243	G4
Brompton Road SW7	242	F5
Brompton Square SW3	242	F4
Bronti Close SE17	245	K7
Brook Drive SE11	245	G5
Brooke Street EC1N	240	F5
Brook Gate W1K	239	H8
Brook Mews North W2	238	D7
Brook's Mews W1K	239	K7
Brook Street W1K	239	K7
Brook Street W2	238	E7
Brown Heart Gardens W1K	239	K7
Browning Mews W1G	239	K5
Browning Street SE17	245	K6
Brownlow Mews WC1N	240	E3
Brownlow Street WC1V	240	E5
Brune Street E1	246	B1
Brunel Road SE16	247	G6
Brune Street E1	246	B1
Brunswick Close SE1	246	A6
Brunswick Gardens W8	242	A1
Brunswick Place N1	241	L2
Brunswick Quay SE16	247	J8
Brunswick Square WC1N	240	D3
Brunswick Street WC1N	240	D3
Brunton Place E14	247	K3
Brushfield Street E1	246	B1
Bruton Lane W1J	239	L8
Bruton Place W1J	239	L7
Bruton Street W1J	239	L8
Bryan Road SE16	247	K6
Bryanston Mews West W1H	239	G5
Bryanston Mews East W1H	239	H5
Bryanston Place W1H	239	G5
Bryanston Square W1H	239	H5
Bryanston Street W1C	239	H7
Buck Hill Walk W2	238	E8
Buckingham Gate SW1E	243	L3
Buckingham Mews SW1E	243	M3
Buckingham Palace SW1A	243	L3
Buckingham Palace Road SW1W	243	L5
Buckingham Place SW1E	243	M4
Buckland Street N1	241	L1
Buckle Street E1	246	C2
Bucknall Street WC2H	240	C6
Buckters Rents SE16	247	J5
Budge's Walk W2	238	D8
Bulleid Way SW1V	243	L5
Bulstrode Street W1U	239	K5
Bunhill Row EC1Y	241	L3
Burdett Estate E14	247	M1
Burdett Road E14	247	L2
Burdett Street SE1	244	F4
Burgess Street E14	247	M1
Burge Street SE1	245	L4
Burlington Arcade W1J	239	M8
Burlington Gardens W1S	239	M8
Burnhouse Place SW1W	243	J6
Burnsall Street SW3	243	G7
Burnside Close SE16	247	J5

Burrell Street SE1	245	H1
Burslem Street E1	246	D3
Burton Grove SE17	245	L7
Burton Street WC1H	240	C3
Burwood Place W2	239	G6
Bury Close SE16	247	H5
Bury Court EC3A	246	A2
Bury Place WC1A	240	D5
Bury Street EC3A	246	A2
Bury Street SW1Y	244	A1
Bury Walk SW3	242	F6
Bushell Street E1W	246	D5
Bush Lane EC4V	241	L7
Butcher Row E14	247	J3
Bute Street SW7	242	E5
Butler Place SW1H	244	B4
Butler's Wharf SE1	246	C6
Buttesland Street N1	241	L2
Byefield Close SE16	247	K6
Bylands Close SE16	247	J5
Byng Place WC1E	240	B4
Byng Street E14	247	M6
Byward Street EC3R	246	A4
Bywater Place SE16	247	K5
Bywater Street SW3	243	G6

C

Cabbell Street NW1	238	F5
Cable Street E1	246	F3
Cadiz Street SE17	245	K7
Cadogan Gardens SW3	243	H5
Cadogan Gate SW1X	243	H5
Cadogan Lane SW1X	243	J4
Cadogan Place SW1X	243	J4
Cadogan Square SW1X	243	H5
Cadogan Street SW3	243	G6
Caledonian Road N1	240	D1
Caledonia Street N1	240	D1
Cale Street SW3	242	F6
Callow Street SW3	242	D7
Calshot Street N1	240	E1
Calthorpe Street WC1X	240	E3
Cambridge Circus WC2H	240	C7
Cambridge Gardens NW6	238	A1
Cambridge Gate NW1	239	L3
Cambridge Road NW6	238	A1
Cambridge Road NW6	238	A2
Cambridge Square W2	238	F6
Cambridge Street SW1V	243	L6
Cambridge Terrace NW1	239	L2
Cambridge Terrace Mews NW1	239	L3
Camdenhurst Street E14	247	K2
Camera Place SW10	242	D8
Camomile Street EC3A	246	A2
Campden Grove W8	242	A2
Campden Hill Road W8	242	A2
Campden Street W8	242	A1
Camperdown Street E1	246	C3
Canada Estate SE16	247	G7
Canada Gate SW1A	243	M3
Canada Street SE16	247	H7
Canada Water ⊖ ⊖ SE16	247	G7
Canada Wharf SE16	247	L5
Canal Street SE5	245	L8
Canary Riverside E14	247	L4
Candle Street E1	247	K1
Canning Place W8	242	C4
Cannon Drive E14	247	M4
Cannon Street EC4N	241	K7
Cannon Street ⇌ ⊖ EC4R	241	K7
Cannon Street Road E1	246	E3
Canon Beck Road SE16	247	G6
Canon Row SW1A	244	D3
Canton Street E14	247	M3
Capeners Close * SW1X	243	J3
Capland Street NW8	238	E3
Capper Street WC1E	240	A4
Capstan Way SE16	247	K5
Carbis Road E14	247	L2
Carburton Street W1W	239	L4
Cardigan Street SE11	244	F6
Cardington Street NW1	240	A2
Carey Street WC2A	240	F6
Carlisle Avenue EC3N	246	B3
Carlisle Lane SE1	244	F4
Carlisle Place SW1P	243	M5
Carlisle Street W1D	240	B6
Carlos Place W1K	239	K7
Carlton Gardens SW1Y	244	B2
Carlton Hill NW6	238	B1
Carlton House Terrace SW1Y	244	B1
Carlton Street W1J	243	L1
Carlton Vale NW6	238	A1
Carlton Vale NW6	238	B1
Carlyle Square SW3	242	F7
Carmelite Street EC4Y	241	G7
Carnaby Street W1F	239	M7
Caroline Place W2	238	B7
Caroline Street E1	247	H3
Caroline Terrace SW1W	243	J5
Carpenter Street W1K	239	K7
Carrington Street W1J	243	L1
Carr Street E14	247	K1
Carteret Street SW1H	244	B3
Carter Lane EC4V	241	H7
Carter Place SE17	245	K7
Carter Street SE17	245	J7
Carthusian Street EC1M	241	J4
Carting Lane WC2R	240	D8
Cartwright Gardens WC1H	240	C2
Cartwright Street E1	246	C4
Casey Close NW8	238	F3
Casson Street E1	246	C1
Castellain Road W9	238	B3
Castlebrook Close SE11	245	G5
Castle Lane SW1E	243	M4
Catesby Street SE17	245	L6
Cathay Street SE16	246	F7
Cathcart Road SW10	242	C8
Cathedral Walk SW1E	243	M4
Catherine Place SW1E	243	M4
Catherine Street WC2E	240	D7
Cato Street W1H	239	G5
Causton Street SW1P	244	B6
Cavell Street E1	246	F1

Cavendish Avenue NW8 ...... 238 E1
Cavendish Place W1G 239 L6
Cavendish Square W1G 239 L6
Cavendish Street N1 ...... 241 L1
Caversham Street SW3 ...... 243 G8
Caxton Street SW1H 244 B4
Cayton Street EC1V 241 K2
Centaur Street SE1 ...... 244 F4
Central Street EC1V 241 J2
Chadwell Street EC1R 241 G1
Chadwick Street SW1P 244 B4
Chagford Street NW1 ...... 239 H4
Chalton Street NW1 ...... 240 B1
Chambers Street SE16 ...... 246 D7
Chamber Street E1 ...... 246 C3
Chambers Wharf SE16 ...... 246 D6
Chancel Street SE1 ...... 245 H1
Chancery Lane WC2A 240 F5
Chancery Lane ⊖ WC1V 240 F5
Chandos Place WC2N 240 C8
Chandos Street W1G 239 L5
Chantry Square W8 ...... 242 B4
Chapel Market N1 ...... 240 F1
Chapel Street NW1 ...... 238 F5
Chapel Street SW1X 243 K3
Chaplin Close SE1 ...... 245 G3
Chapman Street E1 ...... 246 E3
Chapter Road SE17 ...... 245 H7
Chapter Street SW1P 244 B6
Chargrove Close SE16 ...... 247 H6
Charing Cross ⇌ WC2N 244 D1
Charing Cross Road WC2H 240 B6
Charing Cross Road WC2N 240 C7
Charlbert Street NW8 ...... 238 E1
Charles II Street SW1Y 240 B8
Charles Square N1 ...... 241 M2
Charles Street W1J 243 K1
Charleston Street SE17 ...... 245 K6
Charlotte Place EC2A 241 M3
Charlotte Street W1T 240 A4
Charlwood Place SW1V 244 A6
Charlwood Street SW1V 243 M7
Charlwood Street SW1V 244 A6
Charrington Street NW1 ...... 240 B1
Charterhouse Square EC1M 241 H4
Charterhouse Street EC1M 241 G5
Chart Street N1 ...... 241 L2
Chaseley Street E14 ...... 247 J2
Chatham Street SE17 ...... 245 L5
Cheapside EC2V 241 K6
Chelsea Bridge SW1W 243 K8
Chelsea Bridge Road SW1W 243 J7
Chelsea Embankment SW3 ...... 243 G8
Chelsea Manor Gardens SW3 ...... 242 F7
Chelsea Manor Street SW3 ...... 243 G7
Chelsea Park Gardens SW3 ...... 242 E8
Chelsea Physic Garden SW3 ...... 243 H8
Chelsea Square SW3 ...... 242 E7
Cheltenham Terrace SW3 ...... 243 H6
Chenies Mews WC1E 240 B4
Chenies Street WC1E 240 B4
Cheniston Gardens W8 ...... 242 A4
Chepstow Place W2 ...... 238 A7
Chepstow Road W2 ...... 238 A6
Chequer Street EC1Y 241 K3
Cherbury Street N1 ...... 241 L1
Cherry Garden Street SE16 ...... 246 E7
Chesham Close SW1X 243 J4
Chesham Place SW1X 243 J4
Chesham Street SW1X 243 J4
Chester Close SW1X 243 K3
Chester Close North NW1 ...... 239 L2
Chester Close South NW1 ...... 239 L2
Chesterfield Gardens W1J 243 K1
Chesterfield Hill W1J 239 K8
Chesterfield Street W1J 243 K1
Chester Gate NW1 ...... 239 L2
Chester Mews SW1X 243 K3
Chester Place NW1 ...... 239 L1
Chester Road NW1 ...... 239 K2
Chester Row SW1W 243 K5
Chester Square SW1W 243 K5
Chester Square Mews SW1W 243 K4
Chester Street SW1X 243 K3
Chester Terrace NW1 ...... 239 L2
Chester Way SE11 ...... 245 G6
Cheval Place SW7 ...... 243 G4
Cheval Street E14 ...... 247 M7
Cheyne Gardens SW3 ...... 243 G8
Cheyne Row SW3 ...... 242 F8
Cheyne Walk SW3 ...... 242 F8
Chicheley Street SE1 ...... 244 E2
Chichester Road NW6 ...... 238 A1
Chichester Road W2 ...... 238 C5
Chichester Street SW1V 244 A7
Chicksand Street E1 ...... 246 C1
Chigwell Hill E1W 246 E4
Child's Place SW5 ...... 242 A5
Child's Street SW5 ...... 242 A5
Chiltern Street W1U 239 J4
Chilworth Mews W2 ...... 238 D6
Chilworth Street W2 ...... 238 D6
China Hall Mews SE16 ...... 247 G8
Chinatown W1D 240 B7
Chippenham Mews W9 ...... 238 A3
Chiswell Street EC1Y 241 K4
Chitty Street W1T 240 A4
Christchurch Street SW3 ...... 243 G8
Christian Street E1 ...... 246 D3
Christina Street EC2A 241 M3
Christopher Close SE16 ...... 247 H6
Christopher Street EC2A 241 L4
Chudleigh Street E1 ...... 247 H2
Chumleigh Street SE5 ...... 245 M8
Churchill Gardens Road SW1V 243 L7
Churchill War Rooms SW1A 244 C3
Church Street NW8 ...... 238 F4
Church Way NW1 ...... 240 B2
Churchyard Row SE11 ...... 245 H5
Churton Place SW1V 244 A6
Churton Street SW1V 244 A6
Circus Road NW8 ...... 238 D2
Cirencester Square W2 ...... 238 A5
City Garden Row N1 ...... 241 J1
City Road N1 ...... 241 J1
City Road EC1Y 241 L3
City Thameslink ⇌ EC4M 241 H6
Clabon Mews SW1X 243 H5
Clack Street SE16 ...... 247 G7
Clanricarde Gardens W2 ...... 238 A8
Clarkson Row NW1 ...... 239 M1
Claremont Square N1 ...... 240 F1
Clarence Gardens NW1 ...... 239 L2
Clarence Mews SE16 ...... 247 G6
Clarendon Gardens W9 ...... 238 D4
Clarendon Gate W2 ...... 238 F7

Clarendon Place W2 ...... 238 F7
Clarendon Street SW1V 243 L6
Clareville Grove SW7 ...... 242 D6
Clareville Street SW7 ...... 242 D6
Clarges Mews W1J 243 L1
Clarges Street W1J 243 L1
Clark Street E1 ...... 246 F2
Carkson Row NW1 ...... 239 M1
Claverton Street SW1V 244 A7
Clave Street E1W 246 F5
Clay Street W1U 239 H5
Clayton Street SE11 ...... 244 F8
Cleaver Square SE11 ...... 245 G7
Cleaver Street SE11 ...... 245 G7
Clegg Street E1W 246 F5
Clemence Street E14 ...... 247 L2
Clements Lane EC4N 241 L7
Clement's Road SE16 ...... 246 E8
Clenston Mews W1H 239 H6
Clere Street EC2A 241 L3
Clerkenwell Close EC1R 241 G3
Clerkenwell Green EC1R 241 G4
Clerkenwell Road EC1M 241 G4
Cleveland Gardens W2 ...... 238 C6
Cleveland Mews W1T 239 M4
Cleveland Place SW1Y 244 A1
Cleveland Row SW1A 244 A2
Cleveland Square W2 ...... 238 C6
Cleveland Street W1T 239 M4
Cleveland Terrace W2 ...... 238 D6
Clifford Street W1S 239 M7
Clifton Gardens W9 ...... 238 C4
Clifton Place SE16 ...... 247 G6
Clifton Place W2 ...... 238 E7
Clifton Road W9 ...... 238 D3
Clifton Street EC2A 241 M3
Clifton Villas W9 ...... 238 C4
Clink Street SE1 ...... 245 K1
Clipper Close SE16 ...... 247 H6
Clipstone Mews W1W 239 M4
Clipstone Street W1W 239 L4
Cliveden Place SW1W 243 J5
Cloak Lane EC4R 241 K7
Cloth Fair EC1A 241 J5
Cloth Street EC1A 241 J5
Cluny Place SE1 ...... 246 A8
Cobb Street E1 ...... 246 B2
Cobourg Street NW1 ...... 240 A2
Coburg Close SW1P 244 A5
Cochrane Mews NW8 ...... 238 E1
Cochrane Street NW8 ...... 238 E1
Cock Lane EC1A 241 H5
Cockspur Street SW1Y 244 C1
Codling Close * E1W 246 D5
Coin Street SE1 ...... 245 G1
Coke Street E1 ...... 246 D2
Colbeck Mews SW7 ...... 242 C6
Colebrook Row N1 ...... 241 H1
Coleherne Road SW10 ...... 242 B7
Coleman Street EC2R 241 L6
Cole Street SE1 ...... 245 K3
Coley Street WC1X 240 F3
College Hill EC4R 241 K7
College Street EC4R 241 K7
Collett Road SE16 ...... 246 D8
Collier Street N1 ...... 240 E1
Collingham Gardens SW5 ...... 242 B6
Collingham Place SW5 ...... 242 B5
Collingham Road SW5 ...... 242 B5
Colnbrook Street SE1 ...... 245 H4
Colombo Street SE1 ...... 245 H1
Colonnade WC1N 240 D4
Coltman Street E14 ...... 247 K2
Commercial Road E1 ...... 246 D2
Commercial Road E14 ...... 247 K3
Commercial Street E1 ...... 246 B1
Compton Street EC1V 241 H3
Concert Hall Approach SE1 ...... 244 E2
Conder Street E14 ...... 247 K2
Conduit Mews W2 ...... 238 E6
Conduit Place W2 ...... 238 E6
Conduit Street W1S 239 L7
Congreve Street SE17 ...... 245 M5
Connaught Close W2 ...... 238 F7
Connaught Place W2 ...... 239 G7
Connaught Square W2 ...... 239 G6
Connaught Street W2 ...... 239 G6
Cons Street SE1 ...... 245 G2
Constitution Hill SW1A 243 L3
Content Street SE17 ...... 245 K5
Conway Street W1T 239 M4
Cookham Crescent SE16 ...... 247 H6
Cook's Road SE17 ...... 245 H8
Coombs Street N1 ...... 241 J1
Cooper's Lane Estate NW1 ...... 240 B1
Cooper's Row EC3N 246 B3
Copenhagen Place E14 ...... 247 L2
Cope Place W8 ...... 242 A4
Copley Court SE17 ...... 245 J8
Copley Street E1 ...... 247 H2
Copperfield Road E3 ...... 247 K1
Copperfield Street SE1 ...... 245 J2
Copthall Avenue EC2R 241 L6
Coptic Street WC1A 240 C5
Coral Street SE1 ...... 245 G3
Coram Street WC1H 240 C3
Cork Square E1W 246 E5
Cork Street W1S 239 M8
Corlett Street NW1 ...... 238 F5
Cornhill EC3V 241 L6
Cornwall Gardens SW7 ...... 242 C4
Cornwall Mews South SW7 ...... 242 C5
Cornwall Road SE1 ...... 244 F1
Cornwall Road SE1 ...... 245 G2
Cornwall Street E1 ...... 246 E3
Cornwall Terrace Mews NW1 ...... 239 H4
Cornwood Drive E1 ...... 247 G2
Coronet Street N1 ...... 241 M2
Corporation Row EC1R 241 G3
Corsham Street N1 ...... 241 L2
Cosser Street SE1 ...... 244 F4
Cosway Street NW1 ...... 239 G4
Cottage Place SW3 ...... 242 F4
Cottesmore Gardens W8 ...... 242 B4
Cottons Lane SE1 ...... 245 M1
Coulson Street SW3 ...... 243 H6
Counter Street SE1 ...... 245 M1
County Street SE1 ...... 245 K5
Courtenay Square SE11 ...... 244 F7
Courtenay Street SE11 ...... 244 F6
Courtfield Gardens SW5 ...... 242 B5
Courtfield Mews * SW5 ...... 242 C5
Courtfield Road SW7 ...... 242 C5
Court Street E1 ...... 246 E1
'Cousin Lane SE1 ...... 241 K8
Covent Garden ⊖ WC2E 240 D7

Covent Garden WC2E 240 D7
Coventry Street W1D 240 B8
Cowcross Street EC1M 241 H4
Cowper Street EC2A 241 L3
Crail Row SE17 ...... 245 L5
Cramer Street W1U 239 J5
Crampton Street SE17 ...... 245 J6
Cranbourn Street WC2H 240 C7
Cranleigh Street NW1 ...... 240 A1
Cranley Gardens SW7 ...... 242 D6
Cranley Mews SW7 ...... 242 D6
Cranley Place SW7 ...... 242 E6
Cranston Estate N1 ...... 241 L1
Cranwood Street EC1V 241 L2
Craven Hill W2 ...... 238 D7
Craven Hill Gardens W2 ...... 238 C7
Craven Road W2 ...... 238 D7
Craven Street WC2N 244 D1
Craven Terrace W2 ...... 238 D7
Crawford Passage EC1R 241 G3
Crawford Place W1H 239 G5
Crawford Street W1H 239 G5
Creechurch Lane EC3A 246 A3
Creed Lane EC4V 241 H7
Cresswell Place SW10 ...... 242 D6
Cressy Place E1 ...... 247 G1
Crestfield Street WC1H 240 D2
Crimscott Street SE1 ...... 246 A8
Crispin Street E1 ...... 246 B1
Cromer Street WC1H 240 D2
Crompton Street W2 ...... 238 D4
Cranwood Street EC1V 241 L2
Cromwell Mews * SW7 ...... 242 E5
Cromwell Place SW7 ...... 242 E5
Cromwell Road SW5 ...... 242 B5
Cromwell Road SW7 ...... 242 E5
Crondall Court N1 ...... 241 M1
Crondall Street N1 ...... 241 L1
Cropley Street N1 ...... 241 K1
Crosby Row SE1 ...... 245 L3
Cross Lane EC3R 246 A4
Crosswall EC3N 246 B3
Crowder Street E1 ...... 246 E3
Crucifix Lane SE1 ...... 246 A6
Cruikshank Street WC1X 240 F1
Cuba Street E14 ...... 247 M6
Cubitt Street WC1X 240 E2
Culford Gardens SW3 ...... 243 H6
Culling Road SE16 ...... 246 F7
Cullum Street EC3M 246 A4
Culross Street W1K 239 J8
Culworth Street NW8 ...... 238 F1
Cumberland Gardens WC1X 240 F2
Cumberland Gate W2 ...... 239 H7
Cumberland Market NW1 ...... 239 L2
Cumberland Street SW1V 243 L6
Cumberland Terrace NW1 ...... 239 K1
Cumberland Terrace Mews NW1 ...... 239 L1
Cumberland Wharf SE16 ...... 247 G6
Cumming Street N1 ...... 240 E1
Cundy Street SW1W 243 K6
Cunningham Place NW8 ...... 238 E3
Cureton Street SW1P 244 C6
Curlew Street SE1 ...... 246 B6
Cursitor Street EC4A 240 F6
Curtain Road EC2A 241 M3
Curtain Road EC2A 241 M4
Curzon Gate W2 ...... 243 K2
Curzon Street W1J 243 K1
Cuthbert Street W2 ...... 238 E4
Cutler Street EC3A 246 A2
Cynthia Street N1 ...... 240 F1
Cypress Place W1T 240 A4
Cyrus Street EC1V 241 H3

D

Dacre Street SW1H 244 B3
Dakin Place E1 ...... 247 J1
Dallington Street EC1V 241 H3
Damien Street E1 ...... 246 F2
Dane Street WC1R 240 E5
Dansey Place W1D 240 B7
Dante Road SE11 ...... 245 H5
Danvers Street SW3 ...... 242 F8
D'Arblay Street W1F 240 A6
Dartford Street SE17 ...... 245 K8
Dartmouth Street SW1H 244 B3
Darwin Street SE17 ...... 245 L5
Date Street SE17 ...... 245 K7
Davenant Street E1 ...... 246 D1
Daventry Street NW1 ...... 238 F4
Davidge Street SE1 ...... 245 H3
Davies Mews W1K 239 K7
Davies Street W1K 239 K7
Dawes Street SE17 ...... 245 L6
Dawson Place W2 ...... 238 A7
Deal Porters Way SE16 ...... 247 G8
Deal Street E1 ...... 246 D1
Dean Bradley Street SW1P 244 C5
Dean Close SE16 ...... 247 H6
Deancross Street E1 ...... 246 F3
Deanery Street W1K 243 K1
Dean Farrar Street SW1H 244 B3
Dean Ryle Street SW1P 244 C5
Dean's Buildings SE17 ...... 245 L6
Dean Stanley Street SW1P 244 C4
Dean Street W1D 240 B6
Dean's Yard SW1P 244 C4
Decima Street SE1 ...... 245 M4
Deck Close SE16 ...... 247 J6
Defoe Close SE16 ...... 247 K7
Delamere Street W2 ...... 238 C5
Delamere Terrace W2 ...... 238 B4
De Laune Street SE17 ...... 245 H7
Delaware Road W9 ...... 238 B3
Dellow Street E1 ...... 246 F3
Delverton Road SE17 ...... 245 H7
Denbigh Place SW1V 243 M6
Denbigh Street SW1V 243 M6
Denbigh Street SW1V 244 A6
Denman Street W1D 240 B7
Denmark Street WC2H 240 C6
Denny Close SE11 ...... 245 G6
Denny Street SE11 ...... 245 G6
Denyer Street SW3 ...... 243 G5
Derby Gate SW1A 244 D3
Derby Street W1J 243 K1
Dering Street W1S 239 L6
Derry Street W8 ...... 242 B3
De Vere Gardens W8 ...... 242 C3
Deverell Street SE1 ...... 245 L4
Devonport Street E1 ...... 247 G3
Devonshire Close W1G 239 K4

Devonshire Mews South W1G 239 K4
Devonshire Mews West W1G 239 K4
Devonshire Place W1G 239 K4
Devonshire Place Mews W1G 239 K4
Devonshire Row EC2M 246 A2
Devonshire Square EC2M 246 A2
Devonshire Street W1G 239 K4
Devonshire Terrace W2 ...... 238 D7
De Walden Street W1G 239 K5
Dickens Estate SE16 ...... 246 D7
Dickens Square SE1 ...... 245 K4
Dilke Street SW3 ...... 243 H8
Dingley Place EC1V 241 K2
Dingley Road EC1V 241 K2
Disney Place SE1 ...... 245 K2
Distaff Lane EC4V 241 J7
Distin Street SE11 ...... 244 F6
Dockhead SE1 ...... 246 C7
Dock Hill Avenue SE16 ...... 247 J6
Dockley Road SE16 ...... 246 D8
Dock Street E1 ...... 246 D4
Doddington Grove SE17 ...... 245 H7
Doddington Place SE17 ...... 245 H8
Dodson Street SE1 ...... 245 G3
Dod Street E14 ...... 247 M2
Dolben Street SE1 ...... 245 H2
Dolland Street SE11 ...... 244 E7
Dolphin Square SW1V 244 A7
Dolphin Square SW1V 244 B7
Dombey Street WC1N 240 E4
Dominion Drive SE16 ...... 247 H7
Dominion Street EC2A 241 L5
Donegal Street N1 ...... 240 F1
Dongola Road E1 ...... 247 J1
Donne Place SW3 ...... 243 G5
Doon Street SE1 ...... 244 F1
Dora Street E14 ...... 247 L2
Doric Way NW1 ...... 240 B2
Dorset Rise EC4Y 241 G7
Dorset Square NW1 ...... 239 H4
Dorset Street W1U 239 H5
Doughty Mews WC1N 240 E3
Doughty Street WC1N 240 E3
Douglas Street SW1P 244 B6
Douro Place W8 ...... 242 C3
Douthwaite Square * E1W 246 D5
Dovehouse Street SW3 ...... 242 E6
Dover Street W1J 243 L1
Dover Street W1S 239 L8
Dowgate Hill EC4R 241 K7
Downfield Close W9 ...... 238 B4
Downing Street SW1A 244 C2
Down Street W1J 243 K2
Downtown Road SE16 ...... 247 K6
D'Oyley Street SW1X 243 J5
Draco Street SE17 ...... 245 J8
Drake Close SE16 ...... 247 H6
Draycott Avenue SW3 ...... 243 G5
Draycott Place SW3 ...... 243 H6
Draycott Terrace SW3 ...... 243 H5
Drayson Mews W8 ...... 242 A3
Drayton Gardens SW10 ...... 242 D6
Druid Street SE1 ...... 246 A6
Druid Street SE1 ...... 246 B6
Drummond Crescent NW1 ...... 240 B2
Drummond Gate * SW1V 244 B6
Drummond Road SE16 ...... 246 E8
Drummond Street NW1 ...... 240 A3
Drury Lane WC2B 240 D6
Dryden Court SE11 ...... 245 G5
Dryden Street WC2B 240 D6
Duchess Mews W1G 239 L5
Duchess Street W1B 239 L5
Duchy Street SE1 ...... 245 G1
Duckett Street E1 ...... 247 J1
Duck Lane W1F 240 B6
Dufferin Street EC1Y 241 K4
Dufour's Place W1F 240 A6
Duke of Wellington Place SW1W 243 K3
Duke of York Square SW3 ...... 243 H6
Duke of York Street SW1Y 244 A1
Duke Shore Wharf E14 ...... 247 K4
Duke's Lane W8 ...... 242 A2
Duke's Place EC3A 246 B2
Duke's Road WC1H 240 C2
Duke Street W1K 239 K7
Duke Street W1U 239 J6
Duke Street Hill SE1 ...... 245 L1
Duke Street St James's SW1Y 244 A1
Dunbar Wharf E14 ...... 247 L4
Duncannon Street WC2N 240 C8
Duncan Terrace N1 ...... 241 H1
Dundee Street E1W 246 E5
Dundee Wharf E14 ...... 247 L4
Dunelm Street E1 ...... 247 H2
Dunlop Place SE16 ...... 246 C8
Dunraven Street W1K 239 H7
Dunster Court EC3R 246 A3
Duplex Ride SW1X 243 H3
Durand's Wharf SE16 ...... 247 L6
Durham Row E1 ...... 247 J1
Durham Street SE11 ...... 244 E7
Durham Terrace W2 ...... 238 A6
Dyott Street WC1A 240 C6
Dysart Street EC2A 241 M4

E

Eagle Court EC1M 241 H4
Eagle Street WC1R 240 E5
Eamont Street NW8 ...... 239 G1
Eardley Crescent SW5 ...... 242 A7
Earlham Street WC2H 240 C7
Earl's Court ⊖ SW5 ...... 242 A6
Earl's Court Gardens SW5 ...... 242 B6
Earl's Court Road SW5 ...... 242 A6
Earl's Court Square SW5 ...... 242 A6
Earlstoke Street EC1V 241 H2
Earl Street EC2A 241 M4
Earnshaw Street WC2H 240 C6
East Arbour Street E1 ...... 247 H2
Eastbourne Mews W2 ...... 238 D6
Eastbourne Terrace W2 ...... 238 D6
Eastcastle Street W1W 240 A6
Eastcheap EC3M 241 M7
Eastfield Street E14 ...... 247 K1
East India Dock Road E14 ...... 247 M3
East Lane SE16 ...... 246 D6
Easton Street WC1X 240 F3
East Poultry Avenue EC1A 241 H5
East Road N1 ...... 241 L2
East Smithfield E1W 246 C4
East Street SE17 ...... 245 L6
East Tenter Street E1 ...... 246 C3
Eaton Close SW1W 243 J5

Eaton Gate SW1W 243 J5
Eaton Lane SW1W 243 L4
Eaton Mews North SW1W 243 J5
Eaton Mews South SW1W 243 K5
Eaton Mews West SW1W 243 K5
Eaton Place SW1X 243 J4
Eaton Row SW1W 243 K4
Eaton Square SW1W 243 J5
Eaton Terrace SW1W 243 J5
Ebbisham Drive SW8 ...... 244 E8
Ebury Bridge SW1W 243 K6
Ebury Bridge Road SW1W 243 K7
Ebury Mews SW1W 243 K5
Ebury Square SW1W 243 K6
Ebury Street SW1W 243 K5
Eccleston Bridge SW1W 243 L5
Eccleston Mews SW1X 243 K4
Eccleston Place SW1W 243 L5
Eccleston Square SW1V 243 L6
Eccleston Street SW1W 243 K4
Edbrooke Road W9 ...... 238 A3
Edge Street W8 ...... 242 A1
Edgware Road W2 ...... 238 F5
Edgware Road ⊖ NW1 ...... 238 F5
Edinburgh Gate SW1X 243 H3
Edith Grove SW10 ...... 242 C8
Edwards Mews W1H 239 J6
Egerton Crescent SW3 ...... 242 F5
Egerton Gardens SW3 ...... 242 F5
Egerton Terrace SW3 ...... 243 G4
Eglington Court SE17 ...... 245 J7
Elba Place SE17 ...... 245 K5
Eldon Road W8 ...... 242 B4
Eldon Street EC2M 241 L5
Eleanor Close SE16 ...... 247 H6
Elephant & Castle SE1 ...... 245 J4
Elephant & Castle ⇌ ⊖ SE1 ...... 245 J5
Elephant Lane SE16 ...... 246 F6
Elephant Road SE17 ...... 245 J5
Elf Row E1W 247 G3
Elgar Street SE16 ...... 247 K7
Elgin Avenue W9 ...... 238 B2
Elgin Mews North W9 ...... 238 C2
Elgin Mews South W9 ...... 238 C2
Elia Mews N1 ...... 241 H1
Elia Street N1 ...... 241 H1
Elim Estate SE1 ...... 245 M3
Elim Street SE1 ...... 245 M3
Elizabeth Bridge SW1V 243 L6
Elizabeth Street SW1W 243 K5
Ellen Street E1 ...... 246 D3
Elliott's Row SE11 ...... 245 H5
Ellis Street SW1X 243 J5
Elmfield Way W9 ...... 238 A4
Elm Park Gardens SW10 ...... 242 E7
Elm Park Lane SW3 ...... 242 E7
Elm Park Road SW3 ...... 242 E8
Elm Place SW7 ...... 242 E7
Elms Mews W2 ...... 238 D7
Elm Street WC1X 240 F4
Elm Tree Road NW8 ...... 238 E2
Elnathan Mews W9 ...... 238 B4
Elsa Street E1 ...... 247 J1
Elsted Street SE17 ...... 245 L6
Elvaston Mews SW7 ...... 242 D4
Elvaston Place SW7 ...... 242 D4
Elverton Street SW1P 244 B5
Ely Place EC1N 241 G5
Elystan Place SW3 ...... 243 G6
Elystan Street SW3 ...... 242 F6
Embankment ⊖ WC2N 244 D1
Embankment Gardens SW3 ...... 243 H8
Embankment Place WC2N 244 D1
Emba Street SE16 ...... 246 D7
Emerald Street WC1N 240 E4
Emerson Street SE1 ...... 245 J1
Emery Hill Street SW1P 244 A5
Emery Street SE1 ...... 245 G3
Emperor's Gate SW7 ...... 242 C5
Empire Square SE1 ...... 245 L3
Empress Place SW6 ...... 242 A7
Endell Street WC2H 240 C6
Endsleigh Gardens WC1H 240 B3
Endsleigh Place WC1H 240 B3
Endsleigh Street WC1H 240 B3
Enford Street W1H 239 G5
English Grounds SE1 ...... 245 M1
Enid Street SE16 ...... 246 C8
Ennismore Gardens SW7 ...... 242 F3
Ennismore Gardens Mews SW7 ...... 242 F4
Ennismore Mews SW7 ...... 242 F4
Ennismore Street SW7 ...... 242 F4
Ensign Street E1 ...... 246 D4
Epworth Street EC2A 241 L3
Erasmus Street SW1P 244 C6
Errol Street EC1Y 241 K4
Essendine Road W9 ...... 238 A3
Essex Street WC2R 240 F7
Essex Villas W8 ...... 242 A3
Europa Place EC1V 241 J2
Euston ⇌ ⊖ NW1 ...... 240 B2
Euston Road NW1 ...... 240 B3
Euston Square NW1 ...... 240 B2
Euston Square ⊖ NW1 ...... 240 A3
Euston Street NW1 ...... 240 A3
Evelyn Gardens SW7 ...... 242 D7
Evelyn Walk N1 ...... 241 L1
Eversholt Street NW1 ...... 240 A1
Everton Mews NW1 ...... 239 M2
Ewer Street SE1 ...... 245 J2
Ewhurst Close E1 ...... 247 G1
Exchange Square EC2A 241 M4
Exeter Street WC2E 240 D7
Exhibition Road SW7 ...... 242 E3
Exmouth Market EC1R 241 G3
Exon Street SE17 ...... 245 M6
Exton Street SE1 ...... 244 F2
Eyre Street Hill EC1R 240 F4

F

Fairclough Street E1 ...... 246 D3
Fair Street SE1 ...... 246 B6
Falmouth Road SE1 ...... 245 K4
Fann Street EC1M 241 J4
Fanshaw Street N1 ...... 241 M1
Farmer Street W8 ...... 242 A1
Farm Lane SW6 ...... 242 A8
Farm Street W1K 239 K8
Farnham Place SE1 ...... 245 J1
Farrance Street E14 ...... 247 M3
Farringdon ⇌ ⊖ EC1M 241 G4
Farringdon Lane EC1R 241 G4
Farringdon Road EC1R 240 F3

Farringdon Street EC1M....241 H5
Farrins Rents SE16....247 J5
Farrow Place SE16....247 K7
Farthing Fields * E1W....246 F5
Fashion Street E1....246 B1
Faunce Street SE17....245 H7
Fawcett Street SW10....242 C8
Featherstone Street EC1Y....241 L3
Fenchurch Avenue EC3M....246 A3
Fenchurch Buildings EC3M....246 A3
Fenchurch Place EC3M....246 A3
Fenchurch Street ⇌ EC3M....246 A3
Fenchurch Street EC3M....246 A3
Fendall Street SE1....246 B8
Fenning Street SE1....245 M2
Fentiman Road SW8....244 D8
Fernsbury Street WC1X....240 F2
Fetter Lane EC4A....241 G6
Fieldgate Street E1....246 D2
Fielding Street SE17....245 J7
Field Street WC1X....240 E1
Finborough Road SW10....242 B8
Finch Lane EC3V....241 L6
Finland Street SE16....247 K8
Finsbury Circus EC2M....241 L5
Finsbury Estate EC1R....241 G3
Finsbury Market EC2A....241 M4
Finsbury Square EC2A....241 L4
Finsbury Street EC2Y....241 L4
First Street SW3....243 G5
Fishermans Drive SE16....247 J6
Fisher Street WC1R....240 D5
Fisherton Street NW8....238 E3
Fish Street Hill EC3R....241 L7
Fitzalan Street SE11....244 F5
Fitzhardinge Street W1H....239 J6
Fitzroy Square W1T....239 M4
Fitzroy Street W1T....239 M4
Flamborough Street E14....247 J3
Flank Street E1....246 C4
Flaxman Terrace WC1H....240 C3
Fleet Street EC4A....241 G6
Fleming Road SE17....245 H8
Fletcher Street E1....246 D3
Flint Street SE17....245 L6
Flitcroft Street WC2H....240 C6
Flockton Street SE16....246 D7
Flood Street SW3....243 G7
Flood Walk SW3....243 G7
Floral Street WC2E....240 D7
Foley Street W1W....239 M5
Forbes Street E1....246 D3
Fordham Street E1....246 D2
Ford Square E1....246 F2
Fore Street EC2Y....241 K5
Formosa Street W9....238 C4
Forset Street W1H....239 G6
Forsyth Gardens SE17....245 H8
Fort Street E1....246 B1
Fortune Street EC1Y....241 K4
Forum Magnum Square SE1....244 E3
Foster Lane EC2V....241 J6
Foulis Terrace SW7....242 E6
Foundry Close SE16....247 J5
Fournier Street E1....246 C1
Fowey Close E1W....246 E5
Frampton Street NW8....238 E4
Francis Street SW1P....244 A4
Franklin's Row SW3....243 H6
Frazier Street SE1....245 G3
Frean Street SE16....246 C8
Frederick Close W2....239 G7
Frederick Street WC1X....240 E2
Frederic Mews * SW1X....243 J3
Freemantle Street SE17....245 M6
Friday Street EC4V....241 J7
Friend Street EC1V....241 H2
Frith Street W1D....240 B6
Fulbourne Street E1....246 E1
Fulford Street SE16....246 F7
Fulham Road SW10....242 D8
Fulham Road SW3....242 F6
Furnival Street EC4A....240 F5
Fynes Street SW1P....244 B5

G

Gabriel's Wharf SE1....245 G1
Gainsford Street SE1....246 B6
Galleon Close SE16....247 H6
Galsworthy Avenue E14....247 K2
Galway Street EC1V....241 K2
Gambia Street SE1....245 H2
Garden Road NW8....238 D1
Garden Row SE1....245 H4
Garden Street E1....247 H1
Garden Terrace * SW1V....244 B6
Garden Walk EC2A....241 M3
Gard Street EC1V....241 J2
Garford Street E14....247 M4
Garlick Hill EC4R....241 K7
Garnault Place EC1R....241 G3
Garnet Street E1W....246 F4
Garrett Street EC1Y....241 K3
Garrick Street WC2E....240 C7
Garterway SE16....247 H7
Garway Road W2....238 B6
Gaspar Mews SW7....242 C5
Gataker Street * SE16....246 E8
Gate Mews SW7....242 F3
Gateforth Street NW8....238 F3
Gate Mews NW1....239 L3
Gatesborough Street * EC2A....241 M3
Gate Street WC2A....240 E5
Gatliff Road SW1W....243 K7
Gaunt Street SE1....245 J4
Gayfere Street SW1P....244 C4
Gaywood Street SE1....245 H4
Gaza Street SE17....245 H7
Gedling Place SE1....246 C7
Gee Street EC1V....241 J3
George Mathers Road SE11....245 H5
George Row SE16....246 C7
George Street W1H....239 H6
George Yard W1K....239 K7
Geraldine Street SE11....245 H4
Gerald Road SW1W....243 K5
Gerrard Street W1D....240 B7
Gerridge Street SE1....245 G3
Gertrude Street SW10....242 D8
Gibson Road SE11....244 F5
Gilbert Place WC1A....240 C5
Gilbert Road SE11....245 G5
Gilbert Street W1K....239 K7

Gildea Street W1W....239 L5
Gillingham Street SW1V....243 M5
Gill Street E14....247 L3
Gilston Road SW10....242 D7
Giltspur Street EC1A....241 H5
Gladstone Street SE1....245 H4
Glamis Place E1W....247 G4
Glamis Road E1W....247 G4
Glasshill Street SE1....245 J3
Glasshouse Walk SE11....244 D7
Glasshouse Yard EC1....241 J4
Glebe Place SW3....242 F7
Gledhow Road SW5....242 C6
Glentworth Street NW1....239 H4
Globe Pond Road SE16....247 J5
Globe Street SE1....245 K3
Gloucester Court * EC3R....246 A4
Gloucester Gardens W2....238 C6
Gloucester Mews W2....238 D6
Gloucester Mews West W2....238 C6
Gloucester Place NW1....239 H3
Gloucester Place W1U....239 H5
Gloucester Place Mews W1U....239 H5
Gloucester Road SW7....242 C4
Gloucester Road SW7....242 D6
Gloucester Road ⇌ SW7....242 C5
Gloucester Square W2....238 F6
Gloucester Street SW1V....243 M7
Gloucester Terrace W2....238 B5
Gloucester Terrace W2....238 D6
Gloucester Walk W8....242 A2
Gloucester Way EC1R....241 G2
Glyn Street SE11....244 E7
Godfrey Street SW3....243 G6
Goding Street SE11....244 D7
Godliman Street EC4V....241 J7
Godwin Close N1....241 K1
Golden Hinde II SE1....245 L1
Golden Jubilee Bridge WC2N....244 D1
Golden Lane EC1Y....241 J4
Golden Square W1F....240 A7
Golding Street E1....246 E3
Goldney Road W9....238 A4
Goldsmith Street EC2V....241 K6
Gomm Road SE16....247 G8
Goodge Place W1T....240 A5
Goodge Street W1T....240 A5
Goodge Street ⇌ W1T....240 B5
Goodwin Close SE16....246 C8
Gordon Place W8....242 A2
Gordon Square WC1H....240 B3
Gordon Street WC1H....240 B3
Gore Street SW7....242 D4
Goring Street * EC3A....246 A2
Gosfield Street W1W....239 L5
Goslett Yard WC2H....240 B6
Goswell Road EC1V....241 H1
Gough Street WC1X....240 F3
Goulston Street E1....246 B2
Gower Mews WC1E....240 B5
Gower Place NW1....240 A3
Gower Street WC1E....240 B3
Gower's Walk E1....246 D2
Gracechurch Street EC3V....241 M7
Grafton Mews W1T....239 M4
Grafton Place NW1....240 B2
Grafton Street W1S....239 L8
Grafton Way W1T....240 A4
Graham Street N1....241 J1
Graham Terrace SW1W....243 J6
Granby Terrace NW1....239 M1
Grand Avenue EC1A....241 H5
Grange Road SE1....246 B8
Grange Walk SE1....246 A8
Grange Yard SE1....246 B8
Grantully Road W9....238 B2
Granville Place W1H....239 J6
Granville Road NW6....238 A1
Granville Square WC1X....240 F2
Grape Street WC2H....240 C6
Gravel Lane E1....246 B2
Gray's Inn Road WC1X....240 D2
Gray's Inn Square WC1R....240 F5
Gray Street SE1....245 G3
Great Castle Street W1G....239 L6
Great Central Street NW1....239 G4
Great Chapel Street W1D....240 B6
Great College Street SW1P....244 C4
Great Cumberland Place W1H....239 H6
Great Dover Street SE1....245 K3
Great Eastern Street EC2A....241 M3
Great George Street SW1P....244 C3
Great Guildford Street SE1....245 J1
Great James Street WC1N....240 E4
Great Marlborough Street W1F....239 M7
Great Maze Pond SE1....245 L2
Great Newport Street WC2H....240 C7
Greatorex Street E1....246 D1
Great Ormond Street WC1N....240 D4
Great Percy Street WC1X....240 F2
Great Peter Street SW1P....244 B4
Great Portland Street W1W....239 L4
Great Portland Street ⇌ W1W....239 L4
Great Pulteney Street W1F....240 A7
Great Queen Street WC2B....240 D6
Great Russell Street WC1B....240 C5
Great St Helen's EC3A....241 M6
Great Scotland Yard SW1A....244 C1
Great Smith Street SW1P....244 C4
Great Suffolk Street SE1....245 H2
Great Sutton Street EC1V....241 H4
Great Swan Alley EC2R....241 L6
Great Titchfield Street W1W....239 M4
Great Tower Street EC3M....241 M7
Great Tower Street EC3R....246 A4
Great Winchester Street EC2N....241 L6
Great Windmill Street W1D....240 B7
Greek Street W1D....240 B6
Greenacre Square SE16....247 J6
Green Bank E1W....246 E5
Greenberry Street NW8....238 F1
Greencoat Place SW1P....244 A5
Green Coat Row SW1P....244 A4
Greenfield Road E1....246 D2
Greenham Close SE1....244 F3
Green Park ⇌ W1J....243 M1
Green Street W1K....239 J7
Greenwell Street W1W....239 L4
Greet Street SE1....245 G2
Grenade Street E14....247 L4
Grendon Street NW8....238 F3
Grenville Place SW7....242 C5
Gresham Street EC2V....241 J6
Gresse Street W1T....240 B5

Greville Street EC1N....241 G5
Greycoat Place SW1P....244 B4
Greycoat Street SW1P....244 B4
Grigg's Place SE1....246 A8
Grosvenor Bridge SW8....243 L8
Grosvenor Crescent SW1X....243 J3
Grosvenor Crescent Mews SW1X....243 J3
Grosvenor Gardens SW1W....243 L4
Grosvenor Gardens
  Mews East SW1W....243 L4
Grosvenor Gardens
  Mews North SW1W....243 L4
Grosvenor Gardens
  Mews South * SW1W....243 L4
Grosvenor Gate W2....239 H8
Grosvenor Hill W1K....239 L7
Grosvenor Place SW1X....243 K3
Grosvenor Road SW1V....243 L8
Grosvenor Square W1K....239 J7
Grosvenor Street W1K....239 K7
Grosvenor Terrace SE5....245 J8
Grove End Road NW8....238 D2
Guildhouse Street SW1V....243 M5
Guilford Street WC1N....240 D4
Guinness Square SE1....245 M5
Gulliver Street SE16....247 K8
Gunpowder Square EC4A....241 G6
Gun Street E1....246 B1
Gunthorpe Street E1....246 C2
Gutter Lane EC2V....241 J6
Guy Street SE1....245 L3

H

Haberdasher Street N1....241 L2
Haddonhall Estate SE1....245 M4
Hainton Close E1....246 F3
Halcrow Street * E1....246 F2
Half Moon Street W1J....243 L1
Halford Road SW6....242 A8
Halkin Place SW1X....243 J4
Halkin Street SW1X....243 K3
Hallam Street W1W....239 L5
Halley Street E14....247 K1
Hallfield Estate W2....238 C6
Hall Place W2....238 E4
Hall Road NW8....238 D2
Hall Street EC1V....241 H2
Halpin Place SE17....245 M6
Halsey Street SW3....243 G5
Hamilton Close NW8....238 D2
Hamilton Close SE16....247 K7
Hamilton Gardens NW8....238 D2
Hamilton Place W1J....243 K2
Hamilton Terrace NW8....238 C1
Hamlet Way SE1....245 L3
Hammett Street EC3N....246 B4
Hampden Close NW1....240 B1
Hampden Gurney Street W2....239 H6
Hampstead Road NW1....239 M2
Hampton Street SE17....245 J6
Hanbury Street E1....246 C1
Hand Court WC1V....240 E5
Handel Street WC1N....240 D3
Hankey Place SE1....245 L3
Hannibal Road E1....247 G1
Hanover Square W1S....239 L6
Hanover Street W1S....239 L7
Hans Crescent SW3....243 H3
Hanson Street W1W....239 M4
Hans Place SW1X....243 H4
Hans Road SW3....243 G4
Hans Street SW1X....243 H4
Hanway Place W1T....240 B6
Hanway Street W1T....240 B6
Harbet Road W2....238 F5
Harcourt Street W1H....239 G5
Harcourt Terrace SW10....242 C7
Hardinge Street E1W....247 G3
Hardwick Street EC1R....241 G2
Hardwidge Street SE1....245 M2
Hardy Close SE16....247 H6
Harewood Place W1G....239 L6
Harewood Row NW1....239 G4
Harford Street E1....247 J1
Harleyford Road SE11....244 E8
Harley Gardens SW10....242 D7
Harley Place W1G....239 K5
Harley Street W1G....239 L5
Harmsworth Street SE17....245 G7
Harold Estate SE1....246 A8
Harper Road SE1....245 K4
Harpour Street WC1N....240 E4
Harriet Street SW1X....243 H3
Harriet Walk SW1X....243 H3
Harrington Gardens SW7....242 C6
Harrington Road SW7....242 E5
Harrington Square NW1....239 M1
Harrington Street NW1....239 M2
Harrison Street WC1H....240 D2
Harrods SW1X....243 G3
Harrowby Street W1H....239 G6
Harrow Place E1....246 B2
Harrow Road W2....238 A4
Hart Street EC3R....246 A3
Hasker Street SW3....243 G5
Hastings Street WC1H....240 C2
Hatfields SE1....245 G1
Hatherley Grove W2....238 B6
Hatteraick Road SE16....247 G6
Hatton Garden EC1N....241 G4
Hatton Street W2....238 E4
Hatton Wall EC1N....241 G4
Havering Street E1....247 H3
Haverstock Street N1....241 J1
Hawke Place * SE16....247 H6
Haydon Street EC3N....246 B3
Hayes Place NW1....239 G4
Hay Hill W1J....239 L8
Hayles Street SE11....245 H5
Haymarket SW1Y....240 B8
Hayne Street EC1A....241 J4
Hay's Lane SE1....245 M1
Hay's Mews W1J....239 L8
Haywood Place EC1R....241 H3
Headfort Place SW1X....243 K3
Head Street E1....247 H2
Hearnshaw Street E14....247 K2
Hearn Street EC2A....241 M4
Heathcote Street WC1N....240 E3
Heddon Street W1B....239 M7
Heddon Street W1S....240 A7
Hedger Street SE11....245 H5

Heiron Street SE17....245 J8
Hellings Street E1W....246 D5
Helmet Row EC1V....241 K3
Helsinki Square SE16....247 L8
Henderson Drive NW8....238 E3
Heneage Lane EC3A....246 A3
Heneage Street E1....246 C1
Henrietta Place W1G....239 L6
Henrietta Street WC2E....240 D7
Henriques Street E1....246 D2
Henshaw Street SE17....245 L5
Herbal Hill EC1R....241 G4
Herbert Crescent SW1X....243 H4
Herbrand Street WC1H....240 C3
Hercules Road SE1....244 F4
Hereford Road W2....238 A6
Hereford Square SW7....242 D6
Hermitage Street W2....238 E5
Hermitage Wall E1W....246 D5
Hermit Street EC1V....241 H2
Heron Place SE16....247 K5
Heron Quays E14....247 M5
Herrick Street SW1P....244 C6
Hertford Street W1J....243 K2
Hertsmere Road E14....247 M4
Hesper Mews SW5....242 B6
Hessel Street E1....246 E3
Hewett Street EC2A....241 M3
Heygate Street SE17....245 J5
Hide Place SW1P....244 B6
High Holborn WC1V....240 E5
High Street Kensington ⇌ W8....242 A3
Hildyard Road SW6....242 A8
Hilliards Court E1W....246 F5
Hillingdon Street SE17....245 J8
Hill Road NW8....238 D1
Hills Place W1F....239 M6
Hill Street W1J....239 K8
Hinde Street W1U....239 K6
Hind Grove E14....247 M3
Hindgrove Area E14....247 M3
Hithe Grove SE16....247 G8
HMS Belfast SE1....246 A5
Hobart Place SW1W....243 K4
Hobury Street SW10....242 D8
Hogarth Road SW5....242 B6
Holbein Mews SW1W....243 J6
Holbein Place SW1W....243 J6
Holborn EC1N....241 G5
Holborn ⇌ WC2B....240 E5
Holborn Circus EC1N....241 G5
Holborn Viaduct EC1A....241 G5
Holford Street WC1X....240 F2
Holland Street SE1....245 H1
Holland Street W8....242 A3
Hollen Street W1F....240 A6
Holles Street W1C....239 L6
Hollywood Road SW10....242 C8
Holyoak Road SE11....245 H5
Holyrood Street SE1....245 M2
Holyrood Street SE1....246 A6
Holywell Row EC2A....241 M4
Homefield Street * N1....241 M1
Homer Row W1H....239 G5
Homer Street W1H....239 G5
Hooper Street E1....246 D3
Hopetown Street E1....246 C1
Hopkins Street W1F....240 A7
Hopton Street SE1....245 H1
Hopwood Road SE17....245 L8
Hornton Place W8....242 A3
Hornton Street W8....242 A2
Horse & Dolphin Yard W1D....240 B7
Horseferry Road E14....247 J3
Horseferry Road SW1P....244 B4
Horse Guards Avenue SW1A....244 C2
Horse Guards Parade SW1A....244 C2
Horse Guards Road SW1A....244 C2
Horselydown Lane SE1....246 B6
Horsley Street SE17....245 K8
Hosier Lane EC1A....241 H5
Hothfield Place SE16....247 G8
Hotspur Street SE11....244 F6
Houghton Street WC2A....240 E6
Houndsditch EC3A....246 A2
Houses of Parliament SW1A....244 D3
Howick Place SW1E....244 A4
Howland Street W1T....240 A4
Howland Way SE16....247 K7
Howley Place W2....238 D5
Hoxton Square N1....241 M2
Hoxton Street N1....241 M1
Hudson's Place SW1V....243 M5
Hugh Mews SW1V....243 L6
Hugh Street SW1V....243 L6
Hugh Street SW1V....243 L6
Hull Close SE16....247 J6
Hull Street EC1V....241 J2
Hungerford Bridge SE1....244 E1
Hunter Close SE1....245 M4
Hunter Street WC1N....240 D3
Huntley Street WC1E....240 A4
Huntsman Street SE17....245 M6
Huntsworth Mews NW1....239 H3
Hurley Crescent SE16....247 H6
Hutching's Street E14....247 M7
Hutton Street EC4Y....241 G7
Hyde Park W2....243 G1
Hyde Park Corner W1J....243 K2
Hyde Park Corner ⇌ W1J....243 K2
Hyde Park Court SW7....242 D3
Hyde Park Crescent W2....238 F6
Hyde Park Gardens Mews W2....238 F7
Hyde Park Gardens W2....238 F7
Hyde Park Gate SW7....242 C3
Hyde Park Gate SW7....242 D3
Hyde Park Square W2....238 F7
Hyde Park Street W2....238 F7

I

Idol Lane EC3R....241 M7
Ifield Road SW10....242 B8
Iliffe Street SE17....245 J6
Iliffe Yard SE17....245 J6
Imperial College Road SW7....242 D4
Imperial War Museum SE1....245 G4
India Street EC3N....246 B3
Ingestre Place W1F....240 A7
Inglebert Street EC1R....241 F2
Ingram Close SE11....244 E5
Inner Circle NW1....239 J2
Inverness Terrace W2....238 B6
Inverness Terrace Gate W2....238 C8

Invicta Plaza SE1....245 H1
Inville Road SE17....245 L7
Ironmonger Lane EC2V....241 K6
Ironmonger Row EC1V....241 K2
Irving Street WC2N....240 C8
Isambard Place SE16....247 G6
Island Row E14....247 K3
Iverna Court W8....242 A4
Iverna Gardens W8....242 A4
Ives Street SW3....243 G5
Ivor Place NW1....239 G4
Ixworth Place SW3....242 F6

J

Jacob Street SE1....246 C6
Jamaica Gate SE16....246 F8
Jamaica Road SE1....246 C7
Jamaica Road SE16....246 E7
Jamaica Street E1....247 G2
Jamaica Wharf SE1....246 C6
James Street W1U....239 K6
James Street WC2E....240 D7
Jameson Street W8....242 A1
Jamuna Close E14....247 K1
Janeway Street SE16....246 D7
Jardine Road E1W....247 J4
Java Wharf SE1....246 C6
Jay Mews SW7....242 C3
Jermyn Street SW1Y....240 A8
Jerome Crescent NW8....238 F3
Jewery Street EC3N....246 B3
Joan Street SE1....245 G2
Jockey's Fields WC1R....240 E4
Johanna Street SE1....244 F3
John Adam Street WC2N....240 D8
John Carpenter Street EC4Y....241 G7
John Fisher Street E1....246 C4
John Islip Street SW1P....244 C5
John Prince's Street W1G....239 L6
John Roll Way SE16....246 D7
John Ruskin Street SE5....245 J8
John's Mews WC1N....240 E4
Johnson's Place SW1V....244 A7
Johnson Street E1....247 G3
John Street WC1N....240 E4
Joiner Street SE1....245 L1
Jonathan Street SE11....244 E6
Jubilee Place SW3....243 G6
Jubilee Street E1....247 G2
Jubilee Walk W8....242 B1
Judd Street WC1H....240 C2
Junction Mews W2....238 F5
Juxon Street SE11....244 E5

K

Katherine Close SE16....247 H5
Kean Street WC2B....240 E6
Keel Close SE16....247 J6
Keeley Street WC2B....240 E6
Keeton's Road SE16....246 E7
Kell Street SE1....245 H3
Kelso Place W8....242 B4
Kemble Street WC2B....240 E6
Kempsford Gardens SW5....242 A7
Kempsford Road SE11....245 G6
Kendall Place W1U....239 J5
Kendal Street W2....239 G6
Kennet Street E1W....246 D5
Kenning Street SE16....247 G6
Kennings Way SE11....245 G7
Kennington ⇌ SE11....245 H7
Kennington Lane SE11....244 E7
Kennington Oval SE11....244 E8
Kennington Park Gardens SE11....245 G8
Kennington Park Place SE11....245 G8
Kennington Park Road SE11....245 G7
Kennington Road SE1....244 F4
Kennington Road SE11....245 G5
Kennnington Oval SE11....244 F8
Kenrick Place W1U....239 J5
Kensington Church Street W8....242 A1
Kensington Court W8....242 B3
Kensington Gardens W2....242 C1
Kensington Gardens Square W2....238 B6
Kensington Gate W8....242 C4
Kensington Gore SW7....242 C3
Kensington High Street W8....242 A4
Kensington Palace W8....242 B2
Kensington Palace Gardens W8....242 B1
Kensington Palace Gardens W8....242 B2
Kensington Place W8....242 A1
Kensington Road SW7....243 G3
Kensington Road W8....242 B3
Kensington Square W8....242 B3
Kenton Street WC1H....240 C3
Kenway Road SW5....242 A6
Keystone Close N1....240 D1
Keyworth Street SE1....245 H4
Kia Oval (Surrey County
  Cricket Ground) SE11....244 F8
Kilburn Park Road NW6....238 A2
Kildare Terrace W2....238 A6
Killick Street N1....240 E1
Kinburn Street SE16....247 H6
Kinder Street E1....246 E2
King & Queen Wharf SE16....247 H5
King & Queen Street SE17....245 K6
King Charles Street SW1A....244 C2
King David Lane E1....247 G3
Kingdom Street W2....238 C5
King Edward Street EC1A....241 J6
King Edward Walk SE1....245 G4
King James Street SE1....245 H3
Kingly Street W1F....239 M7
King's Bench Street SE1....245 H2
Kingscote Street EC4V....241 H7
King's Cross ⇌ N1C....240 D1
King's Cross Road WC1X....240 E2
King's Cross Square N1C....240 D1
King's Cross St Pancras ⇌ N1C....240 D1
Kingsgate Walk * SW1E....244 A4
King's Head Yard SE1....245 L1
King's Mews WC1N....240 F4
Kingsmill Terrace NW8....238 E1
King Square EC1V....241 J2
King's Road SW3....242 E8
King's Scholars Passage SW1P....243 M5
King's Stairs Close SE16....246 F6
King Street WC2E....240 D7

King Street SW1Y 244 A1
King Street EC2V 241 K6
Kingsway WC2B 240 E6
King William Street EC4N 241 L7
Kinnerton Place North * SW1X 243 J3
Kinnerton Place South * SW1X 243 J3
Kinnerton Street SW1X 243 J3
Kinnerton Yard * SW1X 243 J3
Kipling Estate SE1 .... 245 L3
Kipling Street SE1 .... 245 L3
Kirby Estate SE16 .... 246 D7
Kirby Grove SE1 .... 245 M3
Kirby Street EC1N 241 G4
Knaresborough Place SW5 .... 242 B5
Knightrider Street EC4V 241 H7
Knightsbridge SW1X 243 H3
Knightsbridge SW3 .... 243 H3
Knox Street W1H 239 H4
Kynance Mews SW7 .... 242 C4
Kynance Place SW7 .... 242 C4

L

Lackington Street EC2A 241 L4
Lafone Street SE1 .... 246 B6
Lagado Mews SE16 .... 247 H5
Lambeth Bridge SW1P 244 D5
Lambeth High Street SE1 .... 244 E5
Lambeth Hill EC4V 241 J7
Lambeth North ⊖ SE1 .... 244 F3
Lambeth Palace Road SE1 .... 244 E4
Lambeth Road SE1 .... 244 E4
Lambeth Walk SE11 .... 244 F5
Lamb's Conduit Street WC1N 240 E4
Lamb's Passage EC1Y 241 K4
Lamb Street E1 .... 246 B1
Lamb Way SE1 .... 246 A7
Lamlash Street SE11 .... 245 H5
Lanark Place W9 .... 238 D3
Lanark Road W9 .... 238 B1
Lancaster Gate W2 .... 238 D7
Lancaster Gate W2 .... 238 D8
Lancaster Gate ⊖ W2 .... 238 E7
Lancaster Mews W2 .... 238 D7
Lancaster Place WC2E 240 E7
Lancaster Street SE1 .... 245 H3
Lancaster Terrace W2 .... 238 E7
Lancaster Walk W2 .... 238 D8
Lancelot Place SW7 .... 243 G3
Lancing Street NW1 .... 240 B2
Lanesborough Place * SW1X 243 J3
Langdale Street E1 .... 246 E3
Langford Place NW8 .... 238 D1
Langham Place W1B 239 L5
Langham Street W1W 239 L5
Langham Street W1W 239 M5
Langley Lane SW8 .... 244 D8
Langley Street WC2H 240 C7
Langton Close WC1X 240 E4
Lanhill Road W9 .... 238 A3
Lansdowne Place SE1 .... 245 L4
Lant Street SE1 .... 245 J3
Larcom Street SE17 .... 245 K6
Lauderdale Road W9 .... 238 B3
Laud Street SE11 .... 244 E7
Launcelot Street SE1 .... 244 F3
Launceston Place W8 .... 242 C4
Laurence Pountney Lane EC4V 241 K7
Lavender Grove SE16 .... 247 K5
Lavender Wharf SE16 .... 247 K4
Lavington Street SE1 .... 245 J1
Lawn Lane SW8 .... 244 D8
Lawrence Street SW3 .... 242 F8
Lawrence Wharf SE16 .... 247 L6
Law Street SE1 .... 245 L4
Laxton Place NW1 .... 239 L3
Laystall Street EC1R 240 F4
Leadenhall Street EC3A 246 A3
Leadenhall Street EC3V 241 M6
Leake Street SE1 .... 244 E2
Leather Lane EC1N 241 G4
Leathermarket Street SE1 .... 245 M3
Leeke Street WC1X 240 E2
Lees Place W1K 239 J7
Leicester Square ⊖ WC2H 240 C7
Leicester Square WC2H 240 C7
Leicester Street WC2H 240 B7
Leigh Street WC1H 240 C3
Leinster Gardens W2 .... 238 C6
Leinster Mews W2 .... 238 C7
Leinster Place W2 .... 238 C7
Leinster Square W2 .... 238 C7
Leinster Terrace W2 .... 238 C7
Leman Street E1 .... 246 C3
Lennox Gardens SW1X 243 G4
Lennox Gardens Mews SW1X 243 G5
Leonard Street EC2A 241 L3
Leopold Estate E3 .... 247 M1
Leopold Street E3 .... 247 L1
Leroy Street SE1 .... 245 M5
Lever Street EC1V 241 J2
Lewisham Street SW1H 244 B3
Lexham Gardens W8 .... 242 A5
Lexham Mews W8 .... 242 A5
Lexington Street W1F 240 A7
Leyden Street E1 .... 246 B2
Leydon Close SE16 .... 247 K5
Library Street SE1 .... 245 H3
Lidlington Place NW1 .... 240 A1
Lilestone Street NW8 .... 238 F3
Lilley Close E1W 246 D5
Lillie Road SW6 .... 242 A4
Lillie Yard SW6 .... 242 A4
Limeburner Lane EC4M 241 H6
Lime Close E1W 246 D5
Limehouse Causeway E14 .... 247 L4
Limehouse Link E14 .... 247 L3
Limehouse ≥ E14 .... 247 J3
Limerston Street SW10 .... 242 D8
Lime Street EC3M 241 M7
Lincoln's Inn Fields WC2A 240 E6
Linden Gardens W2 .... 238 A8
Lindley Street E1 .... 246 F1
Lindsay Square SW1V 244 B7
Lindsey Street EC1A 241 H4
Linhope Street NW1 .... 239 G3
Linsey Street SE16 .... 246 D8
Lisle Street WC2H 240 B7
Lisson Green Estate NW8 .... 238 F3
Lisson Grove NW1 .... 239 G4
Lisson Grove NW8 .... 238 F3
Lisson Street NW1 .... 239 G4
Litchfield Street WC2H 240 C7
Little Argyll Street W1F 239 M6

Little Britain EC1A 241 J5
Little Chester Street SW1X 243 K4
Little George Street SW1P 244 C3
Little Marlborough Street W1F 240 A7
Little New Street EC4A 241 G6
Little Portland Street W1G 239 L6
Little Russell Street WC1A 240 C5
Little St James's Street SW1A 243 M2
Little Sanctuary SW1A 244 C3
Little Somerset Street E1 .... 246 B3
Little Titchfield Street W1W 239 M5
Little Trinity Lane EC4R 241 K7
Liverpool Grove SE17 .... 245 K7
Liverpool Street EC2M 241 M5
Liverpool Street ≥ ⊖ EC2M 241 M5
Lizard Street EC1V 241 K3
Llewellyn Street SE16 .... 246 D7
Lloyd Baker Street WC1X 240 F2
Lloyd's Avenue EC3N 246 B3
Lloyd Square WC1X 240 F2
Lloyds Row EC1R 241 G2
Lloyd Street WC1X 240 F2
Locksley Estate E14 .... 247 L2
Locksley Street E14 .... 247 L1
Lockyer Street SE1 .... 245 L3
Lodge Road NW8 .... 238 F3
Loftie Street SE16 .... 246 D7
Logan Place W8 .... 242 A5
Lolesworth Close E1 .... 246 B1
Lollard Street SE11 .... 244 F5
Lollard Street SE11 .... 244 F6
Loman Street SE1 .... 245 J2
Lomas Street E1 .... 246 D1
Lombard Lane EC4Y 241 G6
Lombard Street EC3V 241 L7
London Bridge EC4R 241 L8
London Bridge ≥ ⊖ SE1 .... 245 L1
London Bridge Street SE1 .... 245 L1
London Dungeon SE1 .... 244 E2
London Eye SE1 .... 244 E2
London Mews W2 .... 238 E6
London Road SE1 .... 245 H4
London Street EC3R 246 A3
London Street W2 .... 238 E6
London Transport
    Museum WC2E 240 D7
London Wall EC2M 241 K5
London Zoo ZSL NW1 .... 239 J1
Long Acre WC2E 240 D7
Longford Street NW1 .... 239 L3
Long Lane EC1A 241 J5
Long Lane SE1 .... 245 L3
Longmoore Street SW1V 243 M5
Longridge Road SW5 .... 242 A5
Longville Road SE11 .... 245 H5
Long Walk SE1 .... 246 A8
Long Yard WC1N 240 E4
Lord North Street SW1P 244 C4
Lord's Cricket Ground NW8 .... 238 E2
Lorenzo Street WC1X 240 E1
Lorrimore Road SE17 .... 245 J8
Lorrimore Square SE17 .... 245 H8
Lothbury EC2R 241 L6
Loughborough Street SE11 .... 244 F7
Lovat Lane EC3R 241 M7
Love Lane EC2V 241 K6
Lovell Place SE16 .... 247 K7
Lowell Street E14 .... 247 K2
Lower Belgrave Street SW1W 243 K4
Lower Grosvenor Place SW1W 243 L4
Lower James Street W1F 240 A7
Lower John Street W1F 240 A7
Lower Marsh SE1 .... 244 F3
Lower Road SE16 .... 247 G7
Lower Sloane Street SW1W 243 J6
Lower Thames Street EC3R 246 A4
Lower Thames Street EC3R 241 M8
Lowndes Close * SW1X 243 J4
Lowndes Place SW1X 243 J4
Lowndes Square SW1X 243 H3
Lowndes Street SW1X 243 J4
Lucan Place SW3 .... 242 F5
Lucey Road SE16 .... 246 C8
Ludgate Circus EC4M 241 H6
Ludgate Hill EC4M 241 H6
Luke Street EC2A 241 M3
Lukin Street E1 .... 247 G3
Lumley Street W1K 239 K7
Lupus Street SW1V 243 L7
Lupus Street SW1V 244 B7
Luton Street NW8 .... 238 E4
Luxborough Street W1U 239 J4
Lyall Mews SW1X 243 J4
Lyall Street SW1X 243 J4
Lyons Place NW8 .... 238 E3
Lytham Street SE17 .... 245 K7

M

Macclesfield Road EC1V 241 J2
Macclesfield Street * W1D 240 B7
Mace Street E1W 247 J1
Macklin Street WC2B 240 D6
Mackworth Street NW1 .... 239 M2
Macleod Street SE17 .... 245 K7
Madame Tussauds NW1 .... 239 J4
Maddox Street W1S 239 M7
Magdalen Street SE1 .... 245 M2
Magee Street SE11 .... 244 F8
Maguire Street SE1 .... 246 C6
Maida Avenue W9 .... 238 D4
Maida Vale W9 .... 238 C2
Maida Vale ⊖ W9 .... 238 C2
Maiden Lane SE1 .... 245 K1
Maiden Lane WC2E 240 D7
Major Road SE16 .... 246 D7
Makins Street SW3 .... 243 G6
Malet Street WC1E 240 B4
Mallord Street SW3 .... 242 E8
Mallory Street NW8 .... 238 F3
Mallow Street EC1Y 241 L3
Malta Street EC1V 241 H3
Maltby Street SE1 .... 246 B7
Manchester Square W1U 239 J6
Manchester Street W1U 239 J5
Manciple Street SE1 .... 245 L3
Mandeville Place W1U 239 K6
Manette Street W1D 240 B6
Manilla Street E14 .... 247 M6
Manningford Close EC1V 241 H2
Manor Place SE17 .... 245 J7
Manresa Road SW3 .... 242 F7
Mansell Street E1 .... 246 C3
Mansfield Mews W1G 239 L5

Mansfield Street W1G 239 L5
Mansion House ⊖ EC4V 241 K7
Manson Mews SW7 .... 242 D5
Manson Place SW7 .... 242 D6
Mapleleaf Square SE16 .... 247 J6
Maples Place E1 .... 246 F1
Maple Street W1T 239 M4
Marble Arch ⊖ W1C 239 H7
Marchmont Street WC1H 240 C3
Margaret Street W1W 239 L6
Margaretta Terrace SW3 .... 242 F7
Margery Street WC1X 240 F3
Marigold Street SE16 .... 246 E7
Marine Street SE1 .... 246 C7
Market Mews W1J 243 K1
Market Place W1W 239 M6
Markham Square SW3 .... 243 G6
Markham Street SW3 .... 243 G6
Mark Lane EC3R 246 A4
Marlborough Gate W2 .... 238 E7
Marlborough Place NW8 .... 238 C1
Marlborough Road SW1A 244 A2
Marlborough Street SE1 .... 242 F6
Marloes Road W8 .... 242 B4
Marlow Way SE16 .... 247 H6
Maroon Street E14 .... 247 K2
Marshall Street W1F 240 A7
Marshalsea Road SE1 .... 245 K2
Marsham Street SW1P 244 C5
Marsh Wall E14 .... 247 M5
Martha's Buildings EC1V 241 K3
Martha Street E1 .... 246 F3
Martin Lane EC4V 241 L7
Maryland Road W9 .... 238 A4
Marylands Road W9 .... 238 A4
Marylebone ≥ ⊖ NW1 .... 239 G4
Marylebone Flyover W2 .... 238 E5
Marylebone High Street W1U 239 K5
Marylebone Lane W1U 239 K6
Marylebone Lane W1U 239 K6
Marylebone Road NW1 .... 239 G5
Marylebone Street W1G 239 K5
Marylee Way SE11 .... 244 F6
Masjid Lane E14 .... 247 M2
Mason Street SE17 .... 245 M5
Massinger Street SE17 .... 245 M6
Masters Street E1 .... 247 J1
Matlock Street E14 .... 247 J2
Matthew Parker Street SW1H 244 C3
Maunsel Street SW1P 244 B5
Mayfair Place W1J 243 L1
Mayflower Street SE16 .... 246 F7
Maynards Quay E1W 246 F4
May's Court SE1 .... 240 C8
McAuley Close SE1 .... 244 F4
McLeod's Mews SW7 .... 242 C5
Meadcroft Road SE11 .... 245 G8
Meadcroft Road SE11 .... 245 H8
Meadow Road SW8 .... 244 E8
Meadow Row SE1 .... 245 J5
Mead Row SE1 .... 244 F4
Meakin Estate SE1 .... 245 M4
Mecklenburgh Square WC1N 240 E3
Medway Street SW1P 244 B5
Meeting House Alley E1W 246 E5
Melcombe Place NW1 .... 239 G4
Melcombe Street W1U 239 H4
Melina Place NW8 .... 238 D2
Melior Street SE1 .... 245 M2
Melton Street NW1 .... 240 A2
Memorial Gates SW1W 243 K3
Mepham Street SE1 .... 244 F2
Mercer Street WC2H 240 C7
Merchant Square W2 .... 238 E5
Merlin Street EC1R 240 F2
Mermaid Court SE1 .... 245 K2
Merrick Square SE1 .... 245 K4
Merrington Road SW6 .... 242 A8
Merrow Street SE17 .... 245 L7
Methley Street SE11 .... 245 G7
Meymott Street SE1 .... 245 G2
Micawber Street N1 .... 241 K1
Micklethwaite Road SW6 .... 242 A8
Middlesex Street E1 .... 246 A1
Middlesex Street E1 .... 246 B2
Middle Street EC1A 241 J5
Middle Temple WC2R 240 F7
Middle Temple Lane EC4Y 240 F7
Middleton Drive SE16 .... 247 H6
Midland Road NW1 .... 240 C1
Midship Close SE16 .... 247 H6
Milborne Grove SW10 .... 242 D7
Milcote Street SE1 .... 245 H3
Miles Street SW8 .... 244 D8
Milford Lane WC2R 240 F7
Milk Street EC2V 241 K6
Milk Yard E1W 247 G4
Millbank SW1P 244 D4
Millennium Bridge SE1 .... 241 J8
Millennium Harbour E14 .... 247 M6
Milligan Street E14 .... 247 L4
Millman Mews WC1N 240 E4
Millman Street WC1N 240 E4
Mill Place E14 .... 247 K3
Millstream Road SE1 .... 246 B7
Mill Street SE1 .... 246 C6
Mill Street W1S 239 L7
Milner Street SW3 .... 243 G5
Milton Street EC2Y 241 K4
Milverton Street SE11 .... 245 G7
Mincing Lane EC3M 246 A4
Minera Mews SW1W 243 J5
Minories EC3N 246 B3
Mitchell Street EC1V 241 J3
Mitre Road SE1 .... 245 G2
Mitre Street EC3A 246 A3
Molyneux Street W1H 239 G5
Monck Street SW1P 244 C4
Monkton Street SE11 .... 245 G5
Monkwell Square EC2Y 241 K5
Monmouth Place W2 .... 238 A6
Monmouth Road W2 .... 238 A6
Monmouth Street WC2H 240 C6
Montague Close SE1 .... 245 L1
Montague Place WC1E 240 C5
Montague Street WC1B 240 C5
Montagu Mansions W1U 239 H5
Montagu Mews North W1H 239 H5
Montagu Mews West W1H 239 H5
Montagu Place W1H 239 H5
Montagu Row W1U 239 H5
Montagu Square W1H 239 H5
Montagu Street W1H 239 H5
Montford Place SE11 .... 244 F7
Monthorpe Road E1 .... 246 C1
Montpelier Square SW7 .... 243 G3

Montpelier Street SW7 .... 243 G3
Montpelier Walk SW7 .... 242 G3
Montrose Place SW1X 243 K3
Monument ⊖ EC4R 241 L7
Monument Street EC3R 241 L7
Monument Street EC3R 241 M7
Monza Street E1W 247 G4
Moodkee Street SE16 .... 247 G7
Moore Street SW3 .... 243 H5
Moorfields EC2Y 241 L5
Moorgate EC2R 241 L6
Moorgate ≥ ⊖ EC2Y 241 L5
Moor Lane EC2Y 241 K5
Moor Street W1D 240 C7
Mora Street EC1V 241 K2
Morecambe Street SE17 .... 245 K6
Moreland Street EC1V 241 H2
More London SE1 .... 246 A5
Moreton Place SW1V 244 A6
Moreton Street SW1V 244 B6
Moreton Terrace SW1V 244 A6
Morgan's Lane SE1 .... 245 M2
Morgan's Lane SE1 .... 246 A5
Morley Street SE1 .... 245 G3
Mornington Crescent NW1 .... 239 M1
Mornington Place NW1 .... 239 L1
Mornington Terrace NW1 .... 239 L1
Morocco Street SE1 .... 246 A7
Morpeth Terrace SW1P 243 M5
Morris Street E1 .... 246 F3
Morshead Road W9 .... 238 A2
Mortimer Market WC1E 240 A4
Mortimer Street W1T 240 A5
Mortimer Street W1W 239 M5
Morton Place SE1 .... 244 F4
Morwell Street WC1B 240 B5
Moscow Place W2 .... 238 B7
Moscow Road W2 .... 238 B7
Mossop Street SW3 .... 243 G5
Motcomb Street SW1X 243 J4
Mount Gate W2 .... 242 E2
Mount Mills EC1V 241 J3
Mount Pleasant WC1X 240 F4
Mount Row W1K 239 K8
Mount Street W1K 239 K8
Mount Street Mews W1K 239 K8
Mount Terrace E1 .... 246 E1
Moxon Street W1U 239 J5
Mulberry Street E1 .... 246 D2
Mulberry Walk SW3 .... 242 E8
Mulready Street NW8 .... 238 F4
Mundy Street N1 .... 241 M2
Munster Square NW1 .... 239 L3
Munton Road SE17 .... 245 K5
Murphy Street SE1 .... 244 F3
Murray Grove N1 .... 241 K1
Musbury Street E1 .... 247 G2
Muscovy Street EC3N 246 A4
Museum of London EC2Y 241 J5
Museum Street WC1A 240 C5
Myddelton Passage EC1R 241 G2
Myddelton Square EC1R 241 G1
Myddelton Street EC1R 241 G3
Myrdle Street E1 .... 246 D2

N

Naoroji Street WC1X 240 F2
Napier Grove N1 .... 241 K1
Narrow Street E14 .... 247 K4
Nash Street NW1 .... 239 L2
Nassau Street W1W 239 M5
Nathaniel Close * E1 .... 246 C2
National Portrait
    Gallery WC2H 240 C8
Natural History Museum SW7 .... 242 D4
Neal Street WC2H 240 C6
Neathouse Place * SW1V 243 M5
Neckinger SE1 .... 246 C8
Needleman Street SE16 .... 247 H7
Nelson Close NW6 .... 238 A1
Nelson Place N1 .... 241 H1
Nelson's Column WC2N 240 C8
Nelson Square SE1 .... 245 H2
Nelson Street E1 .... 246 E2
Nelson Terrace N1 .... 241 H1
Neptune Street SE16 .... 247 G7
Nesham Street E1W 246 D4
Netherton Grove SW10 .... 242 D8
Netley Street NW1 .... 239 M2
Nevern Place SW5 .... 242 A6
Nevern Square SW5 .... 242 A6
Neville Street SW7 .... 242 E6
Newark Street E1 .... 246 E2
New Atlas Wharf E14 .... 247 M8
New Bond Street W1S 239 L7
New Bond Street W1S 239 L8
New Bridge Street EC4V 241 H6
New Broad Street EC2M 241 M5
New Burlington Street W1S 239 M7
Newburn Street SE11 .... 244 F7
Newbury Street EC1A 241 J5
Newcastle Place W2 .... 238 E5
New Cavendish Street W1G 239 L5
New Change EC4M 241 J6
New Church Road SE5 .... 245 L8
Newcomen Street SE1 .... 245 K2
New Compton Street WC2H 240 C6
Newcourt Street NW8 .... 238 F1
Newell Street E14 .... 247 L3
New Fetter Lane EC4A 241 G6
Newgate Street EC1A 241 H6
New Globe Walk SE1 .... 241 J8
New Goulston Street E1 .... 246 B2
Newham's Row SE1 .... 246 A7
Newington Butts SE1 .... 245 J4
Newington Causeway SE1 .... 245 J4
New Kent Road SE1 .... 245 K5
Newlands Quay E1W 246 F4
Newman Street W1T 240 A5
New North Place EC2A 241 M3
New North Road N1 .... 241 L1
New North Street WC1N 240 D4
New Oxford Street WC1A 240 C6
Newport Street SE11 .... 244 E5
New Quebec Street W1H 239 H6
New Ride SW7 .... 242 E3
New Road E1 .... 246 E2
New Row WC2N 240 C7
New Spring Gardens Walk SE1 .... 244 D7
New Square WC2A 240 F6
New Street EC2M 246 A2
New Street Square EC4A 241 G6
Newton Road W2 .... 238 A6

Newton Street WC2B 240 D5
New Union Street EC2Y 241 K5
Nicholas Lane EC3V 241 L7
Nicholson Street SE1 .... 245 H1
Nightingale Place SW10 .... 242 D8
Nile Street N1 .... 241 K2
Nine Elms Lane SW8 .... 244 C8
Noble Street EC2V 241 J6
Noel Road N1 .... 241 J1
Noel Street W1F 240 A6
Norbiton Road E14 .... 247 L2
Norfolk Crescent W2 .... 239 G6
Norfolk Place W2 .... 238 E6
Norfolk Square W2 .... 238 E6
Norman Street EC1V 241 J3
Norris Street SW1Y 240 B8
Northampton Road EC1R 241 G3
Northampton Square EC1V 241 H2
North Audley Street W1K 239 J7
North Bank NW8 .... 238 F2
Northburgh Street EC1V 241 H3
North Carriage Drive W2 .... 238 F7
Northdown Street N1 .... 240 D1
Northey Street E14 .... 247 K4
North Gower Street NW1 .... 240 A3
Northington Street WC1N 240 E4
North Mews WC1N 240 E4
North Ride W2 .... 239 G7
North Row W1K 239 J7
North Terrace SW3 .... 242 F5
Northumberland Alley EC3N 246 B3
Northumberland Avenue WC2N 244 C1
Northumberland Place W2 .... 238 A6
Northumberland Street WC2N 244 C1
North Wharf Road W2 .... 238 E5
Northwick Terrace NW8 .... 238 D3
Norway Gate SE16 .... 247 K7
Norway Place E14 .... 247 K3
Norwich Street EC4A 240 F5
Nottingham Place W1U 239 J4
Nottingham Street W1U 239 J4
Notting Hill Gate W11 .... 238 A8
Notting Hill Gate ⊖ W11 .... 242 A1
Nugent Terrace NW8 .... 238 D1
Nutford Place W1H 239 G6

O

Oakden Street SE11 .... 245 G5
Oakington Road W9 .... 238 A3
Oak Lane E14 .... 247 L3
Oakley Close EC1V 241 H1
Oakley Gardens SW3 .... 243 G8
Oakley Square NW1 .... 240 A1
Oakley Street SW3 .... 242 F8
Oak Tree Road NW8 .... 238 F2
Oat Lane EC2V 241 J5
Occupation Road SE17 .... 245 J6
Ocean Square E1 .... 247 J1
Ocean Street E1 .... 247 J1
Odessa Street SE16 .... 247 L7
Ogle Street W1W 239 M5
Old Bailey EC4M 241 H6
Old Barrack Yard SW1X 243 J3
Old Bond Street W1S 239 M8
Old Broad Street EC2N 241 M6
Old Brompton Road SW5 .... 242 C6
Old Brompton Road SW7 .... 242 C6
Old Burlington Street W1S 239 M7
Oldbury Place W1U 239 J4
Old Castle Street E1 .... 246 B2
Old Cavendish Street W1G 239 L6
Old Church Road E1 .... 247 H2
Old Church Street SW3 .... 242 E7
Old Compton Street W1D 240 B7
Old Court Place W8 .... 242 B3
Old Gloucester Street WC1N 240 D4
Old Jamaica Road SE16 .... 246 C7
Old Jewry EC2R 241 K6
Old Kent Road SE1 .... 245 M5
Old Marylebone Road NW1 .... 239 G5
Old Montague Street E1 .... 246 C1
Old North Street WC1X 240 E5
Old Paradise Street SE11 .... 244 E5
Old Park Lane W1J 243 K2
Old Pye Street SW1P 244 B4
Old Queen Street SW1H 244 B3
Old Square WC2A 240 F6
Old Street EC1V 241 K3
Old Street ≥ ⊖ EC1Y 241 L3
Old Street Junction EC1Y 241 L3
Oliver's Yard EC1Y 241 L3
Olney Road SE17 .... 245 J8
O'Meara Street SE1 .... 245 K2
Omega Place N1 .... 240 D1
Onega Gate SE16 .... 247 K8
Ongar Road SW6 .... 242 A8
Onslow Gardens SW7 .... 242 D6
Onslow Square SW7 .... 242 E5
Onslow Square SW7 .... 242 E6
Ontario Street SE1 .... 245 J4
Ontario Way E14 .... 247 M4
Opal Street SE11 .... 245 H6
Orange Place SE16 .... 247 G8
Orange Square SW1W 243 K6
Orange Street WC2H 246 D5
Orange Street WC2H 240 B8
Orb Street SE17 .... 245 L6
Orchardson Street NW8 .... 238 E4
Orchard Street W1H 239 J6
Orde Hall Street WC1N 240 E4
Orient Street SE11 .... 245 H5
Orme Court W2 .... 238 B8
Orme Lane W2 .... 238 B8
Orme Square Gate W2 .... 238 B8
Ormond Close WC1N 240 D4
Ormonde Gate SW3 .... 243 H7
Ormond Yard SW1Y 240 A8
Orsett Mews W2 .... 238 C6
Orsett Street SE11 .... 244 E6
Orsett Terrace W2 .... 238 C5
Orton Street E1W 246 D5
Osbert Street SW1V 244 B6
Osborn Street E1 .... 246 C2
Oslo Square SE16 .... 247 K7
Osnaburgh Street NW1 .... 239 L3
Osnaburgh Terrace NW1 .... 239 L3
Ossington Buildings W1U 239 J5
Ossington Street W2 .... 238 A7
Ossulston Street NW1 .... 240 B1
Osten Mews SW7 .... 242 B4
Oswin Street SE11 .... 245 H5
Othello Close SE1 .... 245 H6
Otto Street SE17 .... 245 H8

Outer Circle NW1 .... 239 H3
Outer Circle NW1 .... 239 K1
Oval ⊖ SE11 .... 244 F8
Oval Way SE11 .... 244 E7
Ovington Square SW3 .... 243 G4
Ovington Street SW3 .... 243 G5
Owen Street EC1V 241 G1
Oxendon Street SW1Y 240 B8
Oxford Circus ⊖ W1B 239 M6
Oxford Road NW6 .... 238 A1
Oxford Square W2 .... 238 F6
Oxford Street W1C 239 L6
Oxford Street WC1A 240 A6

P
Pace Place E1 .... 246 E3
Pacific Wharf SE16 .... 247 H5
Paddington ⊖≷ W2 .... 238 D6
Paddington Green W2 .... 238 E6
Paddington Street W1U 239 J5
Pageant Crescent SE16 .... 247 K5
Page Street SW1P 244 B5
Paget Street EC1V 241 H2
Pakenham Street WC1X 240 E3
Palace Avenue W8 .... 242 B2
Palace Court W2 .... 238 A7
Palace Gardens Terrace W8 .... 242 A1
Palace Gate W8 .... 242 C3
Palace Green W8 .... 242 B2
Palace of Westminster SW1A 244 D3
Palace Place SW1E 243 M4
Palace Street SW1E 243 M4
Pall Mall SW1Y 244 A1
Pall Mall East SW1Y 244 B1
Palmer Street SW1H 244 B3
Pancras Lane EC4N 241 K6
Pancras Road N1C 240 C1
Panton Street SW1Y 240 B8
Paradise Street SE16 .... 246 E7
Paradise Walk SW3 .... 243 H8
Pardoner Street SE1 .... 245 L4
Pardon Street EC1V 241 H3
Parfett Street E1 .... 246 D2
Paris Garden SE1 .... 245 G1
Park Crescent W1B 239 K4
Park Crescent Mews
   West W1G 239 K4
Parker's Row SE1 .... 246 C7
Parker Street WC2B 240 D6
Park Lane W1K 239 H7
Park Lane W1K 243 J1
Park Place SW1A 243 M1
Park Place Villas W2 .... 238 D4
Park Road NW1 .... 239 H3
Park Square East NW1 .... 239 L3
Park Square Mews NW1 .... 239 K3
Park Square West NW1 .... 239 K3
Park Street SE1 .... 245 K1
Park Street W1K 239 J7
Park Village East NW1 .... 239 L1
Park Walk SW10 .... 242 D8
Park West Place W2 .... 239 G6
Parliament Street SW1A 244 C2
Parry Street SW8 .... 244 D8
Passmore Street SW1W 243 J4
Pater Street W8 .... 242 A4
Pattina Walk SE16 .... 247 K5
Paul Street EC2A 241 M3
Paultons Square SW3 .... 242 E8
Paveley Street NW1 .... 239 G3
Pavilion Road SW1X 243 H3
Pavilion Street SW1X 243 H4
Paxton Terrace SW1V 243 L7
Peabody Avenue SW1V 243 L7
Peabody Estate SE1 .... 245 J1
Peacock Street SE17 .... 245 J6
Pearl Street E1W 246 F6
Pearman Street SE1 .... 245 G3
Pear Tree Court EC1R 241 G3
Peartree Lane E1W 247 G4
Pear Tree Street EC1V 241 J3
Peel Street W8 .... 242 A1
Peerless Street EC1V 241 K2
Pelham Crescent SW7 .... 242 F6
Pelham Place SW7 .... 242 F5
Pelham Street SW7 .... 242 F5
Pelier Street SE17 .... 245 K8
Pemberton Row EC4A 241 G6
Pembridge Gardens W2 .... 238 A8
Pembridge Place W2 .... 238 A7
Pembridge Square W2 .... 238 A7
Pembridge Villas W11 .... 238 A7
Pembroke Close SW1X 243 J3
Penang Street E1W 246 F5
Penfold Place NW8 .... 238 F5
Penfold Street NW8 .... 238 E4
Pennant Mews W8 .... 242 B5
Pennington Street E1W 246 D4
Pennyfields E14 .... 247 M4
Penrose Grove SE17 .... 245 J7
Penrose Street SE17 .... 245 J7
Penton Place SE17 .... 245 H6
Penton Rise WC1X 240 E2
Penton Street N1 .... 240 F1
Pentonville Road N1 .... 240 E1
Penywern Road SW5 .... 242 A6
Pepper Street SE1 .... 245 J2
Pepys Street EC3N 246 A4
Percival Street EC1V 241 H3
Percy Circus WC1X 240 F2
Percy Street W1T 240 B5
Perkin's Rents SW1P 244 B4
Perryn Road SE16 .... 246 E7
Petersham Mews SW7 .... 242 D4
Petersham Place SW7 .... 242 C4
Peter Street W1F 240 B7
Peto Place NW1 .... 239 L3
Petticoat Lane E1 .... 246 B2
Petty France SW1H 244 A3
Petty Wales EC3R 246 A4
Petyward SW3 .... 243 G6
Phelp Street SE17 .... 245 L7
Phene Street SW3 .... 243 G8
Phillimore Walk W8 .... 242 A3
Philpot Lane EC3M 241 M7
Philpot Street E1 .... 246 E2
Phipp's Mews SW1W 243 L5
Phipp Street EC2A 241 M3
Phoenix Place WC1X 240 F3
Phoenix Road NW1 .... 240 B1
Phoenix Street WC2H 240 C6
Piccadilly W1J 243 L2

Piccadilly Arcade SW1Y 243 M1
Piccadilly Circus W1B 240 A8
Piccadilly Circus ⊖ W1J 240 B8
Pickard Street EC1V 241 J2
Picton Place W1U 239 K6
Pier Head E1W 246 E6
Pigott Street E14 .... 247 M3
Pilgrimage Street SE1 .... 245 L3
Pimlico ⊖ SW1V 244 B6
Pimlico Road SW1W 243 J6
Pinchin Street E1 .... 246 D3
Pindar Street EC2A 241 M4
Pindock Mews W9 .... 238 B3
Pine Street EC1R 240 F3
Pitfield Street N1 .... 241 M1
Pitsea Street E1 .... 247 H3
Pitt's Head Mews W1J 243 K2
Pitt Street W8 .... 242 A2
Pixley Street E14 .... 247 L2
Platina Street * EC2A 241 L3
Plover Way SE16 .... 247 K8
Plumbers Row E1 .... 246 D2
Plumtree Court EC4A 241 G5
Plympton Street NW8 .... 238 F4
Pocock Street SE1 .... 245 H2
Poland Street W1F 240 A6
Pollen Street W1S 239 L7
Pollitt Drive NW8 .... 238 E3
Polperro Mews SE11 .... 245 G5
Polygon Road NW1 .... 240 B1
Pond Place SW3 .... 242 F6
Ponler Street E1 .... 246 E3
Ponsonby Place SW1P 244 C6
Ponsonby Terrace SW1P 244 C6
Ponton Road SW1V 244 B8
Pont Street SW1X 243 H4
Poolmans Street SE16 .... 247 H6
Pope Street SE1 .... 246 B7
Poplar Place W2 .... 238 B7
Poppin's Court EC4A 241 H6
Porchester Gardens W2 .... 238 B7
Porchester Gate W2 .... 238 C8
Porchester Place W2 .... 239 G6
Porchester Road W2 .... 238 B5
Porchester Square W2 .... 238 B6
Porchester Terrace W2 .... 238 C7
Porchester Terrace
   North W2 .... 238 C6
Porlock Street SE1 .... 245 L3
Porter Street NW1 .... 239 H4
Porteus Road W2 .... 238 D5
Portland Place W1B 239 L4
Portland Place W1B 239 L5
Portland Square E1W 246 E5
Portland Street SE17 .... 245 L7
Portman Close W1H 239 J6
Portman Mews South W1H 239 J6
Portman Square W1H 239 J6
Portman Street W1H 239 J6
Portpool Lane EC1N 240 F4
Portsea Place W2 .... 239 G6
Portsmouth Street WC2A 240 E6
Portsoken Street E1 .... 246 B3
Portugal Street WC2A 240 E6
Potier Street SE1 .... 245 L4
Potters Fields SE1 .... 246 B6
Pottery Street SE16 .... 246 E7
Poultry EC2V 241 K6
Powis Place WC1N 240 D4
Praed Mews W2 .... 238 E6
Praed Street W2 .... 238 E6
Pratt Walk SE1 .... 244 E5
Premier Place E14 .... 247 M4
Prescot Street E1 .... 246 C3
Preston Close SE1 .... 245 M5
Price's Street SE1 .... 245 H1
Prideaux Place WC1X 240 F2
Primrose Street EC2A 246 A1
Prince Albert Road NW8 .... 238 F1
Prince Consort Road SW7 .... 242 D3
Princelet Street E1 .... 246 C1
Prince of Wales Gate SW7 .... 242 F3
Princes Arcade SW1Y 240 A8
Prince's Gardens SW7 .... 242 E3
Prince's Gate Mews SW7 .... 242 E4
Princes Riverside
   Road SE16 .... 247 H5
Prince's Square W2 .... 238 A7
Princess Road NW6 .... 238 A1
Princess Street SE1 .... 245 H4
Princes Street W1B 239 L6
Prince's Street EC2R 241 L6
Princeton Street WC1R 240 E5
Prioress Street SE1 .... 245 L4
Priory Green Estate N1 .... 240 E1
Priory Walk SW10 .... 242 D7
Proctor Street WC1V 240 E5
Prospect Place E1W 247 G5
Prospect Street SE16 .... 246 E7
Provident Court W1K 239 J7
Provost Street N1 .... 241 L1
Prusom Street E1W 246 F5
Pudding Lane EC3R 241 M7
Pumphouse Mews E1 .... 246 D3
Purbrook Street SE1 .... 246 A7
Purcell Street N1 .... 241 M1
Purchese Street NW1 .... 240 B1

Q
Quebec Way SE16 .... 247 J7
Queen Anne's Gate SW1H 244 B3
Queen Anne Street W1G 239 K5
Queen Elizabeth Street SE1 .... 246 B6
Queen Mother Gate W2 .... 243 J2
Queensborough Terrace W2 .... 238 C7
Queensbury Place SW7 .... 242 E5
Queen's Gardens W2 .... 238 C7
Queen's Gate SW7 .... 242 D3
Queen's Gate SW7 .... 242 D4
Queen's Gate Gardens SW7 .... 242 D5
Queen's Gate Mews SW7 .... 242 D4
Queen's Gate Place SW7 .... 242 D4
Queen's Gate
   Place Mews SW7 .... 242 D4
Queen's Gate Terrace SW7 .... 242 C4
Queen's Mews W2 .... 238 B7
Queen Square WC1N 240 D4
Queen's Row SE17 .... 245 K7
Queen Street EC4N 241 K7
Queen Street W1J 239 L1
Queen Street Place EC4R 241 K7
Queen's Walk SE1 .... 246 A5
Queen's Walk SW1A 243 M2

Queensway W2 .... 238 B6
Queensway ⊖ W2 .... 238 B8
Queen Victoria Street EC4V 241 J7
Quick Street N1 .... 241 H1

R
Raby Street E14 .... 247 K2
Radcliffe Road SE1 .... 246 B8
Radcot Street SE11 .... 245 G7
Radnor Mews W2 .... 238 E6
Radnor Place W2 .... 238 F6
Radnor Street EC1V 241 K3
Radnor Walk SW3 .... 243 G7
Railway Approach SE1 .... 245 L1
Railway Avenue SE16 .... 247 G6
Railway Street N1 .... 240 D1
Ralston Street SW3 .... 243 H7
Ramillies Place W1F 239 M6
Ramillies Street W1F 239 M6
Rampart Street E1 .... 246 E2
Rampayne Street SW1V 244 B6
Randall Road SE11 .... 244 D6
Randall Row SE11 .... 244 E6
Randolph Avenue W9 .... 238 B1
Randolph Crescent W9 .... 238 C3
Randolph Gardens NW6 .... 238 B1
Randolph Mews W9 .... 238 D4
Randolph Road W9 .... 238 C4
Ranelagh Grove SW1W 243 K6
Ranelagh Road SW1V 244 A7
Rangoon Street * EC3N 246 B3
Ranston Street NW8 .... 238 F4
Raphael Street SW7 .... 243 G3
Ratcliffe Cross Street E1W 247 J3
Ratcliffe Lane E14 .... 247 J3
Rathbone Place W1T 240 B5
Rathbone Street W1T 240 A5
Raven Row E1 .... 246 F1
Ravensdon Street SE11 .... 245 G7
Ravey Street EC2A 241 M3
Rawlings Street SW3 .... 243 G5
Rawstorne Street EC1V 241 H2
Ray Street EC1R 241 G4
Reardon Place E1W 246 E5
Reardon Street E1W 246 E5
Rectory Square E1 .... 247 H1
Redan Place W2 .... 238 B6
Redburn Street SW3 .... 243 G7
Redcastle Close E1W 247 G4
Redcliffe Gardens SW10 .... 242 B7
Redcliffe Mews SW10 .... 242 C7
Redcliffe Place SW10 .... 242 C8
Redcliffe Road SW10 .... 242 D7
Redcliffe Square SW10 .... 242 B7
Redcliffe Street SW10 .... 242 B8
Redcross Way SE1 .... 245 K2
Redesdale Street SW3 .... 243 G7
Redfield Lane SW5 .... 242 A5
Redhill Street NW1 .... 239 L1
Red Lion Row SE5 .... 245 K8
Red Lion Square WC1R 240 E5
Red Lion Street WC2B 240 E5
Redman's Road E1 .... 247 G1
Red Place W1K 239 J7
Redriff Road SE16 .... 247 J8
Reedworth Street SE11 .... 245 G6
Reeves Mews W1K 239 J8
Regal Close E1 .... 246 D1
Regan Way N1 .... 241 M1
Regency Street SW1P 244 B5
Regent Place W1B 240 A7
Regent's Park ⊖ W1B 239 L4
Regent's Park NW1 .... 239 J1
Regent's Park Estate NW1 .... 239 L2
Regent Square WC1H 240 D2
Regent Street SW1Y 240 B8
Regent Street W1S 239 M7
Relton Mews SW7 .... 243 G4
Remington Street N1 .... 241 H1
Remnant Street WC2A 240 E6
Renforth Street SE16 .... 247 G7
Renfrew Road SE11 .... 245 H5
Rennie Street SE1 .... 245 H1
Rephidim Street SE1 .... 245 M4
Repton Street E14 .... 247 K2
Reveley Square SE16 .... 247 K7
Rex Place W1K 239 J8
Rhodeswell Road E14 .... 247 L2
Rich Street E14 .... 247 M3
Rickett Street SW6 .... 242 A8
Ridgemount Street WC1E 240 B4
Ridgemount Gardens WC1E 240 B4
Riding House Street W1W 239 M5
Riley Road SE1 .... 246 B7
Risborough Street SE1 .... 245 J2
Risdon Street SE16 .... 247 G7
Rissinghill Street N1 .... 240 F1
River Street EC1R 240 F2
Rivington Street EC2A 241 M3
Robert Adam Street W1U 239 J6
Roberts Close SE16 .... 247 J7
Rochester Row SW1P 244 A5
Rochester Street SW1P 244 B5
Rockingham Street SE1 .... 245 J4
Rocliffe Street N1 .... 241 H1
Roding Mews E1W 246 D5
Rodmarton Street W1U 239 H5
Rodney Place SE17 .... 245 K5
Rodney Road SE17 .... 245 K5
Rodney Street N1 .... 240 E1
Roger Street WC1N 240 E4
Roland Gardens SW7 .... 242 D6
Roland Way SE17 .... 245 L7
Romford Street E1 .... 246 E2
Romilly Street W1D 240 B7
Romney Street SW1P 244 C5
Rood Lane EC3M 241 M7
Ropemaker Road SE16 .... 247 K7
Ropemaker Street EC2Y 241 L4
Roper Lane SE1 .... 246 B7
Rope Street SE16 .... 247 K8
Rope Walk Gardens E1 .... 246 E2
Rosary Gardens SW7 .... 242 C6
Roscoe Street EC1Y 241 K3
Rose Alley SE1 .... 245 K1
Rosebery Avenue EC1R 240 F3
Rosemoor Street SW3 .... 243 G6
Rose Street WC2E 240 C7
Rossmore Road NW1 .... 239 G3
Rotary Street SE1 .... 245 H3
Rotherhithe ⊖ SE16 .... 247 G6

Rotherhithe Street SE16 .... 247 G6
Rotherhithe Street SE16 .... 247 J4
Rotherhithe Tunnel SE16 .... 247 H5
Rothsay Street SE1 .... 245 M4
Rotten Row W2 .... 242 F2
Rouel Road SE16 .... 246 C8
Roupell Street SE1 .... 245 G2
Royal Albert Hall SW7 .... 242 E3
Royal Avenue SW3 .... 243 H6
Royal Hospital Road SW3 .... 243 H7
Royal Mint Street E1 .... 246 C4
Royal Oak ⊖ W2 .... 238 B5
Royal Oak Yard SE1 .... 246 A7
Royal Opera House WC2E 240 D7
Royal Road SE17 .... 245 H8
Royal Street SE1 .... 244 E3
Rudolph Road NW6 .... 238 A1
Rugby Street WC1N 240 E4
Rum Close E1W 246 F4
Rupack Street SE16 .... 247 G7
Rupert Street W1D 240 B7
Rushworth Street SE1 .... 245 H2
Russell Court SW1A 244 A2
Russell Square WC1B 240 C4
Russell Square ⊖ WC1B 240 D3
Russell Street WC2B 240 D7
Russia Dock Road SE16 .... 247 K6
Rutherford Street SW1P 244 B5
Rutland Gardens SW7 .... 243 G3
Rutland Gate SW7 .... 242 F3
Rutland Mews SW7 .... 242 F4
Rutland Street SW7 .... 242 F4
Ryder Street SW1Y 244 A1

S
Sackville Street W1S 240 A8
Saffron Hill EC1N 241 G4
Saffron Street EC1N 241 G4
Sail Street SE11 .... 244 F5
St Agnes Place SE11 .... 245 G8
St Alban's Grove W8 .... 242 B4
St Alban's Street SW1Y 240 B8
St Alphage Garden EC2Y 241 K5
St Andrews Hill EC4V 241 H7
St Andrew's Place NW1 .... 239 L3
St Andrew Street EC4A 241 G5
St Anne's Court W1F 240 B6
St Ann's Street SW1P 244 C4
St Barnabas Street SW1W 243 K6
St Botolph Street EC3N 246 B2
St Bride Street EC4A 241 G6
St Chad's Street WC1H 240 D2
St Clare Street EC3N 246 B3
St Clements Lane WC2A 240 E6
St Cross Street EC1N 241 G4
St Dunstan's Hill EC3R 241 M8
St Dunstan's Lane EC3R 241 M7
St Elmos Road SE16 .... 247 J7
St Ermin's Hill SW1H 244 B3
St George's Circus SE1 .... 245 H3
St George's Drive SW1V 243 M6
St George's Estate E1 .... 246 D3
St George's Lane * EC3R 241 M7
St George's Road SE1 .... 245 G4
St George's Square SW1V 244 B7
St George Street W1S 239 L7
St Giles High Street WC2H 240 C6
St Helen's Place EC3A 241 M6
St James Market * SW1Y 240 B8
St James's Park SW1H 244 B3
St James's Park SW1A 244 B3
St James's Place SW1A 243 M2
St James's Road SE16 .... 246 D8
St James's Square SW1Y 244 A1
St James's Street SW1A 243 M1
St James Walk EC1R 241 G3
St John's Lane EC1M 241 H4
St John's Place EC1M 241 H4
St John's Square EC1V 241 H4
St John Street EC1V 241 H2
St John's Wood High Street NW8 .... 238 F1
St John's Wood Road NW8 .... 238 E3
St Katharine's Way E1W 246 C5
St Leonard's Terrace SW3 .... 243 H7
St Loo Avenue SW3 .... 243 G8
St Luke's Close EC1V 241 K3
St Luke's Street SW3 .... 242 F6
St Manningtree E1 .... 246 C2
St Mark Street E1 .... 246 C3
St Martin's Lane WC2N 240 C7
St Martin's le Grand EC1A 241 J6
St Martin's Place WC2N 240 C8
St Mary at Hill EC3R 241 M8
St Mary Axe EC3A 246 A3
St Marychurch Street SE16 .... 247 G6
St Mary's Gardens SE11 .... 245 G5
St Mary's Terrace W2 .... 238 D4
St Mary's Walk SE11 .... 245 G5
St Matthew Street SW1P 244 B4
St Michael's Street W2 .... 238 E6
St Olav's Square SE16 .... 246 F7
St Oswald's Place SE11 .... 244 E7
St Oswulf Street * SW1P 244 C6
St Pancras International ⊖≷ N1C 240 C1
St Paul's ⊖ EC1A 241 J6
St Paul's Avenue SE16 .... 247 J5
St Paul's Cathedral EC4M 241 J6
St Paul's Churchyard EC4M 241 J6
St Paul's Way E3 .... 247 L1
St Petersburgh Mews W2 .... 238 B7
St Petersburgh Place W2 .... 238 B7
St Saviours Wharf SE1 .... 246 C6
St Stephen's Gardens W2 .... 238 A5
St Swithin's Lane EC4N 241 L7
St Thomas Street SE1 .... 245 L2
St Vincent Street W1U 239 J5
Salamanca Street SE1 .... 244 D6
Sale Place W2 .... 238 F5
Salisbury Court EC4Y 241 G6
Salisbury Place W1H 239 H4
Salisbury Street NW8 .... 238 F4
Salmon Lane E14 .... 247 J2
Salter Road SE16 .... 247 J5
Salter Street E14 .... 247 M4
Samford Street NW8 .... 238 F4
Sampson Street E1W 246 E6
Sancroft Street SE11 .... 244 F6
Sandland Street WC1R 240 E5
Sandpiper Close SE16 .... 247 L6
Sandwich Street WC1H 240 C2
Sandy's Row E1 .... 246 B1

Sans Walk EC1R 241 G3
Sardinia Street WC2A 240 E6
Savage Gardens EC3N 246 B3
Savile Row W1S 239 M7
Saville Road WC2R 240 E8
Savoy Hill WC2R 240 D8
Savoy Place WC2R 240 D8
Savoy Street WC2E 240 E7
Sawyer Street SE1 .... 245 J2
Scala Street W1T 240 A5
Scandrett Street E1W 246 E5
Scarborough Street E1 .... 246 C3
Scarsdale Villas W8 .... 242 A4
Schooner Close * SE16 .... 247 H6
Science Museum SW7 .... 242 E4
Scoresby Street SE1 .... 245 H2
Scotch House Junction SW1X 243 H3
Scotland Place SW1A 244 C1
Scott Ellis Gardens NW8 .... 238 E2
Scott Lidgett Crescent SE16 .... 246 D7
Scrutton Street EC2A 241 M3
Seaford Street WC1H 240 D2
Seagrave Road SW6 .... 242 A8
Sea Life London Aquarium SE1 .... 244 E3
Searles Road SE1 .... 245 L5
Sebastian Street EC1V 241 H2
Secker Street SE1 .... 244 F2
Sedan Way SE17 .... 245 M6
Sedding Street SW1X 243 J5
Seddon Street WC1X 240 E3
Seething Lane EC3N 246 A4
Sekforde Street EC1R 241 H3
Selfridges W1A 239 J6
Selsey Street E14 .... 247 M1
Selwood Place SW7 .... 242 E6
Semley Place SW1W 243 K6
Senior Street W2 .... 238 B4
Senrab Street E1 .... 247 H2
Serle Street WC2A 240 F6
Serpentine Bridge W2 .... 242 E1
Serpentine Road W2 .... 242 F2
Seth Street SE16 .... 247 G7
Settles Street E1 .... 246 D2
Seven Dials WC2H 240 C6
Seville Street SW1X 243 H3
Sevington Street W9 .... 238 A3
Seward Street EC1V 241 J3
Seymour Mews W1H 239 J6
Seymour Place W1H 239 G5
Seymour Street W1H 239 H6
Seymour Street W2 .... 239 G7
Seymour Walk SW10 .... 242 C7
Shad Thames SE1 .... 246 B6
Shad Thames SE1 .... 246 C6
Shadwell ⊖ E1 .... 246 F3
Shadwell Gardens E1 .... 246 F3
Shaftesbury Avenue W1D 240 B7
Shaftesbury Avenue WC2H 240 C6
Shaftesbury Street N1 .... 241 K1
Shakespeare's Globe SE1 .... 241 J8
Shand Street SE1 .... 246 A6
Sharsted Street SE17 .... 245 H7
Shaw Crescent E14 .... 247 K2
Shawfield Street SW3 .... 243 G7
Sheffield Terrace W8 .... 242 A2
Sheldon Square W2 .... 238 D5
Shelmerdine Close E3 .... 247 M1
Shelton Street WC2H 240 D6
Shepherdess Walk N1 .... 241 K1
Shepherd Street W1J 243 K1
Sheraton Street W1F 240 B6
Sherborne Lane EC4N 241 L7
Sherwood Street W1D 240 A7
Ship and Mermaid Row SE1 .... 245 M2
Shipwright Road SE16 .... 247 K7
Shirland Road W9 .... 238 A3
Shoe Lane EC4A 241 G5
Shorter Street EC3N 246 B4
Shorts Gardens WC2H 240 C6
Short Street SE1 .... 245 G2
Shoulder of Mutton Alley E14 .... 247 K4
Shouldham Street W1H 239 G5
Shroton Street NW1 .... 238 F4
Siddons Lane W1H 239 H4
Sidmouth Street WC1N 240 D3
Sidney Square E1 .... 246 F2
Sidney Street E1 .... 246 F1
Silex Street SE1 .... 245 H3
Silk Street EC2Y 241 K4
Silver Walk SE16 .... 247 K5
Silvester Street SE1 .... 245 K3
Singer Street EC2A 241 L2
Sir John Soane's Museum WC2A 240 E5
Sir Simon Milton Square SW1V 243 L4
Skinner Place * SW1W 243 J6
Skinners Lane EC4V 241 K7
Skinner Street EC1R 241 G3
Slippers Place SE16 .... 246 F8
Sloane Avenue SW3 .... 243 G6
Sloane Court East SW3 .... 243 J6
Sloane Court West SW3 .... 243 J6
Sloane Gardens SW1W 243 J6
Sloane Square SW1W 243 J6
Sloane Square ⊖ SW1W 243 J6
Sloane Street SW1X 243 H3
Sloane Terrace SW1X 243 J5
Smeaton Street E1W 246 E5
Smithfield Street EC1A 241 H5
Smith Square SW1P 244 C4
Smith Street SW3 .... 243 G7
Smith Terrace SW3 .... 243 G7
Smithy Street E1 .... 247 G1
Snowden Street EC2A 241 M4
Snow Hill EC1A 241 H5
Snowsfields SE1 .... 245 L2
Soho Square W1D 240 B6
Soho Street W1D 240 B6
Somerford Way SE16 .... 247 K7
Somers Crescent W2 .... 238 F6
Somerset House WC2R 240 E7
Somerstown Estate NW1 .... 240 A1
Sondes Street SE17 .... 245 L7
South & West Africa Gate SW1A 244 A3
Southall Place SE1 .... 245 L3
Southampton Buildings WC2A 240 F5
Southampton Place WC1A 240 D5
Southampton Row WC1B 240 D4
Southampton Street WC2E 240 D7
South Audley Street W1K 239 K8
South Carriage Drive SW1X 243 H3
South Carriage Drive SW7 .... 242 F3
South Eaton Place SW1W 243 J5
South Kensington ⊖ SW7 .... 242 E5
South Kensington ⊖ SW7 .... 242 E5
South Lambeth Road SW8 .... 244 D8
South Molton Lane W1K 239 K7

South Molton Street W1K.........239 K7
South Parade SW3.........242 E7
South Place EC2M.........241 L5
South Sea Street SE16.........247 L8
South Square WC1R.........240 F5
South Street W1K.........243 J1
South Tenter Street E1.........246 C3
South Terrace SW7.........242 F5
Southwark ⊖ SE1.........245 H2
Southwark Bridge SE1.........241 K8
Southwark Bridge Road SE1.........245 J3
Southwark Park Road SE16.........246 E8
Southwark Street SE1.........245 H1
Southwell Gardens SW7.........242 C5
South Wharf Road W2.........238 E6
Southwick Mews W2.........238 F6
Southwick Place W2.........238 F6
Southwick Street W2.........238 F6
Sovereign Close E1W.........246 F4
Sovereign Crescent SE16.........247 J4
Spanish Place W1U.........239 J5
Spa Road SE16.........246 C8
Spear Mews SW5.........242 A6
Spelman Street E1.........246 C1
Spence Close SE16.........247 K7
Spencer Street EC1V.........241 H2
Spenser Street SW1E.........244 A4
Spert Street E14.........247 J4
Spital Square E1.........246 A1
Spring Gardens SW1A.........244 C1
Spring Street W2.........238 E6
Spurgeon Street SE1.........245 L4
Spur Road SE1.........244 F3
Stables Way SE11.........244 F7
Stable Yard Road SW1A.........244 A2
Stacey Street WC2H.........240 C6
Stafford Place SW1E.........243 M3
Stafford Road NW6.........238 A2
Stafford Street W1S.........239 M8
Stafford Terrace W8.........242 A3
Stainer Street SE1.........245 L2
Staining Lane EC2V.........241 K6
Stainsby Road E14.........247 M2
Stalham Street SE16.........246 F8
Stamford Street SE1.........245 G1
Stanford Place SE1.........245 M6
Stanford Road W8.........242 B4
Stanford Street * SW1V.........244 B6
Stanhope Close * SE8.........247 H6
Stanhope Gardens SW7.........242 D5
Stanhope Gate W1K.........243 K1
Stanhope Mews SW7.........242 D5
Stanhope Mews East SW7.........242 D5
Stanhope Mews West SW7.........242 D5
Stanhope Place W2.........239 G7
Stanhope Place Gate W2.........239 G7
Stanhope Row W1J.........243 K1
Stanhope Street NW1.........239 M1
Stanhope Terrace SW11.........238 E7
Stannary Street SE11.........245 G7
Staples Close SE16.........247 J5
Staple Street SE1.........245 L3
Starcross Street NW1.........240 A2
Star Street W2.........238 F6
Station Approach SE1.........244 F3
Stave Yard Road SE16.........247 J5
Stead Street SE17.........245 K6
Steedman Street SE17.........245 J5
Steel's Lane E1.........247 G3
Steeres Way SE16.........247 K7
Stephenson Way NW1.........240 A3
Stephen Street W1T.........240 B5
Stepney Green E1.........247 H1
Stepney High Street E1.........247 J1
Stepney Way E1.........246 E1
Sterling Street SW7.........243 G3
Stevedore Street E1W.........246 E5
Stevens Street SE1.........246 A7
Steward Street * E1.........246 B1
Stewart's Grove SW3.........242 F6
Stew Lane EC4V.........241 J7
Stillington Street SW1P.........244 A5
Stockholm Way E1W.........246 D5
Stocks Place E14.........247 M3
Stone Buildings WC2A.........240 F5
Stonecutter Street EC4A.........241 G6
Stoney Lane E1.........246 B2
Stoney Street SE1.........245 K1
Stopford Road SE17.........245 J7
Store Street WC1E.........240 B5
Storey's Gate SW1H.........244 C3
Storks Road SE16.........246 D8
Stoughton Close SE11.........244 E6
Stourcliffe Street W1H.........239 G6
Strafford Street E14.........247 M6
Strand WC2R.........240 D8
Stratford Place W1C.........239 K6
Stratford Road W8.........242 A5
Strathearn Place W2.........238 F7
Stratton Street W1J.........243 L1
Strutton Ground SW1P.........244 B4
Strype Street E1.........246 B2
Stuart Road NW6.........238 A2
Stukeley Street WC2B.........240 D6
Sturgeon Street SE17.........245 J7
Sturge Street SE1.........245 J3
Sturt Street N1.........241 K1
Stutfield Street E1.........246 D3
Sudley Street N1.........241 H1
Sudrey Street SE1.........245 J3
Suffolk Lane EC4V.........241 L7
Suffolk Street SW1Y.........240 B8
Sugar Lane SE16.........246 D7
Sugar Quay Walk EC3R.........246 A4
Sullivan Road SE11.........245 G5
Summercourt Road E1.........247 G2
Summers Street EC1R.........240 F4
Sumner Place SW7.........242 E6
Sumner Street SE1.........245 J1
Sunderland Terrace W2.........238 A6
Sun Passage SE16.........246 D8
Sun Street EC2M.........241 M4
Sun Street Passage EC2M.........241 M5
Surrendale Place W9.........238 A4
Surrey Quays Road SE16.........247 H7
Surrey Row SE1.........245 H2
Surrey Square SE17.........245 M6
Surrey Street WC2E.........240 E7
Surrey Water Road SE16.........247 H6
Sussex Gardens W2.........238 E6
Sussex Mews West W2.........238 E7
Sussex Place NW1.........239 H3
Sussex Place W2.........238 E6
Sussex Square W2.........238 E7
Sussex Street SW1V.........243 L7
Sutherland Avenue W9.........238 A4

Sutherland Row SW1V.........243 L6
Sutherland Square SE17.........245 J7
Sutherland Street SW1V.........243 L7
Sutton Row W1D.........240 B6
Sutton Street E1.........247 G3
Suttons Way EC1Y.........241 K4
Swain Street NW8.........238 F3
Swallow Place W1B.........239 L6
Swallow Street W1B.........240 A8
Swan Lane EC4R.........241 L8
Swan Mead SE1.........245 M4
Swan Road SE16.........247 G6
Swan Street SE1.........245 K3
Swan Walk SW3.........243 H8
Swedenborg Gardens E1.........246 E4
Sweeney Crescent SE1.........246 C7
Swinton Street WC1X.........240 E2
Sydney Place SW7.........242 F6
Sydney Street SW3.........242 F6
Symons Street SW3.........243 H6

T

Tabard Gardens Estate SE1.........245 L3
Tabard Street SE1.........245 L3
Tabernacle Street EC2A.........241 L3
Tachbrook Street SW1V.........244 A6
Talbot Road W2.........238 A6
Talbot Square W2.........238 E6
Talbot Yard SE1.........245 L2
Tallis Street EC4Y.........241 G7
Tamworth Street SW6.........242 A8
Tanner Street SE1.........246 A7
Taplow Street N1.........241 K1
Tarling Street E1.........246 F3
Tarver Road SE17.........245 H7
Tatum Street SE17.........245 M6
Taunton Place NW1.........239 G3
Tavistock Place WC1H.........240 C3
Tavistock Square WC1H.........240 C3
Tavistock Street WC2E.........240 D7
Taviton Street WC1H.........240 B3
Teak Close SE16.........247 K6
Tedworth Square SW3.........243 G7
Telford Terrace SW1V.........243 M7
Temeraire Street SE16.........247 G6
Temple ⊖ WC2R.........240 F7
Temple Avenue EC4Y.........241 G7
Temple Lane EC4Y.........241 G7
Temple Place WC2R.........240 F7
Templeton Place SW5.........242 A5
Tench Street E1W.........246 E5
Tenniel Close W2.........238 C7
Tennis Street SE1.........245 L2
Tenterden Street W1S.........239 L6
Tenterground E1.........246 B1
Teredo Street SE16.........247 J8
Terminus Place SW1V.........243 L4
Thame Road SE16.........247 H6
Thanet Street WC1H.........240 C2
Thavies Inn EC4A.........241 G6
Thayer Street W1U.........239 K5
The Arches WC2N.........240 D8
The Boltons SW10.........242 C7
The British Library NW1.........240 C2
The British Museum WC1B.........240 C5
The Broad Walk W2.........238 B8
The Broad Walk W8.........242 C2
The Cut SE1.........245 G2
Theed Street SE1.........245 G2
The Flower Walk W2.........242 D3
The Grange SE1.........246 B8
The Highway E1W.........246 E4
The Little Boltons SW10.........242 C7
The Mall SW1A.........244 B2
The Mitre E14.........247 L3
The Monument EC3R.........241 L7
The National Gallery WC2N.........240 C8
Theobald's Road WC1X.........240 E4
Theobald Street SE1.........245 L5
The Oval (Surrey County
   Cricket Ground) SE11.........244 F8
The Shard SE1.........245 L2
The Vale SW3.........242 E8
Thirleby Road SW1P.........244 A4
Thomas More Street E1W.........246 D4
Thomas Road E14.........247 M2
Thoresby Street N1.........241 K1
Thorney Street SW1P.........244 C5
Thornton Place W1H.........239 H4
Thrale Street SE1.........245 K1
Thrawl Street E1.........246 C1
Threadneedle Street EC2R.........241 L6
Three Colt Street E14.........247 L3
Three Oak Lane SE1.........246 B6
Throgmorton Avenue EC2N.........241 L6
Throgmorton Street EC2N.........241 L6
Thurland Road SE16.........246 D8
Thurloe Place SW7.........242 F5
Thurloe Square SW7.........242 F5
Thurloe Street SW7.........242 E5
Thurlow Street SE17.........245 M7
Tichbourne Row W2.........238 F6
Tiller Road E14.........247 M8
Tillman Street E1.........246 E3
Tilney Street W1J.........243 K1
Timber Pond Road SE16.........247 J6
Tinsley Road E1.........247 G1
Tinworth Street SE11.........244 D6
Tisdall Place SE17.........245 L6
Tite Street SW3.........243 H8
Tiverton Street SE1.........245 J4
Token House Yard EC2R.........241 L6
Tolmer's Square NW1.........240 A3
Tomlin's Terrace E14.........247 K2
Tonbridge Street WC1H.........240 D2
Tooley Street SE1.........245 L1
Tooley Street SE1.........246 B6
Tor Gardens W8.........242 A2
Torquay Street W2.........238 A5
Torrens Street EC1V.........241 G1
Torrington Place E1W.........246 D5
Torrington Place WC1E.........240 B4
Torrington Square WC1E.........240 B4
Tothill Street SW1H.........244 B3
Tottenham Court Road W1T.........240 A4
Tottenham Court Road ⊖ W1D.........240 B6
Tottenham Street W1T.........240 A5
Toulmin Street SE1.........245 J3
Tower Bridge EC3N.........246 B5
Tower Bridge Approach EC3N.........246 B5
Tower Bridge Road SE1.........246 A7

Tower Bridge Wharf E1W.........246 C5
Tower Gateway ⊖ EC3N.........246 B4
Tower Hill EC3N.........246 B4
Tower Hill ⊖ EC3N.........246 B4
Tower of London EC3N.........246 B4
Tower Place EC3R.........246 A4
Tower Street WC2H.........240 C7
Townsend Street SE17.........245 M5
Toynbee Street E1.........246 B1
Trafalgar Gardens E1.........247 H1
Trafalgar Square WC2N.........240 C8
Trafalgar Street SE17.........245 L7
Transept Street NW1.........238 F5
Trebeck Street W1J.........243 L1
Trebovir Road SW5.........242 A6
Tregunter Road SW10.........242 C7
Trenton Road SE16.........246 E8
Tresham Crescent NW8.........238 F3
Trevor Place SW7.........243 G3
Trevor Square SW7.........243 G3
Trevor Street SW7.........243 G3
Trinidad Street E14.........247 M4
Trinity Church Square SE1.........245 K3
Trinity Square EC3N.........246 B4
Trinity Street SE1.........245 K3
Trump Street EC2V.........241 K6
Tudor Street EC4Y.........241 G7
Tufton Street SW1P.........244 C4
Tunnel Road SE16.........247 G6
Turks Row SW3.........243 J6
Turner's Road E3.........247 L2
Turner Street E1.........246 E2
Turnmill Street EC1N.........241 G4
Turpentine Lane SW1V.........243 L7
Turquand Street SE17.........245 K6
Tyers Gate SE1.........245 M3
Tyers Street SE11.........244 E7
Tyers Terrace SE11.........244 E7
Tyron Street SW3.........243 H6
Tysoe Street EC1R.........241 G3

U

Udall Street SW1P.........244 A5
Ufford Street SE1.........245 G2
Ulster Place NW1.........239 K4
Umberston Street E1.........246 E2
Undershaft EC3A.........246 A2
Underwood Road N1.........241 K2
Underwood Street N1.........241 K1
Union Street SE1.........245 H2
University Street WC1E.........240 A4
Upbrook Mews W2.........238 D6
Upper Belgrave Street SW1X.........243 K4
Upper Berkeley Street W1H.........239 H6
Upper Brook Street W1K.........239 J7
Upper Cheyne Row SW3.........242 F8
Upper Grosvenor Street W1K.........239 J8
Upper Ground SE1.........244 F1
Upper Harley Street NW1.........239 K3
Upper James Street W1F.........240 A7
Upper John Street W1F.........240 A7
Upper Marsh SE1.........244 E3
Upper Montagu Street W1H.........239 H5
Upper St Martin's WC2H.........240 C7
Upper Tachbrook Street SW1V.........244 A5
Upper Thames Street EC4V.........241 J7
Upper Wimpole Street W1G.........239 K4
Upper Woburn Place WC1H.........240 B2
Urlwin Street SE5.........245 J8
Uxbridge Street W8.........242 A1

V

Valentine Place SE1.........245 G3
Vandon Passage SW1H.........244 A3
Vandon Street SW1H.........244 A4
Varden Street E1.........246 E2
Varndell Street NW1.........239 M2
Vauban Street SE16.........246 C8
Vaughan Street SE16.........247 L7
Vaughan Way E1W.........246 D5
Vauxhall ⇌ ⊖ SW8.........244 D7
Vauxhall Bridge SW1V.........244 C7
Vauxhall Bridgefoot SE1.........244 D7
Vauxhall Bridge Road SW1V.........243 M5
Vauxhall Cross SE1.........244 D7
Vauxhall Grove SW8.........244 D8
Vauxhall Street SE11.........244 E6
Vauxhall Walk SE11.........244 E6
Venables Street W2.........238 E4
Vere Street W1G.........239 K6
Vernon Place WC1A.........240 D5
Vernon Rise WC1X.........240 E2
Verulam Street WC1X.........240 F4
Vestry Street N1.........241 L2
Victoria ⇌ ⊖ SW1V.........243 L5
Victoria & Albert Museum SW7.........242 F4
Victoria Embankment SW1A.........244 D2
Victoria Embankment WC2R.........240 F7
Victoria Gate W2.........238 F7
Victoria Road W8.........242 C4
Victoria Square SW1W.........243 L4
Victoria Street SW1E.........243 L4
Victory Place SE17.........245 K5
Victory Way SE16.........247 K7
Vigo Street W1S.........239 M8
Villa Street SE17.........245 L7
Villiers Street WC2N.........240 D8
Vincent Close SE16.........247 K7
Vincent Square SW1P.........244 B5
Vincent Street SW1P.........244 B5
Vincent Terrace N1.........241 H1
Vince Street EC1V.........241 L2
Vine Court E1.........246 D1
Vinegar Street E1W.........246 E5
Vine Hill EC1R.........240 F4
Vine Lane SE1.........246 B6
Vine Street EC3N.........246 B3
Violet Hill NW8.........238 C1
Virgil Street SE1.........244 F4
Virginia Street E1W.........246 D4
Viscount Street EC2Y.........241 J4

W

Wadding Street SE17.........245 K6
Wakefield Street WC1H.........240 D3
Wakeling Street E14.........247 K3
Wakley Street EC1V.........241 H2

Walbrook EC4N.........241 L7
Walcorde Avenue SE17.........245 K6
Walcot Square SE11.........245 G5
Walden Street E1.........246 E2
Waley Street E1.........247 J1
Wallwood Street E14.........247 M1
Walnut Tree Walk SE11.........244 F5
Walpole Street SW3.........243 H6
Walter Terrace E1.........247 H2
Walton Place SW3.........243 H4
Walton Street SW3.........243 G4
Walworth Place SE17.........245 K7
Walworth Road SE17.........245 J5
Wandsworth Road SW8.........244 C8
Wansey Street SE17.........245 K5
Wapping ⊖ E1W.........246 F5
Wapping High Street E1W.........246 D5
Wapping Lane E1.........246 F4
Wapping Wall E1W.........247 G5
Warden's Grove SE1.........245 J2
Wardour Street W1F.........240 B6
Warner Street EC1R.........240 F4
Warren Street W1T.........239 M4
Warren Street ⊖ NW1.........239 M3
Warrington Crescent W9.........238 C3
Warrington Gardens W9.........238 C4
Warwick Avenue W9.........238 B3
Warwick Avenue ⊖ W2.........238 C4
Warwick Crescent W2.........238 C5
Warwick House Street
   SW1Y.........244 B1
Warwick Lane EC4M.........241 H6
Warwick Place W9.........238 C4
Warwick Road SW5.........242 A6
Warwick Row SW1E.........243 L4
Warwick Square SW1V.........243 M6
Warwick Street W1B.........240 A7
Warwick Way SW1V.........243 L6
Waterhouse Square EC1N.........241 G5
Waterloo ⇌ ⊖ SE1.........244 F2
Waterloo Bridge SE1.........244 E1
Waterloo Bridge WC2R.........240 E8
Waterloo East ⇌ SE1.........245 G2
Waterloo Place SW1Y.........244 B1
Waterloo Road SE1.........245 G2
Waterman Way E1W.........246 E5
Waterside Close SE16.........246 D7
Watling Street EC4N.........241 K7
Watney Street E1.........246 F3
Watts Street E1W.........246 E5
Waveney Close E1W.........246 D5
Waverton Street W1J.........239 K8
Weavers Lane SE1.........246 A6
Webber Row SE1.........245 G3
Webber Street SE1.........245 H3
Webb Street SE1.........246 A8
Webster Road SE16.........246 D8
Weighhouse Street W1K.........239 K7
Welbeck Street W1G.........239 K5
Welbeck Way W1G.........239 K6
Welland Mews E1W.........246 E5
Wellclose Square E1.........246 D4
Wellesley Street E1.........247 H2
Wellesley Terrace N1.........241 K2
Wellington Arch W1J.........243 K2
Wellington Square SW3.........243 H6
Wellington Place NW8.........238 E2
Wellington Road NW8.........238 E1
Wellington Street WC2E.........240 D7
Wells Mews W1T.........240 A5
Wells Street W1T.........240 A5
Wells Way SE5.........245 M8
Wenlock Road N1.........241 K1
Wenlock Street N1.........241 K1
Wentworth Street E1.........246 B2
Werrington Street NW1.........240 A1
Wesley Street W1G.........239 K5
West Arbour Street E1.........247 G2
Westbourne Crescent W2.........238 D7
Westbourne Gardens W2.........238 B6
Westbourne Gate W2.........238 E7
Westbourne Grove W2.........238 A6
Westbourne Grove Terrace W2.........238 B6
Westbourne Park Road W2.........238 A5
Westbourne Park Villas W2.........238 A5
Westbourne Street W2.........238 D6
Westbourne Terrace W2.........238 D6
Westbourne Terrace Mews W2.........238 C6
Westbourne Terrace Road W2.........238 C5
West Brompton ⇌ ⊖ SW5.........242 A7
West Carriage Drive W2.........242 E2
Westcott Road SE17.........245 H8
West Cromwell Road SW5.........242 A5
Western Place SE16.........247 G6
Westferry ⊖ E14.........247 M4
Westferry Circus E14.........247 M5
Westferry Road E14.........247 M5
West Gardens SW1W.........246 F4
Westgate Terrace SW10.........242 B7
West Halkin Street SW1X.........243 J4
West Harding Street EC4A.........241 G6
West India Avenue E14.........247 M5
West India Dock Road E14.........247 M3
Westland Place N1.........241 K2
West Lane SE16.........246 E7
Westminster ⊖ SW1A.........244 D3
Westminster Abbey SW1A.........244 C3
Westminster Bridge SE1.........244 D3
Westminster Bridge Road SE1.........244 F3
Westmoreland Place SW1V.........243 L7
Westmoreland Road SE17.........245 K8
Westmoreland Street W1G.........239 K5
Westmoreland Terrace
   SW1V.........243 L7
Weston Rise WC1X.........240 E1
Weston Street SE1.........245 M2
Weston Street SE1.........245 M3
Westport Street E1.........247 H2
West Poultry Avenue EC1A.........241 H5
West Road SW3.........243 H7
West Smithfield EC1A.........241 H5
West Square SE11.........245 H4
West Street WC2H.........240 C7
West Tenter Street E1.........246 C3
West Warwick Place SW1V.........243 M6
Westway W2.........238 B5
Wetherby Gardens SW5.........242 C6
Weyhill Road E1.........246 D2
Weymouth Mews W1G.........239 L5
Weymouth Street W1G.........239 K5
Wharfdale Road N1.........240 D1
Wharfedale Street SW10.........242 B7
Wharf Road N1.........241 J1
Wharton Street WC1X.........240 F2
Wheatley Street W1G.........239 K5

Whetstone Park WC2A.........240 E5
Whidborne Street WC1H.........240 D2
Whiskin Street EC1R.........241 G2
Whitcomb Street WC2H.........240 B8
Whitechapel ⇌ ⊖ E1.........246 E1
Whitechapel Estate E1.........246 C4
Whitechapel High Street E1.........246 C2
Whitechapel Road E1.........246 D1
Whitecross Street EC1Y.........241 K3
Whitefriars Street EC4Y.........241 G6
Whitehall SW1A.........244 C2
Whitehall Court SW1A.........244 D2
Whitehall Place SW1A.........244 D1
White Hart Street SE11.........245 G6
White Hart Yard SE1.........245 L2
Whitehaven Street NW8.........238 F4
Whitehead's Grove SW3.........243 G6
White Horse Lane E1.........247 H1
White Horse Road E1.........247 J3
White Horse Street W1J.........243 L1
White Kennett Street E1.........246 B2
White Lion Hill EC4V.........241 H7
White Lion Street N1.........240 F1
White's Grounds SE1.........246 A7
White's Row E1.........246 B1
White Tower Way E1.........247 J1
Whitfield Place W1T.........240 A4
Whitfield Street W1T.........240 A4
Whitgift Street SE11.........244 E5
Whittaker Street SW1W.........243 J6
Whittlesey Street SE1.........245 G2
Wicker Street E1.........246 E3
Wickham Close E1.........247 G1
Wickham Street SE11.........244 E7
Wicklow Street WC1X.........240 E2
Widegate Street E1.........246 A1
Widley Road W9.........238 A3
Wigmore Place W1G.........239 K5
Wigmore Street W1U.........239 K6
Wigton Place SE11.........245 G7
Wilbraham Place SW1X.........243 J5
Wilcox Place * SW1E.........244 A4
Wild Court WC2B.........240 E6
Wild's Rents SE1.........245 M4
Wild Street WC2B.........240 D6
Wilfred Street SW1E.........243 M4
Wilkes Street E1.........246 B1
William IV Street WC2N.........240 C8
William Mews SW1X.........243 H3
William Road NW1.........239 M3
Willow Place SW1P.........244 A5
Willow Street EC2A.........241 M3
Wilmington Square WC1X.........240 F3
Wilmington Street WC1X.........240 F2
Wilson Grove SE16.........246 E7
Wilson Street EC2A.........241 L4
Wilton Crescent SW1X.........243 J3
Wilton Mews SW1X.........243 K4
Wilton Place SW1X.........243 J3
Wilton Road SW1V.........243 M5
Wilton Row SW1X.........243 J3
Wilton Street SW1X.........243 K4
Wimpole Mews W1G.........239 K5
Wimpole Street W1G.........239 K5
Winchester Street SW1V.........243 L6
Winchester Walk SE1.........245 K1
Wincott Street SE11.........245 G5
Windmill Road SE11.........244 F7
Windmill Street W1T.........240 B5
Windrose Close SE16.........247 H6
Windsor Terrace N1.........241 K1
Wine Close E1W.........246 F5
Winnett Street W1D.........240 B7
Winsland Street W2.........238 E6
Winsley Street W1W.........240 A6
Winthrop Street E1.........246 E1
Woburn Place WC1H.........240 C3
Woburn Square WC1H.........240 C4
Wodeham Gardens E1.........246 E1
Wolfe Crescent SE16.........247 H7
Wolseley Street SE1.........246 C6
Woodbridge Street EC1R.........241 G3
Woodchester Square W9.........238 A4
Woodfall Street SW3.........243 H7
Woodland Crescent SE16.........247 H7
Woodseer Street E1.........246 C1
Woods Mews W1K.........239 J7
Woods Place SE1.........246 A8
Woodstock Street W1C.........239 K6
Wood Street EC2V.........241 K6
Woolaston Close SE1.........245 J5
Wooler Street SE17.........245 L7
Wootton Street SE1.........245 G2
Worgan Street SE11.........244 E6
Worgan Street SE16.........247 H8
Wormwood Street EC2M.........241 M5
Worship Street EC2A.........241 M4
Wren Street WC1X.........240 E3
Wright's Lane W8.........242 A3
Wyatt Close SE16.........247 L7
Wyclif Street EC1V.........241 H2
Wymering Road W9.........238 A2
Wynard Terrace SE11.........244 F7
Wyndham Place W1H.........239 H5
Wyndham Street W1H.........239 G4
Wynnstay Gardens W8.........242 A4
Wynyatt Street EC1V.........241 H2
Wythburn Place W1H.........239 H6

Y

Yalding Road * SE16.........246 C8
Yardley Street WC1X.........240 F2
Yeoman's Row SW3.........243 G4
York Boulevard WC2N.........240 D8
York Bridge NW1.........239 J3
York Gate NW1.........239 J4
York Road SE1.........244 E2
Yorkshire Road E14.........247 K3
York Square E14.........247 J2
York Street W1H.........239 G5
York Street W1U.........239 H5
York Terrace East NW1.........239 J4
York Terrace West NW1.........239 J4
York Way N1.........240 D1
Young Street W8.........242 B3

Z

Zoar Street SE1.........245 J1
ZSL London Zoo NW1.........239 J1

This index lists places appearing in the main map section of the atlas in alphabetical order. The reference following each name gives the atlas page number and grid reference of the square in which the place appears. The map shows counties, unitary authorities and administrative areas, together with a list of the abbreviated name forms used in the index. The top 100 places of tourist interest are indexed in **red**, World Heritage sites in **green**, motorway service areas in **blue**, airports in blue *italic* and National Parks in green *italic*.

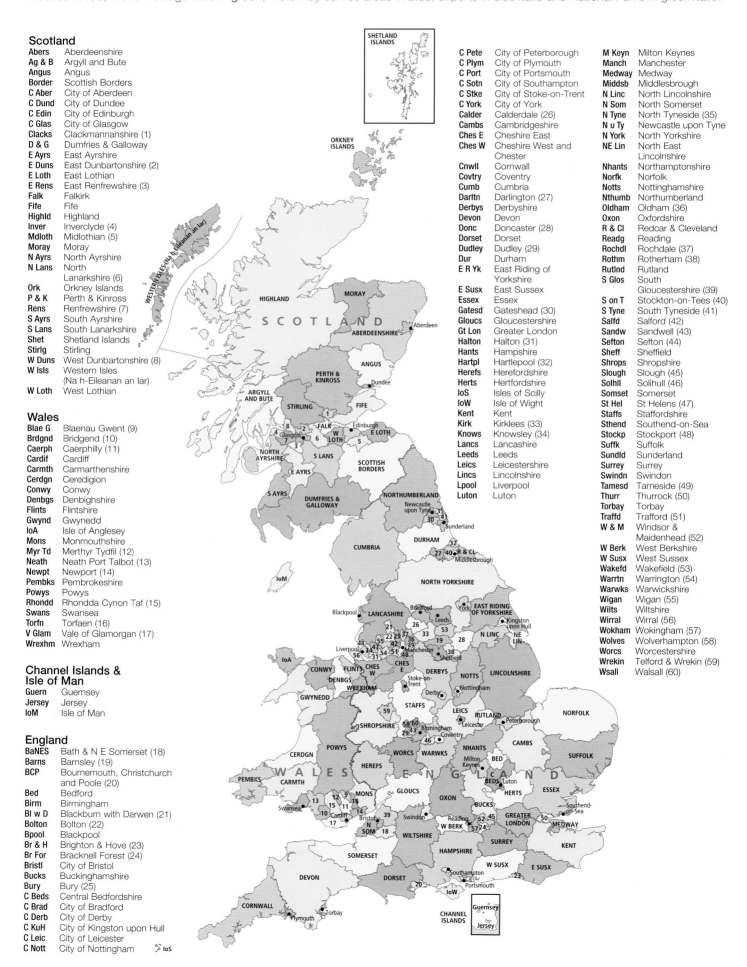

Scotland

Abers	Aberdeenshire
Ag & B	Argyll and Bute
Angus	Angus
Border	Scottish Borders
C Aber	City of Aberdeen
C Dund	City of Dundee
C Edin	City of Edinburgh
C Glas	City of Glasgow
Clacks	Clackmannanshire (1)
D & G	Dumfries & Galloway
E Ayrs	East Ayrshire
E Duns	East Dunbartonshire (2)
E Loth	East Lothian
E Rens	East Renfrewshire (3)
Falk	Falkirk
Fife	Fife
Highld	Highland
Inver	Inverclyde (4)
Mdloth	Midlothian (5)
Moray	Moray
N Ayrs	North Ayrshire
N Lans	North Lanarkshire (6)
Ork	Orkney Islands
P & K	Perth & Kinross
Rens	Renfrewshire (7)
S Ayrs	South Ayrshire
S Lans	South Lanarkshire
Shet	Shetland Islands
Stirlg	Stirling
W Duns	West Dunbartonshire (8)
W Isls	Western Isles (Na h-Eileanan an Iar)
W Loth	West Lothian

Wales

Blae G	Blaenau Gwent (9)
Brdgnd	Bridgend (10)
Caerph	Caerphilly (11)
Cardif	Cardiff
Carmth	Carmarthenshire
Cerdgn	Ceredigion
Conwy	Conwy
Denbgs	Denbighshire
Flints	Flintshire
Gwynd	Gwynedd
IoA	Isle of Anglesey
Mons	Monmouthshire
Myr Td	Merthyr Tydfil (12)
Neath	Neath Port Talbot (13)
Newpt	Newport (14)
Pembks	Pembrokeshire
Powys	Powys
Rhondd	Rhondda Cynon Taf (15)
Swans	Swansea
Torfn	Torfaen (16)
V Glam	Vale of Glamorgan (17)
Wrexhm	Wrexham

Channel Islands & Isle of Man

Guern	Guernsey
Jersey	Jersey
IoM	Isle of Man

England

BaNES	Bath & N E Somerset (18)
Barns	Barnsley (19)
BCP	Bournemouth, Christchurch and Poole (20)
Bed	Bedford
Birm	Birmingham
Bl w D	Blackburn with Darwen (21)
Bolton	Bolton (22)
Bpool	Blackpool
Br & H	Brighton & Hove (23)
Br For	Bracknell Forest (24)
Bristl	City of Bristol
Bucks	Buckinghamshire
Bury	Bury (25)
C Beds	Central Bedfordshire
C Brad	City of Bradford
C Derb	City of Derby
C KuH	City of Kingston upon Hull
C Leic	City of Leicester
C Nott	City of Nottingham

C Pete	City of Peterborough
C Plym	City of Plymouth
C Port	City of Portsmouth
C Sotn	City of Southampton
C Stke	City of Stoke-on-Trent
C York	City of York
Calder	Calderdale (26)
Cambs	Cambridgeshire
Ches E	Cheshire East
Ches W	Cheshire West and Chester
Cnwll	Cornwall
Covtry	Coventry
Cumb	Cumbria
Darltn	Darlington (27)
Derbys	Derbyshire
Devon	Devon
Donc	Doncaster (28)
Dorset	Dorset
Dudley	Dudley (29)
Dur	Durham
E R Yk	East Riding of Yorkshire
E Susx	East Sussex
Essex	Essex
Gatesd	Gateshead (30)
Gloucs	Gloucestershire
Gt Lon	Greater London
Halton	Halton (31)
Hants	Hampshire
Hartpl	Hartlepool (32)
Herefs	Herefordshire
Herts	Hertfordshire
IoS	Isles of Scilly
IoW	Isle of Wight
Kent	Kent
Kirk	Kirklees (33)
Knows	Knowsley (34)
Lancs	Lancashire
Leeds	Leeds
Leics	Leicestershire
Lincs	Lincolnshire
Lpool	Liverpool
Luton	Luton

M Keyn	Milton Keynes
Manch	Manchester
Medway	Medway
Middsb	Middlesbrough
N Linc	North Lincolnshire
N Som	North Somerset
N Tyne	North Tyneside (35)
N u Ty	Newcastle upon Tyne
N York	North Yorkshire
NE Lin	North East Lincolnshire
Nhants	Northamptonshire
Norfk	Norfolk
Notts	Nottinghamshire
Nthumb	Northumberland
Oldham	Oldham (36)
Oxon	Oxfordshire
R & Cl	Redcar & Cleveland
Readg	Reading
Rochdl	Rochdale (37)
Rothm	Rotherham (38)
Rutlnd	Rutland
S Glos	South Gloucestershire (39)
S on T	Stockton-on-Tees (40)
S Tyne	South Tyneside (41)
Salfd	Salford (42)
Sandw	Sandwell (43)
Sefton	Sefton (44)
Sheff	Sheffield
Shrops	Shropshire
Slough	Slough (45)
Solhll	Solihull (46)
Somset	Somerset
St Hel	St Helens (47)
Staffs	Staffordshire
Sthend	Southend-on-Sea
Stockp	Stockport (48)
Suffk	Suffolk
Sundld	Sunderland
Surrey	Surrey
Swindn	Swindon
Tamesd	Tameside (49)
Thurr	Thurrock (50)
Torbay	Torbay
Traffd	Trafford (51)
W & M	Windsor & Maidenhead (52)
W Berk	West Berkshire
W Susx	West Sussex
Wakefd	Wakefield (53)
Warrtn	Warrington (54)
Warwks	Warwickshire
Wigan	Wigan (55)
Wilts	Wiltshire
Wirral	Wirral (56)
Wokham	Wokingham (57)
Wolves	Wolverhampton (58)
Worcs	Worcestershire
Wrekin	Telford & Wrekin (59)
Wsall	Walsall (60)

Abbas Combe – Ansley 255

A

Abbas Combe Somset 20 D10
Abberley Worcs 57 P11
Abberley Common Worcs 57 N11
Abberton Essex 52 H8
Abberton Worcs 47 J4
Abberwick Nthumb 119 M8
Abbess Roding Essex 51 N8
Abbey Devon 10 C2
Abbeycwmhir Powys 55 P10
Abbeydale Sheff 84 D4
Abbey Dore Herefs 45 M8
Abbey Green Staffs 70 H3
Abbey Hill Somset 19 J11
Abbey St Bathans Border 129 K7
Abbeystead Lancs 95 M10
Abbeytown Cumb 110 C10
Abbey Village Lancs 89 J6
Abbey Wood Gt Lon 37 L5
Abbotrule Border 118 B8
Abbots Bickington Devon 16 F9
Abbots Bromley Staffs 71 K10
Abbotsbury Dorset 11 M7
Abbot's Chair Derbys 83 M6
Abbots Deuglie P & K 134 E5
Abbotsham Devon 16 G6
Abbotskerswell Devon 7 M5
Abbots Langley Herts 50 C10
Abbotsleigh Devon 7 L9
Abbots Leigh N Som 31 P10
Abbotsley Cambs 62 B9
Abbots Morton Worcs 47 K3
Abbots Ripton Cambs 62 B5
Abbot's Salford Warwks 47 L4
Abbotstone Hants 22 G8
Abbotswood Hants 22 C10
Abbots Worthy Hants 22 E8
Abbotts Ann Hants 22 B6
Abbott Street Dorset 12 G4
Abcott Shrops 56 F9
Abdon Shrops 57 K7
Abenhall Gloucs 46 C11
Aberaeron Cerdgn 43 J2
Aberaman Rhondd 30 D4
Aberangell Gwynd 55 J2
Aber-arad Carmth 42 F6
Aberarder Highld 147 Q2
Aberargie P & K 134 F4
Aberarth Cerdgn 43 J2
Aberavon Neath 29 K7
Aber-banc Cerdgn 42 G6
Aberbargoed Caerph 30 G4
Aberbeeg Blae G 30 H4
Abercanaid Myr Td 30 E4
Abercarn Caerph 30 H6
Abercastle Pembks 40 G4
Abercegir Powys 55 J4
Aberchalder Highld 147 J7
Aberchirder Abers 158 F7
Aber Clydach Powys 44 G10
Abercorn W Loth 127 K2
Abercraf Powys 29 M2
Abercregan Neath 29 M5
Abercwmboi Rhondd 30 D5
Abercych Pembks 41 P2
Abercynon Rhondd 30 E6
Aberdalgie P & K 134 D3
Aberdare Rhondd 30 D4
Aberdaron Gwynd 66 B9
Aberdeen C Aber 151 N6
Aberdeen Airport C Aber 151 M5
Aberdesach Gwynd 66 G4
Aberdour Fife 134 F10
Aberdulais Neath 29 L5
Aberdyfi Gwynd 54 E5
Aberedw Powys 44 F5
Abereiddy Pembks 40 E4
Abererch Gwynd 66 F7
Aberfan Myr Td 30 E4
Aberfeldy P & K 141 L8
Aberffraw IoA 78 F11
Aberffrwd Cerdgn 54 F9
Aberford Leeds 91 L3
Aberfoyle Stirlg 132 G7
Abergarw Brdgnd 29 P8
Abergarwed Neath 29 M4
Abergavenny Mons 31 J2
Abergele Conwy 80 C9
Aber-giar Carmth 43 K6
Abergorlech Carmth 43 L8
Abergwesyn Powys 44 B4
Abergwili Carmth 42 H10
Abergwydol Powys 54 H4
Abergwynfi Neath 29 N5
Abergwyngregyn Gwynd 79 M10
Abergynolwyn Gwynd 54 F3
Aberhafesp Powys 55 P6
Aberhosan Powys 55 J5
Aberkenfig Brdgnd 29 N8
Aberlady E Loth 128 D4
Aberlemno Angus 143 J6
Aberllefenni Gwynd 54 H3
Aberllynfi Powys 44 H7
Aberlour, Charlestown of Moray 157 P9
Abermagwr Cerdgn 54 F10
Aber-meurig Cerdgn 43 L3
Abermorddu Flints 69 K3
Abermule Powys 56 B6
Abernant Carmth 42 F10
Abernant Rhondd 30 D4
Abernethy P & K 134 F4
Abernyte P & K 142 D11
Aberporth Cerdgn 42 E4
Abersoch Gwynd 66 E9
Abersychan Torfn 31 J4
Aberthin V Glam 30 D10
Abertillery Blae G 30 H4
Abertridwr Caerph 30 F7
Abertridwr Powys 68 D11
Abertysswg Caerph 30 F3
Aberuthven P & K 134 B4
Aberwheeler Denbgs 80 F11
Aberyscir Powys 44 D9
Aberystwyth Cerdgn 54 D8
Abingdon-on-Thames Oxon 34 E5
Abinger Common Surrey 36 D11
Abinger Hammer Surrey 36 C11
Abington Nhants 60 G8
Abington S Lans 116 C6
Abington Pigotts Cambs 50 H2
Abington Services S Lans 116 C6
Abingworth W Susx 24 D7
Ab Kettleby Leics 73 J6
Ab Lench Worcs 47 K4
Ablington Gloucs 33 M3
Ablington Wilts 21 N5
Abney Derbys 83 Q8
Above Church Staffs 71 J4
Aboyne Abers 150 E8
Abhainn Suidhe W Isls 168 f7
Abram Wigan 82 D4
Abriachan Highld 155 Q10
Abridge Essex 51 L11
Abronhill N Lans 126 D2
Abson S Glos 32 D10
Abthorpe Nhants 48 H5
Aby Lincs 87 M5
Acaster Malbis C York 98 B11
Acaster Selby N York 91 P2
Accrington Lancs 89 M5
Acha Ag & B 136 F5
Achahoish Ag & B 123 N4
Achalader P & K 141 R8
Achaleven Ag & B 138 G11
Acha Mor W Isls 168 i5
Achanalt Highld 155 J5
Achandunie Highld 156 A3
Achany Highld 162 D6
Acharacle Highld 138 B4
Acharn Highld 138 C7
Acharn P & K 141 J9
Achavanich Highld 167 L8
Achduart Highld 160 G6
Achfary Highld 164 G9
Achgarve Highld 160 D8
A'Chill Highld 144 C6
Achiltibuie Highld 160 G5
Achina Highld 166 B4
Achinhoan Ag & B 120 E8
Achintee Highld 154 B9
Achintraid Highld 153 Q10
Achlyness Highld 164 F6
Achmelvich Highld 160 H2
Achmore Highld 153 R11
Achmore W Isls 168 i5
Achnacarnin Highld 164 B10
Achnacarry Highld 146 F10
Achnacloich Highld 145 J6
Achnaconeran Highld 147 L4
Achnacroish Ag & B 138 F9
Achnadrish Ag & B 137 M5
Achnafauld P & K 141 L10
Achnagarron Highld 156 B3
Achnaha Highld 137 M2
Achnahaird Highld 160 G4
Achnahannet Highld 148 H2
Achnairn Highld 162 D4
Achnalea Highld 138 F5
Achnamara Ag & B 130 F10
Achnasheen Highld 154 G6
Achnashellach Highld 154 D8
Achnastank Moray 157 P11
Achosnich Highld 137 L2
Achranich Highld 138 C8
Achreamie Highld 166 H3
Achriabhach Highld 139 L4
Achriesgill Highld 164 G6
Achtoty Highld 165 Q4
Achurch Nhants 61 M4
Achvaich Highld 162 G8
Achvarasdal Highld 166 G4
Ackergill Highld 167 Q6
Acklam Middsb 104 E7
Acklam N York 98 F8
Ackleton Shrops 57 P5
Acklington Nthumb 119 P10
Ackton Wakefd 91 L6
Ackworth Moor Top Wakefd 91 L7
Acle Norfk 77 N9
Acock's Green Birm 58 H8
Acol Kent 39 P8
Acomb C York 98 B10
Acomb Nthumb 112 D7
Acombe Somset 10 D2
Aconbury Herefs 45 Q8
Acre Lancs 89 M6
Acrefair Wrexhm 69 J6
Acresford Derbys 59 L2
Acton Ches E 70 A4
Acton Dorset 12 G9
Acton Gt Lon 36 F4
Acton Shrops 56 E8
Acton Staffs 70 E6
Acton Suffk 52 E2
Acton Worcs 58 B11
Acton Wrexhm 69 K4
Acton Beauchamp Herefs 46 C4
Acton Bridge Ches W 82 C9
Acton Burnell Shrops 57 J4
Acton Green Herefs 46 C4
Acton Pigott Shrops 57 J4
Acton Round Shrops 57 L5
Acton Scott Shrops 56 H7
Acton Trussell Staffs 70 G11
Acton Turville S Glos 32 F8
Adbaston Staffs 70 D9
Adber Dorset 19 Q10
Adbolton Notts 72 F3
Adderbury Oxon 48 E7
Adderley Shrops 70 B7
Adderstone Nthumb 119 M4
Addiewell W Loth 126 H5
Addingham C Brad 96 G11
Addington Bucks 49 K9
Addington Gt Lon 37 J8
Addington Kent 37 Q9
Addiscombe Gt Lon 36 H7
Addlestone Surrey 36 C8
Addlestonemoor Surrey 36 C7
Addlethorpe Lincs 87 P7
Adeney Wrekin 70 B11
Adeyfield Herts 50 C9
Adfa Powys 55 P4
Adforton Herefs 56 G10
Adisham Kent 39 M11
Adlestrop Gloucs 47 P9
Adlingfleet E R Yk 92 D6
Adlington Ches E 83 K8
Adlington Lancs 89 J8
Admaston Staffs 71 J10
Admaston Wrekin 57 L2
Admington Warwks 47 P5
Adpar Cerdgn 42 F6
Adsborough Somset 19 J9
Adscombe Somset 18 G7
Adstock Bucks 49 K9
Adstone Nhants 48 G4
Adswood Stockp 83 J7
Adversane W Susx 24 C6
Advie Highld 157 L11
Adwalton Leeds 90 G5
Adwell Oxon 35 J5
Adwick le Street Donc 91 N9
Adwick upon Dearne Donc 91 M10
Ae D & G 109 L3
Ae Bridgend D & G 109 M3
Afan Forest Park Neath 29 N5
Affetside Bury 89 M8
Affleck Abers 158 E9
Affpuddle Dorset 12 D6
Affric Lodge Highld 146 F3
Afon-wen Flints 80 G10
Afon Wen Gwynd 66 G7
Afton Devon 7 L6
Afton IoW 13 P7
Agglethorpe N York 96 G3
Aigburth Lpool 81 M7
Aike E R Yk 99 L11
Aiketgate Cumb 111 J11
Aikhead Cumb 110 D11
Aikton Cumb 110 E10
Ailby Lincs 87 M5
Ailey Herefs 45 L5
Ailsworth C Pete 74 B11
Ainderby Quernhow N York 97 M4
Ainderby Steeple N York 97 M2
Aingers Green Essex 53 K7
Ainsdale Sefton 88 C8
Ainsdale-on-Sea Sefton 88 B8
Ainstable Cumb 111 K11
Ainsworth Bury 89 M8
Ainthorpe N York 105 K9
Aintree Sefton 81 M5
Ainville W Loth 127 L5
Aird Ag & B 130 F7
Aird D & G 106 E5
Aird Highld 145 J7
Aird W Isls 168 k4
Àird a' Mhulaidh W Isls 168 g6
Aird Asaig W Isls 168 g7
Aird Dhubh Highld 153 N9
Airdeny Ag & B 131 K2
Airdrie N Lans 126 D4
Airdriehill N Lans 126 D4
Airds of Kells D & G 108 E6
Àird Uig W Isls 168 f4
Airidh a bhruaich W Isls 168 h6
Airieland D & G 108 G9
Airlie Angus 142 E7
Airmyn E R Yk 92 B6
Airntully P & K 141 Q10
Airor Highld 145 M6
Airth Falk 133 Q10
Airton N York 96 D9
Aisby Lincs 73 Q3
Aisby Lincs 85 Q2
Aisgill Cumb 102 E11
Aish Devon 6 H6
Aish Devon 7 L7
Aisholt Somset 18 G7
Aiskew N York 97 L3
Aislaby N York 98 F3
Aislaby N York 105 N9
Aislaby S on T 104 D8
Aisthorpe Lincs 86 B4
Aith Shet 169 q8
Akeld Nthumb 119 J5
Akeley Bucks 49 K7
Akenham Suffk 53 L2
Albaston Cnwll 5 Q7
Alberbury Shrops 56 F2
Albourne W Susx 24 G7
Albourne Green W Susx 24 G7
Albrighton Shrops 57 Q4
Albrighton Shrops 69 N11
Alburgh Norfk 65 K4
Albury Herts 51 K6
Albury Oxon 35 J3
Albury Surrey 36 B11
Albury End Herts 51 K6
Albury Heath Surrey 36 C11
Alby Hill Norfk 76 H5
Alcaig Highld 155 Q6
Alcaston Shrops 56 H7
Alcester Warwks 47 L3
Alciston E Susx 25 M9
Alcombe Somset 18 C5
Alcombe Wilts 32 F11
Alconbury Cambs 61 Q5
Alconbury Weald Cambs 62 B5
Alconbury Weston Cambs 61 Q5
Aldborough N York 97 P7
Aldborough Norfk 76 H5
Aldbourne Wilts 33 Q9
Aldbrough E R Yk 93 M3
Aldbrough St John N York 103 P8
Aldbury Herts 35 Q2
Aldcliffe Lancs 95 K8
Aldclune P & K 141 L5
Aldeburgh Suffk 65 P10
Aldeby Norfk 65 N3
Aldenham Herts 50 D11
Alderbury Wilts 21 N9
Aldercar Derbys 84 F11
Alderford Norfk 76 G8
Alderholt Dorset 13 K2
Alderley Gloucs 32 E6
Alderley Edge Ches E 82 H9
Aldermans Green Covtry 59 N8
Aldermaston W Berk 34 G11
Alderminster Warwks 47 P5
Alder Moor Staffs 71 N9
Aldersey Green Ches W 69 N3
Aldershot Hants 23 N4
Alderton Gloucs 47 K8
Alderton Nhants 49 K5
Alderton Shrops 69 N10
Alderton Suffk 53 P3
Alderton Wilts 32 F8
Alderwasley Derbys 71 Q4
Aldfield N York 97 L7
Aldford Ches W 69 M3
Aldgate Rutlnd 73 P10
Aldham Essex 52 F6
Aldham Suffk 52 J2
Aldingbourne W Susx 15 P5
Aldingham Cumb 94 F6
Aldington Kent 27 J4
Aldington Worcs 47 L6
Aldington Corner Kent 27 J4
Aldivalloch Moray 150 B2
Aldochlay Ag & B 132 D9
Aldon Shrops 56 G9
Aldoth Cumb 109 P11
Aldreth Cambs 62 F6
Aldridge Wsall 58 G4
Aldringham Suffk 65 N9
Aldro N York 98 G8
Aldsworth Gloucs 33 N3
Aldsworth W Susx 15 L5
Aldunie Moray 150 B2
Aldwark Derbys 84 B9
Aldwark N York 97 Q8
Aldwick W Susx 15 P7
Aldwincle Nhants 61 M4
Aldworth W Berk 34 G9
Alexandria W Duns 125 K2
Aley Somset 18 G7
Alfardisworthy Devon 16 D9
Alfington Devon 10 C5
Alfold Surrey 24 B4
Alfold Bars W Susx 24 B4
Alfold Crossways Surrey 24 B3
Alford Abers 150 F4
Alford Lincs 87 N5
Alford Somset 20 B8
Alfreton Derbys 84 F9
Alfrick Worcs 46 D4
Alfrick Pound Worcs 46 D4
Alfriston E Susx 25 M10
Algarkirk Lincs 74 E3
Alhampton Somset 20 B8
Alkborough N Linc 92 E6
Alkerton Gloucs 32 E3
Alkerton Oxon 48 C6
Alkham Kent 27 N3
Alkington Shrops 69 P7
Alkmonton Derbys 71 M7
Allaleigh Devon 7 L8
Allanaquoich Abers 149 L9
Allanbank N Lans 126 E6
Allanton Border 129 M9
Allanton N Lans 126 E6
Allanton S Lans 126 C7
Allaston Gloucs 32 B4
Allbrook Hants 22 E10
All Cannings Wilts 21 L2
Allendale Nthumb 112 B9
Allen End Warwks 59 J5
Allenheads Nthumb 112 C11
Allensford Dur 112 G10
Allen's Green Herts 51 L7
Allensmore Herefs 45 P7
Allenton C Derb 72 B4
Aller Devon 17 P6
Aller Somset 19 M9
Allerby Cumb 100 E3
Allercombe Devon 9 P6
Aller Cross Devon 17 N6
Allerford Somset 18 B5
Allerston N York 98 H4
Allerthorpe E R Yk 98 F11
Allerton C Brad 90 E4
Allerton Highld 156 D4
Allerton Lpool 81 M7
Allerton Bywater Leeds 91 L5
Allerton Mauleverer N York 97 P9
Allesley Covtry 59 M8
Allestree C Derb 72 A3
Allet Cnwll 3 K4
Allexton Leics 73 L10
Allgreave Ches E 83 L11
Allhallows Medway 38 D6
Allhallows-on-Sea Medway 38 D6
Alligin Shuas Highld 153 Q6
Allimore Green Staffs 70 F11
Allington Dorset 11 K6
Allington Kent 38 C10
Allington Lincs 73 M2
Allington Wilts 21 L2
Allington Wilts 21 P7
Allington Wilts 32 G9
Allithwaite Cumb 94 H5
Alloa Clacks 133 P9
Allonby Cumb 100 E2
Allostock Ches W 82 F10
Alloway S Ayrs 114 F4
Allowenshay Somset 10 H2
All Saints South Elmham Suffk 65 L5
Allscott Shrops 57 N5
Allscott Wrekin 57 L2
All Stretton Shrops 56 H5
Alltami Flints 81 K11
Alltchaorunn Highld 139 M7
Alltmawr Powys 44 F5
Alltsigh Highld 147 M4
Alltwalis Carmth 42 H8
Alltwen Neath 29 K4
Alltyblaca Cerdgn 43 K5
Allwood Green Suffk 64 E7
Almeley Herefs 45 L4
Almeley Wooton Herefs 45 L4
Almer Dorset 12 F5
Almholme Donc 91 P9
Almington Staffs 70 C8
Almodington W Susx 15 M7
Almondbank P & K 134 D2
Almondbury Kirk 90 F8
Almondsbury S Glos 32 B8
Alne N York 97 Q7
Alness Highld 156 B4
Alnham Nthumb 119 J8
Alnmouth Nthumb 119 P8
Alnwick Nthumb 119 N8
Alperton Gt Lon 36 E4
Alphamstone Essex 52 E4
Alpheton Suffk 64 B11
Alphington Devon 9 M6
Alpington Norfk 77 K11
Alport Derbys 84 B8
Alpraham Ches E 69 Q3
Alresford Essex 53 J7
Alrewas Staffs 59 J2
Alsager Ches E 70 D3
Alsagers Bank Staffs 70 D5
Alsop en le Dale Derbys 71 M4
Alston Cumb 111 P11
Alston Devon 10 G4
Alstone Gloucs 47 J8
Alstone Somset 19 K5
Alstonefield Staffs 71 L3
Alston Sutton Somset 19 M4
Alswear Devon 17 N7
Alt Oldham 83 K4
Altandhu Highld 160 F4
Altarnun Cnwll 5 L5
Altass Highld 162 C6
Altcreich Ag & B 138 B10
Altgaltraig Ag & B 124 C3
Altham Lancs 89 M4
Althorne Essex 38 F2
Althorpe N Linc 92 D9
Altnabreac Station Highld 166 H7
Altnaharra Highld 165 N9
Altofts Wakefd 91 K6
Alton Derbys 84 E8
Alton Hants 23 K7
Alton Staffs 71 K6
Alton Wilts 21 N5
Alton Barnes Wilts 21 M2
Alton Pancras Dorset 11 Q4
Alton Priors Wilts 21 M2
Alton Towers Staffs 71 K6
Altrincham Traffd 82 G7
Altskeith Hotel Stirlg 132 F7
Alva Clacks 133 P8
Alvanley Ches W 81 P10
Alvaston C Derb 72 B4
Alvechurch Worcs 58 F10
Alvecote Warwks 59 K4
Alvediston Wilts 21 J10
Alveley Shrops 57 P8
Alverdiscott Devon 17 J6
Alverstoke Hants 14 H7
Alverstone IoW 14 G9
Alverthorpe Wakefd 91 J6
Alverton Notts 73 K2
Alves Moray 157 L5
Alvescot Oxon 33 Q4
Alveston S Glos 32 B7
Alveston Warwks 47 P3
Alvingham Lincs 87 L2
Alvington Gloucs 32 B4
Alwalton C Pete 74 B11
Alweston Dorset 11 P2
Alwinton Nthumb 118 H9
Alwoodley Leeds 90 H2
Alwoodley Gates Leeds 91 J2
Alyth P & K 142 C8
Am Bàgh a Tuath W Isls 168 c17
Ambergate Derbys 84 D10
Amber Hill Lincs 86 H11
Amberley Gloucs 32 G4
Amberley W Susx 24 B8
Amber Row Derbys 84 E9
Amberstone E Susx 25 N8
Amble Nthumb 119 Q10
Amblecote Dudley 58 C7
Ambler Thorn C Brad 90 D5
Ambleside Cumb 101 L10
Ambleston Pembks 41 K5
Ambrosden Oxon 48 H11
Amcotts N Linc 92 E8
America Cambs 62 F5
Amersham Bucks 35 Q5
Amersham Common Bucks 35 Q5
Amersham Old Town Bucks 35 Q5
Amersham on the Hill Bucks 35 Q5
Amerton Staffs 70 H9
Amesbury Wilts 21 N6
Amhuinnsuidhe W Isls 168 f7
Amington Staffs 59 K4
Amisfield D & G 109 M4
Amlwch IoA 78 G6
Ammanford Carmth 28 H2
Amotherby N York 98 E6
Ampfield Hants 22 D10
Ampleforth N York 98 B5
Ampney Crucis Gloucs 33 L4
Ampney St Mary Gloucs 33 L4
Ampney St Peter Gloucs 33 L4
Amport Hants 22 B6
Ampthill C Beds 50 B3
Ampton Suffk 64 B7
Amroth Pembks 41 N9
Amulree P & K 141 L10
Amwell Herts 50 E8
Anaheilt Highld 138 E5
Ancaster Lincs 73 P2
Ancells Farm Hants 23 M3
Anchor Shrops 56 B7
Ancroft Nthumb 129 P11
Ancrum Border 118 B6
Ancton W Susx 15 Q6
Anderby Lincs 87 P5
Anderby Creek Lincs 87 Q5
Andersea Somset 19 K8
Andersfield Somset 18 H8
Anderson Dorset 12 E5
Anderton Ches W 82 D9
Anderton Cnwll 6 C8
Andover Hants 22 C5
Andover Down Hants 22 C5
Andoversford Gloucs 47 K11
Andreas IoM 80 f2
Anelog Gwynd 66 B9
Anerley Gt Lon 36 H7
Anfield Lpool 81 M6
Angarrack Cnwll 2 F6
Angarrick Cnwll 3 K6
Angelbank Shrops 57 K9
Angersleigh Somset 18 G11
Angerton Cumb 110 D9
Angle Pembks 40 G10
Anglesey IoA 78 G8
Anglesey Abbey Cambs 62 H8
Angmering W Susx 24 C10
Angram N York 97 R11
Angram N York 102 G11
Angrouse Cnwll 2 H10
Anick Nthumb 112 D7
Ankerville Highld 156 E3
Ankle Hill Leics 73 K7
Anlaby E R Yk 92 H5
Anmer Norfk 75 P5
Anmore Hants 15 J4
Annan D & G 110 C7
Annandale Water Services D & G 109 P2
Annaside Cumb 94 B3
Annat Highld 154 A7
Annathill N Lans 126 C3
Anna Valley Hants 22 C6
Annbank S Ayrs 114 H3
Anne Hathaway's Cottage Warwks 47 N4
Annesley Notts 84 H10
Annesley Woodhouse Notts 84 G10
Annfield Plain Dur 113 J10
Anniesland C Glas 125 N4
Annitsford N Tyne 113 L6
Annscroft Shrops 56 H3
Ansdell Lancs 88 C5
Ansford Somset 20 B8
Ansley Warwks 59 M6

Anslow *Staffs* 71 N9
Anslow Gate *Staffs* 71 M10
Anslow Lees *Staffs* 71 N10
Ansteadbrook *Surrey* 23 P8
Anstey *Hants* 23 K6
Anstey *Herts* 51 K4
Anstey *Leics* 72 F9
Anstruther *Fife* 135 P7
Ansty *W Susx* 24 G6
Ansty *Warwks* 59 P8
Ansty *Wilts* 21 J9
Ansty Cross *Dorset* 12 C4
An Tairbeart *W Isls* 168 g7
Anthill Common *Hants* 14 H4
Anthonys *Surrey* 36 B8
Anthorn *Cumb* 110 C9
Antingham *Norfk* 77 K5
An t-Ob *W Isls* 168 f9
Antonine Wall 126 E2
Anton's Gowt *Lincs* 87 K11
Antony *Cnwll* 5 Q11
Antrobus *Ches W* 82 D9
Anvil Corner *Devon* 16 F11
Anvil Green *Kent* 27 K2
Anwick *Lincs* 86 F10
Anwoth *D & G* 108 C9
Aperfield *Gt Lon* 37 K9
Apes Dale *Worcs* 58 E10
Apethorpe *Nhants* 73 Q11
Apeton *Staffs* 70 F11
Apley *Lincs* 86 F5
Apperknowle *Derbys* 84 E5
Apperley *Gloucs* 46 G9
Apperley Bridge *C Brad* 90 F3
Apperley Dene *Nthumb* 112 G9
Appersett *N York* 96 C2
Appin *Ag & B* 138 G8
Appleby *Lincs* 92 H9
Appleby-in-Westmorland *Cumb* 102 C6
Appleby Magna *Leics* 59 M3
Appleby Parva *Leics* 59 M3
Appleby Street *Herts* 50 H10
Applecross *Highld* 153 N9
Appledore *Devon* 9 Q2
Appledore *Devon* 16 H5
Appledore *Kent* 26 E6
Appledore Heath *Kent* 26 G5
Appleford *Oxon* 34 F6
Applegarth Town *D & G* 109 P4
Applehaigh *Wakefd* 91 K8
Applemore *Hants* 14 C5
Appleshaw *Hants* 22 B5
Applethwaite *Cumb* 101 J5
Appleton *Halton* 81 Q7
Appleton *Oxon* 34 D4
Appleton *Warrtn* 82 D8
Appleton-le-Moors *N York* 98 E3
Appleton-le-Street *N York* 98 E6
Appleton Roebuck *N York* 91 P2
Appleton Thorn *Warrtn* 82 D8
Appleton Wiske *N York* 104 C10
Appletreehall *Border* 117 Q7
Appletreewick *N York* 96 G8
Appley *Somset* 18 E10
Appley Bridge *Lancs* 88 G9
Apse Heath *IoW* 14 G10
Apsley End *C Beds* 50 D4
Apuldram *W Susx* 15 M6
Arabella *Highld* 156 E2
Arbirlot *Angus* 143 L9
Arborfield *Wokham* 35 L11
Arborfield Cross *Wokham* 35 L11
Arborfield Green *Wokham* 35 L11
Arbourthorne *Sheff* 84 E3
Arbroath *Angus* 143 L9
Arbuthnott *Abers* 143 P2
Arcadia *Kent* 26 E4
Archddu *Carmth* 28 D4
Archdeacon Newton *Darltn* 103 Q7
Archencarroch *W Duns* 132 E11
Archiestown *Moray* 157 N9
Archirondel *Jersey* 11 c1
Arclid *Ches E* 70 D2
Ardallie *Abers* 159 P10
Ardanaiseig Hotel *Ag & B* 131 M3
Ardaneaskan *Highld* 153 Q10
Ardarroch *Highld* 153 Q10
Ardbeg *Ag & B* 122 F10
Ardbeg *Ag & B* 124 D4
Ardbeg *Ag & B* 131 P11
Ardcharnich *Highld* 161 K9
Ardchiavaig *Ag & B* 137 K12
Ardchonnell *Ag & B* 131 K5
Ardchronie *Highld* 162 E9
Ardchullarie More *Stirlg* 132 H5
Arddarroch *Ag & B* 131 Q9
Arddleen *Powys* 69 J11
Ard Dorch *Highld* 145 J2
Ardechive *Highld* 146 E9
Ardeer *N Ayrs* 124 H9
Ardeley *Herts* 50 H5
Ardelve *Highld* 145 Q2
Arden *Ag & B* 132 D11
Ardens Grafton *Warwks* 47 M4
Ardentallen *Ag & B* 130 G3
Ardentinny *Ag & B* 131 P10
Ardentraive *Ag & B* 124 C3
Ardeonaig *Stirlg* 140 G10
Ardersier *Highld* 156 D7
Ardessie *Highld* 160 H9
Ardfern *Ag & B* 130 G7
Ardfernal *Ag & B* 123 J5
Ardgartan *Ag & B* 132 B7
Ardgay *Highld* 162 D8
Ardgour *Highld* 139 J5
Ardgowan *Inver* 124 G3
Ardhallow *Ag & B* 124 F3
Ardhasig *W Isls* 168 g7
Ardheslaig *Highld* 153 P6
Ardindrean *Highld* 161 K9
Ardingly *W Susx* 24 H5
Ardington *Oxon* 34 D7
Ardington Wick *Oxon* 34 D7
Ardlamont *Ag & B* 124 B4
Ardleigh *Essex* 53 J6
Ardleigh Heath *Essex* 52 H5
Ardler *P & K* 142 D9
Ardley *Oxon* 48 F9
Ardley End *Essex* 51 M8
Ardlui *Ag & B* 132 C4
Ardlussa *Ag & B* 130 C10
Ardmair *Highld* 161 J7
Ardmaleish *Ag & B* 124 D4
Ardminish *Ag & B* 123 K10
Ardmolich *Highld* 138 C3

Ardmore *Ag & B* 125 J2
Ardmore *Highld* 162 G9
Ardnadam *Ag & B* 131 P11
Ardnagrask *Highld* 155 P8
Ardnamurchan *Highld* 137 P2
Ardnarff *Highld* 154 A10
Ardnastang *Highld* 138 E5
Ardpatrick *Ag & B* 123 N8
Ardrishaig *Ag & B* 130 H10
Ardross *Highld* 155 R3
Ardrossan *N Ayrs* 124 G9
Ardsley *Barns* 91 K9
Ardslignish *Highld* 137 P3
Ardtalla *Ag & B* 122 G9
Ardtoe *Highld* 138 A3
Arduaine *Ag & B* 130 F5
Ardullie *Highld* 155 Q5
Ardvasar *Highld* 145 K7
Ardvorlich *P & K* 133 J3
Ardvourlie *W Isls* 168 g6
Ardwell *D & G* 106 F8
Ardwick *Manch* 83 J5
Areley Kings *Worcs* 57 P10
Arevegaig *Highld* 138 B4
Arford *Hants* 23 M7
Arglam *E R Yk* 92 C3
Argoed *Caerph* 30 G5
Argoed *Shrops* 69 K10
Argoed Mill *Powys* 44 D2
Argos Hill *E Susx* 25 N5
Argyll Forest Park *Ag & B* 131 Q7
Aribruach *W Isls* 168 h6
Aridhglas *Ag & B* 137 J11
Arileod *Ag & B* 136 F5
Arinagour *Ag & B* 136 G4
Ariogan *Ag & B* 130 H2
Arisaig *Highld* 145 L10
Arisaig House *Highld* 145 L11
Arkendale *N York* 97 N8
Arkesden *Essex* 51 L4
Arkholme *Lancs* 95 M6
Arkleby *Cumb* 100 F3
Arkleton *D & G* 110 G2
Arkle Town *N York* 103 K10
Arkley *Gt Lon* 50 F11
Arksey *Donc* 91 P9
Arkwright Town *Derbys* 84 F6
Arle *Gloucs* 46 H10
Arlecdon *Cumb* 100 D7
Arlescote *Warwks* 48 C5
Arlesey *C Beds* 50 E4
Arleston *Wrekin* 57 M2
Arley *Ches E* 82 E8
Arlingham *Gloucs* 32 D2
Arlington *Devon* 17 L3
Arlington *E Susx* 25 M9
Arlington *Gloucs* 33 M3
Arlington Beccott *Devon* 17 L3
Armadale *Highld* 145 K7
Armadale *Highld* 166 C4
Armadale *W Loth* 126 G4
Armaside *Cumb* 100 G5
Armathwaite *Cumb* 111 K11
Arminghall *Norfk* 77 K11
Armitage *Staffs* 71 K11
Armitage Bridge *Kirk* 90 E8
Armley *Leeds* 90 H4
Armscote *Warwks* 47 P6
Armshead *Staffs* 70 G5
Armston *Nhants* 61 N3
Armthorpe *Donc* 91 Q10
Arnabost *Ag & B* 136 G3
Arnaby *Cumb* 94 D4
Arncliffe *N York* 96 D6
Arncliffe Cote *N York* 96 D6
Arncroach *Fife* 135 N6
Arndilly House *Moray* 157 P8
Arne *Dorset* 12 G7
Arnesby *Leics* 60 D2
Arngask *P & K* 134 E5
Arnisdale *Highld* 145 P5
Arnish *Highld* 153 K8
Arniston *Mdloth* 127 Q5
Arnol *W Isls* 168 i3
Arnold *E R Yk* 93 K2
Arnold *Notts* 85 J11
Arnprior *Stirlg* 133 J9
Arnside *Cumb* 95 K5
Aros *Ag & B* 137 P6
Arowry *Wrexhm* 69 N7
Arrad Foot *Cumb* 94 G4
Arram *E R Yk* 92 H2
Arran *N Ayrs* 120 H4
Arrathorne *N York* 97 K2
Arreton *IoW* 14 F9
Arrina *Highld* 153 N6
Arrington *Cambs* 62 D10
Arrochar *Ag & B* 132 B7
Arrow *Warwks* 47 L3
Arrowfield Top *Worcs* 58 F10
Arscott *Shrops* 56 G3
Artafallie *Highld* 156 A8
Arthington *Leeds* 90 H2
Arthingworth *Nhants* 60 G4
Arthog *Gwynd* 54 E2
Arthrath *Abers* 159 N10
Arthursdale *Leeds* 91 K3
Artrochie *Abers* 159 P11
Arundel *W Susx* 24 B9
Asby *Cumb* 100 E6
Ascog *Ag & B* 124 E5
Ascot *W & M* 35 P11
Ascott *Warwks* 48 B5
Ascott Earl *Oxon* 48 B11
Ascott-under-Wychwood *Oxon* 48 B11
Asenby *N York* 97 N5
Asfordby *Leics* 73 J7
Asfordby Hill *Leics* 73 J7
Asgarby *Lincs* 86 F11
Asgarby *Lincs* 87 K7
Ash *Devon* 7 L9
Ash *Devon* 17 J10
Ash *Dorset* 12 G2
Ash *Kent* 37 P8
Ash *Kent* 39 N10
Ash *Somset* 19 J10
Ash *Somset* 19 N10
Ash *Surrey* 23 P4
Ashampstead *W Berk* 34 G9
Ashampstead Green *W Berk* 34 G9
Ashbocking *Suffk* 64 H11
Ashbourne *Derbys* 71 M5
Ashbrittle *Somset* 18 E10
Ashburnham Place *E Susx* 25 Q8
Ashburton *Devon* 7 K4

Ashbury *Devon* 8 D5
Ashbury *Oxon* 33 Q7
Ashby *N Linc* 92 F8
Ashby by Partney *Lincs* 87 M7
Ashby cum Fenby *NE Lin* 93 N10
Ashby de la Launde *Lincs* 86 E9
Ashby-de-la-Zouch *Leics* 72 B8
Ashby Folville *Leics* 73 J8
Ashby Magna *Leics* 60 C2
Ashby Parva *Leics* 60 B3
Ashby Puerorum *Lincs* 87 K6
Ashby St Ledgers *Nhants* 60 C7
Ashby St Mary *Norfk* 77 L11
Ashchurch *Gloucs* 46 H8
Ashcombe *Devon* 9 M9
Ashcombe *N Som* 19 K2
Ashcott *Somset* 19 M7
Ashdon *Essex* 51 N2
Ashdown Forest *E Susx* 25 L4
Ashe *Hants* 22 F4
Asheldham *Essex* 52 G11
Ashen *Essex* 52 B3
Ashendon *Bucks* 35 K2
Asheridge *Bucks* 35 P4
Ashfield *Hants* 22 C11
Ashfield *Herefs* 46 A10
Ashfield *Stirlg* 133 M7
Ashfield cum Thorpe *Suffk* 65 J9
Ashfield Green *Suffk* 63 N9
Ashfield Green *Suffk* 65 K7
Ashfold Crossways *W Susx* 24 F5
Ashford *Devon* 6 H9
Ashford *Devon* 17 J4
Ashford *Kent* 26 H3
Ashford *Surrey* 36 C6
Ashford Bowdler *Shrops* 57 J10
Ashford Carbonell *Shrops* 57 J10
Ashford Hill *Hants* 22 G2
Ashford in the Water *Derbys* 83 Q11
Ashgill *S Lans* 126 D7
Ash Green *Surrey* 23 P5
Ash Green *Warwks* 59 M8
Ashill *Devon* 10 B2
Ashill *Norfk* 76 B11
Ashill *Somset* 19 K11
Ashingdon *Essex* 38 E3
Ashington *BCP* 12 H5
Ashington *Nthumb* 113 L3
Ashington *Somset* 19 Q10
Ashington *W Susx* 24 D7
Ashkirk *Border* 117 P6
Ashlett *Hants* 14 E6
Ashleworth *Gloucs* 46 F9
Ashleworth Quay *Gloucs* 46 F9
Ashley *Cambs* 63 L8
Ashley *Ches E* 82 G8
Ashley *Devon* 17 M9
Ashley *Dorset* 13 K4
Ashley *Gloucs* 32 H6
Ashley *Hants* 13 N5
Ashley *Hants* 22 C8
Ashley *Kent* 27 P2
Ashley *Nhants* 60 G2
Ashley *Staffs* 70 D7
Ashley *Wilts* 32 F11
Ashley Green *Bucks* 35 Q3
Ashleyhay *Derbys* 71 P4
Ashley Heath *Dorset* 13 K4
Ashley Moor *Herefs* 56 H11
Ash Magna *Shrops* 69 Q7
Ashmansworth *Hants* 22 D3
Ashmansworthy *Devon* 16 E8
Ashmead Green *Gloucs* 32 E5
Ashmill *Devon* 5 P2
Ash Mill *Devon* 17 P7
Ashmore *Dorset* 20 H11
Ashmore Green *W Berk* 34 F11
Ashorne *Warwks* 48 B3
Ashover *Derbys* 84 D8
Ashover Hay *Derbys* 84 D8
Ashow *Warwks* 59 M10
Ash Parva *Shrops* 69 Q7
Ashperton *Herefs* 46 B6
Ashprington *Devon* 7 L7
Ash Priors *Somset* 18 G9
Ashreigney *Devon* 17 L9
Ash Street *Suffk* 52 H2
Ashtead *Surrey* 36 E9
Ash Thomas *Devon* 9 P2
Ashton *C Pete* 74 B9
Ashton *Cnwll* 2 G8
Ashton *Devon* 9 L8
Ashton *Hants* 22 F11
Ashton *Herefs* 45 Q2
Ashton *Inver* 124 G3
Ashton *Nhants* 49 L5
Ashton *Nhants* 61 N3
Ashton *Somset* 19 M5
Ashton Common *Wilts* 20 G3
Ashton Hayes *Ches W* 81 Q11
Ashton Hill *Wilts* 20 H3
Ashton-in-Makerfield *Wigan* 82 C5
Ashton Keynes *Wilts* 33 K6
Ashton-on-Ribble *Lancs* 88 G4
Ashton under Hill *Worcs* 47 J7
Ashton-under-Lyne *Tamesd* 83 K4
Ashton upon Mersey *Traffd* 82 G6
Ashton Vale *Bristl* 31 Q10
Ashurst *Hants* 13 P2
Ashurst *Kent* 25 M3
Ashurst *Lancs* 88 F8
Ashurst *W Susx* 24 E7
Ashurst Wood *W Susx* 25 K3
Ash Vale *Surrey* 23 N4
Ashwater *Devon* 5 P2
Ashwell *Herts* 50 H3
Ashwell *Rutlnd* 73 M8
Ashwell *Somset* 19 L11
Ashwell End *Herts* 50 H2
Ashwellthorpe *Norfk* 64 G2
Ashwick *Somset* 20 B5
Ashwicken *Norfk* 75 P7
Ashwood *Staffs* 58 C7
Askam in Furness *Cumb* 94 E5
Askern *Donc* 91 P8
Askerswell *Dorset* 11 L6
Askett *Bucks* 35 M3
Askham *Cumb* 101 P6
Askham *Notts* 85 M6
Askham Bryan *C York* 98 B11
Askham Richard *C York* 98 A11
Asknish *Ag & B* 131 J9
Askrigg *N York* 96 D2

Askwith *N York* 97 J11
Aslackby *Lincs* 74 A4
Aslacton *Norfk* 64 H3
Aslockton *Notts* 73 J3
Asney *Somset* 19 N7
Aspall *Suffk* 64 H9
Aspatria *Cumb* 100 F2
Aspenden *Herts* 51 J5
Aspenshaw *Derbys* 83 M7
Asperton *Lincs* 74 E3
Aspley *Staffs* 70 E8
Aspley Guise *C Beds* 49 P7
Aspley Heath *C Beds* 49 P8
Aspley Heath *Warwks* 58 G10
Aspull *Wigan* 89 J9
Aspull Common *Wigan* 82 D5
Asselby *E R Yk* 92 B5
Asserby *Lincs* 87 N5
Asserby Turn *Lincs* 87 N5
Assington *Suffk* 52 F4
Assington Green *Suffk* 63 N10
Astbury *Ches E* 70 E2
Astcote *Nhants* 49 J4
Asterby *Lincs* 87 J5
Asterley *Shrops* 56 F3
Asterton *Shrops* 56 F6
Asthall *Oxon* 33 Q2
Asthall Leigh *Oxon* 34 B2
Astle *Highld* 162 G8
Astley *Shrops* 69 P11
Astley *Warwks* 59 M7
Astley *Wigan* 82 F4
Astley *Worcs* 57 P11
Astley Abbotts *Shrops* 57 N5
Astley Bridge *Bolton* 89 L8
Astley Cross *Worcs* 57 Q11
Astley Green *Wigan* 82 F5
Aston *Ches E* 69 R5
Aston *Ches E* 82 C9
Aston *Derbys* 83 Q8
Aston *Flints* 81 L11
Aston *Herefs* 45 P2
Aston *Herts* 50 G6
Aston *Oxon* 34 B4
Aston *Rothm* 84 G3
Aston *Shrops* 69 Q6
Aston *Shrops* 69 P9
Aston *Staffs* 70 D6
Aston *Staffs* 70 F10
Aston *Wokham* 35 L8
Aston *Wrekin* 57 L3
Aston Abbotts *Bucks* 49 M10
Aston Botterell *Shrops* 57 L8
Aston-by-Stone *Staffs* 70 G8
Aston Cantlow *Warwks* 47 M2
Aston Clinton *Bucks* 35 N2
Aston Crews *Herefs* 46 C10
Aston Cross *Gloucs* 46 H8
Aston End *Herts* 50 G6
Aston-Eyre *Shrops* 57 M6
Aston Fields *Worcs* 58 E11
Aston Flamville *Leics* 59 Q6
Aston Heath *Ches W* 82 C9
Aston Ingham *Herefs* 46 C10
Aston juxta Mondrum *Ches E* 70 A3
Aston le Walls *Nhants* 48 E4
Aston Magna *Gloucs* 47 N7
Aston Munslow *Shrops* 57 J7
Aston-on-Carrant *Gloucs* 46 H8
Aston on Clun *Shrops* 56 F8
Aston Pigott *Shrops* 56 E3
Aston Rogers *Shrops* 56 E3
Aston Rowant *Oxon* 35 K5
Aston Sandford *Bucks* 35 L3
Aston Somerville *Worcs* 47 K7
Aston-sub-Edge *Gloucs* 47 M6
Aston Tirrold *Oxon* 34 G7
Aston-upon-Trent *Derbys* 72 C5
Aston Upthorpe *Oxon* 34 G7
Astrope *Herts* 35 N2
Astwick *C Beds* 50 F3
Astwith *Derbys* 84 F8
Astwood *M Keyn* 49 Q5
Astwood *Worcs* 58 D11
Astwood Bank *Worcs* 47 K2
Aswarby *Lincs* 73 R3
Aswardby *Lincs* 87 L6
Atcham *Shrops* 57 J3
Atch Lench *Worcs* 47 K4
Athelhampton *Dorset* 12 C6
Athelington *Suffk* 65 J7
Athelney *Somset* 19 K9
Athelstaneford *E Loth* 128 E4
Atherfield Green *IoW* 14 E11
Atherington *Devon* 17 K7
Atherington *W Susx* 24 B10
Atherstone *Somset* 19 L11
Atherstone *Warwks* 59 M5
Atherstone on Stour *Warwks* 47 P4
Atherton *Wigan* 82 E4
Atley Hill *N York* 103 Q10
Atlow *Derbys* 71 N5
Attadale *Highld* 154 B10
Attenborough *Notts* 72 E4
Atterby *Lincs* 86 C2
Attercliffe *Sheff* 84 E3
Atterley *Shrops* 57 L5
Atterton *Leics* 72 B11
Attingham Park *Shrops* 57 J2
Attleborough *Norfk* 64 E2
Attleborough *Warwks* 59 N6
Attlebridge *Norfk* 76 G8
Attleton Green *Suffk* 63 M10
Atwick *E R Yk* 99 P10
Atworth *Wilts* 32 G11
Auberrow *Herefs* 45 P5
Aubourn *Lincs* 86 B8
Auchbreck *Moray* 149 N2
Auchedly *Abers* 159 L11
Auchenblae *Abers* 143 N2
Auchenbowie *Stirlg* 133 M10
Auchencairn *D & G* 109 L4
Auchencairn *D & G* 108 G10
Auchencairn *N Ayrs* 121 K6
Auchencrow *Border* 129 M7
Auchendinny *Mdloth* 127 P5
Auchengray *S Lans* 126 H7
Auchenhalrig *Moray* 157 R5
Auchenheath *S Lans* 126 E8
Auchenhessnane *D & G* 115 R8
Auchenlochan *Ag & B* 124 B3
Auchenmade *N Ayrs* 125 K8

Auchenmalg *D & G* 106 H7
Auchentiber *N Ayrs* 125 K8
Auchindrain *Ag & B* 131 L7
Auchindrean *Highld* 161 K10
Auchininna *Abers* 158 G8
Auchinleck *E Ayrs* 115 L3
Auchinloch *N Lans* 126 B3
Auchinstarry *N Lans* 126 C2
Auchintore *Highld* 139 K3
Auchiries *Abers* 159 Q10
Auchlean *Highld* 148 F8
Auchlee *Abers* 151 M8
Auchleven *Abers* 150 G3
Auchlochan *S Lans* 126 E10
Auchlossan *Abers* 150 F7
Auchlyne *Stirlg* 132 G2
Auchmillan *E Ayrs* 115 K2
Auchmithie *Angus* 143 M9
Auchmuirbridge *Fife* 134 G2
Auchnacree *Angus* 142 H5
Auchnagatt *Abers* 159 M9
Auchnarrow *Moray* 149 N3
Auchnotteroch *D & G* 106 C5
Auchroisk *Moray* 157 Q7
Auchterarder *P & K* 133 Q5
Auchteraw *Highld* 147 K6
Auchterblair *Highld* 148 G3
Auchtercairn *Highld* 153 Q2
Auchterderran *Fife* 134 G8
Auchterhouse *Angus* 142 E10
Auchterless *Abers* 158 H9
Auchtermuchty *Fife* 134 G5
Auchterneed *Highld* 155 N6
Auchtertool *Fife* 134 G9
Auchtertyre *Highld* 145 P2
Auchtubh *Stirlg* 132 H3
Auckengill *Highld* 167 Q4
Auckley *Donc* 91 Q10
Audenshaw *Tamesd* 83 K5
Audlem *Ches E* 70 B6
Audley *Staffs* 70 D4
Audley End *Essex* 51 M3
Audley End *Essex* 52 D4
Audley End *Suffk* 64 B11
Audley End House & Gardens *Essex* 51 M3
Audmore *Staffs* 70 E10
Audnam *Dudley* 58 C7
Aughertree *Cumb* 101 J3
Aughton *E R Yk* 92 B3
Aughton *Lancs* 88 D9
Aughton *Lancs* 95 M7
Aughton *Rothm* 84 G3
Aughton *Wilts* 21 P3
Aughton Park *Lancs* 88 E9
Auldearn *Highld* 156 G6
Aulden *Herefs* 45 P4
Auldgirth *D & G* 109 K3
Auldhouse *S Lans* 125 Q6
Ault a' chruinn *Highld* 146 A3
Aultbea *Highld* 160 D9
Aultgrishin *Highld* 160 A9
Aultguish Inn *Highld* 155 L1
Ault Hucknall *Derbys* 84 G7
Aultmore *Moray* 158 B7
Aultnagoire *Highld* 147 N3
Aultnamain *Highld* 162 F10
Aunby *Lincs* 73 Q8
Aunk *Devon* 9 P4
Aunsby *Lincs* 73 Q3
Aust *S Glos* 31 Q7
Austendike *Lincs* 74 E6
Austerfield *Donc* 85 L2
Austerlands *Oldham* 90 B9
Austhorpe *Leeds* 91 K4
Austonley *Kirk* 90 E9
Austrey *Warwks* 59 L3
Austwick *N York* 95 R7
Authorpe *Lincs* 87 L4
Authorpe Row *Lincs* 87 P6
Avebury *Wilts* 33 M11
Avebury Trusloe *Wilts* 33 L11
Aveley *Thurr* 37 N4
Avening *Gloucs* 32 G5
Averham *Notts* 85 N10
Aveton Gifford *Devon* 6 H9
Aviemore *Highld* 148 F5
Avington *W Berk* 34 C11
Avoch *Highld* 156 C6
Avon *Hants* 13 K5
Avonbridge *Falk* 126 G3
Avon Dassett *Warwks* 48 D4
Avonmouth *Bristl* 31 P9
Avonwick *Devon* 7 J7
Awbridge *Hants* 22 B10
Awkley *S Glos* 31 Q7
Awliscombe *Devon* 10 C4
Awre *Gloucs* 32 D3
Awsworth *Notts* 72 D2
Axborough *Worcs* 58 C9
Axbridge *Somset* 19 M4
Axford *Hants* 22 H6
Axford *Wilts* 33 P10
Axmansford *Hants* 22 G2
Axminster *Devon* 10 F5
Axmouth *Devon* 10 F6
Axton *Flints* 80 G8
Aycliffe *Dur* 103 Q6
Aydon *Nthumb* 112 F7
Aylburton *Gloucs* 32 B4
Ayle *Nthumb* 111 P11
Aylesbeare *Devon* 9 P6
Aylesbury *Bucks* 35 M2
Aylesby *NE Lin* 93 M9
Aylesford *Kent* 38 B10
Aylesham *Kent* 39 M11
Aylestone *C Leic* 72 F10
Aylestone Park *C Leic* 72 F10
Aylmerton *Norfk* 76 H4
Aylsham *Norfk* 76 H6
Aylton *Herefs* 46 C7
Aylworth *Gloucs* 47 M10
Aymestrey *Herefs* 56 G11
Aynho *Nhants* 48 F8
Ayot Green *Herts* 50 F8
Ayot St Lawrence *Herts* 50 E7
Ayot St Peter *Herts* 50 F7
Ayr *S Ayrs* 114 F3
Aysgarth *N York* 96 H3
Ayshford *Devon* 18 D11
Ayside *Cumb* 94 H4
Ayston *Rutlnd* 73 M10
Aythorpe Roding *Essex* 51 N7
Ayton *Border* 129 N7
Azerley *N York* 97 L6

Babbacombe – Beam Hill 257

B

Babbacombe Torbay 7 N5
Babbington Notts 72 D2
Babbinswood Shrops 69 K9
Babbs Green Herts 51 J7
Babcary Somset 19 Q9
Babel Carmth 44 A7
Babel Green Suffk 63 M11
Babell Flints 80 H10
Babeny Devon 8 G9
Bablock Hythe Oxon 34 D4
Babraham Cambs 62 H10
Babworth Notts 85 L4
Bachau IoA 78 G8
Bache Shrops 56 H8
Bacheldre Powys 56 C6
Bachelor's Bump E Susx 26 D9
Backaland Ork 169 e3
Backbarrow Cumb 94 H4
Backe Carmth 41 Q7
Backfolds Abers 159 P7
Backford Ches W 81 M10
Backford Cross Ches W 81 M10
Backies Highld 163 J6
Back of Keppoch Highld 145 L10
Back o' th' Brook Staffs 71 K4
Back Street Suffk 63 M9
Backwell N Som 31 N11
Backworth N Tyne 113 M6
Bacon's End Solhll 59 J7
Baconsthorpe Norfk 76 G4
Bacton Herefs 45 M8
Bacton Norfk 77 L5
Bacton Suffk 64 F8
Bacton Green Suffk 64 E8
Bacup Lancs 89 P6
Badachro Highld 153 P3
Badanloch Highld 166 C10
Badbury Swindn 33 N8
Badby Nhants 60 C9
Badcall Highld 164 F5
Badcaul Highld 160 G8
Baddeley Edge C Stke 70 G4
Baddeley Green C Stke 70 G4
Baddesley Clinton Warwks 59 K10
Baddesley Ensor Warwks 59 L5
Baddidarrach Highld 160 H2
Baddinsgill Border 127 L7
Badenscoth Abers 158 G10
Badentarbet Highld 160 G5
Badenyon Abers 149 Q4
Badersfield Norfk 77 K7
Badgall Cnwll 5 L4
Badgeney Cambs 74 H11
Badger Shrops 57 P5
Badger's Cross Cnwll 2 D7
Badgers Mount Kent 37 L8
Badgeworth Gloucs 46 H11
Badgworth Somset 19 L4
Badharlick Cnwll 5 M4
Badicaul Highld 145 N2
Badingham Suffk 65 L8
Badlesmere Kent 38 H11
Badlieu Border 116 F7
Badlipster Highld 167 M7
Badluarach Highld 160 F8
Badninish Highld 162 H8
Badrallach Highld 160 H8
Badsey Worcs 47 L6
Badshot Lea Surrey 23 N5
Badsworth Wakefd 91 M8
Badwell Ash Suffk 64 D8
Badwell Green Suffk 64 E8
Bagber Dorset 12 C2
Bagby N York 97 Q4
Bag Enderby Lincs 87 L6
Bagendon Gloucs 33 K3
Bagginswood Shrops 57 M8
Baggrow Cumb 100 G2
Bàgh a' Chaisteil W Isls 168 b18
Bagham Kent 39 J11
Bagillt Flints 81 J9
Baginton Warwks 59 M10
Baglan Neath 29 K6
Bagley Leeds 90 G3
Bagley Shrops 69 M9
Bagley Somset 19 N5
Bagmore Hants 23 J6
Bagnall Staffs 70 G4
Bagnor W Berk 34 E11
Bagshot Surrey 23 P2
Bagshot Wilts 34 B11
Bagstone S Glos 32 C7
Bagthorpe Notts 84 G10
Bagworth Leics 72 C9
Bagwyllydiart Herefs 45 N9
Baildon C Brad 90 F3
Baildon Green C Brad 90 E3
Baile Ailein W Isls 168 h5
Baile a' Mhanaich W Isls 168 c12
Baile Mòr Ag & B 136 H11
Bailey Green Hants 23 J9
Baileyhead Cumb 111 K5
Bailiff Bridge Calder 90 E5
Baillieston C Glas 126 B5
Bailrigg Lancs 95 K9
Bainbridge N York 96 D2
Bainshole Abers 158 F10
Bainton C Pete 74 A9
Bainton E R Yk 99 K10
Bainton Oxon 48 G9
Baintown Fife 135 K7
Bairnkine Border 118 C7
Baker's End Herts 51 J7
Baker Street Thurr 37 P4
Bakewell Derbys 84 B7
Bala Gwynd 68 B7
Balallan W Isls 168 h5
Balbeg Highld 155 M11
Balbeggie P & K 134 F2
Balblair Highld 156 C4
Balby Donc 91 P10
Balcary D & G 108 H11
Balchraggan Highld 155 P9
Balchrick Highld 164 E4
Balcombe W Susx 24 H4
Balcombe Lane W Susx 24 H4
Balcomie Links Fife 135 Q6
Baldersby N York 97 N5
Baldersby St James N York 97 N5
Balderstone Lancs 89 J4
Balderstone Rochdl 89 Q8
Balderton Notts 85 P10
Baldhu Cnwll 3 K5
Baldinnie Fife 135 L5
Baldinnies P & K 134 C4
Baldock Herts 50 F4
Baldock Services Herts 50 F3
Baldovie C Dund 142 H11
Baldrine IoM 80 f5
Baldslow E Susx 26 D9
Baldwin IoM 80 e5
Baldwinholme Cumb 110 F10
Baldwin's Gate Staffs 70 D7
Baldwin's Hill W Susx 25 J3
Bale Norfk 76 E4
Baledgarno P & K 142 D11
Balemartine Ag & B 136 B7
Balerno C Edin 127 M4
Balfarg Fife 134 H7
Balfield Angus 143 J4
Balfour Ork 169 d5
Balfron Stirlg 132 G10
Balgaveny Abers 158 G9
Balgonar Fife 134 C9
Balgowan D & G 106 F9
Balgowan Highld 147 Q9
Balgown Highld 152 F4
Balgracie D & G 106 C5
Balgray S Lans 116 B6
Balham Gt Lon 36 G6
Balhary P & K 142 D8
Balholmie P & K 142 A10
Baligill Highld 166 E3
Balintore Angus 142 D6
Balintore Highld 156 F2
Balintraid Highld 156 C3
Balivanich W Isls 168 c12
Balk N York 97 Q4
Balkeerie Angus 142 E9
Balkholme E R Yk 92 C5
Ballabeg IoM 80 c7
Ballachulish Highld 139 K6
Ballafesson IoM 80 b7
Ballajora IoM 80 g3
Ballakilpheric IoM 80 b7
Ballamodha IoM 80 c7
Ballantrae S Ayrs 114 A11
Ballards Gore Essex 38 F3
Ballards Green Warwks 59 L6
Ballasalla IoM 80 c7
Ballater Abers 150 B8
Ballaugh IoM 80 d3
Ballchraggan Highld 156 D2
Ballencrieff E Loth 128 D4
Ballevullin Ag & B 136 B6
Ball Green C Stke 70 F4
Ball Haye Green Staffs 70 H3
Ball Hill Hants 22 D2
Ballianlay Ag & B 124 C5
Ballidon Derbys 71 N4
Balliekine N Ayrs 120 G4
Balliemore Ag & B 131 N8
Balligmorrie S Ayrs 114 D9
Ballimore Stirlg 132 G4
Ballindalloch Moray 157 M10
Ballindean P & K 134 H2
Ballingdon Suffk 52 E3
Ballinger Common Bucks 35 P4
Ballingham Herefs 46 A8
Ballingry Fife 134 F8
Ballinluig P & K 141 N7
Ballinshoe Angus 142 G7
Ballintuim P & K 141 R6
Balloch Highld 156 C8
Balloch N Lans 126 C3
Balloch P & K 133 N4
Balloch S Ayrs 114 F8
Balloch W Duns 132 D11
Balls Cross W Susx 23 Q9
Balls Green E Susx 25 L3
Ball's Green Gloucs 32 G5
Ballygown Ag & B 137 L7
Ballygrant Ag & B 122 E6
Ballyhaugh Ag & B 136 F4
Balmacara Highld 145 P2
Balmaclellan D & G 108 E5
Balmae D & G 108 E12
Balmaha Stirlg 132 E9
Balmalcolm Fife 135 J6
Balmangan D & G 108 D11
Balmedie Abers 151 P4
Balmer Heath Shrops 69 M8
Balmerino Fife 135 K3
Balmerlawn Hants 13 P4
Balmichael N Ayrs 120 H5
Balmore E Duns 125 P3
Balmuchy Highld 163 K11
Balmule Fife 134 G10
Balmullo Fife 135 L3
Balnacoil Highld 163 J4
Balnacra Highld 154 C8
Balnacroft Abers 149 P9
Balnafoich Highld 156 B10
Balnaguard P & K 141 M7
Balnahard Ag & B 137 M9
Balnain Highld 155 M11
Balnakeil Highld 165 J3
Balne N York 91 P7
Balquharn P & K 141 P10
Balquhidder Stirlg 132 G3
Balsall Common Solhll 59 K9
Balsall Heath Birm 58 G8
Balsall Street Solhll 59 K9
Balscote Oxon 48 C6
Balsham Cambs 63 J10
Baltasound Shet 169 t3
Balterley Staffs 70 D4
Balterley Green Staffs 70 D4
Balterley Heath Staffs 70 C4
Baltersan D & G 107 M5
Balthangie Abers 159 K7
Baltonsborough Somset 19 P8
Balvicar Ag & B 130 F4
Balvraid Highld 145 P4
Balvraid Highld 156 E11
Balwest Cnwll 2 F7
Bamber Bridge Lancs 88 H5
Bamber's Green Essex 51 N6
Bamburgh Nthumb 119 N4
Bamburgh Castle Nthumb 119 N3
Bamford Derbys 84 B4
Bamford Rochdl 89 P8
Bampton Cumb 101 P7
Bampton Devon 18 C10
Bampton Oxon 34 B4
Bampton Grange Cumb 101 P7
Banavie Highld 139 L2
Banbury Oxon 48 E6
Bancffosfelen Carmth 28 E2
Banchory Abers 150 H8
Banchory-Devenick Abers 151 N7
Bancycapel Carmth 28 D2
Bancyfelin Carmth 42 F11
Banc-y-ffordd Carmth 42 H7
Bandirran P & K 142 C11
Bandrake Head Cumb 94 G3
Banff Abers 158 G5
Bangor Gwynd 79 K10
Bangor-on-Dee Wrexhm 69 L5
Bangors Cnwll 5 L2
Bangor's Green Lancs 88 D9
Bangour Village W Loth 127 J3
Bangrove Suffk 64 C7
Banham Norfk 64 F4
Bank Hants 13 N3
Bankend D & G 109 M7
Bankfoot P & K 141 Q10
Bankglen E Ayrs 115 L5
Bank Ground Cumb 101 K11
Bankhead C Aber 151 M5
Bankhead S Lans 116 D2
Bank Newton N York 96 D10
Banknock Falk 126 D2
Banks Cumb 111 L8
Banks Lancs 88 D6
Banks Green Worcs 58 E11
Bankshill D & G 110 C4
Bank Street Worcs 46 B2
Bank Top Calder 90 E6
Bank Top Lancs 88 G9
Banningham Norfk 77 J6
Bannister Green Essex 51 Q6
Bannockburn Stirlg 133 N9
Banstead Surrey 36 G9
Bantham Devon 6 H10
Banton N Lans 126 C2
Banwell N Som 19 L3
Bapchild Kent 38 F9
Bapton Wilts 21 J7
Barabhas W Isls 168 i3
Barassie S Ayrs 125 J11
Barbaraville Highld 156 C3
Barber Booth Derbys 83 P8
Barber Green Cumb 94 H4
Barbieston S Ayrs 114 H4
Barbon Cumb 95 N4
Barbridge Ches E 69 R3
Barbrook Devon 17 N2
Barby Nhants 60 B6
Barcaldine Ag & B 138 H9
Barcheston Warwks 47 Q7
Barclose Cumb 110 H8
Barcombe E Susx 25 K8
Barcombe Cross E Susx 25 K7
Barcroft C Brad 90 C3
Barden N York 96 H2
Barden Park Kent 37 N11
Bardfield End Green Essex 51 P4
Bardfield Saling Essex 51 Q5
Bardney Lincs 86 F7
Bardon Leics 72 C8
Bardon Mill Nthumb 111 Q8
Bardowie E Duns 125 P3
Bardown E Susx 25 Q5
Bardrainney Inver 125 J3
Bardsea Cumb 94 G6
Bardsey Leeds 91 K2
Bardsey Island Gwynd 66 A10
Bardsley Oldham 83 K4
Bardwell Suffk 64 C7
Bare Lancs 95 K8
Bareppa Cnwll 3 K8
Barfad D & G 107 K4
Barford Norfk 76 G10
Barford Warwks 47 Q2
Barford St John Oxon 48 D8
Barford St Martin Wilts 21 L8
Barford St Michael Oxon 48 D8
Barfrestone Kent 39 N11
Bargate Derbys 84 E11
Bargeddie N Lans 126 B5
Bargoed Caerph 30 G5
Bargrennan D & G 107 L2
Barham Cambs 61 P5
Barham Kent 39 M11
Barham Suffk 64 G11
Bar Hill Cambs 62 E8
Barholm Lincs 74 A8
Barkby Leics 72 G9
Barkby Thorpe Leics 72 G9
Barkers Green Shrops 69 P9
Barkestone-le-Vale Leics 73 K4
Barkham Wokham 35 L11
Barking Gt Lon 37 K4
Barking Suffk 64 F11
Barking Riverside Gt Lon 37 L4
Barkingside Gt Lon 37 K3
Barking Tye Suffk 64 F11
Barkisland Calder 90 D7
Barkla Shop Cnwll 3 J3
Barkston Lincs 73 N2
Barkston Ash N York 91 M3
Barkway Herts 51 J3
Barlanark C Glas 126 B5
Barlaston Staffs 70 F7
Barlavington W Susx 23 Q11
Barlborough Derbys 84 G5
Barlby N York 91 Q4
Barlestone Leics 72 C9
Barley Herts 51 K3
Barley Lancs 89 N2
Barleycroft End Herts 51 K5
Barley Hole Rothm 91 K11
Barleythorpe Rutlnd 73 L9
Barling Essex 38 F4
Barlings Lincs 86 E6
Barlochan D & G 108 H9
Barlow Derbys 84 D6
Barlow Gatesd 113 J8
Barlow N York 91 Q5
Barmby Moor E R Yk 98 F11
Barmby on the Marsh E R Yk 92 A5
Barmer Norfk 75 R4
Barming Heath Kent 38 B10
Barmollack Ag & B 120 F3
Barmouth Gwynd 67 L11
Barmpton Darltn 104 B7
Barmston E R Yk 99 P9
Barnaby Green Suffk 65 P5
Barnacarry Ag & B 131 L9
Barnack C Pete 74 A9
Barnacle Warwks 59 N8
Barnard Castle Dur 103 L7
Barnard Gate Oxon 34 D2
Barnardiston Suffk 63 M11
Barnbarroch D & G 108 H9
Barnburgh Donc 91 M10
Barnby Suffk 65 P4
Barnby Dun Donc 91 Q9
Barnby in the Willows Notts 85 Q10
Barnby Moor Notts 85 L4
Barncorkrie D & G 106 E10
Barnehurst Gt Lon 37 L5
Barnes Gt Lon 36 F5
Barnes Street Kent 37 P11
Barnet Gt Lon 50 F11
Barnetby le Wold N Linc 93 J9
Barnet Gate Gt Lon 50 F11
Barney Norfk 76 D5
Barnham Suffk 64 B6
Barnham W Susx 15 Q6
Barnham Broom Norfk 76 F10
Barnhead Angus 143 M6
Barnhill C Dund 142 H11
Barnhill Ches W 69 N4
Barnhill Moray 157 L6
Barnhills D & G 106 C3
Barningham Dur 103 L8
Barningham Suffk 64 D6
Barnoldby le Beck NE Lin 93 M10
Barnoldswick Lancs 96 C11
Barnsdale Bar Donc 91 N8
Barns Green W Susx 24 D5
Barnsley Barns 91 J9
Barnsley Gloucs 33 L4
Barnsole Kent 39 N10
Barnstaple Devon 17 K5
Barnston Essex 51 P7
Barnston Wirral 81 K8
Barnstone Notts 73 J3
Barnt Green Worcs 58 F10
Barnton C Edin 127 M3
Barnton Ches W 82 D10
Barnwell All Saints Nhants 61 M4
Barnwell St Andrew Nhants 61 N4
Barnwood Gloucs 46 G11
Baron's Cross Herefs 45 P3
Baronwood Cumb 101 P2
Barr S Ayrs 114 E9
Barra W Isls 168 b17
Barra Airport W Isls 168 c17
Barrachan D & G 107 L8
Barraigh W Isls 168 b17
Barrananaoil Ag & B 130 G6
Barrapoll Ag & B 136 A7
Barras Cumb 102 F8
Barrasford Nthumb 112 D6
Barregarrow IoM 80 d4
Barrets Green Ches E 69 Q3
Barrhead E Rens 125 M6
Barrhill S Ayrs 114 D11
Barrington Cambs 62 E11
Barrington Somset 19 L11
Barripper Cnwll 2 G6
Barrmill N Ayrs 125 K7
Barrock Highld 167 N2
Barrow Gloucs 46 G10
Barrow Lancs 89 L3
Barrow Rutlnd 73 M7
Barrow Shrops 57 M4
Barrow Somset 20 D8
Barrow Suffk 63 N8
Barroway Drove Norfk 75 L10
Barrow Bridge Bolton 89 K8
Barrow Burn Nthumb 118 G8
Barrowby Lincs 73 M3
Barrow Common N Som 31 P11
Barrowden Rutlnd 73 N10
Barrowford Lancs 89 P3
Barrow Gurney N Som 31 P11
Barrow Haven N Linc 93 J6
Barrow Hill Derbys 84 F5
Barrow-in-Furness Cumb 94 E7
Barrow Island Cumb 94 D7
Barrow Nook Lancs 81 N4
Barrow's Green Ches E 70 B3
Barrows Green Cumb 95 L3
Barrow Street Wilts 20 F8
Barrow-upon-Humber N Linc 93 J6
Barrow upon Soar Leics 72 F7
Barrow upon Trent Derbys 72 B5
Barrow Vale BaNES 20 B2
Barry Angus 143 J11
Barry V Glam 30 F11
Barry Island V Glam 30 F11
Barsby Leics 72 H8
Barsham Suffk 65 M4
Barston Solhll 59 K9
Bartestree Herefs 45 R6
Barthol Chapel Abers 159 K11
Bartholomew Green Essex 52 B7
Barthomley Ches E 70 D4
Bartley Hants 13 P2
Bartley Green Birm 58 F8
Bartlow Cambs 63 J11
Barton Cambs 62 F9
Barton Ches W 69 M4
Barton Gloucs 47 L9
Barton Herefs 45 K3
Barton Lancs 88 D9
Barton Lancs 88 G3
Barton N York 103 P9
Barton Oxon 34 G3
Barton Torbay 7 N5
Barton Warwks 47 M4
Barton Bendish Norfk 75 P9
Barton End Gloucs 32 F5
Barton Green Staffs 71 M11
Barton Hartshorn Bucks 48 H8
Barton Hill N York 98 E8
Barton in Fabis Notts 72 E4
Barton in the Beans Leics 72 B9
Barton-le-Clay C Beds 50 C4
Barton-le-Street N York 98 E6
Barton-le-Willows N York 98 E8
Barton Mills Suffk 63 M6
Barton-on-Sea Hants 13 M6
Barton-on-the-Heath Warwks 47 Q8
Barton St David Somset 19 P8
Barton Seagrave Nhants 61 J5
Barton Stacey Hants 22 D6
Barton Town Devon 17 M3
Barton Turf Norfk 77 M7
Barton-under-Needwood Staffs 71 M11
Barton-upon-Humber N Linc 92 H6
Barton upon Irwell Salfd 82 G5
Barton Waterside N Linc 92 H6
Barugh Barns 91 J9
Barugh Green Barns 91 J9
Barvas W Isls 168 i3
Barway Cambs 63 J5
Barwell Leics 72 C11
Barwick Devon 17 K10
Barwick Herts 51 J7
Barwick Somset 11 M2
Barwick in Elmet Leeds 91 L3
Baschurch Shrops 69 M10
Bascote Warwks 48 D2
Bascote Heath Warwks 48 C2
Base Green Suffk 64 E9
Basford Green Staffs 70 H4
Bashall Eaves Lancs 89 K2
Bashall Town Lancs 89 L2
Bashley Hants 13 M5
Basildon Essex 38 B4
Basingstoke Hants 22 H4
Baslow Derbys 84 C6
Bason Bridge Somset 19 K5
Bassaleg Newpt 31 J7
Bassendean Border 128 G10
Bassenthwaite Cumb 100 H4
Bassett C Sotn 22 D11
Bassingbourn-cum-Kneesworth Cambs 50 H2
Bassingfield Notts 72 G3
Bassingham Lincs 86 B9
Bassingthorpe Lincs 73 P5
Bassus Green Herts 50 H5
Basted Kent 37 P9
Baston Lincs 74 B8
Bastwick Norfk 77 N8
Batch Somset 19 K3
Batchworth Herts 36 C2
Batchworth Heath Herts 36 C2
Batcombe Dorset 11 N4
Batcombe Somset 20 C7
Bate Heath Ches E 82 E9
Batford Herts 50 D7
Bath BaNES 20 D2
Bath BaNES 20 E2
Bathampton BaNES 32 E11
Bathealton Somset 18 E10
Batheaston BaNES 32 E11
Bathford BaNES 32 E11
Bathgate W Loth 126 H4
Bathley Notts 85 N9
Bathpool Cnwll 5 M7
Bathpool Somset 19 J9
Bath Side Essex 53 N5
Bathville W Loth 126 G4
Bathway Somset 19 Q4
Batley Kirk 90 G6
Batsford Gloucs 47 N8
Batson Devon 7 J11
Battersby N York 104 G9
Battersea Gt Lon 36 G5
Battisborough Cross Devon 6 F9
Battisford Suffk 64 F11
Battisford Tye Suffk 64 E11
Battle E Susx 26 C8
Battle Powys 44 E8
Battleborough Somset 19 K4
Battledown Gloucs 47 J10
Battledykes Angus 142 H6
Battlefield Shrops 69 P11
Battlesbridge Essex 38 C3
Battlesden C Beds 49 Q9
Battleton Somset 18 B9
Battlies Green Suffk 64 C9
Battram Leics 72 C9
Battramsley Cross Hants 13 P5
Batt's Corner Hants 23 M6
Baughton Worcs 46 G6
Baughurst Hants 22 G2
Baulds Abers 150 G9
Baulking Oxon 34 B6
Baumber Lincs 86 H6
Baunton Gloucs 33 K4
Baveney Wood Shrops 57 M9
Baverstock Wilts 21 K8
Bawburgh Norfk 76 H10
Bawdeswell Norfk 76 E7
Bawdrip Somset 19 K7
Bawdsey Suffk 53 P3
Bawsey Norfk 75 N6
Bawtry Donc 85 K2
Baxenden Lancs 89 M5
Baxterley Warwks 59 L5
Baxter's Green Suffk 63 N9
Bay Highld 152 D7
Bayble W Isls 168 k4
Baybridge Hants 22 F10
Baybridge Nthumb 112 E10
Baycliff Cumb 94 F6
Baydon Wilts 33 Q9
Bayford Herts 50 H9
Bayford Somset 20 D9
Bayhead W Isls 168 c11
Bay Horse Lancs 95 K10
Bayley's Hill Kent 37 M10
Baylham Suffk 64 G11
Baynard's Green Oxon 48 F9
Baysdale Abbey N York 104 H9
Baysham Herefs 45 R9
Bayston Hill Shrops 56 H3
Baythorne End Essex 52 B3
Bayton Worcs 57 M10
Bayton Common Worcs 57 N10
Bayworth Oxon 34 E4
Beach S Glos 32 D10
Beachampton Bucks 49 L7
Beachamwell Norfk 75 Q9
Beachley Gloucs 31 Q6
Beachy Head E Susx 25 N11
Beacon Devon 10 D3
Beacon End Essex 52 G6
Beacon Hill Kent 26 D5
Beacon Hill Notts 85 P10
Beacon Hill Surrey 23 N7
Beacon's Bottom Bucks 35 L5
Beaconsfield Bucks 35 P6
Beaconsfield Services Bucks 35 Q7
Beadlam N York 98 D4
Beadlow C Beds 50 D3
Beadnell Nthumb 119 P5
Beaford Devon 17 K8
Beal N York 91 N5
Beal Nthumb 119 L2
Bealbury Cnwll 5 P8
Bealsmill Cnwll 5 P6
Beam Hill Staffs 71 N9

Beamhurst Staffs......71 K7
Beaminster Dorset......11 K4
Beamish Dur......113 K10
Beamish - The Living Museum of the North
    Dur......113 K10
Beamsley N York......96 G10
Bean Kent......37 N6
Beanacre Wilts......32 H11
Beanley Nthumb......119 L7
Beardon Devon......8 D8
Beardwood Bl w D......89 K5
Beare Devon......9 N4
Beare Green Surrey......24 E2
Bearley Warwks......47 N2
Bearley Cross Warwks......47 N2
Bearpark Dur......103 P2
Bearsden E Duns......125 N3
Bearstead Kent......38 D10
Bearstone Shrops......70 C7
Bearwood BCP......12 H5
Bearwood Birm......58 F7
Bearwood Herefs......45 M3
Beattock D & G......116 F10
Beauchamp Roding Essex......51 N9
Beauchief Sheff......84 D4
Beaudesert Warwks......59 J11
Beaufort Blae G......30 G2
Beaulieu Essex......52 B10
Beaulieu Hants......14 C6
Beaulieu (National Motor Museum/Palace House) Hants......14 C6
Beaulieu Road Station Hants......13 P3
Beauly Highld......155 P8
Beaumaris IoA......79 L9
Beaumaris Castle IoA......79 L9
Beaumont Cumb......110 F9
Beaumont Essex......53 L7
Beaumont Jersey......11 b2
Beaumont Hill Darltn......103 Q7
Beaumont Leys C Leic......72 F9
Beausale Warwks......59 K10
Beauworth Hants......22 G9
Beaworthy Devon......8 C5
Beazley End Essex......52 B6
Bebington Wirral......81 L8
Bebside Nthumb......113 L4
Beccles Suffk......65 N4
Becconsall Lancs......88 F6
Beckbury Shrops......57 P4
Beckenham Gt Lon......37 J7
Beckermet Cumb......100 D9
Beckett End Norfk......75 Q11
Beckfoot Cumb......94 D3
Beckfoot Cumb......100 G10
Beck Foot Cumb......102 B11
Beckfoot Cumb......109 N11
Beckford Worcs......47 J7
Beckhampton Wilts......33 L11
Beck Hole N York......105 M10
Beckingham Lincs......85 Q10
Beckingham Notts......85 N3
Beckington Somset......20 F4
Beckjay Shrops......56 F9
Beckley E Susx......26 E7
Beckley Hants......13 M5
Beckley Oxon......34 G2
Beck Row Suffk......63 L5
Becks C Brad......96 F11
Beck Side Cumb......94 E4
Beck Side Cumb......94 H4
Beckton Gt Lon......37 K4
Beckwithshaw N York......97 L10
Becontree Gt Lon......37 L3
Becquet Vincent Jersey......11 b1
Bedale N York......97 L3
Bedburn Dur......103 L4
Bedchester Dorset......20 G11
Beddau Rhondd......30 E7
Beddgelert Gwynd......67 K5
Beddingham E Susx......25 K9
Beddington Gt Lon......36 H7
Beddington Corner Gt Lon......36 G7
Bedfield Suffk......65 J8
Bedfield Little Green Suffk......65 J8
Bedford Bed......61 M11
Bedgebury Cross Kent......26 B5
Bedgrove Bucks......35 M2
Bedham W Susx......24 B6
Bedhampton Hants......15 K5
Bedingfield Suffk......64 H8
Bedingfield Green Suffk......64 H8
Bedlam N York......97 L8
Bedlington Nthumb......113 L4
Bedlinog Myr Td......30 E4
Bedminster Bristl......31 Q10
Bedminster Down Bristl......31 Q10
Bedmond Herts......50 C10
Bednall Staffs......70 H11
Bedrule Border......118 B7
Bedstone Shrops......56 F9
Bedwas Caerph......30 G7
Bedwellty Caerph......30 G4
Bedworth Warwks......59 N7
Bedworth Woodlands Warwks......59 M7
Beeby Leics......72 H9
Beech Hants......23 J7
Beech Staffs......70 F7
Beech Hill W Berk......23 J2
Beechingstoke Wilts......21 L3
Beedon W Berk......34 E9
Beedon Hill W Berk......34 E9
Beeford E R Yk......99 N10
Beeley Derbys......84 C7
Beelsby NE Lin......93 M10
Beenham W Berk......34 G11
Beenham's Heath W & M......35 M9
Beeny Cnwll......5 J3
Beer Devon......10 E7
Beer Somset......19 M8
Beercrocombe Somset......19 K10
Beer Hackett Dorset......11 N2
Beesands Devon......7 L10
Beesby Lincs......87 N4
Beeson Devon......7 L10
Beeston C Beds......61 Q11
Beeston Ches W......69 P3
Beeston Leeds......90 H4
Beeston Norfk......76 C8
Beeston Notts......72 E3
Beeston Regis Norfk......76 H3
Beeswing D & G......109 J7
Beetham Cumb......95 K5

Beetham Somset......10 F2
Beetley Norfk......76 D8
Began Cardif......30 H8
Begbroke Oxon......34 E2
Begdale Cambs......75 J9
Begelly Pembks......41 M9
Beggarington Hill Leeds......90 H6
Beggar's Bush Powys......45 K2
Beguildy Powys......56 B9
Beighton Norfk......77 M10
Beighton Sheff......84 F4
Beinn Na Faoghla W Isls......168 d12
Beith N Ayrs......125 K7
Bekesbourne Kent......39 L10
Bekesbourne Hill Kent......39 L10
Belaugh Norfk......77 K8
Belbroughton Worcs......58 D9
Belchalwell Dorset......12 C3
Belchalwell Street Dorset......12 C3
Belchamp Otten Essex......52 C3
Belchamp St Paul Essex......52 C3
Belchamp Walter Essex......52 D3
Belchford Lincs......87 J5
Belford Nthumb......119 M4
Belgrave C Leic......72 F9
Belhaven E Loth......128 H4
Belhelvie Abers......151 N4
Belhinnie Abers......150 D2
Bellabeg Abers......150 B5
Bellamore Herefs......45 M6
Bellanoch Ag & B......130 F9
Bellasize E R Yk......92 D5
Bellaty Angus......142 C6
Bell Bar Herts......50 G9
Bell Busk N York......96 D9
Belleau Lincs......87 M5
Bell End Worcs......58 D9
Bellerby N York......96 H2
Bellever Devon......8 G9
Belle Vue Cumb......110 G9
Belle Vue Wakefd......91 J7
Bellfield S Lans......126 E11
Bellfields Surrey......23 Q4
Bell Heath Worcs......58 D9
Bell Hill Hants......23 K10
Bellingdon Bucks......35 P3
Bellingham Nthumb......112 B4
Belloch Ag & B......120 C4
Bellochantuy Ag & B......120 C5
Bell o' th' Hill Ches W......69 P5
Bellows Cross Dorset......13 J2
Bells Cross Suffk......64 H11
Bellshill N Lans......126 C5
Bellshill Nthumb......119 M4
Bellside N Lans......126 E6
Bellsquarry W Loth......127 K4
Bells Yew Green E Susx......25 P3
Belluton BaNES......20 B2
Belmaduthy Highld......156 A6
Belmesthorpe Rutlnd......73 Q8
Belmont Bl w D......89 K7
Belmont Gt Lon......36 G8
Belmont S Ayrs......114 F4
Belmont Shet......169 s3
Belnacraig Abers......150 B4
Belowda Cnwll......4 F9
Belper Derbys......84 D11
Belper Lane End Derbys......84 D11
Belph Derbys......84 H5
Belsay Nthumb......112 G5
Belses Border......117 R5
Belsize Herts......50 B10
Belstead Suffk......53 K3
Belstone Devon......8 F6
Belthorn Bl w D......89 L6
Beltinge Kent......39 L8
Beltingham Nthumb......111 Q8
Beltoft N Linc......92 D9
Belton Leics......72 C6
Belton Lincs......73 N3
Belton N Linc......92 C9
Belton Norfk......77 P11
Belton House Lincs......73 N3
Belton in Rutland Rutlnd......73 L10
Beltring Kent......37 Q11
Belvedere Gt Lon......37 L5
Belvoir Leics......73 L4
Bembridge IoW......14 H9
Bemerton Wilts......21 M8
Bempton E R Yk......99 P6
Benacre Suffk......65 Q5
Benbecula W Isls......168 d12
Benbecula Airport W Isls......168 c12
Benbuie D & G......115 P8
Benderloch Ag & B......138 G10
Benenden Kent......26 D5
Benfieldside Dur......112 G10
Benfleet Essex......38 C4
Bengate Norfk......77 L6
Bengeo Herts......50 H8
Bengeworth Worcs......47 K6
Benhall Green Suffk......65 M9
Benhall Street Suffk......65 M9
Benholm Abers......143 Q4
Beningbrough N York......98 A9
Benington Herts......50 G6
Benington Lincs......87 L11
Benington Sea End Lincs......87 M11
Benllech IoA......79 J8
Benmore Ag & B......131 N10
Bennacott Cnwll......5 M3
Bennan N Ayrs......121 J7
Bennet Head Cumb......101 M6
Bennetland E R Yk......92 D5
Bennett End Bucks......35 L5
Ben Nevis Highld......139 M3
Benniworth Lincs......86 H4
Benover Kent......26 B2
Ben Rhydding C Brad......96 H11
Benslie N Ayrs......125 J9
Benson Oxon......34 H6
Bentfield Green Essex......51 M5
Benthall Shrops......57 M4
Bentham Gloucs......46 H11
Benthoul C Aber......151 L7
Bentlawnt Shrops......56 E4
Bentley Donc......91 P9
Bentley E R Yk......92 H3
Bentley Hants......23 L6
Bentley Suffk......53 K4
Bentley Warwks......59 L6
Bentley Heath Herts......50 G11
Bentley Heath Solhll......59 J9
Benton Devon......17 M4
Bentpath D & G......110 F2

Bentwichen Devon......17 N5
Bentworth Hants......23 J6
Benvie Angus......142 E11
Benville Dorset......11 L4
Benwick Cambs......62 D2
Beoley Worcs......58 G11
Beoraidbeg Highld......145 L9
Bepton W Susx......23 N11
Berden Essex......51 L5
Berea Pembks......40 E4
Bere Alston Devon......6 C5
Bere Ferrers Devon......6 D6
Berepper Cnwll......2 H9
Bere Regis Dorset......12 D6
Bergh Apton Norfk......77 L11
Berhill Somset......19 M7
Berinsfield Oxon......34 G5
Berkeley Gloucs......32 C5
Berkeley Heath Gloucs......32 C5
Berkeley Road Gloucs......32 D4
Berkhamsted Herts......35 Q3
Berkley Somset......20 F5
Berkswell Solhll......59 K9
Bermondsey Gt Lon......36 H5
Bermuda Warwks......59 N7
Bernera Highld......145 P3
Bernisdale Highld......152 G7
Berrick Prior Oxon......34 H6
Berrick Salome Oxon......34 H6
Berriedale Highld......163 Q2
Berrier Cumb......101 L5
Berriew Powys......56 B4
Berrington Nthumb......119 K2
Berrington Shrops......57 J3
Berrington Worcs......57 K11
Berrington Green Worcs......57 K11
Berrow Somset......19 J4
Berrow Worcs......46 E8
Berrow Green Worcs......46 D3
Berry Brow Kirk......90 E8
Berry Cross Devon......16 H9
Berry Down Cross Devon......17 K3
Berryfield Wilts......20 H2
Berryfields Bucks......49 L11
Berry Hill Gloucs......31 Q2
Berry Hill Pembks......41 L2
Berryhillock Moray......158 C5
Berryhillock Moray......158 D7
Berrynarbor Devon......17 K2
Berry Pomeroy Devon......7 L6
Berry's Green Gt Lon......37 K9
Bersham Wrexhm......69 K5
Bersted W Susx......15 P6
Bertha Park P & K......134 D2
Berthengam Flints......80 G9
Berwick E Susx......25 M9
Berwick Bassett Wilts......33 L10
Berwick Hill Nthumb......113 J5
Berwick St James Wilts......21 L7
Berwick St John Wilts......20 H10
Berwick St Leonard Wilts......20 H8
Berwick Station E Susx......25 M9
Berwick-upon-Tweed Nthumb......129 P9
Bescaby Leics......73 L5
Bescar Lancs......88 D8
Besford Shrops......69 Q9
Besford Worcs......46 H6
Bessacarr Donc......91 Q10
Bessels Leigh Oxon......34 E4
Besses o' th' Barn Bury......89 N9
Bessingby E R Yk......99 P7
Bessingham Norfk......76 H4
Bestbeech Hill E Susx......25 P4
Besthorpe Norfk......64 F2
Besthorpe Notts......85 P8
Bestwood Village Notts......85 J11
Beswick E R Yk......99 L11
Betchcott Shrops......56 G5
Betchworth Surrey......36 F10
Bethania Cerdgn......43 L2
Bethania Gwynd......67 N6
Bethel Gwynd......68 C7
Bethel Gwynd......79 J11
Bethel IoA......78 F10
Bethel Powys......68 F10
Bethersden Kent......26 F3
Bethesda Gwynd......79 L11
Bethesda Gwynd......79 L11
Bethesda Pembks......41 L7
Bethlehem Carmth......43 N9
Bethnal Green Gt Lon......36 H4
Betley Staffs......70 D5
Betsham Kent......37 P6
Betteshanger Kent......39 P11
Bettiscombe Dorset......10 H4
Bettisfield Wrexhm......69 N7
Betton Shrops......70 B7
Betton Strange Shrops......57 J3
Bettws Brdgnd......29 P7
Bettws Newpt......31 J6
Bettws Cedewain Powys......55 Q5
Bettws Ifan Cerdgn......42 F5
Bettws-Newydd Mons......31 L3
Bettyhill Highld......166 H4
Betws Carmth......28 H2
Betws Bledrws Cerdgn......43 L4
Betws Garmon Gwynd......67 J3
Betws Gwerfil Goch Denbgs......68 D5
Betws-y-Coed Conwy......67 P3
Betws-yn-Rhos Conwy......80 C10
Beulah Cerdgn......42 E5
Beulah Powys......44 C4
Bevendean Br & H......24 H9
Bevercotes Notts......85 L6
Beverley E R Yk......92 H3
Beverston Gloucs......32 G6
Bevington Gloucs......32 C5
Bewaldeth Cumb......100 H4
Bewcastle Cumb......111 L6
Bewdley Worcs......57 P9
Bewerley N York......97 J7
Bewholme E R Yk......99 P11
Bewlbridge Kent......26 B4
Bexhill-on-Sea E Susx......26 B10
Bexley Gt Lon......37 L6
Bexleyheath Gt Lon......37 L5
Bexleyhill W Susx......23 P9
Bexon Kent......38 E10
Bexwell Norfk......75 M10
Beyton Suffk......64 C9
Beyton Green Suffk......64 C9
Bhaltos W Isls......168 f4
Bhatarsaigh W Isls......168 b18
Bibstone S Glos......32 C6
Bibury Gloucs......33 M3

Bicester Oxon......48 G10
Bickenhill Solhll......59 J8
Bicker Lincs......74 D3
Bicker Bar Lincs......74 D3
Bicker Gauntlet Lincs......74 D3
Bickershaw Wigan......82 D4
Bickerstaffe Lancs......81 N4
Bickerton Ches E......69 P4
Bickerton Devon......7 L11
Bickerton N York......97 Q10
Bickerton Nthumb......119 J10
Bickford Staffs......58 C2
Bickington Devon......7 L4
Bickington Devon......17 J5
Bickleigh Devon......6 E6
Bickleigh Devon......9 M3
Bickleton Devon......17 J5
Bickley Ches W......69 P5
Bickley Gt Lon......37 K7
Bickley N York......99 J2
Bickley Worcs......57 L10
Bickley Moss Ches W......69 P5
Bicknacre Essex......52 C11
Bicknoller Somset......18 F7
Bicknor Kent......38 E10
Bickton Hants......13 K2
Bicton Herefs......45 P3
Bicton Shrops......56 D8
Bicton Shrops......69 M11
Bidborough Kent......25 N2
Bidden Hants......23 K5
Biddenden Kent......26 E4
Biddenden Green Kent......26 E3
Biddenham Bed......61 M10
Biddestone Wilts......32 G10
Biddisham Somset......19 L4
Biddlesden Bucks......48 H7
Biddlestone Nthumb......119 J9
Biddulph Staffs......70 F3
Biddulph Moor Staffs......70 G3
Bideford Devon......16 H6
Bidford-on-Avon Warwks......47 M4
Bidston Wirral......81 K6
Bielby E R Yk......92 C2
Bieldside C Aber......151 M7
Bierley IoW......14 F11
Bierley Nthumb......49 M11
Bierton Bucks......49 M11
Big Balcraig D & G......107 J8
Bigbury Devon......6 H9
Bigbury-on-Sea Devon......6 H10
Bigby Lincs......93 J9
Biggar Cumb......94 D3
Biggar S Lans......116 E3
Biggin Derbys......71 M3
Biggin Derbys......71 P5
Biggin N York......91 N4
Biggin Hill Gt Lon......37 K9
Biggleswade C Beds......50 E2
Bigholms D & G......110 F4
Bighouse Highld......166 E4
Bighton Hants......22 H8
Biglands Cumb......110 E10
Bignall End Staffs......70 E4
Bignor W Susx......15 Q4
Bigrigg Cumb......100 D8
Big Sand Highld......160 B11
Bigton Shet......169 q11
Bilborough C Nott......72 E2
Bilbrook Somset......18 D6
Bilbrook Staffs......58 C4
Bilbrough N York......98 A11
Bilbster Highld......167 N6
Bildershaw Dur......103 P6
Bildeston Suffk......52 G2
Billacott Cnwll......5 M3
Billericay Essex......37 Q2
Billesdon Leics......73 J10
Billesley Warwks......47 M3
Billingborough Lincs......74 B3
Billinge St Hel......82 B4
Billingford Norfk......64 H6
Billingford Norfk......76 F7
Billingham S on T......104 E6
Billinghay Lincs......86 G10
Billingley Barns......91 L10
Billingshurst W Susx......24 C5
Billingsley Shrops......57 N8
Billington C Beds......49 P10
Billington Lancs......89 L3
Billington Staffs......70 F10
Billockby Norfk......77 N9
Billy Row Dur......103 N3
Bilsborrow Lancs......88 G3
Bilsby Lincs......87 N5
Bilsham W Susx......15 Q6
Bilsington Kent......26 H5
Bilson Green Gloucs......32 C2
Bilsthorpe Notts......85 K8
Bilsthorpe Moor Notts......85 L8
Bilston Mdloth......127 P5
Bilston Wolves......58 E5
Bilstone Leics......72 B9
Bilting Kent......27 J2
Bilton E R Yk......93 L4
Bilton N York......97 M9
Bilton Nthumb......119 P8
Bilton Warwks......59 Q10
Bilton Banks Nthumb......119 P8
Bilton-in-Ainsty N York......97 Q11
Binbrook Lincs......86 H2
Binchester Blocks Dur......103 P4
Bincombe Dorset......11 P8
Binegar Somset......20 B5
Bines Green W Susx......24 E7
Binfield Br For......35 M10
Binfield Heath Oxon......35 K9
Bingfield Nthumb......112 E6
Bingham Notts......73 J3
Bingham's Melcombe Dorset......12 C4
Bingley C Brad......90 E3
Bings Heath Shrops......69 P11
Binham Norfk......76 D4
Binley Covtry......59 N9
Binley Hants......22 D4
Binley Woods Warwks......59 N9
Binnegar Dorset......12 F7
Binniehill Falk......126 F3
Binscombe Surrey......23 Q6
Binsey Oxon......34 E3
Binstead IoW......14 G8
Binsted Hants......23 L6
Binsted W Susx......15 Q5
Binton Warwks......47 M4
Bintree Norfk......76 E7
Binweston Shrops......56 E4
Birch Essex......52 F8

Birch Rochdl......89 P9
Birchall Staffs......70 H4
Bircham Newton Norfk......75 Q4
Bircham Tofts Norfk......75 Q4
Birchanger Essex......51 M6
Birchanger Green Services Essex......51 M6
Birch Cross Staffs......71 L8
Birchencliffe Kirk......90 E7
Bircher Herefs......56 H11
Birchett's Green E Susx......25 Q4
Birchfield Birm......58 G6
Birch Green Essex......52 F8
Birch Green Herts......50 G8
Birch Green Worcs......46 G5
Birchgrove Cardif......30 G9
Birchgrove Swans......29 K5
Birchgrove W Susx......25 K5
Birch Heath Ches W......69 P2
Birch Hill Ches W......81 Q10
Birchington Kent......39 P8
Birchington-on-Sea Kent......39 N8
Birchley Heath Warwks......59 L6
Birchmoor Warwks......59 L4
Birchmoor Green C Beds......49 Q8
Birchover Derbys......84 B8
Birch Services Rochdl......89 N9
Birch Vale Derbys......83 M7
Birch Wood Lincs......86 B7
Birch Wood Somset......10 E2
Birchwood Warrtn......82 E6
Bircotes Notts......85 K2
Birdbrook Essex......52 B3
Birdforth N York......97 Q5
Birdham W Susx......15 M6
Birdingbury Warwks......59 P11
Birdlip Gloucs......32 H2
Birdoswald Cumb......111 M7
Birdsall N York......98 G7
Birds Edge Kirk......90 G9
Birds Green Essex......51 N9
Birdsgreen Shrops......57 P7
Birdsmoorgate Dorset......10 H4
Bird Street Suffk......64 E11
Birdwell Barns......91 J10
Birdwood Gloucs......46 D11
Birgham Border......118 E3
Birichin Highld......162 H8
Birkacre Lancs......88 H8
Birkby N York......104 B10
Birkdale Sefton......88 C8
Birkenbog Abers......158 D4
Birkenhead Wirral......81 L7
Birkenhead (Queensway) Tunnel Lpool......81 L7
Birkenhills Abers......158 H8
Birkenshaw Kirk......90 G5
Birkhall Abers......149 Q9
Birkhill Angus......142 F11
Birkhill D & G......117 J7
Birkholme Lincs......73 P6
Birkin N York......91 N5
Birks Leeds......90 H5
Birkshaw Nthumb......111 Q7
Birley Herefs......45 P4
Birley Carr Sheff......84 D2
Birling Kent......37 Q8
Birling Nthumb......119 P9
Birling Gap E Susx......25 N11
Birlingham Worcs......46 H6
Birmingham Birm......58 G7
Birmingham Airport Solhll......59 J8
Birnam P & K......141 P9
Birness Abers......159 N11
Birse Abers......150 F8
Birsemore Abers......150 E8
Birstall Kirk......90 G5
Birstall Leics......72 F9
Birstwith N York......97 K9
Birthorpe Lincs......74 B4
Birtley Gatesd......113 L9
Birtley Herefs......56 F11
Birtley Nthumb......112 C5
Birts Street Worcs......46 E7
Bisbrooke Rutlnd......73 M11
Biscathorpe Lincs......86 H4
Biscovey Cnwll......3 R3
Bisham W & M......35 M7
Bishampton Worcs......47 J4
Bish Mill Devon......17 N6
Bishop Auckland Dur......103 P5
Bishopbridge Lincs......86 D2
Bishopbriggs E Duns......125 Q3
Bishop Burton E R Yk......92 G3
Bishop Middleham Dur......104 B4
Bishopmill Moray......157 N5
Bishop Monkton N York......97 M7
Bishop Norton Lincs......86 C2
Bishopsbourne Kent......39 L11
Bishops Cannings Wilts......21 K2
Bishop's Castle Shrops......56 E7
Bishop's Caundle Dorset......11 P2
Bishop's Cleeve Gloucs......47 J9
Bishop's Frome Herefs......46 C5
Bishops Gate Surrey......35 Q10
Bishop's Green Essex......51 P7
Bishop's Green Hants......22 F2
Bishop's Hull Somset......18 H10
Bishop's Itchington Warwks......48 C3
Bishops Lydeard Somset......18 G9
Bishop's Norton Gloucs......46 F10
Bishop's Nympton Devon......17 P7
Bishop's Offley Staffs......70 D9
Bishop's Stortford Herts......51 L6
Bishop's Sutton Hants......22 H8
Bishop's Tachbrook Warwks......48 B2
Bishop's Tawton Devon......17 K6
Bishopsteignton Devon......7 N4
Bishopstoke Hants......22 E11
Bishopston Swans......28 G7
Bishopstone Bucks......35 M2
Bishopstone E Susx......25 L10
Bishopstone Herefs......45 N6
Bishopstone Kent......39 M8
Bishopstone Swindn......33 P8
Bishopstone Wilts......21 L9
Bishopstrow Wilts......20 G7
Bishop Sutton BaNES......19 Q3
Bishopswood Somset......10 F2
Bishop's Wood Staffs......58 B3
Bishopsworth Bristl......31 Q11
Bishop Thornton N York......97 L8
Bishopthorpe C York......98 B11
Bishopton Darltn......104 C6
Bishopton Rens......125 L3

Bishopton – Bowscale 259

Bishopton Warwks 47 N3
Bishop Wilton E R Yk 98 F9
Bishton Newpt 31 L7
Bishton Staffs 71 J10
Bisley Gloucs 32 H3
Bisley Surrey 23 Q3
Bisley Camp Surrey 23 P3
Bispham Bpool 88 C2
Bispham Green Lancs 88 F8
Bissoe Cnwll 3 K5
Bisterne Hants 13 K4
Bitchet Green Kent 37 N10
Bitchfield Lincs 73 P5
Bittadon Devon 17 J3
Bittaford Devon 6 H7
Bittering Norfk 76 C8
Bitterley Shrops 57 K9
Bitterne C Sotn 14 E4
Bitteswell Leics 60 B3
Bitton S Glos 32 C11
Bix Oxon 35 K8
Bixter Shet 169 q8
Blaby Leics 72 F11
Blackadder Border 129 L9
Blackawton Devon 7 L8
Blackbeck Cumb 100 D9
Blackborough Devon 10 B3
Blackborough End Norfk 75 N7
Black Bourton Oxon 33 Q4
Blackboys E Susx 25 M6
Blackbrook Derbys 84 D11
Blackbrook St Hel 82 B5
Blackbrook Staffs 70 D7
Blackbrook Surrey 36 E11
Blackburn Abers 151 L5
Blackburn Bl w D 89 K5
Blackburn Rothm 84 E2
Blackburn W Loth 126 H4
Blackburn with Darwen Services Bl w D 89 K6
Black Callerton N u Ty 113 J7
Black Carr Norfk 64 F2
Black Corner W Susx 24 G3
Blackcraig E Ayrs 115 M6
Black Crofts Ag & B 138 G11
Black Cross Cnwll 4 E9
Blackden Heath Ches E 82 G10
Blackdog Abers 151 P5
Black Dog Devon 9 K3
Blackdown Devon 8 D9
Blackdown Dorset 10 H4
Blackdyke Cumb 109 P10
Blacker Barns 91 J9
Blacker Hill Barns 91 K10
Blackfen Gt Lon 37 L6
Blackfield Hants 14 D6
Blackford Cumb 110 G8
Blackford P & K 133 P6
Blackford Somset 19 M5
Blackford Somset 20 C9
Blackfordby Leics 72 A7
Blackgang IoW 14 E11
Blackhall C Edin 127 N3
Blackhall Colliery Dur 104 E3
Blackhall Mill Gatesd 112 H9
Blackhall Rocks Dur 104 E3
Blackham E Susx 25 L2
Blackhaugh Border 117 N3
Blackheath Essex 52 H7
Blackheath Gt Lon 37 J5
Blackheath Sandw 58 E7
Blackheath Suffk 65 N7
Blackheath Surrey 36 B11
Black Heddon Nthumb 112 G5
Blackhill Abers 159 Q6
Blackhill Abers 159 Q9
Blackhill Dur 112 G10
Blackhill of Clackriach Abers 159 M8
Blackjack Lincs 74 E3
Blackland Wilts 33 K11
Black Lane Ends Lancs 89 Q2
Blacklaw D & G 116 E9
Blackley Manch 83 J4
Blacklunans P & K 142 A5
Blackmarstone Herefs 45 Q7
Blackmill Brdgnd 29 P7
Blackmoor Hants 23 L8
Black Moor Leeds 90 H3
Blackmoor N Som 19 N2
Blackmoorfoot Kirk 90 D8
Blackmoor Gate Devon 17 L3
Blackmore Essex 51 P10
Blackmore End Essex 52 B5
Blackmore End Herts 50 E7
Black Mountains 45 K9
Blackness Falk 127 K2
Blacknest Hants 23 L6
Blacknest W & M 35 Q11
Black Notley Essex 52 C7
Blacko Lancs 89 P2
Black Pill Swans 28 H6
Blackpool Bpool 88 C3
Blackpool Devon 7 L4
Blackpool Devon 7 M9
Blackpool Gate Cumb 111 K5
Blackpool Zoo Bpool 88 C3
Blackridge W Loth 126 F4
Blackrock Cnwll 2 H7
Blackrock Mons 30 H2
Blackrod Bolton 89 J8
Blacksboat Moray 157 M10
Blackshaw D & G 109 M7
Blackshaw Head Calder 90 B5
Blacksmith's Green Suffk 64 G8
Blacksnape Bl w D 89 L6
Blackstone W Susx 24 F7
Black Street Suffk 65 Q4
Black Tar Pembks 41 J9
Blackthorn Oxon 48 H11
Blackthorpe Suffk 64 C9
Blacktoft E R Yk 92 D6
Blacktop C Aber 151 M7
Black Torrington Devon 8 C3
Blackwall Derbys 71 P5
Blackwall Tunnel Gt Lon 37 J4
Blackwater Cnwll 3 J4
Blackwater Hants 23 M3
Blackwater IoW 14 F9
Blackwater Somset 19 J11
Blackwaterfoot N Ayrs 120 H6
Blackwell Cumb 110 H10
Blackwell Darltn 103 Q8
Blackwell Derbys 83 P10
Blackwell Derbys 84 F9
Blackwell Warwks 47 P6
Blackwell Worcs 58 E10
Blackwellsend Green Gloucs 46 E9
Blackwood Caerph 30 G5
Blackwood D & G 109 K3
Blackwood S Lans 126 D9
Blackwood Hill Staffs 70 G3
Blacon Ches W 81 M11
Bladbean Kent 27 L2
Bladnoch D & G 107 M7
Bladon Oxon 34 E2
Bladon Somset 19 M10
Blaenannerch Cerdgn 42 D5
Blaenau Ffestiniog Gwynd 67 N5
Blaenau Ffestiniog Gwynd 67 N5
Blaenavon Torfn 31 J3
Blaenavon Industrial Landscape Torfn 30 H3
Blaencwm Rhondd 29 P5
Blaen Dyryn Powys 44 C7
Blaenffos Pembks 41 N3
Blaengarw Brdgnd 29 P6
Blaengeuffordd Cerdgn 54 E8
Blaengwrach Neath 29 N3
Blaengwynfi Neath 29 N5
Blaenllechau Rhondd 30 D5
Blaenpennal Cerdgn 43 M2
Blaenplwyf Cerdgn 54 D9
Blaenporth Cerdgn 42 E5
Blaenrhondda Rhondd 29 P5
Blaenwaun Carmth 41 P5
Blaen-y-coed Carmth 42 F9
Blaen-y-cwm Blae G 30 F2
Blaenycwm Cerdgn 55 J9
Blagdon N Som 19 P3
Blagdon Somset 18 H11
Blagdon Torbay 7 M6
Blagdon Hill Somset 18 H11
Blagill Cumb 111 P11
Blaguegate Lancs 88 F9
Blaich Highld 139 J2
Blain Highld 138 B4
Blaina Blae G 30 H3
Blair Atholl P & K 141 L4
Blair Drummond Stirlg 133 L8
Blairgowrie P & K 142 B8
Blairhall Fife 134 C10
Blairingone P & K 134 B8
Blairlogie Stirlg 133 N8
Blairmore Ag & B 131 P11
Blairmore Highld 164 E5
Blair's Ferry Ag & B 124 B4
Blaisdon Gloucs 46 D11
Blakebrook Worcs 57 Q9
Blakedown Worcs 58 C9
Blake End Essex 52 B7
Blakeley Lane Staffs 70 H5
Blakemere Ches W 82 C10
Blakemere Herefs 45 M6
Blakemore Devon 7 K6
Blakenall Heath Wsall 58 F4
Blakeney Gloucs 32 C3
Blakeney Norfk 76 E3
Blakenhall Ches E 70 C5
Blakenhall Wolves 58 D5
Blakeshall Worcs 58 B8
Blakesley Nhants 48 H4
Blanchland Nthumb 112 E10
Blandford Camp Dorset 12 F3
Blandford Forum Dorset 12 E3
Blandford St Mary Dorset 12 E3
Bland Hill N York 97 K10
Blanefield Stirlg 125 N2
Blankney Lincs 86 E8
Blantyre S Lans 126 B6
Blàr a' Chaorainn Highld 139 L4
Blarghour Ag & B 131 K5
Blargie Highld 147 Q9
Blarmachfoldach Highld 139 K4
Blashford Hants 13 L3
Blaston Leics 73 L11
Blatherwycke Nhants 73 P11
Blawith Cumb 94 F3
Blawquhairn D & G 108 D4
Blaxhall Suffk 65 M10
Blaxton Donc 91 R10
Blaydon Gatesd 113 J8
Bleadney Somset 19 N5
Bleadon N Som 19 K3
Bleak Street Somset 20 E8
Blean Kent 39 K9
Bleasby Lincs 86 F4
Bleasby Notts 85 M11
Bleasdale Lancs 95 M11
Bleatarn Cumb 102 D8
Bleathwood Herefs 57 K10
Blebocraigs Fife 135 L4
Bleddfa Powys 56 C11
Bledington Gloucs 47 P10
Bledlow Bucks 35 L4
Bledlow Ridge Bucks 35 L5
Bleet Wilts 20 G3
Blegbie E Loth 128 D7
Blencarn Cumb 102 B4
Blencogo Cumb 110 C11
Blendworth Hants 15 K4
Blenheim Palace Oxon 48 D11
Blennerhasset Cumb 100 G2
Bletchingdon Oxon 48 F11
Bletchingley Surrey 36 H10
Bletchley M Keyn 49 N8
Bletchley Shrops 69 R8
Bletchley Park Museum M Keyn 49 N8
Bletherston Pembks 41 L6
Bletsoe Bed 61 M9
Blewbury Oxon 34 F7
Blickling Norfk 76 H6
Blidworth Notts 85 J9
Blidworth Bottoms Notts 85 J10
Blindburn Nthumb 118 F8
Blindcrake Cumb 100 F4
Blindley Heath Surrey 37 J11
Blindwells E Loth 128 C5
Blisland Cnwll 5 J7
Blissford Hants 13 L2
Bliss Gate Worcs 57 N10
Blisworth Nhants 49 K4
Blithbury Staffs 71 K11
Blitterlees Cumb 109 P10
Blockley Gloucs 47 N7
Blofield Norfk 77 L10
Blofield Heath Norfk 77 L9
Blo Norton Norfk 64 E6
Bloomfield Border 118 A6
Blore Staffs 70 C8
Blore Staffs 71 L5
Blounce Hants 23 K5
Blounts Green Staffs 71 K8
Blowick Sefton 88 D7
Bloxham Oxon 48 D7
Bloxholm Lincs 86 E10
Bloxwich Wsall 58 E4
Bloxworth Dorset 12 E6
Blubberhouses N York 97 J9
Blue Anchor Cnwll 4 E10
Blue Anchor Somset 18 D6
Blue Bell Hill Kent 38 B9
Blue John Cavern Derbys 83 P8
Blundellsands Sefton 81 L5
Blundeston Suffk 65 Q2
Blunham C Beds 61 Q10
Blunsdon St Andrew Swindn 33 M7
Bluntington Worcs 58 D10
Bluntisham Cambs 62 E6
Blunts Cnwll 5 N9
Blunts Green Warwks 58 H11
Blurton C Stke 70 F6
Blyborough Lincs 86 B2
Blyford Suffk 65 N6
Blymhill Staffs 57 Q2
Blymhill Lawn Staffs 57 Q2
Blyth Notts 85 K3
Blyth Nthumb 113 M4
Blyth Bridge Border 127 L8
Blythburgh Suffk 65 N6
Blythe Border 128 F10
Blythe Bridge Staffs 70 H6
Blythe End Warwks 59 K6
Blythe Marsh Staffs 70 H6
Blyth Services Notts 85 K3
Blyton Lincs 85 Q2
Boarhills Fife 135 P5
Boarhunt Hants 14 H5
Boarley Kent 38 C10
Boarsgreave Lancs 89 N6
Boarshead E Susx 25 M4
Boar's Head Wigan 88 H9
Boars Hill Oxon 34 E4
Boarstall Bucks 34 H2
Boasley Cross Devon 8 D6
Boath Highld 155 Q3
Boat of Garten Highld 148 G4
Bobbing Kent 38 E8
Bobbington Staffs 57 Q6
Bobbingworth Essex 51 M9
Bocaddon Cnwll 5 K10
Bocking Essex 52 C7
Bocking Churchstreet Essex 52 C6
Bockleton Worcs 46 A2
Boconnoc Cnwll 5 J9
Boddam Abers 159 R9
Boddam Shet 169 q12
Boddington Gloucs 46 G9
Bodedern IoA 78 E8
Bodelwyddan Denbgs 80 E9
Bodenham Herefs 45 Q4
Bodenham Wilts 21 N9
Bodenham Moor Herefs 45 Q4
Bodewryd IoA 78 G6
Bodfari Denbgs 80 F10
Bodffordd IoA 78 G9
Bodham Norfk 76 G3
Bodiam E Susx 26 C6
Bodicote Oxon 48 E7
Bodieve Cnwll 4 F7
Bodinnick Cnwll 5 J11
Bodle Street Green E Susx 25 Q8
Bodmin Cnwll 4 H8
Bodmin Moor Cnwll 5 K6
Bodney Norfk 64 A2
Bodorgan IoA 78 F11
Bodsham Kent 27 K2
Boduan Gwynd 66 E7
Bodwen Cnwll 4 G9
Bodymoor Heath Warwks 59 J5
Bogallan Highld 156 A7
Bogbrae Abers 159 P10
Bogend S Ayrs 125 L11
Boggs Holdings E Loth 128 C5
Boghall Mdloth 127 N4
Boghall W Loth 126 H4
Boghead S Lans 126 D9
Bogmoor Moray 157 R5
Bogmuir Abers 143 L3
Bogniebrae Abers 158 E8
Bognor Regis W Susx 15 P7
Bogroy Highld 148 G3
Bogue D & G 108 D4
Bohetherick Cnwll 5 Q8
Bohortha Cnwll 3 M7
Bohuntine Highld 146 H11
Bojewyan Cnwll 2 B7
Bokiddick Cnwll 4 H9
Bolam Dur 103 N6
Bolam Nthumb 112 H4
Bolberry Devon 6 H11
Bold Heath St Hel 82 B7
Boldmere Birm 58 H6
Boldon Colliery S Tyne 113 M8
Boldre Hants 13 P5
Boldron Dur 103 K8
Bole Notts 85 N3
Bolehill Derbys 84 C9
Bole Hill Derbys 84 D6
Bolenowe Cnwll 2 H6
Bolham Devon 18 C11
Bolham Water Devon 10 D2
Bolingey Cnwll 3 K3
Bollington Ches E 83 K9
Bollington Cross Ches E 83 K9
Bollow Gloucs 32 D2
Bolney W Susx 24 G6
Bolnhurst Bed 61 N9
Bolnore W Susx 24 H6
Bolshan Angus 143 L7
Bolsover Derbys 84 G6
Bolster Moor Kirk 90 D7
Bolsterstone Sheff 90 H11
Boltby N York 97 Q3
Bolter End Bucks 35 L6
Bolton Bolton 89 L9
Bolton Cumb 102 B6
Bolton E Loth 128 E6
Bolton E R Yk 98 F10
Bolton Nthumb 119 M8
Bolton Abbey N York 96 G10
Bolton Bridge N York 96 G10
Bolton-by-Bowland Lancs 96 A11
Boltonfellend Cumb 111 J7
Boltongate Cumb 100 H2
Bolton-le-Sands Lancs 95 K7
Bolton Low Houses Cumb 100 H2
Bolton New Houses Cumb 100 H2
Bolton-on-Swale N York 103 Q11
Bolton Percy N York 91 N2
Bolton Town End Lancs 95 K7
Bolton upon Dearne Barns 91 M10
Bolventor Cnwll 5 K6
Bomarsund Nthumb 113 L4
Bomere Heath Shrops 69 N11
Bonar Bridge Highld 162 E8
Bonawe Ag & B 139 J11
Bonby N Linc 92 H7
Boncath Pembks 41 P3
Bonchester Bridge Border 118 A8
Bonchurch IoW 14 G11
Bondleigh Devon 8 G4
Bonds Lancs 88 F2
Bonehill Devon 8 H9
Bonehill Staffs 59 J4
Bo'ness Falk 134 C11
Boney Hay Staffs 58 F2
Bonhill W Duns 125 K2
Boningale Shrops 57 Q4
Bonjedward Border 118 C6
Bonkle N Lans 126 E6
Bonnington Angus 143 K10
Bonnington Kent 27 J4
Bonnybank Fife 135 K7
Bonnybridge Falk 126 E2
Bonnykelly Abers 159 L7
Bonnyrigg Mdloth 127 Q4
Bonnyton Angus 142 E10
Bonsall Derbys 84 C9
Bonshaw Tower D & G 110 D6
Bont Mons 45 M11
Bontddu Gwynd 67 M11
Bont-Dolgadfan Powys 55 K4
Bont-goch Cerdgn 54 F7
Bonthorpe Lincs 87 N6
Bontnewydd Cerdgn 54 E11
Bontnewydd Gwynd 66 H3
Bontuchel Denbgs 68 E3
Bonvilston V Glam 30 E10
Bonwm Denbgs 68 F6
Bon-y-maen Swans 29 J5
Boode Devon 17 J4
Booker Bucks 35 M6
Booley Shrops 69 Q9
Boon Border 128 F10
Boon Hill Staffs 70 E4
Boorley Green Hants 14 F4
Boosbeck R & Cl 105 J7
Boose's Green Essex 52 D5
Boot Cumb 100 G10
Booth Calder 90 C5
Boothby Graffoe Lincs 86 C9
Boothby Pagnell Lincs 73 P4
Boothferry E R Yk 92 B5
Booth Green Ches E 83 K8
Boothstown Salfd 82 F4
Boothtown Calder 90 D5
Boothville Nhants 60 G8
Bootle Cumb 94 C3
Bootle Sefton 81 L5
Boots Green Ches W 82 G10
Boot Street Suffk 53 M2
Booze N York 103 K10
Boraston Shrops 57 L11
Bordeaux Guern 10 c1
Borden Kent 38 E9
Borden W Susx 23 M10
Border Cumb 110 C10
Bordesley Worcs 58 F11
Bordley N York 96 D7
Bordon Hants 23 L7
Boreham Essex 52 C10
Boreham Wilts 20 G6
Boreham Street E Susx 25 Q8
Borehamwood Herts 50 E11
Boreland D & G 110 C2
Boreraig Highld 152 B7
Boreton Shrops 57 J3
Borgh W Isls 168 b17
Borgh W Isls 168 j2
Borgie Highld 165 Q5
Borgue D & G 108 D11
Borgue Highld 167 K11
Borley Essex 52 D3
Borley Green Essex 52 D3
Borley Green Suffk 64 D9
Borneskitaig Highld 152 F3
Borness D & G 108 D11
Boroughbridge N York 97 N7
Borough Green Kent 37 P9
Borras Head Wrexhm 69 L4
Borrowash Derbys 72 C4
Borrowby N York 97 P3
Borrowby N York 105 L7
Borrowdale Cumb 101 J7
Borrowstoun Falk 134 B11
Borstal Medway 38 B8
Borth Cerdgn 54 E6
Borthwick Mdloth 128 B8
Borthwickbrae Border 117 N8
Borthwickshiels Border 117 N7
Borth-y-Gest Gwynd 67 K7
Borve Highld 152 G8
Borve W Isls 168 b17
Borve W Isls 168 f8
Borve W Isls 168 j2
Borwick Lancs 95 L6
Borwick Lodge Cumb 101 K11
Borwick Rails Cumb 94 D5
Bosavern Cnwll 2 B7
Bosbury Herefs 46 C6
Boscarne Cnwll 4 G8
Boscastle Cnwll 4 H3
Boscombe BCP 13 K6
Boscombe Wilts 21 P7
Boscoppa Cnwll 3 Q3
Bosham W Susx 15 M6
Bosham Hoe W Susx 15 M6
Bosherston Pembks 41 J12
Boskednan Cnwll 2 C7
Boskenna Cnwll 2 C9
Bosley Ches E 83 K11
Bosoughan Cnwll 4 D9
Bossall N York 98 E8
Bossiney Cnwll 4 H4
Bossingham Kent 27 L2
Bossington Somset 18 A5
Bostock Green Ches W 82 E11
Boston Lincs 74 F2
Boston Spa Leeds 97 P11
Boswarthan Cnwll 2 C7
Boswinger Cnwll 3 P5
Botallack Cnwll 2 B7
Botany Bay Gt Lon 50 G11
Botcheston Leics 72 D10
Botesdale Suffk 64 E6
Bothal Nthumb 113 K3
Bothampstead W Berk 34 F9
Bothamsall Notts 85 L6
Bothel Cumb 100 G3
Bothenhampton Dorset 11 K6
Bothwell S Lans 126 C6
Bothwell Services (southbound) S Lans 126 C6
Botley Bucks 35 Q4
Botley Hants 14 F4
Botley Oxon 34 E3
Botolph Claydon Bucks 49 K10
Botolphs W Susx 24 E9
Botolph's Bridge Kent 27 K5
Bottesford Leics 73 L3
Bottesford N Linc 92 E9
Bottisham Cambs 62 H8
Bottomcraig Fife 135 K3
Bottom of Hutton Lancs 88 F5
Bottom o' th' Moor Bolton 89 K8
Bottoms Calder 89 Q6
Bottoms Cnwll 2 B9
Botts Green Warwks 59 K6
Botusfleming Cnwll 5 Q9
Botwnnog Gwynd 66 D8
Bough Beech Kent 37 L11
Boughrood Powys 44 G7
Boughspring Gloucs 31 Q5
Boughton Nhants 60 G7
Boughton Norfk 75 P10
Boughton Notts 85 L7
Boughton Aluph Kent 26 H2
Boughton End C Beds 49 Q7
Boughton Green Kent 38 C11
Boughton Lees Kent 26 H2
Boughton Malherbe Kent 26 E2
Boughton Monchelsea Kent 38 C11
Boughton Street Kent 39 J10
Boulby R & Cl 105 L7
Boulder Clough Calder 90 C6
Bouldnor IoW 14 C9
Bouldon Shrops 57 J7
Boulmer Nthumb 119 Q8
Boulston Pembks 41 J8
Boultenstone Abers 150 C5
Boultham Lincs 86 C7
Boundary Staffs 70 H6
Bourn Cambs 62 D9
Bournbrook Birm 58 F8
Bourne Lincs 74 A6
Bournebridge Essex 37 M2
Bourne End Bed 61 M8
Bourne End Bucks 35 N7
Bourne End C Beds 49 Q6
Bourne End Herts 50 B9
Bournemouth BCP 13 J6
Bournemouth Airport BCP 13 K5
Bournes Green Gloucs 32 H4
Bournes Green Sthend 38 F4
Bournheath Worcs 58 E10
Bournmoor Dur 113 M10
Bournstream Gloucs 32 D6
Bournville Birm 58 F8
Bourton Dorset 20 E8
Bourton N Som 19 L2
Bourton Oxon 33 P7
Bourton Shrops 57 K5
Bourton Wilts 21 K2
Bourton on Dunsmore Warwks 59 P10
Bourton-on-the-Hill Gloucs 47 N8
Bourton-on-the-Water Gloucs 47 N10
Bousd Ag & B 136 H3
Boustead Hill Cumb 110 E9
Bouth Cumb 94 G3
Bouthwaite N York 96 H6
Bouts Worcs 47 K3
Boveney Bucks 35 P9
Boveridge Dorset 13 J2
Bovey Tracey Devon 9 K9
Bovingdon Herts 50 B10
Bovingdon Green Bucks 35 M7
Bovinger Essex 51 M9
Bovington Dorset 12 D7
Bovington Camp Dorset 12 D7
Bow Cumb 110 F9
Bow Devon 7 L7
Bow Devon 8 H4
Bow Gt Lon 37 J4
Bow Ork 169 c7
Bowbank Dur 102 H6
Bow Brickhill M Keyn 49 P8
Bowbridge Gloucs 32 G3
Bowburn Dur 104 B3
Bowcombe IoW 14 E9
Bowd Devon 10 C6
Bowden Border 117 R4
Bowden Devon 7 L9
Bowden Hill Wilts 32 H11
Bowdon Traffd 82 G7
Bower Highld 167 M4
Bowerchalke Wilts 21 K10
Bowerhill Wilts 20 H2
Bower Hinton Somset 19 N11
Bower House Tye Suffk 52 G3
Bowermadden Highld 167 M4
Bowers Staffs 70 E7
Bowers Gifford Essex 38 C4
Bowershall Fife 134 D9
Bower's Row Leeds 91 L5
Bowes Dur 103 J8
Bowgreave Lancs 88 F2
Bowhouse D & G 109 M7
Bowithick Cnwll 5 K5
Bowker's Green Lancs 81 N4
Bowland Border 117 P2
Bowland Bridge Cumb 95 J3
Bowley Herefs 45 Q4
Bowley Town Herefs 45 Q4
Bowlhead Green Surrey 23 P7
Bowling C Brad 90 F4
Bowling W Duns 125 L3
Bowling Bank Wrexhm 69 L5
Bowling Green Worcs 46 F4
Bowmanstead Cumb 101 K11
Bowmore Ag & B 122 D8
Bowness-on-Solway Cumb 110 D8
Bowness-on-Windermere Cumb 101 M11
Bow of Fife Fife 135 J5
Bowriefauld Angus 143 J8
Bowscale Cumb 101 L4

Bowsden Nthumb 119 J2
Bowston Cumb 101 N11
Bow Street Cerdgn 54 E7
Bow Street Norfk 64 E2
Bowthorpe Norfk 76 H10
Box Gloucs 32 G4
Box Wilts 32 F11
Boxbush Gloucs 32 D2
Boxbush Gloucs 46 C10
Box End Bed 61 M11
Boxford Suffk 52 G3
Boxford W Berk 34 D10
Boxgrove W Susx 15 P5
Box Hill Surrey 36 E10
Boxley Kent 38 C10
Boxmoor Herts 50 B9
Box's Shop Cnwll 16 C11
Boxted Essex 52 H5
Boxted Suffk 64 A11
Boxted Cross Essex 52 H5
Boxwell Gloucs 32 F6
Boxworth Cambs 62 D8
Boyden End Suffk 63 M9
Boyden Gate Kent 39 M8
Boylestone Derbys 71 M7
Boyndie Abers 158 F5
Boyndlie Abers 159 M5
Boynton E R Yk 99 N7
Boysack Angus 143 L8
Boys Hill Dorset 11 P2
Boythorpe Derbys 84 E7
Boyton Cnwll 5 N3
Boyton Suffk 53 Q2
Boyton Wilts 21 J7
Boyton Cross Essex 51 P9
Boyton End Suffk 52 B3
Bozeat Nhants 61 K9
Braaid IoM 80 d6
Brabling Green Suffk 65 K9
Brabourne Kent 27 K3
Brabourne Lees Kent 27 J3
Brabstermire Highld 167 P3
Bracadale Highld 152 F10
Braceborough Lincs 74 A8
Bracebridge Heath Lincs 86 C7
Bracebridge Low Fields Lincs 86 C7
Braceby Lincs 73 Q3
Bracewell Lancs 96 C11
Brackenfield Derbys 84 E9
Brackenhirst N Lans 126 C4
Brackenthwaite Cumb 110 E11
Brackenthwaite N York 97 L10
Brackla Brdgnd 29 P9
Bracklesham W Susx 15 M7
Brackletter Highld 146 F11
Brackley Nhants 48 G7
Brackley Hatch Nhants 48 H6
Bracknell Br For 35 N11
Braco P & K 133 N6
Bracobrae Moray 158 D7
Bracon Ash Norfk 64 H2
Bracora Highld 145 M9
Bracorina Highld 145 M9
Bradaford Devon 5 P3
Bradbourne Derbys 71 N4
Bradbury Dur 104 B5
Bradden Nhants 48 H5
Braddock Cnwll 5 K9
Bradeley C Stke 70 F4
Bradenham Bucks 35 M5
Bradenstoke Wilts 33 K9
Bradfield Devon 9 Q3
Bradfield Essex 53 K5
Bradfield Norfk 77 K5
Bradfield Sheff 84 C2
Bradfield W Berk 34 H10
Bradfield Combust Suffk 64 B10
Bradfield Green Ches E 70 B3
Bradfield Heath Essex 53 K5
Bradfield St Clare Suffk 64 C10
Bradfield St George Suffk 64 C10
Bradfield Southend W Berk 34 G10
Bradford C Brad 90 F4
Bradford Cnwll 5 J6
Bradford Devon 16 G10
Bradford Nthumb 112 H3
Bradford Nthumb 119 N4
Bradford Abbas Dorset 11 M2
Bradford Leigh Wilts 20 F2
Bradford-on-Avon Wilts 20 F2
Bradford-on-Tone Somset 18 G10
Bradford Peverell Dorset 11 P6
Bradiford Devon 17 K5
Brading IoW 14 H9
Bradley Ches W 69 P5
Bradley Derbys 71 N5
Bradley Hants 22 H6
Bradley Kirk 90 F6
Bradley N York 96 F4
Bradley NE Lin 93 M9
Bradley Staffs 70 F11
Bradley Wolves 58 E5
Bradley Worcs 47 J2
Bradley Wrexhm 69 K4
Bradley Green Somset 19 J7
Bradley Green Warwks 59 L4
Bradley Green Worcs 47 J2
Bradley in the Moors Staffs 71 K6
Bradley Stoke S Glos 32 B8
Bradmore Notts 72 F4
Bradney Somset 19 K7
Bradninch Devon 9 N4
Bradninch Devon 17 L5
Bradnop Staffs 71 J3
Bradnor Green Herefs 45 K3
Bradpole Dorset 11 K6
Bradshaw Bolton 89 L8
Bradshaw Calder 90 D5
Bradshaw Kirk 90 D8
Bradstone Devon 5 P5
Bradwall Green Ches E 70 D2
Bradwell Derbys 83 Q8
Bradwell Devon 17 J3
Bradwell Essex 52 D7
Bradwell M Keyn 49 M6
Bradwell Norfk 77 Q11
Bradwell-on-Sea Essex 52 H10
Bradwell Waterside Essex 52 G10
Bradworthy Devon 16 E9
Brae Highld 156 B5
Brae Shet 169 q7
Braeface Falk 133 M11
Braehead Angus 143 M7
Braehead D & G 107 J7
Braehead S Lans 126 H7

Braeintra Highld 153 R11
Braemar Abers 149 M9
Braemore Highld 161 K11
Braemore Highld 167 J11
Brae Roy Lodge Highld 147 J9
Braeside Inver 124 G3
Braes of Coul Angus 142 D6
Braes of Enzie Moray 158 A6
Braes of Ullapool Highld 161 J8
Braeswick Ork 169 f3
Braevallich Ag & B 131 K6
Braewick Shet 169 p6
Brafferton Darltn 103 Q6
Brafferton N York 97 P6
Brafield-on-the-Green Nhants 60 H9
Bragar W Isls 168 h3
Bragbury End Herts 50 G6
Braidwood S Lans 126 E8
Brailsford Derbys 71 P6
Brailsford Green Derbys 71 P6
Brain's Green Gloucs 32 C3
Braintree Essex 52 C7
Braiseworth Suffk 64 G7
Braishfield Hants 22 C9
Braiswick Essex 52 G6
Braithwaite C Brad 90 C2
Braithwaite Cumb 100 H6
Braithwell Donc 84 H2
Braken Hill Wakefd 91 L7
Bramber W Susx 24 E8
Brambridge Hants 22 E10
Bramcote Notts 72 E3
Bramcote Warwks 59 P7
Bramdean Hants 22 H9
Bramerton Norfk 77 K11
Bramfield Herts 50 G7
Bramfield Suffk 65 M7
Bramford Suffk 53 K2
Bramhall Stockp 83 J8
Bramham Leeds 91 L2
Bramhope Leeds 90 H2
Bramley Hants 23 J3
Bramley Leeds 90 G3
Bramley Rothm 84 G2
Bramley Surrey 24 B2
Bramley Corner Hants 22 H3
Bramley Green Hants 23 J3
Bramley Head N York 96 H9
Bramling Kent 39 M10
Brampford Speke Devon 9 M5
Brampton Cambs 62 B6
Brampton Cumb 102 C6
Brampton Cumb 111 K8
Brampton Lincs 85 P5
Brampton Norfk 77 J7
Brampton Rothm 91 L10
Brampton Suffk 65 N5
Brampton Abbotts Herefs 46 B9
Brampton Ash Nhants 60 G3
Brampton Bryan Herefs 56 F10
Brampton-en-le-Morthen Rothm 84 G3
Bramshall Staffs 71 K8
Bramshaw Hants 21 Q11
Bramshill Hants 23 K2
Bramshott Hants 23 M8
Bramwell Somset 19 M9
Branault Highld 137 N2
Brancaster Norfk 75 Q2
Brancaster Staithe Norfk 75 Q2
Brancepeth Dur 103 P3
Branchill Moray 157 K7
Brand End Lincs 87 L11
Branderburgh Moray 157 N3
Brandesburton E R Yk 99 N11
Brandeston Suffk 65 J9
Brand Green Gloucs 46 D9
Brandis Corner Devon 16 G11
Brandiston Norfk 76 G7
Brandon Dur 103 P2
Brandon Lincs 86 B11
Brandon Nthumb 119 K7
Brandon Suffk 63 N3
Brandon Warwks 59 P9
Brandon Bank Norfk 63 K3
Brandon Creek Norfk 63 K2
Brandon Parva Norfk 76 F10
Brandsby N York 98 B6
Brandy Wharf Lincs 92 H11
Brane Cnwll 2 C8
Bran End Essex 51 Q5
Branksome BCP 12 H6
Branksome Park BCP 13 J6
Bransbury Hants 22 D6
Bransby Lincs 85 Q5
Branscombe Devon 10 D7
Bransford Worcs 46 E4
Bransgore Hants 13 L5
Bransholme C KuH 93 K4
Bransley Shrops 57 M9
Branson's Cross Worcs 58 G10
Branston Leics 73 L5
Branston Lincs 86 D7
Branston Staffs 71 N10
Branston Booths Lincs 86 E7
Branstone IoW 14 G10
Brant Broughton Lincs 86 B10
Brantham Suffk 53 K5
Branthwaite Cumb 100 E6
Branthwaite Cumb 101 J3
Brantingham E R Yk 92 F5
Branton Donc 91 Q10
Branton Nthumb 119 K7
Branton Green N York 97 P8
Branxton Nthumb 118 G3
Brassey Green Ches W 69 P2
Brasside Dur 113 L11
Brassington Derbys 71 N4
Brasted Kent 37 L9
Brasted Chart Kent 37 L10
Brathens Abers 150 H8
Bratoft Lincs 87 N8
Brattleby Lincs 86 B4
Bratton Somset 18 B5
Bratton Wilts 20 H4
Bratton Wrekin 57 L2
Bratton Clovelly Devon 8 C6
Bratton Fleming Devon 17 L4
Bratton Seymour Somset 20 C9
Braughing Herts 51 J5
Braughing Friars Herts 51 K6
Braunston Nhants 60 B7
Braunston Rutlnd 73 L9
Braunstone Town Leics 72 F10
Braunton Devon 16 H4

Brawby N York 98 E5
Brawl Highld 166 D3
Braworth N York 104 F9
Bray W & M 35 P9
Braybrooke Nhants 60 G4
Braydon Wilts 33 L7
Braydon Brook Wilts 33 J6
Braydon Side Wilts 33 K7
Brayford Devon 17 M5
Bray's Hill E Susx 25 Q8
Bray Shop Cnwll 5 N7
Braystones Cumb 100 D9
Braythorn N York 97 K11
Brayton N York 91 Q4
Braywick W & M 35 N9
Braywoodside W & M 35 N9
Brazacott Cnwll 5 M3
Breach Kent 27 L2
Breach Kent 38 C8
Breachwood Green Herts 50 E6
Breacleit W Isls 168 g4
Breaclete W Isls 168 g4
Breaden Heath Shrops 69 M7
Breadsall Derbys 72 B3
Breadstone Gloucs 32 D4
Breage Cnwll 2 G8
Breakachy Highld 155 N9
Breakish Highld 145 L3
Brealangwell Lodge Highld 162 C8
Bream Gloucs 32 B3
Breamore Hants 21 N11
Brean Somset 19 J3
Breanais W Isls 168 e5
Brearley Calder 90 C5
Brearton N York 97 M8
Breascleit W Isls 168 h4
Breasclete W Isls 168 h4
Breaston Derbys 72 D4
Brechfa Carmth 43 K8
Brechin Angus 143 L5
Breckles Norfk 64 D3
Brecon Powys 44 E9
Brecon Beacons National Park 44 E10
Bredbury Stockp 83 K6
Brede E Susx 26 D8
Bredenbury Herefs 46 B3
Bredfield Suffk 65 K11
Bredgar Kent 38 E9
Bredhurst Kent 38 C9
Bredon Worcs 46 H7
Bredon's Hardwick Worcs 46 H7
Bredon's Norton Worcs 46 H7
Bredward Herefs 45 K4
Bredwardine Herefs 45 L6
Breedon on the Hill Leics 72 C6
Breich W Loth 126 H5
Breightmet Bolton 89 L9
Breighton E R Yk 92 B4
Breinton Herefs 45 P7
Breinton Common Herefs 45 P7
Bremhill Wilts 33 J10
Bremridge Devon 17 M6
Brenchley Kent 25 Q2
Brendon Devon 16 F10
Brendon Devon 17 P2
Brendon Hill Somset 18 D8
Brenfield Ag & B 123 P3
Brenish W Isls 168 e5
Brenkley N u Ty 113 K5
Brent Cross Gt Lon 36 F3
Brent Eleigh Suffk 52 F2
Brentford Gt Lon 36 E5
Brentingby Leics 73 K7
Brent Knoll Somset 19 K4
Brent Mill Devon 6 H7
Brent Pelham Herts 51 K4
Brentwood Essex 37 N2
Brenzett Kent 26 H6
Brenzett Green Kent 26 H6
Brereton Staffs 71 K11
Brereton Green Ches E 70 D2
Brereton Heath Ches E 82 H11
Brereton Hill Staffs 71 K11
Bressay Shet 169 s8
Bressingham Norfk 64 F5
Bressingham Common Norfk 64 F5
Bretby Derbys 71 P10
Bretford Warwks 59 P9
Bretforton Worcs 47 L6
Bretherton Lancs 88 F6
Brettabister Shet 169 r8
Brettenham Norfk 64 C5
Brettenham Suffk 64 D11
Bretton C Pete 74 C10
Bretton Derbys 84 B5
Bretton Flints 69 L2
Brewers End Essex 51 N6
Brewer Street Surrey 36 H10
Brewood Staffs 58 C3
Briantspuddle Dorset 12 D6
Brick End Essex 51 N5
Brickendon Herts 50 H9
Bricket Wood Herts 50 D10
Brick Houses Sheff 84 D4
Brickkiln Green Essex 52 B5
Bricklehampton Worcs 47 J6
Bride IoM 80 f1
Bridekirk Cumb 100 F4
Bridell Pembks 41 N2
Brideswell Abers 158 E10
Bridford Devon 8 D7
Bridge Kent 39 L11
Bridge End Cumb 94 D4
Bridge End Cumb 110 G11
Bridge End Devon 6 H9
Bridge End Dur 103 K3
Bridge End Essex 51 Q4
Bridge End Lincs 74 B3
Bridgefoot Angus 142 F10
Bridgefoot Cumb 100 E5
Bridge Green Essex 51 L3
Bridgehampton Somset 19 Q10
Bridge Hewick N York 97 M6
Bridgehill Dur 112 H10
Bridgehouse Gate N York 97 J7
Bridgemary Hants 14 G6
Bridgemere Ches E 70 C5
Bridgend Abers 158 D10
Bridgend Ag & B 120 E4
Bridgend Ag & B 122 G7
Bridgend Ag & B 130 H9
Bridgend Angus 143 J4
Bridgend Brdgnd 29 P9
Bridgend Cerdgn 42 C5

Bridgend Cumb 101 M8
Bridgend D & G 116 F9
Bridgend Devon 6 F9
Bridgend Fife 135 K5
Bridgend Moray 158 A11
Bridgend P & K 134 E3
Bridgend W Loth 127 J2
Bridgend of Lintrathen Angus 142 D7
Bridge of Alford Abers 150 F4
Bridge of Allan Stirlg 133 M8
Bridge of Avon Moray 149 M4
Bridge of Avon Moray 157 M10
Bridge of Balgie P & K 140 H8
Bridge of Brewlands Angus 142 B5
Bridge of Brown Highld 149 L3
Bridge of Cally P & K 142 A7
Bridge of Canny Abers 150 H8
Bridge of Craigisla Angus 142 D7
Bridge of Dee D & G 108 F9
Bridge of Don C Aber 151 N6
Bridge of Dun Angus 143 M6
Bridge of Dye Abers 150 H10
Bridge of Earn P & K 134 E4
Bridge of Ericht P & K 140 D6
Bridge of Feugh Abers 151 J8
Bridge of Gairn Abers 150 B8
Bridge of Gaur P & K 140 D6
Bridge of Marnoch Abers 158 E7
Bridge of Muchalls Abers 151 M9
Bridge of Orchy Ag & B 139 P10
Bridge of Tilt P & K 141 L4
Bridge of Tynet Moray 158 A5
Bridge of Walls Shet 169 p8
Bridge of Weir Rens 125 K4
Bridge Reeve Devon 17 L9
Bridge Sollers Herefs 45 N6
Bridge Street Suffk 52 E2
Bridgetown Cnwll 5 N4
Bridgetown Somset 18 B8
Bridge Trafford Ches W 81 P10
Bridge Yate S Glos 32 C10
Bridgham Norfk 64 D4
Bridgnorth Shrops 57 N6
Bridgwater Somset 19 J7
Bridgwater Services Somset 19 K8
Bridlington E R Yk 99 P7
Bridport Dorset 11 K6
Bridstow Herefs 46 A10
Brierfield Lancs 89 N3
Brierley Barns 91 L8
Brierley Gloucs 46 B11
Brierley Herefs 45 P3
Brierley Hill Dudley 58 D7
Brierton Hartpl 104 E4
Briery Cumb 101 J6
Brigg N Linc 92 H9
Briggate Norfk 77 L6
Briggswath N York 105 N9
Brigham Cumb 100 E4
Brigham Cumb 101 J6
Brigham E R Yk 99 M10
Brighouse Calder 90 E6
Brighstone IoW 14 D10
Brightgate Derbys 84 C9
Brighthampton Oxon 34 C4
Brightholmlee Sheff 90 H11
Brightley Devon 8 F5
Brightling E Susx 25 Q6
Brightlingsea Essex 53 J8
Brighton Br & H 24 H10
Brighton Cnwll 3 N3
Brighton City Airport W Susx 24 E9
Brighton le Sands Sefton 81 L5
Brightons Falk 126 F3
Brightwalton W Berk 34 D9
Brightwalton Green W Berk 34 D9
Brightwalton Holt W Berk 34 D9
Brightwell Suffk 53 N3
Brightwell Baldwin Oxon 35 J5
Brightwell-cum-Sotwell Oxon 34 G6
Brightwell Upperton Oxon 35 J6
Brignall Dur 103 L8
Brig o'Turk Stirlg 132 E5
Brigsley NE Lin 93 N10
Brigsteer Cumb 95 K3
Brigstock Nhants 61 K3
Brill Bucks 35 J2
Brill Cnwll 3 J8
Brilley Herefs 45 K5
Brimfield Herefs 57 J11
Brimfield Cross Herefs 57 J11
Brimington Derbys 84 F6
Brimley Devon 9 K9
Brimpsfield Gloucs 32 H2
Brimpton W Berk 22 G2
Brimpton Common W Berk 22 G2
Brimscombe Gloucs 32 G4
Brimstage Wirral 81 L8
Brincliffe Sheff 84 D4
Brind E R Yk 92 B4
Brindham Somset 19 P7
Brindister Shet 169 p8
Brindle Lancs 88 H5
Brindley Ches E 69 Q4
Brineton Staffs 57 Q2
Bringhurst Leics 60 H2
Bringsty Common Herefs 46 D3
Brington Cambs 61 N5
Briningham Norfk 76 E4
Brinian Ork 169 d4
Brinkely Notts 85 M10
Brinkhill Lincs 87 L6
Brinkley Cambs 63 K10
Brinklow Warwks 59 P9
Brinkworth Wilts 33 K8
Brinscall Lancs 89 J5
Brinscombe Somset 19 M4
Brinsea N Som 19 M2
Brinsley Notts 84 G11
Brinsop Herefs 45 N6
Brinsworth Rothm 84 F3
Brinton Norfk 76 E4
Brisco Cumb 110 H10
Brisley Norfk 76 C7
Brislington Bristl 32 B10
Brissenden Green Kent 26 H4
Bristol Bristl 31 Q10
Bristol Airport N Som 31 P11
Briston Norfk 76 F5
Brisworthy Devon 6 F5

Britannia Lancs 89 P6
Britford Wilts 21 N9
Brithdir Caerph 30 F4
Brithdir Gwynd 67 P11
British Legion Village Kent 38 B10
Briton Ferry Neath 29 K6
Britwell Salome Oxon 35 J6
Brixham Torbay 7 N7
Brixton Devon 6 F8
Brixton Gt Lon 36 H5
Brixton Deverill Wilts 20 G7
Brixworth Nhants 60 F6
Brize Norton Oxon 33 Q3
Brize Norton Airport Oxon 33 Q3
Broad Alley Worcs 58 C11
Broad Blunsdon Swindn 33 M6
Broadbottom Tamesd 83 L6
Broadbridge W Susx 15 M5
Broadbridge Heath W Susx 24 D4
Broad Campden Gloucs 47 N7
Broad Carr Calder 90 D7
Broad Chalke Wilts 21 K9
Broadclyst Devon 9 N5
Broadfield Inver 125 J3
Broadfield Pembks 41 M10
Broad Ford Kent 26 B4
Bradford Bridge W Susx 24 C6
Broadgairhill Border 117 J8
Broadgrass Green Suffk 64 D9
Broad Green Cambs 63 L8
Broad Green Essex 52 E7
Broad Green Worcs 46 E3
Broad Green Worcs 58 E10
Broadhaugh Border 129 M9
Broad Haven Pembks 40 G8
Broadheath Traffd 82 G7
Broadhembury Devon 10 C4
Broadhempston Devon 7 L5
Broad Hill Cambs 63 J5
Broad Hinton Wilts 33 M9
Broadholme Lincs 85 Q6
Broadland Row E Susx 26 D8
Broadlay Carmth 28 C3
Broad Layings Hants 22 D2
Broadley Essex 51 K9
Broadley Lancs 89 P7
Broadley Moray 158 A5
Broadley Common Essex 51 K9
Broad Marston Worcs 47 M5
Broadmayne Dorset 12 B7
Broad Meadow Staffs 70 E5
Broadmere Hants 22 H5
Broadmoor Gloucs 46 B11
Broadmoor Pembks 41 L9
Broadnymett Devon 8 H4
Broad Oak Carmth 43 L10
Broad Oak Cumb 94 C2
Broad Oak Dorset 11 J5
Broad Oak E Susx 25 P6
Broad Oak E Susx 26 D8
Broadoak Gloucs 32 C2
Broad Oak Hants 23 L4
Broad Oak Herefs 45 P10
Broad Oak Kent 39 L9
Broad Oak St Hel 82 B5
Broadoak Wrexhm 69 L3
Broad Road Suffk 65 K6
Broadsands Torbay 7 M7
Broad's Green Essex 51 Q8
Broadstairs Kent 39 Q8
Broadstone BCP 12 H5
Broadstone Mons 31 P4
Broadstone Shrops 57 J7
Broad Street E Susx 26 E8
Broad Street Essex 51 N7
Broad Street Kent 27 K3
Broad Street Kent 38 D10
Broad Street Medway 38 C7
Broad Street Wilts 21 M3
Broad Street Green Essex 52 E10
Broad Town Wilts 33 L9
Broadwas Worcs 46 E3
Broadwater Herts 50 F6
Broadwater W Susx 24 D10
Broadwaters Worcs 58 B9
Broadway Carmth 28 C3
Broadway Carmth 41 Q8
Broadway Pembks 40 G8
Broadway Somset 19 K11
Broadway Suffk 65 M6
Broadway Worcs 47 L7
Broadwell Gloucs 31 Q2
Broadwell Gloucs 47 P9
Broadwell Oxon 33 Q4
Broadwell Warwks 59 Q11
Broadwey Dorset 11 P8
Broadwindsor Dorset 11 J4
Broadwood Kelly Devon 8 F3
Broadwoodwidger Devon 5 Q4
Brobury Herefs 45 L6
Brochel Highld 153 K8
Brochroy Ag & B 139 J11
Brock Lancs 88 G2
Brockamin Worcs 46 E4
Brockbridge Hants 22 H11
Brockdish Norfk 65 J6
Brockencote Worcs 58 C10
Brockenhurst Hants 13 P4
Brocketsbrae S Lans 126 E10
Brockford Green Suffk 64 G8
Brockford Street Suffk 64 G8
Brockhall Nhants 60 D8
Brockhall Village Lancs 89 L3
Brockham Surrey 36 E11
Brockhampton Gloucs 46 H9
Brockhampton Gloucs 47 K10
Brockhampton Hants 15 K5
Brockhampton Herefs 46 A8
Brockhampton Green Dorset 11 Q3
Brockholes Kirk 90 F8
Brockhurst Derbys 84 D8
Brockhurst Warwks 59 Q8
Brocklebank Cumb 101 K2
Brocklesby Lincs 93 K8
Brockley N Som 31 N11
Brockley Suffk 64 A7
Brockley Green Suffk 63 M11
Brockley Green Suffk 64 A11
Brockleymoor Cumb 101 N3
Brockmoor Dudley 58 D7
Brockscombe Devon 8 C5
Brock's Green Hants 22 F2
Brockton Shrops 56 E4

Brockton Shrops 56 E7
Brockton Shrops 57 K6
Brockton Shrops 57 N4
Brockton Staffs 70 E8
Brockweir Gloucs 31 P4
Brockwood Park Hants 22 H9
Brockworth Gloucs 46 G11
Brocton Cnwll 4 G8
Brocton Staffs 70 H11
Brodick N Ayrs 121 K4
Brodie Moray 156 H6
Brodsworth Donc 91 N9
Brogaig Highld 152 H4
Brogborough C Beds 49 Q7
Brokenborough Wilts 32 H7
Broken Cross Ches E 83 J10
Broken Cross Ches W 82 E10
Brokerswood Wilts 20 F4
Bromborough Wirral 81 M8
Brome Suffk 64 G6
Brome Street Suffk 64 H6
Bromeswell Suffk 65 L11
Bromfield Cumb 110 C11
Bromfield Shrops 56 H9
Bromham Bed 61 M10
Bromham Wilts 33 J11
Bromley Barns 91 J11
Bromley Dudley 58 D2
Bromley Gt Lon 37 K7
Bromley Shrops 57 N5
Bromley Common Gt Lon 37 K7
Bromley Cross Bolton 89 L8
Bromley Cross Essex 53 J6
Bromley Green Kent 26 G4
Bromlow Shrops 56 E4
Brompton Medway 38 C8
Brompton N York 104 C11
Brompton-by-Sawdon
  N York 99 J4
Brompton-on-Swale N York 103 P11
Brompton Ralph Somset 18 E8
Brompton Regis Somset 18 C8
Bromsash Herefs 46 C10
Bromsberrow Gloucs 46 D8
Bromsberrow Heath Gloucs 46 D8
Bromsgrove Worcs 58 D10
Bromstead Heath Staffs 70 D11
Bromyard Herefs 46 C4
Bromyard Downs Herefs 46 C3
Bronaber Gwynd 67 N8
Bronant Cerdgn 54 E11
Broncroft Shrops 57 J7
Brongest Cerdgn 42 F5
Bronington Wrexhm 69 N7
Bronllys Powys 44 G8
Bronwydd Carmth 42 H10
Bronydd Powys 45 J5
Bronygarth Shrops 69 J7
Brook Carmth 41 Q9
Brook Hants 13 N2
Brook Hants 22 B9
Brook IoW 14 C10
Brook Kent 27 J3
Brook Surrey 23 P7
Brook Surrey 36 C11
Brooke Norfk 65 K2
Brooke Rutlnd 73 L9
Brookenby Lincs 93 M11
Brook End Bed 61 N8
Brook End C Beds 61 Q11
Brook End Cambs 61 N6
Brook End M Keyn 49 P6
Brookfield Rens 125 L5
Brookhampton Oxon 34 H5
Brookhampton Somset 20 B9
Brook Hill Hants 13 N2
Brookhouse Denbgs 80 F11
Brookhouse Lancs 95 L8
Brookhouse Rothm 84 H3
Brookhouse Green Ches E 70 E2
Brookhouses Derbys 83 M7
Brookland Kent 26 G6
Brooklands Traffd 82 G6
Brookmans Park Herts 50 F10
Brooks Powys 55 Q5
Brooksby Leics 72 H7
Brooks End Kent 39 N8
Brooks Green W Susx 24 D6
Brook Street Essex 37 N2
Brook Street Kent 26 F5
Brook Street Suffk 52 D2
Brook Street W Susx 24 H5
Brookthorpe Gloucs 32 F2
Brookville Norfk 75 P11
Brookwood Surrey 23 Q3
Broom C Beds 50 E2
Broom Rothm 84 F2
Broom Warwks 47 L4
Broombank Worcs 57 M10
Broome Norfk 65 M3
Broome Shrops 56 G8
Broome Worcs 58 D9
Broomedge Warrtn 82 F7
Broome Park Nthumb 119 M8
Broomer's Corner W Susx 24 D6
Broomershill W Susx 24 C7
Broomfield Essex 52 B9
Broomfield Kent 38 D11
Broomfield Kent 39 L8
Broomfield Somset 18 H8
Broomfields Shrops 69 M11
Broomfleet E R Yk 92 E5
Broom Green Norfk 76 D7
Broomhall W & M 35 Q11
Broomhaugh Nthumb 112 F8
Broom Hill Barns 91 L10
Broom Hill Dorset 12 H4
Broom Hill Notts 84 H11
Broomhill Nthumb 119 P10
Broom Hill Worcs 58 D9
Broomhill Green Ches E 70 A5
Broomley Nthumb 112 F8
Broompark Dur 103 P2
Broom's Green Gloucs 46 D8
Broomsthorpe Norfk 76 A6
Broom Street Kent 38 H9
Brora Highld 163 L6
Broseley Shrops 57 M4
Brotherhouse Bar Lincs 74 E8
Brotherlee Dur 102 H3
Brothertoft Lincs 87 J11
Brotherton N York 91 M5
Brotton R & Cl 105 J7
Broubster Highld 166 H5
Brough Cumb 102 E4
Brough Derbys 83 Q7

Brough E R Yk 92 F5
Brough Highld 167 M2
Brough Notts 85 P9
Brough Shet 169 s7
Broughall Shrops 69 Q6
Brough Lodge Shet 169 s4
Brough Sowerby Cumb 102 E4
Broughton Border 116 G3
Broughton Bucks 35 M4
Broughton Cambs 62 C5
Broughton Flints 69 K2
Broughton Hants 22 B8
Broughton Lancs 88 G4
Broughton M Keyn 49 N7
Broughton N Linc 92 G9
Broughton N York 96 D10
Broughton N York 98 F6
Broughton Oxon 48 D7
Broughton Salfd 82 H4
Broughton Staffs 70 D8
Broughton V Glam 29 P10
Broughton Astley Leics 60 B2
Broughton Beck Cumb 94 F4
Broughton Gifford Wilts 20 G2
Broughton Green Worcs 47 J2
Broughton Hackett Worcs 46 H4
Broughton-in-Furness
  Cumb 94 E3
Broughton Mains D & G 107 N8
Broughton Mills Cumb 94 E2
Broughton Moor Cumb 100 E4
Broughton Poggs Oxon 33 P4
Broughton Tower Cumb 94 E3
Broughty Ferry C Dund 142 H11
Brough with St Giles N York 103 P11
Brow End Cumb 94 F6
Brownber Cumb 102 D9
Brown Candover Hants 22 G7
Brown Edge Lancs 88 D8
Brown Edge Staffs 70 G4
Brown Heath Ches W 69 N2
Brownheath Shrops 69 N9
Brownhill Abers 159 L9
Brownhills Fife 135 N4
Brownhills Wsall 58 F3
Brownieside Nthumb 119 N6
Browninghill Green Hants 22 G2
Brown Knowl Ches W 69 N4
Brown Lees Staffs 70 F3
Brownlow Heath Ches E 70 E2
Brownrigg Cumb 100 D3
Brownrigg Cumb 110 C10
Brownsea Island Dorset 12 H7
Brown's Green Birm 58 G6
Brownsham Devon 16 D6
Browns Hill Gloucs 32 G4
Brownsover Warwks 60 B5
Brownston Devon 6 H8
Brown Street Suffk 64 F9
Browston Green Norfk 77 P11
Broxa N York 99 J2
Broxbourne Herts 51 J9
Broxburn E Loth 128 H4
Broxburn W Loth 127 K3
Broxfield Nthumb 119 P7
Broxted Essex 51 N5
Broxton Ches W 69 N4
Broyle Side E Susx 25 L8
Bruan Highld 167 P9
Bruar P & K 141 K4
Bruchag Ag & B 124 E5
Bruera Ches W 69 M2
Bruern Abbey Oxon 47 Q10
Bruichladdich Ag & B 122 C7
Bruisyard Suffk 65 L8
Bruisyard Street Suffk 65 L8
Brumby N Linc 92 F9
Brund Staffs 71 L2
Brundall Norfk 77 L10
Brundish Suffk 65 K8
Brundish Street Suffk 65 K7
Brunery Highld 138 C3
Brunnion Cnwll 2 E6
Brunslow Shrops 56 F9
Brunswick Village N u Ty 113 K6
Bruntcliffe Leeds 90 H5
Brunthwaite C Brad 96 G11
Bruntingthorpe Leics 60 D3
Brunton Fife 135 J3
Brunton Nthumb 119 P6
Brunton Wilts 21 P3
Brushford Devon 17 M10
Brushford Somset 18 B9
Bruton Somset 20 C7
Bryan's Green Worcs 58 C11
Bryanston Dorset 12 E3
Bryant's Bottom Bucks 35 N5
Brydekirk D & G 110 C6
Bryher IoS 2 b2
Brymbo Wrexhm 69 J4
Brympton Somset 19 P11
Bryn Carmth 28 F4
Bryn Ches W 82 D10
Bryn Neath 29 M6
Bryn Shrops 56 D7
Bryn Wigan 82 C4
Brynamman Carmth 29 K2
Brynberian Pembks 41 M3
Brynbryddan Neath 29 L6
Bryn Bwbach Gwynd 67 L7
Bryncae Rhondd 30 C8
Bryncethin Brdgnd 29 P8
Bryncir Gwynd 66 H6
Bryncroes Gwynd 66 C8
Bryncrug Gwynd 54 E4
Bryn Du IoA 78 E10
Bryn-Eden Gwynd 67 N9
Bryneglwys Denbgs 68 F5
Bryneglwys &
  Abergynolwyn Slate
  Landscape Gwynd 54 F3
Brynfields Wrexhm 69 K6
Brynford Flints 80 H10
Bryn Gates Wigan 82 C4
Bryn Golau Rhondd 30 D7
Bryngwran IoA 78 F9
Bryngwyn Mons 31 L3
Bryngwyn Powys 44 H5
Brynhoffnant Cerdgn 42 F4
Bryning Lancs 88 E5
Brynithel Blae G 30 H4
Brynmawr Blae G 30 G3
Bryn-mawr Gwynd 66 C8

Brynmenyn Brdgnd 29 P8
Brynmill Swans 28 H6
Brynna Rhondd 30 C8
Brynnau Gwynion Rhondd 30 C8
Bryn-penarth Powys 55 Q4
Brynrefail Gwynd 67 K2
Brynrefail IoA 78 H7
Brynsadler Rhondd 30 D8
Bryn Saith Marchog Denbgs 68 E4
Brynsiencyn IoA 78 H11
Brynteg IoA 78 H8
Bryn-y-bal Flints 69 J2
Bryn-y-Maen Conwy 79 Q9
Bryn-yr-Eos Wrexhm 69 J6
Bualintur Highld 144 F3
Buarth-draw Flints 80 H9
Bubbenhall Warwks 59 N10
Bubwith E R Yk 92 B3
Buccleuch Border 117 L8
Buchanan Smithy Stirlg 132 F10
Buchanhaven Abers 159 R8
Buchanty P & K 133 Q2
Buchany Stirlg 133 L7
Buchlyvie Stirlg 132 H9
Buckabank Cumb 110 G11
Buckden Cambs 61 Q7
Buckden N York 96 D5
Buckenham Norfk 77 M10
Buckerell Devon 10 C4
Buckfast Devon 7 J5
Buckfastleigh Devon 7 J5
Buckhaven Fife 135 K8
Buckholt Mons 45 Q11
Buckhorn Devon 5 P2
Buckhorn Weston Dorset 20 E10
Buckhurst Hill Essex 37 K2
Buckie Moray 158 B4
Buckingham Bucks 49 J8
Buckland Bucks 35 N2
Buckland Devon 6 H10
Buckland Gloucs 47 L7
Buckland Hants 13 P5
Buckland Herts 51 J4
Buckland Kent 27 P3
Buckland Oxon 34 B5
Buckland Surrey 36 F10
Buckland Brewer Devon 16 G7
Buckland Common Bucks 35 P3
Buckland Dinham Somset 20 E4
Buckland Filleigh Devon 16 H10
Buckland in the Moor
  Devon 7 J4
Buckland Monachorum
  Devon 6 D5
Buckland Newton Dorset 11 P3
Buckland Ripers Dorset 11 P8
Buckland St Mary Somset 10 F2
Buckland-Tout-Saints
  Devon 7 K9
Bucklebury W Berk 34 G10
Bucklers Hard Hants 14 D6
Bucklesham Suffk 53 M3
Buckley Flints 69 J2
Buckley Green Warwks 59 J11
Bucklow Hill Ches E 82 F8
Buckminster Leics 73 M6
Bucknall C Stke 70 G5
Bucknall Lincs 86 G7
Bucknell Oxon 48 G9
Bucknell Shrops 56 F10
Buckpool Moray 158 B4
Bucksburn C Aber 151 M6
Buck's Cross Devon 16 F7
Bucks Green W Susx 24 C4
Buckshaw Village Lancs 88 H6
Bucks Hill Herts 50 C10
Bucks Horn Oak Hants 23 M6
Buck's Mills Devon 16 F7
Buckton E R Yk 99 P6
Buckton Herefs 56 F10
Buckton Nthumb 119 L3
Buckworth Cambs 61 P5
Budby Notts 85 K7
Buddileigh Staffs 70 C5
Bude Cnwll 16 C10
Budge's Shop Cnwll 5 N10
Budlake Devon 9 N4
Budle Nthumb 119 N3
Budleigh Salterton Devon 9 Q8
Budlett's Common E Susx 25 L6
Budock Water Cnwll 3 K7
Buerton Ches E 70 B6
Bugbrooke Nhants 60 E9
Bugford Devon 7 L8
Buglawton Ches E 70 F2
Bugle Cnwll 4 G10
Bugley Dorset 20 E10
Bugthorpe E R Yk 98 F9
Buildwas Shrops 57 L4
Builth Road Powys 44 E4
Builth Wells Powys 44 E4
Bulbourne Herts 35 P2
Bulbridge Wilts 21 L8
Bulby Lincs 73 R5
Bulcote Notts 85 H2
Bulford Wilts 21 N6
Bulford Camp Wilts 21 N6
Bulkeley Ches E 69 P4
Bulkington Warwks 59 N7
Bulkington Wilts 20 H3
Bulkworthy Devon 16 F9
Bullamoor N York 97 N2
Bull Bay IoA 78 G6
Bullbridge Derbys 84 E10
Bullbrook Br For 35 N11
Bullen's Green Herts 50 F9
Bulley Gloucs 46 E11
Bullgill Cumb 100 E3
Bullinghope Herefs 45 Q7
Bullington Hants 22 E6
Bullington Lincs 86 E5
Bullockstone Kent 39 L8
Bull's Green Herts 50 G7
Bull's Green Norfk 65 N3
Bulmer Essex 52 D3
Bulmer N York 98 D7
Bulmer Tye Essex 52 D4
Bulphan Thurr 37 P3
Bulstone Devon 10 D7
Bulstrode Herts 50 B10
Bulverhythe E Susx 26 C10
Bulwark Abers 159 M8
Bulwell C Nott 72 E2
Bulwick Nhants 61 L2
Bumble's Green Essex 51 K9

Bunacaimb Highld 145 L10
Bunarkaig Highld 146 F10
Bunbury Ches E 69 Q3
Bunbury Heath Ches E 69 Q3
Bunchrew Highld 155 R8
Buncton W Susx 24 D8
Bundalloch Highld 145 Q2
Bunessan Ag & B 137 K11
Bungay Suffk 65 L4
Bunker's Hill Lincs 87 J10
Bunnahabhain Ag & B 122 F5
Bunny Notts 72 F5
Buntait Highld 155 M11
Buntingford Herts 51 J5
Bunwell Norfk 64 G3
Bunwell Hill Norfk 64 G3
Bupton Derbys 71 N7
Burbage Derbys 83 M10
Burbage Leics 59 P6
Burbage Wilts 21 P2
Burcher Herefs 45 L2
Burcombe Wilts 21 L8
Burcot Oxon 34 G5
Burcot Worcs 58 E10
Burcote Shrops 57 N5
Burcott Bucks 49 M11
Burcott Bucks 49 N10
Burdale N York 98 H8
Bures Essex 52 F5
Burford Oxon 33 Q2
Burford Shrops 57 K11
Burg Ag & B 137 K6
Burgate Suffk 64 F6
Burgates Hants 23 L9
Burge End Herts 50 D4
Burgess Hill W Susx 24 H7
Burgh Suffk 65 J11
Burgh by Sands Cumb 110 F9
Burgh Castle Norfk 77 P10
Burghclere Hants 22 E2
Burghead Moray 157 L4
Burghfield W Berk 35 J11
Burghfield Common W Berk 35 J11
Burgh Heath Surrey 36 F9
Burghill Herefs 45 P6
Burgh Island Devon 6 G10
Burgh le Marsh Lincs 87 P7
Burgh next Aylsham Norfk 77 J6
Burgh on Bain Lincs 86 H3
Burgh St Margaret Norfk 77 N9
Burgh St Peter Norfk 65 P3
Burghwallis Donc 91 N8
Burham Kent 38 B9
Buriton Hants 23 K11
Burland Ches E 69 R4
Burlawn Cnwll 4 F7
Burleigh Gloucs 32 G4
Burlescombe Devon 18 E11
Burleston Dorset 12 C6
Burlestone Devon 7 L9
Burley Hants 13 M4
Burley Rutlnd 73 M8
Burley Shrops 56 H8
Burleydam Ches E 69 R6
Burley Gate Herefs 45 R5
Burley in Wharfedale C Brad 97 J11
Burley Lawn Hants 13 M4
Burley Street Hants 13 M4
Burley Wood Head C Brad 90 F2
Burlingham Green Norfk 77 M9
Burlingjobb Powys 45 K3
Burlington Shrops 57 P2
Burlton Shrops 69 N9
Burmarsh Kent 27 K5
Burmington Warwks 47 Q7
Burn N York 91 P5
Burnage Manch 83 J6
Burnaston Derbys 71 P8
Burnbanks Cumb 101 P7
Burnbrae N Lans 126 F6
Burn Bridge N York 97 L10
Burnby E R Yk 98 G11
Burn Cross Sheff 91 J11
Burndell W Susx 15 Q6
Burnden Bolton 89 L9
Burnedge Rochdl 89 Q8
Burneside Cumb 101 P11
Burneston N York 97 M4
Burnett BaNES 32 C11
Burnfoot Border 117 N8
Burnfoot Border 117 Q7
Burnfoot D & G 110 L2
Burnfoot D & G 110 F3
Burnfoot P & K 134 B7
Burnham Bucks 35 P8
Burnham N Linc 93 J7
Burnham Deepdale Norfk 75 Q3
Burnham Green Herts 50 G7
Burnham Market Norfk 76 A3
Burnham Norton Norfk 76 A3
Burnham-on-Crouch Essex 38 F2
Burnham-on-Sea Somset 19 L5
Burnham Overy Norfk 76 A3
Burnham Overy Staithe
  Norfk 76 A3
Burnham Thorpe Norfk 76 B3
Burnhead D & G 116 B11
Burnhervie Abers 151 L4
Burnhill Green Staffs 57 P4
Burnhope Dur 113 J11
Burnhouse N Ayrs 125 K7
Burniston N York 99 L2
Burnley Lancs 89 N4
Burnmouth Border 129 P7
Burn Naze Lancs 88 C2
Burn of Cambus Stirlg 133 L7
Burnopfield Dur 113 J9
Burnrigg Cumb 111 J9
Burnsall N York 96 F8
Burnside Angus 142 G6
Burnside Angus 143 J7
Burnside Fife 134 F6
Burnside Moray 157 M4
Burnside W Loth 127 K2
Burnside of Duntrune
  Angus 142 G11
Burntcommon Surrey 36 B10
Burntheath Derbys 71 N8
Burnt Heath Essex 53 J6
Burnt Hill W Berk 34 G10
Burnthouse Cnwll 3 K6
Burnt Houses Dur 103 M6
Burntisland Fife 134 G10

Burnt Oak E Susx 25 M5
Burnton E Ayrs 115 J6
Burntwood Flints 69 J2
Burntwood Staffs 58 G3
Burntwood Green Staffs 58 G3
Burnt Yates N York 97 L8
Burnworthy Somset 18 G11
Burpham Surrey 36 B10
Burpham W Susx 24 B9
Burradon N Tyne 113 L6
Burradon Nthumb 119 J9
Burrafirth Shet 169 t2
Burras Cnwll 2 H7
Burraton Cnwll 5 Q8
Burravoe Shet 169 s5
Burray Village Ork 169 d7
Burrells Cumb 102 C7
Burrelton P & K 142 C10
Burridge Devon 10 G3
Burridge Devon 17 K4
Burridge Hants 14 F4
Burrill N York 97 K3
Burringham N Linc 92 D9
Burrington Devon 17 L8
Burrington Herefs 56 G10
Burrington N Som 19 N3
Burrough End Cambs 63 K9
Burrough Green Cambs 63 K9
Burrough on the Hill Leics 73 K8
Burrow Lancs 95 N6
Burrow Somset 18 B6
Burrow Bridge Somset 19 L8
Burrowhill Surrey 23 Q2
Burrows Cross Surrey 36 C11
Burry Swans 28 E6
Burry Green Swans 28 E6
Burry Port Carmth 28 D4
Burscough Lancs 88 E8
Burscough Bridge Lancs 88 E8
Bursea E R Yk 92 D4
Burshill E R Yk 99 M11
Bursledon Hants 14 E5
Burslem C Stke 70 F5
Burstall Suffk 53 J3
Burstock Dorset 11 J4
Burston Norfk 64 G5
Burston Staffs 70 G8
Burstow Surrey 24 H2
Burstwick E R Yk 93 M5
Burtersett N York 96 C3
Burtholme Cumb 111 K8
Burthorpe Green Suffk 63 N8
Burthwaite Cumb 110 H11
Burthy Cnwll 4 E10
Burtle Somset 19 L6
Burtle Hill Somset 19 L6
Burtoft Lincs 74 E3
Burton BCP 13 L6
Burton Ches W 69 P2
Burton Ches W 81 L10
Burton Dorset 11 P6
Burton Nthumb 119 N4
Burton Pembks 41 J9
Burton Somset 11 L2
Burton Somset 18 G6
Burton Wilts 20 F8
Burton Wilts 32 F9
Burton Agnes E R Yk 99 N8
Burton Bradstock Dorset 11 K7
Burton-by-Lincoln Lincs 86 C6
Burton Coggles Lincs 73 P5
Burton Dassett Warwks 48 C4
Burton End Essex 51 M6
Burton End Suffk 63 L11
Burton Fleming E R Yk 99 M6
Burton Green Warwks 59 L9
Burton Green Wrexhm 69 K3
Burton Hastings Warwks 59 P7
Burton Hill Wilts 32 H7
Burton-in-Kendal Cumb 95 L5
Burton-in-Kendal Services
  Cumb 95 L5
Burton in Lonsdale N York 95 P6
Burton Joyce Notts 72 G2
Burton Latimer Nhants 61 K6
Burton Lazars Leics 73 K7
Burton Leonard N York 97 M8
Burton on the Wolds Leics 72 F6
Burton Overy Leics 72 H11
Burton Pedwardine Lincs 74 B2
Burton Pidsea E R Yk 93 M4
Burton Salmon N York 91 M5
Burton's Green Essex 52 D6
Burton upon Stather N Linc 92 E7
Burton upon Trent Staffs 71 N10
Burton Waters Lincs 86 B6
Burtonwood Warrtn 82 C6
Burtonwood Services
  Warrtn 82 C6
Burwardsley Ches W 69 P3
Burwarton Shrops 57 L7
Burwash E Susx 25 Q6
Burwash Common E Susx 25 P6
Burwash Weald E Susx 25 Q6
Burwell Cambs 63 J7
Burwell Lincs 87 L5
Burwen IoA 78 G6
Burwick Ork 169 d8
Bury Bury 89 N8
Bury Cambs 62 C4
Bury Somset 18 B9
Bury W Susx 24 B8
Bury End C Beds 50 D3
Bury Green Herts 51 L6
Bury St Edmunds Suffk 64 B9
Burythorpe N York 98 F8
Busby E Rens 125 P6
Busby Stoop N York 97 N4
Buscot Oxon 33 P5
Bush Abers 143 P4
Bush Cnwll 16 C10
Bush Bank Herefs 45 P4
Bushbury Wolves 58 D4
Bushby Leics 72 H10
Bushey Herts 50 D11
Bushey Heath Herts 36 D2
Bush Green Norfk 65 J4
Bush Green Suffk 64 C10
Bushley Worcs 46 G8
Bushley Green Worcs 46 G8
Bushmead Bed 61 P8
Bushmoor Shrops 56 G7
Bushton Wilts 33 L9
Busk Cumb 102 B2
Buslingthorpe Lincs 86 E3

Bussage Gloucs 32 G4
Bussex Somset 19 L7
Butcher's Cross E Susx 25 N5
Butcombe N Som 19 P2
Bute Ag & B 124 C4
Butleigh Somset 19 P8
Butleigh Wootton Somset 19 P7
Butler's Cross Bucks 35 M3
Butler's Hill Notts 84 H11
Butlers Marston Warwks 48 B4
Butley Suffk 65 M11
Butley High Corner Suffk ...53 Q2
Buttercrambe N York 98 H9
Butterdean Border 129 K7
Butterknowle Dur 103 M5
Butterleigh Devon 9 N3
Buttermere Cumb 100 G9
Buttermere Wilts 22 B2
Buttershaw C Brad 90 E5
Butterstone P & K 141 Q8
Butterton Staffs 70 E6
Butterton Staffs 71 K3
Butterwick Dur 104 C4
Butterwick Lincs 87 L11
Butterwick N York 98 E5
Butterwick N York 99 K6
Butt Green Ches E 70 B4
Buttington Powys 56 C3
Buttonbridge Shrops 57 N9
Buttonoak Shrops 57 P9
Buttsash Hants 14 D5
Buttsbear Cross Cnwll 16 D11
Butt's Green Essex 52 C11
Buxhall Suffk 64 E10
Buxhall Fen Street Suffk 64 E10
Buxted E Susx 25 L6
Buxton Derbys 83 N10
Buxton Norfk 77 J7
Buxton Heath Norfk 76 H7
Buxworth Derbys 83 M8
Bwlch Powys 44 H10
Bwlchgwyn Wrexhm 69 J4
Bwlchllan Cerdgn 43 L3
Bwlchnewydd Carmth 42 G10
Bwlchtocyn Gwynd 66 E9
Bwlch-y-cibau Powys 68 G11
Bwlch-y-Ddar Powys 68 G10
Bwlchyfadfa Cerdgn 42 H5
Bwlch-y-ffridd Powys 55 P5
Bwlch-y-groes Pembks 41 P3
Bwlchymyrdd Swans 28 G5
Bwlch-y-sarnau Powys 55 N10
Byermoor Gatesd 113 J9
Byers Green Dur 103 P4
Byfield Nhants 48 F4
Byfleet Surrey 36 C8
Byford Herefs 45 M6
Bygrave Herts 50 G3
Byker N u Ty 113 L8
Byland Abbey N York 98 A8
Bylaugh Norfk 76 E8
Bylchau Conwy 68 C2
Byley Ches W 82 F11
Bynea Carmth 28 F5
Byram N York 91 M5
Byrness Nthumb 118 F8
Bystock Devon 9 P8
Bythorn Cambs 61 N5
Byton Herefs 45 M2
Bywell Nthumb 112 F8
Byworth W Susx 23 Q10

C

Cabbacott Devon 16 G7
Cabourne Lincs 93 K10
Cabrach Ag & B 122 G7
Cabrach Moray 150 B2
Cabus Lancs 95 K11
Cackle Street E Susx 25 L5
Cackle Street E Susx 25 Q7
Cackle Street E Susx 26 D8
Cadbury Devon 9 M3
Cadbury Barton Devon 17 M8
Cadbury World Birm 58 F8
Cadder E Duns 125 Q3
Caddington C Beds 50 C7
Caddonfoot Border 117 P3
Cadeby Donc 91 N10
Cadeby Leics 72 C10
Cadeleigh Devon 9 M3
Cade Street E Susx 25 P6
Cadgwith Cnwll 3 J11
Cadham Fife 134 H7
Cadishead Salfd 82 F6
Cadle Swans 28 H5
Cadley Lancs 88 G4
Cadley Wilts 21 P4
Cadley Wilts 33 P11
Cadmore End Bucks 35 L6
Cadnam Hants 13 P2
Cadney N Linc 92 H10
Cadole Flints 68 H2
Cadoxton V Glam 30 F11
Cadoxton Juxta-Neath
  Neath 29 L5
Cadwst Denbgs 68 D7
Caeathro Gwynd 67 J2
Caehopkin Powys 29 M2
Caenby Lincs 86 C3
Caerau Brdgnd 29 N6
Caerau Cardif 30 F9
Cae'r-bont Powys 29 M2
Cae'r bryn Carmth 28 G2
Caerdeon Gwynd 67 M11
Caergeiliog IoA 78 E9
Caergwrle Flints 69 K3
Caerhun Conwy 79 P10
Caerlanrig Border 117 M10
Caerleon Newpt 31 K6
Caernarfon Gwynd 66 H2
Caernarfon Castle Gwynd ...66 H2
Caerphilly Caerph 30 G7
Caersws Powys 55 N6
Caerwedros Cerdgn 42 G3
Caerwent Mons 31 N6
Caerwys Flints 80 G10
Caerynwch Gwynd 67 P11
Caggle Street Mons 45 M11
Caim IoA 79 L8
Caio Carmth 43 N7
Cairinis W Isls 168 d11

Cairnbaan Ag & B 130 G9
Cairnbulg Abers 159 P4
Cairncross Border 129 M11
Cairncurran Inver 125 J3
Cairndow Ag & B 131 P5
Cairneyhill Fife 134 C10
Cairngarroch D & G 106 E8
Cairngorms National Park .149 K7
Cairnie Abers 158 C9
Cairnorrie Abers 159 L9
Cairnryan D & G 106 E4
Cairnty Moray 157 Q7
Caister-on-Sea Norfk 77 Q9
Caistor Lincs 93 K10
Caistor St Edmund Norfk ...77 J11
Cakebole Worcs 58 C10
Cake Street Suffk 64 F3
Calais Street Suffk 52 G4
Calanais W Isls 168 h4
Calbourne IoW 14 D9
Calceby Lincs 87 L5
Calcoed Flints 80 H10
Calcot Gloucs 33 L2
Calcot W Berk 35 J10
Calcot Row W Berk 35 J10
Calcots Moray 157 P5
Calcott Kent 39 L9
Calcott Shrops 56 H2
Calcutt N York 97 M9
Calcutt Wilts 33 M6
Caldbeck Cumb 101 K2
Caldbergh N York 96 G3
Caldecote Cambs 61 P3
Caldecote Cambs 62 D9
Caldecote Herts 50 F3
Caldecott Nhants 61 L7
Caldecott Oxon 34 E5
Caldecott Rutlnd 61 J2
Caldecotte M Keyn 49 N7
Calder Cumb 100 D10
Calderbank N Lans 126 D5
Calder Bridge Cumb 100 D9
Calderbrook Rochdl 89 Q7
Caldercruix N Lans 126 E4
Calder Grove Wakefd 91 J7
Caldermore Rochdl 89 Q7
Calder Vale Lancs 95 L11
Calderwood S Lans 126 B6
Caldey Island Pembks 41 M11
Caldicot Cnwll 31 N7
Caldmore Wsall 58 F5
Caldwell N York 103 N8
Caldy Wirral 81 J7
Calenick Cnwll 3 L5
Calford Green Suffk 63 M11
Calfsound Ork 169 e3
Calgary Ag & B 137 K5
Califer Moray 157 K6
California Falk 126 G2
California Norfk 77 Q8
California Cross Devon 7 J8
Calke Derbys 72 B6
Calke Abbey Derbys 72 B6
Callakille Highld 153 M6
Callander Stirlg 133 J6
Callanish W Isls 168 h4
Callaughton Shrops 57 L5
Callerton N u Ty 113 J7
Callestick Cnwll 3 K3
Calligarry Highld 145 K7
Callington Cnwll 5 P8
Callingwood Staffs 71 N10
Callow Herefs 45 P8
Callow End Worcs 46 F4
Callow Hill Wilts 33 K8
Callow Hill Worcs 47 K2
Callow Hill Worcs 57 N10
Callows Grave Worcs 57 K11
Calmore Hants 13 P2
Calmsden Gloucs 33 K3
Calne Wilts 33 J10
Calow Derbys 84 F6
Calshot Hants 14 E6
Calstock Cnwll 6 C5
Calstone Wellington Wilts ..33 K11
Calthorpe Norfk 76 H5
Calthorpe Street Norfk 77 N6
Calthwaite Cumb 101 N2
Calton N York 96 D9
Calton Staffs 71 L5
Calveley Ches E 69 Q3
Calver Derbys 84 B6
Calverhall Shrops 69 R7
Calver Hill Herefs 45 M5
Calverleigh Devon 9 M4
Calverley Leeds 90 G3
Calver Sough Derbys 84 B6
Calvert Bucks 49 J10
Calverton M Keyn 49 L7
Calverton Notts 85 K11
Calvine P & K 141 K4
Calvo Cumb 109 P10
Calzeat Border 116 G3
Cam Gloucs 32 E5
Camasachoirie Highld 138 D5
Camasine Highld 138 D5
Camas Luinie Highld 146 A2
Camastianavaig Highld 43 J10
Camault Muir Highld 155 P9
Camber E Susx 26 G8
Camberley Surrey 23 N2
Camberwell Gt Lon 36 H5
Camblesforth N York 91 Q5
Cambo Nthumb 112 F3
Cambois Nthumb 113 M4
Camborne Cnwll 2 G5
Camborne & Redruth
  Mining District Cnwll 2 G5
Cambourne Cambs 62 D9
Cambridge Cambs 62 G9
Cambridge Gloucs 32 D4
Cambridge Airport Cambs ...62 G9
Cambrose Cnwll 2 H4
Cambus Clacks 133 P9
Cambusavie Highld 162 H7
Cambusbarron Stirlg 133 M9
Cambuskenneth Stirlg 133 N9
Cambuslang S Lans 125 Q5
Cambus o' May Abers 150 C8
Cambuswallace S Lans 116 E3
Camden Town Gt Lon 36 G4
Cameley BaNES 20 B3

Camelford Cnwll 5 J5
Camelon Falk 133 P11
Camerory Highld 157 J11
Camer's Green Worcs 46 E7
Camerton BaNES 20 C3
Camerton Cumb 100 D4
Camghouran P & K 140 E6
Camieston Border 117 R4
Cammachmore Abers 151 N8
Cammeringham Lincs 86 B4
Camore Highld 162 H9
Campbeltown Ag & B 120 D7
Campbeltown Airport
  Ag & B 120 C7
Camperdown N Tyne 113 L6
Cample D & G 109 J2
Campmuir P & K 142 C10
Camps W Loth 127 K4
Campsall Donc 91 N8
Camps End Cambs 51 P2
Campton C Beds 50 D3
Camptown Border 118 C8
Camrose Pembks 40 H6
Camserney P & K 141 K8
Camusnagaul Highld 139 K3
Camusnagaul Highld 160 H9
Camusteel Highld 153 N9
Camusterrach Highld 153 N9
Canada Hants 21 Q11
Canal Foot Cumb 94 G5
Canaston Bridge Pembks ...41 L7
Candacraig Abers 149 Q8
Candlesby Lincs 87 N7
Candover Green Shrops 57 J3
Candy Mill Border 116 F2
Cane End Oxon 35 J9
Canewdon Essex 38 F3
Canford Bottom Dorset 12 H4
Canford Cliffs BCP 13 J7
Canford Heath BCP 12 H6
Canford Magna BCP 12 H5
Canhams Green Suffk 64 F8
Canisbay Highld 167 P2
Canklow Rothm 84 F2
Canley Covtry 59 M9
Cann Dorset 20 G10
Canna Highld 144 B6
Cann Common Dorset 20 G10
Cannich Highld 155 K11
Cannington Somset 19 J7
Canning Town Gt Lon 37 K4
Cannock Staffs 58 E2
Cannock Chase Staffs 70 H11
Cannock Wood Staffs 58 F2
Cannon Bridge Herefs 45 N6
Canonbie D & G 110 G5
Canon Frome Herefs 46 B6
Canon Pyon Herefs 45 P5
Canons Ashby Nhants 48 G4
Canonstown Cnwll 2 E6
Canterbury Kent 39 K10
Canterbury Cathedral Kent .39 L10
Cantley Norfk 77 M11
Cantlop Shrops 57 J3
Canton Cardif 30 G9
Cantraywood Highld 156 D8
Cantsfield Lancs 95 N6
Canvey Island Essex 38 C5
Canwick Lincs 86 C7
Canworthy Water Cnwll 5 L3
Caol Highld 139 L2
Caolas Scalpaigh W Isls ..168 h8
Caoles Ag & B 136 D6
Caonich Highld 146 D9
Capel Kent 25 P2
Capel Surrey 24 E2
Capel Bangor Cerdgn 54 F9
Capel Betws Lleucu Cerdgn .43 M3
Capel Coch IoA 78 H8
Capel Curig Conwy 67 N3
Capel Cynon Cerdgn 42 G5
Capel Dewi Carmth 43 J10
Capel Dewi Cerdgn 43 J6
Capel-Dewi Cerdgn 54 E8
Capel Garmon Conwy 67 Q3
Capel Green Suffk 53 Q2
Capel Gwyn Carmth 43 J10
Capel Gwyn IoA 78 E9
Capel Gwynfe Carmth 43 P10
Capel Hendre Carmth 28 G2
Capel Isaac Carmth 43 L9
Capel Iwan Carmth 41 Q3
Capel-le-Ferne Kent 27 N4
Capelles Guern 10 c1
Capel Llanilltern Cardif 30 E9
Capel Mawr IoA 78 G10
Capel Parc IoA 78 G7
Capel St Andrew Suffk 53 Q2
Capel St Mary Suffk 53 J4
Capel Seion Cerdgn 54 E9
Capel Trisant Cerdgn 54 G9
Capeluchaf Gwynd 66 G5
Capelulo Conwy 79 N9
Capel-y-ffin Powys 45 K8
Capel-y-graig Gwynd 79 J11
Capenhurst Ches W 81 M10
Capernwray Lancs 95 L6
Cape Wrath Highld 164 G1
Capheaton Nthumb 112 F4
Caplaw E Rens 125 L6
Capon's Green Suffk 65 K8
Capstone Medway 38 C8
Capton Devon 7 L8
Capton Somset 18 E7
Caputh P & K 141 Q9
Caradon Mining District
  Cnwll 5 M7
Caradon Town Cnwll 5 M7
Carbeth Stirlg 125 N2
Carbis Cnwll 4 G10
Carbis Bay Cnwll 2 E6
Carbost Highld 152 F11
Carbost Highld 152 G8
Carbrook Sheff 84 E3
Carbrooke Norfk 76 C11
Carburton Notts 85 K6
Carclaze Cnwll 3 Q3
Car Colston Notts 73 J2
Carcroft Donc 91 N9
Cardenden Fife 134 G8
Cardeston Shrops 56 F2
Cardewlees Cumb 110 G10
Cardiff Cardif 30 G9
Cardiff Airport V Glam 30 E11
Cardiff Gate Services Cardif .30 H8
Cardiff West Services Cardif .30 E9
Cardigan Cerdgn 42 C5
Cardinal's Green Cambs 63 K11
Cardington Bed 61 N11
Cardington Shrops 57 J5
Cardinham Cnwll 5 J8
Cardrain D & G 106 F11
Cardrona Border 117 L3
Cardross Ag & B 125 J2
Cardryne D & G 106 F11
Cardurnock Cumb 110 C9
Careby Lincs 73 Q7
Careston Angus 143 J5
Carew Pembks 41 K10
Carew Cheriton Pembks 41 K10
Carew Newton Pembks 41 K10
Carey Herefs 45 R8
Carfin N Lans 126 D6
Carfraemill Border 128 E9
Cargate Green Norfk 77 M9
Cargenbridge D & G 109 L6
Cargill P & K 142 B10
Cargo Cumb 110 G9
Cargreen Cnwll 6 C6
Cargurrel Cnwll 3 M6
Carham Nthumb 118 E3
Carhampton Somset 18 D6
Carharrack Cnwll 3 J5
Carie P & K 140 F6
Carinish W Isls 168 d11
Carisbrooke IoW 14 E9
Cark Cumb 94 H5
Carkeel Cnwll 5 Q9
Càrlabhagh W Isls 168 h3
Carland Cross Cnwll 3 L3
Carlbury Darltn 103 P7
Carlby Lincs 73 Q8
Carlcroft Nthumb 118 F8
Carlecotes Barns 83 Q4
Carleen Cnwll 2 G7
Carlesmoor N York 97 K6
Carleton Cumb 100 D9
Carleton Cumb 101 P5
Carleton Cumb 110 H10
Carleton Lancs 88 C3
Carleton Wakefd 91 M6
Carleton Forehoe Norfk 76 F10
Carleton-in-Craven N York ..96 E11
Carleton Rode Norfk 64 G3
Carleton St Peter Norfk 77 L11
Carlidnack Cnwll 3 K8
Carlincraig Abers 158 G9
Carlingcott BaNES 20 C3
Carlin How R & Cl 105 K7
Carlisle Cumb 110 H9
Carlisle Lake District
  Airport 111 J8
Carloggas Cnwll 4 D8
Carlops Border 127 M6
Carloway W Isls 168 h3
Carlton Barns 91 K8
Carlton Bed 61 L9
Carlton Cambs 63 K10
Carlton Leeds 91 J5
Carlton Leics 72 B10
Carlton N York 91 Q6
Carlton N York 96 G4
Carlton N York 98 C3
Carlton Notts 72 G2
Carlton S on T 104 C6
Carlton Suffk 65 M9
Carlton Colville Suffk 65 Q4
Carlton Curlieu Leics 72 H11
Carlton Green Cambs 63 K10
Carlton Husthwaite N York ..97 Q5
Carlton-in-Cleveland
  N York 104 F10
Carlton in Lindrick Notts ...85 J4
Carlton-le-Moorland Lincs ..86 B9
Carlton Miniott N York 97 N4
Carlton-on-Trent Notts 85 N8
Carlton Scroop Lincs 86 B11
Carluke S Lans 126 E7
Carlyon Bay Cnwll 3 R3
Carmacoup S Lans 115 Q2
Carmarthen Carmth 42 H10
Carmel Carmth 43 L11
Carmel Flints 80 H9
Carmel Gwynd 66 H4
Carmichael S Lans 116 C3
Carmunnock C Glas 125 P6
Carmyle C Glas 125 Q5
Carmyllie Angus 143 J9
Carnaby E R Yk 99 N7
Carnbee Fife 135 N6
Carnbo P & K 134 D7
Carn Brea Cnwll 2 H5
Carnbrogie Abers 151 M2
Carndu Highld 145 Q2
Carnduff S Lans 126 B8
Carne Cnwll 3 K9
Carne Cnwll 3 M6
Carne Cnwll 4 F10
Carnell E Ayrs 125 M11
Carnewas Cnwll 4 D8
Carnforth Lancs 95 K6
Carn-gorm Highld 146 B3
Carnhedryn Pembks 40 F5
Carnhell Green Cnwll 2 G6
Carnie Abers 151 L6
Carnkie Cnwll 2 H5
Carnkie Cnwll 3 J7
Carnkief Cnwll 3 J3
Carno Powys 55 M5
Carnock Fife 134 C10
Carnon Downs Cnwll 3 K5
Carnousie Abers 158 G7
Carnoustie Angus 143 K11
Carnsmerry Cnwll 3 Q2
Carnwath S Lans 126 H8
Carnyorth Cnwll 2 B7
Carol Green Solhll 59 L9
Carpalla Cnwll 3 P3
Carperby N York 96 F3
Carpley Green N York 96 F3
Carr Rothm 84 H2
Carradale Ag & B 120 F4
Carradale Village Ag & B ...120 E4
Carrbridge Highld 148 G3
Carrbrook Tamesd 83 L4
Carrefour Jersey 11 b1
Carreglefn IoA 78 F7
Carr Gate Wakefd 91 J5
Carrhouse N Linc 92 C9

Carrick Ag & B 131 J10
Carrick Castle Ag & B 131 P9
Carriden Falk 134 C11
Carrington Lincs 87 K9
Carrington Mdloth 127 Q5
Carrington Traffd 82 F6
Carrog Conwy 67 P5
Carrog Denbgs 68 F6
Carron Falk 133 P11
Carron Moray 157 N9
Carronbridge D & G 116 B10
Carron Bridge Stirlg 133 L11
Carronshore Falk 133 P11
Carrow Hill Mons 31 M6
Carr Shield Nthumb 112 B11
Carrutherstown D & G 110 P6
Carruth House Inver 125 K4
Carr Vale Derbys 84 G7
Carsaig Ag & B 137 N11
Carseriggan D & G 107 K4
Carsethorn D & G 109 L9
Carshalton Gt Lon 36 G8
Carsington Derbys 71 P4
Carskey Ag & B 120 C10
Carsluith D & G 107 N7
Carsphairn D & G 115 L9
Carstairs S Lans 126 G8
Carstairs Junction S Lans ..126 H8
Carswell Marsh Oxon 34 B5
Carter's Clay Hants 22 B10
Carters Green Essex 51 M8
Carterton Oxon 33 Q3
Carterway Heads Nthumb ..112 F10
Carthew Cnwll 4 G10
Carthorpe N York 97 M4
Cartington Nthumb 119 K10
Cartland S Lans 126 F8
Cartledge Derbys 84 D5
Cartmel Cumb 94 H5
Cartmel Fell Cumb 95 J3
Carway Carmth 28 E3
Carwinley Cumb 110 H6
Cashe's Green Gloucs 32 F3
Cashmoor Dorset 12 G2
Cassington Oxon 34 E2
Cassop Dur 104 B3
Castallack Cnwll 2 D8
Castel Guern 10 b2
Castell Conwy 79 P11
Castell-y-bwch Torfn 31 J6
Casterton Cumb 95 N5
Castle Cnwll 4 H10
Castle Acre Norfk 75 R7
Castle Ashby Nhants 61 J9
Castlebay W Isls 168 b18
Castle Bolton N York 96 F2
Castle Bromwich Solhll 58 H7
Castle Bytham Lincs 73 P7
Castlebythe Pembks 41 K5
Castle Caereinion Powys 56 B3
Castle Camps Cambs 51 P2
Castle Carrock Cumb 111 K9
Castlecary N Lans 126 D2
Castle Cary Somset 20 B8
Castle Combe Wilts 32 F9
Castlecraig Highld 156 E4
Castle Donington Leics 72 C5
Castle Douglas D & G 108 G8
Castle Eaton Swindn 33 M5
Castle Eden Dur 104 D3
Castle End C Pete 74 B9
Castleford Wakefd 91 L5
Castle Frome Herefs 46 C5
Castle Gate Cnwll 2 D7
Castle Green Cumb 95 L2
Castle Green Surrey 23 Q2
Castle Gresley Derbys 71 P11
Castle Hedingham Essex 52 C4
Castlehill Border 117 J3
Castlehill Highld 167 L3
Castle Hill Kent 25 Q2
Castle Hill Suffk 53 K2
Castlehill W Duns 125 K2
Castle Howard N York 98 E6
Castle Kennedy D & G 106 F6
Castle Lachlan Ag & B 131 L8
Castlemartin Pembks 40 H11
Castlemilk C Glas 125 P6
Castle Morris Pembks 40 H4
Castlemorton Worcs 46 E7
Castlemorton Common
  Worcs 46 E7
Castle O'er D & G 110 D2
Castle Rising Norfk 75 N6
Castleside Dur 112 G11
Castle Stuart Highld 156 C8
Castlethorpe M Keyn 49 M6
Castlethorpe N Linc 92 G9
Castleton Ag & B 130 H11
Castleton Border 111 K3
Castleton Derbys 83 Q8
Castleton N York 105 J9
Castleton Newpt 31 J8
Castleton Rochdl 89 P8
Castletown Ches W 69 M4
Castletown Dorset 11 P10
Castletown Highld 167 L3
Castletown IoM 80 c8
Castletown Sundld 113 N9
Castley N York 97 L11
Caston Norfk 64 D2
Castor C Pete 74 B11
Caswell Bay Swans 28 G7
Catacol N Ayrs 123 R10
Cat and Fiddle Derbys 83 M10
Catbrain S Glos 31 Q8
Catbrook Mons 31 P4
Catch Flints 81 J10
Catchall Cnwll 2 C8
Catchem's Corner Solhll 59 L9
Catchgate Dur 113 J10
Catcliffe Rothm 84 F3
Catcomb Wilts 33 K9
Catcott Somset 19 L7
Caterham Surrey 36 H9
Catfield Norfk 77 M7
Catfield Common Norfk 77 N7
Catford Gt Lon 37 J6
Catforth Lancs 88 F3
Cathcart C Glas 125 P5
Cathedine Powys 44 G9
Catherine-de-Barnes
  Solhll 59 J8
Catherine Slack C Brad 90 D5
Catherington Hants 15 J4

Catherston Leweston
Dorset...............................10 H6
Catherton Shrops................57 M9
Catisfield Hants..................14 G5
Catley Herefs.......................46 C6
Catley Lane Head Rochdl......89 P7
Catlodge Highld.................147 Q9
Catlow Lancs.......................89 P3
Catlowdy Cumb..................111 J5
Catmere End Essex..............51 L3
Catmore W Berk...................34 E8
Caton Devon.........................7 K4
Caton Lancs........................95 L8
Caton Green Lancs...............95 M7
Cator Court Devon.................8 G9
Catrine E Ayrs...................115 K2
Cat's Ash Mons...................31 L6
Catsfield E Susx..................26 B9
Catsfield Stream E Susx........26 B9
Catsgore Somset..................19 P9
Catsham Somset...................19 Q8
Catshill Worcs....................58 E10
Catstree Shrops...................57 N5
Cattadale Ag & B................120 C9
Cattal N York......................97 P10
Cattawade Suffk...................53 K5
Catterall Lancs....................88 F2
Catteralslane Shrops............69 Q6
Catterick N York.................103 P11
Catterick Bridge N York.......103 P11
Catterick Garrison N York....103 N11
Catterlen Cumb..................101 N4
Catterline Abers.................143 R2
Catterton N York..................97 R11
Catteshall Surrey..................23 Q6
Catthorpe Leics...................60 C5
Cattishall Suffk....................64 B8
Cattistock Dorset..................11 M5
Catton N York......................97 N5
Catton Nthumb...................112 B9
Catwick E R Yk....................99 N11
Catworth Cambs...................61 N6
Caudle Green Gloucs.............32 H2
Caulcott C Beds....................50 B2
Caulcott Oxon......................48 F10
Cauldcots Angus.................143 M8
Cauldhame Stirlg.................133 J9
Cauldmill Border.................117 Q7
Cauldon Staffs......................71 K5
Cauldon Lowe Staffs.............71 K5
Cauldwell Derbys..................71 P11
Caulkerbush D & G..............109 K9
Caulside D & G...................110 H4
Caundle Marsh Dorset...........11 P2
Caunsall Worcs....................58 C8
Caunton Notts......................85 M8
Causeway Hants....................23 N10
Causeway End Cumb.............95 K3
Causeway End D & G...........107 M6
Causeway End Essex..............51 Q7
Causewayend S Lans............116 E3
Causewayhead Cumb............109 P10
Causewayhead Stirlg............133 N8
Causeyend Abers.................151 N4
Causey Park Nthumb............113 J2
Causey Park Bridge Nthumb..113 J2
Cavendish Suffk....................63 P11
Cavenham Suffk....................63 N6
Caversfield Oxon..................48 G9
Caversham Readg..................35 K10
Caverswall Staffs...................70 H6
Caverton Mill Border...........118 D5
Cavil E R Yk..........................92 C4
Cawdor Highld....................156 E7
Cawkwell Lincs....................87 J5
Cawood N York......................91 P3
Cawsand Cnwll.......................5 C8
Cawston Norfk......................76 G7
Cawston Warwks...................59 Q10
Cawthorn N York...................98 F3
Cawthorne Barns...................90 H9
Cawton N York......................98 C5
Caxton Cambs.......................62 D9
Caxton End Cambs.................62 D9
Caxton Gibbet Cambs.............62 C8
Caynham Shrops...................57 K10
Caythorpe Lincs....................86 B11
Caythorpe Notts....................85 L11
Cayton N York.......................99 M4
Ceannabeinne Highld...........165 K3
Ceann a Bhaigh W Isls..........168 c11
Ceannacroc Lodge Highld......146 G5
Cearsiadar W Isls.................168 i6
Ceciliford Mons....................31 P4
Cefn Newpt..........................31 J7
Cefn Berain Conwy................80 D11
Cefn-brith Conwy..................68 B4
Cefn-bryn-brain Carmth.........29 K2
Cefn Byrle Powys...................29 M2
Cefn Canel Powys...................68 H8
Cefn Coch Powys....................68 F9
Cefn-coed-y-cymmer
Myr Td..............................30 D3
Cefn Cribwr Brdgnd...............29 N8
Cefn Cross Brdgnd.................29 N8
Cefn-ddwysarn Gwynd............68 C7
Cefn-Einion Shrops................56 D7
Cefneithin Carmth..................28 G2
Cefngorwydd Powys...............44 C5
Cefn-mawr Wrexhm................69 J6
Cefnpennar Rhondd...............30 D4
Cefn-y-bedd Flints.................69 K3
Cefn-y-pant Carmth................41 N5
Ceint IoA............................78 H9
Cellan Cerdgn.......................43 M5
Cellardyke Fife....................135 P7
Cellarhead Staffs...................70 H5
Celleron Cumb....................101 N5
Celynen Caerph.....................30 H5
Cemaes IoA...........................78 F6
Cemmaes Powys....................55 J3
Cemmaes Road Powys............55 J4
Cenarth Cerdgn.....................41 Q2
Cerbyd Pembks......................40 F5
Ceres Fife.........................135 L5
Cerne Abbas Dorset...............11 N4
Cerney Wick Gloucs................33 L5
Cerrigceinwen IoA.................78 G10
Cerrigydrudion Conwy............68 C5
Cess Norfk...........................77 N8
Ceunant Gwynd......................67 J2
Chaceley Gloucs.....................46 G8
Chacewater Cnwll....................3 K5
Chackmore Bucks...................49 J7
Chacombe Nhants..................48 E6
Chadbury Worcs......................47 K5

Chadderton Oldham................89 Q9
Chadderton Fold Oldham.........89 Q9
Chaddesden C Derb................72 B3
Chaddesley Corbett Worcs.......58 C10
Chaddlehanger Devon...............8 C9
Chaddleworth W Berk..............34 D9
Chadlington Oxon..................48 B10
Chadshunt Warwks..................48 B4
Chadwell Leics......................73 K6
Chadwell Shrops.....................57 P2
Chadwell End Bed...................61 N7
Chadwell Heath Gt Lon...........37 L3
Chadwell St Mary Thurr...........37 P5
Chadwick Worcs......................58 B11
Chadwick End Solhll...............59 K10
Chadwick Green St Hel............82 B5
Chaffcombe Somset.................10 H2
Chafford Hundred Thurr...........37 P5
Chagford Devon........................8 H7
Chailey E Susx......................25 J7
Chainbridge Cambs.................74 H10
Chainhurst Kent.....................26 B2
Chalbury Dorset.....................12 H3
Chalbury Common Dorset.........12 H3
Chaldon Surrey......................36 H9
Chaldon Herring Dorset..........12 C8
Chale IoW...........................14 E11
Chale Green IoW....................14 E11
Chalfont Common Bucks..........36 B2
Chalfont St Giles Bucks...........35 Q6
Chalfont St Peter Bucks..........36 B2
Chalford Gloucs.....................32 G4
Chalford Oxon.......................35 K4
Chalford Wilts......................20 G4
Chalgrave C Beds...................50 B5
Chalgrove Oxon......................34 H5
Chalk Kent...........................37 Q6
Chalk End Essex.....................51 P8
Chalkhouse Green Oxon...........35 K9
Chalkway Somset....................10 H3
Chalkwell Kent......................38 E9
Challaborough Devon.................6 H10
Challacombe Devon.................17 M3
Challoch D & G....................107 L4
Challock Kent.......................38 H11
Chalmington Dorset................11 M4
Chalton C Beds......................50 B5
Chalton C Beds......................61 P10
Chalton Hants.......................23 K11
Chalvey Slough......................35 Q9
Chalvington E Susx.................25 M9
Chambers Green Kent..............26 F3
Chandler's Cross Herts...........50 C11
Chandlers Cross Worcs...........46 E7
Chandler's Ford Hants............22 D11
Channel's End Bed..................61 P9
Channel Tunnel Terminal
Kent................................27 L4
Chantry Somset......................20 D5
Chantry Suffk........................53 K3
Chapel Cumb........................100 H4
Chapel Fife.........................134 H9
Chapel Allerton Leeds.............91 J3
Chapel Allerton Somset...........19 M4
Chapel Amble Cnwll...................4 F6
Chapel Brampton Nhants.........60 F7
Chapelbridge Cambs................62 C2
Chapel Chorlton Staffs...........70 E7
Chapel Cross E Susx...............25 P6
Chapel End Bed......................61 P9
Chapel End C Beds..................50 C2
Chapel End Cambs...................61 P4
Chapel End Warwks.................59 M6
Chapelend Way Essex...............52 B4
Chapel-en-le-Frith Derbys........83 N8
Chapel Field Bury...................89 M9
Chapelgate Lincs....................74 H6
Chapel Green Warwks..............48 E2
Chapel Green Warwks..............59 L7
Chapel Haddlesey N York.........91 P5
Chapelhall N Lans.................126 D5
Chapel Hill Abers.................159 Q10
Chapel Hill Lincs...................86 H10
Chapel Hill Mons...................31 P5
Chapel Hill N York.................97 M11
Chapelhope Border.................117 J7
Chapelknowe D & G...............110 F6
Chapel Lawn Shrops................56 E9
Chapel-le-Dale N York............95 Q5
Chapel Leigh Somset...............18 F9
Chapel Milton Derbys.............83 N8
Chapel of Garioch Abers........151 J3
Chapel Rossan D & G.............106 F9
Chapel Row E Susx..................25 P8
Chapel Row Essex...................52 C11
Chapel Row W Berk.................34 G11
Chapels Cumb........................94 E4
Chapel St Leonards Lincs.........87 Q6
Chapel Stile Cumb................101 K9
Chapelton Abers...................151 M9
Chapelton Angus...................143 L8
Chapelton Devon.....................17 K6
Chapelton S Lans..................126 B8
Chapel Town Cnwll...................4 D10
Chapeltown Moray.................149 N3
Chapeltown Sheff....................91 K11
Chapmanslade Wilts................20 F5
Chapmans Well Devon................5 P3
Chapmore End Herts................50 H7
Chappel Essex........................52 E6
Charaton Cnwll........................5 N8
Chard Somset.........................10 G3
Chard Junction Somset............10 G4
Chardleigh Green Somset.........10 G2
Chardstock Devon....................10 G4
Charfield S Glos.....................32 D6
Chargrove Gloucs....................46 H11
Charing Kent.........................26 G2
Charing Heath Kent.................26 F2
Charing Hill Kent...................38 G11
Charingworth Gloucs...............47 N7
Charlbury Oxon......................48 C11
Charlcombe BaNES...................32 D11
Charlcutt Wilts......................33 J9
Charlecote Warwks..................47 Q3
Charlemont Sandw...................58 F6
Charles Devon........................17 M5
Charleshill Surrey..................23 N6
Charleston Angus..................142 F8
Charlestown C Aber...............151 N7
Charlestown C Brad.................90 F3
Charlestown Calder.................90 B5
Charlestown Cnwll....................3 Q3
Charlestown Cnwll....................3 Q3
Charlestown Derbys.................83 M6

Charlestown Dorset................11 P9
Charlestown Fife..................134 D11
Charlestown Highld...............153 Q3
Charlestown Highld...............156 A8
Charlestown Salfd..................82 H4
Charlestown of Aberlour
Moray..............................157 P9
Charles Tye Suffk..................64 E11
Charlesworth Derbys...............83 M6
Charlinch Somset....................18 H7
Charlottetown Fife................134 H5
Charlton Gt Lon.....................37 K5
Charlton Hants.......................22 C5
Charlton Herts.......................50 E5
Charlton Nhants.....................48 F7
Charlton Nthumb...................112 B4
Charlton Oxon........................34 D7
Charlton Somset.....................19 J9
Charlton Somset.....................20 B6
Charlton Somset.....................20 C4
Charlton Surrey......................36 C7
Charlton W Susx.....................15 N4
Charlton Wilts.......................20 H10
Charlton Wilts.......................33 J7
Charlton Worcs.......................47 K5
Charlton Worcs.......................58 B10
Charlton Wrekin......................57 K2
Charlton Abbots Gloucs...........47 K10
Charlton Adam Somset.............19 P9
Charlton All Saints Wilts.........21 N10
Charlton Down Dorset..............11 P5
Charlton Hill Shrops...............57 K3
Charlton Horethorne
Somset.............................20 C10
Charlton Kings Gloucs.............47 J10
Charlton Mackrell Somset.........19 P9
Charlton Marshall Dorset.........12 F4
Charlton Musgrove Somset........20 D9
Charlton-on-Otmoor Oxon........48 G11
Charlton on the Hill Dorset.......12 E4
Charlton St Peter Wilts............21 M3
Charlwood Hants.....................23 J8
Charlwood Surrey....................24 F2
Charminster Dorset.................11 P6
Charmouth Dorset...................10 H6
Charndon Bucks......................49 J10
Charney Bassett Oxon..............34 C6
Charnock Green Lancs..............88 H7
Charnock Richard Lancs............88 H7
Charnock Richard Services
Lancs.............................88 G7
Charsfield Suffk.....................65 K10
Chart Corner Kent...................38 C11
Charter Alley Hants.................22 G3
Charterhall Border................129 K10
Charterhouse Somset...............19 N3
Chartershall Stirlg.................133 M9
Charterville Allotments
Oxon..............................34 B2
Chartham Kent.......................39 K11
Chartham Hatch Kent...............39 K10
Chart Hill Kent......................26 C2
Chartridge Bucks....................35 P4
Chart Sutton Kent...................26 D2
Chartway Street Kent...............38 D11
Charvil Wokham......................35 L9
Charwelton Nhants..................60 B9
Chase Cross Gt Lon.................37 M2
Chase Terrace Staffs................58 F3
Chasetown Staffs....................58 F3
Chastleton Oxon.....................47 P9
Chasty Devon.........................16 E11
Chatburn Lancs......................89 M2
Chatcull Staffs......................70 D8
Chatham Caerph......................30 H7
Chatham Medway.....................38 C8
Chatham Green Essex...............52 B8
Chathill Nthumb...................119 N5
Chatley Worcs........................46 G2
Chatsworth Derbys..................84 C6
Chattenden Medway.................38 C7
Chatter End Essex...................51 L5
Chatteris Cambs.....................62 E3
Chatterton Lancs....................89 M7
Chattisham Suffk....................53 J3
Chatto Border.......................118 E7
Chatton Nthumb....................119 L5
Chaul End C Beds....................50 C6
Chawleigh Devon.....................17 N9
Chawley Oxon........................34 E4
Chawston Bed........................61 Q9
Chawton Hants.......................23 K7
Chaxhill Gloucs......................32 D2
Chazey Heath Oxon.................35 J9
Cheadle Staffs.......................71 J6
Cheadle Stockp......................83 J7
Cheadle Heath Stockp.............83 J7
Cheadle Hulme Stockp............83 J7
Cheam Gt Lon........................36 F8
Cheapside W & M....................35 P11
Chearsley Bucks.....................35 K2
Chebsey Staffs.......................70 F9
Checkendon Oxon....................35 J8
Checkley Ches E......................70 C5
Checkley Herefs......................46 A7
Checkley Staffs......................71 J7
Checkley Green Ches E.............70 C5
Chedburgh Suffk.....................63 N9
Cheddar Somset......................19 M4
Cheddington Bucks..................49 P11
Cheddleton Staffs...................70 H4
Cheddleton Heath Staffs..........70 H4
Cheddon Fitzpaine Somset.......18 H9
Chedglow Wilts......................32 H6
Chedgrave Norfk.....................65 M2
Chedington Dorset..................11 K3
Chediston Suffk......................65 M6
Chediston Green Suffk.............65 M6
Chedworth Gloucs...................33 L2
Chedzoy Somset......................19 K7
Cheeseman's Green Kent...........26 H4
Cheetham Hill Manch...............82 H4
Cheldon Devon.........................8 H2
Chelford Ches E......................82 H10
Chellaston C Derb...................72 B4
Chellington Bed.....................61 L9
Chelmarsh Shrops...................57 N7
Chelmer Village Essex..............52 B10
Chelmick Shrops.....................56 H6
Chelmondiston Suffk...............53 M4
Chelmorton Derbys..................83 P11
Chelmsford Essex....................52 B10
Chelmsley Wood Solhll............59 J7
Chelsea Gt Lon.......................36 G5
Chelsfield Gt Lon...................37 L7
Chelsham Surrey.....................37 J9

Chelston Somset......................18 G10
Chelsworth Suffk....................52 G2
Cheltenham Gloucs..................46 H10
Chelveston Nhants..................61 L7
Chelvey N Som........................31 N11
Chelwood BaNES......................20 B2
Chelwood Common E Susx.........25 K5
Chelwood Gate E Susx.............25 K4
Chelworth Wilts......................33 J6
Chelworth Lower Green
Wilts..............................33 L6
Chelworth Upper Green
Wilts..............................33 L6
Cheney Longville Shrops..........56 G8
Chenies Bucks........................50 B11
Chepstow Mons......................31 P6
Chequerbent Bolton................89 K9
Chequers Corner Norfk...........75 J9
Cherhill Wilts.......................33 K10
Cherington Gloucs..................32 H5
Cherington Warwks..................47 Q7
Cheriton Devon........................17 N2
Cheriton Hants.......................22 G9
Cheriton Kent........................27 M4
Cheriton Pembks.....................41 J11
Cheriton Swans......................28 E6
Cheriton Bishop Devon..............9 J6
Cheriton Fitzpaine Devon...........9 P11
Cherrington Wrekin.................70 B11
Cherry Burton E R Yk...............92 G2
Cherry Hinton Cambs...............62 G9
Cherry Orchard Worcs..............46 G4
Cherry Willingham Lincs..........86 D6
Chertsey Surrey......................36 B7
Cherwell Valley Services
Oxon...............................48 F9
Cheselbourne Dorset...............12 C5
Chesham Bucks.......................35 Q4
Chesham Bury.........................89 N8
Chesham Bois Bucks................35 Q5
Cheshunt Herts.......................51 J10
Chesil Beach Dorset.................11 N9
Chesley Kent.........................38 E9
Cheslyn Hay Staffs..................58 E3
Chessetts Wood Warwks...........59 J10
Chessington Gt Lon.................36 E8
Chessington World of
Adventures Gt Lon...............36 E8
Chester Ches W......................81 N11
Chesterblade Somset................20 C6
Chesterfield Derbys.................84 E6
Chesterfield Staffs..................58 G3
Chesterhill Mdloth................128 B7
Chester-le-Street Dur.............113 L10
Chester Moor Dur.................113 L11
Chesters Border....................118 B6
Chesters Border....................118 B8
Chester Services Ches W.....81 P9
Chesterton Cambs...................62 G8
Chesterton Cambs...................74 B11
Chesterton Gloucs...................33 K4
Chesterton Oxon.....................48 G10
Chesterton Shrops...................57 P5
Chesterton Staffs....................70 E5
Chesterton Green Warwks.........48 C3
Chesterwood Nthumb.............112 B7
Chester Zoo Ches W............81 N10
Chestfield Kent......................39 K8
Chestnut Street Kent...............38 E9
Cheston Devon.........................6 H7
Cheswardine Shrops................70 C8
Cheswick Nthumb..................129 Q10
Cheswick Green Solhll..............58 H9
Chetnole Dorset......................11 N3
Chettiscombe Devon..................9 N2
Chettisham Cambs...................62 H4
Chettle Dorset.......................12 G2
Chetton Shrops......................57 M6
Chetwode Bucks......................48 H9
Chetwynd Wrekin....................70 C10
Chetwynd Aston Wrekin...........70 D11
Cheveley Cambs......................63 L8
Chevening Kent......................37 L9
Cheverton IoW.......................14 E10
Chevington Suffk....................63 N9
Chevithorne Devon..................18 C11
Chew Magna BaNES..................19 Q2
Chew Moor Bolton...................89 K9
Chew Stoke BaNES...................19 Q2
Chewton Keynsham BaNES.........32 C11
Chewton Mendip Somset...........19 Q4
Chicacott Devon.......................8 F5
Chicheley M Keyn....................49 P5
Chichester W Susx...................15 N6
Chickerell Dorset....................11 N8
Chickering Suffk.....................65 J6
Chicklade Wilts......................20 H8
Chicksands C Beds...................50 D3
Chickward Herefs....................45 K4
Chidden Hants........................23 J11
Chiddingfold Surrey................23 Q7
Chiddingly E Susx...................25 M8
Chiddingstone Kent.................25 M2
Chiddingstone Causeway
Kent...............................37 M11
Chiddingstone Hoath Kent.......25 L2
Chideock Dorset......................11 J6
Chidham W Susx.....................15 L6
Chidswell Kirk.......................90 H6
Chieveley W Berk....................34 E10
Chieveley Services W Berk....34 E10
Chignall St James Essex...........51 Q8
Chignall Smealy Essex..............51 Q8
Chigwell Essex.......................37 K2
Chigwell Row Essex.................37 L2
Chilbolton Hants....................22 C6
Chilcomb Hants......................22 F9
Chilcombe Dorset....................11 L6
Chilcompton Somset................20 B4
Chilcote Leics.......................59 L2
Childer Thornton Ches W..........81 M9
Childrey Oxon.......................34 C7
Child's Ercall Shrops...............70 B9
Childswickham Worcs..............47 L7
Childwall Lpool......................81 N7
Childwick Bury Herts...............50 D8
Chilfrome Dorset....................11 M5
Chilgrove W Susx....................15 M4
Chilham Kent.........................39 J11
Chilla Devon...........................8 B4
Chillaton Devon........................8 B8
Chillenden Kent......................39 N11
Chillerton IoW.......................14 E10

Chillesford Suffk....................65 M11
Chillingham Nthumb..............119 L5
Chillington Devon.....................7 K10
Chillington Somset.................10 H2
Chilmark Wilts.......................21 J8
Chilmington Green Kent..........26 G3
Chilson Oxon........................48 B11
Chilsworthy Cnwll....................5 Q7
Chilsworthy Devon..................16 E10
Chiltern Green C Beds.............50 D7
Chiltern Hills.......................35 L5
Chilthorne Domer Somset........19 P11
Chilton Bucks........................35 J2
Chilton Devon.........................9 L4
Chilton Dur..........................103 Q5
Chilton Kent.........................27 N3
Chilton Oxon........................34 E7
Chilton Suffk........................52 E3
Chilton Candover Hants...........22 G6
Chilton Cantelo Somset...........19 Q10
Chilton Foliat Wilts.................34 B10
Chilton Polden Somset............19 L6
Chilton Street Suffk................63 N11
Chilton Trinity Somset............19 J7
Chilwell Notts.......................72 E3
Chilworth Hants.....................22 D11
Chilworth Surrey....................36 B11
Chimney Oxon........................34 C4
Chineham Hants......................23 J3
Chingford Gt Lon....................37 J2
Chinley Derbys.......................83 M8
Chinnor Oxon.........................35 L4
Chipchase Castle Nthumb.......112 C5
Chipnall Shrops......................70 C8
Chippenham Cambs..................63 L7
Chippenham Wilts...................32 H10
Chipperfield Herts...................50 B10
Chipping Herts.......................51 J4
Chipping Lancs.......................89 J2
Chipping Campden Gloucs........47 N7
Chipping Hill Essex.................52 D8
Chipping Norton Oxon.............48 B9
Chipping Ongar Essex..............51 N10
Chipping Sodbury S Glos.........32 D8
Chipping Warden Nhants.........48 E5
Chipshop Devon........................8 B9
Chipstable Somset...................18 D9
Chipstead Kent......................37 M9
Chipstead Surrey....................36 G9
Chirbury Shrops.....................56 D5
Chirk Wrexhm........................69 J7
Chirnside Border...................129 M8
Chirnsidebridge Border..........129 M8
Chirton Wilts........................21 L3
Chisbury Wilts.......................33 Q11
Chiselborough Somset.............11 K2
Chiseldon Swindn...................33 N8
Chiselhampton Oxon...............34 G5
Chiserley Calder....................90 C5
Chisholme Border..................117 N8
Chislehurst Gt Lon.................37 K6
Chislet Kent.........................39 M9
Chiswell Green Herts...............50 D10
Chiswick Gt Lon.....................36 F5
Chiswick End Cambs...............62 E11
Chisworth Derbys...................83 L6
Chitcombe E Susx...................26 D7
Chithurst W Susx....................23 M10
Chittering Cambs....................62 G7
Chitterne Wilts......................21 J6
Chittlehamholt Devon.............17 M7
Chittlehampton Devon.............17 L6
Chittoe Wilts........................33 J11
Chivelstone Devon....................7 K11
Chivenor Devon......................17 J5
Chiverton Cross Cnwll...............3 J4
Chlenry D & G......................106 F5
Chobham Surrey.....................23 Q2
Cholderton Wilts....................21 P6
Cholesbury Bucks...................35 P3
Chollerford Nthumb..............112 D6
Chollerton Nthumb...............112 D6
Cholmondeston Ches E............70 A3
Cholsey Oxon.........................34 G7
Cholstrey Herefs.....................45 P3
Chop Gate N York..................104 G11
Choppington Nthumb.............113 L4
Chopwell Gatesd...................112 H9
Chorley Ches E.......................69 Q4
Chorley Lancs........................88 H7
Chorley Shrops......................57 M8
Chorley Staffs.......................58 G2
Chorleywood Herts..................50 B11
Chorleywood West Herts..........50 B11
Chorlton Ches E......................70 C4
Chorlton-cum-Hardy Manch......82 H6
Chorlton Lane Ches W.............69 N5
Choulton Shrops.....................56 F7
Chowley Ches W......................69 N3
Chrishall Essex......................51 K3
Chrisswell Inver...................124 G3
Christchurch BCP....................13 L6
Christchurch Cambs................75 J11
Christchurch Gloucs................31 Q2
Christchurch Newpt.................31 K7
Christian Malford Wilts...........33 J9
Christleton Ches W..................81 N11
Christmas Common Oxon..........35 K6
Christmas Pie Surrey...............23 P5
Christon N Som......................19 L3
Christon Bank Nthumb...........119 P6
Christow Devon........................9 K7
Christ's Hospital W Susx..........24 D5
Chuck Hatch E Susx................25 L4
Chudleigh Devon......................9 L9
Chudleigh Knighton Devon........9 K9
Chulmleigh Devon...................17 M9
Chunal Derbys.......................83 M6
Church Lancs.........................89 L5
Churcham Gloucs....................46 E11
Church Aston Wrekin...............70 C11
Church Brampton Nhants..........60 F7
Church Brough Cumb..............102 E8
Church Broughton Derbys.........71 N8
Church Cove Cnwll....................3 J11
Church Crookham Hants...........23 M4
Churchdown Gloucs.................46 G11
Church Eaton Staffs................70 E11
Church End Bed......................61 N9
Church End Bed......................61 P9
Church End Bucks....................35 K3
Church End C Beds..................49 Q10
Church End C Beds..................49 Q8
Church End C Beds..................50 B4
Church End C Beds..................50 B7
Church End C Beds..................50 E3

Place	Page	Grid
Church End C Beds	61	Q10
Church End Cambs	61	N6
Church End Cambs	62	B4
Church End Cambs	62	D5
Churchend Essex	38	H3
Church End Essex	51	P6
Church End Essex	52	B6
Church End Essex	52	B8
Church End Gloucs	46	G7
Church End Gt Lon	36	F2
Church End Herts	50	D8
Church End Herts	50	G4
Church End Herts	51	K6
Church End Lincs	74	D4
Church End Lincs	93	R11
Church End Suffk	53	M4
Church End Warwks	59	K6
Church End Warwks	59	L6
Church Enstone Oxon	48	C9
Church Fenton N York	91	N3
Churchfield Sandw	58	F6
Churchgate Herts	50	H10
Churchgate Street Essex	51	L8
Church Green Devon	10	D5
Church Gresley Derbys	71	P11
Church Hanborough Oxon	34	D2
Church Hill Staffs	58	F2
Church Houses N York	105	J11
Churchill Devon	10	F4
Churchill Devon	17	K3
Churchill N Som	19	M3
Churchill Oxon	47	Q10
Churchill Worcs	46	H4
Churchill Worcs	58	C9
Churchinford Somset	10	E2
Church Knowle Dorset	12	F8
Church Laneham Notts	85	P5
Church Langton Leics	60	F2
Church Lawford Warwks	59	Q9
Church Lawton Ches E	70	E3
Church Leigh Staffs	71	J7
Church Lench Worcs	47	K4
Church Mayfield Staffs	71	M6
Church Minshull Ches E	70	B2
Church Norton W Susx	15	N7
Churchover Warwks	60	B4
Church Preen Shrops	57	J5
Church Pulverbatch Shrops	56	G4
Churchstanton Somset	10	D2
Churchstoke Powys	56	D6
Churchstow Devon	7	J9
Church Stowe Nhants	60	D9
Church Street Essex	52	C3
Church Street Kent	38	B7
Church Street Suffk	65	P5
Church Stretton Shrops	56	H6
Churchthorpe Lincs	93	P11
Churchtown Bpool	88	C2
Churchtown Cnwll	4	H6
Churchtown Derbys	84	C8
Churchtown Devon	17	M3
Churchtown IoM	80	f3
Churchtown Lancs	88	F2
Churchtown N Linc	92	C9
Churchtown Sefton	88	D7
Church Village Rhondd	30	E7
Church Warsop Notts	85	J7
Church Wilne Derbys	72	C4
Churnsike Lodge Nthumb	111	N5
Churston Ferrers Torbay	7	N7
Churt Surrey	23	N7
Churton Ches W	69	M3
Churwell Leeds	90	H5
Chwilog Gwynd	66	G7
Chyandour Cnwll	2	D7
Chyanvounder Cnwll	2	H9
Chyeowling Cnwll	2	K5
Chyvarloe Cnwll	2	H9
Cil Powys	56	B4
Cilcain Flints	80	H11
Cilcennin Cerdgn	43	K2
Cilcewydd Powys	56	C4
Cilfrew Neath	29	L4
Cilfynydd Rhondd	30	E6
Cilgerran Pembks	41	N2
Cilgwyn Carmth	43	P9
Cilgwyn Gwynd	66	H4
Ciliau-Aeron Cerdgn	43	K3
Cilmaengwyn Neath	29	K3
Cilmery Powys	44	E4
Cilrhedyn Pembks	41	Q4
Cilsan Carmth	43	L10
Ciltalgarth Gwynd	68	A6
Cilycwm Carmth	43	Q7
Cimla Neath	29	L5
Cinderford Gloucs	32	C2
Cinder Hill Wolves	58	D6
Cippenham Slough	35	Q8
Cirencester Gloucs	33	K4
Citadilla N York	103	P11
City Gt Lon	36	H4
City V Glam	30	C9
City Airport Gt Lon	37	K4
City Dulas IoA	78	H7
Clabhach Ag & B	136	F4
Clachaig Ag & B	131	N11
Clachaig Inn Highld	139	L6
Clachan Ag & B	123	N8
Clachan Ag & B	130	F4
Clachan Ag & B	131	M7
Clachan Ag & B	138	F9
Clachan Highld	153	J10
Clachan-a-Luib W Isls	168	d11
Clachan Mor Ag & B	136	B6
Clachan na Luib W Isls	168	d11
Clachan of Campsie E Duns	125	Q2
Clachan-Seil Ag & B	130	F4
Clachnaharry Highld	156	A8
Clachtoll Highld	164	B11
Clacket Lane Services Surrey	37	K10
Clackmannan Clacks	133	Q9
Clackmannanshire Bridge Fife	133	Q10
Clackmarras Moray	157	N6
Clacton-on-Sea Essex	53	L8
Cladich Ag & B	131	M3
Cladswell Worcs	47	L3
Claggan Highld	138	C8
Claigan Highld	152	C7
Clandown BaNES	20	C3
Clanfield Hants	23	J11
Clanfield Oxon	33	Q4
Clannaborough Devon	8	H4
Clanville Hants	22	B5
Clanville Somset	20	B8
Claonaig Ag & B	123	Q8
Clapgate Dorset	12	H4
Clapgate Herts	51	K6
Clapham Bed	61	M10
Clapham Devon	9	L7
Clapham Gt Lon	36	G5
Clapham N York	95	Q3
Clapham W Susx	24	C9
Clapham Green Bed	61	M10
Clap Hill Kent	27	J4
Clappersgate Cumb	101	L11
Clapton Somset	11	J3
Clapton Somset	20	B4
Clapton-in-Gordano N Som	31	N10
Clapton-on-the-Hill Gloucs	47	N11
Clapworthy Devon	17	M7
Clarach Cerdgn	54	E8
Claravale Gatesd	112	H8
Clarbeston Pembks	41	L6
Clarbeston Road Pembks	41	K6
Clarborough Notts	85	M4
Clare Suffk	63	N11
Clarebrand D & G	108	G7
Clarencefield D & G	109	N7
Clarewood Nthumb	112	F7
Clarilaw Border	117	Q7
Clark's Green Surrey	24	E3
Clarkston E Rens	125	P6
Clashmore Highld	162	G9
Clashmore Highld	164	B10
Clashnessie Highld	164	C10
Clashnoir Moray	149	N3
Clathy P & K	134	B3
Clathymore P & K	134	C3
Clatt Abers	150	E2
Clatter Powys	55	M6
Clatterford End Essex	51	P8
Clatworthy Somset	18	E9
Claughton Lancs	88	G2
Claughton Lancs	95	M7
Claughton Wirral	81	L7
Clavelshay Somset	19	J8
Claverdon Warwks	59	J11
Claverham N Som	31	N11
Clavering Essex	51	L4
Claverley Shrops	57	P6
Claverton BaNES	20	E2
Claverton Down BaNES	20	E2
Clawdd-coch V Glam	30	E9
Clawdd-newydd Denbgs	68	E4
Clawthorpe Cumb	95	L5
Clawton Devon	5	P2
Claxby Lincs	86	F2
Claxby Lincs	87	N6
Claxton N York	98	D9
Claxton Norfk	77	L11
Claybrooke Magna Leics	59	Q7
Clay Common Suffk	65	P5
Clay Coton Nhants	60	C5
Clay Cross Derbys	84	E8
Claydon Oxon	48	E5
Claydon Suffk	53	K2
Clay End Herts	50	H4
Claygate D & G	110	G5
Claygate Kent	26	B3
Claygate Surrey	36	E8
Claygate Cross Kent	37	P9
Clayhall Gt Lon	37	K2
Clayhanger Devon	18	D10
Clayhanger Wsall	58	F4
Clayhidon Devon	18	G11
Clayhill E Susx	26	D7
Clayhill Hants	13	P3
Clayhithe Cambs	62	H8
Clayock Highld	167	L5
Claypit Hill Cambs	62	E10
Claypits Gloucs	32	E3
Claypole Lincs	85	P11
Claythorpe Lincs	87	M5
Clayton C Brad	90	E4
Clayton Donc	91	M9
Clayton W Susx	24	G8
Clayton Green Lancs	88	H6
Clayton-le-Moors Lancs	89	M4
Clayton-le-Woods Lancs	88	H6
Clayton West Kirk	90	H8
Clayworth Notts	85	M3
Cleadale Highld	144	G10
Cleadon S Tyne	113	N8
Cleadon Park S Tyne	113	N8
Clearbrook Devon	6	E5
Clearwell Gloucs	31	Q3
Cleasby N York	103	Q8
Cleat Ork	169	d8
Cleatlam Dur	103	M7
Cleator Cumb	100	D8
Cleator Moor Cumb	100	D7
Cleckheaton Kirk	90	F5
Cleedownton Shrops	57	K8
Cleehill Shrops	57	K9
Cleekhimin N Lans	126	C6
Clee St Margaret Shrops	57	K8
Cleestanton Shrops	57	K9
Cleethorpes NE Lin	93	P9
Cleeton St Mary Shrops	57	L9
Cleeve N Som	31	N11
Cleeve Oxon	34	H8
Cleeve Hill Gloucs	47	J9
Cleeve Prior Worcs	47	L5
Cleghornie E Loth	128	F3
Clehonger Herefs	45	N7
Cleish P & K	134	D8
Cleland N Lans	126	D6
Clement's End C Beds	50	B8
Clement Street Kent	37	M6
Clenamacrie Ag & B	131	J2
Clench Common Wilts	33	N11
Clenchwarton Norfk	75	L6
Clenerty Abers	159	J5
Clent Worcs	58	D9
Cleobury Mortimer Shrops	57	M9
Cleobury North Shrops	57	L7
Cleongart Ag & B	120	C5
Clephanton Highld	156	F7
Clerkhill D & G	117	K11
Cleuch-head D & G	115	R7
Clevancy Wilts	33	L9
Clevedon N Som	31	M10
Cleveley Oxon	48	C10
Cleveleys Lancs	88	C2
Cleverton Wilts	33	J7
Clewer Somset	19	M4
Cley next the Sea Norfk	76	E3
Cliburn Cumb	101	Q5
Cliddesden Hants	22	H5
Cliff Warwks	59	K5
Cliffe Lancs	89	L4
Cliffe Medway	38	B6
Cliffe N York	91	R4
Cliffe N York	103	P7
Cliff End E Susx	26	E9
Cliffe Woods Medway	38	B7
Clifford Herefs	45	J5
Clifford Leeds	91	L2
Clifford Chambers Warwks	47	N4
Clifford's Mesne Gloucs	46	D10
Cliffsend Kent	39	P9
Clifton Bristl	31	Q10
Clifton C Beds	50	E3
Clifton C Nott	72	E4
Clifton C York	98	B10
Clifton Calder	90	F6
Clifton Cumb	101	P5
Clifton Derbys	71	M6
Clifton Devon	17	L3
Clifton Donc	91	N11
Clifton Lancs	88	F4
Clifton N York	97	J11
Clifton Nthumb	113	K4
Clifton Oxon	48	D8
Clifton Salfd	82	G4
Clifton Worcs	46	F5
Clifton Campville Staffs	59	L2
Clifton Hampden Oxon	34	F5
Clifton Reynes M Keyn	49	P4
Clifton upon Dunsmore Warwks	60	B5
Clifton upon Teme Worcs	46	D2
Cliftonville Kent	39	Q7
Climping W Susx	15	Q6
Clink Somset	20	E5
Clint N York	97	L9
Clint Green Norfk	76	E9
Clintmains Border	118	B4
Clipiau Gwynd	55	J2
Clippesby Norfk	77	N9
Clipsham Rutlnd	73	P7
Clipston Nhants	60	F4
Clipston Notts	72	G4
Clipstone C Beds	49	P9
Clipstone Notts	85	J8
Clitheroe Lancs	89	L2
Clive Shrops	69	P10
Cliveden Bucks	35	P7
Clixby Lincs	93	J10
Cloatley Wilts	33	L6
Clocaenog Denbgs	68	E4
Clochan Moray	158	B5
Clock Face St Hel	82	B6
Cloddiau Powys	56	C3
Clodock Herefs	45	L9
Cloford Somset	20	D6
Clola Abers	159	P7
Clophill C Beds	50	C3
Clopton Nhants	61	N4
Clopton Suffk	65	J11
Clopton Corner Suffk	65	J11
Clopton Green Suffk	63	N10
Clopton Green Suffk	64	D10
Clos du Valle Guern	10	c1
Closeburn D & G	109	J2
Closeburnmill D & G	109	K2
Closeclark IoM	80	c6
Closworth Somset	11	M2
Clothall Herts	50	G4
Clotton Ches W	69	P2
Cloudesley Bush Warwks	59	Q7
Clouds Herefs	46	A7
Clough Oldham	89	Q9
Clough Foot Calder	89	Q6
Clough Head Calder	90	D7
Cloughton N York	99	L2
Cloughton Newlands N York	105	N11
Clousta Shet	169	q8
Clova Angus	142	G3
Clovelly Devon	16	E7
Clovenfords Border	117	P3
Clovulin Highld	139	J5
Clow Bridge Lancs	89	N5
Clowne Derbys	84	G5
Clows Top Worcs	57	N10
Cloy Wrexhm	69	L6
Cluanie Inn Highld	146	D5
Cluanie Lodge Highld	146	D5
Clubworthy Cnwll	5	M3
Clugston D & G	107	L6
Clun Shrops	56	E8
Clunas Highld	156	F8
Clunbury Shrops	56	F8
Clunderwen Carmth	41	M7
Clune Highld	148	D2
Clunes Highld	146	H10
Clungunford Shrops	56	F9
Clunie P & K	141	R8
Clunton Shrops	56	E8
Cluny Fife	134	H8
Clutton BaNES	20	B3
Clutton Ches W	69	N4
Clutton Hill BaNES	20	B3
Clwt Conwy	68	C2
Clwt-y-bont Gwynd	67	K2
Clydach Mons	30	H2
Clydach Swans	29	J4
Clydach Vale Rhondd	30	C6
Clydebank W Duns	125	M3
Clydey Pembks	41	Q3
Clyffe Pypard Wilts	33	L9
Clynder Ag & B	131	Q11
Clyne Neath	29	M4
Clynnog Fawr Gwynd	66	G5
Clyro Powys	45	J6
Clyst Honiton Devon	9	N6
Clyst Hydon Devon	9	N5
Clyst St George Devon	9	N7
Clyst St Lawrence Devon	9	N5
Clyst St Mary Devon	9	N6
Cnoc W Isls	168	j4
Cnwch Coch Cerdgn	54	F10
Coad's Green Cnwll	5	M6
Coal Aston Derbys	84	E5
Coalbrookvale Blae G	30	G3
Coalburn S Lans	126	E11
Coalburns Gatesd	112	H8
Coaley Gloucs	32	E4
Coalhill Essex	38	C2
Coalmoor Wrekin	57	M3
Coalpit Heath S Glos	32	C8
Coalport Wrekin	57	M4
Coalsnaughton Clacks	133	P8
Coal Street Suffk	65	J7
Coaltown of Balgonie Fife	134	H8
Coaltown of Wemyss Fife	135	J8
Coalville Leics	72	C8
Coanwood Nthumb	111	N9
Coat Somset	19	N10
Coatbridge N Lans	126	C4
Coatdyke N Lans	126	C4
Coate Swindn	33	N8
Coate Wilts	21	K7
Coates Cambs	74	F11
Coates Gloucs	33	J4
Coates Lincs	86	B4
Coates Notts	85	P4
Coates W Susx	23	Q11
Coatham R & Cl	104	G5
Coatham Mundeville Darltn	103	Q6
Cobbaton Devon	17	L6
Coberley Gloucs	47	J11
Cobhall Common Herefs	45	P7
Cobham Kent	37	Q7
Cobham Surrey	36	D8
Cobham Services Surrey	36	D9
Coblers Green Essex	51	Q7
Cobley Dorset	21	K10
Cobnash Herefs	45	P2
Cobo Guern	10	b1
Cobridge C Stke	70	F5
Coburby Abers	159	M5
Cockayne N York	104	H11
Cock Bank Wrexhm	69	L5
Cock Bevington Warwks	47	L4
Cock Bridge Abers	149	P6
Cockburnspath Border	129	K5
Cock Clarks Essex	52	D11
Cock & End Suffk	63	M10
Cockenzie and Port Seton E Loth	128	C4
Cocker Bar Lancs	88	G6
Cocker Brook Lancs	89	L5
Cockerham Lancs	95	K10
Cockermouth Cumb	100	F4
Cockernhoe Herts	50	D6
Cockersdale Leeds	90	G5
Cockett Swans	28	H5
Cockfield Dur	103	M6
Cockfield Suffk	64	C11
Cockfosters Gt Lon	50	G11
Cock Green Essex	51	Q7
Cocking W Susx	23	N11
Cocking Causeway W Susx	23	N11
Cockington Torbay	7	M6
Cocklake Somset	19	M5
Cockley Beck Cumb	100	H10
Cockley Cley Norfk	75	Q10
Cock Marling E Susx	26	E8
Cockpole Green Wokham	35	L8
Cocks Cnwll	3	K3
Cockshutford Shrops	57	K7
Cockshutt Shrops	69	M9
Cock Street Kent	38	C11
Cockthorpe Norfk	76	D3
Cockwells Cnwll	2	E7
Cockwood Devon	9	N8
Cockwood Somset	18	H6
Cockyard Derbys	83	M9
Cockyard Herefs	45	N8
Coddenham Suffk	64	G11
Coddington Ches W	69	N3
Coddington Herefs	46	D6
Coddington Notts	85	P10
Codford St Mary Wilts	21	J7
Codford St Peter Wilts	21	J7
Codicote Herts	50	F7
Codmore Hill W Susx	24	C6
Codnor Derbys	84	F11
Codrington S Glos	32	D9
Codsall Staffs	58	C4
Codsall Wood Staffs	58	B4
Coed Darcy Neath	29	K5
Coedely Rhondd	30	D7
Coed Hirwaun Neath	29	M8
Coedkernew Newpt	31	J8
Coed Morgan Mons	31	L2
Coedpoeth Wrexhm	69	J4
Coed Talon Flints	69	J3
Coedway Powys	69	K11
Coed-y-Bryn Cerdgn	42	G5
Coed-y-caerau Newpt	31	L6
Coed-y-Cwm Rhondd	30	E6
Coed-y-paen Mons	31	K5
Coed-yr-ynys Powys	44	H10
Coed Ystumgwern Gwynd	67	K10
Coelbren Powys	29	N2
Coffinswell Devon	7	M5
Coffle End Bed	61	M9
Cofton Devon	9	N8
Cofton Hackett Worcs	58	F9
Cogan V Glam	30	G10
Cogenhoe Nhants	60	H8
Cogges Oxon	34	C3
Coggeshall Essex	52	E7
Coggin's Mill E Susx	25	N5
Coignafearn Highld	148	C4
Coilacriech Abers	149	Q8
Coilantogle Stirlg	132	H6
Coillore Highld	152	F10
Coity Brdgnd	29	P8
Col W Isls	168	j4
Colaboll Highld	162	D4
Colan Cnwll	4	D9
Colaton Raleigh Devon	10	B7
Colbost Highld	152	C8
Colburn N York	103	N11
Colby Cumb	102	C6
Colby IoM	80	b7
Colby Norfk	77	J5
Colchester Essex	52	G6
Colchester Zoo Essex	52	G7
Cold Ash W Berk	34	F11
Cold Ashby Nhants	60	E5
Cold Ashton S Glos	32	E10
Cold Aston Gloucs	47	M11
Coldbackie Highld	165	P4
Cold Blow Pembks	41	M8
Cold Brayfield M Keyn	49	P4
Cold Cotes N York	95	Q6
Coldean Br & H	24	H9
Coldeast Devon	7	L4
Colden Calder	90	B5
Colden Common Hants	22	E10
Coldfair Green Suffk	65	N9
Coldham Cambs	74	H10
Cold Hanworth Lincs	86	D4
Coldharbour Cnwll	3	K4
Coldharbour Devon	9	Q2
Coldharbour Gloucs	31	Q4
Cold Harbour Herts	50	D7
Cold Harbour Oxon	34	H9
Coldharbour Surrey	24	D2
Cold Hatton Wrekin	70	A10
Cold Hatton Heath Wrekin	70	A10
Cold Hesledon Dur	113	P11
Cold Hiendley Wakefd	91	K8
Cold Higham Nhants	49	J4
Coldingham Border	129	N6
Cold Kirby N York	98	A4
Coldmeece Staffs	70	F8
Cold Newton Leics	73	J9
Cold Northcott Cnwll	5	L4
Cold Norton Essex	52	E11
Cold Overton Leics	73	L8
Coldred Kent	27	N2
Coldridge Devon	17	M10
Coldstream Border	118	F3
Coldwaltham W Susx	24	B7
Coldwell Herefs	45	N7
Coldwells Abers	159	N10
Cold Weston Shrops	57	K8
Cole Somset	20	C8
Colebatch Shrops	56	E7
Colebrook C Plym	6	E7
Colebrook Devon	9	P3
Colebrooke Devon	9	J5
Coleby Lincs	86	C8
Coleby N Linc	92	E7
Cole End Warwks	59	K7
Coleford Devon	9	J4
Coleford Gloucs	31	Q2
Coleford Somset	20	C5
Coleford Water Somset	18	F8
Colegate End Norfk	64	H4
Cole Green Herts	50	G8
Cole Green Herts	51	K4
Cole Henley Hants	22	E4
Colehill Dorset	12	H4
Coleman Green Herts	50	E8
Coleman's Hatch E Susx	25	K4
Colemere Shrops	69	M8
Colemore Hants	23	K8
Colemore Green Shrops	57	N5
Colenden P & K	134	C7
Coleorton Leics	72	C7
Colerne Wilts	32	F10
Colesbourne Gloucs	33	K2
Cole's Cross Devon	7	K9
Coles Cross Dorset	10	H4
Colesden Bed	61	P9
Coles Green Suffk	53	K3
Coleshill Bucks	35	P5
Coleshill Oxon	33	P6
Coleshill Warwks	59	K7
Colestocks Devon	10	B4
Coley BaNES	19	Q3
Colgate W Susx	24	F4
Colinsburgh Fife	135	M7
Colinton C Edin	127	N4
Colintraive Ag & B	124	C3
Colkirk Norfk	76	C6
Coll Ag & B	136	G4
Coll W Isls	168	j4
Collace P & K	142	C11
Collafirth Shet	169	q5
Coll Airport Ag & B	136	F4
Collaton Devon	7	J11
Collaton St Mary Torbay	7	M6
College of Roseisle Moray	157	L4
College Town Br For	23	N2
Collessie Fife	134	H5
Colleton Mills Devon	17	M8
Collier Row Gt Lon	37	M2
Collier's End Herts	51	J6
Collier's Green E Susx	26	C7
Colliers Green Kent	26	C4
Collier Street Kent	26	B2
Colliery Row Sundld	113	M11
Colliesdon Abers	151	Q2
Collin D & G	109	M5
Collingbourne Ducis Wilts	21	P4
Collingbourne Kingston Wilts	21	P3
Collingham Leeds	97	N11
Collingham Notts	85	P8
Collington Herefs	46	B2
Collingtree Nhants	60	G9
Collins Green Warrtn	82	C6
Collins Green Worcs	46	D3
Colliston Angus	143	L8
Colliton Devon	10	B4
Collyweston Nhants	73	P10
Colmonell S Ayrs	114	B10
Colmworth Bed	61	P9
Colnabaichin Abers	149	P6
Colnbrook Slough	36	B5
Colne Cambs	62	E5
Colne Lancs	89	P3
Colne Bridge Kirk	90	F6
Colne Edge Lancs	89	P2
Colne Engaine Essex	52	D5
Colney Norfk	76	H10
Colney Heath Herts	50	F9
Colney Street Herts	50	E10
Coln Rogers Gloucs	33	L3
Coln St Aldwyns Gloucs	33	M3
Coln St Dennis Gloucs	33	L2
Colonsay Ag & B	136	b2
Colonsay Airport Ag & B	136	b3
Colpy Abers	158	F11
Colquhar Border	117	L2
Colquite Cnwll	4	H7
Colscott Devon	16	F9
Colsterdale N York	96	H4
Colsterworth Lincs	73	N6
Colston Bassett Notts	73	J4
Colt Hill Hants	23	L4
Coltishall Norfk	77	K8
Colton Cumb	94	G3
Colton Leeds	91	K4
Colton N York	91	K4
Colton Norfk	76	G10
Colton Staffs	71	J10
Colt's Hill Kent	25	P2
Columbjohn Devon	9	N5
Colva Powys	44	H4
Colvend D & G	109	J10
Colwall Herefs	46	E6
Colwell Nthumb	112	E5
Colwich Staffs	71	J10
Colwick Notts	72	G2

Colwinston V Glam 29 P9
Colworth W Susx 15 P6
Colwyn Bay Conwy 80 B9
Colyford Devon 10 F6
Colyton Devon 10 E6
Combe Devon 7 J11
Combe Herefs 45 L2
Combe Oxon 48 D11
Combe W Berk 22 C2
Combe Almer Dorset 12 G5
Combe Common Surrey 23 P7
Combe Down BaNES 20 E2
Combe Fishacre Devon 7 L5
Combe Florey Somset 18 G8
Combe Hay BaNES 20 D3
Combeinteignhead Devon 7 N4
Combe Martin Devon 17 K2
Combe Raleigh Devon 10 D4
Comberbach Ches W 82 D9
Comberford Staffs 59 J3
Comberton Cambs 62 E9
Comberton Herefs 56 H11
Combe St Nicholas Somset 10 G2
Combpyne Devon 10 F6
Combridge Staffs 71 K7
Combrook Warwks 48 B4
Combs Derbys 83 M9
Combs Suffk 64 E10
Combs Ford Suffk 64 E10
Combwich Somset 19 J6
Comers Abers 150 H6
Cometytrowe Somset 18 H10
Comhampton Worcs 58 B11
Commercial End Cambs 63 J8
Commins Coch Powys 55 J4
Commondale N York 105 J8
Common Edge Bpool 88 C4
Common End Cumb 100 D6
Common Moor Cnwll 5 L8
Common Platt Wilts 33 M7
Commonside Ches W 82 B10
Commonside Derbys 71 N6
Common Side Derbys 84 D5
Commonwood Shrops 69 N9
Commonwood Wrexhm 69 L4
Compass Somset 19 J8
Compstall Stockp 83 L6
Compstonend D & G 108 E7
Compton Devon 7 M6
Compton Hants 22 C9
Compton Hants 22 E9
Compton Staffs 57 Q8
Compton Surrey 23 Q5
Compton W Berk 34 F8
Compton W Susx 15 L4
Compton Wilts 21 M4
Compton Abbas Dorset 20 G11
Compton Abdale Gloucs 47 L11
Compton Bassett Wilts 33 K10
Compton Beauchamp Oxon 33 Q7
Compton Bishop Somset 19 L3
Compton Chamberlayne
    Wilts 21 K9
Compton Dando BaNES 20 B2
Compton Dundon Somset 19 N8
Compton Durville Somset 19 M11
Compton Greenfield S Glos 31 Q8
Compton Martin BaNES 19 P3
Compton Pauncefoot
    Somset 20 B9
Compton Valence Dorset 11 M6
Comrie Fife 134 C10
Comrie P & K 133 M3
Conaglen House Highld 139 J4
Conchra Highld 145 Q2
Concraigie P & K 141 Q9
Conder Green Lancs 95 K9
Conderton Worcs 47 J7
Condicote Gloucs 47 N9
Condorrat N Lans 126 C3
Condover Shrops 56 H3
Coney Hill Gloucs 46 G11
Coneyhurst W Susx 24 D6
Coneysthorpe N York 98 E6
Coneythorpe N York 97 N9
Coney Weston Suffk 64 D6
Conford Hants 23 M8
Congdon's Shop Cnwll 5 M6
Congerstone Leics 72 B9
Congham Norfk 75 P6
Congleton Ches E 70 F2
Congl-y-wal Gwynd 67 N6
Congresbury N Som 19 M2
Congreve Staffs 58 D2
Conheath D & G 109 L7
Conicavel Moray 156 H7
Coningsby Lincs 86 H9
Conington Cambs 61 Q3
Conington Cambs 62 D7
Conisbrough Donc 91 N11
Conisholme Lincs 93 R11
Coniston Cumb 101 K11
Coniston E R Yk 93 L3
Coniston Cold N York 96 D10
Conistone N York 96 E7
Connah's Quay Flints 81 K11
Connel Ag & B 138 G11
Connel Park E Ayrs 115 M5
Connor Downs Cnwll 2 F6
Conon Bridge Highld 155 P6
Cononley N York 96 E11
Consall Staffs 71 H5
Consett Dur 112 H10
Constable Burton N York 97 J2
Constable Lee Lancs 89 N6
Constantine Cnwll 3 J8
Constantine Bay Cnwll 4 D7
Contin Highld 155 N6
Conwy Conwy 79 P9
Conwy Castle Conwy 79 P9
Conyer Kent 38 G9
Conyer's Green Suffk 64 B8
Cooden E Susx 26 B10
Cookbury Devon 16 H10
Cookbury Wick Devon 16 F10
Cookham W & M 35 N7
Cookham Dean W & M 35 N7
Cookham Rise W & M 35 N7
Cookhill Worcs 47 L3
Cookley Suffk 65 L6
Cookley Worcs 58 B8
Cookley Green Oxon 35 J6
Cookney Abers 151 M9
Cooksbridge E Susx 25 K8
Cooksey Green Worcs 58 D11
Cook's Green Essex 53 L8

Cooks Green Suffk 64 D11
Cookshill Staffs 70 G6
Cooksland Cnwll 4 H8
Cooksmill Green Essex 51 P9
Cookson Green Ches W 82 C10
Coolham W Susx 24 D6
Cooling Medway 38 C6
Cooling Street Medway 38 B7
Coombe Cnwll 2 C2
Coombe Cnwll 3 L5
Coombe Cnwll 3 N3
Coombe Devon 7 N4
Coombe Devon 9 K8
Coombe Devon 10 C6
Coombe Gloucs 32 E6
Coombe Hants 23 J10
Coombe Wilts 21 M4
Coombe Bissett Wilts 21 M9
Coombe Cellars Devon 7 N4
Coombe Cross Hants 23 J10
Coombe Hill Gloucs 46 G9
Coombe Keynes Dorset 12 D8
Coombe Pafford Torbay 7 N5
Coombes W Susx 24 E9
Coombes-Moor Herefs 45 M3
Coombe Street Somset 20 E8
Coombeswood Dudley 58 E7
Coopersale Common Essex 51 L10
Coopersale Street Essex 51 L10
Cooper's Corner Kent 37 L11
Coopers Green E Susx 25 L6
Coopers Green Herts 50 E9
Cooper Street Kent 39 P9
Cooper Turning Bolton 89 J9
Cootham W Susx 24 C8
Copdock Suffk 53 K3
Copford Essex 52 F7
Copford Green Essex 52 F7
Copgrove N York 97 M8
Copister Shet 169 r6
Cople Bed 61 P11
Copley Dur 103 L5
Copley Tamesd 83 L5
Coplow Dale Derbys 83 Q9
Copmanthorpe C York 98 B11
Copmere End Staffs 70 E9
Copp Lancs 88 E3
Coppathorne Cnwll 16 C11
Coppenhall Staffs 70 G11
Coppenhall Moss Ches E 70 C3
Copperhouse Cnwll 2 F6
Coppicegate Shrops 57 N6
Coppingford Cambs 61 Q5
Coppins Corner Kent 26 F2
Copplestone Devon 9 J4
Coppull Lancs 88 H8
Coppull Moor Lancs 88 H8
Copsale W Susx 24 E6
Copster Green Lancs 89 K4
Copston Magna Warwks 59 Q8
Cop Street Kent 39 N9
Copthall Green Essex 51 K10
Copt Heath Solhll 59 J9
Copt Hewick N York 97 M6
Copthorne Cnwll 5 M3
Copthorne W Susx 24 H3
Copt Oak Leics 72 D8
Copy's Green Norfk 76 C4
Copythorne Hants 13 P2
Coram Street Suffk 52 H3
Corbets Tey Gt Lon 37 N3
Corbière Jersey 11 a2
Corbridge Nthumb 112 E8
Corby Nhants 61 J3
Corby Glen Lincs 73 Q6
Corby Hill Cumb 111 J9
Cordon N Ayrs 121 K5
Cordwell Derbys 84 D5
Coreley Shrops 57 L10
Cores End Bucks 35 P7
Corfe Somset 18 H11
Corfe Castle Dorset 12 G8
Corfe Mullen Dorset 12 G5
Corfton Shrops 56 H7
Corgarff Abers 149 P6
Corhampton Hants 22 H10
Corks Pond Kent 25 Q2
Corlae D & G 115 N8
Corley Warwks 59 M7
Corley Ash Warwks 59 L7
Corley Moor Warwks 59 L8
Corley Services Warwks 59 M7
Cormuir Angus 142 E4
Cornard Tye Suffk 52 F3
Corndon Devon 8 G7
Corner Row Lancs 88 E4
Corney Cumb 94 C2
Cornforth Dur 104 B4
Cornhill Abers 158 E6
Cornhill-on-Tweed Nthumb 118 E3
Cornholme Calder 89 Q5
Cornish Hall End Essex 51 Q3
Cornoigmore Ag & B 136 B6
Cornriggs Dur 102 F2
Cornsay Dur 103 M2
Cornsay Colliery Dur 103 N2
Corntown Highld 155 Q6
Corntown V Glam 29 P9
Cornwall Airport Newquay
    Cnwll 4 D9
Cornwell Oxon 47 Q9
Cornwood Devon 6 G7
Cornworthy Devon 7 L7
Corpach Highld 139 K2
Corpusty Norfk 76 G6
Corrachree Abers 150 D7
Corran Highld 139 J5
Corran Highld 145 N6
Corrany IoM 80 g4
Corrie D & G 110 D3
Corrie N Ayrs 121 K3
Corriecravie N Ayrs 120 H7
Corriegills N Ayrs 121 K4
Corriegour Lodge Hotel
    Highld 146 H9
Corriemoille Highld 155 L5
Corrimony Highld 155 L11
Corringham Lincs 85 Q2
Corringham Thurr 38 B5
Corris Gwynd 54 H3
Corris Uchaf Gwynd 54 G3
Corrow Ag & B 131 P7
Corry Highld 145 K3
Corscombe Devon 8 F5
Corscombe Dorset 11 L3

Corse Gloucs 46 E9
Corse Lawn Gloucs 46 F8
Corsham Wilts 32 G10
Corsindae Abers 150 H6
Corsley Wilts 20 F5
Corsley Heath Wilts 20 F5
Corsock D & G 108 G5
Corston BaNES 32 C11
Corston Wilts 32 H8
Corstorphine C Edin 127 M3
Cors-y-Gedol Gwynd 67 L10
Cortachy Angus 142 F6
Corton Suffk 65 Q2
Corton Wilts 20 H6
Corton Denham Somset 20 B10
Coruanan Highld 139 K4
Corwen Denbgs 68 E6
Coryates Dorset 11 N7
Coryton Devon 8 C8
Coryton Thurr 38 B5
Cosby Leics 72 E11
Coseley Dudley 58 D6
Cosford Shrops 57 Q3
Cosgrove Nhants 49 L6
Cosham C Port 15 J5
Cosheston Pembks 41 K10
Coshieville P & K 141 J8
Cossall Notts 72 D2
Cossall Marsh Notts 72 D2
Cossington Leics 72 G8
Cossington Somset 19 L6
Costessey Norfk 76 H9
Costock Notts 72 F6
Coston Leics 73 L6
Coston Norfk 76 F10
Cote Oxon 34 C4
Cote Somset 19 K6
Cotebrook Ches W 82 C11
Cotehill Cumb 111 J10
Cotes Cumb 95 K3
Cotes Leics 72 F6
Cotes Staffs 70 E8
Cotesbach Leics 60 B4
Cotes Heath Staffs 70 E8
Cotford St Luke Somset 18 G9
Cotgrave Notts 72 G3
Cothal Abers 151 M4
Cotham Notts 85 N11
Cothelstone Somset 18 G8
Cotherstone Dur 103 K7
Cothill Oxon 34 E5
Cotleigh Devon 10 E4
Cotmanhay Derbys 72 D2
Coton Cambs 62 E9
Coton Nhants 60 E6
Coton Shrops 69 P8
Coton Staffs 59 J4
Coton Staffs 70 E10
Coton Staffs 70 H8
Coton Clanford Staffs 70 F10
Coton Hayes Staffs 70 H8
Coton Hill Shrops 56 H2
Coton in the Clay Staffs 71 L9
Coton in the Elms Derbys 71 N11
Coton Park Derbys 71 P11
Cotswold Airport Wilts 33 J5
Cotswolds 33 J3
Cotswold Wildlife Park &
    Gardens Oxon 33 P3
Cott Devon 7 K6
Cottam E R Yk 99 K7
Cottam Lancs 88 G4
Cottam Notts 85 P5
Cottenham Cambs 62 F8
Cotterdale N York 96 B2
Cottered Herts 50 H5
Cotteridge Birm 58 F8
Cotterstock Nhants 61 M2
Cottesbrooke Nhants 60 F6
Cottesmore Rutlnd 73 N8
Cottingham E R Yk 92 H4
Cottingham Nhants 60 H2
Cottingley C Brad 90 E3
Cottisford Oxon 48 G8
Cotton Suffk 64 F8
Cotton End Bed 61 N11
Cottown Abers 150 E2
Cottown Abers 151 K4
Cottown of Gight Abers 159 K9
Cotts Devon 6 C5
Cotwall Wrekin 69 R11
Cotwalton Staffs 70 G6
Couch's Mill Cnwll 5 J10
Coughton Herefs 46 A10
Coughton Warwks 47 L2
Coulaghailtro Ag & B 123 M6
Coulags Highld 154 C9
Coulby Newham Middsb 104 F8
Coulderton Cumb 100 C9
Coull Abers 150 E7
Coulport Ag & B 131 Q10
Coulsdon Gt Lon 36 G9
Coulston Wilts 21 J4
Coulter S Lans 116 E4
Coultershaw Bridge W Susx 23 Q11
Coultings Somset 18 H6
Coulton N York 98 C6
Coultra Fife 135 K3
Cound Shrops 57 K3
Coundlane Shrops 57 K4
Coundon Dur 103 P5
Coundon Grange Dur 103 P5
Countersett N York 96 D3
Countess Wilts 21 N6
Countess Cross Essex 52 E5
Countess Wear Devon 9 M7
Countesswells C Aber 151 M7
Countesthorpe Leics 72 F11
Countisbury Devon 17 N2
Coupar Angus P & K 142 C10
Coupe Green Lancs 88 H5
Coupland Cumb 102 D7
Coupland Nthumb 118 H4
Cour Ag & B 123 P10
Courteachan Highld 145 L8
Courteenhall Nhants 49 L4
Court Henry Carmth 43 L10
Courtsend Essex 38 H3
Courtway Somset 18 H8
Cousland Mdloth 128 B6
Cousley Wood E Susx 25 Q4
Cove Ag & B 131 Q11
Cove Border 129 K5
Cove Devon 18 C11

Cove Hants 23 N3
Cove Highld 160 C8
Cove Bay C Aber 151 P7
Cove Bottom Suffk 65 P6
Covehithe Suffk 65 Q5
Coven Staffs 58 D3
Coveney Cambs 62 G4
Covenham St
    Bartholomew Lincs 87 K2
Covenham St Mary Lincs 87 K2
Coven Heath Staffs 58 D3
Coventry Covtry 59 M9
Coverack Cnwll 3 K10
Coverack Bridges Cnwll 2 H7
Coverham N York 96 H3
Covington Cambs 61 N6
Covington S Lans 116 D3
Cowan Bridge Lancs 95 N5
Cowbeech E Susx 25 P8
Cowbit Lincs 74 E7
Cowbridge V Glam 30 C10
Cowdale Derbys 83 N10
Cowden Kent 25 L2
Cowdenbeath Fife 134 F9
Cowden Pound Kent 25 L2
Cowden Station Kent 25 L2
Cowers Lane Derbys 71 Q5
Cowes IoW 14 E7
Cowesby N York 97 Q3
Cowesfield Green Wilts 21 Q10
Cowfold W Susx 24 F6
Cowgill Cumb 95 R3
Cow Green Suffk 64 F8
Cowhill S Glos 32 B6
Cowie Stirlg 133 N10
Cowlam E R Yk 99 K7
Cowley Devon 9 M5
Cowley Gloucs 33 J2
Cowley Gt Lon 36 C4
Cowley Oxon 34 F4
Cowling Lancs 88 H7
Cowling N York 90 B2
Cowling N York 97 K3
Cowlinge Suffk 63 M10
Cowmes Kirk 90 F7
Cowpe Lancs 89 N6
Cowpen Nthumb 113 L4
Cowpen Bewley S on T 104 E6
Cowplain Hants 15 J4
Cowshill Dur 102 G2
Cowslip Green N Som 19 N2
Cowthorpe N York 97 P10
Coxall Herefs 56 F10
Coxbank Ches E 70 B6
Coxbench Derbys 72 B2
Coxbridge Somset 19 P7
Cox Common Suffk 65 N5
Coxford Cnwll 5 K2
Coxford Norfk 76 B6
Coxgreen Staffs 57 Q7
Cox Green Surrey 24 C4
Coxheath Kent 38 B11
Coxhoe Dur 104 B3
Coxley Somset 19 P6
Coxley Wakefd 90 H7
Coxley Wick Somset 19 P6
Coxpark Cnwll 5 Q8
Coxwold N York 98 A5
Coychurch Brdgnd 29 P9
Coylton S Ayrs 114 H4
Coylumbridge Highld 148 G5
Coytrahen Brdgnd 29 N7
Crabbs Cross Worcs 58 F11
Crab Orchard Dorset 13 J3
Crabtree W Susx 24 F5
Crabtree Green Wrexhm 69 K6
Crackenthorpe Cumb 102 C6
Crackington Haven Cnwll 5 J2
Crackley Staffs 70 E4
Crackley Warwks 59 L10
Crackleybank Shrops 57 P2
Crackpot N York 103 J11
Cracoe N York 96 E8
Craddock Devon 10 B2
Cradle End Herts 51 L6
Cradley Dudley 58 D7
Cradley Herefs 46 D5
Cradley Heath Sandw 58 D7
Cradoc Powys 44 E8
Crafthole Cnwll 5 P11
Crafton Bucks 49 N11
Crag Foot Lancs 95 K6
Craggan Highld 149 J2
Cragganmore Moray 157 M10
Cragg Hill Leeds 90 G3
Cragg Vale Calder 90 C6
Craghead Dur 113 K10
Cragside Nthumb 119 L10
Crai Powys 44 B10
Craibstone Moray 158 C6
Craichie Angus 143 J8
Craig Angus 143 M6
Craig Highld 154 D8
Craigbank E Ayrs 115 L5
Craigburn Border 127 N7
Craig-cefn-parc Swans 29 J4
Craigcleuch D & G 110 F3
Craigdam Abers 159 K11
Craigdhu Ag & B 130 G6
Craigearn Abers 151 J5
Craigellachie Moray 157 P9
Craigend P & K 134 E3
Craigend Rens 125 M3
Craigendoran Ag & B 132 C11
Craigends Rens 125 L4
Craigens Ag & B 122 D6
Craighat Stirlg 132 C10
Craighlaw D & G 107 K5
Craighouse Ag & B 122 H6
Craigie P & K 141 R9
Craigie S Ayrs 125 L11
Craigiefold Abers 159 M4
Craiglockhart C Edin 127 M3
Craigmillar C Edin 127 N3
Craignant Shrops 69 J7
Craigneston D & G 115 Q10
Craigneuk N Lans 126 D4
Craigneuk N Lans 126 D5
Craignure Ag & B 138 C10
Craigo Angus 143 M5
Craig Penllyn V Glam 29 P9
Craigrothie Fife 135 K5
Craigruie Stirlg 132 F3
Craig's End Essex 52 B4
Craigton Angus 143 J10

Craigton C Aber 151 L7
Craigton E Rens 125 M7
Craigton of Airlie Angus 142 F9
Craig-y-Duke Neath 29 K4
Craig-y-nos Powys 44 A11
Craik Border 117 L9
Crail Fife 135 Q6
Crailing Border 118 C6
Craiselound N Linc 92 C11
Crakehall N York 97 K3
Crakehill N York 97 P6
Crakemarsh Staffs 71 K7
Crambe N York 98 E6
Crambeck N York 98 E7
Cramlington Nthumb 113 L5
Cramond C Edin 127 M2
Cramond Bridge C Edin 127 M2
Crampmoor Hants 22 C10
Cranage Ches E 82 G11
Cranberry Staffs 70 E7
Cranborne Dorset 13 J2
Cranbourne Br For 35 P10
Cranbrook Devon 9 N6
Cranbrook Kent 26 C4
Cranbrook Common Kent 26 C4
Crane Moor Barns 91 J10
Crane's Corner Norfk 76 C9
Cranfield C Beds 49 Q6
Cranford Devon 16 E7
Cranford Gt Lon 36 D5
Cranford St Andrew Nhants 61 K5
Cranford St John Nhants 61 K5
Cranham Gloucs 32 G2
Cranham Gt Lon 37 N3
Cranhill Warwks 47 M4
Crank St Hel 81 Q5
Cranleigh Surrey 24 C3
Cranmer Green Suffk 64 E7
Cranmore IoW 14 C8
Cranmore Somset 20 C6
Cranoe Leics 73 K11
Cransford Suffk 65 L9
Cranshaws Border 128 H7
Cranstal IoM 80 g1
Cranswick E R Yk 99 L10
Crantock Cnwll 4 B9
Cranwell Lincs 86 D11
Cranwich Norfk 63 N2
Cranworth Norfk 76 D11
Craobh Haven Ag & B 130 F6
Crapstone Devon 6 E5
Crarae Ag & B 131 K8
Crask Inn Highld 162 C2
Crask of Aigas Highld 155 N9
Craster Nthumb 119 Q7
Craswall Herefs 45 K7
Crateford Staffs 58 D3
Cratfield Suffk 65 L6
Crathes Abers 151 K8
Crathie Abers 149 P8
Crathie Highld 147 P9
Crathorne N York 104 D9
Craven Arms Shrops 56 G8
Crawcrook Gatesd 112 H8
Crawford Lancs 88 P4
Crawford S Lans 116 D6
Crawfordjohn S Lans 116 B6
Crawley Hants 22 D8
Crawley Oxon 34 B2
Crawley W Susx 24 G3
Crawley Down W Susx 24 H3
Crawleyside Dur 103 J2
Crawshawbooth Lancs 89 N5
Crawton Abers 143 R2
Craxe's Green Essex 52 F8
Cray N York 96 D5
Cray P & K 142 A5
Crayford Gt Lon 37 M5
Crayke N York 98 B6
Craymere Beck Norfk 76 F5
Crays Hill Essex 38 B3
Cray's Pond Oxon 34 H8
Craythorne Staffs 71 N9
Craze Lowman Devon 9 N2
Crazies Hill Wokham 35 L8
Creacombe Devon 17 Q8
Creagan Inn Ag & B 138 H9
Creag Ghoraidh W Isls 168 c13
Creagorry W Isls 168 c13
Creaguaineach Lodge
    Highld 139 Q4
Creamore Bank Shrops 69 P8
Creaton Nhants 60 F6
Creca D & G 110 D6
Credenhill Herefs 45 P6
Crediton Devon 9 K4
Creebank D & G 107 K2
Creebridge D & G 107 M4
Creech Dorset 12 F8
Creech Heathfield Somset 19 J9
Creech St Michael Somset 19 J9
Creed Cnwll 3 N4
Creekmoor BCP 12 H6
Creekmouth Gt Lon 37 L4
Creeksea Essex 38 F2
Creeting St Mary Suffk 64 F10
Creeting St Peter Suffk 64 F10
Creeton Lincs 73 Q6
Creetown D & G 107 N6
Cregneash IoM 80 a8
Creg ny Baa IoM 80 e5
Cregrina Powys 44 G4
Creich Fife 135 J3
Creigiau Cardif 30 E8
Cremyll Cnwll 6 C8
Cressage Shrops 57 K4
Cressbrook Derbys 83 Q10
Cresselly Pembks 41 L9
Cressex Bucks 35 M6
Cressing Essex 52 C7
Cresswell Nthumb 113 L2
Cresswell Pembks 41 L9
Cresswell Staffs 70 H7
Creswell Derbys 84 H6
Creswell Green Staffs 58 G2
Cretingham Suffk 65 J9
Cretshengan Ag & B 123 M6
Crewe Ches E 70 C3
Crewe-by-Farndon Ches W 69 M4
Crewe Green Ches E 70 C3
Crew Green Powys 69 K11
Crewkerne Somset 11 J3
Crews Hill Gt Lon 50 H11
Crewton C Derb 71 Q4
Crianlarich Stirlg 132 D2
Cribyn Cerdgn 43 K4

266 Criccieth – Darwell Hole

- Criccieth Gwynd 66 H7
- Crich Derbys 84 D10
- Crich Carr Derbys 84 D10
- Crichton Mdloth 128 B7
- Crick Mons 31 N6
- Crick Nhants 60 C6
- Crickadarn Powys 44 F6
- Cricket St Thomas Somset 10 H3
- Crickheath Shrops 69 J10
- Crickhowell Powys 45 J11
- Cricklade Wilts 33 L6
- Cricklewood Gt Lon 36 F3
- Cridling Stubbs N York 91 N6
- Crieff P & K 133 P3
- Criggan Cnwll 4 G9
- Criggion Powys 69 J11
- Crigglestone Wakefd 91 J7
- Crimble Rochdl 89 P8
- Crimond Abers 159 Q6
- Crimplesham Norfk 75 N10
- Crimscote Warwks 47 P5
- Crinaglack Highld 155 M9
- Crinan Ag & B 130 F9
- Crindledyke N Lans 126 E6
- Cringleford Norfk 76 H10
- Cringles C Brad 96 F11
- Crinow Pembks 41 M8
- Cripplesease Cnwll 2 E6
- Cripplestyle Dorset 13 J2
- Cripp's Corner E Susx 26 C7
- Croachy Highld 148 B2
- Croanford Cnwll 4 G7
- Crockenhill Kent 37 M7
- Crocker End Oxon 35 K7
- Crockerhill W Susx 15 P5
- Crockernwell Devon 9 J6
- Crocker's Ash Herefs 45 Q11
- Crockerton Wilts 20 G6
- Crocketford D & G 108 H6
- Crockey Hill C York 98 C11
- Crockham Hill Kent 37 K10
- Crockhurst Street Kent 37 P11
- Crockleford Heath Essex 52 H6
- Crock Street Somset 10 G2
- Croeserw Neath 29 N5
- Croes-goch Pembks 40 F4
- Croes-lan Cerdgn 42 G6
- Croesor Gwynd 67 L6
- Croesyceiliog Carmth 42 H11
- Croesyceiliog Torfn 31 K5
- Croes-y-mwyalch Torfn 31 K6
- Croes-y-pant Mons 31 K4
- Croft Leics 72 E11
- Croft Lincs 87 P8
- Croft Warrtn 82 D6
- Croftamie Stirlg 132 F10
- Croft Mitchell Cnwll 2 H6
- Crofton Cumb 110 F10
- Crofton Wakefd 91 K7
- Crofton Wilts 21 Q2
- Croft-on-Tees N York 103 Q9
- Croftown Highld 161 K10
- Crofts Moray 157 P7
- Crofts Bank Traffd 82 G5
- Crofts of Dipple Moray 157 Q6
- Crofts of Haddo Abers 159 K10
- Crofts of Savoch Abers 159 P5
- Crofty Swans 28 F6
- Crogen Gwynd 68 D7
- Croggan Ag & B 130 E2
- Croglin Cumb 111 L11
- Croick Highld 162 B8
- Cromarty Highld 156 D4
- Crombie Fife 134 D11
- Cromdale Highld 149 K2
- Cromer Herts 50 G5
- Cromer Norfk 77 J3
- Cromford Derbys 84 C9
- Cromhall S Glos 32 C6
- Cromhall Common S Glos 32 C7
- Cromor W Isls 168 j5
- Cromore W Isls 168 j5
- Crompton Fold Oldham 89 Q9
- Cromwell Notts 85 N8
- Cronberry E Ayrs 115 M3
- Crondall Hants 23 L5
- Cronkbourne IoM 80 e6
- Cronk-y-Voddy IoM 80 d4
- Cronton Knows 81 P7
- Crook Cumb 101 N11
- Crook Dur 103 N3
- Crookdake Cumb 100 G2
- Crooke Wigan 88 H9
- Crooked End Gloucs 46 B11
- Crookedholm E Ayrs 125 M10
- Crooked Soley Wilts 34 B10
- Crookes Sheff 84 D3
- Crookhall Dur 112 H10
- Crookham Nthumb 118 H3
- Crookham W Berk 22 F2
- Crookham Village Hants 23 L4
- Crook Inn Border 116 G5
- Crooklands Cumb 95 L4
- Crook of Devon P & K 134 C7
- Cropper Derbys 71 N7
- Cropredy Oxon 48 E5
- Cropston Leics 72 F8
- Cropthorne Worcs 47 J5
- Cropton N York 98 F3
- Cropwell Bishop Notts 72 H3
- Cropwell Butler Notts 72 H3
- Cros W Isls 168 k1
- Crosbost W Isls 168 i5
- Crosby Cumb 100 E3
- Crosby IoM 80 d6
- Crosby N Linc 92 E8
- Crosby Sefton 81 L5
- Crosby Garret Cumb 102 D9
- Crosby Ravensworth Cumb 102 B8
- Crosby Villa Cumb 100 E3
- Croscombe Somset 19 Q6
- Crosemere Shrops 69 M9
- Crosland Edge Kirk 90 E8
- Crosland Hill Kirk 90 E8
- Cross Somset 19 M4
- Crossaig Ag & B 123 P9
- Crossapol Ag & B 136 B7
- Cross Ash Mons 45 N11
- Cross-at-Hand Kent 26 C2
- Crossbost W Isls 168 i5
- Crossbush W Susx 24 B9
- Crosscanonby Cumb 100 E3
- Cross Coombe Cnwll 3 J3
- Crossdale Street Norfk 77 J4
- Cross End Bed 61 N9
- Cross End Essex 52 E5
- Crossens Sefton 88 D6
- Cross Flatts C Brad 90 E2
- Crossford Fife 134 D10
- Crossford S Lans 126 E8
- Crossgate Cnwll 5 N4
- Crossgate Lincs 74 D5
- Crossgate Staffs 70 G7
- Crossgatehall E Loth 128 B6
- Crossgates E Ayrs 125 K9
- Crossgates Fife 134 E10
- Cross Gates Leeds 91 K4
- Crossgates N York 99 L4
- Crossgates Powys 44 F2
- Crossgill Lancs 95 M8
- Cross Green Devon 5 P4
- Cross Green Leeds 91 J4
- Cross Green Staffs 58 D3
- Cross Green Suffk 64 A11
- Cross Green Suffk 64 B10
- Cross Green Suffk 64 D11
- Cross Hands Carmth 28 G2
- Crosshands Carmth 41 N6
- Crosshands E Ayrs 125 M11
- Cross Hands Pembks 41 L8
- Cross Hill Derbys 84 F11
- Crosshill Fife 134 F8
- Crosshill S Ayrs 114 F6
- Cross Hills N York 96 F11
- Crosshouse E Ayrs 125 K10
- Cross Houses Shrops 57 J3
- Cross Houses Shrops 57 M6
- Cross in Hand E Susx 25 N6
- Cross Inn Cerdgn 42 G3
- Cross Inn Cerdgn 43 K2
- Cross Inn Pembks 41 M9
- Cross Inn Rhondd 30 E8
- Cross Keys Ag & B 132 C10
- Crosskeys Caerph 30 H6
- Cross Keys Wilts 32 G10
- Crosskirk Highld 166 H3
- Crosslands Cumb 94 G3
- Cross Lane IoW 14 F9
- Cross Lane Head Shrops 57 N5
- Cross Lanes Cnwll 2 H9
- Cross Lanes Cnwll 3 K5
- Cross Lanes N York 98 A8
- Crosslanes Shrops 69 K11
- Cross Lanes Wrexhm 69 L5
- Crosslee Rens 125 L4
- Crossley Kirk 90 G6
- Crossmichael D & G 108 F7
- Cross Oak Powys 44 G10
- Cross of Jackston Abers 158 H11
- Cross o' th' hands Derbys 71 P5
- Crosspost W Susx 24 G6
- Crossroads Abers 150 F6
- Crossroads Abers 151 K9
- Cross Roads C Brad 90 D3
- Cross Street Suffk 64 H6
- Crosston Angus 143 J6
- Cross Town Ches E 82 G9
- Crossway Mons 45 N11
- Crossway Powys 44 F3
- Crossway Green Mons 31 P6
- Crossway Green Worcs 58 B11
- Crossways Dorset 12 C7
- Crosswell Pembks 41 M3
- Crosthwaite Cumb 95 J2
- Croston Lancs 88 F7
- Crostwick Norfk 77 K8
- Crostwight Norfk 77 L6
- Crouch Kent 37 P9
- Crouch Kent 39 J10
- Crouch End Gt Lon 36 H3
- Croucheston Wilts 21 L9
- Crouch Hill Dorset 11 Q2
- Crough House Green Kent 37 K11
- Croughton Nhants 48 F8
- Crovie Abers 159 K4
- Crow Hants 13 L4
- Crowan Cnwll 2 G7
- Crowborough E Susx 25 M4
- Crowborough Warren E Susx 25 M4
- Crowcombe Somset 18 F7
- Crowdecote Derbys 83 P11
- Crowden Derbys 83 N5
- Crowden Devon 8 C5
- Crowdhill Hants 22 E10
- Crowdleham Kent 37 N9
- Crow Edge Barns 83 Q4
- Crowell Oxon 35 K5
- Crow End Cambs 62 D9
- Crowfield Nhants 48 H6
- Crowfield Suffk 64 G10
- Crowfield Green Suffk 64 G10
- Crowgate Street Norfk 77 L7
- Crow Green Essex 51 N11
- Crowhill E Loth 129 J5
- Crow Hill Herefs 46 B9
- Crowhole Derbys 84 D5
- Crowhurst E Susx 26 C9
- Crowhurst Surrey 37 J11
- Crowhurst Lane End Surrey 37 J11
- Crowland Lincs 74 D8
- Crowland Suffk 64 E7
- Crowlas Cnwll 2 E7
- Crowle N Linc 92 C8
- Crowle Worcs 46 H3
- Crowle Green Worcs 46 H3
- Crowmarsh Gifford Oxon 34 H7
- Crown Corner Suffk 65 K7
- Crownhill C Plym 6 D7
- Crownpits Surrey 23 Q6
- Crownthorpe Norfk 76 F11
- Crowntown Cnwll 2 G7
- Crows-an-Wra Cnwll 2 B8
- Crow's Green Essex 51 Q5
- Crowshill Norfk 76 D10
- Crow's Nest Cnwll 5 M8
- Crowsnest Shrops 56 F4
- Crowthorne Wokham 23 M2
- Crowton Ches W 82 C10
- Croxall Staffs 59 J2
- Croxby Lincs 93 L11
- Croxdale Dur 103 Q3
- Croxden Staffs 71 K7
- Croxley Green Herts 50 C11
- Croxteth Lpool 81 N5
- Croxton Cambs 62 B8
- Croxton N Linc 93 J8
- Croxton Norfk 64 B4
- Croxton Norfk 76 D5
- Croxton Staffs 70 D8
- Croxtonbank Staffs 70 D8
- Croxton Green Ches E 69 Q4
- Croxton Kerrial Leics 73 L5
- Croy Highld 156 D8
- Croy N Lans 126 C2
- Croyde Devon 16 G4
- Croyde Bay Devon 16 G4
- Croydon Cambs 62 D11
- Croydon Gt Lon 36 H7
- Crubenmore Highld 148 B9
- Cruckmeole Shrops 56 G3
- Cruckton Shrops 56 G2
- Cruden Bay Abers 159 Q10
- Crudgington Wrekin 70 A11
- Crudie Abers 159 J6
- Crudwell Wilts 33 J6
- Cruft Devon 8 D5
- Crûg Powys 56 B10
- Crugmeer Cnwll 4 E6
- Crugybar Carmth 43 N7
- Crug-y-byddar Powys 56 B8
- Crumlin Caerph 30 H5
- Crumplehorn Cnwll 5 L11
- Crumpsall Manch 82 H4
- Crundale Kent 27 J2
- Crundale Pembks 41 J7
- Crunwere Pembks 41 N8
- Cruwys Morchard Devon 9 L2
- Crux Easton Hants 22 D3
- Cruxton Dorset 11 N5
- Crwbin Carmth 28 E2
- Cryers Hill Bucks 35 N5
- Crymych Pembks 41 N4
- Crynant Neath 29 L4
- Crystal Palace Gt Lon 36 H6
- Cuaig Highld 153 N6
- Cuan Ag & B 130 F5
- Cubbington Warwks 59 M11
- Cubert Cnwll 4 B10
- Cubley Barns 90 G10
- Cublington Bucks 49 M10
- Cublington Herefs 45 N7
- Cuckfield W Susx 24 H5
- Cucklington Somset 20 E9
- Cuckney Notts 85 J6
- Cuckoo Bridge Lincs 74 D6
- Cuckoo's Corner Hants 23 K6
- Cuckoo's Nest Ches W 69 L2
- Cuddesdon Oxon 34 G4
- Cuddington Bucks 35 K2
- Cuddington Ches W 82 C10
- Cuddington Heath Ches W 69 N5
- Cuddy Hill Lancs 88 F3
- Cudham Gt Lon 37 K9
- Cudliptown Devon 8 D9
- Cudnell BCP 13 J5
- Cudworth Barns 91 K9
- Cudworth Somset 10 H2
- Cuerdley Cross Warrtn 82 B7
- Cufaude Hants 23 J3
- Cuffley Herts 50 H10
- Cuil Highld 138 H6
- Culbokie Highld 155 R6
- Culbone Somset 17 Q2
- Culburnie Highld 155 N9
- Culcabock Highld 156 B9
- Culcharry Highld 156 F7
- Culcheth Warrtn 82 E6
- Culdrain Abers 158 D11
- Culduie Highld 153 N9
- Culford Suffk 64 A7
- Culgaith Cumb 102 B5
- Culham Oxon 34 F5
- Culkein Highld 164 B10
- Culkein Drumbeg Highld 164 D10
- Culkerton Gloucs 32 H5
- Cullen Moray 158 D4
- Cullercoats N Tyne 113 N6
- Cullerlie Abers 151 K7
- Cullicudden Highld 156 A5
- Cullingworth C Brad 90 D3
- Cuillin Hills Highld 144 G3
- Cullipool Ag & B 130 E5
- Cullivoe Shet 169 s3
- Culloden Highld 156 C8
- Cullompton Devon 9 P3
- Cullompton Services Devon 9 P3
- Culm Davy Devon 18 F11
- Culmington Shrops 56 H8
- Culmstock Devon 10 C2
- Culnacraig Highld 160 H6
- Culnaightrie D & G 108 G10
- Culnaknock Highld 153 J5
- Culpho Suffk 53 M2
- Culrain Highld 162 D8
- Culross Fife 134 B10
- Culroy S Ayrs 114 F5
- Culsalmond Abers 158 G11
- Culscadden D & G 107 N8
- Culshabbin D & G 107 K7
- Culswick Shet 169 p9
- Cultercullen Abers 151 N3
- Cults C Aber 151 M7
- Culverstone Green Kent 37 P8
- Culverthorpe Lincs 73 Q2
- Culworth Nhants 48 F5
- Culzean Castle & Country Park S Ayrs 114 D5
- Cumbernauld N Lans 126 D3
- Cumbernauld Village N Lans 126 D2
- Cumberworth Lincs 87 P6
- Cumdivock Cumb 110 F11
- Cuminestown Abers 159 K7
- Cumledge Border 129 K8
- Cummersdale Cumb 110 G10
- Cummertrees D & G 109 P7
- Cummingston Moray 157 L4
- Cumnock E Ayrs 115 L3
- Cumnor Oxon 34 E4
- Cumrew Cumb 111 L10
- Cumrue D & G 109 N3
- Cumwhinton Cumb 111 J10
- Cumwhitton Cumb 111 K10
- Cundall N York 97 P6
- Cunninghamhead N Ayrs 125 K9
- Cunningsburgh Shet 169 r10
- Cupar Fife 135 K5
- Cupar Muir Fife 135 K5
- Curbar Derbys 84 C6
- Curbridge Hants 14 F4
- Curbridge Oxon 34 B3
- Curdridge Hants 14 F4
- Curdworth Warwks 59 J6
- Curland Somset 19 J11
- Curridge W Berk 34 E10
- Currie C Edin 127 M4
- Curry Mallet Somset 19 K10
- Curry Rivel Somset 19 L9
- Curteis Corner Kent 26 E4
- Curtisden Green Kent 26 B3
- Curtisknowle Devon 7 J8
- Cury Cnwll 2 H9
- Cushnie Abers 150 E5
- Cushuish Somset 18 G8
- Cusop Herefs 45 J6
- Cusworth Donc 91 N10
- Cutcloy D & G 107 N11
- Cutcombe Somset 18 B7
- Cutgate Rochdl 89 P8
- Cuthill Highld 162 H9
- Cutiau Gwynd 67 L11
- Cutler's Green Essex 51 N4
- Cutmadoc Cnwll 4 H9
- Cutmere Cnwll 5 N9
- Cutnall Green Worcs 58 C11
- Cutsdean Gloucs 47 L8
- Cutthorpe Derbys 84 D6
- Cuttivett Cnwll 5 P9
- Cuxham Oxon 35 J5
- Cuxton Medway 38 B8
- Cuxwold Lincs 93 L10
- Cwm Blae G 30 G3
- Cwm Denbgs 80 F9
- Cwmafan Neath 29 L6
- Cwmaman Rhondd 30 D5
- Cwmann Carmth 43 L5
- Cwmavon Torfn 31 J3
- Cwmbach Carmth 28 E4
- Cwmbach Carmth 41 Q5
- Cwmbâch Powys 44 H7
- Cwmbach Rhondd 30 D4
- Cwmbach Llechrhyd Powys 44 E4
- Cwmbelan Powys 55 L8
- Cwmbran Torfn 31 J6
- Cwmbrwyno Cerdgn 54 G8
- Cwm Capel Carmth 28 E4
- Cwmcarn Caerph 30 H6
- Cwmcarvan Mons 31 N3
- Cwm-celyn Blae G 30 H3
- Cwm-Cewydd Gwynd 55 K2
- Cwm-cou Cerdgn 41 Q2
- Cwm Crawnon Powys 44 G11
- Cwmdare Rhondd 30 C4
- Cwmdu Carmth 43 M8
- Cwmdu Powys 44 H10
- Cwmdu Swans 28 H6
- Cwmduad Carmth 42 G8
- Cwm Dulais Swans 28 H4
- Cwmdwr Carmth 43 P8
- Cwmfelin Brdgnd 29 N7
- Cwmfelin Myr Td 30 E4
- Cwmfelin Boeth Carmth 41 N7
- Cwmfelinfach Caerph 30 G6
- Cwmfelin Mynach Carmth 41 P6
- Cwmffrwd Carmth 42 H11
- Cwmgiedd Powys 29 L2
- Cwmgorse Carmth 29 K2
- Cwm Gwaun Pembks 41 K4
- Cwmgwili Carmth 28 G2
- Cwmgwrach Neath 29 N4
- Cwmhiraeth Carmth 42 F7
- Cwmifor Carmth 43 N9
- Cwm Irfon Powys 44 B5
- Cwmisfael Carmth 43 J11
- Cwm Llinau Powys 55 J3
- Cwmllynfell Neath 29 K2
- Cwmmawr Carmth 28 F2
- Cwm Morgan Carmth 41 Q4
- Cwmparc Rhondd 29 P5
- Cwmpengraig Carmth 42 G7
- Cwm Penmachno Conwy 67 P5
- Cwmpennar Rhondd 30 D4
- Cwmrhos Powys 44 H10
- Cwmrhydyceirw Swans 29 J5
- Cwmsychbant Cerdgn 43 J5
- Cwmtillery Blae G 30 H3
- Cwm-twrch Isaf Powys 29 L2
- Cwm-twrch Uchaf Powys 29 L2
- Cwm-y-glo Carmth 28 G2
- Cwm-y-glo Gwynd 67 K2
- Cwmyoy Mons 45 K10
- Cwmystwyth Cerdgn 54 H10
- Cwrt Gwynd 54 F5
- Cwrtnewydd Cerdgn 43 J5
- Cwrt-y-gollen Powys 45 J11
- Cyfarthfa Castle Museum Myr Td 30 D3
- Cyffylliog Denbgs 68 E3
- Cyfronydd Powys 55 Q3
- Cylibebyll Neath 29 K4
- Cymau Flints 69 J3
- Cymmer Neath 29 N5
- Cymmer Rhondd 30 D6
- Cyncoed Cardif 30 G8
- Cynghordy Carmth 43 R6
- Cynheidre Carmth 28 E3
- Cynonville Neath 29 M5
- Cynwyd Denbgs 68 E6
- Cynwyl Elfed Carmth 42 G9

D

- Daccombe Devon 7 N5
- Dacre Cumb 101 N5
- Dacre N York 97 J8
- Dacre Banks N York 97 J8
- Daddry Shield Dur 102 G3
- Dadford Bucks 49 J7
- Dadlington Leics 72 C11
- Dafen Carmth 28 F4
- Daffy Green Norfk 76 D10
- Dagenham Gt Lon 37 M4
- Daglingworth Gloucs 33 J3
- Dagnall Bucks 49 Q11
- Dagworth Suffk 64 E9
- Dail bho Dheas W Isls 168 j1
- Dailly S Ayrs 114 E7
- Dainton Devon 7 M5
- Dairsie Fife 135 L4
- Daisy Hill Bolton 82 E4
- Daisy Hill Leeds 90 H5
- Dalabrog W Isls 168 c15
- Dalavich Ag & B 131 K5
- Dalbeattie D & G 108 H8
- Dalbury Derbys 71 P8
- Dalby IoM 80 b6
- Dalby Lincs 87 M7
- Dalby N York 98 C6
- Dalcapon P & K 141 N7
- Dalchalm Highld 163 L5
- Dalchreichart Highld 146 H5
- Dalchruin P & K 133 L4
- Dalcrue P & K 134 C2
- Dalderby Lincs 87 J7
- Dalditch Devon 9 P8
- Dale Cumb 101 P2
- Dale Pembks 40 F9
- Dale Abbey Derbys 72 C3
- Dale Bottom Cumb 101 J6
- Dale End Derbys 84 B8
- Dale End N York 96 E11
- Dale Hill E Susx 26 B5
- Dalehouse N York 105 L7
- Dalelia Highld 138 C4
- Dalgarven N Ayrs 124 H8
- Dalgety Bay Fife 134 F11
- Dalgig E Ayrs 115 L5
- Dalginross P & K 133 M3
- Dalguise P & K 141 N8
- Dalhalvaig Highld 166 E6
- Dalham Suffk 63 M8
- Daliburgh W Isls 168 c15
- Dalkeith Mdloth 127 Q4
- Dallas Moray 157 L7
- Dallinghoo Suffk 65 K10
- Dallington E Susx 25 Q7
- Dallington Nhants 60 F8
- Dallow N York 97 J6
- Dalmally Ag & B 131 P2
- Dalmary Stirlg 132 G8
- Dalmellington E Ayrs 115 J6
- Dalmeny C Edin 127 L2
- Dalmore Highld 156 B4
- Dalmuir W Duns 125 M3
- Dalnabreck Highld 138 C4
- Dalnacardoch P & K 140 H3
- Dalnahaitnach Highld 148 F4
- Dalnaspidal P & K 140 F3
- Dalnawillan Lodge Highld 166 H8
- Dalness Highld 139 M7
- Dalqueich P & K 134 D7
- Dalquhairn S Ayrs 114 F8
- Dalreavoch Highld 162 H5
- Dalry N Ayrs 124 H8
- Dalrymple E Ayrs 114 G5
- Dalserf S Lans 126 D7
- Dalsmeran Ag & B 120 B9
- Dalston Cumb 110 G10
- Dalston Gt Lon 36 H4
- Dalswinton D & G 109 K3
- Dalton Cumb 95 L5
- Dalton D & G 109 P6
- Dalton Lancs 88 F9
- Dalton N York 97 P5
- Dalton N York 103 M9
- Dalton Nthumb 112 H6
- Dalton Rothm 84 G2
- Dalton-in-Furness Cumb 94 E6
- Dalton-le-Dale Dur 113 P11
- Dalton Magna Rothm 84 G2
- Dalton-on-Tees N York 103 Q9
- Dalton Parva Rothm 84 G2
- Dalton Piercy Hartpl 104 E4
- Dalveich Stirlg 133 J3
- Dalwhinnie Highld 147 Q11
- Dalwood Devon 10 E4
- Damask Green Herts 50 G5
- Damerham Hants 21 M11
- Damgate Norfk 77 N10
- Dam Green Norfk 64 E4
- Damnaglaur D & G 106 F10
- Danaway Kent 38 E9
- Danbury Essex 52 C10
- Danby N York 105 K9
- Danby Bottom N York 105 J10
- Danby Wiske N York 104 B11
- Dandaleith Moray 157 P8
- Danderhall Mdloth 127 Q4
- Danebridge Ches E 83 L11
- Dane End Herts 50 H6
- Danegate E Susx 25 N4
- Danehill E Susx 25 K5
- Dane Hills C Leic 72 F10
- Danemoor Green Norfk 76 F10
- Danesford Shrops 57 N6
- Danesmoor Derbys 84 F8
- Dane Street Kent 39 J11
- Daniel's Water Kent 26 G3
- Danshillock Abers 158 H6
- Danskine E Loth 128 F6
- Danthorpe E R Yk 93 N4
- Danzey Green Warwks 58 H11
- Dapple Heath Staffs 71 J9
- Darby Green Hants 23 M2
- Darcy Lever Bolton 89 L9
- Dardy Powys 45 J11
- Darenth Kent 37 N6
- Daresbury Halton 82 C8
- Darfield Barns 91 L10
- Darfoulds Notts 85 J5
- Dargate Kent 39 J9
- Dargavel Rens 125 L3
- Darite Cnwll 5 M8
- Darland Medway 38 C8
- Darland Wrexhm 69 L3
- Darlaston Wsall 58 E5
- Darlaston Green Wsall 58 E5
- Darley N York 97 K9
- Darley Abbey C Derb 72 B3
- Darley Bridge Derbys 84 C8
- Darley Dale Derbys 84 C8
- Darley Green Solhll 59 J10
- Darleyhall Herts 50 D6
- Darley Head N York 97 J9
- Darlingscott Warwks 47 P6
- Darlington Darltn 103 Q8
- Darliston Shrops 69 Q8
- Darlton Notts 85 N6
- Darnford Staffs 58 H3
- Darnick Border 117 Q4
- Darowen Powys 55 J4
- Darra Abers 158 H8
- Darracott Devon 16 C8
- Darracott Devon 16 H4
- Darras Hall Nthumb 113 J6
- Darrington Wakefd 91 M7
- Darsham Suffk 65 N8
- Darshill Somset 20 B6
- Dartford Kent 37 M6
- Dartford Crossing Kent 37 N5
- Dartington Devon 7 K6
- Dartmeet Devon 6 H4
- *Dartmoor National Park* Devon 8 G9
- Dartmouth Devon 7 M8
- Darton Barns 91 J8
- Darvel E Ayrs 125 P10
- Darwell Hole E Susx 25 Q7

Darwen Bl w D..........89 K6
Datchet W & M..........35 Q9
Datchworth Herts..........50 G7
Datchworth Green Herts..........50 G7
Daubhill Bolton..........89 L9
Daugh of Kinermony Moray ... 157 N9
Dauntsey Wilts..........33 J8
Dava Highld..........157 J10
Davenport Ches W..........82 E10
Davenport Stockp..........83 K7
Davenport Green Ches E..........82 H9
Davenport Green Traffd..........82 H7
Daventry Nhants..........60 C8
Davidson's Mains C Edin..........127 N2
Davidstow Cnwll..........5 K4
David Street Kent..........37 P8
Davington D & G..........117 J10
Davington Kent..........38 H9
Daviot Abers..........151 J2
Daviot Highld..........156 C10
Daviot House Highld..........156 C9
Davis's Town E Susx..........25 M7
Davoch of Grange Moray..........158 C7
Davyhulme Traffd..........82 G5
Daw End Wsall..........58 F4
Dawesgreen Surrey..........36 F11
Dawley Wrekin..........57 M3
Dawlish Devon..........9 N9
Dawlish Warren Devon..........9 N9
Dawn Conwy..........80 B10
Daws Green Somset..........18 G10
Daws Heath Essex..........38 D4
Daw's House Cnwll..........5 N5
Dawsmere Lincs..........74 H4
Daybrook Notts..........85 J11
Day Green Ches E..........70 D3
Dayhills Staffs..........70 H8
Dayhouse Bank Worcs..........58 E9
Daylesford Gloucs..........47 P9
Ddol Flints..........80 G10
Ddol-Cownwy Powys..........68 D11
Deal Kent..........39 Q11
Dean Cumb..........100 E5
Dean Devon..........7 J6
Dean Devon..........17 L2
Dean Devon..........17 N2
Dean Dorset..........21 J11
Dean Hants..........22 D8
Dean Hants..........22 G11
Dean Lancs..........89 P5
Dean Oxon..........48 B10
Dean Somset..........20 C6
Dean Bottom Kent..........37 N7
Deanburnhaugh Border..........117 M8
Deancombe Devon..........7 J6
Dean Court Oxon..........34 E3
Deane Bolton..........89 K9
Deane Hants..........22 F4
Dean End Dorset..........21 J11
Dean Head Barns..........90 H10
Deanland Kirk..........90 C7
Deanland Dorset..........21 J11
Deanlane End W Susx..........15 K4
Dean Prior Devon..........7 J6
Deanraw Nthumb..........112 B8
Dean Row Ches E..........83 J8
Deans W Loth..........127 J4
Deanscales Cumb..........100 E5
Deanshanger Nhants..........49 L7
Deanshaugh Moray..........157 R7
Deanston Stirlg..........133 L7
Dean Street Kent..........38 B11
Dearham Cumb..........100 E3
Dearnley Rochdl..........89 Q7
Debach Suffk..........65 J11
Debden Essex..........51 K11
Debden Essex..........51 N4
Debden Green Essex..........51 N4
Debenham Suffk..........64 H9
Deblin's Green Worcs..........46 F5
Dechmont W Loth..........127 J3
Deddington Oxon..........48 E8
Dedham Essex..........53 J5
Dedham Heath Essex..........53 J5
Dedworth W & M..........35 P9
Deene Nhants..........61 K2
Deenethorpe Nhants..........61 L2
Deepcar Sheff..........90 H11
Deepcut Surrey..........23 P3
Deepdale Cumb..........95 Q4
Deepdale N York..........96 C5
Deeping Gate C Pete..........74 B9
Deeping St James Lincs..........74 C9
Deeping St Nicholas Lincs..........74 D7
Deerhurst Gloucs..........46 G8
Deerhurst Walton Gloucs..........46 G9
Deerton Street Kent..........38 G9
Defford Worcs..........46 H6
Defynnog Powys..........44 C9
Deganwy Conwy..........79 P9
Degnish Ag & B..........130 F5
Deighton C York..........91 Q2
Deighton N York..........104 C10
Deiniolen Gwynd..........67 K2
Delabole Cnwll..........4 H5
Delamere Ches W..........82 C11
Delamere Park Ches W..........82 C10
Delfrigs Abers..........151 P3
Delley Devon..........17 J7
Delliefure Highld..........157 K11
Dell Quay W Susx..........15 M6
Delly End Oxon..........34 C2
Delnabo Moray..........149 M4
Delny Highld..........156 C3
Delph Oldham..........90 B9
Delves Dur..........112 H11
Delvin End Essex..........52 C4
Dembleby Lincs..........73 Q3
Demelza Cnwll..........4 F9
Denaby Donc..........91 M11
Denaby Main Donc..........91 M11
Denbies Surrey..........36 D10
Denbigh Denbgs..........80 F11
Denbrae Fife..........135 K4
Denbury Devon..........7 L5
Denby Derbys..........84 E11
Denby Bottles Derbys..........84 E11
Denby Dale Kirk..........90 G9
Denchworth Oxon..........34 C6
Dendron Cumb..........94 E6
Denel End C Beds..........50 B3
Denfield P & K..........134 B4
Denford Nhants..........61 L5
Dengie Essex..........52 G11
Denham Bucks..........36 B3
Denham Suffk..........64 N8

Denham Suffk..........64 H7
Denham End Suffk..........63 N8
Denham Green Bucks..........36 B3
Denham Green Suffk..........64 H7
Denhead Abers..........159 N7
Denhead Fife..........135 M6
Denhead of Gray C Dund..........142 E11
Denholm Border..........117 R7
Denholme C Brad..........90 D4
Denholme Clough C Brad..........90 D4
Denio Gwynd..........66 F7
Denmead Hants..........15 J4
Denne Park W Susx..........24 E5
Dennington Suffk..........65 K8
Denny Falk..........133 N11
Dennyloanhead Falk..........133 N11
Den of Lindores Fife..........134 H4
Denshaw Oldham..........90 B8
Denside of Durris Abers..........151 L8
Densole Kent..........27 M3
Denston Suffk..........63 N10
Denstone Staffs..........71 K6
Denstroude Kent..........39 K9
Dent Cumb..........95 Q3
Denton Cambs..........61 Q3
Denton Darltn..........103 P7
Denton E Susx..........25 L10
Denton Kent..........27 M2
Denton Kent..........37 Q6
Denton Lincs..........73 M4
Denton N York..........96 H11
Denton Nhants..........60 H9
Denton Norfk..........65 K4
Denton Oxon..........34 G4
Denton Tamesd..........83 K5
Denver Norfk..........75 M10
Denwick Nthumb..........119 P8
Deopham Norfk..........76 E11
Deopham Green Norfk..........64 E2
Depden Suffk..........63 N9
Depden Green Suffk..........63 N9
Deptford Gt Lon..........37 J5
Deptford Wilts..........21 K7
Derby C Derb..........72 B3
Derby Devon..........17 K5
Derbyhaven IoM..........80 c8
Dereham Norfk..........76 D9
Deri Caerph..........30 F4
Derril Devon..........16 E11
Derringstone Kent..........27 M2
Derrington Staffs..........70 F10
Derriton Devon..........16 E11
Derry Hill Wilts..........33 J10
Derrythorpe N Linc..........92 D9
Dersingham Norfk..........75 N4
Dervaig Ag & B..........137 L5
Derwen Denbgs..........68 E4
Derwenlas Powys..........54 G5
Derwent Valley Mills
    Derbys..........84 D9
Derwent Water Cumb..........101 J6
Derwydd Carmth..........43 M11
Desborough Nhants..........60 H4
Desford Leics..........72 D10
Detchant Nthumb..........119 L3
Detling Kent..........38 C10
Deuxhill Shrops..........57 M7
Devauden Mons..........31 N5
Devil's Bridge Cerdgn..........54 G9
Devitts Green Warwks..........59 L6
Devizes Wilts..........21 K2
Devonport C Plym..........6 C7
Devonside Clacks..........133 Q8
Devoran Cnwll..........3 K6
Devoran & Perran Cnwll..........3 K6
Dewarton Mdloth..........128 C5
Dewlish Dorset..........12 C7
Dewsbury Kirk..........90 G6
Dewsbury Moor Kirk..........90 G6
Deytheur Powys..........68 H11
Dial N Som..........31 P11
Dial Green W Susx..........23 P9
Dial Post W Susx..........24 E7
Dibberford Dorset..........11 K4
Dibden Hants..........14 D5
Dibden Purlieu Hants..........14 D5
Dickens Heath Solhll..........58 H9
Dickleburgh Norfk..........64 H5
Didbrook Gloucs..........47 L8
Didcot Oxon..........34 F6
Diddington Cambs..........61 Q8
Diddlebury Shrops..........57 J7
Didley Herefs..........45 P8
Didling W Susx..........23 M11
Didmarton Gloucs..........32 F7
Didsbury Manch..........82 H6
Didworthy Devon..........6 H6
Digby Lincs..........86 E10
Digg Highld..........152 H4
Diggle Oldham..........90 C9
Digmoor Lancs..........88 F9
Digswell Herts..........50 F7
Digswell Water Herts..........50 G8
Dihewyd Cerdgn..........43 J3
Dilham Norfk..........77 L6
Dilhorne Staffs..........70 H6
Dill Hall Lancs..........89 M5
Dillington Cambs..........61 Q8
Dilston Nthumb..........112 E8
Dilton Wilts..........20 G5
Dilton Marsh Wilts..........20 F5
Dilwyn Herefs..........45 N4
Dimple Bolton..........89 L7
Dimple Derbys..........84 C8
Dinas Carmth..........41 J7
Dinas Cnwll..........4 E7
Dinas Gwynd..........66 D3
Dinas Gwynd..........66 H3
Dinas Rhondd..........30 D6
Dinas Cross Pembks..........41 K3
Dinas Dinlle Gwynd..........66 G3
Dinas-Mawddwy Gwynd..........67 R11
Dinas Powys V Glam..........30 G10
Dinder Somset..........19 Q6
Dinedor Herefs..........45 Q7
Dingestow Mons..........31 N2
Dingle Lpool..........81 M7
Dingleden Kent..........26 D5
Dingley Nhants..........60 G3
Dingwall Highld..........155 P6
Dinmael Conwy..........68 D6
Dinnet Abers..........150 D8
Dinnington N u Ty..........113 K6
Dinnington Rothm..........84 H3

Dinnington Somset..........11 J2
Dinorwig Gwynd..........67 K2
Dinorwig Slate Landscape
    Gwynd..........67 K2
Dinton Bucks..........35 L2
Dinton Wilts..........21 K8
Dinwoodie D & G..........109 P2
Dinworthy Devon..........16 E8
Dipford Somset..........18 H10
Dipley Hants..........23 K3
Dippen Ag & B..........120 F4
Dippenhall Surrey..........23 M5
Dippermill Devon..........8 B3
Dippertown Devon..........8 B8
Dippin N Ayrs..........121 K7
Dipple Moray..........157 Q6
Dipple S Ayrs..........114 D7
Diptford Devon..........7 J7
Dipton Dur..........113 J10
Diptonmill Nthumb..........112 D8
Dirleton E Loth..........128 E3
Dirt Pot Nthumb..........112 C11
Discoed Powys..........45 K2
Diseworth Leics..........72 D6
Dishforth N York..........97 N6
Disley Ches E..........83 L8
Diss Norfk..........64 G5
Disserth Powys..........44 E3
Distington Cumb..........100 D6
Ditchampton Wilts..........21 L8
Ditcheat Somset..........20 B7
Ditchingham Norfk..........65 L3
Ditchling E Susx..........24 H7
Ditherington Shrops..........57 J2
Ditteridge Wilts..........32 F11
Dittisham Devon..........7 M7
Ditton Kent..........38 B10
Ditton Green Cambs..........63 L9
Ditton Priors Shrops..........57 L7
Dixton Gloucs..........47 J8
Dixton Mons..........31 P2
Dizzard Cnwll..........5 K2
Dobcross Oldham..........90 B9
Dobwalls Cnwll..........5 L8
Doccombe Devon..........9 J7
Dochgarroch Highld..........155 R9
Dockenfield Surrey..........23 M6
Docker Lancs..........95 M6
Docking Norfk..........75 Q3
Docklow Herefs..........45 R3
Dockray Cumb..........101 L6
Dockray Cumb..........110 E11
Dodbrooke Devon..........7 J10
Doddinghurst Essex..........51 N11
Doddington Cambs..........62 F2
Doddington Kent..........38 F10
Doddington Lincs..........85 Q6
Doddington Nthumb..........119 J4
Doddington Shrops..........57 L9
Doddiscombsleigh Devon..........9 J4
Dodd's Green Ches E..........69 R6
Doddshill Norfk..........75 N4
Doddy Cross Cnwll..........5 N9
Dodford Nhants..........60 D8
Dodford Worcs..........58 D10
Dodington S Glos..........32 E8
Dodington Somset..........18 G6
Dodleston Ches W..........69 L2
Dodscott Devon..........17 J8
Dodside E Rens..........125 N7
Dod's Leigh Staffs..........71 J6
Dodworth Barns..........91 J9
Dodworth Bottom Barns..........91 J10
Dodworth Green Barns..........91 J10
Doe Bank Birm..........58 H5
Doe Lea Derbys..........84 G7
Dogdyke Lincs..........86 H9
Dogley Lane Kirk..........90 F8
Dogmersfield Hants..........23 L4
Dogridge Wilts..........33 L7
Dogsthorpe C Pete..........74 C10
Dog Village Devon..........9 N5
Dolanog Powys..........55 P2
Dolau Powys..........55 Q11
Dolaucothi Carmth..........43 N6
Dolbenmaen Gwynd..........67 J6
Doley Staffs..........70 C9
Dolfach Powys..........55 L4
Dol-fôr Powys..........55 J3
Dolfor Powys..........55 Q7
Dolgarrog Conwy..........79 P11
Dolgellau Gwynd..........67 N11
Dolgoch Gwynd..........54 F4
Dol-gran Carmth..........42 H8
Doll Highld..........163 K6
Dollar Clacks..........134 B8
Dollarfield Clacks..........134 B8
Dolley Green Powys..........56 D11
Dollwen Cerdgn..........54 F8
Dolphin Flints..........80 H10
Dolphinholme Lancs..........95 L10
Dolphinton S Lans..........127 L8
Dolton Devon..........17 K9
Dolwen Conwy..........80 B10
Dolwyddelan Conwy..........67 N4
Dolybont Cerdgn..........54 E7
Dolyhir Powys..........45 J3
Domgay Powys..........69 J11
Donaldson's Lodge Nthumb..........118 G2
Doncaster Donc..........91 P10
Doncaster Carr Donc..........91 P10
Doncaster North Services
    Donc..........91 R8
Doncaster Sheffield
    Airport Donc..........91 R11
Donhead St Andrew Wilts..........20 H10
Donhead St Mary Wilts..........20 H10
Donibristle Fife..........134 F10
Doniford Somset..........18 E6
Donington Lincs..........74 D3
Donington on Bain Lincs..........86 H4
Donington Park Services
    Leics..........72 D5
Donington Southing Lincs..........74 D4
Donisthorpe Leics..........59 M2
Donkey Street Kent..........27 K5
Donkey Town Surrey..........23 P2
Donnington Gloucs..........47 N9
Donnington Herefs..........46 D8
Donnington Shrops..........57 K3
Donnington W Berk..........34 E11
Donnington W Susx..........15 N6
Donnington Wrekin..........57 N2
Donnington Wood Wrekin..........57 N2
Donyatt Somset..........10 G2
Doomsday Green W Susx..........24 E5

Doonfoot S Ayrs..........114 F4
Dora's Green Hants..........23 M5
Dorback Lodge Highld..........149 K4
Dorchester Dorset..........11 P6
Dorchester-on-Thames
    Oxon..........34 G6
Dordon Warwks..........59 L4
Dore Sheff..........84 D4
Dores Highld..........155 Q11
Dorking Surrey..........36 E11
Dorking Tye Suffk..........52 F4
Dormansland Surrey..........25 J2
Dormans Park Surrey..........25 J2
Dormington Herefs..........46 A6
Dormston Worcs..........47 J3
Dorn Gloucs..........47 P8
Dorney Bucks..........35 P9
Dorney Reach Bucks..........35 P9
Dornie Highld..........145 Q2
Dornoch Highld..........162 H9
Dornock D & G..........110 D7
Dorrery Highld..........167 J5
Dorridge Solhll..........59 J10
Dorrington Lincs..........86 E10
Dorrington Shrops..........56 H4
Dorrington Shrops..........70 C6
Dorsington Warwks..........47 M5
Dorstone Herefs..........45 L6
Dorton Bucks..........35 J2
Dosthill Staffs..........59 K5
Dothan IoA..........78 F10
Dottery Dorset..........11 K5
Doublebois Cnwll..........5 K9
Doughton Gloucs..........32 G6
Douglas IoM..........80 e6
Douglas S Lans..........116 A4
Douglas and Angus C Dund..........142 G11
Douglas Pier Ag & B..........131 P8
Douglastown Angus..........142 G8
Douglas Water S Lans..........116 B3
Douglas West S Lans..........126 E11
Doulting Somset..........20 B6
Dounby Ork..........169 b4
Doune Highld..........161 Q6
Doune Highld..........133 L7
Dounepark S Ayrs..........114 C8
Dounie Highld..........162 G8
Dousland Devon..........6 E5
Dovaston Shrops..........69 L10
Dove Dale Derbys..........71 L4
Dove Green Notts..........84 G10
Dove Holes Derbys..........83 N9
Dovenby Cumb..........100 E4
Dover Kent..........27 P3
Dover Wigan..........82 D4
Dover Castle Kent..........27 P3
Dovercourt Essex..........53 M5
Doverdale Worcs..........58 C11
Doveridge Derbys..........71 L8
Doversgreen Surrey..........36 G11
Dowally P & K..........141 P8
Dowbridge Lancs..........88 E4
Dowdeswell Gloucs..........47 K11
Dowlais Myr Td..........30 E4
Dowland Devon..........17 K9
Dowlish Ford Somset..........10 H2
Dowlish Wake Somset..........10 H2
Down Ampney Gloucs..........33 L5
Downderry Cnwll..........5 N11
Downe Gt Lon..........37 K8
Downend Gloucs..........32 F5
Downend IoW..........14 F9
Downend S Glos..........32 C9
Downend Berk..........34 E9
Downfield C Dund..........142 F11
Downgate Cnwll..........5 M7
Downgate Cnwll..........5 P7
Downham Essex..........38 B2
Downham Gt Lon..........37 J6
Downham Lancs..........89 M2
Downham Market Norfk..........75 M10
Down Hatherley Gloucs..........46 G10
Downhead Somset..........19 Q9
Downhead Somset..........20 C5
Downhill P & K..........134 D2
Downholland Cross Lancs..........88 D8
Downholme N York..........103 M11
Downicarey Devon..........5 P3
Downies Abers..........151 N9
Downing Flints..........80 H9
Downley Bucks..........35 M5
Down St Mary Devon..........8 H4
Downside Somset..........20 B4
Downside Somset..........20 B6
Downside Surrey..........36 D9
Down Thomas Devon..........6 E8
Downton Hants..........13 N6
Downton Wilts..........21 N10
Dowsby Lincs..........74 B5
Dowsdale Lincs..........74 E8
Doxey Staffs..........70 F10
Doxford Nthumb..........119 N6
Doynton S Glos..........32 D10
Draethen Caerph..........30 H7
Draffan S Lans..........126 D8
Dragonby N Linc..........92 H7
Dragons Green W Susx..........24 D6
Drakeholes Notts..........85 M2
Drakelow Worcs..........57 Q8
Drakemyre N Ayrs..........124 H7
Drakes Broughton Worcs..........46 H5
Drakewalls Cnwll..........6 C4
Draughton N York..........96 F10
Draughton Nhants..........60 G5
Drax N York..........92 A5
Drax Hales N York..........91 R5
Draycote Warwks..........59 P10
Draycot Foliat Swindn..........33 N9
Draycott Derbys..........72 C4
Draycott Gloucs..........47 N7
Draycott Shrops..........58 Q6
Draycott Somset..........19 N4
Draycott Somset..........19 Q10
Draycott Worcs..........46 G5
Draycott in the Clay Staffs..........71 M9
Draycott in the Moors
    Staffs..........70 H6
Drayford Devon..........9 J2
Drayton C Port..........15 J5
Drayton Leics..........73 H2
Drayton Lincs..........74 D3
Drayton Norfk..........76 H9
Drayton Oxon..........34 E6
Drayton Oxon..........48 D6
Drayton Somset..........19 M10

Drayton Somset..........19 N11
Drayton Worcs..........58 D9
Drayton Bassett Staffs..........59 J4
Drayton Beauchamp Bucks..........35 P2
Drayton Manor Resort
    Staffs..........59 J4
Drayton Parslow Bucks..........49 M9
Drayton St Leonard Oxon..........34 G5
Drebley N York..........96 G9
Dreemskerry IoM..........80 g3
Dreen Hill Pembks..........40 H8
Drefach Carmth..........28 F7
Drefach Carmth..........42 G7
Drefach Cerdgn..........43 J5
Drefelin Carmth..........42 G7
Dreghorn N Ayrs..........125 K10
Drellingore Kent..........27 M3
Drem E Loth..........128 E4
Dresden C Stke..........70 G6
Drewsteignton Devon..........8 H6
Driby Lincs..........87 L6
Driffield E R Yk..........99 L9
Driffield Gloucs..........33 L5
Driffield Cross Roads
    Gloucs..........33 L5
Drift Cnwll..........2 C8
Drigg Cumb..........100 E11
Drighlington Leeds..........90 G5
Drimnin Highld..........137 P5
Drimpton Dorset..........11 J4
Drimsallie Highld..........138 H2
Dringhouses C York..........98 B11
Drinkstone Suffk..........64 D9
Drinkstone Green Suffk..........64 D9
Drive End Dorset..........11 M3
Driver's End Herts..........50 F6
Drointon Staffs..........71 J9
Droitwich Spa Worcs..........46 G2
Dron P & K..........134 E4
Dronfield Derbys..........84 E5
Dronfield Woodhouse
    Derbys..........84 D5
Drongan E Ayrs..........114 H4
Dronley Angus..........142 E10
Droop Dorset..........12 C3
Dropping Well Rothm..........84 E2
Droxford Hants..........22 H11
Droylsden Tamesd..........83 K5
Druid Denbgs..........68 D6
Druidston Pembks..........40 G7
Druimarbin Highld..........139 K3
Druimavuic Ag & B..........139 J8
Druimdrishaig Ag & B..........123 M5
Druimindarroch Highld..........145 L11
Drum Ag & B..........124 A2
Drum P & K..........134 C7
Drumalbin S Lans..........116 C3
Drumbeg Highld..........164 D10
Drumblade Abers..........158 E9
Drumbreddon D & G..........106 E9
Drumbuie Highld..........153 P11
Drumburgh Cumb..........110 E9
Drumburn D & G..........109 J10
Drumburn D & G..........109 L8
Drumchapel C Glas..........125 N3
Drumchastle P & K..........140 G6
Drumclog S Lans..........125 Q10
Drumeldrie Fife..........135 L7
Drumelzier Border..........116 G4
Drumfearn Highld..........145 L4
Drumfrennie Abers..........151 J8
Drumgley Angus..........142 G7
Drumguish Highld..........148 D8
Drumin Moray..........157 M11
Drumjohn D & G..........115 K8
Drumlamford S Ayrs..........107 J2
Drumlasie Abers..........150 G6
Drumleaning Cumb..........110 E10
Drumlemble Ag & B..........120 C8
Drumlithie Abers..........151 K11
Drummoddie D & G..........107 L8
Drummore D & G..........106 F10
Drummuir Moray..........158 A9
Drumnadrochit Highld..........155 P11
Drumnagorrach Moray..........158 D7
Drumoak Abers..........151 K8
Drumpark D & G..........109 J5
Drumrunie Highld..........161 K5
Drumshang S Ayrs..........114 E5
Drumuie Highld..........152 H8
Drumuillie Highld..........148 G3
Drumvaich Stirlg..........133 K7
Drunzie P & K..........134 E6
Druridge Nthumb..........119 Q11
Drury Flints..........69 J2
Drws-y-coed Gwynd..........67 J4
Drybeck Cumb..........102 C7
Drybridge Moray..........158 B5
Drybridge N Ayrs..........125 K10
Drybrook Gloucs..........46 B11
Dryburgh Border..........118 A4
Dry Doddington Lincs..........85 Q11
Dry Drayton Cambs..........62 E8
Dryhill Kent..........37 L10
Drymen Stirlg..........132 F10
Drymuir Abers..........159 M8
Drynoch Highld..........152 G11
Dry Sandford Oxon..........34 E4
Dryslwyn Carmth..........43 L10
Dry Street Essex..........37 Q3
Dryton Shrops..........57 K3
Dubford Abers..........159 J5
Dublin Suffk..........64 H8
Duchally Highld..........161 P3
Duck End Bed..........50 C2
Duck End Cambs..........62 B8
Duck End Essex..........51 Q5
Duck End Essex..........51 Q5
Duckend Green Essex..........52 B7
Duckington Ches W..........69 N4
Ducklington Oxon..........34 C3
Duck's Cross Bed..........61 P9
Duddenhoe End Essex..........51 L3
Duddington C Edin..........127 P3
Duddington Nhants..........73 P10
Duddlestone Somset..........18 H10
Duddleswell E Susx..........25 L5
Duddlewick Shrops..........57 M8
Duddo Nthumb..........118 H2
Duddon Ches W..........69 P2
Duddon Bridge Cumb..........94 D3
Duddon Common Ches W..........81 Q11
Dudleston Shrops..........69 K7
Dudleston Heath Shrops..........69 L7
Dudley Dudley..........58 D6
Dudley N Tyne..........113 L6

268 Dudley Hill – Ebchester

Dudley Hill C Brad 90 F4
Dudley Port Sandw 58 E6
Dudnill Shrops 57 L10
Dudsbury Dorset 13 J5
Dudswell Herts 35 Q3
Duffield Derbys 72 A2
Duffryn Neath 29 M5
Dufftown Moray 157 Q9
Duffus Moray 157 M4
Dufton Cumb 102 C5
Duggleby N York 98 H7
Duirinish Highld 153 P11
Duisdalemore Highld 145 M5
Duisky Highld 139 J2
Dukestown Blae G 30 F2
Duke Street Suffk 53 J3
Dukinfield Tamesd 83 K5
Dulas IoA 78 H7
Dulcote Somset 19 Q6
Dulford Devon 9 Q3
Dull P & K 141 K8
Dullatur N Lans 126 C2
Dullingham Cambs 63 K9
Dullingham Ley Cambs 63 K9
Dulnain Bridge Highld 148 H3
Duloe Bed 61 Q8
Duloe Cnwll 5 L10
Dulsie Bridge Highld 156 G9
Dulverton Somset 18 B9
Dulwich Gt Lon 36 H6
Dumbarton W Duns 125 L2
Dumbleton Gloucs 47 K7
Dumfries D & G 109 L5
Dumgoyne Stirlg 132 G11
Dummer Hants 22 G5
Dumpton Kent 39 Q8
Dun Angus 143 M6
Dunalastair P & K 140 H6
Dunan Highld 145 J2
Dunan P & K 140 C6
Dunaverty Ag & B 120 C10
Dunball Somset 19 K6
Dunbar E Loth 128 H4
Dunbeath Highld 167 L11
Dunbeg Ag & B 138 F11
Dunblane Stirlg 133 M7
Dunbog Fife 134 H4
Dunbridge Hants 22 B9
Duncanston Highld 155 Q6
Duncanstone Abers 150 F2
Dunchideock Devon 9 L7
Dunchurch Warwks 59 Q10
Duncote Nhants 49 J4
Duncow D & G 109 L4
Duncrievie P & K 134 E6
Duncton W Susx 23 Q11
Dundee C Dund 142 G11
Dundee Airport C Dund 135 K2
Dundon Somset 19 N8
Dundonald S Ayrs 125 K11
Dundonnell Highld 160 H9
Dundraw Cumb 110 D11
Dundreggan Highld 147 J5
Dundrennan D & G 108 F11
Dundry N Som 31 Q11
Dunecht Abers 151 K6
Dunfermline Fife 134 D10
Dunfield Gloucs 33 M5
Dunford Bridge Barns 83 Q4
Dungate Kent 38 F10
Dungavel S Lans 126 B10
Dunge Wilts 20 G4
Dungeness Kent 27 J8
Dungworth Sheff 84 C3
Dunham Massey Traffd 82 F7
Dunham-on-the-Hill Ches W 81 P10
Dunham-on-Trent Notts 85 P6
Dunhampstead Worcs 46 H2
Dunhampton Worcs 58 B11
Dunham Town Traffd 82 F7
Dunham Woodhouses Traffd 82 F7
Dunholme Lincs 86 D5
Dunino Fife 135 N5
Dunipace Falk 133 N11
Dunkeld P & K 141 P9
Dunkerton BaNES 20 D3
Dunkeswell Devon 10 C3
Dunkeswick N York 97 M11
Dunkirk Ches W 81 M10
Dunkirk Kent 39 J10
Dunkirk S Glos 32 E7
Dunkirk Wilts 21 J2
Dunk's Green Kent 37 P10
Dunlappie Angus 143 K4
Dunley Hants 22 E4
Dunley Worcs 57 P11
Dunlop E Ayrs 125 L8
Dunmaglass Highld 147 P3
Dunmere Cnwll 4 G8
Dunmore Falk 133 P10
Dunnet Highld 167 M2
Dunnichen Angus 143 J8
Dunning P & K 134 C5
Dunnington C York 98 D10
Dunnington E R Yk 99 P10
Dunnington Warwks 47 L4
Dunnockshaw Lancs 89 N5
Dunn Street Kent 38 C9
Dunoon Ag & B 124 F2
Dunphail Moray 157 J8
Dunragit D & G 106 G6
Duns Border 129 K9
Dunsa Derbys 84 B6
Dunsby Lincs 74 B5
Dunscar Bolton 89 L8
Dunscore D & G 109 J4
Dunscroft Donc 91 Q9
Dunsdale R & Cl 104 H7
Dunsden Green Oxon 35 K9
Dunsdon Devon 16 E10
Dunsfold Surrey 24 B3
Dunsford Devon 9 K7
Dunshalt Fife 134 G5
Dunshillock Abers 159 N8
Dunsill Notts 84 G8
Dunsley N York 105 N8
Dunsley Staffs 58 C8
Dunsmore Bucks 35 N3
Dunsop Bridge Lancs 95 P11
Dunstable C Beds 50 B6
Dunstall Staffs 71 M10
Dunstall Common Worcs 46 G6
Dunstall Green Suffk 63 M8
Dunstan Nthumb 119 P7
Dunstan Steads Nthumb 119 P6
Dunster Somset 18 C6
Duns Tew Oxon 48 E9
Dunston Gatesd 113 K8
Dunston Lincs 86 E8
Dunston Norfk 77 J11
Dunston Staffs 70 G11
Dunstone Devon 6 F8
Dunstone Devon 8 H9
Dunston Heath Staffs 70 G11
Dunsville Donc 91 Q9
Dunswell E R Yk 93 J3
Dunsyre S Lans 127 K8
Dunterton Devon 5 P6
Dunthrop Oxon 48 C9
Duntisbourne Abbots Gloucs 33 J3
Duntisbourne Leer Gloucs 33 J3
Duntisbourne Rouse Gloucs 33 J3
Duntish Dorset 11 P3
Duntocher W Duns 125 M3
Dunton Bucks 49 M10
Dunton C Beds 50 F2
Dunton Norfk 76 B5
Dunton Bassett Leics 60 B2
Dunton Green Kent 37 M9
Dunton Wayletts Essex 37 Q2
Duntulm Highld 152 G3
Dunure S Ayrs 114 E4
Dunvant Swans 28 G6
Dunvegan Highld 152 D8
Dunwich Suffk 65 P7
Dunwood Staffs 70 G3
Durdar Cumb 110 H10
Durgan Cnwll 3 K8
Durgates E Susx 25 P4
Durham Dur 103 Q2
Durham Cathedral Dur 103 Q2
Durham Services Dur 104 B3
Durisdeer D & G 116 B10
Durisdeermill D & G 116 B10
Durkar Wakefd 91 J7
Durleigh Somset 19 J7
Durley Hants 22 F11
Durley Wilts 21 P2
Durley Street Hants 22 F11
Durlock Kent 39 N10
Durlock Kent 39 P9
Durlow Common Herefs 46 B7
Durn Rochdl 89 Q7
Durness Highld 165 K3
Durno Abers 151 J2
Duror Highld 138 H6
Durran Ag & B 131 K6
Durrington W Susx 24 D9
Durrington Wilts 21 N6
Dursley Gloucs 32 E5
Dursley Cross Gloucs 46 C10
Durston Somset 19 J9
Durweston Dorset 12 E3
Duston Nhants 60 F8
Duthil Highld 148 G3
Dutlas Powys 56 C9
Duton Hill Essex 51 P5
Dutson Cnwll 5 N4
Dutton Ches W 82 C9
Duxford Cambs 62 G11
Duxford Oxon 34 C5
Duxford IWM Cambs 62 G11
Dwygyfylchi Conwy 79 N9
Dwyran IoA 78 G11
Dyce C Aber 151 M5
Dyer's End Essex 52 B4
Dyfatty Carmth 28 E4
Dyffrydan Gwynd 54 F2
Dyffryn Brdgnd 29 N6
Dyffryn Myr Td 30 E4
Dyffryn V Glam 30 E10
Dyffryn Ardudwy Gwynd 67 K10
Dyffryn Castell Cerdgn 54 H8
Dyffryn Cellwen Neath 29 N2
Dyke Lincs 74 B6
Dyke Moray 156 H6
Dykehead Angus 142 C7
Dykehead Angus 142 F6
Dykehead N Lans 126 F6
Dykehead Stirlg 132 H8
Dykelands Abers 143 N4
Dykends Angus 142 D6
Dykeside Abers 158 H9
Dykes of Gray C Dund 142 E11
Dylife Powys 55 K6
Dymchurch Kent 27 K6
Dymock Gloucs 46 D8
Dynamic Earth C Edin 127 P3
Dyrham S Glos 32 D9
Dysart Fife 135 J9
Dyserth Denbgs 80 F9

E

Eachway Worcs 58 E9
Eachwick Nthumb 112 H6
Eagland Hill Lancs 95 J11
Eagle Lincs 85 Q7
Eagle Barnsdale Lincs 85 Q7
Eagle Moor Lincs 85 Q7
Eaglescliffe S on T 104 D7
Eaglesfield Cumb 100 E5
Eaglesfield D & G 110 D6
Eaglesham E Rens 125 P7
Eagley Bolton 89 L8
Eairy IoM 80 c6
Eakring Notts 85 L8
Ealand N Linc 92 C8
Ealing Gt Lon 36 E4
Eals Nthumb 111 N9
Eamont Bridge Cumb 101 P5
Earby Lancs 96 D11
Earcroft Bl w D 89 K6
Eardington Shrops 57 N6
Eardisland Herefs 45 N3
Eardisley Herefs 45 L5
Eardiston Shrops 69 L9
Eardiston Worcs 57 M11
Earith Cambs 62 E5
Earle Nthumb 119 J5
Earlestown St Hel 82 C5
Earley Wokham 35 K10
Earlham Norfk 76 H10
Earlish Highld 152 F5
Earls Barton Nhants 61 J8
Earls Colne Essex 52 E6
Earls Common Worcs 47 J3
Earl's Croome Worcs 46 G6
Earlsditton Shrops 57 L9
Earlsdon Covtry 59 M9
Earl's Down E Susx 25 P7
Earlsferry Fife 135 M7
Earlsfield Gt Lon 36 G6
Earlsford Abers 159 K11
Earl's Green Suffk 64 E8
Earlsheaton Kirk 90 H6
Earl Shilton Leics 72 D11
Earl Soham Suffk 65 J9
Earl Sterndale Derbys 83 N11
Earlston Border 117 R3
Earlston E Ayrs 125 L10
Earl Stonham Suffk 64 G10
Earlswood Surrey 36 G11
Earlswood Warwks 58 H10
Earlswood Common Mons 31 N6
Earnley W Susx 15 M7
Earnshaw Bridge Lancs 88 G6
Earsdon N Tyne 113 M6
Earsdon Nthumb 113 J2
Earsham Norfk 65 L4
Earswick C York 98 C9
Eartham W Susx 15 P5
Earthcott S Glos 32 C7
Easby N York 104 G9
Easdale Ag & B 130 E4
Easebourne W Susx 23 N10
Easenhall Warwks 59 Q9
Eashing Surrey 23 P6
Easington Bucks 35 J2
Easington Dur 104 D2
Easington E R Yk 93 Q7
Easington Nthumb 119 M4
Easington Oxon 35 J5
Easington R & Cl 105 K7
Easington Colliery Dur 104 D2
Easington Lane Sundld 113 N11
Easingwold N York 98 A7
Easole Street Kent 39 N11
Eassie and Nevay Angus 142 E9
East Aberthaw V Glam 30 D11
East Allington Devon 7 K9
East Anstey Devon 17 R6
East Anton Hants 22 C5
East Appleton N York 103 P11
East Ardsley Leeds 91 J5
East Ashey IoW 14 G9
East Ashling W Susx 15 M5
East Aston Hants 22 D5
East Ayton N York 99 K3
East Balsdon Cnwll 5 M2
East Bank Blae G 30 H3
East Barkwith Lincs 86 G4
East Barming Kent 38 B11
East Barnby N York 105 M8
East Barnet Gt Lon 50 G11
East Barns E Loth 129 J4
East Barsham Norfk 76 C5
East Beckham Norfk 76 H4
East Bedfont Gt Lon 36 C6
East Bergholt Suffk 53 J5
East Bierley Kirk 90 F5
East Bilney Norfk 76 D8
East Blatchington E Susx 25 L10
East Bloxworth Dorset 12 E6
East Boldon S Tyne 113 N8
East Boldre Hants 14 C6
East Bolton Nthumb 119 M7
Eastbourne Darltn 104 B8
Eastbourne E Susx 25 P11
East Bower Somset 19 K7
East Bradenham Norfk 76 C10
East Brent Somset 19 K4
Eastbridge Suffk 65 P8
East Bridgford Notts 72 H2
East Briscoe Dur 103 J7
Eastbrook V Glam 30 G10
East Buckland Devon 17 M5
East Budleigh Devon 9 Q8
Eastburn C Brad 90 C2
Eastburn E R Yk 99 K9
East Burnham Bucks 35 Q8
East Burton Dorset 12 D7
Eastbury W Berk 34 B9
East Butsfield Dur 112 H11
East Butterwick N Linc 92 D9
Eastby N York 96 F10
East Calder W Loth 127 K4
East Carleton Norfk 76 H11
East Carlton Leeds 90 G2
East Carlton Nhants 60 H3
East Chaldon Dorset 12 C8
East Challow Oxon 34 C7
East Charleton Devon 7 K10
East Chelborough Dorset 11 M3
East Chiltington E Susx 25 J7
East Chinnock Somset 11 K2
East Chisenbury Wilts 21 M4
East Cholderton Hants 21 Q5
Eastchurch Kent 38 G7
East Clandon Surrey 36 C10
East Claydon Bucks 49 K9
East Clevedon N Som 31 M10
East Coker Somset 11 L2
Eastcombe Gloucs 32 G4
Eastcombe Somset 18 G8
East Compton Somset 20 B6
East Cornworthy Devon 7 L7
East Cote Cumb 109 P9
Eastcote Gt Lon 36 D3
Eastcote Nhants 49 J4
Eastcote Solhll 59 J9
Eastcott Cnwll 16 D8
Eastcott Wilts 21 K3
East Cottingwith E R Yk 92 B2
Eastcourt Wilts 21 P2
Eastcourt Wilts 33 J6
East Cowes IoW 14 F7
East Cowick E R Yk 91 R6
East Cowton N York 104 B10
East Cramlington Nthumb 113 L5
East Cranmore Somset 20 C6
East Creech Dorset 12 F8
East Curthwaite Cumb 110 F11
East Dean E Susx 25 N11
East Dean Gloucs 46 C10
East Dean Hants 21 Q9
East Dean W Susx 15 P4
Eastdown Devon 7 L9
East Down Devon 17 L3
East Drayton Notts 85 N5
East Dulwich Gt Lon 36 H5
East Dundry N Som 31 Q11
East Ella C KuH 93 J5
East End Bed 61 P9
East End C Beds 49 Q6
East End E R Yk 93 L4
East End E R Yk 93 N5
Eastend Essex 38 F3
East End Essex 51 K8
East End Hants 14 C7
East End Hants 22 D2
East End Herts 51 L5
East End Kent 26 D4
East End Kent 38 G7
East End M Keyn 49 P6
East End Oxon 48 C11
East End Somset 20 C5
East End Suffk 53 K4
Easter Balmoral Abers 149 P9
Easter Compton S Glos 31 Q8
Easter Dalziel Highld 156 D7
Eastergate W Susx 15 P5
Easterhouse C Glas 126 B4
Easter Howgate Mdloth 127 N5
Easter Kinkell Highld 155 Q6
Easter Moniack Highld 155 Q9
Eastern Green Covtry 59 L9
Easter Ord Abers 151 L7
Easter Pitkierie Fife 135 P6
Easter Skeld Shet 169 q9
Easter Softlaw Border 118 E4
Easterton Wilts 21 K4
Eastertown Somset 19 K4
East Everleigh Wilts 21 P4
East Farleigh Kent 38 B11
East Farndon Nhants 60 F4
East Ferry Lincs 92 D11
Eastfield N Lans 126 F5
Eastfield N York 99 L4
East Firsby Lincs 86 D3
East Fortune E Loth 128 E4
East Garforth Leeds 91 L4
East Garston W Berk 34 C9
Eastgate Dur 103 J3
Eastgate Lincs 74 B7
Eastgate Norfk 76 G7
East Ginge Oxon 34 D7
East Goscote Leics 72 G8
East Grafton Wilts 21 Q2
East Green Suffk 65 N8
East Grimstead Wilts 21 P9
East Grinstead W Susx 25 J3
East Guldeford E Susx 26 F7
East Haddon Nhants 60 E7
East Hagbourne Oxon 34 F7
East Halton N Linc 93 K7
East Ham Gt Lon 37 K4
Eastham Wirral 81 M8
Eastham Ferry Wirral 81 M8
Easthampton Herefs 45 N2
East Hanney Oxon 34 D6
East Hanningfield Essex 52 C11
East Hardwick Wakefd 91 M7
East Harling Norfk 64 D4
East Harlsey N York 104 D11
East Harnham Wilts 21 M9
East Harptree BaNES 19 Q3
East Hartford Nthumb 113 L5
East Harting W Susx 23 L11
East Hatch Wilts 20 H9
East Hatley Cambs 62 C10
East Hauxwell N York 97 J2
East Haven Angus 143 K10
Eastheath Wokham 35 L11
East Heckington Lincs 74 C2
East Hedleyhope Dur 103 N2
East Helmsdale Highld 163 N3
East Hendred Oxon 34 E7
East Heslerton N York 99 J5
East Hewish N Som 19 L2
East Hoathly E Susx 25 M7
East Holme Dorset 12 E7
East Hope Dur 103 K9
Easthope Shrops 57 K5
Easthorpe Essex 52 F7
Easthorpe Notts 85 M10
East Horrington Somset 19 Q5
East Horsley Surrey 36 C10
East Horton Nthumb 119 K4
East Howe BCP 13 J5
East Huntspill Somset 19 K5
East Hyde C Beds 50 D7
East Ilkerton Devon 17 N2
East Ilsley W Berk 34 E8
Eastington Devon 8 H3
Eastington Gloucs 32 E3
Eastington Gloucs 33 M2
East Keal Lincs 87 L8
East Kennett Wilts 33 M11
East Keswick Leeds 91 K2
East Kilbride S Lans 125 Q7
East Kimber Devon 8 C5
East Kirkby Lincs 87 K8
East Knighton Dorset 12 D7
East Knowstone Devon 17 Q7
East Knoyle Wilts 20 G8
East Lambrook Somset 19 M11
Eastlands D & G 108 H6
East Langdon Kent 27 P2
East Langton Leics 60 F2
East Lavant W Susx 15 N5
East Lavington W Susx 23 P11
East Layton N York 103 N9
Eastleach Martin Gloucs 33 P4
Eastleach Turville Gloucs 33 N3
East Leake Notts 72 F5
East Learmouth Nthumb 118 G3
East Leigh Devon 6 H8
East Leigh Devon 7 K7
East Leigh Devon 8 G3
Eastleigh Devon 16 H6
Eastleigh Hants 22 E11
East Lexham Norfk 76 B8
Eastling Kent 38 G10
East Linton E Loth 128 F4
East Liss Hants 23 L9
East Lockinge Oxon 34 D7
East Lound N Linc 92 C11
East Lulworth Dorset 12 E8
East Lutton N York 99 J7
East Lydeard Somset 18 G9
East Lydford Somset 19 Q8
East Malling Kent 38 B10
East Malling Heath Kent 37 Q9
East Marden W Susx 15 M4
East Markham Notts 85 M6
East Martin Hants 21 L11
East Marton N York 96 D10
East Meon Hants 23 J10
East Mere Devon 18 C11
East Mersea Essex 52 H9
East Midlands Airport Leics 72 D5
East Molesey Surrey 36 D7
Eastmoor Norfk 75 P10
East Morden Dorset 12 F6
East Morton C Brad 90 D2
East Morton D & G 116 B10
East Ness N York 98 D5
East Newton E R Yk 93 N3
Eastney C Port 15 J7
Eastnor Herefs 46 D7
East Norton Leics 73 K10
Eastoft N Linc 92 D7
East Ogwell Devon 7 L4
Easton Cambs 61 P6
Easton Cumb 110 E9
Easton Devon 8 H7
Easton Dorset 11 P10
Easton Hants 22 F8
Easton Lincs 73 N5
Easton Norfk 76 G9
Easton Somset 19 P5
Easton Suffk 65 K10
Easton W Berk 34 D10
Easton Wilts 32 G10
Easton Grey Wilts 32 G7
Easton-in-Gordano N Som 31 P9
Easton Maudit Nhants 61 J9
Easton-on-the-Hill Nhants 73 Q10
Easton Royal Wilts 21 P2
East Orchard Dorset 20 F11
East Ord Nthumb 129 P9
East Panson Devon 5 P3
East Parley BCP 13 J5
East Peckham Kent 37 Q11
East Pennard Somset 19 Q7
East Portlemouth Devon 7 K11
East Prawle Devon 7 K11
East Preston W Susx 24 C10
East Pulham Dorset 11 Q3
East Putford Devon 16 F8
East Quantoxhead Somset 18 F6
East Rainham Medway 38 D8
East Rainton Sundld 113 M11
East Ravendale NE Lin 93 M11
East Raynham Norfk 76 B6
Eastrea Cambs 74 E11
Eastriggs D & G 110 D7
East Rigton Leeds 91 K2
Eastrington E R Yk 92 C5
East Rolstone N Som 19 L2
Eastrop Swindn 33 P6
East Rounton N York 104 D10
East Rudham Norfk 76 A6
East Runton Norfk 76 H3
East Ruston Norfk 77 L6
Eastry Kent 39 P11
East Saltoun E Loth 128 D6
Eastshaw W Susx 23 N10
East Sheen Gt Lon 36 F6
East Shefford W Berk 34 C10
East Sleekburn Nthumb 113 L4
East Somerton Norfk 77 P8
East Stockwith Lincs 85 N2
East Stoke Dorset 12 E7
East Stoke Notts 85 N11
East Stour Dorset 20 F10
East Stour Common Dorset 20 F10
East Stourmouth Kent 39 N9
East Stowford Devon 17 L6
East Stratton Hants 22 F6
East Studdal Kent 27 P2
East Sutton Kent 26 D2
East Taphouse Cnwll 5 K9
East-the-Water Devon 16 H6
East Thirston Nthumb 119 N10
East Tilbury Thurr 37 Q5
East Tilbury Village Thurr 37 Q5
East Tisted Hants 23 K8
East Torrington Lincs 86 F4
East Tuddenham Norfk 76 F9
East Tytherley Hants 21 Q9
East Tytherton Wilts 33 J10
East Village Devon 9 K3
Eastville Bristl 32 B10
Eastville Lincs 87 M9
East Wall Shrops 57 J6
East Walton Norfk 75 P7
East Water Somset 19 P4
East Week Devon 8 G6
Eastwell Leics 73 K5
East Wellow Hants 22 B10
East Wemyss Fife 135 J8
East Whitburn W Loth 126 H4
Eastwick Herts 51 K8
East Wickham Gt Lon 37 L5
East Williamston Pembks 41 L10
East Winch Norfk 75 N7
East Winterslow Wilts 21 P8
East Wittering W Susx 15 L7
East Witton N York 96 H3
Eastwood Notts 84 G11
Eastwood Sthend 38 D4
East Woodburn Nthumb 112 D3
Eastwood End Cambs 62 F2
East Woodhay Hants 22 D2
East Woodlands Somset 20 E6
East Worldham Hants 23 L7
East Worthing W Susx 24 E10
East Wretham Norfk 64 C3
East Youlstone Devon 16 D8
Eathorpe Warwks 59 N11
Eaton Ches E 83 J11
Eaton Ches W 69 Q2
Eaton Leics 73 K5
Eaton Norfk 77 J10
Eaton Notts 85 M5
Eaton Oxon 34 D4
Eaton Shrops 56 F7
Eaton Shrops 57 J7
Eaton Bishop Herefs 45 N7
Eaton Bray C Beds 49 Q10
Eaton Constantine Shrops 57 K3
Eaton Ford Cambs 61 Q9
Eaton Green C Beds 49 Q10
Eaton Hastings Oxon 33 Q5
Eaton Mascott Shrops 57 J3
Eaton Socon Cambs 61 Q9
Eaton upon Tern Shrops 70 B10
Eaves Brow Warrtn 82 D6
Eaves Green Solhll 59 L8
Ebberston N York 98 H4
Ebbesborne Wake Wilts 21 J10
Ebbsfleet Kent 37 P6
Ebbw Vale Blae G 30 G3
Ebchester Dur 112 H9

Ebdon – Farleys End 269

Ebdon N Som 19 L2
Ebernoe W Susx 23 Q9
Ebford Devon 9 N7
Ebley Gloucs 32 F3
Ebnal Ches W 69 N5
Ebnall Herefs 45 P3
Ebrington Gloucs 47 N6
Ebsworthy Devon 8 D6
Ecchinswell Hants 22 E3
Ecclaw Border 129 K6
Ecclefechan D & G 110 C6
Eccles Border 118 E2
Eccles Kent 38 B9
Eccles Salfd 82 G5
Ecclesall Sheff 84 D4
Ecclesfield Sheff 84 E2
Eccles Green Herefs 45 M5
Eccleshall Staffs 70 E9
Eccleshill C Brad 90 F3
Ecclesmachan W Loth 127 K3
Eccles on Sea Norfk 77 N6
Eccles Road Norfk 64 E4
Eccleston Ches W 69 M2
Eccleston Lancs 88 G7
Eccleston St Hel 81 P5
Eccleston Green Lancs 88 G7
Echt Abers 151 J6
Eckford Border 118 D5
Eckington Derbys 84 F5
Eckington Worcs 46 H6
Ecton Nhants 60 H8
Ecton Staffs 71 K3
Edale Derbys 83 P7
Eday Ork 169 e3
Eday Airport Ork 169 e3
Edburton W Susx 24 F8
Edderside Cumb 109 P11
Edderton Highld 162 G10
Eddington Cambs 62 F9
Eddington Kent 39 L8
Eddleston Border 127 N8
Eddlewood S Lans 126 C7
Edenbridge Kent 37 K11
Edenfield Lancs 89 N7
Edenhall Cumb 101 Q4
Edenham Lincs 73 R6
Eden Mount Cumb 95 J5
Eden Park Gt Lon 37 J7
Eden Project Cnwll 3 Q3
Edensor Derbys 84 B7
Edentaggart Ag & B 132 C9
Edenthorpe Donc 91 Q9
Edern Gwynd 66 D7
Edgarley Somset 19 P7
Edgbaston Birm 58 G8
Edgcott Bucks 49 J10
Edgcott Somset 17 Q4
Edgcumbe Cnwll 3 J7
Edge Gloucs 32 F3
Edge Shrops 56 F3
Edgebolton Shrops 69 Q10
Edge End Gloucs 31 Q2
Edgefield Norfk 76 F5
Edgefield Green Norfk 76 F5
Edgefold Bolton 89 L9
Edge Green Ches W 69 N4
Edgehill Warwks 48 C5
Edgerley Shrops 69 L11
Edgerton Kirk 90 E7
Edgeside Lancs 89 N6
Edgeworth Gloucs 32 H3
Edgeworthy Devon 9 K2
Edginswell Torbay 7 M5
Edgiock Worcs 47 K2
Edgmond Wrekin 70 C11
Edgmond Marsh Wrekin 70 C10
Edgton Shrops 56 F7
Edgware Gt Lon 36 E2
Edgworth Bl w D 89 L7
Edinbane Highld 152 E7
Edinburgh C Edin 127 P3
Edinburgh Airport C Edin 127 L3
Edinburgh Castle C Edin 127 P3
Edinburgh Old & New Town C Edin 127 P3
Edinburgh Zoo RZSS C Edin 127 N3
Edingale Staffs 59 K2
Edingham D & G 108 H8
Edingley Notts 85 L9
Edingthorpe Norfk 77 L5
Edingthorpe Green Norfk 77 L5
Edington Border 129 M9
Edington Nthumb 113 J4
Edington Somset 19 L7
Edington Wilts 20 H4
Edingworth Somset 19 L4
Edistone Devon 16 D7
Edithmead Somset 19 K5
Edith Weston Rutlnd 73 N9
Edlesborough Bucks 49 Q11
Edlingham Nthumb 119 M9
Edlington Lincs 86 H6
Edmond Castle Cumb 111 J9
Edmondsham Dorset 13 J2
Edmondsley Dur 113 K11
Edmondstown Rhondd 30 D6
Edmondthorpe Leics 73 M7
Edmonton Cnwll 4 F7
Edmonton Gt Lon 36 H2
Edmundbyers Dur 112 F10
Ednam Border 118 D3
Ednaston Derbys 71 N6
Edney Common Essex 51 Q10
Edradynate P & K 141 L7
Edrom Border 129 L8
Edstaston Shrops 69 P8
Edstone Warwks 47 N2
Edvin Loach Herefs 46 C3
Edwalton Notts 72 F3
Edwardstone Suffk 52 F3
Edwardsville Myr Td 30 E5
Edwinsford Carmth 43 M8
Edwinstowe Notts 85 K7
Edworth C Beds 50 F2
Edwyn Ralph Herefs 46 B3
Edzell Angus 143 L4
Edzell Woods Abers 143 L4
Efail-fach Neath 29 L5
Efail Isaf Rhondd 30 E8
Efailnewydd Gwynd 66 F7
Efail-Rhyd Powys 68 G9
Efailwen Carmth 41 M5
Efenechtyd Denbgs 68 F3
Effgill D & G 110 F2
Effingham Surrey 36 D10
Effingham Junction Surrey 36 D9
Efflinch Staffs 71 M11
Efford Devon 9 L4
Egbury Hants 22 D4
Egdean W Susx 23 Q10
Egerton Bolton 89 L8
Egerton Kent 26 F2
Egerton Forstal Kent 26 E2
Eggborough N York 91 P6
Eggbuckland C Plym 6 E7
Eggesford Devon 17 M9
Eggington C Beds 49 Q9
Egginton Derbys 71 P9
Egglescliffe S on T 104 D8
Eggleston Dur 103 J6
Egham Surrey 36 B6
Egham Wick Surrey 35 Q10
Egleton Rutlnd 73 M9
Eglingham Nthumb 119 M7
Egloshayle Cnwll 4 G7
Egloskerry Cnwll 5 M4
Eglwysbach Conwy 79 Q10
Eglwys-Brewis V Glam 30 D11
Eglwys Cross Wrexhm 69 N6
Eglwys Fach Cerdgn 54 F5
Eglwyswrw Pembks 41 M3
Egmanton Notts 85 M7
Egremont Cumb 100 D8
Egremont Wirral 81 L6
Egton N York 105 M9
Egton Bridge N York 105 M10
Egypt Bucks 35 Q7
Egypt Hants 22 E6
Eigg Highld 144 G10
Eight Ash Green Essex 52 F6
Eilanreach Highld 145 P4
Eilean Donan Castle Highld 145 Q2
Eisgein W Isls 168 i6
Eishken W Isls 168 i6
Eisteddfa Gurig Cerdgn 54 H8
Elan Valley Powys 55 K11
Elan Village Powys 44 C2
Elberton S Glos 32 B7
Elbridge W Susx 15 P6
Elburton C Plym 6 E8
Elcombe Swindn 33 M8
Elcot W Berk 34 C11
Eldernell Cambs 74 F11
Eldersfield Worcs 46 E8
Elderslie Rens 125 L5
Elder Street Essex 51 N4
Eldon Dur 103 P5
Eldwick C Brad 90 E2
Elerch Cerdgn 54 F7
Elfhill Abers 151 L10
Elford Nthumb 119 N4
Elford Staffs 59 J2
Elgin Moray 157 N5
Elgol Highld 144 H5
Elham Kent 27 L3
Elie Fife 135 M7
Elilaw Nthumb 119 J9
Elim IoA 78 F8
Eling Hants 14 C4
Elkesley Notts 85 L5
Elkstone Gloucs 33 J2
Ella Abers 158 F6
Ellacombe Torbay 7 N6
Elland Calder 90 E6
Elland Lower Edge Calder 90 E6
Ellary Ag & B 123 M4
Ellastone Staffs 71 L6
Ellel Lancs 95 K9
Ellemford Border 129 J7
Ellenabeich Ag & B 130 E4
Ellenborough Cumb 100 D3
Ellenbrook Salfd 82 F4
Ellenhall Staffs 70 E9
Ellen's Green Surrey 24 C3
Ellerbeck N York 104 D11
Ellerby N York 105 L8
Ellerdine Heath Wrekin 69 R10
Ellerhayes Devon 9 N4
Elleric Ag & B 139 J8
Ellerker E R Yk 92 F5
Ellers N York 90 C2
Ellerton E R Yk 92 B3
Ellerton N York 103 Q11
Ellerton Shrops 70 C9
Ellesborough Bucks 35 M3
Ellesmere Shrops 69 L8
Ellesmere Port Ches W 81 N9
Ellicombe Somset 18 C6
Ellingham Hants 13 K3
Ellingham Norfk 65 M3
Ellingham Nthumb 119 N5
Ellingstring N York 97 J4
Ellington Cambs 61 Q6
Ellington Nthumb 113 L2
Ellington Thorpe Cambs 61 Q6
Elliots Green Somset 20 E5
Ellisfield Hants 22 H5
Ellishader Highld 153 J4
Ellistown Leics 72 C8
Ellon Abers 159 N11
Ellonby Cumb 101 M3
Ellough Suffk 65 N4
Elloughton E R Yk 92 F5
Ellwood Gloucs 31 Q3
Elm Cambs 75 J9
Elmbridge Worcs 58 D11
Elmdon Essex 51 L3
Elmdon Solhll 59 J8
Elmdon Heath Solhll 59 J8
Elmer W Susx 15 Q6
Elmers End Gt Lon 37 J7
Elmer's Green Lancs 88 G9
Elmesthorpe Leics 72 D11
Elm Green Essex 52 C10
Elmhurst Staffs 58 H2
Elmington Nhants 61 N3
Elmley Castle Worcs 47 J6
Elmley Lovett Worcs 58 C11
Elmore Gloucs 46 E11
Elmore Back Gloucs 46 E11
Elm Park Gt Lon 37 M3
Elmscott Devon 16 C7
Elmsett Suffk 53 J2
Elms Green Worcs 57 N11
Elmstead Heath Essex 53 J7
Elmstead Market Essex 53 J7
Elmstead Row Essex 53 J7
Elmsted Kent 27 K3
Elmstone Kent 39 N9
Elmstone Hardwicke Gloucs 46 H9
Elmswell E R Yk 99 K9
Elmswell Suffk 64 D9
Elmton Derbys 84 H6
Elphin Highld 161 L4
Elphinstone E Loth 128 B6
Elrick Abers 151 L6
Elrig D & G 107 K8
Elrington Nthumb 112 C8
Elsdon Nthumb 112 D2
Elsecar Barns 91 K11
Elsenham Essex 51 M5
Elsfield Oxon 34 F2
Elsham N Linc 92 H8
Elsing Norfk 76 F8
Elslack N York 96 D11
Elson Hants 14 H6
Elson Shrops 69 L7
Elsrickle S Lans 116 F2
Elstead Surrey 23 P6
Elsted W Susx 23 M11
Elsted Marsh W Susx 23 M10
Elsthorpe Lincs 73 R6
Elstob Dur 104 B6
Elston Lancs 88 H4
Elston Notts 85 N11
Elston Wilts 21 L6
Elstone Devon 17 M8
Elstow Bed 61 N11
Elstree Herts 50 E11
Elstronwick E R Yk 93 M4
Elswick Lancs 88 E3
Elswick N u Ty 113 K8
Elsworth Cambs 62 D8
Elterwater Cumb 101 K10
Eltham Gt Lon 37 K6
Eltisley Cambs 62 C9
Elton Bury 89 M8
Elton Cambs 61 N2
Elton Ches W 81 P9
Elton Derbys 84 B8
Elton Gloucs 32 D2
Elton Herefs 56 H10
Elton S on T 104 D7
Elton Green Ches W 81 P10
Elton-on-the-Hill Notts 73 K3
Eltringham Nthumb 112 G8
Elvanfoot S Lans 116 D7
Elvaston Derbys 72 C4
Elveden Suffk 63 P4
Elvetham Heath Hants 23 M3
Elvingston E Loth 128 D5
Elvington C York 98 E11
Elvington Kent 39 N11
Elwell Devon 17 M5
Elwick Hartpl 104 E4
Elwick Nthumb 119 M3
Elworth Ches E 70 C2
Elworthy Somset 18 E8
Ely Cambs 62 H4
Ely Cardif 30 F9
Emberton M Keyn 49 N5
Embleton Cumb 100 G4
Embleton Dur 104 D5
Embleton Nthumb 119 P6
Embo Highld 163 J8
Emborough Somset 20 B4
Embo Street Highld 163 J8
Embsay N York 96 F10
Emery Down Hants 13 N3
Emley Kirk 90 G8
Emley Moor Kirk 90 G8
Emmbrook Wokham 35 M11
Emmer Green Readg 35 K9
Emmett Carr Derbys 84 G5
Emmington Oxon 35 K4
Emneth Norfk 75 J9
Emneth Hungate Norfk 75 K9
Empingham Rutlnd 73 N9
Empshott Hants 23 L8
Empshott Green Hants 23 K8
Emsworth Hants 15 K5
Enborne W Berk 34 D11
Enborne Row W Berk 22 D2
Enchmarsh Shrops 57 J5
Enderby Leics 72 E11
Endmoor Cumb 95 L4
Endon Staffs 70 G4
Endon Bank Staffs 70 G4
Enfield Gt Lon 51 J11
Enfield Lock Gt Lon 51 J11
Enfield Wash Gt Lon 51 J11
Enford Wilts 21 M4
Engine Common S Glos 32 C8
England's Gate Herefs 45 Q4
Englefield W Berk 34 H10
Englefield Green Surrey 35 Q10
Engleseabrook Ches E 70 D4
English Bicknor Gloucs 46 A11
Englishcombe BaNES 20 D2
English Frankton Shrops 69 N9
Engollan Cnwll 4 D7
Enham Alamein Hants 22 C5
Enmore Somset 18 H7
Enmore Green Dorset 20 G10
Ennerdale Bridge Cumb 100 E7
Enniscaven Cnwll 4 F10
Enochdhu P & K 141 Q5
Ensay Ag & B 137 K6
Ensbury BCP 13 J5
Ensdon Shrops 69 M11
Ensis Devon 17 K6
Enson Staffs 70 G9
Enstone Oxon 48 C10
Enterkinfoot D & G 116 B10
Enterpen N York 104 E9
Enville Staffs 58 B7
Eochar W Isls 168 c13
Eòlaigearraidh W Isls 168 c17
Eoligarry W Isls 168 c17
Eòropaidh W Isls 168 k1
Eoropie W Isls 168 k1
Epney Gloucs 32 E2
Epperstone Notts 85 L11
Epping Essex 51 L10
Epping Green Essex 51 K9
Epping Green Herts 50 G9
Epping Upland Essex 51 K10
Eppleby N York 103 N8
Eppleworth E R Yk 92 H4
Epsom Surrey 36 F8
Epwell Oxon 48 C6
Epworth N Linc 92 C10
Epworth Turbary N Linc 92 C10
Erbistock Wrexhm 69 L6
Erdington Birm 58 H6
Eridge Green E Susx 25 N3
Eridge Station E Susx 25 M4
Erines Ag & B 123 Q4
Eriska Ag & B 138 G9
Eriskay W Isls 168 c17
Eriswell Suffk 63 M5
Erith Gt Lon 37 M5
Erlestoke Wilts 21 J4
Ermington Devon 6 G8
Ernesettle C Plym 6 D6
Erpingham Norfk 76 H5
Erriottwood Kent 38 F10
Errogie Highld 147 P3
Errol P & K 134 G3
Erskine Rens 125 M3
Erskine Bridge Rens 125 M3
Ervie D & G 106 D4
Erwarton Suffk 53 M5
Erwood Powys 44 F6
Eryholme N York 104 B9
Eryrys Denbgs 68 H3
Escalls Cnwll 2 B8
Escomb Dur 103 N4
Escott Somset 18 E7
Escrick N York 91 Q2
Esgair Carmth 42 G9
Esgair Cerdgn 54 D11
Esgairgeiliog Powys 54 H3
Esgerdawe Carmth 43 M6
Esgyryn Conwy 79 Q9
Esh Dur 103 N2
Esher Surrey 36 D8
Esholt C Brad 90 F2
Eshott Nthumb 119 P11
Eshton N York 96 D9
Esh Winning Dur 103 N2
Eskadale Highld 155 N9
Eskbank Mdloth 127 Q4
Eskdale Green Cumb 100 F10
Eskdalemuir D & G 117 K11
Eske E R Yk 93 J2
Eskham Lincs 93 Q11
Eskholme Donc 91 Q7
Esperley Lane Ends Dur 103 M6
Esprick Lancs 88 E3
Essendine Rutlnd 73 Q8
Essendon Herts 50 G9
Essich Highld 156 A10
Essington Staffs 58 E4
Esslemont Abers 151 N2
Eston R & Cl 104 F7
Etal Nthumb 118 H3
Etchilhampton Wilts 21 K2
Etchingham E Susx 26 B6
Etchinghill Kent 27 L4
Etchinghill Staffs 71 J11
Etchingwood E Susx 25 M6
Etling Green Norfk 76 E9
Etloe Gloucs 32 C3
Eton W & M 35 Q9
Eton Wick W & M 35 P9
Etruria C Stke 70 F5
Etteridge Highld 148 B9
Ettersgill Dur 102 G5
Ettiley Heath Ches E 70 C2
Ettingshall Wolves 58 D5
Ettington Warwks 47 Q5
Etton C Pete 74 B9
Etton E R Yk 92 G2
Ettrick Border 117 K8
Ettrickbridge Border 117 M6
Ettrickhill Border 117 K8
Etwall Derbys 71 P8
Eudon George Shrops 57 M7
Euston Suffk 64 B6
Euximoor Drove Cambs 75 J11
Euxton Lancs 88 H7
Evancoyd Powys 45 K2
Evanton Highld 155 R4
Evedon Lincs 86 E11
Evelith Shrops 57 N3
Evelix Highld 162 H8
Evenjobb Powys 45 K2
Evenley Nhants 48 G8
Evenlode Gloucs 47 P9
Evenwood Dur 103 N6
Evenwood Gate Dur 103 N6
Evercreech Somset 20 B7
Everingham E R Yk 92 D2
Everleigh Wilts 21 P4
Everley N York 99 K3
Eversholt C Beds 49 Q8
Evershot Dorset 11 M4
Eversley Hants 23 L2
Eversley Cross Hants 23 L2
Everthorpe E R Yk 92 F4
Everton C Beds 62 B10
Everton Hants 13 N6
Everton Lpool 81 L6
Everton Notts 85 L2
Evertown D & G 110 G5
Evesbatch Herefs 46 C5
Evesham Worcs 47 K6
Evington C Leic 72 G10
Ewden Village Sheff 90 H11
Ewell Surrey 36 F8
Ewell Minnis Kent 27 N3
Ewelme Oxon 34 H6
Ewen Gloucs 33 K5
Ewenny V Glam 29 P9
Ewerby Lincs 86 F11
Ewerby Thorpe Lincs 86 F11
Ewhurst Surrey 24 C2
Ewhurst Green E Susx 26 C7
Ewhurst Green Surrey 24 C3
Ewloe Flints 81 L11
Ewloe Green Flints 81 K11
Ewood Bl w D 89 K5
Ewood Bridge Lancs 89 M6
Eworthy Devon 8 B5
Ewshot Hants 23 M5
Ewyas Harold Herefs 45 M9
Exbourne Devon 8 F4
Exbury Hants 14 D6
Exceat E Susx 25 M11
Exebridge Somset 18 B10
Exelby N York 97 L3
Exeter Devon 9 M6
Exeter Airport Devon 9 N6
Exeter Services Devon 9 N6
Exford Somset 17 R4
Exfordsgreen Shrops 56 H3
Exhall Warwks 47 M3
Exhall Warwks 59 N7
Exlade Street Oxon 35 J8
Exley Head C Brad 90 C2
Exminster Devon 9 M7
Exmoor National Park 17 R4
Exmouth Devon 9 P8
Exning Suffk 63 K7
Exted Kent 27 L3
Exton Devon 9 N7
Exton Hants 22 H10
Exton Rutlnd 73 N8
Exton Somset 18 B8
Exwick Devon 9 M6
Eyam Derbys 84 B5
Eydon Nhants 48 F5
Eye C Pete 74 D10
Eye Herefs 45 P2
Eye Suffk 64 G7
Eye Green C Pete 74 D10
Eyemouth Border 129 N7
Eyeworth C Beds 62 C11
Eyhorne Street Kent 38 D11
Eyke Suffk 65 L11
Eynesbury Cambs 61 Q9
Eynsford Kent 37 M7
Eynsham Oxon 34 D3
Eype Dorset 11 J6
Eyre Highld 152 G7
Eythorne Kent 27 N2
Eyton Herefs 45 P2
Eyton Shrops 56 F2
Eyton Shrops 56 F7
Eyton Shrops 69 M10
Eyton Wrexhm 69 L6
Eyton on Severn Shrops 57 K3
Eyton upon the Weald Moors Wrekin 57 M2

F

Faccombe Hants 22 C3
Faceby N York 104 E10
Fachwen Powys 68 D11
Facit Lancs 89 P7
Fackley Notts 84 G8
Faddiley Ches E 69 Q4
Fadmoor N York 98 D3
Faerdre Swans 29 J4
Faifley W Duns 125 M3
Failand N Som 31 P10
Failford S Ayrs 115 J2
Failsworth Oldham 83 J4
Fairbourne Gwynd 54 E2
Fairburn N York 91 M5
Fairfield Derbys 83 N10
Fairfield Kent 26 G6
Fairfield Worcs 58 D9
Fairfield Park Herts 50 F4
Fairford Gloucs 33 N4
Fairford Park Gloucs 33 N4
Fairgirth D & G 109 J9
Fair Green Norfk 75 N7
Fairhaven Lancs 88 C5
Fair Isle Shet 169 t14
Fair Isle Airport Shet 169 t14
Fairlands Surrey 23 Q4
Fairlie N Ayrs 124 G7
Fairlight E Susx 26 E9
Fairlight Cove E Susx 26 E9
Fairmile Devon 10 B5
Fairmile Surrey 36 D8
Fairmilehead C Edin 127 N4
Fairnilee Border 117 P4
Fair Oak Hants 22 E11
Fairoak Staffs 70 D8
Fair Oak Green Hants 23 J2
Fairseat Kent 37 P8
Fairstead Essex 52 C8
Fairstead Norfk 75 M6
Fairstead Norfk 77 K7
Fairwarp E Susx 25 L5
Fairwater Cardif 30 F9
Fairy Cross Devon 16 G7
Fakenham Norfk 76 C6
Fakenham Magna Suffk 64 C6
Fala Mdloth 128 C7
Fala Dam Mdloth 128 C7
Falcut Nhants 48 G6
Faldingworth Lincs 86 E4
Faldouët Jersey 11 c2
Falfield S Glos 32 C6
Falkenham Suffk 53 N4
Falkirk Falk 133 P11
Falkirk Wheel Falk 133 P11
Falkland Fife 134 H6
Fallburn S Lans 116 D3
Fallgate Derbys 84 E8
Fallin Stirlg 133 N9
Fallodon Nthumb 119 N6
Fallowfield Manch 83 J6
Fallowfield Nthumb 112 D7
Falmer E Susx 25 J9
Falmouth Cnwll 3 L7
Falnash Border 117 M9
Falsgrave N York 99 L3
Falstone Nthumb 111 P3
Fanagmore Highld 164 E7
Fancott C Beds 50 B5
Fanellan Highld 155 N9
Fangdale Beck N York 98 B2
Fangfoss E R Yk 98 F10
Fanmore Ag & B 137 L7
Fannich Lodge Highld 154 H4
Fans Border 118 B2
Far Bletchley M Keyn 49 N8
Farcet Cambs 62 B2
Far Cotton Nhants 60 G9
Farden Shrops 57 K9
Fareham Hants 14 G5
Farewell Staffs 58 G2
Far Forest Worcs 57 N9
Farforth Lincs 87 K5
Far Green Gloucs 32 E4
Faringdon Oxon 33 Q5
Farington Lancs 88 G5
Farlam Cumb 111 L9
Farleigh N Som 31 P11
Farleigh Surrey 37 J8
Farleigh Hungerford Somset 20 F3
Farleigh Wallop Hants 22 H5
Farlesthorpe Lincs 87 N6
Farleton Cumb 95 L4
Farleton Lancs 95 M7
Farley Derbys 84 C8
Farley Staffs 71 K6
Farley Wilts 21 P9
Farley Green Suffk 63 M10
Farley Green Surrey 36 C11
Farley Hill Wokham 23 K2
Farleys End Gloucs 32 E2

Farlington C Port....15 J5
Farlington N York....98 C7
Farlow Shrops....57 L8
Farmborough BaNES....20 C2
Farmbridge End Essex....51 P8
Farmcote Gloucs....47 L9
Farmcote Shrops....57 P6
Farmington Gloucs....47 M11
Farmoor Oxon....34 E3
Far Moor Wigan....82 B4
Farms Common Cnwll....2 H7
Farm Town Leics....72 B7
Farmtown Moray....158 D7
Farnah Green Derbys....84 D11
Farnborough Gt Lon....37 K8
Farnborough Hants....23 N4
Farnborough W Berk....34 D8
Farnborough Warwks....48 D5
Farnborough Park Hants....23 N3
Farncombe Surrey....23 Q6
Farndish Bed....61 K8
Farndon Ches W....69 M4
Farndon Notts....85 N10
Farne Islands Nthumb....119 P3
Farnell Angus....143 L6
Farnham Dorset....21 J11
Farnham Essex....51 L6
Farnham N York....97 M8
Farnham Suffk....65 M9
Farnham Surrey....23 M5
Farnham Common Bucks....35 Q7
Farnham Green Essex....51 L5
Farnham Royal Bucks....35 Q8
Farningham Kent....37 M7
Farnley Leeds....90 H4
Farnley N York....97 K11
Farnley Tyas Kirk....90 F8
Farnsfield Notts....85 K9
Farnworth Bolton....89 L9
Farnworth Halton....81 Q7
Far Oakridge Gloucs....32 H4
Farr Highld....148 E7
Farr Highld....156 B11
Farr Highld....166 B4
Farraline Highld....147 P3
Farringdon Devon....9 P6
Farrington Gurney BaNES....20 B3
Far Sawrey Cumb....101 L11
Farsley Leeds....90 G3
Farther Howegreen Essex....52 D11
Farthing Green Kent....26 D2
Farthinghoe Nhants....48 F7
Farthingloe Kent....27 N3
Farthingstone Nhants....48 H4
Farthing Street Gt Lon....37 K8
Fartown Kirk....90 F7
Farway Devon....10 D5
Fasnacloich Ag & B....139 J8
Fasnakyle Highld....147 J2
Fassfern Highld....139 J2
Fatfield Sundld....113 M10
Faugh Cumb....111 K10
Fauld Staffs....71 M9
Fauldhouse W Loth....126 G5
Faulkbourne Essex....52 C8
Faulkland Somset....20 D4
Fauls Shrops....69 Q8
Faversham Kent....38 H9
Fawdington N York....97 P6
Fawdon N u Ty....113 K7
Fawdon Nthumb....119 K7
Fawfieldhead Staffs....71 K2
Fawkham Green Kent....37 N7
Fawler Oxon....48 C11
Fawley Bucks....35 L7
Fawley Hants....14 E6
Fawley W Berk....34 C8
Fawley Chapel Herefs....46 A9
Fawnog Flints....81 J11
Fawsley Nhants....60 C9
Faxfleet E R Yk....92 E6
Faygate W Susx....24 F4
Fazakerley Lpool....81 M5
Fazeley Staffs....59 K4
Fearby N York....97 J4
Fearn Highld....156 F3
Fearnbeg Highld....153 N6
Fearnhead Warrtn....82 D6
Fearnmore Highld....153 N5
Fearnoch Ag & B....124 A2
Featherstone Staffs....58 D3
Featherstone Wakefd....91 L7
Feckenham Worcs....47 K2
Feering Essex....52 E7
Feetham N York....103 J11
Feizor N York....96 A7
Felbridge Surrey....25 J3
Felbrigg Norfk....77 J4
Felcourt Surrey....25 J2
Felden Herts....50 B10
Felindre Carmth....42 G7
Felindre Carmth....43 L10
Felindre Carmth....43 P9
Felindre Cerdgn....43 L3
Felindre Powys....44 H10
Felindre Powys....56 B8
Felindre Swans....28 H4
Felindre Farchog Pembks....41 M3
Felinfach Cerdgn....43 K3
Felinfach Powys....44 F8
Felinfoel Carmth....28 F4
Felingwmisaf Carmth....43 K10
Felingwmuchaf Carmth....43 K10
Felin-newydd Powys....44 G7
Felixkirk N York....97 Q4
Felixstowe Suffk....53 P5
Felixstowe Ferry Suffk....53 P4
Felkington Nthumb....118 H2
Felkirk Wakefd....91 K8
Felling Gatesd....113 L8
Fell Lane C Brad....90 C2
Fell Side Cumb....101 K3
Felmersham Bed....61 L9
Felmingham Norfk....77 K6
Felpham W Susx....15 P7
Felsham Suffk....64 C10
Felsted Essex....51 Q6
Feltham Gt Lon....36 D6
Felthamhill Surrey....36 C6
Felthorpe Norfk....76 H8
Felton Herefs....46 A5
Felton N Som....31 P11
Felton Nthumb....119 N10
Felton Butler Shrops....69 L11
Feltwell Norfk....63 M2

Fenay Bridge Kirk....90 F7
Fence Lancs....89 N3
Fence Rothm....84 F3
Fence Houses Sundld....113 M11
Fencott Oxon....48 G11
Fendike Corner Lincs....87 N8
Fen Ditton Cambs....62 G8
Fen Drayton Cambs....62 D7
Fen End Lincs....74 D6
Fen End Solhll....59 K10
Fenham Nthumb....119 L2
Feniscliffe Bl w D....89 K5
Feniscowles Bl w D....89 J5
Feniton Devon....10 B5
Feniton Court Devon....10 C5
Fenn Green Shrops....57 P8
Fenn Street Medway....38 C6
Fenny Bentley Derbys....71 M5
Fenny Bridges Devon....10 C5
Fenny Compton Warwks....48 D4
Fenny Drayton Leics....72 B11
Fenny Stratford M Keyn....49 N8
Fenrother Nthumb....113 J2
Fenstanton Cambs....62 D7
Fenstead End Suffk....63 P10
Fen Street Norfk....64 D2
Fen Street Suffk....64 H9
Fenton C Stke....70 F6
Fenton Cambs....62 D5
Fenton Cumb....111 K9
Fenton Lincs....85 P5
Fenton Lincs....85 Q10
Fenton Notts....85 N4
Fenton Nthumb....119 J4
Fenton Barns E Loth....128 E3
Fenwick Donc....91 P7
Fenwick E Ayrs....125 M9
Fenwick Nthumb....112 G6
Fenwick Nthumb....119 L2
Feock Cnwll....3 L6
Feolin Ferry Ag & B....122 F6
Fergushill N Ayrs....125 J9
Feriniquarrie Highld....152 B7
Fermain Bay Guern....10 c2
Fern Angus....142 H5
Ferndale Rhondd....30 C5
Ferndown Dorset....13 J4
Ferness Highld....156 H8
Fernham Oxon....33 Q6
Fernhill Heath Worcs....46 G3
Fernhurst W Susx....23 N9
Fernie Fife....135 J4
Ferniegair S Lans....126 C7
Fernilea Highld....152 F11
Fernilee Derbys....83 M9
Fernwood Notts....85 P10
Ferrensby N York....97 N8
Ferriby Sluice N Linc....92 G6
Ferrindonald Highld....145 L6
Ferring W Susx....24 C10
Ferrybridge Wakefd....91 M6

Ferrybridge Services
  Wakefd....91 M6
Ferryden Angus....143 N6
Ferryhill Dur....103 Q4
Ferryhill Station Dur....103 Q4
Ferry Point Highld....162 G9
Ferryside Carmth....28 C2
Fersfield Norfk....64 F5
Fersit Highld....139 R2
Feshiebridge Highld....148 F7
Fetcham Surrey....36 D9
Fetlar Shet....169 t4
Fetterangus Abers....159 N7
Fettercairn Abers....143 M3
Fewcott Oxon....48 F9
Fewston N York....97 J10
Ffairfach Carmth....43 M10
Ffair Rhos Cerdgn....54 G11
Ffald-y-Brenin Carmth....43 M6
Ffarmers Carmth....43 N6
Ffawyddog Powys....45 J11
Ffestiniog Railway Gwynd....67 L7
Ffordd-las Denbgs....68 F2
Fforest Carmth....28 G4
Fforest Gôch Neath....29 K4
Ffostrasol Cerdgn....42 G5
Ffrith Flints....69 J3
Ffynnonddewi Cerdgn....42 G4
Ffynnongroyw Flints....80 G8
Ffynnon-oer Cerdgn....43 K4
Fickleshole Surrey....37 J8
Fiddington Gloucs....46 H8
Fiddington Somset....18 H6
Fiddleford Dorset....12 D2
Fiddlers Green Cnwll....4 C10
Fiddlers Hamlet Essex....51 L10
Field Staffs....71 J8
Field Broughton Cumb....94 H4
Field Dalling Norfk....76 D4
Fieldhead Cumb....101 N3
Field Head Leics....72 D9
Fifehead Magdalen Dorset....20 E10
Fifehead Neville Dorset....12 D2
Fifehead St Quintin Dorset....12 C2
Fife Keith Moray....158 B7
Fifield Oxon....47 P11
Fifield W & M....35 P9
Fifield Wilts....21 M4
Figheldean Wilts....21 N5
Filands Wilts....32 H7
Filby Norfk....77 P9
Filey N York....99 N4
Filgrave M Keyn....49 N5
Filkins Oxon....33 P4
Filleigh Devon....8 H2
Filleigh Devon....17 M6
Fillingham Lincs....86 B3
Fillongley Warwks....59 L7
Filmore Hill Hants....23 J9
Filton S Glos....32 B9
Fimber E R Yk....98 H8
Finavon Angus....142 H6
Finberry Kent....26 H4
Fincham Norfk....75 N9
Finchampstead Wokham....23 L2
Fincharn Ag & B....131 J2
Finchdean Hants....15 K4
Finchingfield Essex....51 Q4
Finchley Gt Lon....36 G2
Findern Derbys....71 Q8
Findhorn Moray....157 J5
Findhorn Bridge Highld....148 E2
Findochty Moray....158 C4
Findo Gask P & K....134 C2
Findon Abers....151 N8

Findon W Susx....24 D9
Findon Mains Highld....155 R5
Findon Valley W Susx....24 D9
Findrack House Abers....150 G7
Finedon Nhants....61 K6
Fingal Street Suffk....65 J8
Fingask P & K....134 F2
Fingest Bucks....35 L6
Finghall N York....97 J3
Fingland Cumb....110 E9
Fingland D & G....115 Q4
Finglesham Kent....39 P11
Fingringhoe Essex....52 H7
Finkle Green Essex....52 B3
Finkle Street Barns....91 J11
Finlake Devon....9 K9
Finlarig Stirlg....140 E11
Finmere Oxon....48 H8
Finnart P & K....140 D6
Finningham Suffk....64 F8
Finningley Donc....91 R11
Finsbay W Isls....168 f9
Finstall Worcs....58 E10
Finsthwaite Cumb....94 H3
Finstock Oxon....48 C11
Finstown Ork....169 c5
Fintry Abers....159 J7
Fintry Stirlg....133 J10
Finzean Abers....150 G9
Fionnphort Ag & B....137 J11
Fionnsbhagh W Isls....168 f9
Firbank Cumb....95 M2
Firbeck Rothm....85 J3
Firby N York....97 L3
Firby N York....98 E7
Firgrove Rochdl....89 Q8
Firle E Susx....25 L9
Firsby Lincs....87 N8
Firsdown Wilts....21 P8
Fir Tree Dur....103 M4
Fishbourne IoW....14 G8
Fishbourne W Susx....15 M6

Fishbourne Roman Palace
  W Susx....15 M6
Fishburn Dur....104 C4
Fishcross Clacks....133 P8
Fisher W Susx....15 N6
Fisherford Abers....158 G10
Fisherrow E Loth....127 Q3
Fisher's Pond Hants....22 E10
Fisher's Row Lancs....95 J11
Fisherstreet W Susx....23 P8
Fisherton Highld....156 C7
Fisherton S Ayrs....114 E4
Fisherton de la Mere Wilts....21 K7
Fisherwick Staffs....59 J3
Fishery W & M....35 N9
Fishguard Pembks....41 J3
Fishlake Donc....91 R8
Fishleigh Devon....8 D3
Fishmere End Lincs....74 E3
Fishnish Pier Ag & B....138 B9
Fishpond Bottom Dorset....10 H5
Fishponds Bristl....32 B9
Fishtoft Lincs....74 G2
Fishtoft Drove Lincs....87 K11
Fishwick Lancs....88 H5
Fiskavaig Highld....152 E11
Fiskerton Lincs....86 D6
Fiskerton Notts....85 M10
Fitling E R Yk....93 N4
Fittleton Wilts....21 M5
Fittleworth W Susx....24 B7
Fitton End Cambs....74 H8
Fitz Shrops....69 M11
Fitzhead Somset....18 F9
Fitzroy Somset....18 G9
Fitzwilliam Wakefd....91 L7
Five Ash Down E Susx....25 L6
Five Ashes E Susx....25 N5
Five Bells Somset....18 E6
Five Bridges Herefs....46 B5
Fivecrosses Ches W....82 B9
Fivehead Somset....19 L10
Fivelanes Cnwll....5 L5
Five Lanes Mons....31 M6
Five Oak Green Kent....37 P11
Five Oaks Jersey....11 c2
Five Oaks W Susx....24 C5
Five Roads Carmth....28 E3
Five Wents Kent....38 D11
Flack's Green Essex....52 C9
Flackwell Heath Bucks....35 N7
Fladbury Worcs....47 J5
Fladdabister Shet....169 r10
Flagg Derbys....83 P11
Flamborough E R Yk....99 Q6
Flamborough Head E R Yk....99 R6

Flamingo Land Resort
  N York....98 F5
Flamstead Herts....50 C8
Flamstead End Herts....50 H10
Flansham W Susx....15 Q6
Flanshaw Wakefd....91 J6
Flappit Spring C Brad....90 D3
Flasby N York....96 D9
Flash Staffs....83 M11
Flashader Highld....152 E7
Flaunden Herts....50 B10
Flawborough Notts....73 K2
Flawith N York....97 Q7
Flax Bourton N Som....31 P11
Flaxby N York....97 N9
Flaxley Gloucs....46 C11
Flaxmere Ches W....82 C10
Flaxpool Somset....18 F7
Flaxton N York....98 D8
Fleckney Leics....60 D2
Flecknoe Warwks....60 B8
Fledborough Notts....85 P6
Fleet Dorset....11 N8
Fleet Hants....15 K6
Fleet Hants....23 M4
Fleet Lincs....74 G6
Fleetend Hants....14 F5
Fleet Hargate Lincs....74 G6
Fleet Services Hants....23 L3
Fleetwood Lancs....94 G11
Fleggburgh Norfk....77 N9
Flemingston V Glam....30 D11
Flemington S Lans....126 B6
Flempton Suffk....63 P7
Fletchersbridge Cnwll....5 J8
Fletcher's Green Kent....37 M11
Fletchertown Cumb....100 H2
Fletching E Susx....25 K6

Fleur-de-lis Caerph....30 G5
Flexbury Cnwll....16 C10
Flexford Surrey....23 P4
Flimby Cumb....100 D3
Flimwell E Susx....26 B5
Flint Flints....81 J10
Flintham Notts....85 M11
Flint Mountain Flints....81 J10
Flinton E R Yk....93 M3
Flint's Green Solhll....59 L8
Flishinghurst Kent....26 C4
Flitcham Norfk....75 P5
Flitton C Beds....50 C3
Flitwick C Beds....50 B4
Flixborough N Linc....92 E8
Flixborough Stather N Linc....92 E8
Flixton N York....99 L5
Flixton Suffk....65 L4
Flixton Traffd....82 F6
Flockton Kirk....90 G8
Flockton Green Kirk....90 H7
Flodden Nthumb....118 H3
Flodigarry Highld....152 H3
Flookburgh Cumb....94 H5
Flordon Norfk....64 H2
Flore Nhants....60 D8
Flotterton Nthumb....119 J10
Flowers Green E Susx....25 P8
Flowton Suffk....53 J2
Flushdyke Wakefd....90 H6
Flushing Cnwll....3 L7
Fluxton Devon....10 B6
Flyford Flavell Worcs....47 J3
Fobbing Thurr....38 B5
Fochabers Moray....157 Q6
Fochriw Caerph....30 F3
Fockerby N Linc....92 D7
Foddington Somset....19 Q9
Foel Powys....55 M2
Foelgastell Carmth....28 F2
Foel y Dyffryn Brdgnd....29 N6
Foggathorpe E R Yk....92 C3
Fogo Border....129 K10
Fogwatt Moray....157 N6
Foindle Highld....164 E7
Folda Angus....142 B5
Fole Staffs....71 J7
Foleshill Covtry....59 N8
Folke Dorset....11 P2
Folkestone Kent....27 M4

Folkestone Services Kent....27 K4
Folkingham Lincs....73 R4
Folkington E Susx....25 N10
Folksworth Cambs....61 P3
Folkton N York....99 M5
Folla Rule Abers....158 H11
Follifoot N York....97 M10
Folly Gate Devon....8 E5
Folly Hill Surrey....23 M5
Fonmon V Glam....30 D11
Fonthill Bishop Wilts....20 H8
Fonthill Gifford Wilts....20 H8
Fontmell Magna Dorset....20 G11
Fontmell Parva Dorset....12 D2
Fontwell W Susx....15 P5
Font-y-gary V Glam....30 E11
Foolow Derbys....83 Q9
Foots Cray Gt Lon....37 L6
Forbestown Abers....150 B5
Forcett N York....103 N8
Ford Ag & B....130 H1
Ford Bucks....35 L3
Ford Derbys....84 F4
Ford Devon....6 G8
Ford Devon....7 K10
Ford Devon....16 G7
Ford Gloucs....47 J9
Ford Nthumb....118 H3
Ford Shrops....56 G2
Ford Somset....18 E9
Ford Somset....19 Q4
Ford Staffs....71 K4
Ford W Susx....15 Q6
Ford Wilts....21 N8
Ford Wilts....32 F9
Forda Devon....8 D6
Fordcombe Kent....25 M2
Fordell Fife....134 F10
Forden Powys....56 C4
Ford End Essex....51 Q7
Forder Green Devon....7 K5
Fordgate Lancs....95 K11
Fordham Cambs....63 K6
Fordham Essex....52 F6
Fordham Norfk....75 M11
Fordham Heath Essex....52 F6
Ford Heath Shrops....56 G2
Fordingbridge Hants....13 K2
Fordon E R Yk....99 L5
Fordoun Abers....143 N2
Ford's Green Suffk....64 F8
Fordstreet Essex....52 F6
Ford Street Somset....18 G11
Fordton Devon....9 K5
Fordwells Oxon....34 B2
Fordwich Kent....39 L10
Fordyce Abers....158 E5
Forebridge Staffs....70 G10
Foremark Derbys....72 A5
Forest Guern....10 b2
Forest N York....103 Q10
Forest Becks Lancs....96 A10
Forestburn Gate Nthumb....119 L11
Forest Chapel Ches E....83 L10
Forest Coal Pit Mons....45 K10
Forest Gate Gt Lon....37 K3
Forest Green Surrey....24 D2
Forest Hall N Tyne....113 L7
Forest Hill Gt Lon....37 J6
Forest Hill Oxon....34 G3
Forest-in-Teesdale Dur....102 G4
Forest Lane Head N York....97 M9
Forest Mill Clacks....134 B9
Forest of Bowland Lancs....95 N10
Forest of Dean Gloucs....32 B2
Forest Row E Susx....25 K4
Forest Side IoW....14 E9
Forestside W Susx....15 L4
Forest Town Notts....85 J8
Forfar Angus....142 H7
Forgandenny P & K....134 D4
Forge Powys....54 H5
Forge Hammer Torfn....31 J5
Forge Side Torfn....30 H3

Forgie Moray....158 A7
Forgieside Moray....158 B7
Forgue Abers....158 F8
Forhill Worcs....58 G9
Formby Sefton....88 C9
Forncett End Norfk....64 G3
Forncett St Mary Norfk....64 H3
Forncett St Peter Norfk....64 H3
Fornham All Saints Suffk....64 A8
Fornham St Genevieve
  Suffk....64 A8
Fornighty Highld....156 G7
Forres Moray....157 J6
Forsbrook Staffs....70 H6
Forse Highld....167 M10
Forshaw Heath Warwks....58 G10
Forsinard Highld....166 E8
Forss Highld....166 H3
Forston Dorset....11 P5
Fort Augustus Highld....147 K6
Forteviot P & K....134 D4
Forth S Lans....126 G7
Forthampton Gloucs....46 G8
Forth Rail Bridge C Edin....127 L2
Forth Road Bridge Fife....127 L2
Fortingall P & K....140 H8
Forton Hants....22 D6
Forton Lancs....95 K10
Forton Shrops....69 M11
Forton Somset....10 G3
Forton Staffs....70 D10
Fort Richmond Guern....10 b2
Fortrie Abers....158 G8
Fortrose Highld....156 C6
Fortuneswell Dorset....11 P10
Fort William Highld....139 L3
Forty Green Bucks....35 P6
Forward Green Suffk....64 G10
Fosbury Wilts....22 B3
Foscot Oxon....47 P10
Foscote Nhants....49 J5
Fosdyke Lincs....74 F4
Fosdyke Bridge Lincs....74 F4
Foss P & K....141 J6
Fossebridge Gloucs....33 L2
Foss-y-ffin Cerdgn....42 H2
Fosterhouses Donc....91 R8
Foster Street Essex....51 L9
Foston Derbys....71 M8
Foston Leics....60 D2
Foston Lincs....73 M2
Foston N York....98 D7
Foston on the Wolds E R Yk....99 N9
Fotherby Lincs....87 K2
Fothergill Cumb....100 D4
Fotheringhay Nhants....61 N2
Foula Shet....169 k10
Foula Airport Shet....169 k10
Foul Anchor Cambs....75 J7
Foulbridge Cumb....110 H11
Foulby Wakefd....91 K7
Foulden Border....129 N8
Foulden Norfk....75 Q11
Foul End Warwks....59 K6
Foul Mile E Susx....25 P7
Foulness Island Essex....38 G3
Foulridge Lancs....89 P2
Foulsham Norfk....76 E7
Fountainhall Border....128 C10
Four Ashes Solhll....59 J9
Four Ashes Staffs....57 Q7
Four Ashes Staffs....58 D3
Four Ashes Suffk....64 E7
Four Cabots Guern....10 b2
Four Crosses Powys....69 J11
Four Crosses Staffs....58 D3
Four Elms Kent....37 L11
Four Foot Somset....19 Q8
Four Forks Somset....18 H7
Four Gates Bolton....89 J9
Four Gotes Cambs....75 J7
Four Lane End Barns....90 H10
Four Lane Ends Ches W....69 Q2
Four Lanes Cnwll....2 H6
Fourlanes End Ches E....70 E3
Four Marks Hants....23 J7
Four Mile Bridge IoA....78 D7
Four Oaks Birm....58 H5
Four Oaks E Susx....26 E7
Four Oaks Gloucs....46 C9
Four Oaks Solhll....59 K8
Fourpenny Highld....163 J8
Four Points W Berk....34 G9
Four Roads Carmth....28 D3
Four Shire Stone Warwks....47 P8
Fourstones Nthumb....112 C7
Four Throws Kent....26 C6
Four Wents Kent....37 P10
Fovant Wilts....21 K9
Foveran Abers....151 P3
Fowey Cnwll....5 J11
Fowley Common Warrtn....82 E5
Fowlhall Kent....37 Q11
Fowlis Angus....142 E11
Fowlis Wester P & K....133 Q3
Fowlmere Cambs....62 F11
Fownhope Herefs....46 A8
Foxbar Rens....125 M5
Foxcombe Devon....8 C7
Fox Corner Surrey....23 Q4
Foxcote Gloucs....47 K11
Foxcote Somset....10 D3
Foxdale IoM....80 c6
Foxearth Essex....52 D3
Foxendown Kent....37 P7
Foxfield Cumb....94 E3
Foxham Wilts....33 J9
Fox Hatch Essex....51 N11
Foxhills Hants....13 P2
Foxhole Cnwll....3 P3
Foxholes N York....99 L6
Foxhunt Green E Susx....25 M7
Foxley Norfk....76 E7
Foxley Wilts....32 G7
Foxlydiate Worcs....58 F11
Fox Street Essex....53 J6
Foxt Staffs....71 J5
Foxton Cambs....62 F11
Foxton Dur....104 C6
Foxton Leics....60 F3
Foxton N York....104 D11
Foxup N York....96 C5

Foxwist Green – Glenlivet 271

Foxwist Green Ches W 82 D11
Foxwood Shrops 57 L9
Foy Herefs 46 A9
Foyers Highld 147 M3
Foynesfield Highld 156 F7
Fraddam Cnwll 2 F7
Fraddon Cnwll 4 E10
Fradley Staffs 59 J2
Fradswell Staffs 70 H8
Fraisthorpe E R Yk 99 P8
Framfield E Susx 25 L6
Framingham Earl Norfk 77 K11
Framingham Pigot Norfk 77 K11
Framlingham Suffk 65 K9
Frampton Dorset 11 N5
Frampton Lincs 74 F3
Frampton Cotterell S Glos 32 C8
Frampton Mansell Gloucs 32 H4
Frampton-on-Severn Gloucs 32 D3
Frampton West End Lincs 74 F2
Framsden Suffk 64 H10
Framwellgate Moor Dur 103 Q2
Franche Worcs 57 Q9
Frandley Ches W 82 D9
Frankaborough Devon 5 P3
Frankby Wirral 81 J7
Frankfort Norfk 77 L7
Franklands Gate Herefs 45 Q5
Frankley Worcs 58 E8
Frankley Services Worcs 58 E8
Franksbridge Powys 44 G3
Frankton Warwks 59 P10
Frant E Susx 25 N3
Fraserburgh Abers 159 N4
Frating Essex 53 J7
Frating Green Essex 53 J7
Fratton C Port 15 J6
Freathy Cnwll 5 P11
Freckenham Suffk 63 L6
Freckleton Lancs 88 E5
Freebirch Derbys 84 D6
Freeby Leics 73 L6
Freefolk Hants 22 E5
Freehay Staffs 71 J6
Freeland Oxon 34 D2
Freethorpe Norfk 77 N10
Freethorpe Common Norfk 77 N11
Freiston Lincs 74 G2
Fremington Devon 17 J5
Fremington N York 103 K11
Frenchay S Glos 32 B9
Frenchbeer Devon 8 G7
French Street Kent 37 L10
Frenich P & K 141 K6
Frensham Surrey 23 M6
Freshfield Sefton 88 B9
Freshford Wilts 20 E2
Freshwater IoW 13 P7
Freshwater Bay IoW 13 P7
Freshwater East Pembks 41 K11
Fressingfield Suffk 65 K6
Freston Suffk 53 L4
Freswick Highld 167 Q3
Fretherne Gloucs 32 D2
Frettenham Norfk 77 J8
Freuchie Fife 134 H6
Freystrop Pembks 41 J8
Friar Park Sandw 58 F6
Friar's Gate E Susx 25 L4
Friars' Hill N York 98 E3
Friar Waddon Dorset 11 N7
Friday Bridge Cambs 75 J10
Friday Street Suffk 65 J10
Friday Street Suffk 65 L11
Friday Street Suffk 65 M9
Friday Street Surrey 36 D11
Fridaythorpe E R Yk 98 H9
Friden Derbys 71 M2
Friendly Calder 90 D6
Friern Barnet Gt Lon 36 G2
Friesthorpe Lincs 86 E4
Frieston Lincs 86 B11
Frieth Bucks 35 L6
Friezeland Notts 84 G10
Frilford Oxon 34 D5
Frilsham W Berk 34 F10
Frimley Surrey 23 N3
Frimley Green Surrey 23 N3
Frindsbury Medway 38 B8
Fring Norfk 75 P4
Fringford Oxon 48 H9
Frinsted Kent 38 E10
Frinton-on-Sea Essex 53 M7
Friockheim Angus 143 K8
Friog Gwynd 54 E2
Frisby on the Wreake Leics 72 H7
Friskney Lincs 87 N9
Friskney Eaudike Lincs 87 N9
Friston E Susx 25 N11
Friston Suffk 65 N9
Fritchley Derbys 84 E10
Fritham Hants 13 M2
Frith Bank Lincs 87 K11
Frith Common Worcs 57 M11
Frithelstock Devon 16 H8
Frithelstock Stone Devon 16 H8
Frithend Hants 23 M7
Frithsden Herts 50 B9
Frithville Lincs 87 K10
Frittenden Kent 26 D3
Frittiscombe Devon 7 L10
Fritton Norfk 65 J3
Fritton Norfk 77 P11
Fritwell Oxon 48 F9
Frizinghall C Brad 90 E3
Frizington Cumb 100 D7
Frocester Gloucs 32 E4
Frodesley Shrops 57 J4
Frodsham Ches W 81 Q9
Frogden Border 118 E5
Frog End Cambs 62 E11
Frog End Cambs 62 H9
Froggatt Derbys 84 B5
Froghall Staffs 71 J5
Frogham Hants 13 L2
Frogham Kent 39 N11
Frogmore Devon 7 K10
Frognall Lincs 74 C8
Frogpool Cnwll 3 K5
Frog Pool Worcs 57 Q11
Frogwell Cnwll 5 N8
Frolesworth Leics 60 B2
Frome Somset 20 E5
Frome St Quintin Dorset 11 M4
Fromes Hill Herefs 46 C5
Fron Gwynd 66 F7
Fron Gwynd 67 J4
Fron Powys 56 B5
Fron Powys 56 C4
Froncysyllte Wrexhm 69 J6
Fron-goch Gwynd 68 B7
Fron Isaf Wrexhm 69 J6
Frostenden Suffk 65 P5
Frosterley Dur 103 K3
Froxfield C Beds 49 Q8
Froxfield Wilts 33 Q11
Froxfield Green Hants 23 K9
Fryern Hill Hants 22 D10
Fryerning Essex 51 P10
Fryton N York 98 D6
Fuinary Highld 137 Q6
Fulbeck Lincs 86 B10
Fulbourn Cambs 62 H9
Fulbrook Oxon 33 Q2
Fulflood Hants 22 E8
Fulford C York 98 C11
Fulford Somset 18 H9
Fulford Staffs 70 H7
Fulham Gt Lon 36 G5
Fulking W Susx 24 F8
Fullaford Devon 17 M4
Fullarton N Ayrs 125 J10
Fuller's End Essex 51 M5
Fuller's Moor Ches W 69 N4
Fuller Street Essex 52 B8
Fuller Street Kent 37 N9
Fullerton Hants 22 C7
Fulletby Lincs 87 J6
Fullready Warwks 47 Q5
Full Sutton E R Yk 98 E9
Fullwood E Ayrs 125 L7
Fulmer Bucks 35 Q7
Fulmodeston Norfk 76 D5
Fulnetby Lincs 86 E5
Fulney Lincs 74 E6
Fulstone Kirk 90 F9
Fulstow Lincs 93 P11
Fulwell Oxon 48 C10
Fulwell Sundld 113 N9
Fulwood Lancs 88 G4
Fulwood Notts 84 G9
Fulwood Sheff 84 D3
Fulwood Somset 18 H10
Fundenhall Norfk 64 H2
Funtington W Susx 15 M5
Funtley Hants 14 G5
Funtullich P & K 133 M2
Furley Devon 10 F4
Furnace Ag & B 131 L7
Furnace Carmth 28 F4
Furnace Cerdgn 54 F5
Furnace End Warwks 59 K6
Furner's Green E Susx 25 K5
Furness Vale Derbys 83 M8
Furneux Pelham Herts 51 K5
Further Quarter Kent 26 E4
Furtho Nhants 49 L6
Furzehill Devon 17 N2
Furzehill Dorset 12 H4
Furzehills Lincs 87 J6
Furzeley Corner Hants 15 J4
Furze Platt W & M 35 N8
Furzley Hants 21 Q11
Fyfett Somset 10 E2
Fyfield Essex 51 N9
Fyfield Hants 21 Q5
Fyfield Oxon 34 D5
Fyfield Wilts 21 N2
Fyfield Wilts 33 M11
Fyfield Bavant Wilts 21 K9
Fylingthorpe N York 105 P10
Fyning W Susx 23 M10
Fyvie Abers 159 J10

G

Gabroc Hill E Ayrs 125 M7
Gaddesby Leics 72 H8
Gaddesden Row Herts 50 C8
Gadfa IoA 78 H7
Gadgirth S Ayrs 114 H3
Gadlas Shrops 69 L7
Gaer Powys 44 H10
Gaerllwyd Mons 31 M5
Gaerwen IoA 78 H10
Gagingwell Oxon 48 D9
Gailes N Ayrs 125 J10
Gailey Staffs 58 D2
Gainford Dur 103 N7
Gainsborough Lincs 85 P3
Gainsborough Suffk 53 L3
Gainsford End Essex 52 B4
Gairloch Highld 153 Q2
Gairlochy Highld 146 F11
Gairneybridge P & K 134 E8
Gaisgill Cumb 102 B9
Gaitsgill Cumb 110 G11
Galashiels Border 117 P3
Galgate Lancs 95 K9
Galhampton Somset 20 B9
Gallanachbeg Ag & B 130 G2
Gallanachmore Ag & B 130 G2
Gallantry Bank Ches E 69 P4
Gallatown Fife 134 H9
Galley Common Warwks 59 M6
Galleywood Essex 52 B11
Gallovie Highld 147 P10
Galloway Forest Park 114 H10
Gallowfauld Angus 142 G9
Gallowhill P & K 142 B10
Gallows Green Essex 52 F6
Gallows Green Worcs 46 H2
Gallowstree Common Oxon 35 J8
Galltair Highld 145 P3
Gallt-y-foel Gwynd 67 K2
Gallypot Street E Susx 25 L3
Galmisdale Highld 144 G11
Galmpton Devon 6 H10
Galmpton Torbay 7 M7
Galphay N York 97 L6
Galston E Ayrs 125 N10
Gamballs Green Staffs 83 M11
Gamblesby Cumb 102 B3
Gambles Green Essex 52 C9
Gamelsby Cumb 110 E10
Gamesley Derbys 83 M6
Gamlingay Cambs 62 B10
Gamlingay Cinques Cambs 62 B10
Gamlingay Great Heath Cambs 62 B10
Gammersgill N York 96 G4
Gamrie Abers 159 J5
Gamston Notts 72 F3
Gamston Notts 85 M5
Ganarew Herefs 45 Q11
Ganavan Bay Ag & B 138 F11
Gang Cnwll 5 N8
Ganllwyd Gwynd 67 N10
Gannachy Angus 143 K3
Ganstead E R Yk 93 K4
Ganthorpe N York 98 D6
Ganton N York 99 K5
Ganwick Corner Herts 50 G11
Gappah Devon 9 L9
Garbity Moray 157 Q7
Garboldisham Norfk 64 E5
Garbole Highld 148 D3
Garchory Abers 149 Q5
Garden City Flints 81 L11
Gardeners Green Wokham 35 M11
Gardenstown Abers 159 K5
Garden Village Sheff 90 H11
Garderhouse Shet 169 q9
Gardham E R Yk 92 G2
Gare Hill Somset 20 E6
Garelochhead Ag & B 131 Q9
Garford Oxon 34 D5
Garforth Leeds 91 L4
Gargrave N York 96 D10
Gargunnock Stirlg 133 L9
Garlic Street Norfk 65 J5
Garlieston D & G 107 N8
Garlinge Kent 39 P8
Garlinge Green Kent 39 K11
Garlogie Abers 151 K6
Garmond Abers 159 K7
Garmouth Moray 157 Q5
Garmston Shrops 57 L3
Garnant Carmth 29 J2
Garndolbenmaen Gwynd 66 H6
Garnett Bridge Cumb 101 P11
Garnfadryn Gwynd 66 D8
Garnlydan Blae G 30 G2
Garnswllt Swans 28 H3
Garn-yr-erw Torfn 30 H3
Garrabost W Isls 168 k4
Garrallan E Ayrs 115 K4
Garras Cnwll 3 J9
Garreg Gwynd 67 L6
Garrigill Cumb 102 D2
Garriston N York 97 J2
Garroch D & G 108 C4
Garrochtrie D & G 106 F10
Garrochty Ag & B 124 D7
Garros Highld 152 H5
Garsdale Cumb 95 Q3
Garsdale Head Cumb 96 A2
Garsdon Wilts 33 J7
Garshall Green Staffs 70 H8
Garsington Oxon 34 G4
Garstang Lancs 95 K11
Garston Herts 50 D10
Garston Lpool 81 N8
Garswood St Hel 82 C5
Gartachossan Ag & B 122 D7
Gartcosh N Lans 126 B4
Garth Brdgnd 29 N6
Garth Mons 31 K6
Garth Powys 44 D5
Garth Powys 56 D10
Garth Wrexhm 69 J6
Garthamlock C Glas 126 B4
Garthbrengy Powys 44 E8
Gartheli Cerdgn 43 L3
Garthmyl Powys 56 B5
Garthorpe Leics 73 L6
Garthorpe N Linc 92 D7
Garth Row Cumb 101 P11
Garths Cumb 95 L3
Gartly Abers 158 D11
Gartmore Stirlg 132 G8
Gartness N Lans 126 D5
Gartness Stirlg 132 G10
Gartocharn W Duns 132 E10
Garton E R Yk 93 N3
Garton-on-the-Wolds E R Yk 99 K9
Gartymore Highld 163 N4
Garva Bridge Highld 147 N9
Garvald Border 127 L8
Garvald E Loth 128 F5
Garvan Highld 138 H2
Garvard Ag & B 136 b3
Garve Highld 155 L5
Garvellachs Ag & B 130 D5
Garvestone Norfk 76 E10
Garvock Inver 124 H3
Garway Herefs 45 P10
Garway Common Herefs 45 P10
Garway Hill Herefs 45 N9
Garynahine W Isls 168 h4
Garyvard W Isls 168 i6
Gasper Wilts 20 E8
Gastard Wilts 32 G11
Gasthorpe Norfk 64 D5
Gaston Green Essex 51 L7
Gatcombe IoW 14 E9
Gateacre Lpool 81 N7
Gatebeck Cumb 95 L3
Gate Burton Lincs 85 P4
Gateford Notts 85 J4
Gateforth N York 91 P5
Gatehead E Ayrs 125 K10
Gate Helmsley N York 98 D9
Gatehouse Nthumb 111 Q3
Gatehouse of Fleet D & G 108 C9
Gateley Norfk 76 D7
Gatenby N York 97 M3
Gatesgarth Cumb 100 G7
Gateshaw Border 118 E6
Gateshead Gatesd 113 L8
Gates Heath Ches W 69 N2
Gateside Angus 142 G9
Gateside E Rens 125 M6
Gateside Fife 134 F6
Gateside N Ayrs 125 K7
Gateslack D & G 116 B10
Gathurst Wigan 88 G9
Gatley Stockp 82 H7
Gatton Surrey 36 G10
Gattonside Border 117 Q3
Gatwick Airport W Susx 24 G2
Gaufron Powys 55 M11
Gaulby Leics 72 H10
Gauldry Fife 135 K3
Gauldswell P & K 142 C7
Gaulkthorn Lancs 89 M5
Gaultree Norfk 75 J9
Gaunton's Bank Ches E 69 Q5
Gaunt's Common Dorset 12 H3
Gaunt's End Essex 51 N5
Gautby Lincs 86 G6
Gavinton Border 129 K9
Gawber Barns 91 J9
Gawcott Bucks 49 J8
Gawsworth Ches E 83 J11
Gawthorpe Wakefd 90 H6
Gawthrop Cumb 95 P3
Gawthwaite Cumb 94 F4
Gay Bowers Essex 52 C11
Gaydon Warwks 48 C4
Gayhurst M Keyn 49 M5
Gayle N York 96 C3
Gayles N York 103 M9
Gay Street W Susx 24 C6
Gayton Nhants 49 K4
Gayton Norfk 75 P7
Gayton Staffs 70 H9
Gayton Wirral 81 K8
Gayton le Marsh Lincs 87 M4
Gayton Thorpe Norfk 75 P7
Gaywood Norfk 75 M6
Gazeley Suffk 63 M8
Gear Cnwll 3 J9
Gearraidh Bhaird W Isls 168 i6
Gearraidh na h-Aibhne W Isls 168 h4
Geary Highld 152 D5
Gedding Suffk 64 C10
Geddington Nhants 61 J4
Gedling Notts 72 G2
Gedney Lincs 74 H6
Gedney Broadgate Lincs 74 H6
Gedney Drove End Lincs 75 J5
Gedney Dyke Lincs 74 H5
Gedney Hill Lincs 74 F8
Gee Cross Tamesd 83 L6
Geeston Rutlnd 73 P10
Geirinis W Isls 168 c13
Geldeston Norfk 65 M3
Gelli Rhondd 30 C6
Gelli Torfn 31 J6
Gellideg Myr Td 30 D3
Gellifor Denbgs 68 F2
Gelligaer Caerph 30 F5
Gelligroes Caerph 30 G6
Gelligron Neath 29 K4
Gellilydan Gwynd 67 M7
Gellinudd Neath 29 K4
Gelly Pembks 41 L7
Gellyburn P & K 141 Q10
Gellywen Carmth 41 Q6
Gelston D & G 108 G9
Gelston Lincs 86 B11
Gembling E R Yk 99 N9
Gentleshaw Staffs 58 G2
Georgefield D & G 110 E2
George Green Bucks 35 Q8
Georgeham Devon 16 H4
Georgemas Junction Station Highld 167 L5
George Nympton Devon 17 N7
Georgetown Blae G 30 G3
Georgia Cnwll 2 D6
Georth Ork 169 c4
Gerinish W Isls 168 c13
Gerlan Gwynd 79 L11
Germansweek Devon 8 B6
Germoe Cnwll 2 F8
Gerrans Cnwll 3 M6
Gerrards Cross Bucks 36 B3
Gerrick R & Cl 105 K8
Gestingthorpe Essex 52 D4
Gethsemane Pembks 41 L2
Geuffordd Powys 56 C2
Gib Hill Ches W 82 D9
Gibraltar Lincs 87 Q9
Gibsmere Notts 85 M11
Giddeahall Wilts 32 G10
Giddy Green Dorset 12 D7
Gidea Park Gt Lon 37 M2
Gidleigh Devon 8 G7
Giffnock E Rens 125 P6
Gifford E Loth 128 E6
Giffordtown Fife 134 H5
Giggleswick N York 96 B8
Gigha Ag & B 123 K10
Gilberdyke E R Yk 92 D5
Gilbert's End Worcs 46 F6
Gilbert Street Hants 22 H8
Gilchriston E Loth 128 D6
Gilcrux Cumb 100 F3
Gildersome Leeds 90 G5
Gildingwells Rothm 85 J3
Gilesgate Moor Dur 103 Q2
Gileston V Glam 30 D11
Gilfach Caerph 30 G5
Gilfach Goch Brdgnd 30 C6
Gilfachrheda Cerdgn 42 H3
Gilgarran Cumb 100 D6
Gill Cumb 101 M5
Gillamoor N York 98 D3
Gillan Cnwll 3 K8
Gillen Highld 152 D6
Gillesbie D & G 110 C2
Gilling East N York 98 C5
Gillingham Dorset 20 F9
Gillingham Medway 38 C8
Gillingham Norfk 65 N3
Gilling West N York 103 N9
Gillock Highld 167 M5
Gillow Heath Staffs 70 F3
Gills Highld 167 P2
Gill's Green Kent 26 C5
Gilmanscleuch Border 117 L6
Gilmerton C Edin 127 P4
Gilmerton P & K 133 P3
Gilmonby Dur 103 J8
Gilmorton Leics 60 C3
Gilsland Nthumb 111 M7
Gilson Warwks 59 J7
Gilstead C Brad 90 E3
Gilston Border 128 C8
Gilston Herts 51 K8
Gilston Park Herts 51 K8
Giltbrook Notts 84 G11
Gilwern Mons 30 H2
Gimingham Norfk 77 K4
Ginclough Ches E 83 L9
Gingers Green E Susx 25 P8
Gipping Suffk 64 F9
Gipsey Bridge Lincs 87 J11
Girdle Toll N Ayrs 125 J9
Girlington C Brad 90 E4
Girlsta Shet 169 r8
Girsby N York 104 C9
Girtford C Beds 61 Q11
Girthon D & G 108 D10
Girton Cambs 62 F8
Girton Notts 85 P7
Girvan S Ayrs 114 C8
Gisburn Lancs 96 B11
Gisleham Suffk 65 Q4
Gislingham Suffk 64 F7
Gissing Norfk 64 G4
Gittisham Devon 10 C5
Givons Grove Surrey 36 E10
Gladestry Powys 45 J3
Gladsmuir E Loth 128 D5
Glais Swans 29 K4
Glaisdale N York 105 L9
Glamis Angus 142 F8
Glanaber Gwynd 67 L4
Glanaman Carmth 29 J2
Glandford Norfk 76 E3
Glan-Duar Carmth 43 K6
Glandwr Pembks 41 N5
Glan-Dwyfach Gwynd 66 H6
Glandy Cross Carmth 41 M5
Glandyfi Cerdgn 54 F5
Glangrwyney Powys 45 J11
Glanllynfi Brdgnd 29 N6
Glanmule Powys 56 B6
Glanrhyd Pembks 41 M2
Glan-rhyd Powys 29 L3
Glanton Nthumb 119 L8
Glanton Pike Nthumb 119 L8
Glanvilles Wootton Dorset 11 P3
Glan-y-don Flints 80 H9
Glan-y-llyn Cardif 30 F8
Glan-y-nant Powys 55 L8
Glan-yr-afon Gwynd 68 B6
Glan-yr-afon Gwynd 68 D6
Glan-yr-afon IoA 79 L8
Glan-yr-afon Swans 28 H3
Glan-y-wern Gwynd 67 L8
Glapthorn Nhants 61 M2
Glapwell Derbys 84 G7
Glasbury Powys 44 H7
Glascoed Denbgs 80 D10
Glascoed Mons 31 K4
Glascote Staffs 59 K4
Glascwm Powys 44 H4
Glasfryn Conwy 68 B4
Glasgow C Glas 125 P4
Glasgow Airport Rens 125 M4
Glasgow Prestwick Airport S Ayrs 114 G2
Glasgow Science Centre C Glas 125 P4
Glasinfryn Gwynd 79 K11
Glasnacardoch Bay Highld 145 L8
Glasnakille Highld 144 H5
Glasphein Highld 152 B8
Glaspwll Powys 54 G5
Glassenbury Kent 26 C4
Glassford S Lans 126 C8
Glasshoughton Wakefd 91 L6
Glasshouse Gloucs 46 D10
Glasshouse Hill Gloucs 46 D10
Glasshouses N York 97 J8
Glasslaw Abers 159 L6
Glasson Cumb 110 E8
Glassonby Cumb 101 Q3
Glasson Dock Lancs 95 J9
Glasterlaw Angus 143 K7
Glaston Rutlnd 73 M10
Glastonbury Somset 19 P7
Glatton Cambs 61 Q3
Glazebrook Warrtn 82 E6
Glazebury Warrtn 82 E5
Glazeley Shrops 57 N7
Gleadless Sheff 84 E4
Gleadsmoss Ches E 82 H11
Gleaston Cumb 94 F6
Glebe Highld 147 N4
Gledhow Leeds 91 J3
Gledpark D & G 108 D10
Gledrid Shrops 69 K7
Glemsford Suffk 52 D2
Glen Achulish Highld 139 K6
Glenallachie Moray 157 P9
Glenancross Highld 145 L9
Glenaros House Ag & B 137 P7
Glen Auldyn IoM 80 f3
Glenbarr Ag & B 120 C4
Glenbarry Abers 158 E7
Glenbeg Highld 137 P3
Glenbervie Abers 151 K11
Glenboig N Lans 126 C4
Glenborrodale Highld 137 Q3
Glenbranter Ag & B 131 N8
Glenbreck Border 116 F6
Glenbrittle Highld 144 F3
Glenbuck E Ayrs 115 P2
Glencally Angus 142 F5
Glencaple D & G 109 L7
Glencarse P & K 134 F3
Glencoe Highld 139 L6
Glencothe Border 116 F5
Glencraig Fife 134 F9
Glencrosh D & G 115 Q10
Glendale Highld 152 B8
Glendaruel Ag & B 131 K11
Glendevon P & K 134 B7
Glendoe Lodge Highld 147 L6
Glendoick P & K 134 G3
Glenduckie Fife 134 H4
Glenegedale Ag & B 122 D9
Glenelg Highld 145 P4
Glenerney Moray 157 J8
Glenfarg P & K 134 E5
Glenfield Leics 72 E9
Glenfinnan Highld 145 R11
Glenfintaig Lodge Highld 146 G10
Glenfoot P & K 134 F4
Glenfyne Lodge Ag & B 131 Q4
Glengarnock N Ayrs 125 J7
Glengolly Highld 167 K3
Glengorm Castle Ag & B 137 L4
Glengrasco Highld 152 G9
Glenholm Border 116 G4
Glenhoul D & G 115 M10
Glenkin Ag & B 131 N11
Glenkindie Abers 150 C5
Glenlivet Moray 149 M2

Glenlochar D & G......108 F8
Glenlomond P & K......134 F7
Glenluce D & G......106 G6
Glenmassen Ag & B......131 N10
Glenmavis N Lans......126 D4
Glen Maye IoM......80 b6
Glen Mona IoM......80 g4
Glenmore Highld......152 G8
Glenmore Lodge Highld......148 H6
Glen Nevis House Highld......139 L3
Glenochil Clacks......133 P8
Glen Parva Leics......72 F11
Glenquiech Angus......142 G5
Glenralloch Ag & B......123 Q6
Glenridding Cumb......101 L7
Glenrothes Fife......134 H7
Glenshero Lodge Highld......147 P9
Glenstriven Ag & B......124 D2
Glentham Lincs......86 D2
Glentrool D & G......107 L2
Glen Trool Lodge D & G......114 H11
Glentruim Highld......148 N8
Glentworth Lincs......86 B3
Glenuig Highld......138 B2
Glenvarragill Highld......152 H10
Glen Vine IoM......80 d6
Glenwhilly D & G......106 G3
Glespin S Lans......115 R2
Glewstone Herefs......45 R10
Glinton C Pete......74 C9
Glooston Leics......73 K11
Glossop Derbys......83 M6
Gloster Hill Nthumb......119 Q10
Gloucester Gloucs......46 F11
Gloucester Services Gloucs......32 F2
Gloucestershire Airport
Gloucs......46 G10
Glusburn N York......96 F11
Glutt Lodge Highld......166 H9
Gluvian Cnwll......4 E9
Glympton Oxon......48 D10
Glynarthen Cerdgn......42 F5
Glyn Ceiriog Wrexhm......68 H7
Glyncoch Rhondd......30 E6
Glyncorrwg Neath......29 N5
Glynde E Susx......25 L9
Glyndebourne E Susx......25 L8
Glyndyfrdwy Denbgs......68 F6
Glynneath Neath......29 N3
Glynogwr Brdgnd......30 C7
Glyntaff Rhondd......30 E7
Glyntawe Powys......44 A11
Glynteg Carmth......42 G7
Gnosall Staffs......70 E10
Gnosall Heath Staffs......70 E10
Goadby Leics......73 K11
Goadby Marwood Leics......73 K5
Goatacre Wilts......33 K9
Goatham Green E Susx......26 D7
Goathill Dorset......20 C11
Goathland N York......105 M10
Goathurst Somset......19 J8
Goathurst Common Kent......37 L10
Goat Lees Kent......26 H2
Gobowen Shrops......69 K8
Godalming Surrey......23 Q6
Goddard's Corner Suffk......65 K8
Goddard's Green Kent......26 D5
Goddards Green W Susx......24 G6
Godden Green Kent......37 N9
Godford Cross Devon......10 C4
Godington Oxon......48 H9
Godley Tamesd......83 L5
Godmanchester Cambs......62 B6
Godmanstone Dorset......11 P5
Godmersham Kent......39 J11
Godney Somset......19 N6
Godolphin Cross Cnwll......2 G7
Godre'r-graig Neath......29 L3
Godshill Hants......21 N11
Godshill IoW......14 F10
Godstone Staffs......71 J8
Godstone Surrey......37 J10
Godsworthy Devon......8 D9
Godwinscroft Hants......13 L5
Goetre Mons......31 K3
Goff's Oak Herts......50 H10
Gogar C Edin......127 M3
Goginan Cerdgn......54 F8
Golan Gwynd......67 J6
Golant Cnwll......5 J11
Golberdon Cnwll......5 N7
Golborne Wigan......82 D5
Golcar Kirk......90 D7
Goldcliff Newpt......31 L8
Golden Cross E Susx......25 M8
Golden Green Kent......37 P11
Golden Grove Carmth......43 L11
Goldenhill C Stke......70 F4
Golden Hill Pembks......41 J10
Golden Pot Hants......23 K6
Golden Valley Derbys......84 F10
Golders Green Gt Lon......36 F3
Goldfinch Bottom W Berk......22 F2
Goldhanger Essex......52 F10
Gold Hill Cambs......62 H2
Gold Hill Dorset......12 D2
Golding Shrops......57 J4
Goldington Bed......61 N10
Goldsborough N York......97 N9
Goldsborough N York......105 M8
Goldsithney Cnwll......2 E7
Goldstone Kent......39 N9
Goldstone Shrops......70 C9
Goldthorpe Barns......91 M10
Goldworthy Devon......16 F7
Golford Kent......26 C4
Golford Green Kent......26 C4
Gollanfield Highld......156 E7
Gollinglith Foot N York......96 H4
Golly Wrexhm......69 K3
Golsoncott Somset......18 D7
Golspie Highld......163 J6
Gomeldon Wilts......21 N7
Gomersal Kirk......90 G5
Gomshall Surrey......36 C11
Gonalston Notts......85 L11
Gonerby Hill Foot Lincs......73 N3
Gonerby Moor Lincs......73 M3
Gonfirth Shet......169 q7
Goodameavy Devon......6 E6
Good Easter Essex......51 P8
Gooderstone Norfk......75 Q10
Goodleigh Devon......17 L5
Goodmanham E R Yk......92 E2
Goodmayes Gt Lon......37 L3

Goodnestone Kent......38 H9
Goodnestone Kent......39 N11
Goodrich Herefs......45 R11
Goodrington Torbay......7 M7
Goodshaw Lancs......89 N5
Goodshaw Fold Lancs......89 N5
Goodstone Devon......7 K4
Goodwick Pembks......40 H3
Goodwood W Susx......15 N5
Goodworth Clatford Hants......22 C6
Goodyers End Warwks......59 M7
Goole E R Yk......92 B6
Goole Fields E R Yk......92 C6
Goom's Hill Worcs......47 K4
Goonbell Cnwll......3 J4
Goonhavern Cnwll......3 K3
Goonvrea Cnwll......3 J4
Goosecruives Abers......151 K11
Gooseford Devon......8 G6
Goose Green Essex......53 K6
Goose Green Kent......26 D4
Goose Green Kent......37 P10
Goose Green S Glos......32 C10
Goose Green W Susx......24 D7
Goose Green Wigan......82 C4
Gooseham Cnwll......16 C8
Gooseham Mill Cnwll......16 C8
Goosehill Green Worcs......46 H2
Goose Pool Herefs......45 P7
Goosey Oxon......34 C6
Goosnargh Lancs......88 H3
Goostrey Ches E......82 G10
Gorddinog Conwy......79 M10
Gordon Border......118 D3
Gordon Arms Hotel Border......117 L5
Gordonstown Abers......158 G6
Gordonstown Abers......158 H10
Gore Powys......45 K3
Gorebridge Mdloth......127 Q5
Gorefield Cambs......74 H8
Gore Pit Essex......52 E8
Gores Wilts......21 M3
Gore Street Kent......39 N8
Gorey Jersey......11 c2
Goring Oxon......34 H8
Goring-by-Sea W Susx......24 D10
Goring Heath Oxon......35 J9
Gorleston-on-Sea Norfk......77 Q11
Gorrachie Abers......158 H6
Gorran Churchtown Cnwll......3 P5
Gorran Haven Cnwll......3 Q5
Gorran High Lanes Cnwll......3 P5
Gorrig Cerdgn......42 H6
Gors Cerdgn......54 E9
Gorseddau Slate
   Landscape Gwynd......67 K6
Gorse Hill Swindn......33 N7
Gorseinon Swans......28 G5
Gorseybank Derbys......71 P4
Gorsgoch Cerdgn......43 J4
Gorslas Carmth......28 G2
Gorsley Gloucs......46 C9
Gorsley Common Herefs......46 C9
Gorstage Ches W......82 D10
Gorstan Highld......155 L5
Gorstella Ches W......69 L2
Gorsten Ag & B......138 C11
Gorst Hill Worcs......57 N10
Gorsty Hill Staffs......71 L9
Gorthleck Highld......147 N3
Gorton Manch......83 J5
Gosbeck Suffk......64 H10
Gosberton Lincs......74 D4
Gosberton Clough Lincs......74 C5
Gosfield Essex......52 C6
Gosford Devon......10 C5
Gosford Oxon......34 E2
Gosforth Cumb......100 E10
Gosforth N u Ty......113 K7
Gosling Street Somset......19 P8
Gosmore Herts......50 E5
Gospel End Staffs......58 C6
Gospel Green W Susx......23 P8
Gosport Hants......14 H7
Gossard's Green C Beds......49 Q6
Gossington Gloucs......32 D4
Goswick Nthumb......119 L2
Gotham Notts......72 E4
Gotherington Gloucs......47 J9
Gotton Somset......18 H9
Goudhurst Kent......26 B4
Goulceby Lincs......87 J5
Gourdas Abers......159 J9
Gourdie C Dund......142 F11
Gourdon Abers......143 Q3
Gourock Inver......124 G2
Govan C Glas......125 N4
Goveton Devon......7 K9
Govilon Mons......31 J2
Gowdall E R Yk......91 Q6
Gower Highld......155 P6
Gower Swans......28 F6
Gowerton Swans......28 G5
Gowkhall Fife......134 D10
Gowthorpe E R Yk......98 F10
Goxhill E R Yk......93 L2
Goxhill N Linc......93 K6
Goytre Neath......29 L7
Grabhair W Isls......168 i6
Graby Lincs......74 A5
Grade Cnwll......3 J11
Gradeley Green Ches E......69 Q4
Graffham W Susx......23 P11
Grafham Cambs......61 Q7
Grafham Surrey......23 Q7
Grafton Herefs......45 P7
Grafton N York......97 P8
Grafton Oxon......33 Q4
Grafton Shrops......69 M11
Grafton Worcs......46 A2
Grafton Worcs......47 J2
Grafton Flyford Worcs......47 J3
Grafton Regis Nhants......49 L5
Grafton Underwood Nhants......61 K4
Grafty Green Kent......26 E2
Graianrhyd Denbgs......68 H3
Graig Conwy......79 Q10
Graig Denbgs......80 F10
Graigfechan Denbgs......68 F4
Grain Medway......38 E6
Grains Bar Oldham......90 B9
Grainsby Lincs......93 N11
Grainthorpe Lincs......93 Q11
Grampound Cnwll......3 N4
Grampound Road Cnwll......3 N3

Gramsdal W Isls......168 d12
Gramsdale W Isls......168 d12
Granborough Bucks......49 L9
Granby Notts......73 K3
Grandborough Warwks......59 Q11
Grand Chemins Jersey......11 c2
Grandes Rocques Guern......10 b1
Grandtully P & K......141 M7
Grange Cumb......101 J7
Grange Medway......38 C8
Grange P & K......134 H2
Grange Wirral......81 J7
Grange Crossroads Moray......158 C7
Grange Hall Moray......157 K5
Grangehall S Lans......116 D2
Grangemill Derbys......84 B9
Grangemouth Falk......133 Q11
Grange of Lindores Fife......134 H4
Grange-over-Sands Cumb......95 J5
Grangepans Falk......134 C11
Grange Park Nhants......60 G9
Grangetown R & Cl......104 F6
Grangetown Sundld......113 P10
Grange Villa Dur......113 K10
Gransmoor E R Yk......99 N9
Granston Pembks......40 G4
Grantchester Cambs......62 F9
Grantham Lincs......73 N3
Granton C Edin......127 N2
Grantown-on-Spey Highld......149 J2
Grantsfield Herefs......45 Q2
Grantshouse Border......129 L6
Grappenhall Warrtn......82 D7
Grasby Lincs......93 J10
Grasmere Cumb......101 K9
Grasscroft Oldham......83 L4
Grassendale Lpool......81 M7
Grassgarth Cumb......101 K2
Grass Green Essex......52 B4
Grassington N York......96 F8
Grassmoor Derbys......84 F7
Grassthorpe Notts......85 N7
Grateley Hants......21 Q6
Gratwich Staffs......71 J8
Graveley Cambs......62 C8
Graveley Herts......50 F5
Gravelly Hill Birm......58 H6
Gravelsbank Shrops......56 E4
Graveney Kent......39 J9
Gravesend Kent......37 Q6
Gravir W Isls......168 i6
Grayingham Lincs......92 F11
Grayrigg Cumb......101 Q11
Grays Thurr......37 P5
Grayshott Hants......23 N7
Grayson Green Cumb......100 C5
Grayswood Surrey......23 P8
Graythorpe Hartpl......104 F5
Grazeley Wokham......35 J11
Greasbrough Rothm......91 L11
Greasby Wirral......81 K7
Greasley Notts......84 G11
Great Abington Cambs......62 H11
Great Addington Nhants......61 L7
Great Alne Warwks......47 M3
Great Altcar Lancs......88 C9
Great Amwell Herts......51 J8
Great Asby Cumb......102 C8
Great Ashfield Suffk......64 D8
Great Ayton N York......104 F8
Great Baddow Essex......52 B11
Great Badminton S Glos......32 F8
Great Bardfield Essex......51 Q4
Great Barford Bed......61 P10
Great Barr Sandw......58 F5
Great Barrington Gloucs......33 P2
Great Barrow Ches W......81 P11
Great Barton Suffk......64 B8
Great Barugh N York......98 E5
Great Bavington Nthumb......112 E4
Great Bealings Suffk......53 M2
Great Bedwyn Wilts......21 Q2
Great Bentley Essex......53 K7
Great Billing Nhants......60 H8
Great Bircham Norfk......75 Q4
Great Blakenham Suffk......64 H11
Great Blencow Cumb......101 N4
Great Bolas Wrekin......70 A10
Great Bookham Surrey......36 D10
Great Bosullow Cnwll......2 C7
Great Bourton Oxon......48 E5
Great Bowden Leics......60 F3
Great Bradley Suffk......63 L10
Great Braxted Essex......52 E9
Great Bricett Suffk......64 E11
Great Brickhill Bucks......49 P8
Great Bridge Sandw......58 E6
Great Bridgeford Staffs......70 F9
Great Brington Nhants......60 E7
Great Bromley Essex......53 J6
Great Broughton Cumb......100 E4
Great Broughton N York......104 F9
Great Budworth Ches W......82 E9
Great Burdon Darltn......104 B7
Great Burstead Essex......37 Q2
Great Busby N York......104 F9
Great Canfield Essex......51 N7
Great Carlton Lincs......87 M3
Great Casterton Rutlnd......73 Q9
Great Chalfield Wilts......20 G2
Great Chart Kent......26 G3
Great Chatwell Staffs......57 P2
Great Chell C Stke......70 F4
Great Chesterford Essex......51 M2
Great Cheverell Wilts......21 J4
Great Chishill Cambs......51 K3
Great Clacton Essex......53 L8
Great Cliff Wakefd......91 J7
Great Clifton Cumb......100 D5
Great Coates NE Lin......93 M9
Great Comberton Worcs......47 J6
Great Comp Kent......37 P9
Great Corby Cumb......111 J10
Great Cornard Suffk......52 E3
Great Cowden E R Yk......93 M2
Great Coxwell Oxon......33 Q6
Great Cransley Nhants......60 H5
Great Cressingham Norfk......76 B11
Great Crosthwaite Cumb......101 J6
Great Cubley Derbys......71 M7
Great Cumbrae Island
   N Ayrs......124 F6
Great Dalby Leics......73 J8

Great Denham Bed......61 M11
Great Doddington Nhants......61 J8
Great Doward Herefs......45 Q11
Great Dunham Norfk......76 B9
Great Dunmow Essex......51 P6
Great Durnford Wilts......21 M7
Great Easton Essex......51 P5
Great Easton Leics......60 H2
Great Eccleston Lancs......88 E2
Great Edstone N York......98 E4
Great Ellingham Norfk......64 E2
Great Elm Somset......20 D5
Great Everdon Nhants......60 C9
Great Eversden Cambs......62 E10
Great Fencote N York......97 L2
Greatfield Wilts......33 L7
Great Finborough Suffk......64 E10
Greatford Lincs......74 A8
Great Fransham Norfk......76 B9
Great Gaddesden Herts......50 B8
Greatgate Staffs......71 K7
Great Gidding Cambs......61 P4
Great Givendale E R Yk......98 G10
Great Glemham Suffk......65 L9
Great Glen Leics......72 H11
Great Gonerby Lincs......73 M3
Great Gransden Cambs......62 C9
Great Green Cambs......50 G2
Great Green Norfk......65 K4
Great Green Norfk......64 C10
Great Green Suffk......64 C8
Great Habton N York......98 F5
Great Hale Lincs......74 B2
Great Hallingbury Essex......51 M7
Greatham Hants......23 L8
Greatham Hartpl......104 E5
Greatham W Susx......24 B7
Great Hampden Bucks......35 M4
Great Harrowden Nhants......61 J6
Great Harwood Lancs......89 L4
Great Haseley Oxon......34 H4
Great Hatfield E R Yk......93 L2
Great Haywood Staffs......71 H10
Great Heck N York......91 P6
Great Henny Essex......52 E4
Great Hinton Wilts......20 H3
Great Hockham Norfk......64 D3
Great Holland Essex......53 M8
Great Hollands Br For......35 N11
Great Horkesley Essex......52 G5
Great Hormead Herts......51 K5
Great Horton C Brad......90 E4
Great Horwood Bucks......49 L8
Great Houghton Barns......91 L9
Great Houghton Nhants......60 G9
Great Hucklow Derbys......83 Q9
Great Kelk E R Yk......99 N9
Great Kimble Bucks......35 M3
Great Kingshill Bucks......35 N5
Great Langdale Cumb......101 J9
Great Langton N York......103 Q11
Great Leighs Essex......52 B8
Great Limber Lincs......93 K9
Great Linford M Keyn......49 N6
Great Livermere Suffk......64 B7
Great Longstone Derbys......84 B6
Great Lumley Dur......113 L11
Great Lyth Shrops......56 H3
Great Malvern Worcs......46 E5
Great Maplestead Essex......52 D5
Great Marton Bpool......88 C3
Great Massingham Norfk......75 Q6
Great Melton Norfk......76 G10
Great Meols Wirral......81 J6
Great Milton Oxon......34 H4
Great Missenden Bucks......35 N4
Great Mitton Lancs......89 L3
Great Mongeham Kent......39 Q11
Great Moulton Norfk......64 H3
Great Munden Herts......51 J6
Great Musgrave Cumb......102 E8
Great Ness Shrops......69 L11
Great Notley Essex......52 B7
Great Oak Mons......31 L2
Great Oakley Essex......53 L6
Great Oakley Nhants......61 J3
Great Offley Herts......50 D5
Great Ormside Cumb......102 D7
Great Orton Cumb......110 F10
Great Ouseburn N York......97 P8
Great Oxendon Nhants......60 F4
Great Oxney Green Essex......51 Q9
Great Palgrave Norfk......76 A9
Great Parndon Essex......51 K9
Great Pattenden Kent......26 B3
Great Paxton Cambs......62 B8
Great Plumpton Lancs......88 D4
Great Plumstead Norfk......77 L9
Great Ponton Lincs......73 N4
Great Potheridge Devon......17 J9
Great Preston Leeds......91 L5
Great Purston Nhants......48 F7
Great Raveley Cambs......62 C4
Great Rissington Gloucs......47 N11
Great Rollright Oxon......48 B8
Great Ryburgh Norfk......76 D6
Great Ryle Nthumb......119 K8
Great Ryton Shrops......56 H4
Great Saling Essex......51 Q5
Great Salkeld Cumb......101 Q3
Great Sampford Essex......51 P3
Great Saredon Staffs......58 E3
Great Saughall Ches W......81 M11
Great Saxham Suffk......63 N8
Great Shefford W Berk......34 C9
Great Shelford Cambs......62 G10
Great Smeaton N York......104 B10
Great Snoring Norfk......76 C5
Great Somerford Wilts......33 J8
Great Soudley Shrops......70 C9
Great Stainton Darltn......104 B6
Great Stambridge Essex......38 E3
Great Staughton Cambs......61 P8
Great Steeping Lincs......87 M8
Great Stonar Kent......39 P10
Greatstone-on-Sea Kent......27 J7
Great Strickland Cumb......101 Q6
Great Stukeley Cambs......62 B6
Great Sturton Lincs......86 H5
Great Sutton Ches W......81 M9
Great Sutton Shrops......57 J8
Great Swinburne Nthumb......112 D5
Great Tew Oxon......48 D9
Great Tey Essex......52 E6
Great Thurlow Suffk......63 L10
Great Torrington Devon......16 H8

Great Tosson Nthumb......119 K10
Great Totham Essex......52 E9
Great Totham Essex......52 E9
Great Tows Lincs......86 H2
Great Urswick Cumb......94 F6
Great Wakering Essex......38 F4
Great Waldingfield Suffk......52 F3
Great Walsingham Norfk......76 C4
Great Waltham Essex......51 Q8
Great Warford Ches E......82 H9
Great Warley Essex......37 N2
Great Washbourne Gloucs......47 J8
Great Weeke Devon......8 H7
Great Welnetham Suffk......64 B10
Great Wenham Suffk......53 J4
Great Whittington Nthumb......112 F6
Great Wigborough Essex......52 G8
Great Wilbraham Cambs......63 J9
Great Wilne Derbys......72 C4
Great Wishford Wilts......21 L7
Great Witchingham Norfk......76 G7
Great Witcombe Gloucs......32 H2
Great Witley Worcs......57 P11
Great Wolford Warwks......47 Q8
Greatworth Nhants......48 G6
Great Wratting Suffk......63 L11
Great Wymondley Herts......50 F5
Great Wyrley Staffs......58 E3
Great Wytheford Shrops......69 Q11
Great Yarmouth Norfk......77 Q10
Great Yeldham Essex......52 C4
Grebby Lincs......87 M7
Greeba IoM......80 d5
Green Denbgs......80 F11
Green Bank Cumb......94 H4
Greenbottom Cnwll......3 K4
Greenburn W Loth......126 G5
Greencroft Hall Dur......113 J11
Green Cross Surrey......23 N7
Green Down Somset......19 Q4
Green End Bed......61 M11
Green End Bed......61 N8
Green End Bed......61 P10
Green End Bed......61 P8
Green End Cambs......61 Q4
Green End Cambs......62 B6
Green End Cambs......62 E9
Green End Cambs......62 G7
Green End Cambs......62 G8
Green End Herts......50 G4
Green End Herts......50 H4
Green End Herts......50 H6
Greenend Oxon......48 B10
Green End Warwks......59 L7
Greenfield Ag & B......131 Q9
Greenfield C Beds......50 C4
Greenfield Flints......80 H9
Greenfield Highld......146 G2
Greenfield Oldham......83 L4
Greenfield Oxon......35 K6
Greenford Gt Lon......36 D4
Greengairs N Lans......126 D3
Greengates C Brad......90 F3
Greengill Cumb......100 F3
Greenhalgh Lancs......88 E3
Greenham Somset......18 E10
Greenham W Berk......34 E11
Green Hammerton N York......97 Q9
Greenhaugh Nthumb......111 Q3
Green Head Cumb......110 G11
Greenhead Nthumb......111 N7
Green Heath Staffs......58 E2
Greenheys Salfd......82 F4
Greenhill D & G......109 P5
Greenhill Falk......126 E2
Greenhill Herefs......46 B2
Greenhill Kent......39 L8
Greenhill Leics......72 C8
Green Hill Wilts......33 L7
Greenhillocks Derbys......84 F11
Greenhills S Lans......125 Q7
Greenhithe Kent......37 N5
Greenholm E Ayrs......125 N10
Greenholme Cumb......101 Q9
Greenhouse Border......117 R6
Greenhow Hill N York......96 H8
Greenland Highld......167 M3
Greenland Sheff......84 E3
Greenlands Bucks......35 L7
Green Lane Devon......9 J9
Green Lane Worcs......47 L2
Greenlaw Border......129 J10
Greenlea D & G......109 M5
Greenloaning P & K......133 N6
Green Moor Barns......90 H11
Greenmount Bury......89 M8
Green Oak E R Yk......92 D5
Greenock Inver......124 H2
Greenodd Cumb......94 G4
Green Ore Somset......19 Q4
Green Park Readg......35 K10
Green Quarter Cumb......101 N10
Greensgate Norfk......76 G8
Greenshields S Lans......116 E2
Greenside Gatesd......112 H8
Greenside Kirk......90 F7
Greens Norton Nhants......49 J5
Greenstead Green Essex......52 D6
Greensted Essex......51 M10
Green Street E Susx......26 C9
Green Street Gloucs......46 G11
Green Street Herts......50 E11
Green Street Herts......51 L6
Green Street Worcs......46 G5
Green Street Green Gt Lon......37 L8
Green Street Green Kent......37 N6
Greenstreet Green Suffk......52 H2
Green Tye Herts......51 K7
Greenway Gloucs......47 D8
Greenway Somset......19 K10
Greenway V Glam......30 E10
Greenway Worcs......57 N10
Greenwich Gt Lon......37 J5
Greenwich Maritime Gt Lon......37 J5
Greet Gloucs......47 K8
Greete Shrops......57 K10
Greetham Lincs......87 K6
Greetham Rutlnd......73 N8
Greetland Calder......90 D6
Gregson Lane Lancs......88 H5
Greinton Somset......19 M7
Grenaby IoM......80 c7
Grendon Nhants......61 J8
Grendon Warwks......59 L5
Grendon Green Herefs......45 A3

Grendon Underwood Bucks....49 J10
Grenofen Devon....6 D4
Grenoside Sheff....84 D2
Greosabhagh W Isls....168 g8
Gresford Wrexhm....69 K4
Gresham Norfk....76 H4
Greshornish Highld....152 E7
Gressenhall Norfk....76 D8
Gressenhall Green Norfk....76 D8
Gressingham Lancs....95 M8
Gresty Green Ches E....70 C4
Greta Bridge Dur....103 L8
Gretna D & G....110 F7
Gretna Green D & G....110 F7
Gretna Services D & G....110 F7
Gretton Gloucs....47 K8
Gretton Nhants....61 J2
Gretton Shrops....57 J5
Grewelthorpe N York....97 K5
Grey Friars Suffk....65 P7
Greygarth N York....97 J6
Grey Green N Linc....92 C9
Greylake Somset....19 L8
Greylees Lincs....73 Q2
Greyrigg D & G....109 N3
Greys Green Oxon....35 K8
Greysouthen Cumb....100 E5
Greystoke Cumb....101 M4
Greystone Angus....143 J9
Greywell Hants....23 K4
Gribb Dorset....10 H4
Gribthorpe E R Yk....92 C3
Griff Warwks....59 N7
Griffithstown Torfn....31 J5
Griffydam Leics....72 C7
Griggs Green Hants....23 M8
Grimeford Village Lancs....89 J8
Grimesthorpe Sheff....84 E3
Grimethorpe Barns....91 L9
Grimister Shet....169 r4
Grimley Worcs....46 F2
Grimmet S Ayrs....114 F5
Grimoldby Lincs....87 L3
Grimpo Shrops....69 L9
Grimsargh Lancs....88 H4
Grimsby NE Lin....93 N8
Grimscote Nhants....49 J4
Grimscott Cnwll....16 D10
Grimshader W Isls....168 j5
Grimshaw Bl w D....89 L6
Grimshaw Green Lancs....88 F8
Grimsthorpe Lincs....73 Q6
Grimston E R Yk....93 N3
Grimston Leics....72 H6
Grimston Norfk....75 P6
Grimstone Dorset....11 N6
Grimstone End Suffk....64 C8
Grinacombe Moor Devon....5 Q3
Grindale E R Yk....99 N6
Grindle Shrops....57 P4
Grindleford Derbys....84 B5
Grindleton Lancs....95 R11
Grindley Brook Shrops....69 P6
Grindlow Derbys....83 Q9
Grindon Nthumb....118 H2
Grindon S on T....104 C5
Grindon Staffs....71 K4
Grindon Hill Nthumb....112 H8
Grindonrigg Nthumb....118 H2
Gringley on the Hill Notts....85 M2
Grinsdale Cumb....110 G9
Grinshill Shrops....69 P10
Grinton N York....103 K11
Griomsiadar W Isls....168 j5
Grishipoll Ag & B....136 F4
Grisling Common E Susx....25 K6
Gristhorpe N York....99 M4
Griston Norfk....64 C2
Gritley Ork....169 e6
Grittenham Wilts....33 K8
Grittleton Wilts....32 G8
Grizebeck Cumb....94 E4
Grizedale Cumb....94 G2
Groby Leics....72 E9
Groes Conwy....68 D2
Groes-faen Rhondd....30 E8
Groesffordd Gwynd....66 D7
Groesffordd Powys....44 F9
Groesffordd Marli Denbgs....80 E10
Groeslon Gwynd....66 H3
Groeslon Gwynd....67 J2
Groes-lwyd Powys....56 C2
Groes-Wen Caerph....30 F7
Grogarry W Isls....168 c14
Grogport Ag & B....120 F3
Groigearraidh W Isls....168 c14
Gromford Suffk....65 M10
Gronant Flints....80 F8
Groombridge E Susx....25 M3
Grosebay W Isls....168 g8
Grosmont Mons....45 N10
Grosmont N York....105 M9
Groton Suffk....52 G3
Grotton Oldham....83 L4
Grouville Jersey....11 c2
Grove Bucks....49 P10
Grove Dorset....11 P10
Grove Kent....39 M9
Grove Notts....85 M5
Grove Oxon....34 D6
Grove Pembks....41 J10
Grove Green Kent....38 C10
Grovenhurst Kent....26 B3
Grove Park Gt Lon....37 K6
Grovesend S Glos....32 C7
Grovesend Swans....28 G4
Grubb Street Kent....37 N7
Gruinard Highld....160 E9
Gruinart Ag & B....122 C6
Grula Highld....144 E2
Gruline Ag & B....137 N7
Grumbla Cnwll....2 C8
Grundisburgh Suffk....65 J11
Gruting Shet....169 p9
Grutness Shet....169 r12
Gualachulain Highld....139 L8
Guanockgate Lincs....74 G9
Guardbridge Fife....135 M4
Guarlford Worcs....46 F5
Guay P & K....141 P8
Guernsey Guern....10 b2
Guernsey Airport Guern....10 b2
Guestling Green E Susx....26 E9
Guestling Thorn E Susx....26 E9
Guestwick Norfk....76 F6
Guide Bridge Tamesd....83 K5

Guide Post Nthumb....113 L3
Guilden Morden Cambs....50 G2
Guilden Sutton Ches W....81 N11
Guildford Surrey....23 Q5
Guildstead Kent....38 D9
Guildtown P & K....142 A11
Guilsborough Nhants....60 E6
Guilsfield Powys....56 C2
Guilton Kent....39 N10
Guiltreehill S Ayrs....114 G5
Guineaford Devon....17 K4
Guisborough R & Cl....104 H7
Guiseley Leeds....90 F2
Guist Norfk....76 E6
Guiting Power Gloucs....47 L10
Gullane E Loth....128 D3
Gulling Green Suffk....64 A10
Gulval Cnwll....2 D7
Gulworthy Devon....6 D4
Gumfreston Pembks....41 M10
Gumley Leics....60 E3
Gummow's Shop Cnwll....4 D10
Gunby E R Yk....92 B3
Gunby Lincs....73 N6
Gundleton Hants....22 H8
Gun Green Kent....26 C5
Gun Hill E Susx....25 N8
Gun Hill Warwks....59 L7
Gunn Devon....17 L5
Gunnerside N York....103 J11
Gunnerton Nthumb....112 D6
Gunness N Linc....92 D8
Gunnislake Cnwll....6 C4
Gunnista Shet....169 s9
Gunthorpe C Pete....74 C10
Gunthorpe N Linc....92 D11
Gunthorpe Norfk....76 E5
Gunthorpe Notts....72 H2
Gunton Suffk....65 Q2
Gunwalloe Cnwll....2 H9
Gupworthy Somset....18 C8
Gurnard IoW....14 E7
Gurnett Ches E....83 K10
Gurney Slade Somset....20 B5
Gurnos Powys....29 L3
Gushmere Kent....38 H10
Gussage All Saints Dorset....12 H2
Gussage St Andrew Dorset....12 G2
Gussage St Michael Dorset....12 G2
Guston Kent....27 P3
Gutcher Shet....169 s4
Guthrie Angus....143 K7
Guyhirn Cambs....74 H10
Guyhirn Gull Cambs....74 G10
Guy's Marsh Dorset....20 F10
Guyzance Nthumb....119 P10
Gwaenysgor Flints....80 F8
Gwalchmai IoA....78 F9
Gwastadnant Gwynd....67 L3
Gwaun-Cae-Gurwen
  Carmth....29 J2
Gwbert on Sea Cerdgn....42 C4
Gwealavellan Cnwll....2 G5
Gweek Cnwll....3 J8
Gwehelog Mons....31 L4
Gwenddwr Powys....44 F6
Gwennap Cnwll....3 J5
Gwennap Mining District
  Cnwll....3 K5
Gwenter Cnwll....3 J10
Gwernaffield Flints....81 J11
Gwernesney Mons....31 M4
Gwernogle Carmth....43 K8
Gwernymynydd Flints....68 H2
Gwersyllt Wrexhm....69 K4
Gwespyr Flints....80 G8
Gwindra Cnwll....3 P3
Gwinear Cnwll....2 F6
Gwithian Cnwll....2 F5
Gwredog IoA....78 G2
Gwrhay Caerph....30 G5
Gwyddelwern Denbgs....68 E5
Gwyddgrug Carmth....43 J7
Gwynfryn Wrexhm....69 J4
Gwystre Powys....55 P11
Gwytherin Conwy....68 A2
Gyfelia Wrexhm....69 K5
Gyrn Goch Gwynd....66 G5

H

Habberley Shrops....56 F4
Habberley Worcs....57 Q9
Habergham Lancs....89 N4
Habertoft Lincs....87 P7
Habin W Susx....23 M10
Habrough NE Lin....93 K8
Hacconby Lincs....74 B5
Haceby Lincs....73 Q3
Hacheston Suffk....65 L10
Hackbridge Gt Lon....36 G7
Hackenthorpe Sheff....84 F4
Hackford Norfk....76 F11
Hackforth N York....97 K2
Hack Green Ches E....70 A5
Hackland Ork....169 c4
Hackleton Nhants....60 H9
Hacklinge Kent....39 P11
Hackman's Gate Worcs....58 C9
Hackness N York....99 K2
Hackness Somset....19 K5
Hackney Gt Lon....36 H4
Hackthorn Lincs....86 C4
Hackthorpe Cumb....101 P6
Hadden Border....118 E3
Haddenham Bucks....35 K3
Haddenham Cambs....62 G5
Haddington E Loth....128 E5
Haddington Lincs....86 B8
Haddiscoe Norfk....65 N2
Haddon Cambs....61 P2
Hade Edge Kirk....83 P4
Hadfield Derbys....83 M5
Hadham Cross Herts....51 K7
Hadham Ford Herts....51 K6
Hadleigh Essex....38 D4
Hadleigh Suffk....52 H3
Hadley Worcs....46 F9
Hadley Wrekin....57 M2
Hadley End Staffs....71 L10
Hadley Wood Gt Lon....50 G11
Hadlow Kent....37 P11

Hadlow Down E Susx....25 M6
Hadnall Shrops....69 P10
Hadrian's Wall....112 E7
Hadstock Essex....51 N2
Hadston Nthumb....119 Q11
Hady Derbys....46 H2
Haffenden Quarter Kent....26 E3
Hafodunos Conwy....80 B11
Hafod-y-bwch Wrexhm....69 K5
Hafod-y-coed Blae G....30 H4
Hafodyrynys Caerph....30 H5
Haggate Lancs....89 P3
Haggbeck Cumb....111 J6
Haggersta Shet....169 q9
Haggerston Nthumb....119 K2
Haggington Hill Devon....17 K2
Haggs Falk....126 D2
Hagley Herefs....45 R6
Hagley Worcs....58 D8
Hagmore Green Suffk....52 G4
Hagnaby Lincs....87 K8
Hagnaby Lincs....87 N5
Hagworthingham Lincs....87 K7
Haigh Wigan....89 J9
Haighton Green Lancs....88 H4
Haile Cumb....100 D9
Hailes Gloucs....47 K8
Hailey Herts....51 J8
Hailey Oxon....34 C2
Hailey Oxon....34 H7
Hailsham E Susx....25 N9
Hail Weston Cambs....61 Q8
Hainault Gt Lon....37 L2
Haine Kent....39 Q8
Hainford Norfk....77 J8
Hainton Lincs....86 G4
Hainworth C Brad....90 D3
Haisthorpe E R Yk....99 N8
Hakin Pembks....40 G9
Halam Notts....85 L10
Halbeath Fife....134 E10
Halberton Devon....9 P2
Halcro Highld....167 M4
Hale Cumb....95 L5
Hale Halton....81 P8
Hale Hants....21 N11
Hale Somset....20 D9
Hale Surrey....23 M5
Hale Traffd....82 G7
Hale Bank Halton....81 P8
Hale Barns Traffd....82 G7
Hale Green E Susx....25 N8
Hale Nook Lancs....88 D2
Hales Norfk....65 M2
Hales Staffs....70 C8
Halesgate Lincs....74 F5
Hales Green Derbys....71 M6
Halesowen Dudley....58 E8
Hales Place Kent....39 K10
Hale Street Kent....37 Q11
Halesville Essex....38 F3
Halesworth Suffk....65 M6
Halewood Knows....81 P7
Halford Devon....7 L4
Halford Shrops....56 G8
Halford Warwks....47 Q5
Halfpenny Cumb....95 L3
Halfpenny Green Staffs....58 B6
Halfpenny Houses N York....97 K4
Halfway Carmth....43 M8
Halfway Carmth....44 A8
Halfway Sheff....84 F4
Halfway W Berk....34 D11
Halfway Bridge W Susx....23 P10
Halfway House Shrops....56 E2
Halfway Houses Kent....38 F7
Halifax Calder....90 D5
Halket E Ayrs....125 L7
Halkirk Highld....167 K5
Halkyn Flints....81 J10
Hall E Rens....125 L7
Hallam Fields Derbys....72 D3
Halland E Susx....25 L7
Hallaton Leics....73 K11
Hallatrow BaNES....20 B3
Hallbankgate Cumb....111 L9
Hallbeck Cumb....95 N3
Hall Cliffe Wakefd....90 H7
Hall Cross Lancs....88 E4
Hall Dunnerdale Cumb....100 H11
Hallen S Glos....31 Q8
Hall End Bed....61 M11
Hall End C Beds....50 C3
Hallfield Gate Derbys....84 E9
Hallgarth Dur....104 B2
Hallglen Falk....126 F2
Hall Green Birm....58 H8
Hallin Highld....152 D6
Halling Medway....38 B9
Hallington Lincs....87 K3
Hallington Nthumb....112 E5
Halliwell Bolton....89 K8
Halloughton Notts....85 L10
Hallow Worcs....46 F3
Hallow Heath Worcs....46 F3
Hallsands Devon....7 L11
Hall's Green Essex....51 K9
Hall's Green Herts....50 H5
Hallthwaites Cumb....94 D3
Hallworthy Cnwll....5 K4
Hallyne Border....116 H2
Halmer End Staffs....70 D5
Halmond's Frome Herefs....46 C5
Halmore Gloucs....32 D4
Halnaker W Susx....15 P5
Halsall Lancs....88 D8
Halse Nhants....48 G6
Halse Somset....18 F9
Halsetown Cnwll....2 E6
Halsham E R Yk....93 M5
Halsinger Devon....17 J4
Halstead Essex....52 D5
Halstead Kent....37 L8
Halstead Leics....73 K9
Halstock Dorset....11 L3
Halsway Somset....18 F7
Haltcliff Bridge Cumb....101 L3
Haltham Lincs....86 H8
Haltoft End Lincs....87 L11
Halton Bucks....35 N3
Halton Halton....81 N8
Halton Lancs....95 L8
Halton Leeds....91 K4
Halton Nthumb....112 E7
Halton Wrexhm....69 K7
Halton East N York....96 F10

Halton Fenside Lincs....87 M8
Halton Gill N York....96 C5
Halton Green Lancs....95 L7
Halton Holegate Lincs....87 M7
Halton Lea Gate Nthumb....111 M9
Halton Quay Cnwll....5 Q8
Halton Shields Nthumb....112 F7
Halton West N York....96 B10
Haltwhistle Nthumb....111 P8
Halvana Cnwll....5 L6
Halvergate Norfk....77 N10
Halwell Devon....7 K8
Halwill Devon....8 B5
Halwill Junction Devon....8 B4
Ham Devon....10 E4
Ham Gloucs....32 C5
Ham Gloucs....47 J10
Ham Gt Lon....36 E6
Ham Kent....39 P11
Ham Somset....19 J9
Ham Somset....20 C5
Ham Wilts....22 B2
Hambleden Bucks....35 L7
Hambledon Hants....14 H4
Hambledon Surrey....23 Q7
Hamble-le-Rice Hants....14 E5
Hambleton Lancs....88 D2
Hambleton N York....91 P4
Hambleton Moss Side Lancs....88 D2
Hambridge Somset....19 L10
Hambrook Gloucs....32 B9
Hambrook W Susx....15 L5
Ham Common Dorset....20 F9
Hameringham Lincs....87 K7
Hamerton Cambs....61 P5
Ham Green Herefs....46 E6
Ham Green Kent....26 E6
Ham Green Kent....38 D8
Ham Green N Som....31 P9
Ham Green Worcs....47 K2
Ham Hill Kent....37 Q8
Hamilton S Lans....126 C6
Hamilton Services
  (northbound) S Lans....126 C6
Hamlet Dorset....11 M3
Hammer W Susx....23 N8
Hammerpot W Susx....24 C9
Hammersmith Gt Lon....36 F5
Hammer Vale Hants....23 N8
Hammerwich Staffs....58 G3
Hammerwood E Susx....25 K3
Hammond Street Herts....50 H10
Hammoon Dorset....12 D2
Hamnavoe Shet....169 q10
Hampden Park E Susx....25 P10
Hamperden End Essex....51 N4
Hampnett Gloucs....47 L11
Hampole Donc....91 N8
Hampreston Dorset....13 J5
Hampsfield Cumb....95 J4
Hampson Green Lancs....95 K10
Hampstead Gt Lon....36 G3
Hampstead Norreys W Berk....34 F9
Hampsthwaite N York....97 L9
Hampton Devon....10 F5
Hampton Gt Lon....36 D7
Hampton Kent....39 L8
Hampton Shrops....57 N7
Hampton Swindn....33 N6
Hampton Worcs....47 K6
Hampton Bishop Herefs....45 R7
Hampton Court Palace
  Gt Lon....36 E7
Hampton Fields Gloucs....32 G5
Hampton Green Ches W....69 P5
Hampton Hargate C Pete....61 Q2
Hampton Heath Ches W....69 P5
Hampton-in-Arden Solhll....59 K8
Hampton Loade Shrops....57 N7
Hampton Lovett Worcs....58 C11
Hampton Lucy Warwks....47 Q3
Hampton Magna Warwks....59 L11
Hampton on the Hill
  Warwks....47 Q2
Hampton Park Wilts....21 N8
Hampton Poyle Oxon....48 F11
Hampton Vale C Pete....61 Q2
Hampton Wick Gt Lon....36 E7
Hamptworth Wilts....21 P11
Hamrow Norfk....76 C7
Hamsey E Susx....25 K8
Hamsey Green Surrey....37 J9
Hamstall Ridware Staffs....71 K11
Hamstead Birm....58 G6
Hamstead IoW....14 D8
Hamstead Marshall W Berk....34 D11
Hamsterley Dur....103 M4
Hamsterley Dur....112 H9
Hamsterley Mill Dur....112 H9
Hamstreet Kent....26 H5
Ham Street Somset....19 Q8
Hamwood N Som....19 L3
Hamworthy BCP....12 G6
Hanbury Staffs....71 M9
Hanbury Worcs....47 J2
Hanby Lincs....73 Q4
Hanchet End Suffk....63 K11
Hanchurch Staffs....70 E6
Handa Island Highld....164 D7
Handale R & Cl....105 K7
Hand and Pen Devon....9 P5
Handbridge Ches W....81 N11
Handcross W Susx....24 G5
Handforth Ches E....83 J8
Hand Green Ches W....69 P2
Handley Ches W....69 N3
Handley Derbys....84 E8
Handley Green Essex....51 Q9
Handsacre Staffs....71 K11
Handsworth Birm....58 F7
Handsworth Sheff....84 F3
Handy Cross Bucks....35 N6
Hanford C Stke....70 F6
Hanford Dorset....12 D2
Hanging Heaton Kirk....90 H6
Hanging Houghton Nhants....60 G6
Hanging Langford Wilts....21 L7
Hangleton Br & H....24 G9
Hangleton W Susx....24 C10
Hanham S Glos....32 B10
Hankelow Ches E....70 B5
Hankerton Wilts....33 J6
Hankham E Susx....25 P9
Hanley C Stke....70 F5
Hanley Broadheath Worcs....57 M11
Hanley Castle Worcs....46 F6

Hanley Child Worcs....57 M11
Hanley Swan Worcs....46 F6
Hanley William Worcs....57 M11
Hanlith N York....96 C8
Hanmer Wrexhm....69 N7
Hannaford Devon....17 L6
Hannah Lincs....87 N5
Hannington Hants....22 F3
Hannington Nhants....60 H6
Hannington Swindn....33 N6
Hannington Wick Swindn....33 N5
Hanscombe End C Beds....50 D4
Hanslope M Keyn....49 M5
Hanthorpe Lincs....74 A6
Hanwell Gt Lon....36 E5
Hanwell Oxon....48 D6
Hanwood Shrops....56 G3
Hanworth Gt Lon....36 D6
Hanworth Norfk....76 H4
Happendon S Lans....116 B4
Happisburgh Norfk....77 M5
Happisburgh Common
  Norfk....77 M6
Hapsford Ches W....81 P10
Hapton Lancs....89 M4
Hapton Norfk....64 H2
Harberton Devon....7 K7
Harbertonford Devon....7 K7
Harbledown Kent....39 K10
Harborne Birm....58 F8
Harborough Magna Warwks....59 Q9
Harbottle Nthumb....118 H10
Harbourneford Devon....7 J6
Harbours Hill Worcs....58 E11
Harbridge Hants....13 K2
Harbridge Green Hants....13 K2
Harburn W Loth....127 J5
Harbury Warwks....48 C3
Harby Leics....73 J4
Harby Notts....85 Q6
Harcombe Devon....9 L8
Harcombe Devon....10 D6
Harcombe Bottom Devon....10 G5
Harden C Brad....90 D3
Harden Wsall....58 F4
Hardendale Cumb....101 Q8
Hardenhuish Wilts....32 H10
Hardgate Abers....151 K7
Hardgate D & G....108 H7
Hardgate N York....97 L8
Hardgate W Duns....125 N3
Hardham W Susx....24 B7
Hardhorn Lancs....88 D3
Hardingham Norfk....76 E11
Hardingstone Nhants....60 G9
Hardington Somset....20 D4
Hardington Mandeville
  Somset....11 L2
Hardington Marsh Somset....11 L3
Hardington Moor Somset....11 L2
Hardisworthy Devon....16 C7
Hardley Hants....14 D6
Hardley Street Norfk....77 M11
Hardmead M Keyn....49 P5
Hardraw N York....96 C2
Hardsough Lancs....89 M6
Hardstoft Derbys....84 F8
Hardway Hants....14 H6
Hardway Somset....20 D8
Hardwick Bucks....49 M11
Hardwick Cambs....62 E9
Hardwick Nhants....60 H7
Hardwick Nhants....65 J4
Hardwick Oxon....34 C3
Hardwick Oxon....48 G9
Hardwick Rothm....84 G3
Hardwick Wsall....58 G5
Hardwicke Gloucs....32 E2
Hardwicke Gloucs....46 H9
Hardwick Village Notts....85 K5
Hardy's Green Essex....52 F7
Harebeating E Susx....25 N8
Hareby Lincs....87 K7
Hare Croft C Brad....90 D3
Harefield Gt Lon....36 C2
Hare Green Essex....53 K6
Hare Hatch Wokham....35 M9
Harehill Derbys....71 M7
Harehills Leeds....91 J4
Harehope Nthumb....119 L6
Harelaw Border....117 Q6
Harelaw D & G....110 H5
Harelaw Dur....113 J10
Hareplain Kent....26 D4
Haresceugh Cumb....102 B2
Harescombe Gloucs....32 F2
Haresfield Gloucs....32 F2
Harestock Hants....22 E8
Hare Street Essex....51 K9
Hare Street Essex....51 M10
Hare Street Herts....51 J5
Harewood Leeds....97 M11
Harewood End Herefs....45 Q9
Harford Devon....6 G7
Hargate Norfk....64 G3
Hargatewall Derbys....83 P9
Hargrave Ches W....69 N2
Hargrave Nhants....61 M6
Hargrave Suffk....63 N9
Harker Cumb....110 G8
Harkstead Suffk....53 L5
Harlaston Staffs....59 K2
Harlaxton Lincs....73 M4
Harlech Gwynd....67 K8
Harlech Castle Gwynd....67 K8
Harlescott Shrops....69 N11
Harlesden Gt Lon....36 F4
Harlesthorpe Derbys....84 G5
Harleston Devon....7 K9
Harleston Norfk....65 J5
Harleston Suffk....64 E9
Harlestone Nhants....60 F8
Harle Syke Lancs....89 P3
Harley Rothm....91 K11
Harley Shrops....57 K4
Harlington C Beds....50 B4
Harlington Donc....91 M10
Harlington Gt Lon....36 C5
Harlosh Highld....152 D9
Harlow Essex....51 K8
Harlow Hill Nthumb....112 H6
Harlthorpe E R Yk....92 B3
Harlton Cambs....62 E10
Harlyn Cnwll....4 D6

Harman's Cross Dorset...12 G8
Harmby N York...96 H3
Harmer Green Herts...50 G7
Harmer Hill Shrops...69 N10
Harmondsworth Gt Lon...36 C5
Harmston Lincs...86 C8
Harnage Shrops...57 K4
Harnham Nthumb...112 G4
Harnhill Gloucs...33 L4
Harold Hill Gt Lon...37 M2
Haroldston West Pembks...40 G7
Haroldswick Shet...169 t2
Harold Wood Gt Lon...37 N2
Harome N York...98 C4
Harpenden Herts...50 D8
Harpford Devon...10 B6
Harpham E R Yk...99 M8
Harpley Norfk...75 Q5
Harpley Worcs...46 C2
Harpole Nhants...60 E8
Harpsdale Highld...167 K5
Harpsden Oxon...35 L8
Harpswell Lincs...86 B3
Harpurhey Manch...83 J4
Harpur Hill Derbys...83 N10
Harraby Cumb...110 H10
Harracott Devon...17 K6
Harrapool Highld...145 L3
Harras Cumb...100 C7
Harrietfield P & K...134 B2
Harrietsham Kent...38 E11
Harringay Gt Lon...36 H3
Harrington Cumb...100 C5
Harrington Lincs...87 L6
Harrington Nhants...60 G4
Harringworth Nhants...73 N11
Harris W Isls...168 f8
Harriseahead Staffs...70 F3
Harriston Cumb...100 G2
Harrogate N York...97 M9
Harrold Bed...61 K9
Harrop Dale Oldham...90 C9
Harrow Gt Lon...36 E3
Harrowbarrow Cnwll...5 Q7
Harrowden Bed...61 N11
Harrowgate Village Darltn...103 Q7
Harrow Green Suffk...64 B11
Harrow Hill Gloucs...46 C11
Harrow on the Hill Gt Lon...36 E3
Harrow Weald Gt Lon...36 E2
Harston Cambs...62 F10
Harston Leics...73 L4
Harswell E R Yk...92 D2
Hart Hartpl...104 E3
Hartburn Nthumb...112 G3
Hartburn S on T...104 D7
Hartest Suffk...64 A11
Hartfield E Susx...25 L3
Hartford Cambs...62 C6
Hartford Ches W...82 D10
Hartford Somset...18 C9
Hartfordbridge Hants...23 L3
Hartford End Essex...51 Q7
Harthill N York...103 N9
Hartgrove Dorset...20 F11
Harthill Ches W...69 N3
Harthill N Lans...126 G5
Harthill Rothm...84 G4
Harthope D & G...116 E8
Hartington Derbys...71 L2
Hartington Nthumb...112 F3
Hartland Devon...16 D7
Hartland Quay Devon...16 C7
Hartlebury Worcs...58 B10
Hartlepool Hartpl...104 F4
Hartley Cumb...102 E9
Hartley Kent...26 C5
Hartley Kent...37 P7
Hartley Nthumb...113 M5
Hartley Green Kent...37 P7
Hartley Green Staffs...70 H9
Hartley Wespall Hants...23 J3
Hartley Wintney Hants...23 L3
Hartlip Kent...38 D9
Hartoft End N York...98 E2
Harton N York...98 E8
Harton S Tyne...113 N7
Harton Shrops...56 H7
Hartpury Gloucs...46 E10
Hartshead Kirk...90 F6
Hartshead Moor Services Calder...90 F6
Hartshead Moor Top Kirk...90 F5
Hartshill C Stke...70 F5
Hartshill Warwks...59 M6
Hartshorne Derbys...71 Q10
Hartside Nthumb...119 J7
Hartsop Cumb...101 M8
Hart Station Hartpl...104 E3
Hartswell Somset...18 E9
Hartwell Nhants...49 L4
Hartwith N York...97 K8
Hartwood N Lans...126 E6
Hartwoodmyres Border...117 N6
Harvel Kent...37 Q8
Harvington Worcs...47 L5
Harvington Worcs...58 C10
Harwell Notts...85 L2
Harwell Oxon...34 E7
Harwich Essex...53 N5
Harwood Bolton...89 L8
Harwood Dur...102 F4
Harwood Nthumb...112 F2
Harwood Dale N York...105 Q11
Harwood Lee Bolton...89 L8
Harworth Notts...85 K2
Hasbury Dudley...58 E8
Hascombe Surrey...24 B3
Haselbech Nhants...60 F5
Haselbury Plucknett Somset...11 L2
Haseley Warwks...59 K11
Haseley Green Warwks...59 K11
Haseley Knob Warwks...59 K10
Haselor Warwks...47 M3
Hasfield Gloucs...46 F9
Hasguard Pembks...40 G9
Hasholme E R Yk...92 D4
Haskayne Lancs...88 D9
Hasketon Suffk...65 J11
Hasland Derbys...84 E7
Haslemere Surrey...23 P8
Haslingden Lancs...89 M6
Haslingfield Cambs...62 F10
Haslington Ches E...70 C3
Hassall Ches E...70 D3
Hassall Green Ches E...70 D3

Hassell Street Kent...27 J2
Hassingham Norfk...77 M10
Hassness Cumb...100 G7
Hassocks W Susx...24 H7
Hassop Derbys...84 B6
Haste Hill Surrey...23 P8
Haster Highld...167 P6
Hastingleigh Kent...27 J2
Hasthorpe Lincs...87 N7
Hastings E Susx...26 D10
Hastings Somset...19 K11
Hastingwood Essex...51 L9
Hastoe Herts...35 P3
Haswell Dur...104 C2
Haswell Plough Dur...104 C2
Hatch C Beds...61 Q11
Hatch Beauchamp Somset...19 K10
Hatch End Bed...61 N8
Hatch End Gt Lon...36 D2
Hatchet Gate Hants...14 C6
Hatching Green Herts...50 D8
Hatchmere Ches W...82 C10
Hatch Warren Hants...22 H5
Hatcliffe NE Lin...93 M10
Hatfield Donc...91 R9
Hatfield Herefs...46 A3
Hatfield Herts...50 F9
Hatfield Worcs...46 G4
Hatfield Broad Oak Essex...51 M7
Hatfield Heath Essex...51 M7
Hatfield Peverel Essex...52 C9
Hatfield Woodhouse Donc...92 A9
Hatford Oxon...34 B6
Hatherden Hants...22 B4
Hatherleigh Devon...8 D4
Hathern Leics...72 E6
Hatherop Gloucs...33 N3
Hathersage Derbys...84 B4
Hathersage Booths Derbys...84 B4
Hatherton Ches E...70 B5
Hatherton Staffs...58 E2
Hatley St George Cambs...62 C10
Hatt Cnwll...5 P9
Hattersley Tamesd...83 L6
Hattingley Hants...22 H7
Hatton Abers...159 Q10
Hatton Angus...142 H9
Hatton Derbys...71 N8
Hatton Gt Lon...36 C5
Hatton Lincs...86 G5
Hatton Shrops...56 H6
Hatton Warrtn...82 C8
Hatton Warwks...59 K11
Hatton Heath Ches W...69 N2
Hatton of Fintray Abers...151 L4
Hatton Park Warwks...59 L11
Haugh E Ayrs...115 J2
Haugh Lincs...87 M5
Haugh Rochdl...89 Q8
Haugham Lincs...87 K4
Haughhead E Duns...125 Q2
Haugh Head Nthumb...119 K5
Haughley Suffk...64 E9
Haughley Green Suffk...64 E9
Haugh of Glass Moray...158 B10
Haugh of Urr D & G...108 H7
Haughs of Kinnaird Angus...143 L6
Haughton Ches E...69 Q3
Haughton Notts...85 L6
Haughton Powys...69 K11
Haughton Shrops...57 M5
Haughton Shrops...57 N3
Haughton Shrops...69 L9
Haughton Shrops...69 Q11
Haughton Staffs...70 F10
Haughton Green Tamesd...83 K6
Haughton le Skerne Darltn...104 B7
Haultwick Herts...50 H6
Haunton Staffs...59 K2
Hautes Croix Jersey...11 b1
Hauxton Cambs...62 F10
Havannah Ches E...70 F2
Havant Hants...15 K5
Haven Herefs...45 N4
Haven Bank Lincs...86 H10
Haven Side E R Yk...93 L5
Havenstreet IoW...14 G8
Havercroft Wakefd...91 K8
Haverfordwest Pembks...41 J7
Haverhill Suffk...63 L11
Havering-atte-Bower Gt Lon...37 M2
Haversham M Keyn...49 M6
Haverthwaite Cumb...94 G4
Haverton Hill S on T...104 E6
Havyatt N Som...19 N2
Havyatt Somset...19 P7
Hawarden Flints...81 L11
Hawbridge Worcs...46 H5
Hawbush Green Essex...52 C7
Hawcoat Cumb...94 E6
Hawen Cerdgn...42 F5
Hawes N York...96 C3
Hawe's Green Norfk...65 J2
Hawford Worcs...46 F2
Hawick Border...117 Q8
Hawkchurch Devon...10 G4
Hawkedon Suffk...63 N10
Hawkenbury Kent...26 D2
Hawkeridge Wilts...20 G4
Hawkerland Devon...9 Q7
Hawker's Cove Cnwll...4 E6
Hawkesbury S Glos...32 E7
Hawkesbury Warwks...59 N8
Hawkesbury Upton S Glos...32 E7
Hawkes End Covtry...59 L8
Hawk Green Stockp...83 L7
Hawkhead Rens...125 N5
Hawkhill Nthumb...119 P8
Hawkhurst Kent...26 C5
Hawkhurst Common E Susx...25 M7
Hawkinge Kent...27 M4
Hawkley Hants...23 K9
Hawkley Wigan...82 C4
Hawkridge Somset...17 R5
Hawksdale Cumb...110 G11
Hawkshaw Bury...89 M7
Hawkshead Cumb...101 L11
Hawkshead Hill Cumb...101 K11
Hawksland S Lans...116 A3
Hawkspur Green Essex...51 Q4
Hawkstone Shrops...69 Q8
Hawkswick N York...96 E6
Hawksworth Leeds...90 F2
Hawksworth Notts...73 K2

Hawkwell Essex...38 E3
Hawkwell Nthumb...112 G6
Hawley Hants...23 N3
Hawley Kent...37 M6
Hawling Gloucs...47 L10
Hawnby N York...98 A3
Haworth C Brad...90 C3
Hawridge Bucks...35 P3
Hawstead Suffk...64 B10
Hawstead Green Suffk...64 B10
Hawthorn Dur...113 P11
Hawthorn Hants...23 J8
Hawthorn Rhondd...30 E7
Hawthorn Hill Br For...35 N10
Hawthorn Hill Lincs...86 H9
Hawthorpe Lincs...73 Q5
Hawton Notts...85 N10
Haxby C York...98 C9
Haxby Gates C York...98 C9
Haxey N Linc...92 C11
Haxey Carr N Linc...92 C10
Haxted Surrey...37 K11
Haxton Wilts...21 M5
Hay Cnwll...3 P3
Hay Cnwll...4 F7
Haydock St Hel...82 C5
Haydon BaNES...20 C4
Haydon Dorset...20 C11
Haydon Somset...19 J10
Haydon Bridge Nthumb...112 B8
Haydon Wick Swindn...33 M7
Haye Cnwll...5 P7
Hayes Gt Lon...36 C4
Hayes Gt Lon...37 K7
Hayes End Gt Lon...36 C4
Hayfield Ag & B...131 M3
Hayfield Derbys...83 M7
Hayfield Green Donc...91 R11
Haygate Wrekin...57 L2
Hay Green Norfk...75 K7
Hayhillock Angus...143 J9
Hayle Cnwll...2 F6
Hayle Port Cnwll...2 F6
Hayley Green Dudley...58 E8
Hayling Island Hants...15 K6
Haymoor Green Ches E...70 B4
Hayne Devon...9 J7
Hayne Devon...18 C11
Haynes C Beds...50 C2
Haynes Church End C Beds...50 C2
Haynes West End C Beds...50 C2
Hay-on-Wye Powys...45 J4
Hayscastle Pembks...40 G5
Hayscastle Cross Pembks...40 H5
Hay Street Herts...51 J5
Hayton Cumb...100 C7
Hayton Cumb...111 K9
Hayton E R Yk...98 G3
Hayton Notts...85 M4
Hayton's Bent Shrops...57 J8
Haytor Vale Devon...9 J9
Haytown Devon...16 F9
Haywards Heath W Susx...24 H6
Haywood Donc...91 P8
Haywood Herefs...45 P8
Haywood Oaks Notts...85 K9
Hazards Green E Susx...25 Q8
Hazelbank S Lans...126 E8
Hazelbury Bryan Dorset...12 B3
Hazeleigh Essex...52 D11
Hazeley Hants...23 K3
Hazelford Notts...85 M11
Hazel Grove Stockp...83 K7
Hazelhurst Tamesd...83 L4
Hazelslade Staffs...58 F2
Hazel Street Kent...25 Q3
Hazel Stub Suffk...51 Q2
Hazelton Walls Fife...135 J3
Hazelwood Derbys...84 D11
Hazlemere Bucks...35 N5
Hazlerigg N u Ty...113 K6
Hazles Staffs...71 J5
Hazleton Gloucs...47 L11
Heacham Norfk...75 N3
Headbourne Worthy Hants...22 E8
Headbrook Herefs...45 K3
Headcorn Kent...26 D3
Headingley Leeds...90 H3
Headington Oxon...34 F3
Headlam Dur...103 N7
Headlesscross N Lans...126 G6
Headless Cross Worcs...58 F11
Headley Hants...22 F2
Headley Hants...23 M7
Headley Surrey...36 F10
Headley Down Hants...23 M7
Headley Heath Worcs...58 G9
Headon Devon...16 F11
Headon Notts...85 M5
Heads Nook Cumb...111 K10
Heage Derbys...84 E10
Healaugh N York...91 R11
Healaugh N York...103 K11
Heald Green Stockp...82 H7
Heale Devon...17 L2
Heale Somset...18 H10
Heale Somset...19 L9
Healey N York...97 J4
Healey Nthumb...112 F9
Healey Rochdl...89 P7
Healey Wakefd...90 H7
Healeyfield Dur...112 G11
Healing NE Lin...93 M8
Heamoor Cnwll...2 D7
Heanor Derbys...84 F11
Heanton Punchardon Devon...17 J4
Heapham Lincs...85 Q3
Hearn Hants...23 M7
Heart of Scotland Services N Lans...126 G5
Hearts Delight Kent...38 E9
Heasley Mill Devon...17 N5
Heaste Highld...145 K4
Heath Derbys...84 F7
Heath Wakefd...91 K6
Heath and Reach C Beds...49 P9
Heath Common W Susx...24 D7
Heathcote Derbys...71 L2
Heathcote Shrops...69 B9
Heath End Bucks...35 N5
Heath End Hants...22 D2
Heath End Leics...72 B6
Heath End Warwks...59 K10
Heather Leics...72 B8
Heathfield Cambs...62 G11
Heathfield Devon...9 K9

Heathfield E Susx...25 N6
Heathfield N York...96 H7
Heathfield Somset...18 G9
Heathfield Village Oxon...48 F11
Heath Green Worcs...58 G10
Heath Hall D & G...109 L5
Heath Hayes & Wimblebury Staffs...58 F2
Heath Hill Shrops...57 P2
Heath House Somset...19 M5
Heathrow Airport Gt Lon...36 C5
Heathstock Devon...10 C4
Heathton Shrops...57 Q6
Heath Town Wolves...58 D5
Heathwaite N York...104 E10
Heatley Staffs...71 K9
Heatley Warrtn...82 F7
Heaton Bolton...89 K9
Heaton C Brad...90 E3
Heaton Lancs...95 J8
Heaton N u Ty...113 L7
Heaton Staffs...70 H2
Heaton Chapel Stockp...83 J6
Heaton Mersey Stockp...83 J6
Heaton Norris Stockp...83 J6
Heaton's Bridge Lancs...88 E8
Heaverham Kent...37 N9
Heaviley Stockp...83 K7
Heavitree Devon...9 M6
Hebburn S Tyne...113 M8
Hebden N York...96 F8
Hebden Bridge Calder...90 B5
Hebden Green Ches W...82 D11
Hebing End Herts...50 H6
Hebron Carmth...41 N5
Hebron IoA...78 G9
Hebron Nthumb...113 K2
Heckfield Hants...23 K2
Heckfield Green Suffk...64 H6
Heckfordbridge Essex...52 F7
Heckington Lincs...74 B2
Heckmondwike Kirk...90 G6
Heddington Wilts...33 J11
Heddon-on-the-Wall Nthumb...112 H7
Hedenham Norfk...65 L3
Hedge End Hants...14 E4
Hedgerley Bucks...35 Q7
Hedgerley Green Bucks...35 Q7
Hedging Somset...19 K9
Hedley on the Hill Nthumb...112 G9
Hednesford Staffs...58 E2
Hedon E R Yk...93 L5
Hedsor Bucks...35 P7
Heeley Sheff...84 E4
Hegdon Hill Herefs...46 A4
Heglibister Shet...169 q8
Heighington Darltn...103 P6
Heighington Lincs...86 D7
Heightington Worcs...57 P10
Heiton Border...118 D4
Hele Devon...7 J4
Hele Devon...9 N4
Hele Devon...17 J2
Hele Somset...18 G10
Helebridge Cnwll...16 C11
Hele Lane Devon...9 J2
Helensburgh Ag & B...132 B11
Helenton S Ayrs...125 K11
Helford Cnwll...3 K8
Helford Passage Cnwll...3 K8
Helhoughton Norfk...76 B7
Helions Bumpstead Essex...51 Q2
Hellaby Rothm...84 H2
Helland Cnwll...4 H7
Hellandbridge Cnwll...4 H7
Hell Corner W Berk...22 C2
Hellescott Cnwll...5 M4
Hellesdon Norfk...77 J9
Hellesveor Cnwll...2 E5
Hellidon Nhants...60 B9
Hellifield N York...96 C9
Hellingly E Susx...25 N8
Hellington Norfk...77 L11
Helm Nthumb...119 N11
Helmdon Nhants...48 G6
Helme Kirk...90 D8
Helmingham Suffk...64 H10
Helmington Row Dur...103 N3
Helmsdale Highld...163 N3
Helmshore Lancs...89 M6
Helmsley N York...98 C4
Helperby N York...97 P7
Helperthorpe N York...99 K6
Helpringham Lincs...74 B2
Helpston C Pete...74 B9
Helsby Ches W...81 P9
Helsey Lincs...87 P6
Helston Cnwll...2 H8
Helstone Cnwll...4 H5
Helton Cumb...101 P6
Helwith N York...103 L10
Helwith Bridge N York...96 B7
Hemblington Norfk...77 L9
Hembridge Somset...19 Q7
Hemel Hempstead Herts...50 C9
Hemerdon Devon...6 F7
Hemingbrough N York...91 R4
Hemingby Lincs...86 H6
Hemingfield Barns...91 K10
Hemingford Abbots Cambs...62 C6
Hemingford Grey Cambs...62 C6
Hemingstone Suffk...64 G11
Hemington Leics...72 D5
Hemington Nhants...61 N3
Hemington Somset...20 D4
Hemley Suffk...53 N3
Hemlington Middsb...104 F8
Hempholme E R Yk...99 M10
Hempnall Norfk...65 J3
Hempnall Green Norfk...65 J3
Hempriggs Moray...157 L5
Hempstead Essex...51 P3
Hempstead Medway...38 C9
Hempstead Norfk...76 G4
Hempstead Norfk...77 N6
Hempsted Gloucs...46 F11
Hempton Norfk...76 C6
Hempton Oxon...48 D8
Hemsby Norfk...77 P8
Hemswell Lincs...86 B3
Hemswell Cliff Lincs...86 B3
Hemsworth Wakefd...91 K8
Hemyock Devon...10 C2
Henbury Bristl...31 Q9
Henbury Ches E...83 J10

Hendham Devon...7 J8
Hendomen Powys...56 C5
Hendon Gt Lon...36 F3
Hendon Sundld...113 P9
Hendra Cnwll...3 J6
Hendra Cnwll...4 G6
Hendre Brdgnd...29 P8
Hendre Flints...80 H11
Hendredenny Caerph...30 F7
Hendy Carmth...28 G4
Heneglwys IoA...78 G9
Henfield W Susx...24 F7
Henford Devon...5 P3
Henfynyw Cerdgn...43 J2
Henghurst Kent...26 G4
Hengoed Caerph...30 G6
Hengoed Powys...45 J4
Hengoed Shrops...69 J8
Hengrave Suffk...63 P7
Henham Essex...51 M5
Heniarth Powys...55 Q3
Henlade Somset...19 J10
Henley Dorset...11 P4
Henley Gloucs...46 H11
Henley Shrops...56 H7
Henley Shrops...57 J9
Henley Somset...19 M8
Henley Suffk...64 H11
Henley W Susx...23 N9
Henley Green Covtry...59 N8
Henley-in-Arden Warwks...59 J11
Henley-on-Thames Oxon...35 L8
Henley Park Surrey...23 P4
Henley's Down E Susx...26 B9
Henley Street Kent...37 Q7
Henllan Cerdgn...42 G6
Henllan Denbgs...80 E11
Henllan Amgoed Carmth...41 N7
Henllys Torfn...31 J6
Henlow C Beds...50 E3
Henlow Camp C Beds...50 E3
Hennock Devon...9 K8
Henny Street Essex...52 E4
Henryd Conwy...79 P10
Henry's Moat (Castell Hendre) Pembks...41 K5
Hensall N York...91 P6
Henshaw Nthumb...111 Q8
Hensingham Cumb...100 C7
Henstead Suffk...65 P4
Hensting Hants...22 E10
Henstridge Somset...20 D11
Henstridge Ash Somset...20 D10
Henstridge Marsh Somset...20 D10
Henton Oxon...35 L4
Henton Somset...19 N5
Henwick Worcs...46 F3
Henwood Cnwll...5 M7
Henwood Oxon...34 E4
Heogarrig Myr Td...30 D3
Heol-las Swans...29 J5
Heol Senni Powys...44 C10
Heol-y-Cyw Brdgnd...29 P8
Hepburn Nthumb...119 L6
Hepple Nthumb...119 J10
Hepscott Nthumb...113 K4
Heptonstall Calder...90 B5
Hepworth Kirk...90 F9
Hepworth Suffk...64 D7
Herbrandston Pembks...40 G9
Hereford Herefs...45 Q7
Hereson Kent...39 Q8
Heribusta Highld...152 F3
Heriot Border...128 C9
Hermiston C Edin...127 M3
Hermitage Border...117 Q11
Hermitage Dorset...11 P3
Hermitage W Berk...34 F10
Hermitage W Susx...15 L5
Hermit Hill Barns...91 J10
Hermon Carmth...42 G8
Hermon IoA...78 F11
Hermon Pembks...41 P4
Herne Kent...39 L8
Herne Bay Kent...39 L8
Herne Common Kent...39 L8
Herne Hill Gt Lon...36 H6
Herne Pound Kent...37 Q10
Herner Devon...17 K6
Hernhill Kent...39 J9
Herodsfoot Cnwll...5 L8
Heronden Kent...39 N11
Herongate Essex...37 P2
Heronsford S Ayrs...114 B11
Heronsgate Herts...36 B2
Herriard Hants...23 J5
Herringfleet Suffk...65 P2
Herring's Green Bed...50 C2
Herringswell Suffk...63 M6
Herringthorpe Rothm...84 F2
Herrington Sundld...113 N10
Hersden Kent...39 M9
Hersham Cnwll...16 D10
Hersham Surrey...36 D8
Herstmonceux E Susx...25 P8
Herston Dorset...12 H9
Herston Ork...169 d7
Hertford Herts...50 H8
Hertford Heath Herts...51 H8
Hertingfordbury Herts...50 H8
Hesketh Bank Lancs...88 E6
Hesketh Lane Lancs...89 J2
Hesket Newmarket Cumb...101 K3
Heskin Green Lancs...88 G7
Hesleden Dur...104 D3
Hesleden N York...96 C6
Hesley Donc...85 K2
Hesleyside Nthumb...112 B4
Heslington C York...98 C10
Hessay C York...97 R10
Hessenford Cnwll...5 N10
Hessett Suffk...64 C9
Hessle E R Yk...92 H5
Hessle Wakefd...91 K7
Hest Bank Lancs...95 K8
Hestley Green Suffk...64 H8
Heston Gt Lon...36 D5
Heston Services Gt Lon...36 D5
Hestwall Ork...169 b5
Heswall Wirral...81 K8
Hethe Oxon...48 G9
Hethersett Norfk...76 G11
Hethersgill Cumb...111 J7
Hetherside Cumb...110 H7
Hetherson Green Ches W...69 P4
Hethpool Nthumb...118 G5

Hett Dur 103 Q3
Hetton N York 96 E9
Hetton-le-Hole Sundld 113 N11
Hetton Steads Nthumb 119 K3
Heugh Nthumb 112 G6
Heughhead Abers 150 B5
Heugh Head Border 129 M7
Heveningham Suffk 65 L7
Hever Kent 37 L11
Heversham Cumb 95 K4
Hevingham Norfk 76 H7
Hewas Water Cnwll 3 P4
Hewelsfield Gloucs 31 Q4
Hewenden C Brad 90 D3
Hewish N Som 19 M2
Hewish Somset 11 J3
Hewood Dorset 10 H4
Hexham Nthumb 112 D8
Hextable Kent 37 M6
Hexthorpe Donc 91 P10
Hexton Herts 50 D4
Hexworthy Cnwll 5 P5
Hexworthy Devon 6 H4
Hey Lancs 89 P2
Heybridge Essex 51 P11
Heybridge Essex 52 E10
Heybridge Basin Essex 52 E10
Heybrook Bay Devon 6 D9
Heydon Cambs 51 K3
Heydon Norfk 76 H5
Heydour Lincs 73 Q3
Hey Houses Lancs 88 C5
Heylipoll Ag & B 136 B7
Heylor Shet 169 p5
Heyrod Tamesd 83 L5
Heysham Lancs 95 J8
Heyshaw N York 97 J8
Heyshott W Susx 23 N11
Heyside Oldham 89 Q9
Heytesbury Wilts 20 H6
Heythrop Oxon 48 C9
Heywood Rochdl 89 P8
Heywood Wilts 20 G4
Hibaldstow N Linc 92 G10
Hickleton Donc 91 M9
Hickling Norfk 77 N7
Hickling Notts 72 H5
Hickling Green Norfk 77 N7
Hickling Heath Norfk 77 N7
Hickling Pastures Notts 72 H5
Hickmans Green Kent 39 J10
Hicks Forstal Kent 39 L9
Hickstead W Susx 24 G6
Hidcote Bartrim Gloucs 47 N6
Hidcote Boyce Gloucs 47 N6
High Ackworth Wakefd 91 L7
Higham Barns 91 J9
Higham Derbys 84 E9
Higham Kent 37 P11
Higham Kent 38 B7
Higham Lancs 89 N3
Higham Suffk 52 H4
Higham Suffk 63 M7
Higham Dykes Nthumb 112 H5
Higham Ferrers Nhants 61 L7
Higham Gobion C Beds 50 D4
Higham Hill Gt Lon 37 J2
Higham on the Hill Leics 72 B11
Highampton Devon 8 C4
Highams Park Gt Lon 37 J2
High Angerton Nthumb 112 G3
High Ardwell D & G 106 E8
High Auldgirth D & G 109 K3
High Bankhill Cumb 101 Q2
High Barnet Gt Lon 50 G11
High Beach Essex 51 K11
High Bentham N York 95 P7
High Bewaldeth Cumb 100 H4
High Bickington Devon 17 L7
High Biggins Cumb 95 N5
High Birkwith N York 96 B5
High Blantyre S Lans 126 B6
High Bonnybridge Falk 126 E2
High Borrans Cumb 101 M10
High Bradley N York 96 F11
High Bray Devon 17 M5
Highbridge Hants 22 E10
Highbridge Somset 19 K5
Highbrook W Susx 25 J4
High Brooms Kent 25 N2
High Bullen Devon 17 J7
Highburton Kirk 90 F8
Highbury Gt Lon 36 H3
Highbury Somset 20 C5
High Buston Nthumb 119 P9
High Callerton Nthumb 113 J6
High Casterton Cumb 95 N5
High Catton E R Yk 98 E10
Highclere Hants 22 D3
Highcliffe BCP 13 M6
High Close Dur 103 N7
High Cogges Oxon 34 C3
High Common Norfk 76 D10
High Coniscliffe Darltn 103 P7
High Crosby Cumb 111 J9
High Cross Cnwll 3 J8
High Cross E Ayrs 125 L3
High Cross Hants 23 K9
High Cross Herts 51 J7
Highcross Lancs 88 C3
High Cross W Susx 24 F7
High Cross Warwks 59 K11
High Drummore D & G 106 F10
High Dubmire Sundld 113 M11
High Easter Essex 51 P8
High Eggborough N York 91 P6
High Ellington N York 97 J4
Higher Alham Somset 20 C6
Higher Ansty Dorset 12 C4
Higher Ballam Lancs 88 G4
Higher Bartle Lancs 88 G4
Higher Berry End C Beds 49 Q8
Higher Bockhampton
　Dorset 12 B6
Higher Brixham Torbay 7 N8
Higher Burrowton Devon 9 J4
Higher Burwardsley Ches W 69 P3
High Ercall Wrekin 69 Q11
Higher Chillington Somset 10 H2
Higher Clovelly Devon 16 E7
Highercombe Somset 18 B8
Higher Coombe Dorset 11 L6
Higher Disley Ches E 83 L8
Higher Folds Wigan 82 E4
Higherford Lancs 89 P2
Higher Gabwell Devon 7 N5

Higher Halstock Leigh
　Dorset 11 L3
Higher Harpers Lancs 89 N3
Higher Heysham Lancs 95 J8
Higher Hurdsfield Ches E 83 K10
Higher Irlam Salfd 82 F5
Higher Kingcombe Dorset 11 L5
Higher Kinnerton Flints 69 K2
Higher Marston Ches W 82 E9
Higher Muddiford Devon 17 K4
Higher Nyland Dorset 20 D10
Higher Ogden Rochdl 90 B8
Higher Pentire Cnwll 2 H8
Higher Penwortham Lancs 88 G5
Higher Prestacott Devon 5 P2
Higher Studfold N York 96 B6
Higher Town Cnwll 3 L5
Higher Town Cnwll 4 G9
Higher Town IoS 2 c1
Higher Tregantle Cnwll 5 Q11
Higher Walton Lancs 88 H5
Higher Walton Warrtn 82 C7
Higher Wambrook Somset 10 F3
Higher Waterston Dorset 11 Q5
Higher Whatcombe Dorset 12 D4
Higher Wheelton Lancs 89 J6
Higher Whitley Ches W 82 D8
Higher Wincham Ches W 82 E9
Higher Wraxall Dorset 11 M4
Higher Wych Ches W 69 N6
High Etherley Dur 103 N5
High Ferry Lincs 87 L11
Highfield E R Yk 92 B3
Highfield Gatesd 112 H9
Highfield N Ayrs 125 J7
Highfields Donc 91 N9
Highfields Caldecote Cambs 62 E9
High Flats Kirk 90 G9
High Garrett Essex 52 C6
Highgate E Susx 25 K4
Highgate Gt Lon 36 G3
Highgate Kent 26 C5
Highgate Lincs 87 M11
High Grange Dur 103 N4
High Grantley N York 97 K7
High Green Cumb 101 M10
High Green Kirk 90 G8
High Green Norfk 64 H4
High Green Norfk 76 G10
High Green Sheff 91 J11
High Green Shrops 57 N8
High Green Suffk 64 B9
High Green Worcs 46 G5
Highgreen Manor Nthumb 112 B2
High Halden Kent 26 E4
High Halstow Medway 38 C6
High Ham Somset 19 M8
High Harrington Cumb 100 D5
High Harrogate N York 97 M9
High Haswell Dur 104 C2
High Hatton Shrops 69 R10
High Hauxley Nthumb 119 Q10
High Hawsker N York 105 P9
High Hesket Cumb 101 N2
High Hoyland Barns 90 H9
High Hunsley E R Yk 92 G3
High Hurstwood E Susx 25 L5
High Hutton N York 98 F7
High Ireby Cumb 100 H3
High Kelling Norfk 76 G3
High Kilburn N York 97 R5
High Killerby N York 99 M4
High Knipe Cumb 101 P7
High Lands Dur 103 M5
Highlane Ches E 83 J11
Highlane Derbys 84 F4
High Lane Stockp 83 L7
High Lanes Cnwll 2 F6
High Laver Essex 51 M9
Highlaws Cumb 109 P11
Highleadon Gloucs 46 E10
High Legh Ches E 82 F8
Highleigh W Susx 15 M7
High Leven S on T 104 E8
Highley Shrops 57 N8
High Littleton BaNES 20 B3
High Lorton Cumb 100 G5
High Marishes N York 98 G5
High Marnham Notts 85 P6
High Melton Donc 91 N10
High Mickley Nthumb 112 G8
Highmoor Cumb 110 E11
Highmoor Oxon 35 K8
Highmoor Cross Oxon 35 K8
Highmoor Hill Mons 31 N7
High Moorsley Sundld 113 M11
Highnam Gloucs 46 E10
High Newport Sundld 113 N10
Highnam Gloucs 95 J4
High Newton-by-the-Sea
　Nthumb 119 P5
High Nibthwaite Cumb 94 F3
High Offley Staffs 70 D9
High Ongar Essex 51 N10
High Onn Staffs 70 E11
High Park Corner Essex 52 H7
High Pennyvenie E Ayrs 115 J6
High Pittington Dur 104 B2
High Post Wilts 21 N7
Highridge N Som 31 Q11
High Roding Essex 51 P7
High Row Cumb 101 L3
High Row Cumb 101 L6
High Salter Lancs 95 N8
High Salvington W Susx 24 D9
High Scales Cumb 110 C11
High Seaton Cumb 100 D4
High Shaw N York 96 C2
High Side Cumb 100 H4
High Spen Gatesd 112 H9
Highstead Kent 39 M8
Highsted Kent 38 F9
High Stoop Dur 103 M2
High Street Cnwll 3 L4
High Street Kent 26 B5
Highstreet Kent 39 J9
High Street Suffk 65 N10
High Street Suffk 65 N7
Highstreet Green Essex 52 C5
Highstreet Green Surrey 23 Q7
Hightae D & G 109 N5
Highter's Heath Birm 58 G9
High Throston Hartpl 104 E4
Hightown Ches E 70 F2
Hightown Hants 13 L4
Hightown Sefton 81 L4

High Town Staffs 58 E2
Hightown Green Suffk 64 D10
High Toynton Lincs 87 J7
High Trewhitt Nthumb 119 K9
High Urpeth Dur 113 K10
High Valleyfield Fife 134 C10
High Warden Nthumb 112 D7
Highway Herefs 45 P5
Highway Wilts 33 K10
Highweek Devon 7 L4
High Westwood Dur 112 H9
Highwood Essex 51 P10
Highwood Staffs 71 K8
Highwood W Susx 24 E4
Highwood Hill Gt Lon 36 F2
Highwoods Essex 52 H6
High Woolaston Gloucs 31 Q5
High Worsall N York 104 C9
Highworth Swindn 33 P6
High Wray Cumb 101 L11
High Wych Herts 51 L8
High Wycombe Bucks 35 N6
Hilborough Norfk 75 R10
Hilcote Derbys 84 G9
Hilcott Wilts 21 M3
Hildenborough Kent 37 N11
Hilden Park Kent 37 N11
Hildersham Cambs 62 H11
Hilderstone Staffs 70 H8
Hilderthorpe E R Yk 99 P7
Hilfield Dorset 11 N3
Hilgay Norfk 75 M11
Hill S Gloucs 32 B5
Hill Warwks 59 Q11
Hillam N York 91 N5
Hillbeck Cumb 102 E7
Hillborough Kent 39 M8
Hill Brow Hants 23 L9
Hillbutts Dorset 12 G4
Hill Chorlton Staffs 70 D7
Hillclifflane Derbys 71 P5
Hill Common Norfk 77 N7
Hill Common Somset 18 F9
Hill Deverill Wilts 20 G6
Hilldyke Lincs 87 K11
Hill End Dur 103 K3
Hill End Fife 134 C8
Hillend Fife 134 E11
Hill End Gloucs 46 H7
Hillend Mdloth 127 P4
Hillend N Lans 126 E4
Hillend Swans 28 D6
Hillersland Gloucs 31 Q2
Hillerton Devon 8 H5
Hillesden Bucks 49 J9
Hillesley Gloucs 32 E7
Hillfarrance Somset 18 G10
Hill Green Kent 38 D9
Hillgrove W Susx 23 P9
Hillhampton Herefs 46 A5
Hillhead Abers 158 E10
Hillhead Devon 7 N8
Hill Head Hants 14 F6
Hillhead S Lans 116 D2
Hillhead of Cocklaw Abers 159 Q9
Hilliard's Cross Staffs 59 J2
Hilliclay Highld 167 L4
Hillingdon Gt Lon 36 C4
Hillington C Glas 125 N5
Hillington Norfk 75 P5
Hillis Corner IoW 14 E8
Hillmorton Warwks 60 B6
Hillock Vale Lancs 89 M5
Hill of Beath Fife 134 F9
Hill of Fearn Highld 163 J11
Hillowton D & G 108 G8
Hillpool Worcs 58 C9
Hillpound Hants 22 G11
Hill Ridware Staffs 71 K11
Hillside Abers 151 N8
Hillside Angus 143 N5
Hillside Devon 7 J6
Hill Side Kirk 90 F7
Hill Side Worcs 46 E2
Hills Town Derbys 84 G7
Hillstreet Hants 22 B11
Hillswick Shet 169 p6
Hill Top Dur 103 J6
Hill Top Hants 14 D6
Hill Top Kirk 90 D8
Hill Top Rothm 84 E2
Hill Top Sandw 58 E6
Hill Top Wakefd 91 J7
Hillwell Shet 169 q12
Hilmarton Wilts 33 K9
Hilperton Wilts 20 G3
Hilperton Marsh Wilts 20 G3
Hilsea C Port 15 J6
Hilston E R Yk 93 N4
Hiltingbury Hants 22 D10
Hilton Border 129 M9
Hilton Cambs 62 C7
Hilton Cumb 102 D6
Hilton Derbys 71 N8
Hilton Dorset 12 C4
Hilton Dur 103 N6
Hilton S on T 104 E8
Hilton Shrops 57 P5
Hilton of Cadboll Highld 156 F3
Hilton Park Services Staffs 58 E4
Himbleton Worcs 46 H3
Himley Staffs 58 C6
Hincaster Cumb 95 L4
Hinchley Wood Surrey 36 E7
Hinckley Leics 59 P6
Hinderclay Suffk 64 E6
Hinderwell N York 105 L7
Hindford Shrops 69 K8
Hindhead Surrey 23 N7
Hindhead Tunnel Surrey 23 N7
Hindle Fold Lancs 89 L4
Hindley Nthumb 112 F9
Hindley Wigan 82 D4
Hindley Green Wigan 82 D4
Hindlip Worcs 46 G3
Hindolveston Norfk 76 E6
Hindon Wilts 20 H8
Hindringham Norfk 76 D4
Hingham Norfk 76 E11
Hinksford Staffs 58 C7
Hinstock Shrops 70 B9
Hintlesham Suffk 53 J3
Hinton Gloucs 32 C4
Hinton Hants 13 M5
Hinton Herefs 45 L7
Hinton Nhants 48 F4

Hinton S Gloss 32 D9
Hinton Shrops 56 G3
Hinton Shrops 57 M8
Hinton Admiral Hants 13 M5
Hinton Ampner Hants 22 H9
Hinton Blewett BaNES 19 Q3
Hinton Charterhouse BaNES 20 E3
Hinton Cross Worcs 47 K6
Hinton-in-the-Hedges
　Nhants 48 G7
Hinton Marsh Hants 22 G9
Hinton Martell Dorset 12 H3
Hinton on the Green Worcs 47 K6
Hinton Parva Swindn 33 P8
Hinton St George Somset 11 J2
Hinton St Mary Dorset 20 E11
Hinton Waldrist Oxon 34 C5
Hints Shrops 57 L10
Hints Staffs 59 J4
Hinwick Bed 61 K8
Hinxhill Kent 26 H3
Hinxton Cambs 62 G11
Hinxworth Herts 50 F2
Hipperholme Calder 90 E5
Hipsburn Nthumb 119 P8
Hipswell N York 103 N11
Hirn Abers 151 J7
Hirnant Powys 68 D10
Hirst Nthumb 113 L3
Hirst Courtney N York 91 Q6
Hirwaen Denbgs 68 F2
Hirwaun Rhondd 30 C3
Hiscott Devon 17 J6
Histon Cambs 62 F8
Hitcham Suffk 64 D11
Hitcham Causeway Suffk 64 D11
Hitcham Street Suffk 64 D11
Hitchin Herts 50 E5
Hither Green Gt Lon 37 J6
Hittisleigh Devon 8 H5
Hive E R Yk 92 D4
Hixon Staffs 71 J9
Hoaden Kent 39 N10
Hoar Cross Staffs 71 L10
Hoarwithy Herefs 45 Q9
Hoath Kent 39 M9
Hoathly Kent 25 Q3
Hobarris Shrops 56 E9
Hobbles Green Suffk 63 M10
Hobbs Cross Essex 51 L11
Hobbs Cross Essex 51 L8
Hobkirk Border 118 A6
Hobland Hall Norfk 77 Q11
Hobsick Notts 84 G11
Hobson Dur 113 J9
Hoby Leics 72 H7
Hoccombe Somset 18 F9
Hockering Norfk 76 F9
Hockerton Notts 85 M9
Hockley Ches E 83 K8
Hockley Covtry 59 L9
Hockley Essex 38 D3
Hockley Staffs 59 K4
Hockley Heath Solhll 59 J10
Hockliffe Beds 49 Q9
Hockwold cum Wilton Norfk 63 M3
Hockworthy Devon 18 D11
Hoddesdon Herts 51 J9
Hoddlesden Bl w D 89 L6
Hoddom Cross D & G 110 C6
Hoddom Mains D & G 110 C6
Hodgehill Ches E 82 H11
Hodgeston Pembks 41 K11
Hodnet Shrops 69 R9
Hodsock Notts 85 K3
Hodsoll Street Kent 37 P8
Hodson Swindn 33 N8
Hodthorpe Derbys 84 H5
Hoe Hants 22 G11
Hoe Norfk 76 D8
Hoe Benham W Berk 34 D11
Hoe Gate Hants 14 H4
Hoff Cumb 102 C7
Hogben's Hill Kent 38 H10
Hoggards Green Suffk 64 B10
Hoggeston Bucks 49 M10
Hoggrill's End Warwks 59 K6
Hog Hill E Susx 26 E8
Hoghton Lancs 89 J5
Hoghton Bottoms Lancs 89 J5
Hognaston Derbys 71 N4
Hogsthorpe Lincs 87 P6
Holbeach Lincs 74 G6
Holbeach Bank Lincs 74 G5
Holbeach Clough Lincs 74 G5
Holbeach Drove Lincs 74 F8
Holbeach Hurn Lincs 74 G5
Holbeach St Johns Lincs 74 G7
Holbeach St Mark's Lincs 74 G4
Holbeach St Matthew Lincs 74 H4
Holbeck Notts 84 H6
Holbeck Woodhouse Notts 84 H6
Holberrow Green Worcs 47 K3
Holbeton Devon 6 G8
Holborn Gt Lon 36 H4
Holbrough Kent 37 Q8
Holbrook Derbys 72 B2
Holbrook Sheff 84 F4
Holbrook Suffk 53 L4
Holbrook Moor Derbys 84 E11
Holbrooks Covtry 59 M8
Holburn Nthumb 119 K3
Holbury Hants 14 D6
Holcombe Devon 7 P4
Holcombe Somset 20 C5
Holcombe Rogus Devon 18 E11
Holcot Nhants 60 G7
Holden Lancs 96 A11
Holdenby Nhants 60 E7
Holden Gate Calder 89 P6
Holder's Green Essex 51 P5
Holdgate Shrops 57 K7
Holdingham Lincs 86 E11
Holditch Dorset 10 G4
Holdsworth Calder 90 D5
Holehouse Derbys 83 M6
Hole-in-the-Wall Herefs 46 B9
Holemoor Devon 16 G10
Hole Street W Susx 24 D8
Holford Somset 18 G6
Holgate C York 98 B10
Holker Cumb 94 H5
Holkham Norfk 76 B3
Hollacombe Devon 16 F11
Holland Fen Lincs 86 H11
Holland Lees Lancs 88 G9

Holland-on-Sea Essex 53 L8
Hollandstoun Ork 169 g1
Hollee D & G 110 C8
Hollesley Suffk 53 Q3
Hollicombe Torbay 7 M6
Hollingbourne Kent 38 D10
Hollingbury Br & H 24 H9
Hollingdon Bucks 49 N9
Hollingrove E Susx 25 Q6
Hollingthorpe Leeds 91 K4
Hollington Derbys 71 N7
Hollington Staffs 71 K7
Hollingworth Tamesd 83 M9
Hollins Bury 89 N9
Hollins Derbys 84 D6
Hollins Staffs 70 H5
Hollinsclough Staffs 83 N11
Hollins End Sheff 84 E4
Hollins Green Warrtn 82 E6
Hollins Lane Lancs 95 K10
Hollinswood Wrekin 57 N3
Hollinwood Shrops 69 P7
Hollocombe Devon 17 L9
Holloway Derbys 84 D9
Holloway Gt Lon 36 H3
Holloway Wilts 20 G8
Hollowell Nhants 60 E6
Hollowmoor Heath Ches W 81 P11
Hollows D & G 110 G5
Hollybush Caerph 30 G4
Hollybush E Ayrs 114 G4
Hollybush Herefs 46 E7
Holly End Norfk 75 J9
Holly Green Worcs 46 G6
Hollyhurst Ches E 69 Q6
Hollym E R Yk 93 P5
Hollywater Hants 23 M8
Hollywood Worcs 58 G9
Holmbridge Kirk 90 E9
Holmbury St Mary Surrey 24 D2
Holmbush Cnwll 3 Q3
Holmcroft Staffs 70 G10
Holme Cambs 61 Q3
Holme Cumb 95 L5
Holme Kirk 90 E9
Holme N Linc 92 F9
Holme N York 97 N4
Holme Notts 85 P9
Holme Chapel Lancs 89 P5
Holme Green N York 91 P2
Holme Hale Norfk 76 B10
Holme Lacy Herefs 45 R7
Holme Marsh Herefs 45 L4
Holme next the Sea Norfk 75 P2
Holme on the Wolds E R Yk 99 K11
Holme Pierrepont Notts 72 G3
Holmer Herefs 45 Q6
Holmer Green Bucks 35 P5
Holme St Cuthbert Cumb 109 P11
Holmes Chapel Ches E 82 G11
Holmesfield Derbys 84 D5
Holmes Hill E Susx 25 M8
Holmeswood Lancs 88 E7
Holmethorpe Surrey 36 G10
Holme upon Spalding
　Moor E R Yk 92 D3
Holmewood Derbys 84 F7
Holmfield Calder 90 D5
Holmfirth Kirk 90 E9
Holmgate Derbys 84 E8
Holmhead E Ayrs 115 L3
Holmpton E R Yk 93 Q6
Holmrook Cumb 100 E11
Holmshurst E Susx 25 P5
Holmside Dur 113 K11
Holmwrangle Cumb 111 K11
Holne Devon 7 J5
Holnest Dorset 11 P3
Holnicote Somset 18 B5
Holsworthy Devon 16 E11
Holsworthy Beacon Devon 16 F10
Holt Dorset 12 H4
Holt Norfk 76 F4
Holt Wilts 20 G2
Holt Worcs 46 F2
Holt Wrexhm 69 M4
Holtby C York 98 D10
Holt End Worcs 58 G11
Holt Fleet Worcs 46 F2
Holt Green Lancs 88 D9
Holt Heath Dorset 13 J4
Holt Heath Worcs 46 F2
Holton Oxon 34 H3
Holton Somset 20 C9
Holton Suffk 65 N6
Holton cum Beckering Lincs 86 F4
Holton Heath Dorset 12 F6
Holton le Clay Lincs 93 N10
Holton le Moor Lincs 93 J11
Holton St Mary Suffk 53 J4
Holt Street Kent 39 N11
Holtye E Susx 25 L3
Holway Flints 80 H9
Holwell Dorset 11 P2
Holwell Herts 50 E4
Holwell Leics 73 J6
Holwell Oxon 33 P3
Holwick Dur 102 H5
Holworth Dorset 12 C8
Holybourne Hants 23 K6
Holy Cross Worcs 58 D9
Holyfield Essex 51 J10
Holyhead IoA 78 C8
Holy Island IoA 78 D8
Holy Island Nthumb 119 M2
Holy Island Nthumb 119 M2
Holymoorside Derbys 84 D7
Holyport W & M 35 N9
Holystone Nthumb 119 J10
Holytown N Lans 126 D5
Holywell C Beds 50 B7
Holywell Cambs 62 D6
Holywell Cnwll 4 B10
Holywell Dorset 11 M4
Holywell Flints 80 H9
Holywell Nthumb 113 M6
Holywell Warwks 59 K11
Holywell Green Calder 90 D7
Holywell Lake Somset 18 F10
Holywell Row Suffk 63 M5
Holywood D & G 109 L4
Homer Shrops 57 L4
Homer Green Sefton 81 L4
Homersfield Suffk 65 K4

Homescales Cumb	95	M3
Hom Green Herefs	46	A10
Homington Wilts	21	M9
Honeyborough Pembks	40	H9
Honeybourne Worcs	47	M6
Honeychurch Devon	8	F4
Honey Hill Kent	39	K9
Honeystreet Wilts	21	M2
Honey Tye Suffk	52	G4
Honiley Warwks	59	K10
Honing Norfk	77	L6
Honingham Norfk	76	G9
Honington Lincs	73	N2
Honington Suffk	64	C7
Honington Warwks	47	Q6
Honiton Devon	10	D4
Honley Kirk	90	E8
Honnington Wrekin	70	C11
Hoo Kent	39	N9
Hoobrook Worcs	58	B10
Hood Green Barns	91	J10
Hood Hill Rothm	91	K11
Hooe C Plym	6	E8
Hooe E Susx	25	Q8
Hoo End Herts	50	E6
Hoo Green Ches E	82	F8
Hoohill Bpool	88	C3
Hook Cambs	62	F2
Hook Devon	10	G3
Hook E R Yk	92	C5
Hook Gt Lon	36	E8
Hook Hants	14	F5
Hook Hants	23	K4
Hook Pembks	41	J8
Hook Wilts	33	L8
Hook-a-Gate Shrops	56	H3
Hook Bank Worcs	46	F6
Hooke Dorset	11	L4
Hook End Essex	51	N10
Hookgate Staffs	70	C7
Hook Green Kent	25	Q3
Hook Green Kent	37	P6
Hook Norton Oxon	48	C8
Hook Street Gloucs	32	C5
Hook Street Wilts	33	L8
Hookway Devon	9	L5
Hookwood Surrey	24	G2
Hooley Surrey	36	G9
Hooley Bridge Rochdl	89	P8
Hoo Meavy Devon	6	E5
Hoo St Werburgh Medway	38	C7
Hooton Ches W	81	M9
Hooton Levitt Rothm	84	H2
Hooton Pagnell Donc	91	M9
Hooton Roberts Rothm	91	M11
Hopcrofts Holt Oxon	48	E9
Hope Derbys	83	Q8
Hope Devon	6	H10
Hope Flints	69	K3
Hope Powys	56	D3
Hope Shrops	56	E4
Hope Staffs	71	L4
Hope Bagot Shrops	57	K10
Hope Bowdler Shrops	56	H6
Hope End Green Essex	51	N6
Hopehouse Border	117	K7
Hopeman Moray	157	L4
Hope Mansell Herefs	46	B11
Hopesay Shrops	56	F8
Hopetown Wakefd	91	K6
Hope under Dinmore Herefs	45	Q4
Hopgrove C York	98	C10
Hopperton N York	97	P9
Hop Pole Lincs	74	C8
Hopsford Warwks	59	P8
Hopstone Shrops	57	P6
Hopton Derbys	71	P4
Hopton Shrops	69	L10
Hopton Staffs	70	G9
Hopton Suffk	64	D6
Hopton Cangeford Shrops	57	J8
Hopton Castle Shrops	56	F9
Hoptonheath Shrops	56	F9
Hopton on Sea Norfk	65	Q2
Hopton Wafers Shrops	57	L9
Hopwas Staffs	59	J4
Hopwood Rochdl	89	P9
Hopwood Worcs	58	F9
Hopwood Park Services Worcs	58	F10
Horam E Susx	25	N7
Horbling Lincs	74	B3
Horbury Wakefd	90	H7
Horcott Gloucs	33	N4
Horden Dur	104	D2
Horderley Shrops	56	G7
Hordle Hants	13	N5
Hordley Shrops	69	L8
Horeb Carmth	28	E3
Horeb Cerdgn	42	G6
Horfield Bristl	31	Q9
Horham Suffk	65	J7
Horkesley Heath Essex	52	G6
Horkstow N Linc	92	G7
Horley Oxon	48	D6
Horley Surrey	24	G2
Hornblotton Green Somset	19	Q8
Hornby Lancs	95	M7
Hornby N York	97	K2
Hornby N York	104	C9
Horncastle Lincs	87	J7
Hornchurch Gt Lon	37	M3
Horncliffe Nthumb	129	N10
Horndean Border	129	N10
Horndean Hants	15	K4
Horndon Devon	8	D8
Horndon on the Hill Thurr	37	Q4
Horne Surrey	24	H2
Horner Somset	18	B5
Horne Row Essex	52	C11
Horners Green Suffk	52	G3
Horney Common E Susx	25	L5
Horn Hill Bucks	36	B2
Horning Norfk	77	L8
Horninghold Leics	73	L11
Horninglow Staffs	71	N9
Horningsea Cambs	62	G8
Horningsham Wilts	20	F6
Horningtoft Norfk	76	C7
Horningtops Cnwll	5	M9
Hornsbury Somset	10	G2
Hornsby Cumb	111	K10
Hornsbygate Cumb	111	K10
Horns Cross Devon	16	F7
Horns Cross E Susx	26	D7
Hornsea E R Yk	99	P11

Hornsey Gt Lon	36	H3
Horn's Green Gt Lon	37	L9
Horn Street Kent	27	L4
Hornton Oxon	48	C5
Horpit Swindn	33	P8
Horrabridge Devon	6	E5
Horringer Suffk	64	A9
Horringford IoW	14	F9
Horrocks Fold Bolton	89	L8
Horrocksford Lancs	89	M2
Horsacott Devon	17	J5
Horsebridge Devon	5	Q6
Horsebridge E Susx	25	N8
Horsebridge Hants	22	B8
Horsebridge Shrops	56	F3
Horsebridge Staffs	70	H4
Horsebrook Staffs	58	C2
Horsecastle N Som	31	M11
Horsedown Cnwll	2	G7
Horsehay Wrekin	57	M3
Horseheath Cambs	63	K11
Horsehouse N York	96	F4
Horsell Surrey	23	Q3
Horseman's Green Wrexhm	69	M6
Horsenden Bucks	35	L4
Horsey Norfk	77	P7
Horsey Somset	19	K7
Horsey Corner Norfk	77	P7
Horsford Norfk	76	H8
Horsforth Leeds	90	G3
Horsham W Susx	24	E4
Horsham Worcs	46	D3
Horsham St Faith Norfk	77	J8
Horsington Lincs	86	G7
Horsington Somset	20	D10
Horsley Derbys	72	B2
Horsley Gloucs	32	F5
Horsley Nthumb	112	G7
Horsley Nthumb	118	F11
Horsley Cross Essex	53	K6
Horsleycross Street Essex	53	K6
Horsley-Gate Derbys	84	D5
Horsleyhill Border	117	Q7
Horsley's Green Bucks	35	L4
Horsley Woodhouse Derbys	72	B2
Horsmonden Kent	26	B3
Horspath Oxon	34	G3
Horstead Norfk	77	K8
Horsted Keynes W Susx	25	J5
Horton Bucks	49	P11
Horton Dorset	12	H3
Horton Lancs	96	C10
Horton Nhants	49	M4
Horton S Glos	32	E8
Horton Shrops	69	N9
Horton Somset	10	G2
Horton Staffs	70	G3
Horton Surrey	36	E8
Horton Swans	28	E7
Horton W & M	36	B5
Horton Wilts	21	K2
Horton Wrekin	57	M2
Horton Cross Somset	19	K11
Horton-cum-Studley Oxon	34	G2
Horton Green Ches W	69	N5
Horton Heath Hants	22	E11
Horton-in-Ribblesdale N York	96	B6
Horton Kirby Kent	37	N7
Horwich Bolton	89	J8
Horwich End Derbys	83	M8
Horwood Devon	17	J6
Hoscar Lancs	88	F8
Hoscote Border	117	M8
Hose Leics	73	J5
Hosey Hill Kent	37	L10
Hosh P & K	133	P3
Hoswick Shet	169	r11
Hotham E R Yk	92	E4
Hothfield Kent	26	G3
Hoton Leics	72	F6
Hott Nthumb	111	Q3
Hough Ches E	70	C4
Hough Ches E	83	J9
Hougham Lincs	73	M2
Hough End Leeds	90	G4
Hough Green Halton	81	P7
Hough-on-the-Hill Lincs	86	B11
Houghton Cambs	62	C6
Houghton Cumb	110	H9
Houghton Hants	22	B8
Houghton Nthumb	112	H7
Houghton Pembks	41	J9
Houghton W Susx	24	B8
Houghton Conquest C Beds	50	B2
Houghton Gate Dur	113	M10
Houghton Green E Susx	26	F7
Houghton Green Warrtn	82	D6
Houghton le Side Darltn	103	P6
Houghton-le-Spring Sundld	113	M11
Houghton on the Hill Leics	72	H10
Houghton Regis C Beds	50	B6
Houghton St Giles Norfk	76	C4
Houlton Warwks	60	C6
Hound Green Hants	23	K3
Houndslow Border	128	G10
Houndsmoor Somset	18	F9
Houndwood Border	129	L7
Hounslow Gt Lon	36	D5
Househill Highld	156	F6
Houses Hill Kirk	90	F7
Housieside Abers	151	M2
Houston Rens	125	L4
Houstry Highld	167	L10
Houton Ork	169	c6
Hove Br & H	24	G10
Hove Edge Calder	90	E6
Hoveringham Notts	85	L11
Hoveton Norfk	77	L8
Hovingham N York	98	D5
Howbrook Barns	91	J11
How Caple Herefs	46	B8
Howden E R Yk	92	B5
Howden-le-Wear Dur	103	N4
Howe IoM	167	P4
Howe IoM	80	a8
Howe N York	97	N4
Howe Norfk	65	K2
Howe Bridge Wigan	82	E4
Howe Green Essex	52	B11
Howegreen Essex	52	D11
How End C Beds	50	B2
Howe of Teuchar Abers	159	J8
Howes D & G	110	C7
Howe Street Essex	51	Q4

Howe Street Essex	51	Q8
Howey Powys	44	F3
Howgate Cumb	100	C6
Howgate Mdloth	127	N6
Howgill Lancs	96	B11
Howick Nthumb	119	Q7
Howle Wrekin	70	B10
Howle Hill Herefs	46	B10
Howlett End Essex	51	N4
Howley Somset	10	F3
How Mill Cumb	111	K9
Howmore W Isls	168	c14
Hownam Border	118	E7
Howrigg Cumb	110	F11
Howsham N Linc	92	H10
Howsham N York	98	E8
Howtel Nthumb	118	G4
Howt Green Kent	38	E8
Howton Herefs	45	N9
Howtown Cumb	101	M7
How Wood Herts	50	D10
Howwood Rens	125	K5
Hoxa Ork	169	d7
Hoxne Suffk	64	H6
Hoy Ork	169	b7
Hoylake Wirral	81	J7
Hoyland Barns	91	K10
Hoyland Common Barns	91	K10
Hoylandswaine Barns	90	H10
Hoyle W Susx	23	P11
Hoyle Mill Barns	91	K9
Hubberholme N York	96	D5
Hubberston Pembks	40	G9
Hubbert's Bridge Lincs	74	E2
Huby N York	97	L11
Huby N York	98	B7
Huccaby Devon	6	H4
Hucclecote Gloucs	46	G11
Hucking Kent	38	D10
Hucknall Notts	84	H11
Huddersfield Kirk	90	E7
Huddington Worcs	46	H3
Hudnall Herts	50	B8
Hudswell N York	103	M10
Huggate E R Yk	98	H9
Hugglescote Leics	72	C8
Hughenden Valley Bucks	35	N5
Hughley Shrops	57	K5
Hugh Town IoS	2	c2
Huish Devon	17	J9
Huish Wilts	21	M2
Huish Champflower Somset	18	E9
Huish Episcopi Somset	19	M9
Hùisinis W Isls	168	e6
Huisinish W Isls	168	e6
Hulcote C Beds	49	P7
Hulcote Nhants	49	K5
Hulcott Bucks	49	N11
Hulham Devon	9	P8
Hulland Derbys	71	N5
Hulland Ward Derbys	71	P5
Hullavington Wilts	32	G8
Hull Bridge E R Yk	93	J2
Hullbridge Essex	38	D2
Hull, Kingston upon C KuH	93	J5
Hulme Manch	82	H5
Hulme Staffs	70	G5
Hulme Warrtn	82	D6
Hulme End Staffs	71	L3
Hulme Walfield Ches E	82	H11
Hulse Heath Ches E	82	F8
Hulton Lane Ends Bolton	89	K9
Hulverstone IoW	14	C10
Hulver Street Norfk	76	C9
Hulver Street Suffk	65	P4
Humber Devon	9	L9
Humber Herefs	45	Q3
Humber Bridge N Linc	92	H6
Humberside Airport N Linc	93	J8
Humberston NE Lin	93	P9
Humberstone C Leic	72	G9
Humberton N York	97	P7
Humbie E Loth	128	D7
Humbleton E R Yk	93	M4
Humbleton Nthumb	119	J5
Humby Lincs	73	Q4
Hume Border	118	D2
Humshaugh Nthumb	112	D6
Huna Highld	167	Q2
Huncoat Lancs	89	M4
Huncote Leics	72	E11
Hundalee Border	118	B7
Hundall Derbys	84	E5
Hunderthwaite Dur	103	J6
Hundleby Lincs	87	L7
Hundle Houses Lincs	86	H10
Hundleton Pembks	41	J10
Hundon Suffk	63	M11
Hundred End Lancs	88	E6
Hundred House Powys	44	G4
Hungarton Leics	72	H9
Hungerford Hants	13	L2
Hungerford Somset	18	D6
Hungerford W Berk	34	B11
Hungerford Newtown W Berk	34	C10
Hunger Hill Bolton	89	K9
Hunger Hill Lancs	88	G8
Hungerstone Herefs	45	N7
Hungerton Lincs	73	M5
Hungryhatton Shrops	70	B9
Hunmanby N York	99	M5
Hunningham Warwks	59	N11
Hunnington Worcs	58	E8
Hunsbury Hill Nhants	60	F9
Hunsdon Herts	51	K8
Hunsdonbury Herts	51	K8
Hunsingore N York	97	P10
Hunslet Leeds	91	J4
Hunsonby Cumb	101	Q3
Hunstanton Norfk	75	N2
Hunstanworth Dur	112	D11
Hunsterson Ches E	70	B5
Hunston Suffk	64	D8
Hunston W Susx	15	N6
Hunstone Green Suffk	64	D8
Hunstrete BaNES	20	B2
Hunsworth Kirk	90	F5
Hunt End Worcs	47	K2
Hunter's Inn Devon	17	M2
Hunter's Quay Ag & B	124	F2
Huntham Somset	19	K9
Hunthill Lodge Angus	142	H3
Huntingdon Cambs	62	B6
Huntingfield Suffk	65	L7
Huntingford Dorset	20	F9

Huntington C York	98	C9
Huntington Ches W	69	M2
Huntington E Loth	128	D5
Huntington Herefs	45	K4
Huntington Herefs	45	P6
Huntington Staffs	58	E2
Huntingtowerfield P & K	134	D2
Huntley Gloucs	46	D11
Huntly Abers	158	D10
Hunton Hants	22	E6
Hunton Kent	26	B2
Hunton N York	97	J2
Hunton Bridge Herts	50	C10
Hunt's Corner Norfk	64	E4
Huntscott Somset	18	B6
Hunt's Cross Lpool	81	N7
Hunts Green Bucks	35	N4
Hunts Green Warwks	59	J5
Huntsham Devon	18	D10
Huntshaw Devon	17	J7
Huntshaw Cross Devon	17	J7
Huntspill Somset	19	K5
Huntstile Somset	19	J8
Huntworth Somset	19	K8
Hunwick Dur	103	N4
Hunworth Norfk	76	F4
Hurcott Somset	19	L11
Hurdcott Wilts	21	N8
Hurdsfield Ches E	83	K10
Hurley W & M	35	M8
Hurley Warwks	59	K5
Hurley Bottom W & M	35	M8
Hurley Common Warwks	59	K5
Hurlford E Ayrs	125	M10
Hurliness Ork	—	—
Hurlston Green Lancs	88	D8
Hurn BCP	13	K5
Hurn's End Lincs	87	M11
Hursley Hants	22	D9
Hurst Dorset	12	C6
Hurst N York	103	K10
Hurst Somset	19	N11
Hurst Wokham	35	L10
Hurstbourne Priors Hants	22	D5
Hurstbourne Tarrant Hants	22	C4
Hurst Green Essex	53	J6
Hurst Green E Susx	26	B6
Hurst Green Lancs	89	K3
Hurst Green Surrey	37	K10
Hurst Hill Dudley	58	D6
Hurstley Herefs	45	M5
Hurstpierpoint W Susx	24	G7
Hurst Wickham W Susx	24	G7
Hurstwood Lancs	89	P4
Hurtiso Ork	169	e6
Hurtmore Surrey	23	P5
Hurworth Burn Dur	104	D4
Hurworth-on-Tees Darltn	104	B8
Hurworth Place Darltn	103	Q9
Hury Dur	103	J7
Husbands Bosworth Leics	60	D4
Husborne Crawley C Beds	49	Q7
Husthwaite N York	97	R6
Hutcherleigh Devon	7	J6
Hut Green N York	91	P6
Huthwaite Notts	84	G9
Huttoft Lincs	87	P5
Hutton Border	129	N9
Hutton Cumb	101	M5
Hutton E R Yk	99	L10
Hutton Essex	37	P2
Hutton Lancs	88	F5
Hutton N Som	19	L3
Hutton Bonville N York	104	B10
Hutton Buscel N York	99	K4
Hutton Conyers N York	97	M6
Hutton Cranswick E R Yk	99	L10
Hutton End Cumb	101	N3
Hutton Hang N York	97	J3
Hutton Henry Dur	104	D3
Hutton-le-Hole N York	98	E2
Hutton Lowcross R & Cl	104	G8
Hutton Magna Dur	103	M8
Hutton Mulgrave N York	105	M9
Hutton Roof Cumb	95	M5
Hutton Roof Cumb	101	L4
Hutton Rudby N York	104	E9
Hutton Sessay N York	97	Q5
Hutton Wandesley N York	97	R10
Huxham Devon	9	M5
Huxham Green Somset	19	Q7
Huxley Ches W	69	P2
Huyton Knows	81	N6
Hycemoor Cumb	94	B3
Hyde Gloucs	32	G4
Hyde Hants	13	L2
Hyde Tamesd	83	K6
Hyde Heath Bucks	35	P4
Hyde Lea Staffs	70	G11
Hydestile Surrey	23	Q6
Hykeham Moor Lincs	86	B7
Hylands Estate Essex	51	Q10
Hyndford Bridge S Lans	116	C2
Hynish Ag & B	136	B8
Hyssington Powys	56	E6
Hystfield Gloucs	32	C5
Hythe Essex	52	H6
Hythe Hants	14	D5
Hythe Kent	27	L5
Hythe Somset	19	M4
Hythe End W & M	36	B6
Hyton Cumb	94	B3

I

Ibberton Dorset	12	C3
Ible Derbys	84	B9
Ibsley Hants	13	L3
Ibstock Leics	72	C9
Ibstone Bucks	35	L6
Ibthorpe Hants	22	C4
Iburndale N York	105	N9
Ibworth Hants	22	G4
Icelton N Som	31	L11
Ichrachan Ag & B	139	J11
Ickburgh Norfk	75	R11
Ickenham Gt Lon	36	C3
Ickford Bucks	34	H3
Ickham Kent	39	M10
Ickleford Herts	50	E4
Icklesham E Susx	26	E8
Ickleton Cambs	51	L2
Icklingham Suffk	63	N6
Ickornshaw N York	90	B2
Ickwell Green C Beds	61	Q11

Icomb Gloucs	47	P10
Idbury Oxon	47	P11
Iddesleigh Devon	17	K10
Ide Devon	9	L6
Ideford Devon	9	L9
Ide Hill Kent	37	L10
Iden E Susx	26	F7
Iden Green Kent	26	B4
Iden Green Kent	26	D5
Idle C Brad	90	F3
Idless Cnwll	3	L4
Idlicote Warwks	47	Q6
Idmiston Wilts	21	N7
Idole Carmth	42	H11
Idridgehay Derbys	71	P5
Idrigill Highld	152	F5
Idstone Oxon	33	Q8
Iffley Oxon	34	F4
Ifield W Susx	24	G3
Ifold W Susx	24	B4
Iford BCP	13	K6
Iford E Susx	25	K9
Ifton Mons	31	N7
Ifton Heath Shrops	69	K7
Ightfield Shrops	69	Q7
Ightham Kent	37	N9
Iken Suffk	65	N10
Ilam Staffs	71	L4
Ilchester Somset	19	P10
Ilderton Nthumb	119	K6
Ilford Gt Lon	37	K3
Ilford Somset	19	L11
Ilfracombe Devon	17	J2
Ilkeston Derbys	72	D2
Ilketshall St Andrew Suffk	65	M4
Ilketshall St John Suffk	65	M4
Ilketshall St Lawrence Suffk	65	M5
Ilketshall St Margaret Suffk	65	L4
Ilkley C Brad	96	H11
Illand Cnwll	5	M6
Illey Dudley	58	E8
Illidge Green Ches E	70	D2
Illingworth Calder	90	D5
Illogan Cnwll	2	H7
Illston on the Hill Leics	73	J11
Ilmer Bucks	35	L3
Ilmington Warwks	47	P6
Ilminster Somset	10	H2
Ilsington Devon	9	J9
Ilsington Dorset	12	C6
Ilston Swans	28	G6
Ilton N York	97	J5
Ilton Somset	19	L11
Imachar N Ayrs	120	G3
Immingham NE Lin	93	L8
Immingham Dock NE Lin	93	L7
Impington Cambs	62	F8
Ince Ches W	81	P9
Ince Blundell Sefton	81	L4
Ince-in-Makerfield Wigan	82	C4
Inchbae Lodge Highld	155	M4
Inchbare Angus	143	L4
Inchberry Moray	157	Q6
Incheril Highld	154	D5
Inchinnan Rens	125	M4
Inchlaggan Highld	146	F7
Inchmichael P & K	134	G2
Inchmore Highld	155	Q8
Inchnadamph Highld	161	M2
Inchture P & K	134	H2
Inchyra P & K	134	F3
Indian Queens Cnwll	4	E10
Ingatestone Essex	51	P11
Ingbirchworth Barns	90	G9
Ingerthorpe N York	97	L9
Ingestre Staffs	70	H10
Ingham Lincs	86	B4
Ingham Norfk	77	M6
Ingham Suffk	64	B7
Ingham Corner Norfk	77	M6
Ingleborough Norfk	75	J7
Ingleby Derbys	72	A5
Ingleby Arncliffe N York	104	D10
Ingleby Barwick S on T	104	D8
Ingleby Cross N York	104	E10
Ingleby Greenhow N York	104	G9
Ingleigh Green Devon	8	F3
Inglesbatch BaNES	20	D2
Inglesham Swindn	33	P5
Ingleston D & G	109	L7
Ingleton Dur	103	N6
Ingleton N York	95	P6
Inglewhite Lancs	88	G3
Ingmanthorpe N York	97	P10
Ingoe Nthumb	112	F6
Ingol Lancs	88	G4
Ingoldisthorpe Norfk	75	N4
Ingoldmells Lincs	87	Q7
Ingoldsby Lincs	73	Q5
Ingram Nthumb	119	K7
Ingrave Essex	37	P2
Ingrow C Brad	90	D3
Ings Cumb	101	M11
Ingst S Glos	31	Q7
Ingthorpe RutInd	73	P9
Ingworth Norfk	76	H6
Inkberrow Worcs	47	K3
Inkerman Dur	103	M3
Inkersall Green Derbys	84	F6
Inkhorn Abers	159	M10
Inkpen W Berk	22	C2
Inkstack Highld	167	N2
Inmarsh Wilts	20	H2
Innellan Ag & B	124	F3
Innerleithen Border	117	K2
Innerleven Fife	135	K7
Innermessan D & G	106	E5
Innerwick E Loth	129	J5
Innesmill Moray	157	P5
Innsworth Gloucs	46	G10
Insch Abers	150	G2
Insh Highld	148	E7
Inshes Highld	156	B9
Inskip Lancs	88	F3
Inskip Moss Side Lancs	88	F3
Instow Devon	16	H5
Insworke Cnwll	6	C8
Intake Sheff	84	E4
Inver Abers	149	N9
Inver Highld	163	K10
Inver P & K	141	P9
Inverailort Highld	145	N11
Inverallligin Highld	153	Q6
Inverallochy Abers	159	P4
Inveran Highld	162	D4
Inveraray Ag & B	131	M6

Inverarish Highld 153 K10
Inverarity Angus 142 H9
Inveraran Stirlg 132 C4
Inverarnie Highld 156 B11
Inverasdale Highld 160 C10
Inverbeg Ag & B 132 C8
Inverbervie Abers 143 Q3
Inverboyndie Abers 158 G5
Invercreran Lodge Ag & B 139 J8
Inverdruie Highld 148 F5
Inveresk E Loth 127 Q3
Inveresragan Ag & B 138 H10
Inverey Abers 149 K10
Inverfarigaig Highld 147 N3
Inverfolla Ag & B 138 H9
Invergarry Highld 147 J7
Invergeldie P & K 133 L2
Invergloy Highld 146 G10
Invergordon Highld 156 C4
Invergowrie P & K 142 E11
Inverguseran Highld 145 M6
Inverhadden P & K 140 G6
Inverie Highld 145 N7
Inverinan Ag & B 131 K4
Inverinate Highld 145 R3
Inverkeilor Angus 143 M8
Inverkeithing Fife 134 E11
Inverkeithny Abers 158 F8
Inverkip Inver 124 G3
Inverkirkaig Highld 160 H3
Inverlael Highld 161 K9
Inverlair Highld 139 Q2
Inverliever Lodge Ag & B 130 H6
Inverlochy Ag & B 131 P2
Invermark Angus 150 C11
Invermoriston Highld 147 L4
Invernaver Highld 166 B4
Inverneill Ag & B 123 P3
Inverness Highld 156 B8
Inverness Airport Highld 156 D7
Invernettie Abers 159 R9
Invernoaden Ag & B 131 N8
Inveroran Hotel Ag & B 139 P9
Inverquharity Angus 142 H6
Inverquhomery Abers 159 P8
Inverroy Highld 146 H11
Inversanda Highld 138 G6
Invershiel Highld 146 A4
Invershin Highld 162 D7
Invershore Highld 167 M9
Inversnaid Hotel Stirlg 132 C6
Inverugie Abers 159 Q8
Inveruglas Ag & B 132 C6
Inveruglass Highld 148 E7
Inverurie Abers 151 K3
Inwardleigh Devon 8 E5
Inworth Essex 52 E8
Iochdar W Isls 168 c13
Iona Ag & B 136 H10
Iping W Susx 23 N10
iPort Logistics Park Donc 91 Q11
Ipplepen Devon 7 L5
Ipsden Oxon 34 H7
Ipstones Staffs 71 J5
Ipswich Suffk 53 L3
Irby Wirral 81 K8
Irby in the Marsh Lincs 87 N8
Irby upon Humber NE Lin 93 L10
Irchester Nhants 61 K7
Ireby Cumb 100 H3
Ireby Lancs 95 P2
Ireland C Beds 50 D2
Ireleth Cumb 94 E5
Ireshopeburn Dur 102 G3
Ireton Wood Derbys 71 P5
Irlam Salfd 82 F6
Irnham Lincs 73 Q5
Iron Acton S Glos 32 C8
Iron Bridge Cambs 75 J11
Ironbridge Wrekin 57 M4
Ironbridge Gorge Wrekin 57 M4
Iron Cross Warwks 47 L4
Ironmacannie D & G 108 E5
Irons Bottom Surrey 36 F11
Ironville Derbys 84 F10
Irstead Norfk 77 M7
Irthington Cumb 111 J8
Irthlingborough Nhants 61 K6
Irton N York 99 L4
Irvine N Ayrs 125 L4
Isauld Highld 166 G3
Isbister Shet 169 q4
Isbister Shet 169 s7
Isfield E Susx 25 K7
Isham Nhants 61 J6
Isington Hants 23 L4
Islandpool Worcs 58 C8
Islay Ag & B 122 B8
Islay Airport Ag & B 122 D9
Isle Abbotts Somset 19 L10
Isle Brewers Somset 19 L10
Isleham Cambs 63 K6
Isle of Dogs Gt Lon 37 J5
Isle of Grain Medway 38 E6
Isle of Lewis W Isls 168 i4
Isle of Man IoM 80 e4
Isle of Man Ronaldsway Airport IoM 80 c8
Isle of Mull Ag & B 137 Q8
Isle of Purbeck Dorset 12 H8
Isle of Sheppey Kent 38 G8
Isle of Skye Highld 152 G10
Isle of Thanet Kent 39 P8
Isle of Walney Cumb 94 D7
Isle of Whithorn D & G 107 N10
Isle of Wight IoW 14 F9
Isleornsay Highld 145 M5
Isles of Scilly IoS 2 c2
Isles of Scilly St Mary's Airport IoS 2 c2
Islesteps D & G 109 L6
Islet Village Guern 10 c1
Isleworth Gt Lon 36 E5
Isley Walton Leics 72 C6
Islibhig W Isls 168 f5
Islington Gt Lon 36 H4
Islip Nhants 61 L5
Islip Oxon 34 F2
Islivig W Isls 168 f5
Isombridge Wrekin 57 L2
Istead Rise Kent 37 P6
Itchen Abbas Hants 22 F8
Itchen Stoke Hants 22 G8
Itchingfield W Susx 24 D5
Itchington S Glos 32 C7
Itteringham Norfk 76 G5

Itton Devon 8 G5
Itton Mons 31 N5
Itton Common Mons 31 N5
Ivegill Cumb 101 M2
Ivelet N York 102 H11
Iver Bucks 36 B4
Iver Heath Bucks 36 B4
Iveston Dur 112 H10
Ivinghoe Bucks 49 P11
Ivinghoe Aston Bucks 49 Q11
Ivington Herefs 45 P3
Ivington Green Herefs 45 P3
Ivybridge Devon 6 G7
Ivychurch Kent 26 H6
Ivy Cross Dorset 20 G10
Ivy Hatch Kent 37 N10
Ivy Todd Norfk 76 B10
Iwade Kent 38 F8
Iwerne Courtney Dorset 12 E2
Iwerne Minster Dorset 12 E2
Ixworth Suffk 64 C7
Ixworth Thorpe Suffk 64 C7

J

Jack Green Lancs 88 H5
Jack Hill N York 97 J10
Jack-in-the-Green Devon 9 P5
Jack's Bush Hants 21 Q7
Jacksdale Notts 84 F10
Jackson Bridge Kirk 90 F9
Jackton S Lans 125 P7
Jacobstow Cnwll 5 K2
Jacobstowe Devon 8 E4
Jacobs Well Surrey 23 Q4
Jameston Pembks 41 L11
Jamestown Highld 155 N6
Jamestown W Duns 132 D11
Janetstown Highld 167 L10
Jardine D & G 109 P3
Jarrow S Tyne 113 M8
Jarvis Brook E Susx 25 M5
Jasper's Green Essex 52 B6
Jawcraig Falk 126 E2
Jaywick Essex 53 L9
Jealott's Hill Br For 35 N10
Jeater Houses N York 97 P2
Jedburgh Border 118 B6
Jeffreyston Pembks 41 L9
Jemimaville Highld 156 C4
Jerbourg Guern 10 c2
Jersey Jersey 11 b1
Jersey Airport Jersey 11 a2
Jersey Marine Neath 29 K6
Jerusalem Lincs 86 B6
Jesmond N u Ty 113 L7
Jevington E Susx 25 N10
Jingle Street Mons 31 N2
Jockey End Herts 50 B8
Jodrell Bank Ches E 82 G10
Jodrell Bank Ches E 82 G10
Johnby Cumb 101 M4
John Lennon Airport Lpool 81 N8
John o' Groats Highld 167 Q2
Johns Cross E Susx 26 B7
Johnshaven Abers 143 P4
Johnston Pembks 40 H8
Johnstone D & G 117 J10
Johnstone Rens 125 L5
Johnstonebridge D & G 109 P2
Johnstown Carmth 42 G11
Johnstown Wrexhm 69 K5
Joppa C Edin 127 Q3
Joppa Cerdgn 54 D11
Joppa S Ayrs 114 H4
Jordans Bucks 35 Q6
Jordanston Pembks 40 H4
Jordanthorpe Sheff 84 E4
Joyden's Wood Kent 37 M6
Jubilee Corner Kent 26 D2
Jump Barns 91 K10
Jumper's Town E Susx 25 L4
Juniper Nthumb 112 D9
Juniper Green C Edin 127 M4
Jura Ag & B 122 H3
Jurassic Coast Devon 10 G7
Jurby IoM 80 e2
Jurston Devon 8 G8

K

Kaber Cumb 102 E8
Kaimend S Lans 126 H8
Kames Ag & B 124 B3
Kames E Ayrs 115 N2
Kea Cnwll 3 L5
Keadby N Linc 92 D8
Keal Cotes Lincs 87 L8
Kearby Town End N York 97 M11
Kearsley Bolton 82 G4
Kearsley Nthumb 112 F5
Kearsney Kent 27 N3
Kearstwick Cumb 95 N5
Kearton N York 103 J11
Keasden N York 95 Q7
Keaton Devon 6 G8
Keckwick Halton 82 D7
Keddington Lincs 87 K3
Keddington Corner Lincs 87 L3
Kedington Suffk 63 M11
Kedleston Derbys 71 Q6
Keelby Lincs 93 L8
Keele Staffs 70 E5
Keele Services Staffs 70 E6
Keele University Staffs 70 E5
Keeley Green Bed 61 M11
Keelham C Brad 90 D4
Keeres Green Essex 51 N8
Keeston Pembks 40 H7
Keevil Wilts 20 H3
Kegworth Leics 72 D5
Kehelland Cnwll 2 G5
Keig Abers 150 G4
Keighley C Brad 90 D2
Keilarsbrae Clacks 133 P9
Keillour P & K 134 B2
Keiloch Abers 149 M9
Keils Ag & B 122 H6
Keinton Mandeville Somset 19 P8
Keir Mill D & G 109 J2
Keirsleywell Row Nthumb 111 Q10

Keisby Lincs 73 Q5
Keisley Cumb 102 D6
Keiss Highld 167 P4
Keith Moray 158 B7
Keithick P & K 142 C10
Keithock Angus 143 L5
Keithtown Highld 155 P6
Kelbrook Lancs 89 Q3
Kelby Lincs 73 Q2
Keld N York 102 G10
Keld Cumb 101 Q8
Keld Head N York 98 F4
Keldholme N York 98 E3
Kelfield N Linc 92 D10
Kelfield N York 91 Q4
Kelham Notts 85 N9
Kellacott Devon 5 Q4
Kellamergh Lancs 88 E5
Kellas Angus 142 H10
Kellas Moray 157 M7
Kellaton Devon 7 L11
Kelleth Cumb 102 C9
Kelling Norfk 76 F3
Kellingley N York 91 N6
Kellington N York 91 P6
Kelloe Dur 104 B3
Kelloholm D & G 115 P5
Kells Cumb 100 C7
Kelly Devon 5 P5
Kelly Bray Cnwll 5 P7
Kelmarsh Nhants 60 F5
Kelmscott Oxon 33 P5
Kelsale Suffk 65 M8
Kelsall Ches W 81 Q11
Kelshall Herts 50 H4
Kelsick Cumb 110 C10
Kelso Border 118 D4
Kelstedge Derbys 84 D8
Kelstern Lincs 86 H3
Kelsterton Flints 81 K10
Kelston BaNES 32 D11
Keltneyburn P & K 141 J8
Kelton D & G 109 L6
Kelty Fife 134 E9
Kelvedon Essex 52 E8
Kelvedon Hatch Essex 51 N11
Kelynack Cnwll 2 B8
Kemacott Devon 17 M2
Kemback Fife 135 L5
Kemberton Shrops 57 N4
Kemble Gloucs 33 J5
Kemble Wick Gloucs 33 J5
Kemerton Worcs 47 J7
Kemeys Commander Mons 31 K4
Kemnay Abers 151 J4
Kempe's Corner Kent 26 H2
Kempley Gloucs 46 C9
Kempley Green Gloucs 46 C9
Kemps Green Warwks 58 H10
Kempsey Worcs 46 F5
Kempsford Gloucs 33 N5
Kempshott Hants 22 H4
Kempston Bed 61 M11
Kempston Hardwick Bed 50 B2
Kempton Shrops 56 F7
Kemp Town Br & H 24 H10
Kemsing Kent 37 N9
Kemsley Kent 38 F8
Kemsley Street Kent 38 D9
Kenardington Kent 26 G5
Kenchester Herefs 45 N6
Kencot Oxon 33 Q4
Kendal Cumb 95 L2
Kenderchurch Herefs 45 N9
Kendleshire S Glos 32 C9
Kenfig Brdgnd 29 M8
Kenfig Hill Brdgnd 29 M8
Kenilworth Warwks 59 L10
Kenley Gt Lon 36 H8
Kenley Shrops 57 K4
Kenmore Highld 153 P6
Kenmore P & K 141 J8
Kenn Devon 9 M7
Kenn N Som 31 M11
Kennacraig Ag & B 123 P7
Kennall Vale Cnwll 3 J6
Kennards House Cnwll 5 M5
Kenneggy Cnwll 2 F8
Kennerleigh Devon 9 K3
Kennet Clacks 133 Q9
Kennethmont Abers 150 E2
Kennett Cambs 63 L7
Kennford Devon 9 M7
Kenninghall Norfk 64 E4
Kennington Kent 26 H2
Kennington Oxon 34 F4
Kennington Lees Kent 26 H2
Kennoway Fife 135 K7
Kenny Somset 19 K11
Kenny Hill Suffk 63 L5
Kennythorpe N York 98 F7
Kenovay Ag & B 136 B6
Kensaleyre Highld 152 G7
Kensington Gt Lon 36 G5
Kensington Palace Gt Lon 36 G4
Kensworth C Beds 50 B7
Kensworth Common C Beds 50 B7
Kentallen Highld 139 J6
Kentchurch Herefs 45 N9
Kentford Suffk 63 M7
Kent Green Ches E 70 E3
Kentisbeare Devon 9 Q3
Kentisbury Devon 17 L3
Kentisbury Ford Devon 17 L3
Kentish Town Gt Lon 36 G4
Kentmere Cumb 101 N10
Kenton Devon 9 N8
Kenton Gt Lon 36 E3
Kenton N u Ty 113 K7
Kenton Suffk 64 H8
Kenton Bankfoot N u Ty 113 K7
Kentra Highld 138 B4
Kents Bank Cumb 94 H5
Kentsboro Hants 22 B7
Kent's Green Gloucs 46 D10
Kent's Oak Hants 22 B10
Kent Street E Susx 26 C8
Kent Street Kent 37 Q10
Kenwick Shrops 69 M8
Kenwyn Cnwll 3 L4
Kenyon Warrtn 82 D5
Keoldale Highld 165 J3
Keppoch Highld 145 Q3
Kepwick N York 97 Q2
Keresley Covtry 59 M8

Kermincham Ches E 82 H11
Kernborough Devon 7 K10
Kerne Bridge Herefs 46 A11
Kerrera Ag & B 130 G2
Kerridge Ches E 83 K9
Kerridge-end Ches E 83 K9
Kerris Cnwll 2 C8
Kerry Powys 55 Q6
Kerrycroy Ag & B 124 E5
Kersall Notts 85 M8
Kersbrook Devon 9 Q8
Kerscott Devon 17 L6
Kersey Suffk 52 H3
Kersey Tye Suffk 52 G3
Kersey Upland Suffk 52 G3
Kershader W Isls 168 i6
Kershopefoot Cumb 111 J4
Kersoe Worcs 47 J6
Kerswell Devon 10 B3
Kerswell Green Worcs 46 G5
Kerthen Wood Cnwll 2 F7
Kesgrave Suffk 53 M2
Kessingland Suffk 65 Q4
Kessingland Beach Suffk 65 Q4
Kestle Cnwll 3 P4
Kestle Mill Cnwll 3 C10
Keston Gt Lon 37 K8
Keswick Cumb 101 J6
Keswick Norfk 77 J11
Ketsby Lincs 87 L5
Kettering Nhants 61 J5
Ketteringham Norfk 76 H11
Kettins P & K 142 C10
Kettlebaston Suffk 64 D11
Kettlebridge Fife 135 J6
Kettlebrook Staffs 59 K4
Kettleburgh Suffk 65 K9
Kettle Green Herts 51 K7
Kettleholm D & G 109 P5
Kettleness N York 105 M7
Kettleshulme Ches E 83 L9
Kettlesing N York 97 K9
Kettlesing Bottom N York 97 K9
Kettlestone Norfk 76 D5
Kettlethorpe Lincs 85 P5
Kettletoft Ork 169 f3
Kettlewell N York 96 E6
Ketton Rutlnd 73 P10
Kew Gt Lon 36 E5
Kew Royal Botanic Gardens Gt Lon 36 E5
Kewstoke N Som 19 K2
Kexbrough Barns 91 J9
Kexby C York 98 E10
Kexby Lincs 85 Q3
Key Green Ches E 70 F2
Key Green N York 105 M10
Keyham Leics 72 H9
Keyhaven Hants 13 P6
Keyingham E R Yk 93 M5
Keymer W Susx 24 H7
Keynsham BaNES 32 C11
Keysoe Bed 61 N8
Keysoe Row Bed 61 N8
Keyston Cambs 61 M5
Key Street Kent 38 E9
Keyworth Notts 72 G4
Kibbear Somset 18 H10
Kibblesworth Gatesd 113 K9
Kibworth Beauchamp Leics 60 E2
Kibworth Harcourt Leics 60 E2
Kidbrooke Gt Lon 37 K5
Kidburngill Cumb 100 C6
Kiddemore Green Staffs 58 C3
Kidderminster Worcs 58 B9
Kiddington Oxon 48 D10
Kidd's Moor Norfk 76 G11
Kidlington Oxon 34 E2
Kidmore End Oxon 35 J9
Kidsdale D & G 107 M10
Kidsgrove Staffs 70 E4
Kidstones N York 96 E4
Kidwelly Carmth 28 D3
Kiel Crofts Ag & B 138 G10
Kielder Nthumb 111 M2
Kielder Forest Nthumb 111 M3
Kiells Ag & B 122 F6
Kilbarchan Rens 125 L5
Kilbeg Highld 145 L6
Kilberry Ag & B 123 M7
Kilbirnie N Ayrs 125 J7
Kilbride Ag & B 123 M4
Kilbride Ag & B 124 C4
Kilbuiack Moray 157 K5
Kilburn Derbys 84 E11
Kilburn Gt Lon 36 F4
Kilburn N York 97 R5
Kilby Leics 72 G11
Kilchamaig Ag & B 123 P7
Kilchattan Ag & B 124 E7
Kilchattan Ag & B 136 b2
Kilcheran Ag & B 138 E10
Kilchoan Highld 137 M3
Kilchoman Ag & B 122 B7
Kilchrenan Ag & B 131 L3
Kilconquhar Fife 135 M7
Kilcot Gloucs 46 C9
Kilcoy Highld 155 Q7
Kilcreggan Ag & B 131 Q11
Kildale N York 104 H9
Kildalloig Ag & B 120 E8
Kildary Highld 156 D3
Kildavaig Ag & B 124 B4
Kildavanan Ag & B 124 C4
Kildonan Highld 163 L2
Kildonan N Ayrs 121 K7
Kildonan Lodge Highld 163 L2
Kildonnan Highld 144 G10
Kildrochet House D & G 106 E6
Kildrummy Abers 150 D4
Kildwick N York 96 F11
Kilfinan Ag & B 124 A2
Kilfinnan Highld 146 G9
Kilford Denbgs 80 F11
Kilgetty Pembks 41 M9
Kilgrammie S Ayrs 114 E4
Kilgwrrwg Common Mons 31 N5
Kilham E R Yk 99 M8
Kilham Nthumb 118 G3
Kilkenneth Ag & B 136 A7
Kilkenzie Ag & B 120 C7
Kilkerran Ag & B 120 D8
Kilkhampton Cnwll 16 D9
Killamarsh Derbys 84 G4
Killay Swans 28 H6
Killean Ag & B 123 L8
Killearn Stirlg 132 G10

Killen Highld 156 B6
Killerby Darltn 103 N7
Killerton Devon 9 N4
Killichonan P & K 140 D6
Killiechonate Highld 146 G11
Killiechronan Ag & B 137 N7
Killiecrankie P & K 141 M5
Killilan Highld 154 B11
Killimster Highld 167 P5
Killin Stirlg 140 E11
Killinghall N York 97 L9
Killington Cumb 95 N3
Killingworth N Tyne 113 L6
Killington Lake Services Cumb 95 M2
Killiow Cnwll 3 L5
Killochyett Border 128 D10
Kilmacolm Inver 125 K3
Kilmahog Stirlg 133 J6
Kilmahumaig Ag & B 130 F9
Kilmaluag Highld 152 G3
Kilmany Fife 135 K3
Kilmarnock E Ayrs 125 L10
Kilmartin Ag & B 130 G8
Kilmaurs E Ayrs 125 L9
Kilmelford Ag & B 130 H5
Kilmeston Hants 22 G9
Kilmichael Ag & B 120 C7
Kilmichael Glassary Ag & B 130 H9
Kilmichael of Inverlussa Ag & B 130 F10
Kilmington Devon 10 F5
Kilmington Wilts 20 E7
Kilmington Common Wilts 20 E7
Kilmington Street Wilts 20 E7
Kilmorack Highld 155 N9
Kilmore Ag & B 130 H2
Kilmore Highld 145 L6
Kilmory Ag & B 123 M5
Kilmory Highld 137 N2
Kilmory N Ayrs 121 J7
Kilmuir Highld 152 D8
Kilmuir Highld 152 F3
Kilmuir Highld 156 B8
Kilmuir Highld 156 D3
Kilmun Ag & B 131 P11
Kilnave Ag & B 122 C5
Kilncadzow S Lans 126 F8
Kilndown Kent 26 B4
Kiln Green Wokham 35 M9
Kilnhill Cumb 100 H4
Kilnhurst Rothm 91 M11
Kilninver Ag & B 130 G3
Kiln Pit Hill Nthumb 112 F9
Kilnsea E R Yk 93 R7
Kilnsey N York 96 E7
Kilnwick E R Yk 99 K11
Kilnwick Percy E R Yk 98 G10
Kilnwood Vale W Susx 24 F4
Kiloran Ag & B 136 b2
Kilpatrick N Ayrs 120 H6
Kilpeck Herefs 45 N8
Kilpin E R Yk 92 C5
Kilpin Pike E R Yk 92 C5
Kilrenny Fife 135 P7
Kilsby Nhants 60 C6
Kilspindie P & K 134 G2
Kilstay D & G 106 F10
Kilsyth N Lans 126 C2
Kiltarlity Highld 155 P9
Kilton R & Cl 105 K7
Kilton Somset 18 G6
Kilton Thorpe R & Cl 105 J7
Kilvaxter Highld 152 F4
Kilve Somset 18 F6
Kilvington Notts 73 L2
Kilwinning N Ayrs 125 J9
Kimberley Norfk 76 F11
Kimberley Notts 72 D2
Kimberworth Rothm 84 F2
Kimblesworth Dur 113 L11
Kimble Wick Bucks 35 M3
Kimbolton Cambs 61 P7
Kimbolton Herefs 45 Q2
Kimcote Leics 60 C3
Kimmeridge Dorset 12 F9
Kimmerston Nthumb 119 J3
Kimpton Hants 21 Q5
Kimpton Herts 50 E7
Kimworthy Devon 16 E9
Kinbrace Highld 166 E10
Kinbuck Stirlg 133 M6
Kincaple Fife 135 M4
Kincardine Fife 133 Q10
Kincardine Highld 162 E9
Kincardine Bridge Fife 133 Q10
Kincardine O'Neil Abers 150 F8
Kinclaven P & K 142 B10
Kincorth C Aber 151 N7
Kincorth House Moray 157 J5
Kincraig Highld 148 E6
Kincraigie P & K 141 N8
Kindallachan P & K 141 N8
Kineraarach Ag & B 123 L9
Kineton Gloucs 47 L9
Kineton Warwks 48 B4
Kinfauns P & K 134 F2
Kingarth Ag & B 124 D6
Kingcausie Abers 151 M8
Kingcoed Mons 31 M3
Kingerby Lincs 86 E2
Kingford Devon 16 D10
Kingham Oxon 47 Q10
Kingholm Quay D & G 109 L6
Kinghorn Fife 134 H10
Kinglassie Fife 134 G8
Kingoodie P & K 135 J2
King's Acre Herefs 45 P6
Kingsand Cnwll 6 C6
Kingsash Bucks 35 N3
Kingsbarns Fife 135 P5
Kingsborough Kent 38 G7
Kingsbridge Devon 7 J10
Kingsbridge Somset 18 C7
Kingsbridge Swans 28 G5
King's Bromley Staffs 71 L11
Kingsbrook Bucks 35 M2
Kingsburgh Highld 152 F6
Kingsbury Gt Lon 36 F3
Kingsbury Warwks 59 K5
Kingsbury Episcopi Somset 19 M10
King's Caple Herefs 45 N4
Kingsclere Hants 22 F3
King's Cliffe Nhants 73 Q11

Kings Clipstone Notts...85 K8
Kingscote Gloucs...32 F5
Kingscott Devon...17 J8
King's Coughton Warwks...47 L3
Kingscross N Ayrs...121 K6
Kingsdon Somset...19 P9
Kingsdown Kent...27 Q2
Kingsdown Swindn...33 N7
Kingsdown Wilts...32 F11
Kingseat Abers...151 N4
Kingseat Fife...134 E9
Kingsey Bucks...35 K3
Kingsfold W Susx...24 E3
Kingsford C Aber...151 M6
Kingsford E Ayrs...125 L8
Kingsford Worcs...57 Q8
Kingsgate Kent...39 Q7
Kings Green Gloucs...46 E8
Kingshall Street Suffk...64 C9
Kingsheanton Devon...17 K4
King's Heath Birm...58 G8
King's Hill Kent...37 Q9
King's Hill Wsall...58 E5
Kings House Hotel Highld...139 P7
Kingshurst Solhll...59 J7
Kingside Hill Cumb...110 C10
Kingskerswell Devon...7 M5
Kingskettle Fife...135 J6
Kingsland Dorset...11 K5
Kingsland Herefs...45 N2
Kingsland IoA...78 D8
Kings Langley Herts...50 C10
Kingsley Ches W...82 C10
Kingsley Hants...23 L7
Kingsley Staffs...71 J5
Kingsley Green W Susx...23 N8
Kingsley Holt Staffs...71 J5
Kingsley Park Nhants...60 G8
Kingslow Shrops...57 P5
King's Lynn Norfk...75 M6
Kings Meaburn Cumb...102 B6
Kingsmead Hants...14 G4
King's Mills Guern...10 b2
King's Moss St Hel...81 Q4
Kingsmuir Angus...142 H8
Kings Muir Border...117 K3
Kingsmuir Fife...135 N6
Kings Newnham Warwks...59 Q9
King's Newton Derbys...72 B5
Kingsnorth Kent...26 H4
King's Norton Birm...58 G9
King's Norton Leics...72 H10
Kings Nympton Devon...17 M8
King's Pyon Herefs...45 N4
Kings Ripton Cambs...62 C5
King's Somborne Hants...22 C8
King's Stag Dorset...11 Q2
King's Stanley Gloucs...32 F4
King's Sutton Nhants...48 E7
Kingstanding Birm...58 G6
Kingsteignton Devon...7 M4
Kingsthorne Herefs...45 P8
Kingsthorpe Nhants...60 G8
Kingston Cambs...62 D9
Kingston Cnwll...5 P6
Kingston Devon...6 G9
Kingston Devon...9 J2
Kingston Dorset...12 C3
Kingston Dorset...12 G9
Kingston E Loth...128 E3
Kingston Hants...13 L4
Kingston IoW...14 E10
Kingston Kent...39 L11
Kingston W Susx...24 C10
Kingston Bagpuize Oxon...34 D5
Kingston Blount Oxon...35 K5
Kingston by Sea W Susx...24 F9
Kingston Deverill Wilts...20 F7
Kingstone Herefs...45 N7
Kingstone Somset...10 H2
Kingstone Staffs...71 K9
Kingstone Winslow Oxon...33 Q7
Kingston Lacy Dorset...12
Kingston Lisle Oxon...34 B7
Kingston near Lewes E Susx...25 J9
Kingston on Soar Notts...72 E5
Kingston on Spey Moray...157 Q4
Kingston Russell Dorset...11 M5
Kingston St Mary Somset...18 H9
Kingston Seymour N Som...31 M11
Kingston Stert Oxon...35 K4
Kingston upon Hull C KuH...93 J5
Kingston upon Thames Gt Lon...36 E7
Kingston Cumb...110 G9
King's Walden Herts...50 E6
Kingswear Devon...7 M8
Kingswells C Aber...151 M6
Kingswinford Dudley...58 C7
Kingswood Bucks...49 J11
Kingswood C KuH...93 J4
Kingswood Gloucs...32 D6
Kingswood Kent...38 D11
Kingswood Powys...56 C4
Kingswood S Glos...32 B10
Kingswood Somset...18 F7
Kingswood Surrey...36 F9
Kingswood Warwks...59 J10
Kingswood Brook Warwks...59 J10
Kingswood Common Herefs...45 K4
Kingswood Common Staffs...58 B4
Kings Worthy Hants...22 E8
Kingthorpe Lincs...86 F5
Kington Herefs...45 K3
Kington S Glos...32 B6
Kington Worcs...47 J3
Kington Langley Wilts...32 H9
Kington Magna Dorset...20 E10
Kington St Michael Wilts...32 H9
Kingussie Highld...148 D7
Kingweston Somset...19 P8
Kinharrachie Abers...159 M11
Kinharvie D & G...109 K7
Kinkell Bridge P & K...133 Q4
Kinknockie Abers...159 P9
Kinleith C Edin...127 M4
Kinlet Shrops...57 N8
Kinloch Highld...144 F8
Kinloch Highld...164 H10
Kinloch Highld...165 N6
Kinloch P & K...142 A9
Kinlochard Stirlg...132 F7
Kinlochbervie Highld...164 F5

Kinlocheil Highld...138 H2
Kinlochewe Highld...154 D5
Kinloch Hourn Highld...146 B6
Kinlochlaggan Highld...147 N10
Kinlochleven Highld...139 M5
Kinlochmoidart Highld...138 C3
Kinlochnanuagh Highld...145 M11
Kinloch Rannoch P & K...140 G6
Kinloss Moray...157 K5
Kinmel Bay Conwy...80 D8
Kinmuck Abers...151 L4
Kinmundy Abers...151 M4
Kinnabus Ag & B...122 C11
Kinnadie Abers...159 N9
Kinnaird P & K...141 N6
Kinneff Abers...143 Q2
Kinnelhead D & G...116 E10
Kinnell Angus...143 L7
Kinnerley Shrops...69 K10
Kinnersley Herefs...45 L5
Kinnersley Worcs...46 G6
Kinnerton Powys...45 J2
Kinnerton Shrops...56 F5
Kinnerton Green Flints...69 K2
Kinnesswood P & K...134 F7
Kinninvie Dur...103 L6
Kinnordy Angus...142 F6
Kinoulton Notts...72 H4
Kinross P & K...134 E7
Kinrossie P & K...142 B11
Kinross Services P & K...134 E7
Kinsbourne Green Herts...50 D7
Kinsey Heath Ches E...70 B6
Kinsham Herefs...56 F11
Kinsham Worcs...46 H7
Kinsley Wakefd...91 L8
Kinson BCP...13 J5
Kintail Highld...146 B4
Kintbury W Berk...34 C11
Kintessack Moray...157 J5
Kintillo P & K...134 E4
Kinton Herefs...56 G10
Kinton Shrops...69 L11
Kintore Abers...151 K4
Kintour Ag & B...122 G9
Kintra Ag & B...122 D10
Kintra Ag & B...137 J10
Kintraw Ag & B...130 G7
Kintyre Ag & B...120 D4
Kinveachy Highld...148 G4
Kinver Staffs...58 B8
Kiplin N York...103 Q11
Kippax Leeds...91 L4
Kippen Stirlg...133 J9
Kippford D & G...108 H10
Kipping's Cross Kent...25 P2
Kirbister Ork...169 c6
Kirby Bedon Norfk...77 K10
Kirby Bellars Leics...73 J7
Kirby Cane Norfk...65 M3
Kirby Corner Covtry...59 L9
Kirby Cross Essex...53 M7
Kirby Fields Leics...72 E10
Kirby Green Norfk...65 M3
Kirby Grindalythe N York...99 J7
Kirby Hill N York...97 N7
Kirby Hill N York...103 M9
Kirby Knowle N York...97 Q3
Kirby-le-Soken Essex...53 M7
Kirby Misperton N York...98 F5
Kirby Muxloe Leics...72 E10
Kirby Sigston N York...97 P2
Kirby Underdale E R Yk...98 G9
Kirby Wiske N York...97 N4
Kirdford W Susx...24 B5
Kirk Highld...167 N5
Kirkabister Shet...169 r10
Kirkandrews D & G...108 D11
Kirkandrews upon Eden Cumb...110 G9
Kirkbampton Cumb...110 F9
Kirkbean D & G...109 L9
Kirk Bramwith Donc...91 Q8
Kirkbride Cumb...110 D9
Kirkbuddo Angus...143 J9
Kirkburn Border...117 K3
Kirkburn E R Yk...99 K9
Kirkburton Kirk...90 F8
Kirkby Knows...81 N5
Kirkby Lincs...86 E2
Kirkby N York...104 F9
Kirkby Fleetham N York...97 L2
Kirkby Green Lincs...86 E9
Kirkby-in-Ashfield Notts...84 H9
Kirkby-in-Furness Cumb...94 E4
Kirkby la Thorpe Lincs...86 E11
Kirkby Lonsdale Cumb...95 N5
Kirkby Malham N York...96 C8
Kirkby Mallory Leics...72 D10
Kirkby Malzeard N York...97 K6
Kirkby Mills N York...98 E3
Kirkbymoorside N York...98 D3
Kirkby on Bain Lincs...86 H8
Kirkby Overblow N York...97 M11
Kirkby Stephen Cumb...102 E8
Kirkby Thore Cumb...102 B5
Kirkby Underwood Lincs...73 R5
Kirkby Wharf N York...91 N2
Kirkby Woodhouse Notts...84 G10
Kirkcaldy Fife...134 H9
Kirkcambeck Cumb...111 K7
Kirkchrist D & G...108 E10
Kirkcolm D & G...106 C4
Kirkconnel D & G...115 P5
Kirkconnell D & G...109 L7
Kirkcowan D & G...107 K5
Kirkcudbright D & G...108 E10
Kirkdale Lpool...81 L6
Kirk Deighton N York...97 N10
Kirk Ella E R Yk...92 H5
Kirkfieldbank S Lans...116 B2
Kirkgunzeon D & G...109 J7
Kirk Hallam Derbys...72 D2
Kirkham Lancs...88 E4
Kirkham N York...98 E7
Kirkhamgate Wakefd...90 H6
Kirk Hammerton N York...97 Q9
Kirkharle Nthumb...112 F4
Kirkhaugh Nthumb...111 N11
Kirkheaton Kirk...90 F7
Kirkheaton Nthumb...112 F5
Kirkhill Highld...155 Q7
Kirkhope S Lans...116 D9
Kirkhouse Cumb...111 L9
Kirkhouse Green Donc...91 Q8

Kirkibost Highld...145 J4
Kirkinch P & K...142 E9
Kirkinner D & G...107 M7
Kirkintilloch E Duns...126 B3
Kirkland Cumb...100 E11
Kirkland Cumb...102 A4
Kirkland D & G...109 M3
Kirkland D & G...115 P5
Kirkland D & G...115 R9
Kirkland Guards Cumb...100 G2
Kirk Langley Derbys...71 P7
Kirkleatham R & CI...104 G6
Kirklevington S on T...104 D9
Kirkley Suffk...65 Q3
Kirklington N York...97 M4
Kirklington Notts...85 L9
Kirklinton Cumb...110 H7
Kirkliston C Edin...127 L3
Kirkmabreck D & G...107 N6
Kirkmaiden D & G...106 F10
Kirk Merrington Dur...103 Q4
Kirk Michael IoM...80 d3
Kirkmichael P & K...141 Q6
Kirkmichael S Ayrs...114 F6
Kirkmuirhill S Lans...126 D9
Kirknewton Nthumb...118 H4
Kirknewton W Loth...127 L4
Kirkney Abers...158 D11
Kirk of Shotts N Lans...126 E6
Kirkoswald Cumb...101 Q2
Kirkoswald S Ayrs...114 D6
Kirkpatrick D & G...109 K2
Kirkpatrick Durham D & G...108 G6
Kirkpatrick-Fleming D & G...110 E6
Kirk Sandall Donc...91 Q9
Kirksanton Cumb...94 C4
Kirk Smeaton N York...91 N7
Kirkstall Leeds...90 H3
Kirkstead Lincs...86 G8
Kirkstile Abers...158 D10
Kirkstile D & G...110 G2
Kirkstone Pass Inn Cumb...101 M9
Kirkstyle Highld...167 P2
Kirkthorpe Wakefd...91 K6
Kirkton Abers...150 G2
Kirkton D & G...109 L4
Kirkton Fife...135 K2
Kirkton Highld...145 P2
Kirkton Highld...154 B9
Kirkton P & K...134 B4
Kirkton Manor Border...117 J3
Kirkton of Airlie Angus...142 E7
Kirkton of Auchterhouse Angus...142 E10
Kirkton of Barevan Highld...156 E8
Kirkton of Collace P & K...142 B11
Kirkton of Durris Abers...151 K8
Kirkton of Glenbuchat Abers...150 B4
Kirkton of Glenisla Angus...142 C5
Kirkton of Kingoldrum Angus...142 E6
Kirkton of Lethendy P & K...142 A9
Kirkton of Logie Buchan Abers...151 P2
Kirkton of Maryculter Abers...151 M8
Kirkton of Menmuir Angus...143 J5
Kirkton of Monikie Angus...143 J10
Kirkton of Rayne Abers...158 G11
Kirkton of Skene Abers...151 L6
Kirkton of Tealing Angus...142 G10
Kirkton of Tough Abers...150 G6
Kirktown Abers...159 N4
Kirktown Abers...159 Q7
Kirktown of Alvah Abers...158 G5
Kirktown of Bourtie Abers...151 L2
Kirktown of Deskford Moray...158 D5
Kirktown of Fetteresso Abers...151 M10
Kirktown of Mortlach Moray...157 Q10
Kirktown of Slains Abers...151 Q2
Kirkurd Border...116 G2
Kirkwall Ork...169 d5
Kirkwall Airport Ork...169 d6
Kirkwhelpington Nthumb...112 F4
Kirk Yetholm Border...118 F5
Kirmington N Linc...93 K8
Kirmond le Mire Lincs...86 G2
Kirn Ag & B...124 F2
Kirriemuir Angus...142 F7
Kirstead Green Norfk...65 K2
Kirtlebridge D & G...110 D6
Kirtling Cambs...63 L9
Kirtling Green Cambs...63 L9
Kirtlington Oxon...48 E11
Kirtomy Highld...166 B4
Kirton Lincs...74 F3
Kirton Notts...85 L7
Kirton Suffk...53 N3
Kirton End Lincs...74 E2
Kirtonhill W Duns...125 K2
Kirton Holme Lincs...74 E2
Kirton in Lindsey N Linc...92 H11
Kirwaugh D & G...107 M7
Kishorn Highld...153 Q10
Kislingbury Nhants...60 F8
Kitebrook Warwks...47 P8
Kite Green Warwks...59 J11
Kites Hardwick Warwks...59 Q11
Kitleigh Cnwll...5 L2
Kitt Green Wigan...88 G9
Kittisford Somset...18 E10
Kittle Swans...28 G7
Kitt's Green Birm...59 J7
Kittybrewster C Aber...151 N6
Kitwood Hants...23 J8
Kivernoll Herefs...45 P8
Kiveton Park Rothm...84 G4
Knaith Lincs...85 P4
Knaith Park Lincs...85 P3
Knap Corner Dorset...20 F10
Knaphill Surrey...23 Q3
Knapp Somset...19 K9
Knapp Hill Hants...22 D10
Knapthorpe Notts...85 M9
Knapton C York...98 B10
Knapton N York...98 H5
Knapton Green Herefs...45 N4
Knapwell Cambs...62 D8
Knaresborough N York...97 N9
Knarsdale Nthumb...111 N10
Knaven Abers...159 L9
Knayton N York...97 P3
Knebworth Herts...50 G6

Knedlington E R Yk...92 B5
Kneesall Notts...85 M8
Kneeton Notts...85 M11
Knelston Swans...28 E7
Knenhall Staffs...70 G7
Knightacott Devon...17 M4
Knightcote Warwks...48 D4
Knightley Staffs...70 E10
Knightley Dale Staffs...70 E10
Knighton BCP...13 J5
Knighton C Leic...72 G10
Knighton Devon...6 E9
Knighton Dorset...11 N2
Knighton Powys...56 D10
Knighton Somset...18 G6
Knighton Staffs...70 C6
Knighton Staffs...70 D9
Knighton Wilts...33 Q10
Knighton on Teme Worcs...57 L11
Knightsbridge Gloucs...46 G9
Knightsmill Cnwll...4 H5
Knightwick Worcs...46 D3
Knill Herefs...45 K2
Knipoch Ag & B...130 G3
Knipton Leics...73 L4
Knitsley Dur...112 H11
Kniveton Derbys...71 N4
Knock Cumb...102 C5
Knock Highld...145 L6
Knock Moray...158 D7
Knock W Isls...168 j4
Knockally Highld...167 K11
Knockan Highld...161 L4
Knockando Moray...157 M9
Knockbain Highld...155 Q9
Knockbain Highld...156 A6
Knock Castle N Ayrs...124 F5
Knockdee Highld...167 L4
Knockdow Ag & B...124 E3
Knockdown Wilts...32 F7
Knockeen S Ayrs...114 F8
Knockenkelly N Ayrs...121 K6
Knockentiber E Ayrs...125 L10
Knockhall Kent...37 N6
Knockholt Kent...37 L9
Knockholt Pound Kent...37 L9
Knockin Shrops...69 K10
Knockinlaw E Ayrs...125 L10
Knockmill Kent...37 N8
Knocknain D & G...106 C5
Knockrome Ag & B...123 J5
Knocksharry IoM...80 c4
Knocksheen D & G...108 C4
Knockvennie Smithy D & G...108 G6
Knodishall Suffk...65 N9
Knodishall Common Suffk...65 N9
Knole Somset...19 N9
Knole Park S Glos...31 Q8
Knolls Green Ches E...82 H9
Knolton Wrexhm...69 L7
Knook Wilts...20 H6
Knossington Leics...73 L9
Knott End-on-Sea Lancs...94 H11
Knotting Bed...61 M8
Knotting Green Bed...61 M8
Knottingley Wakefd...91 N6
Knotty Ash Lpool...81 N6
Knotty Green Bucks...35 P6
Knowbury Shrops...57 K9
Knowe D & G...107 K3
Knowehead D & G...115 M9
Knoweside S Ayrs...114 E5
Knowes of Elrick Abers...158 F7
Knowle Bristl...32 B10
Knowle Devon...9 J4
Knowle Devon...9 P3
Knowle Devon...9 Q8
Knowle Devon...16 H4
Knowle Shrops...57 K10
Knowle Solhll...59 J9
Knowle Somset...18 C6
Knowle Cross Devon...9 P5
Knowlefield Cumb...110 H9
Knowle Green Lancs...89 J3
Knowle Hill Surrey...35 Q11
Knowle St Giles Somset...10 G2
Knowle Village Hants...14 G5
Knowle Wood Calder...89 Q6
Knowl Green Essex...52 C3
Knowl Hill W & M...35 M9
Knowlton Dorset...12 H3
Knowlton Kent...39 N11
Knowsley Knows...81 N5
Knowsley Safari Knows...81 P6
Knowstone Devon...17 Q7
Knox N York...97 L9
Knox Bridge Kent...26 C3
Knoydart Highld...145 P7
Knucklas Powys...56 D10
Knuston Nhants...61 K7
Knutsford Ches E...82 F9
Knutsford Services Ches E...82 F9
Knutton Staffs...70 E5
Krumlin Calder...90 D7
Kuggar Cnwll...3 J10
Kyleakin Highld...145 N2
Kyle of Lochalsh Highld...145 N2
Kylerhea Highld...145 N3
Kylesku Highld...164 F10
Kylesmorar Highld...145 P9
Kyles Scalpay W Isls...168 h8
Kylestrome Highld...164 F10
Kynaston Herefs...46 B7
Kynaston Shrops...69 L11
Kynnersley Wrekin...70 B11
Kyre Green Worcs...46 B2
Kyre Park Worcs...46 B2
Kyrewood Worcs...57 K11
Kyrle Somset...18 E10

L

La Bellieuse Guern...10 b2
Lacasaigh W Isls...168 i5
Lacasdal W Isls...168 j4
Laceby NE Lin...93 M9
Lacey Green Bucks...35 M4
Lach Dennis Ches W...82 F10
Lackenby R & CI...104 E7
Lackford Suffk...63 N6
Lackford Green Suffk...63 N6
Lacock Wilts...32 H11
Ladbroke Warwks...48 D3
Ladderedge Staffs...70 H4
Laddingford Kent...37 Q11
Lade Bank Lincs...87 L10
Ladock Cnwll...3 M3
Lady Ork...169 f2
Ladybank Fife...135 J6
Ladycross Cnwll...5 N4
Ladygill S Lans...116 C5
Lady Hall Cumb...94 D3
Ladykirk Border...129 M10
Ladyridge Herefs...46 A8
Lady's Green Suffk...63 N9
Ladywood Birm...58 G7
Ladywood Worcs...46 G2
La Fontenelle Guern...10 c1
La Fosse Guern...10 b2
Lag D & G...109 J3
Laga Highld...138 A5
Lagavulin Ag & B...122 F10
Lagg N Ayrs...121 J7
Laggan Highld...146 H8
Laggan Highld...147 Q9
Lagganlia Highld...148 F7
La Greve Guern...10 c1
La Grève de Lecq Jersey...11 a1
La Hougue Bie Jersey...11 c2
La Houguette Guern...10 b2
Laid Highld...165 K5
Laide Highld...160 E8
Laig Highld...144 G10
Laigh Clunch E Ayrs...125 M8
Laigh Fenwick E Ayrs...125 M9
Laigh Glenmuir E Ayrs...115 M3
Laighstonehall S Lans...126 C7
Laindon Essex...37 Q3
Lairg Highld...162 D5
Laisterdyke C Brad...90 F4
Laithes Cumb...101 N4
Lake Devon...8 D7
Lake Devon...17 J6
Lake IoW...14 G10
Lake Wilts...21 M7
Lake District Cumb...100 H8
Lake District National Park Cumb...100 H8
Lakenham Norfk...77 J10
Lakenheath Suffk...63 M4
Laker's Green Surrey...24 C3
Lakes End Norfk...75 K11
Lakeside Cumb...94 H3
Laleham Surrey...36 C7
Laleston Brdgnd...29 N9
Lamanva Cnwll...3 K7
Lamarsh Essex...52 E4
Lamas Norfk...77 J7
Lambden Border...118 D2
Lamberhurst Kent...25 Q3
Lamberhurst Down Kent...25 Q3
Lamberton Border...129 P8
Lambeth Gt Lon...36 H5
Lambfair Green Suffk...63 M10
Lambley Notts...85 K11
Lambley Nthumb...111 N9
Lambourn W Berk...34 B9
Lambourne End Essex...37 L2
Lambourn Woodlands W Berk...34 B9
Lamb Roe Lancs...89 L3
Lambs Green W Susx...24 F3
Lambston Pembks...40 H7
Lamellion Cnwll...5 L9
Lamerton Devon...8 C9
Lamesley Gatesd...113 L9
Lamington S Lans...116 D4
Lamlash N Ayrs...121 K5
Lamonby Cumb...101 M3
Lamorick Cnwll...4 G8
Lamorna Cnwll...2 C9
Lamorran Cnwll...3 M5
Lampen Cnwll...5 K8
Lampeter Cerdgn...43 L5
Lampeter Velfrey Pembks...41 N8
Lamphey Pembks...41 K10
Lamplugh Cumb...100 E6
Lamport Nhants...60 G6
Lamyatt Somset...20 C7
Lana Devon...5 N2
Lana Devon...16 E10
Lanark S Lans...116 B2
Lancaster Lancs...95 K8
Lancaster Services Lancs...95 L10
Lancaut Gloucs...31 P5
Lanchester Dur...113 J11
Lancing W Susx...24 E10
L'Ancresse Guern...10 c1
Landbeach Cambs...62 G7
Landcross Devon...16 H7
Landerberry Abers...151 J7
Landford Wilts...21 Q11
Land-hallow Highld...167 L10
Landimore Swans...28 E6
Landkey Devon...17 K5
Landore Swans...28 H5
Landrake Cnwll...5 P9
Landscove Devon...7 K5
Land's End Cnwll...2 A8
Land's End Airport Cnwll...2 B8
Landshipping Pembks...41 K8
Landue Cnwll...5 P6
Landulph Cnwll...6 C6
Landwade Suffk...63 K7
Lane Cnwll...4 C9
Laneast Cnwll...5 L5
Lane Bottom Lancs...89 P3
Lane End Bucks...35 M6
Lane End Cnwll...4 G8
Lane End Hants...22 G9
Lane End Kent...37 N6
Lane End Lancs...96 C11
Lane End Warrtn...82 E6
Lane End Wilts...20 F5
Lane Ends Derbys...71 N8
Lane Ends Lancs...89 M4
Lane Ends N York...90 B2
Lane Green Staffs...58 C4
Laneham Notts...85 P5
Lanehead Dur...102 F2
Lane Head Dur...103 M8
Lanehead Nthumb...111 Q3
Lane Head Wigan...82 D5
Lane Head Wsall...58 E4
Lane Heads Lancs...88 E3
Lanercost Cumb...111 L8
Laneshaw Bridge Lancs...89 Q2
Lane Side Lancs...89 M6
Langaford Devon...5 Q2

Langal Highld 138 C4
Langaller Somset 19 J9
Langar Notts 73 J4
Langbank Rens 125 K3
Langbar N York 96 G10
Langbaurgh N York 104 G8
Langcliffe N York 96 B8
Langdale End N York 99 J2
Langdon Cnwll 5 N4
Langdon Beck Dur 102 C4
Langdon Hills Essex 37 Q3
Langdown Hants 14 D5
Langdyke Fife 135 J7
Langenhoe Essex 52 H8
Langford C Beds 50 E2
Langford Devon 9 P4
Langford Essex 52 D10
Langford N Som 19 N2
Langford Notts 85 P9
Langford Oxon 33 P4
Langford Somset 18 H9
Langford Budville Somset 18 F10
Langham Dorset 20 E9
Langham Essex 52 H5
Langham Norfk 76 E3
Langham Rutlnd 73 L8
Langham Suffk 64 D8
Langho Lancs 89 L4
Langholm D & G 110 G4
Langland Swans 28 H7
Langlee Border 117 Q3
Langley Ches E 83 K10
Langley Derbys 84 F11
Langley Gloucs 47 K9
Langley Hants 14 D6
Langley Herts 50 F6
Langley Kent 38 D11
Langley Nthumb 112 B8
Langley Oxon 47 Q11
Langley Rochdl 89 P9
Langley Slough 36 B5
Langley Somset 18 E9
Langley W Susx 23 M9
Langley Warwks 47 N2
Langley Burrell Wilts 32 H9
Langley Castle Nthumb 112 B8
Langley Common Derbys 71 P7
Langley Green Derbys 71 P7
Langley Green Essex 52 E7
Langley Green Warwks 47 N2
Langley Heath Kent 38 D11
Langley Lower Green Essex 51 K4
Langley Marsh Somset 18 E9
Langley Mill Derbys 84 F11
Langley Moor Dur 103 Q2
Langley Park Dur 113 K11
Langley Street Norfk 77 M11
Langley Upper Green Essex 51 K4
Langley Vale Surrey 36 F9
Langney E Susx 25 P10
Langold Notts 85 J3
Langore Cnwll 5 M4
Langport Somset 19 M9
Langrick Lincs 87 J11
Langridge BaNES 32 D11
Langridgeford Devon 17 K7
Langrigg Cumb 110 C11
Langrish Hants 23 K10
Langsett Barns 90 G10
Langside P & K 133 M7
Langstone Hants 15 K6
Langstone Newpt 31 L7
Langthorne N York 97 K2
Langthorpe N York 97 N7
Langthwaite N York 103 K10
Langtoft E R Yk 99 L7
Langtoft Lincs 74 B8
Langton Dur 103 N7
Langton Lincs 86 H7
Langton Lincs 87 L6
Langton N York 98 F7
Langton by Wragby Lincs 86 F5
Langton Green Kent 25 M3
Langton Green Suffk 64 G7
Langton Herring Dorset 11 N8
Langton Long Blandford Dorset 12 F3
Langton Matravers Dorset 12 H9
Langtree Devon 16 H8
Langtree Week Devon 16 H8
Langwathby Cumb 101 Q4
Langwell Highld 161 K6
Langwell House Highld 163 N2
Langwith Derbys 84 H7
Langwith Junction Derbys 84 H7
Langworth Lincs 86 E5
Lanhydrock Cnwll 4 H9
Lanivet Cnwll 4 G9
Lanjeth Cnwll 3 P3
Lank Cnwll 4 H6
Lanlivery Cnwll 4 H10
Lanner Cnwll 3 J6
Lanoy Cnwll 5 M6
Lanreath Cnwll 5 K10
Lansallos Cnwll 5 K11
Lanteglos Cnwll 4 H5
Lanteglos Highway Cnwll 5 J11
Lanton Border 118 B6
Lanton Nthumb 118 H4
La Passee Guern 10 b1
Lapford Devon 8 H3
Laphroaig Ag & B 122 C10
Lapley Staffs 58 C2
La Pulente Jersey 11 a2
Lapworth Warwks 59 J10
Larachbeg Highld 138 B8
Larbert Falk 133 P11
Larbreck Lancs 88 E2
Largie Abers 158 F11
Largiemore Ag & B 131 J2
Largoward Fife 135 M6
Largs N Ayrs 124 G6
Largybeg N Ayrs 121 K7
Largymore N Ayrs 121 K7
Larkbeare Devon 9 Q5
Larkfield Inver 124 G2
Larkfield Kent 38 B10
Larkhall S Lans 126 D7
Larkhill Wilts 21 M6
Larling Norfk 64 D4
La Rocque Jersey 11 c2
La Rousaillerie Guern 10 b1
Lartington Dur 103 K8
Lasborough Gloucs 32 F6
Lasham Hants 23 J6
Lashbrook Devon 8 B3

Lashbrook Devon 16 G10
Lashenden Kent 26 D3
Lask Edge Staffs 70 G3
Lasswade Mdloth 127 Q4
Lastingham N York 98 E2
Latcham Somset 19 M5
Latchford Herts 51 J6
Latchford Oxon 35 J4
Latchford Warrtn 82 D7
Latchingdon Essex 52 E11
Latchley Cnwll 5 Q7
Lately Common Warrtn 82 E5
Lathbury M Keyn 49 N6
Latheron Highld 167 M10
Latheronwheel Highld 167 L10
Lathom Lancs 88 F8
Lathones Fife 135 M6
Latimer Bucks 50 B11
Latteridge S Glos 32 C8
Lattiford Somset 20 C9
Latton Wilts 33 L5
Lauder Border 128 E10
Laugharne Carmth 28 B2
Laughterton Lincs 85 P5
Laughton E Susx 25 L8
Laughton Leics 60 E3
Laughton Lincs 74 A4
Laughton Lincs 92 D11
Laughton Common Rothm 84 H3
Laughton-en-le-Morthen Rothm 84 H3
Launcells Cnwll 16 C10
Launcells Cross Cnwll 16 C10
Launceston Cnwll 5 N5
Launton Oxon 48 H10
Laurencekirk Abers 143 N3
Laurieston D & G 108 E8
Laurieston Falk 126 G2
Lavendon M Keyn 49 P4
Lavenham Suffk 52 F2
Lavernock V Glam 30 G11
Laversdale Cumb 111 J8
Laverstock Wilts 21 N8
Laverstoke Hants 22 E5
Laverton Gloucs 47 L7
Laverton N York 97 K6
Laverton Somset 20 E4
La Villette Guern 10 b2
Lavister Wrexhm 69 L3
Law S Lans 126 E7
Lawers P & K 140 G12
Lawford Essex 53 J5
Lawford Somset 18 F7
Law Hill S Lans 126 E7
Lawhitton Cnwll 5 P5
Lawkland N York 95 R7
Lawkland Green N York 96 A7
Lawley Wrekin 57 M3
Lawnhead Staffs 70 E9
Lawrence Weston Bristl 31 P9
Lawrenny Pembks 41 K9
Lawrenny Quay Pembks 41 K9
Lawshall Suffk 64 B11
Lawshall Green Suffk 64 B11
Lawton Herefs 45 N3
Laxay W Isls 168 i5
Laxdale W Isls 168 j4
Laxey IoM 80 f5
Laxfield Suffk 65 K7
Laxford Bridge Highld 164 F7
Laxo Shet 169 r7
Laxton E R Yk 92 C5
Laxton Nhants 73 P11
Laxton Notts 85 M7
Laycock C Brad 90 C2
Layer Breton Essex 52 F8
Layer-de-la-Haye Essex 52 G7
Layer Marney Essex 52 F8
Layham Suffk 52 H3
Laymore Dorset 10 H4
Layter's Green Bucks 35 Q4
Laytham E R Yk 92 B3
Laythes Cumb 110 D9
Lazenby R & Cl 104 G7
Lazonby Cumb 101 P3
Lea Derbys 84 D9
Lea Herefs 46 C10
Lea Lincs 85 P3
Lea Shrops 56 F7
Lea Shrops 56 G3
Lea Wilts 33 J7
Leachkin Highld 156 A8
Leadburn Border 127 N6
Leadenham Lincs 86 B10
Leaden Roding Essex 51 N8
Leadgate Cumb 102 D2
Leadgate Dur 112 H10
Leadgate Nthumb 112 H9
Leadhills S Lans 116 B7
Leadingcross Green Kent 38 E11
Leadmill Derbys 84 B4
Leafield Oxon 48 B11
Leagrave Luton 50 C6
Leagreen Ches W 70 B2
Lea Heath Staffs 71 J9
Leake N York 97 P2
Leake Common Side Lincs 87 L10
Lealholm N York 105 L9
Lealholm Side N York 105 L9
Lealt Highld 153 J4
Leam Derbys 84 B5
Lea Marston Warwks 59 K6
Leamington Hastings Warwks 59 P11
Leamington Spa Warwks 59 M11
Leamside Dur 113 M11
Leap Cross E Susx 25 N8
Learney Abers 150 G7
Leasgill Cumb 95 K4
Leasingham Lincs 86 E11
Leasingthorne Dur 103 Q4
Leatherhead Surrey 36 E9
Leathley N York 97 K11
Leaton Shrops 69 N11
Leaton Wrekin 57 L2
Lea Town Lancs 88 F4
Leaveland Kent 38 H11
Leavenheath Suffk 52 G4
Leavening N York 98 F8
Leaves Green Gt Lon 37 K8
Lea Yeat Cumb 95 R3
Lebberston N York 99 M4
Le Bigard Guern 10 b2
Le Bourg Guern 10 b2
Le Bourg Jersey 11 c2
Lechlade on Thames Gloucs 33 P5

Lecht Gruinart Ag & B 122 C6
Leck Lancs 95 N5
Leckbuie P & K 140 H9
Leckford Hants 22 C7
Leckhampstead Bucks 49 K7
Leckhampstead W Berk 34 D9
Leckhampstead Thicket W Berk 34 D9
Leckhampton Gloucs 46 H11
Leckmelm Highld 161 K9
Leckwith V Glam 30 G10
Leconfield E R Yk 92 H2
Ledaig Ag & B 138 G10
Ledburn Bucks 49 P10
Ledbury Herefs 46 D7
Ledgemoor Herefs 45 N4
Ledicot Herefs 45 N2
Ledmore Highld 161 L4
Ledsham Ches W 81 M10
Ledsham Leeds 91 M5
Ledston Leeds 91 L5
Ledstone Devon 7 J9
Ledston Luck Leeds 91 L4
Ledwell Oxon 48 D9
Lee Devon 16 H2
Lee Gt Lon 37 J5
Lee Hants 22 C11
Lee Shrops 69 M8
Leebotwood Shrops 56 H5
Lee Brockhurst Shrops 69 P9
Leece Cumb 94 E7
Lee Chapel Essex 37 Q3
Lee Clump Bucks 35 P4
Lee Common Bucks 35 P4
Leeds Kent 38 D11
Leeds Leeds 90 H4
Leeds Bradford Airport Leeds 90 G2
Leeds Castle Kent 38 D11
Leeds Skelton Lake Services Leeds 91 K4
Leedstown Cnwll 2 G7
Lee Green Ches E 70 B2
Leek Staffs 70 H3
Leek Wootton Warwks 59 L11
Lee Mill Devon 6 F7
Leeming C Brad 90 C4
Leeming N York 97 L3
Leeming Bar N York 97 L3
Leeming Bar Rest Area N York 97 L3
Lee Moor Devon 6 F6
Lee-on-the-Solent Hants 14 G6
Lees C Brad 90 C3
Lees Derbys 71 P7
Lees Oldham 83 L4
Lees Green Derbys 71 P7
Leesthorpe Leics 73 K8
Leeswood Flints 69 J2
Leetown P & K 134 G3
Leftwich Ches W 82 E10
Legar Powys 45 J11
Legbourne Lincs 87 L4
Legburthwaite Cumb 101 K7
Legerwood Border 118 A2
Legoland W & M 35 P10
Le Gron Guern 10 b2
Legsby Lincs 86 F3
Le Haguais Jersey 11 c2
Le Hocq Jersey 11 c2
Leicester C Leic 72 F10
Leicester Forest East Leics 72 E10
Leicester Forest East Services Leics 72 E10
Leigh Devon 17 N9
Leigh Dorset 11 N3
Leigh Gloucs 46 G9
Leigh Kent 37 M11
Leigh Shrops 56 F4
Leigh Surrey 36 F11
Leigh Wigan 82 E5
Leigh Wilts 33 L6
Leigh Worcs 46 E4
Leigh Beck Essex 38 D5
Leigh Delamere Wilts 32 G9
Leigh Delamere Services Wilts 32 G9
Leigh Green Kent 26 F5
Leigh Knoweglass S Lans 125 Q7
Leighland Chapel Somset 18 D7
Leigh-on-Sea Sthend 38 D4
Leigh Park Dorset 12 H5
Leigh Park Hants 15 K5
Leigh Sinton Worcs 46 E4
Leighswood Wsall 58 G4
Leighterton Gloucs 32 F6
Leighton N York 97 J5
Leighton Powys 56 C3
Leighton Shrops 57 L3
Leighton Somset 20 D6
Leighton Bromswold Cambs 61 P5
Leighton Buzzard C Beds 49 P9
Leigh upon Mendip Somset 20 C5
Leigh Woods N Som 31 Q10
Leinthall Earls Herefs 56 G11
Leinthall Starkes Herefs 56 G11
Leintwardine Herefs 56 G10
Leire Leics 60 B3
Leiston Suffk 65 N9
Leith C Edin 127 P2
Leitholm Border 118 E2
Lelant Cnwll 2 E6
Lelley E R Yk 93 M4
Lem Hill Worcs 57 N9
Lempitlaw Border 118 E4
Lemreway W Isls 168 i6
Lemsford Herts 50 F8
Lenchwick Worcs 47 K5
Lendalfoot S Ayrs 114 B9
Lendrick Stirlg 132 H6
Lenham Kent 38 E11
Lenham Heath Kent 38 F2
Lenie Highld 147 N2
Lennel Border 118 G2
Lennox Plunton D & G 108 D10
Lennoxtown E Duns 125 Q2
Lent Bucks 35 P8
Lenton C Nott 72 F3
Lenton Lincs 73 Q4
Lenwade Norfk 76 F8
Lenzie E Duns 126 B3
Leochel-Cushnie Abers 150 E5
Leomansley Staffs 58 H3
Leominster Herefs 45 P3

Leonard Stanley Gloucs 32 F4
Leoville Jersey 11 a1
Lepe Hants 14 D7
Lephin Highld 152 B8
Leppington N York 98 F8
Lepton Kirk 90 G7
Lerags Ag & B 130 H2
L'Erée Guern 10 a2
Lerryn Cnwll 5 J10
Lerwick Shet 169 r9
Les Arquêts Guern 10 b2
Lesbury Nthumb 119 P8
Les Hubits Guern 10 c2
Leslie Abers 150 F3
Leslie Fife 134 H7
Les Lohiers Guern 10 b2
Lesmahagow S Lans 126 E10
Les Murchez Guern 10 b2
Lesnewth Cnwll 5 J3
Les Nicolles Guern 10 b2
Les Quartiers Guern 10 c1
Les Quennevais Jersey 11 a2
Les Sages Guern 10 b2
Lessingham Norfk 77 M6
Lessonhall Cumb 110 D10
Lesstowder Cnwll 3 K9
Les Villets Guern 10 b2
Leswalt D & G 106 D5
L'Etacq Jersey 11 a1
Letchmore Heath Herts 50 E11
Letchworth Garden City Herts 50 F4
Letcombe Bassett Oxon 34 C8
Letcombe Regis Oxon 34 C7
Letham Angus 143 J8
Letham Border 118 C9
Letham Falk 133 P10
Letham Fife 135 J5
Letham Grange Angus 143 L8
Lethenty Abers 150 F3
Lethenty Abers 159 K9
Letheringham Suffk 65 K10
Letheringsett Norfk 76 F4
Lettaford Devon 8 H8
Letterewe Highld 154 C3
Letterfearn Highld 145 Q3
Letterfinlay Lodge Hotel Highld 146 H9
Letters Highld 161 K9
Lettershaw S Lans 116 B6
Letterston Pembks 40 H5
Lettoch Highld 149 J4
Lettoch Highld 157 L11
Letton Herefs 45 L5
Letton Herefs 56 F10
Lett's Green Kent 37 L9
Letty Green Herts 50 G8
Letwell Rothm 85 J3
Leuchars Fife 135 M3
Leumrabhagh W Isls 168 i6
Leurbost W Isls 168 i5
Levalsa Meor Cnwll 3 Q4
Levan Inver 124 G2
Levedale Staffs 70 F11
Level's Green Essex 51 L6
Leven E R Yk 99 N11
Leven Fife 135 K7
Levens Cumb 95 K3
Levens Green Herts 51 J6
Levenshulme Manch 83 J6
Levenwick Shet 169 r11
Leverburgh W Isls 168 f9
Leverington Cambs 74 H8
Leverstock Green Herts 50 C9
Leverton Lincs 87 M11
Le Villocq Guern 10 b1
Levington Suffk 53 M4
Levisham N York 98 G2
Lew Oxon 34 B3
Lewannick Cnwll 5 M5
Lewdown Devon 8 C7
Lewes E Susx 25 K8
Leweston Pembks 40 H6
Lewisham Gt Lon 37 J6
Lewiston Highld 147 N2
Lewistown Brdgnd 29 P7
Lewis Wych Herefs 45 L3
Lewknor Oxon 35 K5
Leworthy Devon 16 E11
Leworthy Devon 17 M4
Lewson Street Kent 38 G9
Lewth Lancs 88 F3
Lewtrenchard Devon 8 C7
Lexden Essex 52 G6
Lexworthy Somset 18 J7
Ley Cnwll 5 K8
Leybourne Kent 37 Q9
Leyburn N York 96 H2
Leycett Staffs 70 D5
Leygreen Herts 50 E6
Ley Hill Bucks 35 Q4
Leyland Lancs 88 G6
Leyland Green St Hel 82 C4
Leylodge Abers 151 K5
Leys Abers 159 P7
Leys P & K 142 D10
Leysdown-on-Sea Kent 38 H7
Leysmill Angus 143 L8
Leys of Cossans Angus 142 F8
Leysters Herefs 45 R2
Leyton Gt Lon 37 J3
Leytonstone Gt Lon 37 J3
Lezant Cnwll 5 N6
Lezerea Cnwll 2 H7
Leziate Norfk 75 N7
Lhanbryde Moray 157 P5
Libanus Powys 44 D9
Libberton S Lans 116 D2
Libbery Worcs 47 J3
Liberton C Edin 127 P4
Lichfield Staffs 58 H3
Lickey Worcs 58 E10
Lickey End Worcs 58 E10
Lickey Rock Worcs 58 E10
Lickfold W Susx 23 P9
Liddaton Green Devon 8 C8
Liddesdale Highld 138 D6
Liddington Swindn 33 P8
Lidgate Derbys 84 D5
Lidgate Suffk 63 M9
Lidget Donc 85 R10
Lidgett Notts 85 K7
Lidham Hill E Susx 26 D8
Lidlington C Beds 49 Q7
Lidsey W Susx 15 P6
Lidsing Kent 38 C9

Liff Angus 142 E11
Lifford Birm 58 G8
Lifton Devon 5 P4
Liftondown Devon 5 P4
Lighthorne Warwks 48 B3
Lighthorne Heath Warwks 48 C3
Lightwater Surrey 23 P2
Lightwater Valley Family Adventure Park N York 97 L5
Lightwood C Stke 70 G6
Lightwood Green Ches E 70 A6
Lightwood Green Wrexhm 69 L6
Lilbourne Nhants 60 C5
Lilburn Tower Nthumb 119 K6
Lilford Nhants 61 M4
Lilleshall Wrekin 70 C11
Lilley Herts 50 D5
Lilley W Berk 34 D9
Lilliesleaf Border 117 Q5
Lillingstone Dayrell Bucks 49 K7
Lillingstone Lovell Bucks 49 K6
Lillington Dorset 11 N2
Lilliput BCP 12 H7
Lilstock Somset 18 G5
Lilyhurst Shrops 57 N2
Limbrick Lancs 89 J7
Limbury Luton 50 C6
Limebrook Herefs 56 F11
Limefield Bury 89 N8
Limekilnburn S Lans 126 C7
Limekilns Fife 134 D11
Limerigg Falk 126 F3
Limerstone IoW 14 D10
Limestone Brae Nthumb 111 Q11
Lime Street Worcs 46 F8
Limington Somset 19 P10
Limmerhaugh E Ayrs 115 M2
Limpenhoe Norfk 77 M11
Limpley Stoke Wilts 20 E2
Limpsfield Surrey 37 K10
Limpsfield Chart Surrey 37 K10
Linby Notts 84 H10
Linchmere W Susx 23 N8
Lincluden D & G 109 L5
Lincoln Lincs 86 C6
Lincomb Worcs 57 Q11
Lincombe Devon 7 J10
Lincombe Devon 16 H2
Lindale Cumb 95 J4
Lindal in Furness Cumb 94 E5
Lindfield W Susx 24 H5
Lindford Hants 23 M7
Lindley Kirk 90 E7
Lindley N York 97 K11
Lindores Fife 134 H4
Lindow End Ches E 82 H9
Lindridge Worcs 57 M11
Lindsell Essex 51 P5
Lindsey Suffk 52 G2
Lindsey Tye Suffk 52 G2
Liney Somset 19 L7
Linford Hants 13 L3
Linford Thurr 37 Q5
Lingbob C Brad 90 D3
Lingdale R & Cl 105 J7
Lingen Herefs 56 F11
Lingfield Surrey 25 J2
Lingfield Common Surrey 25 J2
Lingwood Norfk 77 M10
Liniclate W Isls 168 c13
Linicro Highld 152 F4
Linkend Worcs 46 F8
Linkenholt Hants 22 C3
Linkhill Kent 26 D6
Linkinhorne Cnwll 5 N7
Linktown Fife 134 H9
Linkwood Moray 157 N5
Linley Shrops 56 F6
Linley Green Herefs 46 C4
Linleygreen Shrops 57 M5
Linlithgow W Loth 126 H2
Linshiels Nthumb 118 G9
Linsidemore Highld 162 C7
Linslade C Beds 49 P9
Linstead Parva Suffk 65 L6
Linstock Cumb 110 H9
Linthurst Worcs 58 E10
Linthwaite Kirk 90 E8
Lintlaw Border 129 L8
Lintmill Moray 158 D4
Linton Cambs 63 J11
Linton Derbys 71 P11
Linton Herefs 46 C9
Linton Kent 38 C11
Linton Leeds 97 N11
Linton N York 96 E8
Linton Nthumb 113 L2
Linton Heath Derbys 71 P11
Linton Hill Herefs 46 C10
Linton-on-Ouse N York 97 Q8
Linwood Hants 13 L3
Linwood Lincs 86 F3
Linwood Rens 125 L5
Lionacleit W Isls 168 c13
Lional W Isls 168 k1
Lions Green E Susx 25 N7
Liphook Hants 23 M8
Lipley Shrops 70 C8
Liscard Wirral 81 K6
Liscombe Somset 18 A8
Liskeard Cnwll 5 M9
Lismore Ag & B 138 E9
Liss Hants 23 L9
Lissett E R Yk 99 N9
Liss Forest Hants 23 L9
Lissington Lincs 86 F4
Liston Essex 52 E3
Lisvane Cardif 30 G8
Liswerry Newpt 31 K7
Litcham Norfk 76 B8
Litchborough Nhants 48 H4
Litchfield Hants 22 E4
Litherland Sefton 81 L5
Litlington Cambs 50 H2
Litlington E Susx 25 M10
Little Abington Cambs 62 H11
Little Addington Nhants 61 L6
Little Airies D & G 107 M8
Little Almshoe Herts 50 F5
Little Alne Warwks 47 M2
Little Altcar Sefton 88 C9
Little Amwell Herts 51 J8
Little Asby Cumb 102 C9
Little Aston Staffs 58 G5
Little Atherfield IoW 14 E11

Place	County	Page	Grid
Little Ayton	N York	104	G8
Little Baddow	Essex	52	C10
Little Badminton	S Glos	32	F8
Little Bampton	Cumb	110	E9
Little Bardfield	Essex	51	Q4
Little Barford	Bed	61	Q9
Little Barningham	Norfk	76	G5
Little Barrington	Gloucs	33	P2
Little Barrow	Ches W	81	P11
Little Barugh	N York	98	F5
Little Bavington	Nthumb	112	E5
Little Bealings	Suffk	53	M2
Littlebeck	N York	105	N10
Little Bedwyn	Wilts	33	Q11
Little Bentley	Essex	53	K6
Little Berkhamsted	Herts	50	G9
Little Billing	Nhants	60	H8
Little Billington	C Beds	49	P10
Little Birch	Herefs	45	Q8
Little Bispham	Bpool	88	C2
Little Blakenham	Suffk	53	K2
Little Blencow	Cumb	101	N4
Little Bloxwich	Wsall	58	F4
Little Bognor	W Susx	24	B6
Little Bolehill	Derbys	71	P4
Little Bollington	Ches E	82	F7
Little Bookham	Surrey	36	D10
Littleborough	Devon	9	K2
Littleborough	Notts	85	P4
Littleborough	Rochdl	89	Q7
Littlebourne	Kent	39	M10
Little Bourton	Oxon	48	E6
Little Bowden	Leics	60	F3
Little Bradley	Suffk	63	L10
Little Brampton	Herefs	45	L2
Little Brampton	Shrops	56	F8
Little Braxted	Essex	52	D9
Little Brechin	Angus	143	K5
Littlebredy	Dorset	11	M7
Little Brickhill	M Keyn	49	P8
Little Bridgeford	Staffs	70	F9
Little Brington	Nhants	60	E8
Little Bromley	Essex	53	J6
Little Broughton	Cumb	100	E4
Little Budworth	Ches W	82	C11
Littleburn	Highld	156	A7
Little Burstead	Essex	37	Q2
Littlebury	Essex	51	M3
Littlebury Green	Essex	51	L3
Little Bytham	Lincs	73	Q7
Little Canfield	Essex	51	N6
Little Carlton	Lincs	87	L3
Little Carlton	Notts	85	N9
Little Casterton	RutInd	73	Q9
Little Catwick	E R Yk	93	K2
Little Catworth	Cambs	61	P6
Little Cawthorpe	Lincs	87	L4
Little Chalfont	Bucks	35	Q5
Little Chart	Kent	26	F2
Little Chesterford	Essex	51	M2
Little Cheveney	Kent	26	B3
Little Cheverell	Wilts	21	J4
Little Chishill	Cambs	51	K3
Little Clacton	Essex	53	L8
Little Clanfield	Oxon	33	Q4
Little Clifton	Cumb	100	E5
Little Coates	NE Lin	93	M9
Little Comberton	Worcs	47	J6
Little Common	E Susx	26	B10
Little Comp	Kent	37	P9
Little Compton	Warwks	47	Q8
Little Corby	Cumb	111	J9
Little Cornard	Suffk	52	F4
Littlecott	Wilts	21	M4
Little Cowarne	Herefs	46	B4
Little Coxwell	Oxon	33	Q6
Little Crakehall	N York	97	K2
Little Cransley	Nhants	60	H5
Little Cressingham	Norfk	76	B11
Little Crosby	Sefton	81	L4
Little Crosthwaite	Cumb	100	H5
Little Cubley	Derbys	71	M7
Little Dalby	Leics	73	K8
Littledean	Gloucs	32	C2
Little Dewchurch	Herefs	45	Q8
Little Ditton	Cambs	63	L9
Little Doward	Herefs	45	Q11
Little Downham	Cambs	62	H4
Little Driffield	E R Yk	99	L9
Little Dunham	Norfk	76	B9
Little Dunkeld	P & K	141	P9
Little Dunmow	Essex	51	Q6
Little Durnford	Wilts	21	M8
Little Easton	Essex	51	P6
Little Eaton	Derbys	72	B2
Little Ellingham	Norfk	64	E2
Little Elm	Somset	20	D5
Little Everdon	Nhants	60	C9
Little Eversden	Cambs	62	E10
Little Faringdon	Oxon	33	Q4
Little Fencote	N York	97	L2
Little Fenton	N York	91	N3
Littleferry	Highld	163	J7
Little Fransham	Norfk	76	C9
Little Gaddesden	Herts	35	Q2
Little Garway	Herefs	45	N10
Little Gidding	Cambs	61	P4
Little Glemham	Suffk	65	L10
Little Gorsley	Herefs	46	C10
Little Gransden	Cambs	62	C9
Little Green	Notts	73	J2
Little Green	Somset	20	D5
Little Grimsby	Lincs	87	K2
Little Gringley	Notts	85	M4
Little Habton	N York	98	E5
Little Hadham	Herts	51	K6
Little Hale	Lincs	74	B2
Little Hallam	Derbys	72	D2
Little Hallingbury	Essex	51	M7
Littleham	Devon	9	P8
Littleham	Devon	16	G7
Little Hampden	Bucks	35	N4
Littlehampton	W Susx	24	B10
Little Hanford	Dorset	12	D2
Little Harrowden	Nhants	61	J6
Little Haseley	Oxon	34	H4
Little Hatfield	E R Yk	93	L2
Little Hautbois	Norfk	77	K7
Little Haven	Pembks	40	G8
Littlehaven	W Susx	24	D2
Little Hay	Staffs	58	H4
Little Hayfield	Derbys	83	M7
Little Haywood	Staffs	71	J10
Little Heath	Staffs	70	F11
Little Heath	W Berk	35	J10
Littlehempston	Devon	7	L6
Little Hereford	Herefs	57	K11
Little Horkesley	Essex	52	G5
Little Hormead	Herts	51	K5
Little Horsted	E Susx	25	L7
Little Horton	C Brad	90	F4
Little Horton	Wilts	21	K2
Little Horwood	Bucks	49	L8
Little Houghton	Barns	91	L9
Little Houghton	Nhants	60	H9
Littlehoughton	Nthumb	119	P7
Little Hucklow	Derbys	83	Q9
Little Hulton	Salfd	82	F4
Little Hungerford	W Berk	34	F10
Little Hutton	N York	97	Q5
Little Irchester	Nhants	61	K7
Little Kelk	E R Yk	99	M9
Little Keyford	Somset	20	E5
Little Kimble	Bucks	35	M3
Little Kineton	Warwks	48	B4
Little Kingshill	Bucks	35	N5
Little Knox	D & G	108	H8
Little Langdale	Cumb	101	K10
Little Langford	Wilts	21	K7
Little Laver	Essex	51	M9
Little Leigh	Ches W	82	D9
Little Leighs	Essex	52	B8
Little Lever	Bolton	89	M9
Little Linford	M Keyn	49	M6
Little Load	Somset	19	N10
Little London	Bucks	34	H2
Little London	Cambs	74	H11
Little London	E Susx	25	N6
Little London	Essex	51	L5
Little London	Essex	51	Q3
Little London	Gloucs	46	D11
Little London	Hants	22	C5
Little London	Hants	22	H3
Little London	Leeds	90	G3
Little London	Lincs	74	D6
Little London	Lincs	74	H6
Little London	Lincs	87	K6
Little London	Norfk	75	L6
Little London	Powys	55	N7
Little Longstone	Derbys	83	Q10
Little Madeley	Staffs	70	D5
Little Malvern	Worcs	46	E6
Little Mancot	Flints	81	L11
Little Maplestead	Essex	52	D5
Little Marcle	Herefs	46	C7
Little Marland	Devon	17	J9
Little Marlow	Bucks	35	N7
Little Massingham	Norfk	75	Q6
Little Melton	Norfk	76	H10
Littlemill	Abers	149	Q8
Littlemill	Highld	156	G2
Little Mill	Mons	31	K4
Little Milton	Oxon	34	H4
Little Missenden	Bucks	35	P5
Little Mongeham	Kent	39	P11
Littlemoor	Derbys	84	E8
Little Moor	Somset	19	K8
Littlemore	Oxon	34	F4
Little Musgrave	Cumb	102	E8
Little Ness	Shrops	69	M11
Little Neston	Ches W	81	K9
Little Newcastle	Pembks	41	J5
Little Newsham	Dur	103	M7
Little Norton	Somset	19	N11
Little Oakley	Essex	53	M6
Little Oakley	Nhants	61	J3
Little Odell	Bed	61	L9
Little Offley	Herts	50	D5
Little Ormside	Cumb	102	D7
Little Orton	Cumb	110	G9
Little Ouse	Cambs	63	K3
Little Ouseburn	N York	97	P8
Littleover	C Derb	72	A4
Little Oxendon	Nhants	60	F4
Little Packington	Warwks	59	K8
Little Pattenden	Kent	26	B2
Little Paxton	Cambs	61	Q8
Little Petherick	Cnwll	4	E7
Little Plumpton	Lancs	88	D4
Little Plumstead	Norfk	77	L9
Little Ponton	Lincs	73	N4
Littleport	Cambs	63	J3
Littleport Bridge	Cambs	63	J3
Little Posbrook	Hants	14	F6
Little Potheridge	Devon	17	J9
Little Preston	Leeds	91	K4
Little Preston	Nhants	48	G4
Littler	Ches W	82	D11
Little Raveley	Cambs	62	C5
Little Reedness	E R Yk	92	D6
Little Ribston	N York	97	N10
Little Rissington	Gloucs	47	N10
Little Rollright	Oxon	47	Q8
Little Rowsley	Derbys	84	C12
Little Ryburgh	Norfk	76	D6
Little Ryle	Nthumb	119	L9
Little Ryton	Shrops	56	H4
Little Salkeld	Cumb	101	Q3
Little Sampford	Essex	51	Q4
Little Sandhurst	Br For	23	M2
Little Saredon	Staffs	58	D3
Little Saughall	Ches W	81	M11
Little Saxham	Suffk	63	P8
Little Scatwell	Highld	155	L6
Little Shelford	Cambs	62	G10
Little Shrewley	Warwks	59	K11
Little Silver	Devon	9	M3
Little Singleton	Lancs	88	D3
Little Skipwith	N York	91	R3
Little Smeaton	N York	91	N7
Little Snoring	Norfk	76	D5
Little Sodbury	S Glos	32	E8
Little Sodbury End	S Glos	32	E8
Little Somborne	Hants	22	C8
Little Somerford	Wilts	33	J8
Little Soudley	Shrops	70	C9
Little Stainforth	N York	96	B7
Little Stainton	Darltn	104	B6
Little Stanion	Nhants	61	J3
Little Stanney	Ches W	81	N10
Little Staughton	Bed	61	N8
Little Steeping	Lincs	87	M8
Littlestoke	Staffs	70	G8
Littlestone-on-Sea	Kent	27	J4
Little Stonham	Suffk	64	G9
Little Stretton	Leics	72	H10
Little Stretton	Shrops	56	G6
Little Strickland	Cumb	101	Q7
Little Stukeley	Cambs	62	B5
Little Sugnall	Staffs	70	E8
Little Sutton	Ches W	81	M9
Little Sutton	Shrops	57	J8
Little Swinburne	Nthumb	112	D5
Little Sypland	D & G	108	F10
Little Tew	Oxon	48	C9
Little Tey	Essex	52	E7
Little Thetford	Cambs	62	H5
Little Thirkleby	N York	97	Q5
Little Thornage	Norfk	76	F4
Little Thornton	Lancs	88	D2
Little Thorpe	Dur	104	D2
Littlethorpe	Leics	72	E11
Littlethorpe	N York	97	M7
Little Thurlow	Suffk	63	L10
Little Thurlow Green	Suffk	63	L10
Little Thurrock	Thurr	37	P5
Littleton	BaNES	19	Q2
Littleton	Ches W	81	N11
Littleton	D & G	108	D9
Littleton	Dorset	12	E4
Littleton	Hants	22	E8
Littleton	Somset	19	N8
Littleton	Surrey	23	Q5
Littleton	Surrey	36	C7
Littleton Drew	Wilts	32	F8
Littleton of Airlie	Angus	142	E7
Littleton-on-Severn	S Glos	31	Q7
Littleton Panell	Wilts	21	J4
Little Torrington	Devon	16	H8
Little Totham	Essex	52	E9
Little Town	Cumb	100	H7
Littletown	Dur	104	B2
Little Town	Lancs	89	K3
Little Town	Warrtn	82	D6
Little Twycross	Leics	72	A9
Little Urswick	Cumb	94	F6
Little Wakering	Essex	38	F4
Little Walden	Essex	51	M2
Little Waldingfield	Suffk	52	F2
Little Walsingham	Norfk	76	C4
Little Waltham	Essex	52	B9
Little Warley	Essex	37	P2
Little Washbourne	Gloucs	47	J8
Little Weighton	E R Yk	92	G4
Little Welnetham	Suffk	64	B10
Little Welton	Lincs	87	K3
Little Wenham	Suffk	53	J4
Little Wenlock	Wrekin	57	L3
Little Weston	Somset	20	B9
Little Whitefield	IoW	14	G9
Little Whittingham Green	Suffk	65	K6
Little Whittington	Nthumb	112	E7
Littlewick Green	W & M	35	M9
Little Wilbraham	Cambs	62	H9
Littlewindsor	Dorset	11	J4
Little Witcombe	Gloucs	46	H11
Little Witley	Worcs	46	E2
Little Wittenham	Oxon	34	G6
Little Wolford	Warwks	47	Q7
Littlewood	Staffs	58	E3
Little Woodcote	Gt Lon	36	G8
Littleworth	Bucks	49	N10
Littleworth	Oxon	34	B5
Littleworth	Staffs	58	F2
Littleworth	Staffs	70	G10
Littleworth	W Susx	24	E6
Littleworth	Worcs	46	G4
Littleworth	Worcs	47	J2
Littleworth Common	Bucks	35	P7
Little Wratting	Suffk	63	L11
Little Wymington	Bed	61	L8
Little Wymondley	Herts	50	F5
Little Wyrley	Staffs	58	F3
Little Wytheford	Shrops	69	Q11
Little Yeldham	Essex	52	C4
Littley Green	Essex	51	Q7
Litton	Derbys	83	Q10
Litton	N York	96	D6
Litton	Somset	19	Q4
Litton Cheney	Dorset	11	L6
Liurbost	W Isls	168	i5
Liverpool	Lpool	81	L6
Liversedge	Kirk	90	F6
Liverton	Devon	9	K9
Liverton	R & Cl	105	K7
Liverton Mines	R & Cl	105	K7
Liverton Street	Kent	38	E11
Livingston	W Loth	127	K4
Livingston Village	W Loth	127	J4
Lixwm	Flints	80	H10
Lizard	Cnwll	3	J11
Llaingoch	IoA	78	C7
Llaithddu	Powys	55	P8
Llan	Powys	55	K8
Llanaber	Gwynd	67	L11
Llanaelhaearn	Gwynd	66	F6
Llanafan	Cerdgn	54	F10
Llanafan-Fawr	Powys	44	D3
Llanallgo	IoA	79	J7
Llanarmon	Gwynd	66	G7
Llanarmon Dyffryn Ceiriog	Wrexhm	68	G8
Llanarmon-yn-Ial	Denbgs	68	G3
Llanarth	Cerdgn	42	H3
Llanarth	Mons	31	L2
Llanarthne	Carmth	43	K11
Llanasa	Flints	80	G8
Llanbabo	IoA	78	F6
Llanbadarn Fawr	Cerdgn	54	E8
Llanbadarn Fynydd	Powys	55	P9
Llanbadarn-y-garreg	Powys	44	G5
Llanbadoc	Mons	31	L5
Llanbadrig	IoA	78	F4
Llanbeder	Newpt	31	L6
Llanbedr	Gwynd	67	K9
Llanbedr	Powys	44	G5
Llanbedr	Powys	45	J10
Llanbedr-Dyffryn-Clwyd	Denbgs	68	F3
Llanbedrgoch	IoA	79	J8
Llanbedrog	Gwynd	66	E8
Llanbedr-y-Cennin	Conwy	79	P11
Llanberis	Gwynd	67	K2
Llanbethêry	V Glam	30	D11
Llanbister	Powys	55	Q10
Llanblethian	V Glam	30	C10
Llanboidy	Carmth	41	P6
Llanbradach	Caerph	30	F6
Llanbrynmair	Powys	55	M5
Llancadle	V Glam	30	D11
Llancarfan	V Glam	30	D10
Llancayo	Mons	31	L4
Llancloudy	Herefs	45	P10
Llancynfelyn	Cerdgn	54	E6
Llandaff	Cardif	30	G9
Llandanwg	Gwynd	67	K9
Llandarcy	Neath	29	K5
Llanddaniel Fab	IoA	78	H10
Llanddarog	Carmth	43	K11
Llanddeiniol	Cerdgn	54	D10
Llanddeiniolen	Gwynd	67	J11
Llandderfel	Gwynd	68	C7
Llanddeusant	Carmth	43	Q10
Llanddeusant	IoA	78	E7
Llanddew	Powys	44	F8
Llanddewi	Swans	28	E7
Llanddewi Brefi	Cerdgn	43	N3
Llanddewi'r Cwm	Powys	44	E5
Llanddewi Rhydderch	Mons	31	L2
Llanddewi Velfrey	Pembks	41	M7
Llanddewi Ystradenni	Powys	55	Q11
Llanddoged	Conwy	67	Q2
Llanddona	IoA	79	K9
Llanddowror	Carmth	41	Q8
Llanddulas	Conwy	80	C9
Llanddwywe	Gwynd	67	K10
Llanddyfnan	IoA	79	J9
Llandecwyn	Gwynd	67	L7
Llandefaelog	Powys	44	E8
Llandefaelog-Tre'r-Graig	Powys	44	G9
Llandefalle	Powys	44	G7
Llandegfan	IoA	79	K10
Llandegla	Denbgs	68	G4
Llandegley	Powys	44	G2
Llandegveth	Mons	31	K5
Llandegwning	Gwynd	66	D9
Llandeilo	Carmth	43	M10
Llandeilo Graban	Powys	44	F6
Llandeilo'r Fan	Powys	44	B8
Llandeloy	Pembks	40	G5
Llandenny	Mons	31	M4
Llandevaud	Newpt	31	M6
Llandevenny	Mons	31	M7
Llandinabo	Herefs	45	Q9
Llandinam	Powys	55	N7
Llandissilio	Pembks	41	M6
Llandogo	Mons	31	P4
Llandough	V Glam	30	C10
Llandough	V Glam	30	G10
Llandovery	Carmth	43	Q8
Llandow	V Glam	29	P10
Llandre	Carmth	43	N6
Llandre	Cerdgn	54	E7
Llandre Isaf	Pembks	41	M5
Llandrillo	Denbgs	68	D7
Llandrillo-yn-Rhôs	Conwy	79	Q8
Llandrindod Wells	Powys	44	F2
Llandrinio	Powys	69	J11
Llandudno	Conwy	79	P8
Llandudno Junction	Conwy	79	P9
Llandulas	Powys	44	B6
Llandwrog	Gwynd	66	H3
Llandybie	Carmth	43	M11
Llandyfaelog	Carmth	28	D2
Llandyfan	Carmth	43	M11
Llandyfriog	Cerdgn	42	F6
Llandyfrydog	IoA	78	G7
Llandygai	Gwynd	79	K10
Llandygwydd	Cerdgn	41	P2
Llandynan	Denbgs	68	G5
Llandyrnog	Denbgs	80	G11
Llandyssil	Powys	56	B5
Llandysul	Cerdgn	42	H6
Llanedeyrn	Cardif	30	H8
Llanedi	Carmth	28	G3
Llaneglwys	Powys	44	F7
Llanegryn	Gwynd	54	E3
Llanegwad	Carmth	43	K10
Llaneilian	IoA	78	H6
Llanelian-yn-Rhôs	Conwy	68	B9
Llanelidan	Denbgs	68	F4
Llanelieu	Powys	44	H8
Llanellen	Mons	31	K2
Llanelli	Carmth	28	F4
Llanelltyd	Gwynd	67	N11
Llanelly	Mons	30	H2
Llanelly Hill	Mons	30	H2
Llanelwedd	Powys	44	E4
Llanenddwyn	Gwynd	67	K10
Llanengan	Gwynd	66	D9
Llanerch	Gwynd	68	A11
Llanerch	Powys	56	E6
Llanerchymedd	IoA	78	G8
Llanerfyl	Powys	55	N3
Llanfabon	Caerph	30	F6
Llanfachraeth	IoA	78	E8
Llanfachreth	Gwynd	67	P10
Llanfaelog	IoA	78	E8
Llanfaelrhys	Gwynd	66	C9
Llanfaenor	Mons	45	N11
Llanfaes	IoA	79	L9
Llanfaes	Powys	44	E9
Llanfaethlu	IoA	78	E7
Llanfair	Gwynd	67	K9
Llanfair Caereinion	Powys	55	Q3
Llanfair Clydogau	Cerdgn	43	M4
Llanfair Dyffryn Clwyd	Denbgs	68	F3
Llanfairfechan	Conwy	79	M10
Llanfair Kilgeddin	Mons	31	L3
Llanfair-Nant-Gwyn	Pembks	41	N3
Llanfairpwllgwyngyll	IoA	79	J10
Llanfair Talhaiarn	Conwy	80	C10
Llanfair Waterdine	Shrops	56	C9
Llanfairynghornwy	IoA	78	E6
Llanfair-yn-Neubwll	IoA	78	E9
Llanfallteg	Carmth	41	N6
Llanfallteg West	Carmth	41	M7
Llanfarian	Cerdgn	54	D9
Llanfechain	Powys	68	G10
Llanfechan	Powys	44	D4
Llanfechell	IoA	78	F6
Llanferres	Denbgs	68	G2
Llan Ffestiniog	Gwynd	67	N6
Llanfflewyn	IoA	78	F7
Llanfigael	IoA	78	E8
Llanfihangel-ar-arth	Carmth	43	J7
Llanfihangel Glyn Myfyr	Conwy	68	C5
Llanfihangel Nant Bran	Powys	44	C8
Llanfihangel-nant-Melan	Powys	44	H3
Llanfihangel Rhydithon	Powys	56	B11
Llanfihangel Rogiet	Mons	31	N7
Llanfihangel Tal-y-llyn	Powys	44	G9
Llanfihangel-uwch-Gwili	Carmth	43	J10
Llanfihangel-y-Creuddyn	Cerdgn	54	F9
Llanfihangel-yng-Ngwynfa	Powys	68	E11
Llanfihangel yn Nhowyn	IoA	78	E9
Llanfihangel-y-pennant	Gwynd	54	F3
Llanfihangel-y-pennant	Gwynd	67	J6
Llanfilo	Powys	44	G8
Llanfoist	Mons	31	J2
Llanfor	Gwynd	68	B7
Llanfrechfa	Torfn	31	K6
Llanfrothen	Gwynd	67	L6
Llanfrynach	Powys	44	F9
Llanfwrog	Denbgs	68	F3
Llanfwrog	IoA	78	E8
Llanfyllin	Powys	68	F11
Llanfynydd	Carmth	43	L9
Llanfynydd	Flints	69	J3
Llanfyrnach	Pembks	41	P4
Llangadfan	Powys	55	N2
Llangadog	Carmth	28	D3
Llangadog	Carmth	43	P9
Llangadwaladr	IoA	78	F11
Llangadwaladr	Powys	68	G8
Llangaffo	IoA	78	G11
Llangain	Carmth	42	G11
Llangammarch Wells	Powys	44	C5
Llangan	V Glam	30	C9
Llangarron	Herefs	45	Q10
Llangasty-Talyllyn	Powys	44	G9
Llangathen	Carmth	43	L10
Llangattock	Powys	45	J11
Llangattock Lingoed	Mons	45	M10
Llangattock-Vibon-Avel	Mons	45	P11
Llangedwyn	Powys	68	G10
Llangefni	IoA	78	H9
Llangeinor	Brdgnd	29	P7
Llangeitho	Cerdgn	43	M3
Llangeler	Carmth	42	G7
Llangelynin	Gwynd	54	D3
Llangennech	Carmth	28	G4
Llangennith	Swans	28	D6
Llangenny	Powys	45	J11
Llangernyw	Conwy	80	B11
Llangian	Gwynd	66	D9
Llangiwg	Neath	29	K3
Llangloffan	Pembks	40	H4
Llanglydwen	Carmth	41	N5
Llangoed	IoA	79	L9
Llangoedmor	Cerdgn	42	D5
Llangollen	Denbgs	68	H6
Llangolman	Pembks	41	M5
Llangors	Powys	44	G9
Llangorwen	Cerdgn	54	E8
Llangovan	Mons	31	N3
Llangower	Gwynd	68	B8
Llangrannog	Cerdgn	42	F4
Llangristiolus	IoA	78	G10
Llangrove	Herefs	45	Q11
Llangua	Mons	45	M9
Llangunllo	Powys	56	C10
Llangunnor	Carmth	42	H10
Llangurig	Powys	55	L9
Llangwm	Conwy	68	C6
Llangwm	Mons	31	M5
Llangwm	Pembks	41	J9
Llangwnnadl	Gwynd	66	C8
Llangwyfan	Denbgs	68	G11
Llangwyllog	IoA	78	G9
Llangwyryfon	Cerdgn	54	D10
Llangybi	Cerdgn	43	M4
Llangybi	Gwynd	66	G6
Llangybi	Mons	31	L5
Llangyfelach	Swans	28	H5
Llangynhafal	Denbgs	68	F2
Llangynidr	Powys	44	H11
Llangynin	Carmth	41	Q7
Llangynllo	Cerdgn	42	G6
Llangynog	Carmth	28	B2
Llangynog	Powys	68	E9
Llangynwyd	Brdgnd	29	N7
Llanhamlach	Powys	44	F9
Llanharan	Rhondd	30	D8
Llanharry	Rhondd	30	D8
Llanhennock	Mons	31	L6
Llanhilleth	Blae G	30	H4
Llanidan	IoA	78	H11
Llanidloes	Powys	55	M8
Llaniestyn	Gwynd	66	D8
Llanigon	Powys	44	J7
Llanilar	Cerdgn	54	E9
Llanilid	Rhondd	30	C8
Llanina	Cerdgn	42	H3
Llanio	Cerdgn	43	M3
Llanishen	Cardif	30	G8
Llanishen	Mons	31	N4
Llanllechid	Gwynd	79	L11
Llanlleonfel	Powys	44	C4
Llanllowell	Mons	31	L5
Llanllugan	Powys	55	P4
Llanllwch	Carmth	42	G11
Llanllwchaiarn	Powys	55	Q6
Llanllwni	Carmth	43	J7
Llanllyfni	Gwynd	66	H4
Llanmadoc	Swans	28	D6
Llanmaes	V Glam	30	C11
Llanmartin	Newpt	31	L7
Llanmerewig	Powys	56	B6
Llanmihangel	V Glam	30	C10
Llanmiloe	Carmth	41	P9
Llanmorlais	Swans	28	F5
Llannefydd	Conwy	80	D10
Llannon	Carmth	28	G3
Llannor	Gwynd	66	F7
Llanon	Cerdgn	54	C11
Llanover	Mons	31	K3
Llanpumsaint	Carmth	42	H9
Llanrhaeadr-ym-Mochnant	Powys	68	F9
Llanrhian	Pembks	40	F4
Llanrhidian	Swans	28	E6
Llanrhos	Conwy	79	P8
Llanrhychwyn	Conwy	67	P2
Llanrhyddlad	IoA	78	E7
Llanrhystud	Cerdgn	54	C11
Llanrothal	Herefs	45	P11
Llanrug	Gwynd	67	J2

Llanrumney Cardif...30 H8
Llanrwst Conwy...67 Q2
Llansadurnen Carmth...41 Q8
Llansadwrn Carmth...43 N8
Llansadwrn IoA...79 K9
Llansaint Carmth...28 C3
Llansamlet Swans...29 J5
Llansanffraid Glan Conwy
  Conwy...79 Q9
Llansannan Conwy...80 C11
Llansannor V Glam...30 C9
Llansantffraed Powys...44 G10
Llansantffraed-
  Cwmdeuddwr Powys...55 M11
Llansantffraed-in-Elvel
  Powys...44 F4
Llansantffraid Cerdgn...54 C11
Llansantffraid-ym-
  Mechain Powys...68 H10
Llansawel Carmth...43 M7
Llansilin Powys...68 H9
Llansoy Mons...31 M4
Llanspyddid Powys...44 E9
Llanstadwell Pembks...40 H10
Llansteffan Carmth...28 C2
Llanstephan Powys...44 G6
Llantarnam Torfn...31 K6
Llanthewy Skirrid Mons...45 L11
Llanthony Mons...45 K9
Llantilio-Crossenny Mons...31 L2
Llantilio Pertholey Mons...45 L11
Llantood Pembks...41 N2
Llantrisant IoA...78 F8
Llantrisant Mons...31 L5
Llantrisant Rhondd...30 D8
Llantrithyd V Glam...30 D10
Llantwit Fardre Rhondd...30 E7
Llantwit Major V Glam...30 C11
Llantysilio Denbgs...68 G6
Llanuwchllyn Gwynd...68 A8
Llanvaches Newpt...31 M6
Llanvair Discoed Mons...31 M6
Llanvapley Mons...31 L2
Llanvetherine Mons...45 M11
Llanveynoe Herefs...45 L8
Llanvihangel Crucorney
  Mons...45 L10
Llanvihangel Gobion Mons...31 K3
Llanvihangel-Ystern-
  Llewern Mons...31 M2
Llanwarne Herefs...45 Q9
Llanwddyn Powys...68 D11
Llanwenarth Mons...31 J2
Llanwenog Cerdgn...43 J5
Llanwern Newpt...31 L7
Llanwinio Carmth...41 Q5
Llanwnda Gwynd...66 H3
Llanwnda Pembks...40 H3
Llanwnnen Cerdgn...43 K5
Llanwnog Powys...55 N6
Llanwonno Rhondd...30 D5
Llanwrda Carmth...43 P8
Llanwrin Powys...54 H4
Llanwrthwl Powys...44 D2
Llanwrtyd Powys...44 B5
Llanwrtyd Wells Powys...44 B5
Llanwyddelan Powys...55 P4
Llanyblodwel Shrops...68 H10
Llanybri Carmth...28 B2
Llanybydder Carmth...43 K6
Llanycefn Pembks...41 L6
Llanychaer Pembks...41 J3
Llanycil Gwynd...68 B8
Llanycrwys Carmth...43 M5
Llanymawddwy Gwynd...68 B11
Llanymynech Powys...68 J10
Llanynghenedl IoA...78 E8
Llanynys Denbgs...68 F2
Llan-y-pwll Wrexhm...69 L4
Llanyre Powys...44 E2
Llanystumdwy Gwynd...66 H7
Llanywern Powys...44 G9
Llawhaden Pembks...41 L7
Llawnt Shrops...68 H8
Llawryglyn Powys...55 L6
Llay Wrexhm...69 K3
Llechcynfarwy IoA...78 F8
Llechfaen Powys...44 F9
Llechrhyd Caerph...30 F3
Llechryd Cerdgn...41 P2
Llechylched IoA...78 E9
Lledrod Cerdgn...54 E10
Llidiardau Gwynd...68 A7
Llidiartnenog Carmth...43 K7
Llidiart-y-parc Denbgs...68 F6
Llithfaen Gwynd...66 F6
Lloc Flints...80 G9
Llowes Powys...44 H6
Llwydcoed Rhondd...30 C4
Llwydiarth Powys...68 D11
Llwyn Denbgs...68 E2
Llwyncelyn Cerdgn...42 H3
Llwyndafydd Cerdgn...42 G3
Llwynderw Powys...56 C4
Llwyn-drain Pembks...41 Q4
Llwyndyrys Gwynd...66 F6
Llwyngwril Gwynd...54 D3
Llwynhendy Carmth...28 F5
Llwynmawr Wrexhm...68 H7
Llwyn-on Myr Td...30 D2
Llwyn-y-brain Carmth...41 N8
Llwyn-y-groes Cerdgn...43 L3
Llwynypia Rhondd...30 C6
Llynclys Shrops...69 J10
Llynfaes IoA...78 G9
Llŷn Peninsula Gwynd...66 E7
Llyn-y-pandy Flints...81 J11
Llysfaen Conwy...80 B9
Llyswen Cerdgn...43 J2
Llyswen Powys...44 G7
Llysworney V Glam...30 C10
Llys-y-frân Pembks...41 K6
Llywel Powys...44 B8
Load Brook Sheff...84 C3
Loan Falk...126 F4
Loanend Nthumb...129 N9
Loanhead Mdloth...127 P4
Loaningfoot D & G...109 L9
Loans S Ayrs...125 J11
Lobb Devon...16 H4
Lobhillcross Devon...8 C7
Lochailort Highld...145 N11
Lochaline Highld...138 B9
Lochans D & G...106 E6

Locharbriggs D & G...109 L4
Lochavich Ag & B...131 J4
Lochawe Ag & B...131 N2
Loch Baghasdail W Isls...168 c16
Lochboisdale W Isls...168 c16
Lochbuie Ag & B...137 Q10
Lochcarron Highld...154 A10
Lochdon Ag & B...138 C11
Lochdonhead Ag & B...138 C11
Lochead Ag & B...123 N4
Lochearnhead Stirlg...132 H3
Lochee C Dund...142 F11
Loch Eil Highld...139 K2
Locheilside Station Highld...138 H2
Lochend Highld...155 Q10
Locheport W Isls...168 d11
Loch Euphort W Isls...168 d11
Lochfoot D & G...109 J6
Lochgair Ag & B...131 J9
Lochgelly Fife...134 F9
Lochgilphead Ag & B...130 H10
Lochgoilhead Ag & B...131 Q7
Lochieheads Fife...134 H5
Lochill Moray...157 P5
Lochindorb Lodge Highld...156 H10
Lochinver Highld...160 H2
Loch Lomond and The
  Trossachs National
  Park...132 E5
Loch Loyal Lodge Highld...165 P7
Lochluichart Highld...155 K5
Lochmaben D & G...109 N4
Lochmaddy W Isls...168 e11
Loch nam Madadh W Isls...168 e11
Loch Ness Highld...147 N2
Lochore Fife...134 F8
Loch Portain W Isls...168 e10
Lochportain W Isls...168 e10
Lochranza N Ayrs...124 J2
Loch Sgioport W Isls...168 d14
Lochside Abers...143 N5
Lochside D & G...109 L5
Lochside Highld...156 E7
Lochskipport W Isls...168 d14
Lochslin Highld...163 J10
Lochton S Ayrs...107 J2
Lochty Angus...143 J5
Lochty Fife...135 N6
Lochuisge Highld...138 D6
Lochwinnoch Rens...125 K6
Lochwood D & G...116 F11
Lockengate Cnwll...4 G9
Lockerbie D & G...109 P4
Lockeridge Wilts...33 M11
Lockerley Hants...22 B9
Locking N Som...19 L3
Locking Stumps Warrtn...82 D6
Lockington E R Yk...99 K11
Lockington Leics...72 D5
Lockleywood Shrops...70 B9
Locksbottom Gt Lon...37 K7
Locksgreen IoW...14 D8
Locks Heath Hants...14 F5
Lockton N York...98 G3
Loddington Leics...73 K10
Loddington Nhants...60 H5
Loddiswell Devon...7 J9
Loddon Norfk...65 M2
Lode Cambs...62 H8
Lode Heath Solhll...59 J8
Loders Dorset...11 K6
Lodsworth W Susx...23 P10
Lofthouse Leeds...91 J5
Lofthouse N York...96 H6
Lofthouse Gate Wakefd...91 J6
Loftus R & Cl...105 K7
Logan E Ayrs...115 L3
Loganbeck Cumb...94 D2
Loganlea W Loth...126 H5
Loggerheads Staffs...70 C7
Logie Angus...143 M5
Logie Fife...135 L3
Logie Moray...157 J7
Logie Coldstone Abers...150 C7
Logie Newton Abers...158 G10
Logie Pert Angus...143 M5
Logierait P & K...141 N7
Logierieve Abers...151 N2
Login Carmth...41 N6
Lolworth Cambs...62 E8
Lonbain Highld...153 M7
Londesborough E R Yk...98 H11
London Gt Lon...36 H4
London Apprentice Cnwll...3 Q4
London Ashford Airport
  Kent...27 J7
London Beach Kent...26 E4
London City Airport Gt Lon...37 K4
London Colney Herts...50 E10
Londonderry N York...97 M3
London Gateway Services
  Gt Lon...36 E2
London Gatwick Airport
  W Susx...24 G2
London Heathrow Airport
  Gt Lon...36 C5
London Luton Airport Luton...50 D6
London Oxford Airport
  Oxon...48 E11
London Southend Airport
  Essex...38 E4
London Stansted Airport
  Essex...51 N6
London Zoo ZSL Gt Lon...36 G4
Londonthorpe Lincs...73 P3
Lonemore Highld...160 D10
Lonemore Highld...153 P2
Long Ashton N Som...31 P10
Long Bank Worcs...57 P10
Long Bennington Lincs...73 L2
Longbenton N Tyne...113 L7
Longborough Gloucs...47 N9
Long Bredy Dorset...11 M6
Longbridge Birm...58 F9
Longbridge Warwks...47 Q2
Longbridge Deverill Wilts...20 G6
Long Buckby Nhants...60 D7
Longburgh Cumb...110 F9
Longburton Dorset...11 N2
Long Cause Devon...7 K6
Long Clawson Leics...73 J5
Longcliffe Derbys...84 B9
Longcombe Devon...7 L7
Long Common Hants...14 F4
Long Compton Staffs...70 F10
Long Compton Warwks...47 Q8

Longcot Oxon...33 Q6
Long Crendon Bucks...35 J3
Long Crichel Dorset...12 G2
Longcroft Cumb...110 D9
Longcross Surrey...35 Q11
Longden Shrops...56 G3
Longden Common Shrops...56 G3
Long Ditton Surrey...36 E7
Longdon Staffs...58 G2
Longdon Worcs...46 F7
Longdon Green Staffs...58 G2
Longdon Heath Worcs...46 F7
Longdon upon Tern Wrekin...69 R11
Longdown Devon...9 L6
Longdowns Cnwll...3 J7
Long Drax N York...92 A5
Long Duckmanton Derbys...84 F6
Long Eaton Derbys...72 D4
Longfield Kent...37 P7
Longford Covtry...59 N8
Longford Derbys...71 N7
Longford Gloucs...46 F10
Longford Gt Lon...36 C5
Longford Kent...37 M9
Longford Shrops...70 A8
Longford Wrekin...70 C11
Longformacus Border...128 H8
Longframlington Nthumb...119 M10
Long Green Ches W...81 P10
Long Green Worcs...46 F8
Longham Dorset...13 J5
Longham Norfk...76 C8
Long Hanborough Oxon...34 D2
Longhaven Abers...159 R10
Long Hedges Lincs...87 L11
Longhirst Nthumb...113 K3
Longhope Gloucs...46 C11
Longhope Ork...169 c7
Longhorsley Nthumb...112 H2
Longhoughton Nthumb...119 P7
Long Itchington Warwks...59 P11
Longlands Cumb...101 J3
Longlane Derbys...71 N7
Long Lawford Warwks...59 Q9
Longleat Wilts...20 F6
Longlevens Gloucs...46 G11
Longley Calder...90 D6
Longley Kirk...90 E9
Longley Green Worcs...46 D4
Longleys P & K...142 D9
Long Load Somset...19 N10
Longmanhill Abers...158 H5
Long Marston Herts...49 N11
Long Marston N York...97 R10
Long Marston Warwks...47 N5
Long Marton Cumb...102 C6
Long Meadowend Shrops...56 G8
Long Melford Suffk...52 E2
Longmoor Camp Hants...23 L8
Longmorn Moray...157 N6
Longmoss Ches E...83 J10
Long Newnton Gloucs...32 H6
Longnewton Border...118 A5
Long Newton E Loth...128 E7
Longnewton on T...104 C7
Longney Gloucs...32 E2
Longniddry E Loth...128 C4
Longnor Shrops...56 H4
Longnor Staffs...71 K2
Longparish Hants...22 D5
Longpark Cumb...110 H8
Long Preston N York...96 B9
Longridge Lancs...89 J3
Longridge Staffs...70 G11
Longridge W Loth...126 G5
Long Riston E R Yk...93 K2
Longrock Cnwll...2 E7
Longsdon Staffs...70 H4
Longshaw Wigan...82 B4
Longside Abers...159 P8
Long Sight Oldham...89 Q9
Longslow Shrops...70 B7
Longstanton Cambs...62 E7
Longstock Hants...22 C7
Longstone Pembks...41 M9
Longstowe Cambs...62 D10
Long Stratton Norfk...64 H3
Long Street M Keyn...49 L5
Longstreet Wilts...21 M4
Long Sutton Hants...23 K5
Long Sutton Lincs...75 H6
Long Sutton Somset...19 N9
Longthorpe C Pete...74 C11
Long Thurlow Suffk...64 E8
Longthwaite Cumb...101 M6
Longton C Stke...70 G6
Longton Lancs...88 F5
Longtown Cumb...110 G7
Longtown Herefs...45 L9
Longueville Jersey...11 c2
Longville in the Dale Shrops...57 J6
Long Waste Wrekin...69 R11
Long Whatton Leics...72 D6
Longwick Bucks...35 L3
Long Wittenham Oxon...34 F6
Longwitton Nthumb...112 H3
Longwood D & G...108 F8
Longworth Oxon...34 C5
Longyester E Loth...128 E7
Lôn-las Swans...29 K5
Lonmay Abers...159 P6
Lonmore Highld...152 D8
Looe Cnwll...5 M11
Loose Kent...38 C11
Loosebeare Devon...8 H3
Loosegate Lincs...74 F5
Loosley Row Bucks...35 M4
Lootcherbrae Abers...158 F7
Lopcombe Corner Wilts...21 Q7
Lopen Somset...11 J2
Loppington Shrops...69 N9
Lorbottle Nthumb...119 M9
Lordington W Susx...15 L5
Lordshill C Sotn...22 C11
Lords Wood Medway...38 C9
Lornty P & K...142 B8
Loscoe Derbys...84 F11
Loscombe Dorset...11 K5
Losgaintir W Isls...168 f8
Lossiemouth Moray...157 N3
Lostford Shrops...69 R8
Lostock Gralam Ches W...82 E10

Lostock Green Ches W...82 E10
Lostock Hall Lancs...88 G5
Lostock Hall Fold Bolton...89 K9
Lostock Junction Bolton...89 K9
Lostwithiel Cnwll...5 J10
Lothbeg Highld...163 L4
Lothersdale N York...96 E11
Lothmore Highld...163 M4
Loudwater Bucks...35 P6
Loudwater Herts...50 C11
Loughborough Leics...72 E7
Loughor Swans...28 G5
Loughton Essex...51 K11
Loughton M Keyn...49 M7
Loughton Shrops...57 L8
Lound Lincs...73 R7
Lound Notts...85 L3
Lound Suffk...65 Q2
Lounston Devon...9 J9
Lount Leics...72 B7
Louth Lincs...87 K3
Loveclough Lancs...89 N5
Lovedean Hants...15 J4
Lover Wilts...21 P10
Loversall Donc...91 P11
Loves Green Essex...51 P10
Lovesome Hill N York...104 C11
Loveston Pembks...41 L9
Lovington Somset...19 Q8
Low Ackworth Wakefd...91 M7
Low Angerton Nthumb...112 G4
Lowbands Gloucs...46 E8
Low Barbeth D & G...106 D4
Low Barlings Lincs...86 E6
Low Bell End N York...105 K11
Low Bentham N York...95 N7
Low Biggins Cumb...95 N5
Low Borrowbridge Cumb...102 B10
Low Bradfield Sheff...84 C2
Low Bradley N York...96 F11
Low Braithwaite Cumb...101 M2
Low Burnham N Linc...92 C10
Low Buston Nthumb...119 P9
Lowca Cumb...100 C6
Low Catton E R Yk...98 E10
Low Coniscliffe Darltn...103 Q8
Low Crosby Cumb...110 H9
Lowdham Notts...85 L11
Low Dinsdale Darltn...104 B8
Lowe Shrops...69 N8
Lowe Hill Staffs...70 H3
Low Ellington N York...97 K4
Lower Aisholt Somset...18 H7
Lower Ansty Dorset...12 C4
Lower Apperley Gloucs...46 G9
Lower Arboll Highld...163 K10
Lower Arncott Oxon...48 H11
Lower Ashton Devon...9 K8
Lower Assendon Oxon...35 K8
Lower Badcall Highld...164 E8
Lower Ballam Lancs...88 D4
Lower Bartle Lancs...88 F4
Lower Basildon W Berk...34 H9
Lower Bearwood Herefs...45 M3
Lower Beeding W Susx...24 F5
Lower Benefield Nhants...61 L3
Lower Bentley Worcs...58 E11
Lower Beobridge Shrops...57 P6
Lower Birchwood Derbys...84 F10
Lower Boddington Nhants...48 E4
Lower Boscaswell Cnwll...2 B7
Lower Bourne Surrey...23 M6
Lower Brailes Warwks...48 B7
Lower Breakish Highld...145 L3
Lower Bredbury Stockp...83 K6
Lower Broadheath Worcs...46 F3
Lower Broxwood Herefs...45 M4
Lower Buckenhill Herefs...46 B8
Lower Bullingham Herefs...45 Q7
Lower Bullington Hants...21 N1
Lower Burrowton Devon...9 P5
Lower Burton Herefs...45 N3
Lower Caldecote C Beds...61 Q11
Lower Cam Gloucs...32 D4
Lower Canada N Som...19 L3
Lower Catesby Nhants...60 B9
Lower Chapel Powys...44 E7
Lower Chicksgrove Wilts...21 J9
Lower Chute Wilts...22 B4
Lower Clapton Gt Lon...36 H3
Lower Clent Worcs...58 D9
Lower Common Hants...23 L2
Lower Compton Wilts...33 K10
Lower Creedy Devon...9 K4
Lower Crossings Derbys...83 M8
Lower Cumberworth Kirk...90 G9
Lower Darwen Bl w D...89 K5
Lower Dean Bed...61 N7
Lower Denby Kirk...90 G9
Lower Diabaig Highld...153 P5
Lower Dicker E Susx...25 N8
Lower Dinchope Shrops...56 H8
Lower Down Shrops...56 E9
Lower Dunsforth N York...97 P8
Lower Egleton Herefs...46 B5
Lower Elkstone Staffs...71 L1
Lower Ellastone Staffs...71 L6
Lower End Bucks...35 J3
Lower End M Keyn...49 P7
Lower End Nhants...61 H9
Lower End Nhants...61 J8
Lower Everleigh Wilts...21 N4
Lower Exbury Hants...14 D7
Lower Eythorne Kent...27 N2
Lower Failand N Som...31 P10
Lower Faintree Shrops...57 M7
Lower Farringdon Hants...23 K7
Lower Feltham Gt Lon...36 C6
Lower Fittleworth W Susx...24 B7
Lower Foxdale IoM...80 c6
Lower Frankton Shrops...69 L8
Lower Freystrop Pembks...41 J8
Lower Froyle Hants...23 L5
Lower Gabwell Devon...7 N5
Lower Gledfield Highld...162 D6
Lower Godney Somset...19 N6
Lower Gornal Dudley...58 D6
Lower Gravenhurst
  C Beds...50 D3
Lower Green Herts...50 E4
Lower Green Herts...51 K4
Lower Green Kent...25 N2
Lower Green Kent...25 P2
Lower Green Norfk...76 D4
Lower Green Staffs...58 D3
Lower Green Suffk...63 M7
Lower Hacheston Suffk...65 L10

Lower Halstock Leigh
  Dorset...11 L3
Lower Halstow Kent...38 E8
Lower Hamworthy BCP...12 G6
Lower Hardres Kent...39 L11
Lower Harpton Herefs...45 K2
Lower Hartlip Kent...38 D9
Lower Hartshay Derbys...84 E10
Lower Hartwell Bucks...35 L2
Lower Hatton Staffs...70 E7
Lower Hawthwaite Cumb...94 E3
Lower Hergest Herefs...45 K3
Lower Heyford Oxon...48 E10
Lower Heysham Lancs...95 J8
Lower Higham Kent...38 B7
Lower Holbrook Suffk...53 L4
Lower Hordley Shrops...69 L9
Lower Horncroft W Susx...24 B7
Lowerhouse Lancs...89 N4
Lower Houses Kirk...90 F7
Lower Howsell Worcs...46 E5
Lower Irlam Salfd...82 F6
Lower Kilburn Derbys...72 B2
Lower Kilcott Gloucs...32 E7
Lower Killeyan Ag & B...122 C11
Lower Kingcombe Dorset...11 M5
Lower Kingswood Surrey...36 F10
Lower Kinnerton Ches W...69 K2
Lower Langford N Som...19 N2
Lower Largo Fife...135 L7
Lower Leigh Staffs...71 J7
Lower Lemington Gloucs...47 P8
Lower Llanfadog Powys...55 M11
Lower Lovacott Devon...17 J6
Lower Loxhore Devon...17 L4
Lower Lydbrook Gloucs...46 A11
Lower Lye Herefs...56 G11
Lower Machen Newpt...30 H7
Lower Maes-coed Herefs...45 L8
Lower Mannington Dorset...13 J4
Lower Marston Somset...20 E6
Lower Meend Gloucs...31 Q4
Lower Merridge Somset...18 H8
Lower Middleton Cheney
  Nhants...48 F6
Lower Milton Somset...19 P5
Lower Moor Worcs...47 J5
Lower Morton S Glos...32 B6
Lower Nazeing Essex...51 J9
Lower Norton Warwks...47 P2
Lower Nyland Dorset...20 E10
Lower Oddington Gloucs...47 P9
Lower Penarth V Glam...30 G11
Lower Penn Staffs...58 C5
Lower Pennington Hants...13 P6
Lower Penwortham Lancs...88 G5
Lower Peover Ches E...82 F10
Lower Place Rochdl...89 Q8
Lower Pollicott Bucks...35 K2
Lower Quinton Warwks...47 N5
Lower Rainham Medway...38 D8
Lower Raydon Suffk...52 H4
Lower Roadwater Somset...18 D7
Lower Salter Lancs...95 N8
Lower Seagry Wilts...33 J8
Lower Sheering Essex...51 L8
Lower Shelton C Beds...49 Q6
Lower Shiplake Oxon...35 L9
Lower Shuckburgh Warwks...48 E2
Lower Slaughter Gloucs...47 N10
Lower Soothill Kirk...90 H6
Lower Soudley Gloucs...32 C3
Lower Standen Kent...27 M3
Lower Stanton St Quintin
  Wilts...32 H8
Lower Stoke Medway...38 D6
Lower Stondon C Beds...50 E3
Lower Stone Gloucs...32 C6
Lower Stonnall Staffs...58 G4
Lower Stow Bedon Norfk...64 D3
Lower Street Dorset...12 D5
Lower Street E Susx...26 B9
Lower Street Norfk...77 K4
Lower Street Suffk...63 N10
Lower Street Suffk...65 G11
Lower Stretton Warrtn...82 D8
Lower Stroud Dorset...11 K5
Lower Sundon C Beds...50 C5
Lower Swanwick Hants...14 E5
Lower Swell Gloucs...47 N9
Lower Tadmarton Oxon...48 D7
Lower Tale Devon...9 Q4
Lower Tasburgh Norfk...64 H2
Lower Tean Staffs...71 J7
Lower Thurlton Norfk...65 N2
Lower Town Cnwll...2 H8
Lower Town Devon...7 J4
Lower Town Herefs...46 B6
Lower Town IoS...2 c1
Lower Town Pembks...41 J3
Lower Trebullett Cnwll...5 N6
Lower Treluswell Cnwll...3 K6
Lower Tysoe Warwks...48 B5
Lower Ufford Suffk...65 K11
Lower Upcott Devon...9 L8
Lower Upham Hants...22 F11
Lower Upnor Medway...38 C7
Lower Vexford Somset...18 F7
Lower Walton Warrtn...82 D7
Lower Waterston Dorset...12 B5
Lower Weare Somset...19 M4
Lower Weedon Nhants...60 D9
Lower Welson Herefs...45 K4
Lower Westmancote Worcs...46 H7
Lower Whatcombe Dorset...12 D4
Lower Whatley Somset...20 D5
Lower Whitley Ches W...82 D9
Lower Wick Gloucs...32 D5
Lower Wick Worcs...46 F4
Lower Wield Hants...22 H6
Lower Willingdon E Susx...25 N10
Lower Withington Ches E...82 H11
Lower Woodend Bucks...35 M7
Lower Woodford Wilts...21 M7
Lower Wraxall Dorset...11 M4
Lower Wyche Worcs...46 E6
Lower Wyke C Brad...90 F5
Lowesby Leics...73 J9
Lowestoft Suffk...65 Q3
Loweswater Cumb...100 F6
Low Etherley Dur...103 N5
Low Fell Gatesd...113 L9
Lowfield Heath W Susx...24 G3
Low Gartachorrans Stirlg...132 D10
Low Gate Nthumb...112 D8

Low Gettbridge Cumb....111 K9
Lowgill Cumb....102 B11
Lowgill Lancs....95 P8
Low Grantley N York....97 K6
Low Green N York....97 K9
Low Habberley Worcs....57 Q9
Low Ham Somset....19 M9
Low Harrogate N York....97 L9
Low Hawsker N York....105 P9
Low Hesket Cumb....111 J11
Low Hutton N York....98 F7
Lowick Cumb....94 F3
Lowick Nhants....61 L4
Lowick Nthumb....119 K3
Lowick Bridge Cumb....94 F3
Lowick Green Cumb....94 F3
Low Knipe Cumb....101 P7
Low Laithe N York....97 J8
Lowlands Dur....103 M5
Lowlands Torfn....31 J5
Low Langton Lincs....86 G5
Low Leighton Derbys....83 M7
Low Lorton Cumb....100 G5
Low Marishes N York....98 G5
Low Marnham Notts....85 P7
Low Middleton Nthumb....119 M3
Low Mill N York....105 J11
Low Moor C Brad....90 F5
Low Moorsley Sundld....113 M11
Low Moresby Cumb....100 C6
Low Newton Cumb....95 J4
Low Newton-by-the-Sea
Nthumb....119 P6
Low Pittington Dur....104 B2
Low Row Cumb....100 G2
Low Row Cumb....101 L3
Low Row Cumb....111 L8
Low Row N York....103 J11
Low Salchrie D & G....106 D4
Low Santon N Linc....92 F8
Lowsonford Warwks....59 J11
Low Street Norfk....77 L7
Low Street Thurr....37 Q5
Low Tharston Norfk....64 H2
Lowther Cumb....101 P6
Lowthorpe E R Yk....99 M8
Lowton Devon....8 G4
Lowton Somset....18 G11
Lowton Wigan....82 D5
Lowton Common Wigan....82 D5
Lowton St Mary's Wigan....82 D5
Low Torry Fife....134 C10
Low Toynton Lincs....87 J6
Low Valley Barns....91 L10
Low Wood Cumb....94 G4
Low Worsall N York....104 C9
Low Wray Cumb....101 L10
Loxbeare Devon....18 B11
Loxhill Surrey....24 B3
Loxhore Devon....17 L4
Loxhore Cott Devon....17 L4
Loxley Warwks....47 Q4
Loxley Green Staffs....71 K8
Loxter Herefs....46 D6
Loxton N Som....19 L3
Loxwood W Susx....24 B4
Lubenham Leics....60 F3
Lucasgate Lincs....87 M11
Lucas Green Surrey....23 P2
Luccombe Somset....18 B6
Luccombe Village IoW....14 G11
Lucker Nthumb....119 N4
Luckett Cnwll....5 P7
Lucking Street Essex....52 D5
Luckington Wilts....32 F8
Lucklawhill Fife....135 L3
Lucknam Wilts....32 F10
Luckwell Bridge Somset....18 B7
Lucton Herefs....45 N2
Lucy Cross N York....103 P8
Ludag W Isls....168 c16
Ludborough Lincs....93 N11
Ludbrook Devon....6 H8
Ludchurch Pembks....41 M8
Luddenden Calder....90 C5
Luddenden Foot Calder....90 C5
Luddenham Court Kent....38 G9
Luddington N Linc....92 D7
Luddington Warwks....47 N4
Luddington in the Brook
Nhants....61 P4
Ludford Lincs....86 G3
Ludford Shrops....57 J10
Ludgershall Bucks....49 J11
Ludgershall Wilts....21 Q4
Ludgvan Cnwll....2 E7
Ludham Norfk....77 M8
Ludlow Shrops....57 J9
Ludney Somset....10 H2
Ludwell Wilts....20 H10
Ludworth Dur....104 C2
Luffenhall Herts....50 G5
Luffincott Devon....5 N3
Luffness E Loth....128 D4
Lugar E Ayrs....115 L3
Luggate Burn E Loth....128 F5
Lugg Green Herefs....45 N2
Luggiebank N Lans....126 D3
Lugton E Ayrs....125 L7
Lugwardine Herefs....45 R6
Luib Highld....145 J2
Luing Ag & B....130 E5
Lulham Herefs....45 N6
Lullington Derbys....59 K2
Lullington E Susx....25 M10
Lullington Somset....20 E4
Lulsgate Bottom N Som....31 P11
Lulsley Worcs....46 D3
Lulworth Camp Dorset....12 D8
Lumb Calder....90 C6
Lumb Lancs....89 N6
Lumbutts Calder....90 B6
Lumby N York....91 M4

Lundy Green Norfk....65 J3
Lunga Ag & B....130 E6
Lunna Shet....169 r7
Lunsford Kent....37 Q9
Lunsford's Cross E Susx....26 B9
Lunt Sefton....81 L4
Luntley Herefs....45 M3
Luppitt Devon....10 D3
Lupridge Devon....7 J8
Lupset Wakefd....91 J7
Lupton Cumb....95 M4
Lurgashall W Susx....23 P9
Lurley Devon....18 B11
Lusby Lincs....87 K7
Luscombe Devon....7 K7
Luskentyre W Isls....168 f8
Luson Devon....6 G8
Luss Ag & B....132 D9
Lussagiven Ag & B....130 C10
Lusta Highld....152 D6
Lustleigh Devon....9 J8
Luston Herefs....45 P2
Luthermuir Abers....143 M4
Luthrie Fife....135 J4
Lutley Dudley....58 D8
Luton Devon....9 M9
Luton Devon....10 B4
Luton Luton....50 C6
Luton Medway....38 C8
Luton Airport Luton....50 D6
Lutterworth Leics....60 B4
Lutton Devon....6 F7
Lutton Devon....6 H6
Lutton Lincs....74 H5
Lutton Nhants....61 P3
Luxborough Somset....18 C7
Luxulyan Cnwll....4 H10
Luxulyan Valley Cnwll....4 H10
Luzley Tamesd....83 L4
Lybster Highld....167 M9
Lydbury North Shrops....56 F7
Lydcott Devon....17 M4
Lydd Kent....26 H7
Lydd Airport Kent....27 J7
Lydden Kent....27 N2
Lydden Kent....39 Q8
Lyddington Rutlnd....73 M11
Lydd-on-Sea Kent....27 J8
Lydeard St Lawrence
Somset....18 F8
Lyde Green Hants....23 K3
Lyde Green S Glos....32 C9
Lydford Devon....8 D7
Lydford on Fosse Somset....19 Q8
Lydgate Calder....89 Q5
Lydgate Rochdl....90 B7
Lydham Shrops....56 E6
Lydiard Green Wilts....33 L7
Lydiard Millicent Wilts....33 L7
Lydiard Tregoze Swindn....33 M8
Lydiate Sefton....81 M4
Lydiate Ash Worcs....58 E9
Lydlinch Dorset....12 B2
Lydney Gloucs....32 B4
Lydstep Pembks....41 L11
Lye Dudley....58 D8
Lye Cross N Som....19 N2
Lye Green Bucks....35 Q4
Lye Green E Susx....25 M4
Lye Green Warwks....59 J11
Lye Head Worcs....57 P10
Lye's Green Wilts....20 F5
Lyford Oxon....34 C6
Lymbridge Green Kent....27 K3
Lyme Regis Dorset....10 G6
Lyminge Kent....27 L3
Lymington Hants....13 P5
Lyminster W Susx....24 B10
Lymm Warrtn....82 E7
Lymm Services Warrtn....82 E8
Lympne Kent....27 K4
Lympsham Somset....19 K4
Lympstone Devon....9 N8
Lynbridge Devon....17 N2
Lynchat Highld....148 D7
Lynch Green Norfk....76 H10
Lyndhurst Hants....13 P3
Lyndon Rutlnd....73 N10
Lyndon Green Birm....58 H7
Lyne Border....117 J2
Lyne Surrey....36 B7
Lyneal Shrops....69 M8
Lyne Down Herefs....46 B8
Lyneham Oxon....47 Q10
Lyneham Wilts....33 K9
Lyneholmford Cumb....111 K6
Lynemouth Nthumb....113 L2
Lyne of Skene Abers....151 K5
Lynesack Dur....103 L5
Lyness Ork....169 c7
Lyng Norfk....76 F8
Lyng Somset....19 K9
Lynmouth Devon....17 N2
Lynn Staffs....58 G4
Lynn Wrekin....70 D11
Lynsted Kent....38 F9
Lynstone Cnwll....16 C10
Lynton Devon....17 N2
Lynton Cross Devon....17 J3
Lyon's Gate Dorset....11 P3
Lyonshall Herefs....45 L3
Lytchett Matravers Dorset....12 F5
Lytchett Minster Dorset....12 G6
Lyth Highld....167 N4
Lytham Lancs....88 D5
Lytham St Annes Lancs....88 C5
Lythbank Shrops....56 H3
Lythe N York....105 M8
Lythmore Highld....167 J3

Machynys Carmth....28 F5
Mackworth Derbys....71 Q7
Macmerry E Loth....128 C5
Maddaford Devon....8 D6
Madderty P & K....134 B3
Maddington Wilts....21 L6
Maddiston Falk....126 G2
Madehurst W Susx....15 M4
Madeley Staffs....70 D6
Madeley Wrekin....57 M4
Madeley Heath Staffs....70 D5
Madeley Park Wood Staffs....70 D6
Madford Devon....10 C2
Madingley Cambs....62 E8
Madley Herefs....45 N7
Madresfield Worcs....46 F5
Madron Cnwll....2 D7
Maenaddwyn IoA....78 H8
Maenan Conwy....79 P11
Maenclochog Pembks....41 L5
Maendy V Glam....30 D9
Maenporth Cnwll....3 K8
Maentwrog Gwynd....67 M6
Maen-y-groes Cerdgn....42 G3
Maer Cnwll....16 C10
Maer Staffs....70 D7
Maerdy Carmth....43 N9
Maerdy Conwy....68 D6
Maerdy Rhondd....30 C5
Maesbrook Shrops....69 K10
Maesbury Shrops....69 K9
Maesbury Marsh Shrops....69 K9
Maes-glas Newpt....31 J7
Maesgwynne Carmth....41 P6
Maeshafn Denbgs....68 H2
Maesllyn Cerdgn....42 G6
Maesmynis Powys....44 E5
Maesmynis Powys....44 E5
Maesteg Brdgnd....29 N6
Maesybont Carmth....43 L11
Maesycwmmer Caerph....30 G6
Magdalen Laver Essex....51 M9
Maggieknockater Moray....157 Q8
Maggots End Essex....51 L5
Magham Down E Susx....25 P8
Maghull Sefton....81 M4
Magna Park Leics....60 B8
Magor Mons....31 M7
Magor Services Mons....31 M7
Maidenbower W Susx....24 G3
Maiden Bradley Wilts....20 F7
Maidencombe Torbay....7 N5
Maidenhayne Devon....10 F5
Maiden Head N Som....31 Q11
Maidenhead W & M....35 N8
Maiden Law Dur....113 J11
Maiden Newton Dorset....11 M5
Maidens S Ayrs....114 C4
Maiden's Green Br For....35 P10
Maidenwell Lincs....87 K5
Maiden Wells Pembks....41 J11
Maidford Nhants....48 H4
Maids Moreton Bucks....49 K7
Maidstone Kent....38 C10
Maidstone Services Kent....38 D10
Maidwell Nhants....60 F5
Mail Shet....169 r9
Maindee Newpt....31 K7
Mainland Ork....169 d6
Mainland Shet....169 r8
Mainsforth Dur....104 B4
Mains of Balhall Angus....143 J5
Mains of Balnakettle Abers....143 L3
Mains of Dalvey Highld....157 L11
Mains of Haulkerton Abers....143 N3
Mains of Lesmoir Abers....150 D2
Mains of Melgunds Angus....143 J6
Mainsriddle D & G....109 K9
Mainstone Shrops....56 D7
Maisemore Gloucs....46 F9
Major's Green Worcs....58 H9
Makeney Derbys....72 B2
Malborough Devon....7 J11
Malcoff Derbys....83 N8
Malden Rushett Gt Lon....36 E8
Maldon Essex....52 E10
Malham N York....96 D8
Maligar Highld....152 H5
Mallaig Highld....145 L8
Mallaigvaig Highld....145 L8
Malleny Mills C Edin....127 M4
Mallows Green Essex....51 L5
Malltraeth IoA....78 G11
Mallwyd Gwynd....55 K2
Malmesbury Wilts....32 H7
Malmsmead Devon....17 P2
Malpas Ches W....69 N5
Malpas Cnwll....3 L5
Malpas Newpt....31 K6
Malshanger Hants....22 G4
Malswick Gloucs....46 D10
Maltby Lincs....87 K4
Maltby Rothm....84 H2
Maltby S on T....104 E8
Maltby le Marsh Lincs....87 N4
Malting Green Essex....52 G7
Maltman's Hill Kent....26 F3
Malton N York....98 F6
Malvern Worcs....46 E5
Malvern Hills....46 E6
Malvern Link Worcs....46 E5
Malvern Wells Worcs....46 E6
Mamble Worcs....57 M10
Mamhilad Mons....31 K4
Manaccan Cnwll....3 K9
Manafon Powys....55 Q4
Mànais W Isls....168 g9
Manaton Devon....9 J8
Manby Lincs....87 L3
Mancetter Warwks....59 M5
Manchester Manch....82 H5
Manchester Airport Manch....82 H8
Mancot Flints....81 L11
Mandally Highld....146 H7
Manea Cambs....62 G3
Maney Birm....58 H5
Manfield N York....103 P8
Mangersta W Isls....168 f4
Mangerton Dorset....11 K5
Mangotsfield S Glos....32 C9
Mangrove Green Herts....50 D6
Mangurstadh W Isls....168 f4
Manhay Cnwll....2 H7
Manish W Isls....168 g9
Mankinholes Calder....90 B6
Manley Ches W....81 Q10

Manmoel Caerph....30 G4
Mannal Ag & B....136 B7
Manningford Bohune Wilts....21 M3
Manningford Bruce Wilts....21 M3
Manningham C Brad....90 E3
Mannings Heath W Susx....24 F5
Mannington Dorset....13 J3
Manningtree Essex....53 K5
Mannofield C Aber....151 N7
Manorbier Pembks....41 L11
Manorbier Newton Pembks....41 K10
Manordeilo Carmth....43 N9
Manorhill Border....118 C4
Manorowen Pembks....40 H3
Manor Park Gt Lon....37 K3
Mansell Gamage Herefs....45 M6
Mansell Lacy Herefs....45 N5
Mansergh Cumb....95 N4
Mansfield E Ayrs....115 M5
Mansfield Notts....84 H8
Mansfield Woodhouse Notts....84 H8
Mansriggs Cumb....94 F4
Manston Dorset....20 F11
Manston Kent....39 P8
Manston Leeds....91 K4
Manswood Dorset....12 G3
Manthorpe Lincs....73 N3
Manthorpe Lincs....73 R7
Manton N Linc....92 F10
Manton Notts....85 K5
Manton Rutlnd....73 M10
Manton Wilts....33 N11
Manuden Essex....51 L5
Manwood Green Essex....51 M8
Maperton Somset....20 C9
Maplebeck Notts....85 M8
Maple Cross Herts....36 B2
Mapledurham Oxon....35 J9
Mapledurwell Hants....23 J4
Maplehurst W Susx....24 E6
Maplescombe Kent....37 N8
Mapleton Derbys....71 M5
Mapleton Kent....37 L11
Mapperley Derbys....72 C2
Mapperley Park C Nott....72 F2
Mapperton Dorset....11 L5
Mappleborough Green
Warwks....58 G11
Mappleton E R Yk....93 M2
Mapplewell Barns....91 J8
Mappowder Dorset....12 B3
Màraig W Isls....168 h7
Marazanvose Cnwll....3 K3
Marazion Cnwll....2 E7
Marbhig W Isls....168 j6
Marbury Ches E....69 Q5
March Cambs....74 H11
March S Lans....116 D8
Marcham Oxon....34 D3
Marchamley Shrops....69 Q9
Marchamley Wood Shrops....69 Q8
Marchington Staffs....71 L8
Marchington Woodlands
Staffs....71 L9
Marchwiel Wrexhm....69 L5
Marchwood Hants....14 C4
Marcross V Glam....29 P11
Marden Herefs....45 Q5
Marden Kent....26 B3
Marden Wilts....21 L3
Marden Ash Essex....51 N10
Marden Beech Kent....26 B3
Marden's Hill E Susx....25 M4
Marden Thorn Kent....26 C3
Mardlebury Herts....50 G7
Mardy Mons....45 L11
Marefield Leics....73 J9
Mareham le Fen Lincs....87 J8
Mareham on the Hill Lincs....87 J7
Marehay Derbys....84 E11
Marehill W Susx....24 C7
Maresfield E Susx....25 L6
Marfleet C KuH....93 K5
Marford Wrexhm....69 L3
Margam Neath....29 L7
Margaret Marsh Dorset....20 F11
Margaret Roding Essex....51 N8
Margaretting Essex....51 Q10
Margaretting Tye Essex....51 Q10
Margate Kent....39 Q7
Margnaheglish N Ayrs....121 K5
Margrie D & G....108 C10
Margrove Park R & Cl....105 J7
Marham Norfk....75 P9
Marhamchurch Cnwll....16 C11
Marham Park Suffk....64 A8
Marholm C Pete....74 B10
Marian-glas IoA....79 J8
Mariansleigh Devon....17 N7
Marine Town Kent....38 F7
Marionburgh Abers....151 L4
Marishader Highld....152 H5
Maristow Devon....6 D6
Marjoriebanks D & G....109 N4
Mark Somset....19 L5
Markbeech Kent....25 L2
Markby Lincs....87 N5
Mark Causeway Somset....19 L5
Mark Cross E Susx....25 N4
Markeaton C Derb....72 A3
Market Bosworth Leics....72 C10
Market Deeping Lincs....74 B8
Market Drayton Shrops....70 B8
Market Harborough Leics....60 F3
Market Lavington Wilts....21 K4
Market Overton Rutlnd....73 M7
Market Rasen Lincs....86 F3
Market Stainton Lincs....86 H5
Market Warsop Notts....85 J7
Market Weighton E R Yk....92 E2
Market Weston Suffk....64 D6
Markfield Leics....72 D9
Markham Caerph....30 G4
Markham Moor Notts....85 M6
Markinch Fife....134 H5
Markington N York....97 L7
Markle E Loth....128 F4
Marksbury BaNES....20 C2
Mark's Corner IoW....14 E8
Marks Tey Essex....52 F7
Markwell Cnwll....5 P10
Markyate Herts....50 C7
Marlborough Wilts....33 N11
Marlbrook Herefs....45 Q4
Marlbrook Worcs....58 E10
Marlcliff Warwks....47 L4

Marldon Devon....7 M6
Marle Green E Susx....25 N7
Marlesford Suffk....65 L10
Marley Kent....39 L11
Marley Kent....39 P11
Marley Green Ches E....69 Q5
Marley Hill Gatesd....113 K9
Marlingford Norfk....76 G10
Marloes Pembks....40 E9
Marlow Bucks....35 M7
Marlow Herefs....56 G9
Marlow Bottom Bucks....35 M7
Marlpit Hill Kent....37 K11
Marlpits E Susx....25 L5
Marlpits E Susx....26 B9
Marlpool Derbys....84 F11
Marnhull Dorset....20 E11
Marple Stockp....83 L7
Marple Bridge Stockp....83 L7
Marr Donc....91 N9
Marrick N York....103 L11
Marros Carmth....41 P9
Marsden Kirk....90 C8
Marsden S Tyne....113 N8
Marsden Height Lancs....89 P3
Marsett N York....96 D3
Marsh Bucks....35 M3
Marsh C Brad....90 C3
Marsh Devon....10 F2
Marshall's Heath Herts....50 E8
Marshalswick Herts....50 E9
Marsham Norfk....76 H7
Marsh Baldon Oxon....34 G5
Marsh Benham W Berk....34 D11
Marshborough Kent....39 P10
Marshbrook Shrops....56 G7
Marshchapel Lincs....93 Q11
Marsh Farm Luton....50 C5
Marshfield Newpt....31 J8
Marshfield S Glos....32 E10
Marshgate Cnwll....5 K3
Marsh Gibbon Bucks....48 H10
Marsh Green Devon....9 P6
Marsh Green E Susx....25 K2
Marsh Green Kent....37 L2
Marsh Green Wrekin....69 Q11
Marshland St James Norfk....75 K9
Marsh Lane Derbys....84 F5
Marsh Lane Gloucs....31 Q3
Marshside Sefton....88 D7
Marsh Street Somset....18 C6
Marshwood Dorset....10 H5
Marske N York....103 M10
Marske-by-the-Sea R & Cl....104 H6
Marsland Green Wigan....82 E9
Marston Ches W....82 E9
Marston Herefs....45 M3
Marston Lincs....73 M2
Marston Oxon....34 F3
Marston Staffs....58 B2
Marston Staffs....70 G9
Marston Warwks....59 K6
Marston Wilts....21 J3
Marston Green Solhll....59 J7
Marston Jabbet Warwks....59 N7
Marston Magna Somset....19 Q10
Marston Meysey Wilts....33 M5
Marston Montgomery
Derbys....71 L7
Marston Moretaine C Beds....49 Q6
Marston on Dove Derbys....71 N9
Marston St Lawrence
Nhants....48 F6
Marston Stannett Herefs....45 R3
Marston Trussell Nhants....60 E3
Marstow Herefs....45 R11
Marsworth Bucks....35 P2
Marten Wilts....21 Q2
Marthall Ches E....82 G9
Martham Norfk....77 P8
Martin Hants....21 L11
Martin Kent....27 P2
Martin Lincs....86 F9
Martin Lincs....86 H7
Martindale Cumb....101 M7
Martin Dales Lincs....86 G8
Martin Drove End Hants....21 L10
Martinhoe Devon....17 M2
Martin Hussingtree Worcs....46 G2
Martinscroft Warrtn....82 E7
Martinstown Dorset....11 N7
Martlesham Suffk....53 M2
Martlesham Heath Suffk....53 M2
Martletwy Pembks....41 K8
Martley Worcs....46 E2
Martock Somset....19 N11
Marton Ches E....83 J11
Marton Ches W....82 D11
Marton Cumb....94 E5
Marton E R Yk....93 L3
Marton E R Yk....99 Q7
Marton Lincs....85 P4
Marton Middsb....104 F7
Marton N York....98 E4
Marton Shrops....56 D4
Marton Warwks....59 P11
Marton-cum-Grafton
N York....97 P8
Marton-le-Moor N York....97 N6
Martyr's Green Surrey....36 C9
Martyr Worthy Hants....22 F8
Marvig W Isls....168 j6
Marwell Zoo Hants....22 F10
Marwick Ork....169 b4
Marwood Devon....17 J4
Marybank Highld....155 N7
Maryburgh Highld....155 P6
Marygold Border....129 L8
Maryhill C Glas....125 P4
Marykirk Abers....143 M4
Maryland Mons....31 P3
Marylebone Gt Lon....36 G4
Marylebone Wigan....88 H9
Marypark Moray....157 M10
Maryport Cumb....100 D3
Maryport D & G....106 F11
Marystow Devon....8 B8
Mary Tavy Devon....8 D9
Maryton Angus....142 F7
Maryton Angus....143 M6
Marywell Abers....150 F8
Marywell Abers....151 N8
Marywell Angus....143 M9
Masham N York....97 K4
Mashbury Essex....51 Q8
Masongill N York....95 P5
Mastin Moor Derbys....84 G5

Matching Essex 51 M8
Matching Green Essex 51 M8
Matching Tye Essex 51 M8
Matfen Nthumb 112 F6
Matfield Kent 25 Q2
Mathern Mons 31 P6
Mathon Herefs 46 D5
Mathry Pembks 40 G4
Matlask Norfk 76 H5
Matlock Derbys 84 D9
Matlock Bank Derbys 84 D8
Matlock Bath Derbys 84 C9
Matlock Dale Derbys 84 C9
Matson Gloucs 46 G11
Matterdale End Cumb 101 L6
Mattersey Notts 85 L3
Mattersey Thorpe Notts 85 L3
Mattingley Hants 23 K3
Mattishall Norfk 76 F9
Mattishall Burgh Norfk 76 F9
Mauchline E Ayrs 115 J2
Maud Abers 159 M8
Maufant Jersey 11 c1
Maugersbury Gloucs 47 P9
Maughold IoM 80 g3
Mauld Highld 155 M10
Maulden C Beds 50 C3
Maulds Meaburn Cumb 102 B2
Maunby N York 97 N3
Maund Bryan Herefs 45 R4
Maundown Somset 18 E9
Mautby Norfk 77 P9
Mavesyn Ridware Staffs 71 K11
Mavis Enderby Lincs 87 L7
Mawbray Cumb 109 N11
Mawdesley Lancs 88 F8
Mawdlam Brdgnd 29 M8
Mawgan Cnwll 3 J8
Mawgan Porth Cnwll 4 D8
Maw Green Ches E 70 C3
Mawla Cnwll 3 J4
Mawnan Cnwll 3 K8
Mawnan Smith Cnwll 3 K8
Mawsley Nhants 60 H5
Mawthorpe Lincs 87 N6
Maxey C Pete 74 B9
Maxstoke Warwks 59 K7
Maxted Street Kent 27 K3
Maxton Border 118 B4
Maxton Kent 27 P3
Maxwelltown D & G 109 L5
Maxworthy Cnwll 5 M3
Mayals Swans 28 H7
May Bank Staffs 70 F5
Maybole S Ayrs 114 G6
Maybury Surrey 36 B9
Mayes Green Surrey 24 D3
Mayfield E Susx 25 N5
Mayfield Mdloth 128 B7
Mayfield Staffs 71 M5
Mayford Surrey 23 Q3
May Hill Gloucs 46 D10
Mayland Essex 52 F11
Maylandsea Essex 52 F11
Maynard's Green E Susx 25 N7
Maypole Birm 58 G9
Maypole Kent 39 M9
Maypole Mons 45 P11
Maypole Green Norfk 65 N2
Maypole Green Suffk 64 C10
Maypole Green Suffk 65 K8
May's Green Oxon 35 K8
May's Green Surrey 36 C9
Mead Devon 16 C8
Meadgate BaNES 20 C3
Meadle Bucks 35 M3
Meadowfield Dur 103 P3
Meadowtown Shrops 56 E4
Meadwell Devon 5 Q5
Meaford Staffs 70 F7
Mealabost W Isls 168 j4
Meal Bank Cumb 101 P11
Mealrigg Cumb 109 P11
Mealsgate Cumb 100 H2
Meanwood Leeds 90 H3
Mearbeck N York 96 B8
Meare Somset 19 N6
Meare Green Somset 19 J10
Meare Green Somset 19 K9
Mearns E Rens 125 N6
Mears Ashby Nhants 60 H7
Measham Leics 72 A8
Meath Green Surrey 24 G2
Meathop Cumb 95 J4
Meaux E R Yk 93 J3
Meavaig W Isls 168 f4
Meavy Devon 6 E5
Medbourne Leics 60 H2
Medburn Nthumb 112 H6
Meddon Devon 16 D8
Meden Vale Notts 85 J7
Medlam Lincs 87 K9
Medlar Lancs 88 E3
Medmenham Bucks 35 M8
Medomsley Dur 112 H10
Medstead Hants 23 J7
Medway Services Medway 38 D9
Meerbrook Staffs 70 H2
Meer Common Herefs 45 M4
Meesden Herts 51 K4
Meeson Wrekin 70 A10
Meeth Devon 17 J10
Meeting Green Suffk 63 N9
Meeting House Hill Norfk 77 L6
Meidrim Carmth 41 Q6
Meifod Powys 56 B2
Meigle P & K 142 D9
Meikle Carco D & G 116 B5
Meikle Earnock S Lans 126 C7
Meikle Ferry Highld 162 G9
Meikle Kilmory Ag & B 124 D5
Meikle Obney P & K 141 P10
Meikleour P & K 142 B10
Meikle Wartle Abers 158 H11
Meinciau Carmth 28 E2
Meir C Stke 70 G6
Meir Heath Staffs 70 G6
Melbost W Isls 168 j4
Melbourn Cambs 51 J2
Melbourne Derbys 72 B5
Melbourne E R Yk 92 C2
Melbourne Essex 51 Q9
Melbur Cnwll 3 N3
Melbury Devon 16 F8
Melbury Abbas Dorset 20 G10
Melbury Bubb Dorset 11 M3

Melbury Osmond Dorset 11 M3
Melbury Sampford Dorset 11 M3
Melchbourne Bed 61 M7
Melcombe Bingham Dorset 12 C4
Meldon Devon 8 E6
Meldon Nthumb 112 H4
Meldon Park Nthumb 112 H3
Meldreth Cambs 62 E11
Meldrum Stirlg 133 L8
Melfort Ag & B 130 G5
Meliden Denbgs 80 F8
Melinau Pembks 41 N8
Melin-byrhedyn Powys 55 J5
Melin-y-coed Conwy 67 Q2
Melin-y-ddol Powys 55 P3
Melin-y-wig Denbgs 68 Q5
Melkinthorpe Cumb 101 Q5
Melkridge Nthumb 111 P8
Melksham Wilts 20 H2
Mellangoose Cnwll 2 H8
Mell Green W Berk 34 E9
Mellguards Cumb 110 H11
Melling Lancs 95 M6
Melling Sefton 81 M4
Melling Mount Sefton 81 N4
Mellis Suffk 64 F7
Mellon Charles Highld 160 C5
Mellon Udrigle Highld 160 D7
Mellor Lancs 89 K4
Mellor Stockp 83 L7
Mellor Brook Lancs 89 J4
Mells Somset 20 D5
Mells Suffk 65 N6
Melmerby Cumb 102 B3
Melmerby N York 96 G3
Melmerby N York 97 M5
Melness Highld 165 N4
Melon Green Suffk 64 A10
Melplash Dorset 11 K5
Melrose Border 117 Q4
Melsetter Ork 169 b8
Melsonby N York 103 N9
Meltham Kirk 90 E8
Meltham Mills Kirk 90 E8
Melton E R Yk 92 G5
Melton Suffk 65 L11
Meltonby E R Yk 98 F10
Melton Constable Norfk 76 E5
Melton Mowbray Leics 73 K7
Melton Ross N Linc 93 J8
Melvaig Highld 160 A9
Melverley Shrops 69 K11
Melverley Green Shrops 69 K11
Melvich Highld 166 F4
Membury Devon 10 F4
Membury Services W Berk 34 B9
Memsie Abers 159 N5
Memus Angus 142 G6
Menabilly Cnwll 4 H11
Menagissey Cnwll 3 J4
Menai Bridge IoA 79 K10
Mendham Suffk 65 K5
Mendip Hills 19 P4
Mendlesham Suffk 64 G8
Mendlesham Green Suffk 64 F9
Menheniot Cnwll 5 M9
Menithwood Worcs 57 N11
Menna Cnwll 3 N3
Mennock D & G 115 R6
Menston C Brad 90 F2
Menstrie Clacks 133 P8
Menthorpe N York 92 B4
Mentmore Bucks 49 P11
Meoble Highld 145 N10
Meole Brace Shrops 56 H2
Meonstoke Hants 22 H11
Meon Vale Warwks 47 N5
Meopham Kent 37 P7
Meopham Green Kent 37 P7
Meopham Station Kent 37 P7
Mepal Cambs 62 F4
Meppershall C Beds 50 D3
Merbach Herefs 45 L5
Mere Ches E 82 F8
Mere Wilts 20 F8
Mere Brow Lancs 88 E7
Mereclough Lancs 89 P4
Mere Green Birm 58 H5
Mere Green Worcs 47 J2
Mere Heath Ches W 82 E10
Meresborough Medway 38 D9
Mereworth Kent 37 Q10
Meriden Solhll 59 K8
Merkadale Highld 152 F11
Merley BCP 12 H5
Merlin's Bridge Pembks 40 H8
Merrington Shrops 69 N10
Merrion Pembks 40 H11
Merriott Somset 11 J2
Merrivale Devon 8 D9
Merrow Surrey 36 B10
Merry Field Hill Dorset 12 H4
Merry Hill Herts 36 D2
Merryhill Wolves 58 C5
Merry Lees Leics 72 D9
Merrymeet Cnwll 5 M8
Mersea Island Essex 52 H8
Mersey Gateway Bridge Halton 82 B8
Mersham Kent 27 J3
Merstham Surrey 36 G10
Merston W Susx 15 N6
Merstone IoW 14 F9
Merther Cnwll 3 M5
Merthyr Carmth 42 G10
Merthyr Cynog Powys 44 D7
Merthyr Dyfan V Glam 30 F11
Merthyr Mawr Brdgnd 29 N9
Merthyr Tydfil Myr Td 30 D3
Merthyr Vale Myr Td 30 E5
Merton Devon 17 J9
Merton Gt Lon 36 G6
Merton Norfk 64 C2
Merton Oxon 48 G11
Meshaw Devon 17 P8
Messing Essex 52 E8
Messingham N Linc 92 E10
Metal Bridge Dur 103 Q4
Metfield Suffk 65 K5
Metherell Cnwll 5 Q8
Metheringham Lincs 86 E8
Methil Fife 135 K8
Methilhill Fife 135 K8
Methley Leeds 91 K5
Methley Junction Leeds 91 K5

Methlick Abers 159 L10
Methven P & K 134 C2
Methwold Norfk 63 M2
Methwold Hythe Norfk 63 M2
Mettingham Suffk 65 M4
Metton Norfk 76 J4
Mevagissey Cnwll 3 N6
Mexborough Donc 91 M10
Mey Highld 167 N2
Meysey Hampton Gloucs 33 M4
Miabhaig W Isls 168 f4
Michaelchurch Herefs 45 Q9
Michaelchurch Escley Herefs 45 L8
Michaelchurch-on-Arrow Powys 45 J4
Michaelstone-y-Fedw Newpt 30 H8
Michaelston-le-Pit V Glam 30 G10
Michaelstow Cnwll 4 H5
Michaelwood Services Gloucs 32 D5
Michelcombe Devon 6 H5
Micheldever Hants 22 F7
Micheldever Station Hants 22 F6
Michelmersh Hants 22 B9
Mickfield Suffk 64 G9
Micklebring Donc 84 H2
Mickleby N York 105 M8
Micklefield Leeds 91 L4
Micklefield Green Herts 50 B11
Mickleham Surrey 36 E10
Mickleover C Derb 71 Q8
Micklethwaite C Brad 90 E2
Micklethwaite Cumb 110 E10
Mickleton Dur 103 J6
Mickleton Gloucs 47 N6
Mickletown Leeds 91 L5
Mickle Trafford Ches W 81 N11
Mickley Derbys 84 D5
Mickley N York 97 L5
Mickley Green Suffk 64 A10
Mickley Square Nthumb 112 G8
Mid Ardlaw Abers 159 M5
Midbea Ork 169 d2
Mid Beltie Abers 150 G7
Mid Bockhampton BCP 13 L5
Mid Calder W Loth 127 K4
Mid Clyth Highld 167 N9
Middle Assendon Oxon 35 K7
Middle Aston Oxon 48 E9
Middle Barton Oxon 48 D9
Middlebie D & G 110 E5
Middlebridge P & K 141 L4
Middle Chinnock Somset 11 K2
Middle Claydon Bucks 49 K9
Middlecliffe Barns 91 L9
Middlecott Devon 8 H7
Middlecroft Derbys 84 F6
Middle Duntisbourne Gloucs 33 J3
Middleham N York 96 H3
Middle Handley Derbys 84 F5
Middle Harling Norfk 64 D4
Middlehill Cnwll 5 M8
Middlehill Wilts 32 F11
Middlehope Shrops 56 H7
Middle Kames Ag & B 131 J10
Middle Littleton Worcs 47 L5
Middle Madeley Staffs 70 D5
Middle Maes-coed Herefs 45 L8
Middlemarsh Dorset 11 P3
Middle Mayfield Staffs 71 L6
Middle Mill Pembks 40 F5
Middlemoor Devon 6 D4
Middle Quarter Kent 26 E4
Middle Rasen Lincs 86 E3
Middle Rocombe Devon 7 N5
Middle Salter Lancs 95 N8
Middlesbrough Middsb 104 E7
Middlesceugh Cumb 101 M3
Middleshaw Cumb 95 M3
Middlesmoor N York 96 G6
Middle Stoford Somset 18 G10
Middle Stoke Medway 38 D6
Middlestone Dur 103 Q4
Middlestone Moor Dur 103 P4
Middle Stoughton Somset 19 M5
Middlestown Wakefd 90 H7
Middle Street Gloucs 32 E4
Middle Taphouse Cnwll 5 K9
Middlethird Border 118 C2
Middleton Ag & B 136 A7
Middleton Cumb 95 N3
Middleton Derbys 71 M2
Middleton Derbys 84 C9
Middleton Essex 52 E4
Middleton Hants 22 D6
Middleton Herefs 57 J11
Middleton Lancs 95 J9
Middleton Leeds 91 J5
Middleton N York 96 H11
Middleton N York 98 F3
Middleton Nhants 60 H3
Middleton Norfk 75 M7
Middleton Nthumb 112 H4
Middleton Nthumb 119 M3
Middleton P & K 134 E6
Middleton Rochdl 89 P9
Middleton Shrops 57 J9
Middleton Shrops 69 K9
Middleton Suffk 65 N8
Middleton Swans 28 J5
Middleton Warwks 59 J5
Middleton Cheney Nhants 48 E6
Middleton Green Staffs 70 H7
Middleton-in-Teesdale Dur 102 H5
Middleton Moor Suffk 65 N8
Middleton One Row Darltn 104 C8
Middleton-on-Leven N York 104 E9
Middleton-on-Sea W Susx 15 Q6
Middleton on the Hill Herefs 45 Q2
Middleton on the Wolds E R Yk 99 J11
Middleton Park C Aber 151 N5
Middleton Priors Shrops 57 L6
Middleton Quernhow N York 97 M5
Middleton St George Darltn 104 C8
Middleton Scriven Shrops 57 M7
Middleton Stoney Oxon 48 F10
Middleton Tyas N York 103 P9
Middletown Cumb 100 C8
Middle Town IoS 2 b3

Middletown N Som 31 N10
Middletown Powys 56 E2
Middle Tysoe Warwks 48 B6
Middle Wallop Hants 21 Q7
Middlewich Ches E 82 F11
Middle Winterslow Wilts 21 P8
Middlewood Cnwll 5 M6
Middlewood Herefs 45 K6
Middle Woodford Wilts 21 M7
Middlewood Green Suffk 64 F9
Middle Yard Gloucs 32 F4
Middlezoy Somset 19 L8
Middridge Dur 103 P5
Midford BaNES 20 E2
Midge Hall Lancs 88 G6
Midgeholme Cumb 111 M9
Midgham W Berk 34 G11
Midgley Calder 90 C5
Midgley Wakefd 90 H8
Mid Holmwood Surrey 36 E11
Midhopestones Sheff 90 G11
Midhurst W Susx 23 N10
Mid Lavant W Susx 15 N5
Midlem Border 117 Q5
Mid Mains Highld 155 M10
Midney Somset 19 N9
Midpark Ag & B 124 C6
Midsomer Norton BaNES 20 C4
Midtown Highld 165 N4
Midville Lincs 87 L9
Midway Ches E 83 K8
Mid Yell Shet 169 s4
Migdale Highld 162 E8
Migvie Abers 150 C6
Milborne Port Somset 20 C11
Milborne St Andrew Dorset 12 D5
Milborne Wick Somset 20 C10
Milbourne Nthumb 112 H5
Milbourne Wilts 33 J7
Milburn Cumb 102 C5
Milbury Heath S Glos 32 C6
Milby N York 97 P7
Milcombe Oxon 48 D8
Milden Suffk 52 G2
Mildenhall Suffk 63 M6
Mildenhall Wilts 33 P11
Milebrook Powys 56 E10
Milebush Kent 26 C2
Mile Elm Wilts 33 J11
Mile End Gloucs 31 Q2
Mile End Suffk 65 L4
Mileham Norfk 76 C8
Mile Oak Br & H 24 F9
Mile Oak Kent 25 Q2
Mile Oak Staffs 59 J4
Miles Green Staffs 70 D5
Miles Hope Herefs 45 R2
Milesmark Fife 134 D10
Mile Town Kent 38 F7
Milfield Nthumb 118 H4
Milford Derbys 84 E11
Milford Devon 16 C7
Milford Powys 55 P6
Milford Staffs 70 H10
Milford Surrey 23 P6
Milford Haven Pembks 40 H9
Milford on Sea Hants 13 N6
Milkwall Gloucs 31 Q3
Millais Jersey 11 a1
Milland W Susx 23 M9
Milland Marsh W Susx 23 M9
Mill Bank Calder 90 C6
Millbeck Cumb 101 J5
Millbreck Abers 159 P9
Millbridge Surrey 23 M6
Millbrook C Beds 50 B3
Millbrook C Sotn 22 C11
Millbrook Cnwll 6 C8
Millbrook Jersey 11 b2
Millbrook Tamesd 83 L5
Mill Brow Stockp 83 L7
Millbuie Abers 151 K6
Millbuie Highld 155 Q7
Millcombe Devon 7 L9
Mill Common Norfk 77 L11
Mill Common Suffk 65 N5
Millcorner E Susx 26 D7
Millcraig Highld 156 B3
Milldale Staffs 71 L4
Mill End Bucks 35 L7
Millend Gloucs 32 D5
Mill End Herts 50 H4
Millerhill Mdloth 127 Q4
Miller's Dale Derbys 83 P10
Millers Green Derbys 71 P4
Miller's Green Essex 51 N9
Millerston C Glas 125 Q4
Millgate Lancs 89 P7
Mill Green Cambs 63 K11
Mill Green Essex 51 P10
Mill Green Herts 50 F8
Mill Green Lincs 74 D6
Mill Green Norfk 64 G5
Mill Green Shrops 70 B9
Mill Green Staffs 71 K10
Mill Green Suffk 64 D10
Mill Green Suffk 64 G9
Mill Green Suffk 65 L9
Millhalf Herefs 45 K5
Millhayes Devon 10 E4
Millhead Lancs 95 K6
Millheugh S Lans 126 C7
Mill Hill E Susx 25 P9
Mill Hill Gt Lon 36 F2
Millhouse Ag & B 124 B3
Millhouse Cumb 101 L3
Millhousebridge D & G 109 P3
Millhouse Green Barns 90 G9
Millhouses Barns 91 L10
Millhouses Sheff 84 D4
Milliken Park Rens 125 L5
Millin Cross Pembks 41 J8
Millington E R Yk 98 G10
Mill Lane Hants 23 L4
Millmeece Staffs 70 E8
Millness Cumb 95 L4
Mill of Drummond P & K 133 N4
Mill of Haldane W Duns 132 D11
Millom Cumb 94 D4
Millook Cnwll 5 K2
Millpool Cnwll 2 F7
Millpool Cnwll 5 J7

Millport N Ayrs 124 F7
Mill Side Cumb 95 J4
Mill Street Kent 37 Q9
Mill Street Norfk 76 F8
Mill Street Suffk 64 F7
Millthorpe Derbys 84 D5
Millthrop Cumb 95 P2
Milltimber C Aber 151 M7
Milltown Abers 149 M6
Milltown Abers 150 D4
Milltown Cnwll 5 J10
Milltown D & G 110 F5
Milltown Derbys 84 E8
Milltown Devon 17 K4
Milltown Highld 153 N9
Milltown of Auchindoun Moray 157 R9
Milltown of Campfield Abers 150 H7
Milltown of Edinvillie Moray 157 P9
Milltown of Rothiemay Moray 158 D8
Milnathort P & K 134 E7
Milngavie E Duns 125 P3
Milnrow Rochdl 89 Q8
Milnthorpe Cumb 95 K4
Milnthorpe Wakefd 91 J7
Milovaig Highld 152 B8
Milson Shrops 57 L10
Milstead Kent 38 F10
Milston Wilts 21 N5
Milthorpe Nhants 48 G5
Milton C Stke 70 G4
Milton Cambs 62 G8
Milton Cumb 111 L8
Milton D & G 106 H7
Milton D & G 108 H6
Milton Derbys 71 Q9
Milton Highld 155 N11
Milton Highld 155 Q8
Milton Highld 156 D3
Milton Highld 167 P6
Milton Inver 125 K4
Milton Kent 37 Q6
Milton Moray 149 M4
Milton Moray 157 D5
Milton N Som 19 K2
Milton Newpt 31 L7
Milton Notts 85 M6
Milton Oxon 34 E6
Milton Oxon 48 E7
Milton P & K 141 Q5
Milton Pembks 41 K10
Milton Somset 19 N10
Milton Stirlg 132 G7
Milton W Duns 125 L3
Milton Abbas Dorset 12 D4
Milton Abbot Devon 6 Q6
Milton Bridge Mdloth 127 P5
Milton Bryan C Beds 49 Q8
Milton Clevedon Somset 20 C7
Milton Combe Devon 6 D5
Milton Common Oxon 35 J4
Milton Damerel Devon 16 F9
Milton End Gloucs 32 D2
Milton End Gloucs 33 M4
Milton Ernest Bed 61 M9
Milton Green Ches W 69 N3
Milton Hill Oxon 34 E6
Milton Keynes M Keyn 49 N7
Milton Lilbourne Wilts 21 N2
Milton Malsor Nhants 60 F9
Milton Morenish P & K 140 F10
Milton of Auchinhove Abers 150 F7
Milton of Balgonie Fife 135 J7
Milton of Buchanan Stirlg 132 E9
Milton of Campsie E Duns 126 B2
Milton of Finavon Angus 142 H6
Milton of Leys Highld 156 B9
Milton of Murtle C Aber 151 M7
Milton on Stour Dorset 20 E9
Milton Regis Kent 38 F9
Milton Street E Susx 25 M10
Milton-under-Wychwood Oxon 47 Q11
Milverton Somset 18 F9
Milverton Warwks 59 M11
Milwich Staffs 70 H8
Milwr Flints 80 H10
Minard Ag & B 131 K8
Minchington Dorset 12 G2
Minchinhampton Gloucs 32 G4
Mindenhurst Surrey 23 P3
Mindrum Nthumb 118 F4
Minehead Somset 18 C5
Minera Wrexhm 69 J4
Minety Wilts 33 K6
Minffordd Gwynd 67 K7
Mingarrypark Highld 138 B4
Miningsby Lincs 87 K8
Minions Cnwll 5 M7
Minishant S Ayrs 114 F5
Minllyn Gwynd 55 K2
Minnigaff D & G 107 M4
Minnonie Abers 159 J5
Minshull Vernon Ches E 70 B2
Minskip N York 97 N8
Minstead Hants 13 N2
Minsted W Susx 23 N10
Minster Kent 39 P9
Minsterley Shrops 56 F3
Minster Lovell Oxon 34 B2
Minster-on-Sea Kent 38 G7
Minsterworth Gloucs 46 E11
Minterne Magna Dorset 11 P4
Minterne Parva Dorset 11 P4
Minting Lincs 86 G6
Mintlaw Abers 159 N8
Minto Border 117 R6
Minton Shrops 56 G6
Minwear Pembks 41 K8
Minworth Birm 59 J6
Mirehouse Cumb 100 C7
Mireland Highld 167 P4
Mirfield Kirk 90 G6
Miserden Gloucs 32 H3
Miskin Rhondd 30 D5
Miskin Rhondd 30 D8
Misson Notts 85 L2
Misterton Leics 60 C4
Misterton Notts 85 N2
Misterton Somset 11 K3
Mistley Essex 53 J5
Mistley Heath Essex 53 K5
Mitcham Gt Lon 36 G7

Mitcheldean Gloucs 46 C11
Mitchell Cnwll 3 M3
Mitchellslacks D & G 116 D11
Mitchel Troy Mons 31 N2
Mitford Nthumb 113 J3
Mithian Cnwll 3 J3
Mitton Staffs 70 F11
Mixbury Oxon 48 H8
Mixenden Calder 90 D5
Moats Tye Suffk 64 E10
Mobberley Ches E 82 G9
Mobberley Staffs 71 J6
Moccas Herefs 45 M6
Mochdre Conwy 79 Q9
Mochdre Powys 55 P7
Mochrum D & G 107 K8
Mockbeggar Hants 13 L3
Mockbeggar Kent 26 B2
Mockerkin Cumb 100 E6
Modbury Devon 6 H8
Moddershall Staffs 70 G7
Moelfre IoA 79 J7
Moelfre Powys 68 G9
Moel Tryfan Gwynd 67 J3
Moffat D & G 116 F9
Mogador Surrey 36 F10
Moggerhanger C Beds 61 P11
Moira Leics 71 Q11
Molash Kent 38 H11
Mol-chlach Highld 144 G5
Mold Flints 68 H2
Moldgreen Kirk 90 F7
Molehill Green Essex 51 N6
Molehill Green Essex 52 B7
Molescroft E R Yk 92 H2
Molesden Nthumb 112 H4
Molesworth Cambs 61 N5
Moll Highld 153 K11
Molland Devon 17 Q6
Mollington Ches W 81 M10
Mollington Oxon 48 D5
Mollinsburn N Lans 126 C3
Monachty Cerdgn 43 K2
Mondynes Abers 143 P2
Monewden Suffk 65 J10
Moneydie P & K 134 D2
Moneyrow Green W & M 35 N9
Moniaive D & G 115 Q9
Monifieth Angus 142 H11
Monikie Angus 142 H10
Monimail Fife 134 H5
Monington Pembks 41 M2
Monk Bretton Barns 91 K9
Monken Hadley Gt Lon 50 F11
Monk Fryston N York 91 N5
Monkhide Herefs 46 B6
Monkhill Cumb 110 F9
Monkhopton Shrops 57 L6
Monkland Herefs 45 P3
Monkleigh Devon 16 H7
Monknash V Glam 29 P10
Monkokehampton Devon 8 E3
Monkseaton N Tyne 113 M6
Monks Eleigh Suffk 52 G2
Monk's Gate W Susx 24 F5
Monks Heath Ches E 82 H10
Monk Sherborne Hants 22 H3
Monks Horton Kent 27 K3
Monksilver Somset 18 E7
Monks Kirby Warwks 59 Q8
Monk Soham Suffk 65 J8
Monkspath Solhll 58 H9
Monks Risborough Bucks 35 M4
Monksthorpe Lincs 87 M7
Monk Street Essex 51 P5
Monkswood Mons 31 K4
Monkton Devon 10 D4
Monkton Kent 39 N9
Monkton S Ayrs 114 G2
Monkton S Tyne 113 M8
Monkton V Glam 29 P10
Monkton Combe BaNES 20 E2
Monkton Deverill Wilts 20 G7
Monkton Farleigh Wilts 32 F11
Monkton Heathfield Somset 19 J9
Monkton Up Wimborne Dorset 12 H2
Monkton Wyld Dorset 10 G5
Monkwearmouth Sundld 113 N9
Monkwood Hants 23 J8
Monmore Green Wolves 58 D5
Monmouth Mons 31 P2
Monnington on Wye Herefs 45 M6
Monreith D & G 107 L9
Montacute Somset 19 N11
Montcliffe Bolton 89 K8
Montford Shrops 56 G2
Montford Bridge Shrops 69 M11
Montgarrie Abers 150 F4
Montgomery Powys 56 C5
Monton Salfd 82 G5
Montrose Angus 143 N6
Mont Saint Guern 10 b2
Monxton Hants 22 B6
Monyash Derbys 83 Q11
Monymusk Abers 150 H4
Monzie P & K 133 P2
Moodiesburn N Lans 126 B3
Moonzie Fife 135 J4
Moor Allerton Leeds 91 J3
Moorbath Dorset 11 J5
Moorby Lincs 87 J8
Moorcot Herefs 45 M3
Moor Crichel Dorset 12 G3
Moordown BCP 13 J6
Moore Halton 82 C8
Moor End C Beds 49 Q10
Moor End Calder 90 D5
Moor End Devon 17 M10
Moorend Gloucs 32 D4
Moor End Lancs 88 D2
Moor End N York 91 Q3
Moorends Donc 92 A7
Moorgreen Hants 22 E11
Moor Green Herts 50 H5
Moorgreen Notts 84 G11
Moorhall Derbys 84 D6
Moorhampton Herefs 45 M5
Moorhead C Brad 90 E3
Moor Head Leeds 90 G6
Moorhouse Cumb 110 E10
Moorhouse Cumb 110 F9
Moorhouse Donc 91 M8
Moorhouse Notts 85 N7
Moorhouse Bank Surrey 37 K10
Moorland Somset 19 K8

Moorlinch Somset 19 L7
Moor Monkton N York 97 R9
Moor Row Cumb 100 D8
Moor Row Cumb 110 D11
Moorsholm R & Cl 105 J8
Moorside Dorset 20 E11
Moorside Dur 112 G11
Moor Side Lancs 88 E4
Moor Side Lancs 88 F3
Moorside Leeds 90 G3
Moor Side Lincs 87 J9
Moorside Oldham 89 Q9
Moorstock Kent 27 K4
Moor Street Medway 38 D8
Moorswater Cnwll 5 L9
Moorthorpe Wakefd 91 M8
Moortown Devon 6 E4
Moortown Hants 13 L4
Moortown IoW 14 D10
Moortown Leeds 90 H3
Moortown Lincs 93 J11
Moortown Wrekin 69 R11
Morangie Highld 162 H10
Morar Highld 145 L9
Morborne Cambs 61 P2
Morchard Bishop Devon 9 J3
Morchard Road Devon 9 J3
Morcombelake Dorset 11 J6
Morcott Rutlnd 73 N10
Morda Shrops 69 J9
Morden Dorset 12 F5
Morden Gt Lon 36 G7
Mordiford Herefs 45 R7
Mordon Dur 104 B5
More Shrops 56 E6
Morebath Devon 18 C9
Morebattle Border 118 E6
Morecambe Lancs 95 J8
Moredon Swindn 33 M7
Morefield Highld 161 J7
Morehall Kent 27 M4
Moreleigh Devon 7 K8
Morenish P & K 140 F10
Moresby Parks Cumb 100 C7
Morestead Hants 22 F9
Moreton Dorset 12 D7
Moreton Essex 51 M9
Moreton Herefs 45 Q2
Moreton Oxon 35 J4
Moreton Staffs 70 D11
Moreton Staffs 71 L9
Moreton Wirral 81 K7
Moreton Corbet Shrops 69 Q10
Moreton Hall Suffk 64 B9
Moretonhampstead Devon 9 J7
Moreton-in-Marsh Gloucs 47 P8
Moreton Jeffries Herefs 46 B5
Moretonmill Shrops 69 Q10
Moreton Morrell Warwks 48 B3
Moreton on Lugg Herefs 45 Q5
Moreton Paddox Warwks 48 B4
Moreton Pinkney Nhants 48 G5
Moreton Say Shrops 70 A8
Moreton Valence Gloucs 32 E3
Morfa Cerdgn 42 F4
Morfa Bychan Gwynd 67 J7
Morfa Dinlle Gwynd 66 G3
Morfa Glas Neath 29 N3
Morfa Nefyn Gwynd 66 D6
Morganstown Cardif 30 F8
Morgan's Vale Wilts 21 N10
Moriah Cerdgn 54 E9
Morland Cumb 102 B6
Morley Ches E 82 H8
Morley Derbys 72 B2
Morley Dur 103 M5
Morley Leeds 90 H5
Morley Green Ches E 82 H8
Morley St Botolph Norfk 64 F2
Mornick Cnwll 5 N7
Morningside C Edin 127 N3
Morningside N Lans 126 E6
Morningthorpe Norfk 65 J3
Morpeth Nthumb 113 J3
Morphie Abers 143 N5
Morrey Staffs 71 L11
Morridge Side Staffs 71 J4
Morriston Swans 29 J5
Morston Norfk 76 E3
Mortehoe Devon 16 H2
Morthen Rothm 84 G3
Mortimer W Berk 23 J2
Mortimer Common W Berk 35 J11
Mortimer's Cross Herefs 45 N2
Mortimer West End Hants 22 H2
Mortlake Gt Lon 36 F5
Morton Cumb 101 N3
Morton Cumb 110 G10
Morton Derbys 84 F8
Morton IoW 14 H9
Morton Lincs 74 A6
Morton Lincs 85 P2
Morton Lincs 85 Q8
Morton Notts 85 M10
Morton Shrops 69 J10
Morton-on-Swale N York 97 N2
Morton on the Hill Norfk 76 G8
Morton Tinmouth Dur 103 N6
Morvah Cnwll 2 C6
Morval Cnwll 5 M10
Morvich Highld 146 B3
Morville Shrops 57 M6
Morville Heath Shrops 57 M6
Morwenstow Cnwll 16 C8
Mosborough Sheff 84 F4
Moscow E Ayrs 125 M9
Mose Shrops 57 P6
Mosedale Cumb 101 L4
Moseley Birm 58 G8
Moseley Wolves 58 D5
Moseley Wolves 58 F3
Moses Gate Bolton 89 L9
Moss Ag & B 136 B7
Moss Donc 91 P8
Moss Wrexhm 69 K4
Mossat Abers 150 D4
Mossbank Shet 169 r6
Moss Bank St Hel 81 Q5
Mossbay Cumb 100 C5
Mossblown S Ayrs 114 H3
Mossbrow Traffd 82 F7
Mossburnford Border 118 C7
Mossdale D & G 108 E6
Mossdale E Ayrs 115 J7
Moss Edge Lancs 88 E2

Moss End Ches E 82 E9
Mossend N Lans 126 C5
Mosser Mains Cumb 100 F5
Mossley Ches E 70 F2
Mossley Tamesd 83 L4
Mosspaul Inn Border 117 M11
Moss Side Cumb 110 C10
Moss-side Highld 156 F6
Moss Side Lancs 88 D4
Moss Side Sefton 81 M4
Mosstodloch Moray 157 Q6
Mossy Lea Lancs 88 G8
Mossyard D & G 107 P7
Mosterton Dorset 11 K3
Moston Manch 83 J4
Moston Shrops 69 Q9
Moston Green Ches E 70 C2
Mostyn Flints 80 H8
Motcombe Dorset 20 G9
Mothecombe Devon 6 G9
Motherby Cumb 101 M5
Motherwell N Lans 126 C6
Motspur Park Gt Lon 36 F7
Mottingham Gt Lon 37 K6
Mottisfont Hants 22 B9
Mottistone IoW 14 D10
Mottram in Longdendale Tamesd 83 L5
Mottram St Andrew Ches E 83 J9
Mouilpied Guern 10 b2
Mouldsworth Ches W 81 Q10
Moulin P & K 141 M6
Moulsecoomb Br & H 24 H9
Moulsford Oxon 34 G8
Moulsoe M Keyn 49 P6
Moultavie Highld 156 A3
Moulton Ches W 82 E11
Moulton Lincs 74 F6
Moulton N York 103 P10
Moulton Nhants 60 G7
Moulton Suffk 63 L8
Moulton V Glam 30 L11
Moulton Chapel Lincs 74 E7
Moulton St Mary Norfk 77 M10
Moulton Seas End Lincs 74 F5
Mount Cnwll 4 B10
Mount Cnwll 5 J8
Mount Kirk 90 D7
Mountain C Brad 90 D4
Mountain Ash Rhondd 30 D5
Mountain Cross Border 127 M8
Mountain Street Kent 39 J11
Mount Ambrose Cnwll 3 J5
Mount Bures Essex 52 F5
Mountfield E Susx 26 B7
Mountgerald Highld 155 Q5
Mount Hawke Cnwll 3 J4
Mount Hermon Cnwll 2 H10
Mountjoy Cnwll 4 D9
Mount Lothian Mdloth 127 P6
Mountnessing Essex 51 P11
Mounton Mons 31 P6
Mount Pleasant Ches E 70 E3
Mount Pleasant Derbys 71 P11
Mount Pleasant Derbys 84 D11
Mount Pleasant Dur 103 Q4
Mount Pleasant E R Yk 93 N3
Mount Pleasant E Susx 25 K7
Mount Pleasant Norfk 64 D3
Mount Pleasant Suffk 63 M11
Mount Pleasant Sundld 113 M10
Mount Pleasant Worcs 47 K2
Mountsorrel Leics 72 F8
Mount Sorrel Wilts 21 K10
Mount Tabor Calder 90 D5
Mousehole Cnwll 2 D8
Mouswald D & G 109 N6
Mow Cop Ches E 70 F3
Mowhaugh Border 118 F6
Mowmacre Hill C Leic 72 F9
Mowsley Leics 60 D3
Moy Highld 147 L11
Moy Highld 156 D11
Moyle Highld 145 Q4
Moylegrove Pembks 41 M2
Muasdale Ag & B 120 C3
Muchalls Abers 151 N9
Much Birch Herefs 45 Q8
Much Cowarne Herefs 46 B5
Much Dewchurch Herefs 45 P8
Muchelney Somset 19 M10
Muchelney Ham Somset 19 M10
Much Hadham Herts 51 K7
Much Hoole Lancs 88 F6
Much Hoole Town Lancs 88 F6
Muchlarnick Cnwll 5 L10
Much Marcle Herefs 46 C8
Much Wenlock Shrops 57 L5
Muck Highld 144 F12
Mucking Thurr 37 Q4
Muckleburgh Military Collection Norfk 76 G3
Muckleford Dorset 11 N6
Mucklestone Staffs 70 C7
Muckley Shrops 57 L5
Muckton Lincs 87 L4
Muddiford Devon 17 K4
Muddles Green E Susx 25 M8
Mudeford BCP 13 L6
Mudford Somset 19 Q11
Mudford Sock Somset 19 Q11
Mudgley Somset 19 N5
Mud Row Kent 38 H7
Mugdock Stirlg 125 P2
Mugeary Highld 152 G10
Mugginton Derbys 71 P6
Muggintonlane End Derbys 71 P6
Muggleswick Dur 112 F11
Muirden Abers 158 H7
Muirdrum Angus 143 K10
Muiresk Abers 158 G8
Muirhead Angus 142 E11
Muirhead Fife 134 H6
Muirhead N Lans 126 B4
Muirhouses Falk 134 C11
Muirkirk E Ayrs 115 N2
Muirmill Stirlg 133 L11
Muir of Fowlis Abers 150 F5
Muir of Miltonduff Moray 157 M6
Muir of Ord Highld 155 P7
Muirshearlich Highld 146 E11
Muirtack Abers 159 N10
Muirton P & K 133 Q5
Muirton Mains Highld 155 N7
Muirton of Ardblair P & K 142 B9

Muker N York 102 H11
Mulbarton Norfk 76 H11
Mulben Moray 157 R7
Mulfra Cnwll 2 D7
Mull Ag & B 137 Q9
Mullacott Cross Devon 17 J3
Mullardoch Highld 154 H11
Mullion Cnwll 2 H10
Mullion Cove Cnwll 2 H10
Mumby Lincs 87 P6
Munderfield Row Herefs 46 B4
Munderfield Stocks Herefs 46 C4
Mundesley Norfk 77 L4
Mundford Norfk 63 P2
Mundham Norfk 65 L2
Mundon Essex 52 E11
Mungrisdale Cumb 101 L4
Munlochy Highld 156 A7
Munnoch N Ayrs 124 H8
Munsley Herefs 46 C6
Munslow Shrops 57 J7
Murchington Devon 8 G7
Murcot Worcs 47 L6
Murcott Oxon 48 G11
Murcott Wilts 33 J6
Murkle Highld 167 L3
Murlaggan Highld 146 C9
Murrell Green Hants 23 K3
Murroes Angus 142 H10
Murrow Cambs 74 G9
Mursley Bucks 49 M9
Murston Kent 38 F9
Murthill Angus 142 H6
Murthly P & K 141 R10
Murton C York 98 C10
Murton Cumb 102 D6
Murton Dur 113 N11
Murton N Tyne 113 M6
Murton Nthumb 129 P10
Murton Swans 28 G7
Musbury Devon 10 F6
Muscoates N York 98 D5
Musselburgh E Loth 127 Q3
Muston Leics 73 L3
Muston N York 99 M5
Mustow Green Worcs 58 C10
Muswell Hill Gt Lon 36 G3
Mutehill D & G 108 E11
Mutford Suffk 65 P4
Muthill P & K 133 P4
Mutterton Devon 9 P3
Muxton Wrekin 57 N2
Mybster Highld 167 L6
Myddfai Carmth 43 Q8
Myddle Shrops 69 N10
Mydroilyn Cerdgn 43 J3
Myerscough Lancs 88 F3
Myland Essex 52 G6
Mylor Cnwll 3 L6
Mylor Bridge Cnwll 3 L6
Mynachlog ddu Pembks 41 M4
Myndd-llan Flints 80 H10
Myndtown Shrops 56 F7
Mynydd Bach Cerdgn 54 G9
Mynydd-bach Mons 31 N6
Mynydd-Bach Swans 29 J5
Mynyddgarreg Carmth 28 D3
Mynydd Isa Flints 69 J2
Mynydd Llandygai Gwynd 79 L11
Mynydd Mechell IoA 78 F6
Mynytho Gwynd 66 E8
Myrebird Abers 151 J8
Myredykes Border 118 A11
Mytchett Surrey 23 N3
Mytholm Calder 90 B5
Mytholmroyd Calder 90 C5
Mythop Lancs 88 D4
Myton-on-Swale N York 97 P7

N

Naast Highld 160 C10
Nab's Head Lancs 89 J5
Na Buirgh W Isls 168 f8
Naburn C York 98 B11
Naccolt Kent 27 J3
Nackington Kent 39 L11
Nacton Suffk 53 M3
Nafferton E R Yk 99 M9
Nag's Head Gloucs 32 G5
Nailbridge Gloucs 46 B11
Nailsbourne Somset 18 H9
Nailsea N Som 31 N10
Nailstone Leics 72 C9
Nailsworth Gloucs 32 F5
Nairn Highld 156 F6
Nalderswood Surrey 36 F11
Nancegollan Cnwll 2 H8
Nancledra Cnwll 2 D6
Nanhoron Gwynd 66 D8
Nannerch Flints 80 H11
Nanpantan Leics 72 E7
Nanpean Cnwll 4 F10
Nanquidno Cnwll 2 B8
Nanstallon Cnwll 4 G8
Nant-ddu Powys 30 D2
Nanternis Cerdgn 42 G3
Nantgaredig Carmth 43 J10
Nantgarw Rhondd 30 F7
Nant-glas Powys 55 M11
Nantglyn Denbgs 68 D2
Nantgwyn Powys 55 M9
Nant Gwynant Gwynd 67 L4
Nantile Gwynd 67 J4
Nantlle Valley Slate Landscape Gwynd 67 J4
Nantmawr Shrops 69 J10
Nantmel Powys 55 N11
Nantmor Gwynd 67 L5
Nant Peris Gwynd 67 L3
Nantwich Ches E 70 B4
Nant-y-Bwch Blae G 30 F2
Nantycaws Carmth 43 J11
Nant-y-derry Mons 31 K3
Nant-y-ffin Carmth 43 L9
Nantyffyllon Brdgnd 29 N6
Nantyglo Blae G 30 G2
Nant-y-gollen Shrops 68 H9
Nant-y-moel Brdgnd 29 P6
Nant-y-pandy Conwy 79 L10
Naphill Bucks 35 M5
Napleton Worcs 46 G5
Nappa N York 96 C10

Napton on the Hill Warwks 48 E2
Narberth Pembks 41 M8
Narborough Leics 72 E11
Narborough Norfk 75 P8
Narkurs Cnwll 5 N10
Nasareth Gwynd 66 H5
Naseby Nhants 60 E5
Nash Bucks 49 L8
Nash Gt Lon 37 K8
Nash Herefs 45 L2
Nash Newpt 31 K8
Nash Shrops 57 L10
Nash End Worcs 57 P8
Nashes Green Hants 23 J5
Nash Lee Bucks 35 M3
Nash Street Kent 37 P7
Nassington Nhants 73 R11
Nastend Gloucs 32 E3
Nasty Herts 51 J6
Nateby Cumb 102 E9
Nateby Lancs 88 F2
National Memorial Arboretum Staffs 59 J2
National Space Centre C Leic 72 F9
Natland Cumb 95 L3
Naughton Suffk 52 H2
Naunton Gloucs 47 M10
Naunton Worcs 46 G7
Naunton Beauchamp Worcs 47 J4
Navenby Lincs 86 C9
Navestock Essex 51 M11
Navestock Side Essex 51 N11
Navidale Highld 163 N3
Navity Highld 156 D5
Nawton N York 98 D4
Nayland Suffk 52 G5
Nazeing Essex 51 K9
Nazeing Gate Essex 51 K9
Neacroft Hants 13 L5
Neal's Green Warwks 59 M8
Neap Shet 169 s8
Near Cotton Staffs 71 K5
Near Sawrey Cumb 101 L11
Neasden Gt Lon 36 F3
Neasham Darltn 104 B8
Neath Neath 29 L5
Neatham Hants 23 K6
Neatishead Norfk 77 L7
Nebo Cerdgn 54 C11
Nebo Conwy 67 Q3
Nebo Gwynd 66 H4
Nebo IoA 78 H6
Necton Norfk 76 B10
Nedd Highld 164 D10
Nedderton Nthumb 113 K4
Nedging Suffk 52 G2
Nedging Tye Suffk 52 H2
Needham Norfk 65 J5
Needham Market Suffk 64 F10
Needham Street Suffk 63 M7
Needingworth Cambs 62 D6
Neen Savage Shrops 57 M9
Neen Sollars Shrops 57 M10
Neenton Shrops 57 L7
Nefyn Gwynd 66 E6
Neilston E Rens 125 M6
Nelson Caerph 30 F5
Nelson Lancs 89 P3
Nemphlar S Lans 126 B2
Nempnett Thrubwell BaNES 19 P2
Nenthall Cumb 111 Q11
Nenthead Cumb 102 E2
Nenthorn Border 118 C3
Neopardy Devon 9 J5
Nep Town W Susx 24 F7
Nerabus Ag & B 122 B8
Nercwys Flints 68 H2
Nerston S Lans 125 Q6
Nesbit Nthumb 119 J4
Nesfield N York 96 G11
Ness Ches W 81 L9
Nesscliffe Shrops 69 L11
Neston Ches W 81 K9
Neston Wilts 32 G11
Netchwood Shrops 57 L6
Nether Abington S Lans 116 C6
Nether Alderley Ches E 82 H9
Netheravon Wilts 21 M5
Nether Blainslie Border 117 Q2
Netherbrae Abers 159 J6
Nether Broughton Leics 72 H5
Netherburn S Lans 126 D8
Netherbury Dorset 11 K5
Netherby Cumb 110 G6
Netherby N York 97 M11
Nether Cerne Dorset 11 P5
Nethercleuch D & G 109 P3
Nether Compton Dorset 19 Q11
Nethercote Warwks 60 B8
Nethercott Devon 5 P2
Nethercott Devon 16 H4
Nether Crimond Abers 151 L3
Nether Dallachy Moray 157 R5
Netherend Gloucs 31 Q4
Nether Exe Devon 9 M4
Netherfield E Susx 26 B8
Netherfield Leics 72 F7
Netherfield Notts 72 G2
Nether Fingland S Lans 116 C8
Nethergate N Linc 92 C11
Nethergate Norfk 76 F6
Netherhampton Wilts 21 M9
Nether Handley Derbys 84 F5
Nether Handwick Angus 142 F9
Nether Haugh Rothm 91 L11
Netherhay Dorset 11 J3
Nether Headon Notts 85 M5
Nether Heage Derbys 84 E10
Nether Heyford Nhants 60 E9
Nether Kellet Lancs 95 L7
Nether Kinmundy Abers 159 Q9
Netherland Green Staffs 71 L8
Nether Langwith Notts 84 H6
Netherley Abers 151 M9
Netherley Lpool 81 N7
Nethermill D & G 109 M3
Nethermuir Abers 159 M9
Netherne-on-the-Hill Surrey 36 G9
Netheroyd Hill Kirk 90 E7
Nether Padley Derbys 84 B5
Nether Poppleton C York 98 B10
Nether Row Cumb 101 K3
Nethersele Derbys 59 L2
Nether Silton N York 97 Q2

Nether Skyborry Shrops....56 D10
Nether Stowey Somset....18 G7
Nether Street Essex....51 N8
Netherstreet Wilts....21 J2
Netherthird E Ayrs....115 L4
Netherthong Kirk....90 E9
Netherthorpe Derbys....84 F6
Netherton Angus....143 J6
Netherton Devon....7 M4
Netherton Dudley....58 D7
Netherton Hants....22 C3
Netherton Herefs....45 Q9
Netherton Kirk....90 E8
Netherton N Lans....126 D7
Netherton Nthumb....119 J9
Netherton Oxon....34 D5
Netherton P & K....142 A7
Netherton Sefton....81 M5
Netherton Shrops....57 N8
Netherton Stirlg....125 P2
Netherton Wakefd....90 H7
Netherton Worcs....47 J6
Nethertown Cumb....100 C9
Nethertown Highld....167 Q1
Nethertown Lancs....89 L3
Nethertown Staffs....71 L11
Netherurd Border....116 G2
Nether Wallop Hants....22 B7
Nether Wasdale Cumb....100 F10
Nether Welton Cumb....110 G11
Nether Westcote Gloucs....47 P10
Nether Whitacre Warwks....59 K6
Nether Whitecleuch S Lans..116 A7
Nether Winchendon Bucks....35 K2
Netherwitton Nthumb....112 G2
Nethy Bridge Highld....149 J3
Netley Hants....14 E5
Netley Marsh Hants....13 P2
Nettlebed Oxon....35 J7
Nettlebridge Somset....20 B5
Nettlecombe Dorset....11 L5
Nettlecombe IoW....14 F11
Nettleden Herts....50 B8
Nettleham Lincs....86 D5
Nettlestead Kent....37 Q10
Nettlestead Green Kent....37 Q10
Nettlestone IoW....14 H8
Nettlesworth Dur....113 L11
Nettleton Lincs....93 K10
Nettleton Wilts....32 F9
Nettleton Shrub Wilts....32 F9
Netton Devon....6 F9
Netton Wilts....21 M7
Neuadd Carmth....43 P10
Neuadd-ddu Powys....55 L9
Nevendon Essex....38 C3
Nevern Pembks....41 L2
Nevill Holt Leics....60 H2
New Abbey D & G....109 L7
New Aberdour Abers....159 L5
New Addington Gt Lon....37 J8
Newall Leeds....97 J11
New Alresford Hants....22 G8
New Alyth P & K....142 C8
Newark C Pete....74 D10
Newark Ork....169 g2
Newark-on-Trent Notts....85 N10
New Arley Warwks....59 L7
New Arram E R Yk....92 H2
Newarthill N Lans....126 D6
New Ash Green Kent....37 P7
New Balderton Notts....85 P10
Newbarn Kent....27 L3
New Barn Kent....37 P7
New Barnet Gt Lon....50 G11
New Barnetby N Linc....93 J8
New Barton Nhants....61 J8
Newbattle Mdloth....127 Q4
New Bewick Nthumb....119 L6
Newbie D & G....110 C7
Newbiggin Cumb....94 B2
Newbiggin Cumb....94 F7
Newbiggin Cumb....101 N5
Newbiggin Cumb....102 B5
Newbiggin Cumb....111 L11
Newbiggin Dur....102 H5
Newbiggin Dur....112 H11
Newbiggin N York....96 E2
Newbiggin N York....96 F3
Newbiggin-by-the-Sea
    Nthumb....113 M3
Newbigging Angus....142 D9
Newbigging Angus....142 G10
Newbigging Angus....142 H10
Newbigging S Lans....127 J8
Newbiggin-on-Lune Cumb..102 D10
New Bilton Warwks....59 Q9
Newbold Derbys....84 E6
Newbold Leics....72 C7
Newbold on Avon Warwks....59 Q9
Newbold on Stour Warwks....47 P5
Newbold Pacey Warwks....47 Q3
Newbold Revel Warwks....59 Q8
Newbold Verdon Leics....72 C10
New Bolingbroke Lincs....87 K9
Newborough C Pete....74 D9
Newborough IoA....78 G11
Newborough Staffs....71 L9
Newbottle Nhants....48 F7
Newbottle Sundld....113 M10
New Boultham Lincs....86 C6
Newbourne Suffk....53 N3
New Bradwell M Keyn....49 M6
New Brampton Derbys....84 E6
New Brancepeth Dur....103 P2
Newbridge C Edin....127 L3
Newbridge Caerph....30 H5
Newbridge Cerdgn....43 K3
Newbridge Cnwll....2 C7
Newbridge Cnwll....3 K5
Newbridge D & G....109 L5
Newbridge Hants....21 Q11
Newbridge IoW....14 D9
New Bridge N York....98 G3
Newbridge Oxon....34 D4
Newbridge Wrexhm....69 J6
Newbridge Green Worcs....46 F7
Newbridge-on-Usk Mons....31 L6
Newbridge-on-Wye Powys....44 E3
New Brighton Flints....81 K11
New Brighton Wirral....81 L6
New Brinsley Notts....84 G10
New Broughton Wrexhm....69 K4
New Buckenham Norfk....64 F3
Newbuildings Devon....9 J4

Newburgh Abers....151 P2
Newburgh Abers....159 N6
Newburgh Fife....134 G4
Newburgh Lancs....88 F8
Newburn N u Ty....113 J7
New Bury Bolton....82 F4
Newbury Somset....20 C5
Newbury W Berk....34 E11
Newbury Wilts....20 F6
Newbury Park Gt Lon....37 K3
Newby Cumb....101 Q6
Newby Lancs....96 B11
Newby N York....95 Q7
Newby N York....99 L3
Newby N York....104 F8
Newby Bridge Cumb....94 H3
Newby Cross Cumb....110 G10
Newby East Cumb....111 J9
Newby Head Cumb....101 Q6
New Byth Abers....159 K7
Newby West Cumb....110 G10
Newby Wiske N York....97 N3
Newcastle Mons....45 N11
Newcastle Shrops....56 D8
Newcastle Airport Nthumb....113 J6
Newcastle Emlyn Carmth....42 F6
Newcastle Great Park
    N u Ty....113 K6
Newcastleton Border....111 J3
Newcastle-under-Lyme
    Staffs....70 E5
Newcastle upon Tyne N u Ty..113 K8
Newchapel Pembks....41 P3
Newchapel Staffs....70 F4
Newchapel Surrey....25 J2
Newchurch Blae G....30 G2
Newchurch Herefs....45 M4
Newchurch IoW....14 G9
Newchurch Kent....27 J5
Newchurch Mons....31 N5
Newchurch Powys....45 J4
Newchurch Staffs....71 L10
Newchurch in Pendle Lancs..89 N3
New Costessey Norfk....76 H9
New Cowper Cumb....109 P11
Newcraighall C Edin....127 Q3
New Crofton Wakefd....91 K7
New Cross Cerdgn....54 E9
New Cross Gt Lon....37 J5
New Cross Somset....19 M11
New Cumnock E Ayrs....115 M5
New Cut E Susx....26 D8
New Deer Abers....159 L8
New Delaval Nthumb....113 L6
New Delph Oldham....90 B9
New Denham Bucks....36 B4
Newdigate Surrey....24 E2
New Duston Nhants....60 F8
New Earswick C York....98 C9
New Eastwood Notts....84 G11
New Edlington Donc....91 N11
New Elgin Moray....157 N5
New Ellerby E R Yk....93 L3
Newell Green Br For....35 N10
New Eltham Gt Lon....37 K6
New End Worcs....47 L2
Newenden Kent....26 D6
New England C Pete....74 C10
New England Essex....52 B3
Newent Gloucs....46 D9
New Farnley Leeds....90 H4
New Ferry Wirral....81 L7
Newfield Dur....103 P4
Newfield Dur....113 K10
Newfield Highld....156 D2
New Fletton C Pete....74 C11
New Forest National Park....13 N3
Newfound Hants....22 G4
New Fryston Wakefd....91 M5
Newgale Pembks....40 G6
New Galloway D & G....108 D5
Newgate Norfk....76 E3
Newgate Street Herts....50 H9
New Gilston Fife....135 L6
New Grimsby IoS....2 b1
Newhall Ches E....69 R5
Newhall Derbys....71 P10
Newham Nthumb....119 N5
New Hartley Nthumb....113 M5
Newhaven C Edin....127 P2
Newhaven Derbys....71 M2
New Haven E Susx....25 K10
New Haw Surrey....36 C8
New Hedges Pembks....41 M10
New Herrington Sundld....113 M10
Newhey Rochdl....89 Q8
New Holkham Norfk....76 B4
New Holland N Linc....93 J6
Newholm N York....105 N8
New Houghton Derbys....84 G7
New Houghton Norfk....75 Q5
Newhouse N Lans....126 D5
New Houses N York....96 B6
New Hutton Cumb....95 M2
New Hythe Kent....38 B10
Newick E Susx....25 K6
Newingreen Kent....27 K4
Newington Kent....27 L4
Newington Kent....38 E9
Newington Oxon....34 H5
Newington Shrops....56 G8
Newington Bagpath Gloucs..32 F6
New Inn Carmth....43 J7
New Inn Pembks....41 L4
New Inn Torfn....31 K5
New Invention Shrops....56 D9
New Lanark S Lans....116 B2
New Lanark Village S Lans..116 B2
Newland C KuH....93 J4
Newland Cumb....94 G5
Newland E R Yk....92 D5
Newland Gloucs....31 Q3
Newland N York....92 A6
Newland Oxon....34 C3
Newland Somset....17 Q4
Newland Worcs....46 E5
Newlandrig Mdloth....128 B7
Newlands Border....111 K2
Newlands Cumb....101 K3
Newlands Nthumb....112 G9
Newlands of Dundurcas
    Moray....157 P7
New Lane Lancs....88 E8
New Lane End Warrtn....82 D6
New Langholm D & G....110 G4
New Leake Lincs....87 M9

New Leeds Abers....159 N7
New Lodge Barns....91 K9
New Longton Lancs....88 G5
New Luce D & G....106 G5
Newlyn Cnwll....2 D8
Newmachar Abers....151 M4
Newmains N Lans....126 E6
New Malden Gt Lon....36 F7
Newman's End Essex....51 M8
Newman's Green Suffk....52 E3
Newmarket Suffk....63 K8
Newmarket W Isls....168 j4
New Marske R & Cl....104 H6
New Marston Oxon....34 F3
New Marton Shrops....69 K8
New Mill Abers....151 K11
Newmill Border....117 P8
New Mill Cnwll....2 D7
New Mill Herts....35 P2
New Mill Kirk....90 F9
Newmillerdam Wakefd....91 J7
Newmills C Edin....127 M4
New Mills Cnwll....3 M3
New Mills Derbys....83 M7
New Mills Fife....134 C10
Newmills Mons....31 P3
New Mills Powys....55 P4
New Mills P & K....142 A11
Newmiln P & K....142 A11
Newmilns E Ayrs....125 N10
New Milton Hants....13 M5
New Mistley Essex....53 K5
New Moat Pembks....41 L5
Newmore Highld....156 C9
Newnes Shrops....69 L8
Newney Green Essex....51 Q9
Newnham Hants....23 K4
Newnham Herts....50 F3
Newnham Kent....38 G10
Newnham Nhants....60 C9
Newnham on Severn Gloucs....32 C2
New Ollerton Notts....85 L7
New Oscott Birm....58 G6
New Pitsligo Abers....159 L6
New Polzeath Cnwll....4 E6
Newport Cnwll....5 N4
Newport Dorset....12 E5
Newport E R Yk....92 E4
Newport Essex....51 M4
Newport Gloucs....32 D5
Newport Highld....163 Q2
Newport IoW....14 F9
Newport Newpt....31 K7
Newport Norfk....77 Q8
Newport Pembks....41 L3
Newport Wrekin....70 C11
Newport-on-Tay Fife....135 L2
Newport Pagnell M Keyn....49 N6
Newport Pagnell Services
    M Keyn....49 N6
Newpound Common W Susx..24 C5
New Prestwick S Ayrs....114 F3
New Quay Cerdgn....42 G3
Newquay Cnwll....4 C9
New Quay Essex....52 H7
Newquay Zoo Cnwll....4 C9
New Rackheath Norfk....77 K9
New Radnor Powys....45 J2
New Rent Cumb....101 N3
New Ridley Nthumb....112 G9
New Road Side N York....90 B2
New Romney Kent....27 J7
New Rossington Donc....91 Q11
New Row Cerdgn....54 G10
New Row Lancs....89 J3
New Sauchie Clacks....133 P9
Newsbank Ches E....82 H11
Newseat Abers....158 H11
Newsham Lancs....88 G3
Newsham N York....97 N4
Newsham N York....103 M8
Newsham Nthumb....113 M5
New Sharlston Wakefd....91 K7
Newsholme E R Yk....92 B5
Newsholme Lancs....96 B10
New Shoreston Nthumb....119 N4
New Silksworth Sundld....113 N10
New Skelton R & Cl....105 J7
Newsome Kirk....90 F8
New Somerby Lincs....73 N3
New Springs Wigan....88 H9
Newstead Border....117 R4
Newstead Notts....84 H10
Newstead Nthumb....119 N5
New Stevenston N Lans....126 D6
New Street Herefs....45 L3
New Swanage Dorset....12 H8
New Swannington Leics....72 C7
Newthorpe N York....91 M4
Newthorpe Notts....84 G11
New Thundersley Essex....38 C4
Newtimber W Susx....24 G8
Newtoft Lincs....86 D3
Newton Ag & B....131 L8
Newton Border....118 B6
Newton Brdgnd....29 M9
Newton C Beds....50 F2
Newton Cambs....62 F11
Newton Cambs....74 H8
Newton Cardif....30 H9
Newton Ches W....69 P3
Newton Ches W....81 N11
Newton Ches W....82 B9
Newton Cumb....94 E6
Newton Derbys....84 F9
Newton Herefs....45 L8
Newton Herefs....45 Q4
Newton Herefs....56 F11
Newton Highld....155 Q7
Newton Highld....156 D4
Newton Highld....156 D4
Newton Highld....167 P7
Newton Lancs....88 A8
Newton Lancs....95 M6
Newton Lincs....73 Q3
Newton Lincs....73 Q3
Newton Mdloth....127 Q4
Newton Moray....157 M5
Newton Moray....157 Q5
Newton N York....98 H6
Newton Nhants....61 J4
Newton Norfk....76 A9
Newton Notts....72 H2
Newton Nthumb....112 F8
Newton Nthumb....118 H9
Newton S Lans....116 C4

Newton S Lans....126 B5
Newton Sandw....58 F6
Newton Shrops....69 M8
Newton Somset....18 F7
Newton Staffs....71 J9
Newton Suffk....52 F3
Newton W Loth....127 K2
Newton Warwks....60 B5
Newton Wilts....21 P10
Newton Abbot Devon....7 M4
Newton Arlosh Cumb....110 D9
Newton Aycliffe Dur....103 Q6
Newton Bewley Hartpl....104 E5
Newton Blossomville
    M Keyn....49 P4
Newton Bromswold Nhants..61 L7
Newton Burgoland Leics....72 B9
Newton by Toft Lincs....86 D3
Newton Ferrers Devon....6 F9
Newton Ferry W Isls....168 d10
Newton Flotman Norfk....65 J2
Newtongrange Mdloth....127 Q5
Newton Green Mons....31 P6
Newton Harcourt Leics....72 G11
Newton Heath Manch....83 J4
Newtonhill Abers....151 N9
Newton Hill Wakefd....91 J6
Newton-in-Bowland Lancs..95 P10
Newton Kyme N York....91 M2
Newton-le-Willows N York..97 K3
Newton-le-Willows St Hel..82 C5
Newtonloan Mdloth....127 Q5
Newton Longville Bucks....49 M8
Newton Mearns E Rens....125 N6
Newtonmill Angus....143 L5
Newton Morrell N York....103 P9
Newton Mountain Pembks..41 J9
Newton Mulgrave N York..105 L7
Newton of Balcanquhal
    P & K....134 F5
Newton of Balcormo Fife....135 N7
Newton of Belltrees Rens..125 K6
Newton-on-Ayr S Ayrs....114 F3
Newton-on-Ouse N York....97 R9
Newton-on-Rawcliffe
    N York....98 G2
Newton on the Hill Shrops..69 N10
Newton-on-the-Moor
    Nthumb....119 N9
Newton on Trent Lincs....85 P6
Newton Poppleford Devon....6 B7
Newton Purcell Oxon....48 H6
Newton Regis Warwks....59 L3
Newton Reigny Cumb....101 N4
Newton St Cyres Devon....9 L5
Newton St Faith Norfk....77 J8
Newton St Loe BaNES....20 D2
Newton St Petrock Devon....16 G7
Newton Solney Derbys....71 P9
Newton Stacey Hants....22 D6
Newton Stewart D & G....107 M4
Newton Tony Wilts....21 P6
Newton Tracey Devon....17 J6
Newton under Roseberry
    R & Cl....104 G8
Newton Underwood Nthumb..112 H3
Newton upon Derwent
    E R Yk....98 E11
Newton Valence Hants....23 K8
Newton Wamphray D & G..109 P2
Newton with Scales Lancs....88 F4
Newtown BCP....12 H6
Newtown Blae G....30 G3
Newtown Ches W....82 B9
Newtown Cnwll....2 F8
Newtown Cnwll....5 M6
Newtown Cumb....101 P6
Newtown Cumb....109 P11
Newtown Cumb....111 G8
Newtown Cumb....111 K8
Newtown D & G....115 Q5
Newtown Derbys....83 L8
Newtown Devon....9 Q5
Newtown Devon....17 P6
Newtown Devon....11 K4
New Town Dorset....12 G3
New Town Dorset....21 J11
New Town Dorset....21 J11
New Town E Susx....25 L6
Newtown Gloucs....32 C4
Newtown Hants....13 M7
Newtown Hants....14 H4
Newtown Hants....22 E2
Newtown Herefs....45 P3
Newtown Herefs....45 Q9
Newtown Herefs....46 B5
Newtown Highld....147 K7
Newtown IoW....14 D8
Newtown Nthumb....119 J4
Newtown Nthumb....119 K10
Newtown Nthumb....119 L8
Newtown Powys....55 Q6
Newtown Rhondd....30 E5
Newtown Shrops....69 M10
Newtown Shrops....69 N8
Newtown Somset....10 E4
Newtown Staffs....58 E4
Newtown Staffs....70 G2
Newtown Wigan....82 C4
Newtown Wilts....20 H9
Newtown Wilts....21 Q2
Newtown Worcs....46 G3
Newtown Worcs....58 D9
Newtown-in-St Martin
    Cnwll....3 J9
Newtown Linford Leics....72 E9
Newtown St Boswells
    Border....117 R4
Newtown Unthank Leics....72 D10
New Tredegar Caerph....30 F4
New Trows S Lans....126 E10
New Tupton Derbys....84 E7
Newtyle Angus....142 D9
New Walsoken Cambs....75 J9
New Waltham NE Lin....93 N10
New Whittington Derbys....84 E5
New Winton E Loth....128 C5
New Yatt Oxon....34 C2
Newyears Green Gt Lon....36 C3
Newyork Ag & B....131 K5
New York Lincs....86 H9
New York N Tyne....113 M6
New York N York....97 J8
New Zealand Wilts....33 K9
Nextend Herefs....45 L3

Neyland Pembks....41 J9
Niarbyl IoM....80 b6
Nibley Gloucs....32 C3
Nibley S Glos....32 C8
Nibley Green Gloucs....32 D5
Nicholashayne Devon....18 F11
Nicholaston Swans....28 G7
Nickies Hill Cumb....111 K7
Nidd N York....97 M8
Nigg C Aber....151 N7
Nigg Highld....156 E3
Nigg Ferry Highld....156 D4
Nimlet BaNES....32 D10
Ninebanks Nthumb....111 Q10
Nine Elms Swindn....33 M7
Nine Wells Pembks....40 E6
Ninfield E Susx....26 B9
Ningwood IoW....14 C5
Nisbet Border....118 C5
Nisbet Hill Border....129 K9
Niton IoW....14 F11
Nitshill C Glas....125 N5
Noah's Ark Kent....37 N9
Noak Bridge Essex....37 Q2
Noak Hill Gt Lon....37 M2
Noblethorpe Barns....90 H9
Nobold Shrops....56 H2
Nobottle Nhants....60 E8
Nocton Lincs....86 E8
Nogdam End Norfk....77 M11
Noke Oxon....34 F2
Nolton Pembks....40 G7
Nolton Haven Pembks....40 G7
No Man's Heath Ches W....69 P5
No Man's Heath Warwks....59 L3
No Man's Land Cnwll....5 M10
Nomansland Devon....9 K2
Nomansland Wilts....21 Q11
Noneley Shrops....69 N9
Nonington Kent....39 N11
Nook Cumb....95 L4
Nook Cumb....111 J5
Norbiton Gt Lon....36 E7
Norbreck Bpool....88 C2
Norbridge Herefs....46 D6
Norbury Ches E....69 Q5
Norbury Derbys....71 L6
Norbury Gt Lon....36 H7
Norbury Shrops....56 F6
Norbury Staffs....70 D10
Norbury Common Ches E....69 Q5
Norbury Junction Staffs....70 D10
Norchard Worcs....58 B11
Norcott Brook Ches W....82 D8
Norcross Lancs....88 C2
Nordelph Norfk....75 L10
Norden Rochdl....89 P8
Nordley Shrops....57 M5
Norfolk Broads Norfk....77 P10
Norham Nthumb....129 N10
Norland Calder....90 D6
Norley Ches W....82 C10
Norleywood Hants....14 C7
Norlington E Susx....25 K8
Normanby Lincs....86 C3
Normanby N Linc....92 E7
Normanby N York....98 E4
Normanby R & Cl....104 F7
Normanby le Wold Lincs....93 K11
Norman Cross Cambs....61 Q2
Normandy Surrey....23 P4
Normans Bay E Susx....25 Q9
Norman's Green Devon....9 Q4
Normanton C Derb....72 A4
Normanton Leics....73 L2
Normanton Notts....85 M10
Normanton Rutlnd....73 N9
Normanton Wakefd....91 K6
Normanton Wilts....21 M6
Normanton le Heath Leics..72 B8
Normanton on Cliffe Lincs..86 B11
Normanton on Soar Notts....72 E6
Normanton on the Wolds
    Notts....72 G4
Normanton on Trent Notts....85 N7
Normoss Lancs....88 C3
Norney Surrey....23 P6
Norrington Common Wilts....20 G2
Norris Green Cnwll....5 Q8
Norris Green Lpool....81 M6
Norris Hill Leics....72 A7
Norristhorpe Kirk....90 G6
Northacre Norfk....64 D2
Northall Bucks....49 Q10
Northallerton N York....97 N2
Northall Green Norfk....76 D9
Northam C Sotn....14 D4
Northam Devon....16 H6
Northampton Nhants....60 G8
Northampton Worcs....58 B11
Northampton Services
    Nhants....60 F9
North Anston Rothm....84 H4
North Ascot Br For....35 P11
North Aston Oxon....48 E9
Northaw Herts....50 G10
Northay Somset....10 F2
North Baddesley Hants....22 C10
North Ballachulish Highld..139 K5
North Barrow Somset....20 B9
North Barsham Norfk....76 C4
Northbay W Isls....168 c17
North Benfleet Essex....38 C4
North Berwick E Loth....128 E3
North Bitchburn Dur....103 N4
North Blyth Nthumb....113 M4
North Boarhunt Hants....14 H4
North Bockhampton BCP....13 L5
Northborough C Pete....74 C9
Northbourne Kent....39 P11
North Bovey Devon....8 H8
North Bradley Wilts....20 G3
North Brentor Devon....8 C8
North Brewham Somset....20 D7
North Bridge Surrey....23 Q7
Northbridge Street E Susx..26 B7
Northbrook Hants....22 H7
Northbrook Oxon....48 E10
North Brook End Cambs....50 G2
North Buckland Devon....16 H3
North Burlingham Norfk....77 M10
North Cadbury Somset....20 B9
North Carlton Lincs....86 B5
North Carlton Notts....85 J4
North Cave E R Yk....92 E4
North Cerney Gloucs....33 K3

North Chailey E Susx ...25 J6
Northchapel W Susx ...23 Q9
North Charford Hants ...21 N11
North Charlton Nthumb ...119 N6
North Cheam Gt Lon ...36 F7
North Cheriton Somset ...20 C9
North Chideock Dorset ...11 J6
Northchurch Herts ...35 Q3
North Cliffe E R Yk ...92 H5
North Clifton Notts ...85 P6
North Close Dur ...103 Q4
North Cockerington Lincs ...87 L2
North Connel Ag & B ...138 G11
North Cornelly Brdgnd ...29 M8
North Corner Cnwll ...3 K10
North Cotes Lincs ...93 P10
Northcott Devon ...5 N3
Northcott Devon ...10 B2
Northcott Devon ...10 C3
North Country Cnwll ...2 H5
Northcourt Oxon ...34 E5
North Cove Suffk ...65 P4
North Cowton N York ...103 Q10
North Crawley M Keyn ...49 P6
North Cray Gt Lon ...37 L6
North Creake Norfk ...76 B4
North Curry Somset ...19 K9
North Dalton E R Yk ...99 J10
North Deighton N York ...97 N10
Northdown Kent ...39 Q7
North Downs ...38 F10
North Duffield N York ...92 A3
Northedge Derbys ...84 E7
North Elham Kent ...27 L3
North Elkington Lincs ...87 J2
North Elmham Norfk ...76 D7
North Elmsall Wakefd ...91 M8
Northend Bucks ...35 K6
North End C Port ...15 J6
North End Cumb ...110 F9
North End Dorset ...20 F9
North End E R Yk ...93 L2
North End E R Yk ...93 N4
North End Essex ...51 Q7
North End Hants ...21 M11
North End Hants ...22 G9
North End Leics ...72 F7
North End Lincs ...74 D2
North End Lincs ...87 M3
North End Lincs ...92 H11
North End Lincs ...93 P10
North End Lincs ...93 K6
North End N Linc ...31 M11
North End N Som ...19 L7
North End Norfk ...64 D3
North End Nthumb ...119 M10
North End Sefton ...81 L4
North End W Susx ...15 Q6
North End W Susx ...24 D9
Northend Warwks ...48 C4
Northenden Manch ...82 H7
Northend Woods Bucks ...35 P7
North Erradale Highld ...160 A10
North Evington C Leic ...72 G10
North Fambridge Essex ...38 E2
North Featherstone Wakefd ...91 L6
North Ferriby E R Yk ...92 G5
Northfield Birm ...58 F9
Northfield C Aber ...151 N6
Northfield E R Yk ...92 H5
Northfields Lincs ...73 Q9
Northfleet Kent ...37 P6
North Frodingham E R Yk ...99 N10
Northgate Lincs ...74 C5
North Gorley Hants ...13 L2
North Green Norfk ...65 J4
North Green Suffk ...65 L9
North Green Suffk ...65 M8
North Greetwell Lincs ...86 D6
North Grimston N York ...98 G7
North Halling Medway ...38 B8
North Hayling Hants ...15 K6
North Hazelrigg Nthumb ...119 L4
North Heasley Devon ...17 N5
North Heath W Susx ...24 C6
North Hele Devon ...18 D10
North Hill Cnwll ...5 M6
North Hillingdon Gt Lon ...36 C4
North Hinksey Village Oxon ...34 E3
North Holmwood Surrey ...36 E11
North Huish Devon ...7 J7
North Hykeham Lincs ...86 B7
Northiam E Susx ...26 D7
Northill C Beds ...61 P11
Northington Gloucs ...32 D3
Northington Hants ...22 G7
North Kelsey Lincs ...92 H10
North Kessock Highld ...156 B8
North Killingholme N Linc ...93 K7
North Kilvington N York ...97 P3
North Kilworth Leics ...60 D4
North Kingston Hants ...13 L4
North Kyme Lincs ...86 G10
North Lancing W Susx ...24 E9
North Landing E R Yk ...99 Q6
Northlands Lincs ...87 K10
Northleach Gloucs ...33 M2
North Lee Bucks ...35 M3
North Lees N York ...97 L6
Northleigh Devon ...10 D5
Northleigh Devon ...17 L5
North Leigh Kent ...27 K2
North Leigh Oxon ...34 C2
North Leverton with Habblesthorpe Notts ...85 N4
Northlew Devon ...8 D5
North Littleton Worcs ...47 L5
Northload Bridge Somset ...19 N7
North Lopham Norfk ...64 E5
North Luffenham Rutlnd ...73 N10
North Marden W Susx ...23 M11
North Marston Bucks ...49 L10
North Middleton Mdloth ...128 B8
North Middleton Nthumb ...119 L9
North Millbrex Abers ...159 K9
North Milmain D & G ...106 E7
North Molton Devon ...17 N6
Northmoor Oxon ...34 D4
North Moreton Oxon ...34 G7
Northmuir Angus ...142 F6
North Mundham W Susx ...15 N6
North Muskham Notts ...85 N9
North Newbald E R Yk ...92 F3
North Newington Oxon ...48 D6
North Newnton Wilts ...21 M3
North Newton Somset ...19 K8

Northney Hants ...15 K6
North Nibley Gloucs ...32 D5
North Oakley Hants ...22 G4
North Ockendon Gt Lon ...37 N3
Northolt Gt Lon ...36 D4
Northolt Airport Gt Lon ...36 C3
Northop Flints ...81 J11
Northop Hall Flints ...81 K11
North Ormesby Middsb ...104 F7
North Ormsby Lincs ...87 J2
Northorpe Kirk ...90 G6
Northorpe Lincs ...74 A7
Northorpe Lincs ...74 D3
Northorpe Lincs ...92 E11
North Otterington N York ...97 N3
Northover Somset ...19 N7
Northover Somset ...19 P10
North Owersby Lincs ...86 F2
Northowram Calder ...90 E5
North Perrott Somset ...11 L3
North Petherton Somset ...19 J8
North Petherwin Cnwll ...5 M4
North Pickenham Norfk ...76 B10
North Piddle Worcs ...47 J4
North Poorton Dorset ...11 L5
Northport Dorset ...12 F7
North Poulner Hants ...13 L3
North Queensferry Fife ...134 E11
North Radworthy Devon ...17 P5
North Rauceby Lincs ...86 D11
Northrepps Norfk ...77 J4
North Reston Lincs ...87 L4
North Rigton N York ...97 L11
North Ripley Hants ...13 L5
North Rode Ches E ...83 J11
North Roe Shet ...169 q5
North Ronaldsay Ork ...169 g1
North Ronaldsay Airport Ork ...169 g1
North Row Cumb ...100 H4
North Runcton Norfk ...75 M7
North Scale Cumb ...94 D7
North Scarle Lincs ...85 P7
North Seaton Nthumb ...113 L3
North Seaton Colliery Nthumb ...113 L3
North Shian Ag & B ...138 G9
North Shields N Tyne ...113 N7
North Shoebury Sthend ...38 F4
North Shore Bpool ...88 C3
North Side C Pete ...74 E11
North Side Cumb ...100 C5
North Skelton R & Cl ...105 J8
North Somercotes Lincs ...93 R11
North Stainley N York ...97 L5
North Stainmore Cumb ...102 F7
North Stifford Thurr ...37 P4
North Stoke BaNES ...32 D11
North Stoke Oxon ...34 H7
North Stoke W Susx ...24 B8
Northstowe Cambs ...62 F7
North Street Cambs ...63 J7
North Street Hants ...21 N11
North Street Hants ...22 H8
North Street Kent ...38 H10
North Street Medway ...38 D7
North Street W Berk ...34 H10
North Sunderland Nthumb ...119 P4
North Tamerton Cnwll ...5 M4
North Tawton Devon ...8 G4
North Third Stirlg ...133 M10
North Thoresby Lincs ...93 N11
North Togston Nthumb ...119 P10
North Tolsta W Isls ...168 k3
Northton W Isls ...168 e9
North Town Devon ...17 J10
North Town Somset ...19 Q6
North Town W & M ...35 N8
North Tuddenham Norfk ...76 E9
North Uist W Isls ...168 c10
Northumberland National Park Nthumb ...111 Q4
North Walbottle N u Ty ...113 J7
North Walsham Norfk ...77 K5
North Waltham Hants ...22 G5
North Warnborough Hants ...23 K4
Northway Somset ...18 F9
North Weald Bassett Essex ...51 L10
North Wheatley Notts ...85 N3
North Whilborough Devon ...7 M5
Northwich Ches W ...82 E10
North Wick BaNES ...31 Q11
Northwick S Glos ...31 Q7
Northwick Somset ...19 L5
Northwick Worcs ...46 F3
North Widcombe BaNES ...19 Q3
North Willingham Lincs ...86 G3
North Wingfield Derbys ...84 F7
North Witham Lincs ...73 N6
Northwold Norfk ...75 Q11
Northwood C Stke ...70 F5
Northwood Derbys ...84 C8
Northwood Gt Lon ...36 C2
Northwood IoW ...14 E8
Northwood Shrops ...69 N8
Northwood Worcs ...57 P9
Northwood Green Gloucs ...46 D11
North Wootton Dorset ...11 P2
North Wootton Norfk ...75 M6
North Wootton Somset ...19 Q6
North Wraxall Wilts ...32 F9
North Wroughton Swindn ...33 M8
North York Moors National Park ...105 K10
Norton Donc ...91 N7
Norton E Susx ...25 L10
Norton Gloucs ...46 G10
Norton Halton ...82 C8
Norton Hants ...22 E6
Norton Herts ...50 F4
Norton IoW ...13 P7
Norton Mons ...45 N10
Norton N Som ...19 K2
Norton Nhants ...60 C8
Norton Notts ...85 J6
Norton Powys ...56 E11
Norton S on T ...104 D6
Norton Sheff ...84 E4
Norton Shrops ...56 H8
Norton Shrops ...57 K3
Norton Shrops ...57 L8
Norton Shrops ...57 N4
Norton Suffk ...64 D8
Norton Swans ...28 H7
Norton W Susx ...15 P5
Norton Wilts ...32 G8

Norton Worcs ...46 G4
Norton Worcs ...47 K5
Norton Bavant Wilts ...20 H6
Norton Bridge Staffs ...70 E7
Norton Canes Staffs ...58 F3
Norton Canes Services Staffs ...58 F3
Norton Canon Herefs ...45 M5
Norton Corner Norfk ...76 F6
Norton Disney Lincs ...85 Q9
Norton Ferris Wilts ...20 E7
Norton Fitzwarren Somset ...18 G9
Norton Green IoW ...13 P7
Norton Hawkfield BaNES ...19 Q2
Norton Heath Essex ...51 P10
Norton in Hales Shrops ...70 C7
Norton-Juxta-Twycross Leics ...59 M3
Norton-le-Clay N York ...97 P6
Norton-le-Moors C Stke ...70 F4
Norton Lindsey Warwks ...47 P2
Norton Little Green Suffk ...64 D8
Norton Malreward BaNES ...20 B2
Norton Mandeville Essex ...51 N10
Norton-on-Derwent N York ...98 F6
Norton St Philip Somset ...20 E3
Norton Subcourse Norfk ...65 N2
Norton sub Hamdon Somset ...19 N11
Norton Wood Herefs ...45 M5
Norwell Notts ...85 N8
Norwell Woodhouse Notts ...85 M8
Norwich Norfk ...77 J10
Norwich Airport Norfk ...77 J9
Norwick Shet ...169 t2
Norwood Clacks ...133 P9
Norwood Derbys ...84 G4
Norwood Kent ...27 J5
Norwood End Essex ...51 N9
Norwood Green Calder ...90 E5
Norwood Green Gt Lon ...36 D5
Norwood Hill Surrey ...24 F2
Norwoodside Cambs ...74 H11
Noseley Leics ...73 J4
Noss Mayo Devon ...6 F9
Nosterfield N York ...97 L4
Nosterfield End Cambs ...51 P2
Nostie Highld ...145 Q2
Notgrove Gloucs ...47 M10
Nottage Brdgnd ...29 M9
Notter Cnwll ...5 P9
Nottingham C Nott ...72 F3
Nottington Dorset ...11 P8
Notton Wakefd ...91 J8
Notton Wilts ...32 H11
Nounsley Essex ...52 C9
Noutard's Green Worcs ...57 Q11
Nowton Suffk ...64 B9
Nox Shrops ...56 G2
Nuffield Oxon ...35 J7
Nunburnholme E R Yk ...98 G11
Nuncargate Notts ...84 H10
Nunclose Cumb ...111 J11
Nuneaton Warwks ...59 N6
Nuneham Courtenay Oxon ...34 G5
Nunhead Gt Lon ...36 H5
Nunkeeling E R Yk ...99 N11
Nun Monkton N York ...97 R9
Nunney Somset ...20 D6
Nunney Catch Somset ...20 D6
Nunnington Herefs ...45 N4
Nunnington N York ...98 D5
Nunsthorpe NE Lin ...93 N9
Nunthorpe C York ...98 C10
Nunthorpe Middsb ...104 F8
Nunthorpe Village Middsb ...104 F8
Nunton Wilts ...21 N9
Nunwick N York ...97 M6
Nunwick Nthumb ...112 C6
Nupdown S Glos ...32 B5
Nup End Bucks ...49 N11
Nupend Gloucs ...32 E3
Nuptown Br For ...35 N10
Nursling Hants ...22 C11
Nursted Hants ...23 L10
Nursteed Wilts ...21 K2
Nurton Staffs ...58 B5
Nutbourne W Susx ...15 L5
Nutbourne W Susx ...24 C7
Nutfield Surrey ...36 H10
Nuthall Notts ...72 E2
Nuthampstead Herts ...51 K4
Nuthurst W Susx ...24 E5
Nutley E Susx ...25 K5
Nutley Hants ...22 H6
Nuttall Bury ...89 M7
Nutwell Donc ...91 Q10
Nybster Highld ...167 Q4
Nyetimber W Susx ...15 N7
Nyewood W Susx ...23 M10
Nymans W Susx ...24 G5
Nymet Rowland Devon ...17 N10
Nymet Tracey Devon ...8 H4
Nympsfield Gloucs ...32 F4
Nynehead Somset ...18 F10
Nythe Somset ...19 M8
Nyton W Susx ...15 P5

O

Oadby Leics ...72 G10
Oad Street Kent ...38 E9
Oakall Green Worcs ...46 F2
Oakamoor Staffs ...71 J6
Oakbank W Loth ...127 K4
Oak Cross Devon ...8 D5
Oakdale Caerph ...30 G5
Oake Somset ...18 G9
Oaken Staffs ...58 C4
Oakenclough Lancs ...95 L11
Oakengates Wrekin ...57 N2
Oakenholt Flints ...81 K10
Oakenshaw Dur ...103 N3
Oakenshaw Kirk ...90 F5
Oakerthorpe Derbys ...84 E10
Oakford Cerdgn ...43 J3
Oakford Devon ...18 B10
Oakfordbridge Devon ...18 B10
Oakgrove Ches E ...83 K11
Oakham Rutlnd ...73 M9
Oakhanger Ches E ...70 D4
Oakhanger Hants ...23 L7
Oakhill Somset ...20 B5
Oakhurst Kent ...37 N10
Oakington Cambs ...62 F8

Oaklands Herts ...50 F7
Oaklands Powys ...44 E4
Oakle Street Gloucs ...46 E11
Oakley BCP ...12 H5
Oakley Bed ...61 M10
Oakley Bucks ...34 H2
Oakley Fife ...134 C10
Oakley Hants ...22 G4
Oakley Oxon ...35 L4
Oakley Suffk ...64 H6
Oakley Green W & M ...35 P9
Oakley Park Powys ...55 M7
Oaks Lancs ...89 K4
Oaks Shrops ...56 G4
Oaksey Wilts ...33 J6
Oaks Green Derbys ...71 M8
Oakshaw Ford Cumb ...111 K5
Oakshott Hants ...23 K9
Oakthorpe Leics ...59 M2
Oak Tree Darltn ...104 C8
Oakwood C Derb ...72 B3
Oakwood Nthumb ...112 D7
Oakworth C Brad ...90 C3
Oare Kent ...38 H9
Oare Somset ...17 P2
Oare Wilts ...21 N2
Oasby Lincs ...73 Q3
Oath Somset ...19 L9
Oathlaw Angus ...142 H6
Oatlands Park Surrey ...36 C7
Oban Ag & B ...130 H2
Oban Airport Ag & B ...138 G10
Obley Shrops ...56 E9
Obney P & K ...141 P10
Oborne Dorset ...20 C11
Obthorpe Lincs ...74 A8
Occold Suffk ...64 H7
Occumster Highld ...167 N9
Ochiltree E Ayrs ...115 K3
Ockbrook Derbys ...72 C3
Ocker Hill Sandw ...58 E6
Ockeridge Worcs ...46 E2
Ockham Surrey ...36 C9
Ockle Highld ...137 P1
Ockley Surrey ...24 D2
Ocle Pychard Herefs ...46 A5
Octon E R Yk ...99 L7
Odcombe Somset ...19 P11
Odd Down BaNES ...20 D2
Oddendale Cumb ...101 Q8
Oddingley Worcs ...46 H3
Oddington Oxon ...48 G11
Odell Bed ...61 L9
Odham Devon ...8 C4
Odiham Hants ...23 K4
Odsal C Brad ...90 F5
Odsey Cambs ...50 G3
Odstock Wilts ...21 M9
Odstone Leics ...72 B9
Offchurch Warwks ...59 N11
Offenham Worcs ...47 L5
Offerton Stockp ...83 K7
Offerton Sundld ...113 M9
Offham E Susx ...25 K8
Offham Kent ...37 Q9
Offham W Susx ...24 B9
Offleymarsh Staffs ...70 D9
Offord Cluny Cambs ...62 B7
Offord D'Arcy Cambs ...62 B7
Offton Suffk ...53 J2
Offwell Devon ...10 D5
Ogbourne Maizey Wilts ...33 N10
Ogbourne St Andrew Wilts ...33 N10
Ogbourne St George Wilts ...33 P10
Ogden Calder ...90 D4
Ogle Nthumb ...112 H5
Oglet Lpool ...81 N8
Ogmore V Glam ...29 N10
Ogmore-by-Sea V Glam ...29 N9
Ogmore Vale Brdgnd ...29 P6
Ogwen Bank Gwynd ...79 L11
Okeford Fitzpaine Dorset ...12 D2
Okehampton Devon ...8 E5
Oker Side Derbys ...84 C8
Okewood Hill Surrey ...24 D3
Olchard Devon ...9 L7
Old Nhants ...60 G6
Old Aberdeen C Aber ...151 N6
Old Alresford Hants ...22 G8
Oldany Highld ...164 C10
Old Arley Warwks ...59 L6
Old Auchenbrack D & G ...115 Q7
Old Basford C Nott ...72 F2
Old Basing Hants ...23 J4
Old Beetley Norfk ...76 D8
Old Bewick Nthumb ...119 L6
Old Bolingbroke Lincs ...87 L7
Old Boxted Essex ...52 G5
Old Bramhope Leeds ...90 G2
Old Brampton Derbys ...84 D6
Old Bridge of Urr D & G ...108 G7
Old Buckenham Norfk ...64 F3
Old Burghclere Hants ...22 E3
Oldbury Kent ...37 N9
Oldbury Sandw ...58 E6
Oldbury Shrops ...57 N6
Oldbury Warwks ...59 M6
Oldbury Naite S Glos ...32 B6
Oldbury-on-Severn S Glos ...32 B6
Oldbury on the Hill Gloucs ...32 F7
Old Byland N York ...98 B3
Old Cantley Donc ...91 Q10
Old Cassop Dur ...104 B3
Oldcastle Mons ...45 L10
Oldcastle Heath Ches W ...69 N5
Old Catton Norfk ...77 J9
Old Churchstoke Powys ...56 D6
Old Clee NE Lin ...93 N9
Old Cleeve Somset ...18 D6
Old Colwyn Conwy ...80 B9
Oldcotes Notts ...85 J3
Old Coulsdon Gt Lon ...36 H9
Old Dailly S Ayrs ...114 D8
Old Dalby Leics ...72 H6
Old Dam Derbys ...83 P9
Old Deer Abers ...159 N8
Old Ditch Somset ...19 P5
Old Edlington Donc ...91 N11
Old Eldon Dur ...103 P5
Old Ellerby E R Yk ...93 L3
Old Felixstowe Suffk ...53 P4
Oldfield C Brad ...90 C3
Oldfield Worcs ...46 F2
Old Fletton C Pete ...74 C11

Oldford Somset ...20 E4
Old Forge Herefs ...45 R11
Old Furnace Herefs ...45 P10
Old Glossop Derbys ...83 M6
Old Goole E R Yk ...92 B6
Old Grimsby IoS ...2 b1
Old Hall Green Herts ...51 J6
Oldhall Green Suffk ...64 B10
Old Hall Street Norfk ...77 L5
Oldham Oldham ...83 K4
Oldhamstocks E Loth ...129 J6
Old Harlow Essex ...51 L8
Old Heath Essex ...52 H7
Old Hunstanton Norfk ...75 N2
Old Hurst Cambs ...62 D5
Old Hutton Cumb ...95 M3
Old Kea Cnwll ...3 L5
Old Kilpatrick W Duns ...125 M3
Old Knebworth Herts ...50 F6
Old Lakenham Norfk ...77 J10
Oldland S Glos ...32 C10
Old Langho Lancs ...89 L3
Old Laxey IoM ...80 f5
Old Leake Lincs ...87 M10
Old Malton N York ...98 F6
Oldmeldrum Abers ...151 L2
Oldmill Cnwll ...5 P7
Old Milverton Warwks ...59 L11
Oldmixon N Som ...19 K3
Old Newton Suffk ...64 F9
Old Oxted Surrey ...37 J10
Old Portlethen Abers ...151 N8
Old Quarrington Dur ...104 B3
Old Radford C Nott ...72 F2
Old Radnor Powys ...45 K3
Old Rayne Abers ...150 H2
Old Romney Kent ...26 H7
Old Shoreham W Susx ...24 F9
Oldshoremore Highld ...164 F5
Old Soar Kent ...37 P10
Old Sodbury S Glos ...32 E8
Old Somerby Lincs ...73 P4
Oldstead N York ...98 A5
Old Stratford Nhants ...49 L6
Old Struan P & K ...141 K4
Old Swarland Nthumb ...119 N10
Old Swinford Dudley ...58 D8
Old Thirsk N York ...97 P4
Old Town Calder ...90 C5
Old Town Cumb ...95 M4
Old Town Cumb ...101 N2
Old Town E Susx ...25 N11
Old Town IoS ...2 c2
Old Trafford Traffd ...82 H5
Old Tupton Derbys ...84 E7
Oldwall Cumb ...111 J8
Oldwalls Swans ...28 E6
Old Warden C Beds ...50 D2
Oldways End Somset ...17 R7
Old Weston Cambs ...61 N5
Old Wick Highld ...167 Q7
Old Windsor W & M ...35 Q10
Old Wives Lees Kent ...39 J11
Old Woking Surrey ...36 B9
Old Wolverton M Keyn ...49 M6
Old Woodhall Lincs ...86 H7
Old Woods Shrops ...69 N10
Olgrinmore Highld ...167 J6
Olive Green Staffs ...71 L11
Oliver's Battery Hants ...22 E9
Ollaberry Shet ...169 q5
Ollach Highld ...153 J10
Ollerton Ches E ...82 G9
Ollerton Notts ...85 L7
Ollerton Shrops ...70 A9
Olmarch Cerdgn ...43 M3
Olmstead Green Cambs ...51 P2
Olney M Keyn ...49 N4
Olrig House Highld ...167 L3
Olton Solhll ...58 H8
Olveston S Glos ...32 B7
Ombersley Worcs ...46 F2
Ompton Notts ...85 L7
Once Brewed Nthumb ...111 P7
Onchan IoM ...80 e6
Onecote Staffs ...71 J3
Onehouse Suffk ...64 E10
Onen Mons ...31 M2
Ongar Street Herefs ...56 F11
Onibury Shrops ...56 H9
Onich Highld ...139 J5
Onllwyn Neath ...29 M2
Onneley Staffs ...70 D6
Onslow Green Essex ...51 Q7
Onslow Village Surrey ...23 Q5
Onston Ches W ...82 C10
Openwoodgate Derbys ...84 E11
Opinan Highld ...153 N3
Orbliston Moray ...157 Q6
Orbost Highld ...152 D9
Orby Lincs ...87 N7
Orchard Portman Somset ...18 H10
Orcheston Wilts ...21 L5
Orcop Herefs ...45 P9
Orcop Hill Herefs ...45 P9
Ord Abers ...158 F6
Ordhead Abers ...150 H5
Ordie Abers ...150 D7
Ordiequish Moray ...157 Q6
Ordley Nthumb ...112 E9
Ordsall Notts ...85 M5
Ore E Susx ...26 D9
Oreleton Common Herefs ...56 H11
Oreton Shrops ...57 M8
Orford Suffk ...65 N11
Orford Warrtn ...82 D6
Organford Dorset ...12 F6
Orgreave Staffs ...71 L11
Orkney Islands Ork ...169 d6
Orkney Neolithic Ork ...169 c5
Orlestone Kent ...26 H5
Orleton Herefs ...56 H11
Orleton Worcs ...57 N11
Orlingbury Nhants ...61 J6
Ormathwaite Cumb ...101 J5
Ormesby R & Cl ...104 F7
Ormesby St Margaret Norfk ...77 P9
Ormesby St Michael Norfk ...77 P9
Ormiscaig Highld ...160 D8
Ormiston E Loth ...128 C6
Ormsaigmore Highld ...137 M3
Ormsary Ag & B ...123 M5
Ormskirk Lancs ...88 F9
Ornsby Hill Dur ...113 J11

Oronsay Ag & B 136 b4
Orphir Ork 169 c6
Orpington Gt Lon 37 L7
Orrell Sefton 81 L5
Orrell Wigan 82 B4
Orrell Post Wigan 88 G9
Orrisdale IoM 80 d3
Orroland D & G 108 G11
Orsett Thurr 37 P4
Orsett Heath Thurr 37 P4
Orslow Staffs 70 E11
Orston Notts 73 K2
Orthwaite Cumb 101 J4
Ortner Lancs 95 L10
Orton Cumb 102 B9
Orton Nhants 60 H5
Orton Staffs 58 C5
Orton Longueville C Pete 74 C11
Orton-on-the-Hill Leics 59 M4
Orton Rigg Cumb 110 F10
Orton Waterville C Pete 74 C11
Orwell Cambs 62 E10
Osbaldeston Lancs 89 J4
Osbaldeston Green Lancs 89 J4
Osbaldwick C York 98 C10
Osbaston Leics 72 C10
Osbaston Mons 31 P2
Osbaston Shrops 69 K10
Osborne IoW 14 F8
Osborne IoW 14 F8
Osbournby Lincs 73 R3
Oscroft Ches W 81 Q11
Ose Highld 152 E9
Osgathorpe Leics 72 C7
Osgodby Lincs 86 E2
Osgodby N York 91 Q4
Osgodby N York 99 M4
Oskaig Highld 153 J10
Oskamull Ag & B 137 M7
Osmaston Derbys 71 M6
Osmington Dorset 11 Q8
Osmington Mills Dorset 12 B8
Osmondthorpe Leeds 91 J4
Osmotherley N York 104 E11
Osney Oxon 34 E3
Ospringe Kent 38 H9
Ossett Wakefd 90 H6
Ossington Notts 85 N8
Ostend Essex 38 F2
Osterley Gt Lon 36 E5
Oswaldkirk N York 98 C5
Oswaldtwistle Lancs 89 L5
Oswestry Shrops 69 J9
Otairnis W Isls 168 e10
Otford Kent 37 M9
Otham Kent 38 C11
Otham Hole Kent 38 D11
Othery Somset 19 L8
Otley Leeds 97 K11
Otley Suffk 65 J10
Otley Green Suffk 65 K10
Otterbourne Hants 22 E10
Otterburn N York 96 C9
Otterburn Nthumb 112 C2
Otter Ferry Ag & B 131 J11
Otterham Cnwll 5 K3
Otterhampton Somset 18 H6
Otterham Quay Kent 38 D8
Otterham Station Cnwll 5 K4
Otternish W Isls 168 e10
Ottershaw Surrey 36 B8
Otterswick Shet 169 s5
Otterton Devon 10 B7
Otterwood Hants 14 D6
Ottery St Mary Devon 10 C5
Ottinge Kent 27 L3
Ottringham E R Yk 93 N6
Oughterby Cumb 110 E9
Oughtershaw N York 96 C4
Oughterside Cumb 100 F2
Oughtibridge Sheff 84 D2
Oughtrington Warrtn 82 E7
Oulston N York 98 A6
Oulton Cumb 110 D10
Oulton Leeds 91 K5
Oulton Norfk 76 G6
Oulton Staffs 70 D10
Oulton Staffs 70 G7
Oulton Suffk 65 Q3
Oulton Broad Suffk 65 H6
Oulton Street Norfk 76 M3
Oundle Nhants 61 M3
Ounsdale Staffs 58 C6
Ousby Cumb 102 B4
Ousden Suffk 63 M9
Ousefleet E R Yk 92 D6
Ouston Dur 113 L10
Outchester Nthumb 119 M4
Out Elmstead Kent 39 M11
Outgate Cumb 101 L11
Outhgill Cumb 102 G10
Outhill Warwks 58 H11
Outlands Staffs 70 D8
Outlane Kirk 90 D7
Out Newton E R Yk 93 Q6
Out Rawcliffe Lancs 88 E2
Outwell Norfk 75 K10
Outwick Hants 21 M11
Outwood Surrey 36 H11
Outwood Wakefd 91 J6
Outwood Gate Bury 89 M9
Outwoods Leics 72 C7
Outwoods Staffs 70 D11
Ouzlewell Green Leeds 91 J5
Ovenden Calder 90 D5
Over Cambs 62 E6
Over Ches W 82 D11
Over Gloucs 46 F11
Over S Glos 31 Q8
Over Burrows Derbys 71 P7
Overbury Worcs 47 J2
Overcombe Dorset 11 P8
Over Compton Dorset 19 Q11
Over End Cambs 61 N2
Overgreen Derbys 84 D6
Over Green Warwks 59 J6
Over Haddon Derbys 84 B7
Over Hulton Bolton 82 E4
Over Kellet Lancs 95 L7
Over Kiddington Oxon 48 D10
Overleigh Somset 19 N7
Overley Staffs 71 M11
Over Monnow Mons 31 P2
Over Norton Oxon 48 B9
Over Peover Ches E 82 G10

Overpool Ches W 81 M9
Overscaig Highld 161 Q2
Overseal Derbys 71 P11
Over Silton N York 97 P2
Oversland Kent 39 J10
Oversley Green Warwks 47 L3
Overstone Nhants 60 G7
Over Stowey Somset 18 F7
Overstrand Norfk 77 J3
Over Stratton Somset 19 M11
Overstreet Wilts 21 L7
Over Tabley Ches E 82 F9
Overthorpe Nhants 48 E6
Overton C Aber 151 M5
Overton Ches W 81 Q9
Overton Hants 22 F5
Overton Lancs 95 J9
Overton N York 98 B9
Overton Shrops 57 J10
Overton Swans 28 E7
Overton Wakefd 90 H7
Overton Wrexhm 69 L6
Overton Bridge Wrexhm 69 L6
Overton Green Ches E 70 E2
Overtown Lancs 89 P5
Overtown Lancs 95 N5
Overtown N Lans 126 E7
Overtown Swindn 33 N9
Overtown Wakefd 91 K7
Over Wallop Hants 21 Q7
Over Whitacre Warwks 59 L6
Over Woodhouse Derbys 84 G6
Over Worton Oxon 48 D9
Overy Oxon 34 G6
Oving Bucks 49 L10
Oving W Susx 15 P6
Ovingdean Br & H 25 J10
Ovingham Nthumb 112 G8
Ovington Dur 103 M8
Ovington Essex 52 C3
Ovington Hants 22 G8
Ovington Norfk 76 C11
Ovington Nthumb 112 G8
Ower Hants 14 E6
Ower Hants 22 B11
Owermoigne Dorset 12 C7
Owlbury Shrops 56 E6
Owlerton Sheff 84 D3
Owlpen Gloucs 32 E5
Owl's Green Suffk 65 K8
Owlsmoor Br For 23 M2
Owlswick Bucks 35 L3
Owmby Lincs 86 D3
Owmby Lincs 93 J10
Owslebury Hants 22 F10
Owston Donc 91 P8
Owston Leics 73 K9
Owston Ferry N Linc 92 D10
Owstwick E R Yk 93 N4
Owthorne E R Yk 93 P5
Owthorpe Notts 72 H4
Owton Manor Hartpl 104 E6
Oxborough Norfk 75 P10
Oxbridge Dorset 11 K5
Oxcombe Lincs 87 K5
Oxcroft Derbys 84 G6
Oxen End Essex 51 Q5
Oxenholme Cumb 95 L3
Oxenhope C Brad 90 C4
Oxen Park Cumb 94 G3
Oxenpill Somset 19 M6
Oxenton Gloucs 47 J8
Oxenwood Wilts 22 B3
Oxford Oxon 34 F3
Oxford Airport Oxon 48 E11
Oxford Services Oxon 34 H4
Oxgangs C Edin 127 N4
Oxhey Herts 50 D11
Oxhill Dur 113 J10
Oxhill Warwks 48 B5
Oxley Wolves 58 D4
Oxley Green Essex 52 F9
Oxley's Green E Susx 25 Q6
Oxlode Cambs 62 G3
Oxnam Border 118 C7
Oxnead Norfk 77 J7
Oxshott Surrey 36 D8
Oxshott Heath Surrey 36 D8
Oxspring Barns 90 H10
Oxted Surrey 37 J10
Oxton Border 128 D9
Oxton N York 91 N2
Oxton Notts 85 K10
Oxton Wirral 81 L7
Oxwich Swans 28 E7
Oxwich Green Swans 28 E7
Oxwick Norfk 76 C6
Oykel Bridge Highld 161 P6
Oyne Abers 150 H2
Oystermouth Swans 28 H7
Ozleworth Gloucs 32 E6

P

Pabail W Isls 168 k4
Packers Hill Dorset 11 Q2
Packington Leics 72 B8
Packmoor C Stke 70 F4
Packmores Warwks 59 L11
Padanaram Angus 142 G7
Padbury Bucks 49 K8
Paddington Gt Lon 36 G4
Paddington Warrtn 82 D7
Paddlesworth Kent 27 L4
Paddlesworth Kent 37 Q8
Paddock Wood Kent 25 Q2
Paddolgreen Shrops 69 P8
Padfield Derbys 83 M5
Padgate Warrtn 82 D7
Padhams Green Essex 51 P11
Padiham Lancs 89 M4
Padside N York 97 J9
Padstow Cnwll 4 E6
Padworth W Berk 34 H11
Page Bank Dur 103 P3
Pagham W Susx 15 N7
Paglesham Essex 38 F3
Paignton Torbay 7 M6
Pailton Warwks 59 Q8
Paine's Cross E Susx 25 P6
Painleyhill Staffs 71 J8
Painscastle Powys 44 H5
Painshawfield Nthumb 112 G8
Painsthorpe E R Yk 98 G9

Painswick Gloucs 32 G3
Painter's Forstal Kent 38 G10
Paisley Rens 125 M5
Pakefield Suffk 65 Q3
Pakenham Suffk 64 C8
Pale Gwynd 68 C7
Pale Green Essex 51 Q2
Palestine Hants 21 Q6
Paley Street W & M 35 N9
Palfrey Wsall 58 F5
Palgrave Suffk 64 G6
Pallington Dorset 12 C6
Palmarsh Kent 27 K5
Palmers Green Gt Lon 36 H2
Palmerston E Ayrs 115 K4
Palmerstown V Glam 30 F11
Palnackie D & G 108 H9
Palnure D & G 107 N5
Palterton Derbys 84 G7
Pamber End Hants 22 H3
Pamber Green Hants 22 H3
Pamber Heath Hants 22 H2
Pamington Gloucs 46 H8
Pamphill Dorset 12 G4
Pampisford Cambs 62 G11
Panborough Somset 19 N5
Panbride Angus 143 K10
Pancrasweek Devon 16 D10
Pancross V Glam 30 D11
Pandy Caerph 54 E4
Pandy Gwynd 68 A9
Pandy Mons 45 L10
Pandy Powys 55 L4
Pandy Wrexhm 68 G7
Pandy Wrexhm 69 K4
Pandy'r Capel Denbgs 68 E4
Pandy Tudur Conwy 67 R2
Panfield Essex 52 B6
Pangbourne W Berk 34 H9
Pangdean W Susx 24 G8
Panks Bridge Herefs 46 B5
Pannal N York 97 M10
Pannal Ash N York 97 L10
Pant Shrops 69 J10
Pantasaph Flints 80 H9
Panteg Pembks 40 H4
Pantersbridge Cnwll 5 K8
Pant Glas Gwynd 66 H5
Pantglas Powys 54 H5
Pant-Gwyn Carmth 43 L9
Pant-lasau Swans 29 J4
Pant Mawr Powys 55 J8
Panton Lincs 86 G5
Pant-pastynog Denbgs 68 D2
Pantperthog Gwynd 54 G4
Pantside Caerph 30 H5
Pant-y-caws Carmth 41 M5
Pant-y-dwr Powys 55 M10
Pant-y-ffridd Powys 56 B4
Pantyffynnon Carmth 28 H2
Pantygaseg Torfn 31 J5
Pantygelli Mons 45 L11
Pant-y-gog Brdgnd 29 P6
Pantymwyn Flints 68 G2
Panxworth Norfk 77 M9
Papcastle Cumb 100 F4
Papigoe Highld 167 Q6
Papple E Loth 128 F5
Papplewick Notts 84 H10
Papworth Everard Cambs 62 C8
Papworth St Agnes Cambs 62 C8
Par Cnwll 3 R3
Paramour Street Kent 39 N9
Parbold Lancs 88 F8
Parbrook Somset 19 Q7
Parbrook W Susx 24 C5
Parc Gwynd 68 A8
Parcllyn Cerdgn 42 D4
Parc Seymour Newpt 31 M6
Pardown Hants 22 G5
Pardshaw Cumb 100 E6
Parham Suffk 65 L9
Park D & G 109 K2
Park Nthumb 111 N8
Park Bottom Cnwll 2 H5
Park Bridge Tamesd 83 K4
Park Corner E Susx 25 M3
Park Corner Oxon 35 J7
Park Corner W & M 35 N8
Park End Bed 49 Q4
Parkend Gloucs 32 B3
Park End Nthumb 112 C5
Parker's Green Kent 37 P11
Parkeston Essex 53 M5
Parkeston Quay Essex 53 M5
Park Farm Kent 26 H4
Parkgate Ches W 81 K9
Parkgate Cumb 110 D11
Parkgate D & G 109 M3
Parkgate E Susx 26 B9
Parkgate Essex 51 Q5
Park Gate Hants 14 F5
Parkgate Kent 26 E5
Park Gate Kent 37 M8
Park Gate Leeds 90 F2
Parkgate Surrey 24 F2
Park Gate Worcs 58 D10
Park Green Essex 51 L5
Park Green Suffk 64 G9
Parkhall W Duns 125 M3
Parkham Devon 16 F7
Parkham Ash Devon 16 F7
Park Head Derbys 84 E10
Parkhill Dur 104 B3
Park Hill Gloucs 32 Q5
Parkhouse Mons 31 P4
Parkmill Swans 28 F7
Park Royal Gt Lon 36 F4
Parkside N Lans 126 E6
Parkside Wrexhm 69 L3
Parkstone BCP 13 H6
Park Street Herts 50 D10
Park Street W Susx 24 D4
Parkway BCP 13 K5
Parley Green BCP 13 K5
Parmoor Bucks 35 M7
Parracombe Devon 17 M2
Parrog Pembks 41 L3
Parsonby Cumb 100 F3
Parson Cross Sheff 84 D2

Parson Drove Cambs 74 G9
Parson's Heath Essex 52 H6
Parson's Hill Derbys 71 P9
Partick C Glas 125 N4
Partington Traffd 82 F6
Partney Lincs 87 M7
Parton Cumb 100 C6
Partridge Green W Susx 24 E7
Partrishow Powys 45 K10
Parwich Derbys 71 M4
Paslow Wood Common Essex 51 N10
Passenham Nhants 49 L7
Passfield Hants 23 M8
Passingford Bridge Essex 51 M11
Paston C Pete 74 C10
Paston Norfk 77 L5
Pasturefields Staffs 70 H10
Patchacott Devon 8 C5
Patcham Br & H 24 H9
Patchetts Green Herts 50 D11
Patching W Susx 24 C9
Patchole Devon 17 L3
Patchway S Glos 32 B8
Pateley Bridge N York 97 J7
Paternoster Heath Essex 52 F8
Pathe Somset 19 L8
Pathhead Fife 134 H9
Pathhead Mdloth 128 B7
Pathlow Warwks 47 N3
Path of Condie P & K 134 D5
Patmore Heath Herts 51 K5
Patna E Ayrs 114 H5
Patney Wilts 21 L3
Patrick IoM 80 b5
Patrick Brompton N York 97 K2
Patricroft Salfd 82 G5
Patrington E R Yk 93 P6
Patrington Haven E R Yk 93 P6
Patrixbourne Kent 39 L10
Patterdale Cumb 101 L7
Pattingham Staffs 57 Q5
Pattishall Nhants 49 J4
Pattiswick Green Essex 52 D7
Patton Shrops 57 K5
Patton Bridge Cumb 101 Q11
Paul Cnwll 2 D8
Paulerspury Nhants 49 K5
Paull E R Yk 93 L5
Paulton BaNES 20 C3
Paultons Park Hants 22 B11
Paunton Herefs 46 C4
Pauperhaugh Nthumb 119 M11
Pave Lane Wrekin 70 D11
Pavenham Bed 61 L9
Pawlett Somset 19 J6
Pawston Nthumb 118 G4
Paxford Gloucs 47 N7
Paxton Border 129 N9
Payden Street Kent 38 F11
Payhembury Devon 10 B4
Paynter's Lane End Cnwll 2 H5
Paythorne Lancs 96 B10
Paytoe Herefs 56 G10
Peacehaven E Susx 25 K10
Peak Dale Derbys 83 N9
Peak District National Park 83 Q6
Peak Forest Derbys 83 P9
Peak Hill Lincs 74 E7
Peakirk C Pete 74 C9
Pearson's Green Kent 25 Q2
Peartree Green Herefs 46 A8
Peasedown St John BaNES 20 D3
Peasehill Derbys 84 F11
Peaseland Green Norfk 76 F8
Peasemore W Berk 34 E9
Peasenhall Suffk 65 M8
Pease Pottage W Susx 24 G4
Pease Pottage Services W Susx 24 G4
Peaslake Surrey 24 C2
Peasley Cross St Hel 81 Q6
Peasmarsh E Susx 26 E7
Peasmarsh Somset 10 G2
Peasmarsh Surrey 23 Q5
Peathill Abers 159 M4
Peat Inn Fife 135 M6
Peatling Magna Leics 60 C2
Peatling Parva Leics 60 C3
Peaton Shrops 57 J7
Pebmarsh Essex 52 E5
Pebsham E Susx 26 C10
Pebworth Worcs 47 M5
Pecket Well Calder 90 B5
Peckforton Ches E 69 P3
Peckham Gt Lon 36 H5
Peckleton Leics 72 D10
Pedairffordd Powys 68 F8
Pedlinge Kent 27 K4
Pedmore Dudley 58 D8
Pedwell Somset 19 M7
Peebles Border 117 K2
Peel IoM 80 b5
Peel Lancs 88 D4
Peel Common Hants 14 G6
Peene Kent 27 L4
Peening Quarter Kent 26 E6
Peggs Green Leics 72 C7
Pegsdon C Beds 50 D4
Pegswood Nthumb 113 K3
Pegwell Kent 39 Q9
Peinchorran Highld 153 J11
Peinlich Highld 152 G6
Pelcomb Pembks 40 H7
Pelcomb Bridge Pembks 40 H7
Pelcomb Cross Pembks 40 H7
Peldon Essex 52 G8
Pell Green E Susx 25 P4
Pelsall Wsall 58 F4
Pelsall Wood Wsall 58 F4
Pelton Dur 113 L10
Pelton Fell Dur 113 L10
Pelutho Cumb 109 P11
Pelynt Cnwll 5 L10
Pemberton Carmth 28 F4
Pemberton Wigan 82 C4
Pembles Cross Kent 26 E2
Pembrey Carmth 28 D4
Pembridge Herefs 45 M3
Pembroke Pembks 41 J10
Pembroke Dock Pembks 41 J10
Pembrokeshire Coast National Park Pembks 40 F6
Pembury Kent 25 P2
Pen-allt Herefs 45 R9

Penallt Mons 31 P2
Penally Pembks 41 M11
Penare Cnwll 3 P5
Penarth V Glam 30 G10
Penblewin Pembks 41 M7
Pen-bont Rhydybeddau Cerdgn 54 F8
Penbryn Cerdgn 42 E4
Pencader Carmth 42 H7
Pencaenewydd Gwynd 66 G6
Pencaitland E Loth 128 C6
Pencarnisiog IoA 78 F10
Pencarreg Carmth 43 L5
Pencarrow Cnwll 5 J5
Pencelli Powys 44 F9
Penclawdd Swans 28 F5
Pencoed Brdgnd 30 C8
Pencombe Herefs 46 A4
Pencoyd Herefs 45 Q9
Pencraig Herefs 45 R10
Pencraig Powys 68 D9
Pendeen Cnwll 2 B7
Penderyn Rhondd 29 P3
Pendine Carmth 41 P9
Pendlebury Salfd 82 G4
Pendleton Lancs 89 M3
Pendock Worcs 46 E8
Pendoggett Cnwll 4 G6
Pendomer Somset 11 L2
Pendoylan V Glam 30 E9
Penegoes Powys 54 H4
Penelewey Cnwll 3 L5
Pen-ffordd Pembks 41 L6
Pengam Caerph 30 G5
Pengam Cardif 30 H9
Penge Gt Lon 37 J6
Pengelly Cnwll 4 H5
Pengenffordd Powys 44 H9
Pengorffwysfa IoA 78 H6
Pengover Green Cnwll 5 M8
Pen-groes-oped Mons 31 K3
Pengwern Denbgs 80 E9
Penhale Cnwll 2 H10
Penhale Cnwll 4 E10
Penhale Cnwll 4 G11
Penhale Cnwll 5 Q11
Penhallow Cnwll 3 K3
Penhalurick Cnwll 3 J6
Penhalvean Cnwll 3 J6
Penhill Swindn 33 N7
Penhow Newpt 31 M6
Penhurst E Susx 25 Q7
Peniarth Gwynd 54 E3
Penicuik Mdloth 127 N6
Peniel Carmth 42 H10
Peniel Denbgs 68 D2
Penifiler Highld 152 H9
Peninver Ag & B 120 E7
Penisarwaun Gwynd 67 K2
Penistone Barns 90 G10
Penjerrick Cnwll 3 K7
Penketh Warrtn 82 C7
Penkill S Ayrs 114 D8
Penkridge Staffs 58 D2
Penlean Cnwll 5 L2
Penleigh Wilts 20 G4
Penley Wrexhm 69 M6
Penllergaer Swans 28 H5
Pen-llyn IoA 78 F8
Penllyn V Glam 30 C9
Pen-lôn IoA 78 G11
Penmachno Conwy 67 P4
Penmaen Caerph 30 G5
Penmaen Swans 28 F7
Penmaenan Conwy 79 N9
Penmaenmawr Conwy 79 N9
Penmaenpool Gwynd 67 M11
Penmark V Glam 30 E11
Penmon IoA 79 L8
Penmorfa Gwynd 67 J6
Penmynydd IoA 79 J10
Penn Bucks 35 P6
Penn Wolves 58 C5
Pennal Gwynd 54 F4
Pennan Abers 159 K4
Pennant Cerdgn 43 K2
Pennant Denbgs 68 D8
Pennant Powys 55 K6
Pennant-Melangell Powys 68 D9
Pennar Pembks 41 J10
Pennard Swans 28 G7
Pennerley Shrops 56 F5
Pennicott Devon 9 L4
Pennines 90 B3
Pennington Cumb 94 F5
Pennington Hants 13 P5
Pennington Green Wigan 89 J9
Pennorth Powys 44 G9
Penn Street Bucks 35 P5
Pennsylvania S Glos 32 D10
Penny Bridge Cumb 94 G4
Pennycross Ag & B 137 N10
Pennygate Norfk 77 L7
Pennyghael Ag & B 137 N10
Pennyglen S Ayrs 114 E5
Penny Green Derbys 84 H5
Penny Hill Lincs 74 E5
Pennymoor Devon 9 L2
Pennywell Sundld 113 N9
Penparc Cerdgn 42 D5
Penparcau Cerdgn 54 D8
Penpedairheol Caerph 30 G5
Penpedwal Mons 31 K4
Penpergwm Mons 31 K4
Penperlleni Mons 31 K4
Penpethy Cnwll 4 H4
Penpillick Cnwll 4 H10
Penpol Cnwll 3 L6
Penpoll Cnwll 5 J11
Penponds Cnwll 2 G6
Penpont Cnwll 4 H7
Penpont D & G 108 H2
Penpont Powys 44 D9
Penquit Devon 6 H8
Penrest Cnwll 5 N6
Penrherber Carmth 41 Q3
Pen-rhiw Pembks 41 P2
Penrhiwceiber Rhondd 30 E5
Pen Rhiwfawr Neath 29 K2
Penrhiwgoch Carmth 43 L11
Penrhiwllan Cerdgn 42 F5
Penrhiwpal Cerdgn 42 F5
Penrhos Gwynd 66 F8
Penrhos IoA 78 D8
Penrhos Mons 31 M2
Penrhos Powys 29 M2

Penrhos garnedd Gwynd ...79 K10
Penrhyn Bay Conwy ...79 Q8
Penrhyn-coch Cerdgn ...54 E8
Penrhyndeudraeth Gwynd ...67 L7
Penrhyn-side Conwy ...79 Q8
Penrhyn Slate Landscape Gwynd ...79 L11
Penrhys Rhondd ...30 D6
Penrice Swans ...28 E7
Penrioch N Ayrs ...120 G3
Penrith Cumb ...101 P4
Penrose Cnwll ...4 D7
Penruddock Cumb ...101 M5
Penryn Cnwll ...3 K7
Pensarn Conwy ...80 D9
Pensax Worcs ...57 N11
Pensby Wirral ...81 K8
Penselwood Somset ...20 E8
Pensford BaNES ...20 B2
Pensham Worcs ...46 H6
Penshaw Sundld ...113 M10
Penshurst Kent ...25 M2
Penshurst Station Kent ...37 M11
Pensilva Cnwll ...5 M7
Pensnett Dudley ...58 D7
Penstone Devon ...9 J4
Penstrowed Powys ...55 P6
Pentewan Cnwll ...3 Q4
Pentir Gwynd ...79 K11
Pentire Cnwll ...4 B9
Pentlepoir Pembks ...41 M9
Pentlow Essex ...52 D3
Pentlow Street Essex ...63 P11
Pentney Norfk ...75 P8
Pentonbridge Cumb ...110 H5
Penton Grafton Hants ...22 B5
Penton Mewsey Hants ...22 B5
Pentraeth IoA ...79 J9
Pentre Denbgs ...68 E2
Pentre Flints ...81 L11
Pentre Mons ...31 K3
Pentre Mons ...31 M4
Pentre Powys ...55 P7
Pentre Powys ...56 B7
Pentre Powys ...56 D6
Pentre Rhondd ...30 C5
Pentre Shrops ...69 L11
Pentre Wrexhm ...69 J6
Pentre-bâch Cerdgn ...43 L5
Pentre Bach Flints ...81 J9
Pentrebach Myr Td ...30 E4
Pentre-bach Powys ...44 C8
Pentrebeirdd Powys ...56 B2
Pentre Berw IoA ...78 H10
Pentre-bont Conwy ...67 N4
Pentre-cagel Carmth ...42 F6
Pentrecelyn Denbgs ...68 F4
Pentre-celyn Powys ...55 K3
Pentre-chwyth Swans ...29 J6
Pentre-clawdd Shrops ...69 J8
Pentre-cwrt Carmth ...42 G7
Pentredwr Denbgs ...68 G5
Pentrefelin Gwynd ...67 J7
Pentrefelin IoA ...78 G6
Pentre Ffwrndan Flints ...81 K10
Pentrefoelas Conwy ...67 R4
Pentregalar Pembks ...41 N4
Pentregat Cerdgn ...42 G4
Pentre-Gwenlais Carmth ...43 M11
Pentre Gwynfryn Gwynd ...67 K9
Pentre Halkyn Flints ...81 J10
Pentre Hodrey Shrops ...56 E9
Pentre Isaf Conwy ...80 D10
Pentre Llanrhaeadr Denbgs ...68 E2
Pentre Llifior Powys ...56 B5
Pentre-llwyn-llwyd Powys ...44 D4
Pentre-llyn Cerdgn ...54 E9
Pentre-llyn-cymmer Conwy ...68 C4
Pentre-Maw Powys ...55 K4
Pentre Meyrick V Glam ...30 C9
Pentre-piod Torfn ...31 J4
Pentre-poeth Newpt ...31 J7
Pentre'rbryn Cerdgn ...42 G4
Pentre'r-felin Cerdgn ...43 M5
Pentre'r Felin Conwy ...79 Q11
Pentre'r-felin Powys ...44 C8
Pentre Saron Denbgs ...68 D2
Pentre-tafarn-y-fedw Conwy ...67 Q2
Pentre ty gwyn Carmth ...43 R7
Pentrich Derbys ...84 E10
Pentridge Dorset ...21 K11
Pen-twyn Caerph ...30 H4
Pentwyn Cardif ...30 H8
Pen-twyn Mons ...31 P3
Pen-twyn Torfn ...31 J4
Pentwynmaur Caerph ...30 G5
Pentyrch Cardif ...30 F8
Penwithick Cnwll ...4 G10
Penwood Hants ...22 D2
Penwyllt Powys ...44 B11
Penybanc Carmth ...43 M10
Penybont Powys ...44 G2
Pen-y-bont Powys ...68 H10
Penybontfawr Powys ...68 E10
Pen-y-bryn Pembks ...41 N2
Pen-y-cae Powys ...29 M2
Penycae Wrexhm ...69 J5
Pen-y-cae-mawr Mons ...31 M5
Penycaerau Gwynd ...66 B9
Pen-y-cefn Flints ...80 G9
Pen-y-clawdd Mons ...31 N3
Pen-y-coedcae Rhondd ...30 E7
Penycwm Pembks ...40 G6
Pen-y-fai Brdgnd ...29 N8
Pen-y-felin Flints ...80 H11
Penyffordd Flints ...69 K2
Pen-y-ffordd Flints ...80 G8
Penyffridd Gwynd ...67 J3
Pen-y-garn Cerdgn ...54 E7
Pen-y-Garnedd Powys ...68 F10
Pen-y-graig Gwynd ...66 C8
Penygraig Rhondd ...30 D6
Penygroes Carmth ...28 G2
Penygroes Gwynd ...66 H4
Pen-y-groeslon Gwynd ...66 C8
Pen-y-Gwryd Gwynd ...67 M3
Pen-y-lan V Glam ...30 C9
Pen-y-Mynydd Carmth ...28 G3
Penymynydd Flints ...69 K2
Pen-yr-Heol Mons ...31 M2
Penysarn IoA ...78 H6
Pen-y-stryt Denbgs ...68 H4
Penywaun Rhondd ...30 C4
Penzance Cnwll ...2 D7

Peopleton Worcs ...46 H4
Peover Heath Ches E ...82 G10
Peper Harow Surrey ...23 P6
Peplow Shrops ...70 A10
Pepper's Green Essex ...51 P8
Pepperstock C Beds ...50 C7
Perceton N Ayrs ...125 K9
Percyhorner Abers ...159 N4
Perelle Guern ...10 b2
Perham Down Wilts ...21 Q5
Periton Somset ...18 C5
Perivale Gt Lon ...36 E4
Perkins Village Devon ...9 P6
Perkinsville Dur ...113 L10
Perlethorpe Notts ...85 K6
Perranarworthal Cnwll ...3 K3
Perranporth Cnwll ...3 K3
Perranuthnoe Cnwll ...2 E8
Perranwell Cnwll ...3 K3
Perranwell Cnwll ...3 K6
Perran Wharf Cnwll ...3 K6
Perranzabuloe Cnwll ...3 K3
Perrott's Brook Gloucs ...33 K3
Perry Birm ...58 G6
Perry Cambs ...61 P7
Perry Barr Birm ...58 G6
Perry Green Essex ...52 D7
Perry Green Herts ...51 K7
Perry Green Wilts ...33 J7
Perrystone Hill Herefs ...46 B9
Perry Street Somset ...10 G3
Pershall Staffs ...70 E9
Pershore Worcs ...46 H5
Pertenhall Bed ...61 N7
Perth P & K ...134 E3
Perthy Shrops ...69 L8
Perton Herefs ...46 A6
Perton Staffs ...58 C5
Pertwood Wilts ...20 G7
Peterborough C Pete ...74 C11
Peterborough Services Cambs ...61 P2
Peterchurch Herefs ...45 L7
Peterculter C Aber ...151 L7
Peterhead Abers ...159 R8
Peterlee Dur ...104 D2
Petersfield Hants ...23 K10
Peter's Green Herts ...50 D7
Petersham Gt Lon ...36 E4
Peters Marland Devon ...16 H9
Peterstone Wentlooge Newpt ...31 J9
Peterston-super-Ely V Glam ...30 E9
Peterstow Herefs ...45 R10
Peters Village Kent ...38 B9
Peter Tavy Devon ...8 D9
Petham Kent ...39 K11
Petherwin Gate Cnwll ...5 M4
Petrockstow Devon ...17 J10
Petsoe End M Keyn ...49 N5
Pett E Susx ...26 E9
Pettaugh Suffk ...64 H10
Pett Bottom Kent ...39 L11
Petterden Angus ...142 G10
Pettinain S Lans ...116 D2
Pettistree Suffk ...65 L10
Petton Devon ...18 D10
Petton Shrops ...69 M9
Petts Wood Gt Lon ...37 L7
Pettycur Fife ...134 H10
Petty France S Glos ...32 E7
Pettymuk Abers ...151 N3
Petworth W Susx ...23 Q10
Pevensey E Susx ...25 P9
Pevensey Bay E Susx ...25 Q10
Pewsey Wilts ...21 N2
Pewsham Wilts ...32 H10
Pheasant's Hill Bucks ...35 L7
Phepson Worcs ...46 H3
Philadelphia Sundld ...113 M10
Philham Devon ...16 D7
Philiphaugh Border ...117 N5
Phillack Cnwll ...2 F6
Philleigh Cnwll ...3 M6
Philpot End Essex ...51 P7
Philpstoun W Loth ...127 K2
Phocle Green Herefs ...46 B9
Phoenix Green Hants ...23 L3
Pibsbury Somset ...19 M9
Pica Cumb ...100 D6
Piccadilly Warwks ...59 K5
Piccotts End Herts ...50 B9
Pickburn Donc ...91 N9
Pickering N York ...98 F4
Picket Piece Hants ...22 C5
Picket Post Hants ...13 L3
Picket Twenty Hants ...22 C5
Pickford Covtry ...59 L8
Pickford Green Covtry ...59 L8
Pickhill N York ...97 M4
Picklescott Shrops ...56 G5
Pickmere Ches E ...82 E9
Pickney Somset ...18 G9
Pickstock Wrekin ...70 C10
Pickup Bank Bl w D ...89 L6
Pickwell Devon ...16 H3
Pickwell Leics ...73 K8
Pickwick Wilts ...32 G10
Pickworth Lincs ...73 Q4
Pickworth Rutlnd ...73 P8
Picton Ches W ...81 N10
Picton Flints ...80 G8
Picton N York ...104 D9
Piddinghoe E Susx ...25 K10
Piddington Bucks ...35 M6
Piddington Nhants ...49 M4
Piddington Oxon ...48 H11
Piddlehinton Dorset ...11 Q5
Piddletrenthide Dorset ...11 Q5
Pidley Cambs ...62 D5
Piercebridge Darltn ...103 P7
Pierowall Ork ...169 d2
Piff's Elm Gloucs ...46 H9
Pigdon Nthumb ...113 J3
Pigeon Green Warwks ...47 P2
Pig Oak Dorset ...12 H4
Pig Street Herefs ...45 M5
Pikehall Derbys ...71 M3
Pilford Dorset ...12 H4
Pilgrims Hatch Essex ...51 N11
Pilham Lincs ...85 Q2
Pill N Som ...31 P9
Pillaton Cnwll ...5 P9
Pillatonmill Cnwll ...5 P9
Pillerton Hersey Warwks ...47 Q5

Pillerton Priors Warwks ...47 Q5
Pilleth Powys ...56 D11
Pilley Barns ...91 J10
Pilley Hants ...13 P5
Pilley Bailey Hants ...13 P5
Pillgwenlly Newpt ...31 K7
Pillhead Devon ...16 H6
Pilling Lancs ...95 J11
Pilling Lane Lancs ...94 H11
Pilning S Glos ...31 Q7
Pilot Inn Kent ...27 J8
Pilsbury Derbys ...71 L2
Pilsdon Dorset ...11 J5
Pilsgate C Pete ...73 R9
Pilsley Derbys ...84 B6
Pilsley Derbys ...84 F8
Pilson Green Norfk ...77 M9
Piltdown E Susx ...25 K5
Pilton Devon ...17 K5
Pilton Nhants ...61 M4
Pilton Rutlnd ...73 N10
Pilton Somset ...19 Q6
Pilton Green Swans ...28 D7
Pimbo Lancs ...81 P4
Pimlico Herts ...50 C9
Pimlico Lancs ...89 L2
Pimlico Nhants ...48 H6
Pimperne Dorset ...12 F3
Pinchbeck Lincs ...74 D5
Pinchbeck Bars Lincs ...74 C5
Pincheon Green Donc ...91 R7
Pinchinthorpe R & Cl ...104 G8
Pincock Lancs ...88 G7
Pinfold Lancs ...88 D8
Pinford End Suffk ...64 A10
Pinged Carmth ...28 D4
Pingewood W Berk ...35 J11
Pin Green Herts ...50 G5
Pinhoe Devon ...9 N6
Pinkett's Booth Covtry ...59 L8
Pinkney Wilts ...32 G7
Pinkneys Green W & M ...35 N8
Pinley Covtry ...59 N9
Pinley Green Warwks ...59 K11
Pin Mill Suffk ...53 M4
Pinminnoch S Ayrs ...114 C9
Pinmore S Ayrs ...114 D9
Pinn Devon ...10 C7
Pinner Gt Lon ...36 D3
Pinner Green Gt Lon ...36 D2
Pinsley Green Ches E ...69 Q5
Pinvin Worcs ...47 J5
Pinwherry S Ayrs ...114 C10
Pinxton Derbys ...84 G10
Pipe and Lyde Herefs ...45 Q6
Pipe Aston Herefs ...56 H10
Pipe Gate Shrops ...70 C6
Pipehill Staffs ...58 G3
Piperdam Angus ...142 D11
Piperhill Highld ...156 F7
Pipers Pool Cnwll ...5 M5
Pipewell Nhants ...60 H3
Pippacott Devon ...17 J4
Pippin Street Lancs ...88 H6
Pipton Powys ...44 H7
Pirbright Surrey ...23 P3
Pirbright Camp Surrey ...23 P3
Pirnie Border ...118 C5
Pirnmill N Ayrs ...120 G3
Pirton Herts ...50 D4
Pirton Worcs ...46 G5
Pisgah Cerdgn ...54 F7
Pishill Oxon ...35 K7
Pistyll Gwynd ...66 E6
Pitblae Abers ...159 N5
Pitcairngreen P & K ...134 D2
Pitcalnie Highld ...156 E3
Pitcaple Abers ...151 J2
Pitcarity Angus ...142 E4
Pitchcombe Gloucs ...32 G3
Pitchcott Bucks ...49 L10
Pitcher Row Lincs ...74 E4
Pitchford Shrops ...57 J4
Pitch Green Bucks ...35 L4
Pitch Place Surrey ...23 N7
Pitch Place Surrey ...23 P4
Pitchroy Moray ...157 M10
Pitcombe Somset ...20 C8
Pitcot V Glam ...29 N10
Pitcox E Loth ...128 G5
Pitfichie Abers ...150 H4
Pitglassie Abers ...158 G9
Pitgrudy Highld ...162 H8
Pitlessie Fife ...135 J6
Pitlochry P & K ...141 M6
Pitmachie Abers ...150 H1
Pitmain Highld ...148 C7
Pitmedden Abers ...151 M2
Pitmedden Garden Abers ...151 M2
Pitminster Somset ...18 H11
Pitmuies Angus ...143 K8
Pitmunie Abers ...150 H5
Pitney Somset ...19 N9
Pitroddie P & K ...134 G2
Pitscottie Fife ...135 L5
Pitsea Essex ...38 B4
Pitses Oldham ...83 K4
Pitsford Nhants ...60 G7
Pitstone Bucks ...49 P11
Pitt Devon ...11 D11
Pitt Hants ...22 E9
Pittarrow Abers ...143 N3
Pitt Court Gloucs ...32 D5
Pittentrail Highld ...162 G6
Pittenweem Fife ...135 M7
Pittodrie House Hotel Abers ...150 H3
Pitton Wilts ...21 P8
Pitt's Wood Kent ...37 P11
Pittulie Abers ...159 N4
Pityme Cnwll ...4 F6
Pity Me Dur ...113 L11
Pivington Kent ...26 F2
Pixey Green Suffk ...65 J6
Pixham Surrey ...36 E10
Plains N Lans ...126 D4
Plain Street Cnwll ...4 F6
Plaish Shrops ...57 J5
Plaistow Gt Lon ...37 K4
Plaistow W Susx ...23 Q9
Plaitford Hants ...21 Q11
Plank Lane Wigan ...82 D5
Plas Cymyran IoA ...78 D9
Plastow Green Hants ...22 F2
Platt Bridge Wigan ...82 D4
Platt Lane Shrops ...69 P7

Platts Heath Kent ...38 E11
Plawsworth Dur ...113 L11
Plaxtol Kent ...37 P10
Playden E Susx ...26 F7
Playford Suffk ...53 M2
Play Hatch Oxon ...35 K9
Playing Place Cnwll ...3 L5
Playley Green Gloucs ...46 E8
Plealey Shrops ...56 G3
Plean Stirlg ...133 N10
Pleasance Fife ...134 G5
Pleasington Bl w D ...89 J5
Pleasley Derbys ...84 H8
Pleasleyhill Notts ...84 H8
Pleasurewood Hills Suffk ...65 Q2
Pleck Dorset ...11 Q2
Pledgdon Green Essex ...51 N5
Pledwick Wakefd ...91 J7
Pleinheaume Guern ...10 b1
Plemont Jersey ...11 a1
Plemstall Ches W ...81 P10
Plenmeller Nthumb ...111 P8
Pleshey Essex ...51 Q8
Plockton Highld ...153 Q11
Plowden Shrops ...56 F7
Plox Green Shrops ...56 F4
Pluckley Kent ...26 F3
Pluckley Station Kent ...26 F3
Pluckley Thorne Kent ...26 F3
Plucks Gutter Kent ...39 N9
Plumbland Cumb ...100 G3
Plumgarths Cumb ...95 K2
Plumley Ches E ...82 F10
Plump Hill Gloucs ...46 C11
Plumpton Cumb ...101 N3
Plumpton E Susx ...25 J8
Plumpton Nhants ...48 G5
Plumpton End Nhants ...49 K6
Plumpton Green E Susx ...25 J7
Plumpton Head Cumb ...101 P3
Plumstead Gt Lon ...37 K5
Plumstead Norfk ...76 G5
Plumstead Green Norfk ...76 G4
Plumtree Notts ...72 G4
Plumtree Green Kent ...26 D2
Plungar Leics ...73 K4
Plurenden Kent ...26 F4
Plush Dorset ...11 Q4
Plusha Cnwll ...5 M5
Plushabridge Cnwll ...5 N7
Plwmp Cerdgn ...42 G4
Plymouth C Plym ...6 D6
Plympton C Plym ...6 E7
Plymstock C Plym ...6 E8
Plymtree Devon ...9 Q4
Pockley N York ...98 C3
Pocklington E R Yk ...98 G11
Pode Hole Lincs ...74 D6
Podimore Somset ...19 P10
Podington Bed ...61 K8
Podmore Staffs ...70 D7
Point Clear Essex ...53 K9
Pointon Lincs ...74 B4
Pokesdown BCP ...13 K6
Polbain Highld ...160 F4
Polbathic Cnwll ...5 N10
Polbeth W Loth ...127 J5
Polbrock Cnwll ...4 G8
Poldark Mine Cnwll ...2 H7
Polebrook Nhants ...61 N3
Pole Elm Worcs ...46 F4
Polegate E Susx ...25 N10
Pole Moor Kirk ...90 D7
Polesden Lacey Surrey ...36 D10
Polesworth Warwks ...59 L4
Polgigga Cnwll ...2 B9
Polglass Highld ...160 G5
Polgooth Cnwll ...3 P3
Polgown D & G ...115 P7
Poling W Susx ...24 B10
Poling Corner W Susx ...24 B9
Polkerris Cnwll ...4 H11
Pollard Street Norfk ...77 L5
Pollington E R Yk ...91 Q7
Polloch Highld ...138 C4
Pollok C Glas ...125 N5
Pollokshaws C Glas ...125 P5
Pollokshields C Glas ...125 P5
Polmassick Cnwll ...3 P4
Polmear Cnwll ...4 H11
Polmont Falk ...126 G2
Polnish Highld ...145 N11
Polperro Cnwll ...5 L11
Polruan Cnwll ...5 J11
Polsham Somset ...19 P6
Polstead Suffk ...52 G4
Polstead Heath Suffk ...52 G3
Poltalloch Ag & B ...130 G8
Poltescoe Cnwll ...3 J10
Poltimore Devon ...9 N5
Polton Mdloth ...127 P5
Polwarth Border ...129 J9
Polyphant Cnwll ...5 M5
Polzeath Cnwll ...4 E6
Pomathorn Mdloth ...127 N6
Pomeroy Derbys ...83 P11
Ponde Powys ...44 G7
Pondersbridge Cambs ...62 C2
Ponders End Gt Lon ...51 J11
Ponsanooth Cnwll ...3 K6
Ponsonby Cumb ...100 D9
Ponsongath Cnwll ...3 K10
Ponsworthy Devon ...7 J4
Pont Abraham Services Carmth ...28 G3
Pontac Jersey ...11 c2
Pontamman Carmth ...28 H2
Pontantwn Carmth ...28 D2
Pontardawe Neath ...29 K4
Pontarddulais Swans ...28 G4
Pont-ar-gothi Carmth ...43 K10
Pont-ar-Hydfer Powys ...44 B9
Pont-ar-Ilechau Carmth ...43 P10
Pontarsais Carmth ...42 H9
Pontblyddyn Flints ...69 J2
Pont Cyfyng Conwy ...67 N3
Pontcysyllte Aqueduct Wrexhm ...69 J6
Pont Dolgarrog Conwy ...79 P11
Pontdolgoch Powys ...55 N6
Pont-Ebbw Newpt ...31 J7
Pontefract Wakefd ...91 M6
Ponteland Nthumb ...113 J6
Ponterwyd Cerdgn ...54 G8
Pontesbury Shrops ...56 F3

Pontesbury Hill Shrops ...56 F3
Pontesford Shrops ...56 G3
Pontfadog Wrexhm ...68 H7
Pontfaen Pembks ...41 K4
Pont-faen Powys ...44 D8
Pontgarreg Cerdgn ...42 F4
Pontgarreg Pembks ...41 M2
Pont Henri Carmth ...28 E3
Ponthir Torfn ...31 K6
Ponthirwaun Cerdgn ...42 E5
Pontllanfraith Caerph ...30 G5
Pontlliw Swans ...28 H4
Pontllyfni Gwynd ...66 G4
Pontlottyn Caerph ...30 F3
Pont Morlais Carmth ...28 F3
Pontnêddfechan Neath ...29 P3
Pontnewydd Torfn ...31 J5
Pontnewynydd Torfn ...31 J4
Pont Pen-y-benglog Gwynd ...67 M2
Pontrhydfendigaid Cerdgn ...54 G11
Pont Rhyd-sarn Gwynd ...67 R9
Pont Rhyd-y-cyff Brdgnd ...29 N7
Ponthydyfen Neath ...29 L6
Pont-rhyd-y-groes Cerdgn ...54 G10
Pontrhydyrun Torfn ...31 J5
Pontrilas Herefs ...45 M9
Pont Robert Powys ...55 Q2
Pont-rug Gwynd ...67 J2
Ponts Green E Susx ...25 Q7
Pontshill Herefs ...46 B10
Pontsian Cerdgn ...42 H5
Pontsticill Myr Td ...30 E2
Pont Walby Neath ...29 N3
Pontwelly Carmth ...42 H6
Pontyates Carmth ...28 E3
Pontyberem Carmth ...28 F2
Pont-y-blew Wrexhm ...69 K7
Pontybodkin Flints ...69 J3
Pontyclun Rhondd ...30 D8
Pontycymer Brdgnd ...29 P6
Pontyglasier Pembks ...41 M3
Pontygwaith Rhondd ...30 D6
Pontygynon Pembks ...41 M3
Pontymister Caerph ...30 H6
Pont-y-pant Conwy ...67 P4
Pontypool Torfn ...31 J4
Pontypridd Rhondd ...30 E7
Pont-yr-hafod Pembks ...40 H5
Pont-yr-Rhyl Brdgnd ...29 P7
Pontywaun Caerph ...30 H6
Pool Cnwll ...2 H5
Poole BCP ...12 H6
Poole Keynes Gloucs ...33 J5
Poolewe Highld ...160 D10
Pooley Bridge Cumb ...101 N6
Pooley Street Norfk ...64 F5
Poolfold Staffs ...70 F3
Pool Head Herefs ...45 R4
Poolhill Gloucs ...46 D9
Pool in Wharfedale Leeds ...97 K11
Pool of Muckhart Clacks ...134 C7
Pool Quay Powys ...56 D2
Pool Street Essex ...52 C4
Pootings Kent ...37 L11
Popes Hill Gloucs ...32 C2
Popham Hants ...22 G6
Poplar Gt Lon ...37 J4
Poplar Street Suffk ...65 N8
Porchfield IoW ...14 D8
Porin Highld ...155 M7
Poringland Norfk ...77 K11
Porkellis Cnwll ...2 H7
Porlock Somset ...18 A5
Porlock Weir Somset ...17 R2
Portachoillan Ag & B ...123 N4
Port-an-Eorna Highld ...153 P11
Port Appin Ag & B ...138 G8
Port Askaig Ag & B ...122 F6
Portavadie Ag & B ...124 A4
Port Bannatyne Ag & B ...124 D4
Portbury N Som ...31 P9
Port Carlisle Cumb ...110 D4
Port Charlotte Ag & B ...122 C8
Portchester Hants ...14 H5
Port Clarence S on T ...104 E6
Port Driseach Ag & B ...124 B3
Port Ellen Ag & B ...122 E10
Port Elphinstone Abers ...151 K3
Portencalzie D & G ...106 D3
Portencross N Ayrs ...124 F8
Port Erin IoM ...80 a8
Portesham Dorset ...11 N7
Portessie Moray ...158 B4
Port e Vullen IoM ...80 g3
Port Eynon Swans ...28 E7
Portfield Gate Pembks ...40 H7
Portgate Devon ...5 Q4
Port Gaverne Cnwll ...4 G5
Port Glasgow Inver ...125 J3
Portgordon Moray ...158 A5
Portgower Highld ...163 N4
Porth Cnwll ...4 C9
Porth Rhondd ...30 D6
Porthallow Cnwll ...3 K9
Porthallow Cnwll ...5 L11
Porthcawl Brdgnd ...29 M9
Porthcothan Cnwll ...4 D7
Porthcurno Cnwll ...2 B9
Port Henderson Highld ...153 P3
Porthgain Pembks ...40 F4
Porthgwarra Cnwll ...2 B9
Porthill Staffs ...70 E5
Porthkea Cnwll ...3 L5
Porthkerry V Glam ...30 E11
Porthleven Cnwll ...2 G8
Porthllechog Gwynd ...67 K7
Porthmadog Gwynd ...67 K7
Porthmeor Cnwll ...2 C6
Porth Navas Cnwll ...3 K8
Portholland Cnwll ...3 P5
Porthoustock Cnwll ...3 L9
Porthpean Cnwll ...3 Q3
Porthtowan Cnwll ...2 H4
Porthwgan Wrexhm ...69 L5
Porthyrhyd Carmth ...43 K11
Porth-y-Waen Shrops ...69 J10
Portincaple Ag & B ...131 Q9
Portinfer Jersey ...11 a1
Portington E R Yk ...92 C4
Portinnisherrich Ag & B ...131 K5
Portinscale Cumb ...101 J6
Port Isaac Cnwll ...4 F5
Portishead N Som ...31 N9
Portknockie Moray ...158 C4
Portland Dorset ...11 P10
Portlethen Abers ...151 N8

Portling D & G ... 109 J10
Portloe Cnwll ... 3 N6
Port Logan D & G ... 106 E9
Portlooe Cnwll ... 5 L11
Portmahomack Highld ... 163 L10
Port Mary D & G ... 108 F11
Portmeirion Gwynd ... 67 K7
Portmellon Cnwll ... 3 Q5
Port Mòr Highld ... 144 F12
Portmore Hants ... 13 P5
Port Mulgrave N York ... 105 L7
Portnaguran W Isls ... 168 k4
Portnahaven Ag & B ... 122 A9
Portnalong Highld ... 152 E11
Portnancon Highld ... 165 K4
Port nan Giùran W Isls ... 168 k4
Port nan Long W Isls ... 168 d10
Port Nis W Isls ... 168 k1
Portobello C Edin ... 127 Q3
Portobello Gatesd ... 113 L9
Portobello Wolves ... 58 L5
Port of Menteith Stirlg ... 132 H7
Port o Ness W Isls ... 168 k1
Porton Wilts ... 21 N7
Portontown Devon ... 5 Q6
Portpatrick D & G ... 106 C7
Port Quin Cnwll ... 4 F5
Port Ramsay Ag & B ... 138 F8
Portreath Cnwll ... 2 H4
Portreath Harbour Cnwll ... 2 H4
Portree Highld ... 152 H9
Port Righ Ag & B ... 120 F4
Port St Mary IoM ... 80 b8
Portscatho Cnwll ... 3 M6
Portsea C Port ... 14 H6
Portskerra Highld ... 166 E3
Portskewett Mons ... 31 N7
Portslade Br & H ... 24 L6
Portslade-by-Sea Br & H ... 24 L6
Portslogan D & G ... 106 C6
Portsmouth C Port ... 14 H7
Portsmouth Calder ... 89 Q5
Portsmouth Arms Devon ... 17 L8
Portsmouth Historic
　Dockyard C Port ... 14 H6
Port Soderick IoM ... 80 d7
Port Solent C Port ... 14 H5
Portsonachan Hotel Ag & B ... 131 L3
Port Sunlight Wirral ... 81 L8
Portswood C Sotn ... 14 D4
Port Talbot Neath ... 29 L7
Port Tennant Swans ... 29 J6
Portuairk Highld ... 137 L2
Portway Herefs ... 45 P6
Portway Herefs ... 45 P7
Portway Sandw ... 58 E7
Portway Worcs ... 58 G10
Port Wemyss Ag & B ... 122 A9
Port William D & G ... 107 K9
Portwrinkle Cnwll ... 5 P11
Portyerrock D & G ... 107 N10
Posbury Devon ... 9 K5
Posenhall Shrops ... 57 M4
Poslingford Suffk ... 52 N11
Posso Border ... 117 J4
Postbridge Devon ... 8 G9
Postcombe Oxon ... 35 K4
Post Green Dorset ... 12 G6
Postling Kent ... 27 K4
Postwick Norfk ... 77 K10
Potarch Abers ... 150 H7
Potsgrove C Beds ... 49 Q8
Potten End Herts ... 50 B9
Potten Street Kent ... 39 N8
Potter Brompton N York ... 99 K5
Pottergate Street Norfk ... 64 H3
Potterhanworth Lincs ... 86 E7
Potterhanworth Booths
　Lincs ... 86 E7
Potter Heigham Norfk ... 77 N8
Potterne Wilts ... 21 J3
Potterne Wick Wilts ... 21 J3
Potter Row Bucks ... 35 P4
Potters Bar Herts ... 50 F10
Potters Brook Lancs ... 95 K10
Potters Corner Kent ... 26 G3
Potter's Cross Staffs ... 58 B8
Potters Crouch Herts ... 50 D9
Potter's Forstal Kent ... 26 E2
Potters Green Covtry ... 59 N8
Potter's Green E Susx ... 25 M6
Potter's Green Herts ... 51 J6
Pottersheath Herts ... 50 F7
Potters Marston Leics ... 72 D11
Potter Somersal Derbys ... 71 L7
Potterspury Nhants ... 49 L6
Potter Street Essex ... 51 L9
Potterton Abers ... 151 N4
Potterton Leeds ... 91 L3
Potthorpe Norfk ... 76 C7
Pottle Street Wilts ... 20 F6
Potto N York ... 104 E10
Potton C Beds ... 62 B11
Pott Row Norfk ... 75 P6
Pott's Green Essex ... 52 F7
Pott Shrigley Ches E ... 83 K9
Poughill Cnwll ... 16 C10
Poughill Devon ... 9 L3
Poulner Hants ... 13 L3
Poulshot Wilts ... 21 J3
Poulton Gloucs ... 33 L4
Poulton Wirral ... 81 L6
Poulton-le-Fylde Lancs ... 88 C3
Poulton Priory Gloucs ... 33 L5
Pound Bank Worcs ... 57 N10
Poundbury Dorset ... 11 P6
Poundffald Swans ... 28 G6
Poundgate E Susx ... 25 L5
Pound Green E Susx ... 25 M6
Pound Green Suffk ... 63 M10
Pound Green Worcs ... 57 P9
Pound Hill W Susx ... 24 G3
Poundon Bucks ... 48 H9
Poundsbridge Kent ... 25 M2
Poundsgate Devon ... 7 J4
Poundstock Cnwll ... 5 L2
Pound Street Hants ... 22 E2
Pounsley E Susx ... 25 L6
Pouton D & G ... 107 N8
Pouy Street Suffk ... 65 M7
Povey Cross Surrey ... 24 G2
Powburn Nthumb ... 119 L6
Powderham Devon ... 9 N8
Powerstock Dorset ... 11 L5

Powfoot D & G ... 109 P7
Pow Green Herefs ... 46 D6
Powhill Cumb ... 110 E9
Powick Worcs ... 46 F4
Powmill P & K ... 134 C8
Poxwell Dorset ... 12 B8
Poyle Slough ... 36 B5
Poynings W Susx ... 24 G8
Poyntington Dorset ... 20 C10
Poynton Ches E ... 83 K8
Poynton Wrekin ... 69 Q11
Poynton Green Wrekin ... 69 Q11
Poystreet Green Suffk ... 64 D10
Praa Sands Cnwll ... 2 F8
Pratt's Bottom Gt Lon ... 37 L8
Praze-an-Beeble Cnwll ... 2 G6
Predannack Wollas Cnwll ... 2 H10
Prees Shrops ... 69 Q8
Preesall Lancs ... 94 H11
Prees Green Shrops ... 69 Q8
Preesgweene Shrops ... 69 J7
Prees Heath Shrops ... 69 Q7
Prees Higher Heath Shrops ... 69 Q7
Prees Lower Heath Shrops ... 69 Q8
Prendwick Nthumb ... 119 K6
Pren-gwyn Cerdgn ... 42 H6
Prenteg Gwynd ... 67 K6
Prenton Wirral ... 81 L7
Prescot Knows ... 81 P6
Prescott Devon ... 10 B2
Prescott Shrops ... 57 M8
Prescott Shrops ... 69 M10
Presnerb Angus ... 142 B4
Pressen Nthumb ... 118 F3
Prestatyn Denbgs ... 80 F8
Prestbury Ches E ... 83 J9
Prestbury Gloucs ... 47 J2
Presteigne Powys ... 45 L2
Prestleigh Somset ... 20 B6
Prestolee Bolton ... 89 M9
Preston Border ... 129 K8
Preston Br & H ... 24 H9
Preston Devon ... 7 M4
Preston Dorset ... 11 Q8
Preston E R Yk ... 93 L4
Preston Gloucs ... 33 M4
Preston Herts ... 50 E6
Preston Kent ... 38 H9
Preston Kent ... 39 M9
Preston Lancs ... 88 G5
Preston Nthumb ... 119 N5
Preston Rutlnd ... 73 M10
Preston Shrops ... 57 J2
Preston Somset ... 18 E7
Preston Torbay ... 7 M6
Preston Wilts ... 33 K9
Preston Wilts ... 33 Q10
Preston Bagot Warwks ... 59 J11
Preston Bissett Bucks ... 49 J9
Preston Bowyer Somset ... 18 F9
Preston Brockhurst Shrops ... 69 P10
Preston Brook Halton ... 82 C8
Preston Candover Hants ... 22 H6
Preston Capes Nhants ... 48 G4
Preston Crowmarsh Oxon ... 34 H6
Preston Deanery Nhants ... 60 G9
Preston Green Warwks ... 59 J11
Preston Gubbals Shrops ... 69 N11
Preston Montford Shrops ... 56 G2
Preston on Stour Warwks ... 47 P5
Preston on Tees S on T ... 104 D7
Preston on the Hill Halton ... 82 C8
Preston on Wye Herefs ... 45 M6
Prestonpans E Loth ... 128 B5
Preston Patrick Cumb ... 95 L4
Preston Plucknett Somset ... 19 P11
Preston St Mary Suffk ... 64 C11
Preston Street Kent ... 39 N9
Preston-under-Scar N York ... 96 H2
Preston upon the Weald
　Moors Wrekin ... 70 B11
Preston Wynne Herefs ... 45 R5
Prestwich Bury ... 82 H4
Prestwick Nthumb ... 113 J6
Prestwick S Ayrs ... 114 G2
Prestwick Airport S Ayrs ... 114 G2
Prestwold Leics ... 72 F7
Prestwood Bucks ... 35 N4
Prestwood Staffs ... 58 C7
Price Town Brdgnd ... 29 P6
Prickwillow Cambs ... 63 J4
Priddy Somset ... 19 P4
Priestacott Devon ... 8 B3
Priestcliffe Derbys ... 83 P10
Priestcliffe Ditch Derbys ... 83 P10
Priest Hutton Lancs ... 95 L6
Priestland E Ayrs ... 125 P10
Priestley Green Calder ... 90 E5
Priest Weston Shrops ... 56 D5
Priestwood Green Kent ... 37 Q8
Primethorpe Leics ... 60 B2
Primrose Green Norfk ... 76 F8
Primrosehill Border ... 129 K8
Primrose Hill Cambs ... 62 E3
Primrose Hill Derbys ... 84 F9
Primrose Hill Dudley ... 58 D7
Primrose Hill Lancs ... 88 D9
Primsidemill Border ... 118 F5
Prince of Wales Bridge
　Mons ... 31 P7
Princes Gate Pembks ... 41 M8
Princes Risborough Bucks ... 35 M4
Princethorpe Warwks ... 59 P10
Princetown Devon ... 6 F4
Prinsted W Susx ... 15 L5
Prion Denbgs ... 68 E2
Prior Rigg Cumb ... 111 J7
Priors Halton Shrops ... 56 H9
Priors Hardwick Warwks ... 48 E3
Priorslee Wrekin ... 57 N2
Priors Marston Warwks ... 48 E3
Priors Norton Gloucs ... 46 G10
Priors Park Gloucs ... 46 G8
Priory Wood Herefs ... 45 K5
Prisk V Glam ... 30 D9
Priston BaNES ... 20 C2
Pristow Green Norfk ... 64 G4
Prittlewell Sthend ... 38 E4
Privett Hants ... 23 J9
Prixford Devon ... 17 K4
Probus Cnwll ... 3 M4
Prora E Loth ... 128 C4
Prospect Cumb ... 100 F2
Prospidnick Cnwll ... 2 G7
Protstonhill Abers ... 159 K5
Prudhoe Nthumb ... 112 G8

Prussia Cove Cnwll ... 2 F8
Pubil P & K ... 140 C9
Publow BaNES ... 20 B2
Puckeridge Herts ... 51 J6
Puckington Somset ... 19 L11
Pucklechurch S Glos ... 32 C9
Puckrup Gloucs ... 46 G7
Puddinglake Ches W ... 82 F11
Puddington Ches W ... 81 L10
Puddington Devon ... 9 K2
Puddledock Norfk ... 64 F3
Puddletown Dorset ... 12 C6
Pudleston Herefs ... 45 R3
Pudsey Leeds ... 90 G4
Pulborough W Susx ... 24 B7
Puleston Wrekin ... 70 C10
Pulford Ches W ... 69 L3
Pulham Dorset ... 11 Q3
Pulham Market Norfk ... 64 H4
Pulham St Mary Norfk ... 65 J4
Pullens Green S Glos ... 32 B6
Pulloxhill C Beds ... 50 C4
Pulverbatch Shrops ... 56 G4
Pumpherston W Loth ... 127 K4
Pumsaint Carmth ... 43 N6
Puncheston Pembks ... 41 K5
Puncknowle Dorset ... 11 L6
Punnett's Town E Susx ... 25 P6
Purbrook Hants ... 15 J5
Purfleet-on-Thames Thurr ... 37 N5
Puriton Somset ... 19 L7
Purleigh Essex ... 52 D11
Purley Gt Lon ... 36 H8
Purley on Thames W Berk ... 35 J9
Purlogue Shrops ... 56 D9
Purlpit Wilts ... 32 G11
Purls Bridge Cambs ... 62 G3
Purse Caundle Dorset ... 20 C11
Purshull Green Worcs ... 58 C10
Purslow Shrops ... 56 F8
Purston Jaglin Wakefd ... 91 L7
Purtington Somset ... 10 H3
Purton Gloucs ... 32 C3
Purton Gloucs ... 32 C4
Purton Wilts ... 33 L7
Purton Stoke Wilts ... 33 L6
Pury End Nhants ... 49 K5
Pusey Oxon ... 34 C5
Putley Herefs ... 46 B7
Putley Green Herefs ... 46 B7
Putloe Gloucs ... 32 E3
Putney Gt Lon ... 36 F6
Putsborough Devon ... 16 G3
Puttenham Herts ... 35 N2
Puttenham Surrey ... 23 P5
Puttock End Essex ... 52 D3
Putton Dorset ... 11 N8
Putts Corner Devon ... 10 C3
Puxley Nhants ... 49 L6
Puxton N Som ... 19 M2
Pwll Carmth ... 28 E4
Pwllcrochan Pembks ... 40 H10
Pwll-du Mons ... 30 H2
Pwll-glâs Denbgs ... 68 F4
Pwllgloyw Powys ... 44 E8
Pwllheli Gwynd ... 66 F7
Pwll-trap Carmth ... 41 Q7
Pwll-y-glaw Neath ... 29 L6
Pydew Conwy ... 79 Q9
Pye Bridge Derbys ... 84 F10
Pyecombe W Susx ... 24 H8
Pye Corner Newpt ... 31 K7
Pye Green Staffs ... 58 E2
Pyle Brdgnd ... 29 M8
Pyleigh Somset ... 18 F8
Pylle Somset ... 20 B7
Pymoor Cambs ... 62 G3
Pymore Dorset ... 11 K6
Pyrford Surrey ... 36 B9
Pyrton Oxon ... 35 J5
Pytchley Nhants ... 61 J6
Pyworthy Devon ... 16 E11

Quabbs Shrops ... 56 C8
Quadring Lincs ... 74 D4
Quadring Eaudike Lincs ... 74 D4
Quainton Bucks ... 49 K10
Quaker's Yard Myr Td ... 30 E5
Quaking Houses Dur ... 113 J10
Quantock Hills Somset ... 18 G7
Quarff Shet ... 169 r10
Quarley Hants ... 21 Q6
Quarndon Derbys ... 72 A2
Quarr Hill IoW ... 14 G8
Quarrier's Village Inver ... 125 K4
Quarrington Lincs ... 73 R2
Quarrington Hill Dur ... 104 B3
Quarrybank Ches W ... 82 C11
Quarry Bank Dudley ... 58 D7
Quarrywood Moray ... 157 M5
Quarter N Ayrs ... 124 F5
Quarter S Lans ... 126 C7
Quatford Shrops ... 57 N6
Quatt Shrops ... 57 P7
Quebec Dur ... 103 N2
Quedgeley Gloucs ... 32 F2
Queen Adelaide Cambs ... 63 J4
Queenborough Kent ... 38 F7
Queen Camel Somset ... 19 Q10
Queen Charlton BaNES ... 32 B11
Queen Dart Devon ... 17 Q8
Queen Elizabeth Forest
　Park Stirlg ... 132 G7
Queen Elizabeth II Bridge
　Thurr ... 37 N5
Queenhill Worcs ... 46 G7
Queen Oak Dorset ... 20 E8
Queen's Bower IoW ... 14 G10
Queensbury C Brad ... 90 E4
Queensferry Flints ... 81 L11
Queen's Head Shrops ... 69 K9
Queen's Hills Norfk ... 76 H9
Queenslie C Glas ... 126 B4
Queen's Park Bed ... 61 M11
Queen's Park Essex ... 51 Q3
Queen's Park Nhants ... 60 G8
Queen Street Kent ... 37 Q11
Queen Street Wilts ... 33 K7
Queenzieburn N Lans ... 126 B2
Quendon Essex ... 51 M4

Queniborough Leics ... 72 G8
Quenington Gloucs ... 33 M4
Quernmore Lancs ... 95 L9
Queslett Birm ... 58 G6
Quethiock Cnwll ... 5 N9
Quick's Green W Berk ... 34 G9
Quidenham Norfk ... 64 E4
Quidhampton Hants ... 22 F4
Quidhampton Wilts ... 21 M8
Quina Brook Shrops ... 69 P8
Quinbury End Nhants ... 48 H4
Quinton Dudley ... 58 E8
Quinton Nhants ... 49 L4
Quinton Green Nhants ... 49 L4
Quintrell Downs Cnwll ... 4 C9
Quixhall Staffs ... 71 L6
Quixwood Border ... 129 K7
Quoditch Devon ... 5 Q2
Quoig P & K ... 133 N3
Quoisley Ches E ... 69 P5
Quorn Leics ... 72 F7
Quothquan S Lans ... 116 D3
Quoyburray Ork ... 169 e6
Quoyloo Ork ... 169 b4

R

Raasay Highld ... 153 K9
Rabbit's Cross Kent ... 26 C2
Rableyheath Herts ... 50 F7
Raby Cumb ... 110 C10
Raby Wirral ... 81 L9
Rachan Mill Border ... 116 G4
Rachub Gwynd ... 79 L11
Rackenford Devon ... 17 R8
Rackham W Susx ... 24 B8
Rackheath Norfk ... 77 K9
Racks D & G ... 109 M6
Rackwick Ork ... 169 b7
Radbourne Derbys ... 71 P7
Radcliffe Bury ... 89 M9
Radcliffe Nthumb ... 119 Q10
Radcliffe on Trent Notts ... 72 G3
Radclive Bucks ... 49 J8
Radcot Oxon ... 33 Q5
Raddery Highld ... 156 C6
Raddington Somset ... 18 D9
Radernie Fife ... 135 M6
Radford Covtry ... 59 M8
Radford Semele Warwks ... 48 B2
Radlet Somset ... 18 H7
Radlett Herts ... 50 E10
Radley Devon ... 17 N7
Radley Oxon ... 34 F5
Radley W Berk ... 34 C11
Radley Green Essex ... 51 P9
Radmore Green Ches E ... 69 Q3
Radnage Bucks ... 35 L5
Radstock BaNES ... 20 C4
Radstone Nhants ... 48 G6
Radway Warwks ... 48 C5
Radwell Bed ... 61 M9
Radwell Herts ... 50 F3
Radwinter Essex ... 51 P3
Radwinter End Essex ... 51 P3
Radyr Cardif ... 30 F7
RAF College (Cranwell)
　Lincs ... 86 D11
Rafford Moray ... 157 K6
RAF Museum Cosford
　Shrops ... 57 P3
RAF Museum London Gt Lon ... 36 F2
Ragdale Leics ... 72 H7
Ragdon Shrops ... 56 H6
Raginnis Cnwll ... 2 D8
Raglan Mons ... 31 M3
Ragnall Notts ... 85 P6
Raigbeg Highld ... 148 E2
Rainbow Hill Worcs ... 46 G3
Rainford St Hel ... 81 P4
Rainford Junction St Hel ... 81 P4
Rainham Gt Lon ... 37 M4
Rainham Medway ... 38 D8
Rainhill St Hel ... 81 P6
Rainhill Stoops St Hel ... 81 Q6
Rainow Ches E ... 83 K9
Rainsough Bury ... 82 H4
Rainton N York ... 97 N5
Rainworth Notts ... 85 J9
Raisbeck Cumb ... 102 B9
Raise Cumb ... 111 P11
Raisthorpe N York ... 98 H8
Rait P & K ... 134 G2
Raithby Lincs ... 87 K4
Raithby Lincs ... 87 L7
Raithwaite N York ... 105 N8
Rake Hants ... 23 M9
Rakewood Rochdl ... 89 Q8
Ralia Highld ... 148 C8
Ram Carmth ... 43 L5
Ramasaig Highld ... 152 B9
Rame Cnwll ... 2 H7
Rame Cnwll ... 6 C9
Ram Hill S Glos ... 32 C9
Ram Lane Kent ... 26 G2
Rampisham Dorset ... 11 M4
Rampside Cumb ... 94 E7
Rampton Cambs ... 62 F7
Rampton Notts ... 85 P5
Ramsbottom Bury ... 89 M7
Ramsbury Wilts ... 33 Q10
Ramscraigs Highld ... 167 K11
Ramsdean Hants ... 23 K10
Ramsdell Hants ... 22 G3
Ramsden Oxon ... 48 C11
Ramsden Worcs ... 46 H5
Ramsden Bellhouse Essex ... 38 B3
Ramsden Heath Essex ... 38 B2
Ramsey Cambs ... 62 C3
Ramsey Essex ... 53 M5
Ramsey IoM ... 80 g3
Ramsey Forty Foot Cambs ... 62 D3
Ramsey Heights Cambs ... 62 B4
Ramsey Island Pembks ... 40 D6
Ramsey Mereside Cambs ... 62 C3
Ramsey St Mary's Cambs ... 62 C3
Ramsgate Kent ... 39 Q8
Ramsgill N York ... 96 H6
Ramshaw Dur ... 103 M5
Ramshaw Dur ... 112 E11
Ramsholt Suffk ... 53 P3
Ramshope Nthumb ... 118 D10
Ramshorn Staffs ... 71 K5
Ramsley Devon ... 8 G6
Ramsnest Common Surrey ... 23 P8

Ranby Lincs ... 86 H5
Ranby Notts ... 85 L4
Rand Lincs ... 86 F5
Randwick Gloucs ... 32 F3
Ranfurly Rens ... 125 K4
Rangemore Staffs ... 71 M10
Rangeworthy S Glos ... 32 C7
Rankinston E Ayrs ... 115 J5
Ranksborough Rutlnd ... 73 L8
Rank's Green Essex ... 52 B8
Rannoch Station P & K ... 140 D9
Ranscombe Somset ... 18 B6
Ranskill Notts ... 85 L3
Ranton Staffs ... 70 F10
Ranton Green Staffs ... 70 E10
Ranworth Norfk ... 77 M9
Raploch Stirlg ... 133 M9
Rapness Ork ... 169 e2
Rapps Somset ... 19 K11
Rascarrel D & G ... 108 G11
Rashfield Ag & B ... 131 N11
Rashwood Worcs ... 58 D11
Raskelf N York ... 97 Q6
Rassau Blae G ... 30 G2
Rastrick Calder ... 90 E6
Ratagan Highld ... 145 R4
Ratby Leics ... 72 E9
Ratcliffe Culey Leics ... 72 A11
Ratcliffe on Soar Notts ... 72 D5
Ratcliffe on the Wreake
　Leics ... 72 G8
Rathen Abers ... 159 N5
Rathillet Fife ... 135 K3
Rathmell N York ... 96 B9
Ratho C Edin ... 127 L3
Ratho Station C Edin ... 127 L3
Rathven Moray ... 158 B4
Ratlake Hants ... 22 D10
Ratley Warwks ... 48 C5
Ratling Kent ... 39 M11
Ratlinghope Shrops ... 56 G5
Rattar Highld ... 167 N2
Ratten Row Cumb ... 101 K2
Ratten Row Cumb ... 110 G11
Ratten Row Lancs ... 88 E2
Rattery Devon ... 7 J6
Rattlesden Suffk ... 64 D10
Ratton Village E Susx ... 25 N10
Rattray P & K ... 142 B8
Raughton Cumb ... 110 G11
Raughton Head Cumb ... 110 G11
Raunds Nhants ... 61 L6
Ravenfield Rothm ... 91 M11
Ravenglass Cumb ... 100 E11
Ravenhills Green Worcs ... 46 D4
Raveningham Norfk ... 65 M2
Ravenscar N York ... 105 Q10
Ravenscraig N Lans ... 126 D6
Ravensdale IoM ... 80 e3
Ravensden Bed ... 61 N10
Ravenseat N York ... 102 G10
Ravenshead Notts ... 85 J10
Ravensmoor Ches E ... 69 R4
Ravensthorpe Kirk ... 90 G6
Ravensthorpe Nhants ... 60 E6
Ravenstone Leics ... 72 C8
Ravenstone M Keyn ... 49 M4
Ravenstonedale Cumb ... 102 D10
Ravenstruther S Lans ... 126 G8
Ravensworth N York ... 103 M9
Raw N York ... 105 P9
Rawcliffe C York ... 98 B10
Rawcliffe E R Yk ... 92 A6
Rawcliffe Bridge E R Yk ... 92 A6
Rawdon Leeds ... 90 G3
Rawling Street Kent ... 38 F10
Rawmarsh Rothm ... 91 L11
Rawnsley Staffs ... 58 F2
Rawreth Essex ... 38 C3
Rawridge Devon ... 10 E3
Rawtenstall Lancs ... 89 N6
Raydon Suffk ... 52 H4
Raylees Nthumb ... 112 D2
Rayleigh Essex ... 38 D3
Raymond's Hill Devon ... 10 G5
Rayne Essex ... 52 B7
Raynes Park Gt Lon ... 36 F7
Reach Cambs ... 63 J7
Read Lancs ... 89 M4
Reading Readg ... 35 K10
Reading Services W Berk ... 35 J11
Reading Street Kent ... 26 F5
Reading Street Kent ... 39 Q8
Reagill Cumb ... 102 B7
Rearquhar Highld ... 162 G8
Rearsby Leics ... 72 H8
Rease Heath Ches E ... 70 A4
Reawla Cnwll ... 2 G6
Reay Highld ... 166 G4
Reculver Kent ... 39 M8
Red Ball Devon ... 18 E11
Redberth Pembks ... 41 L10
Redbourn Herts ... 50 D8
Redbourne N Linc ... 92 G11
Redbrook Gloucs ... 31 P3
Redbrook Wrexhm ... 69 P6
Redbrook Street Kent ... 26 F4
Redburn Highld ... 156 G8
Redburn Nthumb ... 111 Q8
Redcar R & Cl ... 104 H6
Redcastle D & G ... 108 G11
Redcastle Highld ... 155 Q8
Red Dial Cumb ... 110 E11
Redding Falk ... 126 G2
Reddingmuirhead Falk ... 126 G2
Reddish Stockp ... 83 J6
Redditch Worcs ... 58 F11
Rede Suffk ... 63 P9
Redenhall Norfk ... 65 K5
Redenham Hants ... 22 B5
Redesmouth Nthumb ... 112 C4
Redford Abers ... 143 P3
Redford Angus ... 143 K9
Redford W Susx ... 23 N9
Redgate Rhondd ... 30 D7
Redgorton P & K ... 134 D2
Redgrave Suffk ... 64 E6
Redhill Abers ... 151 K7
Red Hill BCP ... 13 J5
Redhill Herts ... 50 H4
Redhill N Som ... 19 N2
Redhill Surrey ... 36 G10
Red Hill Warwks ... 47 M3
Redisham Suffk ... 65 N5
Redland Bristl ... 31 Q9

Redland Ork....169 c4
Redlingfield Suffk....64 H7
Redlingfield Green Suffk....64 H7
Red Lodge Suffk....63 M6
Red Lumb Rochdl....89 N7
Redlynch Somset....20 D8
Redlynch Wilts....21 P10
Redmain Cumb....100 F4
Redmarley Worcs....57 P11
Redmarley D'Abitot Gloucs....46 E8
Redmarshall S on T....104 C6
Redmile Leics....73 K3
Redmire N York....96 F2
Redmyre Abers....143 P2
Rednal Birm....58 F9
Rednal Shrops....69 L9
Redpath Border....118 A3
Red Point Highld....153 N4
Red Post Cnwll....16 D10
Red Rice Hants....22 B6
Red Rock Wigan....88 H9
Red Roses Carmth....41 P8
Red Row Nthumb....119 Q11
Redruth Cnwll....2 H5
Redstocks Wilts....20 H2
Redstone P & K....142 B11
Redstone Cross Pembks....41 M7
Red Street Staffs....70 E4
Redvales Bury....89 N9
Red Wharf Bay IoA....79 J8
Redwick Newpt....31 M8
Redwick S Glos....31 P7
Redworth Darltn....103 P6
Reed Herts....51 J3
Reedham Norfk....77 N11
Reedness E R Yk....92 C6
Reeds Beck Lincs....86 H7
Reeds Holme Lancs....89 N6
Reepham Lincs....86 D6
Reepham Norfk....76 G7
Reeth N York....103 K11
Reeves Green Solhll....59 L9
Regaby IoM....80 f2
Regil N Som....19 P2
Reiff Highld....160 F4
Reigate Surrey....36 G10
Reighton N York....99 N5
Reinigeadal W Isls....168 h7
Reisque Abers....151 M4
Reiss Highld....167 P6
Rejerrah Cnwll....4 B10
Releath Cnwll....2 H7
Relubbus Cnwll....2 F7
Relugas Moray....156 H8
Remenham Wokham....35 L8
Remenham Hill Wokham....35 L8
Rempstone Notts....72 F6
Rendcomb Gloucs....33 K3
Rendham Suffk....65 L9
Rendlesham Suffk....65 L11
Renfrew Rens....125 N4
Renhold Bed....61 N10
Renishaw Derbys....84 G5
Rennington Nthumb....119 P7
Renton W Duns....125 K2
Renwick Cumb....101 Q2
Repps Norfk....77 N8
Repton Derbys....71 Q9
Reraig Highld....145 P2
Resaurie Highld....156 C8
Rescassa Cnwll....3 P5
Rescorla Cnwll....3 P4
Resipole Burn Highld....138 C5
Reskadinnick Cnwll....2 G5
Resolis Highld....156 B4
Resolven Neath....29 M4
Rest and be thankful Ag & B....131 Q6
Reston Border....129 M7
Restronguet Cnwll....3 L6
Reswallie Angus....143 J7
Reterth Cnwll....4 E9
Retford Notts....85 M4
Retire Cnwll....4 G9
Rettendon Common Essex....38 C2
Rettendon Village Essex....38 C2
Retyn Cnwll....4 D10
Revesby Lincs....87 J8
Rew Devon....7 J11
Rew Devon....7 K4
Rewe Devon....9 M5
Rew Street IoW....14 E8
Rexon Devon....5 Q4
Reydon Suffk....65 P6
Reymerston Norfk....76 E10
Reynalton Pembks....41 L9
Reynoldston Swans....28 E7
Rezare Cnwll....5 P6
Rhadyr Mons....31 L4
Rhandirmwyn Carmth....43 Q6
Rhayader Powys....55 M11
Rheindown Highld....155 P8
Rhenigidale W Isls....168 h7
Rhes-y-cae Flints....80 H10
Rhewl Denbgs....68 F2
Rhewl Denbgs....68 G6
Rhewl Mostyn Flints....80 H8
Rhicarn Highld....164 C11
Rhiconich Highld....164 G6
Rhicullen Highld....156 B3
Rhigos Rhondd....29 P3
Rhives Highld....163 J6
Rhiwbina Cardif....30 G8
Rhiwbryfdir Gwynd....67 M5
Rhiwderyn Newpt....31 J7
Rhiwen Gwynd....67 K2
Rhiwinder Rhondd....30 D7
Rhiwlas Gwynd....68 B7
Rhiwlas Gwynd....79 K11
Rhiwlas Powys....68 G8
Rhiwsaeson Rhondd....30 E8
Rhode Somset....19 J8
Rhoden Green Kent....37 Q11
Rhodesia Notts....85 J5
Rhodes Minnis Kent....27 L3
Rhodiad-y-brenin Pembks....40 E5
Rhonehouse D & G....108 F9
Rhoose V Glam....30 E11
Rhos Carmth....42 G7
Rhos Denbgs....68 F2
Rhos Neath....29 K4
Rhosaman Carmth....29 K2
Rhosbeirio IoA....78 F6
Rhoscefnhir IoA....79 J9
Rhoscolyn IoA....78 D9
Rhoscrowther Pembks....40 H10
Rhosesmor Flints....81 J11

Rhos-fawr Gwynd....66 F7
Rhosgadfan Gwynd....67 J3
Rhosgoch IoA....78 G2
Rhosgoch Powys....44 H5
Rhos Haminiog Cerdgn....43 K3
Rhoshill Pembks....41 N2
Rhoshirwaun Gwynd....66 C9
Rhoslan Gwynd....66 H6
Rhoslefain Gwynd....54 D3
Rhoslanerchrugog Wrexhm....69 J5
Rhôs Lligwy IoA....78 H7
Rhosmaen Carmth....43 M10
Rhosmeirch IoA....78 H9
Rhosneigr IoA....78 E10
Rhosnesni Wrexhm....69 L4
Rhôs-on-Sea Conwy....79 Q8
Rhosrobin Wrexhm....69 K4
Rhossili Swans....28 D7
Rhostrehwfa IoA....78 G10
Rhostryfan Gwynd....66 H3
Rhostyllen Wrexhm....69 K5
Rhosybol IoA....78 G2
Rhos-y-brithdir Powys....68 F10
Rhosygadfa Shrops....69 K8
Rhos-y-garth Cerdgn....54 E10
Rhos-y-gwaliau Gwynd....68 B8
Rhos-y-llan Gwynd....66 C7
Rhosymedre Wrexhm....69 J6
Rhos-y-meirch Powys....56 D11
RHS Garden Harlow Carr N York....97 L10
RHS Garden Wisley Surrey....36 C9
Rhu Ag & B....132 B11
Rhuallt Denbgs....80 F9
Rhubodach Ag & B....124 C3
Rhuddall Heath Ches W....69 Q2
Rhuddlan Cerdgn....43 J6
Rhuddlan Denbgs....80 E9
Rhue Highld....161 J7
Rhulen Powys....44 G5
Rhunahaorine Ag & B....123 M10
Rhyd Gwynd....67 L6
Rhydargaeau Carmth....42 H9
Rhydcymerau Carmth....43 L7
Rhydd Worcs....46 F5
Rhyd-Ddu Gwynd....67 K4
Rhydding Neath....29 K5
Rhydgaled Conwy....68 C2
Rhydlanfair Conwy....67 Q4
Rhydlewis Cerdgn....42 F5
Rhydlios Gwynd....66 B9
Rhydlydan Conwy....68 A4
Rhydowen Cerdgn....42 H5
Rhydroser Cerdgn....54 D11
Rhydspence Herefs....45 J5
Rhydtalog Flints....68 H4
Rhyd-uchaf Gwynd....68 B7
Rhyd-y-clafdy Gwynd....66 E8
Rhydycroesau Shrops....68 H8
Rhydyfelin Cerdgn....54 D9
Rhydyfelin Rhondd....30 E8
Rhyd-y-foel Conwy....80 C9
Rhydyfro Neath....29 K3
Rhyd-y-groes Gwynd....79 K11
Rhydymain Gwynd....67 Q10
Rhyd-y-meirch Mons....31 K3
Rhydymwyn Flints....81 J11
Rhyd-y-pennau Cerdgn....54 E7
Rhyd-yr-onnen Gwynd....54 E4
Rhyd-y-sarn Gwynd....67 M6
Rhyl Denbgs....80 E8
Rhymney Caerph....30 F3
Rhynd P & K....134 F3
Rhynie Abers....150 D2
Rhynie Highld....163 J11
Ribbesford Worcs....57 P10
Ribbleton Lancs....88 H4
Ribby Lancs....88 E4
Ribchester Lancs....89 K3
Riber Derbys....84 D9
Riby Lincs....93 L9
Riccall N York....91 Q3
Riccarton Border....111 K2
Riccarton E Ayrs....125 L10
Richards Castle Herefs....56 H11
Richings Park Bucks....36 B5
Richmond Gt Lon....36 E6
Richmond N York....103 N10
Richmond Sheff....84 F3
Rich's Holford Somset....18 F8
Rickerscote Staffs....70 G10
Rickford N Som....19 N3
Rickham Devon....7 K11
Rickinghall Suffk....64 E6
Rickling Essex....51 L4
Rickling Green Essex....51 M5
Rickmansworth Herts....36 C2
Riddell Border....117 Q6
Riddings Derbys....84 F10
Riddlecombe Devon....17 L9
Riddlesden C Brad....90 D2
Ridge BaNES....19 Q3
Ridge Dorset....12 F7
Ridge Herts....50 F10
Ridge Wilts....21 J8
Ridgebourne Powys....44 F2
Ridge Green Surrey....36 H11
Ridge Lane Warwks....59 L6
Ridge Row Kent....27 M3
Ridgeway Derbys....84 F4
Ridgeway Worcs....47 K2
Ridgeway Cross Herefs....46 D5
Ridgewell Essex....52 B3
Ridgewood E Susx....25 L7
Ridgmont C Beds....49 Q7
Riding Mill Nthumb....112 F8
Ridley Kent....37 P8
Ridley Nthumb....111 Q8
Ridley Green Ches E....69 Q4
Ridlington Norfk....77 L5
Ridlington Rutlnd....73 L10
Ridlington Street Norfk....77 L5
Ridsdale Nthumb....112 D4
Rievaulx N York....98 B3
Rigg D & G....110 E7
Riggend N Lans....126 D3
Righoul Highld....156 F7
Rigmadon Park Cumb....95 N4
Rigsby Lincs....87 M5
Rigside S Lans....116 B3
Riley Green Lancs....89 J5
Rileyhill Staffs....58 H2
Rilla Mill Cnwll....5 M7
Rillaton Cnwll....5 M7
Rillington N York....98 H5
Rimington Lancs....96 B11

Rimpton Somset....20 B10
Rimswell E R Yk....93 P5
Rinaston Pembks....41 J5
Rindleford Shrops....57 N5
Ringford D & G....108 E9
Ringinglow Sheff....84 C4
Ringland Norfk....76 G9
Ringles Cross E Susx....25 L6
Ringlestone Kent....38 E10
Ringley Bolton....89 M9
Ringmer E Susx....25 K8
Ringmore Devon....6 H9
Ringmore Devon....7 N4
Ringorm Moray....157 P9
Ring's End Cambs....74 G10
Ringsfield Suffk....65 N4
Ringsfield Corner Suffk....65 N4
Ringshall Herts....35 Q2
Ringshall Suffk....64 E11
Ringshall Stocks Suffk....64 F11
Ringstead Nhants....61 L5
Ringstead Norfk....75 P2
Ringwood Hants....13 L3
Ringwould Kent....27 Q2
Rinmore Abers....150 C4
Rinsey Cnwll....2 F8
Rinsey Croft Cnwll....2 G8
Ripe E Susx....25 M8
Ripley Derbys....84 E10
Ripley Hants....13 L5
Ripley N York....97 L8
Ripley Surrey....36 C9
Riplingham E R Yk....92 G4
Riplington Hants....23 J10
Ripon N York....97 M6
Rippingale Lincs....74 A5
Ripple Kent....39 Q1
Ripple Worcs....46 G7
Ripponden Calder....90 C7
Risabus Ag & B....122 D11
Risbury Herefs....45 Q4
Risby N Linc....92 F8
Risby Suffk....63 P7
Risca Caerph....30 H6
Rise E R Yk....93 L2
Riseden E Susx....25 P4
Riseden Kent....26 B4
Risegate Lincs....74 D5
Riseholme Lincs....86 C5
Risehow Cumb....100 D4
Riseley Bed....61 M8
Riseley Wokham....23 K2
Rishangles Suffk....64 H8
Rishton Lancs....89 L4
Rishworth Calder....90 C7
Rising Bridge Lancs....89 M5
Risley Derbys....72 D3
Risley Warrtn....82 E6
Risplith N York....97 K7
Rivar Wilts....22 B2
Rivenhall End Essex....52 D8
River Kent....27 N3
River W Susx....23 P10
River Bank Cambs....62 H7
Riverford Highld....155 P7
Riverhead Kent....37 M9
Rivers Corner Dorset....12 C2
Rivington Lancs....89 J8
Rivington Services Lancs....89 J8
Roachill Devon....17 N7
Roade Nhants....49 L4
Road Green Norfk....65 L2
Roadhead Cumb....111 K6
Roadmeetings S Lans....126 F6
Roadside E Ayrs....115 L4
Roadside Highld....167 L4
Roadwater Somset....18 D7
Roag Highld....152 D9
Roa Island Cumb....94 E7
Roan of Craigoch S Ayrs....114 E7
Roast Green Essex....51 L4
Roath Cardif....30 G9
Roberton Border....117 N8
Roberton S Lans....116 C5
Robertsbridge E Susx....26 B7
Roberttown Kirk....90 F6
Robeston Wathen Pembks....41 L7
Robgill Tower D & G....110 D6
Robin Hill Staffs....70 G3
Robin Hood Lancs....88 G8
Robin Hood Leeds....91 J5
Robinhood End Essex....52 B4
Robin Hood's Bay N York....105 Q9
Roborough Devon....6 E6
Roborough Devon....17 K8
Robroyston C Glas....125 Q4
Roby Knows....81 N6
Roby Mill Lancs....88 G9
Rocester Staffs....71 L7
Roch Pembks....40 G6
Rochdale Rochdl....89 N8
Roche Cnwll....4 F9
Rochester Medway....38 B8
Rochester Nthumb....118 F11
Rochford Essex....38 E3
Rochford Worcs....57 L11
Roch Gate Pembks....40 G6
Rock Cnwll....4 E6
Rock Neath....29 L6
Rock Nthumb....119 P6
Rock W Susx....24 D8
Rock Worcs....57 N10
Rockbeare Devon....9 P6
Rockbourne Hants....21 M11
Rockcliffe Cumb....110 G8
Rockcliffe D & G....108 H10
Rockcliffe Cross Cumb....110 F8
Rock End Staffs....70 F3
Rockend Torbay....7 N6
Rock Ferry Wirral....81 L7
Rockfield Highld....163 L10
Rockfield Mons....31 N2
Rockford Devon....17 P2
Rockford Hants....13 L3
Rockgreen Shrops....57 J9
Rockhampton S Glos....32 C6
Rockhead Cnwll....4 H5
Rockhill Shrops....56 D9
Rock Hill Worcs....58 E11
Rockingham Nhants....61 L2
Rockland All Saints Norfk....64 D2
Rockland St Mary Norfk....77 L11
Rockland St Peter Norfk....64 D2
Rockley Notts....85 M6
Rockley Wilts....33 N10
Rockliffe Lancs....89 P5

Rockville Ag & B....131 Q9
Rockwell End Bucks....35 L7
Rockwell Green Somset....18 F10
Rodborough Gloucs....32 F4
Rodbourne Swindn....33 M7
Rodbourne Wilts....32 H8
Rodd Herefs....45 L2
Roddam Nthumb....119 K6
Rodden Dorset....11 N8
Roddymoor Dur....103 N3
Rode Somset....20 F4
Rode Heath Ches E....70 E3
Rode Heath Ches E....83 J11
Rodel W Isls....168 f9
Roden Wrekin....69 Q11
Rodhuish Somset....18 D7
Rodington Wrekin....57 K2
Rodington Heath Wrekin....57 K2
Rodley Gloucs....32 D2
Rodley Leeds....90 G3
Rodmarton Gloucs....32 H5
Rodmell E Susx....25 K9
Rodmersham Kent....38 F9
Rodmersham Green Kent....38 F9
Rodney Stoke Somset....19 N5
Rodsley Derbys....71 N6
Rodway Somset....19 J6
Roecliffe N York....97 N7
Roe Cross Tamesd....83 L5
Roe Green Herts....50 F9
Roe Green Herts....50 H4
Roe Green Salfd....82 F4
Roehampton Gt Lon....36 F6
Roffey W Susx....24 E4
Rogart Highld....162 G6
Rogate W Susx....23 M10
Roger Ground Cumb....101 L11
Rogerstone Newpt....31 J7
Roghadal W Isls....168 f9
Rogiet Mons....31 N7
Roke Oxon....34 H6
Roker Sundld....113 P9
Rolleston Leics....73 J10
Rolleston Notts....85 M10
Rollestone Wilts....21 L5
Rolleston on Dove Staffs....71 N9
Rolston E R Yk....93 M2
Rolstone N Som....19 L2
Rolvenden Kent....26 D5
Rolvenden Layne Kent....26 E5
Romaldkirk Dur....103 J6
Romanby N York....97 N1
Romanno Bridge Border....127 M8
Romansleigh Devon....17 N7
Romden Castle Kent....26 E3
Romesdal Highld....152 G7
Romford Dorset....13 J3
Romford Gt Lon....37 M3
Romiley Stockp....83 K6
Romney Street Kent....37 N8
Romsey Cambs....62 G9
Romsey Hants....22 C10
Romsley Shrops....57 P8
Romsley Worcs....58 E8
Rona Highld....153 L6
Ronachan Ag & B....123 M9
Rood Ashton Wilts....20 G3
Rookhope Dur....102 H2
Rookley IoW....14 F10
Rookley Green IoW....14 F10
Rooks Bridge Somset....19 L4
Rooks Nest Somset....18 E9
Rookwith N York....97 K3
Roos E R Yk....93 N4
Roose Cumb....94 E7
Roosebeck Cumb....94 E7
Roothams Green Bed....61 N9
Ropley Hants....22 H8
Ropley Dean Hants....22 H8
Ropley Soke Hants....23 J8
Ropsley Lincs....73 P4
Rora Abers....159 Q7
Rorrington Shrops....56 E3
Rosarie Moray....158 A7
Rose Cnwll....3 K3
Roseacre Lancs....88 E3
Rose Ash Devon....17 P7
Rosebank S Lans....126 E8
Rosebush Pembks....41 L5
Rosecare Cnwll....5 K2
Rosecliston Cnwll....4 C10
Rosedale Abbey N York....105 K11
Rose Green Essex....52 F6
Rose Green Suffk....52 F4
Rose Green Suffk....52 G3
Rose Green W Susx....15 P7
Rosehall Highld....162 B6
Rosehearty Abers....159 M4
Rose Hill E Susx....25 L7
Rose Hill Lancs....89 N4
Rosehill Shrops....69 N11
Roseisle Moray....157 L4
Roselands E Susx....25 P10
Rosemarket Pembks....41 J9
Rosemarkie Highld....156 C6
Rosemary Lane Devon....10 D2
Rosemount P & K....142 B9
Rosenannon Cnwll....4 F8
Rosenithon Cnwll....3 L9
Roser's Cross E Susx....25 M6
Rosevean Cnwll....4 G10
Rosevine Cnwll....3 M6
Rosewarne Cnwll....2 G6
Rosewell Mdloth....127 P5
Roseworth S on T....104 D6
Roseworthy Cnwll....2 G6
Rosgill Cumb....101 P7
Roskestal Cnwll....2 B9
Roskhill Highld....152 D9
Roskorwell Cnwll....3 K9
Rosley Cumb....110 F11
Roslin Mdloth....127 P5
Rosliston Derbys....71 N11
Rosneath Ag & B....132 B11
Ross D & G....108 D12
Ross Nthumb....119 M3
Rossett Wrexhm....69 L3
Rossett Green N York....97 L10
Rossington Donc....91 Q11
Ross-on-Wye Herefs....46 A10
Roster Highld....167 N9
Rosthorne Ches E....82 F7
Rosthwaite Cumb....101 J8
Roston Derbys....71 N6
Rosudgeon Cnwll....2 F8

Rosyth Fife....134 E11
Rothbury Nthumb....119 L10
Rotherby Leics....72 H7
Rotherfield E Susx....25 N5
Rotherfield Greys Oxon....35 K8
Rotherfield Peppard Oxon....35 K8
Rotherham Rothm....84 F2
Rothersthorpe Nhants....60 F9
Rotherwick Hants....23 K3
Rothes Moray....157 P8
Rothesay Ag & B....124 D5
Rothiebrisbane Abers....158 H10
Rothiemurchus Lodge Highld....148 H6
Rothienorman Abers....158 H10
Rothley Leics....72 F8
Rothley Nthumb....112 F3
Rothmaise Abers....158 G11
Rothwell Leeds....91 J5
Rothwell Lincs....93 K11
Rothwell Nhants....60 H4
Rotsea E R Yk....99 M10
Rottal Lodge Angus....142 F4
Rottingdean Br & H....25 J10
Rottington Cumb....100 C8
Roucan D & G....109 M5
Roud IoW....14 F10
Rougham Norfk....76 A7
Rougham Suffk....64 C9
Rough Close Staffs....70 G7
Rough Common Kent....39 K10
Roughlee Lancs....89 N2
Roughpark Abers....149 Q5
Roughton Lincs....86 H8
Roughton Norfk....77 J4
Roughton Shrops....57 P6
Roughway Kent....37 P10
Roundbush Essex....52 E11
Round Bush Herts....50 D11
Roundbush Green Essex....51 N8
Round Green Luton....50 D6
Roundham Somset....11 J3
Roundhay Leeds....91 J3
Rounds Green Sandw....58 E7
Round Street Kent....37 Q7
Roundstreet Common W Susx....24 C5
Roundswell Devon....17 J5
Roundway Wilts....21 K2
Roundyhill Angus....142 F7
Rousay Ork....169 c3
Rousdon Devon....10 F6
Rousham Oxon....48 E10
Rous Lench Worcs....47 K4
Routenburn N Ayrs....124 F5
Routh E R Yk....93 J2
Rout's Green Bucks....35 L5
Row Cnwll....4 H6
Row Cumb....95 K3
Row Cumb....102 B4
Rowanburn D & G....110 H5
Rowardennan Stirlg....132 D8
Rowarth Derbys....83 M7
Row Ash Hants....14 F4
Rowberrow Somset....19 N3
Rowborough IoW....14 E10
Rowde Wilts....21 J2
Rowden Devon....8 F5
Rowen Conwy....79 P10
Rowfields Derbys....71 M5
Rowfoot Nthumb....111 N8
Rowford Devon....18 H9
Row Green Essex....52 B7
Rowhedge Essex....52 H7
Rowhook W Susx....24 D4
Rowington Warwks....59 K11
Rowland Derbys....84 B6
Rowland's Castle Hants....15 K4
Rowlands Gill Gatesd....113 J9
Rowledge Surrey....23 M6
Rowley Dur....112 G11
Rowley E R Yk....92 G4
Rowley Shrops....56 E3
Rowley Hill Kirk....90 F8
Rowley Regis Sandw....58 E7
Rowlstone Herefs....45 M9
Rowly Surrey....24 B2
Rowner Hants....14 G6
Rowney Green Worcs....58 F10
Rownhams Hants....22 C11
Rownhams Services Hants....22 C11
Rowrah Cumb....100 E7
Rowsham Bucks....49 M11
Rowsley Derbys....84 C7
Rowstock Oxon....34 E7
Rowston Lincs....86 E9
Rowthorne Derbys....84 G8
Rowton Ches W....69 M2
Rowton Shrops....57 F2
Rowton Shrops....56 G8
Rowton Wrekin....69 R11
Row Town Surrey....36 B8
Roxburgh Border....118 C4
Roxby N Linc....92 F7
Roxby N York....105 L7
Roxton Bed....61 Q10
Roxwell Essex....51 P9
Royal Botanic Garden Edinburgh C Edin....127 N2
Royal Leamington Spa Warwks....59 M11
Royal Oak Darltn....103 P6
Royal Oak Lancs....81 N4
Royal's Green Ches E....69 R6
Royal Sutton Coldfield Birm....58 H5
Royal Tunbridge Wells Kent....25 N3
Royal Wootton Bassett Wilts....33 L8
Royal Yacht Britannia C Edin....127 P2
Roy Bridge Highld....146 H11
Roydhouse Kirk....90 G8
Roydon Essex....51 K8
Roydon Norfk....64 G5
Roydon Norfk....75 P6
Roydon Hamlet Essex....51 K9
Royston Barns....91 K8
Royston Herts....51 J2
Royton Oldham....89 Q9
Rozel Jersey....11 c1
Ruabon Wrexhm....69 K6
Ruaig Ag & B....136 D6
Ruan High Lanes Cnwll....3 M5
Ruan Lanihorne Cnwll....3 M5
Ruan Major Cnwll....3 J10
Ruan Minor Cnwll....3 J10
Ruardean Gloucs....46 B11
Ruardean Hill Gloucs....46 B11

Ruardean Woodside – Saxtead Little Green

291

Ruardean Woodside Gloucs 46 B11
Rubery Birm 58 E9
Rubha Ban W Isls 168 c16
Ruckcroft Cumb 101 P2
Ruckhall Herefs 45 P7
Ruckinge Kent 26 H5
Ruckland Lincs 87 K5
Ruckley Shrops 57 J4
Rudbaxton Pembks 41 J6
Rudby N York 104 E9
Rudchester Nthumb 112 H7
Ruddington Notts 72 F4
Ruddle Gloucs 32 C2
Ruddlemoor Cnwll 3 Q3
Rudford Gloucs 46 E10
Rudge Somset 20 F4
Rudgeway S Glos 32 B7
Rudgwick W Susx 24 C4
Rudhall Herefs 46 B9
Rudheath Ches W 82 E10
Rudheath Woods Ches E 82 F10
Rudley Green Essex 52 D11
Rudloe Wilts 32 F10
Rudry Caerph 30 H7
Rudston E R Yk 99 M7
Rudyard Staffs 70 H3
Ruecastle Border 118 B6
Rufford Lancs 88 F7
Rufford Abbey Notts 85 K8
Rufforth C York 98 A10
Rug Denbgs 68 E6
Rugby Warwks 60 B5
Rugby Services Warwks 60 B5
Rugeley Staffs 71 J11
Ruigh'riabhach Highld 160 G7
Ruisgarry W Isls 168 e9
Ruishton Somset 19 J9
Ruisigearraidh W Isls 168 e9
Ruislip Gt Lon 36 C3
Rùm Highld 144 E8
Rumbach Moray 158 A7
Rumbling Bridge P & K 134 C8
Rumburgh Suffk 65 L5
Rumby Hill Dur 103 N4
Rumford Cnwll 4 D7
Rumford Falk 126 G2
Rumney Cardif 30 H9
Rumwell Somset 18 G10
Runcorn Halton 81 Q8
Runcton W Susx 15 N6
Runcton Holme Norfk 75 M9
Runfold Surrey 23 N5
Runhall Norfk 76 F10
Runham Norfk 77 P9
Runham Norfk 77 Q10
Runnington Somset 18 F10
Runsell Green Essex 52 C10
Runshaw Moor Lancs 88 G7
Runswick N York 105 M7
Runtaleave Angus 142 D4
Runwell Essex 38 C3
Ruscombe Wokham 35 L9
Rushall Herefs 46 B7
Rushall Norfk 64 H5
Rushall Wilts 21 M3
Rushall Wsall 58 F4
Rushbrooke Suffk 64 B9
Rushbury Shrops 57 J6
Rushden Herts 50 H4
Rushden Nhants 61 L7
Rushenden Kent 38 F7
Rusher's Cross E Susx 25 P5
Rushford Devon 8 C9
Rushford Norfk 64 C5
Rush Green Essex 53 L8
Rush Green Gt Lon 37 M3
Rush Green Herts 50 F6
Rush Green Warrtn 82 E7
Rushlake Green E Susx 25 P7
Rushmere Suffk 65 P4
Rushmere St Andrew Suffk 53 L2
Rushmoor Surrey 23 N6
Rushock Herefs 45 L3
Rushock Worcs 58 C10
Rusholme Manch 83 J6
Rushton Ches W 69 Q2
Rushton Nhants 60 H4
Rushton Shrops 57 L3
Rushton Spencer Staffs 70 G2
Rushwick Worcs 46 F4
Rushyford Dur 103 Q5
Ruskie Stirlg 133 J7
Ruskington Lincs 86 E10
Rusland Cross Cumb 94 G3
Rusper W Susx 24 F3
Ruspidge Gloucs 32 C2
Russell Green Essex 52 B9
Russell's Water Oxon 35 K7
Russel's Green Suffk 65 K7
Russ Hill Surrey 24 F2
Rusthall Kent 25 N3
Rustington W Susx 24 B10
Ruston N York 99 K4
Ruston Parva E R Yk 99 M8
Ruswarp N York 105 N9
Ruthall Shrops 57 K6
Rutherford Border 118 B4
Rutherglen S Lans 125 Q5
Ruthernbridge Cnwll 4 G8
Ruthin Denbgs 68 F3
Ruthrieston C Aber 151 N7
Ruthven Abers 158 D8
Ruthven Angus 142 D8
Ruthven Highld 148 D8
Ruthven Highld 156 E11
Ruthvoes Cnwll 4 E9
Ruthwaite Cumb 100 H3
Ruthwell D & G 109 N7
Ruxley Gt Lon 37 L6
Ruxton Green Herefs 45 Q11
Ruyton-XI-Towns Shrops 69 L10
Ryal Nthumb 112 F6
Ryall Dorset 11 J5
Ryall Worcs 46 G6
Ryarsh Kent 37 Q8
Rycote Oxon 35 J3
Rydal Cumb 101 L9
Ryde IoW 14 G8
Rye E Susx 26 F7
Ryebank Shrops 69 P8
Ryeford Herefs 46 B10
Rye Foreign E Susx 26 E7
Rye Harbour E Susx 26 F8
Ryehill E R Yk 93 M5
Ryeish Green Wokham 35 K11
Rye Street Worcs 46 E7
Ryhall Rutlnd 73 Q8
Ryhill Wakefd 91 K8
Ryhope Sundld 113 P10
Rylah Derbys 84 G7
Ryland Lincs 86 D5
Rylands Notts 72 E3
Rylstone N York 96 E9
Ryme Intrinseca Dorset 11 M2
Ryther N York 91 P3
Ryton Gatesd 113 J8
Ryton N York 98 F5
Ryton Shrops 57 P4
Ryton Warwks 59 P7
Ryton-on-Dunsmore Warwks 59 N10
Ryton Woodside Gatesd 112 H8
RZSS Edinburgh Zoo C Edin 127 N3

S

Sabden Lancs 89 M3
Sabine's Green Essex 51 M11
Sacombe Herts 50 H7
Sacombe Green Herts 50 H7
Sacriston Dur 113 K11
Sadberge Darltn 104 B7
Saddell Ag & B 120 E5
Saddington Leics 60 E2
Saddlebow Norfk 75 M7
Saddlescombe W Susx 24 G8
Sadgill Cumb 101 N9
Saffron Walden Essex 51 M3
Sageston Pembks 41 L10
Saham Hills Norfk 76 C11
Saham Toney Norfk 76 B11
Saighton Ches W 69 M2
St Abbs Border 129 N6
St Agnes Border 128 H7
St Agnes Cnwll 3 J3
St Agnes IoS 2 b3
St Agnes Mining District Cnwll 3 J4
St Albans Herts 50 D9
St Allen Cnwll 3 L3
St Andrew Guern 10 b2
St Andrews Fife 135 N4
St Andrews Botanic Garden Fife 135 N4
St Andrews Major V Glam 30 F10
St Andrews Well Dorset 11 K6
St Anne's Lancs 88 C5
St Ann's D & G 109 N2
St Ann's Chapel Cnwll 5 Q7
St Ann's Chapel Devon 6 H9
St Anthony-in-Meneage Cnwll 3 K8
St Anthony's Hill E Susx 25 P10
St Arvans Mons 31 P5
St Asaph Denbgs 80 E10
St Athan V Glam 30 D11
St Aubin Jersey 11 b2
St Austell Cnwll 3 Q3
St Bees Cumb 100 C8
St Blazey Cnwll 3 R3
St Blazey Gate Cnwll 3 R3
St Boswells Border 118 A4
St Brelade Jersey 11 a2
St Brelade's Bay Jersey 11 a2
St Breock Cnwll 4 F7
St Breward Cnwll 4 H6
St Briavels Gloucs 31 Q4
St Brides Pembks 40 F8
St Brides Major V Glam 29 N10
St Brides Netherwent Mons 31 M7
St Brides-super-Ely V Glam 30 E9
St Brides Wentlooge Newpt 31 J8
St Budeaux C Plym 6 D7
Saintbury Gloucs 47 M7
St Buryan Cnwll 2 C8
St Catherine BaNES 32 E11
St Catherines Ag & B 131 N6
St Chloe Gloucs 32 F4
St Clears Carmth 41 Q7
St Cleer Cnwll 5 L8
St Clement Cnwll 3 M5
St Clement Jersey 11 c2
St Clether Cnwll 5 L5
St Colmac Ag & B 124 C4
St Columb Major Cnwll 4 E9
St Columb Minor Cnwll 4 C9
St Columb Road Cnwll 4 E10
St Combs Abers 159 Q5
St Cross South Elmham Suffk 65 K5
St Cyrus Abers 143 N5
St David's P & K 133 Q3
St Davids Pembks 40 E5
St Davids Cathedral Pembks 40 E5
St Day Cnwll 3 J5
St Decumans Somset 18 E6
St Dennis Cnwll 4 F10
St Devereux Herefs 45 N8
St Dogmaels Pembks 42 C5
St Dogwells Pembks 41 J5
St Dominick Cnwll 5 Q8
St Donats V Glam 29 P11
St Edith's Marsh Wilts 21 J2
St Endellion Cnwll 4 F6
St Enoder Cnwll 4 D10
St Erme Cnwll 3 L4
St Erney Cnwll 5 P10
St Erth Cnwll 2 F6
St Erth Praze Cnwll 2 F6
St Ervan Cnwll 4 D7
St Eval Cnwll 4 D8
St Ewe Cnwll 3 P4
St Fagans Cardif 30 F9
St Fagans National Museum of History Cardif 30 F9
St Fergus Abers 159 Q7
St Fillans P & K 133 K3
St Florence Pembks 41 L10
St Gennys Cnwll 5 J2
St George Conwy 80 D9
St Georges N Som 19 L2
St George's V Glam 30 F9
St George's Hill Surrey 36 C8
St Germans Cnwll 5 P10
St Giles in the Wood Devon 17 J8
St Giles-on-the-Heath Devon 5 P3
St Gluvia's Cnwll 3 K7
St Harmon Powys 55 M10
St Helen Auckland Dur 103 N5
St Helens Cumb 100 D4
St Helen's E Susx 26 D9
St Helens IoW 14 H9
St Helens St Hel 81 Q5
St Helier Gt Lon 36 G7
St Helier Jersey 11 b2
St Hilary Cnwll 2 E7
St Hilary V Glam 30 D10
Saint Hill Devon 10 B3
Saint Hill W Susx 25 J3
St Illtyd Blae G 30 H4
St Ippolyts Herts 50 E5
St Ishmael's Pembks 40 F9
St Issey Cnwll 4 E7
St Ive Cnwll 5 N8
St Ive Cross Cnwll 5 N8
St Ives Cambs 62 D6
St Ives Cnwll 2 E5
St Ives Dorset 13 K4
St James Norfk 77 K7
St James's End Nhants 60 F8
St James South Elmham Suffk 65 L5
St Jidgey Cnwll 4 E8
St John Cnwll 5 Q11
St John Jersey 11 b1
St Johns Dur 103 L4
St John's E Susx 25 M4
St John's IoM 80 c5
St John's Kent 37 M9
St Johns Surrey 23 Q3
St Johns Worcs 46 F4
St John's Chapel Devon 17 J6
St John's Chapel Dur 102 G3
St John's Fen End Norfk 75 K8
St John's Highway Norfk 75 K8
St John's Kirk S Lans 116 D3
St John's Town of Dalry D & G 108 D4
St John's Wood Gt Lon 36 G4
St Judes IoM 80 e2
St Just Cnwll 2 B7
St Just-in-Roseland Cnwll 3 L6
St Just Mining District Cnwll 2 B7
St Katherines Abers 159 J11
St Keverne Cnwll 3 K9
St Kew Cnwll 4 G6
St Kew Highway Cnwll 4 G6
St Keyne Cnwll 5 L9
St Lawrence Cnwll 4 G8
St Lawrence Essex 52 G11
St Lawrence IoW 14 F11
St Lawrence Jersey 11 b1
St Lawrence Kent 39 Q8
St Lawrence Bay Essex 52 G10
St Leonards Bucks 35 P3
St Leonards Dorset 13 K4
St Leonards E Susx 26 D10
St Leonard's Street Kent 37 Q9
St Levan Cnwll 2 B9
St Luke's Park Essex 38 C2
St Lythans V Glam 30 F10
St Mabyn Cnwll 4 G7
St Madoes P & K 134 F3
St Margarets Herefs 45 M8
St Margarets Herts 51 J8
St Margaret's at Cliffe Kent 27 Q3
St Margaret's Hope Ork 169 d7
St Margaret South Elmham Suffk 65 L5
St Marks IoM 80 c7
St Martin Cnwll 3 J9
St Martin Cnwll 5 M10
St Martin Guern 10 b2
St Martin Jersey 11 c1
St Martin's IoS 2 c1
St Martin's P & K 142 B11
St Martin's Shrops 69 K7
St Martin's Moor Shrops 69 K7
St Mary Jersey 11 a1
St Mary Bourne Hants 22 D4
St Marychurch Torbay 7 N5
St Mary Church V Glam 30 D10
St Mary Cray Gt Lon 37 L7
St Mary Hill V Glam 30 C9
St Mary in the Marsh Kent 27 J6
St Mary's IoS 2 c2
St Mary's Ork 169 d6
St Mary's Bay Kent 27 J6
St Mary's Hoo Medway 38 D6
St Mary's Platt Kent 37 P9
St Maughans Mons 45 P11
St Maughans Green Mons 45 P11
St Mawes Cnwll 3 L7
St Mawgan Cnwll 4 D8
St Mellion Cnwll 5 P8
St Mellons Cardif 30 H8
St Merryn Cnwll 4 D7
St Mewan Cnwll 3 P3
St Michael Caerhays Cnwll 3 P5
St Michael Church Somset 19 K8
St Michael Penkevil Cnwll 3 M5
St Michaels Kent 26 E4
St Michaels Worcs 57 K11
St Michael's Mount Cnwll 2 E8
St Michael's on Wyre Lancs 88 F2
St Michael South Elmham Suffk 65 L5
St Minver Cnwll 4 F6
St Monans Fife 135 N7
St Neot Cnwll 5 K8
St Neots Cambs 61 Q8
St Newlyn East Cnwll 4 C10
St Nicholas Pembks 40 H3
St Nicholas V Glam 30 E10
St Nicholas-at-Wade Kent 39 N8
St Ninians Stirlg 133 M9
St Olaves Norfk 65 P2
St Osyth Essex 53 K8
St Ouen Jersey 11 a1
St Owen's Cross Herefs 45 Q10
St Paul's Cray Gt Lon 37 L7
St Paul's Walden Herts 50 E6
St Peter Jersey 11 a1
St Peter Port Guern 10 c2
St Peter's Guern 10 b2
St Peter's Kent 39 Q8
St Peter's Hill Cambs 62 B6
St Petrox Pembks 41 J11
St Pinnock Cnwll 5 L9
St Quivox S Ayrs 114 G3
St Ruan Cnwll 3 J10
St Sampson Guern 10 c1
St Saviour Guern 10 b2
St Saviour Jersey 11 b2
St Stephen Cnwll 3 N3
St Stephens Cnwll 5 N4
St Stephens Cnwll 5 Q10
St Teath Cnwll 4 H5
St Thomas Devon 9 M6
St Margaret's Bay Kent 27 Q3
St Tudy Cnwll 4 H6
St Twynnells Pembks 41 J11
St Veep Cnwll 5 J10
St Vigeans Angus 143 L9
St Wenn Cnwll 4 F9
St Weonards Herefs 45 P10
St Winnow Cnwll 5 J10
St y-Nyll V Glam 30 E9
Salcombe Devon 7 J11
Salcombe Regis Devon 10 D7
Salcott-cum-Virley Essex 52 F9
Sale Traffd 82 G6
Saleby Lincs 87 N5
Sale Green Worcs 46 H3
Salehurst E Susx 26 C7
Salem Carmth 43 M9
Salem Cerdgn 54 F8
Salen Ag & B 137 P7
Salen Highld 138 B5
Salesbury Lancs 89 K4
Salford C Beds 49 P7
Salford Oxon 47 Q9
Salford Salfd 82 H5
Salford Priors Warwks 47 L4
Salfords Surrey 36 G11
Salhouse Norfk 77 L9
Saline Fife 134 C9
Salisbury Wilts 21 M8
Salisbury Plain Wilts 21 L6
Salkeld Dykes Cumb 101 P3
Sallachy Highld 162 C5
Salle Norfk 76 G7
Salmonby Lincs 87 K6
Salperton Gloucs 47 L10
Salph End Bed 61 N10
Salsburgh N Lans 126 E5
Salt Staffs 70 H9
Salta Cumb 109 N11
Saltaire C Brad 90 E3
Saltaire C Brad 90 E3
Saltash Cnwll 6 C7
Saltburn Highld 156 C3
Saltburn-by-the-Sea R & Cl 105 J6
Saltby Leics 73 M5
Salt Coates Cumb 110 C10
Saltcoats Cumb 100 E11
Saltcoats N Ayrs 124 G9
Saltcotes Lancs 88 D5
Saltdean Br & H 25 J10
Salterbeck Cumb 100 C5
Salterforth Lancs 96 C11
Salterswall Ches W 82 D11
Salterton Wilts 21 M7
Saltfleet Lincs 87 N2
Saltfleetby All Saints Lincs 87 N2
Saltfleetby St Clement Lincs 87 N2
Saltfleetby St Peter Lincs 87 M3
Saltford BaNES 32 C11
Salthouse Norfk 76 F3
Saltley Birm 58 H7
Saltmarsh Newpt 31 K8
Saltmarshe E R Yk 92 C6
Saltney Flints 69 L2
Salton N York 98 E5
Saltrens Devon 16 H7
Saltwick Nthumb 113 J4
Saltwood Kent 27 L4
Salvington W Susx 24 D9
Salwarpe Worcs 46 G2
Salway Ash Dorset 11 K5
Sambourne Warwks 47 L2
Sambrook Wrekin 70 C10
Samlesbury Lancs 88 H4
Samlesbury Bottoms Lancs 89 J5
Sampford Arundel Somset 18 F11
Sampford Brett Somset 18 E6
Sampford Courtenay Devon 8 F4
Sampford Moor Somset 18 F11
Sampford Peverell Devon 9 P2
Sampford Spiney Devon 6 E4
Samsonlane Ork 169 f4
Samson's Corner Essex 53 J8
Samuelston E Loth 128 D5
Sanaigmore Ag & B 122 B5
Sancreed Cnwll 2 C8
Sancton E R Yk 92 E3
Sand Somset 19 M5
Sandaig Highld 145 M7
Sandale Cumb 100 H2
Sandal Magna Wakefd 91 J7
Sanday Ork 169 f2
Sanday Airport Ork 169 f2
Sandbach Ches E 70 D2
Sandbach Services Ches E 70 D2
Sandbank Ag & B 131 P11
Sandbanks BCP 12 H7
Sandend Abers 158 E4
Sanderstead Gt Lon 36 H8
Sandford Cumb 102 D7
Sandford Devon 9 K4
Sandford Dorset 12 F7
Sandford Hants 13 L4
Sandford IoW 14 F10
Sandford N Som 19 M3
Sandford S Lans 126 C9
Sandford Shrops 69 K10
Sandford Shrops 69 Q8
Sandford-on-Thames Oxon 34 F4
Sandford Orcas Dorset 20 B10
Sandford St Martin Oxon 48 D9
Sandgate Kent 27 M4
Sandhaven Abers 159 N4
Sandhead D & G 106 E8
Sandhill Rothm 91 L11
Sandhills Dorset 11 M4
Sandhills Dorset 11 P2
Sand Hills Leeds 91 K3
Sandhills Oxon 34 G3
Sandhills Surrey 23 P7
Sandhoe Nthumb 112 E7
Sandhole Ag & B 131 L8
Sand Hole E R Yk 92 D3
Sandholme E R Yk 92 D4
Sandholme Lincs 74 F3
Sandhurst Br For 23 M2
Sandhurst Gloucs 46 F10
Sandhurst Kent 26 D6
Sandhurst Cross Kent 26 C6
Sandhutton N York 97 N4
Sand Hutton N York 98 D9
Sandiacre Derbys 72 D3
Sandilands Lincs 87 P4
Sandiway Ches W 82 D10
Sandleheath Hants 21 M11
Sandleigh Oxon 34 E4
Sandley Dorset 20 E10
Sandling Kent 38 C10
Sandlow Green Ches E 82 G11
Sandness Shet 169 n8
Sandon Essex 52 B11
Sandon Herts 50 H4
Sandon Staffs 70 G9
Sandon Bank Staffs 70 G9
Sandown IoW 14 G10
Sandplace Cnwll 5 M10
Sandridge Herts 50 E8
Sandridge Wilts 32 H11
Sandringham Norfk 75 N5
Sands Bucks 35 M6
Sandsend N York 105 N8
Sand Side Cumb 94 E4
Sandside Cumb 95 K4
Sandtoft N Linc 92 B9
Sandway Kent 38 E11
Sandwich Kent 39 P10
Sandwich Bay Kent 39 Q10
Sandwick Cumb 101 M7
Sandwick Shet 169 r11
Sandwick W Isls 168 j4
Sandwith Cumb 100 C8
Sandwith Newtown Cumb 100 C8
Sandy C Beds 61 Q11
Sandy Bank Lincs 87 J9
Sandycroft Flints 81 L11
Sandy Cross E Susx 25 N6
Sandy Cross Herefs 46 C3
Sandyford D & G 110 D2
Sandygate Devon 7 M4
Sandygate IoM 80 e2
Sandy Haven Pembks 40 G9
Sandyhills D & G 109 J9
Sandylands Lancs 95 J8
Sandy Lane C Brad 90 E3
Sandylane Staffs 70 C7
Sandylane Swans 28 G7
Sandy Lane Wilts 33 J11
Sandy Lane Wrexhm 69 M6
Sandy Park Devon 8 H7
Sandysike Cumb 110 G7
Sandyway Herefs 45 P9
Sangobeg Highld 165 K3
Sangomore Highld 165 K3
Sankey Bridges Warrtn 82 C7
Sankyn's Green Worcs 57 P11
Sanna Highld 137 L2
Sanndabhaig W Isls 168 j4
Sannox N Ayrs 124 C8
Sanquhar D & G 115 Q6
Santon Cumb 100 F10
Santon IoM 80 d7
Santon Bridge Cumb 100 F10
Santon Downham Suffk 63 P3
Sapcote Leics 59 Q6
Sapey Common Herefs 46 D2
Sapiston Suffk 64 C6
Sapley Cambs 62 B6
Sapperton Derbys 71 M8
Sapperton Gloucs 32 H4
Sapperton Lincs 73 Q4
Saracen's Head Lincs 74 F5
Sarclet Highld 167 P8
Sarisbury Hants 14 F5
Sarn Brdgnd 29 P8
Sarn Powys 56 C6
Sarnau Carmth 42 F11
Sarnau Cerdgn 42 F4
Sarnau Gwynd 68 C7
Sarnau Powys 44 E8
Sarnau Powys 68 H11
Sarn Bach Gwynd 66 E9
Sarnesfield Herefs 45 M4
Sarn Mellteyrn Gwynd 66 C8
Sarn Park Services Brdgnd 29 P8
Sarn-wen Powys 69 J11
Saron Carmth 28 H2
Saron Carmth 42 G7
Saron Gwynd 66 H3
Saron Gwynd 79 J11
Sarratt Herts 50 B11
Sarre Kent 39 N8
Sarsden Oxon 47 Q10
Sarson Hants 22 B6
Satley Dur 103 M2
Satmar Kent 27 N4
Satron N York 102 H11
Satterleigh Devon 17 M7
Satterthwaite Cumb 94 G2
Satwell Oxon 35 K8
Sauchen Abers 151 J5
Saucher P & K 142 B11
Sauchieburn Abers 143 M4
Saul Gloucs 32 D3
Saundby Notts 85 N3
Saundersfoot Pembks 41 M10
Saunderton Bucks 35 L4
Saunderton Station Bucks 35 M5
Saunton Devon 16 H4
Sausthorpe Lincs 87 L7
Saverley Green Staffs 70 H7
Savile Town Kirk 90 G6
Sawbridge Warwks 60 B7
Sawbridgeworth Herts 51 L8
Sawdon N York 99 J4
Sawley Derbys 72 D4
Sawley Lancs 96 A11
Sawley N York 97 K7
Sawston Cambs 62 G11
Sawtry Cambs 61 Q4
Saxby Leics 73 L7
Saxby Lincs 86 D3
Saxby All Saints N Linc 92 G7
Saxelbye Leics 72 H6
Saxham Street Suffk 64 F9
Saxilby Lincs 85 Q5
Saxlingham Norfk 76 E4
Saxlingham Green Norfk 65 J2
Saxlingham Nethergate Norfk 65 J2
Saxlingham Thorpe Norfk 65 J2
Saxmundham Suffk 65 M9
Saxondale Notts 72 H3
Saxon Street Cambs 63 L9
Saxtead Suffk 65 K8
Saxtead Green Suffk 65 K9
Saxtead Little Green Suffk 65 J8

Saxthorpe Norfk 76 G5
Saxton N York 91 M3
Sayers Common W Susx 24 G7
Scackleton N York 98 C6
Scadabay W Isls 168 g8
Scadabhagh W Isls 168 g8
Scafell Pike Cumb 100 H9
Scaftworth Notts 85 L2
Scagglethorpe N York 98 G6
Scalasaig Ag & B 136 b3
Scalby E R Yk 92 D5
Scalby N York 99 L2
Scald End Bed 61 M9
Scaldwell Nhants 60 G6
Scaleby Cumb 110 H8
Scalebyhill Cumb 110 H8
Scale Houses Cumb 111 L11
Scales Cumb 94 F6
Scales Cumb 101 K5
Scalesceugh Cumb 110 H11
Scalford Leics 73 K6
Scaling N York 105 K8
Scaling Dam R & Cl 105 K8
Scalloway Shet 169 r10
Scalpay Highld 153 L11
Scalpay W Isls 168 h8
Scambleby Lincs 87 J5
Scammonden Kirk 90 D7
Scamodale Highld 138 E3
Scampston N York 98 H5
Scampton Lincs 86 C5
Scaniport Highld 156 A10
Scapegoat Hill Kirk 90 D7
Scarba Ag & B 130 D7
Scarborough N York 99 L3
Scarcewater Cnwll 3 N3
Scarcliffe Derbys 84 G7
Scarcroft Leeds 91 K2
Scarfskerry Highld 167 N2
Scargill Dur 103 L8
Scarinish Ag & B 136 C7
Scarisbrick Lancs 88 D8
Scarness Cumb 100 H4
Scarning Norfk 76 D9
Scarrington Notts 73 J2
Scarth Hill Lancs 88 E9
Scarthingwell N York 91 M3
Scartho NE Lin 93 N9
Scatsta Airport Shet 169 q6
Scaur D & G 108 H10
Scawby N Linc 92 G9
Scawsby Donc 91 N10
Scawthorpe Donc 91 P9
Scawton N York 98 A4
Scayne's Hill W Susx 25 J6
Scethrog Powys 44 G9
Scholar Green Ches E 70 E3
Scholes Kirk 90 F5
Scholes Kirk 90 F9
Scholes Leeds 91 K3
Scholes Rothm 91 K11
Scholes Wigan 88 H9
School Aycliffe Dur 103 Q6
School Green C Brad 90 E4
School Green Ches W 70 A2
Schoolgreen Wokham 35 K11
School House Dorset 10 H4
Scissett Kirk 90 G8
Scleddau Pembks 40 H4
Scofton Notts 85 K4
Scole Norfk 64 H6
Scone P & K 134 E2
Sconser Highld 153 J11
Scoonie Fife 135 K7
Scopwick Lincs 86 E9
Scoraig Highld 160 G7
Scorborough E R Yk 99 L11
Scorrier Cnwll 3 J5
Scorriton Devon 7 J5
Scorton Lancs 95 L11
Scorton N York 103 Q10
Sco Ruston Norfk 77 K7
Scotby Cumb 110 H9
Scotch Corner N York 103 P9
Scotch Corner Rest Area
  N York 103 P9
Scotforth Lancs 95 K9
Scot Hay Staffs 70 D5
Scothern Lincs 86 D5
Scotland Lincs 73 Q4
Scotland Gate Nthumb 113 L4
Scotlandwell P & K 134 F7
Scot Lane End Bolton 89 J9
Scotscalder Station Highld 167 J5
Scotsdike Cumb 110 G6
Scot's Gap Nthumb 112 F3
Scotsmill Abers 150 F4
Scotstoun C Glas 125 N4
Scotswood N u Ty 113 K8
Scotter Lincs 92 E10
Scotterthorpe Lincs 92 E10
Scottish Seabird Centre
  E Loth 128 F2
Scottlethorpe Lincs 73 R6
Scotton Lincs 92 E11
Scotton N York 97 M9
Scotton N York 103 N11
Scottow Norfk 77 K7
Scott Willoughby Lincs 73 R3
Scoulton Norfk 76 D11
Scounslow Green Staffs 71 K9
Scourie Highld 164 E8
Scourie More Highld 164 D8
Scousburgh Shet 169 q12
Scouthead Oldham 90 B9
Scrabster Highld 167 K2
Scraesburgh Border 118 C7
Scrafield Lincs 87 K7
Scrainwood Nthumb 119 J9
Scrane End Lincs 74 G2
Scraptoft Leics 72 G9
Scratby Norfk 77 Q8
Scrayingham N York 98 E9
Scrays E Susx 26 C8
Scredington Lincs 74 A2
Scremby Lincs 87 M7
Scremerston Nthumb 129 Q10
Screveton Notts 73 J2
Scrivelsby Lincs 87 J7
Scriven N York 97 M9
Scrooby Notts 85 L2
Scropton Derbys 71 M8
Scrub Hill Lincs 86 H9
Scruton N York 97 L1
Scuggate Cumb 110 H6
Scullomie Highld 165 P4

Sculthorpe Norfk 76 B5
Scunthorpe N Linc 92 F8
Scurlage Swans 28 E7
Sea Somset 10 G2
Seaborough Dorset 11 J3
Seabridge Staffs 70 E6
Seabrook Kent 27 L4
Seaburn Sundld 113 P9
Seacombe Wirral 81 L6
Seacroft Leeds 91 K3
Seacroft Lincs 87 Q8
Seadyke Lincs 74 F3
Seafield W Loth 127 J4
Seaford E Susx 25 L11
Seaforth Sefton 81 L5
Seagrave Leics 72 G7
Seagry Heath Wilts 33 J8
Seaham Dur 113 P11
Seahouses Nthumb 119 P4
Seal Kent 37 N9
Sealand Flints 81 M11
Seale Surrey 23 N5
Seamer N York 99 L4
Seamer N York 104 E8
Seamill N Ayrs 124 G8
Sea Palling Norfk 77 N6
Searby Lincs 93 J9
Seasalter Kent 39 J9
Seascale Cumb 100 D10
Seathwaite Cumb 100 H11
Seathwaite Cumb 100 H4
Seatle Cumb 94 H4
Seatoller Cumb 100 H8
Seaton Cnwll 5 N11
Seaton Cumb 100 D4
Seaton Devon 10 E6
Seaton Dur 113 N11
Seaton E R Yk 99 P11
Seaton Kent 39 M10
Seaton Nthumb 113 M5
Seaton Rutlnd 73 N11
Seaton Burn N Tyne 113 K6
Seaton Carew Hartpl 104 F5
Seaton Delaval Nthumb 113 M5
Seaton Ross E R Yk 92 C2
Seaton Sluice Nthumb 113 M5
Seatown Dorset 11 J6
Seatown Moray 157 N3
Seave Green N York 104 D9
Seaview IoW 14 H8
Seaville Cumb 110 C10
Seavington St Mary Somset 11 J2
Seavington St Michael
  Somset 19 M11
Sebastopol Torfn 31 J5
Sebergham Cumb 101 L2
Seckington Warwks 59 L3
Second Severn Crossing
  Mons 31 P7
Sedbergh Cumb 95 P2
Sedbury Gloucs 31 P6
Sedbusk N York 96 C2
Sedgeberrow Worcs 47 K7
Sedgebrook Lincs 73 M3
Sedge Fen Suffk 63 L4
Sedgefield Dur 104 C5
Sedgeford Norfk 75 P3
Sedgehill Wilts 20 G9
Sedgemoor Services
  Somset 19 L4
Sedgley Dudley 58 D6
Sedgley Park Bury 82 H4
Sedgwick Cumb 95 L3
Sedlescombe E Susx 26 C8
Sedrup Bucks 35 M2
Seed Kent 38 F10
Seend Wilts 20 H2
Seend Cleeve Wilts 20 H2
Seer Green Bucks 35 Q6
Seething Norfk 65 L2
Sefton Sefton 81 M4
Seghill Nthumb 113 L6
Seighford Staffs 70 F9
Seion Gwynd 79 J11
Seisdon Staffs 58 B5
Selattyn Shrops 69 J8
Selborne Hants 23 K8
Selby N York 91 Q4
Selham W Susx 23 P10
Selhurst Gt Lon 36 H7
Selkirk Border 117 P5
Sellack Herefs 45 R9
Sellafield Station Cumb 100 D10
Sellafirth Shet 169 s4
Sellan Cnwll 2 C7
Sellick's Green Somset 18 H11
Sellindge Kent 27 J4
Selling Kent 38 H10
Sells Green Wilts 20 H2
Selly Oak Birm 58 F8
Selmeston E Susx 25 M9
Selsdon Gt Lon 37 J8
Selsey W Susx 15 N8
Selsfield Common W Susx 24 H4
Selside Cumb 101 P11
Selside N York 96 A5
Selsley Gloucs 32 F4
Selsted Kent 27 M3
Selston Notts 84 G10
Selworthy Somset 18 B5
Semer Suffk 52 G2
Semington Wilts 20 G2
Semley Wilts 20 G9
Sempringham Lincs 74 B4
Send Surrey 36 B9
Send Marsh Surrey 36 B9
Senghenydd Caerph 30 F6
Sennen Cnwll 2 B8
Sennen Cove Cnwll 2 B8
Sennybridge Powys 44 C9
Serlby Notts 85 K3
Sessay N York 97 Q5
Setchey Norfk 75 M8
Setley Hants 13 P4
Seton Mains E Loth 128 C4
Settle N York 96 B8
Settrington N York 98 G6
Seven Ash Somset 18 G8
Sevenhampton Gloucs 47 K10
Sevenhampton Swindn 33 P6
Seven Kings Gt Lon 37 L3
Sevenoaks Kent 37 M9
Sevenoaks Weald Kent 37 M10
Seven Sisters Neath 29 M3
Seven Springs Gloucs 47 J11
Seven Star Green Essex 52 F6

Severn Beach S Glos 31 P8
Severn Bridge S Glos 31 Q6
Severn Stoke Worcs 46 G6
Severn View Services S Glos 31 Q7
Sevick End Bed 61 N10
Sevington Kent 26 H3
Sewards End Essex 51 N3
Sewardstonebury Essex 51 J11
Sewell C Beds 49 Q10
Sewerby E R Yk 99 P7
Seworgan Cnwll 3 J7
Sewstern Leics 73 M6
Sexhow N York 104 E9
Sgalpaigh W Isls 168 h8
Sgiogarstaigh W Isls 168 k1
Shabbington Bucks 35 J3
Shackerley Shrops 57 Q3
Shackerstone Leics 72 B9
Shacklecross Derbys 72 C4
Shackleford Surrey 23 P5
Shade Calder 89 Q6
Shader W Isls 168 j1
Shadforth Dur 104 B2
Shadingfield Suffk 65 N5
Shadoxhurst Kent 26 G4
Shadwell Leeds 91 J3
Shadwell Norfk 64 C5
Shaftenhoe End Herts 51 K3
Shaftesbury Dorset 20 G10
Shaftholme Donc 91 P9
Shafton Barns 91 K8
Shafton Two Gates Barns 91 K8
Shakerley Wigan 82 H4
Shalbourne Wilts 22 B2
Shalcombe IoW 14 C9
Shalden Hants 23 J6
Shalden Green Hants 23 K6
Shaldon Devon 7 N4
Shalfleet IoW 14 D9
Shalford Essex 52 B6
Shalford Surrey 36 B11
Shalford Green Essex 52 B6
Shallowford Staffs 70 F9
Shalmsford Street Kent 39 J11
Shalstone Bucks 48 H7
Shamley Green Surrey 24 B2
Shandford Angus 142 H5
Shandon Ag & B 132 B10
Shandwick Highld 156 E4
Shangton Leics 73 J11
Shankhouse Nthumb 113 L5
Shanklin IoW 14 G10
Shantron Ag & B 132 C10
Shap Cumb 101 Q7
Shapinsay Ork 169 e5
Shapwick Dorset 12 F4
Shapwick Somset 19 M7
Shard End Birm 59 J7
Shardlow Derbys 72 C4
Shareshill Staffs 58 D3
Sharlston Wakefd 91 K7
Sharlston Common Wakefd 91 K7
Sharmans Cross Solhll 58 H9
Sharnal Street Medway 38 C7
Sharnbrook Bed 61 L9
Sharneyford Lancs 89 P6
Sharnford Leics 59 Q6
Sharnhill Green Dorset 11 Q3
Sharoe Green Lancs 88 G4
Sharow N York 97 M6
Sharpenhoe C Beds 50 C4
Sharperton Nthumb 119 J10
Sharp Green Norfk 77 M7
Sharpness Gloucs 32 C4
Sharpthorne W Susx 25 J4
Sharptor Cnwll 5 M7
Sharpway Gate Worcs 58 E11
Sharrington Norfk 76 E4
Shatterford Worcs 57 P8
Shatterling Kent 39 N10
Shatton Derbys 84 B4
Shaugh Prior Devon 6 E6
Shave Cross Dorset 11 J5
Shavington Ches E 70 B4
Shaw C Brad 90 C3
Shaw Oldham 89 Q9
Shaw Swindn 33 M7
Shaw W Berk 34 E11
Shaw Wilts 32 G11
Shawbirch Wrekin 57 L2
Shawbost W Isls 168 h3
Shawbury Shrops 69 Q10
Shawclough Rochdl 89 P8
Shaw Common Gloucs 46 C9
Shawdon Hill Nthumb 119 L8
Shawell Leics 60 B4
Shawford Hants 22 E9
Shawforth Lancs 89 P6
Shaw Green Herts 50 H4
Shaw Green Lancs 88 G7
Shaw Green N York 97 L10
Shawhead D & G 109 J3
Shaw Mills N York 97 L8
Shawsburn S Lans 126 D7
Shear Cross Wilts 20 G6
Shearington D & G 109 M7
Shearsby Leics 60 D2
Shearston Somset 19 J8
Shebbear Devon 16 G10
Shebdon Staffs 70 D9
Shebster Highld 166 H4
Shedfield Hants 14 G4
Sheen Staffs 71 L2
Sheepbridge Derbys 84 E6
Sheep Hill Dur 113 J9
Sheepridge Kirk 90 F7
Sheepscar Leeds 91 J4
Sheepscombe Gloucs 32 G2
Sheepstor Devon 6 F5
Sheepwash Devon 16 G10
Sheepwash Nthumb 113 L3
Sheepway N Som 31 N9
Sheepy Magna Leics 72 A10
Sheepy Parva Leics 72 A10
Sheering Essex 51 M8
Sheerness Kent 38 F7
Sheerwater Surrey 36 B8
Sheet Hants 23 L10
Sheffield Cnwll 2 C8
Sheffield Sheff 84 E3
Sheffield Bottom W Berk 34 H11
Sheffield Green E Susx 25 K5
Sheffield Park & Garden
  E Susx 25 K6
Shefford C Beds 50 D3
Shefford Woodlands W Berk 34 C10

Sheigra Highld 164 E4
Sheinton Shrops 57 L4
Shelderton Shrops 56 G9
Sheldon Birm 58 J8
Sheldon Derbys 83 Q11
Sheldon Devon 10 C3
Sheldwich Kent 38 H10
Sheldwich Lees Kent 38 H10
Shelf Calder 90 E5
Shelfanger Norfk 64 G5
Shelfield Warwks 47 M2
Shelfield Wsall 58 F4
Shelfield Green Warwks 47 M2
Shelford Notts 72 H2
Shelford Warwks 59 P7
Shellacres Nthumb 118 G2
Shelley Essex 51 N9
Shelley Kirk 90 G8
Shelley Suffk 52 H4
Shelley Far Bank Kirk 90 G8
Shellingford Oxon 34 B6
Shellow Bowells Essex 51 P9
Shelsley Beauchamp Worcs 46 D2
Shelsley Walsh Worcs 46 D2
Shelton Bed 61 M7
Shelton Norfk 65 J3
Shelton Notts 73 K2
Shelton Shrops 56 H2
Shelton Green Norfk 65 J3
Shelton Lock C Derb 72 B4
Shelton Under Harley Staffs 70 E7
Shelve Shrops 56 E5
Shelwick Herefs 45 Q6
Shenfield Essex 51 P11
Shenington Oxon 48 C6
Shenley Herts 50 E10
Shenley Brook End M Keyn 49 M7
Shenleybury Herts 50 E10
Shenley Church End M Keyn 49 M7
Shenmore Herefs 45 M7
Shennanton D & G 107 K5
Shenstone Staffs 58 H4
Shenstone Worcs 58 C10
Shenstone Woodend Staffs 58 H4
Shenton Leics 72 B11
Shenval Moray 149 N2
Shepeau Stow Lincs 74 F8
Shephall Herts 50 G6
Shepherd's Bush Gt Lon 36 F4
Shepherd's Green Oxon 35 K8
Shepherds Patch Gloucs 32 D4
Shepherdswell Kent 27 N2
Shepley Kirk 90 F9
Shepperdine S Glos 32 B5
Shepperton Surrey 36 C7
Shepperton Green Surrey 36 C7
Shepreth Cambs 62 E11
Shepshed Leics 72 D7
Shepton Beauchamp
  Somset 19 M11
Shepton Mallet Somset 20 B6
Shepton Montague Somset 20 C8
Shepway Kent 38 C11
Sheraton Dur 104 D3
Sherborne Dorset 20 B11
Sherborne Gloucs 33 N2
Sherborne Somset 19 Q3
Sherborne St John Hants 22 H3
Sherbourne Warwks 47 Q2
Sherburn Dur 104 B2
Sherburn N York 99 K5
Sherburn Hill Dur 104 B2
Sherburn in Elmet N York 91 M4
Shere Surrey 36 C11
Shereford Norfk 76 B6
Sherfield English Hants 21 Q10
Sherfield on Loddon Hants 23 J3
Sherfin Lancs 89 M5
Sherford Devon 6 C4
Sherford Devon 7 K10
Sherford Dorset 12 F6
Sheriffhales Shrops 57 P2
Sheriff Hutton N York 98 D7
Sheringham Norfk 76 H3
Sherington M Keyn 49 N5
Shermanbury W Susx 24 F7
Shernborne Norfk 75 P4
Sherrington Wilts 21 J7
Sherston Wilts 32 G7
Sherwood C Nott 72 F2
Sherwood Forest Notts 85 K8
Shetland Islands Shet 169 r8
Shettleston C Glas 125 Q5
Shevington Wigan 88 G4
Shevington Moor Wigan 88 G3
Shevington Vale Wigan 88 G9
Sheviock Cnwll 5 P10
Shibden Head C Brad 90 D5
Shide IoW 14 F9
Shidlaw Nthumb 118 F3
Shiel Bridge Highld 146 A4
Shieldaig Highld 153 R7
Shieldhill D & G 109 M3
Shieldhill Falk 126 F2
Shieldhill House Hotel
  S Lans 116 F7
Shields N Lans 126 D6
Shielfoot Highld 138 B3
Shielhill Angus 142 G6
Shielhill Inver 124 G3
Shifford Oxon 34 C4
Shifnal Shrops 57 N3
Shilbottle Nthumb 119 N9
Shildon Dur 103 P5
Shillford E Rens 125 M6
Shillingford Devon 18 C10
Shillingford Oxon 34 G6
Shillingford Abbot Devon 9 M7
Shillingford St George
  Devon 9 M7
Shillingstone Dorset 12 D2
Shillington C Beds 50 D4
Shillmoor Nthumb 118 H8
Shilton Oxon 33 Q3
Shilton Warwks 59 P8
Shimpling Norfk 64 H5
Shimpling Suffk 64 B11
Shimpling Street Suffk 64 B11
Shincliffe Dur 103 Q2
Shiney Row Sundld 113 M10
Shinfield Wokham 35 K11
Shingay Cambs 62 D11
Shingle Street Suffk 53 Q3
Shinnersbridge Devon 7 K6
Shinness Highld 162 C4
Shipbourne Kent 37 N10

Shipdham Norfk 76 D10
Shipham Somset 19 M4
Shiphay Torbay 7 M5
Shiplake Oxon 35 L9
Shiplake Row Oxon 35 K9
Shiplate N Som 19 L3
Shipley C Brad 90 F3
Shipley Derbys 72 C2
Shipley Shrops 57 Q5
Shipley W Susx 24 D6
Shipley Bridge Surrey 24 H2
Shipley Hatch Kent 26 H4
Shipmeadow Suffk 65 M3
Shippea Hill Station Cambs 63 K4
Shippon Oxon 34 E5
Shipston-on-Stour Warwks 47 Q6
Shipton Bucks 49 L9
Shipton Gloucs 47 K11
Shipton N York 98 B9
Shipton Shrops 57 K6
Shipton Bellinger Hants 21 P5
Shipton Gorge Dorset 11 K6
Shipton Green W Susx 15 M7
Shipton Moyne Gloucs 32 G7
Shipton-on-Cherwell Oxon 48 E11
Shiptonthorpe E R Yk 92 E2
Shipton-under-Wychwood
  Oxon 47 Q11
Shirburn Oxon 35 J5
Shirdley Hill Lancs 88 D8
Shire Cumb 102 B3
Shirebrook Derbys 84 H7
Shiregreen Sheff 84 E2
Shirehampton Bristl 31 P9
Shiremoor N Tyne 113 M6
Shirenewton Mons 31 N6
Shire Oak Wsall 58 G4
Shireoaks Notts 85 J4
Shirkoak Kent 26 F4
Shirland Derbys 84 F9
Shirlett Shrops 57 L5
Shirley C Sotn 14 D4
Shirley Derbys 71 N6
Shirley Gt Lon 37 J7
Shirley Solhll 58 H9
Shirl Heath Herefs 45 N3
Shirrell Heath Hants 14 G4
Shirwell Devon 17 L4
Shiskine N Ayrs 120 H6
Shittlehope Dur 103 K3
Shobdon Herefs 45 N2
Shobley Hants 13 L3
Shobrooke Devon 9 L4
Shoby Leics 72 H6
Shocklach Ches W 69 M5
Shocklach Green Ches W 69 M5
Shoeburyness Sthend 38 F4
Sholden Kent 39 Q11
Sholing C Sotn 14 E4
Shoot Hill Shrops 56 G2
Shop Cnwll 4 D7
Shop Cnwll 16 C9
Shopwyke W Susx 15 N5
Shore Rochdl 89 Q7
Shoreditch Gt Lon 36 H4
Shoreditch Somset 18 H10
Shoreham Kent 37 M8
Shoreham-by-Sea W Susx 24 F9
Shoreswood Nthumb 129 N10
Shorley Hants 22 G9
Shorncote Gloucs 33 K5
Shorne Kent 37 Q6
Shortacross Cnwll 5 M10
Shortbridge E Susx 25 L6
Shortfield Common Surrey 23 M6
Shortgate E Susx 25 L7
Short Heath Birm 58 G6
Shortheath Hants 23 L7
Short Heath Wsall 58 E4
Shortlanesend Cnwll 3 L4
Shortlees E Ayrs 125 L10
Shortstown Bed 61 N11
Shorwell IoW 14 E10
Shoscombe BaNES 20 D3
Shotesham Norfk 65 J2
Shotgate Essex 38 C3
Shotley Suffk 53 M4
Shotley Bridge Dur 112 G10
Shotleyfield Nthumb 112 G10
Shotley Gate Suffk 53 M5
Shottenden Kent 38 H11
Shottery Warwks 47 N4
Shotteswell Warwks 48 D5
Shottisham Suffk 53 P3
Shottle Derbys 71 Q5
Shottlegate Derbys 71 Q5
Shotton Dur 104 C5
Shotton Dur 104 D3
Shotton Flints 81 L11
Shotton Nthumb 113 K5
Shotton Nthumb 118 F4
Shotton Colliery Dur 104 C2
Shotts N Lans 126 F6
Shotwick Ches W 81 L10
Shougle Moray 157 N6
Shouldham Norfk 75 N9
Shouldham Thorpe Norfk 75 N9
Shoulton Worcs 46 F3
Shover's Green E Susx 25 Q4
Shraleybrook Staffs 70 D5
Shrawardine Shrops 69 L11
Shrawley Worcs 57 Q11
Shreding Green Bucks 36 B4
Shrewley Warwks 59 K11
Shrewsbury Shrops 56 H2
Shrewton Wilts 21 L6
Shripney W Susx 15 P6
Shrivenham Oxon 33 P7
Shropham Norfk 64 D3
Shroton Dorset 12 E2
Shrub End Essex 52 G6
Shucknall Herefs 46 A6
Shudy Camps Cambs 51 P2
Shuna Ag & B 130 F6
Shurdington Gloucs 46 H11
Shurlock Row W & M 35 M10
Shurnock Worcs 47 K2
Shurrery Highld 166 H5
Shurrery Lodge Highld 166 H5
Shurton Somset 18 H6
Shustoke Warwks 59 K6
Shute Devon 9 L4
Shute Devon 10 F5
Shutford Oxon 48 C6
Shut Heath Staffs 70 F10

Shuthonger Gloucs 46 G7
Shutlanger Nhants 49 K5
Shutterton Devon 9 N9
Shutt Green Staffs 58 C3
Shuttington Warwks 59 L3
Shuttlewood Derbys 84 G6
Shuttleworth Bury 89 N7
Siabost W Isls 168 h3
Siadar W Isls 168 i2
Sibbertoft Nhants 60 E4
Sibdon Carwood Shrops 56 G8
Sibford Ferris Oxon 48 C7
Sibford Gower Oxon 48 C7
Sible Hedingham Essex 52 C5
Sibley's Green Essex 51 P5
Siblyback Cnwll 5 L7
Sibsey Lincs 87 L10
Sibsey Fenside Lincs 87 K10
Sibson Cambs 74 A11
Sibson Leics 72 B10
Sibster Highld 167 P6
Sibthorpe Notts 85 M6
Sibthorpe Notts 85 N11
Sibton Suffk 65 M8
Sicklesmere Suffk 64 B9
Sicklinghall N York 97 N11
Sidbrook Somset 19 J9
Sidbury Devon 10 C6
Sidbury Shrops 57 M7
Sid Cop Barns 91 K9
Sidcot N Som 19 M3
Sidcup Gt Lon 37 L6
Siddick Cumb 100 D4
Siddington Ches E 82 H10
Siddington Gloucs 33 K5
Sidemoor Worcs 58 E10
Sidestrand Norfk 77 K4
Sidford Devon 10 C6
Sidlesham W Susx 15 N7
Sidlesham Common W Susx 15 N7
Sidley E Susx 26 B10
Sidmouth Devon 10 C7
Siefton Shrops 56 H8
Sigford Devon 7 K4
Sigglesthorne E R Yk 99 P11
Sigingstone V Glam 30 C10
Signet Oxon 33 P2
Silchester Hants 22 H2
Sileby Leics 72 G7
Silecroft Cumb 94 C4
Silfield Norfk 64 G2
Silian Cerdgn 43 L4
Silkstead Hants 22 D11
Silkstone Barns 90 H9
Silkstone Common Barns 90 H10
Silk Willoughby Lincs 73 R2
Silloth Cumb 109 P10
Silpho N York 99 K2
Silsden C Brad 96 F11
Silsoe C Beds 50 C3
Silton Dorset 20 E9
Silverburn Mdloth 127 N5
Silverdale Lancs 95 K6
Silverdale Staffs 70 E5
Silver End Essex 52 D8
Silverford Abers 159 J5
Silvergate Norfk 76 H6
Silver Jubilee Bridge Halton 81 L7
Silverlace Green Suffk 65 L9
Silverley's Green Suffk 65 K6
Silverstone Nhants 49 J6
Silver Street Kent 38 E9
Silver Street Somset 19 P8
Silverton Devon 9 N4
Silverwell Cnwll 3 J4
Silvington Shrops 57 L9
Simister Bury 89 N9
Simmondley Derbys 83 M6
Simonburn Nthumb 112 C6
Simonsbath Somset 17 P4
Simonsburrow Devon 18 F11
Simonstone Lancs 89 M4
Simonstone N York 96 C2
Simprim Border 129 L11
Simpson M Keyn 49 N7
Simpson Cross Pembks 40 G7
Sinclair's Hill Border 129 L9
Sinclairston E Ayrs 115 J4
Sinderby N York 97 M4
Sinderhope Nthumb 112 B10
Sinderland Green Traffd 82 F7
Sindlesham Wokham 35 L11
Sinfin C Derb 72 A4
Singleborough Bucks 49 L8
Single Street Gt Lon 37 K9
Singleton Kent 26 H3
Singleton Lancs 88 D3
Singleton W Susx 15 N4
Singlewell Kent 37 Q6
Sinkhurst Green Kent 26 D3
Sinnahard Abers 150 D5
Sinnington N York 98 E3
Sinope Leics 72 C7
Sinton Worcs 46 F2
Sinton Worcs 46 F2
Sinton Green Worcs 46 F2
Sipson Gt Lon 36 C5
Sirhowy Blae G 30 F2
Sissinghurst Kent 26 C4
Siston S Glos 32 C9
Sitcott Devon 5 P3
Sithney Cnwll 2 G8
Sithney Common Cnwll 2 G8
Sithney Green Cnwll 2 G8
Sittingbourne Kent 38 F9
Six Ashes Shrops 57 P7
Six Bells Blae G 30 H4
Six Hills Leics 72 G6
Sixhills Lincs 86 G3
Six Mile Bottom Cambs 63 J9
Sixmile Cottages Kent 27 K3
Sixpenny Handley Dorset 21 J11
Six Rues Jersey 11 b1
Sizewell Suffk 65 P9
Skaill Ork 169 e6
Skara Brae Ork 169 b5
Skares E Ayrs 115 K4
Skateraw Abers 151 N7
Skateraw E Loth 129 J5
Skeabost Highld 152 G8
Skeeby N York 103 N10
Skeffington Leics 73 J10
Skeffling E R Yk 93 Q7
Skegby Notts 84 G8
Skegby Notts 85 N7
Skegness Lincs 87 Q8

Skelbo Highld 162 H7
Skelbo Street Highld 162 H8
Skelbrooke Donc 91 N8
Skeldyke Lincs 74 F3
Skellingthorpe Lincs 86 B6
Skellorn Green Ches E 83 K8
Skellow Donc 91 N8
Skelmanthorpe Kirk 90 G8
Skelmersdale Lancs 88 F9
Skelmorlie N Ayrs 124 F4
Skelpick Highld 166 B5
Skelston D & G 108 H3
Skelton C York 98 B9
Skelton Cumb 101 M3
Skelton E R Yk 92 C5
Skelton on Ure N York 97 N7
Skelwith Bridge Cumb 101 K10
Skendleby Lincs 87 M7
Skene House Abers 151 K5
Skenfrith Mons 45 P10
Skerne E R Yk 99 L9
Skerray Highld 165 Q4
Skerricha Highld 164 F6
Skerton Lancs 95 K8
Sketchley Leics 59 P6
Sketty Swans 28 H6
Skewen Neath 29 K5
Skewsby N York 98 C6
Skeyton Norfk 77 J6
Skeyton Corner Norfk 77 K6
Skiall Highld 166 H3
Skidbrooke Lincs 87 M2
Skidbrooke North End Lincs 93 R11
Skidby E R Yk 92 H4
Skigersta W Isls 168 k1
Skilgate Somset 18 C9
Skillington Lincs 73 M5
Skinburness Cumb 109 P9
Skinflats Falk 133 Q11
Skinidin Highld 152 C8
Skinners Green W Berk 34 D11
Skinningrove R & Cl 105 K7
Skipness Ag & B 123 R8
Skipper's Bridge D & G 110 G4
Skiprigg Cumb 110 G11
Skipsea E R Yk 99 P10
Skipsea Brough E R Yk 99 P10
Skipton N York 96 E10
Skipton-on-Swale N York 97 N5
Skipwith N York 91 R3
Skirbeck Lincs 74 F2
Skirlaugh E R Yk 93 K3
Skirling Border 116 F3
Skirmett Bucks 35 L6
Skirpenbeck E R Yk 98 E9
Skirwith Cumb 102 B4
Skirwith N York 95 Q6
Skirza Highld 167 Q3
Skitby Cumb 110 H7
Skittle Green Bucks 35 L4
Skokholm Island Pembks 40 D10
Skomer Island Pembks 40 D9
Skulamus Highld 145 L3
Skyborry Green Shrops 56 D10
Skye Green Essex 52 E7
Skye of Curr Highld 148 H3
Skyreholme N York 96 G9
Slack Calder 90 B5
Slackbuie Highld 156 B9
Slackcote Oldham 90 B9
Slack Head Cumb 95 K5
Slackholme End Lincs 87 P6
Slacks of Cairnbanno Abers 159 K8
Slad Gloucs 32 G3
Slade Devon 10 J2
Slade Devon 17 J2
Slade Devon 17 Q6
Slade End Oxon 34 G6
Slade Green Gt Lon 37 M5
Slade Heath Staffs 58 D3
Slade Hooton Rothm 84 H3
Sladesbridge Cnwll 4 G7
Slades Green Worcs 46 F8
Slaggyford Nthumb 111 N10
Slaidburn Lancs 95 Q10
Slaithwaite Kirk 90 D8
Slaley Derbys 84 C9
Slaley Nthumb 112 E9
Slamannan Falk 126 F3
Slapton Bucks 49 P10
Slapton Devon 7 L9
Slapton Nhants 48 H5
Slattocks Rochdl 89 P9
Slaugham W Susx 24 G5
Slaughterford Wilts 32 F10
Slawston Leics 60 G2
Sleaford Hants 23 M7
Sleaford Lincs 86 E11
Sleagill Cumb 101 Q7
Sleap Shrops 69 N9
Sleapford Wrekin 70 A11
Sleapshyde Herts 50 E9
Sleasdairidh Highld 162 E7
Slebech Pembks 41 K7
Sledge Green Worcs 46 F8
Sledmere E R Yk 99 J8
Sleetbeck Cumb 111 K5
Sleight Dorset 12 G5
Sleightholme Dur 103 J8
Sleights N York 105 N9
Slepe Dorset 12 F6
Slickly Highld 167 N3
Sliddery N Ayrs 120 H7
Sligachan Highld 144 G2
Sligrachan Ag & B 131 P9
Slindon Staffs 70 E8
Slindon W Susx 15 Q5
Slinfold W Susx 24 D4
Sling Gloucs 31 Q3
Sling Gwynd 79 L11
Slingsby N York 98 D6
Slip End C Beds 50 C7
Slip End Herts 50 G3
Slipton Nhants 61 L5
Slitting Mill Staffs 71 J11
Slochd Highld 148 E3
Slockavullin Ag & B 130 G8
Sloley Norfk 77 K7
Sloncombe Devon 8 H7
Sloothby Lincs 87 N6
Slough Slough 35 Q9
Slough Green Somset 19 J11
Slough Green W Susx 24 G5

Slumbay Highld 154 A10
Slyfield Surrey 23 Q4
Slyne Lancs 95 K7
Smailholm Border 118 B3
Smallbridge Rochdl 89 Q7
Smallbrook Devon 9 L5
Smallbrook Gloucs 31 Q4
Smallburgh Norfk 77 L7
Smallburn E Ayrs 115 N2
Smalldale Derbys 83 N9
Smalldale Derbys 83 Q8
Small Dole W Susx 24 F8
Smalley Derbys 72 C2
Smalley Common Derbys 72 C2
Smalley Green Derbys 72 C2
Smallfield Surrey 24 H2
Smallford Herts 50 E9
Small Heath Birm 58 H7
Small Hythe Kent 26 E5
Smallridge Devon 10 G4
Smallthorne C Stke 70 F4
Smallways N York 103 M8
Small Wood Hey Lancs 94 H11
Smallworth Norfk 64 E5
Smannell Hants 22 C5
Smardale Cumb 102 D9
Smarden Kent 26 E3
Smarden Bell Kent 26 E3
Smart's Hill Kent 25 M2
Smeafield Nthumb 119 L3
Smeatharpe Devon 10 D2
Smeeth Kent 27 J4
Smeeton Westerby Leics 60 E2
Smelthouses N York 97 J8
Smerral Highld 167 L10
Smestow Staffs 58 C6
Smethwick Sandw 58 F7
Smethwick Green Ches E 70 E2
Smirisary Highld 138 A2
Smisby Derbys 72 A7
Smith End Green Worcs 46 E4
Smithfield Cumb 110 H7
Smith Green Lancs 95 K9
Smithies Barns 91 J9
Smithincott Devon 9 Q2
Smith's End Herts 51 K3
Smith's Green Essex 51 N6
Smith's Green Essex 51 Q2
Smithstown Highld 160 B11
Smithton Highld 156 C8
Smithy Bridge Rochdl 89 Q7
Smithy Green Ches E 82 F10
Smithy Green Stockp 83 J7
Smithy Houses Derbys 84 E11
Smockington Leics 59 Q7
Smoo Highld 165 K3
Smythe's Green Essex 52 F8
Snade D & G 108 H3
Snailbeach Shrops 56 F4
Snailwell Cambs 63 K7
Snainton N York 99 J4
Snaith E R Yk 91 Q6
Snake Pass Inn Derbys 83 P6
Snape N York 97 L4
Snape Suffk 65 M10
Snape Green Lancs 88 D8
Snape Street Suffk 65 M10
Snaresbrook Gt Lon 37 K3
Snarestone Leics 72 A9
Snarford Lincs 86 D4
Snargate Kent 26 G6
Snave Kent 26 H6
Sneachill Worcs 46 H4
Snead Powys 56 E6
Sneath Common Norfk 64 H4
Sneaton N York 105 N9
Sneatonthorpe N York 105 P9
Snelland Lincs 86 E4
Snelson Ches E 82 H10
Snelston Derbys 71 M6
Snetterton Norfk 64 D3
Snettisham Norfk 75 N4
Snibston Leics 72 C8
Snig's End Gloucs 46 E9
Snitter Nthumb 119 K10
Snitterby Lincs 86 C2
Snitterfield Warwks 47 P3
Snitton Derbys 84 C8
Snitton Shrops 57 K9
Snoadhill Kent 26 F3
Snodhill Herefs 45 L6
Snodland Kent 38 B9
Snoll Hatch Kent 37 Q11
Snowden Hill Barns 90 H10
Snowdon Gwynd 67 L4
Snowdonia National Park 67 Q9
Snow End Herts 51 K4
Snowshill Gloucs 47 L8
Snow Street Norfk 64 F5
Soake Hants 15 J4
Soar Cardif 30 E8
Soar Devon 7 J11
Soar Powys 44 D8
Soay Highld 144 F5
Soberton Hants 22 H11
Soberton Heath Hants 14 H4
Sockbridge Cumb 101 N5
Sockburn Darltn 104 B9
Sodom Denbgs 80 F10
Sodylt Bank Shrops 69 K7
Soham Cambs 63 J6
Soham Cotes Cambs 63 J5
Solas W Isls 168 d10
Solbury Pembks 40 G8
Soldon Devon 16 E9
Soldon Cross Devon 16 E9
Soldridge Hants 23 J7
Sole Street Kent 27 J2
Sole Street Kent 37 Q7
Solihull Solhll 59 J9
Sollas W Isls 168 d10
Sollers Dilwyn Herefs 45 N3
Sollers Hope Herefs 46 B8
Sollom Lancs 88 F7
Solva Pembks 40 F6
Solwaybank D & G 110 F5
Somerby Leics 73 K8
Somerby Lincs 93 J9
Somercotes Derbys 84 F10
Somerford BCP 13 L6
Somerford Keynes Gloucs 33 K5
Somerley W Susx 15 M7
Somerleyton Suffk 65 P2
Somersal Herbert Derbys 71 L7

Somersby Lincs 87 K6
Somersham Cambs 62 E5
Somersham Suffk 53 J2
Somerton Oxon 48 E9
Somerton Somset 19 N9
Somerton Suffk 63 P10
Somerwood Shrops 57 K2
Sompting W Susx 24 E9
Sompting Abbotts W Susx 24 E9
Sonning Wokham 35 L9
Sonning Common Oxon 35 K8
Sonning Eye Oxon 35 K9
Sontley Wrexhm 69 K5
Sopley Hants 13 L5
Sopwell Herts 50 E9
Sopworth Wilts 32 F7
Sorbie D & G 107 M8
Sordale Highld 167 K4
Sorisdale Ag & B 136 H3
Sorn E Ayrs 115 L2
Sornhill E Ayrs 125 N11
Sortat Highld 167 N4
Sotby Lincs 86 H5
Sots Hole Lincs 86 F8
Sotterley Suffk 65 N5
Soughton Flints 81 J11
Soulbury Bucks 49 N9
Soulby Cumb 101 N5
Soulby Cumb 102 D8
Souldern Oxon 48 F8
Souldrop Bed 61 L8
Sound Ches E 70 A5
Sound Muir Moray 157 R7
Soundwell S Glos 32 C9
Sourton Devon 8 D6
Soutergate Cumb 94 E4
South Acre Norfk 75 R8
South Alkham Kent 27 M3
Southall Gt Lon 36 D5
South Allington Devon 7 K11
South Alloa Falk 133 P9
Southam Gloucs 47 J9
Southam Warwks 48 D2
South Ambersham W Susx 23 P10
Southampton C Sotn 14 D4
Southampton Airport Hants 22 E11
South Anston Rothm 84 H4
South Ascot W & M 35 P11
South Ashford Kent 26 H3
South Baddesley Hants 14 C7
South Bank C York 98 B10
South Bank R & Cl 104 F6
South Barrow Somset 20 B9
South Beddington Gt Lon 36 G8
South Beer Cnwll 5 N3
South Benfleet Essex 38 C4
South Bockhampton BCP 13 L5
Southborough Gt Lon 37 K7
Southborough Kent 25 N2
Southbourne BCP 13 K6
Southbourne W Susx 15 L5
South Bowood Dorset 11 J5
South Bramwith Donc 91 Q8
South Brent Devon 6 H6
South Brewham Somset 20 D7
South Broomhill Nthumb 119 P11
Southburgh Norfk 76 E10
South Burlingham Norfk 77 M10
Southburn E R Yk 99 K10
South Cadbury Somset 20 B9
South Carlton Lincs 86 B5
South Carlton Notts 85 J4
South Cave E R Yk 92 F4
South Cerney Gloucs 33 K5
South Chailey E Susx 25 J7
South Chard Somset 10 G3
South Charlton Nthumb 119 N6
South Cheriton Somset 20 C10
South Church Dur 103 P5
Southchurch Sthend 38 F4
South Cleatlam Dur 103 M7
South Cliffe E R Yk 92 E4
South Clifton Notts 85 P6
South Cockerington Lincs 87 L3
South Cornelly Brdgnd 29 M8
Southcott Cnwll 5 K2
Southcott Devon 8 D7
Southcott Devon 9 J8
Southcott Devon 16 D8
Southcott Wilts 21 N3
Southcourt Bucks 35 M2
South Cove Suffk 65 P5
South Creake Norfk 76 B4
South Crosland Kirk 90 E8
South Croxton Leics 72 H8
South Dalton E R Yk 99 K11
South Darenth Kent 37 N7
South Dell W Isls 168 j1
South Downs National Park 25 J9
South Duffield N York 92 A4
South Earlswood Surrey 36 G11
Southease E Susx 25 K9
South Elkington Lincs 87 J3
South Elmsall Wakefd 91 M8
Southend Ag & B 120 C10
South End E R Yk 93 Q7
South End Herefs 46 D6
South End N Linc 93 K6
South End Norfk 64 D3
Southend Wilts 33 N10
Southend Airport Essex 38 E4
Southend-on-Sea Sthend 38 E4
Southernby Cumb 101 L3
Southernden Kent 26 E2
Southerndown V Glam 29 N10
Southerness D & G 109 L10
South Erradale Highld 153 N3
Southerton Devon 10 D4
Southery Norfk 63 K2
South Fambridge Essex 38 E3
South Fawley W Berk 34 C8
South Ferriby N Linc 92 G6
South Field E R Yk 92 H5
Southfleet Kent 37 P6
Southford IoW 14 F11
Southgate Gt Lon 36 G2
Southgate Norfk 75 N6
Southgate Norfk 76 B4
Southgate Norfk 76 G7
Southgate Swans 28 G7
South Godstone Surrey 37 J11
South Gorley Hants 13 L3
South Gosforth N u Ty 113 K7

South Green Essex 37 Q2
South Green Essex 52 H8
South Green Kent 38 E9
South Green Norfk 76 E9
South Green Suffk 64 H6
South Gyle C Edin 127 M3
South Hanningfield Essex 38 B2
South Harting W Susx 23 L11
South Hayling Hants 15 K7
South Hazelrigg Nthumb 119 L4
South Heath Bucks 35 P4
South Heighton E Susx 25 K10
South Hetton Dur 113 N11
South Hiendley Wakefd 91 K8
South Hill Cnwll 5 N7
South Hill Somset 19 N9
South Hinksey Oxon 34 F4
South Hole Devon 16 C7
South Holmwood Surrey 24 E2
South Hornchurch Gt Lon 37 M4
South Horrington Somset 19 Q5
South Huish Devon 6 H10
South Hykeham Lincs 86 B8
South Hylton Sundld 113 N9
Southill C Beds 50 E2
Southington Hants 22 F5
South Kelsey Lincs 92 H11
South Kessock Highld 156 B8
South Killingholme N Linc 93 K7
South Kilvington N York 97 P4
South Kilworth Leics 60 D4
South Kirkby Wakefd 91 L8
South Knighton Devon 7 L4
South Kyme Lincs 86 G11
Southleigh Devon 10 E6
South Leigh Oxon 34 C3
South Leverton Notts 85 N4
South Littleton Worcs 47 L5
South Lopham Norfk 64 E5
South Luffenham Rutlnd 73 N10
South Lynn Norfk 75 M7
South Malling E Susx 25 K8
South Marston Swindn 33 N7
South Merstham Surrey 36 G10
South Middleton Nthumb 119 J6
South Milford N York 91 M4
South Milton Devon 6 J10
South Mimms Herts 50 F10
South Mimms Services Herts 50 F10
Southminster Essex 38 G2
South Molton Devon 17 N6
South Moor Dur 113 J10
Southmoor Oxon 34 C5
South Moreton Oxon 34 G7
Southmuir Angus 142 F7
South Mundham W Susx 15 N6
South Muskham Notts 85 N9
South Newbald E R Yk 92 F3
South Newington Oxon 48 D8
South Newsham Nthumb 113 M5
South Newton Wilts 21 L8
South Nitshill C Glas 125 N6
South Normanton Derbys 84 F9
South Norwood Gt Lon 36 H7
South Nutfield Surrey 36 H11
South Ockendon Thurr 37 N4
Southoe Cambs 61 Q8
Southolt Suffk 64 H8
South Ormsby Lincs 87 L5
Southorpe C Pete 74 A10
South Ossett Wakefd 90 H7
South Otterington N York 97 N3
Southover Devon 11 N6
Southover E Susx 25 Q5
South Owersby Lincs 86 G2
Southowram Calder 90 E6
South Park Surrey 36 F11
South Perrott Dorset 11 K3
South Petherton Somset 19 M11
South Petherwin Cnwll 5 N5
South Pickenham Norfk 76 B11
South Pill Cnwll 5 Q10
South Pool Devon 7 K10
South Poorton Dorset 11 L5
Southport Sefton 88 C7
South Queensferry C Edin 127 L2
South Radworthy Devon 17 N5
South Rauceby Lincs 86 D11
South Raynham Norfk 76 B7
South Reddish Stockp 83 J6
South Repps Norfk 77 K4
South Reston Lincs 87 M4
Southrey Lincs 86 F7
South Ronaldsay Ork 169 d8
Southrop Gloucs 33 N4
Southrope Hants 23 J6
South Runcton Norfk 75 M9
South Scarle Notts 85 P8
Southsea C Port 15 J7
Southsea Wrexhm 69 K4
South Shian Ag & B 138 G9
South Shields S Tyne 113 N7
South Shore Bpool 88 C4
Southside Dur 103 M5
South Somercotes Lincs 87 M2
South Stainley N York 97 M8
South Stifford Thurr 37 N5
South Stoke BaNES 20 D2
South Stoke Oxon 34 G8
South Stoke W Susx 24 B9
South Stour Kent 26 H4
South Street Kent 37 P8
South Street Kent 39 J9
South Street Kent 39 K8
South Tarrance S Lans 127 J7
South Tawton Devon 8 G6
South Tehidy Cnwll 2 H5
South Thoresby Lincs 87 M5
South Town Hants 23 J7
Southtown Norfk 77 Q10
Southtown Somset 19 K11
South Uist W Isls 168 d14
Southwaite Cumb 110 H11
Southwaite Services Cumb 110 H11
South Walsham Norfk 77 M9
Southwark Gt Lon 36 H5
South Warnborough Hants 23 K5
Southwater W Susx 24 E5
Southwater Street W Susx 24 E5
Southway C Plym 6 D6
Southway Somset 19 P6
South Weald Essex 37 N2
Southwell Dorset 11 P10
Southwell Notts 85 L10

South Weston Oxon....35 K5
South Wheatley Cnwll....5 L3
South Wheatley Notts....85 N3
Southwick Hants....14 H5
Southwick Nhants....61 M2
Southwick Somset....19 L5
Southwick Sundld....113 N9
Southwick W Susx....24 F9
Southwick Wilts....20 F3
South Widcombe BaNES....19 Q3
South Wigston Leics....72 F11
South Willingham Lincs....86 G4
South Wingate Dur....104 D4
South Wingfield Derbys....84 E9
South Witham Lincs....73 N7
Southwold Suffk....65 Q6
South Wonston Hants....22 E7
Southwood Norfk....77 M10
Southwood Somset....19 Q8
South Woodham Ferrers
Essex....38 D2
South Wootton Norfk....75 M6
South Wraxall Wilts....20 F2
South Zeal Devon....8 G6
Sovereign Harbour E Susx....25 P10
Sowerby Calder....90 C6
Sowerby N York....97 P4
Sowerby Bridge Calder....90 D6
Sowerby Row Cumb....101 L2
Sower Carr Lancs....88 D2
Sowerhill Somset....18 A10
Sowhill Torfn....31 J4
Sowley Green Suffk....63 M10
Sowood Calder....90 D7
Sowton Devon....6 E5
Sowton Devon....9 N6
Soyland Town Calder....90 C6
Spa Common Norfk....77 K5
Spain's End Essex....51 Q3
Spalding Lincs....74 D6
Spaldington E R Yk....92 C4
Spaldwick Cambs....61 P6
Spalford Notts....85 P7
Spanby Lincs....74 A3
Spanish Green Hants....23 J3
Sparham Norfk....76 F8
Sparhamill Norfk....76 F8
Spark Bridge Cumb....94 G4
Sparket Cumb....101 M5
Sparkford Somset....20 B9
Sparkhill Birm....58 H8
Sparkwell Devon....6 F7
Sparrow Green Norfk....76 C9
Sparrowpit Derbys....83 N8
Sparrows Green E Susx....25 P4
Sparsholt Hants....22 D8
Sparsholt Oxon....34 B7
Spartylea Nthumb....112 C11
Spath Staffs....71 K7
Spaunton N York....98 E3
Spaxton Somset....18 H7
Spean Bridge Highld....146 G11
Spear Hill W Susx....24 D7
Spearywell Hants....22 B9
Speen Bucks....35 M5
Speen W Berk....34 E11
Speeton N York....99 P6
Speke Lpool....81 N8
Speldhurst Kent....25 N2
Spellbrook Herts....51 L7
Spelmonden Kent....26 B4
Spelsbury Oxon....48 B10
Spen Kirk....90 F5
Spencers Wood Wokham....35 K11
Spen Green Ches E....70 E2
Spennithorne N York....96 H3
Spennymoor Dur....103 Q4
Spernall Warwks....47 L2
Spetchley Worcs....46 G4
Spetisbury Dorset....12 F4
Spexhall Suffk....65 M5
Spey Bay Moray....157 R4
Speybridge Highld....149 J2
Speyview Moray....157 P9
Spilsby Lincs....87 M7
Spindlestone Nthumb....119 N4
Spinkhill Derbys....84 G5
Spinningdale Highld....162 G7
Spion Kop Notts....85 J7
Spirthill Wilts....33 J9
Spital Wirral....81 L8
Spital Hill Donc....85 K2
Spital in the Street Lincs....86 C2
Spithurst E Susx....25 K7
Spittal E Loth....128 D4
Spittal E R Yk....98 F10
Spittal Highld....167 L6
Spittal Nthumb....129 Q9
Spittal Pembks....41 J6
Spittalfield P & K....141 R9
Spittal of Glenmuick Abers....149 Q10
Spittal of Glenshee P & K....141 R4
Spittal-on-Rule Border....118 A7
Spixworth Norfk....77 J8
Splatt Cnwll....4 D4
Splatt Cnwll....5 L4
Splatt Cnwll....8 F3
Splayne's Green E Susx....25 K6
Splott Cardif....30 H9
Spofforth N York....97 N10
Spondon C Derb....72 C3
Spon Green Flints....69 J2
Spooner Row Norfk....64 F2
Sporle Norfk....76 A9
Spott E Loth....128 H4
Spottiswoode Border....128 G10
Spratton Nhants....60 F7
Spreakley Surrey....23 M6
Spreyton Devon....8 G5
Spriddlestone Devon....6 E8
Spridlington Lincs....86 D4
Springburn C Glas....125 Q4
Springfield D & G....110 F7
Springfield Essex....52 B10
Springfield Fife....135 J5
Springhill Staffs....58 E4
Springhill Staffs....58 G3
Springholm D & G....108 H6
Springside N Ayrs....125 K10
Springthorpe Lincs....85 Q3
Spring Vale Barns....90 H10
Springwell Sundld....113 L9
Sproatley E R Yk....93 L4
Sproston Green Ches W....82 F11
Sprotbrough Donc....91 N10
Sproughton Suffk....53 K3

Sprouston Border....118 E3
Sprowston Norfk....77 K9
Sproxton Leics....73 M6
Sproxton N York....98 C4
Spunhill Shrops....69 M8
Spurstow Ches E....69 Q3
Spyway Dorset....11 L6
Square and Compass
Pembks....40 F4
Stableford Shrops....57 P5
Stableford Staffs....70 E7
Stacey Bank Sheff....84 C2
Stackhouse N York....96 B7
Stackpole Pembks....41 J11
Stackpole Elidor Pembks....41 J11
Stacksford Norfk....64 F3
Stacksteads Lancs....89 P6
Staddiscombe C Plym....6 D7
Staddlethorpe E R Yk....92 D5
Staden Derbys....83 N10
Stadhampton Oxon....34 H5
Stadhlaigearraidh W Isls....168 c14
Staffield Cumb....101 P2
Staffin Highld....152 H4
Stafford Staffs....70 G10
Stafford Services
(northbound) Staffs....70 F8
Stafford Services
(southbound) Staffs....70 F8
Stagsden Bed....49 Q5
Stainborough Barns....91 J10
Stainburn Cumb....100 D5
Stainburn N York....97 L11
Stainby Lincs....73 N6
Staincross Barns....91 J8
Staindrop Dur....103 M6
Staines-upon-Thames
Surrey....36 B6
Stainfield Lincs....74 A4
Stainfield Lincs....86 F6
Stainforth Donc....91 Q8
Stainforth N York....96 B7
Staining Lancs....88 C3
Stainland Calder....90 D7
Stainsacre N York....105 P9
Stainsby Derbys....84 G7
Stainton Cumb....95 L3
Stainton Cumb....101 N5
Stainton Cumb....110 Q9
Stainton Donc....85 J2
Stainton Dur....103 L7
Stainton Middsb....104 E8
Stainton N York....103 M11
Stainton by Langworth
Lincs....86 E5
Staintondale N York....105 Q11
Stainton Grove Dur....103 L7
Stainton le Vale Lincs....86 G2
Stainton with Adgarley
Cumb....94 E6
Stair Cumb....100 H6
Stair E Ayrs....114 H3
Stairfoot Barns....91 K9
Stairhaven D & G....106 H7
Staithes N York....105 L7
Stakeford Nthumb....113 L3
Stake Pool Lancs....95 J11
Stakes Hants....15 J5
Stalbridge Dorset....20 D11
Stalbridge Weston Dorset....20 D11
Stalham Norfk....77 M6
Stalham Green Norfk....77 M7
Stalisfield Green Kent....38 G11
Stalland Common Norfk....64 E2
Stallen Dorset....20 B11
Stallingborough NE Lin....93 L8
Stalling Busk N York....96 D3
Stallington Staffs....70 G7
Stalmine Lancs....94 H11
Stalmine Moss Side Lancs....94 H11
Stalybridge Tamesd....83 L5
Stambourne Essex....52 B4
Stambourne Green Essex....51 Q3
Stamford Lincs....73 Q9
Stamford Nthumb....119 P7
Stamford Bridge Ches W....81 P11
Stamford Bridge E R Yk....98 E9
Stamfordham Nthumb....112 G6
Stamford Hill Gt Lon....36 H3
Stanah Lancs....88 D2
Stanborough Herts....50 F8
Stanbridge C Beds....49 Q10
Stanbridge Dorset....12 H4
Stanbury C Brad....90 C3
Stand Bury....89 M9
Stand N Lans....126 D4
Standburn Falk....126 G3
Standeford Staffs....58 D3
Standen Kent....26 E3
Standen Street Kent....26 D5
Standerwick Somset....20 F4
Standford Hants....23 M8
Standingstone Cumb....100 E4
Standish Gloucs....32 E3
Standish Wigan....88 H8
Standish Lower Ground
Wigan....88 H9
Standlake Oxon....34 C4
Standon Hants....22 D9
Standon Herts....51 J6
Standon Staffs....70 E7
Standon Green End Herts....51 J7
Standwell Green Suffk....64 G8
Stane N Lans....126 F6
Stanfield Norfk....76 C7
Stanford C Beds....50 E2
Stanford Kent....27 K4
Stanford Shrops....56 G2
Stanford Bishop Herefs....46 C4
Stanford Bridge Worcs....57 N11
Stanford Bridge Wrekin....70 C10
Stanford Dingley W Berk....34 G10
Stanford in the Vale Oxon....34 B6
Stanford le Hope Thurr....37 Q4
Stanford on Avon Nhants....60 C5
Stanford on Soar Notts....72 G6
Stanford on Teme Worcs....57 N11
Stanford Rivers Essex....51 M10
Stanfree Derbys....84 G6
Stanghow R & Cl....105 J7
Stanground C Pete....74 D11
Stanhill Lancs....89 L5
Stanhoe Norfk....75 R3
Stanhope Border....116 G5
Stanhope Dur....103 J3
Stanhope Kent....26 H3

Stanhope Bretby Derbys....71 P10
Stanion Nhants....61 K3
Stanklin Worcs....58 C10
Stanley Derbys....72 C2
Stanley Dur....113 J10
Stanley Notts....84 G8
Stanley P & K....141 R11
Stanley Shrops....57 N4
Stanley Staffs....70 G4
Stanley Wakefd....91 J6
Stanley Common Derbys....72 C2
Stanley Crook Dur....103 N3
Stanley Ferry Wakefd....91 K6
Stanley Gate Lancs....88 E9
Stanley Moor Staffs....70 G4
Stanley Pontlarge Gloucs....47 K8
Stanmer Br & H....24 H9
Stanmore Gt Lon....36 E2
Stanmore Hants....22 E9
Stanmore W Berk....34 E9
Stannersburn Nthumb....111 P3
Stanningfield Suffk....64 B10
Stanningley Leeds....90 H4
Stannington Nthumb....113 K5
Stannington Sheff....84 D3
Stannington Station Nthumb....113 K4
Stansbatch Herefs....45 L2
Stansfield Suffk....63 N10
Stanshope Staffs....71 L4
Stanstead Suffk....52 D2
Stanstead Abbotts Herts....51 J8
Stansted Kent....37 P8
Stansted Airport Essex....51 N6
Stansted Mountfitchet
Essex....51 M5
Stanton Derbys....71 P11
Stanton Gloucs....47 L8
Stanton Mons....45 L10
Stanton Nthumb....112 H2
Stanton Staffs....71 L5
Stanton Suffk....64 D7
Stanton by Bridge Derbys....72 B5
Stanton by Dale Derbys....72 D3
Stanton Cross Nhants....61 K7
Stanton Drew BaNES....19 Q2
Stanton Fitzwarren Swindn....33 N6
Stanton Harcourt Oxon....34 D3
Stanton Hill Notts....84 G8
Stanton in Peak Derbys....84 B8
Stanton Lacy Shrops....56 H9
Stanton Lees Derbys....84 C8
Stanton Long Shrops....57 K6
Stanton-on-the-Wolds
Notts....72 G4
Stanton Prior BaNES....20 C2
Stanton St Bernard Wilts....21 L2
Stanton St John Oxon....34 G3
Stanton St Quintin Wilts....32 H9
Stanton Street Suffk....64 D8
Stanton under Bardon Leics....72 D8
Stanton upon Hine Heath
Shrops....69 Q10
Stanton Wick BaNES....20 B2
Stantway Gloucs....32 C3
Stanwardine in the Field
Shrops....69 M10
Stanwardine in the Wood
Shrops....69 M9
Stanway Essex....52 F7
Stanway Gloucs....47 L8
Stanway Green Essex....52 G7
Stanway Green Suffk....65 J7
Stanwell Surrey....36 C6
Stanwell Moor Surrey....36 B6
Stanwick Nhants....61 L6
Stanwick St John N York....103 N8
Stanwix Cumb....110 H9
Staoinebrig W Isls....168 c14
Stape N York....98 F2
Stapehill Dorset....13 J4
Stapeley Ches E....70 B5
Stapenhill Staffs....71 P10
Staple Kent....39 N10
Staple Cross Devon....18 D10
Staplecross E Susx....26 C7
Staplefield W Susx....24 G5
Staple Fitzpaine Somset....19 J11
Stapleford Cambs....62 G10
Stapleford Herts....50 H7
Stapleford Leics....73 L7
Stapleford Lincs....85 Q9
Stapleford Notts....72 D3
Stapleford Wilts....21 L7
Stapleford Abbotts Essex....37 M2
Stapleford Tawney Essex....51 M11
Staplegrove Somset....18 H9
Staplehay Somset....18 H10
Staple Hill Worcs....58 E10
Staplehurst Kent....26 C3
Staplers IoW....14 F9
Staplestreet Kent....39 J9
Stapleton Cumb....111 K6
Stapleton Herefs....56 E11
Stapleton Leics....72 C11
Stapleton N York....103 Q8
Stapleton Shrops....56 H4
Stapleton Somset....19 N10
Stapley Somset....10 D2
Staploe Bed....61 Q8
Staplow Herefs....46 C6
Star Fife....135 J7
Star IoA....79 J10
Star Pembks....41 P4
Star Somset....19 M3
Starbeck N York....97 M9
Starbotton N York....96 E6
Starcross Devon....9 N8
Stareton Warwks....59 M10
Starkholmes Derbys....84 D9
Starlings Green Essex....51 L4
Starr's Green E Susx....26 C8
Starston Norfk....65 J5
Start Devon....7 L10
Startforth Dur....103 K7
Startley Wilts....32 H8
Statenborough Kent....39 N10
Statham Warrtn....82 E7
Stathe Somset....19 L9
Stathern Leics....73 K5
Station Town Dur....104 D3
Staughton Green Cambs....61 Q7
Staughton Highway Cambs....61 P8
Staunton Gloucs....31 Q2
Staunton Gloucs....46 E9
Staunton in the Vale Notts....73 L2
Staunton on Arrow Herefs....45 M2

Staunton on Wye Herefs....45 M6
Staveley Cumb....101 N11
Staveley Derbys....84 F6
Staveley N York....97 N8
Staveley-in-Cartmel Cumb....94 H3
Staverton Devon....7 K6
Staverton Gloucs....46 G10
Staverton Nhants....60 B8
Staverton Wilts....20 G2
Staverton Bridge Gloucs....46 G10
Stawell Somset....19 L7
Stawley Somset....18 E10
Staxigoe Highld....167 Q6
Staxton N York....99 L5
Staylittle Cerdgn....54 E7
Staylittle Powys....55 K6
Staynall Lancs....88 D2
Staythorpe Notts....85 N10
Stead C Brad....96 H11
Stean N York....96 G6
Stearsby N York....98 C6
Steart Somset....19 J5
Stebbing Essex....51 Q6
Stebbing Green Essex....51 Q6
Stechford Birm....58 H7
Stede Quarter Kent....26 E4
Stedham W Susx....23 N10
Steel Nthumb....112 D9
Steel Cross E Susx....25 M4
Steelend Fife....134 C9
Steele Road Border....111 K2
Steel Green Cumb....94 D5
Steel Heath Shrops....69 P7
Steen's Bridge Herefs....45 Q3
Steep Hants....23 K9
Steephill IoW....14 F11
Steep Lane Calder....90 C6
Steeple Dorset....12 F8
Steeple Essex....52 F11
Steeple Ashton Wilts....20 H3
Steeple Aston Oxon....48 E9
Steeple Barton Oxon....48 D10
Steeple Bumpstead Essex....51 Q2
Steeple Claydon Bucks....49 K9
Steeple Gidding Cambs....61 P4
Steeple Langford Wilts....21 K7
Steeple Morden Cambs....50 G2
Steep Marsh Hants....23 L9
Steeton C Brad....90 C2
Stein Highld....152 D6
Stella Gatesd....113 J8
Stelling Minnis Kent....27 K2
Stembridge Somset....19 M10
Stenalees Cnwll....4 G10
Stenhouse D & G....115 R9
Stenhousemuir Falk....133 P11
Stenigot Lincs....86 H4
Stenness Ork....169 c5
Stenscholl Highld....152 H4
Stenson Fields Derbys....72 A4
Stenton E Loth....128 G5
Steòrnabhagh W Isls....168 j4
Stepaside Pembks....41 M9
Stepford D & G....109 J4
Stepney Gt Lon....37 J4
Stepping Hill Stockp....83 K7
Steppingley C Beds....50 B3
Stepps N Lans....126 B4
Sternfield Suffk....65 M9
Stert Wilts....21 K3
Stetchworth Cambs....63 K9
Stevenage Herts....50 F5
Steven's Crouch E Susx....26 B8
Stevenston N Ayrs....124 H9
Steventon Hants....22 F5
Steventon Oxon....34 E6
Steventon End Essex....51 N2
Stevington Bed....49 Q4
Stewartby Bed....50 B2
Stewartfield S Lans....125 Q6
Stewarton Ag & B....120 C8
Stewarton E Ayrs....125 L8
Stewkley Bucks....49 N9
Stewley Somset....19 K11
Stewton Lincs....87 L3
Steyne Cross IoW....14 H9
Steyning W Susx....24 E8
Steynton Pembks....40 H9
Stibb Cnwll....16 C9
Stibbard Norfk....76 D6
Stibb Cross Devon....16 G9
Stibb Green Wilts....21 P2
Stibbington Cambs....74 A11
Stichill Border....118 D3
Sticker Cnwll....3 P3
Stickford Lincs....87 L8
Sticklepath Devon....8 F6
Sticklepath Somset....18 D7
Stickling Green Essex....51 L4
Stickney Lincs....87 K9
Stiffkey Norfk....76 D3
Stifford Clays Thurr....37 P4
Stifford's Bridge Herefs....46 D5
Stiff Street Kent....38 E9
Stile Bridge Kent....26 C2
Stileway Somset....19 N6
Stilligarry W Isls....168 c14
Stillingfleet N York....91 P2
Stillington N York....98 B7
Stillington S on T....104 C6
Stilton Cambs....61 Q3
Stinchcombe Gloucs....32 D5
Stinsford Dorset....11 Q6
Stiperstones Shrops....56 F4
Stirchley Birm....58 G8
Stirchley Wrekin....57 M3
Stirling Abers....159 R9
Stirling Stirlg....133 M9
Stirling Castle Stirlg....133 M9
Stirling Services Stirlg....133 N10
Stirtloe Cambs....61 Q7
Stirton N York....96 E10
Stisted Essex....52 D7
Stitchcombe Wilts....33 P11
Stithians Cnwll....3 J6
St Michaels Fife....135 L3
Stoak Ches W....81 N10
Stobo Border....116 H3
Stoborough Dorset....12 F7
Stoborough Green Dorset....12 F7
Stobs Castle Border....117 Q3
Stobswood Nthumb....119 P11
Stock Essex....51 Q11
Stock N Som....19 N2

Stockbridge Hants....22 C7
Stockbridge W Susx....15 N6
Stockbriggs S Lans....126 D10
Stockbury Kent....38 D9
Stockcross W Berk....34 D11
Stockdalewath Cumb....110 G11
Stocker's Head Kent....38 G11
Stockerston Leics....73 L11
Stock Green Worcs....47 J3
Stocking Herefs....46 B8
Stockingford Warwks....59 M6
Stocking Pelham Herts....51 L5
Stockland Devon....10 E4
Stockland Bristol Somset....18 H6
Stockland Green Kent....25 N2
Stockleigh English Devon....9 L3
Stockleigh Pomeroy Devon....9 L4
Stockley Wilts....33 J11
Stockley Hill Herefs....45 M7
Stocklinch Somset....19 L11
Stockmoor Herefs....45 M4
Stockport Stockp....83 J6
Stocksbridge Sheff....90 H11
Stocksfield Nthumb....112 G8
Stocksmoor Kirk....90 F8
Stockton Herefs....45 Q2
Stockton Norfk....65 M3
Stockton Shrops....56 D4
Stockton Shrops....57 N5
Stockton Warwks....48 C9
Stockton Wilts....21 J7
Stockton Wrekin....70 D11
Stockton Brook Staffs....70 G4
Stockton Heath Warrtn....82 D7
Stockton-on-Tees S on T....104 D7
Stockton on Teme Worcs....57 N11
Stockton on the Forest
C York....98 D9
Stockwell Gloucs....32 H2
Stockwell End Wolves....58 C4
Stockwell Heath Staffs....71 K10
Stockwood Bristl....32 B11
Stockwood Dorset....11 M3
Stock Wood Worcs....47 K3
Stodday Lancs....95 K9
Stodmarsh Kent....39 M9
Stody Norfk....76 F4
Stoer Highld....164 B11
Stoford Somset....11 M2
Stoford Wilts....21 L7
Stogumber Somset....18 E8
Stogursey Somset....18 H6
Stoke Covtry....59 N9
Stoke Devon....16 C7
Stoke Hants....15 K6
Stoke Hants....22 D4
Stoke Medway....38 D7
Stoke Abbott Dorset....11 K4
Stoke Albany Nhants....60 H3
Stoke Ash Suffk....64 G7
Stoke Bardolph Notts....72 G2
Stoke Bliss Worcs....46 C2
Stoke Bruerne Nhants....49 K5
Stoke-by-Clare Suffk....52 B3
Stoke-by-Nayland Suffk....52 G4
Stoke Canon Devon....9 M5
Stoke Charity Hants....22 E7
Stoke Climsland Cnwll....5 P7
Stoke Cross Herefs....46 B4
Stoke D'Abernon Surrey....36 D9
Stoke Doyle Nhants....61 M3
Stoke Dry Rutlnd....73 M11
Stoke Edith Herefs....46 B6
Stoke End Warwks....59 J5
Stoke Farthing Wilts....21 L9
Stoke Ferry Norfk....75 P10
Stoke Fleming Devon....7 M9
Stokeford Dorset....12 E7
Stoke Gabriel Devon....7 M7
Stoke Gifford S Glos....32 B9
Stoke Golding Leics....72 B11
Stoke Goldington M Keyn....49 M5
Stoke Green Bucks....35 Q8
Stokeham Notts....85 N5
Stoke Hammond Bucks....49 N9
Stoke Heath Shrops....70 B8
Stoke Heath Worcs....58 D11
Stoke Holy Cross Norfk....77 J11
Stokeinteignhead Devon....7 N4
Stoke Lacy Herefs....46 B5
Stoke Lyne Oxon....48 G9
Stoke Mandeville Bucks....35 M2
Stokenchurch Bucks....35 L5
Stoke Newington Gt Lon....36 H3
Stokenham Devon....7 L10
Stoke-on-Trent C Stke....70 F5
Stoke Orchard Gloucs....46 H9
Stoke Poges Bucks....35 Q8
Stoke Pound Worcs....58 E11
Stoke Prior Herefs....45 Q3
Stoke Prior Worcs....58 D11
Stoke Rivers Devon....17 L4
Stoke Rochford Lincs....73 N5
Stoke Row Oxon....35 J8
Stoke St Gregory Somset....19 K9
Stoke St Mary Somset....19 J10
Stoke St Michael Somset....20 C5
Stoke St Milborough Shrops....57 K8
Stokesay Shrops....56 G8
Stokesby Norfk....77 N9
Stokesley N York....104 F9
Stoke sub Hamdon Somset....19 N11
Stoke Talmage Oxon....35 J5
Stoke Trister Somset....20 D9
Stoke upon Tern Shrops....70 A9
Stoke-upon-Trent C Stke....70 F5
Stoke Wake Dorset....12 C3
Stoke Wharf Worcs....58 E11
Stolford Somset....18 H5
Stondon Massey Essex....51 N10
Stone Bucks....35 L2
Stone Gloucs....32 C5
Stone Kent....37 N6
Stone Rothm....85 J3
Stone Somset....19 Q8
Stone Staffs....70 G8
Stone Worcs....58 C9
Stonea Cambs....62 G2
Stone Allerton Somset....19 L4
Ston Easton Somset....20 B4
Stonebridge N Som....19 L3
Stonebridge Warwks....59 K8
Stone Bridge Corner C Pete....74 E10
Stonebroom Derbys....84 F9
Stone Chair Calder....90 E5

Stone Cross – Tallarn Green 295

Stone Cross E Susx 25 M5
Stone Cross E Susx 25 P10
Stone Cross E Susx 25 P4
Stone Cross Kent 25 M3
Stone Cross Kent 26 H4
Stone Cross Kent 39 P10
Stonecross Green Suffk 63 P9
Stonecrouch Kent 26 B5
Stone-edge-Batch N Som 31 N10
Stoneferry C KuH 93 K4
Stonefield Castle Hotel Ag & B 123 Q5
Stonegate E Susx 25 Q5
Stonegate N York 105 L9
Stonegrave N York 98 D5
Stonehall Worcs 46 G5
Stonehaugh Nthumb 111 Q5
Stonehaven Abers 151 M10
Stonehenge Wilts 21 M6
Stone Hill Donc 92 A9
Stonehouse C Plym 6 D8
Stone House Cumb 95 R3
Stonehouse Gloucs 32 F3
Stonehouse Nthumb 111 N9
Stonehouse S Lans 126 D8
Stone in Oxney Kent 26 F6
Stoneleigh Warwks 59 M10
Stoneley Green Ches E 69 R4
Stonely Cambs 61 P7
Stoner Hill Hants 23 K9
Stonesby Leics 73 L6
Stonesfield Oxon 48 C11
Stones Green Essex 53 L6
Stone Street Kent 37 N10
Stone Street Suffk 52 G4
Stone Street Suffk 52 H3
Stone Street Suffk 65 M5
Stonestreet Green Kent 27 J4
Stonethwaite Cumb 101 J8
Stonewells Moray 157 P4
Stonewood Kent 37 N6
Stoneybridge W Isls 168 c14
Stoneybridge Worcs 58 D9
Stoneyburn W Loth 126 H5
Stoney Cross Hants 13 N2
Stoneygate C Leic 72 G10
Stoneyhills Essex 38 G2
Stoneykirk D & G 106 E7
Stoney Middleton Derbys 84 B5
Stoney Stanton Leics 59 Q6
Stoney Stoke Somset 20 D8
Stoney Stratton Somset 20 C7
Stoney Stretton Shrops 56 F3
Stoneywood C Aber 151 M5
Stoneywood Falk 133 M11
Stonham Aspal Suffk 64 G10
Stonnall Staffs 58 G4
Stonor Oxon 35 K7
Stonton Wyville Leics 73 J11
Stonybreck Shet 169 t14
Stony Cross Herefs 46 D5
Stony Cross Herefs 57 J11
Stonyford Hants 22 B11
Stony Houghton Derbys 84 G7
Stony Stratford M Keyn 49 L6
Stonywell Staffs 58 G2
Stoodleigh Devon 17 M5
Stoodleigh Devon 18 B11
Stopham W Susx 24 B7
Stopsley Luton 50 D6
Stoptide Cnwll 4 E6
Storeton Wirral 81 L8
Storeyard Green Herefs 46 D6
Storey Arms Powys 44 D10
Stornoway W Isls 168 j4
Stornoway Airport W Isls 168 j4
Storridge Herefs 46 E5
Storrington W Susx 24 C8
Storth Cumb 95 K5
Storwood E R Yk 92 B2
Stotfield Moray 157 N3
Stotfold C Beds 50 F3
Stottesdon Shrops 57 M8
Stoughton Leics 72 G10
Stoughton Surrey 23 Q4
Stoughton W Susx 15 M4
Stoulton Worcs 46 H5
Stourbridge Dudley 58 C8
Stourhead Wilts 20 E8
Stourpaine Dorset 12 E3
Stourport-on-Severn Worcs 57 Q10
Stour Provost Dorset 20 E10
Stour Row Dorset 20 F10
Stourton Leeds 91 J4
Stourton Staffs 58 C8
Stourton Warwks 47 Q7
Stourton Wilts 20 E8
Stourton Caundle Dorset 20 D11
Stout Somset 19 M8
Stove Shet 169 r11
Stoven Suffk 65 N5
Stow Border 117 P2
Stow Lincs 85 Q4
Stow Bardolph Norfk 75 M9
Stow Bedon Norfk 64 D2
Stowbridge Norfk 75 M9
Stow-cum-Quy Cambs 62 H8
Stowe Gloucs 31 Q3
Stowe Shrops 56 E10
Stowe-by-Chartley Staffs 71 J9
Stowehill Nhants 60 D9
Stowell Somset 20 C10
Stowey BaNES 19 Q3
Stowford Devon 8 B5
Stowford Devon 8 B7
Stowford Devon 10 C7
Stowford Devon 17 M3
Stowlangtoft Suffk 64 D8
Stow Longa Cambs 61 P6
Stow Maries Essex 38 D2
Stowmarket Suffk 64 E10
Stow-on-the-Wold Gloucs 47 N9
Stowting Kent 27 K3
Stowting Common Kent 27 K3
Stowupland Suffk 64 F9
Straad Ag & B 124 C5
Straanruie Highld 148 H4
Strachan Abers 150 H9
Strachur Ag & B 131 M7
Stradbroke Suffk 65 J7
Stradbrook Wilts 20 H4
Stradishall Suffk 63 N10
Stradsett Norfk 75 N9
Stragglethorpe Lincs 86 B10
Stragglethorpe Notts 72 H3
Straight Soley Wilts 34 B10
Straiton Mdloth 127 P4
Straiton S Ayrs 114 G7
Straloch Abers 151 M3
Straloch P & K 141 P5
Stramshall Staffs 71 K7
Strang IoM 80 e6
Strangeways Salfd 82 H5
Strangford Herefs 46 A9
Stranraer D & G 106 E5
Strata Florida Cerdgn 54 G11
Stratfield Mortimer W Berk 23 J2
Stratfield Saye Hants 23 J2
Stratfield Turgis Hants 23 J3
Stratford C Beds 61 Q11
Stratford Gt Lon 37 J4
Stratford St Andrew Suffk 65 M9
Stratford St Mary Suffk 52 H5
Stratford sub Castle Wilts 21 M8
Stratford Tony Wilts 21 L9
Stratford-upon-Avon Warwks 47 P3
Strath Highld 160 B11
Strathan Highld 148 H2
Strathan Highld 165 N4
Strathaven S Lans 126 C9
Strathblane Stirlg 125 P2
Strathcanaird Highld 161 K6
Strathcarron Highld 154 B9
Strathcoil Ag & B 138 B11
Strathdon Abers 150 B5
Strathkinness Fife 135 M4
Strathloanhead W Loth 126 G3
Strathmashie House Highld 147 P9
Strathmiglo Fife 134 G6
Strathpeffer Highld 155 N6
Strathtay P & K 141 M7
Strathwhillan N Ayrs 121 K4
Strathy Highld 166 D4
Strathy Inn Highld 166 D3
Strathyre Stirlg 132 H4
Stratton Cnwll 16 C10
Stratton Dorset 11 P6
Stratton Gloucs 33 K4
Stratton Audley Oxon 48 H9
Stratton-on-the-Fosse Somset 20 C4
Stratton St Margaret Swindn 33 N7
Stratton St Michael Norfk 65 J3
Stratton Strawless Norfk 77 J7
Stream Somset 18 E7
Streat E Susx 25 J7
Streatham Gt Lon 36 H6
Streatley C Beds 50 C5
Streatley W Berk 34 G8
Street Devon 10 D7
Street Lancs 95 L10
Street N York 105 K10
Street Somset 19 N7
Street Ashton Warwks 59 Q8
Street Dinas Shrops 69 K7
Street End E Susx 25 P6
Street End Kent 39 K11
Street End W Susx 15 N7
Street Gate Gatesd 113 K9
Streethay Staffs 58 H2
Street Houses N York 98 A11
Streetlam N York 104 B11
Street Lane Derbys 84 E11
Streetly Wsall 58 G5
Streetly End Cambs 63 K11
Street on the Fosse Somset 20 B7
Strefford Shrops 56 G7
Strelitz P & K 142 B10
Strelley Notts 72 E2
Strensall C York 98 C8
Strensham Worcs 46 H6
Strensham Services (northbound) Worcs 46 G6
Strensham Services (southbound) Worcs 46 H6
Stretcholt Somset 19 J6
Strete Devon 7 L9
Stretford Herefs 45 N3
Stretford Herefs 45 Q3
Stretford Traffd 82 G6
Strethall Essex 51 L3
Stretham Cambs 62 H6
Strettington W Susx 15 N5
Stretton Ches W 69 M4
Stretton Derbys 84 E8
Stretton Rutlnd 73 N7
Stretton Staffs 58 C2
Stretton Staffs 71 P9
Stretton Warrtn 82 D8
Stretton en le Field Leics 59 M2
Stretton Grandison Herefs 46 B6
Stretton-on-Dunsmore Warwks 59 P10
Stretton on Fosse Warwks 47 P7
Stretton Sugwas Herefs 45 P6
Stretton under Fosse Warwks 59 Q8
Stretton Westwood Shrops 57 K5
Strichen Abers 159 M6
Strines Stockp 83 L7
Stringston Somset 18 G6
Strixton Nhants 61 K8
Stroat Gloucs 31 Q5
Strollamus Highld 145 J2
Stroma Highld 167 Q1
Stromeferry Highld 153 R11
Stromness Ork 169 b6
Stronaba Highld 146 G11
Stronachlachar Stirlg 132 E5
Stronafian Ag & B 131 L11
Stronchrubie Highld 161 L3
Strone Ag & B 131 P11
Strone Highld 146 E11
Strone Highld 147 N2
Stronmilchan Ag & B 131 P2
Stronsay Ork 169 f4
Stronsay Airport Ork 169 f4
Strontian Highld 138 E5
Strood Kent 26 E5
Strood Medway 38 B8
Strood Green Surrey 36 F11
Strood Green W Susx 24 B6
Stroud Gloucs 32 G3
Stroud Hants 23 K10
Stroude Surrey 36 B7
Stroud Green Essex 38 E3
Stroud Green Gloucs 32 F3
Stroxton Lincs 73 N4
Struan Highld 152 E10
Struan P & K 141 K4
Strubby Lincs 87 N4
Strumpshaw Norfk 77 L10
Strutherhill S Lans 126 D8
Struthers Fife 135 K6
Struy Highld 155 M9
Stryd-y-Facsen IoA 78 E8
Stuartfield Abers 159 N8
Stubbers Green Wsall 58 F4
Stubbington Hants 14 G6
Stubbins Lancs 89 M7
Stubbs Cross Kent 26 G4
Stubbs Green Norfk 65 K2
Stubhampton Dorset 12 F2
Stubley Derbys 84 D5
Stubshaw Cross Wigan 82 C5
Stubton Lincs 85 Q11
Stuckton Hants 13 L2
Studfold N York 96 B7
Stud Green W & M 35 N9
Studham C Beds 50 B7
Studholme Cumb 110 E9
Studland Dorset 12 H8
Studlands Park Suffk 63 K7
Studley Warwks 47 L2
Studley Wilts 33 J10
Studley Common Warwks 47 L2
Studley Roger N York 97 L7
Studley Royal N York 97 L6
Studley Royal Park & Fountains Abbey N York 97 L7
Stuntney Cambs 63 J5
Stunts Green E Susx 25 P8
Sturbridge Staffs 70 E8
Sturgate Lincs 85 Q3
Sturmer Essex 51 Q2
Sturminster Common Dorset 12 C2
Sturminster Marshall Dorset 12 G4
Sturminster Newton Dorset 12 C2
Sturry Kent 39 L9
Sturton N Linc 92 G10
Sturton by Stow Lincs 85 Q4
Sturton le Steeple Notts 85 N4
Stuston Suffk 64 G6
Stutton N York 91 M2
Stutton Suffk 53 L5
Styal Ches E 82 H8
Stydd Lancs 89 K3
Stynie Moray 157 Q5
Styrrup Notts 85 K2
Succoth Ag & B 132 B6
Suckley Worcs 46 D4
Suckley Green Worcs 46 D4
Sudborough Nhants 61 L4
Sudbourne Suffk 65 N11
Sudbrook Lincs 73 P2
Sudbrook Mons 31 P7
Sudbrooke Lincs 86 D5
Sudbury Derbys 71 M8
Sudbury Gt Lon 36 E3
Sudbury Suffk 52 E3
Sudden Rochdl 89 P8
Sudgrove Gloucs 32 H3
Suffield N York 99 K2
Suffield Norfk 77 J5
Sugdon Wrekin 69 R11
Sugnall Staffs 70 D8
Sugwas Pool Herefs 45 P6
Suisnish Highld 145 J4
Sulby IoM 80 e3
Sulgrave Nhants 48 G6
Sulham W Berk 34 H10
Sulhamstead W Berk 34 H11
Sulhamstead Abbots W Berk 34 H11
Sulhamstead Bannister W Berk 34 H11
Sullington W Susx 24 C8
Sullom Shet 169 q6
Sullom Voe Shet 169 r6
Sully V Glam 30 G11
Sumburgh Airport Shet 169 q12
Summerbridge N York 97 K8
Summercourt Cnwll 4 D10
Summerfield Norfk 75 Q3
Summerfield Worcs 58 B10
Summer Heath Bucks 35 K6
Summerhill Pembks 41 N9
Summerhill Staffs 58 G3
Summer Hill Wrexhm 69 K4
Summerhouse Darltn 103 P7
Summerlands Cumb 95 L3
Summerley Derbys 84 E5
Summersdale W Susx 15 N5
Summerseat Bury 89 M8
Summertown Oxon 34 F3
Summit Oldham 89 Q9
Summit Rochdl 89 Q7
Sunbiggin Cumb 102 C9
Sunbury-on-Thames Surrey 36 D7
Sundaywell D & G 108 H4
Sunderland Ag & B 122 B7
Sunderland Cumb 100 G3
Sunderland Lancs 95 J9
Sunderland Sundld 113 N9
Sunderland Bridge Dur 103 Q3
Sundhope Border 117 L5
Sundon Park Luton 50 C5
Sundridge Kent 37 L9
Sunk Island E R Yk 93 N7
Sunningdale W & M 35 Q11
Sunninghill W & M 35 P11
Sunningwell Oxon 34 E4
Sunniside Dur 103 M3
Sunniside Gatesd 113 K9
Sunny Brow Dur 103 N4
Sunnyhill C Derb 72 A4
Sunnyhurst Bl w D 89 K6
Sunnylaw Stirlg 133 M8
Sunnymead Oxon 34 F3
Sunton Wilts 21 P4
Surbiton Gt Lon 36 E7
Surfleet Lincs 74 E5
Surfleet Seas End Lincs 74 E5
Surlingham Norfk 77 L10
Surrex Essex 52 E7
Sustead Norfk 76 H4
Susworth Lincs 92 D10
Sutcombe Devon 16 E9
Sutcombemill Devon 16 E9
Suton Norfk 64 F2
Sutterby Lincs 87 L6
Sutterton Lincs 74 E3
Sutton C Beds 62 B11
Sutton C Pete 74 A11
Sutton Cambs 62 F5
Sutton Devon 7 J10
Sutton Devon 8 H4
Sutton Donc 91 P8
Sutton E Susx 25 L11
Sutton Gt Lon 36 G8
Sutton Kent 27 P2
Sutton N York 91 M5
Sutton Norfk 77 M7
Sutton Notts 73 K3
Sutton Oxon 34 D3
Sutton Pembks 40 H7
Sutton Shrops 57 J2
Sutton Shrops 57 N7
Sutton Shrops 69 L9
Sutton Shrops 70 B8
Sutton St Hel 82 B6
Sutton Staffs 70 D10
Sutton Suffk 53 P2
Sutton W Susx 23 Q11
Sutton Abinger Surrey 36 D11
Sutton-at-Hone Kent 37 N7
Sutton Bassett Nhants 60 G2
Sutton Benger Wilts 32 H9
Sutton Bingham Somset 11 L2
Sutton Bonington Notts 72 E6
Sutton Bridge Lincs 75 J6
Sutton Cheney Leics 72 C10
Sutton Coldfield Birm 58 H5
Sutton Courtenay Oxon 34 F6
Sutton Crosses Lincs 74 H6
Sutton cum Lound Notts 85 L4
Sutton Fields Notts 72 D5
Sutton Green Surrey 36 B10
Sutton Green Wrexhm 69 M5
Sutton Heath Suffk 53 P2
Sutton Howgrave N York 97 M5
Sutton-in-Ashfield Notts 84 G9
Sutton-in-Craven N York 90 C2
Sutton in the Elms Leics 60 B2
Sutton Lane Ends Ches E 83 K10
Sutton Maddock Shrops 57 N4
Sutton Mallet Somset 19 L7
Sutton Mandeville Wilts 21 J9
Sutton Manor St Hel 81 Q6
Sutton Marsh Herefs 45 R6
Sutton Montis Somset 20 B10
Sutton-on-Hull C KuH 93 K4
Sutton on Sea Lincs 87 P4
Sutton-on-the-Forest N York 98 B8
Sutton on the Hill Derbys 71 N8
Sutton on Trent Notts 85 N7
Sutton Poyntz Dorset 11 Q8
Sutton St Edmund Lincs 74 G8
Sutton St James Lincs 74 G7
Sutton St Nicholas Herefs 45 Q5
Sutton Scotney Hants 22 E7
Sutton Street Kent 38 D10
Sutton-under-Brailes Warwks 48 B7
Sutton-under-Whitestonecliffe N York 97 Q4
Sutton upon Derwent E R Yk 98 E11
Sutton Valence Kent 26 D2
Sutton Veny Wilts 20 H6
Sutton Waldron Dorset 20 G11
Sutton Weaver Ches W 82 B9
Sutton Wick BaNES 19 Q3
Sutton Wick Oxon 34 E6
Swaby Lincs 87 L5
Swadlincote Derbys 71 P11
Swaffham Norfk 75 R9
Swaffham Bulbeck Cambs 63 J8
Swaffham Prior Cambs 63 J8
Swafield Norfk 77 K5
Swainby N York 104 E10
Swainshill Herefs 45 P6
Swainsthorpe Norfk 77 J11
Swainswick BaNES 32 E11
Swalcliffe Oxon 48 C7
Swalecliffe Kent 39 K8
Swallow Lincs 93 L10
Swallow Beck Lincs 86 B7
Swallowcliffe Wilts 21 J9
Swallowfield Wokham 23 K2
Swallownest Rothm 84 G3
Swallows Cross Essex 51 P11
Swampton Hants 22 D4
Swanage Dorset 12 H9
Swanbourne Bucks 49 M9
Swanbridge V Glam 30 G11
Swancote Shrops 57 N6
Swan Green Ches W 82 F10
Swanland E R Yk 92 G5
Swanley Kent 37 M7
Swanley Village Kent 37 M7
Swanmore Hants 22 G11
Swannington Leics 72 C7
Swannington Norfk 76 G8
Swanpool Lincs 86 C7
Swanscombe Kent 37 P6
Swansea Swans 29 J6
Swansea Airport Swans 28 G6
Swansea West Services Swans 28 H5
Swan Street Essex 52 E6
Swanton Abbot Norfk 77 K6
Swanton Morley Norfk 76 E8
Swanton Novers Norfk 76 E5
Swanton Street Kent 38 E10
Swan Valley Nhants 60 F9
Swan Village Sandw 58 E6
Swanwick Derbys 84 F10
Swanwick Hants 14 F5
Swarby Lincs 73 Q2
Swardeston Norfk 77 J11
Swarkestone Derbys 72 B5
Swarland Nthumb 119 N10
Swarraton Hants 22 G7
Swartha C Brad 96 G11
Swarthmoor Cumb 94 F5
Swaton Lincs 74 B3
Swavesey Cambs 62 E7
Sway Hants 13 N5
Swayfield Lincs 73 P6
Swaythling C Sotn 22 D11
Sweet Green Worcs 46 B2
Sweetham Devon 9 L5
Sweethaws E Susx 25 M5
Sweetlands Corner Kent 26 C2
Sweets Cnwll 5 K2
Sweetshouse Cnwll 4 H9
Swefling Suffk 65 L9
Swepstone Leics 72 B8
Swerford Oxon 48 C8
Swettenham Ches E 82 H11
Swffryd Blae G 30 H5
Swift's Green Kent 26 E3
Swilland Suffk 64 H11
Swillbrook Lancs 88 F4
Swillington Leeds 91 K4
Swimbridge Devon 17 L5
Swimbridge Newland Devon 17 L5
Swinbrook Oxon 33 Q2
Swincliffe Kirk 90 G5
Swincliffe N York 97 K9
Swincombe Devon 17 M3
Swindale Cumb 101 P8
Swinden N York 96 C10
Swinderby Lincs 85 Q8
Swindon Gloucs 46 H9
Swindon Nthumb 119 J11
Swindon Staffs 58 C6
Swindon Swindn 33 M8
Swine E R Yk 93 K3
Swinefleet E R Yk 92 C6
Swineford S Glos 32 C11
Swineshead Bed 61 N7
Swineshead Lincs 74 D2
Swineshead Bridge Lincs 74 D2
Swiney Highld 167 M9
Swinford Leics 60 C5
Swinford Oxon 34 D3
Swingate Notts 72 E2
Swingfield Minnis Kent 27 M3
Swingfield Street Kent 27 M3
Swingleton Green Suffk 52 G2
Swinhoe Nthumb 119 P5
Swinhope Lincs 93 M11
Swinithwaite N York 96 F3
Swinmore Common Herefs 46 C6
Swinscoe Staffs 71 L5
Swinside Cumb 100 H6
Swinstead Lincs 73 Q6
Swinthorpe Lincs 86 E4
Swinton Border 129 L10
Swinton N York 97 K5
Swinton N York 98 F6
Swinton Rothm 91 M11
Swinton Salfd 82 G4
Swiss Valley Carmth 28 F4
Swithland Leics 72 F8
Swordale Highld 155 Q4
Swordland Highld 145 N9
Swordly Highld 166 B4
Sworton Heath Ches E 82 E8
Swyddffynnon Cerdgn 54 F11
Swyncombe Oxon 35 J6
Swynnerton Staffs 70 F7
Swyre Dorset 11 L7
Sycharth Powys 68 H9
Sychnant Powys 55 M9
Sychtyn Powys 55 M3
Sydallt Wrexhm 69 K3
Syde Gloucs 33 J2
Sydenham Gt Lon 37 J6
Sydenham Oxon 35 K4
Sydenham Damerel Devon 5 Q6
Sydenhurst Surrey 23 Q8
Syderstone Norfk 76 A5
Sydling St Nicholas Dorset 11 N5
Sydmonton Hants 22 E3
Sydnal Lane Shrops 57 Q3
Syerston Notts 85 M11
Syke Rochdl 89 P7
Sykehouse Donc 91 Q7
Syleham Suffk 65 J6
Sylen Carmth 28 F3
Symbister Shet 169 s7
Symington S Ayrs 125 K11
Symington S Lans 116 D3
Symondsbury Dorset 11 J6
Symonds Yat (East) Herefs 45 R11
Symonds Yat (West) Herefs 45 R11
Sympson Green C Brad 90 F3
Synderford Dorset 10 H4
Synod Inn Cerdgn 42 H4
Syre Highld 165 Q8
Syreford Gloucs 47 K10
Syresham Nhants 48 H6
Syston Leics 72 G8
Syston Lincs 73 N2
Sytchampton Worcs 58 B11
Sywell Nhants 60 H7

T

Tabley Hill Ches E 82 F9
Tackley Oxon 48 E11
Tacolneston Norfk 64 G2
Tadcaster N York 91 M2
Taddington Derbys 83 P10
Taddington Gloucs 47 L8
Taddiport Devon 16 H8
Tadley Hants 22 H2
Tadlow Cambs 62 C11
Tadmarton Oxon 48 C7
Tadpole Swindn 33 M6
Tadwick BaNES 32 D10
Tadworth Surrey 36 F9
Tafarnaubach Blae G 30 F2
Tafarn-y-bwlch Pembks 41 L4
Tafarn-y-Gelyn Denbgs 68 G2
Taff's Well Cardif 30 F8
Tafolwern Powys 55 K4
Taibach Neath 29 L7
Tain Highld 162 H10
Tain Highld 167 M3
Tai'n Lôn Gwynd 66 G4
Tai'r Bull Powys 44 D9
Tairgwaith Neath 29 K2
Takeley Essex 51 N6
Takeley Street Essex 51 M6
Talachddu Powys 44 F8
Talacre Flints 80 G8
Talaton Devon 9 Q5
Talbenny Pembks 40 F8
Talbot Green Rhondd 30 D8
Talbot Village BCP 13 J6
Taleford Devon 10 B5
Talerddig Powys 55 L4
Talgarreg Cerdgn 42 H4
Talgarth Powys 44 H8
Talisker Highld 152 E11
Talke Staffs 70 E4
Talke Pits Staffs 70 E4
Talkin Cumb 111 L9
Talladale Highld 154 B3
Talla Linnfoots Border 116 G6
Tallaminnock S Ayrs 114 H8
Tallarn Green Wrexhm 69 M6

296 Tallentire – Tile Hill

Tallentire Cumb 100 F3
Talley Carmth 43 M8
Tallington Lincs 74 A9
Tallwrn Wrexhm 69 J5
Talmine Highld 165 N4
Talog Carmth 42 F9
Talsarn Cerdgn 43 K3
Talsarnau Gwynd 67 L7
Talskiddy Cnwll 4 E8
Talwrn IoA 78 H9
Talwrn Wrexhm 69 L5
Tal-y-bont Cerdgn 54 F7
Tal-y-Bont Conwy 79 P11
Talybont Gwynd 67 K10
Tal-y-bont Gwynd 79 L10
Talybont-on-Usk Powys 44 G10
Tal-y-Cafn Conwy 79 P10
Tal-y-coed Mons 45 N11
Tal-y-garn Rhondd 30 D9
Tal-y-llyn Gwynd 54 G3
Talysarn Gwynd 66 H4
Tal-y-Waun Torfn 31 J4
Talywern Powys 55 J4
Tamar Valley Mining District Devon 6 C5
Tamer Lane End Wigan 82 D4
Tamerton Foliot C Plym 6 D6
Tamworth Staffs 59 K4
Tamworth Green Lincs 74 G2
Tamworth Services Warwks 59 K4
Tancred N York 97 Q9
Tancredston Pembks 40 G5
Tandridge Surrey 37 J10
Tanfield Dur 113 J9
Tanfield Lea Dur 113 J10
Tangasdale W Isls 168 b17
Tangiers Pembks 41 J7
Tangley Hants 22 B4
Tangmere W Susx 15 P5
Tan Hill N York 102 G9
Tankerness Ork 169 e6
Tankersley Barns 91 J11
Tankerton Kent 39 K8
Tannach Highld 167 P7
Tannachie Abers 151 K11
Tannadice Angus 142 H6
Tanner's Green Worcs 58 G10
Tannington Suffk 65 J8
Tannochside N Lans 126 C5
Tansley Derbys 84 D9
Tansor Nhants 61 N2
Tantobie Dur 113 J10
Tanton N York 104 F8
Tanwood Worcs 58 D10
Tanworth in Arden Warwks 58 H10
Tan-y-Bwlch Gwynd 67 M6
Tan-y-fron Conwy 68 C2
Tan-y-fron Wrexhm 69 J4
Tan-y-grisiau Gwynd 67 M5
Tan-y-groes Cerdgn 42 E5
Taobh Tuath W Isls 168 e9
Taplow Bucks 35 P8
Tarbert Ag & B 123 L9
Tarbert Ag & B 123 Q6
Tarbert W Isls 168 g7
Tarbet Ag & B 132 C7
Tarbet Highld 145 N9
Tarbet Highld 164 E7
Tarbock Green Knows 81 P7
Tarbolton S Ayrs 114 H2
Tarbrax S Lans 127 J6
Tardebigge Worcs 58 E11
Tarfside Angus 142 H2
Tarland Abers 150 D7
Tarleton Lancs 88 F6
Tarlscough Lancs 88 E8
Tarlton Gloucs 33 J5
Tarnock Somset 19 L4
Tarns Cumb 109 P11
Tarnside Cumb 95 J2
Tarporley Ches W 69 Q2
Tarr Somset 17 R5
Tarrant Crawford Dorset 12 F4
Tarrant Gunville Dorset 12 F2
Tarrant Hinton Dorset 12 F2
Tarrant Keyneston Dorset 12 F4
Tarrant Launceston Dorset 12 F3
Tarrant Monkton Dorset 12 F3
Tarrant Rawston Dorset 12 F3
Tarrant Rushton Dorset 12 F3
Tarring Neville E Susx 25 K10
Tarrington Herefs 46 B6
Tarskavaig Highld 145 J5
Tarves Abers 159 L11
Tarvin Ches W 81 P11
Tarvin Sands Ches W 81 P11
Tasburgh Norfk 65 J2
Tasley Shrops 57 M6
Taston Oxon 48 C10
Tatenhill Staffs 71 N10
Tathall End M Keyn 49 M5
Tatham Lancs 95 N7
Tathwell Lincs 87 K4
Tatsfield Surrey 37 K9
Tattenhall Ches W 69 N3
Tatterford Norfk 76 B6
Tattersett Norfk 76 A6
Tattershall Lincs 86 H9
Tattershall Bridge Lincs 86 G9
Tattershall Thorpe Lincs 86 H9
Tattingstone Suffk 53 K4
Tattingstone White Horse Suffk 53 K4
Tatton Park Ches E 82 F8
Tatworth Somset 10 G3
Tauchers Moray 157 R8
Taunton Somset 18 H10
Taunton Deane Services Somset 18 G10
Taverham Norfk 76 H9
Taverners Green Essex 51 N7
Tavernspite Pembks 41 N8
Tavistock Devon 6 D4
Tavistock Devon 6 D4
Taw Green Devon 8 G5
Tawstock Devon 17 K6
Taxal Derbys 83 M9
Tay Bridge C Dund 135 L2
Taychreggan Hotel Ag & B 131 L3
Tay Forest Park P & K 141 J5
Tayinloan Ag & B 123 L10
Taynton Gloucs 46 D10
Taynton Oxon 33 P2
Taynuilt Ag & B 139 J11
Tayport Fife 135 M2
Tayvallich Ag & B 130 E10
Tealby Lincs 86 G2
Tealing Angus 142 G10
Team Valley Gatesd 113 K9
Teangue Highld 145 L6
Teanord Highld 155 Q5
Tebay Cumb 102 B10
Tebay Services Cumb 102 B9
Tebworth C Beds 49 Q9
Tedburn St Mary Devon 9 K6
Teddington Gloucs 47 J8
Teddington Gt Lon 36 E6
Tedstone Delamere Herefs 46 C3
Tedstone Wafer Herefs 46 C3
Teesport R & Cl 104 F6
Teesside International Airport S on T 104 C8
Teesside Park S on T 104 E7
Teeton Nhants 60 E6
Teffont Evias Wilts 21 J8
Teffont Magna Wilts 21 J8
Tegryn Pembks 41 P4
Teigh Rutlnd 73 M7
Teigncombe Devon 8 G7
Teigngrace Devon 7 M4
Teignmouth Devon 7 N4
Teindside Border 117 N9
Telford Wrekin 57 M3
Telford Services Shrops 57 N3
Telham E Susx 26 C9
Tellisford Somset 20 F3
Telscombe E Susx 25 K10
Telscombe Cliffs E Susx 25 K10
Tempar P & K 140 G6
Templand D & G 109 N3
Temple Cnwll 5 J7
Temple Mdloth 127 Q6
Temple Balsall Solhll 59 K9
Temple Bar Cerdgn 43 K4
Temple Cloud BaNES 20 B3
Templecombe Somset 20 D10
Temple End Suffk 63 L10
Temple Ewell Kent 27 N3
Temple Grafton Warwks 47 M3
Temple Guiting Gloucs 47 L9
Temple Herdewyke Warwks 48 C4
Temple Hirst N York 91 Q6
Temple Normanton Derbys 84 F7
Temple of Fiddes Abers 151 L11
Temple Sowerby Cumb 102 B5
Templeton Devon 9 L2
Templeton Pembks 41 M8
Templetown Dur 112 H10
Tempsford C Beds 61 Q10
Tenbury Wells Worcs 57 K11
Tenby Pembks 41 M10
Tendring Essex 53 K7
Tendring Green Essex 53 K6
Tendring Heath Essex 53 K6
Ten Mile Bank Norfk 75 L11
Tenpenny Heath Essex 53 J7
Tenterden Kent 26 E5
Terling Essex 52 C8
Tern Wrekin 69 R11
Ternhill Shrops 70 A8
Terregles D & G 109 K5
Terrington N York 98 D6
Terrington St Clement Norfk 75 L6
Terrington St John Norfk 75 K8
Terry's Green Warwks 58 H10
Teston Kent 38 B11
Testwood Hants 14 C4
Tetbury Gloucs 32 G6
Tetbury Upton Gloucs 32 G5
Tetchill Shrops 69 L8
Tetcott Devon 5 N2
Tetford Lincs 87 K6
Tetney Lincs 93 P10
Tetney Lock Lincs 93 P10
Tetsworth Oxon 35 J4
Tettenhall Wolves 58 C4
Tettenhall Wood Wolves 58 C5
Teversal Notts 84 G8
Teversham Cambs 62 G9
Teviothead Border 117 N9
Tewin Herts 50 G8
Tewin Wood Herts 50 G7
Tewkesbury Gloucs 46 G8
Teynham Kent 38 G9
Thackley C Brad 90 F3
Thackthwaite Cumb 100 F6
Thackthwaite Cumb 101 M5
Thainstone Abers 151 K4
Thakeham W Susx 24 D7
Thame Oxon 35 K3
Thames Ditton Surrey 36 E7
Thamesmead Gt Lon 37 L4
Thamesport Medway 38 E7
Thanington Kent 39 K10
Thankerton S Lans 116 D3
Tharston Norfk 64 H3
Thatcham W Berk 34 F11
Thatto Heath St Hel 81 Q6
Thaxted Essex 51 P4
Theakston N York 97 M3
Thealby N Linc 92 E7
Theale Somset 19 N5
Theale W Berk 34 H10
Thearne E R Yk 93 J3
The Bank Ches E 70 E3
The Beeches Gloucs 33 K4
Theberton Suffk 65 N8
The Blythe Staffs 71 J9
The Bog Shrops 56 F5
The Bourne Worcs 47 J3
The Braes Highld 153 J11
The Bratch Staffs 58 C6
The Bridge Kent 37 M5
The Broad Herefs 45 P2
The Broads 77 P10
The Brunt E Loth 128 H5
The Bryn Mons 31 K3
The Bungalow IoM 80 e4
The Burf Worcs 57 Q11
The Camp Gloucs 32 H3
The Chequer Wrexhm 69 N6
The City Bed 61 P9
The City Bucks 35 L5
The Common Oxon 47 Q9
The Common Wilts 21 P8
The Common Wilts 33 K7
The Corner Kent 26 B3
The Cronk IoM 80 d2
Theddingworth Leics 60 E3
Theddlethorpe All Saints Lincs 87 N3
Theddlethorpe St Helen Lincs 87 N3
The Deep C KuH 93 J5
The Den N Ayrs 125 J7
The Forge Herefs 45 L3
The Forstal Kent 26 H4
The Fouralls Shrops 70 B8
The Green Cumb 94 D4
The Green Essex 52 C8
The Green N York 105 L9
The Green Wilts 20 G8
The Grove Dur 112 G10
The Grove Worcs 46 G6
The Haven W Susx 24 C4
The Haw Gloucs 46 F9
The Hendre Mons 31 N2
The Hill Cumb 94 D4
The Holt Wokham 35 M9
The Hundred Herefs 45 Q2
Thelbridge Cross Devon 9 J2
The Leacon Kent 26 G5
The Lee Bucks 35 P4
The Lhen IoM 80 e1
Thelnetham Suffk 64 E6
The Lochs Moray 157 Q5
Thelveton Norfk 64 H5
Thelwall Warrtn 82 E7
The Marsh Powys 56 E5
Themelthorpe Norfk 76 F7
The Middles Dur 113 K10
The Moor Kent 26 C6
The Mumbles Swans 28 H7
The Murray S Lans 125 Q7
The Mythe Gloucs 46 G8
The Narth Mons 31 P3
The Neuk Abers 151 J8
Thenford Nhants 48 F6
Theobald's Green Wilts 33 K11
The Quarry Gloucs 32 D5
The Quarter Kent 26 E3
The Reddings Gloucs 46 H10
Therfield Herts 50 H3
The Rhôs Powys 44 H8
The Ross P & K 133 M3
The Sands Surrey 23 N5
The Shoe Wilts 32 F10
The Smithies Shrops 57 M5
The Spring Warwks 59 L10
The Square Torfn 31 J5
The Stair Kent 37 P11
The Stocks Kent 26 F6
The Straits Hants 23 L7
The Strand Wilts 20 H3
Thetford Norfk 64 B5
Thetford Forest Park 63 P3
Thethwaite Cumb 101 L2
The Towans Cnwll 2 F6
The Town IoS 2 b1
The Vauld Herefs 45 Q5
The Wyke Shrops 57 N3
Theydon Bois Essex 51 K11
Theydon Mount Essex 51 L11
Thicket Priory N York 92 A2
Thickwood Wilts 32 F10
Thimbleby Lincs 86 H6
Thimbleby N York 104 D11
Thingwall Wirral 81 K8
Thirkleby N York 97 Q5
Thirlby N York 97 Q4
Thirlestane Border 128 F10
Thirn N York 97 K3
Thirsk N York 97 P4
Thirtleby E R Yk 93 L4
Thistleton Lancs 88 E3
Thistleton Rutlnd 73 N7
Thistley Green Suffk 63 L5
Thixendale N York 98 G8
Thockrington Nthumb 112 E5
Tholomas Drove Cambs 74 H9
Tholthorpe N York 97 Q7
Thomas Chapel Pembks 41 M9
Thomas Close Cumb 101 M2
Thomastown Abers 158 E10
Thompson Norfk 64 C2
Thomshill Moray 157 N6
Thong Kent 37 Q6
Thongsbridge Kirk 90 F9
Thoralby N York 96 F3
Thoresby Notts 85 K6
Thoresthorpe Lincs 87 N5
Thoresway Lincs 93 L11
Thorganby Lincs 93 M11
Thorganby N York 92 A2
Thorgill N York 105 K11
Thorington Suffk 65 N7
Thorington Street Suffk 52 H4
Thorlby N York 96 E10
Thorley Herts 51 L7
Thorley IoW 14 C9
Thorley Houses Herts 51 L6
Thorley Street IoW 14 C9
Thormanby N York 97 Q6
Thornaby-on-Tees S on T 104 E7
Thornage Norfk 76 F4
Thornborough Bucks 49 K8
Thornborough N York 97 L5
Thornbury C Brad 90 F4
Thornbury Devon 16 G10
Thornbury Herefs 46 B3
Thornbury S Glos 32 B6
Thornby Cumb 110 E10
Thornby Nhants 60 E5
Thorncliff Staffs 71 J3
Thorncombe Dorset 10 H4
Thorncombe Street Surrey 23 Q6
Thorncott Green C Beds 61 Q11
Thorncross IoW 14 D10
Thorndon Suffk 64 G8
Thorndon Cross Devon 8 D6
Thorne Donc 92 A8
Thorne Coffin Somset 19 P11
Thornecroft Devon 7 K5
Thornehillhead Devon 16 G8
Thorner Leeds 91 K2
Thornes Staffs 58 G4
Thornes Wakefd 91 J7
Thorne St Margaret Somset 18 F10
Thorney Bucks 36 B5
Thorney C Pete 74 E10
Thorney Notts 85 Q6
Thorney Somset 19 M10
Thorney Hill Hants 13 M5
Thorney Island W Susx 15 L6
Thorney Toll Cambs 74 F10
Thornfalcon Somset 19 J10
Thornford Dorset 11 N2
Thorngrafton Nthumb 111 Q7
Thorngrove Somset 19 L8
Thorngumbald E R Yk 93 M5
Thornham Norfk 75 P2
Thornham Magna Suffk 64 G7
Thornham Parva Suffk 64 G7
Thornhaugh C Pete 73 R10
Thornhill C Sotn 14 E4
Thornhill Caerph 30 G8
Thornhill Cumb 100 D9
Thornhill D & G 116 B11
Thornhill Derbys 83 Q8
Thornhill Kirk 90 H7
Thornhill Stirlg 133 K7
Thornhill Lees Kirk 90 G7
Thornhills Calder 90 F6
Thornholme E R Yk 99 N8
Thornicombe Dorset 12 E4
Thornington Nthumb 118 G4
Thornley Dur 103 M3
Thornley Dur 104 C3
Thornley Gate Nthumb 112 B9
Thornliebank E Rens 125 P6
Thorns Suffk 63 M9
Thornsett Derbys 83 M7
Thorns Green Ches E 82 G8
Thornthwaite Cumb 100 H5
Thornthwaite N York 97 J9
Thornton Angus 142 F8
Thornton Bucks 49 K7
Thornton C Brad 90 D4
Thornton E R Yk 98 F11
Thornton Fife 134 H8
Thornton Lancs 88 C2
Thornton Leics 72 D9
Thornton Lincs 86 H7
Thornton Middsb 104 E8
Thornton Nthumb 129 P10
Thornton Pembks 40 H9
Thornton Sefton 81 L4
Thornton Curtis N Linc 93 J7
Thorntonhall S Lans 125 P6
Thornton Heath Gt Lon 36 H7
Thornton Hough Wirral 81 L8
Thornton-in-Craven N York 96 D11
Thornton in Lonsdale N York 95 P6
Thornton-le-Beans N York 97 N2
Thornton-le-Clay N York 98 D7
Thornton-le-Dale N York 98 G4
Thornton le Moor Lincs 92 H11
Thornton-le-Moor N York 97 N3
Thornton-le-Moors Ches W 81 N10
Thornton-le-Street N York 97 P3
Thorntonloch E Loth 129 K5
Thornton Rust N York 96 E3
Thornton Steward N York 97 J3
Thornton Watlass N York 97 K3
Thornwood Common Essex 51 L10
Thornydykes Border 128 G10
Thornythwaite Cumb 101 L6
Thoroton Notts 73 K2
Thorp Arch Leeds 97 P11
Thorpe Derbys 71 M4
Thorpe E R Yk 99 K11
Thorpe Lincs 87 N4
Thorpe N York 96 F8
Thorpe Norfk 65 N2
Thorpe Notts 85 N11
Thorpe Surrey 36 B7
Thorpe Abbotts Norfk 64 H6
Thorpe Acre Leics 72 E7
Thorpe Arnold Leics 73 K6
Thorpe Audlin Wakefd 91 M7
Thorpe Bassett N York 98 H6
Thorpe Bay Sthend 38 F4
Thorpe by Water Rutlnd 73 M11
Thorpe Common Rothm 91 K11
Thorpe Constantine Staffs 59 L3
Thorpe End Norfk 77 K9
Thorpe Green Essex 53 L7
Thorpe Green Lancs 88 H6
Thorpe Green Suffk 64 C11
Thorpe Hesley Rothm 91 K11
Thorpe in Balne Donc 91 P8
Thorpe Langton Leics 60 F2
Thorpe Larches Dur 104 C5
Thorpe Lea Surrey 36 B6
Thorpe le Fallows Lincs 86 B4
Thorpe-le-Soken Essex 53 L7
Thorpe le Street E R Yk 92 D2
Thorpe Malsor Nhants 60 H5
Thorpe Mandeville Nhants 48 F6
Thorpe Market Norfk 77 J4
Thorpe Marriot Norfk 76 H8
Thorpe Morieux Suffk 64 C11
Thorpeness Suffk 65 P10
Thorpe on the Hill Leeds 91 J5
Thorpe on the Hill Lincs 86 B7
Thorpe Park Resort Surrey 36 B7
Thorpe St Andrew Norfk 77 K10
Thorpe St Peter Lincs 87 N8
Thorpe Salvin Rothm 84 H4
Thorpe Satchville Leics 73 J8
Thorpe Thewles S on T 104 C6
Thorpe Tilney Lincs 86 F9
Thorpe Underwood N York 97 Q9
Thorpe Underwood Nhants 60 G4
Thorpe Waterville Nhants 61 M4
Thorpe Willoughby N York 91 P4
Thorpland Norfk 75 M9
Thorrington Essex 53 J8
Thorverton Devon 9 M4
Thrales End C Beds 50 D7
Thrandeston Suffk 64 G6
Thrapston Nhants 61 L5
Threapland Cumb 100 G3
Threapland N York 96 E8
Threapwood Ches W 69 M5
Threapwood Staffs 71 J6
Threapwood Head Staffs 71 J6
Threave S Ayrs 114 F6
Three Ashes Herefs 45 Q10
Three Bridges W Susx 24 G3
Three Burrows Cnwll 3 K4
Three Chimneys Kent 26 D4
Three Cocks Powys 44 H7
Three Crosses Swans 28 G6
Three Cups Corner E Susx 25 P6
Three Gates Worcs 46 C2
Threehammer Common Norfk 77 L8
Three Hammers Cnwll 5 L4
Three Holes Norfk 75 K10
Threekingham Lincs 74 A3
Three Leg Cross E Susx 25 Q4
Three Legged Cross Dorset 13 J3
Three Mile Cross Wokham 35 K11
Threemilestone Cnwll 3 K4
Threemiletown W Loth 127 K2
Three Oaks E Susx 26 D9
Threlkeld Cumb 101 K5
Threshers Bush Essex 51 L9
Threshfield N York 96 E8
Thrigby Norfk 77 P9
Thringarth Dur 102 H6
Thringstone Leics 72 C7
Thrintoft N York 97 M2
Thriplow Cambs 62 F11
Throapham Rothm 84 H3
Throckenhalt Lincs 74 G9
Throcking Herts 50 H4
Throckley N u Ty 113 J7
Throckmorton Worcs 47 J4
Throop BCP 13 K5
Throop Dorset 12 D6
Throphill Nthumb 112 H3
Thropton Nthumb 119 K10
Throsk Stirlg 133 P9
Througham Gloucs 32 H3
Throughgate D & G 109 J4
Throwleigh Devon 8 G6
Throwley Kent 38 G10
Throwley Forstal Kent 38 G11
Thrumpton Notts 72 E4
Thrumpton Notts 85 M4
Thrumster Highld 167 P7
Thrunscoe NE Lin 93 P9
Thrunton Nthumb 119 L8
Thrup Oxon 33 Q5
Thrupp Gloucs 32 G4
Thrupp Oxon 48 E11
Thrushelton Devon 8 B7
Thrussington Leics 72 H7
Thruxton Hants 21 Q5
Thruxton Herefs 45 N8
Thrybergh Rothm 91 M11
Thulston Derbys 72 C4
Thundersley Essex 38 C4
Thurcaston Leics 72 F8
Thurcroft Rothm 84 G3
Thurdon Cnwll 16 D9
Thurgarton Norfk 76 H5
Thurgarton Notts 85 L11
Thurgoland Barns 90 H10
Thurlaston Leics 72 E11
Thurlaston Warwks 59 Q10
Thurlbear Somset 19 J10
Thurlby Lincs 74 A7
Thurlby Lincs 86 B8
Thurlby Lincs 87 N5
Thurleigh Bed 61 N9
Thurlestone Devon 6 H10
Thurloxton Somset 19 J8
Thurlstone Barns 90 G10
Thurlton Norfk 65 N2
Thurlwood Ches E 70 E3
Thurmaston Leics 72 G9
Thurnby Leics 72 G10
Thurne Norfk 77 N8
Thurnham Kent 38 D10
Thurning Nhants 61 N4
Thurning Norfk 76 F6
Thurnscoe Barns 91 M9
Thurrock Services Thurr 37 N5
Thursby Cumb 110 F10
Thursden Lancs 89 Q4
Thursford Norfk 76 D5
Thursley Surrey 23 P7
Thurso Highld 167 K3
Thurstaston Wirral 81 J8
Thurston Suffk 64 C8
Thurston Clough Oldham 90 B9
Thurstonfield Cumb 110 F9
Thurstonland Kirk 90 F8
Thurston Planche Suffk 64 C9
Thurton Norfk 77 L11
Thurvaston Derbys 71 N7
Thuxton Norfk 76 E10
Thwaite N York 102 G11
Thwaite Suffk 64 G8
Thwaite Head Cumb 94 G2
Thwaites C Brad 90 D2
Thwaite St Mary Norfk 65 L2
Thwaites Brow C Brad 90 D2
Thwing E R Yk 99 L6
Tibbermore P & K 134 C3
Tibbers D & G 116 B11
Tibberton Gloucs 46 E10
Tibberton Worcs 46 H3
Tibberton Wrekin 70 B10
Tibenham Norfk 64 G4
Tibshelf Derbys 84 F8
Tibshelf Services Derbys 84 F8
Tibthorpe E R Yk 99 K9
Ticehurst E Susx 25 Q4
Tichborne Hants 22 G8
Tickencote Rutlnd 73 P9
Tickenham N Som 31 N10
Tickford End M Keyn 49 N6
Tickhill Donc 85 J2
Ticklerton Shrops 56 H6
Ticknall Derbys 72 B6
Tickton E R Yk 93 J2
Tidbury Green Solhll 58 H9
Tidcombe Wilts 21 Q3
Tiddington Oxon 34 H4
Tiddington Warwks 47 P3
Tiddleywink Wilts 32 G9
Tidebrook E Susx 25 P4
Tideford Cnwll 5 P10
Tideford Cross Cnwll 5 N9
Tidenham Gloucs 31 Q5
Tideswell Derbys 83 Q9
Tidmarsh W Berk 34 H10
Tidmington Warwks 47 Q7
Tidpit Hants 21 L11
Tidworth Wilts 21 P5
Tiers Cross Pembks 40 H8
Tiffield Nhants 49 K4
Tigerton Angus 143 J5
Tigh a' Ghearraidh W Isls 168 c10
Tigharry W Isls 168 c10
Tighnabruaich Ag & B 124 B3
Tigley Devon 7 K6
Tilbrook Cambs 61 N7
Tilbury Thurr 37 P5
Tilbury Dock Thurr 37 P5
Tilbury Green Essex 52 B3
Tilbury Juxta Clare Essex 52 C3
Tile Cross Birm 59 J7
Tile Hill Covtry 59 L9

Tilehouse Green – Trois Bois 297

Tilehouse Green Solhll 59 J9
Tilehurst Readg 35 J10
Tilford Surrey 23 N6
Tilgate W Susx 24 G4
Tilgate Forest Row W Susx 24 G4
Tilham Street Somset 19 Q7
Tillers Green Gloucs 46 C8
Tilley Shrops 69 P9
Tillicoultry Clacks 133 Q8
Tillietudlem S Lans 126 E8
Tillingham Essex 52 G11
Tillington Herefs 45 P6
Tillington W Susx 23 Q10
Tillington Common Herefs 45 P5
Tillybirloch Abers 150 H6
Tillyfourie Abers 150 G5
Tillygreig Abers 151 M3
Tillyrie P & K 134 E6
Tilmanstone Kent 39 P11
Tilney All Saints Norfk 75 L7
Tilney High End Norfk 75 L7
Tilney St Lawrence Norfk 75 K8
Tilshead Wilts 21 K5
Tilstock Shrops 69 P7
Tilston Ches W 69 N4
Tilstone Bank Ches W 69 Q3
Tilstone Fearnall Ches W 69 Q2
Tilsworth C Beds 49 Q10
Tilton on the Hill Leics 73 J9
Tiltups End Gloucs 32 F5
Tilty Essex 51 N5
Timberland Lincs 86 F9
Timbersbrook Ches E 70 F2
Timberscombe Somset 18 C6
Timble N York 97 J10
Timewell Devon 18 C9
Timpanheck D & G 110 F6
Timperley Traffd 82 G7
Timsbury BaNES 20 C3
Timsbury Hants 22 B10
Timsgarry W Isls 168 f4
Timsgearraidh W Isls 168 f4
Timworth Suffk 64 B8
Timworth Green Suffk 64 B8
Tincleton Dorset 12 C6
Tindale Cumb 111 M9
Tingewick Bucks 49 J8
Tingley Leeds 90 H5
Tingrith C Beds 50 B4
Tingwall Airport Shet 169 r9
Tingwell Ork 169 d4
Tinhay Devon 5 P4
Tinker's Hill Hants 22 D5
Tinkersley Derbys 84 C8
Tinsley Sheff 84 F2
Tinsley Green W Susx 24 G3
Tintagel Cnwll 4 H4
Tintern Mons 31 P4
Tintinhull Somset 19 N11
Tintwistle Derbys 83 M5
Tinwald D & G 109 M4
Tinwell Rutlnd 73 Q9
Tippacott Devon 17 P2
Tipp's End Norfk 75 K11
Tiptoe Hants 13 N5
Tipton Sandw 58 E6
Tipton Green Sandw 58 E6
Tipton St John Devon 10 B6
Tiptree Essex 52 E8
Tiptree Heath Essex 52 E8
Tirabad Powys 44 B6
Tircoed Swans 28 H4
Tiree Ag & B 136 C7
Tiree Airport Ag & B 136 C7
Tiretigan Ag & B 123 M7
Tirley Gloucs 46 F9
Tiroran Ag & B 137 M10
Tirphil Caerph 30 F4
Tirril Cumb 101 P5
Tir-y-fron Flints 69 J3
Tisbury Wilts 20 H9
Tisman's Common W Susx 24 C4
Tissington Derbys 71 M4
Titchberry Devon 16 C6
Titchfield Hants 14 F5
Titchfield Common Hants 14 F5
Titchmarsh Nhants 61 M5
Titchwell Norfk 75 Q2
Tithby Notts 72 H3
Tithebarn Devon 9 N6
Titley Herefs 45 L2
Titmore Green Herts 50 F5
Titsey Surrey 37 K10
Titson Cnwll 16 C11
Tittensor Staffs 70 F7
Tittleshall Norfk 76 B7
Titton Worcs 58 B11
Tiverton Ches W 69 Q2
Tiverton Devon 9 N2
Tivetshall St Margaret Norfk 64 H4
Tivetshall St Mary Norfk 64 H4
Tivington Somset 18 B5
Tivy Dale Barns 90 H9
Tixall Staffs 70 H10
Tixover Rutlnd 73 P10
Toab Shet 169 q12
Toadhole Derbys 84 E9
Toadmoor Derbys 84 D10
Tobermory Ag & B 137 N4
Toberonochy Ag & B 130 E6
Tobha Mòr W Isls 168 c14
Tocher Abers 158 G11
Tochieneal Moray 158 D4
Tockenham Wilts 33 K9
Tockenham Wick Wilts 33 K8
Tocketts R & Cl 104 H7
Tockholes Bl w D 89 K6
Tockington S Glos 32 B7
Tockwith N York 97 Q10
Todber Dorset 20 E11
Todburn Nthumb 119 M11
Toddington C Beds 50 B5
Toddington Gloucs 47 K8
Toddington Services C Beds 50 B5
Todds Green Herts 50 F5
Todenham Gloucs 47 P7
Todhills Angus 142 G10
Todhills Cumb 110 G8
Todhills Dur 103 P4
Todhills Rest Area Cumb 110 G8
Todmorden Calder 89 Q6
Todwick Rothm 84 G4
Toft Cambs 62 E9
Toft Ches E 82 G9
Toft Lincs 73 R7
Toft Shet 169 r6
Toft Warwks 59 Q10
Toft Hill Dur 103 N5
Toft Hill Lincs 86 H8
Toft Monks Norfk 65 N3
Toft next Newton Lincs 86 D3
Toftrees Norfk 76 B6
Toftwood Norfk 76 D9
Togston Nthumb 119 P10
Tokavaig Highld 145 K5
Tokers Green Oxon 35 K9
Tolastadh bho Thuath W Isls 168 k3
Toldish Cnwll 4 E10
Tolland Somset 18 F8
Tollard Farnham Dorset 21 J11
Tollard Royal Wilts 20 H11
Toll Bar Donc 91 P9
Tollbar End Covtry 59 N9
Toller Fratrum Dorset 11 M5
Toller Porcorum Dorset 11 M5
Tollerton N York 97 R8
Tollerton Notts 72 G4
Toller Whelme Dorset 11 L4
Tollesbury Essex 52 G9
Tolleshunt D'Arcy Essex 52 F9
Tolleshunt Knights Essex 52 F9
Tolleshunt Major Essex 52 F9
Tollingham E R Yk 92 D3
Toll of Birness Abers 159 P11
Tolpuddle Dorset 12 C6
Tolworth Gt Lon 36 E7
Tomatin Highld 148 E2
Tomchrasky Highld 146 H5
Tomdoun Highld 146 F7
Tomich Highld 147 J2
Tomich Highld 155 P8
Tomich Highld 156 B3
Tomich Highld 162 E5
Tomintoul Moray 149 M4
Tomlow Warwks 48 E2
Tomnacross Highld 155 P9
Tomnavoulin Moray 149 N2
Tompkin Staffs 70 G4
Ton Mons 31 K4
Ton Mons 31 L5
Tonbridge Kent 37 N11
Tondu Brdgnd 29 N8
Tonedale Somset 18 F10
Tonfanau Gwynd 54 D4
Tong C Brad 90 G4
Tong Kent 38 G10
Tong Shrops 57 P3
Tong W Isls 168 j4
Tonge Leics 72 C6
Tong Green Kent 38 G11
Tongham Surrey 23 N5
Tongland D & G 108 E10
Tong Norton Shrops 57 P3
Tongue Highld 165 N5
Tongue End Lincs 74 C7
Tongwynlais Cardif 30 F8
Tonmawr Neath 29 M5
Tonna Neath 29 L5
Ton-teg Rhondd 30 E7
Tonwell Herts 50 H7
Tonypandy Rhondd 30 C6
Tonyrefail Rhondd 30 D7
Toot Baldon Oxon 34 G4
Toot Hill Essex 51 M10
Toothill Hants 22 C11
Toothill Swindn 33 M8
Tooting Gt Lon 36 G6
Tooting Bec Gt Lon 36 G6
Topcliffe N York 97 N5
Topcroft Norfk 65 K3
Topcroft Street Norfk 65 K3
Top End Bed 61 M8
Topham Donc 91 Q7
Top of Hebers Rochdl 89 P9
Toppesfield Essex 52 B4
Toprow Norfk 64 H2
Topsham Devon 9 N7
Top-y-rhos Flints 69 J3
Torbeg N Ayrs 120 G6
Torboll Highld 162 H7
Torbreck Highld 156 A9
Torbryan Devon 7 L5
Torcastle Highld 139 L2
Torcross Devon 7 L10
Tore Highld 155 R7
Torfrey Cnwll 5 J11
Torinturk Ag & B 123 P7
Torksey Lincs 85 P5
Torlundy Highld 139 L2
Tormarton S Glos 32 E9
Tormore N Ayrs 120 G5
Tornagrain Highld 156 D7
Tornaveen Abers 150 G6
Torness Highld 147 P2
Toronto Dur 103 N4
Torpenhow Cumb 100 H3
Torphichen W Loth 126 H3
Torphins Abers 150 G7
Torpoint Cnwll 6 C7
Torquay Torbay 7 N6
Torquhan Border 128 C10
Torr Devon 6 F8
Torran Highld 153 K8
Torrance E Duns 125 Q3
Torranyard N Ayrs 125 K9
Torre Somset 18 D7
Torridon Highld 154 B6
Torridon House Highld 153 R6
Torrin Highld 145 J3
Torrisdale Ag & B 120 E4
Torrisdale Highld 165 Q4
Torrish Highld 163 M3
Torrisholme Lancs 95 K8
Torrobull Highld 162 D6
Torry C Aber 151 N6
Torryburn Fife 134 C10
Torteval Guern 10 a2
Torthorwald D & G 109 M5
Tortington W Susx 24 B9
Torton Worcs 58 B10
Tortworth S Glos 32 D6
Torvaig Highld 152 H9
Torver Cumb 94 F2
Torwood Falk 133 N11
Torwoodlee Border 117 P3
Torworth Notts 85 L3
Tosberry Devon 16 D7
Toscaig Highld 153 N10
Toseland Cambs 62 B8
Tosside Lancs 95 R9
Tostock Suffk 64 D9
Totaig Highld 152 C7
Tote Highld 152 G8
Tote Highld 153 J5
Tote Hill W Susx 23 N10
Totford Hants 22 G7
Tothill Lincs 87 M4
Totland IoW 13 P7
Totley Sheff 84 D5
Totley Brook Sheff 84 D4
Totnes Devon 7 L6
Toton Notts 72 E4
Totronald Ag & B 136 F4
Totscore Highld 152 F4
Tottenham Gt Lon 36 H2
Tottenhill Norfk 75 M8
Totteridge Gt Lon 36 F2
Totternhoe C Beds 49 Q10
Tottington Bury 89 M8
Tottleworth Lancs 89 L4
Totton Hants 14 C4
Touchen End W & M 35 N9
Toulston N York 91 M2
Toulton Somset 18 G8
Toulvaddie Highld 163 K10
Tovil Kent 38 C11
Towan Cnwll 3 Q4
Towan Cnwll 4 D7
Toward Ag & B 124 E4
Toward Quay Ag & B 124 E4
Towcester Nhants 49 J5
Towednack Cnwll 2 D6
Tower of London Gt Lon 36 H4
Towersey Oxon 35 K3
Towie Abers 150 C5
Tow Law Dur 103 M3
Town End Cambs 74 H11
Town End Cumb 95 J4
Town End Cumb 101 K9
Town End Cumb 102 B5
Townend W Duns 125 K2
Towngate Cumb 111 K11
Towngate Lincs 74 B8
Town Green Lancs 88 E9
Town Green Norfk 77 M9
Townhead Barns 83 Q4
Townhead Cumb 100 E3
Town Head Cumb 101 M10
Townhead Cumb 102 B4
Townhead D & G 109 M3
Town Head N York 96 B9
Townhead of Greenlaw D & G 108 F8
Townhill Fife 134 E10
Town Kelloe Dur 104 C3
Townlake Devon 5 Q7
Town Lane Wigan 82 E5
Town Littleworth E Susx 25 K7
Town of Lowton Wigan 82 D5
Town Row E Susx 25 N4
Towns End Hants 22 G3
Townsend Somset 10 H2
Townshend Cnwll 2 F7
Town Street Suffk 63 N3
Townwell S Glos 32 D6
Town Yetholm Border 118 F5
Towthorpe C York 98 C9
Towthorpe E R Yk 98 H8
Towton N York 91 M3
Towyn Conwy 80 D9
Toxteth Lpool 81 M7
Toynton All Saints Lincs 87 L8
Toynton Fen Side Lincs 87 L8
Toynton St Peter Lincs 87 M8
Toy's Hill Kent 37 L10
Trabboch E Ayrs 114 H3
Trabbochburn E Ayrs 115 J3
Traboe Cnwll 3 J9
Tracebridge Somset 18 E10
Tradespark Highld 156 F6
Trafford Park Traffd 82 G5
Trallong Powys 44 D9
Tranent E Loth 128 C5
Tranmere Wirral 81 L7
Trantelbeg Highld 166 E6
Trantlemore Highld 166 E6
Tranwell Nthumb 113 J4
Trap Carmth 43 N11
Traprain E Loth 128 F4
Trap's Green Warwks 58 H11
Trapshill W Berk 22 C2
Traquair Border 117 L4
Trash Green W Berk 35 J11
Trawden Lancs 89 Q3
Trawscoed Cerdgn 54 F10
Trawsfynydd Gwynd 67 N7
Trealaw Rhondd 30 D6
Treales Lancs 88 E4
Trearddur Bay IoA 78 D9
Treator Cnwll 4 E6
Tre Aubrey V Glam 30 D10
Trebanog Rhondd 30 D6
Trebanos Neath 29 K4
Trebartha Cnwll 5 M6
Trebarwith Cnwll 4 H4
Trebeath Cnwll 5 M4
Trebetherick Cnwll 4 E6
Treborough Somset 18 D7
Trebudannon Cnwll 4 D9
Trebullett Cnwll 5 N6
Treburgett Cnwll 4 H6
Treburley Cnwll 5 P6
Treburrick Cnwll 4 D7
Trebyan Cnwll 4 H9
Trecastle Powys 44 B9
Trecogo Cnwll 5 N5
Trecott Devon 8 F4
Trecwn Pembks 41 J4
Trecynon Rhondd 30 C4
Tredaule Cnwll 5 L5
Tredavoe Cnwll 2 D8
Tredegar Blae G 30 F3
Tredethy Cnwll 4 H7
Tredington Gloucs 46 H9
Tredington Warwks 47 Q6
Tredinnick Cnwll 4 E7
Tredinnick Cnwll 4 G10
Tredinnick Cnwll 5 K8
Tredinnick Cnwll 5 L10
Tredinnick Cnwll 5 M10
Tredomen Powys 44 G8
Tredrizzick Cnwll 4 F6
Tredunnock Mons 31 L6
Tredustan Powys 44 G8
Treen Cnwll 2 B9
Treen Cnwll 2 C6
Treesmill Cnwll 4 H10
Treeton Rothm 84 F3
Trefasser Pembks 40 G3
Trefdraeth IoA 78 G10
Trefecca Powys 44 G8
Trefechan Myr Td 30 D3
Trefeglwys Powys 55 M6
Trefenter Cerdgn 54 E11
Treffgarne Pembks 41 J6
Treffgarne Owen Pembks 40 G5
Treffynnon Pembks 40 G5
Trefil Blae G 30 F2
Trefilan Cerdgn 43 K3
Trefin Pembks 40 F4
Treflach Shrops 69 J9
Trefnannau Powys 68 H11
Trefnant Denbgs 80 F10
Trefonen Shrops 69 J9
Trefor Gwynd 66 F5
Trefor IoA 78 F8
Treforest Rhondd 30 E7
Trefrew Cnwll 5 J5
Trefriw Conwy 67 P2
Tregadillett Cnwll 5 M5
Tre-gagle Mons 31 P3
Tregaian IoA 78 H8
Tregare Mons 31 M2
Tregarne Cnwll 3 K9
Tregaron Cerdgn 43 N3
Tregarth Gwynd 79 L11
Tregaswith Cnwll 4 D9
Tregatta Cnwll 4 H4
Tregawne Cnwll 4 G8
Tregeare Cnwll 5 L4
Tregeiriog Wrexhm 68 G8
Tregele IoA 78 F6
Tregellist Cnwll 4 G6
Tregenna Cnwll 3 M5
Tregeseal Cnwll 2 B7
Tregew Cnwll 3 L7
Tre-Gibbon Rhondd 30 C3
Tregidden Cnwll 3 K9
Tregiskey Cnwll 3 Q4
Treglemais Pembks 40 F5
Tregole Cnwll 5 K2
Tregolls Cnwll 3 J6
Tregonce Cnwll 4 E7
Tregonetha Cnwll 4 F9
Tregonning & Gwinear Mining District Cnwll 2 F7
Tregony Cnwll 3 N5
Tregoodwell Cnwll 5 J5
Tregorrick Cnwll 3 Q3
Tregoss Cnwll 4 F9
Tregoyd Powys 44 H7
Tregrehan Mills Cnwll 3 Q3
Tre-groes Cerdgn 42 H6
Tregullon Cnwll 4 H9
Tregunna Cnwll 4 F7
Tregunnon Cnwll 5 L5
Tregurrian Cnwll 4 D8
Tregynon Powys 55 P5
Tre-gynwr Carmth 42 H11
Trehafod Rhondd 30 D6
Trehan Cnwll 5 Q10
Treharris Myr Td 30 E5
Treharrock Cnwll 4 G6
Trehemborne Cnwll 4 D7
Treherbert Carmth 43 L5
Treherbert Rhondd 29 P5
Trehunist Cnwll 5 N9
Trekenner Cnwll 5 N6
Treknow Cnwll 4 H4
Trelan Cnwll 3 J10
Trelash Cnwll 5 K3
Trelassick Cnwll 3 M3
Trelawne Cnwll 5 L11
Trelawnyd Flints 80 F9
Treleague Cnwll 3 K9
Treleaver Cnwll 3 K10
Trelech Carmth 41 Q4
Trelech a'r Betws Carmth 42 F9
Treleddyd-fawr Pembks 40 E5
Trelew Cnwll 3 L6
Trelewis Myr Td 30 F5
Treligga Cnwll 4 G5
Trelights Cnwll 4 F6
Trelill Cnwll 4 G6
Trelinnoe Cnwll 5 N5
Trelion Cnwll 3 N3
Trelissick Cnwll 3 L6
Trellech Mons 31 P3
Trelleck Grange Mons 31 N4
Trelogan Flints 80 G8
Trelow Cnwll 4 E8
Trelowarren Cnwll 3 J9
Trelowia Cnwll 5 M10
Treluggan Cnwll 3 M6
Trelystan Powys 56 D4
Tremadog Gwynd 67 K7
Tremail Cnwll 5 K4
Tremain Cerdgn 42 D5
Tremaine Cnwll 5 L4
Tremar Cnwll 5 M8
Trematon Cnwll 5 P10
Trembraze Cnwll 5 M8
Tremeirchion Denbgs 80 F10
Tremethick Cross Cnwll 2 C7
Tremore Cnwll 4 G9
Tre-Mostyn Flints 80 G9
Trenance Cnwll 3 L9
Trenance Cnwll 4 D8
Trenance Cnwll 4 E7
Trenarren Cnwll 3 Q4
Trench Wrekin 57 M2
Trench Green Oxon 35 J9
Trendeal Cnwll 3 M3
Trendrine Cnwll 2 D6
Treneague Cnwll 4 F7
Trenear Cnwll 2 H7
Treneglos Cnwll 5 L4
Trenerth Cnwll 2 G6
Trenewan Cnwll 5 K11
Trenewth Cnwll 4 H6
Trengune Cnwll 5 K3
Treninnick Cnwll 4 C9
Trenowah Cnwll 4 B10
Trenoweth Cnwll 3 K7
Trent Dorset 19 Q11
Trentham C Stke 70 F6
Trentishoe Devon 17 L2
Trentlock Derbys 72 D4
Trent Port Lincs 85 P4
Trent Vale C Stke 70 F6
Trenwheal Cnwll 2 G7
Treoes V Glam 29 P9
Treorchy Rhondd 30 C5
Trequite Cnwll 4 G6
Tre'r-ddol Cerdgn 54 F6
Trerhyngyll V Glam 30 D9
Trerulefoot Cnwll 5 N10
Tresaith Cerdgn 42 E4
Tresawle Cnwll 3 M4
Tresco IoS 2 b2
Trescott Staffs 58 C5
Trescowe Cnwll 2 F7
Tresean Cnwll 4 B10
Tresham Gloucs 32 E6
Treshnish Isles Ag & B 136 G7
Tresillian Cnwll 3 M4
Tresinney Cnwll 5 J5
Treskinnick Cross Cnwll 5 L2
Tresmeer Cnwll 5 L4
Tresparrett Cnwll 5 J3
Tressait P & K 141 K5
Tresta Shet 169 q8
Tresta Shet 169 t4
Treswell Notts 85 N5
Treswithian Cnwll 2 G5
Tre Taliesin Cerdgn 54 F6
Trethevey Cnwll 4 H4
Trethewey Cnwll 2 B9
Trethomas Caerph 30 G7
Trethosa Cnwll 3 N3
Trethurgy Cnwll 4 G10
Tretio Pembks 40 E5
Tretire Herefs 45 Q10
Tretower Powys 44 H10
Treuddyn Flints 69 J3
Trevadlock Cnwll 5 M6
Trevalga Cnwll 4 H3
Trevalyn Wrexhm 69 L3
Trevanger Cnwll 4 F6
Trevanson Cnwll 4 F7
Trevarrack Cnwll 2 D7
Trevarren Cnwll 4 E9
Trevarrian Cnwll 4 D8
Trevarrick Cnwll 3 P5
Trevarth Cnwll 3 J5
Trevaughan Carmth 41 P7
Tre-vaughan Carmth 42 G10
Treveal Cnwll 2 D5
Treveal Cnwll 4 B10
Treveighan Cnwll 4 H6
Trevellas Downs Cnwll 3 J3
Trevelmond Cnwll 5 L9
Trevemper Cnwll 4 C10
Treveor Cnwll 3 P5
Treverbyn Cnwll 3 M4
Treverbyn Cnwll 4 G10
Treverva Cnwll 3 K7
Trevescan Cnwll 2 B9
Trevethin Torfn 31 J4
Trevia Cnwll 4 H5
Trevigro Cnwll 5 N8
Trevilla Cnwll 3 L6
Trevilson Cnwll 4 C10
Treviscoe Cnwll 4 E10
Treviskey Cnwll 3 N5
Trevithick Cnwll 3 P4
Trevithick Cnwll 4 D9
Trevoll Cnwll 4 C10
Trevone Cnwll 4 D6
Trevor Wrexhm 69 J6
Trevorgans Cnwll 2 C8
Trevorrick Cnwll 4 E7
Trevose Cnwll 4 D6
Trew Cnwll 2 G8
Trewalder Cnwll 4 H5
Trewalkin Powys 44 H8
Trewarmett Cnwll 4 H4
Trewassa Cnwll 5 J4
Trewavas Cnwll 2 F8
Trewavas Mining District Cnwll 2 F8
Treween Cnwll 5 L5
Trewellard Cnwll 2 B7
Trewen Cnwll 5 M5
Trewennack Cnwll 2 H8
Trewent Pembks 41 K11
Trewern Powys 56 D2
Trewetha Cnwll 4 G5
Trewethern Cnwll 4 G6
Trewidland Cnwll 5 M10
Trewillis Cnwll 3 K10
Trewint Cnwll 5 L5
Trewint Cnwll 5 M9
Trewithian Cnwll 3 M6
Trewoodloe Cnwll 5 N7
Trewoon Cnwll 2 H10
Trewoon Cnwll 3 P3
Treworga Cnwll 3 M5
Treworgan Cnwll 3 L4
Treworlas Cnwll 3 M6
Treworld Cnwll 5 J3
Treworthal Cnwll 3 M6
Tre-wyn Mons 45 L10
Treyarnon Cnwll 4 D7
Treyford W Susx 23 M11
Trickett's Cross Dorset 13 J4
Triermain Cumb 111 L7
Triffleton Pembks 41 J6
Trillacott Cnwll 5 M4
Trimdon Dur 104 C4
Trimdon Colliery Dur 104 C3
Trimdon Grange Dur 104 C3
Trimdon Station Dur 104 C3
Trimingham Norfk 77 K4
Trimley Lower Street Suffk 53 N4
Trimley St Martin Suffk 53 N4
Trimley St Mary Suffk 53 N4
Trimpley Worcs 57 P9
Trimsaran Carmth 28 E4
Trims Green Herts 51 L7
Trimstone Devon 17 J3
Trinafour P & K 140 H5
Trinant Caerph 30 H5
Tring Herts 35 P2
Tringford Herts 35 P2
Tring Wharf Herts 35 P2
Trinity Angus 143 L5
Trinity Jersey 11 b1
Trinity Gask P & K 134 B4
Triscombe Somset 18 G7
Trislaig Highld 139 K3
Trispen Cnwll 3 L3
Tritlington Nthumb 113 K2
Troan Cnwll 4 D10
Trochry P & K 141 N9
Troedrhiwfuwch Caerph 30 F4
Troedyraur Cerdgn 42 F5
Troedyrhiw Myr Td 30 E4
Trofarth Conwy 80 B10
Trois Bois Jersey 11 b1

Troon Cnwll 2 H6
Troon S Ayrs 125 J11
Tropical World Leeds Leeds 91 J3
Trossachs Stirlg 132 G6
Trossachs Pier Stirlg 132 F6
Troston Suffk 64 B7
Troswell Cnwll 5 M3
Trotshill Worcs 46 G3
Trottiscliffe Kent 37 P8
Trotton W Susx 23 M10
Troughend Nthumb 112 C2
Trough Gate Lancs 89 P6
Troutbeck Cumb 101 L5
Troutbeck Cumb 101 M10
Troutbeck Bridge Cumb 101 M10
Troway Derbys 84 E5
Trowbridge Wilts 20 G3
Trowell Notts 72 D3
Trowell Services Notts 72 D2
Trowle Common Wilts 20 F3
Trowley Bottom Herts 50 C8
Trowse Newton Norfk 77 J10
Troy Leeds 90 G3
Trudoxhill Somset 20 D6
Trull Somset 18 H10
Trumfleet Donc 91 Q8
Trumpan Highld 152 C5
Trumpet Herefs 46 C7
Trumpington Cambs 62 F10
Trumpsgreen Surrey 35 Q11
Trunch Norfk 77 K5
Trunnah Lancs 88 C2
Truro Cnwll 3 L5
Truscott Cnwll 5 M4
Trusham Devon 9 L8
Trusley Derbys 71 P7
Trusthorpe Lincs 87 P4
Trysull Staffs 58 C6
Tubney Oxon 34 D5
Tuckenhay Devon 7 L7
Tuckhill Shrops 57 P7
Tuckingmill Cnwll 2 H5
Tuckingmill Wilts 20 H9
Tuckton BCP 13 K6
Tucoyse Cnwll 3 P4
Tuddenham Suffk 63 M6
Tuddenham St Martin Suffk 53 L2
Tudeley Kent 37 P11
Tudhoe Dur 103 Q3
Tudorville Herefs 46 A10
Tudweiliog Gwynd 66 C7
Tuesley Surrey 23 Q6
Tuffley Gloucs 32 F2
Tufton Hants 22 E5
Tufton Pembks 41 K5
Tugby Leics 73 K10
Tugford Shrops 57 K7
Tughall Nthumb 119 P5
Tullibody Clacks 133 P8
Tullich Abers 150 B8
Tullich Highld 147 Q2
Tullich Highld 156 F2
Tulliemet P & K 141 P7
Tulloch Abers 159 K11
Tullochgorm Ag & B 131 K8
Tulloch Station Highld 147 K11
Tullymurdoch P & K 142 B7
Tullynessle Abers 150 F4
Tulse Hill Gt Lon 36 H6
Tumble Carmth 28 F2
Tumbler's Green Essex 52 D6
Tumby Lincs 86 H9
Tumby Woodside Lincs 87 J9
Tummel Bridge P & K 141 J6
Tunbridge Wells Kent 25 N3
Tundergarth D & G 110 C4
Tunga W Isls 168 j4
Tungate Norfk 77 K6
Tunley BaNES 20 C3
Tunstall E Stke 70 F4
Tunstall E R Yk 93 P4
Tunstall Kent 38 E9
Tunstall Lancs 95 N6
Tunstall N York 103 N10
Tunstall Norfk 77 N10
Tunstall Staffs 70 D9
Tunstall Suffk 65 M10
Tunstall Sundld 113 N10
Tunstead Derbys 83 P10
Tunstead Norfk 77 K7
Tunstead Milton Derbys 83 M8
Tunworth Hants 23 J5
Tupsley Herefs 45 Q6
Tupton Derbys ... 23 J3
Turgis Green Hants 23 J3
Turkdean Gloucs 47 M11
Tur Langton Leics 73 F2
Turleigh Wilts 20 F2
Turleygreen Shrops 57 P7
Turn Lancs 89 N7
Turnastone Herefs 45 M7
Turnberry S Ayrs 114 D6
Turnchapel C Plym 6 D8
Turnditch Derbys 71 P5
Turner Green Lancs 89 J4
Turner's Green E Susx 25 P7
Turner's Green Warwks 59 J11
Turners Hill W Susx 24 H3
Turners Puddle Dorset 12 D6
...ford Herts 51 J10
...ouse C Edin 127 M3
...orth Dorset 12 D3
... Abers 158 H7
... Bottoms 89 L7
...Cambs 74 F11
...Bed 49 P4
... 35 L6
...Heath 35 K6
...ton Buc 48 H7
...w Inn 117 L7
...Staffs 71 N9
...Worcs 58 E10
...Gloucs 31 P6
...ton Norfk 77 J6
...ump W 34 G10
...Cnwll 5 P6
...Notts 85 M9
...k 169 b4
...et 169 q8
...re E Dun 126 B2
...nk Bo 117 Q4
...uth 129 P9
...uir B 116 G6
...ads 3 K5
...aks 25 Q6
...Gr 82 G1
...cs 74 C6

Twerton BaNES 20 D2
Twickenham Gt Lon 36 E6
Twigworth Gloucs 46 F10
Twineham W Susx 24 G7
Twineham Green W Susx 24 G6
Twinhoe BaNES 20 E3
Twinstead Essex 52 E4
Twitchen Devon 17 P5
Twitchen Shrops 56 H7
Twitham Kent 39 N10
Two Bridges Devon 6 G4
Two Dales Derbys 84 C8
Two Gates Staffs 59 K4
Two Mile Ash W Susx 24 D5
Two Mile Oak Cross Devon 7 L5
Two Pots Devon 17 J3
Two Waters Herts 50 C9
Twycross Leics 72 A10
Twycross Zoo Leics 59 M3
Twyford Bucks 49 J9
Twyford Hants 22 E10
Twyford Leics 73 J8
Twyford Lincs 73 N6
Twyford Norfk 76 E7
Twyford Wokham 35 L9
Twyford Common Herefs 45 Q7
Twyn-carno Caerph 30 F3
Twynholm D & G 108 E10
Twyning Gloucs 46 G7
Twynllanan Carmth 43 Q10
Twyn-yr-Odyn V Glam 30 F10
Twyn-y-Sheriff Mons 31 M3
Twywell Nhants 61 L5
Tyberton Herefs 45 M7
Tyburn Birm 58 H6
Tycroes Carmth 28 H2
Ty Croes IoA 78 D5
Tycrwyn Powys 68 F11
Tydd Gote Lincs 75 J7
Tydd St Giles Cambs 74 H7
Tydd St Mary Lincs 74 H7
Tye Hants 15 K6
Tye Green Essex 51 M4
Tye Green Essex 51 N3
Tye Green Essex 52 C7
Tyersal C Brad 90 F4
Tyldesley Wigan 82 E4
Tyler Hill Kent 39 K9
Tylers Green Bucks 35 P6
Tyler's Green Essex 51 M9
Tylers Green Surrey 37 J10
Tylorstown Rhondd 30 D5
Tylwch Powys 55 M8
Ty-nant Conwy 68 C6
Ty-nant Gwynd 68 B9
Tyncelyn Cerdgn 43 M2
Tyndrum Stirlg 139 Q11
Ty'n-dwr Denbgs 68 H6
Tyneham Dorset 12 E8
Tynemouth N Tyne 113 N7
Tyne Tunnel S Tyne 113 M7
Tynewydd Rhondd 29 P5
Tyninghame E Loth 128 G4
Tynron D & G 115 P9
Ty'n-y-bryn Rhondd 30 D7
Ty'n-y-coedcae Caerph 30 G7
Tynygongl IoA 79 J8
Tynygraig Cerdgn 54 F11
Ty'n-y-Groes Conwy 79 P10
Tyn-y-nant Rhondd 30 E7
Tyrie Abers 159 M5
Tyringham M Keyn 49 N5
Tyseley Birm 58 H8
Tythegston Brdgnd 29 N9
Tytherington Ches E 83 K9
Tytherington S Glos 32 C7
Tytherington Somset 20 E6
Tytherington Wilts 20 H6
Tytherleigh Devon 10 G4
Tytherton Lucas Wilts 32 H10
Tyttenhanger Herts 50 E9
Tywardreath Cnwll 4 H11
Tywardreath Highway Cnwll 4 H10
Tywyn Conwy 79 P9
Tywyn Gwynd 54 D4

U

Ubbeston Green Suffk 65 L7
Ubley BaNES 19 P3
Uckerby N York 103 P10
Uckfield E Susx 25 L6
Uckinghall Worcs 46 G7
Uckington Gloucs 46 H10
Uckington Shrops 57 K2
Uddingston S Lans 126 B5
Uddington S Lans 116 B3
Udimore E Susx 26 E8
Udny Green Abers 151 M2
Udny Station Abers 151 N3
Uffcott Wilts 33 M9
Uffculme Devon 9 Q2
Uffington Lincs 73 R9
Uffington Oxon 34 B7
Uffington Shrops 57 J2
Ufford C Pete 74 A10
Ufford Suffk 65 K11
Ufton Warwks 48 C2
Ufton Nervet W Berk 34 H11
Ugadale Ag & B 120 E6
Ugborough Devon 6 H7
Uggeshall Suffk 65 N5
Ugglebarnby N York 105 N9
Ughill Sheff 84 C2
Ugley Essex 51 M5
Ugley Green Essex 51 M5
Ugthorpe N York 105 L8
Uibhist A Deas W Isls 8 d14
Uibhist A Tuath W Isls c10
Uig Ag & B F5
Uig Highld B7
Uig Highld
Uig Highld
Uig W Isls
Uigshader Highld
Uisken Ag & B
Ulbster Highld
Ulcat Row Cumb
Ulceby Lincs
Ulceby N Linc
Ulceby Skitter N Linc
Ulcombe Kent
Uldale Cumb
Uley Gloucs
Ulgham Nthumb

Ullapool Highld 161 J8
Ullenhall Warwks 58 H11
Ullenwood Gloucs 46 H11
Ulleskelf N York 91 N3
Ullesthorpe Leics 60 B3
Ulley Rothm 84 G3
Ullingswick Herefs 46 A5
Ullock Cumb 100 E6
Ullswater Cumb 101 M6
Ullswater 'Steamers' Cumb 101 L7
Ulpha Cumb 94 D2
Ulpha Cumb 95 K4
Ulrome E R Yk 99 P9
Ulsta Shet 169 r5
Ulting Wick Essex 52 D10
Ulva Ag & B 137 K7
Ulverley Green Solhll 58 H8
Ulverston Cumb 94 F5
Ulwell Dorset 12 H8
Ulzieside D & G 115 Q6
Umberleigh Devon 17 L7
Unapool Highld 164 F10
Underbarrow Cumb 95 K2
Under Burnmouth Border 111 J4
Undercliffe C Brad 90 F4
Underdale Shrops 57 J2
Underling Green Kent 26 C2
Underriver Kent 37 N10
Underwood Newpt 31 L7
Underwood Notts 84 G10
Undley Suffk 63 L4
Undy Mons 31 M7
Union Mills IoM 80 e6
Union Street E Susx 26 B5
Unst Shet 169 s3
Unstone Derbys 84 E5
Unstone Green Derbys 84 E5
Unthank Cumb 101 N3
Unthank Cumb 102 B2
Unthank Cumb 110 G11
Unthank Derbys 84 D5
Unthank Nthumb 129 P10
Upavon Wilts 21 M4
Up Cerne Dorset 11 P4
Upchurch Kent 38 D8
Upcott Devon 17 P6
Upcott Herefs 45 L4
Upend Cambs 63 M9
Up Exe Devon 9 M4
Upgate Norfk 76 G8
Upgate Street Norfk 64 F3
Upgate Street Norfk 65 K3
Uphall Dorset 11 M4
Uphall W Loth 127 K3
Upham Devon 9 L3
Upham Hants 22 F10
Uphampton Herefs 45 M2
Uphampton Worcs 46 F2
Uphill N Som 19 K3
Up Holland Lancs 88 G9
Uplawmoor E Rens 125 L6
Upleadon Gloucs 46 E9
Upleatham R & Cl 104 H7
Uplees Kent 38 H9
Uploders Dorset 11 L6
Uplowman Devon 18 D11
Uplyme Devon 10 G6
Up Marden W Susx 15 L4
Upminster Gt Lon 37 N3
Up Mudford Somset 19 Q11
Up Nately Hants 23 J4
Upottery Devon 10 E3
Upper Affcot Shrops 56 G7
Upper Arley Worcs 57 P8
Upper Arncott Oxon 48 H11
Upper Astrop Nhants 48 F7
Upper Badcall Highld 164 E8
Upper Basildon W Berk 34 G9
Upper Batley Kirk 90 G5
Upper Beeding W Susx 24 E8
Upper Benefield Nhants 61 L3
Upper Bentley Worcs 58 E11
Upper Bighouse Highld 166 E5
Upper Birchwood Derbys 84 F9
Upper Boat Rhondd 30 F7
Upper Boddington Nhants 48 E4
Upper Borth Cerdgn 54 E7
Upper Brailes Warwks 48 B7
Upper Breinton Herefs 45 P6
Upper Broadheath Worcs 46 F3
Upper Broughton Notts 72 H5
Upper Bucklebury W Berk 34 F11
Upper Burgate Hants 21 N11
Upper Bush Medway 37 Q7
Upperby Cumb 110 H10
Upper Caldecote C Beds 61 Q11
Upper Canada N Som 19 L3
Upper Canterton Hants 13 N2
Upper Catesby Nhants 60 B9
Upper Catshill Worcs 58 E10
Upper Chapel Powys 44 E6
Upper Cheddon Somset 18 H9
Upper Chicksgrove Wilts 21 J9
Upper Chute Wilts 21 Q4
Upper Clapton Gt Lon 36 H3
Upper Clatford Hants 22 C6
Upper Coberley Gloucs 47 J11
Upper Cotton Staffs 71 K5
Upper Cound Shrops 57 K3
Upper Cudworth Barns 91 K9
Upper Cumberworth Kirk 90 G9
Upper Dallachy Moray 157 R5
Upper Deal Kent 39 Q11
Upper Dean Bed 61 M7
Upper Denby Kirk 90 G9
Upper Denton Cumb 111 M7
Upper Dicker E Susx 25 N9
Upper Dinchope Shrops 56 H8
Upper Dounreay Highld 166 H3
Upper Dovercourt Essex 53 M5
Upper Drumbane Stirlg 133 K6
Upper Dunsforth N York 97 P8
Upper Eashing Surrey 23 Q6
Upper Eathie Highld 156 D5
Upper Egleton Herefs 46 B6
Upper Elkstone Staffs 71 K3
Upper Ellastone Staffs 71 L6
Upper End Derbys 83 N9
Upper Enham Hants 22 C4
Upper Farmcote Shrops 57 P6
Upper Farringdon Hants 23 K7
Upper Framilode Gloucs 32 E2
Upper Froyle Hants 23 L5
Upper Godney Somset 19 N6

Upper Gravenhurst C Beds 50 D3
Upper Green Mons 45 M11
Upper Green Suffk 63 M8
Upper Green W Berk 22 C2
Upper Grove Common Herefs 45 R9
Upper Hackney Derbys 84 C8
Upper Hale Surrey 23 M5
Upper Halliford Surrey 36 C7
Upper Halling Medway 37 Q8
Upper Hambleton Rutlnd 73 N9
Upper Harbledown Kent 39 K10
Upper Hardres Court Kent 39 L11
Upper Hardwick Herefs 45 N3
Upper Hartfield E Susx 25 L4
Upper Hartshay Derbys 84 E10
Upper Hatherley Gloucs 46 H10
Upper Hatton Staffs 70 E7
Upper Haugh Rothm 91 L11
Upper Hayton Shrops 57 J8
Upper Heaton Kirk 90 F7
Upper Helmsley N York 98 D9
Upper Hergest Herefs 45 K4
Upper Heyford Nhants 60 E9
Upper Heyford Oxon 48 E9
Upper Hill Herefs 45 P4
Upper Hockenden Kent 37 M9
Upper Hopton Kirk 90 F7
Upper Howsell Worcs 46 E5
Upper Hulme Staffs 71 J2
Upper Ifold Surrey 24 B4
Upper Inglesham Swindn 33 P5
Upper Kilcott Gloucs 32 E7
Upper Killay Swans 28 G6
Upper Kinchrackine Ag & B 131 P2
Upper Knockando Moray 157 M9
Upper Lambourn W Berk 34 B8
Upper Landywood Staffs 58 E3
Upper Langford N Som 19 N3
Upper Langwith Derbys 84 H7
Upper Largo Fife 135 L7
Upper Layham Suffk 52 H3
Upper Leigh Staffs 71 J7
Upper Littleton N Som 19 Q2
Upper Lochton Abers 150 H8
Upper Longdon Staffs 58 G2
Upper Ludstone Shrops 57 Q5
Upper Lybster Highld 167 N9
Upper Lydbrook Gloucs 46 B11
Upper Lyde Herefs 45 P6
Upper Lye Herefs 56 F11
Upper Maes-coed Herefs 45 L8
Upper Marham Norfk 75 P9
Upper Midhope Sheff 90 G11
Uppermill Oldham 89 B9
Upper Milton Worcs 57 Q10
Upper Minety Wilts 33 K6
Upper Moor Worcs 47 J5
Upper Moor Side Leeds 90 G4
Upper Mulben Moray 157 R7
Upper Netchwood Shrops 57 L6
Upper Nobut Staffs 71 J7
Upper Norwood W Susx 23 P11
Upper Oddington Gloucs 47 P9
Upper Padley Derbys 84 B5
Upper Pennington Hants 13 P5
Upper Pollicott Bucks 35 K2
Upper Poppleton C York 98 B10
Upper Quinton Warwks 47 N5
Upper Ratley Hants 22 B10
Upper Rissington Gloucs 47 P11
Upper Rochford Worcs 57 L11
Upper Ruscoe D & G 108 C8
Upper Sapey Herefs 46 C2
Upper Saxondale Notts 72 H3
Upper Seagry Wilts 32 H8
Upper Shelton C Beds 49 Q6
Upper Sheringham Norfk 76 G3
Upper Skelmorlie N Ayrs 124 G3
Upper Slaughter Gloucs 47 N10
Upper Soudley Gloucs 32 C2
Upper Spond Herefs 45 L4
Upper Standen Kent 27 M3
Upper Staploe Bed 61 P9
Upper Stoke Norfk 77 K11
Upper Stondon C Beds 50 D3
Upper Stowe Nhants 60 D9
Upper Street Hants 21 N11
Upper Street Norfk 64 H6
Upper Street Norfk 77 L8
Upper Street Norfk 77 M8
Upper Street Suffk 53 K5
Upper Street Suffk 63 N10
Upper Street Suffk 64 G11
Upper Strensham Worcs 46 G7
Upper Sundon C Beds 50 B5
Upper Swell Gloucs 47 N9
Upper Tankersley Barns 91 J11
Upper Tean Staffs 71 J7
Upperthong Kirk 90 E9
Upperthorpe Derbys 84 G4
Upperthorpe N Linc 92 C10
Upper Threapwood Ches W 69 M5
Upperton W Susx 23 Q10
Upper Town Derbys 71 N4
Upper Town Derbys 84 D8
Upper Town Dur 103 L3
Upper Town Herefs 46 A5
Uppertown Highld 167 Q1
Upper Town N Som 31 P11
Upper Town Suffk 64 C8
Upper Tumble Carmth 28 F2
Upper Tysoe Warwks 48 B6
Upper Ufford Suffk 65 K11
Upperup Gloucs 33 K5
Upper Upham Wilts 33 P9
Upper Upnor Medway 38 C7
Upper Victoria Angus 143 J10
Upper Vobster Somset 20 D5
Upper Wardington Oxon 48 E5
Upper Weald M Keyn 49 M7
Upper Weedon Nhants 60 D9
Upper Welland Worcs 46 E6
Upper Wellingham E Susx 25 K8
Upper Weston BaNES 32 D11
Upper Weybread Suffk 65 J6
Upper Wick Worcs 46 F4
Upper Wield Hants 22 H7
Upper Winchendon Bucks 35 K2
Upperwood Derbys 84 C9
Upper Woodford Wilts 21 M7
Upper Woolhampton W Berk 34 G11
Upper Wootton Hants 22 G4
Upper Wraxall Wilts 32 F10

Upper Wyche Worcs 46 E6
Uppincott Devon 9 M3
Uppingham Rutlnd 73 M11
Uppington Dorset 12 H3
Uppington Shrops 57 K3
Upsall N York 97 Q3
Upsettlington Border 129 M10
Upshire Essex 51 K10
Up Somborne Hants 22 C8
Upstreet Kent 39 M9
Up Sydling Dorset 11 N4
Upthorpe Suffk 64 D7
Upton Bucks 35 L2
Upton C Pete 74 B10
Upton Cambs 61 Q5
Upton Ches W 81 N11
Upton Cnwll 5 M7
Upton Cnwll 16 C11
Upton Cumb 101 K3
Upton Devon 7 J10
Upton Devon 10 B4
Upton Dorset 12 B8
Upton Dorset 12 G6
Upton E R Yk 99 N10
Upton Halton 81 P7
Upton Hants 22 C11
Upton Hants 22 C3
Upton Leics 72 B11
Upton Lincs 85 Q3
Upton Nhants 60 F9
Upton Norfk 77 M9
Upton Notts 85 M10
Upton Notts 85 M5
Upton Oxon 33 P2
Upton Oxon 34 F7
Upton Pembks 41 K10
Upton R & Cl 105 K7
Upton Slough 35 Q9
Upton Somset 18 C9
Upton Somset 19 N9
Upton Wakefd 91 M8
Upton Warwks 47 M3
Upton Wilts 20 G8
Upton Wirral 81 K7
Upton Bishop Herefs 46 C9
Upton Cheyney S Glos 32 C10
Upton Cressett Shrops 57 M6
Upton Crews Herefs 46 B9
Upton Cross Cnwll 5 M7
Upton End C Beds 50 D4
Upton Grey Hants 23 J5
Upton Heath Ches W 81 N11
Upton Hellions Devon 9 K4
Upton Lovell Wilts 20 H6
Upton Magna Shrops 57 K2
Upton Noble Somset 20 D7
Upton Pyne Devon 9 M5
Upton St Leonards Gloucs 46 G11
Upton Scudamore Wilts 20 G5
Upton Snodsbury Worcs 46 H4
Upton Towans Cnwll 2 F5
Upton-upon-Severn Worcs 46 G6
Upton Warren Worcs 58 D11
Upwaltham W Susx 15 P4
Upware Cambs 62 H6
Upwell Norfk 75 J10
Upwey Dorset 11 P7
Upwick Green Herts 51 L6
Upwood Cambs 62 C4
Urchfont Wilts 21 K3
Urdimarsh Herefs 45 Q5
Ure Bank N York 97 M6
Urlay Nook S on T 104 D8
Urmston Traffd 82 G6
Urpeth Dur 113 L10
Urquhart Moray 157 P5
Urquhart Castle Highld 147 N2
Urra N York 104 G10
Urray Highld 155 P7
Ury Abers 151 N10
Uryside Abers 151 K3
Usan Angus 143 N7
Ushaw Moor Dur 103 P2
Usk Mons 31 L4
Usselby Lincs 86 E2
Usworth Sundld 113 M9
Utkinton Ches W 82 B11
Utley C Brad 90 D2
Uton Devon 9 K5
Utterby Lincs 87 K2
Uttoxeter Staffs 71 K8
Uwchmynydd Gwynd 66 B9
Uxbridge Gt Lon 36 C4
Uyeasound Shet 169 s3
Uzmaston Pembks 41 J8

V

Vale Guern 10 c1
Valley IoA 78 D9
Valley End Surrey 23 Q2
Valley Truckle Cnwll 4 H5
Valtos Highld 153 J5
Valtos W Isls 168 f4
Vange Essex 38 B4
Varteg Torfn 31 J3
Vatsetter Shet 169 s5
Vatten Highld 152 D9
Vaynor Myr Td 30 D2
Vazon Bay Guern 10 b2
Veensgarth Shet 169 r9
Velindre Powys 44 H7
Vellow Somset 18 E7
Velly Devon 16 D7
Venngreen Devon 16 F9
Vennington Shrops 56 E3
Venn Ottery Devon 10 B6
Venny Tedburn Devon 9 K5
Venterdon Cnwll 5 P7
Ventnor IoW 14 G11
Venton Devon 6 F7
Vernham Dean Hants 22 B3
Vernham Street Hants 22 B3
Vernolds Common Shrops 56 H8
Verwood Dorset 13 J3
Veryan Cnwll 3 N6
Veryan Green Cnwll 3 N5
Vicarage Devon 10 E7
Vickerstown Cumb 94 D7
Victoria Barns 90 F9
Victoria Blae G 30 G3
Victoria Cnwll 4 F9
Vidlin Shet 169 r7
Viewfield Moray 157 P5

Viewpark N Lans 126 C5
Vigo Kent 37 P8
Village de Putron Guern 10 c2
Ville la Bas Jersey 11 a1
Villiaze Guern 10 b2
Vinehall Street E Susx 26 C7
Vines Cross E Susx 25 N7
Virginia Water Surrey 36 B7
Virginstow Devon 5 P3
Vobster Somset 20 D5
Voe Shet 169 r7
Vowchurch Herefs 45 M7
Vulcan Village St Hel 82 C6

W

Waberthwaite Cumb 94 C2
Wackerfield Dur 103 N6
Wacton Norfk 64 H3
Wadborough Worcs 46 H5
Waddesdon Bucks 49 K11
Waddesdon Manor Bucks 49 K11
Waddeton Devon 7 M7
Waddicar Sefton 81 M5
Waddingham Lincs 92 G11
Waddington Lancs 89 L2
Waddington Lincs 86 D2
Waddon Devon 9 L9
Waddon Dorset 11 M7
Waddon Gt Lon 36 H8
Wadebridge Cnwll 4 F7
Wadeford Somset 10 G2
Wadenhoe Nhants 61 N4
Wadesmill Herts 51 J7
Wadhurst E Susx 25 P4
Wadshelf Derbys 84 D6
Wadswick Wilts 32 F11
Wadworth Donc 91 P11
Waen Denbgs 68 C2
Waen Denbgs 80 G11
Waen Powys 68 H11
Waen Fach Powys 68 H11
Waen-pentir Gwynd 79 K11
Waen-wen Gwynd 79 K11
Wagbeach Shrops 56 F4
Wainfelin Torfn 31 J4
Wainfleet All Saints Lincs 87 N9
Wainfleet Bank Lincs 87 N9
Wainfleet St Mary Lincs 87 N9
Wainford Norfk 65 L3
Wainhouse Corner Cnwll 5 K2
Wainscott Medway 38 B7
Wain's Hill N Som 31 L10
Wainstalls Calder 90 C5
Waitby Cumb 102 E9
Waithe Lincs 93 N10
Wakefield Wakefd 91 J6
Wake Green Birm 58 G8
Wakerley Nhants 73 P11
Wakes Colne Essex 52 E6
Walberswick Suffk 65 P7
Walberton W Susx 15 Q5
Walbottle N u Ty 113 J7
Walbutt D & G 108 F7
Walby Cumb 110 H8
Walcombe Somset 19 Q5
Walcot Lincs 73 R3
Walcot N Linc 92 E6
Walcot Shrops 56 F6
Walcot Shrops 57 K2
Walcot Swindn 33 N8
Walcote Leics 60 C4
Walcote Warwks 47 M3
Walcot Green Norfk 64 G5
Walcott Lincs 86 F9
Walcott Norfk 77 M5
Walden N York 96 F4
Walden Head N York 96 E4
Walden Stubbs N York 91 P7
Walderslade Medway 38 C9
Walderton W Susx 15 L4
Walditch Dorset 11 K6
Waldley Derbys 71 L7
Waldridge Dur 113 L11
Waldringfield Suffk 53 N2
Waldron E Susx 25 M7
Wales Rothm 84 G4
Wales Somset 19 Q10
Walesby Lincs 86 F2
Walesby Notts 85 L6
Walford Herefs 46 A10
Walford Herefs 56 F10
Walford Shrops 69 M10
Walford Staffs 70 E8
Walford Heath Shrops 69 M11
Walgherton Ches E 70 B5
Walgrave Nhants 60 H6
Walhampton Hants 13 P5
Walkden Salfd 82 F4
Walker N u Ty 113 L8
Walkerburn Border 117 M3
Walker Fold Lancs 89 K2
Walkeringham Notts 85 N2
Walkerith Lincs 85 N2
Walkern Herts 50 H5
Walker's Green Herefs 45 Q5
Walker's Heath Birm 58 G8
Walkerton Fife 134 G7
Walkford BCP 13 M6
Walkhampton Devon 6 E5
Walkington E R Yk 92 G4
Walkley Sheff 84 D3
Walk Mill Lancs 89 P5
Walkwood Worcs 47 K2
Wall Nthumb 112 F7
Wall Staffs 58 H3
Wallacetown S Ayrs 114 E4
Wallacetown S Ayrs 114 F3
Wallands Park E Susx 25 K8
Wallasey Wirral 81 K6
Wallasey (Kingsway) Tunnel Wirral 81 L6
Wall End Cumb 94 E4
Wall End Herefs 45 N3
Wallend Medway 38 E6
Waller's Green Herefs 46 C7
Wallhead Cumb 111 J8
Wall Heath Dudley 58 C7
Wall Houses Nthumb 112 F7
Wallingford Oxon 34 H7
Wallington Gt Lon 36 G8
Wallington Hants 14 G5
Wallington Herts 50 G4

Wallington Heath Wsall 58 E4
Wallis Pembks 41 K5
Wallisdown BCP 13 J6
Walliswood Surrey 24 D3
Walls Shet 169 p9
Wallsend N Tyne 113 L7
Wallthwaite Cumb 101 L5
Wall under Haywood Shrops 57 J4
Wallyford E Loth 128 B5
Walmer Kent 39 Q11
Walmer Bridge Lancs 88 F6
Walmersley Bury 89 N8
Walmestone Kent 39 N10
Walmley Birm 58 H6
Walmley Ash Birm 58 H6
Walmsgate Lincs 87 L5
Walney Cumb 94 D7
Walpole Somset 19 K6
Walpole Suffk 65 M7
Walpole Cross Keys Norfk 75 K7
Walpole Highway Norfk 75 K8
Walpole St Andrew Norfk 75 K7
Walpole St Peter Norfk 75 K7
Walrow Somset 19 K5
Walsall Wsall 58 F5
Walsall Wood Wsall 58 F4
Walsden Calder 89 Q6
Walsgrave on Sowe Covtry 59 N8
Walsham le Willows Suffk 64 E7
Walshaw Bury 89 M8
Walshford N York 97 P10
Walsoken Norfk 75 J8
Walston S Lans 127 L6
Walsworth Herts 50 E4
Walter's Ash Bucks 35 M5
Walters Green Kent 25 M2
Walterstone Herefs 45 L9
Waltham Kent 27 K2
Waltham NE Lin 93 N10
Waltham Abbey Essex 51 J10
Waltham Chase Hants 14 G4
Waltham Cross Herts 51 J10
Waltham on the Wolds Leics 73 L6
Waltham St Lawrence W & M 35 M9
Waltham's Cross Essex 51 Q4
Walthamstow Gt Lon 37 J3
Walton C Pete 74 C10
Walton Cumb 111 K8
Walton Derbys 84 E7
Walton Leeds 97 P11
Walton Leics 60 C3
Walton M Keyn 49 N7
Walton Powys 45 K3
Walton Shrops 56 H9
Walton Somset 19 N7
Walton Staffs 70 F8
Walton Staffs 70 F9
Walton Suffk 53 N4
Walton W Susx 15 L4
Walton Wakefd 91 K7
Walton Warwks 47 Q4
Walton Wrekin 69 Q11
Walton Cardiff Gloucs 46 H8
Walton East Pembks 41 K6
Walton Elm Dorset 20 E11
Walton Grounds Nhants 48 F8
Walton Highway Norfk 75 J8
Walton-in-Gordano N Som 31 M10
Walton-le-Dale Lancs 88 H5
Walton-on-the-Hill Staffs 70 H10
Walton-on-the-Hill Surrey 36 F9
Walton-on-the-Naze Essex 53 M7
Walton on the Wolds Leics 72 F7
Walton-on-Trent Derbys 71 N11
Walton Park N Som 31 M10
Walton West Pembks 40 G8
Walwen Flints 80 G9
Walwen Flints 80 H10
Walwen Flints 81 J9
Walwick Nthumb 112 D6
Walworth Darltn 103 P7
Walworth Gt Lon 36 H5
Walworth Gate Darltn 103 P6
Walwyn's Castle Pembks 40 G8
Wambrook Somset 10 F3
Wampool Cumb 110 D10
Wanborough Surrey 23 P5
Wanborough Swindn 33 P8
Wandon End Herts 50 D6
Wandsworth Gt Lon 36 G5
Wangford Suffk 65 P6
Wanlip Leics 72 F8
Wanlockhead D & G 116 B8
Wannock E Susx 25 N10
Wansford C Pete 73 R11
Wansford E R Yk 99 M9
Wanshurst Green Kent 26 C2
Wanstead Gt Lon 37 K3
Wanstrow Somset 20 D6
Wanswell Gloucs 32 C4
Wantage Oxon 34 C7
Wants Green Worcs 46 E3
Wapley S Glos 32 D9
Wappenbury Warwks 59 N11
Wappenham Nhants 48 H5
Warbleton E Susx 25 P7
Warborough Oxon 34 G6
Warboys Cambs 62 D4
Warbreck Bpool 88 C3
Warbstow Cnwll 5 L3
Warburton Traffd 82 F7
Warcop Cumb 102 D7
Warden Kent 38 H7
Warden Nthumb 112 D7
Warden Street C Beds 50 D2
Ward End Birm 58 H7
Ward Green Suffk 64 E9
Ward Green Cross Lancs 89 J3
Wardhedges C Beds 50 C3
Wardington Oxon 48 E5
Wardle Ches E 69 R3
Wardle Rochdl 89 Q7
Wardley Gatesd 113 M8
Wardley Rutlnd 73 L10
Wardley Salfd 82 G4
Wardlow Derbys 83 Q10
Wardsend Ches E 83 K8
Wardy Hill Cambs 62 G4
Ware Herts 51 J8
Wareham Dorset 12 F7
Warehorne Kent 26 G5
Warenford Nthumb 119 M5

Waren Mill Nthumb 119 M4
Warenton Nthumb 119 M4
Wareside Herts 51 J7
Waresley Cambs 62 C10
Waresley Worcs 58 B10
Ware Street Kent 38 C10
Warfield Br For 35 N10
Warfleet Devon 7 M8
Wargate Lincs 74 D4
Wargrave Wokham 35 L9
Warham Herefs 45 P7
Warham Norfk 76 D3
Wark Nthumb 112 C5
Wark Nthumb 118 F3
Warkleigh Devon 17 L7
Warkton Nhants 61 J5
Warkworth Nhants 48 E6
Warkworth Nthumb 119 P9
Warlaby N York 97 M2
Warland Calder 89 Q6
Warleggan Cnwll 5 K8
Warleigh BaNES 20 E2
Warley Town Calder 90 D6
Warlingham Surrey 37 J9
Warmbrook Derbys 71 P4
Warmfield Wakefd 91 K6
Warmingham Ches E 70 C2
Warmington Nhants 61 N2
Warmington Warwks 48 D5
Warminster Wilts 20 G5
Warmley S Glos 32 C10
Warmsworth Donc 91 N10
Warmwell Dorset 12 C7
Warndon Worcs 46 G3
Warner Bros. Studio Tour London Herts 50 C10
Warnford Hants 22 H10
Warnham W Susx 24 E4
Warningcamp W Susx 24 B9
Warninglid W Susx 24 F5
Warren Ches E 83 J10
Warren Pembks 40 H11
Warrenby R & Cl 104 G5
Warren Row W & M 35 M8
Warren's Green Herts 50 G5
Warren Street Kent 38 F11
Warrington M Keyn 49 N4
Warrington Warrtn 82 D7
Warriston C Edin 127 P2
Warsash Hants 14 E5
Warslow Staffs 71 K3
Warsop Vale Notts 84 H7
Warter E R Yk 98 H10
Warthermaske N York 97 K5
Warthill N York 98 D9
Wartling E Susx 25 Q9
Wartnaby Leics 73 J6
Warton Lancs 88 E5
Warton Lancs 95 K6
Warton Nthumb 119 K10
Warton Warwks 59 L4
Warwick Warwks 59 L11
Warwick Bridge Cumb 111 J9
Warwick Castle Warwks 47 Q2
Warwick-on-Eden Cumb 111 J9
Warwick Services Warwks 48 B3
Warwicksland Cumb 111 J5
Wasbister Ork 169 c3
Wasdale Head Cumb 100 G9
Wash Derbys 83 N8
Washall Green Herts 51 K4
Washaway Cnwll 4 G8
Washbourne Devon 7 K8
Washbrook Somset 19 M4
Washbrook Suffk 53 K3
Washfield Devon 18 B11
Washfold N York 103 L10
Washford Somset 18 E6
Washford Pyne Devon 9 K2
Washingborough Lincs 86 D6
Washington Sundld 113 M9
Washington W Susx 24 D8
Washington Services Gatesd 113 L9
Washwood Heath Birm 58 H7
Wasing W Berk 22 G2
Waskerley Dur 112 F11
Wasperton Warwks 47 Q3
Wasps Nest Lincs 86 E8
Wass N York 98 B5
Wast Water Cumb 100 G9
Watchet Somset 18 E6
Watchfield Oxon 33 P6
Watchfield Somset 19 K5
Watchgate Cumb 101 P11
Watchill Cumb 100 G2
Watcombe Torbay 7 N5
Watendlath Cumb 101 J7
Water Devon 9 J8
Water Lancs 89 N5
Water Eaton Oxon 34 F2
Water Eaton Staffs 58 D2
Water End Bed 61 P10
Water End C Beds 61 P11
Water End C Beds 50 C3
Water End E R Yk 92 C3
Water End Essex 51 N2
Water End Herts 50 B8
Water End Herts 50 F10
Waterfall Staffs 71 K4
Waterfoot Ag & B 120 F4
Waterfoot E Rens 125 P6
Waterfoot Lancs 89 N6
Waterford Herts 50 H8
Water Fryston Wakefd 91 M5
Watergate Cnwll 5 J5
Waterhead Cumb 101 L10
Waterheads Border 127 N7
Waterhouses Dur 103 N2
Waterhouses Staffs 71 K4
Wateringbury Kent 37 Q10
Waterlane Gloucs 32 H4
Waterloo Cnwll 5 J1
Waterloo Derbys 84 E7
Waterloo Herefs 45 L1
Waterloo Highld 145 L1
Waterloo N Lans 126 E5
Waterloo Norfk 77 K3
Waterloo P & K 141 Q1
Waterloo Pembks 41 J1

Waterloo Sefton 81 L5
Waterloo Cross Devon 9 Q2
Waterloo Port Gwynd 66 H2
Waterlooville Hants 15 J5
Watermead Bucks 49 M11
Watermillock Cumb 101 M6
Water Newton Cambs 74 B11
Water Orton Warwks 59 J6
Waterperry Oxon 34 H3
Waterrow Somset 18 E9
Watersfield W Susx 24 B7
Waterside Bl w D 89 L6
Waterside Bucks 35 Q4
Waterside Donc 91 R8
Waterside E Ayrs 114 H6
Waterside E Ayrs 125 M9
Waterside E Duns 126 B3
Water's Nook Bolton 89 K9
Waterstein Highld 152 A8
Waterstock Oxon 34 H3
Waterston Pembks 40 H9
Water Stratford Bucks 49 J8
Water Street Neath 29 M8
Waters Upton Wrekin 70 A11
Water Yeat Cumb 94 F3
Watford Herts 50 D11
Watford Nhants 60 D7
Watford Gap Services Nhants 60 D7
Wath N York 96 H7
Wath N York 97 M5
Wath upon Dearne Rothm 91 L10
Watlington Norfk 75 M8
Watlington Oxon 35 J6
Watnall Notts 84 H11
Watten Highld 167 M6
Wattisfield Suffk 64 E7
Wattisham Suffk 64 E11
Watton Dorset 11 K6
Watton E R Yk 99 L10
Watton Norfk 76 C11
Watton-at-Stone Herts 50 H7
Watton Green Norfk 76 C11
Wattons Green Essex 51 M11
Wattston N Lans 126 D3
Wattstown Rhondd 30 D6
Wattsville Caerph 30 H6
Wauldby E R Yk 92 G5
Waulkmill Abers 150 G9
Waunarlwydd Swans 28 H5
Waun Fach Powys 44 H9
Waunfawr Cerdgn 54 E8
Waunfawr Gwynd 67 J3
Waungron Swans 28 G4
Waunlwyd Blae G 30 G3
Wavendon M Keyn 49 P7
Waverbridge Cumb 110 D11
Waverley Rothm 84 F3
Waverton Ches W 69 N2
Waverton Cumb 110 D11
Wawne E R Yk 93 J3
Waxham Norfk 77 N6
Waxholme E R Yk 93 P5
Way Kent 39 P8
Waye Devon 7 K4
Wayford Somset 11 J3
Waytown Dorset 11 K5
Way Village Devon 9 L2
Way Wick N Som 19 L2
Weacombe Somset 18 F6
Weald Oxon 34 B4
Wealdstone Gt Lon 36 E3
Weardley Leeds 90 H2
Weare Somset 19 M4
Weare Giffard Devon 16 H7
Wearhead Dur 102 G3
Wearne Somset 19 M9
Weasdale Cumb 102 C10
Weasenham All Saints Norfk 76 A7
Weasenham St Peter Norfk 76 B7
Weaste Salfd 82 H5
Weatheroak Hill Worcs 58 G10
Weaverham Ches W 82 D10
Weaverslake Staffs 71 K11
Weaverthorpe N York 99 K6
Webbington Somset 19 L3
Webb's Heath S Glos 32 C10
Webheath Worcs 58 F11
Webton Herefs 45 N7
Wedderlairs Abers 159 L11
Wedding Hall Fold N York 96 D11
Weddington Kent 39 N10
Weddington Warwks 59 N6
Wedhampton Wilts 21 L3
Wedmore Somset 19 M5
Wednesbury Sandw 58 E5
Wednesfield Wolves 58 D4
Weecar Notts 85 P7
Weedon Bucks 49 M11
Weedon Bec Nhants 60 D9
Weedon Lois Nhants 48 H5
Weeford Staffs 58 H4
Week Devon 7 K6
Week Devon 17 K6
Week Devon 17 N8
Weeke Devon 9 J3
Weeke Hants 22 E8
Weekley Nhants 61 J4
Week St Mary Cnwll 5 L2
Weel E R Yk 93 J3
Weeley Essex 53 K7
Weeley Heath Essex 53 L7
Weem P & K 141 K8
Weeping Cross Staffs 70 G10
Weethley Warwks 47 L3
Weeting Norfk 63 N3
Weeton E R Yk 93 Q6
Weeton Lancs 88 D4
Weeton N York 97 L11
Weetwood Leeds 90 H3
Weir Lancs 89 P5
Weirbrook Shrops 69 K10

Welford W Berk 34 D10
Welford-on-Avon Warwks 47 M4
Welham Leics 60 G2
Welham Notts 85 M4
Welham Bridge E R Yk 92 C4
Welham Green Herts 50 F9
Well Hants 23 L5
Well Lincs 87 M6
Well N York 97 L4
Welland Worcs 46 E6
Wellbank Angus 142 H10
Well End Bucks 35 N7
Well End Herts 50 F11
Wellesbourne Warwks 47 Q3
Wellesbourne Mountford Warwks 47 Q3
Well Head Herts 50 E5
Well Hill Kent 37 L8
Wellhouse W Berk 34 F10
Welling Gt Lon 37 L5
Wellingborough Nhants 61 J7
Wellingham Norfk 76 B7
Wellingore Lincs 86 C9
Wellington Cumb 100 E10
Wellington Herefs 45 P5
Wellington Somset 18 F10
Wellington Wrekin 57 M2
Wellington Heath Herefs 46 D6
Wellington Marsh Herefs 45 P5
Wellow BaNES 20 D3
Wellow IoW 14 C9
Wellow Notts 85 L7
Wellpond Green Herts 51 K6
Wells Somset 19 P5
Wellsborough Leics 72 B10
Wells Green Ches E 70 B4
Wells Head C Brad 90 D4
Wells-next-the-Sea Norfk 76 C3
Wellstye Green Essex 51 P7
Well Town Devon 9 M3
Welltree P & K 134 B3
Wellwood Fife 134 D10
Welney Norfk 62 H2
Welshampton Shrops 69 M7
Welsh Bicknor Herefs 46 A11
Welsh End Shrops 69 P7
Welsh Frankton Shrops 69 L8
Welsh Hook Pembks 40 H5
Welsh Newton Herefs 45 Q11
Welshpool Powys 56 C3
Welsh St Donats V Glam 30 D9
Welton Cumb 101 L2
Welton E R Yk 92 G5
Welton Lincs 86 D5
Welton Nhants 60 C7
Welton le Marsh Lincs 87 N7
Welton le Wold Lincs 87 J3
Welwick E R Yk 93 P6
Welwyn Herts 50 F7
Welwyn Garden City Herts 50 F8
Wem Shrops 69 P9
Wembdon Somset 19 J7
Wembley Gt Lon 36 E3
Wembury Devon 6 E9
Wembworthy Devon 17 M10
Wemyss Bay Inver 124 F4
Wenallt Cerdgn 54 F10
Wendens Ambo Essex 51 M3
Wendlebury Oxon 48 G11
Wendling Norfk 76 C9
Wendover Bucks 35 N3
Wendron Cnwll 2 H7
Wendron Mining District Cnwll 2 H7
Wendy Cambs 62 D11
Wenfordbridge Cnwll 4 H6
Wenhaston Suffk 65 N6
Wennington Cambs 62 B5
Wennington Gt Lon 37 M4
Wennington Lancs 95 N1
Wensley Derbys 84 C8
Wensley N York 96 G3
Wentbridge Wakefd 91 M7
Wentnor Shrops 56 F6
Wentworth Cambs 62 G5
Wentworth Rothm 91 K11
Wenvoe V Glam 30 F10
Weobley Herefs 45 N4
Weobley Marsh Herefs 45 N4
Wepham W Susx 24 B9
Wereham Norfk 75 N10
Wergs Wolves 58 C4
Wern Gwynd 67 J7
Wern Powys 44 G11
Wern Powys 56 D2
Wern Shrops 69 J8
Werneth Low Tamesd 83 L6
Wernffrwd Swans 28 F6
Wern-Gifford Mons 45 L10
Wern-y-gaer Flints 81 J11
Werrington C Pete 74 C10
Werrington Cnwll 5 N4
Werrington Staffs 70 G5
Wervin Ches W 81 N10
Wesham Lancs 88 E4
Wessington Derbys 84 E9
West Aberthaw V Glam 30 D11
West Acre Norfk 75
West Allerdean Nthumb 129
West Alvington
West Amesbury 21
West Anstey D... 1
West Appleton
West Ashby D...
West Ashling
West Ashton V...
West Auckland 1
West Ayton
West Bagborough
West Bank Bla...
West Bank Ha... 81
West Barkwit...
West Barnby 105 M8
West Barns N... 128 F4
West Barsham Norfk 76 C5
West Bay Dorset 11 K6
West Beckham Norfk 76 G4
West Bedfont Surrey 36 C5
West Bergholt Essex 52 G6
West Bexington Dorset 11 L7
West Bilney Norfk 75 P7
West Blatchington Br & H... 24 F9
West Boldon S Tyne 113 N8
Westborough Lincs 73 M2
Westbourne BCP 13 J6

Westbourne W Susx ...15 L5
West Bourton Dorset ...20 E9
West Bowling C Brad ...90 F4
West Brabourne Kent ...27 J3
West Bradenham Norfk ...76 C10
West Bradford Lancs ...89 L2
West Bradley Somset ...19 Q7
West Bretton Wakefd ...90 H8
West Bridgford Notts ...72 F3
West Briscoe Dur ...103 J7
West Bromwich Sandw ...58 F6
Westbrook Kent ...39 P7
Westbrook W Berk ...34 D10
Westbrook Wilts ...33 J11
West Buckland Devon ...17 M5
West Buckland Somset ...18 G10
West Burrafirth Shet ...169 p8
West Burton N York ...96 F3
West Burton W Susx ...15 Q4
Westbury Bucks ...48 H7
Westbury Shrops ...56 F3
Westbury Wilts ...20 G4
Westbury Leigh Wilts ...20 G5
Westbury-on-Severn Gloucs ...32 D2
Westbury-on-Trym Bristl ...31 Q9
Westbury-sub-Mendip
  Somset ...19 P5
West Butsfield Dur ...103 M2
West Butterwick N Linc ...92 D9
Westby Lancs ...88 D4
West Byfleet Surrey ...36 B8
West Cairngaan D & G ...106 F11
West Caister Norfk ...77 Q9
West Calder W Loth ...127 J5
West Camel Somset ...19 Q10
West Chaldon Dorset ...12 C8
West Challow Oxon ...34 C7
West Charleton Devon ...7 K10
West Chelborough Dorset ...11 L3
West Chevington Nthumb ...119 P11
West Chiltington W Susx ...24 C7
West Chinnock Somset ...11 K2
West Chisenbury Wilts ...21 M4
West Clandon Surrey ...36 B10
West Cliffe Kent ...27 P3
Westcliff-on-Sea Sthend ...38 E4
West Clyst Devon ...9 N5
West Coker Somset ...11 L2
West Combe Devon ...7 K4
Westcombe Somset ...20 C7
West Compton Somset ...19 Q6
West Compton Abbas
  Dorset ...11 M6
Westcote Gloucs ...47 P10
Westcote Barton Oxon ...48 D9
Westcott Bucks ...49 K11
Westcott Devon ...9 P4
Westcott Surrey ...36 D11
West Cottingwith N York ...92 A2
Westcourt Wilts ...21 P2
West Cowick E R Yk ...91 Q6
West Cross Swans ...28 H7
West Curry Cnwll ...5 M3
West Curthwaite Cumb ...110 F11
Westdean E Susx ...25 M11
West Dean W Susx ...15 N4
West Dean Wilts ...21 Q9
West Deeping Lincs ...74 B9
West Derby Lpool ...81 M6
West Dereham Norfk ...75 N10
West Ditchburn Nthumb ...119 M6
West Down Devon ...17 J3
Westdown Camp Wilts ...21 K5
Westdowns Cnwll ...4 H5
West Drayton Gt Lon ...36 C5
West Drayton Notts ...85 M6
West Dunnet Highld ...167 M2
Wested Kent ...37 M7
West Ella E R Yk ...92 H5
West End C Beds ...49 Q4
West End Br For ...35 N10
West End Caerph ...30 H5
West End Cumb ...110 F9
West End E R Yk ...92 F4
West End E R Yk ...93 L4
West End E R Yk ...93 N5
Westend Gloucs ...32 E3
West End Hants ...14 E4
West End Hants ...22 H7
West End Herts ...50 G9
West End Herts ...50 H9
West End Lancs ...89 L5
West End Leeds ...90 G3
West End Lincs ...93 Q11
West End N Som ...31 N11
West End N York ...91 N2
West End Norfk ...76 C10
West End Norfk ...77 Q9
West End Oxon ...34 G2
West End S Glos ...32 D7
West End Somset ...20 C8
West End Surrey ...23 P2
West End Surrey ...36 D8
West End W & M ...35 M9
West End W Susx ...24 F7
West End Wilts ...20 H10
West End Wilts ...21 J10
West End Wilts ...33 J9
West End Green Hants ...23 J2
Westend Town Nthumb ...111 Q7
Westenhanger Kent ...27 K4
Wester Aberchalder Highld ...147 P3
Wester Balblair Highld ...155 P8
Westerdale Highld ...167 K6
Westerdale N York ...105 J9
Westerfield Suffk ...53 L2
Westergate W Susx ...15 P5
Wester Hailes C Edin ...127 M3
Westerham Kent ...37 K10
Westerhope N u Ty ...113 J7
Westerland Devon ...7 M6
Westerleigh S Glos ...32 C9
Western Isles W Isls ...168 f8
Wester Ochiltree W Loth ...127 J3
Wester Pitkierie Fife ...135 P6
Wester Ross Highld ...160 F11
Westerton W Susx ...15 N5
Westerton of Rossie Angus ...143 M4
Westerwick Shet ...169 p9
West Ewell Surrey ...36 F8
West Farleigh Kent ...38 B11
West Farndon Nhants ...48 E4
West Felton Shrops ...69 K9
Westfield BaNES ...20 C4
Westfield Cumb ...100 D8
Westfield E Susx ...26 D8

Westfield Highld ...167 J4
Westfield N Lans ...126 C3
Westfield Norfk ...76 D10
Westfield Surrey ...36 B9
Westfield W Loth ...126 G3
Westfields Dorset ...12 B3
Westfields Herefs ...45 P6
Westfields of Rattray P & K ...142 B8
Westfield Sole Kent ...38 C9
West Flotmanby N York ...99 M5
Westford Somset ...18 F10
Westgate Dur ...102 H3
Westgate N Linc ...92 C9
Westgate Norfk ...76 D3
Westgate Hill C Brad ...90 G5
Westgate-on-Sea Kent ...39 P7
Westgate Street Norfk ...76 H7
West Ginge Oxon ...34 D7
West Grafton Wilts ...21 P2
West Green Hants ...23 K3
West Grimstead Wilts ...21 P9
West Grinstead W Susx ...24 E5
West Haddlesey N York ...91 P5
West Haddon Nhants ...60 D6
West Hagbourne Oxon ...34 F7
West Hagley Worcs ...58 D8
Westhall Suffk ...65 N5
West Hallam Derbys ...72 C2
West Hallam Common
  Derbys ...72 C2
West Halton N Linc ...92 F6
Westham Dorset ...11 P9
West Ham Gt Lon ...37 J4
Westham E Susx ...25 P10
Westham Somset ...19 M5
Westhampnett W Susx ...15 N5
West Handley Derbys ...84 E5
West Hanney Oxon ...34 D6
West Hanningfield Essex ...38 B2
West Harnham Wilts ...21 M9
West Harptree BaNES ...19 Q3
West Harting W Susx ...23 L10
West Hatch Somset ...19 J10
West Hatch Wilts ...20 H9
West Haven Angus ...143 K10
Westhay Somset ...19 M6
Westhead Lancs ...88 E9
West Head Norfk ...75 L9
West Heath Birm ...58 F9
West Heath Hants ...22 G3
West Helmsdale Highld ...163 N3
West Hendred Oxon ...34 D7
West Heslerton N York ...99 J5
West Hewish N Som ...19 L2
Westhide Herefs ...46 A6
Westhill Abers ...151 L6
West Hill Devon ...9 Q5
Westhill Highld ...156 C9
West Hoathly W Susx ...25 J4
West Holme Dorset ...12 E7
Westholme Somset ...19 Q6
Westhope Herefs ...45 P4
Westhope Shrops ...56 H7
West Horndon Essex ...37 P3
Westhorp Nhants ...48 F4
Westhorpe Lincs ...74 D4
Westhorpe Suffk ...64 E8
West Horrington Somset ...19 Q5
West Horsley Surrey ...36 C10
West Horton Nthumb ...119 K4
West Hougham Kent ...27 N3
Westhoughton Bolton ...89 K9
Westhouse N York ...95 P6
Westhouses Derbys ...84 F9
West Howe BCP ...13 J5
West Howetown Somset ...18 B8
Westhumble Surrey ...36 E10
West Huntingtower P & K ...134 D3
West Huntspill Somset ...19 K6
West Hyde C Beds ...50 D7
West Hyde Herts ...36 B2
West Hythe Kent ...27 K5
West Ilkerton Devon ...17 N2
West Ilsley W Berk ...34 E8
West Itchenor W Susx ...15 L6
West Keal Lincs ...87 L8
West Kennett Wilts ...33 M11
West Kilbride N Ayrs ...124 G3
West Kingsdown Kent ...37 N8
West Kington Wilts ...32 F9
West Kirby Wirral ...81 J7
West Knapton N York ...98 H5
West Knighton Dorset ...12 B7
West Knoyle Wilts ...20 G8
West Kyloe Nthumb ...119 L2
Westlake Devon ...6 G8
West Lambrook Somset ...19 M11
Westland Green Herts ...51 K6
West Langdon Kent ...27 P2
West Lavington W Susx ...23 N10
West Lavington Wilts ...21 K4
West Layton N York ...103 M8
West Leake Notts ...72 E5
West Learmouth Nthumb ...118 F3
West Lees N York ...104 E10
West Leigh Devon ...8 G3
Westleigh Devon ...16 H6
Westleigh Devon ...18 E11
West Leigh Somset ...18 F8
Westleton Suffk ...65 N8
West Lexham Norfk ...76 A8
Westley Shrops ...56 F3
Westley Suffk ...63 P8
Westley Waterless Cambs ...63 K9
West Lilling N York ...98 C8
Westlington Bucks ...35 L2
West Linton Border ...127 M7
Westlinton Cumb ...110 G8
West Littleton S Glos ...32 E9
West Lockinge Oxon ...34 D7
West Lulworth Dorset ...12 D8
West Lutton N York ...99 J7
West Lydford Somset ...19 Q8
West Lyn Devon ...17 N2
West Lyng Somset ...19 K9
West Lynn Norfk ...75 M6
West Malling Kent ...37 Q9
West Malvern Worcs ...46 E5
West Marden W Susx ...15 L4
West Markham Notts ...85 M6
Westmarsh Kent ...39 N9
West Marsh NE Lin ...93 N3
West Marton N York ...96 C10
West Melbury Dorset ...20 G10
West Melton Rothm ...91 L10
West Meon Hants ...22 H9

West Meon Hut Hants ...23 J9
West Meon Woodlands
  Hants ...22 H9
West Mersea Essex ...52 H9
Westmeston E Susx ...24 H8
West Mickley Nthumb ...112 G8
West Midland Safari Park
  Worcs ...57 Q9
Westmill Herts ...50 H7
Westmill Herts ...51 J5
West Milton Dorset ...11 L5
Westminster Gt Lon ...36 G5
Westminster Abbey &
  Palace Gt Lon ...36 G5
West Molesey Surrey ...36 D7
West Monkton Somset ...19 J9
West Moors Dorset ...13 J4
West Morden Dorset ...12 F5
West Morriston Border ...118 B2
West Morton C Brad ...90 D2
West Mudford Somset ...19 Q10
Westmuir Angus ...142 F7
West Ness N York ...98 D5
Westnewton Cumb ...100 F2
West Newton E R Yk ...93 M3
West Newton Norfk ...75 N5
West Newton Somset ...19 J9
West Norwood Gt Lon ...36 H6
Westoe S Tyne ...113 N7
West Ogwell Devon ...7 L4
Weston BaNES ...32 D11
Weston Ches E ...70 C4
Weston Devon ...10 C4
Weston Devon ...10 D7
Weston Dorset ...11 P10
Weston Halton ...81 Q8
Weston Hants ...23 K10
Weston Herefs ...45 M3
Weston Herts ...50 G4
Weston Lincs ...74 E6
Weston N York ...97 J11
Weston Nhants ...48 G5
Weston Notts ...85 N7
Weston Shrops ...56 E10
Weston Shrops ...57 L6
Weston Shrops ...69 J9
Weston Staffs ...70 H9
Weston Suffk ...65 N4
Weston W Berk ...34 C10
Weston Beggard Herefs ...46 A6
Westonbirt Gloucs ...32 G7
Weston by Welland Nhants ...60 G2
Weston Colley Hants ...22 F7
Weston Colville Cambs ...63 K10
Weston Corbett Hants ...23 J5
Weston Coyney C Stke ...70 G6
Weston Favell Nhants ...60 G8
Weston Green Cambs ...63 K10
Weston Heath Shrops ...57 P2
Weston Hills Lincs ...74 E6
Weston in Arden Warwks ...59 N7
Westoning C Beds ...50 B4
Weston-in-Gordano N Som ...31 M10
Westoning Woodend C Beds ...50 B4
Weston Jones Staffs ...70 D10
Weston Longville Norfk ...76 G8
Weston Lullingfields Shrops ...69 M10
Weston-on-Avon Warwks ...47 N4
Weston-on-the-Green
  Oxon ...48 F11
Weston Park Staffs ...57 Q2
Weston Patrick Hants ...23 J5
Weston Rhyn Shrops ...69 J7
Weston-sub-Edge Gloucs ...47 M6
Weston-super-Mare N Som ...19 K2
Weston Turville Bucks ...35 N2
Weston-under-Lizard Staffs ...57 Q2
Weston under Penyard
  Herefs ...46 B10
Weston-under-Redcastle
  Shrops ...69 Q9
Weston under Wetherley
  Warwks ...59 N11
Weston Underwood Derbys ...71 P6
Weston Underwood M Keyn ...49 N4
Weston-upon-Trent Derbys ...72 C5
Westonzoyland Somset ...19 L8
West Orchard Dorset ...20 F11
West Overton Wilts ...33 M11
Westow N York ...98 F7
West Panson Devon ...5 N3
West Park Abers ...151 K8
West Parley Dorset ...13 J5
West Peckham Kent ...37 P10
West Peeke Devon ...5 N3
West Pelton Dur ...113 K10
West Pennard Somset ...19 P7
West Pentire Cnwll ...4 B9
West Pinchbeck Lincs ...74 D6
West Porlock Somset ...17 R2
Westport Somset ...19 L10
West Pulham Dorset ...11 Q3
West Putford Devon ...16 F8
West Quantoxhead Somset ...18 F6
Westquarter Falk ...126 G2
Westra V Glam ...30 F10
West Raddon Devon ...9 L4
West Rainton Dur ...113 M11
West Rasen Lincs ...86 E3
West Ravendale NE Lin ...93 M11
Westray Ork ...169 d2
Westray Airport Ork ...169 d1
West Raynham Norfk ...76 B6
West Retford Notts ...85 L4
Westridge Green W Berk ...34 G9
Westrigg W Loth ...126 G4
Westrop Swindn ...33 P6
West Rounton N York ...104 D10
West Row Suffk ...63 L5
West Rudham Norfk ...75 R5
West Runton Norfk ...76 H3
Westruther Border ...128 G10
Westry Cambs ...74 H11
West Saltoun E Loth ...128 D6
West Sandford Devon ...9 K4
West Sandwick Shet ...169 r5
West Scrafton N York ...96 G4
West Sleekburn Nthumb ...113 M4
West Somerton Norfk ...77 P7
West Stafford Dorset ...11 Q7
West Stockwith Notts ...92 C11
West Stoke W Susx ...15 M5
West Stonesdale N York ...102 G10
West Stoughton Somset ...19 M5
West Stour Dorset ...20 E10

West Stourmouth Kent ...39 N9
West Stow Suffk ...63 P6
West Stowell Wilts ...21 M2
West Stratton Hants ...22 F6
West Street Kent ...38 F11
West Street Kent ...39 P11
West Street Medway ...38 B6
West Street Suffk ...64 D7
West Tanfield N York ...97 L5
West Taphouse Cnwll ...5 J9
West Tarbert Ag & B ...123 Q6
West Tarring W Susx ...24 D10
West Thirston Nthumb ...119 N11
West Thorney W Susx ...15 L6
Westthorpe Derbys ...84 G5
West Thorpe Notts ...72 G5
West Thurrock Thurr ...37 N5
West Tilbury Thurr ...37 Q5
West Tisted Hants ...23 J9
West Torrington Lincs ...86 F4
West Town BaNES ...19 P2
West Town Hants ...15 K7
West Town Herefs ...45 N2
West Town N Som ...31 N11
West Town Somset ...19 P7
West Town Somset ...20 D6
West Tytherley Hants ...21 Q9
West Walton Norfk ...75 J8
Westward Cumb ...101 J2
Westward Ho! Devon ...16 G6
Westwell Kent ...26 G2
Westwell Oxon ...33 P3
Westwell Leacon Kent ...26 G2
West Wellow Hants ...21 Q11
West Wembury Devon ...6 E9
West Wemyss Fife ...135 J9
Westwick Cambs ...62 F7
Westwick Dur ...103 L7
West Wick N Som ...19 L2
Westwick Norfk ...77 K6
West Wickham Cambs ...63 K11
West Wickham Gt Lon ...37 J7
West Williamston Pembks ...41 K9
West Winch Norfk ...75 M7
West Winterslow Wilts ...21 P8
West Wittering W Susx ...15 L7
West Witton N York ...96 G3
Westwood Devon ...9 P5
Westwood Kent ...37 P6
Westwood Kent ...39 Q8
Westwood Notts ...84 G10
Westwood Nthumb ...111 Q7
Westwood Wilts ...20 F3
West Woodburn Nthumb ...112 C3
West Woodhay W Berk ...22 C2
Westwood Heath Covtry ...59 L9
West Woodlands Somset ...20 E6
Westwoodside N Linc ...92 B10
West Worldham Hants ...23 K7
West Worthing W Susx ...24 D10
West Wratting Cambs ...63 K10
West Wycombe Bucks ...35 M6
West Wylam Nthumb ...112 H8
West Yatton Wilts ...32 G9
West Yoke Kent ...37 P7
West Youlstone Cnwll ...16 D8
Wetham Green Kent ...38 D8
Wetheral Cumb ...111 J10
Wetherby Leeds ...97 P11
Wetherby Services N York ...97 P10
Wetherden Suffk ...64 E9
Wetheringsett Suffk ...64 G8
Wethersfield Essex ...52 B5
Wetherup Street Suffk ...64 G9
Wetley Rocks Staffs ...70 H5
Wettenhall Ches E ...69 R2
Wetton Staffs ...71 L3
Wetwang E R Yk ...99 J9
Wetwood Staffs ...70 D8
Wexcombe Wilts ...21 Q3
Wexham Slough ...35 Q8
Wexham Street Bucks ...35 Q8
Weybourne Norfk ...76 G3
Weybourne Surrey ...23 N5
Weybread Suffk ...65 J5
Weybread Street Suffk ...65 J6
Weybridge Surrey ...36 C8
Weycroft Devon ...10 G5
Weydale Highld ...167 L4
Weyhill Hants ...22 B5
Weymouth Dorset ...11 P9
Whaddon Bucks ...49 M8
Whaddon Cambs ...62 E11
Whaddon Gloucs ...32 F2
Whaddon Wilts ...20 G2
Whaddon Wilts ...21 N9
Whale Cumb ...101 P6
Whaley Derbys ...84 H6
Whaley Bridge Derbys ...83 M8
Whaley Thorns Derbys ...84 H6
Whaligoe Highld ...167 P8
Whalley Lancs ...89 L3
Whalley Banks Lancs ...89 L3
Whalsay Shet ...169 s7
Whalton Nthumb ...112 H4
Whaplode Lincs ...74 F6
Whaplode Drove Lincs ...74 F8
Wharf Warwks ...48 D4
Wharfe N York ...96 A7
Wharles Lancs ...88 E3
Wharley End C Beds ...49 P6
Wharncliffe Side Sheff ...84 C2
Wharram-le-Street N York ...98 H7
Wharton Ches W ...82 E11
Wharton Herefs ...45 Q3
Whashton N York ...103 N9
Whasset Cumb ...95 L4
Whatcote Warwks ...47 Q6
Whateley Warwks ...59 K5
Whatfield Suffk ...52 H2
Whatley Somset ...10 H3
Whatley Somset ...20 D5
Whatley's End S Glos ...32 C8
Whatlington E Susx ...26 C8
Whatsole Street Kent ...27 K3
Whatstandwell Derbys ...84 D10
Whatton-in-the-Vale Notts ...73 J3
Whauphill D & G ...107 M8
Whaw N York ...103 J10
Wheal Peevor Cnwll ...3 J5
Wheal Rose Cnwll ...3 J5
Wheatacre Norfk ...65 P3
Wheatfield Oxon ...35 J5
Wheathampstead Herts ...50 E8
Wheathill Shrops ...57 L8
Wheathill Somset ...19 Q8

Wheatley Hants ...23 L6
Wheatley Oxon ...34 G3
Wheatley Hill Dur ...104 C3
Wheatley Hills Donc ...91 P10
Wheatley Lane Lancs ...89 N3
Wheaton Aston Staffs ...58 C2
Wheddon Cross Somset ...18 B7
Wheelbarrow Town Kent ...27 K2
Wheeler End Bucks ...35 M6
Wheeler's Green Wokham ...35 L10
Wheelerstreet Surrey ...23 P6
Wheelock Ches E ...70 D3
Wheelock Heath Ches E ...70 D3
Wheelton Lancs ...89 J6
Wheldale Wakefd ...91 M5
Wheldrake C York ...92 A2
Whelford Gloucs ...33 N5
Whelpley Hill Bucks ...35 Q4
Whelpo Cumb ...101 K3
Whelston Flints ...81 J9
Whempstead Herts ...50 H6
Whenby N York ...98 C7
Whepstead Suffk ...64 A10
Wherstead Suffk ...53 L3
Wherwell Hants ...22 C6
Wheston Derbys ...83 P9
Whetsted Kent ...37 Q11
Whetstone Gt Lon ...36 G2
Whetstone Leics ...72 F11
Wheyrig Cumb ...110 C11
Whicham Cumb ...94 C4
Whichford Warwks ...48 B8
Whiddon Devon ...8 C5
Whiddon Down Devon ...8 G6
Whigstreet Angus ...142 H9
Whilton Nhants ...60 D8
Whimble Devon ...16 F3
Whimple Devon ...9 P5
Whimpwell Green Norfk ...77 M6
Whinburgh Norfk ...76 E10
Whin Lane End Lancs ...88 D2
Whinnieliggate D & G ...108 F10
Whinnow Cumb ...110 F10
Whinnyfold Abers ...159 Q11
Whinny Hill S on T ...104 C7
Whippingham IoW ...14 F8
Whipsnade C Beds ...50 B7
Whipsnade Zoo ZSL C Beds ...50 B7
Whipton Devon ...9 M6
Whirlow Sheff ...84 D4
Whisby Lincs ...86 B7
Whissendine Rutlnd ...73 L8
Whissonsett Norfk ...76 C7
Whistlefield Ag & B ...131 Q9
Whistlefield Inn Ag & B ...131 N9
Whistley Green Wokham ...35 L10
Whiston Knows ...81 P6
Whiston Nhants ...60 H8
Whiston Rothm ...84 F3
Whiston Staffs ...58 C2
Whiston Staffs ...71 J5
Whiston Cross Shrops ...57 P4
Whiston Eaves Staffs ...71 J5
Whitacre Fields Warwks ...59 L6
Whitbeck Cumb ...94 C4
Whitbourne Herefs ...46 D3
Whitburn S Tyne ...113 P8
Whitburn W Loth ...126 G5
Whitby Ches W ...81 M9
Whitby N York ...105 N8
Whitbyheath Ches W ...81 M10
Whitchester Border ...129 J8
Whitchurch BaNES ...32 B11
Whitchurch Bucks ...49 M10
Whitchurch Cardif ...30 G9
Whitchurch Devon ...6 D4
Whitchurch Hants ...22 E4
Whitchurch Herefs ...45 R11
Whitchurch Oxon ...34 H9
Whitchurch Pembks ...40 F5
Whitchurch Shrops ...69 P6
Whitchurch Canonicorum
  Dorset ...10 H5
Whitchurch Hill Oxon ...34 H9
Whitcombe Dorset ...11 Q7
Whitcott Keysett Shrops ...56 F6
Whiteacre Kent ...27 K2
Whiteacre Heath Warwks ...59 K6
Whiteash Green Essex ...52 C5
White Ball Somset ...18 F11
Whitebridge Highld ...147 M4
Whitebrook Mons ...31 P3
Whitebushes Surrey ...36 G11
Whitecairns Abers ...151 N4
Whitechapel Gt Lon ...36 H4
White Chapel Lancs ...88 H2
Whitechurch Pembks ...41 N3
Whitecliff Gloucs ...31 Q3
White Colne Essex ...52 E6
White Coppice Lancs ...89 J7
Whitecraig E Loth ...127 Q3
Whitecroft Gloucs ...32 B3
Whitecrook D & G ...106 G6
Whitecross Cnwll ...2 E7
White Cross Cnwll ...2 F7
Whitecross Cnwll ...4 F7
Whitecross Falk ...126 H2
White End Worcs ...46 E8
Whiteface Highld ...162 G9
Whitefarland N Ayrs ...120 G3
Whitefaulds S Ayrs ...114 E6
Whitefield Bury ...89 N9
Whitefield Devon ...17 N4
Whitefield Somset ...18 E9
Whitefield Lane End Knows ...81 P7
Whiteford Abers ...151 J2
Whitegate Ches W ...82 D11
Whitehall Ork ...169 f4
Whitehall W Susx ...24 D6
Whitehaven Cumb ...100 C7
Whitehill Hants ...23 L8
Whitehill Kent ...38 H10
Whitehill Leics ...72 C8
Whitehills Abers ...158 G4
Whitehouse Abers ...150 G5
Whitehouse Ag & B ...123 P7
Whitehouse Common Birm ...58 H6
Whitekirk E Loth ...128 F3
White Kirkley Dur ...103 K3
White Lackington Dorset ...11 Q5
Whitelackington Somset ...19 L11
White Ladies Aston Worcs ...46 H4
Whiteleaf Bucks ...35 M4

White-le-Head Dur......113 J10
Whiteley Hants......14 F5
Whiteley Bank IoW......14 G10
Whiteley Green Ches E......83 K9
Whiteley Village Surrey......36 G8
Whitemans Green W Susx......24 H5
White Mill Carmth......43 J10
Whitemire Moray......156 H7
Whitemoor C Nott......72 E2
Whitemoor Cnwll......4 F10
Whitemoor Derbys......84 E11
Whitemoor Staffs......70 F2
Whiteness Shet......169 q9
White Notley Essex......52 C8
Whiteoak Green Oxon......34 B2
White Ox Mead BaNES......20 D3
Whiteparish Wilts......21 P10
White Pit Lincs......87 L5
Whiterashes Abers......151 M3
White Roding Essex......51 N8
Whiterow Highld......167 Q7
Whiterow Moray......157 J6
Whiteshill Gloucs......32 F3
Whitesmith E Susx......25 M8
White Stake Lancs......88 G5
Whitestaunton Somset......10 F2
Whitestone Devon......9 L6
White Stone Herefs......45 R6
Whitestone Warwks......59 N7
Whitestone Cross Devon......9 L6
Whitestreet Green Suffk......52 G4
Whitewall Corner N York......98 F7
White Waltham W & M......35 M9
Whiteway BaNES......20 D2
Whiteway Gloucs......32 H2
Whitewell Lancs......95 P11
Whiteworks Devon......6 G4
Whitfield C Dund......142 G11
Whitfield Kent......27 P2
Whitfield Nhants......48 H7
Whitfield Nthumb......111 N10
Whitfield S Glos......32 C6
Whitfield Hall Nthumb......111 N10
Whitford Devon......10 F5
Whitford Flints......80 G9
Whitgift E R Yk......92 D6
Whitgreave Staffs......70 G9
Whithorn D & G......107 M9
Whiting Bay N Ayrs......121 K6
Whitkirk Leeds......91 K4
Whitland Carmth......41 N7
Whitlaw Border......117 Q8
Whitletts S Ayrs......114 G3
Whitley N York......91 P6
Whitley Readg......35 K10
Whitley Sheff......84 D2
Whitley Wilts......32 G11
Whitley Bay N Tyne......113 N6
Whitley Chapel Nthumb......112 D9
Whitley Heath Staffs......70 E9
Whitley Lower Kirk......90 G7
Whitley Row Kent......37 L10
Whitlock's End Solhll......58 H9
Whitminster Gloucs......32 E3
Whitmore Dorset......13 J3
Whitmore Staffs......70 E6
Whitnage Devon......18 D11
Whitnash Warwks......48 B2
Whitney-on-Wye Herefs......45 K5
Whitrigg Cumb......100 H3
Whitrigg Cumb......110 D9
Whitrigglees Cumb......110 D9
Whitsbury Hants......21 M11
Whitsome Border......129 M9
Whitson Newpt......31 L8
Whitstable Kent......39 K8
Whitstone Cnwll......5 M2
Whittingham Nthumb......119 L8
Whittingslow Shrops......56 G7
Whittington Derbys......84 D6
Whittington Gloucs......47 K10
Whittington Lancs......95 N5
Whittington Norfk......75 P11
Whittington Shrops......69 K8
Whittington Staffs......58 C8
Whittington Staffs......59 J3
Whittington Warwks......59 L5
Whittington Worcs......46 G4
Whittington Moor Derbys......84 E6
Whittlebury Nhants......49 J6
Whittle-le-Woods Lancs......88 H6
Whittlesey Cambs......74 E11
Whittlesford Cambs......62 G11
Whittlestone Head Bl w D......89 L7
Whitton N Linc......92 F6
Whitton Nthumb......119 L10
Whitton Powys......56 D11
Whitton S on T......104 C6
Whitton Shrops......57 K10
Whitton Suffk......53 K2
Whittonditch Wilts......33 Q10
Whittonstall Nthumb......112 G9
Whitway Hants......22 E3
Whitwell Derbys......84 H5
Whitwell Herts......50 E6
Whitwell IoW......14 F11
Whitwell N York......103 N10
Whitwell Rutlnd......73 N9
Whitwell-on-the-Hill
  N York......98 E7
Whitwell Street Norfk......76 G7
Whitwick Leics......72 C7
Whitwood Wakefd......91 L6
Whitworth Lancs......89 P7
Whixall Shrops......69 P8
Whixley N York......97 P9
Whorlton Dur......103 M8
Whorlton N York......104 E10
Whyle Herefs......45 R2
Whyteleafe Surrey......36 H9
Wibdon Gloucs......31 Q5
Wibsey C Brad......90 E4
Wibtoft Warwks......59 Q7
Wichelstowe Swindn......33 M8
Wichenford Worcs......46 E2
Wichling Kent......38 F11
Wick BCP......13 L6
Wick Devon......10 D4
Wick Highld......167 Q6
Wick S Glos......32 D10
Wick Somset......18 H6
Wick Somset......19 M9
Wick V Glam......29 P10
Wick W Susx......24 B10
Wick Wilts......21 N10
Wick Worcs......47 J5

Wicken Cambs......63 J6
Wicken Nhants......49 K7
Wicken Bonhunt Essex......51 L4
Wickenby Lincs......86 E4
Wick End Bed......49 Q4
Wicken Green Village Norfk......76 A5
Wickersley Rothm......84 G2
Wicker Street Green Suffk......52 G3
Wickford Essex......38 B3
Wickham Hants......14 G4
Wickham W Berk......34 C10
Wickham Bishops Essex......52 D9
Wickhambreaux Kent......39 M10
Wickhambrook Suffk......63 N10
Wickhamford Worcs......47 L6
Wickham Green Suffk......64 F8
Wickham Green W Berk......34 D10
Wickham Heath W Berk......34 D11
Wickham Market Suffk......65 L10
Wickhampton Norfk......77 N10
Wickham St Paul Essex......52 D4
Wickham Skeith Suffk......64 F8
Wickham Street Suffk......63 N10
Wickham Street Suffk......64 F8
Wickhurst Green W Susx......24 D4
Wick John o' Groats
  Airport Highld......167 Q6
Wicklewood Norfk......76 F11
Wickmere Norfk......76 H5
Wick St Lawrence N Som......31 L11
Wicksteed Park Nhants......61 J5
Wickstreet E Susx......25 M9
Wickwar S Glos......32 D7
Widdington Essex......51 M4
Widdop Calder......89 Q4
Widdrington Nthumb......119 Q11
Widdrington Station
  Nthumb......113 K2
Widecombe in the Moor
  Devon......8 H9
Widegates Cnwll......5 M10
Widemouth Bay Cnwll......16 C11
Wideopen N Tyne......113 L6
Widford Essex......51 Q10
Widford Herts......51 K7
Widham Wilts......33 L7
Widley Hants......15 J5
Widmer End Bucks......35 N5
Widmerpool Notts......72 G5
Widmore Gt Lon......37 K7
Widnes Halton......81 Q7
Widworthy Devon......10 E5
Wigan Wigan......88 H9
Wigborough Somset......19 M11
Wiggaton Devon......10 C6
Wiggenhall St Germans
  Norfk......75 L8
Wiggenhall St Mary
  Magdalen Norfk......75 L8
Wiggenhall St Mary the
  Virgin Norfk......75 L8
Wiggenhall St Peter Norfk......75 M8
Wiggens Green Essex......51 Q2
Wigginstall Staffs......71 K2
Wiggington Shrops......69 K7
Wigginton C York......98 C9
Wigginton Herts......35 P2
Wigginton Oxon......48 C8
Wigginton Staffs......59 K3
Wigginton Bottom Herts......35 P3
Wigglesworth N York......96 B9
Wiggonby Cumb......110 E10
Wiggonholt W Susx......24 C7
Wighill N York......97 Q11
Wighton Norfk......76 C4
Wightwick Wolves......58 C5
Wigley Derbys......84 D6
Wigley Hants......22 B11
Wigmore Herefs......56 G11
Wigmore Medway......38 C9
Wigsley Notts......85 Q6
Wigsthorpe Nhants......61 M4
Wigston Leics......72 G11
Wigston Fields Leics......72 G10
Wigston Parva Leics......59 Q7
Wigthorpe Notts......85 J4
Wigtoft Lincs......74 E3
Wigton Cumb......110 E11
Wigtown D & G......107 M6
Wigtwizzle Sheff......90 G11
Wike Leeds......91 J2
Wilbarston Nhants......60 H3
Wilberfoss E R Yk......98 E10
Wilburton Cambs......62 G5
Wilby Nhants......61 J7
Wilby Norfk......64 E4
Wilby Suffk......65 J7
Wilcot Wilts......21 M2
Wilcott Shrops......69 L11
Wilcove Cnwll......6 C7
Wilcrick Newpt......31 M7
Wilday Green Derbys......84 D6
Wildboarclough Ches E......83 L11
Wilden Bed......61 N9
Wilden Worcs......58 B10
Wilde Street Suffk......63 M5
Wildhill Herts......50 G9
Wildmanbridge S Lans......126 E7
Wildmill Brdgnd......29 P8
Wildmoor Hants......23 J3
Wildmoor Worcs......58 E9
Wildsworth Lincs......92 D11
Wilford C Nott......72 F3
Wilkesley Ches E......70 A6
Wilkhaven Highld......163 L9
Wilkieston W Loth......127 L4
Wilkin's Green Herts......50 F9
Wilksby Lincs......87 J8
Willand Devon......9 P2
Willards Hill E Susx......26 B7
Willaston Ches E......70 B4
Willaston Ches W......81 L9
Willen M Keyn......49 N6
Willenhall Covtry......59 N9
Willenhall Wsall......58 E5
Willerby E R Yk......92 H4
Willerby N York......99 L5
Willersey Gloucs......47 M7
Willersley Herefs......45 L5
Willesborough Kent......26 H3
Willesborough Lees Kent......26 H3
Willesden Gt Lon......36 F4
Willesleigh Devon......17 L5
Willesley Wilts......32 G7
Willett Somset......18 F8

Willey Shrops......57 M5
Willey Warwks......59 Q8
Willey Green Surrey......23 P4
Williamscot Oxon......48 E5
Williamstown Rhondd......30 D6
Willian Herts......50 F4
Willicote Warwks......47 N5
Willingale Essex......51 N9
Willingdon E Susx......25 N10
Willingham Cambs......62 F6
Willingham by Stow Lincs......85 Q4
Willingham Green Cambs......63 K10
Willingham St Mary Suffk......65 N5
Willington Bed......61 P10
Willington Derbys......71 P9
Willington Dur......103 N3
Willington Kent......38 C11
Willington N Tyne......113 M7
Willington Warwks......47 Q7
Willington Corner Ches W......82 B11
Willitoft E R Yk......92 B4
Williton Somset......18 E6
Willoughby Lincs......87 N6
Willoughby Warwks......60 B7
Willoughby Hills Lincs......87 L11
Willoughby-on-the-Wolds
  Notts......72 G5
Willoughby Waterleys Leics......60 C2
Willoughton Lincs......86 B2
Willow Green Ches W......82 D9
Willows Green Essex......52 B8
Willsbridge S Glos......32 C10
Willsworthy Devon......8 D8
Willtown Somset......19 L10
Wilmcote Warwks......47 N3
Wilmington BaNES......20 C2
Wilmington Devon......10 E5
Wilmington E Susx......25 M10
Wilmington Kent......37 M6
Wilmslow Ches E......82 H8
Wilnecote Staffs......59 K4
Wilpshire Lancs......89 K4
Wilsden C Brad......90 D3
Wilsford Lincs......73 Q2
Wilsford Wilts......21 M3
Wilsford Wilts......21 M7
Wilsham Devon......17 P2
Wilshaw Kirk......90 E9
Wilsill N York......97 J8
Wilsley Green Kent......26 C4
Wilsley Pound Kent......26 C4
Wilson Herefs......45 R10
Wilson Leics......72 C6
Wilsontown S Lans......126 G6
Wilstead Bed......50 C2
Wilsthorpe Lincs......74 A8
Wilstone Herts......35 P2
Wilstone Green Herts......35 P2
Wilton Cumb......100 D8
Wilton Herefs......46 A10
Wilton N York......98 H4
Wilton R & Cl......104 G7
Wilton Wilts......21 L8
Wilton Wilts......21 Q2
Wilton Dean Border......117 P8
Wimbish Essex......51 N3
Wimbish Green Essex......51 P3
Wimbledon Gt Lon......36 F6
Wimblington Cambs......62 F2
Wimboldsley Ches W......70 B2
Wimborne Minster Dorset......12 H5
Wimborne St Giles Dorset......12 H2
Wimbotsham Norfk......75 M9
Wimpole Cambs......62 E11
Wimpstone Warwks......47 P5
Wincanton Somset......20 D9
Winceby Lincs......87 K7
Wincham Ches W......82 E9
Winchburgh W Loth......127 K3
Winchcombe Gloucs......47 K9
Winchelsea E Susx......26 F8
Winchelsea Beach E Susx......26 F8
Winchester Hants......22 E9
Winchester Services Hants......22 F7
Winchet Hill Kent......26 B3
Winchfield Hants......23 L4
Winchmore Hill Bucks......35 P5
Winchmore Hill Gt Lon......36 H2
Wincle Ches E......83 L11
Wincobank Sheff......84 E2
Winder Cumb......100 D7
Windermere Cumb......101 M11
Windermere Jetty Museum
  Cumb......101 M11
Winderton Warwks......48 B6
Windhill Highld......155 P8
Windlehurst Stockp......83 L7
Windlesham Surrey......23 P2
Windmill Cnwll......4 D7
Windmill Derbys......83 Q9
Windmill Hill E Susx......25 P8
Windmill Hill Somset......19 K11
Windrush Gloucs......33 N2
Windsole Abers......158 E5
Windsor W & M......35 Q9
Windsor Castle W & M......35 Q9
Windsoredge Gloucs......32 F4
Windsor Green Suffk......64 B11
Windygates Fife......135 J7
Windyharbour Ches E......82 H10
Windy Hill Wrexhm......69 K4
Wineham W Susx......24 F6
Winestead E R Yk......93 N6
Winewall Lancs......89 Q2
Winfarthing Norfk......64 G4
Winford IoW......14 G10
Winford N Som......19 P2
Winforton Herefs......45 K5
Winfrith Newburgh Dorset......12 D8
Wing Bucks......49 N10
Wing Rutlnd......73 M10
Wingate Dur......104 D3
Wingates Bolton......89 K9
Wingates Nthumb......119 L11
Wingerworth Derbys......84 E7
Wingfield C Beds......50 B5
Wingfield Suffk......65 J6
Wingfield Wilts......20 F3
Wingfield Green Suffk......65 J6
Wingham Kent......39 M10
Wingland Lincs......75 J6
Wingmore Kent......27 L2
Wingrave Bucks......49 N11
Winkburn Notts......85 M9
Winkfield Br For......35 P10
Winkfield Row Br For......35 N10

Winkhill Staffs......71 K4
Winkhurst Green Kent......37 L11
Winkleigh Devon......17 L10
Winksley N York......97 L6
Winkton BCP......13 L5
Winlaton Gatesd......113 J8
Winlaton Mill Gatesd......113 J8
Winless Highld......167 P6
Winllan Powys......68 H10
Winmarleigh Lancs......95 K11
Winnall Hants......22 E9
Winnersh Wokham......35 L10
Winnington Ches W......82 D10
Winscales Cumb......100 D5
Winscombe N Som......19 M3
Winsford Ches W......82 E11
Winsford Somset......18 B8
Winsham Devon......17 J4
Winsham Somset......10 H3
Winshill Staffs......71 P10
Winshwen Swans......29 J5
Winskill Cumb......101 Q4
Winslade Hants......23 J5
Winsley Wilts......20 E2
Winslow Bucks......49 L9
Winson Gloucs......33 L3
Winsor Hants......13 P2
Winstanley Wigan......82 C4
Winster Cumb......95 J2
Winster Derbys......84 B8
Winston Dur......103 M7
Winston Suffk......64 H9
Winstone Gloucs......33 J3
Winston Green Suffk......64 H9
Winswell Devon......16 H9
Winterborne Came Dorset......11 Q7
Winterborne Clenston
  Dorset......12 D4
Winterborne Herringston
  Dorset......11 P7
Winterborne Houghton
  Dorset......12 D4
Winterborne Kingston
  Dorset......12 E5
Winterborne Monkton
  Dorset......11 P7
Winterborne Stickland
  Dorset......12 D4
Winterborne Tomson Dorset......12 E5
Winterborne Whitechurch
  Dorset......12 D4
Winterborne Zelston Dorset......12 E5
Winterbourne S Glos......32 B8
Winterbourne W Berk......34 E10
Winterbourne Abbas Dorset......11 N6
Winterbourne Bassett Wilts......33 L10
Winterbourne Dauntsey
  Wilts......21 N8
Winterbourne Earls Wilts......21 N8
Winterbourne Gunner Wilts......21 N7
Winterbourne Monkton
  Wilts......33 L10
Winterbourne Steepleton
  Dorset......11 N7
Winterbourne Stoke Wilts......21 L6
Winterbrook Oxon......34 H7
Winterburn N York......96 D9
Winteringham N Linc......92 F6
Winterley Ches E......70 C3
Wintersett Wakefd......91 K7
Winterslow Wilts......21 P8
Winterton N Linc......92 F7
Winterton-on-Sea Norfk......77 P8
Winthorpe Lincs......87 Q7
Winthorpe Notts......85 P9
Winton BCP......13 J6
Winton Cumb......102 E8
Winton E Susx......25 M10
Winton N York......104 D11
Wintringham Cambs......62 D9
Wintringham N York......98 H6
Winwick Cambs......61 P4
Winwick Nhants......60 D6
Winwick Warrtn......82 D6
Wirksworth Derbys......71 P4
Wirral......81 K7
Wirswall Ches E......69 P6
Wisbech Cambs......75 J9
Wisbech St Mary Cambs......74 H9
Wisborough Green W Susx......24 C5
Wiseman's Bridge Pembks......41 M9
Wiseton Notts......85 M3
Wishanger Gloucs......32 H3
Wishaw N Lans......126 D6
Wishaw Warwks......59 J6
Wisley Surrey......36 C9
Wispington Lincs......86 H6
Wissenden Kent......26 F3
Wissett Suffk......65 M6
Wissington Norfk......75 N11
Wissington Suffk......52 G5
Wistanstow Shrops......56 G7
Wistanswick Shrops......70 B9
Wistaston Ches E......70 B4
Wistaston Green Ches E......70 B4
Wisterfield Ches E......82 H10
Wiston Pembks......41 K7
Wiston S Lans......116 D4
Wiston W Susx......24 D8
Wistow Cambs......62 C4
Wistow Leics......72 G11
Wistow N York......91 P3
Wiswell Lancs......89 L3
Witcham Cambs......62 G4
Witchampton Dorset......12 G3
Witchford Cambs......62 H5
Witcombe Somset......19 N10
Witham Essex......52 D9
Witham Friary Somset......20 D6
Witham on the Hill Lincs......73 Q7
Witham St Hughs Lincs......85 Q8
Withcall Lincs......87 J4
Withdean Br & H......24 H9
Witherenden Hill E Susx......25 P5
Witheridge Devon......9 K2
Witherley Leics......72 A11
Withern Lincs......87 M4
Withernsea E R Yk......93 P5
Withernwick E R Yk......93 L2
Withersdale Street Suffk......65 L5
Withersfield Suffk......63 L11
Witherslack Cumb......95 J4
Withiel Cnwll......4 F8
Withiel Florey Somset......18 C9
Withielgoose Cnwll......4 G8
Withington Gloucs......47 K11

Withington Herefs......45 R6
Withington Manch......82 H6
Withington Shrops......57 K2
Withington Staffs......71 J7
Withington Green Ches E......82 H10
Withington Marsh Herefs......45 R6
Withleigh Devon......9 M2
Withnell Lancs......89 J6
Withnell Fold Lancs......89 J6
Withybed Green Worcs......58 F10
Withybrook Warwks......59 P8
Withycombe Somset......18 D6
Withyham E Susx......25 L3
Withy Mills BaNES......20 C3
Withypool Somset......17 Q4
Withywood Bristl......31 Q11
Witley Surrey......23 P7
Witnesham Suffk......64 H11
Witney Oxon......34 C2
Wittering C Pete......73 R10
Wittersham Kent......26 F6
Witton Birm......58 G6
Witton Norfk......77 L10
Witton Norfk......77 L5
Witton Gilbert Dur......113 K11
Witton Green Norfk......77 N11
Witton le Wear Dur......103 M4
Witton Park Dur......103 N4
Wiveliscombe Somset......18 E9
Wivelrod Hants......23 J7
Wivelsfield E Susx......24 H6
Wivelsfield Green E Susx......25 J7
Wivelsfield Station W Susx......24 H7
Wivenhoe Essex......52 H7
Wivenhoe Cross Essex......52 H7
Wiveton Norfk......76 E3
Wix Essex......53 L6
Wixams Bed......50 C2
Wixford Warwks......47 L4
Wix Green Essex......53 L6
Wixhill Shrops......69 Q9
Wixoe Suffk......52 B3
Woburn C Beds......49 P8
Woburn Safari Park C Beds......49 Q8
Woburn Sands M Keyn......49 P7
Wokefield Park W Berk......35 J11
Woking Surrey......36 B9
Wokingham Wokham......35 M11
Wolborough Devon......7 M4
Woldingham Surrey......37 J9
Wold Newton E R Yk......99 L6
Wold Newton NE Lin......93 M11
Wolfclyde S Lans......116 E3
Wolferlow Herefs......46 C2
Wolferton Norfk......75 N5
Wolfhampcote Warwks......60 B7
Wolfhill P & K......142 B11
Wolf Hills Nthumb......111 P9
Wolf's Castle Pembks......41 J5
Wolfsdale Pembks......40 H6
Wollaston Dudley......58 C8
Wollaston Nhants......61 K8
Wollaston Shrops......56 E2
Wollaton C Nott......72 E3
Wollaton Hall C Nott......72 E3
Wolleigh Devon......9 K8
Wollerton Shrops......69 R8
Wollescote Dudley......58 D8
Wolseley Bridge Staffs......71 J10
Wolsingham Dur......103 L3
Wolstanton Staffs......70 F5
Wolstenholme Rochdl......89 N8
Wolston Warwks......59 P9
Wolsty Cumb......109 P10
Wolvercote Oxon......34 E2
Wolverhampton Wolves......58 D5
Wolverhampton Halfpenny
  Green Airport Staffs......58 B6
Wolverley Ches E......69 N8
Wolverley Worcs......58 B9
Wolverton Hants......22 G3
Wolverton Kent......27 N3
Wolverton M Keyn......49 M6
Wolverton Warwks......47 P2
Wolverton Wilts......20 E8
Wolverton Common Hants......22 G3
Wolvesnewton Mons......31 N5
Wolvey Warwks......59 P7
Wolvey Heath Warwks......59 P7
Wolviston S on T......104 E5
Wombleton N York......98 E4
Wombourne Staffs......58 C6
Wombwell Barns......91 L10
Womenswold Kent......39 M11
Womersley N York......91 N7
Wonastow Mons......31 N2
Wonersh Surrey......36 B11
Wonford Devon......9 M6
Wonson Devon......8 G7
Wonston Dorset......12 B3
Wonston Hants......22 E7
Wooburn Bucks......35 P7
Wooburn Green Bucks......35 P7
Wooburn Moor Bucks......35 P7
Woodacott Devon......16 F10
Woodale N York......96 F5
Woodall Rothm......84 G4
Woodall Services Rothm......84 G4
Woodbank Ches W......81 M10
Woodbastwick Norfk......77 L8
Woodbeck Notts......85 N5
Wood Bevington Warwks......47 L4
Woodborough Notts......85 K11
Woodborough Wilts......21 M3
Woodbridge Devon......10 D5
Woodbridge Dorset......20 G11
Woodbridge Suffk......53 N2
Wood Burcote Nhants......49 J5
Woodbury Devon......9 P7
Woodbury Salterton Devon......9 P7
Woodchester Gloucs......32 F4
Woodchurch Kent......26 F5
Woodchurch Wirral......81 K7
Woodcombe Somset......18 C5
Woodcote Gt Lon......36 G8
Woodcote Oxon......34 H8
Woodcote Wrekin......70 D11
Woodcote Green Worcs......58 D10
Woodcott Hants......22 D4
Woodcroft Gloucs......31 P5
Woodcutts Dorset......21 J11
Wood Dalling Norfk......76 F6
Woodditton Cambs......63 L9
Woodeaton Oxon......34 F2
Wood Eaton Staffs......70 E11
Wooden Pembks......41 M9

Wood End Bed 61 M11
Wood End Bed 61 N7
Wood End C Beds 49 Q6
Wood End Cambs 62 E5
Wood End Gt Lon 36 D4
Wood End Herts 50 H5
Woodend Highld 138 D5
Woodend Nhants 48 H5
Woodend Staffs 71 M9
Woodend W Loth 126 G4
Woodend W Susx 15 M5
Wood End Warwks 58 H10
Wood End Warwks 59 K5
Wood End Warwks 59 L7
Wood End Wolves 58 D4
Wood Enderby Lincs 87 J8
Woodend Green Essex 51 N5
Woodfalls Wilts 21 N10
Woodford Cnwll 6 C9
Woodford Devon 7 K8
Woodford Gloucs 32 C5
Woodford Gt Lon 37 K2
Woodford Nhants 61 L5
Woodford Stockp 83 J8
Woodford Bridge Gt Lon 37 K2
Woodford Green Gt Lon 37 K2
Woodford Halse Nhants 48 F4
Woodford Wells Gt Lon 37 K2
Woodgate Birm 58 E8
Woodgate Devon 18 F11
Woodgate Norfk 76 B8
Woodgate Norfk 76 E8
Woodgate W Susx 15 P6
Woodgate W Susx 24 Q4
Woodgate Worcs 58 E11
Wood Green Gt Lon 36 H2
Woodgreen Hants 21 N11
Woodgreen Oxon 34 C2
Woodhall N York 96 E2
Woodhall Hill Leeds 90 G3
Woodhall Spa Lincs 86 G8
Woodham Bucks 49 K11
Woodham Dur 103 Q5
Woodham Surrey 36 B8
Woodham Ferrers Essex 38 C2
Woodham Mortimer Essex 52 D11
Woodham Walter Essex 52 D10
Wood Hayes Wolves 58 D4
Woodhead Abers 159 J10
Woodhill Shrops 57 N8
Woodhill Somset 19 L9
Woodhorn Nthumb 113 L3
Woodhorn Demesne
  Nthumb 113 M3
Woodhouse Leeds 90 H4
Woodhouse Leics 72 E8
Woodhouse Sheff 84 F4
Woodhouse Wakefd 91 K6
Woodhouse Eaves Leics 72 E8
Woodhouse Green Staffs 70 G2
Woodhouselee Mdloth 127 N5
Woodhouselees D & G 110 G6
Woodhouse Mill Sheff 84 F3
Woodhouses Cumb 110 F10
Woodhouses Oldham 83 K4
Woodhouses Staffs 58 G3
Woodhouses Staffs 71 M11
Woodhuish Devon 7 N8
Woodhurst Cambs 62 D5
Woodingdean Br & H 25 J9
Woodkirk Leeds 90 H5
Woodland Abers 151 M3
Woodland Devon 6 G7
Woodland Devon 7 K5
Woodland Dur 103 L5
Woodland Kent 27 K3
Woodland S Ayrs 114 C8
Woodland Head Devon 9 J5
Woodlands Donc 91 N9
Woodlands Dorset 13 J3
Woodlands Hants 13 P2
Woodlands Kent 37 N8
Woodlands N York 97 M10
Woodlands Somset 18 G6
Woodlands of Durris Abers 151 K8
Woodlands Park W & M 35 N9
Woodlands St Mary W Berk 34 B9
Woodland Street Somset 19 P7
Woodland View Sheff 84 D3
Wood Lane Shrops 69 M8
Wood Lane Staffs 70 E5
Woodleigh Devon 7 J9
Woodlesford Leeds 91 K5
Woodley Stockp 83 K6
Woodley Wokham 35 L10
Woodmancote Gloucs 32 E5
Woodmancote Gloucs 33 K3
Woodmancote Gloucs 47 J9
Woodmancote W Susx 15 L5
Woodmancote W Susx 24 F8
Woodmancote Worcs 46 H6
Woodmancott Hants 22 G6
Woodmansey E R Yk 93 J3
Woodmansgreen W Susx 23 N9
Woodmansterne Surrey 36 G9
Woodmanton Devon 9 P7
Woodmarsh Wilts 20 G3
Woodmill Staffs 71 L10
Woodminton Wilts 21 K10
Woodnesborough Kent 39 P10
Woodnewton Nhants 61 M2
Woodnook Notts 84 G10
Wood Norton Norfk 76 E6
Woodplumpton Lancs 88 F4
Woodrising Norfk 76 D11
Wood Row Leeds 91 K5
Woodrow Worcs 58 C9
Wood's Corner E Susx 25 Q7
Woods Eaves Herefs 45 K5
Woodseaves Shrops 70 B8
Woodseaves Staffs 70 D9
Woodsend Wilts 33 P9
Woodsetts Rothm 84 H4
Woodsford Dorset 12 C6
Wood's Green E Susx 25 P4
Woodside Br For 35 P10
Woodside Cumb 100 D4
Woodside Essex 51 L10
Woodside Fife 135 L6
Woodside Gt Lon 36 H7
Woodside Hants 13 P6
Woodside Herts 50 F9
Woodside P & K 142 C10
Woodside Green Kent 38 F11
Woodstock Oxon 48 D11
Woodstock Pembks 41 K5

Woodston C Pete 74 C11
Wood Street Norfk 77 M7
Wood Street Village Surrey 23 Q4
Woodthorpe Derbys 84 G6
Woodthorpe Leics 72 E7
Woodthorpe Lincs 87 M4
Woodton Norfk 65 K3
Woodtown Devon 16 G7
Woodvale Sefton 88 C8
Woodville Derbys 71 Q11
Woodwall Green Staffs 70 D8
Wood Walton Cambs 62 B4
Woodyates Dorset 21 K11
Woody Bay Devon 17 M2
Woofferton Shrops 57 J11
Wookey Somset 19 P5
Wookey Hole Somset 19 P5
Wool Dorset 12 D7
Woolacombe Devon 16 H3
Woolage Green Kent 27 M2
Woolage Village Kent 39 M11
Woolaston Gloucs 31 Q5
Woolaston Common Gloucs 31 Q4
Woolavington Somset 19 N10
Woolbeding W Susx 23 N10
Woolbrook Devon 10 C7
Woolcotts Somset 18 C8
Wooldale Kirk 90 F9
Wooler Nthumb 119 J5
Woolfardisworthy Devon 9 K3
Woolfardisworthy Devon 16 E7
Woolfold Bury 89 M8
Woolfords S Lans 127 J6
Woolhampton W Berk 34 G11
Woolhope Herefs 46 B7
Woolland Dorset 12 C3
Woollard BaNES 20 B2
Woollensbrook Herts 51 J9
Woolley BaNES 32 D11
Woolley Cambs 61 Q6
Woolley Cnwll 16 D8
Woolley Derbys 84 E8
Woolley Wakefd 91 J8
Woolley Bridge Derbys 83 M6
Woolley Edge Services
  Wakefd 91 J8
Woolley Green W & M 35 M8
Woolmere Green Worcs 47 J2
Woolmer Green Herts 50 G7
Woolmerston Somset 19 J8
Woolminstone Somset 11 J3
Woolpack Kent 26 E4
Woolpit Suffk 64 D9
Woolpit Green Suffk 64 D9
Woolscott Warwks 60 B7
Woolsgrove Devon 9 J4
Woolsington N u Ty 113 J6
Woolstaston Shrops 56 H5
Woolsthorpe by Belvoir
  Lincs 73 L4
Woolsthorpe-by-
  Colsterworth Lincs 73 N6
Woolston C Sotn 14 D4
Woolston Devon 7 J10
Woolston Devon 7 J8
Woolston Shrops 56 G7
Woolston Shrops 69 K10
Woolston Somset 18 E7
Woolston Somset 20 C9
Woolston Warrtn 82 D7
Woolstone Gloucs 47 J8
Woolstone M Keyn 49 N7
Woolstone Oxon 33 Q7
Woolston Green Devon 7 K5
Woolton Lpool 81 N7
Woolton Hill Hants 22 D2
Woolverstone Suffk 53 L4
Woolverton Somset 20 E4
Woolwich Gt Lon 37 K5
Woonton Herefs 45 M4
Woonton Herefs 45 R2
Wooperton Nthumb 119 K6
Woore Shrops 70 C6
Wootten Green Suffk 65 K6
Wootton Bed 50 B2
Wootton Hants 13 M5
Wootton Herefs 45 L4
Wootton IoW 14 F8
Wootton Kent 27 M2
Wootton N Linc 93 J7
Wootton Nhants 60 G9
Wootton Oxon 34 C4
Wootton Oxon 48 D11
Wootton Shrops 69 K9
Wootton Staffs 70 E9
Wootton Staffs 71 L6
Wootton Bassett Wilts 33 L8
Wootton Bridge IoW 14 F8
Wootton Broadmead Bed 50 B2
Wootton Common IoW 14 F8
Wootton Courtenay Somset 18 B6
Wootton Fitzpaine Dorset 10 H5
Wootton Rivers Wilts 21 N2
Wootton St Lawrence Hants 22 H3
Wootton Wawen Warwks 47 N2
Worcester Worcs 46 G4
Worcester Park Gt Lon 36 F7
Wordsley Dudley 58 C7
Worfield Shrops 57 P5
Worgret Dorset 12 F7
Workhouse End Bed 61 P10
Workhouse Green Suffk 52 F4
Workington Cumb 100 D5
Worksop Notts 85 J5
Worlaby Lincs 87 K5
Worlaby N Linc 92 H8
Worlds End Bucks 35 M8
Worlds End Hants 14 H4
World's End W Berk 34 E9
Worlds End W Susx 24 H6
Worle N Som 19 L2
Worleston Ches E 70 B3
Worlingham Suffk 65 N4
Worlington Devon 9 J2
Worlington Suffk 63 K5
Worlingworth Suffk 65 J8
Wormald Green N York 97 M7
Wormbridge Herefs 45 N7
Wormegay Norfk 75 N8
Wormelow Tump Herefs 45 P8
Wormhill Derbys 83 P10
Wormhill Herefs 45 N7
Wormingford Essex 52 F5
Worminghall Bucks 34 H3
Wormington Gloucs 47 K7
Worminster Somset 19 Q7

Wormit Fife 135 L2
Wormleighton Warwks 48 E4
Wormley Herts 51 J9
Wormley Surrey 23 P7
Wormleybury Herts 51 J9
Wormley Hill Donc 91 R7
Wormshill Kent 38 D10
Wormsley Herefs 45 N5
Worplesdon Surrey 23 Q4
Worrall Sheff 84 D2
Worrall Hill Gloucs 32 B2
Worsbrough Barns 91 K10
Worsbrough Bridge Barns 91 K10
Worsbrough Dale Barns 91 K10
Worsley Salfd 82 G4
Worstead Norfk 77 L6
Worsthorne Lancs 89 P4
Worston Devon 6 F8
Worston Lancs 89 M2
Worth Kent 39 P10
Worth Somset 19 P5
Worth W Susx 24 H3
Wortham Suffk 64 F6
Worthen Shrops 56 E4
Worthenbury Wrexhm 69 M5
Worthing Norfk 76 D8
Worthing W Susx 24 D10
Worthington Leics 72 C6
Worth Matravers Dorset 12 G9
Worthybrook Mons 31 N2
Worting Hants 22 H4
Wortley Barns 91 J11
Wortley Gloucs 32 E6
Wortley Leeds 90 H4
Worton N York 96 E3
Worton Wilts 21 J3
Wortwell Norfk 65 K5
Wothersone Shrops 56 D4
Wothorpe C Pete 73 Q9
Wotter Devon 6 F4
Wotton Surrey 36 D11
Wotton-under-Edge Gloucs 32 D6
Wotton Underwood Bucks 49 J11
Woughton on the Green
  M Keyn 49 N7
Wouldham Kent 38 B9
Woundale Shrops 57 P6
Wrabness Essex 53 L5
Wrafton Devon 16 H4
Wragby Lincs 86 F5
Wragby Wakefd 91 L7
Wramplingham Norfk 76 G10
Wrangaton Devon 6 H7
Wrangbrook Wakefd 91 M8
Wrangle Lincs 87 M10
Wrangle Common Lincs 87 M10
Wrangle Lowgate Lincs 87 M10
Wrangway Somset 18 F2
Wrantage Somset 19 K10
Wrawby N Linc 92 H9
Wraxall N Som 31 N10
Wraxall Somset 20 B7
Wray Lancs 95 N7
Wraysbury W & M 36 B6
Wrayton Lancs 95 N6
Wrea Green Lancs 88 D4
Wreaks End Cumb 94 E3
Wreay Cumb 101 M6
Wreay Cumb 110 H11
Wrecclesham Surrey 23 M6
Wrekenton Gatesd 113 L9
Wrelton N York 98 F3
Wrenbury Ches E 69 Q5
Wrench Green N York 99 K3
Wreningham Norfk 64 H2
Wrentham Suffk 65 P5
Wrenthorpe Wakefd 91 J6
Wrentnall Shrops 56 G4
Wressle E R Yk 92 B4
Wressle N Linc 92 G9
Wrestlingworth C Beds 62 C11
Wretton Norfk 75 N10
Wrexham Wrexhm 69 K4
Wrexham Industrial Estate
  Wrexhm 69 L4
Wribbenhall Worcs 57 P9
Wrickton Shrops 57 L7
Wrightington Bar Lancs 88 G8
Wright's Green Essex 51 M7
Wrinehill Staffs 70 D5
Wrington N Som 19 N2
Writhlington BaNES 20 C4
Writtle Essex 51 Q9
Wrockwardine Wrekin 57 L2
Wroot N Linc 92 B10
Wrose C Brad 90 F3
Wrotham Kent 37 P9
Wrotham Heath Kent 37 P9
Wrottesley Staffs 58 B4
Wroughton Swindn 33 M8
Wroxall IoW 14 G11
Wroxall Warwks 59 K10
Wroxeter Shrops 57 K3
Wroxham Norfk 77 L8
Wroxton Oxon 48 D6
Wyaston Derbys 71 M6
Wyatt's Green Essex 51 N11
Wyberton Lincs 74 F2
Wyboston Bed 61 Q9
Wybunbury Ches E 70 B5
Wychbold Worcs 58 D11
Wych Cross E Susx 25 K4
Wychnor Staffs 71 M11
Wychwood Ches E 70 C4
Wyck Hants 23 L7
Wyck Rissington Gloucs 47 N10
Wycliffe Dur 103 M8
Wycoller Lancs 89 Q3
Wycomb Leics 73 K6
Wycombe Marsh Bucks 35 N6
Wyddial Herts 51 J4
Wye Kent 27 J2
Wyesham Mons 31 P2
Wyfordby Leics 73 K7
Wyke C Brad 90 F5
Wyke Devon 9 L5
Wyke Devon 10 F5
Wyke Dorset 20 E9
Wyke Shrops 57 L4
Wyke Surrey 23 P4
Wyke Champflower Somset 20 C8
Wykeham N York 99 K4
Wyken Covtry 59 N8
Wyken Shrops 57 P5
Wyke Regis Dorset 11 P9
Wykey Shrops 69 L10

Wykin Leics 72 C11
Wylam Nthumb 112 H8
Wylde Green Birm 58 H6
Wylye Wilts 21 K7
Wymeswold Leics 72 G6
Wymington Bed 61 L8
Wymondham Leics 73 L8
Wymondham Norfk 76 G11
Wyndham Brdgnd 29 P6
Wynford Eagle Dorset 11 M5
Wynyard Park S on T 104 D5
Wynyard Village S on T 104 D5
Wyre Piddle Worcs 47 J5
Wysall Notts 72 G5
Wyson Herefs 57 J11
Wythall Worcs 58 G9
Wythall Green Worcs 58 G10
Wytham Oxon 34 E3
Wythburn Cumb 101 M3
Wythenshawe Manch 82 H7
Wythop Mill Cumb 100 G5
Wyton Cambs 62 C4
Wyton E R Yk 93 L4
Wyton on the Hill Cambs 62 C6
Wyverstone Suffk 64 E8
Wyverstone Street Suffk 64 E8
Wyville Lincs 73 M5

Y

Yaddlethorpe N Linc 92 E9
Yafford IoW 14 D10
Yafforth N York 97 M2
Yalberton Torbay 7 M7
Yalding Kent 37 Q10
Yanwath Cumb 101 P5
Yanworth Gloucs 33 L2
Yapham E R Yk 98 F10
Yapton W Susx 15 Q6
Yarborough N Som 19 L3
Yarbridge IoW 14 H9
Yarburgh Lincs 87 L2
Yarcombe Devon 10 E3
Yard Devon 17 P7
Yardley Birm 58 H7
Yardley Gobion Nhants 49 L6
Yardley Hastings Nhants 61 J9
Yardley Wood Birm 58 H9
Yardro Powys 45 J3
Yarford Somset 18 H9
Yarkhill Herefs 46 B4
Yarley Somset 19 P6
Yarlington Somset 20 C9
Yarm S on T 104 D8
Yarmouth IoW 14 C9
Yarnacott Devon 17 L5
Yarnbrook Wilts 20 G4
Yarner Devon 9 J9
Yarnfield Staffs 70 F7
Yarnscombe Devon 17 K7
Yarnton Oxon 34 E2
Yarpole Herefs 45 P2
Yarrow Border 117 M5
Yarrow Somset 19 L5
Yarrow Feus Border 117 L5
Yarrowford Border 117 N4
Yarsop Herefs 45 N5
Yarwell Nhants 73 R11
Yate S Glos 32 D8
Yateley Hants 23 M2
Yatesbury Wilts 33 L10
Yattendon W Berk 34 G10
Yatton Herefs 56 G11
Yatton N Som 31 M11
Yatton Keynell Wilts 32 G9
Yaverland IoW 14 H9
Yawl Devon 10 G6
Yawthorpe Lincs 85 Q2
Yaxham Norfk 76 E9
Yaxley Cambs 61 Q2
Yaxley Suffk 64 G7
Yazor Herefs 45 N5
Yeading Gt Lon 36 D4
Yeadon Leeds 90 G2
Yealand Conyers Lancs 95 L6
Yealand Redmayne Lancs 95 L5
Yealand Storrs Lancs 95 K5
Yealmbridge Devon 6 F8
Yealmpton Devon 6 F8
Yearby R & Cl 104 G6
Yearngill Cumb 100 F2
Yearsley N York 98 B6
Yeaton Shrops 69 M11
Yeaveley Derbys 71 M6
Yeavering Nthumb 118 H4
Yedingham N York 98 H5
Yelford Oxon 34 C4
Yell Shet 169 r5
Yelland Devon 16 H5
Yelling Cambs 62 C8
Yelvertoft Nhants 60 C5
Yelverton Devon 6 E5
Yelverton Norfk 77 K11
Yenston Somset 20 D10
Yeoford Devon 9 J5
Yeolmbridge Cnwll 5 N4
Yeo Mill Devon 17 Q6
Yeo Vale Devon 16 G7
Yeovil Somset 19 Q11
Yeovil Marsh Somset 19 P11
Yeovilton Somset 19 P10
Yerbeston Pembks 41 L9
Yesnaby Ork 169 b5
Yetlington Nthumb 119 K9
Yetminster Dorset 11 M2
Yetson Devon 7 L7
Yettington Devon 9 Q7
Yetts o'Muckhart Clacks 134 C7
Yews Green C Brad 90 D4
Yew Tree Sandw 58 F5
Y Felinheli Gwynd 79 J11
Y Ferwig Cerdgn 42 C5
Y Ffôr Gwynd 66 F7
Yielden Bed 61 M7
Yieldingtree Worcs 58 C9
Yieldshields S Lans 126 F7
Yiewsley Gt Lon 36 C4
Y Nant Wrexhm 69 J4
Ynys Gwynd 67 K8
Ynysboeth Rhondd 30 E5
Ynysddu Caerph 30 G6
Ynysforgan Swans 29 J5
Ynyshir Rhondd 30 D6
Ynyslas Cerdgn 54 E6

Ynysmaerdy Rhondd 30 D8
Ynysmeudwy Neath 29 K3
Ynystawe Swans 29 J4
Ynyswen Powys 29 M2
Ynyswen Rhondd 30 C5
Ynysybwl Rhondd 30 E6
Ynysymaengwyn Gwynd 54 D4
Yockenthwaite N York 96 D5
Yockleton Shrops 56 F2
Yokefleet E R Yk 92 D6
Yoker C Glas 125 N4
York C York 98 C10
York Lancs 89 L4
Yorkletts Kent 39 J9
Yorkley Gloucs 32 B3
Yorkshire Dales National
  Park 96 C5
York Town Surrey 23 N2
Yorton Heath Shrops 69 P10
Youlgreave Derbys 84 B8
Youlthorpe E R Yk 98 F9
Youlton N York 97 Q8
Youngsbury Herts 51 J7
Young's End Essex 52 B8
Yoxall Staffs 71 L11
Yoxford Suffk 65 M8
Y Rhiw Gwynd 66 C9
Ysbyty Cynfyn Cerdgn 54 H9
Ysbyty Ifan Conwy 67 Q5
Ysbyty Ystwyth Cerdgn 54 G10
Ysceifiog Flints 80 H10
Ysgubor-y-Coed Cerdgn 54 F5
Ystalyfera Neath 29 L3
Ystrad Rhondd 30 C5
Ystrad Aeron Cerdgn 43 K3
Ystradfellte Powys 29 P2
Ystrad Ffin Carmth 43 Q5
Ystradgynlais Powys 29 L2
Ystrad Meurig Cerdgn 54 G11
Ystrad Mynach Caerph 30 F6
Ystradowen Carmth 29 L2
Ystradowen V Glam 30 D9
Ystumtuen Cerdgn 54 G9
Ythanbank Abers 159 M11
Ythanwells Abers 158 F10
Ythsie Abers 159 L11

Z

Zeal Monachorum Devon 8 H4
Zeals Wilts 20 E8
Zelah Cnwll 3 L3
Zennor Cnwll 2 D6
Zoar Cnwll 3 K10
Zouch Notts 72 E6
ZSL London Zoo Gt Lon 36 G4
ZSL Whipsnade Zoo C Beds 50 B7